ISSAC 2011

San Jose, California, USA • June 8-11, 2011

Proceedings of the 36th International Symposium on Symbolic and Algebraic Computation

Anton Leykin, Editor

Association for
Computing Machinery

Advancing Computing as a Science & Profession

Association for Computing Machinery

Advancing Computing as a Science & Profession

Foreword

ISSAC 2011 is a continuation of a well-established series of international conferences for the presentation of the latest advances in the field of Symbolic and Algebraic Computation. The first meeting of the series (1966) was held in Washington, DC, and sponsored by the Association for Computing Machinery (ACM). Since then, the abbreviated name of the meeting has evolved from SYMSAM, SYMSAC, EUROSAM, EUROCAL to finally settle on the present name ISSAC. This 36th meeting took place in San Jose, CA, from June 8 to June 11. For the first time, ISSAC was affiliated with the Federated Computing Research Conference (FCRC). FCRC assembles a spectrum of conferences and workshops into a week-long meeting, to foster communication among researchers in different fields in computer science and engineering.

The topics represented at ISSAC include, but are not limited to:

- *Algorithmic aspects:* Exact and symbolic linear, polynomial and differential algebra. Symbolic-numeric, homotopy, and series methods. Computational geometry, group theory, number theory, quantifier elimination and logic. Summation, recurrence equations, integration, ODE & PDE. Theoretical and practical aspects, including algebraic complexity, and techniques for important special cases.

- *Software aspects:* Design of packages and systems, data representation. Parallel and distributed algebraic computing, considerations for modern hardware. User interface issues, and use of computer algebra systems with other software such as systems for digital libraries, simulation and optimization, automated theorem-proving, computer-aided design, automatic differentiation, and courseware.

- *Application aspects:* Applications that stretch the current limits of symbolic and algebraic computation, use it in new ways, or apply it in situations with broad impact, in particular to the natural sciences, life sciences, engineering, economics and finance, and education.

ISSAC 2011 featured invited talks, contributed papers, tutorials, poster sessions and software presentations. This volume contains all the contributed papers which were presented at the meeting as well as the abstracts of the invited talks and of the tutorials.

A total of 83 papers were submitted; each was distributed to members of the program committee and external reviewers. Reviewing included a rebuttal phase for certain papers. An average of 3.5 referee reports was obtained for each submission and 44 papers were selected. They are representative of the various facets of today's research in computer algebra, ranging from purely theoretical results to software development and important applications. They also offer an illustration of the field's vitality after a history of half a century, and of its future prospects.

We want to acknowledge the contributions of all the researchers and educators who submitted papers and all who assisted in the selection process, especially under this year's tight schedule. We would also like to express our sincere gratitude to all the organizers listed in the front material of these proceedings; the success of ISSAC 2011 is in large part due to the efforts of these people. Finally, we thank the ACM and its Special Interest Group on Symbolic and Algebraic Manipulation (SIGSAM) for their sponsorship and for their assistance in the organization.

Éric Schost	**Ioannis Z. Emiris**	**Emil Volcheck**	**Anton Leykin**
General Chair	*Program Chair*	*Local Arrangements Chair*	*Editor*

Table of Contents

ISSAC 2011 Conference Organization

General Chair:	Éric Schost *(The University of Western Ontario, Canada)*
Program Chair:	Ioannis Z. Emiris *(University of Athens, Greece)*
SIGSAM Chair:	Jeremy Johnson *(Drexel University, USA)*
Proceedings Editor:	Anton Leykin *(Georgia Tech, USA)*
Local Arrangements Chair:	Emil Volcheck *(National Security Agency, USA)*
Tutorials Chair:	Mark Giesbrecht *(University of Waterloo, Canada)*
Poster Committee Chair:	Manuel Kauers *(RISC-Linz, Austria)*
Software Exhibits Chair:	Michael Stillman *(Cornell University, USA)*
Publicity Chair:	Jean-Guillaume Dumas *(Université Joseph Fourier, France)*
Treasurer:	Werner Krandick *(Drexel University, USA)*
Fundraiser:	Ilias Kotsireas *(Wilfrid Laurier University, Canada)*
Webmaster:	Guillaume Moroz *(LORIA, France)*
Program Committee:	Hirokazu Anai *(Kyushu University, Japan)*
	Dario Bini *(Università di Pisa, Italy)*
	John Cannon *(University of Sydney, Australia)*
	Ioannis Z. Emiris *(University of Athens, Greece, Chair)*
	Gabriela Jeronimo *(Universidad de Buenos Aires, Argentina)*
	Pascal Koiran *(ENS Lyon, France)*
	Grégoire Lecerf *(École Polytechnique, France)*
	Wen-shin Lee *(University of Antwerp, Belgium)*
	Hongbo Li *(Chinese Academy of Sciences, China)*
	Kurt Mehlhorn *(MPI Saarbrücken, Germany)*
	Marc Moreno Maza *(The University of Western Ontario, Canada)*
	Mohab Safey El Din *(Université Pierre & Marie Curie, France)*
	Josef Schicho *(RICAM Linz, Austria)*
	Rafael Sendra *(Universidad de Alcalà, Spain)*
	Agnes Szanto *(North Carolina State University, USA)*
	Nobuki Takayama *(Kobe University, Japan)*
	Ashish Tiwari *(SRI International, USA)*
	Elias Tsigaridas *(University of Aarhus, Denmark)*
	Jan Verschelde *(University of Illinois at Chicago, USA)*
Poster Committee:	Sharon Hutton *(North Carolina State University, USA)*
	Manuel Kauers *(RISC-Linz, Austria, Chair)*
	Dan Roche *(University of Waterloo, Canada)*
	Sonia L. Rueda *(Universidad Politécnica de Madrid, Spain)*

Additional reviewers (continued):

Scott McCallum
Andrew McLennan
Martín Mereb
Michael Monagan
Antonio Montes
Teo Mora
Guillaume Moroz
Bernard Mourrain
Kosaku Nagasaka
Sam Nelson
Chau Ngo
Andrew Novocin
Kazuhiro Ogata
Victor Y. Pan
Wei Pan
Nikolaos Papaspyrou
Roman Pearce
Clément Pernet
Ludovic Perret
Daniel Perrucci
John Perry
Chris Peterson
Marko Petkovšek
Eckhard Pflügel
Andre Platzer
Sebastian Pokutta
Loïc Pottier
Georg Regensburger
Guénaël Renault
Jim Renegar
Francesco Romani
Lajos Rónyai
Fabrice Rouillier
Marie-Françoise Roy
Sonia L. Rueda
Michael Sagraloff
Tateaki Sasaki
Peter Scheiblechner
Éric Schost
Pascal Schweitzer

David Sevilla
Flavia Stan
Allan Steel
Damien Stehlé
Rainer Steinwandt
Arne Storjohann
Yann Strozecki
Adam Strzebonski
Nico Temme
Andreas Tielmann
Marialaura Torrente
Eugene Tyrtyshnikov
George M. Tzoumas
Joris van der Hoeven
Mark van Hoeij
Anke van Zuylen
Angelina Vidali
Raimundas Vidunas
Gilles Villard
Carlo Viola
Paul Vrbik
Dongming Wang
Mingsheng Wang
Jacques-Arthur Weil
Michael Wibmer
Andrew Wilson
Franz Winkler
Christopher Wolf
Min Wu
Bican Xia
Rong Xiao
Yoshinori Yamazaki
Hitoshi Yanami
Zhengfeng Yang
Kazuhiro Yokoyama
Chun-Ming Yuan
Alberto Zanoni
Lihong Zhi
Eugene Zima

ISSAC 2011 Sponsor & Supporters

Sponsor:

SIGSAM

Special Interest Group on

Symbolic and Algebraic Manipulation

Supporters:

Certicom

Maplesoft

The University of Western Ontario

Office of the Vice-President

(Research & International Relations)

The University of Western Ontario

Faculty of Science

WOLFRAMRESEARCH

MAKERS OF **MATHEMATICA**
AND **WOLFRAM ALPHA**

Wolfram Research

Computational Aspects of Elliptic Curves and Modular Forms

Victor S. Miller
IDA Center for Communications Research
805 Bunn Driv
Princeton, NJ 08540
victor@idaccr.org

"It is possible to write endlessly about Elliptic Curves. This is not a threat!" – Serge Lang

ABSTRACT

The ultimate motivation for much of the study of Number Theory is the solution of Diophantine Equations – finding integer solutions to systems of equations. Elliptic curves comprise a large, and important class of such equations. Throughout the history of their study Elliptic Curves have always had a strong algorithmic component. In the early 1960's Birch and Swinnerton-Dyer developed systematic algorithms to automate a generalization of a procedure called "descent" which went back to Fermat. The data they obtained was instrumental in formulating their famous conjecture, which is now one of the Clay Mathematical Institute's Millenium prizes.

Categories and Subject Descriptors: F.2.1 [Theory of Computation]:Numerical Algorithms and Problems – *Number Theoretic Computations*

General Terms: Experimentation, Theory

1. INTRODUCTION

The study of Diophantine equations is concerned with understanding the solutions of a system of polynomial equations where the values of the variables are restricted to be integers or rational numbers. If C is a curve and R is a ring (usually $\mathbb{Q}$ or a finite field), then $C(R)$ denotes the set of points (solutions to the equations) in C whose coordinates are in R. Understanding $C(R)$ can mean many things:

1. Decide whether or not there *are any solutions*: is $C(R) = \emptyset$?

2. Count the solutions: calculate $\#C(R)$.

3. Describe the set of solutions – such as saying how to generate them.

Elliptic curves constitute a particularly important class of Diophantine equations. The quest for understanding their solutions is quite subtle, and has historically involved experimentation. Once computers came to be available the development of algorithms to collect some of this data became more and more important. Recently, the computer algebra system SAGE [13] was developed specifically to allow large and complicated calculations involving elliptic curves and modular forms (closely related functions to elliptic curves). We quote from a recent paper [1]

> We have a network of heuristics and conjectures regarding rational points, and we have massive data accumulated to exhibit instances of the phenomena. Generally, we would expect that our data support our conjectures, and if not, we lose faith in our conjectures. But here there is a somewhat more surprising interrelation between data and conjecture: they are not exactly in open conflict one with the other, but they are no great comfort to each other either. We discuss various aspects of this story, including recent heuristics and data that attempt to resolve this mystery. We shall try to convince the reader that, despite seeming discrepancy, data and conjecture are, in fact, in harmony.

Until 1985 the study of elliptic curves was restricted to a small but active community of number theorists and algebraic geometers. In that year it was proposed [9, 7] that elliptic curves over finite fields should be used as a basis for an analogue of the Diffie-Hellman cryptosystem which would less vulnerable to attack. In time the study of elliptic curves became a standard part of the cryptography curriculum in computer science and engineering.

2. ELLIPTIC CURVES

Getting back to Diophantine equations, we can look at the case when there is a single equation in two variables $f(x, y) = 0$, where the coefficients of f are in K – a particular field, usually taken to be $\mathbb{Q}$ or a finite field. This is a *plane curve* over K. Such curves might be classified by their degree, but a finer, and more useful invariant is their *genus*. The curves of genus 0 are either straight lines or conics. There are satisfactory ways, going back to Gauss, to understand their solutions. The next step up is genus 1, which will be our topic of discussion. If a curve C of genus 1, and $C(K) \neq \emptyset$, then by a rational change of coordinates C can be put in the form

$$C : y^2 + a_1 xy + a_3 y = x^3 + a_2 x^2 + a_4 x + a_6, \quad (1)$$

ISSAC'11, June 8–11, 2011, San Jose, California, USA.
ACM 978-1-4503-0675-1/11/06.

where $a_i \in K$[1]. We call such a C an *elliptic curve* [2] The first remarkable fact is that C is a commutative algebraic group – there are rational functions in the coordinates which give an associative and commutative group operation. The second remarkable fact[3] is

THEOREM 1 (MORDELL). *If C an elliptic curve, then $C(\mathbb{Q})$ is a finitely generated group.*

Thus, one is led to the problem of finding a set of independent generators of the group. There is a procedure[4] called *descent* which allows one to compute a set of independent generators. The number of generators which have infinite order is called the *rank* of the curve. A particular version of this procedure is available as a program called `mwrank` [5].

By analyzing descent, one can define a group, known as the *Tate-Shafarevich group*, and denoted by Ш whose cardinality is related to running time of the procedure. It has long been a conjecture that this group is finite, but until the work of Rubin [11]and Kolyvagin [8] in 1987, this was not known to be true for a single instance!

Around 1960, Birch and Swinnerton-Dyer figured out a systematic algorithmic theory of descent (which had before that only been calculated by hand), and ran their program on the EDSAC2 computer accumulating a large amount of data. In particular they saw that they could reliably predict the rank, r, of the curve C by looking at plots of the function

$$P(x) := \prod_{p \leq x} \frac{N_p}{p} \qquad (2)$$

where p is a prime number, and N_p denotes the number of points on the curve C when it's reduced modulo p. They conjectured that $P(x) \sim c(\log x)^r$ as $x \to \infty$, for some $c \neq 0$ which depended on the curve. By using standard techniques from analytic number theory they strengthened this conjecture to give a specific value for c [5] which depended on the cardinality of Ш. By standard analytic number theory, the function $P(x)$ was easily related to the r-th derivative at 1 of something known as the *Hasse-Weil L-function* – a function of a complex variable which was only known to be defined, for general elliptic curves C, for $\Re s > \frac{3}{2}$.

In 1972 [15] Tate said about this conjecture:

> This remarkable conjecture relates the behavior of a function L at a point where it is not at present known to be defined to the order of a group Ш which is not known to be finite!

3. MODULARITY

It had been known for a number of years that there *were* particular elliptic curves for which one could prove that the Hasse-Weil L function was defined on the whole complex plane, and even find good approximations to the appropriate derivatives in the Birch Swinnerton-Dyer conjecture (called BSD). All numerical results for these curves agreed with the conjecture. A major conjecture, called the *modularity conjecture* said that *every* elliptic curve over $\mathbb{Q}$ could be parametrized by a class of complex functions called modular functions. This conjecture was finally proved in 1994 by Wiles, Breuil, Diamond, Conrad and Taylor. Even before this conjecture was proved, large computations [5] were performed on the basis of it to give more numerical verfication of BSD. Gross and Zagier had previously [6] shown that if the modularity conjecture was true that one could explicitly construct a known multiple of the generator in the case that the rank= 1.

More and more computing power and deep algorithms are even now being brought to bear on some of the most interesting and exciting conjectures about elliptic curves.

4. REFERENCES

[1] B. Bektemirov, B. Mazur, W. Stein, and M. Watkins. Average ranks of elliptic curves: tension between data and conjecture. *Bull. Amer. Math. Soc. (N.S.)*, 44(2):233–254 (electronic), 2007.

[2] B. J. Birch and H. P. F. Swinnerton-Dyer. Notes on elliptic curves. I. *J. Reine Angew. Math.*, 212:7–25, 1963.

[3] B. J. Birch and H. P. F. Swinnerton-Dyer. Notes on elliptic curves. II. *J. Reine Angew. Math.*, 218:79–108, 1965.

[4] A. Brumer and O. McGuinness. The behavior of the Mordell-Weil group of elliptic curves. *Bull. Amer. Math. Soc. (N.S.)*, 23(2):375–382, 1990.

[5] J. E. Cremona. *Algorithms for modular elliptic curves.* Cambridge University Press, Cambridge, second edition, 1997.

[6] B. Gross and D. Zagier. Points de Heegner et dérivées de fonctions L. *C. R. Acad. Sci. Paris Sér. I Math.*, 297(2):85–87, 1983.

[7] N. Koblitz. Elliptic curve cryptosystems. *Math. Comp.*, 48(177):203–209, 1987.

[8] V. A. Kolyvagin. Finiteness of $E(\mathbb{Q})$ and Ш$(E, \mathbb{Q})$ for a subclass of Weil curves. *Izv. Akad. Nauk SSSR Ser. Mat.*, 52(3):522–540, 670–671, 1988.

[9] V. S. Miller. Use of elliptic curves in cryptography. In *Advances in cryptology—CRYPTO '85*, volume 218 of *Lecture Notes in Comput. Sci.*, pages 417–426. Springer, Berlin, 1986.

[10] V. S. Miller. The Weil pairing, and its efficient calculation. *J. Cryptology*, 17(4):235–261, 2004.

[11] K. Rubin. Tate-Shafarevich groups and L-functions of elliptic curves with complex multiplication. *Invent. Math.*, 89(3):527–559, 1987.

[12] K. Rubin and A. Silverberg. Ranks of elliptic curves. *Bull. Amer. Math. Soc. (N.S.)*, 39(4):455–474 (electronic), 2002.

[13] W. Stein et al. *Sage Mathematics Software (Version 4.6.2).* The Sage Development Team, 2011. http://www.sagemath.org.

[14] W. A. Stein and M. Watkins. A database of elliptic curves—first report. In *Algorithmic number theory (Sydney, 2002)*, volume 2369 of *Lecture Notes in Comput. Sci.*, pages 267–275. Springer, Berlin, 2002.

[15] J. T. Tate. The arithmetic of elliptic curves. *Invent. Math.*, 23:179–206, 1974.

---

[1]There is an additional condition that a particular polynomial in the a_i called the discriminatnt be non-zero, to assume that the genus is not zero

[2]the term derives from the fact that if one writes down an integral to compute the arc-length of an ellipse, one is led to *elliptic functions* which parametrize such curves

[3]The same result was proved for $C(K)$ where K is a number field by André Weil in his thesis. The group $C(K)$ is usually called the *Mordell-Weil* group

[4]In the technical sense – it is a program not proved to always terminate

[5]It was later shown by Goldfeld that their constant c had to be modified by a known factor

Recent Progress in Linear Algebra and Lattice Basis Reduction

Gilles Villard
CNRS, ENS de Lyon, INRIA, UCBL, Université de Lyon
Laboratoire LIP
gilles.villard@ens-lyon.fr

Categories and Subject Descriptors

I.1.2 [**Symbolic and Algebraic Manipulation**]: Algorithms; F.2.1 [**Analysis of Algorithms and Problem Complexity**]: Numerical Algorithms and Problems

General Terms

Algorithms

ABSTRACT

A general goal concerning fundamental linear algebra problems is to reduce the complexity estimates to essentially the same as that of multiplying two matrices (plus possibly a cost related to the input and output sizes). Among the bottlenecks one usually finds the questions of designing a recursive approach and mastering the sizes of the intermediately computed data.

In this talk we are interested in two special cases of lattice basis reduction. We consider bases given by square matrices over $K[x]$ or $\mathbb{Z}$, with, respectively, the notion of *reduced form* and *LLL reduction*. Our purpose is to introduce basic tools for understanding how to generalize the Lehmer and Knuth-Schönhage gcd algorithms for basis reduction. Over $K[x]$ this generalization is a key ingredient for giving a basis reduction algorithm whose complexity estimate is essentially that of multiplying two polynomial matrices. Such a problem relation between integer basis reduction and integer matrix multiplication is not known. The topic receives a lot of attention, and recent results on the subject show that there might be room for progressing on the question.

Fundamental problems in linear algebra. Many matrix problems over a field K can be solved in $O^{\tilde{}}(n^\omega)$ if ω is the exponent for matrix multiplication (see e.g. [2]). Over the last decade it became clear that the corresponding cost bounds, $O^{\tilde{}}(n^\omega \delta)$ and $O^{\tilde{}}(n^\omega \beta)$, for multiplying matrices of degree δ in $K[x]^{n \times n}$ or with entries having bit length β in $\mathbb{Z}^{n \times n}$, may also be reached for symbolic problems. We refer for example to Storjohann's algorithms for the determinant and Smith form [21], and to the applications of polynomial approximant bases in [9]. The cost bounds have been recently improved for the characteristic polynomial [11] or matrix inverse [22]. However, as well as for integer LLL reduction, the question of reaching the bounds $O^{\tilde{}}(n^\omega \beta)$ ($O^{\tilde{}}(n^3 \beta)$ for inversion) remains open for these problems.

Lattices. A polynomial lattice Λ_x of dimension d of $K[x]^n$ is the set of the polynomial combinations of d linearly independent vectors $b_1, \ldots, b_d$ of $K[x]^n$. The latter vectors form a basis of the lattice and define a matrix $B \in K[x]^{n \times d}$. Any lattice admits an infinity of bases, but one may identify special ones, called minimal, with the smallest possible degrees. The matrix corresponding to a minimal basis, with degrees $\delta_1, \ldots, \delta_d$, is said to be in *reduced form* and is "orthogonal". We mean that up to a column scaling its leading coefficient matrix is full rank, and the orthogonality defect is

$$\Delta_x(b_1, \ldots, b_d) = \prod_j 2^{\delta_j} / 2^{\deg \det(\Lambda_x)} = 1.$$

The polynomial situation is simpler than its number theoretic analogue for which it is much harder to compute minimal quantities. A lattice Λ of $\mathbb{Z}^n$ is the set of the integer combinations of a basis $b_1, \ldots, b_d$ in $\mathbb{Z}^n$. We consider the relaxed notion of reduction introduced by Lenstra, Lenstra and Lovász in [14]. The lengths of the vectors of a *LLL reduced* basis are not minimal but fairly small. Among other properties, the lengths and the orthogonality defect satisfy

$$\Delta(b_1, \ldots, b_d) = \prod_j \|b_j\| / \det(\Lambda) \leq 2^{O(d^2)}.$$

The problem of finding a reduced basis of a lattice given by an arbitrary basis is called *basis reduction*. We focus on the two above particular cases for non singular matrices. A more general setting would be reduction for discrete subgroups of $\mathbb{R}^n$ and free modules of finite rank. A rich litterature and the wide spectrum of applications of basis reduction show the importance of the domain. For the polynomial case we may refer to Kailath [10] and system theory references therein. About LLL and stronger reductions we may refer to Lovász [15] and the contributions in [16].

Basis reduction. Two matrices A and B whose columns form a basis of a given lattice are equivalent, i.e. $B = AU$ with U unimodular. A typical approach for computing a reduced B from a non reduced A is to apply successive transformations. Over $K[x]$, the transformations correspond to dependencies in coefficient matrices, and decrease the column degrees. In the integer case, geometrical informations are obtained from orthogonalizations over $\mathbb{R}$ for decreasing the column norms. The basic transformations consist in reducing vectors or matrices against others, and vice versa. Reduction algorithms are seen as generalizations of Euclid's gcd or continued fraction algorithm (see [7] and seminal references therein). The intermediately computed bases play the role of "remainders", and the successive basic transformations performed on the bases play the role of "quotients".

Lehmer's & Knuth-Schönhage algorithms. Lehmer's modification of Euclid's algorithm [13], and Knuth's [12] and Schönhage's [19] algorithms, have been a crucial progress. Their idea is to employ the fact that for small quotients, truncated remainders suffice to compute the quotient sequence. Via an algorithm that multiplies two integers of size β in $\mu(\beta)$ operations, this has led to the bit complexity estimate $O(\mu(\beta)\log\beta)$ for the gcd problem. Through some analogies between recent algorithms over $\mathsf{K}[x]$ and $\mathbb{Z}$, we will see how similar recursive approaches may be developed for reduction.

Reduced form over $\mathsf{K}[x]$. Beckermann and Labahn [1] has given a key generalization of the Knuth-Schönhage algorithm for Padé approximants. As a consequence one may show [9] that reconstructing a univariate and proper matrix fraction CB^{-1} from its expansion, with B column reduced of degree $O(\delta)$, can be done in $O^{\sim}(n^{\omega}\delta)$ field operations. This may be applied to computing a reduced form B of a non singular matrix A, by reconstructing a fraction CB^{-1} from an appropriate (proper) segment of the expansion of A^{-1} [4]. We will see that it follows that the reduction of a non singular $A \in \mathsf{K}[x]^{n \times n}$ of degree δ can be performed within about the same number $O^{\sim}(n^{\omega}\delta)$ of operations as that of multiplying two matrices of degree δ in $\mathsf{K}[x]^{n \times n}$. The corresponding algorithm of Giorgi et al. [4] is randomized. A deterministic algorithm is given in [5] where the problem of reducing A is reduced to the problem of reducing the Hermite form H of A. The latter problem may be solved in $O^{\sim}(n^{\omega}\delta)$ via a partial linearization of H, and using the algorithm designed in [4] for fraction reconstruction via approximants.

These reduction approaches work in two phases. A first phase transforms the problem into a "simpler"—with a small degree solution—matrix approximant problem (either via a fraction or the Hermite normal form). The second phase inherits the approximation method of [1], and works by recurrence on the approximation order. (The process may be decomposed into successive matrix factorizations over K.)

LLL reduction over $\mathbb{Z}$. For an insight into LLL reduction algorithms we may refer to the contributions of Nguyen (Ch. 2), Schnorr (Ch. 4), and Stehlé (Ch. 5) in [16]. We focus on the cost with respect to the integer bit size β, with the aim of obtaining a bit complexity estimate $O^{\sim}(\mathcal{P}oly(n)\beta)$.

We will present the gradual strategy of [8, 17] for designing a Lehmer-like algorithm in the following special case (see also [18]). Assume that B_0 is LLL reduced, and let $\sigma = \mathrm{diag}(\ell, 1, \ldots, 1)$ where $\ell > 1$. We call lift-reduction of B_0 the problem of reducing $\sigma^k B_0$, $k \in \mathbb{N}$. The lift-reduction of [17] is a recurrence on the order k of the lifting, and implements the lift-reduction as k successive elementary steps. (B_{i+1} is a reduced basis of σB_i.) With this setting, the Knuth-Schönhage algorithm may be generalized for the task of lift-reducing [17]. The truncation process of the successive bases ("remainders") relies on an LLL reduction definition that resists perturbation, and takes advantage of the numerical quality of the reduced bases that are fairly well conditioned (see [3]). The multi-dimensionality of lattice reduction leads to the manipulation of significantly differing magnitudes in the transformations themselves. The problem may be solved by truncating also the transformations. (Unlike the integer gcd case where the quotients are not truncated.)

We will see how to use lift-reduction for the LLL reduction of A in time quasi-linear in β [17] (non singular case). Lift-reduction is specialized to reducing a lift/shift of an already reduced basis. For example, appropriate reduced bases for calling the lift-reduction can be created iteratively from the Hermite form of A. The above approach takes a matrix point of view. An alternative approach to LLL reduction in time $O^{\sim}(\mathcal{P}oly(n)\beta)$ has been recently obtained [6], by using the 2-dimensional Knuth-Schönhage algorithm from [20, 23].

Acknowledgment. We are grateful to Damien Stehlé for his help during the preparation of this talk.

References

[1] B. Beckermann and G. Labahn. A uniform approach for the fast computation of matrix-type Padé approximants. *SIAM J. Matrix Anal. Appl.*, 15(3):804–823, July 1994.

[2] P. Bürgisser, M. Clausen, and M. Shokrollahi. *Algebraic Complexity Theory.* Volume 315, Grundlehren der mathematischen Wissenschaften. Springer-Verlag, 1997.

[3] X.-W. Chang, D. Stehlé, and G. Villard. Perturbation analysis of the QR factor R in the context of LLL lattice basis reduction. *Math. Comp.*, to appear.

[4] P. Giorgi, C. Jeannerod, and G. Villard. On the complexity of polynomial matrix computations. In *Proc. ISSAC, Philadelphia, PA*, pages 135–142. ACM Press, Aug. 2003.

[5] S. Gupta, S. Sarkar, A. Storjohann, and J. Valeriote. Triangular x-basis decompositions and derandomization of linear algebra algorithms over $\mathsf{K}[x]$. *J. Symbolic Comput.*, to appear.

[6] G. Hanrot, X. Pujol, and D. Stehlé. Personal communication, Dec. 2010.

[7] J. Hastad, B. Just, J. Lagarias, and C. Schnorr. Polynomial time algorithms for finding integer relations among real numbers. *SIAM J. Comput.*, 18(5):859–881, 1989.

[8] M. van Hoeij and A. Novocin. Gradual sub-lattice reduction and a new complexity for factoring polynomials. In *Proc. LATIN 2010*, volume 6034, pages 539–553, 2010.

[9] C. Jeannerod and G. Villard. Asymptotically fast polynomial matrix algorithms for multivariable systems. *Int. J. Control*, 79(11):1359–1367, 2006.

[10] T. Kailath. *Linear systems.* Prentice Hall, 1980.

[11] E. Kaltofen and G. Villard. On the complexity of computing determinants. *Comput. Complexity*, 13(3-4):91–130, 2005.

[12] D. Knuth. The analysis of algorithms. In *Proc. International Congress of Mathematicians (Nice, 1970)*, volume 3, pages 269–274, 1971.

[13] D. Lehmer. Euclid's algorithm for large numbers. *Amer. Math. Monthly*, 45:227–233, 1938.

[14] A. Lenstra, H. Lenstra, and L. Lovász. Factoring polynomials with rational coefficients. *Math. Ann.*, 261:515–534, 1982.

[15] L. Lovász. *An algorithmic theory of numbers, graphs and convexity.* CBMS-NSF Regional Conferences Series in Applied Mathematics, SIAM, 1986.

[16] P. Q. Nguyen and B. Vallée, editors. *The LLL Algorithm, Survey and Applications.* Springer-Verlag, 2010.

[17] A. Novocin, D. Stehlé, and G. Villard. An LLL-reduction algorithm with quasi-linear time complexity. In *Proc. 43rd ACM STOC, San Jose, CA.* ACM Press, June 2011.

[18] S. Radziszowski and D. Kreher. Solving subset sum problems with the L^3 algorithm. *J. Combin. Math. Combin. Comput.*, 3:49–63, 1988.

[19] A. Schönhage. Schnelle Berechnung von Kettenbruchenwicklungen. *Acta Inform.*, 1:139–144, 1971.

[20] A. Schönhage. Fast reduction and composition of binary quadratic forms. In *Proc. ISSAC, Bonn, Germany*, pages 128–133. ACM Press, 1991.

[21] A. Storjohann. The shifted number system for fast linear algebra on integer matrices. *J. Complexity*, 21(4):609–650, 2005.

[22] A. Storjohann. On the complexity of inverting integer and polynomial matrices. *Comput. Complexity*, to appear.

[23] C. K. Yap. Fast unimodular reduction: planar integer lattices. In *Proc. 33rd IEEE FOCS, Pittsburgh, PA*, pages 437–446, 1992.

Probabilistic Analysis of Condition Numbers

[Tutorial Overview]

Peter Bürgisser
Institute of Mathematics
University of Paderborn
D-33095 Paderborn, Germany
pbuerg@upb.de

ABSTRACT

Condition numbers are well known in numerical linear algebra. It is less known that this concept also plays a crucial part in understanding the efficiency of algorithms in linear programming, convex optimization, and for solving systems of polynomial equations. Indeed, the running time of such algorithms may be often effectively bounded in terms of the condition underlying the problem.

"Smoothed analysis", as suggested by Spielman and Teng, is a blend of worst-case and average-case probabilistic analysis of algorithms. The goal is to prove that for all inputs (even ill-posed ones), and all slight random perturbations of that input, it is unlikely that the running time (or condition number) will be large.

The tutorial will present a unifying view on the notion of condition in linear algebra, convex optimization, and polynomial equations. We will discuss the role of condition for the analysis of algorithms as well as techniques for their probabilistic analysis. For the latter, geometry plays an important role.

Categories and Subject Descriptors

I.1.2 [**Symbolic and Algebraic Manipulation**]: Analysis of Algorithms; F.2.1 [**Analysis of Algorithms and Problem Complexity**]: Numerical Algorithms

General Terms

Algorithms, Theory

Keywords

condition, complexity, smoothed analysis of algorithms, convex optimization, polynomial equation solving, homotopy continuation

Tutorial Outline

Part I: Linear Equalities

- Turing's condition number $\kappa(A)$
- Average probabilistic analysis of $\kappa(A)$
- Smoothed probabilistic analysis of $\kappa(A)$
- Random triangular matrices

Part II: Linear Inequalities

- Interior-point methods
- Condition numbers of linear programming
- Average analysis of GCC condition number
- Smoothed analysis of GCC condition number
- Condition numbers of convex optimization

Part III: Polynomial Equations

- Smale's 17th problem
- Approximate zeros, condition, and homotopy continuation
- Probabilistic analyses
- A near solution to Smale's 17th problem
- Ideas of proof

A monography with the title *Condition* is currently in preparation, jointly with Felipe Cucker (City University of Hong Kong). This book covers the material of this tutorial in detail. We hope to complete this book by the end of 2011.

The Concrete Tetrahedron

Manuel Kauers[*]

RISC
Johannes Kepler University
4040 Linz (Austria)
mkauers@risc.jku.at

ABSTRACT

We give an overview over computer algebra algorithms for dealing with symbolic sums, recurrence equations, generating functions, and asymptotic estimates, and we will illustrate how to apply these algorithms to problems arising in discrete mathematics.

Categories and Subject Descriptors

I.1.2 [**Computing Methodologies**]: Symbolic and Algebraic Manipulation—*Algorithms*; G.2.1 [**Mathematics of Computing**]: Discrete Mathematics—*Combinatorics*

General Terms

Algorithms

Keywords

Symbolic Sums, Recurrence Equations, Generating Functions, Asymptotic Estimates

1. OVERVIEW

Questions arising in discrete mathematics tend to require calculations involving symbolic sums, recurrence equations, generating functions, and asymptotic estimates. These four mathematical concepts do not stand for their own but rather form the four corners of a compound which we call the concrete tetrahedron. We will survey the most important algorithms which are useful for solving problems in this context: algorithms for obtaining symbolic sums from generating functions, for obtaining recurrence equations from symbolic sums, for obtaining asymptotic estimates from recurrence equations, and so on.

Ideally, the tutorial should cover the four parts of the concrete tetrahedron for polynomial sequences, c-finite sequences, hypergeometric terms, algebraic functions, and for holonomic functions; it should cover the algorithms for univariate sequences as well as their generalizations to the multivariate case; and it should cover algorithmic details as well as real world applications. But this will hardly be possible in the available amount of time. Our plan is to present a representative selection of the material and to give a flavor of the underlying algorithmic principles and the way in which they are put to use.

Further details on the material covered in the tutorial can be found in the classical textbook [3]. This book focusses more on traditional paper-and-pencil techniques, whereas the recent introductory textbook [4] follows a more algorithmic approach to the subject. Special books on (hypergeometric) summation are [8, 5]. An introduction to the classical theory of generating function is available in [10]. A standard reference on techniques for computing asymptotic estimates is the volume [2]. The relevant original references are available in these books. Unfortunately, we do not have the space to mention them also here.

Concerning software, most general purpose computer algebra systems nowadays include implementations of hypergeometric summation algorithms (Gosper's and Zeilberger's algorithm) as well as facilities for computing various kinds of series expansions. Tools for univariate holonomic sequences and power series are available for Maple in the gfun package [9] and for Mathematica in the a package of Mallinger [7] (since version 7, Mathematica has also builtin tools). The more general algorithms for holonomic and D-finite functions in several variables were implemented by Chyzak [1] in the Mgfun package for Maple and by Koutschan [6] for Mathematica.

2. REFERENCES

[1] F. Chyzak. *Fonctions holonomes en calcul formel.* PhD thesis, INRIA Rocquencourt, 1998.

[2] Ph. Flajolet and R. Sedgewick. *Analytic Combinatorics.* Cambridge University Press, 2009.

[3] R. L. Graham, D. E. Knuth, and O. Patashnik. *Concrete Mathematics.* Addison-Wesley, 1989/1994.

[4] M. Kauers and P. Paule. *The Concrete Tetrahedron.* Springer, 2011.

[5] W. Koepf. *Hypergeometric Summation.* Vieweg, 1998.

[6] C. Koutschan. *Advanced Applications of the Holonomic Systems Approach.* PhD thesis, RISC, 2009.

[7] C. Mallinger. Algorithmic manipulations and transformations of univariate holonomic functions and sequences. Master's thesis, RISC, 1996.

[8] M. Petkovšek, H. S. Wilf, and D. Zeilberger. *A = B.* AK Peters, 1997.

[9] B. Salvy and P. Zimmermann. Gfun: a Maple package for the manipulation of generating and holonomic functions in one variable. *ACM T. Math. Software*, 20(2):163–177, 1994.

[10] H. S. Wilf. *generatingfunctionology.* AK Peters, 1989.

[*]Supported by the Austrian FWF grant Y464-N18.

Hybrid Symbolic-Numeric Methods for the Solution of Polynomial Systems

[Tutorial Overview]

Agnes Szanto
Department of Mathematics
North Carolina State University
Campus Box 8205
Raleigh, NC, 27695
aszanto@ncsu.edu

ABSTRACT

In this tutorial we will focus on the solution of polynomial systems given with inexact coefficients using hybrid symbolic-numeric methods. In particular, we will concentrate on systems that are over-constrained or have roots with multiplicities. These systems are considered ill-posed or ill-conditioned by traditional numerical methods and they try to avoid them. On the other hand, traditional symbolic methods are not designed to handle inexactness. Ill-conditioned polynomial equation systems arise very frequently in many important applications areas such as geometric modeling, computer vision, fluid dynamics, etc.

Categories and Subject Descriptors

I.1.2 [**Symbolic and Algebraic Manipulation**]: Algorithms; G.1.5 [**Numerical Analysis**]: Roots of Nonlinear Equations

General Terms

Algorithms

Keywords

Hybrid symbolic-numeric computation, ill-conditioned, approximate GCD, multivariate polynomial systems

Introduction

In recent years there has been intensive research on extending the applicability of symbolic and numerical methods to handle problems which are given with limited accuracy and which were traditionally considered "ill-conditioned". The integration of numerical and symbolic techniques resulted in a remarkable progress in the applicability, versatility, robustness and efficiency of the algorithms for the solution of problems such as approximate GCD, approximate polynomial

factorization, solution of under and over-constrained approximate polynomial systems, characterization of the symmetries and the solution of differential equations, just to name a few.

Outline of the Tutorial

- Introduction
    - Motivation
    - Main topics
    - Topics not discussed
- Theoretical framework
    - Polynomials with inexact coefficients
    - Ill-posed and ill-conditioned problems
    - Forward and backward error
    - Certification of the solution
- Univariate Case: Approximate GCD
    - Symbolic methods adapted to inexact input
        * Certification of nearest GCD via subresultant method
        * Structured matrix optimization
    - Iterative root finding methods
        * Karmarkar-Lakshman's optimization formulation for nearest GCD
        * Nearest polynomial with root multiplicities
- Multivariate Case: Over-constrained systems
    - Overview of symbolic methods and their behaviour under coefficient perturbation
        * Gröbner bases
        * Border bases and reduction to an eigen-problem
        * Resultants and subresultants
    - Solution via optimization: nearest system with k common roots
- Multivariate systems near root multiplicities
    - Moment and trace matrices
    - Approximate radical computation
- Open problems

Border Basis Detection is NP-complete

Prabhanjan V. Ananth
Dept. of Computer Science and Automation
Indian Institute of Science
prabhanjan@csa.iisc.ernet.in

Ambedkar Dukkipati
Dept. of Computer Science and Automation
Indian Institute of Science
ambedkar@csa.iisc.ernet.in

ABSTRACT

Border basis detection (BBD) is described as follows: given
a set of generators of an ideal, decide whether that set of generators is a border basis of the ideal with respect to some
order ideal. The motivation for this problem comes from a
similar problem related to Gröbner bases termed as Gröbner
basis detection (GBD) which was proposed by Gritzmann
and Sturmfels (1993). GBD was shown to be NP-hard by
Sturmfels and Wiegelmann (1996). In this paper, we investigate the computational complexity of BBD and show that
it is NP-complete.

Categories and Subject Descriptors

F.0 [**Theory of Computation**]: General

General Terms

Theory

Keywords

Border bases, Zero-dimensional ideals, Complexity,
NP-completeness

1. INTRODUCTION

Gröbner bases play an important role in computational commutative algebra and algebraic geometry as they have been
used to solve classic problems like ideal membership, intersection and saturation of ideals, solving system of polynomial equations and so on. Gröbner bases are defined with
respect to a 'term order' and the choice of the term order
plays a crucial role in time required to compute Gröbner
bases. Gröbner bases are also known to be numerically unstable and hence are not suitable to be used to describe
ideals which are constructed from measured data [7]. Border bases, an alternative to Gröbner bases, is known to show
more numerical stability as compared to Gröbner bases.

The notion of border bases was introduced to find a system
of generators for zero dimensional ideals having some nice

properties. The theory of border bases was used by Auzinger
and Stetter [1] to solve zero dimensional polynomial systems
of equations. Kehrein and Kreuzer [4] gave characterisations
of border bases [4] and also extended Mourrain's idea [8] to
compute border bases [5]. The border bases as computed
by the algorithm were associated with degree compatible
term orderings. Mourrain and Trébuchet in [9] weakened the
monomial ordering requirement and proposed an approach
to construct the quotient algebra. Recently, Mourrain and
Trébuchet extended their work in [10] to give an algorithm
to compute border bases. Brian and Pokutta [2] gave a polyhedral characterisation of order ideals and gave an algorithm
to compute border bases where the associated order ideals
were independent of term orderings. They also showed that
computing a preference optimal order ideal is NP-hard.

Gritzmann and Sturmfels [3] introduced Gröbner basis
detection (GBD) problem and solved this problem using
Minkowski addition of polytopes. Later Sturmfels and Wiegelmann [11] showed that GBD is NP-hard. For this, they introduced a related problem called SGBD (Structural Gröbner basis detection) which was shown to be NP-complete
by a reduction from the set packing problem. Using SGBD
it was proved that GBD is NP-hard. In this paper, we introduce a similar problem related to border bases known as
Border Basis Detection (BBD) and prove that the problem
is NP-complete. Even though the concept of border basis
generalises Gröbner basis, the complexity of GBD does not
easily imply the complexity of BBD for the reason that there
exists order ideals which are not associated with any term
orderings [6].

In § 2, we give preliminaries for border bases and describe
the border basis detection problem. We describe the preliminary observations in § 3. In § 4, we prove that BBD is in
NP and then a polynomial time reduction from 3,4-SAT to
BBD is described in § 5 which will be followed the proof of
the correctness of the reduction. We make the concluding
remarks in § 6,.

2. BORDER BASES

Let $\mathbb{F}[x_1, \ldots, x_n]$ be a polynomial ring, where $\mathbb{F}$ is a field.
$\mathbb{T}^n$ denotes the set of terms* *i.e.*,

$$\mathbb{T}^n = \{x_1{}^{\alpha_1} \cdots x_n{}^{\alpha_n} : (\alpha_1, \ldots, \alpha_n) \in \mathbb{Z}^n_{\geq 0}\}.$$

The total degree of a term $t = x_1{}^{\alpha_1} \cdots x_n{}^{\alpha_n}$ denoted by

---

*In the classical sense, $x_1{}^{\alpha_1} \cdots x_n{}^{\alpha_n}$ is called a monomial
and a term is the product of a field element and a mono-
mial. Here, we prefer to call $x_1{}^{\alpha_1} \cdots x_n{}^{\alpha_n}$ as a term and a
monomial as a product of term and a field element.

deg(t) is $\sum_{i=1}^n \alpha_i$. We represent all the terms of total degree i by $\mathbb{T}_i^n$ and all the terms of total degree less than or equal to i by $\mathbb{T}_{\leq i}^n$. By support of a polynomial we mean, all the terms appearing in that polynomial i.e., support of a polynomial $f = \sum_{i=1}^s c_i t_i$ (denoted by $\mathrm{Supp}(f)$) is $\{t_1, \ldots, t_s\}$, where $t_i \in \mathbb{T}^n$ and each c_i is non-zero and belongs to $\mathbb{F}$. Similarly, support of a set of polynomials is the union of support of all the polynomials in the set i.e., $\mathrm{Supp}(S) = \bigcup_{f \in S} \mathrm{Supp}(f)$.

The following notions are useful for the theory of border basis.

DEFINITION 1. *A non-empty finite set of terms $\mathcal{O} \subset \mathbb{T}^n$ is called an order ideal if it is closed under forming divisors i.e., if $t \in \mathcal{O}$ and $t'|t$ then it implies $t' \in \mathcal{O}$.*

DEFINITION 2. *Let $\mathcal{O}$ be an order ideal. The border of $\mathcal{O}$ is the set*

$$\partial \mathcal{O} = (\mathbb{T}_1^n . \mathcal{O}) \backslash \mathcal{O} = (x_1 \mathcal{O} \cup \ldots \cup x_n \mathcal{O}) \backslash \mathcal{O}.$$

The first border closure of $\mathcal{O}$ is defined as the set $\mathcal{O} \cup \partial \mathcal{O}$ and it is denoted by $\overline{\partial \mathcal{O}}$.

It can be shown that $\overline{\partial \mathcal{O}}$ is also an order ideal.

DEFINITION 3. *Let $\mathcal{O} = \{t_1, \ldots, t_\mu\}$ be an order ideal, and let $\partial \mathcal{O} = \{b_1, \ldots, b_\nu\}$ be its border. A set of polynomials $G = \{g_1, \ldots, g_\nu\}$ is called an $\mathcal{O}$-border prebasis if the polynomials have the form $g_j = b_j - \sum_{i=1}^{\mu} \alpha_{ij} t_i$, where $\alpha_{ij} \in \mathbb{F}$ for $1 \leq i \leq \mu$ and $1 \leq j \leq \nu$.*

Note that the $\mathcal{O}$-border prebasis consists of polynomials which have exactly one term from $\partial \mathcal{O}$ and rest of the terms are in order ideal $\mathcal{O}$.

If a $\mathcal{O}$-border prebasis belongs to an ideal $\mathfrak{a}$ and the order ideal has a nice property with respect to an ideal then that $\mathcal{O}$-border prebasis is termed as $\mathcal{O}$-border basis. The definition of $\mathcal{O}$-border basis is given below.

DEFINITION 4. *Let $\mathcal{O} = \{t_1, \ldots, t_\mu\}$ be an order ideal and $G = \{g_1, \ldots, g_\nu\}$ be an $\mathcal{O}$-border prebasis consisting of polynomials in $\mathfrak{a}$. We say that the set G is an $\mathcal{O}$-**border basis** of $\mathfrak{a}$ if the residue classes of $t_1, \ldots, t_\mu$ form a $\mathbb{F}$-vector space basis of $\mathbb{F}[x_1, \ldots, x_n]/\mathfrak{a}$.*

It can be shown that an $\mathcal{O}$-border basis of an ideal $\mathfrak{a}$ indeed generates $\mathfrak{a}$ [6]. It can also be shown that for a fixed order ideal $\mathcal{O}$, with respect to an ideal $\mathfrak{a}$ there can be at most one $\mathcal{O}$-border basis for $\mathfrak{a}$. In [4], a criterion was stated for an $\mathcal{O}$-border prebasis to be $\mathcal{O}$-border basis termed as "Buchberger criterion for border bases". The following notion is required for stating that criterion.

DEFINITION 5. *Let $G = \{g_1, \ldots, g_\nu\}$ be an $\mathcal{O}$-border prebasis. Two prebasis polynomials g_k, g_l are neighbors, where $k, l \in \{1, \ldots, \nu\}$, if their border terms are related according to $x_i b_k = x_j b_l$ or $x_i b_k = b_l$ for some indeterminates x_i, x_j. Then, the corresponding S-polynomials are*

$$S(g_k, g_l) = x_i g_k - x_j g_l \text{ and } S(g_k, g_l) = x_i g_k - g_l$$

respectively.

We now state the Buchberger criterion for border bases.

THEOREM 2.1. *An $\mathcal{O}$-border prebasis $G = \{g_1, \ldots, g_\nu\}$ is an $\mathcal{O}$-border basis of an ideal $\mathfrak{a}$ if and only if $G \subset \mathfrak{a}$ and, for each pair of neighboring prebasis polynomials g_k, g_l, there are constant coefficients $c_j \in \mathbb{F}$ such that*

$$S(g_k, g_l) = c_1 g_1 + \cdots + c_\nu g_\nu.$$

The proof for the above theorem can be found in [4].

3. PRELIMINARY OBSERVATIONS

BBD is described as follows:

> Given a set of polynomials $\mathcal{F}$ such that $\mathfrak{a} = \langle \mathcal{F} \rangle$ where $\mathfrak{a}$ is an ideal, decide whether $\mathcal{F}$ is a $\mathcal{O}$-border basis of $\mathfrak{a}$ for some order ideal $\mathcal{O}$.

We first describe the input representation of the polynomials for the BBD instance. We follow the "sparse representation" as in [3] to represent the polynomials in $\mathcal{F}$. Let $\mathbb{F}[x_1, \ldots, x_n]$ be the polynomial ring under consideration and let $\mathcal{F}$ be the set of input polynomials in the BBD instance. Consider a polynomial $f = c_1 X^{\alpha_1} + \cdots + c_s X^{\alpha_s} \in \mathcal{F}$ where $c_i \in \mathbb{F}$, $X^{\alpha_i} = x_1^{\alpha_{1i}} \cdots x_n^{\alpha_{ni}}$ for $i \in \{1, \ldots, s\}$ and $\alpha_i = (\alpha_{1i}, \ldots, \alpha_{ni}) \in \mathbb{Z}_{\geq 0}^n$. f is represented by its non-zero field coefficients $c_1, \ldots, c_k$ and its corresponding non-negative exponent vectors $\alpha_1, \ldots, \alpha_s$.

In this section, we show that BBD is NP-complete. The NP-complete problem we have chosen for our reduction is 3,4-SAT. 3,4-SAT denotes the class of instances of the satisfiability problem with exactly three variables per clause and each variable or its complement appears in no more than four clauses. The 3,4-SAT problem was shown to be NP-complete by Tovey [12].

Let $\mathcal{I}$ be an instance for the 3,4-SAT problem. Let $X_1, \ldots, X_n$ be variables and $C_1, \ldots, C_m$ be clauses in $\mathcal{I}$ such that $\mathcal{I} = C_1 \wedge \cdots \wedge C_m$. Each clause is a disjunction of three literals. For example, $(X_i \vee \overline{X}_j \vee X_k)$ represents a clause for $i, j, k \in \{1, \ldots, n\}$. Assume without loss of generality that X_i appears in at least one clause and so does $\overline{X}_i$. Also assume that X_i and $\overline{X}_i$ do not appear in the same clause for any $i \in \{1, \ldots, n\}$. We construct a BBD instance from this 3,4-SAT instance.

Consider the polynomial ring

$$P = \mathbb{F}[x_1, \ldots, x_n, \overline{x}_1, \ldots, \overline{x}_n, c_1, \ldots, c_m, x_{c_1}, \ldots, x_{c_m}, Y],$$

where $\mathbb{F}$ is a field. We will reduce the 3,4-SAT instance $\mathcal{I}$ to a set of polynomials $\mathcal{F} \subset P$. Note that P is a polynomial ring with $N = 2n + 2m + 1$ indeterminates. Before we describe the reduction, we list some definitions and observations that will be useful for our reduction.

- With respect to all the clauses in which $X_i, \overline{X}_i$ appear for $i \in \{1, \ldots, n\}$, we associate the term $t_{C_{x_i}} = \left(\prod_{j \in S} c_j \right) Y^{\alpha}$ where for each $j \in S \subset \{1, \ldots, m\}$ either X_i or $\overline{X}_i$ appears in C_j and $\alpha = 4 - |S|$. Note that $\deg(t_{C_{x_i}}) = 4$.

- With respect to each $X_i, \overline{X}_i$ for $i \in \{1, \ldots, n\}$, we associate the terms $t_{X_i} = x_i \overline{x}_i^2 t_{C_{x_i}}$, $t_{\overline{X}_i} = x_i^2 \overline{x}_i t_{C_{x_i}}$ respectively. Note that $\deg(t_{X_i}) = \deg(t_{\overline{X}_i}) = 7$.

- We define children of a term t to be

  $\text{ch}(t) = \{t'|$ for some indeterminate y, $t'y = t\}$.

  Note that each term can have at most N children.

- Extending the above definition, we define children of a set of terms S to be $\text{ch}(S) = \bigcup_{t \in S} \text{ch}(t)$. It follows that for two sets of terms A and B, $\text{ch}(A \cup B) = \text{ch}(A) \cup \text{ch}(B)$.

- We define parents of a term t to be

  $\text{pt}(t) = \{t'|$ for some indeterminate y, $ty = t'\}$.

  Note that each term has exactly N parents.

- Extending the above definition, we define parents of a set of terms S to be $\text{pt}(S) = \bigcup_{t \in S} \text{pt}(t)$.

- $K_{X_i} = \left\{ \frac{t_{X_i} x_{c_l}}{c_l} \,\middle|\, X_i \text{ appears in clause } C_l \text{ for some } l \in \{1, \ldots, m\} \right\}$ for $i = 1, \ldots, n$. (*Note:* If t', t are two terms such that $t'x = t$ for some indeterminate x then we represent t' as $\frac{t}{x}$.)

- $K_{\overline{X}_i} = \left\{ \frac{t_{\overline{X}_i} x_{c_l}}{c_l} \,\middle|\, \overline{X}_i \text{ appears in clause } C_l \text{ for some } l \in \{1, \ldots, m\} \right\}$ for $i = 1, \ldots, n$.

- $K_i = K_{X_i} \cup K_{\overline{X}_i} \cup \{t_{X_i}, t_{\overline{X}_i}\}$ for $i = 1, \ldots, n$.

- $P_{X_i} = \left\{ t_{X_i} x_{c_l} \,\middle|\, X_i \text{ appears in clause } C_l \text{ for some } l \in \{1, \ldots, m\} \right\}$ for $i = 1, \ldots, n$.

- $P_{\overline{X}_i} = \left\{ t_{\overline{X}_i} x_{c_l} \,\middle|\, \overline{X}_i \text{ appears in clause } C_l \text{ for some } l \in \{1, \ldots, m\} \right\}$ for $i = 1, \ldots, n$.

- $P_i = P_{X_i} \cup P_{\overline{X}_i}$ for $i = 1, \ldots, n$. The number of clauses where X_i or $\overline{X}_i$ appear is $|P_i|$. Hence, $|P_i| \leq 4$.

- We define $I(t)$ to be the number of indeterminates that divide a term t. Note that $I(t) = |\text{ch}(t)|$.

- The region associated with $X_i, \overline{X_i}$ for $i \in \{1, \ldots, n\}$ is defined as

  $R_i = \text{ch}(P_i) = \text{ch}(P_{X_i}) \cup \text{ch}(P_{\overline{X}_i})$.

In other words R_i consists of all the children of P_i and hence $|R_i| \leq 4N$. For $i, j \in \{1, \ldots, n\}$ and $i \neq j$, since every term in R_i contains either x_i or $\overline{x}_i$ (and does not contain $x_j, \overline{x}_j$) and similarly every term in R_j contains either x_j or $\overline{x}_j$ (and does not contain $x_i, \overline{x}_i$) and hence $R_i \cap R_j = \phi$.

We now state and prove a few observations that will be used for the reduction.

LEMMA 3.1. *Two distinct terms can have no more than one common parent i.e., for two distinct terms t_1, t_2, $|\text{pt}(t_1) \cap \text{pt}(t_2)| \leq 1$.*

PROOF. Consider two terms t_1, t_2 such that $t_1 \neq t_2$. Assume that there exists two distinct terms t, t' such that $t_1, t_2 \in \text{ch}(t)$ and $t_1, t_2 \in \text{ch}(t')$. This implies that there exists indeterminates y_1, y_2, y_1', y_2' such that

$$t_1 y_1 = t, \ t_2 y_2 = t, \ t_1 y_1' = t', \ t_2 y_2' = t'.$$

This implies that $y_2' y_1 = y_1' y_2$. Since, $y_1 \neq y_1'$ and $y_1 \neq y_2$, we get a contradiction. $\square$

COROLLARY 3.2. *For two distinct terms t_1, t_2, $|\text{ch}(t_1) \cap \text{ch}(t_2)| \leq 1$.*

PROOF. This follows from the definition and the previous lemma. $\square$

COROLLARY 3.3. *Let S be a set of terms and t be a term such that $t \notin S$. Then $|\text{ch}(t) \cap \text{ch}(S)| \leq |S|$.*

PROOF. Let $S = \bigcup_{i:a_i \in S} \{a_i\}$. We have

$$\text{ch}(t) \cap \text{ch}(S) = \bigcup_{i:a_i \in S} (\text{ch}(t) \cap \text{ch}(a_i)).$$

But,

$$\left| \bigcup_{i:a_i \in S} (\text{ch}(t) \cap \text{ch}(a_i)) \right| \leq \sum_{i:a_i \in S} |(\text{ch}(t) \cap \text{ch}(a_i))|$$
$$\leq |S| \text{ (from the previous corollary).}$$

Hence, $|\text{ch}(t) \cap \text{ch}(S)| \leq |S|$. $\square$

LEMMA 3.4. *No two terms from two different regions can have a common parent i.e., if there are two terms $t_1 \in R_i$, $t_2 \in R_j$ then there exists no term t_3 such that $t_1, t_2 \in \text{ch}(t_3)$.*

PROOF. Let $t_1 \in R_i$ and $t_2 \in R_j$ for some $i, j \in \{1, \ldots, n\}$. Assume without loss of generality that $t_1 \in \text{ch}(t_{X_i} y)$ (a similar argument holds if $t_1 \in \text{ch}(t_{\overline{X}_i} y)$), where y is an indeterminate such that $t_{X_i} y \in P_{X_i}$. Hence, there exists an indeterminate y' such that $t_1 y' = t_{X_i} y$. Now, if we assume that there exists a term t_3 such that $t_1, t_2 \in \text{ch}(t_3)$ then there exists two indeterminates y_1, y_2 such that,

$$t_3 = t_1 y_1 = t_2 y_2 \Rightarrow t_{X_i} y y_1 = t_2 y_2 y'.$$

But, $x_i \overline{x}_i{}^2 | t_{X_i} \Rightarrow x_i \overline{x}_i{}^2 | t_2 y_2 y' \Rightarrow x_i \overline{x}_i{}^2 | y_2 y'$ (since $x_i, \overline{x}_i$ does not divide any term in R_j) and hence a contradiction. $\square$

LEMMA 3.5. *Let $\mathcal{O}$ be an order ideal. If all the children of a term t are in $\partial \mathcal{O}$ then t cannot be in $\partial \mathcal{O}$ and $\mathcal{O}$ i.e., for a term t such that $\text{ch}(t) \subset \partial \mathcal{O}$ then $t \notin \mathcal{O}, t \notin \partial \mathcal{O}$.*

PROOF. Let t be a term such that $\text{ch}(t) \subset \partial \mathcal{O}$. If $t \in \mathcal{O}$ then $\text{ch}(t) \subset \mathcal{O}$ and hence $t \notin \mathcal{O}$. If $t \in \partial \mathcal{O}$ then there exists some indeterminate y' such that for some term $t' \in \mathcal{O}$, we have $t' y' = t$. But $t' \in \text{ch}(t) \Rightarrow t' \in \partial \mathcal{O}$, a contradiction. Hence, $t \notin \partial \mathcal{O}$. $\square$

LEMMA 3.6. *For a term t such that $t \in \text{ch}(P_i)$ where $i \in \{1, \ldots, n\}$, then $I(t) \geq |P_i| + 2$.*

PROOF. For a term $t' \in P_i$, $I(t') = 3 + I(t_{C_{x_i}})$, but

$$I(t_{C_{x_i}}) = \min(|P_i| + 1, 4).$$

We have $I(t') = \min(|P_i| + 1, 4) + 3$ and thus for $t \in \text{ch}(t')$,

$I(t) \geq \min(|P_i|+1, 4) + 2 = \min(|P_i|+3, 6)$ and since $|P_i| \leq 4$,

$I(t) \geq |P_i| + 2$. $\square$

LEMMA 3.7. *Let t_1, t_2 be terms such that $t_1 t = t_2$ where t is a term and $t \neq 1$. If x is an indeterminate such that x divides t then $t_1 \big| \frac{t_2}{x}$.*

PROOF. Since x divides t, x also divides t_2 and hence $\frac{t_2}{x}, \frac{t}{x}$ are valid terms. We have, $t_1 \left(\frac{t}{x} \right) = \frac{t_2}{x}$. Thus, $t_1 \big| \frac{t_2}{x}$. $\square$

In other words, the above lemma states that if a term t_1 divides t_2 and $t_1 \neq t_2$, then there exists a child of t_2, say t_3 such that t_1 divides t_3.

4. BBD IS IN NP

In this section we prove that BBD belongs to the NP complexity class. To prove that, we ask the following question: When is a set of terms a border with respect to an order ideal? It turns out that if the terms in B obey some conditions then there exists an order ideal such that B is it's border.

Let $B \subset \mathbb{T}^N$ be a finite set of terms. Let B' be a subset of B such that every term t in B' obeys the following conditions:
(C1) For indeterminates y, x such that $x|t$ and $y \neq x$, at least one of $ty, \frac{ty}{x}, \frac{t}{x}$ is in B.
(C2) There exists an indeterminate x such that $x|t$ and $\frac{t}{x} \notin B$.
(C3) Let t', t'' be terms such that $t'|t'', t''|t$ and t'' is a parent of t'. If $t' \in B$ then t'' is in B.
If $B = B'$ then we say that "B satisfies the three conditions" else we say that "B does not satisfy the three conditions". We will later prove that the three conditions mentioned before are sufficient and necessary for the existence of an order ideal such that B is it's border. Before that we state an equivalent formulation of third condition.
For a term t in B consider the following set:

$$S_t = \left\{ t'' \in \mathbb{T}^N \;\middle|\; t''|t \text{ and } \exists \text{ a term } t' \in B \text{ such that } t'|t'' \right\}$$

LEMMA 4.1. *All the terms in B obey the third condition if and only if $S_t \subset B$ for all $t \in B$.*

PROOF. If for all $t \in B$, $S_t \subset B$ then B satisfies the third condition.

Assume all terms in B obey (C3). Let t be a term in B and let S'_t be the subset of S_t such that it contains all the terms in S_t and not in B. If $S'_t = \emptyset$ then $S_t \subset B$. Hence assume that $S'_t \neq \emptyset$. Let t'' be a term in S'_t such that no term in S'_t divides t''. Since $t'' \in S_t$, there exists a term t_1 such that $t_1|t''$ and $t_1 \in B$. From lemma 3.7, $t_1|t'$ where $t' \in \text{ch}(t'')$. Since $t_1|t', t'|t$ and $t_1 \in B$, we have $t' \in S_t$. By the choice of t'', $t' \in S'_t$ which means $t' \in B$. We have a situation where there are three terms t, t', t'' such that *(i)* $t'|t'', t''|t$, *(ii)* $t, t' \in B$, $t'' \notin B$ and *(iii)* $t'' \in \text{pt}(t')$. But this contradicts the fact that all the terms in B satisfy the condition (C3). $\square$

From the above lemma, for a term $t \in B$ the (C3) condition can be rephrased as follows:
(C3') For terms t', t'' such that $t' \in B$, $t'|t''$ and $t''|t$ then t'' is in B.

We now give the necessary and sufficient conditions for B to be the border of an order ideal $\mathcal{O}$.

THEOREM 4.2. *There exists an order ideal $\mathcal{O}$ such that $\partial \mathcal{O} = B$ if and only if B satisfies all the conditions.*

PROOF. Let $\mathcal{O}$ be an order ideal such that B is it's border *i.e.* $B = \partial \mathcal{O}$. Assume that B does not satisfy the three conditions which means there exists a term $t \in B$ which does not obey all the three conditions. Consider the following cases:
Case (i) Suppose t does not obey (C1). There exists indeterminates x, y such that $x|t, y \neq x$ and $t_1 = ty \notin B, t_2 = \frac{ty}{x} \notin B, t_3 = \frac{t}{x} \notin B$. Since $t \in \partial \mathcal{O}$, t_3 is in $\mathcal{O}$ which implies that $t_3 y = t_2 \in \mathcal{O}$ since $t_2 \notin \partial \mathcal{O}$. Similarly, $t_2 x = t_1 \in \mathcal{O}$. But $\mathcal{O}$ is an order ideal and since $t|t_1$, t should be in $\mathcal{O}$ and hence a contradiction.
Case (ii) Suppose t does not obey (C2). Then $\text{ch}(t) \subset B = \partial \mathcal{O}$. From lemma 3.5, $t \notin \partial \mathcal{O}$ which is a contradiction.
Case (iii) Suppose t does not obey (C3). There exists two terms t', t'' such that $t' \in B, t'' \in \mathcal{O}$ and $t'|t'', t''|t, t'' \in \text{pt}(t')$. Since $\mathcal{O}$ is an order ideal, $t'' \in \mathcal{O}$ implies that $t' \in \mathcal{O}$, a contradiction.
Hence B has to satisfy the three conditions for it to be the border of the order ideal $\mathcal{O}$.

Assume that B satisfies all the three conditions. Now, consider the following set:

$$\mathcal{O} = \left\{ t \in \mathbb{T}^N \;\middle|\; \exists t' \in B \text{ such that } t|t' \text{ and } t \notin B \right\}$$

Claim. $\mathcal{O}$ is an order ideal.
Proof. Consider a term $t \in \mathcal{O}$. Let t' be a term such that $t'|t$. By the construction of $\mathcal{O}$, there exists a term $t'' \in B$ such that $t|t''$ and this implies that $t'|t''$. Now, if t' was in B then from lemma 4.1, t'' would violate the third condition and hence $t' \notin B$. Hence, $t' \in \mathcal{O}$.

Claim. $B = \partial \mathcal{O}$.
Proof. We will first show that $B \subset \partial \mathcal{O}$. Consider a term $t \in B$ and from the second condition there exists a term $t' \notin B$ such that $t = t'x$ for some indeterminate x. This implies that $t' \in \mathcal{O}$ and hence, $t'x = t \in \partial \mathcal{O}$ since $t \notin \mathcal{O}$. It remains to show that $\partial \mathcal{O} \subset B$. Let $t_1 \in \partial \mathcal{O}$ and hence there exists a term $t \in \mathcal{O}$ such that $tx = t_1 \in \partial \mathcal{O}$ for an indeterminate x. From the construction of $\mathcal{O}$, t divides at least one term in B. Let $t_2 \in B$ such that $t|t_2$ and if there is a term t' such that $t|t'$ and $t'|t_2$ then $t' \in \mathcal{O}$. Since $t|t_2$, from Lemma 3.7 there exists a child of t_2 such that t divides that term. Let x_1 be an indeterminate such that $x_1|t_2$ and $t \big| \frac{t_2}{x_1}$. Consider the following two cases:
Case (i) $x_1 = x$: In this case $t_1|t_2$ and hence $t_1 \in B$ since $t_1 \notin \mathcal{O}$.
Case (ii) $x_1 \neq x$: From the first condition, one of $t_2 x, \frac{t_2 x}{x_1}, \frac{t_2}{x_1}$ has to be in B. Assume that $\frac{t_2}{x_1} \in B$. We have a term $t_2'' = \frac{t_2}{x_1}$ such that $t|t_2'', t_2''|t_2$ and $t_2'' \in B$ which contradicts the choice of t_2. Hence $\frac{t_2}{x_1} \notin B$ which means $\frac{t_2 x}{x_1}$ or $t_2 x$ is in B. Now $t \big| \left(\frac{t_2}{x_1} \right)$ and hence $tx \big| \left(\frac{t_2 x}{x_1} \right)$, $tx \big| t_2 x$ which implies that $tx = t_1$ divides a term in B. This further implies that $t_1 \in \mathcal{O}$ or $t_1 \in B$. Since $t_1 \in \partial \mathcal{O}, t_1 \notin \mathcal{O}$ and thus $t_1 \in B$. $\square$

Let B be a set of terms and let m be the size of binary representation of B. For a term $t \in B$ and a fixed pair of indeterminates (y, x), we can search whether $\frac{ty}{x}, \frac{t}{x}, ty$ are in B in $O(m)^{\dagger}$ time. And since there are $|B| (\leq m)$ terms and

---
†Big-O notation

N^2 pairs of indeterminates (N is the number of indeterminates), condition 1 can be checked in $\mathrm{O}(m^2 N^2)$ time.

For every term t, at most N children are possible. In $\mathrm{O}(Nm)$ time it can be checked whether all the children of the term t are in B or not. Since there are $|B|$ terms, condition 2 can be checked in $\mathrm{O}(Nm^2)$ time.

Every term has exactly N parents. For terms $t', t' \in B$ fixed such that $t'|t$, it takes $\mathrm{O}(Nm)$ time to check whether all the parents of t' dividing t are in B. Since there are $|B|^2$ such terms possible, condition 3 can be checked in $\mathrm{O}(Nm^3)$ time.

Hence, it can be checked in time polynomial in N and m (binary size of B) whether B is the border of some order ideal.

Let B be the border of some order ideal $\mathcal{O}$ i.e. $B = \partial\mathcal{O}$ and let $\mathcal{F}$ be a set of polynomials such that the support of each polynomial in $\mathcal{F}$ contains exactly one term from B and $|B| = |\mathcal{F}|$. We state a lemma that will be helpful in checking whether $\mathcal{F}$ is a $\mathcal{O}$-border prebasis.

LEMMA 4.3. $\mathcal{F}$ is a $\mathcal{O}$-border prebasis if and only if every term in $\mathrm{Supp}(\mathcal{F}\backslash B)$ divides a term in B.

PROOF. Let $\mathcal{F}$ be a $\mathcal{O}$-border prebasis. Then $B' = \mathrm{Supp}(\mathcal{F}\backslash B) \subset \mathcal{O}$. Let $t \in B'$ i.e., $t \in \mathcal{O}$. For an indeterminate x, consider the sequence of terms $t, tx, tx^2, \dots$. Not all the terms in the sequence can be in $\mathcal{O}$ since $\mathcal{O}$ is a finite set of terms. Let i be the least number such that $tx^i \notin \mathcal{O}$ and hence $tx^i \in \partial\mathcal{O}$. Thus, t divides a term in $\partial\mathcal{O}$.

Let t be a term in B' such that t divides a term $t' \in B$. As mentioned before, $\overline{\partial\mathcal{O}}$ is an order ideal and hence $t \in \overline{\partial\mathcal{O}}$. Since, $t \notin \partial\mathcal{O}$, t has to be in $\mathcal{O}$. Thus, $B' \subset \mathcal{O}$. Hence, $|B| = |\mathcal{F}|$ and support of each polynomial in $\mathcal{F}$ contains exactly one term in B and the rest of the terms are in $\mathcal{O}$. Thus, $\mathcal{F}$ is a $\mathcal{O}$-border prebasis. $\square$

We now give the proof that BBD is in NP.

THEOREM 4.4. BBD is in NP.

PROOF. Let $\mathcal{F}$ be a set of input polynomials to the BBD instance such that $\mathfrak{a} = \langle \mathcal{F} \rangle$. Assume that a set $B = \mathrm{Supp}(\mathcal{F})$ containing exactly one term from each polynomial in $\mathcal{F}$ and $|B| = |\mathcal{F}|$, is given as a "YES" certificate[‡] for $\mathcal{F}$ such that $B = \partial\mathcal{O}$ for some order ideal $\mathcal{O}$ and $\mathcal{F}$ is a $\mathcal{O}$-border basis. Let the binary size of representation of $\mathcal{F}, B$ be denoted by $m_{\mathcal{F}}, m_B$ respectively. This certificate can be verified in polynomial time as follows:

We have seen that it can be verified in time polynomial in m_B and N whether B is the border of some order ideal $\mathcal{O}$. In order to check whether $\mathcal{F}$ is a $\mathcal{O}$-border prebasis, from the previous claim we need to check whether each term in $\mathrm{Supp}(\mathcal{F})\backslash B$ divides a term in B. This can be implemented in $\mathrm{O}(m_{\mathcal{F}} m_B)$ time. And in time polynomial in $m_{\mathcal{F}}$, it can be verified whether $\mathcal{F}$ satisfies the Buchberger criterion. Since a "YES" certificate for the BBD instance can be verified in polynomial time, BBD is in NP. $\square$

We now give a polynomial time reduction from 3,4-SAT to BBD.

5. REDUCTION

We are now going to construct a set of polynomials $\mathcal{F}$ as follows:

- With respect to variable X_i for $i \in \{1, \dots, n\}$, associate a polynomial

$$t_{X_i} + t_{\overline{X}_i}.$$

We shall refer to such polynomials as v-**polynomials** (variable polynomials)

$$F_v = \{t_{X_i} + t_{\overline{X}_i} \mid i = 1, \dots, n\}.$$

i.e F_v is a set of v-polynomials.

- With respect to each clause C_l in $\mathcal{I}$ for $l \in \{1, \dots, m\}$, we associate a polynomial. Without loss of generality assume that $C_l = (X_i \vee \overline{X}_j \vee X_k)$, for $i, j, k \in \{1, \dots, n\}$. The polynomial associated with C_l is

$$\frac{t_{X_i} x_{c_l}}{c_l} + \frac{t_{\overline{X}_j} x_{c_l}}{c_l} + \frac{t_{X_k} x_{c_l}}{c_l}.$$

We will refer to the above set of polynomials as c-**polynomials** (clause polynomials).

$$F_c = \left\{ \frac{t_{X_i} x_{c_l}}{c_l} + \frac{t_{X_j} x_{c_l}}{c_l} + \frac{t_{X_k} x_{c_l}}{c_l} \;\middle|\; \right.$$
$$\left. C_l = (X_i \vee X_j \vee X_k) \text{ is a clause in } \mathcal{I} \right\}$$

- The third set of polynomials are those that contain just one term in their support:

$$F_1 = \{t \mid \deg(t) = 8\}, \quad F_2 = \bigcup_{i=1}^{n}(R_i \backslash K_i), \quad \mathcal{F}' = F_1 \cup F_2.$$

We refer to the set of polynomials in $\mathcal{F}'$ as t-**polynomials** (polynomials containing just one term).

From the above set of polynomials, we construct the system of polynomials $\mathcal{F}$ which is an instance to the BBD problem:

$$\mathcal{F} = F_v \cup F_c \cup \mathcal{F}'.$$

Note that all the terms in $\mathrm{Supp}(\mathcal{F})$ have total degree either 7 or 8. Also, for any two polynomials $f, g \in \mathcal{F}$ we have $\mathrm{Supp}(f) \cap \mathrm{Supp}(g) = \emptyset$.

The construction of each polynomial in F_c, F_v can be done in time polynomial in n, m. So F_c, F_v can be constructed in time polynomial in n and m since $|F_c| = m$ and $|F_v| = n$. F_1, F_2 can be computed in time polynomial in $|F_1|$ and $|F_2|$. Also $|F_2|$ is bounded above by $\sum_{i=1}^{n}|R_i|$ ($\leq \sum_{i=1}^{n} 4N \leq 4nN$) and $|F_1| \leq \binom{N+8}{8} \in \mathrm{O}(N^8)$. Hence F_1, F_2 can be constructed in time polynomial in N. Since F_c, F_v, F_1 and F_2 can be constructed in time polynomial in N, the reduction can be performed in polynomial time.

We state a theorem that will be helpful for proving the correctness of reduction in the next section.

THEOREM 5.1. *Let $\mathcal{F}$ be a $\mathcal{O}$-border basis. If X_i appears in C_l for $i \in \{1,\ldots,n\}$, $l \in \{1,\ldots,m\}$ then both t_{X_i} and $\frac{t_{X_i}x_{c_l}}{c_l}$ cannot be in $\partial\mathcal{O}$. Similarly if $\overline{X}_i$ appears in C_l for $i \in \{1,\ldots,n\}$, $l \in \{1,\ldots,m\}$, then both $t_{\overline{X}_i}$ and $\frac{t_{\overline{X}_i}x_{c_l}}{c_l}$ cannot be in $\partial\mathcal{O}$.*

PROOF. Assume that X_i appears in C_l. We have

$$\mathrm{ch}(t_{X_i}x_{c_l}) \cap \mathrm{Supp}(F_c \cup F_v) = \left\{ t_{X_i}, \frac{t_{X_i}x_{c_l}}{c_l} \right\} \text{ and}$$

$$\mathrm{ch}(t_{X_i}x_{c_l}) \backslash \left\{ t_{X_i}, \frac{t_{X_i}x_{c_l}}{c_l} \right\} \subset F_2 \ .$$

Since F_2 contains t-polynomials, every term in the support of F_2 has to be in $\partial\mathcal{O}$ and similarly all the terms in F_1 has to be in $\partial\mathcal{O}$. Hence,

$$t_{X_i}x_{c_l} \in \partial\mathcal{O}, \ \mathrm{ch}(t_{X_i}x_{c_l}) \backslash \left\{ t_{X_i}, \frac{t_{X_i}x_{c_l}}{c_l} \right\} \subset \partial\mathcal{O} \ .$$

Now, both $t_{X_i}, \frac{t_{X_i}x_{c_l}}{c_l}$ cannot be in $\partial\mathcal{O}$ without contradicting the Lemma 3.5. Similarly, it can be argued that if $\overline{X}_i$ appears in C_l then both $t_{\overline{X}_i}$ and $\frac{t_{\overline{X}_i}x_{c_l}}{c_l}$ cannot be in $\partial\mathcal{O}$. $\square$

We now prove the correctness of polynomial time reduction.

THEOREM 5.2. *3,4-SAT instance $\mathcal{I}$ is satisfiable if and only if $\mathcal{F}$ is a $\mathcal{O}$-border basis with respect to some order ideal $\mathcal{O}$.*

PROOF. Suppose $\mathcal{F}$ is an $\mathcal{O}$-border basis of $\mathfrak{a}$ with respect to order ideal $\mathcal{O}$, we will construct an assignment to $\mathcal{I}$ and show that it is a satisfying assignment.
The truth values to variables in instance $\mathcal{I}$ are assigned as follows. Consider the polynomial $t_{X_i} + t_{\overline{X}_i} \in F_v$ for $i \in \{1,\ldots,n\}$. Exactly one among the terms $t_{X_i}, t_{\overline{X}_i}$ has to be in $\mathcal{O}$ and the other term in $\partial\mathcal{O}$. If t_{X_i} is in $\mathcal{O}$, then assign true value to variable X_i and if $t_{\overline{X}_i}$ is in $\mathcal{O}$, then assign false value to X_i.

Claim. The above assignment is a satisfiable assignment to $\mathcal{I}$.
Proof. Assume that the above assignment is not a satisfiable assignment then there exists a clause C_l for $l \in \{1,\ldots,m\}$ such that C_l is not satisfied. Without loss of generality let C_l be of the form $(X_i \vee \overline{X}_j \vee X_k)$, where $i,j,k \in \{1,\ldots,n\}$. Since C_l is not satisfied, all of $t_{X_i}, t_{\overline{X}_j}, t_{X_k}$ are in $\partial\mathcal{O}$. From Corollary 5.1, this implies that $\frac{t_{X_i}x_{c_l}}{c_l}, \frac{t_{\overline{X}_j}x_{c_l}}{c_l}, \frac{t_{X_k}x_{c_l}}{c_l} \in \mathcal{O}$. Consider the polynomial

$$f = \frac{t_{X_i}x_{c_l}}{c_l} + \frac{t_{\overline{X}_j}x_{c_l}}{c_l} + \frac{t_{X_k}x_{c_l}}{c_l} \in F_c \ .$$

All the terms in the support of f are in $\mathcal{O}$. But this is not possible since $\mathcal{F}$ is a border basis and f should contain exactly one term in $\partial\mathcal{O}$, a contradiction.

Suppose that $\mathcal{I}$ is satisfiable. Let A be a satisfying assignment to instance $\mathcal{I}$. Using A, we will construct an order ideal $\mathcal{O}$ such that $\mathcal{F}$ is a $\mathcal{O}$-border basis. For that we first construct sets $\mathcal{O}$ and T and prove the following statements.
i) $\mathcal{O}$ is an order ideal,

ii) T is the border of the order ideal $\mathcal{O}$ i.e. $T = \partial\mathcal{O}$,
iii) $\mathcal{F}$ is a $\mathcal{O}$-border prebasis and
iv) $\mathcal{F}$ is a $\mathcal{O}$-border basis.

We construct the set T as follows.
1) For $i \in \{1,\ldots,n\}$, if X_i is assigned to be false in assignment A then include t_{X_i} in T. If X_i is assigned to be true then include $t_{\overline{X}_i}$ in T
2) Let C_l be a clause in instance $\mathcal{I}$ for $l \in \{1,\ldots,m\}$. Assume that $C_l = (X_i \vee \overline{X}_j \vee X_k)$ for $i,j,k \in \{1,\ldots,n\}$. Associated to this clause, we have the polynomial

$$f = \frac{t_{X_i}x_{c_l}}{c_l} + \frac{t_{\overline{X}_j}x_{c_l}}{c_l} + \frac{t_{X_k}x_{c_l}}{c_l} \in \mathcal{F} \ .$$

If one term among $t_{X_i}, t_{\overline{X}_j}, t_{X_k}$, say t_{X_i}, is not in T (if there are more than one term among $t_{X_i}, t_{\overline{X}_j}, t_{X_k}$ not in T then pick one term arbitrarily) then include $\frac{t_{X_i}x_{c_l}}{c_l}$ in T. Thus, in the support of every clause polynomial no more than one term is included in T.
3) Include all the terms in the support of $F_1 \cup F_2$ to be in T.

Claim. Let $\mathcal{O} = \mathbb{T}^N_{\leq 8} \backslash T$. $\mathcal{O}$ is an order ideal.
Proof. All the terms of total degree 8 are in T (by construction). Thus, $\mathcal{O}$ contains terms of total degree 7 or less. If $t \in \mathcal{O}$ and $t'|t$ then $\deg(t') < \deg(t) \leq 7$ which implies that $\deg(t') < 7$. But since $T \subset \mathrm{Supp}(\mathcal{F})$ and $\mathrm{Supp}(\mathcal{F})$ contains no term of total degree less than 7, all the terms of total degree 6 or less are in $\mathcal{O}$. Therefore, $t' \in \mathcal{O}$.

Claim. T is the border of the order ideal $\mathcal{O}$ i.e. $T = \partial\mathcal{O}$.
Proof. Let $t' \in \partial\mathcal{O}$. There exists a term $t \in \mathcal{O}$ and an indeterminate y such that $t' = ty$. Since all the terms in $\mathcal{O}$ have total degree 7 or less, we have $\deg(t) \leq 7$ which implies that $t' = ty \in \mathbb{T}^N_{\leq 8}$. By our construction of $\mathcal{O}$, this means that $t' \in T$. This proves that $\partial\mathcal{O} \subset T$.
  In order to show $T \subset \partial\mathcal{O}$, it is enough to show that for a term $t \in T$, there exists an indeterminate y such that $y|t$ and $\frac{t}{y} = t' \notin T$ i.e. $t' \in \mathcal{O}$. Now, since all the terms of total degree 6 or less are in $\mathcal{O}$, all the terms of total degree 7 in T are also in $\partial\mathcal{O}$. So, assume that there exists a term t such that $\deg(t) = 8$ and $\mathrm{ch}(t) \subset T$. We prove by contradiction that such a term cannot exist. Since all the terms of total degree 7 in T are in $\cup^n_{i=1}R_i$, $\mathrm{ch}(t) \subset \cup^n_{i=1}R_i$. From Lemma 3.4, $\mathrm{ch}(t)$ should be a subset of R_i for some $i \in \{1,\ldots,n\}$. There are two cases for t as described below.
(i) $t \in P_i$: Assume without loss of generality, $t = t_{X_i}x_{c_l} \in P_{X_i}$ for $i \in \{1,\ldots,n\}, l \in \{1,\ldots,m\}$. By our construction, both t_{X_i} and $\frac{t_{X_i}x_{c_l}}{c_l}$ cannot be in T. Hence at least one child of t is in $\mathcal{O}$ and thus not all terms in $\mathrm{ch}(t)$ is contained in T. So, this case is not possible.
(ii) $t \notin P_i$: From Corollary 3.3, we have

$$\begin{aligned} |\mathrm{ch}(t) \cap R_i| &= |\mathrm{ch}(t)| \leq |(P_{X_i} \cup P_{X_i})| \\ &\Rightarrow |\mathrm{ch}(t)| \leq |P_i| \\ &\Rightarrow I(t) \leq |P_i|. \end{aligned}$$

Now, for any term $t' \in \mathrm{ch}(t)$ we have $I(t') \leq |P_i|$. But from Lemma 3.6, $I(t'') \geq |P_i| + 2$ for any term $t'' \in \mathrm{ch}(P_i) = R_i$. Thus this case is not possible.
From the above two cases we get a contradiction that there exists a term t such that $\mathrm{ch}(t) \subset R_i$ for some $i \in \{1,\ldots,n\}$

and thus $\operatorname{ch}(t) \nsubseteq T$. So, t has at least one child in $\mathcal{O}$. Thus, $T \subset \partial \mathcal{O}$.

Claim. $\mathcal{F}$ is a $\mathcal{O}$-border prebasis.
Proof. In order to show $\mathcal{F}$ is a $\mathcal{O}$-border prebasis, we have to show that each polynomial in $\mathcal{F}$ has exactly one term in $\partial \mathcal{O}$ and the rest of the terms in $\mathcal{O}$. We show this for all the polynomials in $\mathcal{F}$:

- t-polynomials: From our construction, all the terms in the t-polynomials are in T *i.e.* in $\partial \mathcal{O}$ and hence each polynomial has exactly one term in $\partial \mathcal{O}$.

- v-polynomials: Again by our construction, each v-polynomial has exactly one term in T *i.e.* $\partial \mathcal{O}$ and the other term in $\mathcal{O}$.

- c-polynomials: Consider a clause C_l for $l \in \{1, \ldots, m\}$. Assume that $C_l = (X_i \vee \overline{X}_j \vee X_k)$ where $i, j, k \in \{1, \ldots, n\}$ in the instance $\mathcal{I}$. Let f be the polynomial associated with the clause C_l:

$$f = \frac{t_{X_i} x_{c_l}}{c_l} + \frac{t_{\overline{X}_j} x_{c_l}}{c_l} + \frac{t_{X_k} x_{c_l}}{c_l} \in \mathcal{F}.$$

Since all the terms in the support of f have total degree 7, the terms must either be in $\partial \mathcal{O}$ or $\mathcal{O}$. Consider the following cases:
Case (i): More than one term in f is in $\partial \mathcal{O}$: this cannot happen from our construction.
Case (ii): All the terms are in $\mathcal{O}$: This can happen only if all of $t_{X_i}, t_{\overline{X}_j}, t_{X_k}$ are in $\partial \mathcal{O}$ which implies that $X_i, \overline{X}_j, X_k$ are false in assignment A. So, C_l is false. But this is not possible since assignment A satisfies instance $\mathcal{I}$. Hence this case is not possible.
From the above two cases, we deduce that exactly one term in the support of f belongs to $\partial \mathcal{O}$ and from our construction, rest of the terms in f must belong to $\mathcal{O}$.

Since any polynomial in $\mathcal{F}$ must be either a t-polynomial, c-polynomial or v-polynomial, from the above argument we deduce that $\mathcal{F}$ is a $\mathcal{O}$-border prebasis.

Claim. $\mathcal{F}$ is a $\mathcal{O}$-border basis of $\mathfrak{a}$.
Proof. Since $\mathcal{F}$ is a $\mathcal{O}$-border prebasis, if $\mathcal{F}$ satisfies Buchberger criterion for border basis then $\mathcal{F}$ is a $\mathcal{O}$-border basis. Thus we need to show that for any two neighbouring polynomials $f, g \in \mathcal{F}$, $S(f, g)$ can be written as a linear combination of polynomials in $\mathcal{F}$. Before we consider the following cases for f and g we note that any polynomial containing only terms of total degree 8 in it's support can be expressed as a sum of t-polynomials in $F_1 \subset \mathcal{F}$. Thus, in order to prove that $\mathcal{F}$ satisfies Buchberger criterion it is enough to show that the support of $S(f, g)$ contains only terms of total degree 8. Neighbouring polynomials f, g can be of the following cases,
Case (i): f and g are t-polynomials: then $S(f, g) = 0$.
Case (ii): f is a t-polynomial and g is a c-polynomial or a v-polynomial: All the terms in $\operatorname{Supp}(g)$ have total degree 7. Hence for any indeterminate y, all the terms in $\operatorname{Supp}(yg)$ are of total degree 8. If $f \in F_2$, then yf for any indeterminate y is also a t-polynomial of total degree 8. The S-polynomial of f and g can be

$$S(f, g) = f - y_1 g$$

or

$$S(f, g) = y_2 f - y_1 g,$$

for some indeterminates y_1, y_2. In the first case, f has to be in F_1 (if f were to be in F_2, by the way we have written the S-polynomial the border term of total degree 7 in f is equal to $y_1 b$ of total degree 8 where b is the border term in g which is not possible) and hence support of $S(f, g)$ contains only terms of total degree 8. The second case can happen only if $f \in F_2$ and hence support of $S(f, g)$ contains only terms of total degree 8.
Case (iii): f and g are not t-polynomials: S-polynomial of f and g is of the form,

$$S(f, g) = y_1 f - y_2 g,$$

for some indeterminates y_1, y_2. As argued before, all the terms in the support of $y_1 f$ and $y_2 g$ are of total degree 8. Hence, all the terms in the support of $S(f, g)$ contains only terms of total degree 8. From the three cases it follows that $\mathcal{F}$ is a $\mathcal{O}$-border basis of $\mathfrak{a}$. $\square$

Thus, we have proved that I has a satisfying assignment if and only if $\mathcal{F}$ is a $\mathcal{O}$-border basis of $\mathfrak{a} = \langle \mathcal{F} \rangle$ for some order ideal $\mathcal{O}$. There is a polynomial time reduction from 3,4-SAT instance to BBD instance and since 3,4-SAT is NP-complete, we have the result that BBD is NP-complete. We give an example to illustrate the reduction.

Example
Let us consider an instance $\mathcal{I}$ to the 3,4-SAT problem as follows.

$$(X_1 \vee X_2 \vee X_3) \wedge (X_1 \vee \overline{X}_3 \vee X_4) \wedge (\overline{X}_2 \vee X_3 \vee X_4) \wedge$$

$$\wedge (\overline{X}_1 \vee X_2 \vee X_4) \wedge (X_1 \vee X_3 \vee \overline{X}_5).$$

where $X_1, \ldots, X_5$ are the variables. Let $C_1, \ldots, C_5$ be the clauses as they appear in the formula.
The polynomial time reduction procedure transforms the above instance to the following set of polynomials as an input to the BBD problem:

$$f_1 = x_1 \overline{x}_1^2 c_1 c_2 c_4 c_5 + x_1^2 \overline{x}_1 c_1 c_2 c_4 c_5$$

$$f_2 = x_2 \overline{x}_2^2 c_1 c_3 c_4 Y + x_2^2 \overline{x}_2 c_1 c_3 c_4 Y$$

$$f_3 = x_3 \overline{x}_3^2 c_1 c_2 c_3 c_5 + x_3^2 \overline{x}_3 c_1 c_2 c_3 c_5$$

$$f_4 = x_4 \overline{x}_4^2 c_2 c_3 c_4 Y + x_4^2 \overline{x}_4 c_2 c_3 c_4 Y$$

$$f_5 = x_5 \overline{x}_5^2 c_5 Y^3 + x_5^2 \overline{x}_5 c_5 Y^3$$

$$g_1 = x_1 \overline{x}_1^2 x_{c_1} c_2 c_4 c_5 + x_2 \overline{x}_2^2 x_{c_1} c_3 c_4 Y + x_3 \overline{x}_3^2 x_{c_1} c_2 c_3 c_5$$

$$g_2 = x_1 \overline{x}_1^2 c_1 x_{c_2} c_4 c_5 + x_3^2 \overline{x}_3 c_1 x_{c_2} c_3 c_5 + x_4 \overline{x}_4^2 x_{c_2} c_3 c_4 Y$$

$$g_3 = x_2^2 \overline{x}_2 c_1 x_{c_3} c_4 Y + x_3 \overline{x}_3^2 c_1 c_2 x_{c_3} c_5 + x_4 \overline{x}_4^2 c_2 x_{c_3} c_4 Y$$

$$g_4 = x_1^2 \overline{x}_1 c_1 c_2 x_{c_4} c_5 + x_2 \overline{x}_2^2 c_1 c_3 x_{c_4} Y + x_4 \overline{x}_4^2 c_2 c_3 x_{c_4} Y$$

$$g_5 = x_1 \overline{x}_1^2 c_1 c_2 c_4 x_{c_5} + x_3 \overline{x}_3^2 c_1 c_2 c_3 x_{c_5} + x_5^2 \overline{x}_5 x_{c_5} Y^3$$

$$\mathcal{F} = \{f_1, \ldots, f_5, g_1, \ldots, g_5\}$$

We now show the following: If I has a satisfying assignment then an order ideal $\mathcal{O}$ can be found such that $\mathcal{F}$ is a $\mathcal{O}$-border basis. Conversely if $\mathcal{F}$ is a border basis with respect to some order ideal $\mathcal{O}$, we show a satisfying assignment to the instance $\mathcal{I}$.

(1) Consider the following assignment of truth values to the variables.

$$X_1 = \text{true}, X_2 = \text{false}, X_3 = \text{false}, X_4 = \text{true}, X_5 = \text{false}$$

It can be checked that with respect to this assignment the instance $\mathcal{I}$ is satisfied. We show that $\mathcal{F}$ is a border basis with respect to some order ideal. For that we first construct T. Choose all the terms in the support of $\mathcal{F}_1 \cup \mathcal{F}_2$ to be in T. Corresponding to the satisfying assignment we choose the following set of terms from $f_1, \ldots, f_5$ to be in T.

$$\{ x_1{}^2 \overline{x}_1 c_1 c_2 c_4 c_5, \ x_2 \overline{x}_2{}^2 c_1 c_3 c_4 y, \ x_3 \overline{x}_3{}^2 c_1 c_2 c_3 c_5,$$

$$x_4{}^2 \overline{x}_4 c_2 c_3 c_4 y, \ x_5 \overline{x}_5{}^2 c_5 y^3 \}$$

From each of $g_1, \ldots, g_5$, a term has to be chosen to be in T such that not all children of a term are in T. We first consider g_1. The term $x_2 \overline{x}_2{}^2 c_1 c_3 c_4 Y$ cannot included in T because all the children of $x_2 \overline{x}_2{}^2 x_{c_1} c_1 c_3 c_4 Y$ would be in T. But this will not be a problem if we include $x_1 \overline{x}_1{}^2 x_{c_1} c_2 c_4 c_5$ in T. Similarly the following set of terms from g_2, g_3, g_4, g_5 can be included in T.

$$\{ x_4 \overline{x}_4{}^2 x_{c_2} c_3 c_4 Y, \ x_2 \overline{x}_2 c_1 x_{c_3} c_4 Y, \ x_4 \overline{x}_4{}^2 c_2 c_3 x_{c_4} Y, \ x_5{}^2 \overline{x}_5 x_{c_5} Y^3 \}$$

Let $\mathcal{O} = \mathbb{T}^{21}_{\leq 8} \backslash T$. The construction of T and the proof of Theorem 5.2 guarantees that $\mathcal{O}$ is an order ideal and $\mathcal{F}$ is a $\mathcal{O}$-border basis.

(2) Let T be a set such that

$$T = F_1 \cup F_2 \cup \{ x_1 \overline{x}_1{}^2 c_1 c_2 c_4 c_5, \ x_2{}^2 \overline{x}_2 c_1 c_3 c_4 Y,$$

$$x_3{}^2 \overline{x}_3 c_1 c_2 c_3 c_5, \ , \ x_4{}^2 \overline{x}_4 c_2 c_3 c_4 Y, \ x_5 \overline{x}_5{}^2 c_5 Y^3, \ x_2 \overline{x}_2{}^2 x_{c_1} c_3 c_4 Y,$$

$$x_4 \overline{x}_4{}^2 x_{c_2} c_3 c_4 Y, \ x_3 \overline{x}_3{}^2 c_1 c_2 x_{c_3} c_5, \ x_1{}^2 \overline{x}_1 c_1 c_2 x_{c_4} c_5, \ x_5{}^2 \overline{x}_5 x_{c_5} Y^3 \}$$

where F_1 and F_2 are the terms are as defined in 5. Let $\mathcal{O} = \mathbb{T}^{21}_{\leq 8} \backslash T$. It can be verified that $\mathcal{O}$ is an order ideal and $\mathcal{F}$ is a $\mathcal{O}$-border basis. We now construct a satisfying assignment for $\mathcal{I}$ as follows. Since, $x_1 \overline{x}_1{}^2 c_1 c_2 c_4 c_5 \in T$ and hence does not belong to $\mathcal{O}$, we assign X_1 to be false. Similarly, X_2, X_3, X_4 are assigned true and X_5 are assigned false. It can be observed this assignment satisfies the formula.

6. CONCLUDING REMARKS

In this paper, we introduced the border basis detection (BBD) problem on the lines of Gröbner basis detection (GBD). Sturmfels and Wiegelmann proved GBD to be NP-hard by showing the NP-completeness of Structural Gröbner basis detection (SGBD), a variant of GBD. We show BBD to be NP-complete by a reduction from 3,4-SAT.

7. ACKNOWLEDGEMENTS

Authors would like to thank Vikram M. Tankasali and Prashanth Puranik for their useful comments and suggestions on this work.

8. REFERENCES

[1] W. Auzinger and H. J. Stetter. An elimination algorithm for the computation of all zeros of a system of multivariate polynomial equations. In *Numerical mathematics, Singapore 1988*, volume 86 of *Internat. Schriftenreihe Numer. Math.*, pages 11–30. Birkhäuser, Basel, 1988.

[2] G. Braun and S. Pokutta. Border bases and order ideals: a polyhedral characterization. *arXiv:0912.1502v2*, 2010.

[3] P. Gritzmann and B. Sturmfels. Minkowski addition of polytopes: computational complexity and applications to grobner bases. *SIAM J. Discret. Math.*, 6(2):246–269, 1993.

[4] A. Kehrein and M. Kreuzer. Characterizations of border bases. *Journal of Pure and Applied Algebra*, 196:251–270, April 2005.

[5] A. Kehrein and M. Kreuzer. Computing border bases. *Journal of Pure and Applied Algebra*, 205:279–295, May 2006.

[6] A. Kehrein, M. Kreuzer, and L. Robbiano. An algebraist's view on border bases. In *Solving Polynomial Equations*, volume 14 of *Algorithms and Computation in Mathematics*, pages 169–202. Springer Berlin Heidelberg, December 2005.

[7] M. Kreuzer and L. Robbiano. *Computational Commutative Algebra 2*. Springer-Verlag, Heidelberg, 2005.

[8] B. Mourrain. A new criterion for normal form algorithms. In *Lecture Notes In Computer Science; Vol. 1719*, pages 430 – 443. Springer-Verlag, London,UK, 1999.

[9] B. Mourrain and Ph. Trébuchet. Generalized normal forms and polynomial system solving. In *Proceedings of the 2005 international symposium on Symbolic and algebraic computation*, ISSAC '05, pages 253–260, New York, NY, USA, 2005. ACM.

[10] B. Mourrain and Ph. Trébuchet. Stable normal forms for polynomial system solving. *Theor. Comput. Sci.*, 409:229–240, December 2008.

[11] B. Sturmfels and M. Wiegelmann. Structural Gröbner basis detection. *Appl. Algebra Eng. Commun. Comput.*, 8(4):257–263, 1997.

[12] C.A. Tovey. A simplified NP-complete satisfiability problem. *Discrete Applied Mathematics*, 8(1):85–89, 1984.

Formal First Integrals Along Solutions of Differential Systems I

Ainhoa Aparicio-Monforte[*]
Research Institute for Symbolic Computation
Johannes Kepler University
Altenberger Straße 69
A-4040 Linz, Austria
aparicio@risc.uni-linz.ac.at

Moulay Barkatou
XLIM (DMI),
Université de Limoges
123 avenue Albert Thomas
87060 Limoges Cedex, France
moulay.barkatou@unilim.fr

Sergi Simon
Department of Mathematics
University of Portsmouth
Lion Gate Bldg, Lion Terrace
Portsmouth PO1 3HF, UK
sergi.simon@port.ac.uk

Jacques-Arthur Weil
XLIM (DMI),
Université de Limoges
123 avenue Albert Thomas
87060 Limoges Cedex, France
weil@unilim.fr

ABSTRACT

We consider an analytic vector field $\dot{x} = X(x)$ and study, via a variational approach, whether it may possess analytic first integrals. We assume one solution Γ is known and we study the successive variational equations along Γ. Constructions in [MRRS07] show that Taylor expansion coefficients of first integrals appear as rational solutions of the dual linearized variational equations. We show that they also satisfy linear "filter" conditions. Using this, we adapt the algorithms from [Bar99, vHW97] to design new ones optimized to this effect and demonstrate their use. Part of this work stems from the first author's Ph.D. thesis[1] [AM10].

Categories and Subject Descriptors

I.1.2 [**Algorithms**]: Algebraic Algorithms; J.2 [**Physical Sciences and Engineering**]: Mathematics and statistics, Physics, Astronomy

General Terms

Theory, algorithms

Keywords

Computer Algebra, Integrability, First Integrals, Linear Differential Systems, Rational Solutions, Differential Galois

[*]supported both by a FEDER doctoral grant of Région Limousin and by the Austrian FWF grant Y464-N18
[1]   https://sites.google.com/site/ainhoaaparicio/home/recherche/publications-pre-prints

1. INTRODUCTION

Consider an analytic differential vector field

$$\dot{x} = X(x). \tag{1}$$

Let us recall that a *first integral* of (1) is a complex-valued function F defined on a domain $U \subset \mathbb{C}^n$ such that

$$D_X F = 0 \quad \text{where} \quad D_X := \sum_{i=1}^{n} X_i \frac{\partial}{\partial x_i}.$$

This is equivalent to F being constant along every solution of system (1).

The existence of first integrals (meromorphic, rational, polynomial...) is relevant to the study of the integrability of complex analytic vector fields. Since the direct computation of first integrals is in general an open problem, only indirect techniques are available. Among those, the approach we suggest here is variational: assuming one solution of (1) is known, we consider the variational equations along it. Whenever the solution is an equilibrium point, a wide battery of normal form theories is available for us to characterize the behavior of (1) along the solution. No such local tools exist, though, to characterize *formal* first integrals along a *non-equilibrium* solution ϕ.

The aim of our paper is to start filling this gap by means of an algorithmic answer to the following question. Assume the vector field (1) has a first integral which is holomorphic, at least, along a solution ϕ: how would we compute, or recover, its Taylor expansion along ϕ? We first recall that the coefficients of such an expansion are rational solutions of linear differential systems (namely, the *linearized variational equations* LVE_ϕ^m). We prove they are also solutions of linear (algebraic) systems: the filter equations (see Section 3.1). We then adapt the algorithms of [Bar99, vHW97] to design an efficient algorithm for computing such Taylor expansions of (unknown) holomorphic first integrals.

We wish to thank J. J Morales-Ruiz and J.-P. Ramis for fruitful discussions during the preparation of this paper.

2. BACKGROUND

2.1 Taylor Expansions

The *modulus* $|i|$ of a multi-index $i = (i_1, \ldots, i_n) \in \mathbb{N}^n$ is defined as the sum of its entries. Multi-index addition is defined $(i_1, \ldots, i_n) + (j_1 \ldots j_n) := (i_1 + j_1, \ldots, i_n + j_n)$. We use the *standard lexicographic order*, denoted by $<_{\text{lex}}$, where $(i_1, \ldots, i_n) <_{\text{lex}} (j_1, \ldots, j_n)$ means $i_1 = j_1, \ldots, i_{k-1} = j_{k-1}$ and $i_k < j_k$ for some $k \geq 1$.

DEFINITION 1. *Let $F : U \subset \mathbb{C}^n \to \mathbb{C}$ be a complex analytic function over the open set U. We define the* lexicographically sifted differential *of F of order m as the row vector*

$$F^{(m)}(x) := \text{lex}\left(\frac{\partial^m F}{\partial x_1^{i_1} \ldots \partial x_n^{i_n}} \right)_{i_1 + \ldots + i_n = m},$$

where entries are ordered as per $<_{\text{lex}}$ on multi-indices.

Let $F : U \subset \mathbb{C}^n \to \mathbb{C}$ be a holomorphic function and let $\phi : I \subset \mathbb{C} \to U$ be a parametrization of a Riemann surface $\Gamma \subset U$. Then F admits a Taylor expansion along ϕ, $F(\phi + y) = F(\phi) +$

$$\sum_{m=1}^{\infty} \frac{1}{m!} \sum_{i_1 + \ldots + i_n = m} \binom{m}{i_1, \ldots, i_n} \frac{\partial^m F}{\partial x_1^{i_1} \ldots \partial x_n^{i_n}}(\phi) y_1^{i_1} \ldots y_n^{i_n}$$

where y is a vector of n formal variables. Using symmetric powers of vectors (see [AM10], Chapter 2), a compact form is

LEMMA 2. *The Taylor expansion of F along ϕ is*

$$F(\phi + y) = F(\phi) + \sum_{m=1}^{\infty} \frac{1}{m!} \left\langle F^{(m)}(\phi), \text{Sym}^m y \right\rangle$$

PROOF. By construction ([AM10, Ch. 2]), the entry corresponding to multi-index $(i_1, \ldots, i_n)$ in $\text{Sym}^m y$ is exactly $\binom{m}{i_1, \ldots, i_n} y_1^{i_1} \ldots y_n^{i_n}$. Vectors $F^{(m)}(\phi)$ and $\text{Sym}^m y$ have the same dimension

$$d_{m,n} := \binom{n + m - 1}{m}$$

□

2.2 Variational equations (VE_ϕ^m)

The subject matter of this section is described in [MR99, MRRS07, AM10]. Denote by $\Phi(t, z)$ the flow of (1), $(t, z) \in \mathbb{C} \times U$. Consider the Taylor expansion of $\Phi(t, z)$ with respect to the phase variables z at the point (t, x)

$$\Phi(t, z) = \Phi(t, x) + \Phi^{(1)}(t)(z - x) + \ldots + \Phi^{(m)}(t)(z - x)^m + \ldots$$

where $\Phi^{(m)}(t) := \frac{1}{m!} \frac{\partial^m}{\partial x^m} \Phi(t, x)$. Let Γ denote an integral curve of (1) parametrized by $\phi(t)$.

DEFINITION 3. *The* order-m variational equations *of (1) along an integral curve Γ are the differential system satisfied by $(\Phi^{(1)}(t), \ldots, \Phi^{(m)}(t))$ when $x \in \Gamma$.*

All variational systems are non-linear except for the first-order one, $m = 1$, which we express as $\dot{\xi}_1 = A_1 \xi_1$ where

$$A_1 := \left[\frac{\partial X_i}{\partial x_j}(\phi) \right]_{i,j} \in \text{Mat}(n, \boldsymbol{k}),$$

with $\boldsymbol{k} := \mathbb{C}\langle \phi \rangle = \mathbb{C}\left(\phi, \dot{\phi}, \ldots \right)$. By means of tensor constructions, a linear differential system (LVE_ϕ^m) equivalent to (VE_ϕ^m) can be built for each $m \in \mathbb{N}$: we call it m^{th} *order linearized variational equation* along ϕ.

We denote (LVE_ϕ^m), $m \geq 2$ by $\dot{Y}_m = A_m Y_m$, where

$$A_m := \begin{bmatrix} \mathfrak{sym}^m A_1 & 0 \\ B_m & A_{m-1} \end{bmatrix} \in \text{Mat}\left(\sum_{i=1}^m d_{i,n}, \boldsymbol{k} \right). \quad (2)$$

and $\mathfrak{sym}^m$ stands for the mth *symmetric power in the sense of Lie algebras*, implicitly defined for any given linear system $\dot{Y} = AY$, and any fundamental matrix U thereof, by

$$\frac{d}{dt}\left(\text{Sym}^m U \right) = \left(\mathfrak{sym}^m A \right)\left(\text{Sym}^m U \right),$$

$\text{Sym}^m U$ standing for the mth *symmetric power in the sense of Lie groups* of U. For a precise account on symmetric powers see [AM10, Ch. 2], or [FH91].

2.3 First integrals

2.3.1 Junior forms

Let ϕ be a non-constant solution of (1) and F be a first integral. We henceforth normalize F by assuming $F(\phi) = 0$. Following [Aud01], we define the *valuation* of F along ϕ as the integer $\nu \geq 1$ satisfying

$$F(\phi) = 0, \ldots, F^{(\nu-1)}(\phi) = 0 \quad \text{and} \quad F^{(\nu)}(\phi) \neq 0.$$

The *junior form of F* along ϕ is then defined as

$$F^\circ(y) := \frac{1}{\nu!} \left\langle F^{(\nu)}(\phi), \text{Sym}^\nu y \right\rangle;$$

$F^\circ(\phi)$ is the lowest-degree homogeneous polynomial in the Taylor expansion of F, i.e

$$F(y + \phi) = F^\circ(y) + \sum_{i=\nu+1}^{\infty} \frac{1}{i!} \left\langle F^{(i)}(\phi), \text{Sym}^i y \right\rangle$$

DEFINITION 4. *A first integral F of (1) of valuation ν along ϕ is said to be* non-degenerate *along ϕ if $\nu = 1$ (i.e. $F^\circ(y)$ is linear) and* degenerate of order ν *along ϕ if $\nu \geq 2$.*

The following Lemmae deal with classical facts about the valuation of first integrals and junior forms.

LEMMA 5. *[Aud01] Let F_1 and F_2 be first integrals of (1) vanishing along ϕ and having valuations ν_1 and ν_2 respectively along ϕ. We then have*

$$(F_1 F_2)^\circ(y) = F_1^\circ(y) \cdot F_2^\circ(y)$$

and the valuation of $F_1 \cdot F_2$ along ϕ is $\nu_1 + \nu_2$.

The following result (see Chapter 2 of [AM10] for symmetric products of vectors) will be useful in the sequel:

LEMMA 6. *Let ϕ be a non-constant solution of (1) and let $F_1, \ldots, F_k$ be holomorphic first integrals of (1), non-degenerate and vanishing along ϕ. Then,*

1. $(F_1 \cdot F_2)^{(2)}(\phi) = (F_1^{(1)}(\phi) \, \text{Ⓢ} \, F_2^{(1)}(\phi))$,

2. $(F_1^m)^{(m)}(\phi) = \text{Sym}^m(F_1^{(1)}(\phi))$,

3. $(F_1^{m_1} \cdot \ldots \cdot F_k^{m_k})^{(m_1 + \ldots + m_k)}(\phi) = (\text{Sym}^{m_1}(F_1^{(1)}(\phi)) \, \text{Ⓢ} \, \ldots \, \text{Ⓢ} \, \text{Sym}^{m_k}(F_k^{(1)}(\phi)))$

PROOF. 1. Since F_1 and F_2 are non-degenerate, their product $F_1 \cdot F_2$ is a first integral of valuation 2 along ϕ. Now $\frac{\partial^2 (F_1 \cdot F_2)}{\partial x_{i_1} \partial x_{i_2}}(\phi)$ is equal to:

$$\frac{\partial^2 F_1}{\partial x_{i_1} \partial x_{i_2}}(\phi) \cdot F_2(\phi) + \frac{\partial F_1}{\partial x_{i_1}}(\phi) \cdot \frac{\partial F_2}{\partial x_{i_2}}(\phi) +$$

$$\frac{\partial F_1}{\partial x_{i_2}}(\phi) \cdot \frac{\partial F_2}{\partial x_{i_1}}(\phi) + \frac{\partial^2 F_2}{\partial x_{i_1} \partial x_{i_2}}(\phi) \cdot F_1(\phi).$$

Since $F_1(\phi) = F_2(\phi) = 0$, for every $i_1, i_2 = 1, \ldots, n$ we have $\left((F_1 \cdot F_2)^{(2)}(\phi) \right)_{(i_1, i_2)}$ equal to

$$C_{i_1, i_2} = \frac{\partial F_1}{\partial x_{i_1}}(\phi) \cdot \frac{\partial F_2}{\partial x_{i_2}}(\phi) + \frac{\partial F_1}{\partial x_{i_2}}(\phi) \cdot \frac{\partial F_2}{\partial x_{i_1}}(\phi).$$

Computing $(F_1^{(1)}(\phi) \, \text{\textcircled{S}} \, F_2^{(1)}(\phi))$ in the canonical base $\{e_i\}$ yields exactly

$$\left(F_1^{(1)}(\phi) \, \text{\textcircled{S}} \, F_2^{(1)}(\phi) \right)_{(i_1, i_2)} = \sum_{1 \leq i_1 \leq i_2 \leq n} C_{i_1, i_2} e_{i_1} \cdot e_{i_2},$$

hence $(F_1 \cdot F_2)^{(2)}(\phi) = F_1^{(1)}(\phi) \, \text{\textcircled{S}} \, F_2^{(1)}(\phi)$.

2. Since F_1 is non-degenerate along ϕ, F_1^m has valuation m, hence all its partial derivatives of order less than m vanish at ϕ. Thus, the entry in $(F_1^m)^{(m)}(\phi)$ corresponding to any modulus-m multi-index of exponent $(m_1, \ldots, m_n)$ is

$$\frac{\partial^m (F_1^m)}{\partial x_1^{m_1} \ldots \partial x_n^{m_n}}(\phi) = \binom{m}{m_1, \ldots, m_n} \prod_{j=1}^{n} \left(\frac{\partial F}{\partial x_j}(\phi) \right)^{m_j},$$

equal to the entry in $\text{Sym}^m (F_1^{(1)}(\phi))$ corresponding to the same modulus-m exponents multi-index.

3. Follows from the two previous items.

$\square$

2.3.2 Holomorphic first integrals and (LVE_ϕ^m)

Let $\boldsymbol{k} := \mathbb{C} \langle \phi \rangle$ denote our base field; if X is rational, the fact $\dot{\phi} = X(\phi)$ implies $\boldsymbol{k} = \mathbb{C}(\phi)$. Let A_m be the matrix of the order-m variational equations of (1), as written in (2).

The *dual (or adjoint)* m^{th} *order variational equation along* ϕ, denoted by $\left(\text{LVE}_\phi^m \right)^\star$, is defined by $\dot{V} = A_m^\star V$ with

$$A_m^\star := -{}^t A_m \in \text{Mat}\left(\sum_{i=1}^m d_{i,n}, \boldsymbol{k} \right).$$

LEMMA 7. *If F is a holomorphic first integral of (1) and ϕ is a non-constant solution of (1) then*

$$V_m := {}^t (F^{(m)}(\phi), \ldots, F^{(1)}(\phi)) \in \boldsymbol{k}^{\sum_{i=1}^m d_{i,n}}$$

is a (rational) solution of $\left(\text{LVE}_\phi^m \right)^\star$.

PROOF. This is a direct consequence of proof in reference [MRRS07, pp. 859 – 862] which, though originally written in the context of Hamiltonian systems, is still valid for general complex analytic differential systems $\dot{x} = X(x)$. $\square$

We denote the set of rational solutions of $\left(\text{LVE}_\phi^m \right)^\star$ by

$$\text{Sol}_{\boldsymbol{k}}\left(\left(\text{LVE}_\phi^m \right)^\star \right) := \{ W \in \boldsymbol{k}^{\sum_{i=1}^m d_{i,n}} : \dot{W} = A_m^\star W \}.$$

An immediate consequence of Lemma 7 is the following:

COROLLARY 8. *Let F be a holomorphic first integral of (1) with valuation ν along a non-constant solution ϕ, then $F^{(\nu)}(\phi) \in \text{Sol}_{\boldsymbol{k}}((\text{sym}^\nu A_1)^\star)$.*

PROOF. Since F has valuation ν along ϕ, by Lemma 7, we have $V_\nu = (F^{(\nu)}(\phi), 0) \in \text{Sol}_{\boldsymbol{k}}([A_\nu^\star])$. More explicitly, we have that

$$\left[\begin{array}{c} \frac{d}{dt}({}^t F^{(\nu)}(\phi)) \\ 0 \end{array} \right] = \left[\begin{array}{cc} (\text{sym}^\nu A_1)^\star & B_\nu^\star \\ 0 & A_{\nu-1}^\star \end{array} \right] \cdot \left[\begin{array}{c} {}^t F^{(\nu)}(\phi) \\ 0 \end{array} \right]$$

which implies that $\frac{d}{dt}({}^t F^{(\nu)}(\phi)) = (\text{sym}^\nu A_1)^\star \cdot {}^t F^{(\nu)}(\phi)$. $\square$

EXAMPLE 9. *Consider the toy example of the anharmonic oscillator [Aud01]: it is modeled by a two-degree-of-freedom Hamiltonian*

$$H(q, p) = \frac{1}{2}(p_1^2 + p_2^2) + \lambda q_2^2 + (q_1^2 + q_2^2)^2$$

with $(q, p) = (q_1, q_2, p_1, p_2) \in \mathbb{C}^4$, and the Hamiltonian field X_H is given by the equations:

$$\dot{q} = p, \quad \dot{p}_1 = -4q_1 (q_1^2 + q_2^2), \quad \dot{p}_2 = -2q_2 (2\lambda + q_1^2 + q_2^2)$$

This system is integrable, an additional first integral being

$$K = \frac{1}{2} p_1^2 + \frac{1}{2}(q_1 p_2 - q_2 p_1)^2 + q_1^2 (q_1^2 + q_2^2),$$

and has a particular solution $\psi(t) = \left(\frac{\text{i}\sqrt{2}}{2t}, 0, -\frac{\text{i}\sqrt{2}}{2t^2}, 0 \right)$ for which $H(\psi) \equiv 0$. The second-order Taylor expansion of H along ψ is therefore given by:

$$H(\psi + y) = \left(-\frac{\text{i}\sqrt{2}}{t^3} y_1 - \frac{\text{i}\sqrt{2}}{2t^2} y_3 \right) + \qquad (3)$$
$$\left(-\frac{3y_1^2}{t^2} + \frac{(\lambda t^2 - 1) y_2^2}{t^2} + \frac{y_3^2}{2} + \frac{y_4^2}{2} \right) + \text{O}(y^3).$$

which is the same as writing

$$H^{(1)}(\psi) = \left(-\frac{\text{i}\sqrt{2}}{t^3}, 0, -\frac{\text{i}\sqrt{2}}{2t^2}, 0 \right) \quad and$$

$$H^{(2)}(\psi) = \left(-\frac{6}{t^2}, 0, 0, 0, \frac{2(-1 + \lambda t^2)}{t^2}, 0, 0, 1, 0, 1 \right)$$

Given the formal vector of variables $y := (y_1, y_2, y_3, y_4)$ its symmetric square $\text{Sym}^2 y$ is easy to compute:

$${}^t [y_1^2, 2y_1 y_2, 2y_1 y_3, 2y_1 y_4, y_2^2, 2y_2 y_3, 2y_2 y_4, y_3^2, 2y_3 y_4, y_4^2].$$

It is easily checked that we can rewrite (3) as

$$H(\psi + y) = \langle H^{(1)}(\psi), y \rangle + \frac{1}{2} \langle H^{(2)}(\psi), \text{Sym}^2 y \rangle + \text{O}(y^3).$$

Along any solution $\phi = (q_1, q_2, p_1, p_2)$, the matrices for VE_ϕ^1 and LVE_ϕ^2 are, respectively,

$$A_1 = \left[\begin{array}{cccc} 0 & 0 & 1 & 0 \\ 0 & 0 & 0 & 1 \\ a & d & 0 & 0 \\ d & c & 0 & 0 \end{array} \right],$$

and $A_2 := \begin{bmatrix} \mathfrak{sym}^2 A_1 & 0_{10\times 4} \\ X^{(2)}(\psi) & A_1 \end{bmatrix}$, *explicitly written as*

$$\begin{bmatrix}
0 & 0 & 1 & 0 & 0 & 0 & 0 & 0 & 0 & 0 & 0 & 0 & 0 & 0 \\
0 & 0 & 0 & 1 & 0 & 1 & 0 & 0 & 0 & 0 & 0 & 0 & 0 & 0 \\
2a & d & 0 & 0 & 0 & 0 & 0 & 2 & 0 & 0 & 0 & 0 & 0 & 0 \\
2d & c & 0 & 0 & 0 & 0 & 0 & 1 & 0 & 0 & 0 & 0 & 0 & 0 \\
0 & 0 & 0 & 0 & 0 & 1 & 0 & 0 & 0 & 0 & 0 & 0 & 0 & 0 \\
0 & a & 0 & 0 & 2d & 0 & 0 & 1 & 0 & 0 & 0 & 0 & 0 & 0 \\
0 & d & 0 & 0 & 2c & 0 & 0 & 0 & 2 & 0 & 0 & 0 & 0 & 0 \\
0 & 0 & a & 0 & 0 & d & 0 & 0 & 0 & 0 & 0 & 0 & 0 & 0 \\
0 & 0 & d & a & 0 & c & d & 0 & 0 & 0 & 0 & 0 & 0 & 0 \\
0 & 0 & 0 & d & 0 & 0 & c & 0 & 0 & 0 & 0 & 0 & 0 & 0 \\
0 & 0 & 0 & 0 & 0 & 0 & 0 & 0 & 0 & 0 & 0 & 1 & 0 & 0 \\
0 & 0 & 0 & 0 & 0 & 0 & 0 & 0 & 0 & 0 & 0 & 0 & 1 & 0 \\
-24q_1 & -8q_2 & 0 & 0 & -8q_1 & 0 & 0 & 0 & 0 & 0 & a & d & 0 & 0 \\
-8q_2 & -8q_1 & 0 & 0 & -24q_2 & 0 & 0 & 0 & 0 & 0 & d & c & 0 & 0
\end{bmatrix},$$

where $a = -8q_1^2 - 4\left(q_1^2 + q_2^2\right)$, $b = -8q_2^2 - 4\left(q_1^2 + q_2^2\right)$, $c = -2\lambda + b$ *and* $d = -8q_1q_2$.

$$\begin{aligned}
K^\circ(y) &= \frac{1}{2}\langle K^{(2)}(\psi), \mathrm{Sym}^2 y\rangle \qquad (4)\\
&= \left(\frac{(2t-1)^2}{4t^4}y_2^2 + \frac{1}{2t^3}y_2y_4 + \frac{1}{4}\frac{(1+2t^2)}{t^2}y_4^2\right)
\end{aligned}$$

and $K^{(2)}(\psi) \in \mathrm{Sol}_{\boldsymbol{k}}((\mathfrak{sym}^2 A_1)^\star)$ *is equal to*

$${}^t\left(0,0,0,0,0,\frac{(2t-1)^2}{4t^4},0,\frac{1}{2t^3},0,0,14\frac{(1+2t^2)}{t^2}\right).$$

3. ADMISSIBLE SOLUTIONS OF $(\mathrm{LVE}_\phi^M)^\star$

3.1 A filter condition

We prove the existence of an additional set of linear conditions linking the entries of $(F^{(m)}(\phi),\ldots,F^{(1)}(\phi))$ if F is a first integral of (1).

Let us begin with a very simple case. If F is a holomorphic first integral then its Taylor expansion along ϕ reads as

$$\hat{F}(y) = \left\langle F^{(1)}(\phi), y\right\rangle + \frac{1}{2}\left\langle F^{(2)}(\phi), \mathrm{Sym}^2 y\right\rangle + \ldots$$

and ${}^t F^{(1)}(\phi)$ is a rational solution of $(\mathrm{VE}_\phi^1)^\star$; but it satisfies a (non-differential) linear condition as well. Indeed, F being a first integral is equivalent to $\frac{d}{dt}F(\phi(t)) = 0$ for any solution ϕ of (1). Developing the expression we obtain

$$\frac{d}{dt}F(\phi(t)) = \sum_{i=1}^n \frac{\partial F}{\partial x_i}(\phi(t))\,\dot{\phi}_i(t) = \left\langle {}^t\dot{\phi}, {}^t F^{(1)}(\phi)\right\rangle.$$

Thus, among the $V \in \mathrm{Sol}_{\boldsymbol{k}}((\mathrm{VE}_\phi^m)^\star)$ only those satisfying the condition $\left\langle {}^t\dot{\phi}, V\right\rangle = 0$ may be admissible as possible gradients of some holomorphic first integral along ϕ.

DEFINITION 10. *Let ϕ be a non-constant solution of (1), $\boldsymbol{k} := \mathbb{C}\langle\phi\rangle = \mathbb{C}\left(\phi,\dot{\phi},\ldots\right)$, V be a $\boldsymbol{k}$-vector space of finite dimension n, (e_i) be a basis of V and $\dot{\phi} = \left(\dot{\phi}_1,\ldots,\dot{\phi}_n\right)$ denote the expression $\dot{\phi} = \sum_{i=1}^n \dot{\phi}_i \cdot e_i$. Let $(f_{m,j})_{j=1\ldots d_{m,n}}$ be the corresponding canonical basis of $\mathrm{Sym}^m(V)$.*

1. *We define $M_1 := {}^t\dot{\phi}$.*

2. *We define $M_m \in \mathrm{Mat}\left(d_{m-1,n} \times d_{m,n}, \mathbb{C}\left(\dot{\phi}\right)\right)$ as the matrix whose j^{th} row is the symmetric product of $\dot{\phi}$ with the jth basis vector $f_{m-1,j}$: $\dot{\phi}\textcircled{S}f_{m-1,j}$.*

3. *We define the matrices*

$$\mathcal{M}_m \in \mathrm{Mat}\left(\sum_{i=0}^{m-1} d_{i,n} \times \sum_{i=1}^m d_{i,n}, \boldsymbol{k}\right)$$

inductively as follows:

$$\mathcal{M}_1 := M_1, \quad \mathcal{M}_2 = \begin{bmatrix} M_2 & {}^t A_1 \\ 0 & M_1 \end{bmatrix},$$

and

$$\mathcal{M}_m := \left[\begin{array}{c|c|c} M_m & {}^t(\mathfrak{sym}^{m-1}A_1) & {}^t B_{m-1} \\ \hline 0 & \multicolumn{2}{c}{\mathcal{M}_{m-1}} \end{array}\right]$$

where $B_{m-1} \in \mathrm{Mat}\left(d_{m-1,n} \times \sum_{i=1}^{m-1} d_{i,n}, \boldsymbol{k}\right)$ is the sub-diagonal block of the matrix of the order-$m-1$ variational equation of (1),

$$A_{m-1} = \begin{bmatrix} \mathfrak{sym}^m A_1 & 0 \\ B_{m-1} & A_{m-1} \end{bmatrix}.$$

EXAMPLE 11. *This provides an explicit construction of M_m, e.g. $M_1 = \begin{bmatrix} \dot{\phi}_1 & \dot{\phi}_2 & \dot{\phi}_3 & \dot{\phi}_4 \end{bmatrix}$ and*

$$M_2 = \begin{bmatrix}
\dot{\phi}_1 & \dot{\phi}_2 & \dot{\phi}_3 & \dot{\phi}_4 & 0 & 0 & 0 & 0 & 0 & 0 \\
0 & \dot{\phi}_1 & 0 & 0 & \dot{\phi}_2 & \dot{\phi}_3 & \dot{\phi}_4 & 0 & 0 & 0 \\
0 & 0 & \dot{\phi}_1 & 0 & 0 & \dot{\phi}_2 & 0 & \dot{\phi}_3 & \dot{\phi}_4 & 0 \\
0 & 0 & 0 & \dot{\phi}_1 & 0 & 0 & \dot{\phi}_2 & 0 & \dot{\phi}_3 & \dot{\phi}_4
\end{bmatrix}.$$

This has been successfully implemented in Maple for any order m.

The following Theorem characterizes the jets of derivatives of holomorphic first integrals.

THEOREM 12. *Let F be a holomorphic first integral and ϕ be a non-constant solution of (1), then for each $m \geq 1$:*

1. *The above matrices M_m and $\mathcal{M}_m$ have full rank.*

2. *$F^{(m)}(\phi)$ and $F^{(m-1)}(\phi)$ are linked by*

$$M_m \cdot {}^t F^{(m)}(\phi) = \frac{d}{dt}\left({}^t F^{(m-1)}(\phi)\right). \qquad (5)$$

3. *$V_m := {}^t\left(F^{(m)}(\phi),\ldots,F^{(1)}(\phi)\right)$ satisfies*

$$\mathcal{M}_m \cdot V_m = 0$$

PROOF. 1. $\dot{\phi} \neq 0$ by hypothesis. Let $(f_{j,m-1})$ be the basis of $\mathrm{Sym}^{m-1}V$ as in Definition 10. Vectors

$$\left\{(f_{j,m-1}\textcircled{S}\dot{\phi}) \in \mathrm{Sym}^m V\right\}$$

are linearly independent. Thus, the rows of M_m are linearly independent, implying M_m has full rank. Differentiating $F^{(m-1)} \in \mathrm{Sym}^{m-1}V$ yields, on the basis element corresponding to multi-index j,

$$\begin{aligned}
({}^t F^{(m-1)}(\phi))_j &= \sum_{i=1}^n \frac{\partial^m F}{\partial x_1^{j_1}\cdots\partial x_i^{j_i+1}\cdots\partial x_n^{j_n}}(\phi)\cdot\dot{\phi}_i \\
&= \left\langle\dot{\phi}\textcircled{S}f_{j,m-1}, {}^t F^{(m)}(\phi)\right\rangle.
\end{aligned}$$

But $\dot{\phi}\textcircled{S}f_{j,m-1}$ corresponds to the exact expression of row j in matrix M_m, which proves (5).

2. All M_m being full-rank, $\mathcal{M}_m$ is, too, by construction. Let $v_i := F^{(i)}(\phi)$ and $V_m := (v_m,\ldots,v_1)$.

At order 1 the result is already proved. For $m = 2$ the previous item implies $M_2 \cdot v_2 = \dot{v}_1 = A_1^\star \cdot v_1$, since F is a first integral. Therefore, we have

$$M_2 \cdot v_2 + {}^t A_1^\star \cdot v_1 = \mathcal{M}_2 \cdot V_2 = 0.$$

22

Assume $\mathcal{M}_{m-1} \cdot V_{m-1} = 0$ and let us prove it true for m as well. Since F is a first integral we have

$$M_m \cdot v_m = \dot{v}_{m-1} = (\mathfrak{sym}^{m-1} A_1)^\star \cdot v_{m-1} + B_{m-1}^\star \cdot V_{m-2},$$

which implies $[M_m, {}^t\mathfrak{sym}^{m-1} A_1, {}^t B_{m-1}] \cdot V_m = 0$. Since $\mathcal{M}_{m-1} \cdot V_{m-1} = 0$, the result follows.

$\square$

COROLLARY 13. *For $m \in \mathbb{N}$ in the usual notations:*

1. $\dim_{\boldsymbol{k}} (\ker (\mathcal{M}_m)) = d_{m,n} - 1$.

2. $\dim_{\boldsymbol{k}} (\ker (M_m)) = d_{m,n-1}$.

PROOF.   1. By Theorem 12 $\mathcal{M}_m$ has full rank, whence

$$\dim_{\boldsymbol{k}} (\ker (\mathcal{M}_m)) = \sum_{i=1}^{m} d_{i,n} - \sum_{i=0}^{m-1} d_{i,n} = d_{m,n} - 1.$$

2. Again in virtue of the same Theorem, M_m is full-rank, implying $\dim_{\boldsymbol{k}} (\ker (M_m)) = d_{m,n} - d_{m-1,n} = d_{m,n-1}$.

$\square$

In virtue of Theorem 12, given a holomorphic first integral F and a non-constant solution ϕ of (1), the jet of derivatives V_m along ϕ satisfies $V_m \in \mathrm{Sol}_{\boldsymbol{k}} \left((\mathrm{LVE}_\phi^m)^\star \right) \cap \ker(\mathcal{M}_m)$ for every $m \geq 1$. This motivates the following:

DEFINITION 14. *The set of admissible solutions of the system $(\mathrm{LVE}_\phi^m)^\star$ is defined as*

$$\mathrm{Sol}_{\mathrm{adm}} \left((\mathrm{LVE}_\phi^m)^\star \right) := \mathrm{Sol}_{\boldsymbol{k}} \left((\mathrm{LVE}_\phi^m)^\star \right) \cap \ker(\mathcal{M}_m), \quad m \geq 1.$$

EXAMPLE 15. *Let us illustrate Theorem 12 by showing how these filters work. As in Example 9 we consider the anharmonic oscillator $H = \frac{1}{2}(p_1^2 + p_1^2) + \lambda \cdot q_2^2 + (q_1^2 + q_2^2)^2$ as well as, once again, the solution $\psi(t) = \left(\frac{i\sqrt{2}}{2t}, 0, -\frac{i\sqrt{2}}{2t^2}, 0 \right)$, and define the base differential field $\boldsymbol{k} := \mathbb{C}\left(\psi, \dot{\psi} \right) = \mathbb{C}(t)$. Recall that $H(\psi) = 0$.*

$(\mathrm{VE}_\psi^1)^\star$:   *We apply our algorithm from the next Section and compute the rational solutions of $(\mathrm{VE}_\psi^1)^\star$ belonging to $\boldsymbol{k}^4$ and obtain $\mathrm{Sol}_{\boldsymbol{k}} \left(\mathrm{LVE}_\psi^1 \right)^\star$ equal to*

$$\left\{ {}^t\left(-3c_1 t^2 - c_2 \frac{2}{t^3}, 0, c_1 t^3 + c_2 \frac{1}{t^2}, 0 \right) : (c_1, c_2) \in \mathbb{C}^2 \right\},$$

having dimension 2. Let $V_1 \in \mathrm{Sol}_{\boldsymbol{k}}((\mathrm{VE}_\psi^1)^\star)$ be any such vector. Applying filter condition $\mathcal{M}_1 \cdot V_1 = 0$ yields $V_1 = {}^t(-c_2 \frac{2}{t^3}, 0, c_2 \frac{1}{t^2}, 0)$ which is proportional to $H^{(1)}(\psi)$. Thus, $\mathrm{Sol}_{\mathrm{adm}}(\mathrm{VE}_\psi^1)^\star = \mathrm{span}_{\mathbb{C}}(H^{(1)}(\psi))$; this proves that H is the only holomorphic first integral which is not degenerate along ψ.

$(\mathrm{LVE}_\psi^2)^\star$:   *Since $H(\psi) = 0$, H^2 has valuation 2 along ψ. We know there is another first integral degenerate of order 2 along ψ,*

$$K = \frac{1}{2} p_1^2 + \frac{1}{2}(q_1 p_2 - q_2 p_1)^2 + q_1^2(q_1^2 + q_2^2).$$

Therefore, we expect there will be at least 3 admissible solutions for $(\mathrm{LVE}_\psi^2)^\star$:

$$(H^{(2)}(\psi), H^{(1)}(\psi)), \quad ((H^2)^{(2)}(\psi), 0), \quad (K^{(2)}(\psi), 0),$$

stemming respectively from H, H^2 and K. We compute $\mathrm{Sol}_{\boldsymbol{k}} \left((\mathrm{LVE}_\psi^2)^\star \right)$ and its dimension happens to be 6. After due application of the filter condition $\mathcal{M}_2$, $\dim_{\mathbb{C}} \mathrm{Sol}_{\mathrm{adm}}((\mathrm{LVE}_\psi^2)^\star)$ is exactly 3 and we have

$$\mathrm{Sol}_{\mathrm{adm}}((\mathrm{LVE}_\psi^2)^\star) = \mathrm{span}_{\mathbb{C}}\{W_2 (c_1, c_2, c_3) : c_i \in \mathbb{C}\},$$

for a three-parametric vector W_2. Hence, the admissible solutions of $(\mathrm{LVE}_\psi^2)^\star$ correspond to the three first integrals of valuation $\nu \leq 2$ along ψ: H, K and H^2 [2].

Since the valuation of H^2 and K along ψ is 2, both $((H^2)^{(2)}(\psi))$ and $(K^{(2)}(\psi))$ must be admissible solutions of $(\mathfrak{sym}^2 A_1)^\star$. We compute $\mathrm{Sol}_{\boldsymbol{k}}((\mathfrak{sym}^2 A_1)^\star)$; its dimension is 4. Applying the filter M_2 we discard 2 out of 4 solutions. We obtain

$$\mathrm{Sol}_{\mathrm{adm}}((\mathfrak{sym}^2 A_1)^\star) = \{V_2 (c_1, c_3) : c_i \in \mathbb{C}\},$$

thus proving that H^2 and K are the only two holomorphic first integrals degenerate of order 2 along ψ.

$(\mathrm{LVE}_\psi^3)^\star$:   *We perform the same computations at order 3 and obtain that*

$$\dim_{\mathbb{C}} \mathrm{Sol}_{\boldsymbol{k}}((\mathrm{LVE}_\psi^3)^\star) = 12.$$

We expect to get at least 5 admissible solutions: those stemming from

$$H, H^2, K, H^3 \quad and \quad H \cdot K.$$

After applying the filter conditions we conclude that such solutions are indeed the only admissible ones since

$$\dim_{\mathbb{C}} \mathrm{Sol}_{\mathrm{adm}}(\mathrm{LVE}_\psi^3) = 5.$$

We obtain that the admissible solutions of $(\mathfrak{sym}^3 A_1)^\star$ are exactly those stemming from the first integrals degenerate of order 3 along ψ: H^3 and $H \cdot K$ discarding thanks to the filter M_3, 4 solutions out of 6. Therefore, the only first integrals degenerate of order 3 along ψ are H^3 and $H \cdot K$.

$(\mathrm{LVE}_\psi^4)^\star$:   *Similarly at order 4 we obtain that*

$$\dim_{\mathbb{C}} \mathrm{Sol}_{\boldsymbol{k}}((\mathrm{LVE}_\psi^4)^\star) = 21.$$

We expect to get at least 8 admissible solutions: those stemming from

$$H, H^2, H^3, H^4, K, H \cdot K, H^2 \cdot K \quad and \quad K^2.$$

After applying the filter conditions we see that such solutions are indeed the only admissible ones since

$$\dim_{\mathbb{C}} \mathrm{Sol}_{\mathrm{adm}} (\mathrm{LVE}_\psi^4) = 8.$$

Consequently, the admissible solutions of $(\mathfrak{sym}^4 A_1)^\star$ are exactly those stemming from the first integrals degenerate of order 4 along ψ: H^4, $H^2 \cdot K$ and K^2 discarding thanks to the filter M_4, 6 solutions out of nine. Therefore, the only order-four-degenerate first integrals along ψ are H^4, $H^2 \cdot K$ and K^2.

Even assuming no prior knowledge about the existence of K or the integrability of the system, this filter procedure leads us as far as:

---

[2]The values $(1, 0, 0), (0, 1, 0)$ and $(0, 0, 1)$ of (c_1, c_2, c_3) correspond to K, H^2 and H respectively.

1. *computing the germ of a valuation-2 formal first integral along ψ;*

2. *and proving there is no other holomorphic first integral of valuation at most 4 along ψ, which is a strong hint on the non-existence of any other holomorphic first integral, as they would have to be of valuation at least 5 along ψ.*

3.2 Bounds on $\dim_{\mathbb{C}} \mathrm{Sol}_{\mathrm{adm}}((\mathfrak{sym}^m A_1)^\star)$

The number of analytic first integrals which are degenerate at order-m along a non-constant solution ϕ has a lower bound depending on the number of analytic algebraically independent first integrals of the system:

PROPOSITION 16. *Let ϕ be a non-constant solution of (1) and let $\mathcal{F} = \{F_1, \ldots, F_N\}$ with $N \geq 1$ be a family of holomorphic first integrals of (1) satisfying Ziglin's Lemma (i.e their junior forms are algebraically independent) with valuations $\nu_1, \ldots, \nu_N$ along ϕ. Then, for every $m \geq 1$, we have the inequalities*

$$\mathrm{card}\left\{ r \in \mathbb{N}^N : \sum_{i=1}^N r_i \nu_i = m \right\} \leq$$
$$\dim_{\mathbf{k}}(\mathrm{Sol}_{\mathrm{adm}}((\mathfrak{sym}^m A_1)^\star)) \leq d_{m-1,n-1}.$$

PROOF. The upper-bound condition is easy:

$$\dim_{\mathbf{k}} \mathrm{Sol}_{\mathrm{adm}}(\mathfrak{sym}^m A_1)^\star \leq \dim_{\mathbf{k}} \ker M_m$$
$$= d_{m,n} - d_{m-1,n} = d_{m-1,n-1}.$$

Now let $m \in \mathbb{N}$ and consider

$$\mathcal{G}_m := \left\{ G = \prod_{i=1}^N F_i^{m_i} : \nu(G) = m \right\},$$

the family of first integrals of valuation m which are monomials of degree m in $F_1, \ldots, F_N$. For $G \in \mathcal{G}_m$, we have $G^\circ = \prod_{i=1}^N (F_i^\circ)^{m_i}$. And $\prod_{i=1}^N (F_i^\circ)^{m_i}$ are linearly independent (otherwise the F_i° would be algebraically dependent). Therefore, $\dim_{\mathbf{k}}(\mathrm{span}_{\mathbb{C}}(\prod_{i=1}^N (F_i^\circ)^{m_i})_{\sum_i m_i \nu_i = m})$ is equal to $\mathrm{card}\left\{ r \in \mathbb{N}^N : r_1 \nu_1 + \ldots + r_N \nu_N = m \right\}$. Now,

$$\mathrm{span}_{\mathbb{C}}(\prod_{i=1}^N (F_i^\circ))^{m_i} \subset \mathrm{Sol}_{\mathrm{adm}}((\mathfrak{sym}^m A_1)^\star),$$

which proves our point. $\square$

EXAMPLE 17. *Back to the anharmonic oscillator example. The table below summarizes for m ranging from 1 to 4 (first column) the dimension of $\mathrm{Sol}_{\mathrm{adm}}\left((\mathrm{LVE}_\phi^m)^\star\right)$ (second column) as well as the generators of the latter (third column). For each m we find out that the admissible solutions of the $[A_m^\star]$ are generated by*

1	1	$\mathrm{span}_{\mathbb{C}}\{H^{(1)}(\phi)\}$
2	3	$\mathrm{span}_{\mathbb{C}}\{H^{(2)}(\phi), K^{(2)}(\phi), (H^2)^{(2)}(\phi)\}$
3	5	$\mathrm{span}_{\mathbb{C}}\left\{ \begin{array}{c} H^{(3)}(\phi), K^{(3)}(\phi), (H^2)^{(3)}(\phi) \\ (H^3)^{(3)}(\phi), (H \cdot K)^{(3)}(\phi) \end{array} \right\}$
4	8	$\mathrm{span}_{\mathbb{C}}\left\{ \begin{array}{c} H^{(4)}(\phi), K^{(4)}(\phi), (H^2)^{(3)}(\phi) \\ (H^3)^{(4)}(\phi), (HK)^{(4)}(\phi) \\ (H^4)^{(4)}(\phi), (H^2K)^{(4)}(\phi), (K^2)^{(4)}(\phi) \end{array} \right\}$

In light of Proposition 16 consider the table below which summarizes for each value of m ranging from 1 to 4 (first column) the dimension of $\mathrm{Sol}_{\mathrm{adm}}(\mathfrak{sym}^m A_1)^\star)$ (second column) as well as the generators of the latter (third column)

1	1	$\mathrm{span}_{\mathbb{C}}\{H^{(1)}(\phi)\}$
2	2	$\mathrm{span}_{\mathbb{C}}\{K^{(2)}(\phi), (H^2)^{(2)}(\phi)\}$
3	2	$\mathrm{span}_{\mathbb{C}}\{(H^3)^{(3)}(\phi), (HK)^{(3)}(\phi)\}$
4	3	$\mathrm{span}_{\mathbb{C}}\{(H^4)^{(4)}(\phi), (H^2K)^{(4)}(\phi), (K^2)^{(4)}(\phi)\}$

Had the dimension of $\mathrm{Sol}_{\mathrm{adm}}((\mathfrak{sym}^3 A_1)^\star)$ been less than 2 and that of $\mathrm{Sol}_{\mathrm{adm}}((\mathfrak{sym}^4 A_1)^\star)$ less than 3, we could have discarded the possibility of there existing any holomorphic degenerate first integral of order 2 along ψ other than H^2. In this sense, Proposition 16 acts as a non-integrability indicator.

4. GENERAL ALGORITHM

To summarize, we study (1) along an integral curve Γ parametrized by $\phi(t)$. We wish to detect holomorphic (or formal) first integrals and compute their Taylor expansions. The above Theorems show that we should compute admissible solutions of the (LVE_ϕ^m). This is done as follows.

1. Compute rational solutions of (VE_ϕ^1). Apply filter condition from Theorem 12.

2. Order m. Assume we know a parametrized admissible solution $V_{m-1} = \sum c_i V_{i,m-1}$ in $\mathrm{Sol}_{\mathrm{adm}}(\mathrm{LVE}_\phi^{m-1})$.

   (a) Compute rational solutions of $\dot{Y} = \mathfrak{sym}^m(A)Y$ (and filter via Theorem 12); this gives junior forms of first integrals of valuation m along ϕ.

   (b) Compute rational solutions of the inhomogeneous system (with parametrized right-hand side)

   $$\dot{Y} = \mathfrak{sym}^m(A)^\star Y + B_m^\star V_{m-1}.$$

Details on how to optimize this in the case $\mathbf{k} = \mathbb{C}(t)$ are given in the next Section.

5. AN ALGORITHM FOR THE RATIONAL FUNCTION BASE FIELD CASE

Assume now $\mathbf{k} = \mathbb{C}(t)$. We recall Barkatou's algorithm in [Bar99] to compute rational solutions of linear systems and adapt it to a variant of [vHW97] tailored to our context.

DEFINITION 18. *Given $A \in \mathrm{Mat}(n, \mathbf{k})$ and $P \in \mathrm{GL}_n(\mathbf{k})$, $Y = PZ$ transforms system $\dot{Y} = AY$ into $\dot{Z} = P[A]Z$ where*

$$P[A] := P^{-1}(AP - \dot{P}).$$

Such a change of variables is usually called a gauge transformation.

A *universal denominator* (UD in short) is a rational function $r(t)$ such that any rational solution is $Y = r(t)Z$, Z being a vector of polynomials. We briefly recall how such a UD is computed. Consider a system $\dot{Y} = A(t)Y$, with $A \in \mathcal{M}_n(\mathbb{C}(t))$. If Y is a rational solution and $p \in \mathbb{C}$ is a finite pole of Y then p is a pole of A. Moreover for any finite pole p of A one can compute an integer ℓ_p such that for any rational solution Y the function $(t-p)^{-\ell_p}Y$ has no pole at p. A UD is obtained by taking the product

$$\prod_{p \text{ pole of } A} (t-p)^{\ell_p}.$$

In order to compute the bound ℓ_p one must first compute a gauge-equivalent system in a suitable so-called *simple form* from which the indicial polynomial at p can be immediately obtained. ℓ_p is then the smallest integer root of this indicial equation. Simple forms are computed by using an adapted version of the super-reduction algorithm ([HW87, BP09]).

Once a UD $r(t)$ is known, we have rational solutions if, and only if, system $\dot{Z} = (A - \frac{\dot{r}}{r}\mathrm{Id}_n)Z$ has polynomial solutions. To achieve this, [Bar99] computes a gauge transformation P_∞ polynomial in t^{-1} (with P_∞^{-1} polynomial in t) such that $P_\infty[A]$ is in simple form at infinity (note that $P_\infty[A] - \dot{r}/r\,Id_n = P_\infty[A - \dot{r}/r\,Id_n]$) and computes the coefficients of Z from regular solutions at ∞.

In the parametrized right-hand side case $\dot{Y} = AY + \sum c_i V_i$, this algorithm returns the values of the c_i for which the system admits a rational solution, hence is adapted to part (2.b) of our general algorithm.

5.1 Symmetric Powers of Differential Systems

Recall [AM10] that Sym is a group morphism, i.e.

$$\mathrm{Sym}^m(UV) = \mathrm{Sym}^m(U)\,\mathrm{Sym}^m(V),$$

and $\mathfrak{sym}$ is a vector space morphism:

$$\mathfrak{sym}^m(A + \lambda B) = \mathfrak{sym}^m(A) + \lambda\,\mathfrak{sym}^m(B).$$

The following Lemmae, valid for all complex matrices, summarize properties which will be used below.

LEMMA 19.   • Let $\lambda_1, \ldots, \lambda_n$ be the eigenvalues of M. The eigenvalues of $\mathfrak{sym}^m(M)$ (resp. $\mathrm{Sym}^m(M)$) are of the form $\sum_{|i|=m} i_j\lambda_j$ (resp. $\prod_{|i|=m} \lambda_j^{i_j}$).

• If $M \in \mathcal{M}_n(\boldsymbol{k})$ is such that M and $\dot{M}$ commute, then $\mathrm{Sym}^m(e^M) = e^{\mathfrak{sym}^m(M)}$.

LEMMA 20. Given gauge transformation $B = P[A]$,

• $\mathfrak{sym}^m(P[A]) = \mathrm{Sym}^m(P)[\mathfrak{sym}^m(A)]$.

• If A has a regular singularity at $t = 0$ and matrix $P[A] = \frac{A_0}{t} + \cdots$ has a pole of order one, we then have $\mathrm{Sym}^m(P)[\mathfrak{sym}^m(A)]) = \frac{\mathfrak{sym}^m(A_0)}{t} + \cdots$.

5.2 Case in which all singularities are regular

In this Section we consider the regular singular case, as it often occurs in examples and simplifies the exposition.

Any system $\dot{Y} = AY$ with a regular singularity, say at $t = 0$, can be transformed, e.g. using Moser's algorithm (see [Mos60], [BP09]), to a gauge-equivalent system with a first-kind singularity, i.e. $\dot{Z} = BZ$, B having at most a simple pole at 0: $B(t) = \frac{1}{t}B_0 + B_1 + \cdots$. The indicial polynomial coincides with the characteristic polynomial of B_0.

It is well-known that, using a suitable polynomial gauge transformation, one can assume that the eigenvalues of B_0 do not differ by non-zero integers. In this case the system $\dot{Z} = BZ$ has a formal solution matrix at $t = 0$ of the form $\hat{U} = \hat{\Phi}(t) \cdot t^\Lambda$, where $\hat{\Phi} \in \mathcal{M}_n(\mathbb{C}[[t]])$ satisfies $\det \Phi(0) \neq 0$ and $\Lambda \in \mathcal{M}_n(\mathbb{C})$ is the normal Jordan form of B_0. The eigenvalues of B_0 are called the (local) exponents (or local data) at $t = 0$.

For each finite singularity p, one can compute, with the Moser algorithm, a polynomial gauge transformation P_p such that $B = P_p[A] = \frac{1}{t-p}B_{0,p} + \cdots$ and the order of the UD at $t = p$ is the least integer eigenvalue of $B_{0,p}$. We thus have $\mathrm{Sym}^m(P_p)[\mathfrak{sym}^m(A)]) = \frac{\mathfrak{sym}^m(B_{0,p})}{t-p} + \cdots$ hence the

eigenvalues of $\mathfrak{sym}^m(B_{0,p})$ are $\sum_{|i|=m} i_j\lambda_j$, $\lambda_1, \ldots, \lambda_n$ being the eigenvalues of $B_{0,p}$. We may thus compute a UD r_m for system $\dot{Y} = \mathfrak{sym}^m(A).Y$ from the local data computed on $\dot{Y} = AY$. Since ∞ is regular, $P_\infty[A]$ has simple pole at infinity; hence $\mathrm{Sym}(P_\infty)[\mathfrak{sym}^m(A)]$ also has a simple pole at infinity. It follows that the Barkatou algorithm for polynomial solutions may be applied directly to

$$\mathrm{Sym}^m(P_\infty)[\mathfrak{sym}^m(A)^\star] - \frac{\dot{r}_m}{r_m}Id.$$

To summarize, bounds at singularities (for denominators) are computed from local data of (VE^1_ϕ), the transformation to simple form at ∞ is lifted to $\mathfrak{sym}^m(A)^\star$ and polynomial solutions of the latter are then as in [Bar99] or [vHW97]. This gives junior forms of first integrals of valuation m along ϕ. Note that, as in [vHW97], we may reduce the size of computations by means of suitable formal solutions from (VE^1_ϕ) at this stage.

Part 2.b of the algorithm is adapted similarly. The only thing that changes is that we need a min between the "universal bound" computed above (at each singularity) and the valuations of the right-hand side $B_m^\star V_{m-1}$.

5.3 Irregular Singularities

For a singularity, say $t = 0$, which is not regular singular, $\hat{U} = \hat{\Phi}(t)t^\Lambda e^Q$ with notations as above and $Q = \mathrm{diag}\left(q_1(1/t^{\frac{1}{r}}), \ldots, q_n(1/t^{\frac{1}{r}})\right)$ with $q_i \in \mathbb{C}[1/t^{1/r}]$. These exponential parts of $A_1^\star$ may be computed from [Bar97]. Once exponents are computed at p (using [Bar99, §4.3] as above), the corresponding exponents of $\mathfrak{sym}^m(A)$ may be computed from these exponents and the exponential parts using (a small adaptation of) procedure global-bounds in [vHW97, §3 (p. 368)]. Regarding bounds at infinity, the symmetric power of a super-reduced system at infinity may not be simple. However, it will be very close. So if we let $SR(A)$ denote a super-reduced form of A at infinity (see [Bar99, App. A.1, A.2]), then $SR(\mathfrak{sym}^m(SR(A)))$ involves a small calculation once $SR(A)$ is known.

5.4 Further Reduction Strategies

The first part of Lemma 20 shows that whenever we have a gauge transformation $Y = PZ$ which "simplifies" the system, then $\mathrm{Sym}^m(P)$ provides the same simplification on $\mathfrak{sym}^m(A)$. If, say, r linearly independent admissible solutions are computed for (VE^1_ϕ), and an invertible P is built whose first columns are the said admissible solutions, the first r columns of $P[A^\star]$ will vanish and $\mathrm{Sym}^m(P)$ will yield $\binom{r+m-1}{m-1}$ columns of zeroes in $\mathfrak{sym}^m(A^\star)$.

If (VE^1_ϕ) has been put in reduced form [AMW09, AMW10, AM10] then, as shown in [AMCW11] (also [AM10, Ch. 3]), rational solutions of all $\mathfrak{sym}^m(A^\star)$ will have constant coefficients, notably simplifying part 2.a of the algorithm, namely kernel computation on a $\mathfrak{sym}$ power.

6. CONCLUSION

Given a holomorphic vector field X, the vector of the derivatives up to order m of a holomorphic first integral of X appears as a rational solution of $(\mathrm{LVE}^m)^\star$ [MRRS07]. In this work, following [AM10] we have proved that those germs satisfy an additional set of linear conditions and we have introduced the notion of admissible solution to this effect. This construction provides a method allowing us to retrieve those admissible solutions, germs of holomorphic first integrals among them [AM10]. Combining the latter with Barkatou's use of local simple forms for rational solutions, we have introduced an algorithm allowing us to efficiently compute (whenever the base field is $\mathbb{C}(t)$) those admissible solutions.

EXAMPLE 21. *Consider the one-parameter family of classical two-degrees-of-freedom Hamiltonian systems*

$$H_\epsilon(q_1, q_2, p_1, p_2) = \frac{1}{2}(p_1^2 + p_2^2) + V_\epsilon(q_1, q_2),$$

where $V_\epsilon(q_1, q_2) = \frac{1}{4}(q_1^4 + q_2^4) + \frac{\epsilon}{2}(q_1 q_2)^2$ with $\epsilon \in \mathbb{C}$. This family has been proven to be integrable only for the values 0, 1 and 3 of the parameter ϵ [Yos88]. These systems admit

$$\phi = \left(\frac{c_1}{t}, \frac{c_2}{t}, -\frac{c_1}{t^2}, -\frac{c_2}{t^2} \right) \quad i = 1, 2,$$

as solution curves[3]. We pick two particular cases, one integrable ($\epsilon = 3$) and one non-integrable ($\epsilon = 2$).

The table below summarizes, for m ranging from 1 to 3, $\dim \mathrm{Sol}_k((\mathrm{LVE}_\phi^m)^\star)$ (second column for $\epsilon = 3$ fourth column for $\epsilon = 2$) and the dimension of $\mathrm{Sol}_{\mathrm{adm}}((\mathrm{LVE}_\phi^m)^\star)$ (third column for $\epsilon = 3$ and fifth column for $\epsilon = 2$):

1	4	3	2	1
2	14	9	6	3
3	34	19	9	5

For $\epsilon = 3$ the potential is completely integrable. Indeed, the system admits another polynomial first integral $F = p_1 p_2 + q_1 q_2(q_1^2 + q_2^2)$ which, same as H, is non degenerate along all particular solutions ϕ.

The dimension of $\mathrm{Sol}_{\mathrm{adm}}((\mathrm{LVE}_\phi^m)^\star)$ is maximal for all m considered; this suggests H could be superintegrable (the third first integral being non degenerate along ϕ). This is consistent with the superintegrability necessary condition in [MPY08]. In fact a necessary condition for superintegrability for a general Hamiltonian system of dimension 2 is that the set of admissible solutions be of maximal dimension (possibly from a certain order on).

For $\epsilon = 2$, the potential is not meromorphically integrable. In particular, we can affirm that H is the only first integral which is not degenerate along ϕ. At order 2, in addition to the solutions corresponding to H and H^2, there is an additional admissible solution and at order 3 there are 2 additional admissible solutions. Applying the necessary condition given above it is clear that the results obtained for $\epsilon = 2$ do not hint at superintegrability – as expected.

[AM10] conjectured that for each m, $\mathrm{Sol}_{\mathrm{adm}}((\mathrm{LVE}_\phi^m)^\star)$ are but the solutions of a differential submodule of $\nabla_m^\star = \frac{d}{dt} - A_m^\star$. Once proven, this conjecture, together with the algorithm exposed in this work, will pave the way towards an effective theory of formal first integrals of differential systems along a non-constant solution.

7. REFERENCES

[AM10]   Ainhoa Aparicio-Monforte, *Méthodes effectives pour l'intégrabilité des systèmes dynamiques*, Ph.D. thesis, Université de Limoges, December 2010.

[AMCW11] Ainhoa Aparicio-Monforte, Élie Compoint, and Jacques-Arthur Weil, *A characterization of reduced forms of linear differential systems*, Preprint, January 2011.

[AMW09]   Ainhoa Aparicio-Monforte and Jacques-Arthur Weil, *A reduced form for linear differential systems and its application to integrability of hamiltonian systems*, arXiv:0912.3538v1, December 2009.

[AMW10]   _____, *A reduction method for higher order variational equations of hamiltonian systems*, To appear, October 2010.

[Aud01]   Michèle Audin, *Les systèmes hamiltoniens et leur intégrabilité*, Cours Spécialisés,, vol. 8, Société Mathématique de France, Paris, 2001.

[Bar97]   M. A. Barkatou, *An algorithm to compute the exponential part of a formal fundamental matrix solution of a linear differential system*, Appl. Algebra Engrg. Comm. Comput. **8** (1997), no. 1, 1–23.

[Bar99]   Moulay A. Barkatou, *On rational solutions of systems of linear differential equations*, J. Symbolic Comput. **28** (1999), no. 4-5, 547–567.

[BP09]   Moulay A. Barkatou and Eckhard Pflügel, *On the moser- and super-reduction algorithms of systems of linear differential equations and their complexity*, J. Symb. Comput. **44** (2009), no. 8, 1017–1036.

[FH91]   William Fulton and Joe Harris, *Representation theory*, Graduate Texts in Mathematics, vol. 129, Springer-Verlag, New York, 1991.

[HW87]   A. Hilali and A. Wazner, *Formes super–irréductibles des systèmes différentiels linéaires*, Numer. Math. **50** (1987), 429–449.

[Mos60]   J. Moser, *The order of a singularity in Fuchs' theory*, Math. Z. (1960), 379–398.

[MPY08]   Andrzej J. Maciejewski, Maria Przybylska, and Haruo Yoshida, *Necessary conditions for super-integrability of Hamiltonian systems*, Phys. Lett. A **372** (2008), no. 34, 5581–5587.

[MR99]   Juan J. Morales Ruiz, *Differential Galois theory and non-integrability of Hamiltonian systems*, Progress in Mathematics, vol. 179, Birkhäuser Verlag, Basel, 1999.

[MRRS07] Juan J. Morales-Ruiz, Jean-Pierre Ramis, and Carles Simo, *Integrability of Hamiltonian systems and differential Galois groups of higher variational equations*, Ann. Sci. École Norm. Sup. (4) **40** (2007), no. 6, 845–884.

[vHW97]   Mark van Hoeij and Jacques-Arthur Weil, *An algorithm for computing invariants of differential Galois groups*, J. Pure Appl. Algebra **117/118** (1997), 353–379.

[Yos88]   Haruo Yoshida, *Ziglin analysis for proving nonintegrability of Hamiltonian systems*, Finite-dimensional integrable nonlinear dynamical systems (Johannesburg, 1988), World Sci. Publishing, Singapore, 1988, pp. 74–93.

---

[3]Where c_1 and c_2 are defined by algebraic relations.

Virtual Roots of a Real Polynomial and Fractional Derivatives

Daniel Bembé
Mathematisches Institut der Universität München
Theresienstr. 39, D-80333 München, Germany
bembe@math.lmu.de

André Galligo*
Universite de Nice-Sophia Antipolis,
Mathematiques
Parc Valrose 06108 Nice cedex 02, France
galligo@unice.fr

ABSTRACT

After the works of Gonzales-Vega, Lombardi, Mahé [11], and Coste, Lajous, Lombardi, Roy [6], we consider the virtual roots of a univariate polynomial f with real coefficients. Using fractional derivatives, we associate to f a bivariate polynomial $P_f(x,t)$ depending on the choice of an origin a, then two type of plan curves we call the FDcurve and stem of f. We show, in the generic case, how to locate the virtual roots of f on the Budan table and on each of these curves. The paper is illustrated with examples and pictures computed with the computer algebra system Maple.

Categories and Subject Descriptors

I.1.2 [**Computing Methodologies**]: Symbolic and Algebraic Manipulation—*Algorithms*

General Terms

Algorithms.

Keywords

virtual roots; real univariate polynomial; Budan table; fractional derivatives; FDcurve; stem

1. INTRODUCTION

In [13], Rahman and Schmeisser note that rules of signs for calculating the roots of a polynomial are older than calculus. Nowadays subdivision methods, heirs of these rules, are widely applied for calculating good approximations of solutions of polynomial equations or intersections of surfaces in Computer Aided Geometric Design. The geometric dictionary in complex algebraic geometry between invariants readable on equations and features of varieties is ultimately based on the fact that a polynomial of degree n admits n roots. This is not the case for real roots, and make real algebraic geometry more complicated. A natural strategy

---

*and INRIA Mediterrannée, Galaad project team.

for studying properties of real algebraic varieties is to consider simultaneously roots of iterated derivatives of the input. An important progress was achieved by Gonzales-Vega, Lombardi, Mahé when generalizing the real roots, they introduced in [11] the notion of virtual roots of a polynomial. The n virtual roots of a degree n polynomial provide a good substitute to the n complex roots.

Tables containing the signs of all the derivatives of a polynomial f are called in this paper Budan tables. They were used by various mathematicians including R. Thom for separating and labeling the different real roots of a polynomial, see [4]. Relying on Rolle theorem, we analyze the different admissible configurations of successive rows in such a table. Restricting to the generic case where all roots of all derivatives are two by two distinct, we identify the table with an infinite rectangle separated into positive and negative blocs. We study the topology of the positive (resp. negative) blocs components, and characterize the virtuals roots using connected blocs components.

We also view these connected bloc components inside the Budan table as plane surfaces delimited by discretized curves. To further explore this analogy, we consider derivatives with non-integers orders called fractional derivatives. We point out that fractional derivatives of a polynomial admit a bivariate polynomial factor. This bivariate factor is used to construct two kinds of real planes curves attached to f: FDcurves and stem. The roots of all derivatives of f lie on each curve. These curves naturally realize a partition of the plane, hence can be used to geometrically determine the sign of a derivative at any point. We discuss and illustrate with examples, the possibility of using these curves to ease the location of the virtual roots in a Budan table.

The paper is organized as follows. Section 2 presents the virtual roots and give a quick proof of their characterization by jumps in the sign variations, followed by the definition of virtual multiplicity. Then admissible configurations for a table to be a Budan table are identified. Section 3 examinates what happens in the generic case and establishes our main connexity result. Section 4 is devoted to fractional derivatives and its applications to our setting, FDcurves are introduced and illustrated. Section 5 describes intersections of FDcurves (resp. stems) with a Budan table and their use for the location of virtual roots.

2. VIRTUAL ROOTS

In this section let $\mathbb{R}$ be the field of real numbers (more generally a real closed field). In [11] the virtual roots of a monic n-degree polynomial $f \in \mathbb{R}[X]$ were introduced. They provide n root functions $\rho_{n,k}$ $(1 \leq k \leq n)$ on the space of all monic n-degree polynomials. In particular they have the following properties:

1. For every k the $\rho_{n,k} : \mathbb{R}^n \to \mathbb{R}$ is a continuous function of the n coefficients $(a_0, \ldots, a_{n-1}) \in \mathbb{R}^n$ of the monic polynomial $f(X) = X^n + a_{n-1}X^{n-1} + \ldots + a_0$.

2. if $f(a) = 0$ then $a = \rho_{n,k}$ for at least one k,

3. for every k we have $\rho_{n,k} \leq \rho_{n-1,k} \leq \rho_{n,k+1}$, where $\rho_{n-1,k}$ denotes the k-th virtual root of f'.

From an approximate computational point of view, the advantage is that the coefficients need not be known with infinite precision in order to compute the virtual roots with finite precision.

In 2.1 we summarize some of the results of [11] and [6]. The authors of [6] show that the Budan-Fourier count always gives the number of virtual roots (with multiplicities) on an interval (which is our proposition 2.3). Furthermore they present some of our statements in the more general context of **f**-derivatives. In 2.2 we present the Budan table and some claim about the virtual multiplicity [2].

2.1 Definition

DEFINITION 2.1 (VIRTUAL ROOTS). *Let $f \in \mathbb{R}[X]$ monic of degree n and $f^{(i)}$ denote its i-th derivative. Let $\rho_{j,0} = -\infty$ and $\rho_{j,j+1} = \infty$ for $j \in \{0, \ldots, n\}$. For $j \in \{1, \ldots, n\}$ the j virtual roots of $f^{(n-j)}$, $\rho_{j,1} \leq \cdots \leq \rho_{j,j}$, will be defined inductively:*

1. *Let be defined the $\rho_{j-1,k}$ such that for $1 \leq k \leq j$*

$$f^{(n-j+1)}(x)f^{(n-j+1)}(y) \geq 0$$

for all $x,y \in \mathbb{R}_{j-1,k} = [\rho_{j-1,k-1}, \rho_{j-1,k}]$ (resp. the half-open intervals if $k \in \{1, j\}$).

2. *Then for every $1 \leq k \leq j$ $\rho_{j,k} \in \mathbb{R}_{j-1,k}$ is defined by the inequality*

$$|f^{(n-j)}(\rho_{j,k})| \leq |f^{(n-j)}(x)|$$

for all $x \in \mathbb{R}_{j-1,k}$. This is well-defined since $f^{(n-j)}$ is strictly monotone on $\mathbb{R}_{j-1,k}$.
Three cases can appear:

(a) *$\rho_{j-1,k-1} = \rho_{j,k} = \rho_{j-1,k}$,*

(b) *$f^{(n-j)}$ admits a real root in $]\rho_{j-1,k-1}, \rho_{j-1,k}[$ then $\rho_{j,k}$ is equal to this real root,*

(c) *$f^{(n-j)}$ does not admit a real root in $]\rho_{j-1,k-1}, \rho_{j-1,k}[$ then $\rho_{j,k}$ is the point with the least absolute value under $f^{(n-j)}$ (see Figure 1). Hence it is either $\rho_{j-1,k-1}$ or $\rho_{j-1,k}$.*

3. *We get for $1 \leq k \leq j+1$*

$$f^{(n-j)}(x)f^{(n-j)}(y) \geq 0$$

for all $x,y \in [\rho_{j,k-1}, \rho_{j,k}]$ (resp. the half-open intervals if $k \in \{1, j+1\}$).

Before we state a theorem which enables us to determine virtual roots, we consider the simple example with $n = 3$, $f := (x-2)^3 - 3(x-2) + 4$. See Figure 1.
Its virtual roots are: $\rho_{3,1} \approx -0.19$ (case 2.(b)); $\rho_{3,2} = 3$ (case 2.(c)); $\rho_{3,3} = 3$ (case 2.(c)). We also have (case 2.(b)), $\rho_{2,1} = 1$, $\rho_{2,2} = 3$. and $\rho_{1,1} = 2$.

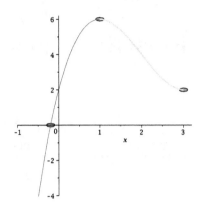

Figure 1: $\rho_{3,1} = -0.19$, $\rho_{2,1} = 1$, $\rho_{3,2} = \rho_{2,2} = 3$.

DEFINITION 2.2. *1. Let $f \in \mathbb{R}[X]$ and $a \in \mathbb{R}$.*

(a) *The real multiplicity $\mathrm{rmult}_f(a)$ denotes the number $m \geq 0$, for which $(X-a)^m$ divides $f(X)$ and $(X-a)^{m+1}$ does not. If $\mathrm{rmult}_f(a) \geq 1$ we say, that a is a real root of f.*

(b) *If $\rho_{n,k} = a$ for some k we say, that a is a virtual root of f, and the virtual multiplicity*

$$\mathrm{vmult}_f(a) := l - k + 1,$$

choosing k minimal, l maximal such that $\rho_{n,k} = a = \rho_{n,l}$.
Otherwise $\mathrm{vmult}_f(a) = 0$.

(c) *If $\mathrm{vmult}_f(a) > \mathrm{rmult}_f(a) = 0$ we denote a as virtual non real root of f.*

2. (a) *For a sequence $(a_0, \ldots, a_n) \in (\mathbb{R} \setminus \{0\})^{n+1}$ the number of sign changes $\mathbf{V}(a_0, \ldots, a_n)$ is defined inductively in the following way:*

$$\mathbf{V}(a_0) := 0; \qquad \mathbf{V}(a_0, \ldots, a_i) :=$$
$$\begin{cases} \mathbf{V}(a_0, \ldots, a_{i-1}) & \text{if } a_{i-1}a_i > 0, \\ \mathbf{V}(a_0, \ldots, a_{i-1}) + 1 & \text{if } a_{i-1}a_i < 0. \end{cases}$$

(b) *To determine the number of sign changes of a sequence $(a_0, \ldots, a_n) \in \mathbb{R}^{n+1}$ delete the zeros in $(a_0, \ldots, a_n)$ and apply case 2a. ($\mathbf{V}$ of the empty sequence equals 0).*

In the previous example, the virtual multiplicity of $a = 3$ is two since $\rho_{3,2} = \rho_{3,3}$.

PROPOSITION 2.3. *Let $f \in \mathbb{R}[X]$ be monic of degree n, $\rho_{n,1} \leq \cdots \leq \rho_{n,n}$ its virtual roots and $\rho_{n,0} = -\infty$, $\rho_{n,n+1} = \infty$. Then we have for $1 \leq k \leq n+1$ with $\rho_{n,k-1} \neq \rho_{n,k}$*

$$x \in [\rho_{n,k-1}, \rho_{n,k}[\Longleftrightarrow$$
$$\mathbf{V}(f(x), f'(x), \ldots, f^{(n)}(x)) = n + 1 - k$$

(resp. for $k = 1$ the interval $x \in]-\infty, \rho_{n,1}[$).

PROOF. By induction on the degree j of $f^{(n-j)}$. Let $\rho_{j,1} \leq \cdots \leq \rho_{j,j}$ denote the virtual roots of $f^{(n-j)}$ and $\rho_{j,0} = -\infty$, $\rho_{j,j+1} = \infty$.
Let $j = 0$. Then $]\rho_{0,0}, \rho_{0,1}[= \mathbb{R}$ and $\mathbf{V}(f^{(n)}(x)) = 0$ for all $x \in \mathbb{R}$.

Let $j > 0$ and the statement be true for $j - 1$. Let $1 \leq k \leq j+1$ with $\rho_{j-1,k-1} \neq \rho_{j-1,k}$ and consider $x \in [\rho_{j-1,k-1}, \rho_{j-1,k}[$. In case 2.(b) of the definition of the virtual roots we get

$$f^{(n-j+1)}(x)f^{(n-j)}(x) < 0 \text{ for } \rho_{j-1,k-1} = x$$
$$f^{(n-j+1)}(x)f^{(n-j)}(x) < 0 \text{ for } \rho_{j-1,k-1} < x < \rho_{j,k},$$
$$f^{(n-j)}(x) = 0 \text{ for } \rho_{j,k} = x$$
$$f^{(n-j+1)}(x)f^{(n-j)}(x) > 0 \text{ for } \rho_{j,k} < x < \rho_{j-1,k},$$

for the smallest $i \geq 1$ with $f^{(n-j+i)}(\rho_{j-1,k-1}) \neq 0$. In case 2.(c) the same argument holds. $\square$

COROLLARY 2.4.   *1. For every k the $\rho_{n,k} : \mathbb{R}^n \to \mathbb{R}$ are continuous functions of $(a_0, \ldots, a_{n-1})$ in $\mathbb{R}^n$, the n coefficients of the monic polynomial f.*

2. For every $a \in \mathbb{R}$

$$\mathrm{rmult}_f(a) \leq \mathrm{vmult}_f(a).$$

3. For every $a \in \mathbb{R}$

$$\mathrm{vmult}_f(a) - \mathrm{rmult}_f(a) \text{ is even.}$$

4. (Budan's theorem) For $x, y \in \mathbb{R}$ with $x < y$

$$0 \leq \sum_{a \in]x,y]} \mathrm{rmult}_f(a)$$
$$\leq \mathbf{V}(f(y) \ldots, f^{(n)}(y)) - \mathbf{V}(f(x) \ldots, f^{(n)}(x)).$$

PROOF.   1. Let $a := \rho_{n,k}(f)$ be the k-th virtual root of f and let be $\epsilon \in \mathbb{R}$, $\epsilon > 0$ such that $f^{(i)}(a-\epsilon)f^{(i)}(a+\epsilon) \neq 0$ for $i \in \{0, \ldots, n\}$. Now let $\tilde{f}$ denote the new polynomial obtained by a small change of the coefficients of f, in such a way that the following holds: $f^{(i)}(a-\epsilon)\tilde{f}^{(i)}(a-\epsilon) > 0$ and $f^{(i)}(a+\epsilon)\tilde{f}^{(i)}(a+\epsilon) > 0$ for $i \in \{0, \ldots, n\}$. From proposition 2.3 we get $\rho_{n,k}(\tilde{f}) \in]a-\epsilon, a+\epsilon[$; and we are done.

2. This follows from the following fact, which can be derived from the mean value theorem, applied inductively on f and its derivatives: Let $g \in \mathbb{R}[X]$ of degree ≥ 1. For every $a \in \mathbb{R}$ exists an $\epsilon > 0$ such that

$$(-1)^{\mathrm{rmult}_g(a)} g(x)g(y) > 0 \tag{1}$$
$$g(y)g'(y) > 0$$

for every $x \in]a-\epsilon, a[$ and $y \in]a, a+\epsilon[$.

3. This follows from (1) and $f^{(n)}(x)f^{(n)}(y) > 0$.

4. This follows from 2. since

$$\mathbf{V}(f(y) \ldots, f^{(n)}(y)) - \mathbf{V}(f(x) \ldots, f^{(n)}(x))$$
$$= \sum_{a \in]x,y]} \mathrm{vmult}_f(a),$$

as desired.

$\square$

REMARK 2.5   (ABOUT BUDAN'S THEOREM).   *Budan's theorem is stated in the appendix of [5]. According to [1], it was published for the first time in 1807, while Fourier published the equivalent result in 1820 ("Le Bulletin des Sciences de la*

Société Philomatique de Paris"). In fact, Budan's counting of roots is today known as "Budan-Fourier count".
Budan proved the non-negativity of the difference by the equivalent claim: For $y > 0$, $f(X) = \sum a_i X^i$ and $f(X + y) = \sum b_i X^i$ we get $\mathbf{V}(a_0, \ldots, a_n) \geq \mathbf{V}(b_0, \ldots, b_n)$. While Budan did not use the sequence of derivatives, it was introduced by Fourier ("Analyse des Équations"), as mentioned in [14]. In the same text an elegant proof of this equivalence, by Taylor series, is presented.

A different proof for the continuity is given in [11]. The following important property is proved.

THEOREM 2.6   ([11]).   *The $\rho_{n,k}$ with $1 \leq k \leq n$ are continuous functions of the n coefficients, $(a_0, \ldots, a_{n-1}) \in \mathbb{R}^n$, of the monic polynomial f. Moreover they are semi algebraic continuous functions defined over $\mathbf{Q}$ and integral over the polynomials.*

2.2   Budan table and multiplicities

In the Budan table we present the roots and signs of $f(x)$ and its derivatives for all $x \in \mathbb{R}$ as an infinite rectangle, formed by $n + 1$ rectangles $L_j := \mathbb{R} \times [j - 0.5, j + 0.5[$ with $0 \leq j \leq n$. A root a of $f^{(n-j)}$ is represented by a bar | positioned at a in the j-th rectangle. Between the bars | the sign of $f^{(n-j)}$ is fixed, if it is $-$ the block is colored, if it is $+$ it remains white. In the picture we often put a small disk at the roots to point them out. Consider figure 2, which shows the Budan table of a 6-degree polynomial f without real roots. The black disks show the tree pairs of virtual roots of f.
The following arguments make it easy to determine the virtual roots in a given Budan table. First, we characterize the behavior of $\mathrm{vmult}_f(a)$ and $\mathrm{rmult}_f(a)$ when integrating f':

PROPOSITION 2.7.   *Let $f \in \mathbb{R}[X]$ be monic, $a \in \mathbb{R}$. Provided as well $\mathrm{vmult}_f(a) - \mathrm{rmult}_f(a)$ as $\mathrm{vmult}_{f'}(a) - \mathrm{rmult}_{f'}(a)$ being even the following cases and only them can appear:*

1. $\mathrm{rmult}_f(a) = 0 = \mathrm{rmult}_{f'}(a)$ and $\mathrm{vmult}_f(a) = \mathrm{vmult}_{f'}(a)$;

2. $\mathrm{rmult}_f(a) = \mathrm{rmult}_{f'}(a) + 1$ and $\mathrm{vmult}_f(a) = \mathrm{vmult}_{f'}(a) + 1$;

3. $\mathrm{rmult}_f(a) = 0 < \mathrm{rmult}_{f'}(a)$ and $\mathrm{vmult}_f(a) - \mathrm{vmult}_{f'}(a) \in \{-1, 0, 1\}$.

PROOF. This follows from the definitons and corresponding examples. $\square$

This leads to the following way to determine if a real root of a derivative of f is a pair of virtual roots of f:

PROPOSITION 2.8.   *Let $f \in \mathbb{R}[X]$ be monic, $a \in \mathbb{R}$. Let m be the number of $i \in \{0, \ldots, n\}$ for which the following holds:*
$f^{(i)}(a) = 0$ and it exists an $\epsilon > 0$ such that

$$f^{(i-1)}(y)f^{(i)}(y) > 0$$
$$f^{(i)}(x)f^{(i)}(y) < 0$$
$$f^{(i+1)}(y)f^{(i)}(y) > 0$$

for every $x \in]a-\epsilon, a[$ and $y \in]a, a+\epsilon[$.
Then

$$\mathrm{vmult}_f(a) = \begin{cases} 2m & \text{if } f(a) \neq 0, \\ 2m+1 & \text{if } f(a) = 0. \end{cases}$$

PROOF. This follows by induction on the degree and proposition 2.7. $\square$

3. GENERICITY AND RANDOMNESS

Genericity is a concept used in algebraic geometry. Often in computer algebra, to choose a generic element we rely on the random function rand(), which produces numbers uniformly distributed in an interval. However, the two notions should not be confused.

3.1 Genericity

The set of degree n polynomials form a real vector space endowed with two natural topologies. The usual inherited form that of $\mathbf{R}$ and the Zariski topology. In the second one a basis of closed sets is formed by algebraic hypersurfaces defined as the zeros of multivariate polynomials. A property is then said generic if it is satisfied by a Zariski-dense subset of polynomials.

In practice, we try to concentrate all the "bad" behaviors that we want to avoid into an algebraic hypersurface (which need not be explicitly computed) and then just say "generically". Here after f generic will mean that all roots of the iterated derivatives of the polynomial f are two by two distinct.

PROPOSITION 1. *For a generic polynomial, all virtual not real roots are double.*

PROOF. As all roots of its iterated derivatives are 2 by 2 distinct, near such a root y of a derivative $f^{(i)}$ there is small positive number e and an interval $[y - e, y + e]$ where all the other derivatives keep a constant sign. So the only possibility for a sign variation between $y - e$ and $y + e$ is 0 or 2. $\square$

For a generic polynomial f, we can use Maple to point-plot the roots of the derivatives together with vertical lines passing by them, as illustrated in Figure 2 with a polynomial of degree 6 having no real root. So we expect 3 double virtual roots. In order to locate these 3 virtual roots, we need to evaluate the signs of the derivatives on each row (i.e. rectangle). We know that all the signs are $+$ at ∞ and alternated $+$ and $-$ at $-\infty$. Since the signs change at each root, the signs in the Budan table can be easily completed. Therefore, we can apply the discussion we made in section 2 of the characterization of the patterns appearing in Budan table at a virtual root. Then, a FDcurve or a stem of f (see below in the next section) can be used to express the propagation of the signs of the derivatives in a 2D picture. Let's now state our main connexity result.

THEOREM 3.1. *Let f be generic monic univariate polynomial of degree n. The Budan table of f is represented by $n + 1$ rectangles of height one $L_i := \mathbb{R} \times [i - 1/2, i + 1/2[$ for i from 0 to n. A rectangle (possibly infinite) corresponding to negative values of a derivative is colored, while one corresponding to positive values remain white. The first rectangle is white. Then:*

- *In this table, the number of connected colored components bounded on the right plus the number of connected white components bounded on the right is equal to the number of pairs of virtual non real roots plus the number of real roots.*

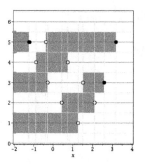

Figure 2: Blocs and roots

- *The rightest blocks of such connected (bounded on the right) components, not on the n-th rectangle, characterize the virtual non real roots.*

PROOF. By genericity, we have $n = 2m + p$ where p is the number of real roots and m the number of (double) virtual non real roots. On the n-th rectangle there are $q := \lceil p/2 \rceil$ (negative) colored blocks bounded on the right and $p - q$ (positive) white blocks bounded on the right. The following argument shows that each of these p blocks are connected to (at least) one of the infinite left ends of the same sign.

By local monotonicity for each i, from 1 to n, and for each root x_0 of $f^{(i-1)}$, the signs of $f^{(i-1)}(x_0 + e)$ and of $f^{(i)}(x_0 + e)$ are the same for small enough $e > 0$. Hence the block of L_{i-1} at the right of x_0 is connected "by the left" to a block of the same sign of L_i. However a block of L_{i-1} can also be connected "by the right" to a block of the same sign of L_i. Let's see when this happens.

For each i, from 1 to n, by Rolle theorem and genericity, there are an odd number of roots on a rectangle L_{i-1} between two successive roots x_1 and x_2 of $f^{(i)}$, let us denote this number by $2r + 1$. Respectively, there are an even number of roots on a rectangle L_{i-1} between $-\infty$ and the first root of $f^{(i)}$, respectively between ∞ and the last root; let us denote this number by $2r$. When $r = 0$, only one connection "by the left" is allowed.

However, when r is a positive integer, r other connections "by the right" appear. See Figures 2 and 10 for an illustration. These connections surround r blocks on L_i with the opposite sign, each of them is limited on the right by a root y of $f^{(i)}$ and is surounded above, below and on the right of that root y, by blocks with the other color. This means that, at that root y, Budan-Fourier count jumps; therefore y is a virtual non real root of f of multiplicity 2.

Such a configuration corresponds to the upper right end of a connected blocks component (bounded on the right); $2m$ among the n left ends at $-\infty$ arrive at such points. The claim follows from this description. $\square$

Figure 2 illustrates an example of degree 6 with 3 virtual non real roots of multiplicity 2. There are 3 "connected colored components bounded on the right" and 0 "connected white components bounded on the right". They characterize 2 virtual roots on the 5-th row and a virtual root on the 3-rd row. See also the example at the end of the paper, where the situation is less simple.

3.2 Randomness

We call random polynomial, a polynomial whose coefficients are obtained by a random distribution, in general image of a classical law (Normal, uniform, Bernouilli). Two kinds of random polynomials have been extensively studied. First, those obtained by choosing a basis of degree n polynomials (x^i or $\sqrt{1/i!}x^i$, etc..) and taking linear combination with random independent coefficients distributed with a classical law. Second, the characteristic polynomials of random matrices whose entries are distributed with a classical law.

A random polynomial f is, with a good probability, generic in the previous algebraic sense; but it is more specific. Indeed, its virtual roots inherit other statistical properties from the distribution of the coefficients of f; when the degree n tends to infinity, some properties are asymptotically almost sure.

For instance, generically the n complex roots of a polynomial are 2 by 2 distinct. But if we consider the characteristic polynomial of a dense random $(128, 128)$ matrix, whose entries are instances of independent centered normal variables with variance v, its complex roots (the eigenvalues) are almost uniformly distributed in a disk of radius $\sqrt{nv}$. This behavior is obviously not generic.

For large degree n (say 100), colored Budan tables look like discretized shapes, exploring this interpretation, it seems worthwhile to also consider the derivation orders as discretized values, hence consider fractional derivatives.

4. FRACTIONAL DERIVATIVES

The idea to introduce and compute with derivatives or antiderivatives of non-integer orders goes back to Leibnitz. In the book [12], the authors relate the history of this concept from 1695 to 1975, the progression is illustrated by historical notes and they included more than a hundred enlightening citations from papers of several great mathematicians: Euler, Lagrange, Laplace, Fourier, Abel, Liouville, Riemann, and many more.

In 1832 Liouville expanded functions in series of exponentials and defined q-th derivatives of such a series by operating term-by-term for q a real number, although Riemann proposed another approach via a definite integral. They give rise to an integral of fractional order called Riemann-Liouville integral for $q < 0$, which depends upon an origin a and generalizes the classical formula for iterated integrations:

$$[\frac{d^q f}{[d(x-a)]^q}]_{R-L} := \frac{1}{\Gamma(-q)} \int_a^x [x-y]^{-q-1} f(y) dy.$$

Then for positive order and any sufficiently derivable function f, one relies on a composition property with $\frac{d^m}{d(x-a)^m}$, for an integer m. So, for any real number $m+q$, one obtains:

$$[\frac{d^{m+q} f}{[d(x-a)]^{m+q}}]_{R-L} := \frac{d^m}{d(x-a)^m} [\frac{d^q f}{[d(x-a)]^q}]_{R-L}.$$

Thanks to properties of the Γ function, this definition is coherent when a change of (q,m) keeping $m+q$ constant. The generalization of this definition to other functions f is discussed in the book [12]. The traditional adjective "fractional" corresponding to the order of derivation is misleading, since it need not be rational.

Let us emphasize that nowadays in mathematics, fractional derivatives are mostly used for the study of PDE in functional analysis. They are presented via Fourier or Laplace transforms. Fractional derivatives are seldom encountered in polynomial algebra or in computer algebra. The second author learned this concept and its history working on [10], then used the following very simple formula, with $q > 0$ and n an integer, attributed to Peacock.

$$\frac{d^q}{[d(x-a)]^q}(x-a)^n := \frac{n!}{(n-q)!}(x-a)^{n-q}.$$

We illustrate it with the monomials of a polynomial, $q = \frac{1}{2}$ and $a = 0$:

$$\frac{d^{1/2}}{[dx]^{1/2}}(x^2 - 2x + 3, x) = (\frac{8}{3}x^2 - 4x + 3)x^{-1/2}\frac{1}{\sqrt{\pi}}.$$

4.1 A bivariate polynomial

LEMMA 1. *Let $f(x)$ be a polynomial of degree n, then*

$$(x-a)^q \Gamma(-q) \frac{d^q f}{[d(x-a)]^q}$$

is a polynomial in x and q.

To interpolate the non vanishing roots of the successive derivatives of a polynomial f, only fractional derivatives, up to a power of $(x-a)$ are needed. We introduce the following notations for a family of univariate polynomials in q and another in $t := n - q$, indexed by their degrees.

For $i = 0, ..., n-1$,

$$l_0 := 1; \quad l_{n-i}(q) := \prod_{j=i+1}^{n} 1 - \frac{q}{j}; \quad \lambda_0 := n!;$$

$$\lambda_{n-i}(t) := n! l_{n-i}(n-t) = i! t(t-1)...(t+i+1-n).$$

DEFINITION 1. *Let $f = \sum a_i(x-a)^i$ be a degree n polynomial. We call monic polynomial factor of a fractional derivative of order q, with respect to the origin a, of f, the bivariate polynomial $(x-a)^q \frac{(n-q)!}{n!} \frac{d^q f}{[d(x-a)]^q}$. It is a polynomial of total degree n in $(x-a)$ and q which is written as*

$$\sum_{i=0}^{n-1} a_i(x-a)^i l_{n-i}(q).$$

It will be convenient to let $t = n - q$, and consider the polynomial obtained with this substitution:

$$P_f(x,t) := \frac{1}{n!} \sum_{i=0}^{n} a_i(x-a)^i \lambda_{n-i}(t).$$

For all $k = 0, ..., n$, we have $P_f(x, n-k) = \frac{(n-k)!}{n!}(x-a)^k f^{(k)}$.

It also holds $(x-a)\frac{\partial}{\partial x} P_f = P_{(x-a)f'}$.

The previous bivariate polynomial realizes an homotopy between the graphs of $f(x)$ and $(x-a)f'(x)$ when t varies between 0 and 1.

4.2 FDcurve

DEFINITION 2. *We call FDcurve, with origin a, of a polynomial f of degree n, the real algebraic curve defined by the bivariate equation $P_f(x,t) = 0$.*

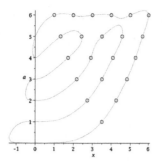

Figure 3: A simple FDcurve

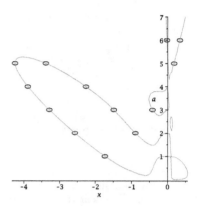

Figure 5: A lonesome component

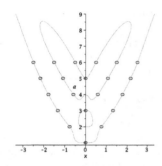

Figure 4: Changing the origin a

Notice that instead of taking the origin at a, we can fix the origin at 0, perform a substitution $x := x - a$ on f and then translate the obtained curve.

Figure 3 shows a simple example with $f := (x - 1)(x - 2)(x - 3)(x - 4)(x - 5)(x - 6)$, $n = 4, a = 0$, an hyperbolic polynomial, hence all its derivatives are hyperbolic. The roots of f and its derivatives are represented by small green disks. In Figure 4 we first performed a substitution with $a = 3.5$. The two curves are quite different, the second has 3 connected components and infinite branches, but both pass through all the roots. The FDcurve corresponding to other values a may have singularities (e.g. double points). So the topologies of the FDcurve can change with a.

In many examples all the connected components cut the axis $x = a$, but it is not always the case: Figure 5 shows the small lonesome component of the example, with $a = 0$,
$f = x^6 + 10.4x^5 + 34.55x^4 + 41.20x^3 + 29.85x^2 - 15.00x - 0.37$. However no root lies on this small component, we do not know if it is always so. In this example f has two real roots, it has also two virtual double roots, their location will be studied in the next section.

In [10], another curve (an algebraic C^0 spline), called the stem of f, is associated to a degree n polynomial f. It is defined as the union of the real curves formed by the roots of all the monic polynomial factors of the derivatives $f^{(i)}$ of f, for i from 0 to $n - 1$ and $0 \le q < 1$. Stems were designed to study the roots of the derivatives of random polynomials of high degrees and exploit their symmetries. To illustrate the differences between these two constructions, Figure 6 shows the stem corresponding to the previous FDcurve with the lonesome component: it is less curved.

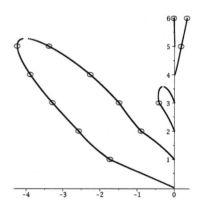

Figure 6: Stem of the previous curve

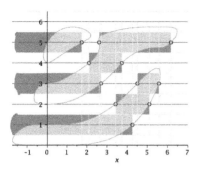

Figure 7: Budan inside and around an FDcurve

5. LOCATION OF VIRTUAL ROOTS

For f a generic monic univariate polynomial of degree n, in this section, we consider partitions of the infinite rectangle R. R is the union of $n+1$ rectangles of height one $\mathbb{R} \times [i-1/2, i+1/2[$ for i from 0 to n. In section 3, we have seen the partition of R corresponding to the Budan table: the rectangles (possibly infinite) corresponding to negative values of a derivative are colored while the ones corresponding to positive values remain white. Theorem 3.1 shows that this partition allows to locate the virtual roots of f. Here, we aim to rely on the ovals of FDcurves or stems to transmit "quickly" the sign information needed for the partition of the Budan table.

For this purpose, let us consider an example where all the roots of the derivatives of f are positive, and choose $a = 0$. This is always possible up to a translation on x. We take the intersection of the negative part of the Budan table and the negative locus of P_f (delimited by the components of the FDcurve). In Figure 7 the intersection zones are colored in grey. These intersection zones are helpful to see that some blocks are connected but not sufficient to guaranty that other blocks are disconnected. So, we also consider the zones colored in blue, shaped as curved triangles in the picture. Two blue zones attached to two separated connected components of the FDcurve may intersect, this happens in Figure 8 with the same example where we changed the origin a, hence the FDcurve. Let's do the same constructions with the stem of Figure 6. In that case, the interiors of the ovals correspond to positive values of an implicit function, so it is better to color the positive blocks. Now, the virtual roots correspond to the leftest blocks. This is illustrated in Figure 9: the 2 virtual roots are immediately located at the leftest roots on the two left ovals.

As a conclusion, we can say that depending on the shape of the stem of f or of an FDcurve, the location of the virtual roots may become very fast. But this possibility should be studied case by case.

5.1 An example of medium degree

We consider a randomly generated polynomial of degree $n = 16$, taking a random linear combination of the so-called Bernstein polynomials, used in Computer Aided Design. It has 6 real roots. In Figure 10, we truncated the picture, and we see only 4 of them. So it remains 5 double virtual roots. In the picture real roots and virtual roots are represented by

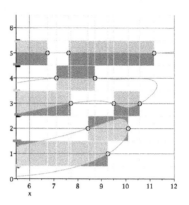

Figure 8: Connecting the components

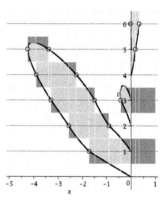

Figure 9: With a stem curve

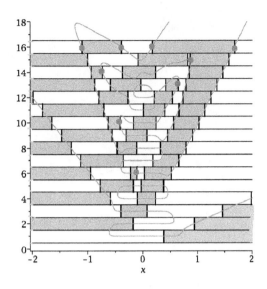

Figure 10: An example of degree 16

blue disks. We colored in grey the negative blocks. Among the 5 virtual roots, 4 correspond to grey blocks components and 1 to a white blocks component.

Notice that the FDcurve is helpful for locating the positive virtual roots (at the end of the ear shaped curves), but not for the negative virtual roots. Therefore it is useful to reduce to positive values and simultaneously consider the polynomial obtained by changing $f(x)$ into $(-1)^n f(-x)$.

6. CONCLUSION

We have characterized the possible patterns between successive rows in a Budan table corresponding to a virtual roots. Restricting to the generic case we have given a global characterization (using connectivity of connected components) of the location of virtual roots in a Budan table. Moreover, we have used fractional derivatives to associate a bivariate polynomial to f, and introduced two types of plane curve associated to f, which help geometrically to see the signs taken by the iterated derivatives of f hence to locate, in many cases, a virtual roots near one of their critical points. We suggest three directions for future researches:

- Investigate what happens when we relax the genericity hypothesis (i.e. specialization to more degenerated cases),

- Study the relationship beteen virtual roots in an interval and pairs of conjugate complex roots which lie in a sector close to this interval counted by Obreschkoff theorem, see [13], chapter 10.

- generalize to other families of functions beyond the polynomials, as initiated in [6].

Acknowledgments

We are grateful to H. Lombardi for valuable discussions. We thank the reviewers for their helpful suggestions. A. Galligo was partially supported by the European ITN Marie Curie network SAGA. D. Bembé was partially supported by the Deutsch-Französische-Hochschule École-Franco-Allemande.

7. REFERENCES

[1] Akritas Alkiviadis G., *Reflections on an pair of theorems by Budan and Fourier*, University of Cansas **22**.

[2] Bembé, D: Budan's theorem and virtual roots of real polynomials Preprint.(2009)

[3] Bharucha-Reid, A. T. and Sambandham, M.: Random Polynomials. Academic Press, N.Y. (1986).

[4] Bochnack, J. and Coste, M. and Roy, M-F.: Real Algebraic Geometry. Springer (1998).

[5] Budan de Boislaurent, *Nouvelle méthode pour la résolution des équations numériques d'un degré quelconque.* Paris (1822). Contains in the appendix a proof of Budan's theorem edited by the Académie des Sciences (1811).

[6] Coste, M and Lajous, T and Lombardi, H and Roy, M-F : Generalized Budan-Fourier theorem and virtual roots. Journal of Complexity, 21, 478-486 (2005).

[7] Edelman,A and Kostlan,E: How many zeros of a random polynomial are real? Bulletin AMS, 32(1):1âĂŞ37, (1995).

[8] Emiris, I and Galligo, A and Tsigaridas, E: Random polynomials and expected complexity of bisection methods for real solving. *Proceedings of the ISSAC'2010 conference,* pp 235-242, ACM NY, (2010).

[9] Farahmand,K: Topics in random polynomials. Pitman research notes in mathematics series 393, Addison Wesley, (1998).

[10] Galligo, A: Roots of the Derivatives of some Random Polynomials. Submitted SNC (2011).

[11] Gonzales-Vega, L and Lombardi, H and Mahé, L : Virtual roots of real polynomials. J. Pure Appl. Algebra,124, pp 147-166,(1998).

[12] Oldham, K and Spanier, J: The fractional calculus. Academic Press Inc. NY, (1974).

[13] Rahman, Q.I and Schmeisser,G: Analytic theory of polynomials, Oxford Univ. press. (2002).

[14] Vincent M,. *Sur la résolution des équations numéricques*, Journal de mathématicques pures et appliquées **44** (1836) 235–372.

Multihomogeneous Polynomial Decomposition using Moment Matrices

Alessandra Bernardi*   Jérôme Brachat*   Pierre Comon+   Bernard Mourrain*

*GALAAD, INRIA Méditerranée
BP 93, 06902 Sophia-Antipolis, France
[FirstName.LastName]@inria.fr

+Laboratoire I3S, CNRS and Univ. of Nice,
Sophia-Antipolis, France
pcomon@i3s.unice.fr

ABSTRACT

In the paper, we address the important problem of tensor decomposition which can be seen as a generalisation of Singular Value Decomposition for matrices. We consider general multilinear and multihomogeneous tensors. We show how to reduce the problem to a truncated moment matrix problem and we give a new criterion for flat extension of Quasi-Hankel matrices. We connect this criterion to the commutation characterisation of border bases. A new algorithm is described: it applies for general multihomogeneous tensors, extending the approach of J.J. Sylvester on binary forms. An example illustrates the algebraic operations involved in this approach and how the decomposition can be recovered from eigenvector computation.

Categories and Subject Descriptors

G.1.5 [**Mathematics of Computing**]: Tensor decomposition; I.1.2 [**Computing Methodologies**]: Symbolic and Algebraic Manipulation—*Algebraic algorithms*

General Terms

Algorithms, Theory

Keywords

Moment matrix, multihomogeneous polynomial decomposition, tensor decomposition.

1. INTRODUCTION

Tensors are objects which appear in many context and applications. The most famous type of tensors corresponds to matrices which are tensors of order two. However in many problems, higher order tensors are naturally used to collect informations which depend on more than two variables. Typically, these data could be observations of some experimentation or of a physical phenomena that depends on several parameters. These observations are stored in a structure called a tensor, according to the dimensional parameters (or modes) of the problem.

The tensor decomposition problem consists to decompose the tensor (e.g. the set of observations) into a minimal sum of indecomposable tensors (i.e. tensors of rank 1). Such a decomposition, which is independent of the coordinate system, allows to extract geometric or invariant properties associated to the observations. For this reason, the tensor decomposition problem has a large impact in many applications. The first well known case for matrices is related to Singular Value Decomposition with applications e.g. to Principal Component Analysis. Its extension to higher order tensors appears in Electrical Engineering [46], in Signal processing [17], [12], in Antenna Array Processing [21] [11] or Telecommunications [48], [10], [43], [24], [20], in Chemometrics [6] or Psychometrics [30], in Data Analysis [14], [9], [22], [29], [44], but also in more theoretical domains such as Arithmetic complexity [31] [4], [45], [32]. Further numerous applications of tensor decompositions may be found in [12], [44].

From a mathematical point of view, the tensors that we will consider are elements of $\mathcal{T} := S^{\delta_1}(E_1) \otimes \cdots \otimes S^{\delta_k}(E_k)$ where $\delta_i \in \mathbb{N}$, E_i are vector spaces of dimension $n_i + 1$ over a field $\mathbb{K}$ (which is of characteristic 0 and algebraically closed), and $S^{\delta_i}(E_i)$ is the δ_i^{th} symmetric power of E_i. The set of tensors of rank 1 form a projective variety which is called the Veronese variety when $k = 1$ or the Segre variety when $\delta_i = 1, i = 1, \ldots, k$. We will call it hereafter the Segre-Veronese variety of $\mathbb{P}(\mathcal{T})$ and denote it $\Xi(\mathcal{T})$. The set of tensors which are the linear combinations of r elements of the Segre-Veronese variety are those which admits a decomposition with at most r terms of rank 1 (ie. in $\Xi(\mathcal{T})$). The closure of this set is called the r-secant variety and denoted $\Xi_r(\mathcal{T})$. More precise definitions of these varieties will be given in Sec. 2.3.

The first method to compute such a decomposition besides the case of matrices or quadratic forms which may go back to the Babylonians, is due to Sylvester for binary forms [47]. Using apolarity, kernels of catalecticant matrices are computed degree by degree until a polynomial with simple roots is found. See also [13], [28]. An extension of this approach for symmetric tensors has been analyzed in [28], and yields a decomposition method in some cases (see [28][p. 187]). Some decomposition methods are also available for specific degrees and dimensions, e.g. using invariant theory [16]. In [3], there is a simplified version of the Sylvester algorithm that uses the mathematical interpretation of the problem in terms of secant varieties of rational normal curves. The same approach is used in [3] to give algorithms for the decompositions of symmetric tensors belonging to $\Xi_2(S^d(E))$ and to $\Xi_3(S^d(E))$. In [1] a complete rank stratification of $\Xi_4(S^d(E))$ is given.

In [5], Sylvester's approach is revisited from an affine point of view and a general decomposition method based on a flat extension criteria is described. In the current paper, we extend this method to more general tensor spaces including classical multilinear tensors and multihomogeneous tensors. We give a new and more flexible criterion for the existence of a decomposition of a given rank, which extend the result in [37] and the characterisation used in [5]. This criterion is a rank condition of an associated Hankel operator. It is used in an algorithm which checks degree by degree if the roots deduced from the kernel of the Hankel operator are simple.

In Sec. 2, we recall the notations, the geometric point related to secants of Segre and Veronese varieties, and the algebraic point of view based on moment matrices. In Sec. 3, we describe the algorithm and the criterion used to solve the truncated moment problem. In Sec. 4, an example of tensor decompositions from Antenna processing illustrates the approach.

2. DUALITY, MOMENT MATRICES AND TENSOR DECOMPOSITION

2.1 Notation and preliminaries

Let $\mathbb{K}$ be an algebraically closed field (e.g. $\mathbb{K} = \mathbb{C}$ the field of complex numbers). We assume that $\mathbb{K}$ is of characteristic 0. For a vector space E, its associated projective space is denoted $\mathbb{P}(E)$. For $\mathbf{v} \in E - \{0\}$ its class in $\mathbb{P}(E)$ is denoted $\overline{\mathbf{v}}$. Let $\mathbb{P}^n$ be the projective space of $E := \mathbb{K}^{n+1}$. For a subset $F = \{f_1, \ldots, f_m\}$ of a vector-space (resp. ring) R, we denote by $\langle F \rangle$ (resp. (F)) the vector space (resp. ideal) generated by F in R.

We consider hereafter the symmetric δ-th power $S^\delta(E)$ where E is a vector space of basis $x_0, \ldots, x_n$. An element of $S^\delta(E)$ is a homogeneous polynomial of degree $\delta \in \mathbb{N}$ in the variables $\mathbf{x} = (x_0, \ldots, x_n)$. For $\mathbf{x}_1 = (x_{0,1}, \ldots, x_{n_1,1})$ $, \ldots, \mathbf{x}_k = (x_{0,k}, \ldots, x_{n_k,k})$, $S^{\delta_1}(E_1) \otimes \cdots \otimes S^{\delta_k}(E_k)$ (with $E_i = \langle x_{0,i}, \ldots, x_{n_i,i} \rangle$) is the vector space of multihomogeneous polynomials of degree δ_i in the variables $\mathbf{x}_i$.

Hereafter, we will consider the dehomogeneization of elements in $S^{\delta_1}(E_1) \otimes \cdots \otimes S^{\delta_k}(E_k)$, obtained by setting $x_{0,i} = 1$ for $i = 1, \ldots, k$. We denote by $R_{\delta_1, \ldots, \delta_k}$ this space, where $R = \mathbb{K}[\underline{\mathbf{x}}_1, \ldots, \underline{\mathbf{x}}_k]$ is the space of polynomials in the variables $\underline{\mathbf{x}}_1 = (x_{1,1}, \ldots, x_{n_1,1}), \ldots, \underline{\mathbf{x}}_k = (x_{1,k}, \ldots, x_{n_k,k})$.

For $\alpha_i = (\alpha_{1,i}, \ldots, \alpha_{n_i,i}) \in \mathbb{N}^{n_i}$ $(i = 1, \ldots, k)$, let $\underline{\mathbf{x}}_i^{\alpha_i} = \prod_{j=1}^{n_i} x_{j,i}^{\alpha_{j,i}}$, $|\alpha_i| = \sum_{j=1}^{n_i} \alpha_{j,i}$, and $\underline{\mathbf{x}}^\alpha = \prod_{j=1}^{n_i} \underline{\mathbf{x}}_i^{\alpha_i}$.

An element f of $R_\delta = R_{\delta_1, \ldots, \delta_k}$ is represented as

$$f = \sum_{\alpha = (\alpha_1, \ldots, \alpha_k); |\alpha_i| \le \delta_i} f_\alpha \underline{\mathbf{x}}_1^{\alpha_1} \cdots \underline{\mathbf{x}}_k^{\alpha_k}.$$

The dimension of $R_\delta := R_{\delta_1, \ldots, \delta_k}$ is $n_{\delta_1, \ldots, \delta_k; n_1, \ldots, n_k} = \prod_{i=1}^k \binom{n_i + \delta_i}{\delta_i}$. For $\delta \in \mathbb{N}, \alpha \in \mathbb{N}^n$ with $|\alpha| \le \delta$, let $\binom{\delta}{\alpha} = \frac{\delta!}{\alpha_1! \cdots \alpha_n!(\delta - |\alpha|)!}$. We define the apolar inner product on $R_{\delta_1, \ldots, \delta_k}$ by $\langle f | g \rangle = \sum_{|\alpha_i| \le \delta_i} f_\alpha \, g_\alpha \binom{\delta_1}{\alpha_1}^{-1} \cdots \binom{\delta_k}{\alpha_k}^{-1}$.

The dual space of a $\mathbb{K}$-vector space E is denoted $E^* = \mathrm{Hom}_{\mathbb{K}}(E, \mathbb{K})$. It is the set of $\mathbb{K}$-linear forms from E to $\mathbb{K}$. A basis of the dual space R_δ^*, is given by the set of linear forms that compute the coefficients of a polynomial in the monomial basis $(\underline{\mathbf{x}}^\alpha)_{\alpha \in \mathbb{N}^{n_1} \times \cdots \times \mathbb{N}^{n_k}; |\alpha_i| \le \delta_i}$. We denote it

by $(\mathbf{d}^\alpha)_{\alpha \in \mathbb{N}^{n_1} \times \cdots \times \mathbb{N}^{n_k}; |\alpha_i| \le \delta_i}$. We identify R^* with the (vector) space of formal power series $\mathbb{K}[[\mathbf{d}]] = \mathbb{K}[[\mathbf{d}_1, \ldots, \mathbf{d}_k]] = \mathbb{K}[[d_{1,1}, \ldots, d_{n_1,1}, \ldots, d_{1,k}, \ldots, d_{n_k,k}]]$. Any element $\Lambda \in R^*$ can be decomposed as

$$\Lambda = \sum_{\alpha \in \mathbb{N}^{n_1} \times \cdots \times \mathbb{N}^{n_k}} \Lambda(\mathbf{x}^\alpha) \, \mathbf{d}^\alpha.$$

Typical elements of R^* are the linear forms that correspond to the evaluation at a point $\zeta = (\zeta_1, \ldots, \zeta_k) \in \mathbb{K}^{n_1} \times \cdots \times \mathbb{K}^{n_k}$:

$$\mathbf{1}_\zeta \; : \; \begin{aligned} R &\to \mathbb{K} \\ p &\mapsto p(\zeta) \end{aligned}$$

The decomposition of $\mathbf{1}_\zeta$ in the basis $\{\mathbf{d}^\alpha\}_{\alpha \in \mathbb{N}^{n_1} \times \cdots \times \mathbb{N}^{n_k}}$ is

$$\mathbf{1}_\zeta = \sum_{\alpha \in \mathbb{N}^{n_1} \times \cdots \times \mathbb{N}^{n_k}} \zeta^\alpha \, \mathbf{d}^\alpha = \sum_{\alpha \in \mathbb{N}^{n_1} \times \cdots \times \mathbb{N}^{n_k}} \prod_{i=1}^k \zeta_i^{\alpha_i} \, \mathbf{d}_i^{\alpha_i}.$$

We recall that the dual space R^* has a natural structure of R-module [23] which is defined as follows: for all $p \in R$, and for all $\Lambda \in R^*$ consider the linear operator

$$p \star \Lambda \; : \; \begin{aligned} R &\to \mathbb{K} \\ q &\mapsto \Lambda(pq). \end{aligned}$$

In particular, we have $x_{i,j} \star \mathbf{d}_1^{\alpha_1} \cdots \mathbf{d}_j^{\alpha_j} \cdots \mathbf{d}_k^{\alpha_k} = \mathbf{d}_1^{\alpha_1} \cdots \mathbf{d}_{j-1}^{\alpha_{j-1}} d_{1,j}^{\alpha_{1,j}} \cdots d_{i-1,j}^{\alpha_{i-1,j}} d_{i,j}^{\alpha_{i,j}-1} d_{i+1,j}^{\alpha_{i+1,j}} \cdots d_{n_j,j}^{\alpha_{n_j,j}} \mathbf{d}_{j+1}^{\alpha_{j+1}} \cdots \mathbf{d}_k^{\alpha_k}$ if $\alpha_{i,j} > 0$ and 0 otherwise.

2.2 Tensor decomposition

In this section, we present different formulations of the tensor decomposition problem, that we consider in this paper.

We will consider hereafter a partially symmetric tensor T which is an element of $S^{\delta_1}(E_1) \otimes \cdots \otimes S^{\delta_k}(E_k)$ where $E_i = \langle x_{0,i}, \ldots, x_{n_i,i} \rangle$. It can be represented by a partially symmetric array of coefficients

$$[T] = (T_{\alpha_1, \ldots, \alpha_k})_{\alpha_i \in \mathbb{N}^{n_i+1}; |\alpha_i| = \delta_i}. \tag{1}$$

For $\alpha_i \in \mathbb{N}^{n_i}$ with $|\alpha_i| \le \delta_i$, we denote $\overline{\alpha}_i = (\delta_i - |\alpha_i|, \alpha_{1,i}, \ldots, \alpha_{n_i,i})$ and, with an abuse of notation, we identify $T_{\alpha_1, \ldots, \alpha_k} := T_{\overline{\alpha_1}, \ldots, \overline{\alpha_k}}$.

Such a tensor is naturally associated to a (multihomogeneous) polynomial in the variables $\mathbf{x}_1 = (x_{0,1}, \ldots, x_{n_1,1})$, $\ldots, \mathbf{x}_k = (x_{0,k}, \ldots, x_{n_k,k})$

$$T(\mathbf{x}) = \sum_{\substack{\alpha = (\alpha_1, \ldots, \alpha_k) \in \mathbb{N}^{n_1} \times \cdots \times \mathbb{N}^{n_k}; \\ |\alpha_i| \le \delta_i}} T_\alpha \mathbf{x}_1^{\overline{\alpha}_1} \cdots \mathbf{x}_k^{\overline{\alpha}_k}.$$

or to an element $\underline{T}(\underline{\mathbf{x}}) \in R_{\delta_1, \ldots, \delta_k}$ obtained by substituting $x_{0,i}$ by 1 in $T(\mathbf{x})$ (for $i = 1, \ldots, k$):

$$\underline{T}(\underline{\mathbf{x}}) = \sum_{\substack{\alpha \in \mathbb{N}^{n_1} \times \cdots \times \mathbb{N}^{n_k}; \\ |\alpha_i| \le \delta_i}} T_\alpha \underline{\mathbf{x}}_1^{\alpha_1} \cdots \underline{\mathbf{x}}_k^{\alpha_k}.$$

An element of $R^* = \mathbb{K}[[\mathbf{d}]]$ can also be associated naturally to T:

$$T^*(\mathbf{d}) = \sum_{\substack{\alpha \in \mathbb{N}^{n_1} \times \cdots \times \mathbb{N}^{n_k}; \\ |\alpha_i| \le \delta_i}} \binom{\delta_1}{\alpha_1}^{-1} \cdots \binom{\delta_k}{\alpha_k}^{-1} T_\alpha \, \mathbf{d}_1^{\alpha_1} \cdots \mathbf{d}_k^{\alpha_k}.$$

so that for all $T' \in R_{\delta_1, \ldots, \delta_k}$,

$$\langle T(\underline{\mathbf{x}}) | T'(\underline{\mathbf{x}}) \rangle = T^*(\mathbf{d})(T'(\underline{\mathbf{x}})).$$

The problem of decomposition of the tensor T can be stated as follows:

Tensor decomposition problem. *Given* $T(\mathbf{x}) \in S^{\delta_1}(E_1) \otimes \cdots \otimes S^{\delta_k}(E_k)$, *find a decomposition of* $T(\mathbf{x})$ *as a sum of products of powers of linear forms in* $\mathbf{x}_j$:

$$T(\mathbf{x}) = \sum_{i=1}^{r} \gamma_i \, \mathbf{l}_{1,i}(\mathbf{x}_1)^{\delta_1} \cdots \mathbf{l}_{k,i}(\mathbf{x}_k)^{\delta_k} \qquad (2)$$

where $\gamma_i \neq 0$, $\mathbf{l}_{j,i}(\mathbf{x}_j) = l_{0,j,i} x_{0,j} + l_{1,j,i} x_{1,j} + \cdots + l_{n_j,j,i} x_{j,n_j}$ *and* r *is the smallest possible integer for such a decomposition.*

DEFINITION 2.1. *The minimal number of terms* r *in a decomposition of the form* (2) *is called the* rank *of* T.

We say that $T(\mathbf{x})$ has an *affine decomposition* if there exists a minimal decomposition of $T(\mathbf{x})$ of the form (2) where r is the rank of T and such that $l_{0,j,i} \neq 0$ for $i = 1, \dots, r$. Notice that by a generic change of coordinates in E_i, we may assume that all $l_{0,j,i} \neq 0$ and thus that T has an affine decomposition. Suppose that $T(\mathbf{x})$ has an affine decomposition. Then by scaling $\mathbf{l}_{j,i}(\mathbf{x}_j)$ and multiplying γ_i by the inverse of the δ_j^{th} power of this scaling factor, we may assume that $l_{0,j,i} = 1$. Thus, the polynomial

$$\underline{T}(\underline{\mathbf{x}}) = \sum_{i=1}^{r} \gamma_i \sum_{|\alpha_i| \leq \delta_i} \binom{\delta_1}{\alpha_1} \cdots \binom{\delta_k}{\alpha_k} \zeta_{1,i}^{\alpha_1} \cdots \zeta_{k,i}^{\alpha_k} \underline{\mathbf{x}}_1^{\alpha_1} \cdots \underline{\mathbf{x}}_k^{\alpha_k}$$

with $T_{\alpha_1, \dots, \alpha_k} = \sum_{i=1}^{r} \gamma_i \sum_{|\alpha_i| \leq \delta_i} \binom{\delta_1}{\alpha_1} \cdots \binom{\delta_k}{\alpha_k} \zeta_{1,i}^{\alpha_1} \cdots \zeta_{k,i}^{\alpha_k}$. Equivalently, we have

$$T^*(\mathbf{d}) = \sum_{i=1}^{r} \gamma_i \sum_{|\alpha_i| \leq \delta_i} \zeta_{1,i}^{\alpha_1} \cdots \zeta_{k,i}^{\alpha_k} \mathbf{d}_1^{\alpha_1} \cdots \mathbf{d}_k^{\alpha_k}$$

so that $T^*(\mathbf{d})$ coincides on $R_{\delta_1, \dots, \delta_k}$ with the linear form

$$\sum_{i=1}^{r} \gamma_i \, \mathbf{1}_{\zeta_{1,i}, \dots, \zeta_{k,i}} = \sum_{i=1}^{r} \gamma_i \, \mathbf{1}_{\zeta_i}$$

with $\zeta_i := (\zeta_{1,i}, \dots, \zeta_{k,i}) \in \mathbb{K}^{n_1} \times \cdots \mathbb{K}^{n_k}$.

The problem of decomposition of T can then be restated as follows:

Interpolation problem. *Given* $T^* \in R^*_{\delta_1, \dots, \delta_k}$ *which admits an affine decomposition, find the minimal number of non-zero vectors* $\zeta_1, \dots, \zeta_r \in \mathbb{K}^{n_1} \times \cdots \times \mathbb{K}^{n_k}$ *and non-zero scalars* $\gamma_1, \dots, \gamma_r \in \mathbb{K} - \{0\}$ *such that*

$$T^* = \sum_{i=1}^{r} \gamma_i \, \mathbf{1}_{\zeta_i} \qquad (3)$$

on $R_{\delta_1, \dots, \delta_k}$.

If such a decomposition exists, we say that $\Lambda = \sum_{i=1}^{r} \gamma_i \, \mathbf{1}_{\zeta_i} \in R^*$ extends $T^* \in R^*_{\delta_1, \dots, \delta_k}$.

2.3 Indecomposable tensors

In this section, we analyze the set of indecomposable tensor (or tensors of rank 1). They naturally form projective varieties, which we are going to describe using the language of projective geometry.

We begin by defining two auxiliary but very classical varieties, namely Segre variety and Veronese variety.

DEFINITION 2.2. *The image of the following map*

$$s_k : \mathbb{P}(E_1) \times \cdots \times \mathbb{P}(E_k) \rightarrow \mathbb{P}(E_1 \otimes \cdots \otimes E_k)$$
$$(\overline{\mathbf{v}_1}, \dots, \overline{\mathbf{v}_k}) \mapsto \overline{\mathbf{v}_1 \otimes \cdots \otimes \mathbf{v}_k}$$

is the so called Segre variety of k *factors. We denote it by* $\Xi(E_1 \otimes \cdots \otimes E_k)$.

From Definition 2.1 of the rank of a tensor and from the Interpolation Problem point of view (3) we see that a Segre variety parametrizes projective classes of rank 1 tensors $T = \mathbf{v}_1 \otimes \cdots \otimes \mathbf{v}_k \in E_1 \otimes \cdots \otimes E_k$ for certain $\mathbf{v}_i \in E_i$, $i = 1, \dots, k$.

DEFINITION 2.3. *Let* (J_1, J_2) *be a partition of the set* $\{1, \dots, k\}$. *If* $J_1 = \{h_1, \dots, h_s\}$ *and* $J_2 = \{1, \dots, k\} \setminus J_1 = \{h'_1, \dots, h'_{k-s}\}$, *the* (J_1, J_2)-Flattening *of* $E_1 \otimes \cdots \otimes E_k$ *is the following:*

$$E_{J_1} \otimes E_{J_2} = (E_{h_1} \otimes \cdots \otimes E_{h_s}) \otimes (E_{h'_1} \otimes \cdots \otimes E_{h'_{k-s}}).$$

Let $E_{J_1} \otimes E_{J_2}$ be any flattening of $E_1 \otimes \cdots \otimes E_k$ as in Definition 2.3 and let $f_{J_1, J_2} : \mathbb{P}(E_1 \otimes \cdots \otimes E_k) \rightarrow \mathbb{P}(E_{J_1} \otimes E_{J_2})$ be the obvious isomorphism. Let $[T]$ be an array associated to a tensor $T \in E_1 \otimes \cdots \otimes E_k$; let $\overline{T'} = f_{J_1, J_2}(\overline{\mathbf{T}}) \in \mathbb{P}(E_{J_1} \otimes E_{J_2})$ and let $[A_{J_1, J_2}]$ be the matrix associated to T'. Then the d-minors of the matrix $[A_{J_1, J_2}]$ are said to be d-minors of $[T]$.

An array $[A] = (x_{i_1, \dots, i_k})_{0 \leq i_j \leq n_j, \, j=1, \dots, k}$ is said to be a generic array of indeterminates of $R = \mathbb{K}[\underline{\mathbf{x}}_1, \dots, \underline{\mathbf{x}}_k]$ if the entries of $[A]$ are the independent variables of R.

It is a classical result due to R. Grone (see [26]) that a set of equations for a Segre variety is given by all the 2-minors of a generic array. In [27] it is proved that, if $[A]$ is a generic array in R of size $(n_1 + 1) \times \cdots \times (n_k + 1)$ and $I_d([A])$ is the ideal generated by the d-minors of $[A]$, then $I_2([A])$ is a prime ideal, therefore:

$$I(\Xi(E_1 \otimes \cdots \otimes E_k)) = I_2([A]).$$

We introduce now the Veronese variety. Classically it is defined to be the d-tuple embedding of $\mathbb{P}^n$ into $\mathbb{P}^{\binom{n+d}{d}-1}$ via the linear system associated to the sheaf $\mathcal{O}(d)$ with $d > 0$. We give here an equivalent definition.

Let E be an $n + 1$ dimensional vector space. With the notation $S^d(E)$ we mean the vector subspace of $E^{\otimes d}$ of symmetric tensors.

DEFINITION 2.4. *The image of the following map*

$$\nu_d : \mathbb{P}(E) \rightarrow \mathbb{P}(S^d(E))$$
$$\overline{\mathbf{v}} \mapsto \overline{\mathbf{v}^{\otimes \mathbf{d}}}$$

is the so called Veronese variety. We indicate it with $\Xi(S^d(E))$.

With this definition it is easy to see that the Veronese variety parametrizes symmetric rank 1 tensors.

Observe that if we take the vector space E to be a vector space of linear forms $\langle x_0, \dots, x_n \rangle$ then the image of the map ν_d above parametrizes homogeneous polynomials that can be written as d-th powers of linear forms.

The Veronese variety $\Xi(S^d(E)) \subset \mathbb{P}(S^d(E))$ can be also viewed as $\Xi(S^d(E)) = \Xi(E^{\otimes d}) \cap \mathbb{P}(S^d(E))$.

Let $[A] = (x_{i_1, \dots, i_d})_{0 \leq i_j \leq n, \, j=1, \dots, d}$ be a generic symmetric array. It is a known result that:

$$I(\Xi(S^d(E))) = I_2([A]). \qquad (4)$$

See [49] for the set theoretical point of view. In [41] the author proved that $I(\Xi(S^d(E)))$ is generated by the 2-minors of a particular catalecticant matrix (for a definition of "Catalecticant matrices" see e.g. either [41] or [25]). A. Parolin, in his PhD thesis ([40]), proved that the ideal generated by the 2-minors of that catalecticant matrix is actually $I_2([A])$.

We are now ready to describe the geometric object that parametrizes partially symmetric tensors $T \in S^{\delta_1}(E_1) \otimes \cdots \otimes S^{\delta_k}(E_k)$. Let us start with the rank 1 partially symmetric tensors.

DEFINITION 2.5. *Let $E_1, \ldots, E_k$ be vector spaces of dimensions $n_1 + 1, \ldots, n_k + 1$ respectively. The Segre-Veronese variety $\Xi(S^{\delta_1}(E_1) \otimes \cdots \otimes S^{\delta_k}(E_k))$ is the embedding of $\mathbb{P}(E_1) \otimes \cdots \otimes \mathbb{P}(E_k)$ into $\mathbb{P}^{N-1} \simeq \mathbb{P}(S^{\delta_1}(E_1) \otimes \cdots \otimes S^{\delta_k}(E_k))$, where $N = \left(\Pi_{i=1}^{k} \binom{n_i + \delta_i}{d_i} \right)$, given by sections of the sheaf $\mathcal{O}(\delta_1, \ldots, \delta_k)$. I.e. $\Xi(S^{\delta_1}(E_1) \otimes \cdots \otimes S^{\delta_k}(E_k))$ is the image of the composition of the following two maps:*

$$\mathbb{P}(E_1) \times \cdots \times \mathbb{P}(E_k) \xrightarrow{\nu_{\delta_1} \times \cdots \times \nu_{\delta_k}} \mathbb{P}^{\binom{n_1 + \delta_1}{\delta_1} - 1} \times \cdots \times \mathbb{P}^{\binom{n_k + \delta_k}{\delta_k} - 1}$$

and $\mathbb{P}^{\binom{n_1 + \delta_1}{\delta_1} - 1} \times \cdots \times \mathbb{P}^{\binom{n_k + \delta_k}{\delta_t} - 1} \xrightarrow{s} \mathbb{P}^{N-1}$, where each ν_{δ_i} is a Veronese embedding of $\mathbb{P}(E_i)$ as in Definition 2.4 then $Im(\nu_{\delta_1} \times \cdots \times \nu_{\delta_k}) = \Xi(S^{\delta_1}(E_1)) \times \cdots \times \Xi(S^{\delta_k}(E_k))$ and $Im(s)$ is the Segre variety of k factors. Therefore the Segre-Veronese variety is the Segre re-embedding of the product of k Veronese varieties.

If $(\delta_1, \ldots, \delta_k) = (1, \ldots, 1)$ then the corresponding Segre-Veronese variety is nothing else than the classical Segre variety of $\mathbb{P}(E_1 \otimes \cdots \otimes E_k)$.

If $k = 1$ then the corresponding Segre-Veronese variety is nothing else than the classical Veronese variety of $\mathbb{P}(S^{\delta_1}(E_1))$.

Observe that $\Xi(S^{\delta_1}(E_1) \otimes \cdots \otimes S^{\delta_k}(E_k))$ can be viewed as the intersection with the Segre variety $\Xi(E_1^{\otimes \delta_1} \otimes \cdots \otimes E_k^{\otimes \delta_k})$ that parametrizes rank one tensors and the projective subspace $\mathbb{P}(S^{\delta_1}(E_1) \otimes \cdots \otimes S^{\delta_k}(E_k)) \subset \mathbb{P}(E_1^{\otimes \delta_1} \otimes \cdots \otimes E_k^{\otimes \delta_k})$ that parametrizes partially symmetric tensors: $\Xi(S^{\delta_1}(E_1) \otimes \cdots \otimes S^{\delta_k}(E_k)) = \Xi(E_1^{\otimes \delta_1} \otimes \cdots \otimes E_k^{\otimes \delta_k}) \cap \mathbb{P}(S^{\delta_1}(E_1) \otimes \cdots \otimes S^{\delta_k}(E_k))$.

In [2] it is proved that if $[A]$ is a generic array of indeterminates associated to the multihomogeneous polynomial ring $S^{\delta_1}(E_1) \otimes \cdots \otimes S^{\delta_k}(E_k)$ (i.e. it is a generic partially symmetric array), the ideal of the Segre-Veronese variety $\Xi(S^{\delta_1}(E_1) \otimes \cdots \otimes S^{\delta_k}(E_k))$ is

$$I(\Xi(S^{\delta_1}(E_1) \otimes \cdots \otimes S^{\delta_k}(E_k))) = I_2([A])$$

with $\delta_i > 0$ for $i = 1, \ldots, k$.

Now if we consider the vector spaces E_i that are vector spaces of linear forms $E_i \simeq S^1(E_i)$ for $i = 1, \ldots, k$, we get that the Segre-Veronese variety $\Xi(S^{\delta_1}(E_1) \otimes \cdots \otimes S^{\delta_k}(E_k))$ parametrizes multihomogenoeus polynomials $F \in S^{\delta_1}(E_1) \otimes \cdots \otimes S^{\delta_k}(E_k)$ of the type $F = \mathbf{l}_1^{\delta_1} \cdots \mathbf{l}_k^{\delta_k}$ where $\mathbf{l}_i$ are linear forms in $S^1(E_i)$ for $i = 1, \ldots, k$.

From this observation we understand that the Tensor decomposition problem of finding a minimal decomposition of type (2) for an element $T \in S^{\delta_1}(E_1) \otimes \cdots \otimes S^{\delta_k}(E_k)$ is equivalent to finding the minimum number of elements belonging to the Segre-Veronese variety $\Xi(S^{\delta_1}(E_1) \otimes \cdots \otimes S^{\delta_k}(E_k))$ whose span contains $\overline{T} \in \mathbb{P}(S^{\delta_1}(E_1) \otimes \cdots \otimes S^{\delta_k}(E_k))$.

The natural geometric objects that are associated to this kind of problems are the higher Secant varieties of the Segre-Veronese varieties that we are going to define.

DEFINITION 2.6. *Let $X \subset \mathbb{P}^N$ be any projective variety and define $X_s^0 := \bigcup_{\overline{\mathbf{P_1}}, \ldots, \overline{\mathbf{P_s}} \in X} \langle \overline{\mathbf{P_1}}, \ldots, \overline{\mathbf{P_s}} \rangle$. The s-th secant variety $X_s \subset \mathbb{P}^N$ of X is the Zariski closure of X_s^0.*

Observe that the generic element of X_s is a point $\overline{\mathbf{P}} \in \mathbb{P}^N$ that can be written as a linear combination of s points of X, in fact a generic element of X_s is an element of X_s^0. Therefore if X is the Segre-Veronese variety, then the generic element of $\Xi_s(S^{\delta_1}(E_1) \otimes \cdots \otimes S^{\delta_k}(E_k))$ is the projective class of a partially symmetric tensor $T \in S^{\delta_1}(E_1) \otimes \cdots \otimes S^{\delta_k}(E_k)$ that can be written as a linear combination of s linearly independent partially symmetric tensors of rank 1. Unfortunately not all the elements of $\Xi_s(S^{\delta_1}(E_1) \otimes \cdots \otimes S^{\delta_k}(E_k))$ are of this form. In fact if $\overline{T} \in \Xi_s(S^{\delta_1}(E_1) \otimes \cdots \otimes S^{\delta_k}(E_k)) \setminus \Xi_s^0(S^{\delta_1}(E_1) \otimes \cdots \otimes S^{\delta_k}(E_k))$ then the rank of T is strictly bigger than s.

DEFINITION 2.7. *The minimum integer s such that $\overline{T} \in \mathbb{P}(S^{\delta_1}(E_1) \otimes \cdots \otimes S^{\delta_k}(E_k))$ belongs to $\Xi_s(S^{\delta_1}(E_1) \otimes \cdots \otimes S^{\delta_k}(E_k))$ is called the border rank of T.*

In order to find the border rank of a tensor $T \in S^{\delta_1}(E_1) \otimes \cdots \otimes S^{\delta_k}(E_k)$ we should need a set of equations for $\Xi_s(S^{\delta_1}(E_1) \otimes \cdots \otimes S^{\delta_k}(E_k))$ for $s > 1$. The knowledge of the generators of the ideals of secant varieties of homogeneous varieties is a very deep problem that is solved only for very particular cases (see eg. [39], [36], [33], [34], [7], [35]).

From a computational point of view, there is a very direct and well known way of getting the equations for the secant variety, which consists of introducing parameters or unknowns for the coefficients of $\mathbf{l}_{i,j}$ and γ_i in (2), to expand the polynomial and identify its coefficients with the coefficients of T. Eliminating the coefficients of $\mathbf{l}_{i,j}$ and γ_i yields the equations of the secant variety.

Unfortunately this procedure is far from being computationally practical, because we have to deal with high degree polynomials in many variables, with a lot of symmetries. This is why we need to introduce moment matrices and to use a different kind of elimination.

2.4 Moment matrices

In this section, we recall the algebraic tools and the properties we need to describe and analyze our algorithm. We refer e.g. to [5], [23], [38].

Let $n := \sum_i n_i$, we have $R \simeq \mathbb{K}[x_1, \ldots, x_n]$. For any $\Lambda \in R^*$, we define the bilinear form Q_Λ, such that $\forall a, b \in R$, $Q(a, b) = \Lambda(ab)$. The matrix of Q_Λ in the monomial basis, of R is $\mathbb{Q}_\Lambda = (\Lambda(\mathbf{x}^{\alpha + \beta}))_{\alpha, \beta}$, where $\alpha, \beta \in \mathbb{N}^n$. Similarly, for any $\Lambda \in R^*$, we define the Hankel operator H_Λ from R to R^* as

$$H_\Lambda \quad : \quad R \to R^*$$
$$p \mapsto p \star \Lambda.$$

The matrix of the linear operator H_Λ in the monomial basis, and in the dual basis, $\{\mathbf{d}^\alpha\}$, is $\mathbb{H}_\Lambda = (\Lambda(\mathbf{x}^{\alpha + \beta}))_{\alpha, \beta}$, where $\alpha, \beta \in \mathbb{N}^n$. The following relates the Hankel operators with the bilinear forms. For all $a, b \in R$, thanks to the R-module structure, it holds

$$Q_\Lambda(a, b) = \Lambda(ab) = a \star \Lambda(b) = H_\Lambda(a)(b).$$

In what follows, we will identify H_Λ and Q_Λ.

DEFINITION 2.8. *Given $B = \{b_1, \ldots, b_r\}, B' = \{b'_1, \ldots, b'_{r'}\} \subset R$, we define*

$$H_\Lambda^{B, B'} : \langle B \rangle \to \langle B' \rangle^*,$$

as the restriction of H_Λ to the vector space $\langle B \rangle$ and inclusion of $\langle B' \rangle^*$ in R^*. Let $\mathbb{H}_\Lambda^{B, B'} = (\Lambda(b_i b'_j))_{1 \le i \le r, 1 \le j \le r'}$. If $B' = B$, we also use the notation H_Λ^B and $\mathbb{H}_\Lambda^{\overline{B}}$.

If B, B' are linearly independent, then $\mathbb{H}_\Lambda^{B,B'}$ is the matrix of $H_\Lambda^{B,B'}$ in this basis $\{b_1, \ldots, b_r\}$ of $\langle B \rangle$ and the dual basis of B' in $\langle B' \rangle^*$. The *catalecticant* matrices of [28] correspond to the case where $k = 1$ and B and B' are, respectively, the set of monomials of degree $\leq i$ and $\leq d - i$ $(i = 0, \ldots, \delta)$.

From the definition of the Hankel operators, we can deduce that a polynomial $p \in R$ belongs to the kernel of $\mathbb{H}_\Lambda$ if and only if $p \star \Lambda = 0$, which in turn holds if and only if for all $q \in R$, $\Lambda(pq) = 0$.

PROPOSITION 2.9   ([5]). *Let I_Λ be the kernel of H_Λ. Then, I_Λ is an ideal of R.*

Let $\mathcal{A}_\Lambda = R/I_\Lambda$ be the quotient algebra of polynomials modulo the ideal I_Λ, which, as Proposition 2.9 states is the kernel of H_Λ. The rank of H_Λ is the dimension of $\mathcal{A}_\Lambda$ as a $\mathbb{K}$-vector space.

DEFINITION 2.10. *For any $B \subset R$, let $B^+ = B \cup x_{1,1}B \cup \cdots \cup x_{n_k,k}B$ and $\partial B = B^+ \setminus B$.*

PROPOSITION 2.11   ([37, 5]). *Assume that $\mathrm{rank}(H_\Lambda) = r < \infty$ and let $B = \{b_1, \ldots, b_r\} \subset R$ such that $\mathbb{H}_\Lambda^B$ is invertible. Then $b_1, \ldots, b_r$ is a basis of $\mathcal{A}_\Lambda$. If $1 \in \langle B \rangle$ the ideal I_Λ is generated by $\ker H_\Lambda^{B^+}$.*

PROPOSITION 2.12   ([23, 5]). *If $\mathrm{rank}(H_\Lambda) = r < \infty$, then $\mathcal{A}_\Lambda$ is of dimension r over $\mathbb{K}$ and there exist $\zeta_1, \ldots, \zeta_d \in \mathbb{K}^n$ where $d \leq r$), and $p_i \in \mathbb{K}[\partial_1, \ldots, \partial_n]$, such that*

$$\Lambda = \sum_{i=1}^{d} \mathbf{1}_{\zeta_i} \circ p_i(\partial). \qquad (5)$$

Moreover the multiplicity of ζ_i is the dimension of the vector space spanned the inverse system generated by $\mathbf{1}_{\zeta_i} \circ p_i(\partial)$.

In characteristic 0, the inverse system of $\mathbf{1}_{\zeta_i} \circ p_i(\partial)$ is isomorphic to the vector space generated by p_i and its derivatives of any order with respect to the variables ∂_i. In general characteristic, we replace the derivatives by the product by the "inverse" of the variables [38], [23].

DEFINITION 2.13. *For $T^* \in R^*_{\delta_1, \ldots, \delta_k}$, we call generalized decomposition of T^* a decomposition such that $T^* = \sum_{i=1}^{d} \mathbf{1}_{\zeta_i} \circ p_i(\partial)$ where the sum for $i = 1, \ldots, d$ of the dimensions of the vector spaces spanned by the inverse system generated by $\mathbf{1}_{\zeta_i} \circ p_i(\partial)$ is minimal. This minimal sum of dimensions is called the length of T^*.*

This definition extends the definition introduced in [28] for binary forms. The length of T^* is the rank of the corresponding Hankel operator H_Λ.

THEOREM 2.14   ([5]). *For any $\Lambda \in R^*$, we have $\Lambda = \sum_{i=1}^{r} \gamma_i \mathbf{1}_{\zeta_i}$ with $\gamma_i \neq 0$ and ζ_i distinct points of $\mathbb{K}^n$ iff $\mathrm{rank}\, H_\Lambda = r$ and I_Λ is a radical ideal.*

In the binary case this rank also corresponds to the border rank of T^*, therefore the r-th minors of the Hankel operator give equations for the r-th secant variety to the rational normal curves [28].

In order to compute the zeroes of an ideal I_Λ when we know a basis of $\mathcal{A}_\Lambda$, we exploit the properties of the operators of multiplication in $\mathcal{A}_\Lambda$: $M_a : \mathcal{A}_\Lambda \to \mathcal{A}_\Lambda$, such that $\forall b \in \mathcal{A}_\Lambda$, $M_a(b) = a\,b$ and its transposed operator $M_a^t : \mathcal{A}_\Lambda^* \to \mathcal{A}_\Lambda^*$, such that for $\forall \gamma \in \mathcal{A}_\Lambda^*$, $M_a^\top(\gamma) = a \star \gamma$.

The following proposition expresses a similar result, based on the properties of the duality.

PROPOSITION 2.15   ([38, 5]). *For any linear form $\Lambda \in R^*$ such that $\mathrm{rank}\, H_\Lambda < \infty$ and any $a \in \mathcal{A}_\Lambda$, we have*

$$H_{a \star \Lambda} = M_a^t \circ H_\Lambda \qquad (6)$$

We have the following well-known theorem:

THEOREM 2.16   ([19, 18, 23]). *Assume that $\mathcal{A}_\Lambda$ is a finite dimensional vector space. Then $\Lambda = \sum_{i=1}^{d} \mathbf{1}_{\zeta_i} \circ p_i(\partial)$ for $\zeta_i \in \mathbb{K}^n$ and $p_i(\partial) \in \mathbb{K}[\partial_1, \ldots, \partial_n]$ and*

- *the eigenvalues of the operators M_a and M_a^t, are given by $\{a(\zeta_1), \ldots, a(\zeta_r)\}$.*
- *the common eigenvectors of the operators $(M_{x_i}^t)_{1 \leq i \leq n}$ are (up to scalar) $\mathbf{1}_{\zeta_i}$.*

Using the previous proposition, one can recover the points $\zeta_i \in \mathbb{K}^n$ by eigenvector computation as follows. Assume that $B \subset R$ with $|B| = \mathrm{rank}(H_\Lambda)$, then equation (6) and its transposition yield

$$\mathbb{H}_{a \star \Lambda}^B = \mathbb{M}_a^t \mathbb{H}_\Lambda^B = \mathbb{H}_\Lambda^B \mathbb{M}_a,$$

where $\mathbb{M}_a$ is the matrix of multiplication by a in the basis B of $\mathcal{A}_\Lambda$. By Theorem 2.16, the common solutions of the generalized eigenvalue problem

$$(\mathbb{H}_{a \star \Lambda} - \lambda\, \mathbb{H}_\Lambda)\mathbf{v} = \mathbb{0} \qquad (7)$$

for all $a \in R$, yield the common eigenvectors $\mathbb{H}_\Lambda^B \mathbf{v}$ of $\mathbb{M}_a^t$, that is the evaluation $\mathbf{1}_{\zeta_i}$ at the roots. Therefore, these common eigenvectors $\mathbb{H}_\Lambda^B \mathbf{v}$ are up to a scalar, the vectors $[b_1(\zeta_i), \ldots, b_r(\zeta_i)]$ $(i = 1, \ldots, r)$. Notice that it is sufficient to compute the common eigenvectors of $(\mathbb{H}_{x_i \star \Lambda}, \mathbb{H}_\Lambda)$ for $i = 1, \ldots, n$

If $\Lambda = \sum_{i=1}^{d} \gamma_i \mathbf{1}_{\zeta_i}$ $(\gamma_i \neq 0)$, then the roots are simple, and one eigenvector computation is enough: for any $a \in R$, $\mathbb{M}_a$ is diagonalizable and the generalized eigenvectors $\mathbb{H}_\Lambda^B \mathbf{v}$ are, up to a scalar, the evaluation $\mathbf{1}_{\zeta_i}$ at the roots.

Coming back to our problem of partially symmetric tensor decomposition, $T^* \in R^*_{\delta_1, \ldots, \delta_k}$ admits an affine decomposition of rank r iff T^* coincide on $R_{\delta_1, \ldots, \delta_k}$ with

$$\Lambda = \sum_{i=1}^{r} \gamma_i\, \mathbf{1}_{\zeta_i},$$

for some distinct $\zeta_1, \ldots, \zeta_r \in \mathbb{K}^{n_1} \times \cdots \times \mathbb{K}^{n_k}$ and some $\gamma_i \in \mathbb{K} - \{0\}$. Then, by theorem 2.14, H_Λ is of rank r and I_Λ is radical.

Conversely, given H_Λ of rank r with I_Λ radical which coincides on $R_{\delta_1, \ldots, \delta_k}$ with T^*, by proposition 2.12, $\Lambda = \sum_{i=1}^{r} \gamma_i \mathbf{1}_{\zeta_i}$ and extends T^*, which thus admits an affine decomposition.

Therefore we can say that if the border rank of T is r then also $\mathrm{rank}(H_\Lambda) = r$. Conversely if $\mathrm{rank}(H_\Lambda) = r$, we can only claim that the border rank of T is at least r.

The problem of decomposition of T^* can thus be reformulated as follows:

Truncated moment problem. *Given $T^* \in R^*_{\delta_1, \ldots, \delta_k}$, find the smallest r such that there exists $\Lambda \in R^*$ which extends T^* with H_Λ of rank r and I_Λ a radical ideal.*

In the next section, we will describe an algorithm to solve the truncated moment problem.

3. ALGORITHM

In this section, we first describe the algorithm from a geometric point of view and the algebraic computation it induces. Then, we characterize under which the conditions T^*

can be extended to $\Lambda \in R^*$ with H_Λ of rank r. The idea of the algorithm is the following:

Given a tensor $T \in S^{\delta_1}(E_1) \otimes \cdots \otimes S^{\delta_k}(E_k)$, set $r = 0$;

1. *Determine if T^* can be extended to $\Lambda \in R^*$ with rank $H_\Lambda = r$; if the answer is YES, go to step 2, otherwise repeat step 1) with $r + 1$.*

2. *Find if there exists r distinct points $P_1, \ldots, P_r \in \Xi(S^{\delta_1}(E_1) \otimes \cdots \otimes S^{\delta_k}(E_k))$ such that $T \in \langle P_1, \ldots, P_r \rangle \simeq \mathbb{P}^{s-1}$ – equivalently compute the roots of $\ker H_\Lambda$ by generalized eigenvector computation (7) and check that the eigenspaces are simple;*

3. *If the answer to 2 is YES, then the rank of T is actually r and we are done;*

4. *If the answer to 3 is NO, then it means that the rank of T is bigger than r. Repeat this procedure from step 3 with $r + 1$.*

This algorithm extends the one in [5] which applies only for symmetric tensors. The approach used in [3] for the rank of tensors in $\Xi_2(S^d(E))$ and in $\Xi_3(S^d(E))$ allows to avoid to loop again at step 4: if one doesn't get simple roots, then it is possible to use other techniques to compute the rank. Unfortunately the mathematical knowledge on the stratification by rank of secant varieties is nowadays not complete, hence these techniques cannot be used now to improve algorithms for higher border ranks.

We are going to characterize now under which conditions T^* can be extended to $\Lambda \in R^*$ with H_Λ of rank r (step 3).

We need the following technical property on the bases of $\mathcal{A}_\Lambda$, that we will consider:

DEFINITION 3.1. *Let B be a subset of monomials in $R \simeq \mathbb{K}[x_1, ..., x_n]$. We say that B is connected to 1 if $\forall m \in B$ either $m = 1$ or there exists $i \in [1, n]$ and $m' \in B$ such that $m = x_i m'$.*

Let $B, B' \subset R_{\delta_1, \ldots, \delta_k}$ be a two sets of monomials connected to 1. We consider the formal Hankel matrix

$$\mathcal{H}_\Lambda^{B, B'} = (h_{\alpha+\beta})_{\alpha \in B', \beta \in B},$$

with $h_\alpha = T^*(\mathbf{x}^\alpha) = c_\alpha$ if $\mathbf{x}^\alpha \in R_{\delta_1, \ldots, \delta_k}$ and otherwise h_α is a variable. The set of these new variables is denoted $\mathbf{h}$.

Suppose that $\mathcal{H}_\Lambda^{B, B'}$ is invertible in $\mathbb{K}(\mathbf{h})$, then we define the formal multiplication operators

$$\mathcal{M}_{i,l}^{B, B'}(\mathbf{h}) := (\mathcal{H}_\Lambda^{B, B'})^{-1} \mathcal{H}_{x_{i,l} \star \Lambda}^{B, B'}$$

for every variable $x_{i,l} \in R$.

We use the following theorems which extend the results of [37] to the cases of distinct sets of monomials indexing the rows and columns of the Hankel operators. They characterizes the cases where $\mathbb{K}[\mathbf{x}] = B \oplus I_\Lambda$:

THEOREM 3.2. *Let $B = \{\mathbf{x}^{\beta_1}, \ldots, \mathbf{x}^{\beta_r}\}$ and $B' = \{\mathbf{x}^{\beta_1'}, \ldots, \mathbf{x}^{\beta_r'}\}$ be two sets of monomials in $R_{\delta_1, \ldots, \delta_k}$, connected to 1 and let Λ be a linear form that belongs to $(\langle B' \cdot B^+ \rangle_{\delta_1, \ldots, \delta_k})^*$. Let $\Lambda(\mathbf{h})$ be the linear form of $\langle B' \cdot B^+ \rangle^*$ defined by $\Lambda(\mathbf{h})(\mathbf{x}^\alpha) = \Lambda(\mathbf{x}^\alpha)$ if $\mathbf{x}^\alpha \in R_{\delta_1, \ldots, \delta_k}$ and $h_\alpha \in \mathbb{K}$ otherwise. Then, $\Lambda(\mathbf{h})$ admits an extension $\tilde{\Lambda} \in R^*$ such that $H_{\tilde{\Lambda}}$ is of rank r with B and B' basis of $A_{\tilde{\Lambda}}$ iff*

$$\mathcal{M}_{i,l}^B(\mathbf{h}) \circ \mathcal{M}_{j,q}^B(\mathbf{h}) - \mathcal{M}_{j,q}^B(\mathbf{h}) \circ \mathcal{M}_{i,l}^B(\mathbf{h}) = 0 \quad (8)$$

$(0 \le l, q \le k, 1 \le i \le n_l, 1 \le j \le n_q)$ and $\det(\mathcal{H}_{\Lambda(\mathbf{h})}^{B', B}) \ne 0$. *Moreover, such a $\tilde{\Lambda}$ is unique.*

We are going to give an equivalent characterization of the extension property, based on rank conditions:

THEOREM 3.3. *Let $B = \{\mathbf{x}^{\beta_1}, \ldots, \mathbf{x}^{\beta_r}\}$ and $B' = \{\mathbf{x}^{\beta_1'}, \ldots, \mathbf{x}^{\beta_r'}\}$ be two sets of monomials in $R_{\delta_1, \ldots, \delta_k}$, connected to 1. Let Λ be a linear form in $(\langle B'^+ * B^+ \rangle_{\delta_1, \ldots, \delta_k})^*$ and $\Lambda(\mathbf{h})$ be the linear form of $\langle B'^+ \cdot B^+ \rangle^*$ defined by $\Lambda(\mathbf{h})(\mathbf{x}^\alpha) = \Lambda(\mathbf{x}^\alpha)$ if $\mathbf{x}^\alpha \in R_{\delta_1, \ldots, \delta_k}$ and $h_\alpha \in \mathbb{K}$ otherwise. Then, $\Lambda(\mathbf{h})$ admits an extension $\tilde{\Lambda} \in R^*$ such that $H_{\tilde{\Lambda}}$ is of rank r with B and B' basis of $A_{\tilde{\Lambda}}$ iff all $(r+1) \times (r+1)$-minors of $\mathcal{H}_{\Lambda(\mathbf{h})}^{B'^+, B^+}$ vanish and $\det(\mathcal{H}_{\Lambda(\mathbf{h})}^{B', B}) \ne 0$.*

4. EXAMPLES AND APPLICATIONS

There exist numerous fields in which decomposing a tensor into a sum of rank-one terms is useful. These fields range from arithmetic complexity [8] to chemistry [44]. One nice application is worth to be emphasized, namely wireless transmissions [42]: one or several signals are wished to be extracted form noisy measurements, received on an array of sensors and disturbed by interferences. The approach is deterministic, which makes the difference compared to approaches based on data statistics [15]. The array of sensors is composed of J subarrays, each containing I sensors. Subarrays do not need to be disjoint, but must be deduced from each other by a translation in space. If the transmission is narrow band and in the far field, then the measurements at time sample t recorded on sensor i of subarray j take the form:

$$T(i, j, t) = \sum_{p=1}^r A_{ip} B_{jp} C_{tp}$$

if r waves impinge on the array. Matrices A and B characterize the geometry of the array (subarray and translations), whereas matrix C contains the signals received on the array. An example with $(I, J) = (4, 4)$ is given in Figure 1. Computing the decomposition of tensor T allows to extract signals of interest as well as interferences, all included in matrix C. Radiating sources can also be localized with the help of matrix A if the exact location of sensors of a subarray are known. Note that this framework applies in radar, sonar or telecommunications.

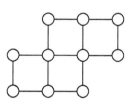

Figure 1: Array of 10 sensors decomposed into 4 subarrays of 4 sensors each.

We consider such an example with 6 time samples, that is an element of $\mathbb{R}^4 \otimes \mathbb{R}^4 \otimes \mathbb{R}^6$: $T :=_{1046} a_1 b_1 c_1 + 959 a_1 b_1 c_2 +$
$660 a_1 b_1 c_3 + 866 a_1 b_1 c_4 + 952 a_1 b_1 c_5 - 1318 a_1 b_2 c_1 - 1222 a_1 b_2 c_2 - 906 a_1 b_2 c_3 -$
$1165 a_1 b_2 c_4 - 1184 a_1 b_2 c_5 - 153 a_1 b_3 c_1 + 52 a_1 b_3 c_2 + 353 a_1 b_3 c_3 + 354 a_1 b_3 c_4 +$
$585 a_1 b_3 c_5 + 852 a_2 b_1 c_1 + 833 a_2 b_1 c_2 + 718 a_2 b_1 c_3 + 903 a_2 b_1 c_4 + 828 a_2 b_1 c_5 -$
$1068 a_2 b_2 c_1 - 1060 a_2 b_2 c_2 - 992 a_2 b_2 c_3 - 1224 a_2 b_2 c_4 - 1026 a_2 b_2 c_5 +$
$256 a_2 b_3 c_1 + 468 a_2 b_3 c_2 + 668 a_2 b_3 c_3 + 748 a_2 b_3 c_4 + 1198 a_2 b_3 c_5 - 614 a_3 b_1 c_1 -$
$495 a_3 b_1 c_2 - 276 a_3 b_1 c_3 - 392 a_3 b_1 c_4 - 168 a_3 b_1 c_5 + 664 a_3 b_2 c_1 + 525 a_3 b_2 c_2 +$
$336 a_3 b_2 c_3 + 472 a_3 b_2 c_4 + 63 a_3 b_2 c_5 + 713 a_3 b_3 c_1 + 737 a_3 b_3 c_2 + 791 a_3 b_3 c_3 +$
$965 a_3 b_3 c_5 + 674 a_3 b_3 c_5 - 95 a_1 b_1 + 88 a_1 b_2 + 193 a_1 b_3 + 320 a_1 c_1 + 285 a_1 c_2 +$
$134 a_1 c_3 + 188 a_1 c_4 + 382 a_1 c_5 - 29 a_2 b_1 - 2 a_2 b_2 + 198 a_2 b_3 + 292 a_2 c_1 +$
$269 a_2 c_2 + 138 a_2 c_3 + 187 a_2 c_4 + 406 a_2 c_5 + 119 a_3 b_1 - 139 a_3 b_2 + 20 a_3 b_3 -$

$222\,a_3\,c_1 - 160\,a_3\,c_2 + 32\,a_3\,c_3 + 9\,a_3\,c_4 - 229\,a_3\,c_5 + 122\,b_1\,c_1 + 119\,b_1\,c_2 +$
$112\,b_1\,c_3 + 140\,b_1\,c_4 + 108\,b_1\,c_5 - 160\,b_2\,c_1 - 163\,b_2\,c_2 - 176\,b_2\,c_3 - 214\,b_2\,c_4 -$
$117\,b_2\,c_5 + 31\,b_3\,c_1 + 57\,b_3\,c_2 + 65\,b_3\,c_3 + 73\,b_3\,c_4 + 196\,b_3\,c_5 - 35\,a_1 - 21\,a_2 +$
$54\,a_3 - 3\,b_1 - 3\,b_2 + 24\,b_3 + 50\,c_1 + 46\,c_2 + 20\,c_3 + 29\,c_4 + 63\,c_5 - 6.$

If we take $B = \{1, a_1, a_2, a_3, b_1, b_2\}$ and $B' = \{1, c_1, c_2, c_3, c_4, c_5\}$ we obtain the following known submatrix of H_Λ:

$$\mathbb{H}_\Lambda^{B',B} = \begin{bmatrix} -6 & -35 & -21 & 54 & -3 & -3 \\ 50 & 320 & 292 & -222 & 122 & -160 \\ 46 & 285 & 269 & -160 & 119 & -163 \\ 20 & 134 & 138 & 32 & 112 & -176 \\ 29 & 188 & 187 & 9 & 140 & -214 \\ 63 & 382 & 406 & -229 & 108 & -117 \end{bmatrix}$$

which is invertible. Thus, the rank is at least 6. Let us find if $H_{\tilde\Lambda}$ can be extended to a rank 6 Hankel matrix H_Λ. If we look at $H_\Lambda^{B'^+,B^+}$, several coefficients are unknown. Yet, as will see, they can be determined by exploiting the commutation relations, as follows.

The columns $\mathbb{H}^{B',\{m\}}$ are also known for $m \in \{b_3, a_1\,b_1, a_2\,b_1, a_3\,b_1, a_1\,b_2, a_2\,b_2, a_3\,b_2\}$. Thus we deduce the relations between these monomials and B by solving the system $\mathbb{H}_\Lambda^{B',B} X = \mathbb{H}_\Lambda^{B',\{m\}}$. This yields the following relations in $\mathcal{A}_\Lambda$: $b_3 \equiv -1. - 0.02486\,a_1 + 1.412\,a_2 + 0.8530\,a_3 - 0.6116\,b_1 + 0.3713\,b_2,$ $a_1\,b_1 \equiv -2. + 6.122\,a_1 - 3.304\,a_2 + .6740\,a_3 + .7901\,b_1 - 1.282\,b_2,$ $a_2\,b_1 \equiv -2. + 4.298\,a_1 - 1.546\,a_2 + 1.364\,a_3 + .5392\,b_1 - 1.655\,b_2,$ $a_3\,b_1 \equiv -2. - 3.337\,a_1 + 5.143\,a_2 + 1.786\,a_3 - 2.291\,b_1 + 1.699\,b_2,$ $a_1\,b_2 \equiv -2. + 0.03867\,a_1 - 0.1967\,a_2 + 1.451\,a_3 - 2.049\,b_1 + 3.756\,b_2,$ $a_2\,b_2 \equiv -2. + 3.652\,a_1 - 3.230\,a_2 + .9425\,a_3 - 2.562\,b_1 + 4.198\,b_2,$ $a_3\,b_2 \equiv -2. + 6.243\,a_1 - 7.808\,a_2 - 1.452\,a_3 + 5.980\,b_1 + 0.03646\,b_2$

Using the first relation on b_3, we can reduce $a_1\,b_3, a_2\,b_3, a_3\,b_3$ and obtain 3 linear dependency relations between the monomials in $B \cup \{a_1^2, a_1 a_2, a_1 a_3, a_2^2, a_2 a_3, a_3^2\}$. Using the commutation relations $\frac{\mathrm{lcm}(m_1,m_2)}{m_1} N(m_1) - \frac{\mathrm{lcm}(m_1,m_2)}{m_2} N(m_2)$, for $(m_1, m_2) \in \{(a_1\,b_1, a_2\,b_1), (a_1\,b_2, a_2\,b_2), (a_2\,b_2, a_3\,b_2)\}$ where $N(m_i)$ is the reduction of m_i with respect to the prevision relations, we obtain 3 new linear dependency relations between the monomials in $B \cup \{a_1^2, a_1 a_2, a_1 a_3, a_2^2, a_2 a_3, a_3^2\}$. From these 6 relations, we deduce the expression of the monomials in $\{a_1^2, a_1 a_2, a_1 a_3, a_2^2, a_2 a_3, a_3^2\}$ as linear combinations of monomials in B:

$a_1^2 \equiv 12.08\,a_1 - 5.107\,a_2 + .2232\,a_3 - 2.161\,b_1 - 2.038\,b_2 - 2.,$ $a_1 a_2 \equiv 8.972\,a_1 - 1.431\,a_2 + 1.392\,a_3 - 3.680\,b_1 - 2.254\,b_2 - 2.,$ $a_1 a_3 \equiv -11.56\,a_1 + 9.209\,a_2 + 2.802\,a_3 + 1.737\,b_1 + .8155\,b_2 - 2.,$ $a_2^2 \equiv -2. + 6.691\,a_1 + 2.173\,a_2 + 2.793\,a_3 - 5.811\,b_1 - 2.846\,b_2,$ $a_2 a_3 \equiv -2. - 11.87\,a_1 + 9.468\,a_2 + 2.117\,a_3 + 3.262\,b_1 + 0.01989\,b_2,$ $a_3^2 \equiv -2. + 16.96\,a_1 - 8.603\,a_2 + 1.349\,a_3 - 6.351\,b_1 - .3558\,b_2.$

Now, we are able to compute the matrix of multiplication by a_1 in B, which is obtained by reducing the monomials $B \cdot a_1 = \{a_1, a_1^2, a_1 a_2, a_1 a_3, a_1 b_1, a_1 b_2\}$ by the computed relations:

$$M_{a_1} := \begin{bmatrix} 0.0 & -2.0 & -2.0 & -2.0 & -2.0 & -2.0 \\ 1.0 & 12.08 & 8.972 & -11.56 & 6.122 & 0.03867 \\ 0.0 & -5.107 & -1.431 & 9.209 & -3.304 & -0.1967 \\ 0.0 & 0.2232 & 1.392 & 2.802 & 0.6740 & 1.451 \\ 0.0 & -2.161 & -3.680 & 1.737 & 0.7901 & -2.049 \\ 0.0 & -2.038 & -2.254 & 0.8155 & -1.282 & 3.756 \end{bmatrix}$$

The eigenvectors of the transposed operator are:

$$\begin{bmatrix} 1.0 \\ 5.0 \\ 7.003 \\ 3.0 \\ 3.0 \\ -4.0 \end{bmatrix}, \begin{bmatrix} 1.0 \\ 2.999 \\ 4.0 \\ -4.999 \\ -2.999 \\ 4.999 \end{bmatrix}, \begin{bmatrix} 1.0 \\ 2.0 \\ 2.0 \\ 2.0 \\ 2.0 \\ 2.0 \end{bmatrix}, \begin{bmatrix} 1.0 \\ 8.001 \\ 6.002 \\ -7.002 \\ 4.001 \\ -5.001 \end{bmatrix}, \begin{bmatrix} 1.0 \\ -1.0 \\ -2.0 \\ 3.0 \\ -1.0 \\ -1.0 \end{bmatrix}, \begin{bmatrix} 1.0 \\ 0.9999 \\ 0.9999 \\ 0.9999 \\ 0.9999 \\ 0.9999 \end{bmatrix}$$

They are normalized so that the first coordinate is 1 and correspond to the vectors of evaluation of the monomial vector B at the roots of I_Λ. Thus we known the coordinates a_1, a_2, a_3, b_1, b_2 of these roots. By expanding the polynomial

$\gamma_1\,(1 + a_1 + a_2 + a_3))\,(1 + b_1 + b_2 + b_3)\,(1 + \cdots) + \gamma_2\,(1 - a_1 - 2\,a_2 + 3\,a_3)\,(1 - b_1 - b_2 - b_3)\,(1 + \cdots) + \gamma_3\,(1 + 2\,a_1 + 2\,a_2 + 2\,a_3)\,(1 + 2\,b_1 + 2\,b_2 + 3\,b_3)\,(1 + \cdots) + \gamma_4\,(1 + 5\,a_1 + 7\,a_2 + 3\,a_3)\,(1 + 3\,b_1 - 4\,b_2 + 8\,b_3)\,(1 + \cdots) + \gamma_5\,(1 + 8\,a_1 + 6\,a_2 - 7\,a_3)\,(1 + 4\,b_1 - 5\,b_2 - 3\,b_3)\,(1 + \cdots) + \gamma_6\,(1 + 3\,a_1 + 4\,a_2 - 5\,a_3)\,(1 - 3\,b_1 + 5\,b_2 + 4\,b_3)\,(1 + \cdots)$

(where the $\cdots$ are terms linear in c_i) and identifying the coefficients of T which do not depend on $c_1, \ldots, c_5$, we obtain a linear system in γ_i, which unique solution is $(2, -1, -2, 3, -5, -3)$. This allows us to compute the value Λ for any monomials in $\{a_1, a_2, a_3, b_1, b_2, b_3\}$. In particular, we can compute the entries of $\mathbb{H}_\Lambda^{B,B}$. Solving the system $\mathbb{H}_\Lambda^{B,B} X = \mathbb{H}_\Lambda^{B,B'}$, we deduce the relations between the monomials in B' and B in $\mathcal{A}_\Lambda$ and in particular $c_1, \ldots, c_5$ as linear combinations of monomials in B. This allows us to recover the missing coordinates and yields the following decomposition:

$T := 2\,(1 + a_1 + a_2 + a_3)\,(1 + b_1 + b_2 + b_3)\,(1 + c_1 + c_2 + c_3 + c_4 + c_5) - (1 - a_1 - 2\,a_2 + 3\,a_3)\,(1 - b_1 - b_2 - b_3)\,(1 - c_1 - 2\,c_2 - 3\,c_3 - 4\,c_4 + 5\,c_5) - 2\,(1 + 2\,a_1 + 2\,a_2 + 2\,a_3)\,(1 + 2\,b_1 + 2\,b_2 + 3\,b_3)\,(1 + 2\,c_1 + 2\,c_2 + 2\,c_3 + 2\,c_4 + 2\,c_5) + 3\,(1 + 5\,a_1 + 7\,a_2 + 3\,a_3)\,(1 + 3\,b_1 - 4\,b_2 + 8\,b_3)\,(1 + 4\,c_1 + 5\,c_2 + 6\,c_3 + 7\,c_4 + 8\,c_5) - 5\,(1 + 8\,a_1 + 6\,a_2 - 7\,a_3)\,(1 + 4\,b_1 - 5\,b_2 - 3\,b_3)\,(1 - 6\,c_1 - 5\,c_2 - 2\,c_3 - 3\,c_4 - 5\,c_5) - 3\,(1 + 3\,a_1 + 4\,a_2 - 5\,a_3)\,(1 - 3\,b_1 + 5\,b_2 + 4\,b_3)\,(1 - 3\,c_1 - 2\,c_2 + 3\,c_3 + 3\,c_4 - 7\,c_5).$

5. REFERENCES

[1] E. Ballico and A. Bernardi. Stratification of the fourth secant variety of veronese variety via symmetric rank. arXiv 1005.3465, 2010.

[2] A. Bernardi. Ideals of varieties parameterized by certain symmetric tensors. *J. Pure Appl. Algebra*, 212(6):1542–1559, 2008.

[3] A. Bernardi, A. Gimigliano, and M. Idà. Computing symmetric rank for symmetric tensors. *J. Symb. Comput.*, 46:34–53, January 2011.

[4] D. Bini, M. Capovani, F. Romani, and G. Lotti. $O(n^{2.77})$ Complexity for $n \times n$ approximate matrix multiplication. *Inform. Process*, 8(5):234–235, 1979.

[5] J. Brachat, P. Comon, B. Mourrain, and E. Tsigaridas. Symmetric tensor decomposition. *Linear Algebra and Applications*, 433:1851–1872, 2010.

[6] R. Bro. Parafac, tutorial and applications. *Chemom. Intel. Lab. Syst.*, 38:149–171, 1997.

[7] J. Buczynski, A. Ginensky, and J.M. Landsberg. Determinental equations for secant varieties and the Eisenbud-Koh-Stillman conjecture. 1007.0192, 2010.

[8] P. Bürgisser, M. Clausen, and M. A. Shokrollahi. *Algebraic complexity theory*, volume 315 of *Grundlehren der Mathematischen Wissenschaften [Fundamental Principles of Mathematical Sciences]*. Springer-Verlag, Berlin, 1997. With the collaboration of Thomas Lickteig.

[9] J. F. Cardoso. Blind signal separation: statistical principles. *Proc. of the IEEE*, 90:2009–2025, October 1998. special issue, R.W. Liu and L. Tong eds.

[10] P. Chevalier. Optimal separation of independent narrow-band sources - concept and performance. *Signal Processing, Elsevier*, 73(1):27–48, February 1999. special issue on blind separation and deconvolution.

[11] P. Chevalier, L. Albera, A. Ferreol, and P. Comon. On the virtual array concept for higher order array

processing. *IEEE Proc.*, 53(4):1254–1271, April 2005.

[12] A. Cichocki and S-I. Amari. *Adaptive Blind Signal and Image Processing*. Wiley, New York, 2002.

[13] G. Comas and M. Seiguer. On the rank of a binary form, 2001.

[14] P. Comon. Independent Component Analysis. In J-L. Lacoume, editor, *Higher Order Statistics*, pages 29–38. Elsevier, Amsterdam, London, 1992.

[15] P. Comon and C. Jutten, editors. *Handbook of Blind Source Separation, Independent Component Analysis and Applications*. Academic Press, Oxford UK, Burlington USA, 2010.

[16] P. Comon and B. Mourrain. Decomposition of quantics in sums of powers of linear forms. *Signal Processing*, 53(2-3):93–107, 1996.

[17] P. Comon and M. Rajih. Blind identification of under-determined mixtures based on the characteristic function. *Signal Processing*, 86(9):2271–2281, 2006.

[18] D. Cox, J. Little, and D. O'Shea. *Ideals, Varieties, and Algorithms*. Undergraduate Texts in Mathematics. Springer-Verlag, New York, 2nd edition, 1997.

[19] D. Cox, J. Little, and D. O'Shea. *Using Algebraic Geometry*. Number 185 in Graduate Texts in Mathematics. Springer, New York, 2nd edition, 2005.

[20] L. de Lathauwer and J. Castaing. Tensor-based techniques for the blind separation of ds-cdma signals. *Signal Processing*, 87(2):322–336, February 2007.

[21] M. C. Dogan and J. Mendel. Applications of cumulants to array processing .I. aperture extension and array calibration. *IEEE Trans. Sig. Proc.*, 43(5):1200–1216, May 1995.

[22] D. L. Donoho and X. Huo. Uncertainty principles and ideal atomic decompositions. *IEEE Trans. Inform. Theory*, 47(7):2845–2862, November 2001.

[23] M. Elkadi and B. Mourrain. *Introduction à la résolution des systèmes polynomiaux*, volume 59 of *Mathḿatiques et Applications*. Springer, 2007.

[24] A. Ferreol and P. Chevalier. On the behavior of current second and higher order blind source separation methods for cyclostationary sources. *IEEE Trans. Sig. Proc.*, 48:1712–1725, June 2000. erratum in vol.50, pp.990, Apr. 2002.

[25] A. V. Geramita. Catalecticant varieties. In *Commutative algebra and algebraic geometry (Ferrara)*, volume 206 of *Lecture Notes in Pure and Appl. Math.*, pages 143–156. Dekker, New York, 1999.

[26] R. Grone. Decomposable tensors as a quadratic variety. *Proc. Amer. Math. Soc.*, 64(2):227–230, 1977.

[27] H. T. Hà. Box-shaped matrices and the defining ideal of certain blowup surfaces. *J. Pure Appl. Algebra*, 167(2-3):203–224, 2002.

[28] A. Iarrobino and V. Kanev. *Power sums, Gorenstein algebras, and determinantal loci*, volume 1721 of *Lecture Notes in Computer Science*. Springer-Verlag, Berlin, 1999.

[29] T. Jiang and N. Sidiropoulos. Kruskal's permutation lemma and the identification of CANDECOMP/PARAFAC and bilinear models. *IEEE Trans. Sig. Proc.*, 52(9):2625–2636, September 2004.

[30] H. A. L. Kiers and W. P. Krijnen. An efficient algorithm for Parafac of three-way data with large numbers of observation units. *Psychometrika*, 56:147, 1991.

[31] J. B. Kruskal. Three-way arrays: Rank and uniqueness of trilinear decompositions. *Linear Algebra and Applications*, 18:95–138, 1977.

[32] J. Landsberg. Geometry and the complexity of matrix multiplication. *Bull. Amer. Math. Soc.*, 45(2):247–284, April 2008.

[33] J. M. Landsberg and L. Manivel. Generalizations of Strassen's equations for secant varieties of Segre varieties. *Comm. Algebra*, 36(2):405–422, 2008.

[34] J. M. Landsberg and G. Ottaviani. Equations for secant varieties to veronese varieties. arXiv 1006.0180, 2010.

[35] J. M. Landsberg and G. Ottaviani. Equations for secant varieties via vector bundles. arXiv 1010.1825, 2010.

[36] J. M. Landsberg and J. Weyman. On the ideals and singularities of secant varieties of Segre varieties. *Bull. Lond. Math. Soc.*, 39(4):685–697, 2007.

[37] M. Laurent and B. Mourrain. A Sparse Flat Extension Theorem for Moment Matrices. *Archiv der Mathematik*, 93:87–98, 2009.

[38] B. Mourrain and V.Y. Pan. Multivariate Polynomials, Duality, and Structured Matrices. *Journal of Complexity*, 16(1):110–180, 2000.

[39] G. Ottaviani. An invariant regarding Waring's problem for cubic polynomials. *Nagoya Math. J.*, 193:95–110, 2009.

[40] A. Parolin. Varietà secanti alle varietà di segre e di veronese e loro applicazioni, tesi di dottorato. *Università di Bologna*, 2003/2004.

[41] M. Pucci. The Veronese variety and catalecticant matrices. *J. Algebra*, 202(1):72–95, 1998.

[42] N. D. Sidiropoulos, R. Bro, and G. B. Giannakis. Parallel factor analysis in sensor array processing. *IEEE Trans. Sig. Proc.*, 48(8):2377–2388, August 2000.

[43] N. D. Sidiropoulos, G. B. Giannakis, and R. Bro. Blind PARAFAC receivers for DS-CDMA systems. *IEEE Trans. on Sig. Proc.*, 48(3):810–823, 2000.

[44] A. Smilde, R. Bro, and P. Geladi. *Multi-Way Analysis*. Wiley, 2004.

[45] V. Strassen. Rank and optimal computation of generic tensors. *Linear Algebra Appl.*, 52:645–685, July 1983.

[46] A. Swami, G. Giannakis, and S. Shamsunder. Multichannel ARMA processes. *IEEE Trans. Sig. Proc.*, 42(4):898–913, April 1994.

[47] J. J. Sylvester. Sur une extension d'un théorème de Clebsch relatif aux courbes du quatrième degré. *Comptes Rendus, Math. Acad. Sci. Paris*, 102:1532–1534, 1886.

[48] A. J. van der Veen and A. Paulraj. An analytical constant modulus algorithm. *IEEE Trans. Sig. Proc.*, 44(5):1136–1155, May 1996.

[49] K. Wakeford. On canonical forms. *Proc. London Math. Soc.*, 18:403–410, 1918-19.

Special Values of Generalized Log-sine Integrals

Jonathan M. Borwein
University of Newcastle
Callaghan, NSW 2308, Australia
jonathan.borwein@newcastle.edu.au

Armin Straub
Tulane University
New Orleans, LA 70118, USA
astraub@tulane.edu

ABSTRACT

We study generalized log-sine integrals at special values. At π and multiples thereof explicit evaluations are obtained in terms of Nielsen polylogarithms at ± 1. For general arguments we present algorithmic evaluations involving Nielsen polylogarithms at related arguments. In particular, we consider log-sine integrals at $\pi/3$ which evaluate in terms of polylogarithms at the sixth root of unity. An implementation of our results for the computer algebra systems *Mathematica* and SAGE is provided.

Categories and Subject Descriptors

I.1.1 [**Symbolic and Algebraic Manipulation**]: Expressions and Their Representation; I.1.2 [**Symbolic and Algebraic Manipulation**]: Algorithms

General Terms

Algorithms, Theory

Keywords

log-sine integrals, multiple polylogarithms, multiple zeta values, Clausen functions

1. INTRODUCTION

For $n = 1, 2, \ldots$ and $k \geq 0$, we consider the (generalized) *log-sine integrals* defined by

$$\mathrm{Ls}_n^{(k)}(\sigma) := -\int_0^\sigma \theta^k \log^{n-1-k} \left| 2 \sin \frac{\theta}{2} \right| \, \mathrm{d}\theta. \quad (1)$$

The modulus is not needed for $0 \leq \sigma \leq 2\pi$. For $k = 0$ these are the (basic) log-sine integrals $\mathrm{Ls}_n(\sigma) := \mathrm{Ls}_n^{(0)}(\sigma)$. Various log-sine integral evaluations may be found in [20, §7.6 & §7.9].

In this paper, we will be concerned with evaluations of the log-sine integrals $\mathrm{Ls}_n^{(k)}(\sigma)$ for special values of σ. Such evaluations are useful for physics [15]: log-sine integrals appeared

for instance in recent work on the ε-expansion of various Feynman diagrams in the calculation of higher terms in the ε-expansion, [8, 16, 9, 11, 14]. Of particular importance are the log-sine integrals at the special values $\pi/3$, $\pi/2$, $2\pi/3$, π. The log-sine integrals also appear in many settings in number theory and analysis: classes of inverse binomial sums can be expressed in terms of generalized log-sine integrals, [10, 4].

In Section 3 we focus on evaluations of log-sine and related integrals at π. General arguments are considered in Section 5 with a focus on the case $\pi/3$ in Section 5.1. Imaginary arguments are briefly discussed in 5.2. The results obtained are suitable for implementation in a computer algebra system. Such an implementation is provided for *Mathematica* and SAGE, and is described in Section 7. This complements existing packages such as lsjk [15] for numerical evaluations of log-sine integrals or HPL [21] as well as [25] for working with multiple polylogarithms.

Further motivation for such evaluations was sparked by our recent study [6] of certain *multiple Mahler measures*. For k functions (typically Laurent polynomials) in n variables the multiple Mahler measure $\mu(P_1, P_2, \ldots, P_k)$, introduced in [18], is defined by

$$\int_0^1 \cdots \int_0^1 \prod_{j=1}^k \log \left| P_j \left(e^{2\pi i t_1}, \ldots, e^{2\pi i t_n} \right) \right| \mathrm{d}t_1 \mathrm{d}t_2 \ldots \mathrm{d}t_n.$$

When $P = P_1 = P_2 = \cdots = P_k$ this devolves to a *higher Mahler measure*, $\mu_k(P)$, as introduced and examined in [18]. When $k = 1$ both reduce to the standard (logarithmic) *Mahler measure* [7].

The multiple Mahler measure

$$\mu_k(1 + x + y_*) := \mu(1 + x + y_1, 1 + x + y_2, \ldots, 1 + x + y_k) \quad (2)$$

was studied by Sasaki [24, Lemma 1] who provided an evaluation of $\mu_2(1 + x + y_*)$. It was observed in [6] that

$$\mu_k(1 + x + y_*) = \frac{1}{\pi} \mathrm{Ls}_{k+1}\left(\frac{\pi}{3}\right) - \frac{1}{\pi} \mathrm{Ls}_{k+1}(\pi). \quad (3)$$

Many other Mahler measures studied in [6, 1] were shown to have evaluations involving generalized log-sine integrals at π and $\pi/3$ as well.

To our knowledge, this is the most exacting such study undertaken — perhaps because it would be quite impossible without modern computational tools and absent a use of the quite recent understanding of multiple polylogarithms and multiple zeta values [3].

2. PRELIMINARIES

In the following, we will denote the *multiple polylogarithm* as studied for instance in [4] and [2, Ch. 3] by

$$\mathrm{Li}_{a_1,\dots,a_k}(z) := \sum_{n_1 > \dots > n_k > 0} \frac{z^{n_1}}{n_1^{a_1} \cdots n_k^{a_k}}.$$

For our purposes, the $a_1, \dots, a_k$ will usually be positive integers and $a_1 \geq 2$ so that the sum converges for all $|z| \leq 1$. For example, $\mathrm{Li}_{2,1}(z) = \sum_{k=1}^{\infty} \frac{z^k}{k^2} \sum_{j=1}^{k-1} \frac{1}{j}$. In particular, $\mathrm{Li}_k(x) := \sum_{n=1}^{\infty} \frac{x^n}{n^k}$ is the *polylogarithm of order* k. The usual notation will be used for repetitions so that, for instance, $\mathrm{Li}_{2,\{1\}^3}(z) = \mathrm{Li}_{2,1,1,1}(z)$.

Moreover, *multiple zeta values* are denoted by

$$\zeta(a_1, \dots, a_k) := \mathrm{Li}_{a_1, \dots, a_k}(1).$$

Similarly, we consider the *multiple Clausen functions* (Cl) and *multiple Glaisher functions* (Gl) of depth k and weight $w = a_1 + \dots + a_k$ defined as

$$\mathrm{Cl}_{a_1,\dots,a_k}(\theta) = \left\{ \begin{array}{ll} \mathrm{Im}\, \mathrm{Li}_{a_1,\dots,a_k}(e^{i\theta}) & \text{if } w \text{ even} \\ \mathrm{Re}\, \mathrm{Li}_{a_1,\dots,a_k}(e^{i\theta}) & \text{if } w \text{ odd} \end{array} \right\}, \quad (4)$$

$$\mathrm{Gl}_{a_1,\dots,a_k}(\theta) = \left\{ \begin{array}{ll} \mathrm{Re}\, \mathrm{Li}_{a_1,\dots,a_k}(e^{i\theta}) & \text{if } w \text{ even} \\ \mathrm{Im}\, \mathrm{Li}_{a_1,\dots,a_k}(e^{i\theta}) & \text{if } w \text{ odd} \end{array} \right\}, \quad (5)$$

in accordance with [20]. Of particular importance will be the case of $\theta = \pi/3$ which has also been considered in [4].

Our other notation and usage is largely consistent with that in [20] and that in the newly published [23] in which most of the requisite material is described. Finally, a recent elaboration of what is meant when we speak about evaluations and "closed forms" is to be found in [5].

3. EVALUATIONS AT π

3.1 Basic log-sine integrals at π

The exponential generating function, [19, 20],

$$-\frac{1}{\pi} \sum_{m=0}^{\infty} \mathrm{Ls}_{m+1}(\pi) \frac{\lambda^m}{m!} = \frac{\Gamma(1+\lambda)}{\Gamma^2 \left(1 + \frac{\lambda}{2}\right)} = \binom{\lambda}{\frac{\lambda}{2}} \quad (6)$$

is well-known and implies the recurrence

$$\frac{(-1)^n}{n!} \mathrm{Ls}_{n+2}(\pi) = \pi\,\alpha(n+1)$$
$$+ \sum_{k=1}^{n-2} \frac{(-1)^k}{(k+1)!}\, \alpha(n-k)\, \mathrm{Ls}_{k+2}(\pi), \quad (7)$$

where $\alpha(m) = (1 - 2^{1-m})\zeta(m)$.

Example 1. (Values of $\mathrm{Ls}_n(\pi)$) We have $\mathrm{Ls}_2(\pi) = 0$ and

$$-\mathrm{Ls}_3(\pi) = \frac{1}{12}\,\pi^3$$
$$\mathrm{Ls}_4(\pi) = \frac{3}{2}\,\pi\,\zeta(3)$$
$$-\mathrm{Ls}_5(\pi) = \frac{19}{240}\,\pi^5$$
$$\mathrm{Ls}_6(\pi) = \frac{45}{2}\,\pi\,\zeta(5) + \frac{5}{4}\,\pi^3\zeta(3)$$
$$-\mathrm{Ls}_7(\pi) = \frac{275}{1344}\,\pi^7 + \frac{45}{2}\,\pi\,\zeta(3)^2$$
$$\mathrm{Ls}_8(\pi) = \frac{2835}{4}\,\pi\,\zeta(7) + \frac{315}{8}\,\pi^3\zeta(5) + \frac{133}{32}\,\pi^5\zeta(3),$$

and so forth. The fact that each integral is a multivariable rational polynomial in π and zeta values follows directly from the recursion (7). Alternatively, these values may be conveniently obtained from (6) by a computer algebra system. For instance, in *Mathematica* the code

```
FullSimplify[D[-Binomial[x,x/2], {x,6}] /.x->0]
```

produces the above evaluation of $\mathrm{Ls}_6(\pi)$. $\diamond$

3.2 The log-sine-cosine integrals

The log-sine-cosine integrals

$$\mathrm{Lsc}_{m,n}(\sigma) := -\int_0^{\sigma} \log^{m-1}\left|2\sin\frac{\theta}{2}\right| \log^{n-1}\left|2\cos\frac{\theta}{2}\right| d\theta \quad (8)$$

appear in physical applications as well, see for instance [9, 14]. They have also been considered by Lewin, [19, 20], and he demonstrates how their values at $\sigma = \pi$ may be obtained much the same as those of the log-sine integrals in Section 3.1. As observed in [1], Lewin's result can be put in the form

$$-\frac{1}{\pi} \sum_{m,n=0}^{\infty} \mathrm{Lsc}_{m+1,n+1}(\pi) \frac{x^m}{m!} \frac{y^n}{n!} = \frac{2^{x+y}}{\pi} \frac{\Gamma\left(\frac{1+x}{2}\right)\Gamma\left(\frac{1+y}{2}\right)}{\Gamma\left(1 + \frac{x+y}{2}\right)}$$
$$= \binom{x}{x/2}\binom{y}{y/2} \frac{\Gamma\left(1 + \frac{x}{2}\right)\Gamma\left(1 + \frac{y}{2}\right)}{\Gamma\left(1 + \frac{x+y}{2}\right)}. \quad (9)$$

The last form makes it clear that this is an extension of (6).

The notation Lsc has been introduced in [9] where evaluations for other values of σ and low weight can be found.

3.3 Log-sine integrals at π

As Lewin [20, §7.9] sketches, at least for small values of n and k, the generalized log-sine integrals $\mathrm{Ls}_n^{(k)}(\pi)$ have closed forms involving zeta values and Kummer-type constants such as $\mathrm{Li}_4(1/2)$. This will be made more precise in Remark 1. Our analysis starts with the generating function identity

$$-\sum_{n,k\geq 0} \mathrm{Ls}_{n+k+1}^{(k)}(\pi) \frac{\lambda^n}{n!} \frac{(i\mu)^k}{k!} = \int_0^{\pi} \left(2\sin\frac{\theta}{2}\right)^{\lambda} e^{i\mu\theta} d\theta$$
$$= i e^{i\pi\frac{\lambda}{2}} B_1\left(\mu - \frac{\lambda}{2}, 1 + \lambda\right) - i e^{i\pi\mu} B_{1/2}\left(\mu - \frac{\lambda}{2}, -\mu - \frac{\lambda}{2}\right) \quad (10)$$

given in [20]. Here B_x is the *incomplete Beta* function:

$$B_x(a,b) = \int_0^x t^{a-1}(1-t)^{b-1} dt.$$

We shall show that with care — because of the singularities at zero — (10) can be differentiated as needed as suggested by Lewin.

Using the identities, valid for $a, b > 0$ and $0 < x < 1$,

$$B_x(a,b) = \frac{x^a(1-x)^{b-1}}{a}\, {}_2F_1\left(\begin{array}{c} 1-b, 1 \\ a+1 \end{array} \middle| \frac{x}{x-1}\right)$$
$$= \frac{x^a(1-x)^b}{a}\, {}_2F_1\left(\begin{array}{c} a+b, 1 \\ a+1 \end{array} \middle| x\right),$$

found for instance in [23, §8.17(ii)], the generating function (10) can be rewritten as

$$i e^{i\pi\frac{\lambda}{2}} \left(B_1\left(\mu - \frac{\lambda}{2}, 1 + \lambda\right) - B_{-1}\left(\mu - \frac{\lambda}{2}, 1 + \lambda\right)\right).$$

Upon expanding this we obtain the following computationally more accessible generating function for $\mathrm{Ls}_{n+k+1}^{(k)}(\pi)$:

THEOREM 1. *For $2|\mu| < \lambda < 1$ we have*

$$-\sum_{n,k \geq 0} \mathrm{Ls}_{n+k+1}^{(k)}(\pi) \frac{\lambda^n}{n!} \frac{(i\mu)^k}{k!}$$

$$= i \sum_{n \geq 0} \binom{\lambda}{n} \frac{(-1)^n e^{i\pi\frac{\lambda}{2}} - e^{i\pi\mu}}{\mu - \frac{\lambda}{2} + n}. \qquad (11)$$

We now show how the log-sine integrals $\mathrm{Ls}_n^{(k)}(\pi)$ can quite comfortably be extracted from (11) by differentiating its right-hand side. The case $n = 0$ is covered by:

PROPOSITION 1. *We have*

$$\frac{\mathrm{d}^k}{\mathrm{d}\mu^k} \frac{\mathrm{d}^m}{\mathrm{d}\lambda^m} i \frac{e^{i\pi\frac{\lambda}{2}} - e^{i\pi\mu}}{\mu - \frac{\lambda}{2}} \bigg|_{\substack{\lambda=0 \\ \mu=0}} = \frac{\pi}{2^m} (i\pi)^{m+k} B(m+1, k+1).$$

PROOF. This may be deduced from

$$\frac{e^x - e^y}{x - y} = \sum_{m,k \geq 0} \frac{x^m y^k}{(k+m+1)!}$$

$$= \sum_{m,k \geq 0} B(m+1, k+1) \frac{x^m}{m!} \frac{y^k}{k!}$$

upon setting $x = i\pi\lambda/2$ and $y = i\pi\mu$. $\square$

The next proposition is most helpful in differentiation of the right-hand side of (11) for $n \geq 1$, Here, we denote a *multiple harmonic number* by

$$H_{n-1}^{[\alpha]} := \sum_{n > i_1 > i_2 > \ldots > i_\alpha} \frac{1}{i_1 i_2 \cdots i_\alpha}. \qquad (12)$$

If $\alpha = 0$ we set $H_{n-1}^{[0]} := 1$.

PROPOSITION 2. *For $n \geq 1$*

$$\frac{(-1)^\alpha}{\alpha!} \left(\frac{\mathrm{d}}{\mathrm{d}\lambda}\right)^\alpha \binom{\lambda}{n} \bigg|_{\lambda=0} = \frac{(-1)^n}{n} H_{n-1}^{[\alpha-1]}. \qquad (13)$$

Note that, for $\alpha \geq 0$,

$$\sum_{n \geq 0} \frac{(\pm 1)^n}{n^\beta} H_{n-1}^{[\alpha]} = \mathrm{Li}_{\beta, \{1\}^\alpha}(\pm 1)$$

which shows that the evaluation of the log-sine integrals will involve Nielsen polylogarithms at ± 1, that is polylogarithms of the type $\mathrm{Li}_{a, \{1\}^b}(\pm 1)$.

Using the Leibniz rule coupled with Proposition 2 to differentiate (11) for $n \geq 1$ and Proposition 1 in the case $n = 0$, it is possible to explicitly write $\mathrm{Ls}_n^{(k)}(\pi)$ as a finite sum of Nielsen polylogarithms with coefficients only being rational multiples of powers of π. The process is now exemplified for $\mathrm{Ls}_4^{(2)}(\pi)$ and $\mathrm{Ls}_5^{(1)}(\pi)$.

Example 2. $(\mathrm{Ls}_4^{(2)}(\pi))$ To find $\mathrm{Ls}_4^{(2)}(\pi)$ we differentiate (11) once with respect to λ and twice with respect to μ. To simplify computation, we exploit the fact that the result will be real which allows us to neglect imaginary parts:

$$-\mathrm{Ls}_4^{(2)}(\pi) = \frac{\mathrm{d}^2}{\mathrm{d}\mu^2} \frac{\mathrm{d}}{\mathrm{d}\lambda} i \sum_{n \geq 0} \binom{\lambda}{n} \frac{(-1)^n e^{i\pi\frac{\lambda}{2}} - e^{i\pi\mu}}{\mu - \frac{\lambda}{2} + n} \bigg|_{\lambda=\mu=0}$$

$$= 2\pi \sum_{n \geq 1} \frac{(-1)^{n+1}}{n^3} = \frac{3}{2} \pi \zeta(3).$$

In the second step we were able to drop the term corresponding to $n = 0$ because its contribution $-i\pi^4/24$ is purely imaginary as follows a priori from Proposition 2. $\diamond$

Example 3. $(\mathrm{Ls}_5^{(1)}(\pi))$ Similarly, setting

$$\mathrm{Li}_{a_1, \ldots, a_n}^{\pm} := \mathrm{Li}_{a_1, \ldots, a_n}(1) - \mathrm{Li}_{a_1, \ldots, a_n}(-1)$$

we obtain $\mathrm{Ls}_5^{(1)}(\pi)$ as

$$-\mathrm{Ls}_5^{(1)}(\pi) = \frac{3}{4} \sum_{n \geq 1} \frac{8(1-(-1)^n)}{n^4} \left(n H_{n-1}^{[2]} - H_{n-1}\right)$$

$$+ \frac{6(1-(-1)^n)}{n^5} - \frac{\pi^2}{n^3}$$

$$= 6 \mathrm{Li}_{3,1,1}^{\pm} - 6 \mathrm{Li}_{4,1}^{\pm} + \frac{9}{2} \mathrm{Li}_5^{\pm} - \frac{3}{4} \pi^2 \zeta(3)$$

$$= -6 \mathrm{Li}_{3,1,1}(-1) + \frac{105}{32} \zeta(5) - \frac{1}{4} \pi^2 \zeta(3).$$

The last form is what is automatically produced by our program, see Example 13, and is obtained from the previous expression by reducing the polylogarithms as discussed in Section 6. $\diamond$

The next example hints at the rapidly growing complexity of these integrals, especially when compared to the evaluations given in Examples 2 and 3.

Example 4. $(\mathrm{Ls}_6^{(1)}(\pi))$ Proceeding as before we find

$$-\mathrm{Ls}_6^{(1)}(\pi) = -24 \mathrm{Li}_{3,1,1}^{\pm} + 24 \mathrm{Li}_{4,1,1}^{\pm} - 18 \mathrm{Li}_{5,1}^{\pm} + 12 \mathrm{Li}_6^{\pm}$$

$$+ 3\pi^2 \zeta(3,1) - 3\pi^2 \zeta(4) + \frac{\pi^6}{480}$$

$$= 24 \mathrm{Li}_{3,1,1,1}(-1) - 18 \mathrm{Li}_{5,1}(-1)$$

$$+ 3\zeta(3)^2 - \frac{3}{1120} \pi^6. \qquad (14)$$

In the first equality, the term $\pi^6/480$ is the one corresponding to $n = 0$ in (11) obtained from Proposition 1. The second form is again the automatically reduced output of our program. $\diamond$

Remark 1. From the form of (11) and (13) we find that the log-sine integrals $\mathrm{Ls}_n^{(k)}(\pi)$ can be expressed in terms of π and Nielsen polylogarithms at ± 1. Using the duality results in [3, §6.3, and Example 2.4] the polylogarithms at -1 may be explicitly reexpressed as multiple polylogarithms at $1/2$. Some examples are given in [6].

Particular cases of Theorem 1 have been considered in [15] where explicit formulae are given for $\mathrm{Ls}_n^{(k)}(\pi)$ where $k = 0, 1, 2$. $\diamond$

3.4 Log-sine integrals at 2π

As observed by Lewin [20, 7.9.8], log-sine integrals at 2π are expressible in terms of zeta values only. If we proceed as in the case of evaluations at π in (10) we find that the resulting integral now becomes expressible in terms of gamma functions:

$$-\sum_{n,k \geq 0} \mathrm{Ls}_{n+k+1}^{(k)}(2\pi) \frac{\lambda^n}{n!} \frac{(i\mu)^k}{k!} = \int_0^{2\pi} \left(2 \sin\frac{\theta}{2}\right)^\lambda e^{i\mu\theta} \, \mathrm{d}\theta$$

$$= 2\pi e^{i\mu\pi} \binom{\lambda}{\frac{\lambda}{2} + \mu} \qquad (15)$$

45

The special case $\mu = 0$, in the light of (20) which gives $\mathrm{Ls}_n(2\pi) = 2\,\mathrm{Ls}_n(\pi)$, recovers (6).

We may now extract log-sine integrals $\mathrm{Ls}_n^{(k)}(2\pi)$ in a similar way as described in Section 3.1.

Example 5. For instance,

$$\mathrm{Ls}_5^{(2)}(2\pi) = -\frac{13}{45}\pi^5.$$

We remark that this evaluation is incorrectly given in [20, (7.144)] as $7\pi^5/30$ underscoring an advantage of automated evaluations over tables (indeed, there are more misprints in [20] pointed out for instance in [9, 15]). ◇

3.5 Log-sine-polylog integrals

Motivated by the integrals $\mathrm{LsLsc}_{k,i,j}$ defined in [14] we show that the considerations of Section 3.3 can be extended to more involved integrals including

$$\mathrm{Ls}_n^{(k)}(\pi; d) := -\int_0^\pi \theta^k \log^{n-k-1}\left(2\sin\frac{\theta}{2}\right)\mathrm{Li}_d(e^{i\theta})\,\mathrm{d}\theta.$$

On expressing $\mathrm{Li}_d(e^{i\theta})$ as a series, rearranging, and applying Theorem 1, we obtain the following exponential generating function for $\mathrm{Ls}_n^{(k)}(\pi; d)$:

COROLLARY 1. *For $d \geq 0$ we have*

$$-\sum_{n,k\geq 0}\mathrm{Ls}_{n+k+1}^{(k)}(\pi; d)\frac{\lambda^n}{n!}\frac{(i\mu)^k}{k!}$$

$$= i\sum_{n\geq 1}H_{n,d}(\lambda)\frac{e^{i\pi\frac{\lambda}{2}} - (-1)^n e^{i\pi\mu}}{\mu - \frac{\lambda}{2} + n} \quad (16)$$

where

$$H_{n,d}(\lambda) := \sum_{k=0}^{n-1}\frac{(-1)^k\binom{\lambda}{k}}{(n-k)^d}. \quad (17)$$

We note for $0 \leq \theta \leq \pi$ that $\mathrm{Li}_{-1}(e^{i\theta}) = -1/\left(2\sin\frac{\theta}{2}\right)^2$, $\mathrm{Li}_0(e^{i\theta}) = -\frac{1}{2} + \frac{i}{2}\cot\frac{\theta}{2}$, while $\mathrm{Li}_1(e^{i\theta}) = -\log\left(2\sin\frac{\theta}{2}\right) + i\frac{\pi-\theta}{2}$, and $\mathrm{Li}_2(e^{i\theta}) = \zeta(2) + \frac{\theta}{2}\left(\frac{\theta}{2} - \pi\right) + i\,\mathrm{Cl}_2(\theta)$.

Remark 2. Corresponding results for an arbitrary Dirichlet series $\mathrm{L}_{\mathbf{a},d}(x) := \sum_{n\geq 1}a_n x^n/n^d$ can be easily derived in the same fashion. Indeed, for

$$\mathrm{Ls}_n^{(k)}(\pi; \mathbf{a}, d) := -\int_0^\pi \theta^k \log^{n-k-1}\left(2\sin\frac{\theta}{2}\right)\mathrm{L}_{\mathbf{a},d}(e^{i\theta})\,\mathrm{d}\theta$$

one derives the exponential generating function (16) with $H_{n,d}(\lambda)$ replaced by

$$H_{n,\mathbf{a},d}(\lambda) := \sum_{k=0}^{n-1}\frac{(-1)^k\binom{\lambda}{k}a_{n-k}}{(n-k)^d}. \quad (18)$$

This allows for $\mathrm{Ls}_n^{(k)}(\pi; \mathbf{a}, d)$ to be extracted for many number theoretic functions. It does not however seem to cover any of the values of the $\mathrm{LsLsc}_{k,i,j}$ function defined in [14] that are not already covered by Corollary 1. ◇

4. QUASIPERIODIC PROPERTIES

As shown in [20, (7.1.24)], it follows from the periodicity of the integrand that, for integers m,

$$\mathrm{Ls}_n^{(k)}(2m\pi) - \mathrm{Ls}_n^{(k)}(2m\pi - \sigma)$$

$$= \sum_{j=0}^k (-1)^{k-j}(2m\pi)^j\binom{k}{j}\mathrm{Ls}_{n-j}^{(k-j)}(\sigma). \quad (19)$$

Based on this quasiperiodic property of the log-sine integrals, the results of Section 3.4 easily generalize to show that log-sine integrals at multiples of 2π evaluate in terms of zeta values. This is shown in Section 4.1. It then follows from (19) that log-sine integrals at general arguments can be reduced to log-sine integrals at arguments $0 \leq \sigma \leq \pi$. This is discussed briefly in Section 4.2.

Example 6. In the case $k = 0$, we have that

$$\mathrm{Ls}_n(2m\pi) = 2m\,\mathrm{Ls}_n(\pi). \quad (20)$$

For $k = 1$, specializing (19) to $\sigma = 2m\pi$ then yields

$$\mathrm{Ls}_n^{(1)}(2m\pi) = 2m^2\pi\,\mathrm{Ls}_{n-1}(\pi)$$

as is given in [20, (7.1.23)]. ◇

4.1 Log-sine integrals at multiples of 2π

For odd k, specializing (19) to $\sigma = 2m\pi$, we find

$$2\,\mathrm{Ls}_n^{(k)}(2m\pi) = \sum_{j=1}^k (-1)^{j-1}(2m\pi)^j\binom{k}{j}\mathrm{Ls}_{n-j}^{(k-j)}(2m\pi)$$

giving $\mathrm{Ls}_n^{(k)}(2m\pi)$ in terms of lower order log-sine integrals.

More generally, on setting $\sigma = 2\pi$ in (19) and summing the resulting equations for increasing m in a telescoping fashion, we arrive at the following reduction. We will use the standard notation

$$H_n^{(a)} := \sum_{k=1}^n k^{-a}$$

for *generalized harmonic sums*.

THEOREM 2. *For integers $m \geq 0$,*

$$\mathrm{Ls}_n^{(k)}(2m\pi) = \sum_{j=0}^k (-1)^{k-j}(2\pi)^j\binom{k}{j}H_m^{(-j)}\mathrm{Ls}_{n-j}^{(k-j)}(2\pi).$$

Summarizing, we have thus shown that the generalized log-sine integrals at multiples of 2π may always be evaluated in terms of integrals at 2π. In particular, $\mathrm{Ls}_n^{(k)}(2m\pi)$ can always be evaluated in terms of zeta values by the methods of Section 3.4.

4.2 Reduction of arguments

A general (real) argument σ can be written uniquely as $\sigma = 2m\pi \pm \sigma_0$ where $m \geq 0$ is an integer and $0 \leq \sigma_0 \leq \pi$. It then follows from (19) and

$$\mathrm{Ls}_n^{(k)}(-\theta) = (-1)^{k+1}\mathrm{Ls}_n^{(k)}(\theta)$$

that $\mathrm{Ls}_n^{(k)}(\sigma)$ equals

$$\mathrm{Ls}_n^{(k)}(2m\pi) \pm \sum_{j=0}^k (\pm 1)^{k-j}(2m\pi)^j\binom{k}{j}\mathrm{Ls}_{n-j}^{(k-j)}(\sigma_0). \quad (21)$$

Since the evaluation of log-sine integrals at multiples of 2π was explicitly treated in Section 4.1 this implies that the evaluation of log-sine integrals at general arguments σ reduces to the case of arguments $0 \leq \sigma \leq \pi$.

5. EVALUATIONS AT OTHER VALUES

In this section we first discuss a method for evaluating the generalized log-sine integrals at arbitrary arguments in terms of Nielsen polylogarithms at related arguments. The gist of our technique originates with Fuchs ([12], [20, §7.10]). Related evaluations appear in [8] for $\mathrm{Ls}_3(\tau)$ to $\mathrm{Ls}_6(\tau)$ as well as in [9] for $\mathrm{Ls}_n(\tau)$ and $\mathrm{Ls}_n^{(1)}(\tau)$.

We then specialize to evaluations at $\pi/3$ in Section 5.1. The polylogarithms arising in this case have been studied under the name of *multiple Clausen and Glaisher values* in [4]. In fact, the next result (22) with $\tau = \pi/3$ is a modified version of [4, Lemma 3.2]. We employ the notation

$$\binom{n}{a_1, \ldots, a_k} := \frac{n!}{a_1! \cdots a_k!(n - a_1 - \ldots - a_k)!}$$

for multinomial coefficients.

THEOREM 3. *For* $0 \leq \tau \leq 2\pi$, *and nonnegative integers* n, k *such that* $n - k \geq 2$,

$$\zeta(n-k, \{1\}^k) - \sum_{j=0}^{k} \frac{(-i\tau)^j}{j!} \mathrm{Li}_{2+k-j, \{1\}^{n-k-2}}(e^{i\tau})$$

$$= \frac{i^{k+1}(-1)^{n-1}}{(n-1)!} \sum_{r=0}^{n-k-1} \sum_{m=0}^{r} \binom{n-1}{k, m, r-m}$$

$$\times \left(\frac{i}{2}\right)^r (-\pi)^{r-m} \mathrm{Ls}_{n-(r-m)}^{(k+m)}(\tau). \quad (22)$$

PROOF. Starting with

$$\mathrm{Li}_{k, \{1\}^n}(\alpha) - \mathrm{Li}_{k, \{1\}^n}(1) = \int_1^{\alpha} \frac{\mathrm{Li}_{k-1, \{1\}^n}(z)}{z} \, dz$$

and integrating by parts repeatedly, we obtain

$$\sum_{j=0}^{k-2} \frac{(-1)^j}{j!} \log^j(\alpha) \mathrm{Li}_{k-j, \{1\}^n}(\alpha) - \mathrm{Li}_{k, \{1\}^n}(1)$$

$$= \frac{(-1)^{k-2}}{(k-2)!} \int_1^{\alpha} \frac{\log^{k-2}(z) \mathrm{Li}_{\{1\}^{n+1}}(z)}{z} \, dz. \quad (23)$$

Letting $\alpha = e^{i\tau}$ and changing variables to $z = e^{i\theta}$, as well as using

$$\mathrm{Li}_{\{1\}^n}(z) = \frac{(-\log(1-z))^n}{n!},$$

the right-hand side of (23) can be rewritten as

$$\frac{(-1)^{k-2}}{(k-2)!} \frac{i}{(n+1)!} \int_0^{\tau} (i\theta)^{k-2} \left(-\log\left(1 - e^{i\theta}\right)\right)^{n+1} d\theta.$$

Since, for $0 \leq \theta \leq 2\pi$ and the principal branch of the logarithm,

$$\log(1 - e^{i\theta}) = \log\left|2\sin\frac{\theta}{2}\right| + \frac{i}{2}(\theta - \pi), \quad (24)$$

this last integral can now be expanded in terms of generalized

log-sine integrals at τ.

$$\zeta(k, \{1\}^n) - \sum_{j=0}^{k-2} \frac{(-i\tau)^j}{j!} \mathrm{Li}_{k-j, \{1\}^n}(e^{i\tau})$$

$$= \frac{(-i)^{k-1}}{(k-2)!} \frac{(-1)^n}{(n+1)!} \sum_{r=0}^{n+1} \sum_{m=0}^{r} \binom{n+1}{r} \binom{r}{m}$$

$$\left(\frac{i}{2}\right)^r (-\pi)^{r-m} \mathrm{Ls}_{n+k-(r-m)}^{(k+m-2)}(\tau). \quad (25)$$

Applying the *MZV duality formula* [3], we have

$$\zeta(k, \{1\}^n) = \zeta(n+2, \{1\}^{k-2}),$$

and a change of variables yields the claim. $\square$

We recall that the real and imaginary parts of the multiple polylogarithms are Clausen and Glaisher functions as defined in (4) and (5).

Example 7. Applying (22) with $n = 4$ and $k = 1$ and solving for $\mathrm{Ls}_4^{(1)}(\tau)$ yields

$$\mathrm{Ls}_4^{(1)}(\tau) = 2\zeta(3, 1) - 2\,\mathrm{Gl}_{3,1}(\tau) - 2\tau\,\mathrm{Gl}_{2,1}(\tau)$$

$$+ \frac{1}{4}\mathrm{Ls}_4^{(3)}(\tau) - \frac{1}{2}\pi\,\mathrm{Ls}_3^{(2)}(\tau) + \frac{1}{4}\pi^2\,\mathrm{Ls}_2^{(1)}(\tau)$$

$$= \frac{1}{180}\pi^4 - 2\,\mathrm{Gl}_{3,1}(\tau) - 2\tau\,\mathrm{Gl}_{2,1}(\tau)$$

$$- \frac{1}{16}\tau^4 + \frac{1}{6}\pi\tau^3 - \frac{1}{8}\pi^2\tau^2.$$

For the last equality we used the trivial evaluation

$$\mathrm{Ls}_n^{(n-1)}(\tau) = -\frac{\tau^n}{n}. \quad (26)$$

It appears that both $\mathrm{Gl}_{2,1}(\tau)$ and $\mathrm{Gl}_{3,1}(\tau)$ are not reducible for $\tau = \pi/2$ or $\tau = 2\pi/3$. Here, reducible means expressible in terms of multi zeta values and Glaisher functions of the same argument and lower weight. In the case $\tau = \pi/3$ such reductions are possible. This is discussed in Example 9 and illustrates how much less simple values at $2\pi/3$ are than those at $\pi/3$. We remark, however, that $\mathrm{Gl}_{2,1}(2\pi/3)$ is reducible to one-dimensional polylogarithmic terms [6]. In [1] explicit reductions for all weight four or less polylogarithms are given. $\diamond$

Remark 3. Lewin [20, 7.4.3] uses the special case $k = n - 2$ of (22) to deduce a few small integer evaluations of the log-sine integrals $\mathrm{Ls}_n^{(n-2)}(\pi/3)$ in terms of classical Clausen functions. $\diamond$

In general, we can use (22) recursively to express the log-sine values $\mathrm{Ls}_n^{(k)}(\tau)$ in terms of multiple Clausen and Glaisher functions at τ.

Example 8. (22) with $n = 5$ and $k = 1$ produces

$$\mathrm{Ls}_5^{(1)}(\tau) = -6\zeta(4, 1) + 6\,\mathrm{Cl}_{3,1,1}(\tau) + 6\tau\,\mathrm{Cl}_{2,1,1}(\tau)$$

$$+ \frac{3}{4}\mathrm{Ls}_5^{(3)}(\tau) - \frac{3}{2}\pi\,\mathrm{Ls}_4^{(2)}(\tau) + \frac{3}{4}\pi^2\,\mathrm{Ls}_3^{(1)}(\tau).$$

Applying (22) three more times to rewrite the remaining log-sine integrals produces an evaluation of $\mathrm{Ls}_5^{(1)}(\tau)$ in terms of multi zeta values and Clausen functions at τ. $\diamond$

5.1 Log-sine integrals at $\pi/3$

We now apply the general results obtained in Section 5 to the evaluation of log-sine integrals at $\tau = \pi/3$. Accordingly, we encounter multiple polylogarithms at the basic 6-th root of unity $\omega := \exp(i\pi/3)$. Their real and imaginary parts satisfy various relations and reductions, studied in [4], which allow us to further treat the resulting evaluations. In general, these polylogarithms are more tractable than those at other values because $\bar{\omega} = \omega^2$.

Example 9. (Values at $\frac{\pi}{3}$) Continuing Example 7 we have

$$-\operatorname{Ls}_4^{(1)}\left(\frac{\pi}{3}\right) = 2\operatorname{Gl}_{3,1}\left(\frac{\pi}{3}\right) + \frac{2}{3}\pi\operatorname{Gl}_{2,1}\left(\frac{\pi}{3}\right) + \frac{19}{6480}\pi^4.$$

Using known reductions from [4] we get:

$$\operatorname{Gl}_{2,1}\left(\frac{\pi}{3}\right) = \frac{1}{324}\pi^3, \quad \operatorname{Gl}_{3,1}\left(\frac{\pi}{3}\right) = -\frac{23}{19440}\pi^4, \quad (27)$$

and so arrive at

$$-\operatorname{Ls}_4^{(1)}\left(\frac{\pi}{3}\right) = \frac{17}{6480}\pi^4. \quad (28)$$

Lewin explicitly mentions (28) in the preface to [20] because of its "queer" nature which he compares to some of Landen's curious 18th century formulas. $\diamond$

Many more reduction besides (27) are known. In particular, the one-dimensional Glaisher and Clausen functions reduce as follows [20]:

$$\operatorname{Gl}_n(2\pi x) = \frac{2^{n-1}(-1)^{1+\lfloor n/2\rfloor}}{n!}B_n(x)\pi^n,$$

$$\operatorname{Cl}_{2n+1}\left(\frac{\pi}{3}\right) = \frac{1}{2}(1-2^{-2n})(1-3^{-2n})\zeta(2n+1). \quad (29)$$

Here, B_n denotes the n-th *Bernoulli polynomial*. Further reductions can be derived for instance from the duality result [4, Theorem 4.4]. For low dimensions, we have built these reductions into our program, see Section 6.

Example 10. (Values of $\operatorname{Ls}_n(\pi/3)$) The log-sine integrals at $\pi/3$ are evaluated by our program as follows:

$$\operatorname{Ls}_2\left(\frac{\pi}{3}\right) = \operatorname{Cl}_2\left(\frac{\pi}{3}\right)$$

$$-\operatorname{Ls}_3\left(\frac{\pi}{3}\right) = \frac{7}{108}\pi^3$$

$$\operatorname{Ls}_4\left(\frac{\pi}{3}\right) = \frac{1}{2}\pi\zeta(3) + \frac{9}{2}\operatorname{Cl}_4\left(\frac{\pi}{3}\right)$$

$$-\operatorname{Ls}_5\left(\frac{\pi}{3}\right) = \frac{1543}{19440}\pi^5 - 6\operatorname{Gl}_{4,1}\left(\frac{\pi}{3}\right)$$

$$\operatorname{Ls}_6\left(\frac{\pi}{3}\right) = \frac{15}{2}\pi\zeta(5) + \frac{35}{36}\pi^3\zeta(3) + \frac{135}{2}\operatorname{Cl}_6\left(\frac{\pi}{3}\right)$$

$$-\operatorname{Ls}_7\left(\frac{\pi}{3}\right) = \frac{74369}{326592}\pi^7 + \frac{15}{2}\pi\zeta(3)^2 - 135\operatorname{Gl}_{6,1}\left(\frac{\pi}{3}\right)$$

As follows from the results of Section 5 each integral is a multivariable rational polynomial in π as well as Cl, Gl, and zeta values. These evaluations confirm those given in [9, Appendix A] for $\operatorname{Ls}_3\left(\frac{\pi}{3}\right)$, $\operatorname{Ls}_4\left(\frac{\pi}{3}\right)$, and $\operatorname{Ls}_6\left(\frac{\pi}{3}\right)$. Less explicitly, the evaluations of $\operatorname{Ls}_5\left(\frac{\pi}{3}\right)$ and $\operatorname{Ls}_7\left(\frac{\pi}{3}\right)$ can be recovered from similar results in [15, 9] (which in part were obtained using PSLQ; we refer to Section 6 for how our analysis relies on PSLQ).

The first presumed-irreducible value that occurs is

$$\operatorname{Gl}_{4,1}\left(\frac{\pi}{3}\right) = \sum_{n=1}^{\infty}\frac{\sum_{k=1}^{n-1}\frac{1}{k}}{n^4}\sin\left(\frac{n\pi}{3}\right)$$

$$= \frac{3341}{1632960}\pi^5 - \frac{1}{\pi}\zeta(3)^2 - \frac{3}{4\pi}\sum_{n=1}^{\infty}\frac{1}{\binom{2n}{n}n^6}. \quad (30)$$

The final evaluation is described in [4]. Extensive computation suggests it is not expressible as a sum of products of one dimensional Glaisher and zeta values. Indeed, conjectures are made in [4, §5] for the number of irreducibles at each depth. Related dimensional conjectures for polylogs are discussed in [26]. $\diamond$

5.2 Log-sine integrals at imaginary values

The approach of Section 5 may be extended to evaluate log-sine integrals at imaginary arguments. In more usual terminology, these are *log-sinh integrals*

$$\operatorname{Lsh}_n^{(k)}(\sigma) := -\int_0^{\sigma}\theta^k\log^{n-1-k}\left|2\sinh\frac{\theta}{2}\right|d\theta \quad (31)$$

which are related to log-sine integrals by

$$\operatorname{Lsh}_n^{(k)}(\sigma) = (-i)^{k+1}\operatorname{Ls}_n^{(k)}(i\sigma).$$

We may derive a result along the lines of Theorem 3 by observing that equation (24) is replaced, when $\theta = it$ for $t > 0$, by the simpler

$$\log(1 - e^{-t}) = \log\left|2\sinh\frac{t}{2}\right| - \frac{t}{2}. \quad (32)$$

This leads to:

THEOREM 4. *For $t > 0$, and nonnegative integers n, k such that $n - k \geq 2$,*

$$\zeta(n-k,\{1\}^k) - \sum_{j=0}^{k}\frac{t^j}{j!}\operatorname{Li}_{2+k-j,\{1\}^{n-k-2}}(e^{-t})$$

$$= \frac{(-1)^{n+k}}{(n-1)!}\sum_{r=0}^{n-k-1}\binom{n-1}{k,r}\left(-\frac{1}{2}\right)^r\operatorname{Lsh}_n^{(k+r)}(t). \quad (33)$$

Example 11. Let $\rho := (1 + \sqrt{5})/2$ be the golden mean. Then, by applying Theorem 4 with $n = 3$ and $k = 1$,

$$\operatorname{Lsh}_3^{(1)}(2\log\rho) = \zeta(3) - \frac{4}{3}\log^3\rho$$

$$- \operatorname{Li}_3(\rho^{-2}) - 2\operatorname{Li}_2(\rho^{-2})\log\rho.$$

This may be further reduced, using $\operatorname{Li}_2(\rho^{-2}) = \frac{\pi^2}{15} - \log^2\rho$ and $\operatorname{Li}_3(\rho^{-2}) = \frac{4}{5}\zeta(3) - \frac{2}{15}\pi^2\log\rho + \frac{2}{3}\log^3\rho$, to yield the well-known

$$\operatorname{Lsh}_3^{(1)}(2\log\rho) = \frac{1}{5}\zeta(3).$$

The interest in this kind of evaluation stems from the fact that log-sinh integrals at $2\log\rho$ express values of alternating inverse binomial sums (the fact that log-sine integrals at $\pi/3$ give inverse binomial sums is illustrated by Example 10 and (30)). In this case,

$$\operatorname{Lsh}_3^{(1)}(2\log\rho) = \frac{1}{2}\sum_{n=1}^{\infty}\frac{(-1)^{n-1}}{\binom{2n}{n}n^3}.$$

More on this relation and generalizations can be found in each of [22, 16, 4, 2]. $\diamond$

6. REDUCING POLYLOGARITHMS

The techniques described in Sections 3.3 and 5 for evaluating log-sine integrals in terms of multiple polylogarithms usually produce expressions that can be considerably reduced as is illustrated in Examples 3, 4, and 9. Relations between polylogarithms have been the subject of many studies [3, 2] with a special focus on (alternating) multiple zeta values [17, 13, 26] and, to a lesser extent, Clausen values [4].

There is a certain deal of choice in how to combine the various techniques that we present in order to evaluate log-sine integrals at certain values. The next example shows how this can be exploited to derive relations among the various polylogarithms involved.

Example 12. For $n = 5$ and $k = 2$, specializing (19) to $\sigma = \pi$ and $m = 1$ yields

$$\mathrm{Ls}_5^{(2)}(2\pi) = 2\,\mathrm{Ls}_5^{(2)}(\pi) - 4\pi\,\mathrm{Ls}_4^{(1)}(\pi) + 4\pi^2\,\mathrm{Ls}_3(\pi).$$

By Example 5 we know that this evaluates as $-13/45\pi^5$. On the other hand, we may use the technique of Section 3.3 to reduce the log-sine integrals at π. This leads to

$$-8\pi\,\mathrm{Li}_{3,1}(1) + 12\pi\,\mathrm{Li}_4(1) - \frac{2}{5}\pi^5 = -\frac{13}{45}\pi^5.$$

In simplified terms, we have derived the famous identity $\zeta(3,1) = \frac{\pi^4}{360}$. Similarly, the case $n = 6$ and $k = 2$ leads to $\zeta(3,1,1) = \frac{3}{2}\zeta(4,1) + \frac{1}{12}\pi^2\zeta(3) - \zeta(5)$ which further reduces to $2\zeta(5) - \frac{\pi^2}{6}\zeta(3)$. As a final example, the case $n = 7$ and $k = 4$ produces $\zeta(5,1) = \frac{\pi^6}{1260} - \frac{1}{2}\zeta(3)^2$. ◇

For the purpose of an implementation, we have built many reductions of multiple polylogarithms into our program. Besides some general rules, such as (29), the program contains a table of reductions at low weight for polylogarithms at the values 1 and −1, as well as Clausen and Glaisher functions at the values $\pi/2$, $\pi/2$, and $2\pi/3$. These correspond to the polylogarithms that occur in the evaluation of the log-sine integrals at the special values $\pi/3$, $\pi/2$, $2\pi/3$, π which are of particular importance for applications as mentioned in the introduction. This table of reductions has been compiled using the integer relation finding algorithm PSLQ [2]. Its use is thus of heuristic nature (as opposed to the rest of the program which is working symbolically from the analytic results in this paper) and is therefore made optional.

7. THE PROGRAM

7.1 Basic usage

As promised, we implemented[1] the presented results for evaluating log-sine integrals for use in the computer algebra systems *Mathematica* and SAGE. The basic usage is very simple and illustrated in the next example for *Mathematica*[2].

Example 13. Consider the log-sine integral $\mathrm{Ls}_5^{(2)}(2\pi)$. The following self-explanatory code evaluates it in terms of polylogarithms:

```
LsToLi[Ls[5,2,2Pi]]
```

This produces the output $-13/45\pi^5$ as in Example 5. As a second example,

```
-LsToLi[Ls[5,0,Pi/3]]
```

results in the output

```
1543/19440*Pi^5 - 6*Gl[{4,1},Pi/3]
```

which agrees with the evaluation in Example 10. Finally,

```
LsToLi[Ls[5,1,Pi]]
```

produces

```
6*Li[{3,1,1},-1] + (Pi^2*Zeta[3])/4
- (105*Zeta[5])/32
```

as in Example 3. ◇

Example 14. Computing

```
LsToLi[Ls[6,3,Pi/3]-2*Ls[6,1,Pi/3]]
```

yields the value $\frac{313}{204120}\pi^6$ and thus automatically proves a result of Zucker [27]. A family of relations between log-sine integrals at $\pi/3$ generalizing the above has been established in [22]. ◇

7.2 Implementation

The conversion from log-sine integrals to polylogarithmic values demonstrated in Example 13 roughly proceeds as follows:

- First, the evaluation of $\mathrm{Ls}_n^{(k)}(\sigma)$ is reduced to the cases of $0 \le \sigma \le \pi$ and $\sigma = 2m\pi$ as described in Section 4.2.

- The cases $\sigma = 2m\pi$ are treated as in Section 3.4 and result in multiple zeta values.

- The other cases σ result in polylogarithmic values at $e^{i\sigma}$ and are obtained using the results of Sections 3.3 and 5.

- Finally, especially in the physically relevant cases, various reductions of the resulting polylogarithms are performed as outlined in Section 6.

---

[1]The packages are freely available for download from
http://arminstraub.com/pub/log-sine-integrals
[2]The interface in the case of SAGE is similar but may change slightly, especially as we hope to integrate our package into the core of SAGE.

7.3 Numerical usage

The program is also useful for numerical computations provided that it is coupled with efficient methods for evaluating polylogarithms to high precision. It complements for instance the C++ library `lsjk` "for arbitrary-precision numeric evaluation of the generalized log-sine functions" described in [15].

Example 15. We evaluate

$$\mathrm{Ls}_5^{(2)}\left(\frac{2\pi}{3}\right) = 4\,\mathrm{Gl}_{4,1}\left(\frac{2\pi}{3}\right) - \frac{8}{3}\pi\,\mathrm{Gl}_{3,1}\left(\frac{2\pi}{3}\right)$$
$$- \frac{8}{9}\pi^2\,\mathrm{Gl}_{2,1}\left(\frac{2\pi}{3}\right) - \frac{8}{1215}\pi^5.$$

Using specialized code[3] such as [25], the right-hand side is readily evaluated to, for instance, two thousand digit precision in about a minute. The first 1024 digits of the result match the evaluation given in [15]. However, due to its implementation `lsjk` currently is restricted to log-sine functions $\mathrm{Ls}_n^{(k)}(\theta)$ with $k \leq 9$. ◇

Acknowledgements.

We are grateful to Andrei Davydychev and Mikhail Kalmykov for several valuable comments on an earlier version of this paper and for pointing us to relevant publications. We also thank the reviewers for their thorough reading and helpful suggestions.

8. REFERENCES

[1] D. Borwein, J. M. Borwein, A. Straub, and J. Wan. Log-sine evaluations of Mahler measures, II. Preprint, March 2011. arXiv:1103.3035.

[2] J. M. Borwein, D. H. Bailey, and R. Girgensohn. *Experimentation in Mathematics: Computational Paths to Discovery*. A. K. Peters, 1st edition, 2004.

[3] J. M. Borwein, D. M. Bradley, D. J. Broadhurst, and P. Lisoněk. Special values of multiple polylogarithms. *Trans. Amer. Math. Soc.*, 353(3):907–941, 2001. arXiv:math/9910045.

[4] J. M. Borwein, D. J. Broadhurst, and J. Kamnitzer. Central binomial sums, multiple Clausen values, and zeta values. *Experimental Mathematics*, 10(1):25–34, 2001. arXiv:hep-th/0004153.

[5] J. M. Borwein and R. E. Crandall. Closed forms: what they are and why we care. *Notices Amer. Math. Soc.*, 2010. In press.

[6] J. M. Borwein and A. Straub. Log-sine evaluations of Mahler measures. *J. Aust Math. Soc.*, Mar 2011. arXiv:1103.3893.

[7] D. W. Boyd. Speculations concerning the range of Mahler's measure. *Canad. Math. Bull.*, 24:453–469, 1981.

[8] A. Davydychev and M. Kalmykov. Some remarks on the ε-expansion of dimensionally regulated Feynman diagrams. *Nuclear Physics B - Proceedings Supplements*, 89(1-3):283–288, Oct. 2000. arXiv:hep-th/0005287.

[9] A. Davydychev and M. Kalmykov. New results for the ε-expansion of certain one-, two- and three-loop Feynman diagrams. *Nuclear Physics B*, 605:266–318, 2001. arXiv:hep-th/0012189.

[10] A. Davydychev and M. Kalmykov. Massive Feynman diagrams and inverse binomial sums. *Nuclear Physics B*, 699(1-2):3–64, 2004. arXiv:hep-th/0303162.

[11] A. I. Davydychev. Explicit results for all orders of the ε expansion of certain massive and massless diagrams. *Phys. Rev. D*, 61(8):087701, Mar 2000. arXiv:hep-ph/9910224.

[12] W. Fuchs. Two definite integrals (solution to a problem posed by L. Lewin). *The American Mathematical Monthly*, 68(6):580–581, 1961.

[13] M. E. Hoffman and Y. Ohno. Relations of multiple zeta values and their algebraic expression. *J. Algebra*, 262:332–347, 2003. arXiv:math/0010140.

[14] M. Kalmykov. About higher order ε-expansion of some massive two- and three-loop master-integrals. *Nuclear Physics B*, 718:276–292, July 2005. arXiv:hep-ph/0503070.

[15] M. Kalmykov and A. Sheplyakov. lsjk - a C++ library for arbitrary-precision numeric evaluation of the generalized log-sine functions. *Comput. Phys. Commun.*, 172(1):45–59, 2005. arXiv:hep-ph/0411100.

[16] M. Kalmykov and O. Veretin. Single scale diagrams and multiple binomial sums. *Phys. Lett. B*, 483(1-3):315–323, 2000. arXiv:hep-th/0004010.

[17] K. S. Kölbig. Closed expressions for $\int_0^1 t^{-1}\log^{n-1}t\log^p(1-t)dt$. *Mathematics of Computation*, 39(160):647–654, 1982.

[18] N. Kurokawa, M. Lalín, and H. Ochiai. Higher Mahler measures and zeta functions. *Acta Arithmetica*, 135(3):269–297, 2008. arXiv:0908.0171.

[19] L. Lewin. On the evaluation of log-sine integrals. *The Mathematical Gazette*, 42:125–128, 1958.

[20] L. Lewin. *Polylogarithms and associated functions*. North Holland, 1981.

[21] D. Maitre. HPL, a Mathematica implementation of the harmonic polylogarithms. *Comput. Phys. Commun.*, 174:222–240, 2006. arXiv:hep-ph/0507152.

[22] Z. Nan-Yue and K. S. Williams. Values of the Riemann zeta function and integrals involving $\log(2\sinh(\theta/2))$ and $\log(2\sin(\theta/2))$. *Pacific J. Math.*, 168(2):271–289, 1995.

[23] F. W. J. Olver, D. W. Lozier, R. F. Boisvert, and C. W. Clark. *NIST Handbook of Mathematical Functions*. Cambridge University Press, 2010.

[24] Y. Sasaki. On multiple higher Mahler measures and multiple L values. *Acta Arithmetica*, 144(2):159–165, 2010.

[25] J. Vollinga and S. Weinzierl. Numerical evaluation of multiple polylogarithms. *Comput. Phys. Commun.*, 167:177, 2005. arXiv:hep-ph/0410259.

[26] S. Zlobin. Special values of generalized polylogarithms. To appear in proceedings of the conference "Diophantine and Analytic Problems in Number Theory", 2007. arXiv:0712.1656.

[27] I. Zucker. On the series $\sum_{k=1}^\infty \binom{2k}{k}^{-1}k^{-n}$ and related sums. *J. Number Theory*, 20:92–102, 1985.

---

[3]The C++ code we used is based on the fast Hölder transform described in [3], and is available on request.

Vector Rational Number Reconstruction

Curtis Bright
cbright@uwaterloo.ca

Arne Storjohann
astorjoh@uwaterloo.ca

David R. Cheriton School of Computer Science
University of Waterloo, Ontario, Canada N2L 3G1

ABSTRACT

The final step of some algebraic algorithms is to reconstruct the common denominator d of a collection of rational numbers $(n_i/d)_{1 \le i \le n}$ from their images $(a_i)_{1 \le i \le n}$ mod M, subject to a condition such as $0 < d \le N$ and $|n_i| \le N$ for a given magnitude bound N. Applying elementwise rational number reconstruction requires that $M \in \Omega(N^2)$. Using the gradual sublattice reduction algorithm of van Hoeij and Novocin [23], we show how to perform the reconstruction efficiently even when the modulus satisfies a considerably smaller magnitude bound $M \in \Omega(N^{1+1/c})$ for c a small constant, for example $2 \le c \le 5$. Assuming $c \in O(1)$ the cost of the approach is $O(n(\log M)^3)$ bit operations using the original LLL lattice reduction algorithm, but is reduced to $O(n(\log M)^2)$ bit operations by incorporating the L^2 variant of Nguyen and Stehlé [17]. As an application, we give a robust method for reconstructing the rational solution vector of a linear system from its image, such as obtained by a solver using p-adic lifting.

Categories and Subject Descriptors

F.2.1 [**Analysis of Algorithms and Problem Complexity**]: Numerical Algorithms and Problems—*Number-theoretic computations*; G.4 [**Mathematical Software**]: Algorithm Design and Analysis; I.1.2 [**Symbolic and Algebraic Manipulation**]: Algorithms

General Terms

Algorithms

Keywords

Rational reconstruction, lattice basis reduction

1. INTRODUCTION

A rational number reconstruction of an integer $a \in \mathbb{Z}$ with respect to a positive modulus $M \in \mathbb{Z}_{>0}$ is a signed fraction

$n/d \in \mathbb{Q}$ with $\gcd(n, d) = 1$ such that $a \equiv n/d \pmod M$. In general, there may be multiple possibilities, for example $a \equiv n_1/d_1 \equiv n_2/d_2 \pmod M$ with $n_1 \not\equiv n_2 \pmod M$.

Assuming a reconstruction exists, its uniqueness can be ensured by stipulating bounds for the magnitudes of the output integers n and d. In addition to a and M, the simplest version of the problem takes as input a bound $N < M$, and asks for output a pair of integers (d, n) such that

$$da \equiv n \pmod M, \qquad |n| \le N, \qquad 0 < d \le N. \qquad (1)$$

Note that if (d, n) is a solution to (1) with $\gcd(n, d) = 1$ then n/d is a rational reconstruction of $a \pmod M$. Since there are $\Theta(N^2)$ coprime pairs (d, n) which satisfy the bounds of (1), a requirement for rational reconstruction uniqueness is $M \in \Omega(N^2)$ by the pigeonhole principle.

In fact, if the bound $M > 2N^2$ is satisfied then there is at most one solution of (1) with $\gcd(n, d) = 1$. Such a solution can be computed effectively using the well known approach based on the extended Euclidean algorithm and the continued fraction expansion of a/M. See for example [11, Theorem 5.1] or the books [8, 21].

Rational number reconstruction is an essential tool in many algorithms that employ a homomorphic imaging scheme to avoid intermediate expression swell, to allow for a simple coarse grain parallelization, or to facilitate an output sensitive approach; explicit examples include solving sparse rational systems [4] and computing gcds of polynomials [7]. Often, the final step of these algorithms is to reconstruct the common denominator $d \in \mathbb{Z}_{>0}$ of a collection of rational numbers $(n_i/d)_{1 \le i \le n}$ from their images $(a_i)_{1 \le i \le n}$ modulo M. The images modulo M are typically computed by combining multiple smaller images, either using Chinese remaindering $(M = p_1 p_2 \cdots p_m)$ or a variation of Newton–Hensel lifting $(M = p^m)$. The cost of an algorithm that uses a homomorphic imaging scheme is highly correlated to m, the number of smaller images computed, which is directly related to the bitlength of the modulus M. Ideally, just enough smaller images are computed to allow reconstruction of the common denominator d. If N is an upper bound for both d and $\max_i |n_i|$, elementwise rational reconstruction can be applied but requires that $M > 2N^2$ to ensure success.

This paper gives a deterministic algorithm for efficiently computing the common denominator d that for some applications requires about half as many image computations as the standard approach. Our specification of the vector version of the problem differs slightly from the scalar case shown in (1). The vector rational reconstruction problem takes as input a vector $\boldsymbol{a} \in \mathbb{Z}^n$ of images modulo M, and asks for a pair $(d, \boldsymbol{n}) \in (\mathbb{Z}, \mathbb{Z}^n)$ such that

$$d\boldsymbol{a} \equiv \boldsymbol{n} \pmod{M}, \qquad 0 < \left\| \left[\, d \mid \boldsymbol{n} \,\right] \right\|_2 \leq N. \qquad (2)$$

Here, we use a common bound for d and $\boldsymbol{n}$ based on the 2-norm because this is a more natural condition for the algorithm we will present, which is based on integer lattice basis reduction. In particular, the problem of computing solutions to (2) is equivalent to finding short nonzero vectors in the lattice generated by the rows of the matrix

$$\left[\begin{array}{c|c} & M\boldsymbol{I}_{n \times n} \\ \hline 1 & \boldsymbol{a} \end{array} \right] \in \mathbb{Z}^{(n+1) \times (n+1)}. \qquad (3)$$

The lattice shown in (3) is a special case of the "knapsack-type" lattices studied by van Hoeij and Novocin [23], who give an algorithm which can be used to compute a "generating set" for (2), that is, a set $(d_i, \boldsymbol{n}_i)_{1 \leq i \leq c}$ corresponding to linearly independent vectors $\left[\, d_i \mid \boldsymbol{n}_i \,\right]_{1 \leq i \leq c}$ such that every solution of (2) can be expressed as a $\mathbb{Z}$-linear combination of the members of the generating set. On the one hand, from the scalar case, we know that a sufficient condition to ensure the existence of a generating set of dimension zero (no solution) or one (a unique minimal denominator solution) is that the modulus M be large enough to satisfy $M > 2N^2$. On the other hand, if c is an integer such that $M > 2^{(c+1)/2} N^{1+1/c}$ is satisfied, it follows from a strengthening of [23, Theorem 2] that the generating set returned will contain at most c vectors. The generating set produced will be LLL reduced, so the 2-norm of the first vector will be at most $2^{(c-1)/2}$ times that of the shortest vector which solves (2).

To apply lattice reduction directly to a lattice with row dimension $n + 1$ would be prohibitively expensive in terms of n when n is large. Instead, van Hoeij and Novocin [23] propose a gradual sublattice reduction algorithm which adds columns to the work lattice one by one, while keeping the row dimension bounded by $c + 1$ by removing vectors which provably can't contribute to a solution of (2). Assuming $c \in O(1)$, this algorithm applied to bases of the form in (3) will run in $O(n^2 (\log M)^3)$ bit operations when the standard LLL algorithm algorithm is used. By using properties of the special basis form (3) and incorporating the L^2 algorithm [17] we show how to reduce the cost to $O(n(\log M)^2)$ bit operations.

The approach is particularly well suited to applications where it is known *a priori* that there can exist at most one linearly independent solution to (2). In Section 5 we consider the problem of solving a nonsingular integer linear system $\boldsymbol{Ax} = \boldsymbol{b}$, which has exactly one rational solution vector with common denominator a factor of $\det \boldsymbol{A}$. As a concrete example, coming from [2], suppose $\boldsymbol{A}$ and $\boldsymbol{b}$ have dimension 10,000 and are filled randomly with single decimal digit integers. The common denominator and the numerators of a typical solution vector for such a system have about 24,044 decimal digits, or of magnitude about $\beta = 10^{24044}$. To apply elementwise rational reconstruction requires $M > 2N^2$ with $N \geq \beta$ to be satisfied, so M needs to have length about 48,088 decimal digits. But by choosing the parameter $c = 5$, the vector algorithm requires only that $M > 2^{(c+1)/2} N^{1+1/c}$ with $N \geq \sqrt{n+1}\beta$ in order to succeed, so M need have only about 28,856 decimal digits. The method we propose is robust in the sense that β need not be known beforehand; if a reconstruction is attempted with N too small, FAIL will be reported, but if N is sufficiently large the algorithm will guarantee to return the correct reconstruction.

Related work.

For the scalar version of the problem, much work has focused on decreasing the running time from $O((\log M)^2)$ to nearly linear in $\log M$ by incorporating fast integer multiplication. For a survey of work in this direction we refer to [15]. An algorithm that doesn't need a priori bounds for the numerator and denominator is described in [16].

Now consider the vector version of the problem. Two approaches are proposed in [12]. The first is a heuristic randomized algorithm to recover a solution d and $\boldsymbol{n}$ that satisfies $d\|\boldsymbol{n}\|_\infty \in O(M)$. The second, based on the good simultaneous Diophantine approximation algorithm in [13], can be applied to find a solution even when $\left\| \left[\, d \mid \boldsymbol{n} \,\right] \right\|_2 \in o(N^2)$ but the algorithm performs lattice reduction directly on $n + 1$ dimensional lattices similar to (3) and seems to be expensive when n is large.

The survey [10] has an overview of using lattices with bases similar to (3) for effectively solving real and p-adic simultaneous Diophantine approximation problems. However, these results are concerned with existence, not uniqueness.

An efficient algorithm for the rational function version of the vector reconstruction problem is given in [20].

Organization.

In Section 2 we illustrate the main ideas of the algorithm with a worked example. In Section 3 we establish our notation and recall the required facts about lattices and the LLL lattice basis reduction algorithm. Section 4 presents the algorithm for vector rational reconstruction, proves its correctness, and provides a simple cost analysis. In Section 5 we show how the vector rational reconstruction algorithm can be incorporated into an algorithm for solving nonsingular linear systems to save on the number of required image computations.

2. OUTLINE OF THE ALGORITHM

As previously noted, the problem of finding solutions to (2) is identical to the problem of finding short nonzero vectors, with respect to the 2-norm, in the lattice generated by the rows of the following matrix:

$$\begin{bmatrix} & & & & M \\ & & & \cdot\cdot & \\ & & M & & \\ & M & & & \\ 1 & a_1 & a_2 & \cdots & a_n \end{bmatrix} \in \mathbb{Z}^{(n+1) \times (n+1)}.$$

The first n rows of the matrix can be used to reduce modulo M the last n entries of any vector in the lattice; in particular, a vector obtained by multiplying the last row by d. The first entry of such a vector will still be d and the ith entry for $2 \leq i \leq n + 1$ will be congruent to $da_{i-1} \pmod{M}$.

For example, consider the lattice basis matrix

$$\boldsymbol{L} = \begin{bmatrix} & & & & 195967 \\ & & & 195967 & \\ & & 195967 & & \\ & 195967 & & & \\ 1 & -23677 & -49539 & 74089 & -21989 \end{bmatrix}$$

where our target length is $N = 10^4$. When n is large it is infeasible to reduce the entire basis at once. Instead, the gradual sublattice reduction algorithm of [23] will keep the row dimension of the lattice constant by adding columns one by one, and removing basis vectors which are provably too big. We continue with our example, which is similar to the example given in [18, Section 2.2].

Consider reducing just the lower-left 2×2 submatrix of $\boldsymbol{L}$:

$$\begin{bmatrix} 0 & 195967 \\ 1 & -23677 \end{bmatrix} \xRightarrow{\text{LLL}} \begin{bmatrix} -389 & -96 \\ -149 & 467 \end{bmatrix}$$

Knowing the reduction of the lower-left 2×2 submatrix can help us reduce the lower-left 3×3 submatrix of $\boldsymbol{L}$. The first step is to find a basis of the lower-left 2×3 submatrix by 'adding a column'.

Though we could have kept track of the third column of $\boldsymbol{L}$ while doing the above reduction, it can also be simply computed afterwards: the third column is just a_2 times the first column, since this property holds in the the lower-left 2×3 submatrix of $\boldsymbol{L}$ and is preserved by the unimodular row operations used in lattice basis reduction.

After determining a basis of the lower-left 2×3 submatrix, the next step is simply to 'add a row' to find a basis of the lower-left 3×3 submatrix. For example, the lattice generated by the lower-left 3×3 submatrix of $\boldsymbol{L}$ has the following basis, which we again reduce:

$$\left[\begin{array}{cc|c} 0 & 0 & 195967 \\ \hline -389 & -96 & 19270671 \\ -149 & 467 & 7381311 \end{array}\right] \xRightarrow{\text{LLL}} \begin{bmatrix} -538 & 371 & 470 \\ 91 & 1030 & -808 \\ 27089 & 13738 & 20045 \end{bmatrix}$$

Now, it happens that the final vector in the Gram–Schmidt orthogonalization of this basis has norm larger than N. It follows [23, Lemma 2] that any vector in the lattice generated by this basis which includes the final basis vector must have norm at least N. Since we are only interested in vectors shorter than this, we can safely discard the last row, and repeat the same augmentation process to find a sublattice which contains all short vectors in the lattice generated by the lower-left 4×4 submatrix of $\boldsymbol{L}$.

If $M > 2^{(c+1)/2}N^{1+1/c}$ for $c \in \mathbb{Z}_{>0}$ then the process described above of adding columns and removing final rows of the lattice will keep the row dimension of the lattice bounded by $c + 1$. For $c \in O(1)$ this leads to a cost estimate that is quadratic in n. To obtain a running time that is linear in n, we avoid computing the basis vectors in $\boldsymbol{L}$ as the reduction proceeds. Instead, we show how to reconstruct the entire basis from only its first column.

3. PRELIMINARIES

For a $k \times n$ matrix $\boldsymbol{L}$ we let $\boldsymbol{L}_S$ be the rows of $\boldsymbol{L}$ which have indices in $S \subseteq \{1, \ldots, k\}$, let $\boldsymbol{L}_R^{\mathrm{T}}$ be the columns of $\boldsymbol{L}$ which have indices in $R \subseteq \{1, \ldots, n\}$, and let $\boldsymbol{L}_{S,R}$ denote $(\boldsymbol{L}_S)_R^{\mathrm{T}}$. We simply write i for $\{i\}$ and $1..i$ for $\{1, \ldots, i\}$. When not used with a subscript, $\boldsymbol{L}^{\mathrm{T}}$ denotes the transpose of $\boldsymbol{L}$. A subscript on a row vector will always refer to entrywise selection, and the norm of a row vector will refer to the 2-norm, $\|\boldsymbol{x}\| := \sqrt{\boldsymbol{x}\boldsymbol{x}^{\mathrm{T}}}$.

Vectors are denoted by lower-case bold variables and matrices by upper-case or Greek bold variables, with the boldface dropped when referring to individual entries. The $\mathrm{rem}_M(x)$ function returns the reduction of $x \pmod{M}$ in the symmetric range, and applies elementwise to vectors and matrices.

3.1 Lattices

A *point lattice* is a discrete additive subgroup of $\mathbb{R}^n$. The elements of the lattice generated by the rank k matrix $\boldsymbol{L} \in$ $\mathbb{Z}^{k \times n}$ are given by

$$\mathcal{L}(\boldsymbol{L}) := \left\{ \sum_{i=1}^{k} r_i \boldsymbol{L}_i : r_i \in \mathbb{Z} \right\},$$

and $\boldsymbol{L}$ is a *basis* of $\mathcal{L}(\boldsymbol{L})$. If $\mathcal{L}(\boldsymbol{S}) \subseteq \mathcal{L}(\boldsymbol{L})$ then $\mathcal{L}(\boldsymbol{S})$ is known as a *sublattice* of $\mathcal{L}(\boldsymbol{L})$; this occurs if and only if there exists an integer matrix $\boldsymbol{B}$ such that $\boldsymbol{S} = \boldsymbol{B}\boldsymbol{L}$.

The set of vectors in $\mathcal{L}(\boldsymbol{L})$ shorter than some target length N is denoted

$$\mathcal{L}_N(\boldsymbol{L}) := \{ \boldsymbol{b} \in \mathcal{L}(\boldsymbol{L}) : \|\boldsymbol{b}\| \leq N \}.$$

We call a basis of a sublattice of $\boldsymbol{L}$ which contains all the elements of $\mathcal{L}_N(\boldsymbol{L})$ a *generating matrix* of $\mathcal{L}_N(\boldsymbol{L})$.

3.2 Linear Algebra

For a lattice basis $\boldsymbol{L} \in \mathbb{Z}^{k \times n}$, let $\boldsymbol{L}^* \in \mathbb{Q}^{k \times n}$ denote its Gram–Schmidt orthogonal $\mathbb{R}$-basis and let $\boldsymbol{\mu} \in \mathbb{Q}^{k \times k}$ denote the associated change-of-basis matrix. That is,

$$\begin{bmatrix} \boldsymbol{L}_1 \\ \boldsymbol{L}_2 \\ \vdots \\ \boldsymbol{L}_k \end{bmatrix} = \begin{bmatrix} 1 & & & \\ \mu_{2,1} & 1 & & \\ \vdots & & \ddots & \\ \mu_{k,1} & \mu_{k,2} & \cdots & 1 \end{bmatrix} \begin{bmatrix} \boldsymbol{L}_1^* \\ \boldsymbol{L}_2^* \\ \vdots \\ \boldsymbol{L}_k^* \end{bmatrix}$$

with $\mu_{i,j} = \boldsymbol{L}_i(\boldsymbol{L}_j^*)^{\mathrm{T}}/\|\boldsymbol{L}_j^*\|^2$. Additionally, let $\boldsymbol{G} = \boldsymbol{L}\boldsymbol{L}^{\mathrm{T}} \in \mathbb{Z}^{k \times k}$ denote the Gramian matrix of $\boldsymbol{L}$.

3.3 LLL Reduction

A lattice basis $\boldsymbol{L} \in \mathbb{Z}^{k \times n}$ (or its Gramian $\boldsymbol{G} \in \mathbb{Z}^{k \times k}$) is said to be *LLL-reduced* if its Gram–Schmidt orthogonalization satisfies the conditions

1. $\|\boldsymbol{\mu} - \boldsymbol{I}_{k \times k}\|_{\max} \leq \frac{1}{2}$,

2. $\|\boldsymbol{L}_i^*\|^2 \geq (\frac{3}{4} - \mu_{i,i-1}^2)\|\boldsymbol{L}_{i-1}^*\|^2$ for $1 < i \leq k$.

Given a lattice basis $\boldsymbol{L} \in \mathbb{Z}^{k \times n}$, the *lattice basis reduction* problem is to compute an LLL-reduced basis $\boldsymbol{L}'$ such that $\mathcal{L}(\boldsymbol{L}) = \mathcal{L}(\boldsymbol{L}')$. Assuming $k \in O(1)$, the L^2 algorithm from [17] accomplishes this in $O(n(\log B)^2)$ bit operations, where $\max_i \|\boldsymbol{L}_i\| \leq B$. A well known and important feature of the LLL algorithm, that we will exploit, is that the sequence of unimodular row operations required to reduce a given lattice can be determined strictly from the $\mu_{i,j}$ and $\|\boldsymbol{L}_i^*\|^2$, or in the case of L^2, the Gramian.

Consider Algorithm 1, which only includes the specification of the input and output. If $\boldsymbol{G}$ is the Gramian for a lattice $\boldsymbol{L}$ with row dimension k and arbitrary column dimension, we could LLL reduce $\boldsymbol{L}$ in-place by calling $\mathsf{InPlaceL}^2(k, \boldsymbol{G}, \boldsymbol{L})$. Alternatively, we could also initialize a matrix $\boldsymbol{U}$ as $\boldsymbol{I}_{k \times k}$, call $\mathsf{InPlaceL}^2(k, \boldsymbol{G}, \boldsymbol{U})$ to capture all required unimodular transformations in $\boldsymbol{U}$, and then compute the reduced lattice as $\boldsymbol{U}\boldsymbol{L}$.

Algorithm 1 The $\mathsf{InPlaceL}^2(k, \boldsymbol{G}, \boldsymbol{U})$ lattice basis reduction algorithm.

Input: The Gramian $\boldsymbol{G} \in \mathbb{Z}^{k \times k}$ of some lattice basis $\boldsymbol{L} \in \mathbb{Z}^{k \times *}$, and a matrix $\boldsymbol{U} \in \mathbb{Z}^{k \times *}$.
Output: Use L^2 to update $\boldsymbol{G}$ to be an LLL-reduced Gramian of $\mathcal{L}(\boldsymbol{L})$ and apply all unimodular row operations to $\boldsymbol{U}$.

The following algorithm, Algorithm 2 from [23] applied to L^2, computes an LLL-reduced generating matrix (for a given target length N) of a lattice by using L^2 and discarding vectors which are too large to contribute to a vector shorter than the target length.

Algorithm 2 The L^2WithRemovals$(k, \boldsymbol{G}, \boldsymbol{U}, N)$ generating matrix algorithm.

Input: The Gramian $\boldsymbol{G} \in \mathbb{Z}^{k \times k}$ of some lattice basis $\boldsymbol{L} \in \mathbb{Z}^{k \times *}$, a target length $N \in \mathbb{Z}_{>0}$, and a matrix $\boldsymbol{U} \in \mathbb{Z}^{k \times *}$.
Output: Use L^2 to update $\boldsymbol{G}$ to be an LLL-reduced Gramian of a generating matrix of $\mathcal{L}_N(\boldsymbol{L})$, update k to be its number of rows, and apply all unimodular row operations to $\boldsymbol{U}$.

---

4. THE VECRECON ALGORITHM

In this section we present our vector rational reconstruction algorithm, which computes an LLL-reduced generating matrix for $\mathcal{L}_N(\boldsymbol{\Lambda}_{\boldsymbol{a}}^M)$, where $\boldsymbol{a} \in \mathbb{Z}^{1 \times n}$, $M \in \mathbb{Z}_{>0}$, and

$$\boldsymbol{\Lambda}_{\boldsymbol{a}}^M := \begin{bmatrix} & & & & M \\ & & & \cdot^{\cdot^{\cdot}} & \\ & & M & & \\ & M & & & \\ 1 & a_1 & a_2 & \cdots & a_n \end{bmatrix} \in \mathbb{Z}^{(n+1) \times (n+1)}.$$

The computed generating matrix contains at most c vectors, where $c \geq 1$ is a small constant such that $M > 2^{(c+1)/2} N^{1+1/c}$ is satisfied. The larger c is chosen, the smaller M is allowed to be (assuming $c < \sqrt{2 \log_2 N}$). However, if c is chosen too large the algorithm may be inefficient, since in the worst case it will reduce bases containing up to $c + 1$ vectors.

As already outlined, the algorithm computes a generating matrix of $\mathcal{L}_N(\boldsymbol{\Lambda}_{\boldsymbol{a}}^M)$ gradually, by computing generating matrices of $\mathcal{L}_N(\boldsymbol{\Lambda}_{\boldsymbol{a}_{1..l}}^M)$ for $l = 1, 2, \ldots, n$. However, for efficiency these intermediate generating matrices will not be explicitly stored during the algorithm; we will only keep track of the first column $\boldsymbol{f}$. The following lemma shows how all sublattices of $\mathcal{L}(\boldsymbol{\Lambda}_{\boldsymbol{a}_{1..l}}^M)$ have bases of a special form which strongly depends on the first basis column.

LEMMA 1. *Any* $\boldsymbol{L} \in \mathbb{Z}^{k \times (l+1)}$ *with* $\mathcal{L}(\boldsymbol{L}) \subseteq \mathcal{L}(\boldsymbol{\Lambda}_{\boldsymbol{a}_{1..l}}^M)$ *is of the form*

$$\left[\boldsymbol{L}_1^{\mathrm{T}} \mid \mathrm{rem}_M(\boldsymbol{L}_1^{\mathrm{T}} \boldsymbol{a}_{1..l}) + M \boldsymbol{R} \right]$$

for some $\boldsymbol{R} \in \mathbb{Z}^{k \times l}$.

PROOF. Let $\boldsymbol{\Lambda}$ denote $\boldsymbol{\Lambda}_{\boldsymbol{a}_{1..l}}^M$. Since $\mathcal{L}(\boldsymbol{L})$ is a sublattice of $\mathcal{L}(\boldsymbol{\Lambda})$ there exists a $\boldsymbol{B} \in \mathbb{Z}^{k \times (l+1)}$ such that

$$\begin{aligned} \boldsymbol{L} &= \boldsymbol{B} \boldsymbol{\Lambda} \\ &= \boldsymbol{B}_{l+1}^{\mathrm{T}} \boldsymbol{\Lambda}_{l+1} + \boldsymbol{B}_{1..l}^{\mathrm{T}} \boldsymbol{\Lambda}_{1..l} \\ &= \left[\boldsymbol{B}_{l+1}^{\mathrm{T}} \mid \boldsymbol{B}_{l+1}^{\mathrm{T}} \boldsymbol{a}_{1..l} + \boldsymbol{B}_{1..l}^{\mathrm{T}} \boldsymbol{\Lambda}_{1..l, 2..l+1} \right], \end{aligned}$$

so $\boldsymbol{B}_{l+1}^{\mathrm{T}} = \boldsymbol{L}_1^{\mathrm{T}}$. The result follows since M divides every entry of $\boldsymbol{\Lambda}_{1..l, 2..l+1}$ and $\mathrm{rem}_M(\boldsymbol{L}_1^{\mathrm{T}} \boldsymbol{a}_{1..l}) = \boldsymbol{L}_1^{\mathrm{T}} \boldsymbol{a}_{1..l} + M \boldsymbol{Q}$ for some $\boldsymbol{Q} \in \mathbb{Z}^{k \times l}$. $\square$

The complete algorithm pseudocode is given as Algorithm 3. Were we explicitly storing the generating matrix $\boldsymbol{L}$, we would require the initialization of $L_{1,1} := 1$ in step 1, and the column/row augmentation in step 3 of

$$\boldsymbol{L} := \left[\begin{array}{c|c} \boldsymbol{0} & M \\ \hline \boldsymbol{L} & \mathrm{rem}_M(a_l \boldsymbol{f}) \end{array} \right] \text{ where } \boldsymbol{f} = \boldsymbol{L}_1^{\mathrm{T}}. \quad (4)$$

The application of rem_M to the new column entries is justified by adding suitable multiples of the first row. It is not strictly necessary, but ensures that the new entries have absolute value at most $M/2$, and allows us to give tighter bounds on the entries of $\boldsymbol{L}$. The following lemma is a strengthening of [23, Lemma 7], due to the special form of bases we are considering.

Algorithm 3 The VecRecon$(n, \boldsymbol{a}, M, N, c)$ generating matrix algorithm using L^2.

Input: $\boldsymbol{a} \in \mathbb{Z}_M^{1 \times n}$ and $N, c \in \mathbb{Z}_{>0}$ with $M > 2^{(c+1)/2} N^{1+1/c}$.
Output: An LLL-reduced generating matrix $\boldsymbol{S} \in \mathbb{Z}^{k \times (n+1)}$ of $\mathcal{L}_N(\boldsymbol{\Lambda}_{\boldsymbol{a}}^M)$ with $k \leq c$.

// Note $\boldsymbol{f} \in \mathbb{Z}^{k \times 1}$, $\boldsymbol{G} \in \mathbb{Z}^{k \times k}$ after each step

1. [Initialization]
   $k := 1$; $f_1 := 1$; $G_{1,1} := 1$;

2. [Iterative lattice augmentation]
   for $l := 1$ to n **do**

   3. [Add new vector to generating matrix]
      $k := k + 1$;
      // Update $\boldsymbol{G}$, due to addition of column $\boldsymbol{g}$ to generating matrix
      $\boldsymbol{G} := \left[\begin{array}{c|c} 0 & \boldsymbol{0} \\ \hline \boldsymbol{0} & \boldsymbol{G} \end{array} \right] + \boldsymbol{g} \boldsymbol{g}^{\mathrm{T}}$ where $\boldsymbol{g} = \left[\dfrac{M}{\mathrm{rem}_M(a_l \boldsymbol{f})} \right]$;
      // Update first column of generating matrix
      $\boldsymbol{f} := \left[\dfrac{0}{\boldsymbol{f}} \right]$;

   4. [LLL reduction with removals]
      L^2WithRemovals$(k, \boldsymbol{G}, \boldsymbol{f}, N)$;
      If $k = 0$, **return** the unique element of $\mathbb{Z}^{0 \times (n+1)}$.

   assert A. $\boldsymbol{L} = \left[\boldsymbol{f} \mid \mathrm{rem}_M(\boldsymbol{f} a_{1..l}) \right]$ is an LLL-reduced generating matrix of $\mathcal{L}_N(\boldsymbol{\Lambda}_{\boldsymbol{a}_{1..l}}^M)$ with Gramian $\boldsymbol{G}$
   B. $k \leq c$.

5. [Complete generating matrix]
   return $\boldsymbol{S} := \left[\boldsymbol{f} \mid \mathrm{rem}_M(\boldsymbol{f} \boldsymbol{a}) \right]$;

LEMMA 2. *At the conclusion of the following steps during Algorithm 3 the following bounds hold:*

- *Step 3:* $\max_i \|\boldsymbol{L}_i\| \leq M$ *if* $k \leq c + 1$
- *Step 4:* $\max_i \|\boldsymbol{L}_i\| < M/2$ *if* $k \leq c$

PROOF. After step 4, LLL reduction with removals (with target length N) will return a basis which satisfies $\|\boldsymbol{L}_i\| \leq 2^{(k-1)/2} N$ by [23, Lemma 3]. Since $k \leq c$, it follows

$$\|\boldsymbol{L}_i\| < 2^{(c+1)/2} N^{1+1/c}/2 < M/2.$$

After step 3, $\|\boldsymbol{L}_1\| = M$ and for $i > 1$ we have $\|\boldsymbol{L}_i\|^2 < (M/2)^2 + (M/2)^2$ by the previous bound (assuming $k \leq c$ at the start of step 3) and the fact the new entries are in the symmetric range. $\square$

We are now ready to show the assertions after step 4 of Algorithm 3 hold, from which the algorithm's correctness immediately follows.

PROPOSITION 1. *Assertion A after step 4 of Algorithm 3 holds.*

PROOF. The fact $\mathcal{L}(\boldsymbol{L})$ is a sublattice of $\mathcal{L}(\boldsymbol{\Lambda}^M_{\boldsymbol{a}_{1..l}})$ follows from the fact every vector in $\boldsymbol{L}$ is a linear combination of the vectors in $\boldsymbol{\Lambda}^M_{\boldsymbol{a}_{1..l}}$ by (4) and LLL reduction does not change this. The fact $\mathcal{L}(\boldsymbol{L})$ contains all vectors in $\mathcal{L}_N(\boldsymbol{\Lambda}^M_{\boldsymbol{a}_{1..l}})$ and that $\boldsymbol{L}$ is LLL-reduced follows from the output of $\mathsf{L}^2\mathsf{WithRemovals}$.

By how $\boldsymbol{f}$ is updated in steps 3 and 4 it is clear that $\boldsymbol{f} = \boldsymbol{L}_1^{\mathrm{T}}$. However, we still must show that $\boldsymbol{L} = \left[\, \boldsymbol{f} \mid \mathrm{rem}_M(\boldsymbol{f}a_{1..l}) \,\right]$, i.e., when $\boldsymbol{L}$ is expressed in the form from Lemma 1, $\boldsymbol{R}$ is the zero matrix. If it were not, then some entry of $\boldsymbol{L}$ would not be in the symmetric range (mod M). In which case there would be an entry $|L_{i,j}| \geq M/2$, so $\|\boldsymbol{L}_i\| \geq M/2$, in contradiction to Lemma 2.

Finally, taking the Gramian of (4) shows that step 3 ensures $\boldsymbol{G} = \boldsymbol{L}\boldsymbol{L}^{\mathrm{T}}$, and $\mathsf{L}^2\mathsf{WithRemovals}$ also keeps $\boldsymbol{G}$ correctly updated. $\square$

The next proposition follows from the method of proof of [23, Theorem 2] taking into account that $\|\boldsymbol{L}_i^*\| \leq M$ by Lemma 2 at the start of (and therefore during) the LLL reduction when $k \leq c + 1$.

PROPOSITION 2. *Assertion B after step 4 of Algorithm 3 holds.*

PROOF. If no vector was discarded during step 4 when $k = c + 1$ we would have a contradiction from bounds on the volume $\sqrt{\det \boldsymbol{G}}$ of the lattice,

$$2^{c(c+1)/2}N^{c+1} < M^c \leq \sqrt{\det \boldsymbol{G}} \leq 2^{c(c+1)/4}N^{c+1}.$$

The upper bound holds for all LLL-reduced bases with final Gram–Schmidt vector shorter than N. The lower bound is derived by noting the volume increases by a factor of M each time a vector is added to the basis, and decreases by a factor of at most M each time a vector is removed from the basis. $\square$

Finally, we analyze the bit complexity of our algorithm for $c \in O(1)$ and $\|\boldsymbol{a}\|_\infty \in O(M)$. During step 3 we have $\|\boldsymbol{f}\|_\infty < M/2$ by Lemma 2, so the bitlength of numbers involved is $O(\log M)$, and thus step 3 executes in $O((\log M)^2)$ bit operations. Step 4 executes $\mathsf{L}^2\mathsf{WithRemovals}$ on a lattice of dimension at most c, with Gramian entries of bitlength $O(\log M)$, at a cost of $O((\log M)^2)$ bit operations. Since the loop runs $O(n)$ times, the total cost is $O(n(\log M)^2)$ bit operations. Step 5 requires $O(n)$ arithmetic operations, all on integers of bitlength $O(\log M)$. This gives the following result.

THEOREM 1. *Algorithm 3 returns an LLL-reduced generating matrix $\boldsymbol{S} \in \mathbb{Z}^{k \times (n+1)}$ of $\mathcal{L}_N(\boldsymbol{\Lambda}^M_{\boldsymbol{a}})$ with $k \leq c$. When $c \in O(1)$ and $\|\boldsymbol{a}\|_\infty \in O(M)$, the running time is $O(n(\log M)^2)$ bit operations.*

5. LINEAR SYSTEM SOLVING

In this section let $\boldsymbol{A} \in \mathbb{Z}^{n \times n}$ be a nonsingular matrix and $\boldsymbol{b} \in \mathbb{Z}^n$ be a vector such that $\left\|\left[\,\boldsymbol{A} \mid \boldsymbol{b}\,\right]\right\|_{\max} \leq B$. Consider the problem of computing $\boldsymbol{x} \in \mathbb{Q}^n$ such that $\boldsymbol{A}\boldsymbol{x} = \boldsymbol{b}$, using for example Dixon's algorithm [5]. This requires reconstructing the solution $\boldsymbol{x}$ from its modular image $\boldsymbol{a} = \mathrm{rem}_M(\boldsymbol{x})$, where $M = p^m$ for some prime $p \nmid \det(\boldsymbol{A})$ and $m \in \mathbb{Z}_{>0}$ is large enough that the reconstruction is unique.

We can use p-adic lifting to recover the image vector $\boldsymbol{a}$ for $m = 2, 3, \ldots$, though it is not necessary that m increase linearly. The cost of the lifting phase of the solver is directly related to the number of lifting steps m, which dictates the precision of the image. Highly optimized implementations of p-adic lifting [3, 4, 6, 9] employ an output sensitive approach to compute the vector rational reconstruction $\boldsymbol{x}$ from $\boldsymbol{a}$ in order to avoid computing more images than required. As m increases, the algorithm periodically attempts to perform a rational reconstruction of the current image vector. The attempted rational reconstruction should either return the unique minimal denominator solution or FAIL. When FAIL is returned more lifting steps are performed before another rational reconstruction is attempted.

Suppose $(d, \boldsymbol{n}) \in (\mathbb{Z}, \mathbb{Z}^n)$ is such that $\boldsymbol{a} = \mathrm{rem}_M(\boldsymbol{n}/d)$, that is, $\boldsymbol{A}\boldsymbol{n} \equiv d\boldsymbol{b} \pmod{M}$. To check if $\boldsymbol{A}\boldsymbol{n} = d\boldsymbol{b}$, that is, if $\boldsymbol{n}/d$ is the actual solution of the system $\boldsymbol{A}\boldsymbol{x} = \boldsymbol{b}$, we could directly check if $\boldsymbol{A}\boldsymbol{n} = d\boldsymbol{b}$ by performing a matrix vector product and scalar vector product. However, this direct check is too expensive. The following idea of Cabay [1] can be used to avoid the direct check, requiring us to only check some magnitude bounds.

LEMMA 3. *If $\|\boldsymbol{n}\|_\infty < M/(2nB)$, $0 < |d| < M/(2B)$, and $\boldsymbol{A}\boldsymbol{n} \equiv d\boldsymbol{b} \pmod{M}$ then $\boldsymbol{x} = \boldsymbol{n}/d$ solves $\boldsymbol{A}\boldsymbol{x} = \boldsymbol{b}$.*

PROOF. Note that $\|\boldsymbol{A}\boldsymbol{n}\|_\infty \leq nB\|\boldsymbol{n}\|_\infty$ and $\|d\boldsymbol{b}\|_\infty \leq B|d|$, so by the given bounds $\|\boldsymbol{A}\boldsymbol{n}\|_\infty < M/2$ and $\|d\boldsymbol{b}\|_\infty < M/2$. Every integer absolutely bounded by $M/2$ falls into a distinct congruence class modulo M, so since the components of $\boldsymbol{A}\boldsymbol{n}$ and $d\boldsymbol{b}$ are in this range and componentwise they share the same congruence classes, $\boldsymbol{A}\boldsymbol{n} = d\boldsymbol{b}$, and the result follows. $\square$

Algorithm 4 shows how Lemma 3 can be combined with the elementwise rational reconstruction approach to get an output sensitive algorithm for the reconstruction of $\boldsymbol{x}$ from its image $\boldsymbol{a}$. Let $\mathsf{RatRecon}(a, M, N)$ be a function which returns the minimal d which solves (1), or FAIL if no solution exists.

The algorithm does not take the target length N as a parameter, but calculates an N such that there will be at most one lowest-terms reconstruction. Lemma 3 may be used following step 4 to guarantee the output in step 5 will be the unique solution vector $\boldsymbol{x}$.

Note that the elementwise approach requires us to choose N to satisfy $M > 2N^2$. If β is the maximum of the magnitudes of the denominator and numerators of the actual solution vector of the system then we need $N \geq \beta$ for the algorithm to succeed, i.e., $M \in \Omega(\beta^2)$. By Hadamard's bound and Cramer's rule we have the a priori bound $\beta \leq n^{n/2}B^n$, but in general this bound is pessimistic and to avoid needless lifting we employ a output sensitive approach, as in [22].

Algorithm 5 shows how Lemma 3 can be combined with $\mathsf{VecRecon}$ instead to get an output sensitive algorithm for the reconstruction. For this algorithm we need only $M > 2^{(c+1)/2}N^{1+1/c}$ to satisfy the precondition of $\mathsf{VecRecon}$. On the one hand, Lemma 4 shows that Algorithm 5 will never return an incorrect answer. On the other hand, Lemma 5 shows that the algorithm will succeed for $M \in \Omega((\sqrt{n}\beta)^{1+1/c})$.

LEMMA 4. *If Algorithm 5 does not return FAIL then the output when run on $\boldsymbol{a} = \mathrm{rem}_M(\boldsymbol{x})$ is the correct solution $\boldsymbol{x} = \boldsymbol{A}^{-1}\boldsymbol{b}$.*

Algorithm 4 An output sensitive LinSolRecon$(n, \boldsymbol{a}, M, B)$ using scalar reconstruction.

Input: The image $\boldsymbol{a} \in \mathbb{Z}_M^n$ of the solution of the linear system $\boldsymbol{A}\boldsymbol{x} = \boldsymbol{b}$, and $B \in \mathbb{Z}_{>0}$, an upper bound on the magnitude of the entries of $\boldsymbol{A}$ and $\boldsymbol{b}$.
Output: Either the solution $\boldsymbol{x} \in \mathbb{Q}^n$ or FAIL.

   // Need $M > 2N^2$ and $M > 2nBN$.

1. [Set an acceptable size bound]
   $N := \lceil \min(\sqrt{M/2}, M/(2nB)) \rceil - 1$;

2. [Simultaneous rational reconstruction]
   $d := 1$;
   for $i := 1$ to n **do**

   3. [Entrywise rational reconstruction]
      $d := d \cdot \mathsf{RatRecon}(\mathrm{rem}_M(da_i), M, N)$;
      If RatRecon returns FAIL then **return** FAIL.

4. [Check reconstruction]
   If $|d| > N$ or $\|\mathrm{rem}_M(d\boldsymbol{a})\|_\infty > N$ then **return** FAIL.

5. [Return solution]
   return $\mathrm{rem}_M(d\boldsymbol{a})/d$;

PROOF. First, note that every entry of $\boldsymbol{S}$ is absolutely bounded by $M/(2nB)$:

$$\|\boldsymbol{S}\|_{\max} \leq \max_i \|\boldsymbol{S}_i\| \qquad \text{(Norm comparison)}$$
$$\leq 2^{(k-1)/2} \|\boldsymbol{S}_k^*\| \qquad \text{(Proposition (1.7) in [14])}$$
$$\leq 2^{(c-1)/2} N \qquad \text{(Output of VecRecon)}$$
$$< M/(2nB) \qquad (M > 2^{(c+1)/2} nBN)$$

Then we can apply Lemma 3 on any row i of $\boldsymbol{S}$, since $\boldsymbol{A}(\boldsymbol{S}_{i,2..n+1})^{\mathrm{T}} \equiv S_{i,1}\boldsymbol{b} \pmod{M}$ by construction of $\boldsymbol{S}$. Therefore every row of $\boldsymbol{S}$ yields a solution $\boldsymbol{x} = \boldsymbol{S}_{i,2..n+1}/S_{i,1}$, but since there is only one solution and the rows of $\boldsymbol{S}$ are linearly independent, $\boldsymbol{S}$ can have at most one row. Assuming the algorithm did not return FAIL, we have $\boldsymbol{x} = \boldsymbol{S}_{2..n+1}/S_1$, as required. $\square$

LEMMA 5. *Let d, $\boldsymbol{n}$ be the minimal denominator and numerators of the system's unique rational solution vector $\boldsymbol{x}$, and suppose $|d|, \|\boldsymbol{n}\|_\infty \leq \beta$. If $M \geq 2^{(c+1)/2}(\sqrt{n+1}\beta)^{1+1/c}$ then Algorithm 5 run on $\boldsymbol{a} = \mathrm{rem}_M(\boldsymbol{x})$ will return $\boldsymbol{x}$, not FAIL.*

PROOF. From the given bounds, $\|[d \mid \boldsymbol{n}]\|^2 \leq (n+1)\beta^2$, so when $\sqrt{n+1}\beta \leq N$ we have that $[d \mid \boldsymbol{n}] \in \mathcal{L}_N(\boldsymbol{\Lambda}_a^M)$, which is guaranteed to be in the lattice $\mathcal{L}(\boldsymbol{S})$ found by VecRecon in step 2.

It is straightforward to check that if M satisfies the given bound then in fact after step 1 we have $N \geq \sqrt{n+1}\beta$, so the algorithm will not return FAIL in this case. By Lemma 4 the output will be the correct solution $\boldsymbol{x}$. $\square$

The running time of Algorithm 5 is simply that of VecRecon, which by Theorem 1 is $O(n(\log M)^2)$ bit operations. Table 1 shows the reduction in required bitlength of $\log M$ by comparing some minimal bounds on $\log M$ for Algorithms 4 and 5 to succeed.

Algorithm 5 An output sensitive LinSolRecon$(n, \boldsymbol{a}, M, B, c)$ using vector reconstruction.

Input: The image $\boldsymbol{a} \in \mathbb{Z}_M^n$ of the solution of the linear system $\boldsymbol{A}\boldsymbol{x} = \boldsymbol{b}$, and $B \in \mathbb{Z}_{>0}$, an upper bound on the magnitude of the entries of $\boldsymbol{A}$ and $\boldsymbol{b}$. Also, a parameter $c \in \mathbb{Z}_{>0}$ controlling the maximum lattice dimension to use in VecRecon.
Output: Either the solution $\boldsymbol{x} \in \mathbb{Q}^n$ or FAIL.

   // Need $M > 2^{(c+1)/2}N^{1+1/c}$ and $M > 2^{(c+1)/2}nBN$.

1. [Set an acceptable size bound]
   $N := \lceil \min(M^{c/(c+1)}/2^{c/2}, M/(2^{(c+1)/2}nB)) \rceil - 1$;

2. [Vector rational reconstruction]
   $\boldsymbol{S} := \mathsf{VecRecon}(n, \boldsymbol{a}, M, N, c) \in \mathbb{Z}^{k \times (n+1)}$;
   If $k = 0$ then **return** FAIL.

assert $k = 1$

3. [Return solution]
   return $\boldsymbol{S}_{2..n+1}/S_1$;

---

n	B	Alg. 4	Alg. 5 $c=2$	Alg. 5 $c=3$	Alg. 5 $c=4$	Alg. 5 $c=5$
200	1	1061	800	712	668	642
400	1	2398	1803	1604	1504	1444
800	1	5349	4017	3571	3349	3215
1600	1	11806	8860	7876	7385	7090
Alg. 5/Alg. 4			$\approx 75\%$	$\approx 67\%$	$\approx 63\%$	$\approx 60\%$

Table 1: **The value of $\log M$ required to guarantee Algorithms 4 and 5 return a solution.**

6. FUTURE WORK

The recent article [19] gives an LLL-like algorithm for lattice basis reduction which is quasi-linear in the bitlength M of the input basis entries, that is, for a lattice with vectors of constant dimension it runs in $O((\log M)^{1+\epsilon})$ bit operations. It would be interesting to see if this quasi-linear algorithm could be employed with VecRecon.

The VecRecon algorithm, based on the L^{2}WithRemovals algorithm of [23], requires that $M \in \Omega(N^{1+1/c})$ for some positive integer c. But according to Lemma 3, when the input $\boldsymbol{a}$ to the vector reconstruction problem is the image of a rational linear system of dimension n with size of entries bounded by B, we only need $M > 2nBN$ to ensure that at most one linearly independent reconstruction $d\boldsymbol{a} \equiv \boldsymbol{n} \pmod{M}$ with $|d|, \|\boldsymbol{n}\|_\infty \leq N$ exists. This raises the following open question: is there a fast algorithm to find d, if it exists, that only requires $M \in O(nBN)$?

7. REFERENCES

[1] S. Cabay. Exact solution of linear systems. In *Proc. Second Symp. on Symbolic and Algebraic Manipulation*, pages 248–253, 1971.

[2] Z. Chen. A BLAS based C library for exact linear algebra on integer matrices. Master's thesis, David R. Cheriton School of Computer Science, University of Waterloo, 2005.

[3] Z. Chen and A. Storjohann. A BLAS based C library for exact linear algebra on integer matrices. In M. Kauers, editor, *Proc. Int'l. Symp. on Symbolic and Algebraic Computation: ISSAC '05*, pages 92–99. ACM Press, New York, 2005.

[4] W. Cook and D. E. Steffy. Solving very sparse rational systems of equations. *ACM Trans. Math. Softw.*, 37:39:1–39:21, February 2011.

[5] J. D. Dixon. Exact solution of linear equations using *p*-adic expansions. *Numerische Mathematik*, 40:137–141, 1982.

[6] J.-G. Dumas, T. Gautier, M. Giesbrecht, P. Giorgi, B. Hovinen, E. Kaltofen, B. D. Saunders, W. J. Turner, and G. Villard. LinBox: A generic library for exact linear algebra. In A. J. Cohen and N. Gao, X.-S. andl Takayama, editors, *Proc. First Internat. Congress Math. Software ICMS 2002, Beijing, China*, pages 40–50, Singapore, 2002. World Scientific.

[7] M. J. Encarnación. Computing gcds of polynomials over algebraic number fields. *J. Symb. Comput.*, 20:299–313, September 1995.

[8] J. von zur Gathen and J. Gerhard. *Modern Computer Algebra*. Cambridge University Press, 2 edition, 2003.

[9] P. Giorgi. *Arithmetic and algorithmic in exact linear algebra for the LinBox library*. PhD thesis, École normale supérieure de Lyon, LIP, Lyon, France, December 2004.

[10] G. Hanrot. LLL: a tool for effective diophantine approximation. In *Conference in honour of the 25th birthday of the LLL algorithm - LLL+25*, Caen France, 2007.

[11] E. Kaltofen and H. Rolletschek. Computing greatest common divisors and factorizations in quadratic number fields. *Math. Comput.*, 53(188), 1989.

[12] E. Kaltofen and Z. Yang. On exact and approximate interpolation of sparse rational functions. In J. P. May, editor, *Proc. Int'l. Symp. on Symbolic and Algebraic Computation: ISSAC '07*, pages 203–210. ACM Press, New York, 2007.

[13] J. C. Lagarias. The computational complexity of simultaneous diophantine approximation problems. *SIAM Journal of Computing*, 14(1):196–209, 1985.

[14] A. K. Lenstra, H. W. Lenstra, and L. Lovász. Factoring polynomials with rational coefficients. *Math. Ann.*, 261:515–534, 1982.

[15] D. Lichtblau. Half-GCD and fast rational recovery. In M. Kauers, editor, *Proc. Int'l. Symp. on Symbolic and Algebraic Computation: ISSAC '05*, pages 231–236. ACM Press, New York, 2005. Extended version available at `http://library.wolfram.com/infocenter/Conferences/7534/HGCD_and_planar_lattices.pdf`.

[16] M. Monagan. Maximal quotient rational reconstruction: an almost optimal algorithm for rational reconstruction. In J. Gutierrez, editor, *Proc. Int'l. Symp. on Symbolic and Algebraic Computation: ISSAC '04*, pages 243–249. ACM Press, New York, 2004.

[17] P. Q. Nguyen and D. Stehlé. An LLL algorithm with quadratic complexity. *SIAM Journal on Computing*, 39(3):874–903, 2009.

[18] A. Novocin. *Factoring Univariate Polynomials over the Rationals*. PhD thesis, Florida State University, 2008.

[19] A. Novocin, D. Stehlé, and G. Villard. An LLL-reduction algorithm with quasi-linear time complexity. *STOC 2011: 43rd ACM Symposium on Theory of Computing*, to appear.

[20] Z. Olesh and A. Storjohann. The vector rational function reconstruction problem. In I. Kotsireas and E. Zima, editors, *Proc. of the Waterloo Workshop on Computer Algebra: devoted to the 60th birthday of Sergei Abramov (WWCA-2006)*, pages 137–149. World Scientific, 2006.

[21] V. Shoup. *A Computational Introduction to Number Theory and Algebra*. Cambridge University Press, 2 edition, 2005.

[22] D. E. Steffy. Exact solutions to linear systems of equations using output sensitive lifting. *SIGSAM Bull.*, 44:160–182, January 2011.

[23] M. van Hoeij and A. Novocin. Gradual sub-lattice reduction and a new complexity for factoring polynomials. In A. López-Ortiz, editor, *LATIN 2010: Theoretical Informatics*, volume 6034 of *Lecture Notes in Computer Science*, pages 539–553. Springer Berlin / Heidelberg, 2010.

Detecting Genus in Vertex Links for the Fast Enumeration of 3-Manifold Triangulations

Benjamin A. Burton[*]
School of Mathematics and Physics
The University of Queensland
Brisbane QLD 4072, Australia
bab@maths.uq.edu.au

ABSTRACT

Enumerating all 3-manifold triangulations of a given size is a difficult but increasingly important problem in computational topology. A key difficulty for enumeration algorithms is that most combinatorial triangulations must be discarded because they do not represent topological 3-manifolds. In this paper we show how to preempt bad triangulations by detecting genus in partially-constructed vertex links, allowing us to prune the enumeration tree substantially.

The key idea is to manipulate the boundary edges surrounding partial vertex links using expected logarithmic time operations. Practical testing shows the resulting enumeration algorithm to be significantly faster, with up to 249× speed-ups even for small problems where comparisons are feasible. We also discuss parallelisation, and describe new data sets that have been obtained using high-performance computing facilities.

Categories and Subject Descriptors

G.2.1 [**Discrete Mathematics**]: Combinatorics—*Combinatorial algorithms*; G.4 [**Mathematical Software**]: Algorithm design and analysis; I.1.2 [**Symbolic and Algebraic Manipulation**]: Algorithms—*Nonalgebraic algorithms*

General Terms

Algorithms, experimentation, performance

Keywords

Computational topology, 3-manifolds, triangulations, census algorithm, combinatorial enumeration

[*]Supported by the Australian Research Council under the Discovery Projects funding scheme (projects DP1094516 and DP110101104).

1. INTRODUCTION

In computational geometry and topology, triangulations are natural and ubiquitous data structures for representing topological spaces. Here we focus on triangulations in 3-manifold topology, an important branch of topology in which many key problems are theoretically decidable but extremely difficult for practical computation [1, 11].

A *census* of 3-manifold triangulations is a list of all triangulations that satisfy some given set of properties. A typical census fixes the number of tetrahedra (the *size* of the triangulation), and enumerates all triangulations up to *isomorphism* (a relabelling of the tetrahedra and their vertices).

Censuses of this type first appeared in the late 1980s [14, 23].[1] These were censuses of *minimal triangulations*, which represent a given 3-manifold using the fewest possible tetrahedra. Such censuses have brought about new insights into the combinatorics of minimal triangulations [9, 18, 20] and the complexities of 3-manifolds [17, 19], and have proven useful for computation and experimentation [4, 10].

A more recent development has been censuses of *all* possible 3-manifold triangulations of a given size, including non-minimal triangulations [11]. These have yielded surprising experimental insights into algorithmic complexity problems and random 3-manifold triangulations [11, 12], both topics which remain extremely difficult to handle theoretically.

The limits of censuses in the literature are fairly small. For closed $\mathbb{P}^2$-irreducible 3-manifolds, all minimal triangulations have been enumerated for only ≤ 10 tetrahedra [8]; for the orientable case only, the list of manifolds (but not triangulations) is known for ≤ 12 tetrahedra [22]. A full list of all closed 3-manifold triangulations (non-minimal included) is known for just ≤ 9 tetrahedra [11]. These small limits are unavoidable because censuses grow exponentially—and sometimes super-exponentially [12]—in size.

Nevertheless, in theory it should be possible to extend these results substantially. Census algorithms are typically based on a recursive search through all possible *combinatorial triangulations*—that is, methods of gluing together faces of tetrahedra in pairs. However, as the number of tetrahedra grows large, almost all combinatorial triangulations are *not* 3-manifold triangulations [13]. The problem is that *vertex links*—boundaries of small neighbourhoods of the vertices of a triangulation—are generally not spheres or discs as they should be, but instead higher-genus surfaces.

To illustrate: for $n = 9$ tetrahedra, if we simply glue

[1]Some authors, following Matveev [23], work in the setting of *special spines* which are dual to triangulations.

together all $4n$ tetrahedron faces in pairs, a very rough estimate (described in the appendix) gives at least 6.44×10^{12} connected *combinatorial* triangulations up to isomorphism. However, just $139\,103\,032$ are *3-manifold* triangulations [11], and a mere $3\,338$ are minimal triangulations of closed $\mathbb{P}^2$-irreducible 3-manifolds [8].

It is clear then that large branches of the combinatorial search tree can be avoided, if one could only identify *which* branches these are. The current challenge for enumeration algorithms is to find new and easily-testable conditions under which such branches can be pruned.

For censuses of minimal triangulations, several such conditions are known: examples include the absence of low-degree edges [6, 14, 20], or of "bad subgraphs" in the underlying 4-valent face pairing graph [8, 16]. Nevertheless, seeing how few minimal triangulations are found in practice, there are likely many more conditions yet to be found.

It is critical that such conditions can be tested quickly, since these tests are run on a continual basis as the search progresses and backtracks. The paper [8] introduces a modified union-find framework through which several minimality tests can be performed in $O(\log n)$ time. Importantly, this framework can also be used with censuses of *all* 3-manifold triangulations (non-minimal included), where it is used to test that: (i) partially-constructed vertex links are orientable, and (ii) fully-constructed edges are not identified with themselves in reverse. Although tests (i) and (ii) are powerful when enumerating *non-orientable* triangulations, they do not help for *orientable* triangulations because they are already enforced by the overall enumeration algorithm.

The main contributions of this paper are:

- We add the following condition to the suite of tests used during enumeration: *all partially-constructed vertex links must be punctured spheres* (not punctured higher-genus surfaces).

  Although this condition is straightforward, it has traditionally required $O(n)$ operations to test, making it impractical for frequent use in the enumeration algorithm. In Section 3 we show how to test this condition *incrementally*, using only expected logarithmic-time operations at each stage of the combinatorial search.

  This condition is extremely powerful in both the orientable and non-orientable cases, and our new incremental test makes it practical for real use. Performance testing in Section 4 shows speed-ups of up to $249\times$ even for small enumeration problems where experimental comparisons are feasible ($n \leq 7$).

- In Section 6 we use this to obtain new census data, including all closed 3-manifold triangulations of size $n \leq 10$ (non-minimal included, improving the previous limit of $n \leq 9$), and all minimal triangulations of closed $\mathbb{P}^2$-irreducible 3-manifolds of size $n \leq 11$ (improving the previous limit of $n \leq 10$). High-performance computing and distributed algorithms play a key role, as outlined in Section 5. All censuses cover both orientable and non-orientable triangulations.

This new census data is already proving useful in ongoing projects, such as studying the structure of minimal triangulations, and mapping out average-case and generic complexities for difficult topological decision problems.

It should be noted that avoiding isomorphisms—often a significant difficulty in combinatorial enumeration—is not a problem here. See the full version of this paper for details.

Looking forward, the techniques of this paper can also be applied to the enumeration of *4-manifold* triangulations. In this higher-dimensional setting, our techniques can be applied to edge links rather than vertex links. Vertices on the other hand become more difficult to handle: each vertex link must be a 3-sphere, and 3-sphere recognition remains a difficult algorithmic problem [12, 19]. Here research into algebraic techniques may yield new heuristics to further prune the search tree.

Throughout this paper we restrict our attention to closed 3-manifolds, although all of the results presented here extend easily to manifolds with boundary.

All algorithms described in this paper can be downloaded as part of *Regina* [5, 7], an open-source software package for the algebraic and combinatorial manipulation of 3-manifolds and their triangulations.

2. PRELIMINARIES

Consider a collection of n tetrahedra (these are abstract objects, and need not be embedded in some $\mathbb{R}^d$). A *combinatorial triangulation* of *size* n is obtained by affinely identifying (or "gluing together") the $4n$ tetrahedron faces in pairs.[2] Specifically, it consists of the following data:

- a partition of the $4n$ tetrahedron faces into $2n$ pairs, indicating which faces are to be identified;

- $2n$ permutations of three elements, indicating which of the six possible rotations or reflections is to be used for each identification.

For instance, consider the following example with $n = 3$ tetrahedra. The tetrahedra are labelled A, B, C, and the four vertices of each tetrahedron are labelled $0, 1, 2, 3$.

Tetrahedron	Face 012	Face 013	Face 023	Face 123
A	$C:013$	$B:012$	$A:312$	$A:230$
B	$A:013$	$C:120$	$C:231$	$C:302$
C	$B:301$	$A:012$	$B:231$	$B:302$

The top-left cell of this table indicates that face 012 of tetrahedron A is identified with face 013 of tetrahedron C, using the rotation or reflection that maps vertices $0, 1, 2$ of tetrahedron A to vertices $0, 1, 3$ of tetrahedron C respectively. For convenience, the same identification is also shown from the other direction in the second cell of the bottom row.

As a consequence of these face identifications, we find that several tetrahedron edges become identified together; each such equivalence class is called an *edge of the triangulation*. Likewise, each equivalence class of identified vertices is called a *vertex of the triangulation*. The triangulation illustrated above has three edges and just one vertex.

The *face pairing graph* of a combinatorial triangulation is the 4-valent multigraph whose nodes represent tetrahedra and whose edges represent face identifications. The face pairing graph for the example above is shown in Figure 1. A combinatorial triangulation is called *connected* if and only if its face pairing graph is connected.

---

[2] A combinatorial triangulation need not be a simplicial complex, and need not represent a topological 3-manifold. The word "combinatorial" indicates that we are only interested in face identifications, with no topological requirements.

Figure 1: An example face pairing graph

The *vertex links* of a triangulation are obtained as follows. In each tetrahedron we place four triangles surrounding the four vertices, as shown in Figure 2. We then glue together the edges of these triangles in a manner consistent with the face identifications of the surrounding tetrahedra, as illustrated in Figure 3.

Figure 2: The triangles that form the vertex links

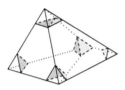

Figure 3: Joining vertex linking triangles along their edges in adjacent tetrahedra

The result is a collection of triangulated closed surfaces, one surrounding each vertex of the triangulation. The surface surrounding vertex V is referred to as the *link of V*. Topologically, this represents the boundary of a small neighbourhood of V in the triangulation.

A *3-manifold triangulation* is a combinatorial triangulation that, when viewed as a topological space, represents a 3-manifold. Equivalently, a 3-manifold triangulation is a combinatorial triangulation in which:

(i) each vertex link is a topological sphere;

(ii) no tetrahedron edge is identified with itself in reverse as a result of the face identifications.[3]

The earlier example is *not* a 3-manifold triangulation, since the link of the (unique) vertex is a torus, not a sphere. For many 3-manifolds M, the size of a minimal triangulation of M corresponds to the Matveev complexity of M [17, 19].

A *partial triangulation* is a combinatorial triangulation in which we identify only $2k$ of the $4n$ tetrahedron faces in pairs, for some $0 \leq 2k \leq 4n$. We define vertices, edges and vertex links as before, noting that vertex links might now be surfaces with boundary (not closed surfaces).

A typical enumeration algorithm works as follows [8, 14]:

ALGORITHM 1. *Suppose we wish to enumerate all connected 3-manifold triangulations of size n satisfying some set of properties P. The main steps are:*

---

[3]An equivalent condition to (ii) is that we can direct the edges of every tetrahedron in a manner consistent with the face identifications.

1. *Enumerate all possible face pairing graphs (i.e., all connected 4-valent multigraphs on n nodes).*

2. *For each graph, recursively try all 6^{2n} possible rotations and reflections for identifying the corresponding tetrahedron faces. Each "partial selection" of rotations and reflections gives a partial triangulation, and recursion and backtracking correspond to gluing and ungluing tetrahedron faces in these partial triangulations.*

3. *Whenever we have a partial triangulation, run a series of tests that can identify situations where, no matter how we glue the remaining faces together, we can never obtain a 3-manifold triangulation satisfying the properties in P. If this is the case, prune the current branch of the search tree and backtrack immediately.*

4. *Whenever we have a complete selection of 6^{2n} rotations and reflections, test whether (i) the corresponding combinatorial triangulation is in fact a 3-manifold triangulation, and (ii) whether this 3-manifold triangulations satisfies the required properties in P.*

There is also the problem of avoiding isomorphisms. This is computationally cheap if the recursion is ordered carefully; for details, see the full version of this paper.

In practice, step 1 is negligible—almost all of the computational work is in the recursive search (steps 2–4). The tests in step 3 are critical: they must be extremely fast, since they are run at every stage of the recursive search. Moreover, if chosen carefully, these tests can prune vast sections of the search tree and speed up the enumeration substantially.

A useful observation is that some graphs can be eliminated immediately after step 1. See [6, 8, 16] for algorithms that incorporate such techniques.

3. TRACKING VERTEX LINKS

In this paper we add the following test to step 3 of the enumeration algorithm:

TEST 2. *Whenever we have a partial triangulation $\mathcal{T}$, test whether all vertex links are spheres with zero or more punctures. If not, prune the current branch of the search tree and backtrack immediately.*

Theoretically, it is simple to show that this test works:

LEMMA 3. *If $\mathcal{T}$ is a partial triangulation and the link of some vertex V is not a sphere with zero or more punctures, then there is no way to glue together the remaining faces of $\mathcal{T}$ to obtain a 3-manifold triangulation.*

PROOF. Suppose we *can* glue the remaining faces together to form a 3-manifold triangulation $\mathcal{T}'$. Let L and L' be the links of V in $\mathcal{T}$ and $\mathcal{T}'$ respectively; since $\mathcal{T}'$ is a 3-manifold triangulation, L' must be a topological sphere.

This link L' is obtained from L by attaching zero or more additional triangles. Therefore L is an embedded subsurface of the sphere, and so L must be a sphere with zero or more punctures. □

The test itself is straightforward; the difficulty lies in performing it *quickly*. A fast implementation is crucial, since it will be called repeatedly throughout the recursive search.

The key idea is to track the 1-dimensional *boundary curves* of the vertex links, which are formed from cycles of edges belonging to vertex-linking triangles. As we glue tetrahedron faces together, we repeatedly split and splice these boundary cycles. To verify Test 2, we must track which triangles belong to the same vertex links and which edges belong to the same boundary cycles, which we can do in expected logarithmic time using union-find and skip lists respectively.

In the sections below, we describe what additional data needs to be stored (Section 3.1), how to manipulate and use this data (Section 3.2), and how skip lists can ensure a small time complexity (Section 3.3).

3.1   Data structures

In a partial triangulation with n tetrahedra, there are $4n$ *vertex linking triangles* that together form the vertex links (four such triangles are shown in Figure 2). These $4n$ triangles are surrounded by a total of $12n$ *vertex linking edges*.

Each time we glue together two tetrahedron faces, we consequently glue together three pairs of vertex linking edges, as shown in Figure 3. This gradually combines the triangles into a collection of larger triangulated surfaces, as illustrated in Figure 4. The boundary curves of these surfaces are drawn in bold in Figure 4; these are formed from the vertex linking edges that have not yet been paired together.

Figure 4: Vertex linking surfaces after gluing several tetrahedron faces

To support Test 2, we store all $12n$ vertex linking edges in a series of cyclic list structures that describe these boundary curves. To simplify the discussion, we begin with a naïve implementation based on doubly-linked lists. However, this leaves us with an $O(n)$ operation to perform, as seen in Section 3.2. To run all operations in expected logarithmic time we use skip lists [25], which we outline in Section 3.3.

We treat the vertex linking edges as *directed edges* (i.e., arrows), with directions chosen arbitrarily at the beginning of the enumeration algorithm. For each vertex linking edge e, we store the following data:

- If e is part of a boundary curve, we store the two edges adjacent to e along this boundary curve, as well as two booleans that tell us whether these adjacent edges point in the same or opposite directions.

- If e is not part of a boundary curve (i.e., it has been glued to some other vertex linking edge and is now internal to a vertex linking surface), we store a snapshot of the above data from the last time that e *was* part of a boundary curve.

To summarise: edges on the boundary curves are stored in a series of doubly-linked lists, and internal edges remember where they *were* in these lists right before they were glued to their current partner.

3.2   Recursion, backtracking and testing

Recall that each time we glue two tetrahedron faces together, we must glue together *three* pairs of vertex linking edges. Each of these edge gluings changes the vertex linking surfaces, and so we process each edge gluing individually.

There are three key operations that we must perform in relation to edge gluings:

(i) gluing two vertex linking edges together (when we step forward in the recursion);

(ii) ungluing two vertex linking edges (when we backtrack);

(iii) verifying Test 2 after gluing two vertex linking edges together (i.e., verifying that all vertex links are spheres with zero or more punctures).

We now present the details of each operation in turn. Throughout this discussion we assume that edges are glued together so that all vertex links are *orientable* surfaces; the paper [8] describes an efficient framework for detecting non-orientable vertex links as soon as they arise.

Recursion: gluing edges together

Suppose we wish to glue together edges x and y, as illustrated in Figure 5. Only local modifications are required: edges p and r become adjacent and must now to link to each other (instead of to x and y); likewise, edges q and s must be adjusted to link to each other. Note that this gluing introduces a change of direction where p and r meet (and likewise for q and s), so as we adjust the direction-related booleans we must perform an extra negation on each side.

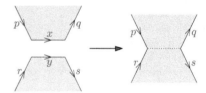

Figure 5: Gluing two vertex linking edges together

We make no changes to the data stored for edges x and y, since these two edges are now internal and their associated data now represents a snapshot from the last time that they were boundary edges (as required by Section 3.1).

All of these local modifications can be performed in $O(1)$ time. The associated list operations are deletion, splitting and splicing; this becomes important when we move to skip lists in Section 3.3.

It is important to remember the special case in which edges x and y are adjacent in the same boundary cycle. Here the local modifications are slightly different (there are only two or possibly zero nearby edges to update instead of four), but these modifications remain $O(1)$ time.

Backtracking: ungluing edges

As with gluing, ungluing a pair of vertex linking edges is a simple matter of local modifications. Here the backtracking context is important: it is essential that we unglue edges in the reverse order to that in which they were glued.

Suppose we are ungluing edges x and y as depicted in Figure 5. The snapshot data stored with edges x and y shows that they *were* adjacent to edges p, q, r and s immediately before this gluing was made (and therefore immediately *after* the ungluing that we are now performing).

This snapshot data therefore gives us access to edges p, q, r and s: now we simply adjust p and q to link to x (instead of r and s), and likewise we adjust r and s to link to y. No modifications to edges x and y are required.

Again we must adjust the direction-related booleans carefully, and we must cater for the case in which edges x and y were adjacent immediately before the gluing was made.

As before, all local modifications can be performed in $O(1)$ time. For the skip list discussion in Section 3.3, the associated list operations are splitting, splicing and insertion.

Testing: verifying that links are punctured spheres

Each time we glue two vertex linking edges together we must ensure that every vertex link is a sphere with zero or more punctures (Test 2). We test this *incrementally*: we assume this is true *before* we glue these edges together, and we verify that our new gluing does not introduce any unwanted genus to the vertex links.

Our incremental test is based on the following two observations:

LEMMA 4. *Let S and S' be distinct triangulated spheres with punctures, and let x and y be boundary edges from S and S' respectively. If we glue x and y together, the resulting surface is again a sphere with punctures.*

LEMMA 5. *Let S be a triangulated sphere with punctures, and let x and y be distinct boundary edges of S. If we glue x and y together in an orientation-preserving manner, the resulting surface is a sphere with punctures if and only if x and y belong to the same boundary cycle of S.*

The proofs of Lemmata 4 and 5 are simple, and we do not give further details here. Figure 6(a) illustrates the scenario of Lemma 4 with two distinct punctured spheres, and Figures 6(b)–6(d) show different scenarios from Lemma 5 in which we join two boundary edges from the same punctured sphere.

In particular, Figure 6(b) shows the case in which x and y belong to different boundary cycles; here we observe that the resulting surface is a twice-punctured torus. Figures 6(c) and 6(d) show cases with x and y on the same boundary cycle; in 6(d), x and y are adjacent along the boundary.

Note that Lemmata 4 and 5 hold even with very short boundaries (for instance, one-edge boundaries consisting of x or y alone).

It is now clear how to incrementally verify Test 2 when we glue together vertex linking edges x and y:

1. Test whether the vertex linking triangles containing x and y belong to the same connected vertex linking surface. If not, the test passes. Otherwise:

2. Test whether x and y belong to the same doubly-linked list of boundary edges (i.e., the same boundary cycle). If so, the test passes. If not, the test fails.

Here we implicitly assume that all gluings are orientation-preserving, as noted at the beginning of Section 3.2.

Step 1 can be performed in $O(\log n)$ time using the modified union-find structure outlined in [8]. The original purpose of this structure was to enforce orientability in vertex linking surfaces, and one of the operations it provides is an

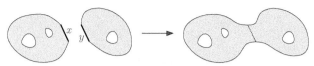

(a) Two distinct spheres with punctures

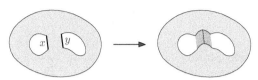

(b) Same sphere, different boundary cycles

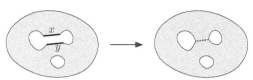

(c) Same boundary cycle, non-adjacent edges

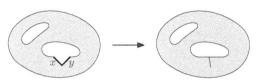

(d) Same boundary cycle, adjacent edges

Figure 6: Different ways of gluing boundary edges together

$O(\log n)$ test for whether two vertex linking triangles belong to the same connected vertex linking surface. This modified union-find supports backtracking; see [8] for further details.

Step 2 is more difficult: a typical implementation might involve walking through the doubly-linked list containing x until we either find y or verify that y is not present, which takes $O(n)$ time to complete. Union-find cannot help us, because of our repeated splitting and splicing of boundary cycles. In the following section we show how to reduce this $O(n)$ running time to expected $O(\log n)$ by extending our doubly-linked lists to become *skip lists*.

It should be noted that Step 2 can in fact be carried out in $O(b)$ time, where b is the number of boundary edges on all vertex linking surfaces. Although $b \in O(n)$ in general, for some face pairing graphs b can be far smaller. For instance, when the face pairing graph is a double-ended chain [6], we can arrange the recursive search so that $b \in O(1)$. See the full version of this paper for details.

3.3 Skip lists and time complexity

From the discussion in Section 3.2, we see that with our naïve doubly-linked list implementation, the three key operations of gluing edges, ungluing edges and verifying Test 2 have $O(1)$, $O(1)$ and $O(n)$ running times respectively. The bottleneck is the $O(n)$ test for whether two vertex linking edges belong to the same doubly-linked list (i.e., the same boundary cycle).

We can improve our situation by extending our doubly-linked list to a *skip list* [25]. Skip lists are essentially linked lists with additional layers of "express pointers" that allow us to move quickly through the list instead of stepping forward one element at a time. Figure 7 shows a typical skip list structure.

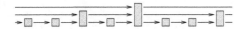

Figure 7: The internal layout of a skip list

The list operations used in Section 3.2 for gluing and ungluing edges are deletion, insertion, splitting and splicing; all of these can be performed on a skip list in expected $O(\log n)$ time [24, 25]. Importantly, it also takes expected $O(\log n)$ time to search forward to the last element of a skip list.[4] We can therefore test whether vertex linking edges x and y belong to the same list by searching forward to the end of each list and testing whether the final elements are the same.

It follows that, with a skip list implementation, all three key operations of gluing edges, ungluing edges and verifying Test 2 run in expected $O(\log n)$ time. Therefore:

THEOREM 6. *It is possible to implement Test 2 by performing expected $O(\log n)$ operations at every stage of the recursive search.*

Note that we must include reverse links at the lowest layer of the skip list (effectively maintaining the original doubly-linked list), since both forward and backward links are required for the gluing and ungluing operations (see Section 3.2). Full details of the skip list implementation can be found in the full version of this paper.

4. PERFORMANCE

Here we measure the performance of our new algorithm experimentally. Specifically, we compare two enumeration algorithms: the *old algorithm*, which includes all of the optimisations described in [8] (including the union-find framework for ensuring that vertex links remain orientable), and the *new algorithm*, which enhances the old algorithm with the new tests described in Section 3.[5]

We run our performance tests by enumerating censuses of all 3-manifold triangulations of size $n \leq 7$. We choose this type of census because a census of minimal triangulations requires significant manual post-processing [8], and because a census of all triangulations is significantly larger and therefore a stronger "stress test". We restrict our tests to $n \leq 7$ because for larger n the old algorithm becomes too slow to run time trials on a single CPU.

Table 1 shows the results of our time trials, split into censuses of orientable and non-orientable triangulations. For $n \leq 4$ both algorithms run in 1 second or less. All trials were carried out on a single 2.93 GHz Intel Xeon X5570 CPU.

The results are extremely pleasing: for $n = 7$ we see a speed-up of $128\times$ in the non-orientable case and $249\times$ in the orientable case (from almost four days of running time down to just 22 minutes). Moreover, the speed-up factors appear to grow exponentially with n. All of this suggests that our

---

[4] Although our lists are cyclic, we can always define an arbitrary endpoint.

[5] We compare the new algorithm against [8] because this allows us to isolate our new techniques, and because the source code and implementation details for alternative algorithms [16, 19] are not readily available.

Census parameters	Triangulations	Old (h:m:s)	New (m:s)	Speed-up
$n = 5$, orientable	4807	0:59	0:03	$20\times$
$n = 5$, non-orient.	377	1:09	0:06	$12\times$
$n = 6$, orientable	52946	1:11:57	1:03	$69\times$
$n = 6$, non-orient.	4807	1:23:30	2:05	$40\times$
$n = 7$, orientable	658474	92:23:39	22:16	$249\times$
$n = 7$, non-orient.	64291	103:24:51	48:27	$128\times$

Table 1: Running times for old and new algorithms

new algorithm can indeed make a concrete difference as to how large a census we can feasibly build.

It is worth noting that speed-ups are consistently better for the orientable case. This may be because the union-find framework introduced in [8] is most effective for non-orientable enumeration (as noted in Section 1), and so the orientable case has more room for gain. Nevertheless, it is pleasing to see that the new algorithm gives substantial improvements for both the orientable and non-orientable cases.

5. PARALLELISATION

As n increases, the output size for a typical census grows exponentially in n, and sometimes super-exponentially—for instance, the growth rate of a census of all 3-manifold triangulations is known to be $\exp(\Theta(n \log n))$ [12]. It is therefore critical that enumeration algorithms be parallelised if we are to make significant progress in obtaining new census data.

Like many combinatorial searches, the enumeration of triangulations is an embarrassingly parallel problem: different branches of the search tree can be processed independently, making the problem well-suited for clusters and server farms. Avoiding isomorphisms causes some minor complications, which we discuss in the full version of this paper.

The main obstacle is that, because of the various pruning techniques (as described in Sections 2 and 3), it is very difficult to estimate in advance how long each branch of the search tree will take to process. Experience shows that there can be orders-of-magnitude differences in running time between subsearches at the same depth in the tree.

For this reason, parallelisation must use a controller / slave model in which a controller process repeatedly hands small pieces of the search space to the next available slave, as opposed to a simple subdivision in which each process handles a fixed portion of the search space. This means that some inter-process communication is required.

For each subsearch, the controller must send $O(n)$ data to the slave: this includes the face pairing graph, the partial triangulation, and the data associated with the vertex linking edges and triangles as described in Section 3. The output for each subsearch can be super-exponentially large, and so it is preferable for slaves to write this data directly to disk (as opposed to communicating it back to the controller). Collating the output from different slaves is a simple task that can be performed after the enumeration has finished.

The enumeration code in *Regina* implements such a model using MPI, and runs successfully on hundreds of simultaneous CPUs with a roughly proportional speed-up in wall time.

6. CENSUS DATA

The new algorithms in this paper have been implemented and run in parallel using high-performance computing facilities to obtain new census data that exceeds the best known limits in the literature. This includes (i) a census of all closed 3-manifold triangulations of size $n \leq 10$, and (ii) a census of all minimal triangulations of closed $\mathbb{P}^2$-irreducible 3-manifolds of size $n \leq 11$.

6.1 All closed 3-manifold triangulations

The first reported census of all closed 3-manifold triangulations appears in [11] for $n \leq 9$, and has been used to study algorithmic complexity and random triangulations [11, 12]. Here we extend this census to $n \leq 10$ with a total of over 2 billion triangulations:

THEOREM 7. *There are precisely* 2 196 546 921 *closed 3-manifold triangulations that can be constructed from* ≤ 10 *tetrahedra, as summarised by Table 2.*

Size (n)	Orientable	Non-orientable	Total
1	4	—	4
2	16	1	17
3	76	5	81
4	532	45	577
5	4 807	377	5 184
6	52 946	4 807	57 753
7	658 474	64 291	722 765
8	8 802 955	984 554	9 787 509
9	123 603 770	15 499 262	139 103 032
10	1 792 348 876	254 521 123	2 046 869 999
Total	1 925 472 456	271 074 465	2 196 546 921

Table 2: All closed 3-manifold triangulations

The total CPU time required to enumerate the 10-tetrahedron census was $\simeq 2.4$ years, divided amongst 192 distinct 2.93 GHz Intel Xeon X5570 CPUs.

The paper [11] makes two conjectures regarding the worst-case and average number of vertex normal surfaces for a closed 3-manifold triangulation of size n. Details and definitions can be found in [11]; in summary, these conjectures are:

CONJECTURE 1. *For all positive* $n \neq 1, 2, 3, 5$, *a tight upper bound on the number of vertex normal surfaces in a closed 3-manifold triangulation of size n is:*

$$
\begin{array}{ll}
17^k + k & \text{if } n = 4k; \\
581 \cdot 17^{k-2} + k + 1 & \text{if } n = 4k + 1; \\
69 \cdot 17^{k-1} + k & \text{if } n = 4k + 2; \\
141 \cdot 17^{k-1} + k + 2 & \text{if } n = 4k + 3,
\end{array}
$$

and so this upper bound grows asymptotically as $\Theta(17^{n/4})$.

CONJECTURE 2. *If $\overline{\sigma}_n$ represents the average number of vertex normal surfaces amongst all closed 3-manifold triangulations (up to isomorphism), then $\overline{\sigma}_n < \overline{\sigma}_{n-1} + \overline{\sigma}_{n-2}$ for all $n \geq 3$, and so $\overline{\sigma}_n \in O(\lceil \frac{1+\sqrt{5}}{2} \rceil^n)$.*

These conjectures were originally based on the census data for $n \leq 9$. With our new census we can now verify these conjectures at the 10-tetrahedron level:

THEOREM 8. *Conjectures 1 and 2 are true for all $n \leq 10$.*

This census contains over 63 GB of data, and so the data files have not been posted online. Readers who wish to work with this data are welcome to contact the author for a copy.

6.2 Closed $\mathbb{P}^2$-irreducible 3-manifolds

A 3-manifold is $\mathbb{P}^2$-*irreducible* if every sphere bounds a ball and there are no embedded two-sided projective planes. Censuses of closed $\mathbb{P}^2$-irreducible 3-manifolds and their minimal triangulations have a long history [2, 3, 8, 9, 15, 16, 21, 22, 23]. The largest reported census of all minimal *triangulations* of these manifolds reaches $n \leq 10$ [8]. If we enumerate *manifolds* but not their triangulations, the censuses reaches $n \leq 12$ in the orientable case [22] but remains at $n \leq 10$ in the non-orientable case.

Here we extend this census of minimal triangulations of closed $\mathbb{P}^2$-irreducible 3-manifolds to $n \leq 11$. As a result, we also extend the census of underlying manifolds to $n \leq 11$ in the non-orientable case, and in the orientable case we confirm that the number of manifolds matches Matveev's census [22].

THEOREM 9. *There are precisely* 13 765 *closed $\mathbb{P}^2$-irreducible 3-manifolds that can be constructed from ≤ 11 tetrahedra. These have a combined total of* 55 488 *minimal triangulations, as summarised by Table 3.*

Size (n)	Minimal triangulations		Distinct 3-manifolds	
	Orientable	Non-orient.	Orientable	Non-orient.
1	4	—	3	—
2	9	—	6	—
3	7	—	7	—
4	15	—	14	—
5	40	—	31	—
6	115	24	74	5
7	309	17	175	3
8	945	59	436	10
9	3 031	307	1 154	33
10	10 244	983	3 078	85
11	36 097	3 282	8 421	230
Total	50 816	4 672	13 399	366

Table 3: All minimal triangulations of closed $\mathbb{P}^2$-irreducible 3-manifolds

The paper [9] raises conjectures for certain classes of non-orientable 3-manifolds regarding the combinatorial structure of every minimal triangulation. Again we refer to the source [9] for details and definitions; in summary:

CONJECTURE 3. *Every minimal triangulation of a non-flat non-orientable torus bundle over the circle is a layered torus bundle.*

CONJECTURE 4. *Every minimal triangulation of a non-flat non-orientable Seifert fibred space over $\mathbb{R}P^2$ or $\bar{D}$ with two exceptional fibres is either a plugged thin I-bundle or a plugged thick I-bundle.*

Layered torus bundles and plugged thin and thick I-bundles are families of triangulations with well-defined combinatorial structures. The original conjectures were based on census data for $n \leq 8$, and in [8] they are shown to hold for all $n \leq 10$. With our new census data we are now able to validate these conjectures at the 11-tetrahedron level:

THEOREM 10. *Conjectures 3 and 4 are true for all minimal triangulations of size $n \leq 11$.*

Data files for this census, including the 3-manifolds and all of their minimal triangulations, can be downloaded from the *Regina* website [5].

7. ACKNOWLEDGMENTS

Computational resources used in this work were provided by the Queensland Cyber Infrastructure Foundation and the Victorian Partnership for Advanced Computing.

8. REFERENCES

[1] I. Agol, J. Hass, and W. Thurston. 3-manifold knot genus is NP-complete. In *STOC '02: Proceedings of the Thiry-Fourth Annual ACM Symposium on Theory of Computing*, pages 761–766. ACM Press, 2002.

[2] G. Amendola and B. Martelli. Non-orientable 3-manifolds of small complexity. *Topology Appl.*, 133(2):157–178, 2003.

[3] G. Amendola and B. Martelli. Non-orientable 3-manifolds of complexity up to 7. *Topology Appl.*, 150(1-3):179–195, 2005.

[4] R. Budney. Embeddings of 3-manifolds in S^4 from the point of view of the 11-tetrahedron census. Preprint, arXiv:0810.2346, Oct. 2008.

[5] B. A. Burton. Regina: Normal surface and 3-manifold topology software. http://regina.sourceforge.net/, 1999–2010.

[6] B. A. Burton. Face pairing graphs and 3-manifold enumeration. *J. Knot Theory Ramifications*, 13(8):1057–1101, 2004.

[7] B. A. Burton. Introducing Regina, the 3-manifold topology software. *Experiment. Math.*, 13(3):267–272, 2004.

[8] B. A. Burton. Enumeration of non-orientable 3-manifolds using face-pairing graphs and union-find. *Discrete Comput. Geom.*, 38(3):527–571, 2007.

[9] B. A. Burton. Observations from the 8-tetrahedron nonorientable census. *Experiment. Math.*, 16(2):129–144, 2007.

[10] B. A. Burton. Converting between quadrilateral and standard solution sets in normal surface theory. *Algebr. Geom. Topol.*, 9(4):2121–2174, 2009.

[11] B. A. Burton. The complexity of the normal surface solution space. In *SCG '10: Proceedings of the Twenty-Sixth Annual Symposium on Computational Geometry*, pages 201–209. ACM, 2010.

[12] B. A. Burton. The Pachner graph and the simplification of 3-sphere triangulations. To appear in SCG '11: Proceedings of the Twenty-Seventh Annual Symposium on Computational Geometry, arXiv:1011.4169, Nov. 2010.

[13] N. M. Dunfield and W. P. Thurston. Finite covers of random 3-manifolds. *Invent. Math.*, 166(3):457–521, 2006.

[14] M. V. Hildebrand and J. R. Weeks. A computer generated census of cusped hyperbolic 3-manifolds. In *Computers and Mathematics (Cambridge, MA, 1989)*, pages 53–59. Springer, New York, 1989.

[15] B. Martelli. Complexity of 3-manifolds. In *Spaces of Kleinian Groups*, volume 329 of *London Math. Soc. Lecture Note Ser.*, pages 91–120. Cambridge Univ. Press, Cambridge, 2006.

[16] B. Martelli and C. Petronio. Three-manifolds having complexity at most 9. *Experiment. Math.*, 10(2):207–236, 2001.

[17] B. Martelli and C. Petronio. A new decomposition theorem for 3-manifolds. *Illinois J. Math.*, 46:755–780, 2002.

[18] B. Martelli and C. Petronio. Complexity of geometric three-manifolds. *Geom. Dedicata*, 108(1):15–69, 2004.

[19] S. Matveev. *Algorithmic Topology and Classification of 3-Manifolds*. Number 9 in Algorithms and Computation in Mathematics. Springer, Berlin, 2003.

[20] S. V. Matveev. Tables of 3-manifolds up to complexity 6. *Max-Planck-Institut für Mathematik Preprint Series*, (67), 1998. available from http://www.mpim-bonn.mpg.de/html/preprints/preprints.html.

[21] S. V. Matveev. Recognition and tabulation of three-dimensional manifolds. *Dokl. Akad. Nauk*, 400(1):26–28, 2005.

[22] S. V. Matveev. Tabulation of three-dimensional manifolds. *Russian Math. Surveys*, 60(4):673–698, 2005.

[23] S. V. Matveev and A. T. Fomenko. Constant energy surfaces of Hamiltonian systems, enumeration of three-dimensional manifolds in increasing order of complexity, and computation of volumes of closed hyperbolic manifolds. *Russian Math. Surveys*, 43(1):3–24, 1988.

[24] W. Pugh. A skip list cookbook. Report UMIACS-TR-89-72.1, Univ. of Maryland Institute for Advanced Computer Studies, College Park, MD, USA, 1990.

[25] W. Pugh. Skip lists: A probabilistic alternative to balanced trees. *Commun. ACM*, 33(6):668–676, 1990.

APPENDIX

In the introduction we claim there are at least 6.44×10^{12} connected combinatorial triangulations of size $n = 9$, up to isomorphism. Here we give the arguments to support this claim.

We begin by placing a lower bound on the number of *labelled* connected combinatorial triangulations. To ensure that each triangulation is connected, we insist that the first face of tetrahedron k is glued to some face chosen from tetrahedra $1, \ldots, k-1$, for all $k > 1$. Of course there are many labelled connected triangulations that do not satisfy this constraint, but since we are computing a lower bound this does not matter.

We initially choose gluings for the first face of each tetrahedron $2, 3, \ldots, n$ in order. For the first face of tetrahedron k there are $2k$ choices for a partner face—these are the $4(k-1)$ faces of tetrahedra $1, \ldots, k-1$ minus the $2(k-2)$ faces already glued—as well as six choices of rotation or reflection. This gives a total of $4 \times 6 \times \ldots \times (2n-2) \times 2n \times 6^{n-1}$ possibilities. From here there are $(2n+1) \times (2n-1) \times \ldots \times 3 \times 1 \times 6^{n+1}$ ways of gluing together the remaining $2n + 2$ faces in pairs, giving a lower bound of at least $(2n + 1)! \times 6^{2n}/2$ labelled connected combinatorial triangulations of size n.

We finish by factoring out isomorphisms. Each isomorphism class has size at most $n! \times 4^n$ (all possible relabellings of tetrahedra and their vertices), and so the total number of connected combinatorial triangulations of size n *up to isomorphism* is at least

$$\frac{(2n + 1)! \times 6^{2n}}{2 \times n! \times 4!^n}.$$

For $n = 9$ this evaluates to approximately 6.4435×10^{12}.

Linear Algebra to Compute Syzygies and Gröbner Bases

Daniel Cabarcas[*]
Dept. of Mathematical Sciences
University of Cincinnati
2600 Clifton ave. Cincinnati, OH 45221
cabarcas@gmail.com

Jintai Ding[†]
Dept. of Mathematical Sciences
University of Cincinnati
2600 Clifton ave. Cincinnati, OH 45221
and South China University of Technology, China
jintai.ding@uc.edu

ABSTRACT

In this paper, we introduce a new method to avoid zero reductions in Gröbner basis computation. We call this method LASyz, which stands for **Lineal Algebra** to compute **Syzygies**. LASyz uses exhaustively the information of both principal syzygies and non-trivial syzygies to avoid zero reductions. All computation is done using linear algebra techniques. LASyz is easy to understand and implement. The method does not require to compute Gröbner bases of subsequences of generators incrementally and it imposes no restrictions on the reductions allowed. We provide a complete theoretical foundation for the LASyz method and we describe an algorithm to compute Gröbner bases for zero dimensional ideals based on this foundation. A qualitative comparison with similar algorithms is provided and the performance of the algorithm is illustrated with experimental data.

Categories and Subject Descriptors

I.1.2 [**Symbolic and Algebraic Manipulation**]: Algorithms—*Algebraic algorithms*; F.2.2 [**Analysis of Algorithms and Problem Complexity**]: Nonnumerical Algorithms and Problems—*Computations on discrete structures*

General Terms

Algorithms, Theory

Keywords

Gröbner Bases, Syzygy, Linear Algebra

[*]Daniel Cabarcas is partially supported by the Distinguished Dissertation Completion Fellowship awarded by the Graduate School of the University of Cincinnati.

[†]Jintai Ding would like to thank partial support of NSF China grant #60973131 and the Taft Research Center.

1. INTRODUCTION

Gröbner bases have become the most important tool of applied algebraic geometry. Efficient computation of Gröbner bases has been the subject of abundant research, ever since the original algorithm was proposed by Buchberger in 1965 [3]. Progress has thrust applications, boosting attention, and subsequent progress.

In a polynomial ring R, a Gröbner basis for an ideal I is a particularly useful basis that can be computed from any set of generators for I. A Gröbner basis solves the ideal membership problem by providing standard representatives for the classes of the quotient ring R/I. Most algorithms to compute Gröbner bases start from any given basis for I and enlarge it with other elements from I until certain saturation condition is met.

Advancement in Gröbner basis computation has been driven, among others, by two ideas, reducing polynomials using linear algebra techniques, and avoiding zero reductions —linearly dependent polynomials. The relation between Linear algebra and Gröbner bases was first studied by Lazard [15] and later transformed into practical algorithms like F_4 [11], XL [7] or MGB [5]. Zero reductions were first studied by Buchberger [4], who proposed criteria to identify s-polynomials that reduce to zero, and later by Möller, Mora and Traverso [18], who proposed computing simultaneously a basis for the module of syzygies —algebraic relations among polynomials. Although impractical, the latest approach laid the foundation for practical implementations like Faugère's F_5 [12].

We propose a new method to avoid zero reductions by keeping a basis for the module of syzygies and using linear algebra techniques. We call this method LASyz, which stands for **Lineal Algebra** to compute **Syzygies**. LASyz uses known syzygies to avoid redundant computation in an exhaustive fashion. The use of linear algebra techniques for both polynomial reduction and syzygy reduction makes LASyz practical. LASyz procedes one degree at a time. Syzygies found at degree d are multiplied by monomials to predict syzygies at degree $d+1$. Principal syzygies are assembled and group together with other known syzygies. All known syzygies are row reduced to avoid redundancies and they are used to discard redundant polynomials. LASyz is easy to understand and implement, and its simplicity makes transparent the complexity of both reduction and syzygy bookkeeping. While some of the previous attempts to prevent zero reductions compute Gröbner bases incrementally by including one polynomial at a time, LASyz does not require incremental computation and it imposes no restrictions on the reductions allowed, offering more flexibility.

The paper is organized as follows. In Section 2, we provide a complete theoretical foundation for LASyz, including a formal statement of the algorithm and results that prove its correctness and effectiveness. In Section 3, we present a toy example that illustrates LASyz proceeding. Then, in Section 4, we describe a Gröbner bases algorithm based on LASyz. In Section 5, LASyz is compared with previous work from a qualitative point of view, and in Section 6, experimental results are presented and analyzed. In Section 7, we state conclusions and propose future work.

2. THEORETICAL FOUNDATION

Let k be a field and $R = k[x_1, \ldots, x_n]$ be the ring of polynomials over k on n variables. For $d \geq 0$ let R_d be the additive subgroup of homogeneous polynomials of degree d, so that $R = \oplus_{d=0}^{\infty} R_d$ is the usual gradation. Let M be the set of all monomials and M_d the set of monomials of degree d. Let P be a sequence of m polynomials. Let $\alpha \in R^m$ be an m-tuple of polynomials. We call *leading entry* of α with respect to P ($\mathrm{LE}_P(\alpha)$ for short) the polynomial in P corresponding to the first non-zero entry of α. For example, if $P = \{p_1, p_2, p_3\}$ and $\alpha = (0, xy - yz, xyz)$, then $\mathrm{LE}_P(\alpha) = p_2$. We often omit the reference to P when it is understood from the context.

Define the R-module homomorphism $v_P : R^m \to R$ by $v_P((\alpha_p)_{p \in P}) = \sum_{p \in P} \alpha_p p$. A *syzygy* of P is any m-tuple $\alpha = (\alpha_1, \ldots, \alpha_m)$ in the kernel of v_P, and we denote by $\mathrm{Syz}(F)$ the R-module of all syzygies. For $f, g \in P$, with $f \neq g$, we denote by $\pi_{f,g}$ the syzygy $g\mathcal{E}_f - f\mathcal{E}_g$, where $\mathcal{E}_f$ denotes the *canonical unit vector* with a single non-zero entry 1 in the position corresponding to f. We call $\pi_{f,g}$ a *principal syzygy* of P (also known as trivial syzygy) and denote by $\mathrm{pSyz}(P)$ the R-module generated by all principal syzygies.

For the rest of this section, assume that for all $p \in P$, p is homogeneous of degree d_p. Then, R^m is a graded R-module with degree d elements defined by

$$R_d^m := \{(\alpha_p)_{p \in P} \in R^m \mid \text{ for } p \in P, \alpha_p = 0 \text{ or } \alpha_p \in R_{d-d_p}\}.$$

With $\mathrm{Syz}_d(P) := \mathrm{Syz}(P) \cap R_d^m$, $\mathrm{Syz}(P) = \oplus_{d=0}^{\infty} \mathrm{Syz}_d(P)$ is a graded module and with $\mathrm{pSyz}_d(P) := \mathrm{pSyz}(P) \cap R_d^m$, $\mathrm{pSyz}(P) = \oplus_{d=0}^{\infty} \mathrm{pSyz}_d(P)$ is also a graded module.

Syzygies have a relative nature that is exploited by the proposed LASyz method. For example, suppose $f_1, f_2, g_1, g_2, h_1, h_2$ are polynomials such that $f_1 g_1 h_1 + f_2 g_2 h_2 = 0$. We can say that $(f_1 g_1, f_2 g_2)$ is a syzygy of (h_1, h_2) or we can say that (f_1, f_2) is a syzygy of $(g_1 h_1, g_2 h_2)$. We are interested in a particular map between modules of syzygies. Consider the family of extension sets defined for $d \geq 0$ by

$$P_d := \{tp \mid t \in \mathrm{M}, p \in P, \deg(tp) = d\},$$

and

$$P_{(d)} := \bigcup_{j=0}^{d} P_j.$$

There is a natural surjective k-module homomorphism

$$\sigma_d : \mathrm{Syz}_d(P_{(d)}) \twoheadrightarrow \mathrm{Syz}_d(P_d),$$

defined by

$$\sum_{p \in P_{(d)}} \left(\sum_{t \in \mathrm{M}} a_{p,t} t\right) \mathcal{E}_p \mapsto \sum_{p \in P_{(d)}} \sum_{t \in \mathrm{M}} a_{p,t} \mathcal{E}_{tp},$$

where for $p \in P_{(d)}$ and $t \in \mathrm{M}$, $a_{p,t} \in k$ and $a_{p,t} \neq 0$ implies $\deg(tp) = d$. The homomorphisms σ_d provides a systematic way to transform syzygies between different extension sets.

Notice that degree d syzygies of P_d have scalar entries and they constitute a vector space. We are particularly interested in syzygies with only scalar entries, because linear algebra techniques can be used for computing with them. The set of all syzygies of P with scalar entries will be denoted by $\mathrm{Syz\text{-}S}(P)$. Using this notation, $\mathrm{Syz}_d(P_d) = \mathrm{Syz\text{-}S}(P_d)$.

The basic linear algebra procedure that we use can be described as follows. Let A be an $m \times n$ matrix in k. Consider the linear map associated with A, $L_A : k^m \to k^n$ defined by $L_A(X) = XA$. Suppose we are interested in finding a basis for the row space of A consisting of a subset of its rows. For this purpose, we can compute a triangular basis $\mathcal{B}$ for the kernel of L_A, and remove from A all rows that correspond to first non-zero entries of elements in $\mathcal{B}$. If we are given a-priori a finite subset B of the kernel of L_A, we can use it to reduce the problem, by first row reducing B to echelon form and removing from A all rows that correspond to first non-zero entries of elements in B.

Given $B \subseteq \mathrm{Syz\text{-}S}(P)$, we call C an *echelon form* of B if $0 \notin C$, $\mathrm{span}(B) = \mathrm{span}(C)$ and for $\alpha_1, \alpha_2 \in C$, $\alpha_1 \neq \alpha_2$ implies $\mathrm{LE}(\alpha_1) \neq \mathrm{LE}(\alpha_2)$.

We describe LASyz as a method to avoid zero reductions in an XL type algorithm [7]. Starting with a finite set of polynomials P, we generate, degree by degree, the extension sets P_d. We discard redundant elements from P_d by using the linear algebra procedure described above. Known kernel elements come from two sources, principal syzygies and redundancies found at previous degrees. We rely on the relativity of syzygies to obtain as many syzygies as possible from previous degrees.

Given a basis for the degree $d-1$ syzygies of P_{d-1}, Algorithm 1 computes a basis for the degree d syzygies of P_d.

Algorithm 1 LASyz$(P, d, \mathcal{B}_{d-1})$

Require: P is a finite subset of homogeneous polynomials.
Require: $\mathcal{B}_{d-1}$ is a basis for $\mathrm{Syz}_{d-1}(P_{d-1})$
1: $A := \{\sigma_d(x \cdot \alpha) \mid x \in \{x_1, \ldots, x_n\}, \alpha \in \mathcal{B}_{d-1}\}$
2: $B := \{\sigma_d(\pi_{f,g}) \mid f, g \in P, \deg(fg) = d\}$
3: $C :=$ an echelon form of $A \cup B$
4: $G := P_d \setminus \mathrm{LE}(C)$
5: $D :=$ a basis for $\mathrm{Syz\text{-}S}(G)$
6: $\mathcal{B}_d := C \cup D$
7: **return** $\mathcal{B}_d$

Note that for $f, g \in P$ and $s, t \in \mathrm{M}$ such that $\deg(stfg) = d$, $\sigma_d(\pi_{(tf, sg)}) = \sigma_d(st\pi_{(f,g)})$, hence, we only need to consider principal syzygies among elements of P and not among elements in extension sets.

The following lemma explains the use of the leading entries of C to discard elements from P_d.

LEMMA 1. *If C is a subset of $\mathrm{Syz\text{-}S}(P)$ in echelon form, then the set $P \setminus \mathrm{LE}(C)$ spans the same space as P does. Moreover, if C spans $\mathrm{Syz\text{-}S}(P)$ then $P \setminus \mathrm{LE}(C)$ is a basis for $\mathrm{span}(P)$.*

PROOF. Suppose that $P = \{p_1, \ldots, p_m\}$ and $C = \{\alpha_1, \ldots, \alpha_s\}$, $s \leq m$. By reordering P if necessary and multiplying by appropriate scalars, we can assume without lost of generality that for $i = 1, \ldots, s$, $\mathrm{LE}(\alpha_i) = p_i$ and that the i-th entry of α_i is 1. Then, for $i = 1, \ldots, s$, p_i belongs to span$\{p_{i+1}, \ldots, p_m\}$. By induction it follows that for $i = 1, \ldots, s$, p_i belongs to span$\{p_{s+1}, \ldots, p_m\}$. It follows that $P \setminus \mathrm{LE}(C) = \{p_{s+1}, \ldots, p_m\}$ spans the same space as P does.

Now suppose that C spans Syz-S(P). Since for $\alpha \neq \alpha' \in C$, $\mathrm{LE}(\alpha) \neq \mathrm{LE}(\alpha')$, C must be a basis. Further suppose that there exist $b_{s+1}, \ldots, b_m \in k$ such that $\sum_{i=s+1}^{m} b_i p_i = 0$. Then $\sum_{i=s+1}^{m} b_i e_i \in$ Syz-S(P) (e_i represents the i-canonical unit vector of R^m). Since C spans Syz-S(P) then there exist $c_1, \ldots, c_s \in k$ such that $\sum_{i=s+1}^{m} b_i e_i = \sum_{j=1}^{s} c_j \alpha_j$. Looking at the first entry of the equality we conclude that if $s > 0$

$$0 = \left(\sum_{i=s+1}^{m} b_i e_i \right)_1 = \left(\sum_{j=1}^{s} c_j \alpha_j \right)_1 = c_1 .$$

By induction on the entries, we can conclude that for $j = 1, \ldots, s$, $c_j = 0$ hence $\sum_{i=s+1}^{m} b_i e_i = \sum_{j=1}^{s} c_j \alpha_j = 0$ and therefore $b_{s+1} = \cdots = b_m = 0$. This shows that $P \setminus \mathrm{LE}(C)$ is a basis for span(P). $\square$

We are now ready to prove the main result of this section, the correctness of LASyz.

THEOREM 1. *Algorithm 1 computes a basis for the degree d syzygies of P_d.*

PROOF. By definition of σ_d, $A \cup B$ is a subset of Syz-S(P_d). By definition of echelon form, span(C) = span$(A \cup B)$ and for $\alpha \neq \alpha' \in C$, $\mathrm{LE}(\alpha) \neq \mathrm{LE}(\alpha')$. Since Syz-S$(P_d)$ is a vector space over k, C is a subset of Syz-S(P_d). Then, by Lemma 1, $G = P_d \setminus \mathrm{LE}(C)$ spans the same space as P_d.

Let $\alpha \in$ Syz$_d(P_d)$. Because C is in echelon form, there exist $\beta \in$ span(C) such that, for all $p \in \mathrm{LE}(C)$, the entry in $\alpha - \beta$ corresponding to p is zero. Then, $\alpha - \beta \in$ Syz-S(G) = span(D), and therefore, $\alpha \in$ span$(\mathcal{B}_d)$, proving that $\mathcal{B}_d$ spans Syz$_d(P_d)$. C and D are bases so in order to show that $\mathcal{B}_d$ is a basis it suffices to show that for any $0 \neq \alpha \in C$, and $0 \neq \beta \in D$, $a, b \in k$, $a\alpha + b\beta = 0$ implies $a = 0 = b$. Indeed, because C is in echelon form, for all $p \in \mathrm{LE}(C)$, the entry in β corresponding to p is zero and the entry in α corresponding to p is non-zero, hence $a = 0$ and therefore $b = 0$. $\square$

We conclude this section with two results that partially prove the effectiveness of LASyz in keeping track of syzygies.

In Algorithm 1, we look only at degree d syzygies of P_d, but it is always possible to track them back to the original set of generators P. For that purpose we define the surjective k-module homomorphism

$$\rho_d : \mathrm{Syz}_d(P_{(d)}) \twoheadrightarrow \mathrm{Syz}_d(P)$$

by

$$\sum_{\substack{s \in M, p \in P \\ sp \in P_{(d)}}} \alpha_{sp} \mathcal{E}_{sp} \longmapsto \sum_{\substack{s \in M, p \in P \\ sp \in P_{(d)}}} \alpha_{sp} s \mathcal{E}_p .$$

Next theorem demonstrates that principal syzygies are used effectively by Algorithm 1, in the sense that, if P only possesses trivial syzygies, then all degree d syzygies of P_d

are caught before Line 5 is executed. It is stated and proved for regular sequences but it can be adapted for semi-regular sequences with degree bounded by the degree of regularity.

THEOREM 2. *If P is a regular sequence of polynomials then* Syz-S$(G) = 0$, *in Algorithm 1.*

PROOF. It suffices to show that every syzygy of P_d with scalar entries belongs to the span of C. In such case, by Lemma 1, G is a basis for span(P_d) hence Syz-S$(G) = 0$. Since P is a regular sequence and the polynomials are homogeneous, pSyz(P) = Syz(P).

Let $\alpha \in$ Syz-S(P_d). Since, pSyz(P) = Syz(P), there exist $a_{t,f,g} \in k$ such that

$$\rho_d(\alpha) = \sum_{f \neq g \in P} \sum_{t \in M} a_{t,f,g} t \pi_{f,g} ,$$

where $a_{t,f,g} \neq 0$ implies $\deg(tfg) = d$. Then, applying σ_d to both sides of the equality we obtain

$$\alpha = \sigma_d(\rho_d(\alpha)) = \sum_{f \neq g \in P} \sum_{t \in M} a_{t,f,g} \sigma_d(t \pi_{f,g}) .$$

With A and B as defined in Algorithm 1, we can split the sum above into two parts, one coming from A and the other from B.

$$\alpha = \sum_{f \neq g \in P} \sum_{1 \neq t \in M} a_{t,f,g} \sigma_d(t \pi_{f,g}) + \sum_{f \neq g \in P} a_{1,f,g} \sigma_d(\pi_{f,g})$$

Note that for $a_{t,f,g} \neq 0$ with $t \neq 1$ there exist $x \in \{x_1, \ldots, x_n\}$ such that $\frac{t}{x} \in M$ thus $\sigma_{d-1}(\frac{t}{x} \pi_{f,g}) \in$ Syz-S(P_{d-1}) = span$(\mathcal{B}_{d-1})$ hence $\sigma_d(t \pi_{f,g}) = \sigma_d(x \sigma_{d-1}(\frac{t}{x} \pi_{f,g})) \in$ span(A). Also, for $a_{1,f,g} \neq 0$, $\sigma_d(\pi_{f,g}) \in B$. Therefore $\alpha \in$ span$(A \cup B)$ = span(C). $\square$

The following theorem shows that syzygies of P_d with scalar entries account for all syzygies, which justifies focusing only on those.

THEOREM 3. *If $\mathcal{B}_d$ is a basis for* Syz-S(P_d) *then $\rho_d(\mathcal{B}_d)$ is a basis for* Syz$_d(P)$.

PROOF. Let $\alpha = \sum_{p \in P} \alpha_p \mathcal{E}_p \in$ Syz$_d(P)$. Since α is a degree d syzygy, $\alpha_p = 0$ whenever $\deg(p) > d$. Hence α can be written as a syzygy of $P_{(d)}$, $\alpha' = \sum_{p \in P_{(d)}} \alpha'_p \mathcal{E}_p$ with $\alpha'_p = \alpha_p$ whenever $p \in P$ and $\alpha'_p = 0$ otherwise.

Consider $\sigma_d(\alpha') \in$ Syz-S(P_d). Because $\mathcal{B}_d$ is a basis for Syz-S(P_d), there exist $A_\beta \in k$ such that

$$\sigma_d(\alpha') = \sum_{\beta \in \mathcal{B}_d} A_\beta \beta .$$

Applying the homomorphism ρ_d on both sides of the equality we obtain

$$\alpha = \rho_d(\sigma_d(\alpha')) = \rho_d \left(\sum_{\beta \in \mathcal{B}_d} A_\beta \beta \right) = \sum_{\beta \in \mathcal{B}_d} A_\beta \rho_d(\beta) .$$

This shows that $\rho_d(\mathcal{B}_d)$ generates Syz$_d(P)$.

Now suppose $\sum_{\beta \in \mathcal{B}_d} A_\beta \rho_d(\beta) = 0$ for some $A_\beta \in k$. Then

$$0 = \sigma \left(\sum_{\beta \in \mathcal{B}_d} A_\beta \rho_d(\beta) \right) = \sum_{\beta \in \mathcal{B}_d} A_\beta \sigma(\rho_d(\beta)) = \sum_{\beta \in \mathcal{B}_d} A_\beta \beta ,$$

and because $\mathcal{B}_d$ is a basis for Syz-S(P_d), it follows that $A_\beta = 0$ for all $\beta \in \mathcal{B}_d$ and therefore $\rho_d(\mathcal{B}_d)$ is a basis. $\square$

3. TOY EXAMPLE

We illustrate how `LASyz` avoids reductions to zero by means of a simple example. Let

$$P = \{p_1 = 22x^2 + 4xz + 20y^2 + 5yz + 14z^2$$
$$p_2 = 15x^2 + 17xy + 7xz + 12y^2 + 3yz + 10z^2$$
$$p_3 = x^2 + 4xy + 8xz + 16y^2 + 18yz + 18z^2$$
$$p_4 = x^2 + 7xy + 22xz + 11y^2 + 2yz + 10z^2\},$$

a set of degree 2 polynomials in the variables x, y, z with coefficients in GF(23). These polynomials are linearly independent. However, the polynomials in P_3 are not —

$$P_3 = \{xp_1, xp_2, xp_3, xp_4, yp_1, yp_2, yp_3, yp_4, zp_1, zp_2, zp_3, zp_4\} \,.$$

Using linear algebra over the matrix that represents P_3, we are able to find two linear relations among the polynomials in P_3,

$$\alpha = (1 \quad 0 \quad 6 \quad 18 \quad 20 \quad 1 \quad 2 \quad 14 \quad 19 \quad 20 \quad 2 \quad 5) \,,$$
$$\beta = (0 \quad 1 \quad 0 \quad 8 \quad 6 \quad 15 \quad 12 \quad 18 \quad 11 \quad 11 \quad 3 \quad 5) \in \text{Syz}(P_3) \,.$$

From these, and by multiplying by x, y, z, we can obtain syzygies among the polynomials in P_4. For example, the syzygy α corresponds to the equation

$$xp_1 + 6xp_3 + 18xp_4 + 20yp_1 + yp_2 + 2yp_3 + \cdots + 5zp_4 = 0 \,.$$

By multiplying it by x we obtain

$$x^2p_1 + 6x^2p_3 + 18x^2p_4 + 20xyp_1 + xyp_2 + 2xyp_3 + \cdots + 5xzp_4 = 0 \,,$$

which corresponds to the syzygy of P_4

$$\mathcal{E}_{x^2p_1} + 6\mathcal{E}_{x^2p_3} + 18\mathcal{E}_{x^2p_4} + 20\mathcal{E}_{xyp_1} + \mathcal{E}_{xyp_2} + 2\mathcal{E}_{xyp_3} + \cdots + 5\mathcal{E}_{xzp_4} \,,$$

where $\mathcal{E}_p$ denotes the *canonical unit vector* with a single non-zero entry 1 in the position corresponding to p. In this fashion, we can obtain six elements of $\text{Syz}(P_4)$ corresponding to $x\alpha, x\beta, y\alpha, y\beta, z\alpha, z\beta$.

We also know a-priori the principal syzygies of P. For example, $p_1\mathcal{E}_{p_2} - p_2\mathcal{E}_{p_1}$ which corresponds to the equation

$$(22x^2 + \cdots + 14z^2)p_2 - (15x^2 + \cdots + 10z^2)p_1 = 0 \,,$$

or equivalently

$$22x^2p_2 + \cdots + 14z^2p_2 - 15x^2p_1 - \cdots - 10z^2p_1 = 0 \,,$$

which corresponds to the syzygy of P_4

$$22\mathcal{E}_{x^2p_2} + \cdots + 14\mathcal{E}_{z^2p_2} - 15\mathcal{E}_{x^2p_1} - \cdots - 10\mathcal{E}_{z^2p_1} \,.$$

Overall, we have obtained twelve elements of $\text{Syz}(P_4)$, six from multiplying elements of $\text{Syz}(P_3)$ by variables, and six principal syzygies. Next, we put these twelve vectors on a matrix and row reduce it to obtain a row echelon form. Each pivot column corresponds to a redundant element of P_4 revealing redundant the polynomials

$$x^2p_1, x^2p_2, x^2p_3, xyp_1, xyp_2, xyp_3, xzp_1, xzp_2, xzp_3, xp_1, xp_2 \,.$$

We can safely remove them to form a smaller set of generators for the span of P_4. In this fashion we are using exhaustively the information of both principal syzygies of P and non-trivial syzygies found at degree three, to avoid redundancies at degree four.

4. NEW GRÖBNER BASES ALGORITHM

Next, we introduce a new algorithm to compute Gröbner bases of zero-dimensional ideals based on the `mutantXL` algorithm [8]. The description is for the ring of boolean functions

$$\mathcal{B} := R/\langle x_1^2 - x_1, \ldots, x_n^2 - x_n \rangle \,,$$

with $R = k[x_1, \ldots, x_n]$ and k the Galois field of order two. We decided to describe the algorithm for this ring due to its importance in cryptography and coding theory.

`mutantXL` can be summarized as follows. Assume a monomial order is fixed and let P be a finite set of elements in $\mathcal{B}$ (usually not homogeneous). `mutantXL` constructs, one degree at a time, an extension set P_d, linearizes it, computes an echelon form, and searches for mutant polynomials, i.e. polynomials of a lower degree than d. If mutants are found, it extends mutants before constructing the next extension set P_{d+1}. The difference between the new algorithm and `mutantXL` is the use of `LASyz` to discard redundant polynomials.

We shall make some precisions in the notation for the particular ring $\mathcal{B}$ and for working with non-homogeneous polynomials:

1. In the quotient ring $\mathcal{B}$, the degree of a class is defined to be the minimum among the degrees of all representatives. In the case of a syzygy, the *degree* of $\alpha = (\alpha_p)_{p \in P} \in \text{Syz}(P)$ is the maximum among the degrees of the $\alpha_p p$. We denote by $\text{Syz}_{(d)}(P)$ the k-module of syzygies of P of degree up to d. Note that this notion of degree does not produce a gradation of $\text{Syz}(P)$ but only a filtration.

2. Just as in Section 2, we are interested in syzygies with scalar entries, because they can be computed using linear algebra. We denote by $\text{Syz-S}(P)$ the k-module of all syzygies of P with scalar entries. There is a natural surjective k-module homomorphism

$$\sigma_d : \text{Syz}_{(d)}(P_{(d)}) \twoheadrightarrow \text{Syz-S}(P_{(d)})$$

defined by

$$\sum_{p \in P_{(d)}} \left(\sum_{t \in M} a_{p,t} t \right) \mathcal{E}_p \mapsto \sum_{p \in P_{(d)}} \sum_{t \in M} a_{p,t} \mathcal{E}_{tp} \,,$$

where for $p \in P_{(d)}$ and $t \in M$, $a_{p,t} \in k$, and $a_{p,t} \neq 0$ implies $\deg(tp) \leq d$.

3. In the ring $\mathcal{B}$, any $p \in \mathcal{B}$ satisfies $p^2 = p$. We include this relations as principal syzygies by extending the notation $\pi_{f,g}$. We denote by $\pi_{p,p}$ the syzygy $(p-1)\mathcal{E}_p$.

4. For any $p \in \mathcal{B}$ of degree d, we denote by p^h the *leading form* of p (the homogeneous part of p of degree d), and by p^{-h} the rest of the polynomial $p - p^h$.

In Algorithm 2, we spelled out the details of the new Gröbner bases algorithm which we call `LASyzGB`.

We now explain the algorithm. The **while** loop of the algorithm produces, one degree at a time, a set G that spans $P_{(d)}$. As termination condition, we can use the conditions in Proposition 3 from [16] which we state below for completeness. This proposition, together with Theorem 1 guarantee that upon termination `LASyzGB` returns a Gröbner basis.

Algorithm 2 LASyzGB(P)

Require: P is a finite subset of polynomials in $\mathcal{B}$.

1: $d := 1$
2: $\mathcal{B}_0 := \emptyset$
3: **while** termination condition **do**
4:     $A := \{\sigma_d(x \cdot \alpha) \mid x \in \{x_1, \ldots, x_n\}, \alpha \in \mathcal{B}_{d-1}\}$
5:     $B := A \cup \{\sigma_d(\pi_{f,g}) \mid f, g \in P, \deg(fg) = d\}$
6:     **repeat**
7:         $C :=$ an echelon form of $B \cup \mathcal{B}_1 \cup \cdots \cup \mathcal{B}_{d-1}$
8:         $G := P_{(d)} \setminus \mathrm{LE}(C)$
9:         $D :=$ an echelon form of Syz-S(G)
10:        $G := G \setminus \mathrm{LE}(D)$
11:        $B := B \cup D$
12:        **for** $i = 1, \ldots, d$ **do**
13:            $\overline{G} := \{g \in G \mid \deg(g) = i\}$
14:            $E :=$ an echelon form of Syz-S($\overline{G}^h$)
15:            **if** $E \neq \emptyset$ **then**
16:                mutants $:= v_{\overline{G}}(E)$
17:                $P := P \cup$ mutants
18:                $B := B \cup E$
19:                break
20:        **until** mutants $= \emptyset$
21:     $\mathcal{B}_d := B$
22:     $d := d + 1$
23: **return** G

PROPOSITION 1   ([16]). *Let G be a finite subset of $\mathcal{B}$ with highest degree D and suppose that the following holds:*

1. $\mathrm{LM}(G) \supseteq \mathrm{LM}(\mathrm{M}_D)$, and

2. *if $H := G \cup \{t \cdot g \mid g \in G, t \in \mathrm{M}$ and $\deg(t) + \deg(g) \leq D + 1\}$, there exists $\widetilde{H}$, a row echelon form of H, such that $\{h \in \widetilde{H} \mid \deg(h) \leq D\} = G$,*

then G is a Gröbner basis for the ideal I generated by G.

The set A in Algorithm 2, Line 4, groups syzygies obtained in previous degrees extended and interpreted as syzygies of $P_{(d)}$ with scalar entries. The set B in Line 5, appends to A all principal syzygies of degree d interpreted as syzygies of $P_{(d)}$ with scalar entries.

The **repeat-until** loop, constructs the set G and verifies whether there are any mutant polynomials, in which case it modifies the set P of original polynomials and reconstructs G accordingly. Lines 7 to 11 compute syzygies using LASyz as described in Algorithm 1.

The **for** loop checks for mutants at each degree i. Note that if $\alpha \in$ Syz-S($\overline{G}^h$) then $v_{\overline{G}}(\alpha)$ is a mutant polynomial of G or zero. In Line 17, the mutant polynomials found at degree i are appended to the original set of polynomials P, and in Line 18 the corresponding relations are appended to the set of syzygies B. If mutants are found the loop is broken.

5. QUALITATIVE COMPARISON

This is by no means the first attempt to avoid zero reductions in Gröbner basis computation. Remarkable work precedes us by Buchberger [4], Möller, Mora and Traverso [18], Faugère [12], among others. It is important to evaluate from a qualitative point of view where our new approach lies in this spectrum of algorithms.

Buchberger's criteria to discard s-polynomials are effective for avoiding zero reductions and can be efficiently implemented [14]. It has been shown that many more zero reductions can be avoided by a syzygy approach [18]. Möller, et. al. claim that their approach "covers both of Buchberger criteria" and "avoids more superfluous reductions". The algorithm proposed here is similar to Möller's in that it maintains a subset of the module of syzygies and uses it to avoid reductions to zero. However, Möller's algorithm is not practical, as the authors claim, "The first results show an ambiguous behavior: many useless pairs are discovered, but this involves a lot of extra computation, so the execution time is increased." LASyz overcomes this problem with a different way to maintain syzygies. Syzygies are kept in reference to the original set of generators and computation is purely based on linear algebra. In this way, all the burden of syzygy bookkeeping is carried by a sparse linear algebra package. As Faugère demonstrated with his F_4 algorithm, linear algebra can make a huge impact in the efficiency.

Faugère's F_5 relies on two criteria to avoid zero reductions, the rewritten criterion and Faugère's criterion [10]. The former uses non-trivial syzygies previously detected, but it is uncertain how effective it is. Faugère's criterion relies on principal syzygies and it has been proved to be effective, but the cost associated still awaits to be fully understood. The hidden cost of Faugère's criterion lies is its incremental nature, which restricts the reductions allowed. We explain this last point with the aid of MatrixF5, a close relative of F_5 that was first mentioned in [1]. Let $P = \{p_1, \ldots, p_m\}$ be homogeneous polynomials of degrees $d_1, \ldots, d_m$ respectively. Define the sets

$$P_{d,i} := \{tp \mid t \in \mathrm{M}, p \in \{p_1, \ldots, p_i\}, \deg(tp) = d\}.$$

Faugère's criterion states that if G is an echelon form of $P_{d-d_i, i-1}$ and t is a leading monomial of G, then, tp_i is redundant in $P_{d,i}$. The problem with the implementation of this criterion is its incremental nature. It is necessary to obtain the leading monomials of an echelon form of $P_{d-d_i, i-1}$ in order to avoid syzygies in $P_{d,i}$, placing a burden on the linear algebra procedure. During the reduction of P_d a strict order must be enforced and only row operations "downward" are allowed. Such restriction may inhibit the choice of the most suitable sparse matrix algorithm to compute an echelon form.

In [13], Gao et. al. propose an incremental Gröbner bases algorithm called G2V, which offers another way to avoid zero reductions using information from the module of syzygies. Given $G = \{g_1, \ldots, g_m\}$ a Gröbner basis for an ideal I and any $g \in R$, G2V computes Gröbner bases for $\langle I, g \rangle$ and $(I : g) = \{u \in R \mid ug \in I\}$. Notice that $u \in (I : g)$ implies that there exist $h_1, \ldots, h_m \in R$ such that $ug = \sum_{i=1}^{m} h_i g_i$, so u can be regarded as some kind of signature for the syzygy $(-h_1, \ldots, -h_m, u)$ of $(g_1, \ldots, g_m, g)$.

The incremental nature of G2V also acts in detriment of its efficiency. Besides a restriction on the reductions allowed, G2V also imposes a strict order in the selection of the pairs. The paper announces a non-incremental version which shall be very interesting, given the simplicity and efficiency achieved already by G2V. It is also important to note that in the execution of G2V, the elements of $(I : g)$ are not reduced among each other, allowing redundancies and missing opportunities for discarding zero reductions.

In this context, our proposed non-incremental algorithm

offers an alternative that is simple, easy to implement an analyze, that offers a comprehensive treatment of both trivial and non-trivial syzygies and that relies entirely on linear algebra procedures with no restrictions. The new algorithm also yields a basis for the module of syzygies.

6. EXPERIMENTAL RESULTS

We have tested LASyz' performance in avoiding zero reductions and we have compared it with other methods. In order to illustrate its capabilities and limitations, we present here details of some experiments. We have implemented the proposed algorithm for computing Gröbner bases in C++ and in Magma [2]. All experiments were run in a personal computer equipped with an Intel(R) core(TM) 2 Duo CPU E6550 @2.33GHz processor, with 2 GB of Ram, and running Windows XP. The first experiment illustrates the behavior of the algorithm in presence of non-trivial syzygies and the second one aims at evaluating the cost of keeping a basis of syzygies and detecting zero reductions. Two more experiments compare LASyz with Faugère's F_5 algorithm.

6.1 Non-trivial Syzygies Experiment

For the purpose of illustrating the behavior of the algorithm in presence of non-trivial syzygies, we chose polynomials coming from an HFE cryptosystem [19]. The cryptosystem is a random HFE with parameters: size of field $q = 2$, extension degree $n = 14$, degree bound $D = 16$. The polynomials are the homogeneous degree two part of the public key and computations were made modulo $\langle x_1^2, \ldots, x_n^2 \rangle$. Three equations were removed, making this an HFE minus system.

The results are presented in Table 6.1. The table shows the number of polynomials produced at each degree by the new algorithm and by Magma's implementation of Faugère's F_4 [2] for comparison.

LASyz				
Degree	2	3	4	5
Number of polynomials in P_d	11	154	1001	4004
Number of polynomials used	11	154	935	2436
Dimension of kernel	0	0	46	434
Number of syzygies			66	1568
Faugère's F_4				
Number of polynomials used	11	336	1958	4756

Table 1: Comparison in number of polynomials produced at each degree on an HFE minus system.

The use of less polynomials translates into less memory. The gain comes from two sources. At degree four, 66 trivial syzygies allow us to ignore 66 polynomials of the extension set P_4. Also, at this same degree, 46 non-trivial syzygies are spotted in the kernel of the set P_4. Then, we put together the 66 trivial plus the 46 non-trivial for a total of 112 syzygies, which are extended to degree five by multiplying by each variable to obtain $112(14) = 1568$ syzygies of degree five. The 1568 syzygies allow us to ignore 1568 polynomials of the extension set P_5.

6.2 Performance Experiment

In order to illustrate the performance of LASyzGB, we used a random system of 22 polynomial equations in 14 variables with coefficients in $GF(2^8)$. We computed a Gröbner basis

for the system using Faugère's F_4 algorithm and the new proposed algorithm implemented in C++. Because the algorithm to compute row echelon forms is critical for performance, and in order to obtain comparable results, we ran both the proposed algorithm and our own home brew (HB) implementation of F_4 using the same row echelon form algorithm as described in [6]. We also run Magma's F_4 for reference.

The most time consuming task in both cases is the row reduction of a large matrix that represents degree five polynomials. Values for those matrices are presented in Table 6.2: number of rows and columns, number of non-zero entries before and after reduction, time and memory used.

	Magma F_4	HB F_4	LASyzGB	Syzygy
rows	12413	14011	9086	3234
cols	8184	9782	11508	14938
nnz before	6074177	13183492	1087961	774396
nnz after	14258890	16051461	12961466	12448862
time(sec)	57.109	606.5	424.5	96.86
mem(MB)	60.2	456.1	339.2	241.7

Table 2: Comparison in matrix size time and memory between new algorithm and F_4.

Note that LASyzGB produces less rows but more columns than F_4. The number of non-zero entries before the reduction takes place is significantly smaller, yet after the reduction it is comparable. Both the time and memory effort are lower for the new algorithm.

The right-most column of Table 6.2 shows the same measures for the matrix that represents the degree five syzygies. Note that the time and memory efforts for this were relatively small compared to the reduction of the matrix that represents degree five polynomials.

6.3 Comparison with Faugère's F_5

We chose a smaller system in order to compare LASyz with available implementations of Faugère's F_5 [12]. We used a random degree 2 homogeneous overdetermined system of 10 polynomials in 8 variables with coefficients in $GF(2^8)$. We computed a Gröbner basis for the system using LASyz and two different implementations of Faugère's F_5, Stegers' [20] written for Magma and Eder and Perry's [9] written for Singular.

In summary, the execution of Stegers' F_5 reports that 506 polynomials were treated, 65314 pairs were avoided, the maximum degree of a critical pair was 16, the maximum degree of a polynomial was 12 and the total number of zero reductions was 138. The total running time was 44.80 seconds. Execution of Eder and Perry' F_5 run for more than 96 hours without terminating.

LASyz generated 1245 polynomials, the maximum degree of a polynomial was 5, the total number of zero reductions was 48 and 405 syzygies were used in avoiding the same number of zero reductions. Using the Magma implementation of LASyz, the total running time was 3.31. The C++ version was faster, terminating in 1.51 seconds.

6.4 A Standard Benchmark

Next we present results for Katsura 6 over $GF(7)$. It is important to note that this system does not have a zero dimensional solution thus the algorithm proposed in Section 4 does not terminate. It was necessary therefore to halt the algorithm artificially at degree 6, where we knew a Gröbner basis was obtained. Also, in this case we used the Magma implementation of LASyz, instead of the C++ implementation used in previous cases.

In summary, the execution of Stegers' F_5 reports that 74 polynomials were treated, 2519 pairs were avoided, the maximum degree of a critical pair was 7, the maximum degree of a polynomial was 7 and the total number of zero reductions was zero. The total running time was 0.469 seconds.

LASyz generated 1572 polynomials, the maximum degree of a polynomial was 6 and the total number of zero reductions was zero. 820 syzygies were used in avoiding the same number of zero reductions. Using the Magma implementation of LASyz, the total running time was 7.047 seconds.

6.5 Analysis of Experimental Results

The Experiments show that LASyz is effective in avoiding zero reductions. The small number of polynomials used in the HFE minus example clearly shows that a significant amount of redundancy is being avoided. Also, in the random example, we can observe a small number of rows compared with F_4.

For overdetermined systems the performance of the proposed algorithm is comparable to Faugère's F_4 and much better than Faugère's F_5. In such cases the incremental nature of F_5 militates against its performance. This is evidenced by the high degree of the operation. A matrix version of F_5 may perform better with overdetermined systems but it is still unknown to the authors the impact in performance of the restrictions in the linear algebra procedures.

LASyz exhibits a poor performance in the katsura benchmark compared to F_5. This is due to lack of a selection strategy, that would filter the polynomials used. Examples of such strategies are s-polynomials [3], symbolic preprocessing [11] and partial enlargement [17]. Other examples show a similar behavior. In order to get a more throughout comparison, it is desirable to use a more efficient implementation of the linear algebra procedures. We are working on optimizing our implementation.

7. CONCLUSIONS AND FUTURE WORK

We have introduced a new method to avoid reductions to zero in Gröbner basis computation called LASyz. We have proved that LASyz works correctly and it effectively uses trivial and non-trivial syzygies to avoid zero reductions. LASyz provides the first mechanism to avoid zero reductions in XL type algorithms that does not require an incremental computation. A comparison with previous alternatives highlights the benefits of the new approach.

LASyz can be used to study syzygies, which is important in algebraic geometry to study geometric properties of algebraic varieties.

A Gröbner basis algorithm based on LASyz was described and tested. The Experiments ratify that using LASyz for avoiding zero reductions is effective and that the use of sparse linear algebra makes it efficient. For overdetermined systems, the performance of the proposed algorithm is comparable to Faugère's F_4 and much better than Faugère's F_5.

LASyz does not replace the need for a selection strategy. We envision that LASyz can be combined with s-polynomial strategy or with any other heuristic method for partial enlargement.

We are making progress in establishing complexity bounds

for LASyz. A possible deficiency of LASyz stems from the lack of sparsity of non-trivial syzygies. LASyz can be adapted to overcome this issue by restricting the use of non-trivial syzygies to predict further syzygies. The resulting trade-off between accuracy and cost can be studied using the framework of this new method. The complexity can be studied thanks to the simplicity of the method. This direction shall be pursued in another paper.

Another possibility offered by the LASyz method is to track other level of syzygies. We can use the same strategy described in this paper, to manage syzygies of syzygies, and so on.

8. REFERENCES

[1] M. Bardet. *Étude des Systèmes Algébriques Surdéterminés. Applications aux Codes Correcteurs et à la Cryptographie*. PhD thesis, Université Paris VI, 2004.

[2] W. Bosma, J. Cannon, and C. Playoust. The Magma Algebra System. I. The User Language. *J. Symbolic Computation*, 24(3-4):235–265, 1997.

[3] B. Buchberger. *Ein Algorithmus zum Auffinden der Basiselemente des Restklassenringes nach einem nulldimensionalen Polynomideal (An Algorithm for Finding the Basis Elements in the Residue Class Ring Modulo a Zero Dimensional Polynomial Ideal)*. PhD thesis, Mathematical Institute, University of Innsbruck, Austria, 1965. (English translation in Journal of Symbolic Computation, 2004).

[4] B. Buchberger. A Criterion for Detecting Unnecessary Reductions in the Construction of Gröbner Bases. In *Proceedings of the EUROSAM 79 Symposium on Symbolic and Algebraic Manipulation*, volume 72 of *Lecture Notes in Computer Science*, pages 3–21. Springer, Berlin - Heidelberg - New York, 1979.

[5] J. Buchmann, D. Cabarcas, J. Ding, and M. S. E. Mohamed. Flexible Partial Enlargement to Accelerate Gröbner Basis Computation over $\mathbb{F}_2$. In *Progress in Cryptology – AFRICACRYPT 2010*, Lecture Notes in Computer Science. Springer-Verlag, Berlin, 2010.

[6] D. Cabarcas. An Implementation of Faugère's F_4 Algorithm for Computing Gröbner Bases. Master's thesis, University of Cincinnati, 2010.

[7] N. Courtois, A. Klimov, J. Patarin, and A. Shamir. Efficient Algorithms for Solving Overdefined Systems of Multivariate Polynomial Equations. In *Advances in Cryptology – EUROCRYPT 2000*, Lecture Notes in Computer Science, pages 392–407. Springer-Verlag, Berlin / Heidelberg, 2000.

[8] J. Ding, J. Buchmann, M. S. E. Mohamed, W. S. A. Moahmed, and R.-P. Weinmann. MutantXL. In *Proceedings of the First International Conference on Symbolic Computation and Cryptography (SCC08)*, pages 16 – 22. LMIB, 2008.

[9] C. Eder and J. Perry. Singular Implementation of Faugère's F5 Algorithm. Available online at http://www.math.usm.edu/perry/Research/f5 library.lib. v 1.1 2009/01/26.

[10] C. Eder and J. Perry. F5C: A Variant of Faugère's F5 algorithm with Reduced Gröbner Bases. *Journal of Symbolic Computation*, 45(12):1442 – 1458, 2010.

[11] J.-C. Faugère. A New Efficient Algorithm for

Computing Gröbner Bases (F_4). *Pure and Applied Algebra*, 139(1-3):61–88, June 1999.

[12] J.-C. Faugère. A New Efficient Algorithm for Computing Gröbner Bases Without Reduction to Zero (F_5). In *Proceedings of the 2002 International Symposium on Symbolic and Algebraic Computation (ISSAC)*, pages 75 – 83. ACM, July 2002.

[13] S. Gao, Y. Guan, and F. V. IV. A New Incremental Algorithm for Computing Groebner Bases. In *Proceedings of The 2010 International Symposium on Symbolic and Algebraic Computation (ISSAC)*. ACM, 2010.

[14] R. Gebauer and H. Möller. On an Installation of Buchberger's Algorithm. *Journal of Symbolic Computation*, 6(2-3):275–286, 1988.

[15] D. Lazard. Gröbner-Bases, Gaussian Elimination and Resolution of Systems of Algebraic Equations. In *EUROCAL '83: Proceedings of the European Computer Algebra Conference on Computer Algebra*, pages 146–156. Springer-Verlag, 1983.

[16] M. S. E. Mohamed, D. Cabarcas, J. Ding, J. Buchmann, and S. Bulygin. MXL3: An Efficient Algorithm for Computing Gröbner Bases of Zero-Dimensional Ideals. In *Proceedings of The 12th International Conference on Information Security and Cryptology, (ICISC 2009)*, Lecture Notes in Computer Science. Springer-Verlag, Berlin, 2009.

[17] M. S. E. Mohamed, W. S. A. E. Mohamed, J. Ding, and J. Buchmann. MXL2: Solving Polynomial Equations over GF(2) Using an Improved Mutant Strategy. In *Proceedings of The Second international Workshop on Post-Quantum Cryptography, (PQCrypto08)*, Lecture Notes in Computer Science, pages 203–215. Springer-Verlag, Berlin, 2008.

[18] H. Möller, F. Mora, and C. Traverso. Gröbner Bases Computation Using Syzygies. In *The 1992 International Symposium on Symbolic and Algebraic Computation (ISSAC)*, pages 320–328. ACM Press, 1992.

[19] J. Patarin. Hidden Fields Equations (HFE) and Isomorphisms of Polynomials (IP): Two New Families of Asymmetric Algorithms. In *Proceeding of International Conference on the Theory and Application of Cryptographic Techniques Advances in Cryptology- Eurocrypt*, volume 1070 of *Lecture Notes in Computer Science*, pages 33–48. Springer, 1996.

[20] T. Stegers. *Faugère's F5 Algorithm Revisited*. PhD thesis, Technische Universität Darmstadt, 2005.

Computing with Semi-Algebraic Sets Represented by Triangular Decomposition

Changbo Chen
University of Western Ontario
cchen252@csd.uwo.ca

James H. Davenport
University of Bath
J.H.Davenport@bath.ac.uk

Marc Moreno Maza
University of Western Ontario
moreno@csd.uwo.ca

Bican Xia
Peking University
xbc@math.pku.edu.cn

Rong Xiao
University of Western Ontario
rong@csd.uwo.ca

ABSTRACT

This article is a continuation of our earlier work [3], which introduced triangular decompositions of semi-algebraic systems and algorithms for computing them. Our new contributions include theoretical results based on which we obtain practical improvements for these decomposition algorithms.

We exhibit new results on the theory of *border polynomials* of parametric semi-algebraic systems: in particular a geometric characterization of its "true boundary" (Definition 2). In order to optimize these algorithms, we also propose a technique, that we call *relaxation*, which can simplify the decomposition process and reduce the number of redundant components in the output. Moreover, we present procedures for basic set-theoretical operations on semi-algebraic sets represented by triangular decomposition. Experimentation confirms the effectiveness of our techniques.

Categories and Subject Descriptors

I.1.2 [**Symbolic and Algebraic Manipulation**]: Algorithms—*Algebraic algorithms, Analysis of algorithms*

General Terms

Algorithms, Experimentation, Theory

Keywords

triangular decomposition, regular semi-algebraic system, border polynomial, effective boundary, relaxation

1. INTRODUCTION

Triangular decompositions of semi-algebraic systems were introduced in [3]. The key notions and notations of this paper are reviewed in the next section.

That paper presents also an algorithm for generating those decompositions. This algorithm can either be *eager*, computing the entire decomposition, or *lazy*, only computing

the decomposition corresponding to the highest (complex) dimensional components, and deferring lower-dimensional components. While a complete decomposition is known to have a worst-case complexity which is doubly-exponential in the number of variables [8], under plausible assumptions the lazy variant has a singly-exponential complexity. Nevertheless, it is still desirable to improve the practical efficiency of both types of decomposition.

The notion of a *border polynomial* [15] is at the core of our work. A strongly related notion, discriminant variety, was introduced in [9] and the link between them was investigated in [14]. Other similar but more restrictive notions like "generalised discriminant" and "generalised resultant" were introduced in [10]. For a squarefree regular chain T, regarded as a real parametric system in its free variables $\mathbf{u}$, the border polynomial $BP(T)$ encodes the locus of the $\mathbf{u}$-values at which T has lower rank or at which T is no longer a squarefree regular chain. (See §2 for the notions related to triangular decomposition and regular chains.) Consequently, for each connected component C of the complement of the real hypersurface defined by $BP(T)$ the number of real solutions of the regular chain T is constant at any point of C. However, $BP(T)$ is not an invariant of the variety $\overline{W(T)}$, which is a bottleneck in designing better algorithms based on the notion of a border polynomial. We overcome this difficulty in two ways.

Firstly, in §3, we prove that among all regular chains T' satisfying $\mathrm{sat}(T') = \mathrm{sat}(T)$ there is one and only one (characterized in Theorem 1) for which $BP(T')$ is minimal w.r.t. inclusion. Secondly, in §4, we introduce the concept of an *effective boundary* of a squarefree semi-algebraic system, see Definition 2. This allows us to identify a subset of $BP(T)$ which is an invariant of $\overline{W(T)}$, that is, unchanged when replacing T by T' as long as $\overline{W(T)} = \overline{W(T')}$ holds. In many ways, our notion of effective boundary is similar to the "better projection" ideas in the classical [7, and many others] approach to cylindrical algebraic decomposition.

In §5, we introduce the technique of *relaxation* which we shall motivate by an example. Consider the semi-algebraic system $sys = [f = 0, x - b > 0]$, where $f = ax^3 + bx - a$ for the variable ordering $a < b < x$. The LazyRealTriangularize algorithm of [3] will compute the border polynomial set $B = \{a, b_1, b_2\}$ and the fingerprint polynomial set (FPS) $F = \{a, b_1, b_2, b, p_1, p_2, p_3\}$. where $b_1 = ab^3 + b^2 - a$, $b_2 = 27a^3 + 4b^3$, $p_1 = 2b^3 + 1$, $p_2 = b^3 - 4$ and $p_3 = b - 1$. Thus the LazyRealTriangularize(sys) will produce 1 regular semi-algebraic system $S_1 = [Q_1, \{f = 0, x - b > 0\}]$, and 7 un-evaluated recursive calls, where

$$Q_1 = (b < 0 \wedge p_1 \neq 0 \wedge b_1 \neq 0 \wedge a \neq 0 \wedge b_2 \neq 0)$$
$$\vee (p_1 > 0 \wedge b_1 > 0 \wedge a < 0 \wedge p_3 > 0 \wedge p_2 \neq 0 \wedge b_2 \neq 0)$$
$$\vee (b > 0 \wedge p_1 > 0 \wedge b_1 \neq 0 \wedge a < 0 \wedge p_3 < 0 \wedge p_2 < 0 \wedge b_2 \neq 0)$$
$$\vee (b > 0 \wedge p_1 > 0 \wedge b_1 < 0 \wedge a > 0 \wedge p_3 < 0 \wedge p_2 < 0 \wedge b_2 > 0)$$

and the 7 calls are made for each $p \in F$ with the form LazyRealTriangularize($[p = 0, f = 0, x - b > 0]$). The key observation is that some of these recursive calls can simply be avoided if some of the strict inequalities in Q_1 can be relaxed, that is, replaced by non-strict inequalities. The results of §5, and in particular Theorem 5 provide criteria for this purpose. Returning to our example, when relaxation techniques are used LazyRealTriangularize(sys) will produce 1 regular semi-algebraic system $S_2 = [Q_2, \{f = 0, x - b > 0\}]$, and 3 un-evaluated recursive calls, where

$$Q_2 = (b \leq 0 \wedge b_1 \neq 0 \wedge a \neq 0 \wedge b_2 \neq 0)$$
$$\vee (p_1 \geq 0 \wedge b_1 > 0 \wedge a < 0 \wedge p_3 \geq 0 \wedge b_2 \neq 0)$$
$$\vee (b \geq 0 \wedge p_1 \geq 0 \wedge b_1 \neq 0 \wedge a < 0 \wedge p_3 \leq 0 \wedge p_2 \leq 0 \wedge b_2 \neq 0)$$
$$\vee (b \geq 0 \wedge p_1 \geq 0 \wedge b_1 < 0 \wedge a > 0 \wedge p_3 \leq 0 \wedge p_2 \leq 0 \wedge b_2 > 0)$$

Moreover, it turns that the the 3 un-evaluated recursive calls are of the form LazyRealTriangularize($[p = 0, f = 0, x - b > 0]$), for $p \in B$. Continuing with that example, one can check that the full triangular decomposition of sys produces 16 and 9 regular semi-algebraic systems, without and with relaxation techniques, respectively. Therefore, relaxation techniques can help simplify the output of our algorithms.

Nevertheless, even with relaxation techniques, our algorithms can produce redundant components, that is, a regular semi-algebraic system S for which there exists another regular semi-algebraic system S' in the same decomposition and such that $Z_\mathbb{R}(S) \subseteq Z_\mathbb{R}(S')$ holds. This is actually the case for our example where 1 out of the 9 regular semi-algebraic systems is redundant.

To perform inclusion test on the zero sets of regular semi-algebraic systems, we have developed algorithms for set-theoretical operations on semi-algebraic sets represented by triangular decomposition, see §7. Those algorithms rely on a new algorithm, presented in §6, for computing triangular decomposition of semi-algebraic systems in an incremental manner, which is a natural adaption of the idea presented in [11] for computing triangular decomposition of algebraic systems incrementally.

The experimentation illustrates the effectiveness of the different techniques presented in this paper. In particular, we observe that with relaxation, the decomposition algorithm will produce output with less redundancy without paying a lot, and accelerate on some hard systems; the incremental algorithm for computing triangular decomposition of semi-algebraic systems often outperforms the one in [3]. Moreover, we observe that our techniques for removing redundant components can usually process in a "reasonable" amount time the output of the systems that RealTriangularize can decompose.

2. TRIANGULAR DECOMPOSITION

We summarize below the notions and notations of [3], including triangular decompositions of semi-algebraic systems.

Zero sets and topology. In this paper, we use "Z" to denote the zero set of a polynomial system, involving equations and inequations, in $\mathbb{C}^n$ and "$Z_\mathbb{R}$" to denote the zero set of a semi-algebraic system in $\mathbb{R}^n$. If a semi-algebraic set S is finite, we denote by $\#(S)$ the number of distinct points in it. In $\mathbb{R}^n$, we use the Euclidean topology; in $\mathbb{C}^n$, we use the Zariski topology. Given a semi-algebraic set S, we denote by ∂S the boundary of S, by $\overline{S}$ the closure of S.

Notations on polynomials. Throughout this paper, all polynomials are in $\mathbb{Q}[\mathbf{x}]$, with ordered variables $\mathbf{x} = x_1 < \cdots < x_n$. We order monomials of $\mathbb{Q}[\mathbf{x}]$ by the lexicographical ordering induced by $x_1 < \cdots < x_n$. Then, we require that the leading coefficient of every polynomial in a regular chain or in a border polynomial set (defined hereafter) is equal to 1. Let $F \subset \mathbb{Q}[\mathbf{x}]$. We denote by $V(F)$ the set of common zeros of F in $\mathbb{C}^n$. Let p be a polynomial in $\mathbb{Q}[\mathbf{x}] \setminus \mathbb{Q}$. Then denote by mvar($p$), init($p$), and mdeg($p$) respectively the greatest variable appearing in p (called the *main variable* of p), the leading coefficient of p w.r.t. mvar(p) (called the *initial* of p), and the degree of p w.r.t. mvar(p) (called the *main degree* of p). Let $v \in \mathbf{x}$. Denote by lc(p, v), deg(p, v), der(p, v), discrim(p, v) respectively the leading coefficient, the degree, the derivative and the discriminant of p w.r.t. v.

Triangular set. Let $T \subset \mathbb{Q}[\mathbf{x}]$ be a *triangular set*, that is, a set of non-constant polynomials with pairwise distinct main variables. Denote by mvar(T) the set of main variables of the polynomials in T. A variable v in $\mathbf{x}$ is called *algebraic* w.r.t. T if $v \in$ mvar(T), otherwise it is said *free* w.r.t. T. If no confusion is possible, we shall always denote by $\mathbf{u} = u_1, \ldots, u_d$ and $\mathbf{y} = y_1, \ldots, y_m$ ($m + d = n$) respectively the free and the main variables of T. When T is regarded as a *parametric system*, the free variables in T are its parameters.

Let h_T be the product of the initials of the polynomials in T. We denote by sat(T) the *saturated ideal* of T: if T is the empty triangular set, then sat(T) is defined as the trivial ideal $\langle 0 \rangle$, otherwise it is the colon ideal $\langle T \rangle : h_T^\infty$. The *quasi-component* $W(T)$ of T is defined as $V(T) \setminus V(h_T)$. Denote by $\overline{W(T)}$ the Zariski closure of $W(T)$, which is equal to $V($sat(T)$)$. Denote by $W_\mathbb{R}(T)$ the set $Z_\mathbb{R}(T) \setminus Z_\mathbb{R}(h_T)$.

Iterated resultant. Let $p, q \in \mathbb{Q}[\mathbf{x}] \setminus \mathbb{Q}$. Let $v = $ mvar(q). Denote by res(p, q, v) the resultant of p, q w.r.t. v. Let $T \subset \mathbb{Q}[\mathbf{x}]$ be a triangular set. We define res(p, T) inductively: if T is empty, then res(p, T) $= p$; otherwise let v be the largest variable occurring in T, then res(p, T) $=$ res(res(p, T_v, v), $T_{<v}$), where T_v and $T_{<v}$ denote respectively the polynomials of T with main variables equal to and less than v.

Regular chain. A triangular set $T \subset \mathbb{Q}[\mathbf{x}]$ is called a *regular chain* if: either T is empty; or (letting t be the polynomial in T with maximum main variable), $T \setminus \{t\}$ is a regular chain, and the initial of t is regular w.r.t. sat($T \setminus \{t\}$). Let $H \subset \mathbb{Q}[\mathbf{x}]$. The pair $[T, H]$ is a *regular system* if each polynomial in H is regular modulo sat(T). A regular chain T or a regular system $[T, H]$, is *squarefree* if for all $t \in T$, der(t) is regular w.r.t. sat(T). Given $u \in \mathbb{R}^d$, we say that a squarefree regular system $[T, H]$ *specializes well* at u if $h_T(u) \neq 0$ and $[T(u), H(u)]$ is a squarefree regular system. A regular chain is called d-*dimensional* if it has d free variables.

Semi-algebraic system. Consider four finite polynomial sets $F = \{f_1, \ldots, f_s\}$, $N = \{n_1, \ldots, n_k\}$, $P = \{p_1, \ldots, p_e\}$, and $H = \{h_1, \ldots, h_\ell\}$ of $\mathbb{Q}[\mathbf{x}]$. Let $N_\geq$ denote the set of non-negative inequalities $\{n_1 \geq 0, \ldots, n_k \geq 0\}$. Let $P_>$ denote the set of positive inequalities $\{p_1 > 0, \ldots, p_e > 0\}$. Let

$H_{\neq}$ denote the set of inequations $\{h_1 \neq 0, \ldots, h_\ell \neq 0\}$. We denote by $\mathfrak{S} = [F, N_\geq, P_>, H_\neq]$ the *semi-algebraic system* (SAS) defined as the conjunction of the constraints $f_1 = \cdots f_s = 0$, $N_\geq$, $P_>$, $H_\neq$. When $N_\geq$, $H_\neq$ are empty, $\mathfrak{S}$ is called a *basic semi-algebraic system* and denoted by $[F, P_>]$.

Regular semi-algebraic system. We call a basic SAS $[T, P_>]$ in $\mathbb{Q}[\mathbf{u}, \mathbf{y}]$ a squarefree semi-algebraic system, SFSAS for short, if $[T, P]$ forms a squarefree regular system. Let $[T, P_>]$ be an SFSAS. Let $\mathcal{Q}$ be a quantifier-free formula of $\mathbb{Q}[\mathbf{u}]$. We say that $R := [\mathcal{Q}, T, P_>]$ is a *regular semi-algebraic system* if
  (i) $\mathcal{Q}$ defines a non-empty open semi-algebraic set S in $\mathbb{R}^d$;
  (ii) $[T, P]$ specializes well at every point of S,
  (iii) at each $u \in S$, the specialized system $[T(u), P(u)_>]$ has at least one real zero.

Border polynomial [15, 16, 3]. We review briefly the notion of *border polynomial* of a regular chain, a regular system, or an SFSAS. Let R be either a squarefree regular chain T, or a squarefree regular system $[T, P]$, or an SFSAS $[T, P_>]$ in $\mathbb{Q}[\mathbf{x}]$. We denote by $B_{sep}(T)$, $B_{ini}(T)$, $B_{ineqs}([T, P])$ the set of irreducible factors of: $\prod_{t \in T} \mathrm{res}(\mathrm{discrim}(t, \mathrm{mvar}(t)), T)$, $\prod_{t \in T} \mathrm{res}(\mathrm{init}(t), T)$, and $\prod_{f \in P} \mathrm{res}(f, T)$, respectively. Denote by $\mathrm{BP}(R)$ the set $B_{sep}(T) \cup B_{ini}(T) \cup B_{ineqs}([T, P])$. Then $\mathrm{BP}(R)$ (resp. the polynomial $\prod_{f \in \mathrm{BP}(R)} f$) is called the *border polynomial set* (resp. *border polynomial*) of R.

LEMMA 1 (LEMMA 2 IN [3]). *Let $R = [T, P_>]$ be an SFSAS of $\mathbb{Q}[\mathbf{x}]$. Let u_1, u_2 be two parameter values in a same connected component of $Z_{\mathbb{R}}(\prod_{f \in \mathrm{BP}(R)} f \neq 0)$ in $\mathbb{R}^d$. Then $\#Z_{\mathbb{R}}(R(u_1)) = \#Z_{\mathbb{R}}(R(u_2))$.*

Fingerprint polynomial set. $R = [B_{\neq}, T, P_>]$ is called a *pre-regular semi-algebraic system*, if for each $p \in \mathrm{BP}([T, P_>])$, p is a factor of some polynomial in B. Suppose R is a pre-regular semi-algebraic system. A polynomial set $D \subset \mathbb{Q}[\mathbf{u}]$ is called a *fingerprint polynomial set* (FPS) of R if:
  (i) $Z_{\mathbb{R}}(D_{\neq}) \subseteq Z_{\mathbb{R}}(B_{\neq})$ holds,
  (ii) for all $\alpha, \beta \in Z_{\mathbb{R}}(D_{\neq})$ with $\alpha \neq \beta$, if the signs of $p(\alpha)$ and $p(\beta)$ are the same for all $p \in D$, then $R(\alpha)$ has real solutions if and only if $R(\beta)$ does.

Open CAD operator [12, 2, 3]. Let $\mathbf{u} = u_1 < \cdots < u_d$ be ordered variables. For a polynomial $p \in \mathbb{Q}[\mathbf{u}]$, denote by $\mathrm{factor}(p)$ the set of the non-constant irreducible factors of p; for $A \subset \mathbb{Q}[\mathbf{u}]$, define $\mathrm{factor}(A) = \cup_{p \in A} \mathrm{factor}(p)$. For a squarefree polynomial p, the *open projection operator* (oproj) w.r.t. a variable $v \in \mathbf{u}$ is defined as below:

$$\mathrm{oproj}(p, v) := \mathrm{factor}(\mathrm{discrim}(p, v) \, \mathrm{lc}(p, v)).$$

If p is not squarefree, then we define $\mathrm{oproj}(p, v) := \mathrm{oproj}(p^*, v)$, where p^* is the squarefree part of p; then for a polynomial set A, we define $\mathrm{oproj}(A, v) := \mathrm{oproj}(\Pi_{f \in A} f, v)$.

Given $A \subset \mathbb{Q}[\mathbf{u}]$ and $x \in \{u_1, \ldots, u_d\}$, denote by $\mathrm{der}(A, x)$ the *derivative closure* of A w.r.t. x. The *open augmented projected factors* of A, denoted by $\mathrm{oaf}(A)$, is defined as follows. Let k be the smallest positive integer such that $A \subset \mathbb{Q}[u_1, \ldots, u_k]$ holds. Let $C = \mathrm{factor}(\mathrm{der}(A, u_k))$; we have:
  1. if $k = 1$, then $\mathrm{oaf}(A) := C$;
  2. if $k > 1$, then $\mathrm{oaf}(A) := C \cup \mathrm{oaf}(\mathrm{oproj}(C, u_k))$.

3. BORDER POLYNOMIAL

The relation "having the same saturated ideal" is an equivalence relation among regular chains of $\mathbb{Q}[\mathbf{x}]$. We show in this section that, for each equivalence class, there exists a unique representative whose border polynomial set is contained in the border polynomial set of any other representative.

To this end, we rely on the concept of *canonical regular chain*. In the field of triangular decompositions, several authors have used this term to refer to different notions. To be precise, we make use of the one defined in [13].

DEFINITION 1 (CANONICAL REGULAR CHAIN). *Let T be a regular chain of $\mathbb{Q}[\mathbf{x}]$. If each polynomial t of T satisfies:*
  1. *the initial of t involves only the free variables of T,*
  2. *for any polynomial $f \in T$ with $\mathrm{mvar}(f) < \mathrm{mvar}(t)$, we have $\deg(t, \mathrm{mvar}(f)) < \mathrm{mdeg}(f)$,*
  3. *t is primitive over $\mathbb{Q}$, w.r.t. its main variable,*
then we say that T is canonical.

REMARK 1. *Let $T = \{t_1, \cdots, t_m\}$ be a regular chain; let $d_k = \mathrm{mdeg}(t_k)$, for $k = 1 \cdots m$. One constructs a canonical regular chain $T^* = \{t_1^*, t_2^*, \ldots, t_m^*\}$ such that $\mathrm{sat}(T) = \mathrm{sat}(T^*)$ in the following way:*
  1. *set t_1^* to be the primitive part of t_1 w.r.t. y_1;*
  2. *for $k = 2, \ldots, m$, let r_k be the iterated resultant $\mathrm{res}(\mathrm{init}(t_k), \{t_1, \ldots, t_{k-1}\})$. Suppose $r_k = a_k \mathrm{init}(t_k) + \sum_{i=1}^{k-1} c_i t_i$. Compute t as the pseudo-reminder of $a_k t_k + (\sum_{i=1}^{k-1} c_i t_i) y_k^{d_k}$ by $\{t_1^*, \ldots, t_{k-1}^*\}$. Set t_k^* to be the primitive part of t w.r.t. y_k.*

A canonical regular chain has the minimal border polynomial set among the family of regular chains having the same saturated ideal, which is stated in the following theorem.

THEOREM 1. *Given a squarefree regular chains T of $\mathbb{Q}[\mathbf{x}]$, there exists a unique canonical regular chain T^* such that $\mathrm{sat}(T) = \mathrm{sat}(T^*)$. Moreover, we have $\mathrm{BP}(T^*) \subseteq \mathrm{BP}(T)$.*

The proof of the above theorem relies on some basic properties of border polynomial set recalled below.

Given a constructible set $\mathcal{C}$ defined by a parametric polynomial system, *the minimal discriminant variety* (MDV) [9] of $\mathcal{C}$, denoted by $\mathrm{mdv}(\mathcal{C})$, is an intrinsic geometric object attached to $\mathcal{C}$ and the parameters. The following results relate the border polynomial of a regular chains T and the discriminant variety of the algebraic variety $V(T)$.

LEMMA 2 ([14]). *Let T be a squarefree regular chain of $\mathbb{Q}[\mathbf{u}, \mathbf{y}]$. Then we have $\mathrm{mdv}(V(T)) = V(\prod_{f \in \mathrm{BP}(T)} f)$.*

LEMMA 3 ([14, LEMMA 17]). *Let T be a squarefree regular chain of $\mathbb{Q}[\mathbf{u}, \mathbf{y}]$. Then we have $\mathrm{mdv}(\overline{W(T)}) \subseteq \mathrm{mdv}(V(T))$ and $\mathrm{mdv}(V(T)) \setminus \mathrm{mdv}(\overline{W(T)}) \subseteq V(\prod_{f \in B_{ini}(T)} f)$.*

LEMMA 4. *Let T_1 and T_2 be squarefree regular chains of $\mathbf{k}[\mathbf{x}]$ such that $\mathrm{sat}(T_1) = \mathrm{sat}(T_2)$. If $B_{ini}(T_1) \subseteq B_{ini}(T_2)$, then we have $\mathrm{BP}(T_1) \subseteq \mathrm{BP}(T_2)$.*

PROOF. Firstly, we have $V(\prod_{f \in B_{ini}(T_i)} f) \subseteq \mathrm{mdv}(V(T_i))$ by Lemma 2. Then with Lemma 3, we have $\mathrm{mdv}(V(T_i)) = V(\prod_{f \in B_{ini}(T_i)} f) \cup \mathrm{mdv}(\overline{W(T_i)})$. Since $\mathrm{sat}(T_1) = \mathrm{sat}(T_2)$, we have $\overline{W(T_1)} = \overline{W(T_2)}$. Therefore we have $\mathrm{mdv}(V(T_2)) \subseteq \mathrm{mdv}(V(T_1))$ by the assumption $B_{ini}(T_1) \subseteq B_{ini}(T_2)$, which implies the lemma. $\square$

Next we prove Theorem 1.

PROOF. By Remark 1, we can always construct a canonical regular chain T^* such that $\mathrm{sat}(T) = \mathrm{sat}(T^*)$. Moreover, for each $t \in T$, we have $\mathrm{init}(t^*)$ divides $\mathrm{res}(\mathrm{init}(t), T)$. Therefore, $B_{ini}(T^*) \subseteq B_{ini}(T)$ holds, which implies $\mathrm{BP}(T^*) \subseteq \mathrm{BP}(T)$ by Lemma 4.

Suppose $T^\diamond$ is any given canonical regular chain such that $\mathrm{sat}(T^\diamond) = \mathrm{sat}(T)$ holds. It is sufficient to show that $T^* = T^\diamond$ holds to complete the proof.

Note that $T^\diamond$, T^* and T have the same set of free and algebraic variables, denoted respectively by $\mathbf{u}$ and $\mathbf{y}$. Given $\mathcal{I}$ an ideal in $\mathbb{Q}[\mathbf{u}, \mathbf{y}]$, denote by $\mathcal{I}^{ext}$ the extension of $\mathcal{I}$ in $\mathbb{Q}(\mathbf{u})[\mathbf{y}]$. Since $\mathfrak{p}^{ext} = \langle 1 \rangle$ holds for any prime ideal $\mathfrak{p}$ in $\mathbb{Q}[\mathbf{u}, \mathbf{y}]$ with $\mathbf{u}$ algebraically dependent, we have $\langle T^* \rangle^{ext} = \langle T^\diamond \rangle^{ext} = \mathrm{sat}(T)^{ext}$ holds. Therefore, the polynomials in T^* (or $T^\diamond$) form a Gröbner basis of $\mathrm{sat}(T)^{ext}$ (w.r.t. the lexicographical ordering on $\mathbf{y}$) since their leading power products are pairwise coprime. Dividing each polynomial in T^* (or $T^\diamond$) by its initial, we obtain the unique reduced Gröbner basis of $\mathrm{sat}(T)^{ext}$. This implies $T^* = T^\diamond$. $\square$

4. EFFECTIVE BOUNDARY AND FPS

In this subsection, we will focus on an SFSAS $\mathfrak{S} = [T, P_>]$ in $\mathbb{Q}[\mathbf{u}, \mathbf{y}]$ where $\mathbf{u} = u_1, \dots, u_d$ are the free variables of T.

DEFINITION 2 (EFFECTIVE BOUNDARY). *Let $\mathbf{h}$ be a $(d-1)$-dimensional hypersurface in the parameter space $\mathbb{R}^d$ of $\mathfrak{S}$. We call $\mathbf{h}$ an effective boundary of $\mathfrak{S}$ if for every hypersurface $\mathcal{H} \not\supseteq \mathbf{h}$ in $\mathbb{R}^d$, there exists a point u^* in $\mathbf{h} \setminus \mathcal{H}$ satisfying: for any open ball $O(u^*)$ of u^*, there exist two points α_1, $\alpha_2 \in O(u^*) \setminus \mathbf{h}$, s.t. $\#Z_{\mathbb{R}}(\mathfrak{S}(\alpha_1)) \neq \#Z_{\mathbb{R}}(\mathfrak{S}(\alpha_2))$. Denote by $\mathcal{E}(\mathfrak{S})$ the union of all effective boundaries of $\mathfrak{S}$.*

Recall that the hypersurface defined by the border polynomial of an SFSAS partitions the parametric space into regions, where the number of real solutions is locally invariant. One might imagine that the effective boundaries are strongly related to the border polynomial set. Indeed, we have the following Lemma stating the relation.

LEMMA 5. *We have $\mathcal{E}(\mathfrak{S}) \subseteq Z_{\mathbb{R}}(\prod_{f \in \mathrm{BP}(\mathfrak{S})} f = 0)$.*

PROOF. Let $\mathbf{h} \in \mathcal{E}(\mathfrak{S})$ such that $\mathbf{h} \not\subseteq Z_{\mathbb{R}}(\prod_{f \in \mathrm{BP}(\mathfrak{S})} f = 0)$ holds. Then for each $u \in \mathbf{h} \setminus Z_{\mathbb{R}}(\prod_{f \in \mathrm{BP}(\mathfrak{S})} f = 0)$, we can choose an open ball $O(u)$ of u contained in a connected component of the set $Z_{\mathbb{R}}(\prod_{f \in B} f \neq 0)$. By Lemma 1, for any two points $\alpha_1, \alpha_2 \in O(u)$, $\#Z_{\mathbb{R}}(\mathfrak{S}(\alpha_1)) = \#Z_{\mathbb{R}}(\mathfrak{S}(\alpha_2))$ holds. That is a contradiction to the assumption of $\mathbf{h}$ being an effective boundary. $\square$

Lemma 5 implies that the set of effective boundaries represented by irreducible polynomials of $\mathbb{Q}[\mathbf{u}]$ is finite and can be given by polynomials from the border polynomial set.

DEFINITION 3. *A polynomial p in $\mathrm{BP}(\mathfrak{S})$ is called an effective border polynomial factor if $Z_{\mathbb{R}}(p = 0)$ is an effective boundary of $\mathfrak{S}$. We denote by $\mathrm{ebf}(\mathfrak{S})$ the set of effective border polynomial factors.*

The example below shows that some of the polynomials in a border polynomial may not be effective. Roughly speaking, the factors in B_{ini} are not effective. This property is formally stated in a soon coming extended version of this article.

EXAMPLE 1. *Consider an SFSAS $R = [\{ax^2 + bx + 1\}, \{ \ \}]$. Its border polynomial set is $\{a, b^2 - 4a\}$. One can verify from Figure 1 that $Z_{\mathbb{R}}(b^2 - 4a = 0)$ is an effective boundary of R, while $Z_{\mathbb{R}}(a = 0)$ is not. Indeed, all a, b-values in the blank (resp. filled) area specialize R to have 2 (resp. 0) real solutions.*

Figure 1: Effective and non-effective boundary

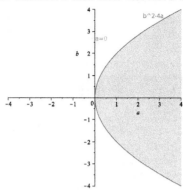

Since $\mathcal{E}(\mathfrak{S})$ can be described by border polynomial factors, we derive the following theorem, which can be viewed as a "computable-version" of Definition 2.

THEOREM 2. *A polynomial p in $\mathrm{BP}(\mathfrak{S})$ is an effective border polynomial factor if and only if there exist two connected components C_1, C_2 of $Z_{\mathbb{R}}(\prod_{f \in \mathrm{BP}(\mathfrak{S})} f \neq 0)$ satisfying*
(1) $\partial C_1 \cap \partial C_2 \cap Z_{\mathbb{R}}(p = 0)$ is of dimension $d-1$,
(2) for all point $\alpha_1 \in C_1$ and for all point $\alpha_2 \in C_2$ we have $\#Z_{\mathbb{R}}(\mathfrak{S}(\alpha_1)) \neq \#Z_{\mathbb{R}}(\mathfrak{S}(\alpha_2))$.

PROOF. "$\Rightarrow$". Suppose p is an effective border polynomial factor. By definition, there exists a point $u^* \in Z_{\mathbb{R}}(p = 0) \setminus Z_{\mathbb{R}}(\prod_{f \in \mathrm{BP}(\mathfrak{S}) \setminus \{p\}} f = 0)$ and a sufficiently small open ball $O(u^*)$ centered at u^* satisfying the properties below:
(i) $O(u^*) \setminus Z_{\mathbb{R}}(p = 0) \subseteq Z_{\mathbb{R}}(\prod_{f \in \mathrm{BP}(\mathfrak{S})} f \neq 0)$;
(ii) $O(u^*) \cap Z_{\mathbb{R}}(\prod_{f \in \mathrm{ebf}(\mathfrak{S})} f = 0) \subseteq Z_{\mathbb{R}}(p = 0)$;
(iii) there exist two points α_1, α_2 in $O(u^*) \setminus Z_{\mathbb{R}}(p = 0)$, such that we have $\#Z_{\mathbb{R}}(\mathfrak{S}(\alpha_1)) \neq \#Z_{\mathbb{R}}(\mathfrak{S}(\alpha_2))$;
(iv) $O(u^*) \setminus Z_{\mathbb{R}}(p = 0) = O(u^*) \cap C_1 \cup O(u^*) \cap C_2$, where C_i is the connected component of $Z_{\mathbb{R}}(\prod_{f \in \mathrm{BP}(\mathfrak{S})} f \neq 0)$ containing α_i, for $i = 1, 2$.

Property (iv) can be achieved by imposing that $Z_{\mathbb{R}}(p = 0)$ is not singular at u^*. Property (iii) and Lemma 1 imply that $O(u^*) \setminus Z_{\mathbb{R}}(p = 0)$ is not a connected set. Since $O(u^*)$ is an open ball, we deduce that $O(u^*) \cap Z_{\mathbb{R}}(p = 0)$ must be $d-1$ dimensional. Then Property (iv) implies $O(u^*) \cap Z_{\mathbb{R}}(p = 0) = \overline{O(u^*) \cap C_1} \cap \overline{O(u^*) \cap C_2}$. and $\overline{O(u^*) \cap C_i} = \overline{O(u^*)} \cap \overline{C_i}$ for $i = 1, 2$. Therefore, we have: $O(u^*) \cap Z_{\mathbb{R}}(p = 0) \subseteq (\partial C_1 \cap \partial C_2) \cap Z_{\mathbb{R}}(p = 0)$. Hence $(\partial C_1 \cap \partial C_2) \cap Z_{\mathbb{R}}(p = 0)$ is also of dimension $d-1$.

"$\Leftarrow$". Suppose there exist two connected components C_1, C_2 of $Z_{\mathbb{R}}(\prod_{f \in \mathrm{BP}(\mathfrak{S})} f \neq 0)$ satisfying the above (1) and (2) in the theorem statement. Let $\mathcal{H}$ be a hypersurface with $\mathcal{H} \not\supseteq Z_{\mathbb{R}}(p = 0)$. Since the dimension of $(\mathcal{H} \cup Z_{\mathbb{R}}(\prod_{f \in \mathrm{BP}(\mathfrak{S}) \setminus \{p\}} f = 0)) \cap Z_{\mathbb{R}}(p = 0)$ cannot be $d-1$, the set S defined by

$$(\partial C_1 \cap \partial C_2 \cap Z_{\mathbb{R}}(p = 0)) \setminus \left(\mathcal{H} \cup Z_{\mathbb{R}}\left(\prod_{f \in \mathrm{BP}(\mathfrak{S}) \setminus \{p\}} f = 0 \right) \right)$$

is not empty. Let u^* be a point of S. Any open ball $O(u^*)$ centered at u^* contains at least one point α_1 (resp. α_2) from C_1 (resp. C_2). From (2) we deduce $\#Z_{\mathbb{R}}(\mathfrak{S}(\alpha_1)) \neq \#Z_{\mathbb{R}}(\mathfrak{S}(\alpha_2))$. That is, $Z_{\mathbb{R}}(p = 0)$ is an effective boundary according to Definition 2. $\square$

The above theorem suggests some practical ways to compute the effective border polynomial factors, using the adjacency information and sample points of the connected components of $Z_\mathbb{R}(\prod_{f \in \mathrm{BP}(\mathfrak{S})} \neq 0)$.

COROLLARY 1. *If two points $\alpha_1, \alpha_2 \in Z_\mathbb{R}(\prod_{f \in \mathrm{BP}(\mathfrak{S})} f \neq 0)$ are in the same connected component of the complement of $\mathcal{E}(\mathfrak{S})$, then $\#Z_\mathbb{R}(\mathfrak{S}(\alpha_1)) = \#Z_\mathbb{R}(\mathfrak{S}(\alpha_2))$ holds.*

PROOF. Let C be a connected component of the complement of $\mathcal{E}(\mathfrak{S})$. Observe that $C \setminus Z_\mathbb{R}(\prod_{f \in \mathrm{BP}(\mathfrak{S})} f = 0)$ is the union of a finite set $\mathcal{O}$ of connected components of $Z_\mathbb{R}(\prod_{f \in \mathrm{BP}(\mathfrak{S})} f \neq 0)$. Indeed, $\mathcal{E}(\mathfrak{S}) \subseteq Z_\mathbb{R}(\prod_{f \in \mathrm{BP}(\mathfrak{S})} f = 0)$ holds by Lemma 5. If $\mathcal{O}$ contains only one element, the conclusion is trivially true.

Assume from now that $\mathcal{O}$ contains more than one elements. We can number the elements of $\mathcal{O}$ such that for any two elements with consecutive numbers, say C_i, C_{i+1}, the dimension of $\partial C_i \cap \partial C_{i+1}$ is $d - 1$. Proceeding by contradiction, assume that the conclusion of the corollary is false. Thus, there exist two consecutive elements of $\mathcal{O}$, say C_i, C_{i+1}, and two points $\alpha_i \in C_i$, $\alpha_{i+1} \in C_{i+1}$, such that $\#Z_\mathbb{R}(\mathfrak{S}(\alpha_i)) \neq \#Z_\mathbb{R}(\mathfrak{S}(\alpha_{i+1}))$ holds. Since C lies in the complement of $\mathcal{E}(\mathfrak{S})$, there exists a non-effective border polynomial factor p such that $\partial C_i \cap \partial C_{i+1} \subseteq Z_\mathbb{R}(p = 0)$ holds. However, this also implies that p is an effective border polynomial factor by Theorem 2, which is a contradiction. $\square$

Given a pre-regular system $R = [B_{\neq}, T, P_>]$, we can rely on $\mathrm{ebf}([T, P_>])$ to compute an FPS of R rather than B (which is often much larger than $\mathrm{ebf}([T, P_>])$).

THEOREM 3. *Given a pre-regular system $R = [B_{\neq}, T, P_>]$, let $D = \mathrm{oaf}(\mathrm{ebf}([T, P_>]))$. Then $D \cup B$ is an FPS of R.*

PROOF. By Theorem 3 in [3] on the property of the oaf operator, each realizable strict sign conditions on D defines a connected components of $Z_\mathbb{R}(\prod_{f \in D} f \neq 0)$. Therefore, for any two points $\alpha_1, \alpha_2 \in Z_\mathbb{R}(\prod_{f \in B} f \neq 0)$ satisfying the same realizable sign condition of D, we have $\#Z_\mathbb{R}(R(\alpha_1)) = \#Z_\mathbb{R}(R(\alpha_2))$ by Corollary 1. Hence $D \cup B$ is an FPS of R by definition. $\square$

THEOREM 4. *Given two SFSASes $R_1 = [T_1, P_>]$ and $R_2 = [T_2, P_>]$ with $\mathrm{sat}(T_1) = \mathrm{sat}(T_2)$, then $\mathcal{E}(R_1) = \mathcal{E}(R_2)$ holds.*

PROOF. Let $B = \mathrm{BP}(R_1) \cup \mathrm{BP}(R_2)$ and let $\mathbf{h}$ be an effective boundary of R_1 defined by a polynomial p in $\mathrm{BP}(R_1)$. Let $\mathcal{H} \not\supseteq \mathbf{h}$ be any hypersurface and denote by S the set $\mathbf{h} \setminus \left(Z_\mathbb{R}(\prod_{f \in B \setminus \{p\}} f = 0) \cup \mathcal{H} \right)$. Observe that S is not empty.

We can find a point $u^* \in S$ satisfying: for any open ball $O(u^*)$ centered at u^*, there exist two points $\alpha_1, \alpha_2 \in O(u^*) \setminus \mathbf{h}$, such that $\#Z_\mathbb{R}(R_1(\alpha_1)) \neq \#Z_\mathbb{R}(R_1(\alpha_2))$ holds.

Since $\mathrm{sat}(T_1) = \mathrm{sat}(T_2)$ holds, for all $u \in Z_\mathbb{R}(\prod_{f \in B} f \neq 0)$, we have $Z_\mathbb{R}(R_1(u)) = Z_\mathbb{R}(R_2(u))$. When an open ball O at u^* is sufficiently small, $O \cap Z_\mathbb{R}(\prod_{f \in B \setminus p} f = 0) = \emptyset$ holds. Therefore, $Z_\mathbb{R}(R_1(u)) = Z_\mathbb{R}(R_2(u))$ holds for any $u \in O \setminus \mathbf{h}$.

From the above arguments and Definition 2, we deduce that $\mathbf{h}$ is also an effective boundary of R_2. This shows $\mathcal{E}(R_1) \subseteq \mathcal{E}(R_2)$. Similarly $\mathcal{E}(R_1) \supseteq \mathcal{E}(R_2)$ can be proved. $\square$

Let $R = [T, P_>]$, $R_i = [T_i, P_>]$ $(i = 1, 2)$ be three SFSASes with $\mathrm{sat}(T) = \mathrm{sat}(T_1) \cap \mathrm{sat}(T_2)$. One can prove that $\mathcal{E}(R) \subseteq \mathcal{E}(R_1) \cup \mathcal{E}(R_2)$ holds. Moreover, one can prove that $\mathrm{ebf}(R_1) \cap \mathrm{ebf}(R_2) = \emptyset$ implies $\mathcal{E}(R) = \mathcal{E}(R_1) \cup \mathcal{E}(R_2)$. These results and their proofs will appear in an extended version of this article.

5. RELAXATION TECHNIQUES

Given a pre-regular semi-algebraic system $R = [B_{\neq}, T, P_>]$ as input, the algorithm GenerateRegularSas in [3] generates an FPS $\mathbf{F} \supseteq B$ of R and a regular semi-algebraic system $[\mathcal{Q}, T, P_>]$ such that $Z_\mathbb{R}(\mathbf{F}_{\neq}) \cap Z_\mathbb{R}(R) = Z_\mathbb{R}([\mathcal{Q}, T, P_>])$. Denote by B^* the polynomial set $\mathrm{oaf}(B)$, which is proved to be an FPS of R by Theorem 4 in [3]. The notations R, B, T, P, $\mathbf{F}$, B^* will be fixed in this section.

Note that if $\mathbf{F} = B$, then we have $Z_\mathbb{R}(R) = Z_\mathbb{R}([\mathcal{Q}, T, P_>])$; otherwise, for each $b \in \mathbf{F} \setminus B$, we have to compute recursively a triangular decomposition of $[T \cup \{b\}, \{\}, P_>, B_{\neq}]$ to obtain a complete triangular decomposition of R. There are two directions to reduce the number of such recursive calls, which will help to produce output with less redundancy:

(i) minimize the number of polynomials in $\mathbf{F}$, where the effective boundary theory in Section 4 can help;

(ii) relax some polynomials in $\mathbf{F} \setminus B$ such that there is no need to make recursive calls for those polynomials, which we will discuss in this section.

The following notions of *sign condition* and *relaxation* appear in [1] in a more general setting. We adapt them to our study of regular semi-algebraic systems. Throughout this subsection, we consider a finite set $F \subset \mathbb{Q}[\mathbf{x}]$ of coprime polynomials.

DEFINITION 4. *We call any semi-algebraic system of the form*

$$\bigwedge_{f \in F} f \, \sigma_f \, 0, \tag{1}$$

where σ_f is one of $>, <, \geq, \leq$, a sign condition on F, or an F-sign condition. An F-sign condition is called strict *if every σ_f involved belongs to $\{>, <\}$. An F-sign condition C is called* realizable *if C has at least one real solution.*

DEFINITION 5 (RELAXATION OF SIGN CONDITION). *For an F-sign condition C given as in (1) and a subset E of F, the (partial) relaxation of C w.r.t. E, denoted by $\widetilde{C}^E$, is defined by*

$$\bigwedge_{p \in F} p \, \widetilde{\sigma}_p \, 0 \quad \text{where } \widetilde{\sigma}_p = \begin{cases} \leq, & \text{if } p \in E \text{ and } \sigma_p \text{ is } <, \\ \geq, & \text{if } p \in E \text{ and } \sigma_p \text{ is } >, \\ \sigma_p, & \text{otherwise.} \end{cases}$$

Let $Q = \vee_{i=1}^e C_i$ be a quantifier free formula, where each C_i is an F-sign condition. The relaxation of Q w.r.t. E, denoted by $\widetilde{Q}^E$, is defined as $\vee_{i=1}^e \widetilde{C_i}^E$. If E contains only one polynomial h, then we also denote the relaxation by $\widetilde{Q}^h$.

Let us fix the following notations as well in the rest of this section. Let $D \subseteq \mathbb{Q}[\mathbf{u}]$ such that $B \subseteq D \subseteq \mathbf{F}$. Let Q_i $(i = 0, 1)$ be a quantifier free formula in disjunctive form such that each conjunction clause C of it is in the following form: $C = \wedge_{f \in \mathbf{F}} f \, \sigma_f \, 0$, where $\sigma_f \in \{>, <\}$ if $f \in D$ and $\sigma_f \in \{\geq, \leq\}$ if $f \in \mathbf{F} \setminus D$. Moreover, assume that for any u such that $D(u) \neq 0$, $R(u)$ has (resp. has no) real solutions if and only if $Q_1(u)$ (resp. $Q_0(u)$) is true. Let h be a polynomial in $D \setminus B$. Denote by D^h the set $D \setminus \{h\}$. Denote by ∂_i $(i = 0, 1)$ the boundary of the set $Z_\mathbb{R}(Q_i)$. Denote by G_i $(i = 0, 1)$ the set $Z_\mathbb{R}(\widetilde{Q_i}^h) \cap \overline{Z_\mathbb{R}(Q_i)}$. Let S_i $(i = 0, 1)$ be the semi-algebraic set such that $Z_\mathbb{R}(\widetilde{Q_i}^h) = G_i \uplus S_i$, where the symbol $\uplus$ denotes disjoint union.

The following Theorem states an criterion for relaxation.

Table 1 The timing and number of components in the output of different algorithms

sys	$\text{RTD}|_{re}$ −relax				$\text{RTD}|_{re}$ +relax				$\text{RTD}|_{inc}$ −relax				$\text{RTD}|_{inc}$ +relax			
	RTD		RR		RTD		RR		RTD		RR		RTD		RR	
8-3-config-Li	418.6	203	1727	45	410.6	203	1688	45	30.5	47	129.5	47	30.4	47	129.1	47
dgp6	65.17	20	17.44	15	64.37	20	17.59	15	47.73	19	22.38	17	47.43	19	22.24	17
Leykin-1	4.9	28	20.1	18	4.9	28	20.8	18	6.5	19	13.9	19	6.5	19	14.0	19
L	14.9	69	94.3	20	14.9	69	96.9	20	2.6	19	11.7	19	2.6	19	11.7	19
Mehta0	1294	21	NA	NA	713.6	15	NA	NA	1558	20	NA	NA	998.9	15	NA	NA
EdgeSquare	247.7	116	NA	NA	725.3	91	NA	NA	116.8	43	NA	NA	629.4	33	NA	NA
Enneper	6.1	18	12.4	13	5.4	13	11.0	12	4.9	17	12.7	12	4.9	12	10.1	11
IBVP	14.1	8	NA	NA	16.8	4	NA	NA	2.5	8	NA	NA	7.6	4	NA	NA
MPV89	2.7	6	84.1	6	2.4	5	53.1	5	2.1	7	73.4	6	2.1	6	53.4	5
SEIT	NA	NA	NA	NA	1411	1	0.00	1	NA	NA	NA	NA	NA	NA	NA	NA
Solotareff-4b	3223	3	229.0	3	3222	3	228.4	3	3424	3	230.0	3	3424	3	228.4	3
Xia	223.7	12	NA	NA	224.8	10	NA	NA	21.4	9	NA	NA	20.5	8	NA	NA
Lanconelli	1.1	7	2.4	6	1.1	7	2.4	6	1.0	7	2.2	6	1.0	7	2.2	6
MacLane	17.4	79	240.5	28	17.3	79	239.5	28	5.8	27	35.8	27	5.8	27	35.6	27
MontesS12	197.8	163	346.5	62	197.4	163	344.7	62	49.9	85	413.9	61	49.7	85	433.8	61
MontesS14	3.4	23	14.1	13	3.4	23	14.1	13	2.8	15	11.0	13	2.9	15	11.1	13
Pappus	750.5	409	NA	NA	748.2	409	NA	NA	29.1	119	1127.6	119	29.0	119	1125	119
Wang168	7.0	16	8.4	10	7.1	16	8.4	10	3.4	11	5.6	10	3.5	11	5.6	10
xia-issac07-1	2.7	13	NA	NA	4.4	11	NA	NA	2.2	12	NA	NA	4.2	10	NA	NA

THEOREM 5. *The following two statements are equivalent:*

(i) $Z_{\mathbb{R}}(\widetilde{Q_1}^h) \cap Z_{\mathbb{R}}(\widetilde{Q_0}^h) = \emptyset$,

(ii) for any $u \in Z_{\mathbb{R}}(D_{\neq}^h)$, $R(u)$ *has real solutions if and only if* $\widetilde{Q_1}^h(u)$ *is true;* $R(u)$ *has no real solutions if and only if* $\widetilde{Q_0}^h(u)$ *is true.*

Before providing the proof, we supply several lemmas on the properties of the objects we defined.

LEMMA 6. $Z_{\mathbb{R}}(Q_0)$ *and* $Z_{\mathbb{R}}(Q_1)$ *are both open sets.*

PROOF. On one hand, $Z_{\mathbb{R}}(D_{\neq}) = Z_{\mathbb{R}}(Q_0) \cup Z_{\mathbb{R}}(Q_1)$. On the other hand, there exists a finite set of connected open sets, $\mathcal{O} = \{C_1, \ldots, C_e\}$, such that $Z_{\mathbb{R}}(D_{\neq}) = \cup_{i=1}^{e} C_i$ holds. By Lemma 1, for each $C_i \in \mathcal{O}$, either $C_i \subseteq Z_{\mathbb{R}}(Q_0)$ or $C_i \subseteq Z_{\mathbb{R}}(Q_1)$ holds. Therefore, both $Z_{\mathbb{R}}(Q_0)$ and $Z_{\mathbb{R}}(Q_1)$ are a union of finitely many elements of $\mathcal{O}$ and thus are open. $\square$

LEMMA 7. *For any* $u \in \overline{Z_{\mathbb{R}}(Q_0)} \cap Z_{\mathbb{R}}(B_{\neq})$, $R(u)$ *has no real solutions; for any* $u \in \overline{Z_{\mathbb{R}}(Q_1)} \cap Z_{\mathbb{R}}(B_{\neq})$, $R(u)$ *has real solutions.*

PROOF. Suppose u is in $\overline{Z_{\mathbb{R}}(Q_0)} \cap Z_{\mathbb{R}}(B_{\neq})$. There exists a connected component C of $Z_{\mathbb{R}}(Q_0)$ and a connected component C' of $Z_{\mathbb{R}}(B_{\neq})$ such that $u \in \overline{C} \cap Z_{\mathbb{R}}(B_{\neq}) \subseteq C'$ holds. Since $C \subseteq Z_{\mathbb{R}}(Q_0) \subseteq Z_{\mathbb{R}}(B_{\neq})$, we have $C \subseteq C'$. Since the number of real solutions of R is constant above C' (by Lemma 1) and R has no real solutions above C, we conclude that $R(u)$ has no real solutions. The other part of the lemma can be proved similarly. $\square$

Note that $G_i = Z_{\mathbb{R}}(\widetilde{Q_i}^h) \cap \overline{Z_{\mathbb{R}}(Q_i)} \subseteq Z_{\mathbb{R}}(B_{\neq}) \cap \overline{Z_{\mathbb{R}}(Q_i)}$ $(i = 0, 1)$ holds. We have the following proposition as a direct consequence of Lemma 7.

PROPOSITION 1. *For any* $u \in G_0$, $R(u)$ *has no real solutions; for any* $u \in G_1$, $R(u)$ *has real solutions.*

LEMMA 8. *The following relations hold:* (i) $\partial_0 \cup \partial_1 = Z_{\mathbb{R}}(\prod_{f \in D} f)$; (ii) $\partial_0 \cap \partial_1 \subseteq Z_{\mathbb{R}}(\prod_{f \in B} f)$.

PROOF. By Lemma 6, both $Z_{\mathbb{R}}(Q_0)$ and $Z_{\mathbb{R}}(Q_1)$ are open sets. We have $\partial_0 \cup \partial_1 = \partial(Z_{\mathbb{R}}(Q_0) \cup Z_{\mathbb{R}}(Q_1))$, since $Z_{\mathbb{R}}(Q_0) \cap$

$Z_{\mathbb{R}}(Q_1) = \emptyset$ holds. Therefore, we have

$$
\begin{aligned}
\partial_0 \cup \partial_1 &= \overline{Z_{\mathbb{R}}(Q_0) \cup Z_{\mathbb{R}}(Q_1)} \setminus (Z_{\mathbb{R}}(Q_0) \cup Z_{\mathbb{R}}(Q_1)) \\
&= \overline{Z_{\mathbb{R}}(D_{\neq})} \setminus (Z_{\mathbb{R}}(D_{\neq})) \\
&= Z_{\mathbb{R}}(\textstyle\prod_{f \in D} f).
\end{aligned}
$$

By Lemma 7, $\overline{Z_{\mathbb{R}}(Q_0)} \cap Z_{\mathbb{R}}(B_{\neq})$ and $\overline{Z_{\mathbb{R}}(Q_1)} \cap Z_{\mathbb{R}}(B_{\neq})$ has no intersection. Therefore $\overline{Z_{\mathbb{R}}(Q_0)} \cap \overline{Z_{\mathbb{R}}(Q_1)} \cap Z_{\mathbb{R}}(B_{\neq}) = \emptyset$. Then the conclusion follows by $\partial_i \subseteq \overline{Z_{\mathbb{R}}(Q_i)}$ $(i = 0, 1)$. $\square$

LEMMA 9. *The following relations hold: (a) for* $(i = 0, 1)$, $\overline{Z_{\mathbb{R}}(Q_i)} \cap Z_{\mathbb{R}}(D_{\neq}^h) \subseteq Z_{\mathbb{R}}(\widetilde{Q_i}^h)$; (b) $Z_{\mathbb{R}}(\widetilde{Q_0}^h) \cup Z_{\mathbb{R}}(\widetilde{Q_1}^h) = Z_{\mathbb{R}}(D_{\neq}^h)$.*

PROOF. Since $Z_{\mathbb{R}}(\widetilde{Q_i}^D)$ is a closed set, we have $\overline{Z_{\mathbb{R}}(Q_i)} \subseteq Z_{\mathbb{R}}(\widetilde{Q_i}^D)$. Therefore, we have

$$
Z_{\mathbb{R}}(D_{\neq}^h) \cap \overline{Z_{\mathbb{R}}(Q_i)} \subseteq Z_{\mathbb{R}}(D_{\neq}^h) \cap Z_{\mathbb{R}}(\widetilde{Q_i}^D) = Z_{\mathbb{R}}(\widetilde{Q_i}^h).
$$

By (a), we have $Z_{\mathbb{R}}(D_{\neq}^h) \cap (\cup_{i=0,1} \overline{Z_{\mathbb{R}}(Q_i)}) \subseteq \cup_{i=0,1} Z_{\mathbb{R}}(\widetilde{Q_i}^h)$, which implies that $Z_{\mathbb{R}}(D_{\neq}^h) \subseteq Z_{\mathbb{R}}(\widetilde{Q_0}^h) \cup Z_{\mathbb{R}}(\widetilde{Q_1}^h)$. And $Z_{\mathbb{R}}(\widetilde{Q_0}^h) \cup Z_{\mathbb{R}}(\widetilde{Q_1}^h) \subseteq Z_{\mathbb{R}}(D_{\neq}^h)$ holds since all polynomials in D^h remain strict after relaxing h. $\square$

PROPOSITION 2. *For* $i = 0, 1$, *we have* $S_i \subseteq Z_{\mathbb{R}}(h = 0) \cap Z_{\mathbb{R}}(\widetilde{Q_i}^h)$ *holds.*

PROOF. Recall that $G_i = Z_{\mathbb{R}}(\widetilde{Q_i}^h) \cap \overline{Z_{\mathbb{R}}(Q_i)}$, $Z_{\mathbb{R}}(\widetilde{Q_i}^h) = G_i \cup S_i$. Therefore, we have $Z_{\mathbb{R}}(Q_i) \subseteq G_i$ and $S_i = Z_{\mathbb{R}}(\widetilde{Q_i}^h) \setminus G_i \subseteq Z_{\mathbb{R}}(\widetilde{Q_i}^h) \setminus Z_{\mathbb{R}}(Q_i) \subseteq Z_{\mathbb{R}}(h = 0)$ hold. Hence, we deduce that $S_i \subseteq Z_{\mathbb{R}}(h = 0) \cap Z_{\mathbb{R}}(\widetilde{Q_i}^h)$ holds. $\square$

LEMMA 10. *Both* $S_1 \subseteq G_0$ *and* $S_0 \subseteq G_1$ *hold.*

PROOF. By Lemma 8, we have $\partial_0 \cup \partial_1 = Z_{\mathbb{R}}(\prod_{f \in D} f = 0)$. Since $h \in D$, we have $Z_{\mathbb{R}}(h = 0) \subseteq \partial_0 \cup \partial_1$, which implies $Z_{\mathbb{R}}(h = 0)$ can be rewriten as

$$
Z_{\mathbb{R}}(h = 0) \cap ((\partial_0 \setminus \partial_1) \cup (\partial_1 \setminus \partial_0) \cup (\partial_0 \cap \partial_1)).
$$

By Lemma 8, we have $\partial_0 \cap \partial_1 \subseteq Z_{\mathbb{R}}(\prod_{f \in B} f = 0)$, which implies that $Z_{\mathbb{R}}(D_{\neq}^h) \cap \partial_0 \cap \partial_1 = \emptyset$. Let S_h be $Z_{\mathbb{R}}(h =$

$0) \cap Z_{\mathbb{R}}(D^h_{\neq})$. Then S_h can be rewriten as $(Z_{\mathbb{R}}(h = 0) \cap Z_{\mathbb{R}}(D^h_{\neq}) \cap (\partial_0 \setminus \partial_1)) \cup (Z_{\mathbb{R}}(h = 0) \cap Z_{\mathbb{R}}(D^h_{\neq}) \cap (\partial_1 \setminus \partial_0))$.

Intersecting both sides of relation (a) of Lemma 9 with $\overline{Z_{\mathbb{R}}(Q_i)}$, we obtain $Z_{\mathbb{R}}(D^h_{\neq}) \cap \overline{Z_{\mathbb{R}}(Q_i)} \subseteq G_i$, which implies that $Z_{\mathbb{R}}(D^h_{\neq}) \cap \partial_i \subseteq G_i$. Therefore, $S_h \subseteq G_0 \cup G_1$ holds.

Since $Z_{\mathbb{R}}(\widetilde{Q_i}^h) \subseteq Z_{\mathbb{R}}(D^h_{\neq})$, we have $Z_{\mathbb{R}}(h=0) \cap Z_{\mathbb{R}}(\widetilde{Q_i}^h) \subseteq S_h$. By Proposition 2, we have $S_i \subseteq Z_{\mathbb{R}}(h = 0) \cap Z_{\mathbb{R}}(\widetilde{Q_i}^h)$. Therefore, $S_i \subseteq S_h$ holds.

We then deduce the conclusion by combining the facts $S_i \cap G_i = \emptyset$, $S_i \subseteq S_h$, and $S_h \subseteq G_0 \cup G_1$. $\square$

COROLLARY 2. *We have* $Z_{\mathbb{R}}(\widetilde{Q_1}^h) \cap Z_{\mathbb{R}}(\widetilde{Q_0}^h) = S_0 \uplus S_1$.

PROOF. We can rewrite $Z_{\mathbb{R}}(\widetilde{Q_1}^h) \cap Z_{\mathbb{R}}(\widetilde{Q_0}^h)$ as the disjoint union $(S_1 \cap G_0) \uplus (S_0 \cap G_1) \uplus (S_1 \cap S_0) \uplus (G_0 \cap G_1)$. By Proposition 1, $G_0 \cap G_1 = \emptyset$. Together with Lemma 10, we have $Z_{\mathbb{R}}(\widetilde{Q_1}^h) \cap Z_{\mathbb{R}}(\widetilde{Q_0}^h) = S_0 \uplus S_1$. $\square$

Next, we complete the proof for Theorem 5.

PROOF. By Lemma 9, $Z_{\mathbb{R}}(\widetilde{Q_0}^h) \cup Z_{\mathbb{R}}(\widetilde{Q_1}^h) = Z_{\mathbb{R}}(D^h_{\neq})$.
$(i) \Rightarrow (ii)$. By Corollary 2, we have $S_0 = S_1 = \emptyset$ and $Z_{\mathbb{R}}(\widetilde{Q_i}^h) = G_i$ $(i = 0, 1)$. Then the conclusion follows from Proposition 1.
$(ii) \Rightarrow (i)$. We prove by contradiction. Assume (i) does not hold. There exists $u \in Z_{\mathbb{R}}(D^h_{\neq})$, such that both $\widetilde{Q_0}^h(u)$ and $\widetilde{Q_1}^h(u)$ are true. This is a contradiction to (ii). $\square$

We have the following remarks on relaxation once (i) of Theorem 5 is checked to be true.
- One can verify that, $\widetilde{Q_i}^h$ $(i = 0, 1)$ and D^h have the same configuration as that we assumed on Q_i $(i = 0, 1)$ and D. So $Z_{\mathbb{R}}(\widetilde{Q_1}^h)$ is still **open** by Lemma 6.
- If $[Q_1, T, P_>]$ is a regular semi-algebraic system, then so is $[\widetilde{Q_1}^h, T, P_>]$.

6. INCREMENTAL DECOMPOSITION

In this section, we present algorithms to compute a full triangular decomposition of a semi-algebraic system in an incremental manner, which serves as a counterpart of the recursive algorithm in our previous paper [3]. Given a semi-algebraic system $\mathfrak{S} := [F, N_\geq, P_>, H_{\neq}]$, the incremental decomposition is realized by passing the empty regular chain $\varnothing$ and $\mathfrak{S}$ to Algorithm 1, whose incrementality is mainly due to its subroutine Triangularize, which computes a Lazard triangular decomposition by solving equations one by one [11].

External algorithms. We recall the specifications of the algorithms BorderPolynomialSet and GenerateRegularSas, (see [3]), Triangularize, Intersect, RegularOnly (see [11]). BorderPolynomialSet computes the border polynomial set of a regular system, whereas GenerateRegularSas decomposes the zero set of a pre-regular semi-algebraic system as a union of zero sets of regular semi-algebraic systems. Let p be a polynomial, F be a polynomial list, and T be a regular chain. The algorithm Triangularize$(F, T, \text{mode} = \text{Lazard})$ computes regular chains T_i, $i = 1, \ldots, e$, such that $V(F) \cap W(T) \subseteq \cup_{i=1}^{e} W(T_i) \subseteq V(F) \cap \overline{W(T)}$. The algorithm Intersect(p, T) is equivalent to Triangularize$(\{p\}, T, \text{mode} = \text{Lazard})$. The algorithm RegularOnly(T, F) computes regular chains T_i, $i = 1, \ldots, e$, s.t. $W(T) \setminus V(\prod_{h \in F} h) = \cup_{i=1}^{e} W(T_i) \setminus V(\prod_{h \in F} h)$ and every polynomial in F is regular modulo $\text{sat}(T_i)$.

The proof of the termination and correctness of the algorithms rely on standard arguments used in the proof of algorithm PCTD in paper [4]. Limited to space, we will not expand the proof here.

Algorithm 1: RealTriangularize$(T, F, N_\geq, P_>, H_{\neq})$

Input: a regular chain T and a semi-algebraic system $\mathfrak{S} = [F, N_\geq, P_>, H_{\neq}]$

Output: a set of regular semi-algebraic systems R_i, $i = 1 \cdots e$, such that $W_{\mathbb{R}}(T) \cap Z_{\mathbb{R}}(\mathfrak{S}) = \cup_{i=1}^{e} Z_{\mathbb{R}}(R_i)$.

$\mathfrak{T} := \text{Triangularize}(F, T, \text{mode} = \text{Lazard})$;

for $C \in \mathfrak{T}$ **do**
$\quad$ output RealTriangularize$(C, N_\geq, P_>, H_{\neq} \cup \text{init}(T)_{\neq})$;

---

7. SET THEORETICAL OPERATIONS

In paper [3], we proved that every semi-algebraic set can be represented by the union of zero sets of finitely many regular semi-algebraic systems. Therefore it is natural to ask how to perform set theoretical operations, such as union, intersection, complement and difference of semi-algebraic sets based on such a representation.

Note that each regular semi-algebraic system can also be seen as a quantifier free formula. So one can implement the set operations naively based on the algorithm RealTriangularize and logic operations. However, an obvious drawback of such an implementation is that it totally neglects the structure of a regular semi-algebraic system.

Indeed, if the structure of the computed object can be exploited, it is possible to obtain more efficient algorithms. One good example of this is the Difference algorithm, which computes the difference of zero sets of two regular systems, presented in [6]. This algorithm exploits the structure of a regular chain and outperforms the naive implementation by several orders of magnitude.

Apart from the algebraic computations, the idea behind the Difference algorithm of paper [6] is to compute the difference $(A_1 \cap A_2) \setminus (B_1 \cap B_2)$ in the following way:

$$(A_1 \cap B_1) \cap (A_2 \setminus B_2) \bigcup (A_1 \setminus B_1) \cap A_2.$$

Observe that if $A_1 \cap B_1 = \emptyset$, then the difference is $(A_1 \cap A_2)$. Moreover, computing $\cap_{i=1}^{s} A_i \setminus \cap_{i=1}^{t} B_i$ $(s, t \geq 2)$ can be reduced to the above base case.

In this section, we present algorithms (Algorithm 4 and 5) which take advantage of the algorithm Difference (also an algorithm Intersection derived from it) and the idea presented above for computing the intersection and difference of semi-algebraic sets represented by regular semi-algebraic systems.

8. EXPERIMENTATION

In this section, we report on the experimental results of the techniques presented in this paper. The systems were tested on a machine with Intel Core 2 Quad CPU (2.40GHz) and 3.0Gb total memory. The time-out is set as 3600 seconds. The memory usage is limited to 60% of total memory. NA means the computation does not finish in the resource (time or memory) limit.

In Table 1, RTD denotes RealTriangularize. The subscripts re and inc denote respectively the recursive and incremental implementation of RealTriangularize. The suffixes $+relax$

Algorithm 2: RealTriangularize($T, N_{\geq}, P_{>}, H_{\neq}$)

Input: a regular chain T and a semi-algebraic system $\mathfrak{S} = [\emptyset, N_{\geq}, P_{>}, H_{\neq}]$

Output: a set of regular semi-algebraic systems R_i, $i = 1, \ldots, e$, such that $W_{\mathbb{R}}(T) \cap Z_{\mathbb{R}}(\mathfrak{S}) = \cup_{i=1}^{e} Z_{\mathbb{R}}(R_i)$.

$H := \mathsf{init}(T) \cup H$;
$\mathfrak{T} := \{[T, \emptyset]\}$; $\mathfrak{T}' := \emptyset$;
for $p \in N$ **do**
$\quad$ **for** $[T', N'] \in \mathfrak{T}$ **do**
$\quad\quad$ $\mathfrak{T}' := \mathfrak{T}' \cup \{[C, N'] \mid C \in \mathsf{Intersect}(p, T')\}$;
$\quad\quad$ $\mathfrak{T}' := \mathfrak{T}' \cup \{[T', N' \cup \{p\}]\}$
$\quad$ $\mathfrak{T} := \mathfrak{T}'$; $\mathfrak{T}' := \emptyset$;
$\mathfrak{T} := \{[T', N' \cup P, H] \mid [T', N'] \in \mathfrak{T}\}$;
while $\mathfrak{T} \neq \emptyset$ **do**
$\quad$ let $[T', P', H] \in \mathfrak{T}$; $\mathfrak{T} := \mathfrak{T} \setminus \{[T', P', H]\}$;
$\quad$ **for** $C \in \mathsf{RegularOnly}(T', P' \cup H)$ **do**
$\quad\quad$ $BP := \mathsf{BorderPolynomialSet}(C, P' \cup H)$;
$\quad\quad$ $(DP, \mathcal{R}) = \mathsf{GenerateRegularSas}(BP, C, P')$;
$\quad\quad$ **if** $\mathcal{R} \neq \emptyset$ **then** output $\mathcal{R}$;
$\quad\quad$ **for** $f \in DP \setminus (P' \cup H)$ **do**
$\quad\quad\quad$ $\mathfrak{T} := \mathfrak{T} \cup \{[D, P', H] \mid D \in \mathsf{Intersect}(f, C)\}$;

Algorithm 3: RealTriangularize($T, \mathcal{Q}$)

Input: T, a regular chain; $\mathcal{Q}$, a quantifier free formula
Output: a set of regular semi-algebraic systems R_i, $i = 1, \ldots, e$, such that $W_{\mathbb{R}}(T) \cap Z_{\mathbb{R}}(\mathcal{Q}) = \cup_{i=1}^{e} Z_{\mathbb{R}}(R_i)$.
for *each conjunctive formula* $F \wedge N_{\geq} \wedge P_{>} \wedge H_{\neq}$ **do**
$\quad$ output RealTriangularize($T, F, N_{\geq}, P_{>}, H_{\neq}$);

Algorithm 4: DifferenceRsas(R, R')

Input: two regular semi-algebraic systems $R = [\mathcal{Q}, T, P_{>}]$ and $R' = [\mathcal{Q}', T', P'_{>}]$
Output: a set of regular semi-algebraic systems R_i, $i = 1, \ldots, e$, such that $Z_{\mathbb{R}}(R) \setminus Z_{\mathbb{R}}(R') = \cup_{i=1}^{e} Z_{\mathbb{R}}(R_i)$.
begin
$\quad$ $\mathcal{Q} := \mathcal{Q} \wedge P_{>}$;
$\quad$ $\mathcal{Q}' := \mathcal{Q}' \wedge P'_{>}$;
$\quad$ $\mathfrak{T} := \mathsf{Difference}(T, T')$;
$\quad$ $\mathfrak{T}' := \mathsf{Intersection}(T, T')$;
$\quad$ **if** $\mathfrak{T}' = \emptyset$ **then** return R;
$\quad$ **for** $[T^*, H^*] \in \mathfrak{T}'$ **do**
$\quad\quad$ $\mathcal{Q}^* = \mathcal{Q} \setminus \mathcal{Q}' \wedge H^*_{\neq}$;
$\quad\quad$ output RealTriangularize($T^*, \mathcal{Q}^*$)
$\quad$ **for** $[T^*, H^*] \in \mathfrak{T}$ **do**
$\quad\quad$ $\mathcal{Q}^* = \mathcal{Q} \wedge H^*_{\neq}$;
$\quad\quad$ output RealTriangularize($T^*, \mathcal{Q}^*$)

Algorithm 5: IntersectionRsas(R, R')

Input: two regular semi-algebraic systems $R = [\mathcal{Q}, T, P_{>}]$ and $R' = [\mathcal{Q}', T', P'_{>}]$
Output: a set of regular semi-algebraic systems R_i, $i = 1, \ldots, e$, such that $Z_{\mathbb{R}}(R) \cap Z_{\mathbb{R}}(R') = \cup_{i=1}^{e} Z_{\mathbb{R}}(R_i)$.
$\mathcal{Q}^* := \mathcal{Q} \wedge P_{>} \wedge \mathcal{Q}' \wedge P'_{>}$;
for $[T^*, H^*] \in \mathsf{Intersection}(T, T')$ **do**
$\quad$ output RealTriangularize($T^*, \mathcal{Q}^* \wedge H^*_{\neq}$)
---

and $-relax$ denote respectively applying and not applying relaxation techniques. The name RR, short name for RemoveRedundantComponents, is an algorithm, implemented based on the algorithm DifferenceRsas, to remove the redundant components in the output of RTD. For each algorithm, the left column records the time (in seconds) while the right one records the number of components in the output.

Table 1 illustrates the effectiveness of the techniques presented in this paper. For system 8-3-config-Li, $RTD|_{inc}$ greatly outperforms $RTD|_{re}$. Moreover, RR helps reduce the number of the output components of $RTD|_{re}$ from 203 to 45. For system Metha0, with the relaxation technique, both timing and the number of components in the output are reduced. For system SEIT, with the help of relaxation, $RTD|_{re}$ can now solve it within half an hour.

To conclude, the algorithms of [3] can, in practice, be often substantially improved by better analysis of the border polynomials, by relaxation (where allowed) and by the incremental approach. The experimentation shows that the latter can sometimes result in a speed-up by more than 10.

Acknowledgments. The authors would like to thank the reviewers for their valuable remarks, the support from MAPLESOFT, MITACS and NSERC of Canada, and the EXACTA project supported by ANR (ANR-09-BLAN-0371-01) and NSFC (60911130369 and 91018012).

9. REFERENCES

[1] S. Basu, R. Pollack, and M-F. Roy. *Algorithms in real algebraic geometry*. Springer-Verlag, 2006.

[2] C. W. Brown. Improved projection for cylindrical algebraic decomposition. *J. Symb. Comput.*, 32(5):447–465, 2001.

[3] C. Chen, J.H. Davenport, J. May, M. Moreno Maza, B. Xia, and R. Xiao. Triangular decomposition of semi-algebraic systems. In *Proc. of ISSAC 2010*, pages 187–194, 2010.

[4] C. Chen, O. Golubitsky, F. Lemaire, M. Moreno Maza, and W. Pan. Comprehensive triangular decomposition. In *Proc. of CASC'07*, volume 4770 of *Lecture Notes in Computer Science*, pages 73–101, 2007.

[5] C. Chen and M. Moreno Maza. Algorithms for Computing Triangular Decompositions of Polynomial Systems In *Proc. of ISSAC 2011*, ACM Press, 2011.

[6] C. Chen, M. Moreno Maza, W. Pan, and Y. Xie. On the verification of polynomial system solvers. *Frontiers of Computer Science in China*, 2(1):55–66, 2008.

[7] G.E. Collins. Quantifier Elimination for Real Closed Fields by Cylindrical Algebraic Decomposition. In *Proc. of 2nd. GI Conference Automata Theory & Formal Languages*, pages 134–183, 1975.

[8] J.H. Davenport and J. Heintz. Real Quantifier Elimination is Doubly Exponential. *J. Symbolic Comp.*, 5:29–35, 1988.

[9] D. Lazard and F. Rouillier. Solving parametric polynomial systems. *J. Symb. Comput.*, 42(6):636–667, 2007.

[10] S. McCallum and C. W. Brown. On delineability of varieties in cad-based quantifier elimination with two equational constraints. In *Proc. of ISSAC 2009*, pages 71–78, 2010.

[11] M. Moreno Maza. On triangular decompositions of algebraic varieties. Technical Report TR 4/99, NAG Ltd, Oxford, UK, 1999. Presented at MEGA-2000, Bath, England.

[12] A. Strzeboński. Solving systems of strict polynomial inequalities. *J. Symb. Comput.*, 29(3):471–480, 2000.

[13] D. M. Wang. *Elimination Methods*. Springer, New York, 2000.

[14] R. Xiao. *Parametric Polynomial System Solving*. PhD thesis, Peking University, Beijing, 2009.

[15] L. Yang, X. Hou, and B. Xia. A complete algorithm for automated discovering of a class of inequality-type theorems. *Science in China, Series* **F**, 44(6):33–49, 2001.

[16] L. Yang and B. Xia. Real solution classifications of a class of parametric semi-algebraic systems. In *Proc. of the A3L'05*, pages 281–289, 2005.

[17] N. Phisanbut, R.J. Bradford, and J.H. Davenport. Geometry of Branch Cuts. *Communications in Computer Algebra*, 44:132–135, 2010.

Algorithms for Computing Triangular Decompositions of Polynomial Systems

Changbo Chen
ORCCA, University of Western Ontario (UWO)
London, Ontario, Canada
cchen252@csd.uwo.ca

Marc Moreno Maza
ORCCA, University of Western Ontario (UWO)
London, Ontario, Canada
moreno@csd.uwo.ca

ABSTRACT

We propose new algorithms for computing triangular decompositions of polynomial systems incrementally. With respect to previous works, our improvements are based on a *weakened* notion of a polynomial GCD modulo a regular chain, which permits to greatly simplify and optimize the sub-algorithms. Extracting common work from similar expensive computations is also a key feature of our algorithms. In our experimental results the implementation of our new algorithms, realized with the `RegularChains` library in MAPLE, outperforms solvers with similar specifications by several orders of magnitude on sufficiently difficult problems.

Categories and Subject Descriptors

I.1.2 [**Symbolic and Algebraic Manipulation**]: Algorithms—*Algebraic algorithms*

General Terms

Algorithms, Experimentation, Theory

Keywords

regular chain, triangular decomposition, incremental algorithm, subresultant, polynomial system, regular GCD

1. INTRODUCTION

The Characteristic Set Method [22] of Wu has freed Ritt's decomposition from polynomial factorization, opening the door to a variety of discoveries in polynomial system solving. In the past two decades the work of Wu has been extended to more powerful decomposition algorithms and applied to different types of polynomial systems or decompositions: differential systems [2, 11], difference systems [10], real parametric systems [23], primary decomposition [18], cylindrical algebraic decomposition [5]. Today, triangular decomposition algorithms provide back-engines for computer algebra system front-end solvers, such as MAPLE's `solve` command.

Permission to make digital or hard copies of all or part of this work for personal or classroom use is granted without fee provided that copies are not made or distributed for profit or commercial advantage and that copies bear this notice and the full citation on the first page. To copy otherwise, to republish, to post on servers or to redistribute to lists, requires prior specific permission and/or a fee.
ISSAC'11, June 8–11, 2011, San Jose, California, USA.
Copyright 2011 ACM 978-1-4503-0675-1/11/06 ...$10.00.

Algorithms computing triangular decompositions of polynomial systems can be classified in several ways. One can first consider the relation between the input system S and the output triangular systems $S_1, \ldots, S_e$. From that perspective, two types of decomposition are essentially different: those for which $S_1, \ldots, S_e$ encode all the points of the zero set S (over the algebraic closure of the coefficient field of S) and those for which $S_1, \ldots, S_e$ represent only the "generic zeros" of the irreducible components of S.

One can also classify triangular decomposition algorithms by the algorithmic principles on which they rely. From this other angle, two types of algorithms are essentially different: those which proceed *by variable elimination*, that is, by reducing the solving of a system in n unknowns to that of a system in $n-1$ unknowns and those which proceed *incrementally*, that is, by reducing the solving of a system in m equations to that of a system in $m-1$ equations.

The Characteristic Set Method and the algorithm in [21] belong to the first type in each classification. Kalkbrener's algorithm [12], which is an elimination method solving in the sense of the "generic zeros", has brought efficient techniques, based on the concept of a *regular chain*. Other works [13, 17] on triangular decomposition algorithms focus on incremental solving. This principle is quite attractive, since it allows to control the properties and size of the intermediate computed objects. It is used in other areas of polynomial system solving such as the probabilistic algorithm of Lecerf [14] based on lifting fibers and the numerical method of Sommese, Verschelde, Wample [19] based on diagonal homotopy.

Incremental algorithms for triangular decomposition rely on a procedure for computing the intersection of an hypersurface and the quasi-component of a regular chain. Thus, the input of this operation can be regarded as well-behaved geometrical objects. However, known algorithms, namely the one of Lazard [13] and the one of the second author [17] are quite involved and difficult to analyze and optimize.

In this paper, we revisit this intersection operation. Let $R = \mathbf{k}[x_1, \ldots, x_n]$ be the ring of multivariate polynomials with coefficients in $\mathbf{k}$ and ordered variables $\mathbf{x} = x_1 < \cdots < x_n$. Given a polynomial $p \in R$ and a regular chain $T \subset \mathbf{k}[x_1, \ldots, x_n]$, the function call $\mathsf{Intersect}(p, T, R)$ returns regular chains $T_1, \ldots, T_e \subset \mathbf{k}[x_1, \ldots, x_n]$ such that we have:

$$V(p) \cap W(T) \subseteq W(T_1) \cup \cdots \cup W(T_e) \subseteq V(p) \cap \overline{W(T)}.$$

(See Section 2 for the notion of a regular chain and related concepts and notations.) We exhibit an algorithm for computing $\mathsf{Intersect}(p, T, R)$ which is conceptually simpler and practically much more efficient than those of [13, 17]. Our improvements result mainly from two new ideas.

Weakened notion of polynomial GCDs modulo regular chain. Modern algorithms for triangular decomposition rely implicitly or explicitly on a notion of GCD for univariate polynomials over an arbitrary commutative ring. A formal definition was proposed in [17] (see Definition 1) and applied to residue class rings of the form $\mathbb{A} = \mathbf{k}[\mathbf{x}]/\mathrm{sat}(T)$ where $\mathrm{sat}(T)$ is the saturated ideal of the regular chain T. A modular algorithm for computing these GCDs appears in [15]: if $\mathrm{sat}(T)$ is known to be radical, the performance (both in theory and practice) of this algorithm are very satisfactory whereas if $\mathrm{sat}(T)$ is not radical, the complexity of the algorithm increases substantially w.r.t. the radical case. In this paper, the ring $\mathbb{A}$ will be of the form $\mathbf{k}[\mathbf{x}]/\sqrt{\mathrm{sat}(T)}$ while our algorithms will not need to compute a basis nor a characteristic set of $\sqrt{\mathrm{sat}(T)}$. For the purpose of polynomial system solving (when retaining the multiplicities of zeros is not required) this weaker notion of a polynomial GCD is clearly sufficient. In addition, this yields a very simple procedure for computing such GCDs, see Theorem 1. To this end, we rely on the *specialization property of subresultants*. The technical report [4] reviews this property and provides corner cases for which we could not find a reference in the literature.

Extracting common work from similar computations. Up to technical details, if T consists of a single polynomial t whose main variable is the same as p, say v, computing $\mathsf{Intersect}(p, T, R)$ can be achieved by successively computing
(s_1) the resultant r of p and t w.r.t. v,
(s_2) a regular GCD of p and t modulo the squarefree part of r.
Observe that Steps (s_1) and (s_2) reduce essentially to computing the subresultant chain of p and t w.r.t. v. The algorithms of Section 4 extend this simple observation for computing $\mathsf{Intersect}(p, T, R)$ with an arbitrary regular chain. In broad terms, the intermediate polynomials computed during the "elimination phasis" of $\mathsf{Intersect}(p, T, R)$ are recycled for performing the "extension phasis" at essentially no cost.

The techniques developed for $\mathsf{Intersect}(p, T, R)$ are applied to other key sub-algorithms, such as the regularity test of a polynomial modulo the saturated of a regular chain, see Section 4. The primary application of the operation $\mathsf{Intersect}$ is to obtain triangular decomposition encoding all the points of the zero set of the input system. However, we also derive from it in Section 6 an algorithm computing triangular decompositions in the sense of Kalkbrener.

Experimental results. We have implemented the algorithms presented in this paper within the `RegularChains` library in MAPLE, leading to a new implementation of the `Triangularize` command. In Section 7, we report on various benchmarks. This new version of `Triangularize` outperforms the previous ones (based on [17]) by several orders of magnitude on sufficiently difficult problems. Other MAPLE commands or packages for solving polynomial systems (the `WSolve` package, the `Groebner:-Solve` command and the `Groebner:-Basis` command for a lexicographical term order) are also outperformed by the implementation of the algorithms presented in this paper both in terms of running time and, in the case of engines based on Gröbner bases, in terms of output size.

2. REGULAR CHAINS

We review hereafter the notion of a regular chain and its related concepts. Then we state basic properties (Proposi-

tions 1, 2, 3, 4, and Corollaries 1, 2) of regular chains, which are at the core of the proofs of the algorithms of Section 4.

Throughout this paper, $\mathbf{k}$ is a field, $\mathbf{K}$ is the algebraic closure of $\mathbf{k}$ and $\mathbf{k}[\mathbf{x}]$ denotes the ring of polynomials over $\mathbf{k}$, with ordered variables $\mathbf{x} = x_1 < \cdots < x_n$. Let $p \in \mathbf{k}[\mathbf{x}]$.

Notations for polynomials. If p is not constant, then the greatest variable appearing in p is called the *main variable* of p, denoted by $\mathrm{mvar}(p)$. Furthermore, the leading coefficient, the degree, the leading monomial, the leading term and the reductum of p, regarded as a univariate polynomial in $\mathrm{mvar}(p)$, are called respectively the *initial*, the *main degree*, the *rank*, the *head* and the *tail* of p; they are denoted by $\mathrm{init}(p)$, $\mathrm{mdeg}(p)$, $\mathrm{rank}(p)$, $\mathrm{head}(p)$ and $\mathrm{tail}(p)$ respectively. Let q be another polynomial of $\mathbf{k}[\mathbf{x}]$. If q is not constant, then we denote by $\mathrm{prem}(p, q)$ and $\mathrm{pquo}(p, q)$ the pseudo-remainder and the pseudo-quotient of p by q as univariate polynomials in $\mathrm{mvar}(q)$. We say that p is less than q and write $p \prec q$ if either $p \in \mathbf{k}$ and $q \notin \mathbf{k}$ or both are non-constant polynomials such that $\mathrm{mvar}(p) < \mathrm{mvar}(q)$ holds, or $\mathrm{mvar}(p) = \mathrm{mvar}(q)$ and $\mathrm{mdeg}(p) < \mathrm{mdeg}(q)$ both hold. We write $p \sim q$ if neither $p \prec q$ nor $q \prec p$ hold.

Notations for polynomial sets. Let $F \subset \mathbf{k}[\mathbf{x}]$. We denote by $\langle F \rangle$ the ideal generated by F in $\mathbf{k}[\mathbf{x}]$. For an ideal $\mathcal{I} \subset \mathbf{k}[\mathbf{x}]$, we denote by $\dim(\mathcal{I})$ its dimension. A polynomial is *regular* modulo $\mathcal{I}$ if it is neither zero, nor a zerodivisor modulo $\mathcal{I}$. Denote by $V(F)$ the *zero set* (or algebraic variety) of F in $\mathbf{K}^n$. Let $h \in \mathbf{k}[\mathbf{x}]$. The *saturated ideal* of $\mathcal{I}$ w.r.t. h, denoted by $\mathcal{I} : h^\infty$, is the ideal $\{q \in \mathbf{k}[\mathbf{x}] \mid \exists m \in \mathbb{N} \text{ s.t. } h^m q \in \mathcal{I}\}$.

Triangular set. Let $T \subset \mathbf{k}[\mathbf{x}]$ be a *triangular set*, that is, a set of non-constant polynomials with pairwise distinct main variables. The set of main variables and the set of ranks of the polynomials in T are denoted by $\mathrm{mvar}(T)$ and $\mathrm{rank}(T)$, respectively. A variable in $\mathbf{x}$ is called *algebraic* w.r.t. T if it belongs to $\mathrm{mvar}(T)$, otherwise it is said *free* w.r.t. T. For $v \in \mathrm{mvar}(T)$, denote by T_v the polynomial in T with main variable v. For $v \in \mathbf{x}$, we denote by $T_{<v}$ (resp. $T_{\geq v}$) the set of polynomials $t \in T$ such that $\mathrm{mvar}(t) < v$ (resp. $\mathrm{mvar}(t) \geq v$) holds. Let h_T be the product of the initials of the polynomials in T. We denote by $\mathrm{sat}(T)$ the *saturated ideal* of T defined as follows: if T is empty then $\mathrm{sat}(T)$ is the trivial ideal $\langle 0 \rangle$, otherwise it is the ideal $\langle T \rangle : h_T^\infty$. The *quasi-component* $W(T)$ of T is defined as $V(T) \setminus V(h_T)$. Denote $\overline{W(T)} = V(\mathrm{sat}(T))$ as the Zariski closure of $W(T)$. For $F \subset \mathbf{k}[\mathbf{x}]$, we write $Z(F, T) := V(F) \cap W(T)$.

Rank of a triangular set. Let $S \subset \mathbf{k}[\mathbf{x}]$ be a triangular set. We say that T has smaller rank than S and write $T \prec S$ if there exists $v \in \mathrm{mvar}(T)$ such that $\mathrm{rank}(T_{<v}) = \mathrm{rank}(S_{<v})$ holds and: (*i*) either $v \notin \mathrm{mvar}(S)$; (*ii*) or $v \in \mathrm{mvar}(S)$ and $T_v \prec S_v$. We write $T \sim S$ if $\mathrm{rank}(T) = \mathrm{rank}(S)$.

Iterated resultant. Let $p, q \in \mathbf{k}[\mathbf{x}]$. Assume q is nonconstant and let $v = \mathrm{mvar}(q)$. We define $\mathrm{res}(p, q, v)$ as follows: if the degree $\deg(p, v)$ of p in v is null, then $\mathrm{res}(p, q, v) = p$; otherwise $\mathrm{res}(p, q, v)$ is the resultant of p and q w.r.t. v. Let T be a triangular set of $\mathbf{k}[\mathbf{x}]$. We define $\mathrm{res}(p, T)$ by induction: if $T = \varnothing$, then $\mathrm{res}(p, T) = p$; otherwise let v be greatest variable appearing in T, then $\mathrm{res}(p, T) = \mathrm{res}(\mathrm{res}(p, T_v, v), T_{<v})$.

Regular chain. A triangular set $T \subset \mathbf{k}[\mathbf{x}]$ is a *regular chain* if: (*i*) either T is empty; (*ii*) or $T \setminus \{T_{\max}\}$ is a regular chain, where $T_{\max}$ is the polynomial in T with maximum rank, and the initial of $T_{\max}$ is regular w.r.t. $\mathrm{sat}(T \setminus \{T_{\max}\})$. The empty regular chain is simply denoted by $\varnothing$.

Triangular decomposition. Let $F \subset \mathbf{k}[\mathbf{x}]$ be finite. Let

$\mathfrak{T} := \{T_1, \ldots, T_e\}$ be a finite set of regular chains of $\mathbf{k}[\mathbf{x}]$. We call $\mathfrak{T}$ a *Kalkbrener triangular decomposition* of $V(F)$ if we have $V(F) = \cup_{i=1}^{e} \overline{W(T_i)}$. We call $\mathfrak{T}$ a *Lazard-Wu triangular decomposition* of $V(F)$ if we have $V(F) = \cup_{i=1}^{e} W(T_i)$.

PROPOSITION 1 ([1]). *Let p and T be respectively a polynomial and a regular chain of $\mathbf{k}[\mathbf{x}]$. Then, $prem(p, T) = 0$ holds if and only if $p \in sat(T)$ holds.*

PROPOSITION 2 ([17]). *Let T and T' be two regular chains of $\mathbf{k}[\mathbf{x}]$ such that $\sqrt{sat(T)} \subseteq \sqrt{sat(T')}$ and $\dim(sat(T)) = \dim(sat(T'))$ hold. Let $p \in \mathbf{k}[\mathbf{x}]$ such that p is regular w.r.t. $sat(T)$. Then p is also regular w.r.t. $sat(T')$.*

PROPOSITION 3 ([1]). *Let $p \in \mathbf{k}[\mathbf{x}]$ and $T \subset \mathbf{k}[\mathbf{x}]$ be a regular chain. Let $v = mvar(p)$ and $r = prem(p, T_{\geq v})$ such that $r \in \sqrt{sat(T_{<v})}$ holds. Then, we have $p \in \sqrt{sat(T)}$.*

COROLLARY 1. *Let T, T' be regular chains of $\mathbf{k}[x_1, \ldots, x_k]$, for $1 \leq k < n$. Let $p \in \mathbf{k}[\mathbf{x}]$ with $mvar(p) = x_{k+1}$ such that $init(p)$ is regular w.r.t. $sat(T)$ and $sat(T')$. We have:*
$$\sqrt{sat(T)} \subseteq \sqrt{sat(T')} \implies \sqrt{sat(T \cup p)} \subseteq \sqrt{sat(T' \cup p)}.$$

PROPOSITION 4 ([3]). *Let $p \in \mathbf{k}[\mathbf{x}]$. Let $T \subset \mathbf{k}[\mathbf{x}]$ be a regular chain. Then the following statements are equivalent:*
 (i) the polynomial p is regular w.r.t. $sat(T)$,
 (ii) for each prime $\mathfrak{p}$ associated with $sat(T)$, we have $p \notin \mathfrak{p}$,
 (iii) the iterated resultant $res(p, T)$ is not zero.

COROLLARY 2. *Let $p \in \mathbf{k}[\mathbf{x}]$ and $T \subset \mathbf{k}[\mathbf{x}]$ be a regular chain. Let $v := mvar(p)$ and $r := res(p, T_{\geq v})$. We have:*
 (1) the polynomial p is regular w.r.t. $sat(T)$ if and only if r is regular w.r.t. $sat(T_{<v})$;
 (2) if $v \notin mvar(T)$ and $init(p)$ is regular w.r.t. $sat(T)$, then p is regular w.r.t. $sat(T)$.

3. REGULAR GCDS

Definition 1 was introduced in [17] as part of a formal framework for algorithms manipulating regular chains [8, 13, 6, 12, 24]. In the present paper, the ring $\mathbb{A}$ will always be of the form $\mathbf{k}[\mathbf{x}]/\sqrt{sat(T)}$. Thus, a regular GCD of p, t in $\mathbb{A}[y]$ is also called a regular GCD of p, t modulo $\sqrt{sat(T)}$.

DEFINITION 1. *Let $\mathbb{A}$ be a commutative ring with unity. Let $p, t, g \in \mathbb{A}[y]$ with $t \neq 0$ and $g \neq 0$. We say that $g \in \mathbb{A}[y]$ is a regular GCD of p, t if:*
 (R_1) the leading coefficient of g in y is a regular element;
 (R_2) g belongs to the ideal generated by p and t in $\mathbb{A}[y]$;
 (R_3) if $\deg(g, y) > 0$, then g pseudo-divides both p and t, that is, $prem(p, g) = prem(t, g) = 0$.

PROPOSITION 5. *For $1 \leq k \leq n$, let $T \subset \mathbf{k}[x_1, \ldots, x_{k-1}]$ be a regular chain, possibly empty. Let $p, t, g \in \mathbf{k}[x_1, \ldots, x_k]$ with main variable x_k. Assume $T \cup \{t\}$ is a regular chain and g is a regular GCD of p, t modulo $\sqrt{sat(T)}$. We have:*
 (i) if $mdeg(g) = mdeg(t)$, then $\sqrt{sat(T \cup t)} = \sqrt{sat(T \cup g)}$ and $W(T \cup t) \subseteq Z(h_g, T \cup t) \cup W(T \cup g)$ both hold,
 (ii) if $mdeg(g) < mdeg(t)$, let $q = pquo(t, g)$, then $T \cup q$ is a regular chain and the following two relations hold:
  (ii.a) $\sqrt{sat(T \cup t)} = \sqrt{sat(T \cup g)} \cap \sqrt{sat(T \cup q)}$,
  (ii.b) $W(T \cup t) \subseteq Z(h_g, T \cup t) \cup W(T \cup g) \cup W(T \cup q)$,
 (iii) $W(T \cup g) \subseteq V(p)$,
 (iv) $Z(p, T \cup t) \subseteq W(T \cup g) \cup Z(\{p, h_g\}, T \cup t)$.

PROOF. We first establish a relation between p, t and g. By definition of pseudo-division, there exist polynomials q, r and a nonnegtive integer e_0 such that
$$h_g^{e_0} t = qg + r \quad \text{and} \quad r \in \sqrt{sat(T)} \tag{1}$$
both hold. Hence, there exists an integer $e_1 \geq 0$ such that:
$$(h_T)^{e_1}(h_g^{e_0} t - qg)^{e_1} \in \langle T \rangle \tag{2}$$
holds, which implies: $t \in \sqrt{sat(T \cup g)}$. We first prove (i). Since $mdeg(t) = mdeg(g)$ holds, we have $q \in \mathbf{k}[x_1, \ldots, x_{k-1}]$, and thus $h_g^{e_0} h_t = q h_g$ holds. Since h_t and h_g are regular modulo $sat(T)$, the same property holds for q. With (2), we obtain $g \in \sqrt{sat(T \cup t)}$. Therefore $\sqrt{sat(T \cup t)} = \sqrt{sat(T \cup g)}$. The inclusion relation in (i) follows from (1).

We prove (ii). Assume $mdeg(t) > mdeg(g)$. With (1) and (2), this hypothesis implies that $T \cup q$ is a regular chain and $t \in \sqrt{sat(T \cup q)}$ holds. Since $t \in \sqrt{sat(T \cup g)}$ also holds, $\sqrt{sat(T \cup t)}$ is contained in $\sqrt{sat(T \cup g)} \cap \sqrt{sat(T \cup q)}$. Conversely, for any $f \in \sqrt{sat(T \cup g)} \cap \sqrt{sat(T \cup q)}$, there exists an integer $e_2 \geq 0$ and $a \in \mathbf{k}[\mathbf{x}]$ such that $(h_g h_q)^{e_2} f^{e_2} - aqg \in sat(T)$ holds. With (1) we deduce that $f \in \sqrt{sat(T \cup t)}$ holds and so does (ii.a). With (1), we have (ii.b) holds.

We prove (iii) and (iv). Definition 1 implies: $prem(p, g) \in \sqrt{sat(T)}$. Thus $p \in \sqrt{sat(T \cup g)}$ holds, that is, $\overline{W(T \cup g)} \subseteq V(p)$, which implies (iii). Moreover, since $g \in \langle p, t, \sqrt{sat(T)} \rangle$, we have $Z(p, T \cup t) \subseteq V(g)$, so we deduce (iv). $\square$

Let p, t be two polynomials of $\mathbf{k}[x_1, \ldots, x_k]$, for $k \geq 1$. Let $m = \deg(p, x_k), n = mdeg(t, x_k)$. Assume that $m, n \geq 1$. Let $\lambda = \min(m, n)$. Let T be a regular chain of $\mathbf{k}[x_1, \ldots, x_{k-1}]$. Let $\mathbb{B} = \mathbf{k}[x_1, \ldots, x_{k-1}]$ and $\mathbb{A} = \mathbb{B}/\sqrt{sat(T)}$.

Let $S_0, \ldots, S_{\lambda-1}$ be the subresulant polynomials [16, 9] of p and t w.r.t. x_k in $\mathbb{B}[x_k]$. Let $s_i = \text{coeff}(S_i, x_k^i)$ be the principle subresultant coefficient of S_i, for $0 \leq i \leq \lambda - 1$. If $m \geq n$, we define $S_\lambda = t$, $S_{\lambda+1} = p$, $s_\lambda = init(t)$ and $s_{\lambda+1} = init(p)$. If $m < n$, we define $S_\lambda = p$, $S_{\lambda+1} = t$, $s_\lambda = init(p)$ and $s_{\lambda+1} = init(t)$.

The following theorem provides sufficient conditions for S_j (with $1 \leq j \leq \lambda+1$) to be a regular GCD of p and t in $\mathbb{A}[x_k]$.

THEOREM 1. *Let j be an integer, with $1 \leq j \leq \lambda + 1$, such that s_j is a regular element of $\mathbb{A}$ and such that for any $0 \leq i < j$, we have $s_i = 0$ in $\mathbb{A}$. Then S_j is a regular GCD of p and t in $\mathbb{A}[x_k]$.*

PROOF. By Definition 1, it suffices to prove that both $prem(p, S_j, x_k) = 0$ and $prem(t, S_j, x_k) = 0$ hold in $\mathbb{A}$. By symmetry we only prove the former equality.

Let $\mathfrak{p}$ be any prime ideal associated with $sat(T)$. Define $\mathbb{D} = \mathbf{k}[x_1, \ldots, x_{k-1}]/\mathfrak{p}$ and let $\mathbb{L}$ be the fraction field of the integral domain $\mathbb{D}$. Let ϕ be the homomorphism from $\mathbb{B}$ to $\mathbb{L}$. By Theorem 4 in the Appendix of [4], we know that $\phi(S_j)$ is a GCD of $\phi(p)$ and $\phi(t)$ in $\mathbb{L}[x_k]$. Therefore there exists a polynomial q of $\mathbb{L}[x_k]$ such that $p = qS_j$ in $\mathbb{L}[x_k]$, which implies that there exists a nonzero element a of $\mathbb{D}$ and a polynomial q' of $\mathbb{D}[x_k]$ such that $ap = q'S_j$ in $\mathbb{D}[x_k]$. Therefore $prem(ap, S_j) = 0$ in $\mathbb{D}[x_k]$, which implies that $prem(p, S_j) = 0$ in $\mathbb{D}[x_k]$. Hence $prem(p, S_j)$ belongs to $\mathfrak{p}$ and thus to $\sqrt{sat(T)}$. So $prem(p, S_j, x_k) = 0$ in $\mathbb{A}$. $\square$

4. THE INCREMENTAL ALGORITHM

In this section, we present an algorithm to compute Lazard-Wu triangular decompositions in an incremental manner.

Algorithm 1: Triangularize(F, R)

---

1   **if** $F = \{\ \}$ **then return** $\{\varnothing\}$
2   Choose a polynomial $p \in F$ with maximal rank
3   **for** $T \in$ Triangularize$(F \setminus \{p\}, R)$ **do**
4   output Intersect(p, T, R)

Algorithm 2: Intersect(p, T, R)

---

1   **if** $\mathrm{prem}(p, T) = 0$ **then return** $\{T\}$
2   **if** $p \in \mathbf{k}$ **then return** $\{\ \}$
3   $r := p$; $P := \{r\}$; $S := \{\ \}$
4   **while** $mvar(r) \in mvar(T)$ **do**
5       $v := mvar(r)$; $src :=$ SubresultantChain(r, T_v, v, R)
6       $S := S \cup \{src\}$; $r :=$ resultant(src)
7   **if** $r = 0$ **then break**
8   **if** $r \in \mathbf{k}$ **then return** $\{\ \}$
9       $P := P \cup \{r\}$
10   $\mathfrak{T} := \{\varnothing\}$; $\mathfrak{T}' := \{\ \}$; $i := 1$
11   **while** $i \leq n$ **do**
12   **for** $C \in \mathfrak{T}$ **do**
13   **if** $x_i \notin mvar(P)$ **and** $x_i \notin mvar(T)$ **then**
14           $\mathfrak{T}' := \mathfrak{T}' \cup$ CleanChain(C, T, x_{i+1}, R)
15   **else if** $x_i \notin mvar(P)$ **then**
16           $\mathfrak{T}' := \mathfrak{T}' \cup$ CleanChain$(C \cup T_{x_i}, T, x_{i+1}, R)$
17   **else if** $x_i \notin mvar(T)$ **then**
18   **for** $D \in$ IntersectFree(P_{x_i}, x_i, C, R) **do**
19             $\mathfrak{T}' := \mathfrak{T}' \cup$ CleanChain(D, T, x_{i+1}, R)
20   **else**
21   **for** $D \in$ IntersectAlgebraic$(P_{x_i}, T, x_i, S_{x_i}, C, R)$
           do
22             $\mathfrak{T}' := \mathfrak{T}' \cup$ CleanChain(D, T, x_{i+1}, R)
23       $\mathfrak{T} := \mathfrak{T}'$; $\mathfrak{T}' := \{\ \}$; $i := i + 1$
24   **return** $\mathfrak{T}$

Algorithm 3: RegularGcd(p, q, v, S, T, R)

---

1   $\mathfrak{T} := \{(T, 1)\}$
2   **while** $\mathfrak{T} \neq \emptyset$ **do**
3   let $(C, i) \in \mathfrak{T}$; $\mathfrak{T} := \mathfrak{T} \setminus \{(C, i)\}$
4   **for** $[f, D] \in$ Regularize(s_i, C, R) **do**
5   **if** $\dim D < \dim C$ **then** output $[0, D]$
6   **else if** $f = 0$ **then** $\mathfrak{T} := \mathfrak{T} \cup \{(D, i+1)\}$
7   **else** output $[S_i, D]$

Algorithm 4: IntersectFree(p, x_i, C, R)

---

1   **for** $[f, D] \in$ Regularize$(init(p), C, R)$ **do**
2   **if** $f = 0$ **then** output Intersect$(tail(p), D, R)$
3   **else**
4   output $D \cup p$
5   **for** $E \in$ Intersect$(init(p), D, R)$ **do**
6   output Intersect$(tail(p), E, R)$

Algorithm 5: IntersectAlgebraic(p, T, x_i, S, C, R)

---

1   **for** $[g, D] \in$ RegularGcd$(p, T_{x_i}, x_i, S, C, R)$ **do**
2   **if** $\dim D < \dim C$ **then**
3   **for** $E \in$ CleanChain(D, T, x_i, R) **do**
4   output IntersectAlgebraic(p, T, x_i, S, E, R)
5   **else**
6   output $D \cup g$
7   **for** $E \in$ Intersect$(init(g), D, R)$ **do**
8   **for** $F \in$ CleanChain(E, T, x_i, R) **do**
9   output IntersectAlgebraic(p, T, x_i, S, F, R)

Algorithm 6: Regularize(p, T, R)

---

1   **if** $p \in \mathbf{k}$ **or** $T = \varnothing$ **then return** $[p, T]$
2   $v := mvar(p)$
3   **if** $v \notin mvar(T)$ **then**
4   **for** $[f, C] \in$ Regularize$(init(p), T, R)$ **do**
5   **if** $f = 0$ **then** output Regularize$(tail(p), C, R)$
6   **else** output $[p, C]$
7   **else**
8       $src :=$ SubresultantChain(p, T_v, v, R);
       $r :=$ resultant(src)
9   **for** $[f, C] \in$ Regularize$(r, T_{<v}, R)$ **do**
10   **if** $\dim C < \dim T_{<v}$ **then**
11   **for** $D \in$ Extend(C, T, v, R) **do**
12   output Regularize(p, D, R)
13   **else if** $f \neq 0$ **then** output $[p, C \cup T_{\geq v}]$
14   **else**
15   **for** $[g, D] \in$ RegularGcd(p, T_v, v, src, C, R) **do**
16   **if** $\dim D < \dim C$ **then**
17   **for** $E \in$ Extend(D, T, v, R) **do**
18   output Regularize(p, E, R)
19   **else**
20   **if** $mdeg(g) = mdeg(T_v)$ **then** output
               $[0, D \cup T_{\geq v}]$; next
21   output $[0, D \cup g \cup T_{>v}]$
22               $q :=$ pquo(T_v, g)
23   output Regularize$(p, D \cup q \cup T_{>v}, R)$
24   **for** $E \in$ Intersect(h_g, D, R) **do**
25   **for** $F \in$ Extend(E, T, v, R) **do**
26   output Regularize(p, F, R)

Algorithm 7: Extend(C, T, x_i, R)

---

1   **if** $T_{\geq x_i} = \varnothing$ **then return** C;
2   let $p \in T$ with greatest main variable; $T' := T \setminus \{p\}$;
3   **for** $D \in$ Extend(C, T', x_i, R) **do**
4   **for** $[f, E] \in$ Regularize$(init(p), D)$ **do**
5   **if** $f \neq 0$ **then** output $E \cup p$;

Algorithm 8: CleanChain(C, T, x_i, R)

---

1   **if** $x_i \notin mvar(T)$ **or** $\dim C = \dim T_{<x_i}$ **then return** C
2   **for** $[f, D] \in$ Regularize$(init(T_{x_i}), C, R)$ **do**
3   **if** $f \neq 0$ **then** output D

We recall the concepts of a *process* and a *regular (delayed) split*, which were introduced as Definitions 9 and 11 in [17]. To serve our purpose, we modify the definitions as below.

DEFINITION 2. *A* process *of* $\mathbf{k}[\mathbf{x}]$ *is a pair* (p, T)*, where* $p \in \mathbf{k}[\mathbf{x}]$ *is a polynomial and* $T \subset \mathbf{k}[\mathbf{x}]$ *is a regular chain. The process* $(0, T)$ *is also written as* T *for short. Given two processes* (p, T) *and* (p', T')*, let* v *and* v' *be respectively the greatest variable appearing in* (p, T) *and* (p', T')*. We say* $(p, T) \prec (p', T')$ *if: (i) either* $v < v'$*; (ii) or* $v = v'$ *and* $\dim T < \dim T'$*; (iii) or* $v = v'$*,* $\dim T = \dim T'$ *and* $T \prec T'$*; (iv) or* $v = v'$*,* $\dim T = \dim T'$*,* $T \sim T'$ *and* $p \prec p'$*. We write* $(p, T) \sim (p', T')$ *if neither* $(p, T) \prec (p', T')$ *nor* $(p', T') \prec (p, T)$ *hold. Clearly any sequence of processes which is strictly decreasing w.r.t.* $\prec$ *is finite.*

DEFINITION 3. *Let* T_i*,* $1 \le i \le e$*, be regular chains of* $\mathbf{k}[\mathbf{x}]$*. Let* $p \in \mathbf{k}[\mathbf{x}]$*. We call* $T_1, \ldots, T_e$ *a regular split of* (p, T) *whenever we have*
(L_1) $\sqrt{sat(T)} \subseteq \sqrt{sat(T_i)}$
(L_2) $W(T_i) \subseteq V(p)$ *(or equivalently* $p \in \sqrt{sat(T_i)}$*)*
(L_3) $V(p) \cap W(T) \subseteq \cup_{i=1}^{e} W(T_i)$
We write as $(p, T) \longrightarrow T_1, \ldots, T_e$*. Observe that the above three conditions are equivalent to the following relation.*

$$V(p) \cap W(T) \subseteq W(T_1) \cup \cdots \cup W(T_e) \subseteq V(p) \cap \overline{W(T)}.$$

Geometrically, this means that we may compute a little more than $V(p) \cap W(T)$*; however,* $W(T_1) \cup \cdots \cup W(T_e)$ *is a "sharp" approximation of the intersection of* $V(p)$ *and* $W(T)$*.*

Next we list the specifications of our triangular decomposition algorithm and its subroutines. We denote by R the polynomial ring $\mathbf{k}[\mathbf{x}]$, where $\mathbf{x} = x_1 < \cdots < x_n$.

Triangularize(F, R)
- **Input:** F, a finite set of polynomials of R
- **Output:** A Lazard-Wu triangular decomposition of $V(F)$.

Intersect(p, T, R)
- **Input:** p, a polynomial of R; T, a regular chain of R
- **Output:** a set of regular chains $\{T_1, \ldots, T_e\}$ such chat $(p, T) \longrightarrow T_1, \ldots, T_e$.

Regularize(p, T, R)
- **Input:** p, a polynomial of R; T, a regular chain of R.
- **Output:** a set of pairs $\{[p_1, T_1], \ldots, [p_e, T_e]\}$ such that for each $i, 1 \le i \le e$: (1) T_i is a regular chain; (2) $p = p_i \bmod \sqrt{sat(T_i)}$; (3) if $p_i = 0$, then $p_i \in \sqrt{sat(T_i)}$ otherwise p_i is regular modulo $\sqrt{sat(T_i)}$; moreover we have $T \longrightarrow T_1, \ldots, T_e$.

SubresultantChain(p, q, v, R)
- **Input:** v, a variable of $\{x_1, \ldots, x_n\}$; p and q, polynomials of R, whose main variables are both v.
- **Output:** a list of polynomials $(S_0, \ldots, S_\lambda)$, where $\lambda = \min(\mathrm{mdeg}(p), \mathrm{mdeg}(q))$, such that S_i is the i-th subresultant of p and q w.r.t. v.

RegularGcd(p, q, v, S, T, R)
- **Input:** v, a variable of $\{x_1, \ldots, x_n\}$,
  - T, a regular chain of R such that $\mathrm{mvar}(T) < v$,
  - p and q, polynomials of R with the same main variable v such that: $\mathrm{init}(q)$ is regular modulo $\sqrt{sat(T)}$; $\mathrm{res}(p, q, v)$ belongs to $\sqrt{sat(T)}$,
  - S, the subresultant chain of p and q w.r.t. v.

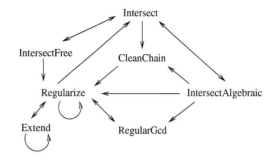

Figure 1: Flow graph of the Algorithms

- **Output:** a set of pairs $\{[g_1, T_1], \ldots, [g_e, T_e]\}$ such that $T \longrightarrow T_1, \ldots, T_e$ and for each T_i: if $\dim T = \dim T_i$, then g_i is a regular GCD of p and q modulo $\sqrt{sat(T_i)}$; otherwise $g_i = 0$, which means undefined.

IntersectFree(p, x_i, C, R)
- **Input:** x_i, a variable of $\mathbf{x}$; p, a polynomial of R with main variable x_i; C, a regular chain of $\mathbf{k}[x_1, \ldots, x_{i-1}]$.
- **Output:** a set of regular chains $\{T_1, \ldots, T_e\}$ such that $(p, C) \longrightarrow (T_1, \ldots, T_e)$.

IntersectAlgebraic(p, T, x_i, S, C, R)
- **Input:** p, a polynomial of R with main variable x_i,
  - T, a regular chain of R, where $x_i \in \mathrm{mvar}(T)$,
  - S, the subresultant chain of p and T_{x_i} w.r.t. x_i,
  - C, a regular chain of $\mathbf{k}[x_1, \ldots, x_{i-1}]$, such that: $\mathrm{init}(T_{x_i})$ is regular modulo $\sqrt{sat(C)}$; the resultant of p and T_{x_i}, which is S_0, belongs to $\sqrt{sat(C)}$.
- **Output:** a set of regular chains $T_1, \ldots, T_e$ such that $(p, C \cup T_{x_i}) \longrightarrow T_1, \ldots, T_e$.

CleanChain(C, T, x_i, R)
- **Input:** T, a regular chain of R; C, a regular chain of $\mathbf{k}[x_1, \ldots, x_{i-1}]$ such that $\sqrt{sat(T_{<x_i})} \subseteq \sqrt{sat(C)}$.
- **Output:** if $x_i \notin \mathrm{mvar}(T)$, return C; otherwise return a set of regular chains $\{T_1, \ldots, T_e\}$ such that $\mathrm{init}(T_{x_i})$ is regular modulo each $sat(T_j)$, $\sqrt{sat(C)} \subseteq \sqrt{sat(T_j)}$ and $W(C) \setminus V(\mathrm{init}(T_{x_i})) \subseteq \cup_{j=1}^{e} W(T_j)$.

Extend(C, T, x_i, R)
- **Input:** C, is a regular chain of $\mathbf{k}[x_1, \ldots, x_{i-1}]$. T, a regular chain of R such that $\sqrt{sat(T_{<x_i})} \subseteq \sqrt{sat(C)}$.
- **Output:** Regular chains $T_1, \ldots, T_e$ of R such that $W(C \cup T_{\ge x_i}) \subseteq \cup_{j=1}^{e} W(T_j)$ and $\sqrt{sat(T)} \subseteq \sqrt{sat(T_j)}$.

Algorithm SubresultantChain is standard, see [9]. The algorithm Triangularize is a *principle algorithm* which was first presented in [17]. We use the following conventions in our pseudo-code: the keyword **return** yields a result and terminates the current function call while the keyword **output** yields a result and keeps executing the current function call.

5. PROOF OF THE ALGORITHMS

THEOREM 2. *All the algorithms in Fig. 1 terminate.*

PROOF. The key observation is that the flow graph of Fig. 1 can be transformed into an equivalent flow graph satisfying the following properties: (1) the algorithms Intersect and Regularize only call each other or themselves; (2) all the other algorithms only call either Intersect or Regularize. Therefore, it suffices to show that Intersect and Regularize terminate.

Note that the input of both functions is a process, say (p, T). One can check that, while executing a call with (p, T)

	sys	Input size				Output size				
		#v	#e	deg	dim	GL	GS	GD	TL	TK
1	4corps-1parameter-homog	4	3	8	1	-	-	21863	-	30738
2	8-3-config-Li	12	7	2	7	67965	-	72698	7538	1384
3	Alonso-Li	7	4	4	3	1270	-	614	2050	374
4	Bezier	5	3	6	2	-	-	32054	-	114109
5	Cheaters-homotopy-1	7	3	7	4	26387452	-	17297	-	285
7	childDraw-2	10	10	2	0	938846	-	157765	-	-
8	Cinquin-Demongeot-3-3	4	3	4	1	1652062	-	680	2065	895
9	Cinquin-Demongeot-3-4	4	3	5	1	-	-	690	-	2322
10	collins-jsc02	5	4	3	1	-	-	28720	2770	1290
11	f-744	12	12	3	1	102082	-	83559	4509	4510
12	Haas5	4	2	10	2	-	-	28	-	548
14	Lichtblau	3	2	11	1	6600095	-	224647	110332	5243
16	Liu-Lorenz	5	4	2	1	47688	123965	712	2339	938
17	Mehta2	11	8	3	3	-	-	1374931	5347	5097
18	Mehta3	13	10	3	3	-	-	-	25951	25537
19	Mehta4	15	12	3	3	-	-	-	71675	71239
21	p3p-isosceles	7	3	3	4	56701	-	1453	9253	840
22	p3p	8	3	3	5	160567	-	1768	-	1712
23	Pavelle	8	4	2	4	17990	-	1552	3351	1086
24	Solotareff-4b	5	4	3	1	2903124	-	14810	2438	872
25	Wang93	5	4	3	1	2772	56383	1377	1016	391
26	Xia	6	3	4	3	63083	2711	672	1647	441
27	xy-5-7-2	6	3	3	3	12750	-	599	-	3267

Table 1 The input and output sizes of systems

as input, any subsequent call to either functions Intersect or Regularize will take a process (p', T') as input such that $(p', T') \prec (p, T)$ holds. Since a descending chain of processes is necessarily finite, both algorithms terminate. $\square$

Since all algorithms terminate, and following the flow graph of Fig. 1, each call to one of our algorithms unfold to a finite dynamic acyclic graph (DAG) where each vertex is a call to one of our algorithms. Therefore, proving the correctness of these algorithms reduces to prove the following two points.

- *Base:* each algorithm call, which makes no subsequent calls to another algorithm or to itself, is correct.
- *Induction:* each algorithm call, which makes subsequent calls to another algorithm or to itself, is correct, as soon as all subsequent calls are themselves correct.

For all algorithms in Fig. 1, proving the base cases is straightforward. Hence we focus on the induction steps.

PROPOSITION 6. IntersectFree *satisfies its specification.*

PROOF. We have the following two key observations:

- $C \longrightarrow D_1, \ldots, D_s$, where D_i are the regular chains in the output of Regularize.
- $V(p) \cap W(D) = W(D, p) \cup V(\mathrm{init}(p), \mathrm{tail}(p)) \cap W(D)$.

Then it is not hard to conclude that $(p, C) \longrightarrow T_1, \ldots, T_e$. $\square$

PROPOSITION 7. IntersectAlgebraic *is correct.*

PROOF. We need to prove: $(p, C \cup T_{x_i}) \longrightarrow T_1, \ldots, T_e$. Let us prove (L_1) now, that is, for each regular chain T_j in the output, we have $\sqrt{\mathrm{sat}(C \cup T_{x_i})} \subseteq \sqrt{\mathrm{sat}(T_j)}$. First by the specifications of the called functions, we have $\sqrt{\mathrm{sat}(C)} \subseteq \sqrt{\mathrm{sat}(D)} \subseteq \sqrt{\mathrm{sat}(E)}$, thus, $\sqrt{\mathrm{sat}(C \cup T_{x_i})} \subseteq \sqrt{\mathrm{sat}(E \cup T_{x_i})}$ by Corollary 1, since $\mathrm{init}(T_{x_i})$ is regular modulo both $\mathrm{sat}(C)$ and $\mathrm{sat}(E)$. Secondly, since g is a regular GCD of p and T_{x_i} modulo $\sqrt{\mathrm{sat}(D)}$, we have $\sqrt{\mathrm{sat}(C \cup T_{x_i})} \subseteq \sqrt{\mathrm{sat}(D \cup g)}$ by Corollaries 1 and Proposition 5.

Next we prove (L_2). It suffices to prove that $W(D \cup g) \subseteq V(p)$ holds. Since g is a regular GCD of p and T_{x_i} modulo $\sqrt{\mathrm{sat}(D)}$, the conclusion follows from (iii) in Proposition 5.

Finally we prove (L_3), that is $Z(p, C \cup T_{x_i}) \subseteq \bigcup_{j=1}^{e} W(T_j)$. Let $D_1, \ldots, D_s$ be the regular chains returned from Algorithm RegularGcd. We have $C \longrightarrow D_1, \ldots, D_s$, which implies $Z(p, C \cup T_{x_i}) \subseteq \bigcup_{j=1}^{e} Z(p, D_j \cup T_{x_i})$. Next since g is a

regular GCD of p and T_{x_i} modulo $\sqrt{\mathrm{sat}(D_j)}$, the conclusion follows from point (iv) of Proposition 5. $\square$

PROPOSITION 8. Intersect *satisfies its specification.*

PROOF. The first while loop can be seen as a projection process. We claim that it produces a nonempty triangular set P such that $V(p) \cap W(T) = V(P) \cap W(T)$. The claim holds before staring the while loop. For each iteration, let P' be the set of polynomials obtained at the previous iteration. We then compute a polynomial r, which is the resultant of a polynomial in P' and a polynomial in T. So $r \in \langle P', T \rangle$. By induction, we have $\langle p, T \rangle = \langle P, T \rangle$. So the claim holds.

Next, we claim that the elements in $\mathfrak{T}$ satisfy the following invariants: at the beginning of the i-th iteration of the second while loop, we have

(1) each $C \in \mathfrak{T}$ is a regular chain; if T_{x_i} exists, then $\mathrm{init}(T_{x_i})$ is regular modulo $\mathrm{sat}(C)$,
(2) for each $C \in \mathfrak{T}$, we have $\sqrt{\mathrm{sat}(T_{<x_i})} \subseteq \sqrt{\mathrm{sat}(C)}$,
(3) for each $C \in \mathfrak{T}$, we have $\overline{W(C)} \subseteq V(P_{<x_i})$,
(4) $V(p) \cap W(T) \subseteq \bigcup_{C \in \mathfrak{T}} Z(P_{\geq x_i}, C \cup T_{\geq x_i})$.

When $i = n+1$, we then have $\sqrt{\mathrm{sat}(T)} \subseteq \sqrt{\mathrm{sat}(C)}$, $W(C) \subseteq V(P) \subseteq V(p)$ for each $C \in \mathfrak{T}$ and $V(p) \cap W(T) \subseteq \bigcup_{C \in \mathfrak{T}} W(C)$. So $(L_1), (L_2), (L_3)$ of Definition 3 all hold. This concludes the correctness of the algorithm.

Now we prove the above claims (1), (2), (3), (4) by induction. The claims clearly hold when $i = 1$ since $C = \varnothing$ and $V(p) \cap W(T) = V(P) \cap W(T)$. Now assume that the loop invariants hold at the beginning of the i-th iteration. We need to prove that it still holds at the beginning of the $(i+1)$-th iteration. Let $C \in \mathfrak{T}$ be an element picked up at the beginning of i-th iteration and let L be the set of the new elements of $\mathfrak{T}'$ generated from C.

Then for any $C' \in L$, claim (1) clearly holds by specification of CleanChain. Next we prove (2).

- if $x_i \notin \mathrm{mvar}(T)$, then $T_{<x_{i+1}} = T_{<x_i}$. By induction and specifications of called functions, we have

$$\sqrt{\mathrm{sat}(T_{<x_{i+1}})} \subseteq \sqrt{\mathrm{sat}(C)} \subseteq \sqrt{\mathrm{sat}(C')}.$$

- if $x_i \in \mathrm{mvar}(T)$, by induction we have $\sqrt{\mathrm{sat}(T_{<x_i})} \subseteq \sqrt{\mathrm{sat}(C)}$ and $\mathrm{init}(T_{x_i})$ is regular modulo both $\mathrm{sat}(C)$

and sat$(T_{<x_i})$. By Corollary 1 we have

$$\sqrt{\mathrm{sat}(T_{<x_{i+1}})} \subseteq \sqrt{\mathrm{sat}(C \cup T_{x_i})} \subseteq \sqrt{\mathrm{sat}(C')}.$$

Therefore (2) holds. Next we prove claim (3). By induction and the specifications of called functions, we have $\overline{W(C')} \subseteq \overline{W(C \cup T_{x_i})} \subseteq V(P_{<x_i})$. Secondly, we have $\overline{W(C')} \subseteq V(P_{x_i})$. Therefore $\overline{W(C')} \subseteq V(P_{<x_{i+1}})$, that is (3) holds. Finally, since $V(P_{x_i}) \cap W(C \cup T_{x_i}) \setminus V(\mathrm{init}(T_{x_{i+1}})) \subseteq \cup_{C' \in L} W(C')$, we have $Z(P_{\geq x_i}, C \cup T_{\geq x_i}) \subseteq \cup_{C' \in L} Z(P_{\geq x_{i+1}}, C' \cup T_{\geq x_{i+1}})$, which implies that (4) holds. This completes the proof. □

PROPOSITION 9. Regularize *satisfies its specification.*

PROOF. If $v \notin \mathrm{mvar}(T)$, the conclusion follows directly from point (2) of Corollary 2. From now on, assume $v \in \mathrm{mvar}(T)$. Let $\mathfrak{L}$ be the set of pairs $[p', T']$ in the output. We aim to prove the following facts
(1) each T' is a regular chain,
(2) if $p' = 0$, then p is zero modulo $\sqrt{\mathrm{sat}(T')}$, otherwise p is regular modulo sat(T),
(3) we have $\sqrt{\mathrm{sat}(T)} \subseteq \sqrt{\mathrm{sat}(T')}$,
(4) we have $W(T) \subseteq \cup_{T' \in \mathfrak{L}} W(T')$.
Statement (1) is due to Proposition 2. Next we prove (2). First, when there are recursive calls, the conclusion is obvious. Let $[f, C]$ be a pair in the output of Regularize$(r, T_{<v}, R)$. If $f \neq 0$, the conclusion follows directly from point (1) of Corollary 2. Otherwise, let $[g, D]$ be a pair in the output of the algorithm RegularGcd(p, T_v, v, src, C, R). If $\mathrm{mdeg}(g) = \mathrm{mdeg}(T_v)$, then by the algorithm of RegularGcd, $g = T_v$. Therefore we have $\mathrm{prem}(p, T_v) \in \sqrt{\mathrm{sat}(C)}$, which implies that $p \in \sqrt{\mathrm{sat}(C \cup T_{\geq v})}$ by Proposition 3.

Next we prove (3). Whenever Extend is called, (3) holds immediately. Otherwise, let $[f, C]$ be a pair returned by Regularize$(r, T_{<v}, R)$. When $f \neq 0$, since $\sqrt{\mathrm{sat}(T_{<v})} \subseteq \sqrt{\mathrm{sat}(C)}$ holds, we conclude $\sqrt{\mathrm{sat}(T)} \subseteq \sqrt{\mathrm{sat}(C \cup T_{\geq v})}$ by Corollary 1. Let $[g, D] \in$ RegularGcd(p, T_v, v, src, C, R). Corollary 1 and point (ii) of Proposition 5 imply that $\sqrt{\mathrm{sat}(T)} \subseteq \sqrt{\mathrm{sat}(D \cup T_{\geq v})}$, $\sqrt{\mathrm{sat}(T)} \subseteq \sqrt{\mathrm{sat}(D \cup g \cup T_{>v})}$ together with $\sqrt{\mathrm{sat}(T)} \subseteq \sqrt{\mathrm{sat}(D \cup q \cup T_{>v})}$ hold. Hence (3) holds.

Finally by point (ii.b) of Proposition 5, we have $W(D \cup T_v) \subseteq Z(h_g, D \cup T_v) \cup W(D \cup g) \cup W(D \cup q)$. So (4) holds. □

PROPOSITION 10. Extend *satisfies its specification.*

PROOF. It clearly holds when $T_{\geq x_i} = \varnothing$, which is the base case. By induction and the specification of Regularize, we know that $\sqrt{\mathrm{sat}(T')} \subseteq \sqrt{\mathrm{sat}(E)}$. Since init$(p)$ is regular modulo both sat(T') and sat(E), by Corollary 1, we have $\sqrt{\mathrm{sat}(T)} \subseteq \sqrt{\mathrm{sat}(E \cup p)}$. On the other hand, we have $W(C \cup T'_{\geq x_i}) \subseteq \cup W(D)$ and $W(D) \setminus V(h_p) \subseteq \cup W(E)$. Therefore $W(C \cup T_{\geq x_i}) \subseteq \cup_{j=1}^e W(T_j)$, where $T_1, \ldots, T_e$ are the regular chains in the output. □

PROPOSITION 11. CleanChain *satisfies its specification.*

PROOF. It follows directly from Proposition 2. □

PROPOSITION 12. RegularGcd *satisfies its specification.*

PROOF. Let $[g_i, T_i]$, $i = 1, \ldots, e$, be the output. First from the specification of Regularize, we have $T \longrightarrow T_1, \ldots, T_e$. When $\dim T_i = \dim T$, by Proposition 2 and Theorem 1, g_i is a regular GCD of p and q modulo $\sqrt{\mathrm{sat}(T)}$. □

6. KALKBRENER DECOMPOSITION

In this section, we adapt the Algorithm Triangularize (Algorithm 1), in order to compute efficiently a Kalkbrener triangular decomposition. The basic technique we rely on follows from Krull's principle ideal theorem.

THEOREM 3. *Let $F \subset \mathbf{k}[\mathbf{x}]$ be finite, with cardinality $\#(F)$. Assume F generates a proper ideal of $\mathbf{k}[\mathbf{x}]$. Then, for any minimal prime ideal $\mathfrak{p}$ associated with $\langle F \rangle$, the height of $\mathfrak{p}$ is less than or equal to $\#(F)$.*

COROLLARY 3. *Let $\mathfrak{T}$ be a Kalkbrener triangular decomposition of $V(F)$. Let T be a regular chain of $\mathfrak{T}$, the height of which is greater than $\#(F)$. Then $\mathfrak{T} \setminus \{T\}$ is also a Kalkbrener triangular decomposition of $V(F)$.*

Based on this corollary, we prune the decomposition tree generated during the computation of a Lazard-Wu triangular decomposition and remove the computation branches in which the height of every generated regular chain is greater than the number of polynomials in F.

Next we explain how to implement this tree pruning technique to the algorithms of Section 4. Inside Triangularize, define $A = \#(F)$ and pass it to every call to Intersect in order to signal Intersect to output only regular chains with height no greater than A. Next, in the second while loop of Intersect, for the i-th iteration, we pass the height $A - \#(T_{\geq x_{i+1}})$ to CleanChain, IntersectFree and IntersectAlgebraic.

In IntersectFree, we pass its input height A to every function call. Besides, Lines 5 to 6 are executed only if the height of D is strictly less than A, since otherwise we would obtain regular chains of height greater than A. In other algorithms, we apply similar strategies as in Intersect and IntersectFree.

7. EXPERIMENTATION

Part of the algorithms presented in this paper are implemented in MAPLE14 while all of them are present in the current development version of MAPLE. Tables 1 and 2 report on our comparison between Triangularize and other MAPLE solvers. The notations used in these tables are defined below.

Notation for Triangularize. We denote by TK and TL the latest implementation of Triangularize for computing, respectively, Kalkbrener and Lazard-Wu decompositions, in the current version of MAPLE. Denote by TK14 and TL14 the corresponding implementation in MAPLE14. Denote by TK13, TL13 the implementation based on the algorithm of [17] in MAPLE13. Finally, STK and STL are versions of TK and TL, enforcing all computed regular chains to be squarefree, by means of the algorithms in the Appendix of [4].

Notation for the other solvers. Denote by GL, GS, GD, respectively the function Groebner:-Basis (plex order), Groebner:-Solve, Groebner:-Basis (tdeg order) in current beta version of MAPLE. Denote by WS the function wsolve of the package Wsolve [20], which decomposes a variety as a union of quasi-components of Wu Characteristic Sets.

The tests were launched on a machine with Intel Core 2 Quad CPU (2.40GHz) and 3.0Gb total memory. The time-out is set as 3600 seconds. The memory usage is limited to 60% of total memory. In both Table 1 and 2, the symbol "-" means either time or memory exceeds the limit we set.

The examples are mainly in positive dimension since other triangular decomposition algorithms are specialized to dimension zero [7]. All examples are in characteristic zero.

sys	Triangularize								Triangularize versus other solvers				
	TK13	TK14	TK	TL13	TL14	TL	STK	STL	GL	GS	WS	TL	TK
1	-	241.7	36.9	-	-	-	62.8	-	-	-	-	-	36.9
2	8.7	5.3	5.9	29.7	24.1	25.8	6.0	26.6	108.7	-	27.8	25.8	5.9
3	0.3	0.3	0.4	14.0	2.4	2.1	0.4	2.2	3.4	-	7.9	2.1	0.4
4	-	-	88.2	-	-	-	-	-	-	-	-	-	88.2
5	0.4	0.5	0.7	-	-	-	451.8	-	2609.5	-	-	-	0.7
7	-	-	-	-	-	-	1326.8	1437.1	19.3	-	-	-	-
8	3.2	0.7	0.6	-	55.9	7.1	0.7	8.8	63.6	-	-	7.1	0.6
9	166.1	5.0	3.1	-	-	-	3.3	-	-	-	-	-	3.1
10	5.8	0.4	0.4	-	1.5	1.5	0.4	1.5	-	-	0.8	1.5	0.4
11	-	29.1	12.7	-	27.7	14.8	12.9	15.1	30.8	-	-	14.8	12.7
12	452.3	454.1	0.3	-	-	-	0.3	-	-	-	-	-	0.3
14	0.7	0.7	0.3	801.7	226.5	143.5	0.3	531.3	125.9	-	-	143.5	0.3
16	0.4	0.4	0.4	4.7	2.6	2.3	0.4	4.4	3.2	2160.1	40.2	2.3	0.4
17	-	2.1	2.2	-	4.5	4.5	2.2	6.2	-	-	5.7	4.5	2.2
18	-	15.6	14.4	-	126.2	51.1	14.5	63.1	-	-	-	51.1	14.4
19	-	871.1	859.4	-	1987.5	1756.3	859.2	1761.8	-	-	-	1756.3	859.4
21	1.2	0.6	0.3	-	1303.1	352.5	0.3	-	6.2	-	792.8	352.5	0.3
22	168.8	5.5	0.3	-	-	-	0.3	-	33.6	-	-	-	0.3
23	0.8	0.9	0.5	-	10.3	7.0	0.4	12.6	1.8	-	-	7.0	0.5
24	1.5	0.7	0.8	-	1.9	1.9	0.9	2.0	35.2	-	9.1	1.9	0.8
25	0.5	0.6	0.7	0.6	0.8	0.8	0.8	0.9	0.2	1580.0	0.8	0.8	0.7
26	0.2	0.3	0.4	4.0	1.9	1.9	0.5	2.7	4.7	0.1	12.5	1.9	0.4
27	3.3	0.9	0.6	-	-	-	0.7	-	0.3	-	-	-	0.6

Table 2 Timings of Triangularize versus other solvers

In Table 1, we provide characteristics of the input systems and the sizes of the output obtained by different solvers. For each polynomial system $F \subset \mathbb{Q}[\mathbf{x}]$, the number of variables appearing in F, the number of polynomials in F, the maximum total degree of a polynomial in F, the dimension of the algebraic variety $V(F)$ are denoted respectively by $\#v$, $\#e$, deg, dim. For each solver, the size of its output is measured by the total number of characters in the output. To be precise, let "dec" and "gb" be respectively the output of the Triangularize and Groebner functions. The MAPLE command we use are length(convert(map(Equations, dec, R), string)) and length(convert(gb, string)). From Table 1, it is clear that Triangularize produces much smaller output than commands based on Gröbner basis computations.

TK, TL, GS, WS (and, to some extent, GL) can all be seen as polynomial system solvers in the sense of that they provide equidimensional decompositions where components are represented by triangular sets. Moreover, they are implemented in MAPLE (with the support of efficient C code in the case of GS and GL). The specification of TK are close to those of GS while TL is related to WS, though the triangular sets returned by WS are not necessarily regular chains.

In Table 2, we provide the timings of different versions of Triangularize and other solvers. From this table, it is clear that the implementations of Triangularize, based on the algorithms presented in this paper (that is TK14, TL14, TK, TL) outperform the previous versions (TK13, TL13), based on [17], by several orders of magnitude. We observe also that TK outperforms GS and GL while TL outperforms WS.

Acknowledgments. The authors would like to thank the support of MAPLESOFT, MITACS and NSERC of Canada.

8. REFERENCES

[1] P. Aubry, D. Lazard, and M. Moreno Maza. On the theories of triangular sets. *J. Symb. Comp.*, 28(1-2):105–124, 1999.

[2] F. Boulier, D. Lazard, F. Ollivier, and M. Petitot. Representation for the radical of a finitely generated differential ideal. In *proceedings of ISSAC'95*, pages 158–166, 1995.

[3] C. Chen, O. Golubitsky, F. Lemaire, M. Moreno Maza, and W. Pan. *Comprehensive Triangular Decomposition*, volume 4770 of *LNCS*, pages 73–101. Springer Verlag, 2007.

[4] C. Chen and M. Moreno Maza. Algorithms for Computing Triangular Decompositions of Polynomial System. *CoRR*, 2011.

[5] C. Chen, M. Moreno Maza, B. Xia, and L. Yang. Computing cylindrical algebraic decomposition via triangular decomposition. In *ISSAC'09*, pages 95–102, 2009.

[6] S.C. Chou and X.S. Gao. Solving parametric algebraic systems. In *Proc. ISSAC'92*, pages 335–341, 1992.

[7] X. Dahan, M. Moreno Maza, É. Schost, W. Wu, and Y. Xie. Lifting techniques for triangular decompositions. In *ISSAC'05*, pages 108–115. ACM Press, 2005.

[8] J. Della Dora, C. Dicrescenzo, and D. Duval. About a new method for computing in algebraic number fields. In *Proc. EUROCAL 85 Vol. 2*, pages 289–290. Springer-Verlag, 1985.

[9] L. Ducos. Optimizations of the subresultant algorithm. *Journal of Pure and Applied Algebra*, 145:149–163, 2000.

[10] X.-S. Gao, J. Van der Hoeven, Y. Luo, and C. Yuan. Characteristic set method for differential-difference polynomial systems. *J. Symb. Comput.*, 44:1137–1163, 2009.

[11] É. Hubert. Factorization free decomposition algorithms in differential algebra. *J. Symb. Comp.*, 29(4-5):641–662, 2000.

[12] M. Kalkbrener. A generalized euclidean algorithm for computing triangular representations of algebraic varieties. *J. Symb. Comp.*, 15:143–167, 1993.

[13] D. Lazard. A new method for solving algebraic systems of positive dimension. *Discr. App. Math*, 33:147–160, 1991.

[14] G. Lecerf. Computing the equidimensional decomposition of an algebraic closed set by means of lifting fibers. *J. Complexity*, 19(4):564–596, 2003.

[15] X. Li, M. Moreno Maza, and W. Pan. Computations modulo regular chains. In *Proc. ISSAC'09*, pages 239–246, New York, NY, USA, 2009. ACM Press.

[16] B. Mishra. *Algorithmic Algebra*. Springer-Verlag, 1993.

[17] M. Moreno Maza. On triangular decompositions of algebraic varieties. Technical Report TR 4/99, NAG Ltd, Oxford, UK, 1999. Presented at the MEGA-2000 Conference, Bath, England.

[18] T. Shimoyama and K. Yokoyama. Localization and primary decomposition of polynomial ideals. *J. Symb. Comput.*, 22(3):247–277, 1996.

[19] A.J. Sommese, J. Verschelde, and C. W. Wampler. Solving polynomial systems equation by equation. In *Algorithms in Algebraic Geometry*, pages 133–152. Springer-Verlag, 2008.

[20] D. K. Wang. The Wsolve package. http://www.mmrc.iss.ac.cn/~dwang/wsolve.txt.

[21] D. M. Wang. *Elimination Methods*. Springer, New York, 2000.

[22] W. T. Wu. A zero structure theorem for polynomial equations solving. *MM Research Preprints*, 1:2–12, 1987.

[23] L. Yang, X.R. Hou, and B. Xia. A complete algorithm for automated discovering of a class of inequality-type theorems. *Science in China, Series* **F**, 44(6):33–49, 2001.

[24] L. Yang and J. Zhang. Searching dependency between algebraic equations: an algorithm applied to automated reasoning. Technical Report IC/89/263, International Atomic Energy Agency, Miramare, Trieste, Italy, 1991.

On the Structure of Compatible Rational Functions[*]

Shaoshi Chen[1,2,3], Ruyong Feng[1], Guofeng Fu[1], Ziming Li[1]
[1]Key Lab of Math.-Mech. AMSS, Chinese Academy of Sciences, Beijing 100190, (China)
[2] Algorithms Project-Team, INRIA, Paris-Rocquencourt, 78513 Le Chesnay, (France)
[3] RISC, Johannes Kepler University, 4040 Linz, (Austria)
{schen, ryfeng}@amss.ac.cn,   {fuguofeng, zmli}@mmrc.iss.ac.cn

ABSTRACT

A finite number of rational functions are compatible if they satisfy the compatibility conditions of a first-order linear functional system involving differential, shift and q-shift operators. We present a theorem that describes the structure of compatible rational functions. The theorem enables us to decompose a solution of such a system as a product of a rational function, several symbolic powers, a hyperexponential function, a hypergeometric term, and a q-hypergeometric term. We outline an algorithm for computing this product, and present an application.

Categories and Subject Descriptors

I.1.2 [**Computing Methodologies**]: Symbolic and Algebraic Manipulation—*Algebraic Algorithms*

General Terms

Algorithms, Theory

Keywords

Compatibility conditions, compatible rational functions, hyperexponential function, (q-)hypergeometric term

1. INTRODUCTION

A linear functional system consists of linear partial differential, shift and q-shift operators. The commutativity of these operators implies that the coefficients of a linear functional system satisfy compatibility conditions.

[*]This work was supported in part by two grants of NSFC No. 60821002/F02 and No. 10901156. The first author was a PhD student in the Chinese Academy of Sciences and IN-RIA, Paris-Rocquencourt when the first draft of this paper was written. He is now a post doctoral fellow at RISC-Linz, and acknowledges the financial support by Austrian FWF grant Y464-N18

A nonzero solution of a first-order linear partial differential system in one unknown function is called a hyperexponential function. Christopher and Zoladek [9, 21] use the compatibility (integrability) conditions to show that a hyperexponential function can be written as a product of a rational function, finitely many power functions, and an exponential function. Their results generalize a well-known fact, namely, for a rational function $r(t)$,

$$\exp\left(\int r(t)dt\right) = f(t)r_1(t)^{e_1} \cdots r_m(t)^{e_m} \exp(g(t)),$$

where $e_1, \ldots, e_m$ are constants, and $f, r_1, \ldots, r_m, g$ are rational functions. The generalization is useful to compute Liouvilian first integrals.

A nonzero solution of a first-order linear partial difference system in one unknown term is called a hypergeometric term. The Ore-Sato Theorem [16, 18] states that a hypergeometric term is a product of a rational function, several power functions and factorial terms. A q-analogue of the Ore-Sato theorem is given in [11, 8]. All these results are based on compatibility conditions. The Ore-Sato theorem was rediscovered in one way or another, and is important for the proofs of a conjecture of Wilf and Zeilberger about holonomic hypergeometric terms [2, 4, 17]. This theorem and its q-analogue also play a crucial role in deriving criteria on the existence of telescopers for hypergeometric and q-hypergeometric terms, respectively [1, 8].

Consider a first-order mixed system

$$\left\{\frac{\partial z(t,x)}{\partial t} = u(t,x)z(t,x), \; z(t,x+1) = v(t,x)z(t,x)\right\},$$

where u and v are rational functions with $v \neq 0$. Its compatibility condition is $\partial v(t,x)/\partial t = v(t,x)(u(t,x+1) - u(t,x))$. By Proposition 5 in [10], a nonzero solution of the above system can be written as a product $f(t,x)r(t)^x \mathcal{E}(t)\mathcal{G}(x)$, where f is a bivariate rational function in t and x, r is a univariate rational function in t, $\mathcal{E}$ is a hyperexponential function in t, and $\mathcal{G}$ is a hypergeometric term in x. This proposition is used to compute Liouvillian solutions of difference-differential systems.

In fact, the above proposition is also fundamental for the criteria on the existence of telescopers when both differential and shift operators are involved [7]. This motivates us to generalize the proposition to include differential, difference and q-difference cases. Such a generalization will enable us to establish the existence of telescopers when both differential (shift) and q-shift operators appear. Next, the proof of the Wilf-Zeilberger conjecture for hypergeometric terms is based on the Ore-Sato theorem. So it is reasonable to expect that a structural theorem on compatible rational functions with respect to differential, shift and q-shift operators helps us study the conjecture in more general cases.

The main result of this paper is Theorem 5.4 which reveals a special structure of compatible rational functions. By the theorem, a hyperexponential-hypergeometric solution, defined in Section 2, is a product of a rational function, several symbolic powers, a hyperexponential function, a hypergeometric term, and a q-hypergeometric term (see Proposition 6.1). This paves the way to decompose such solutions by Christopher-Zoladek's generalization, the Ore-Sato Theorem, and its q-analogue.

This paper is organized as follows. The notion of compatible rational functions is introduced in Section 2. The bivariate case is studied in Section 3. After presenting a few preparation lemmas in Section 4, we prove in Section 5 a theorem that describes the structure of compatible rational functions. Section 6 is about algorithms and applications.

2. COMPATIBLE RATIONAL FUNCTIONS

In the rest of this paper, $\mathbb{F}$ is a field of characteristic zero. Let $\mathbf{t} = (t_1, \ldots, t_l)$, $\mathbf{x} = (x_1, \ldots, x_m)$ and $\mathbf{y} = (y_1, \ldots, y_n)$. Assume that $q_1, \ldots, q_n \in \mathbb{F}$ are neither zero nor roots of unity. For an element f of $\mathbb{F}(\mathbf{t}, \mathbf{x}, \mathbf{y})$, define $\delta_i(f) = \partial f / \partial t_i$ for all i with $1 \leq i \leq l$,

$$\sigma_j(f(\mathbf{t}, \mathbf{x}, \mathbf{y})) = f(\mathbf{t}, x_1, \ldots, x_{j-1}, x_j + 1, x_{j+1}, \ldots, x_m, \mathbf{y})$$

for all j with $1 \leq j \leq m$, and

$$\tau_k(f(\mathbf{t}, \mathbf{x}, \mathbf{y})) = f(\mathbf{t}, \mathbf{x}, y_1, \ldots, y_{k-1}, q_k y_k, y_{k+1}, \ldots, y_n)$$

for all k with $1 \leq k \leq n$. They are called derivations, shift operators, and q-shift operators, respectively.

Let $\Delta = \{\delta_1, \ldots, \delta_l, \sigma_1, \ldots, \sigma_m, \tau_1, \ldots, \tau_n\}$. These operators commute pairwise. The field of constants w.r.t. an operator in Δ consists of all rational functions free of the indeterminate on which the operator acts nontrivially.

By a first-order linear functional system over $\mathbb{F}(\mathbf{t}, \mathbf{x}, \mathbf{y})$, we mean a system consisting of

$$\delta_i(z) = u_i z, \; \sigma_j(z) = v_j z, \; \tau_k(z) = w_k z \qquad (1)$$

for some rational functions $u_i, v_j, w_k \in \mathbb{F}(\mathbf{t}, \mathbf{x}, \mathbf{y})$ and for all i, j, k with $1 \leq i \leq l$, $1 \leq j \leq m$ and $1 \leq k \leq n$. System (1) is said to be *compatible* if

$$v_1 \cdots v_m w_1 \cdots w_n \neq 0 \qquad (2)$$

and the conditions listed in (3)-(8) hold:

$$\delta_i(u_j) = \delta_j(u_i), \quad 1 \leq i < j \leq l, \qquad (3)$$

$$\sigma_i(v_j)/v_j = \sigma_j(v_i)/v_i, \quad 1 \leq i < j \leq m, \qquad (4)$$

$$\tau_i(w_j)/w_j = \tau_j(w_i)/w_i, \quad 1 \leq i < j \leq n, \qquad (5)$$

$$\delta_i(v_j)/v_j = \sigma_j(u_i) - u_i, \quad 1 \leq i \leq l \text{ and } 1 \leq j \leq m, \qquad (6)$$

$$\delta_i(w_k)/w_k = \tau_k(u_i) - u_i, \quad 1 \leq i \leq l \text{ and } 1 \leq k \leq n, \qquad (7)$$

$$\sigma_j(w_k)/w_k = \tau_k(v_j)/v_j, \quad 1 \leq j \leq m \text{ and } 1 \leq k \leq n. \qquad (8)$$

Compatibility conditions (3)-(8) are caused by the commutativity of the maps in Δ. A sequence of rational functions: $u_1, \ldots, u_l, v_1, \ldots, v_m, w_1, \ldots, w_n$ is said to be *compatible* w.r.t. Δ if (2)-(8) hold.

By a Δ-extension of $\mathbb{F}(\mathbf{t}, \mathbf{x}, \mathbf{y})$, we mean a ring extension R of $\mathbb{F}(\mathbf{t}, \mathbf{x}, \mathbf{y})$ s.t. every derivation and automorphism in Δ can be extended to a derivation and a monomorphism from R to R, and, moreover, the extended maps are commutative with each other. Given a finite number of first-order compatible systems, one can construct a Picard-Vessiot Δ-extension of $\mathbb{F}(\mathbf{t}, \mathbf{x}, \mathbf{y})$ that contains "all" solutions of these systems. Moreover, every nonzero solution is invertible. Details on Picard-Vessiot extensions of compatible systems may be found in [5]. More general and powerful extensions are described in [12]. By a *hyperexponential-hypergeometric solution h over* $\mathbb{F}(\mathbf{t}, \mathbf{x}, \mathbf{y})$, we mean a nonzero solution of the system (1). The coefficients u_i, v_j and w_k in (1) are called δ_i-, σ_j-, *and* τ_k-*certificates of h*, respectively. For brevity, we abbreviate "hyperexponential-hypergeometric solution" as "H-solution". An H-solution is a hyperexponential function when $m = n = 0$ in (1), it is a hypergeometric term if $l = n = 0$, and a q-hypergeometric term if $l = m = 0$.

REMARK 2.1. *We opt for the word "solution" rather than "function", since all the t_i, x_j and y_k are regarded as indeterminates. It is more sophisticated to regard hypergeometric terms as functions of integer variables [17, 4, 3].*

As a matter of notation, for an element $f \in \mathbb{F}(\mathbf{t}, \mathbf{x}, \mathbf{y})$, the denominator and numerator of f are denoted den(f) and num(f), respectively. Note that den(f) and num(f) are coprime. For a ring $\mathbb{A}$, $\mathbb{A}^\times$ stands for $\mathbb{A} \setminus \{0\}$, and for a field $\mathbb{E}$, $\overline{\mathbb{E}}$ stands for the algebraic closure of $\mathbb{E}$. For every $\phi \in \Delta$ and $f \in \mathbb{F}(\mathbf{t}, \mathbf{x}, \mathbf{y})^\times$, we denote by $\ell\phi(f)$ the fraction $\phi(f)/f$. When ϕ is a derivation δ_i, $\ell\delta_i(f)$ stands for the logarithmic derivative of f with respect to t_i. This notation allows us to avoid stacking fractions and subscripts.

Let $\mathbb{E}$ be a field and t an indeterminate. A nonzero element f of $\mathbb{E}(t)$ can be written uniquely as $f = p + r$, where $p \in \mathbb{E}[t]$ and r is a proper fraction. We say that p is the polynomial part of f w.r.t. t.

REMARK 2.2. *Let $z \in \{t_1, \ldots, t_l, x_1, \ldots, x_m, y_1, \ldots, y_n\}$ and $f \in \mathbb{F}(\mathbf{t}, \mathbf{x}, \mathbf{y})^\times$. For all i with $1 \leq i \leq l$, the polynomial part of $\ell\delta_i(f)$ w.r.t. z has degree at most zero in z.*

3. BIVARIATE CASE

In this section, we assume that $l = m = n = 1$. For brevity, set $t = t_1$, $x = x_1$, $y = y_1$, $\delta = \delta_1$, $\sigma = \sigma_1$, $\tau = \tau_1$, and $q = q_1$. By (2), (6), (7) and (8), three rational functions u, v, w in $\mathbb{F}(t, x, y)$ are Δ-compatible if $vw \neq 0$,

$$\ell\delta(v) = \sigma(u) - u, \qquad (9)$$

$$\ell\delta(w) = \tau(u) - u, \qquad (10)$$

$$\ell\sigma(w) = \ell\tau(v). \qquad (11)$$

Other compatibility conditions become trivial in this case.

EXAMPLE 3.1. *Let $\alpha \in \mathbb{F}(t, y)^\times$. The system consisting of $\delta(z) = \ell\delta(\alpha) x z$ and $\sigma(z) = \alpha z$ is compatible w.r.t. δ and σ. Denote a solution of this system by α^x, which is irrational if $\alpha \neq 1$.*

The next lemma is immediate from [10, Proposition 5].

LEMMA 3.1. *Let $u, v \in \mathbb{F}(t, x, y)$ with $v \neq 0$. If (9) holds, then $u = \ell\delta(f) + \ell\delta(\alpha) x + \beta$ and $v = \ell\sigma(f) \alpha\lambda$ for some f in $\mathbb{F}(t, x, y)$, α, β in $\mathbb{F}(t, y)$, and λ in $\mathbb{F}(x, y)$.*

Assume that an H-solution h has δ-certificate u and σ-certificate v. By Lemma 3.1, $h = cf\alpha^x \mathcal{E}\mathcal{G}$ in some Δ-ring, where c is a constant w.r.t. δ and σ, $\mathcal{E}$ is hyperexponential with certificate β, and $\mathcal{G}$ is hypergeometric with certificate λ.

We shall prove two similar results: one is about differential and q-shift variables; the other about shift and q-shift ones. To this end, we recall some terminologies from [2, 4, 12].

Let $\mathbb{A} = \mathbb{F}(t, y)$ and $p \in \mathbb{A}[x]^{\times}$. The σ-*dispersion* of p is defined to be the largest nonnegative integer i s.t. for some r in $\overline{\mathbb{A}}$, r and $r + i$ are roots of p. Let $f \in \mathbb{A}(x)^{\times}$. We say that f is σ-*reduced* if $\text{den}(f)$ and $\sigma^i(\text{num}(f))$ are coprime for every integer i; and that f is σ-*standard* if zero is the σ-dispersion of $\text{num}(f)\text{den}(f)$. A σ-standard rational function is a σ-reduced one, but the converse is false. By Lemma 6.2 in [12], $f = \ell\sigma(a)\,b$ for some a, b in $\mathbb{A}(x)$ with b being σ-standard or σ-reduced.

Let $\mathbb{B} = \mathbb{F}(t, x)$ and $p \in \mathbb{B}[y]^{\times}$. The τ-*dispersion* of p is defined to be the largest nonnegative integer i s.t. for some *nonzero* $r \in \overline{\mathbb{B}}$, r and $q^i r$ are roots of p. In addition, the τ-dispersion of p is set to be zero if $p = cy^k$ for some $c \in \mathbb{B}$. Let $f \in \mathbb{B}(y)^{\times}$. The *polar* τ-*dispersion* is the τ-dispersion of $\text{den}(f)$. The notion of τ-reduced and τ-standard rational functions are defined likewise. One can write $f = \ell\tau(a)\,b$, where $a, b \in \mathbb{B}(y)^{\times}$ and b is τ-standard or τ-reduced.

Now, we prove a q-analogue of Lemma 3.1.

LEMMA 3.2. *Let* $u, w \in \mathbb{F}(t, x, y)$ *with* $w \neq 0$. *If (10) holds, then* $u = \ell\delta(f) + a$ *and* $w = \ell\tau(f)\,b$ *for some* f *in* $\mathbb{F}(t, x, y)$, a *in* $\mathbb{F}(t, x)$, *and* b *in* $\mathbb{F}(x, y)$.

PROOF. Set $w = \ell\tau(f)\,b$ for some f, b in $\mathbb{F}(t, x, y)$ with b being τ-standard. Set $b = y^k P/Q$, where $P, Q \in \mathbb{F}(x)[t, y]$ are coprime, and neither is divisible by y. Since b is τ-standard, so is P/Q. Assume $u = \ell\delta(f) + a$. By (10),

$$\ell\delta(P/Q) = \tau(a) - a. \tag{12}$$

Since P/Q is τ-standard, the τ-dispersion of PQ is zero, and so is the polar τ-dispersion of the left-hand side in (12), which, together with [12, Lemma 6.3], implies that a belongs to $\mathbb{F}(t, x)[y, y^{-1}]$. Moreover, a is free of positive powers of y by Remark 2.2 (setting $z = y$); and a is free of negative powers of y, because neither P nor Q is divisible by y. We conclude that a is in $\mathbb{F}(t, x)$. Consequently, $\tau(a) = a$. It follows from (12) that $\delta(P/Q) = 0$, i.e., b is in $\mathbb{F}(x, y)$. □

By the above lemma, an H-solution h can be written as a product of a constant w.r.t. δ and τ, a rational function, a hyperexponential function, and a q-hypergeometric term.

The last lemma is a q-analogue of [4, Theorem 9]. Our proof is based on an easy consequence of [20, Lemma 2.1].

FACT 3.1. *Let* $a, b \in \mathbb{F}(t, x, y)^{\times}$. *If* $\sigma(a) = ba$, *and* P *is an irreducible factor of* $\text{den}(b)$ *with* $\deg_x P > 0$, *then* $\sigma^i(P)$ *is a factor of* $\text{num}(b)$ *for some nonzero integer* i.

The same is true if we swap $\text{den}(b)$ *and* $\text{num}(b)$ *in the above assertion.*

LEMMA 3.3. *Let* $v, w \in \mathbb{F}(t, x, y)^{\times}$. *If (11) holds, then* $v = \ell\sigma(f)\,a$ *and* $w = \ell\tau(f)\,b$ *for some* f *in* $\mathbb{F}(t, x, y)$, a *in* $\mathbb{F}(t, x)$, *and* b *in* $\mathbb{F}(t, y)$.

PROOF. In this proof, $P \mid Q$ means that $P, Q \in \mathbb{F}(t)[x, y]^{\times}$ and $Q = PR$ for some $R \in \mathbb{F}(t)[x, y]$.

Set $v = \ell\sigma(f)\,a$, where $f, a \in \mathbb{F}(t, x, y)$ and a is σ-reduced. Assume $w = \ell\tau(f)\,b$. By (11), $\ell\sigma(b) = \ell\tau(a)$, that is,

$$\sigma(b) = gb, \quad \text{where } g = \frac{\tau(\text{num}(a))\,\text{den}(a)}{\tau(\text{den}(a))\,\text{num}(a)}. \tag{13}$$

First, we show that a is the product of an element in $\mathbb{F}(t, x)$ and an element in $\mathbb{F}(t, y)$. Suppose the contrary. Then there is an irreducible polynomial $P \in \mathbb{F}(t)[x, y]$ with $\deg_x P > 0$ and $\deg_y P > 0$ s.t. P divides $\text{den}(a)\text{num}(a)$ in $\mathbb{F}(t)[x, y]$. Assume that $P \mid \text{num}(a)$. If $P \nmid \text{den}(g)$, then $P \mid \tau(\text{num}(a))$ since $\text{num}(a)$ and $\text{den}(a)$ are coprime. So $\tau^{-1}(P) \mid \text{num}(a)$. If $P \mid \text{den}(g)$, then $\sigma^i(P) \mid \text{num}(g)$ for some integer i by (13) and Fact 3.1. Thus, $\sigma^i(P) \mid \tau(\text{num}(a))$, because $\text{num}(g)$ is a factor of $\tau(\text{num}(a))\text{den}(a)$ and a is σ-reduced. This implies $\sigma^i\tau^{-1}(P) \mid \text{num}(a)$. In either case, we have that

$$\sigma^j\tau^{-1}(P) \mid \text{num}(a) \quad \text{for some integer } j.$$

Assume $P \mid \text{den}(a)$. Then the same argument implies

$$\sigma^k\tau^{-1}(P) \mid \text{den}(a) \quad \text{for some integer } k.$$

Hence, there exists an integer m_1 s.t. $P_1 := \sigma^{m_1}\tau^{-1}(P_0)$ is an irreducible factor of $\text{den}(a)\text{num}(a)$, where $P_0 = P$. A repeated use of the above reasoning leads to an infinite sequence of irreducible polynomials $P_0, P_1, P_2, \ldots$ in $\mathbb{F}(t)[x, y]$ s.t. $P_i = \sigma^{m_i}\tau^{-1}(P_{i-1})$ and $P_i \mid \text{den}(a)\text{num}(a)$. Therefore, there are two $\mathbb{F}(t)$-linearly dependent members in the sequence. Using these two members, we get $P_0 = c\sigma^m\tau^n(P_0)$ for some c in $\mathbb{F}(t)$ and m, n in $\mathbb{Z}$ with $n \neq 0$. Write

$$P_0 = p_d(x)y^d + p_{d-1}(x)y^{d-1} + \cdots + p_0(x),$$

where $d > 0$, $p_i \in \mathbb{F}(t)[x]$ and $p_d \neq 0$. Then

$$p_d(x) = cp_d(x + m)q^{-dn} \quad \text{and} \quad p_0(x) = cp_0(x + m).$$

Since P_0 is irreducible and of positive degree in x, p_0 is also nonzero. We see that $1 = cq^{-dn}$ and $1 = c$ when comparing the leading coefficients in the above two equalities. Consequently, q is a root of unity, a contradiction. This proves that all irreducible factors of $\text{den}(a)\text{num}(a)$ are either in $\mathbb{F}(t)[x]$ or $\mathbb{F}(t)[y]$. Therefore, a is a product of an element in $\mathbb{F}(t, x)$ and an element in $\mathbb{F}(t, y)$.

So we can write $a = a_1 a_2$ for some a_1 in $\mathbb{F}(t, x)$ and a_2 in $\mathbb{F}(t, y)$. By $\ell\sigma(b) = \ell\tau(a)$, the equation $\sigma(z) = \ell\tau(a_2)z$ has a rational solution b. Since $\ell\tau(a_2)$ is a constant w.r.t. σ, we conclude $\ell\tau(a_2) = 1$, for otherwise, $\sigma(z) = \ell\tau(a_2)z$ would have no rational solution. So $b \in \mathbb{F}(t, y)$ and $a \in \mathbb{F}(t, x)$. □

Similar to Lemmas 3.1 and 3.2, the above lemma implies that an H-solution h can be written as a product of a constant w.r.t. σ and τ, a rational function, a hypergeometric term, and a q-hypergeometric term.

We shall extend these lemmas to multivariate cases in Section 5. Before closing this section, we present three examples to illustrate calculations involving compatibility conditions. These calculations are useful in Section 5.

EXAMPLE 3.2. *Assume*

$$u = \ell\delta(f) + \ell\delta(a)\,x + b \quad \text{and} \quad v = \ell\sigma(f)\,a\,c,$$

where $f, c \in \mathbb{F}(t, x, y)^{\times}$, $a \in \mathbb{F}(t, y)^{\times}$, *and* $b \in \mathbb{F}(t, x, y)$. *By the logarithmic derivative identity: for all* r, s *in* $\mathbb{F}(t, x, y)^{\times}$, $\ell\delta(r\,s) = \ell\delta(r) + \ell\delta(s)$, *we get*

$$\ell\delta(v) = \ell\delta \circ \ell\sigma(f) + \ell\delta(a) + \ell\delta(c).$$

Since $\ell\delta(a)$ *is constant w.r.t.* σ, *and* $\sigma \circ \ell\delta = \ell\delta \circ \sigma$, *we have*

$$\begin{aligned}
\sigma(u) - u &= \sigma \circ \ell\delta(f) - \ell\delta(f) + \ell\delta(a) + \sigma(b) - b \\
&= \ell\delta \circ \ell\sigma(f) + \ell\delta(a) + \sigma(b) - b.
\end{aligned}$$

If (9) holds, then $\ell\delta(c)=\sigma(b)-b$. Hence, $\delta(c)=0$ iff $\sigma(b)=b$, i.e., $c \in \mathbb{F}(x,y)$ iff $b \in \mathbb{F}(t,y)$.

EXAMPLE 3.3. *Assume* $u = \ell\delta(f) + a$ *and* $w = \ell\tau(f)\,b$, *where* $a \in \mathbb{F}(t,x,y)$ *and* $f,b \in \mathbb{F}(t,x,y)^\times$. *If* (10) *holds, then a similar calculation as above yields* $\ell\delta(b) = \tau(a) - a$. *Hence,* $\delta(b) = 0$ *iff* $\tau(a) = a$, *i.e.,* $b \in \mathbb{F}(x,y)$ *iff* $a \in \mathbb{F}(t,x)$.

EXAMPLE 3.4. *Assume* $v = \ell\sigma(f)\,a$ *and* $w = \ell\tau(f)\,b$, *where* $f,a,b \in \mathbb{F}(t,x,y)^\times$. *Applying* $\ell\sigma, \ell\tau$ *to* w,v, *respectively, we see that*

$$\ell\sigma(w) = \ell\sigma \circ \ell\tau(f)\,\ell\sigma(b), \quad \ell\tau(v) = \ell\tau \circ \ell\sigma(f)\,\ell\tau(a).$$

If (11) *holds, then* $\ell\sigma(b) = \ell\tau(a)$, *because* $\ell\sigma \circ \ell\tau = \ell\tau \circ \ell\sigma$. *Hence,* $\sigma(b) = b$ *iff* $\tau(a) = a$, *i.e.,* $b \in \mathbb{F}(t,y)$ *iff* $a \in \mathbb{F}(t,x)$.

4. PREPARATION LEMMAS

To extend Lemmas 3.1, 3.2, and 3.3 to multivariate cases, we will proceed by induction on the number of variables. There arise different expressions for a rational function in our induction. Lemmas given in this section will be used to eliminate redundant indeterminates in these expressions.

We define a few additive subgroups of $\mathbb{F}(\mathbf{t},\mathbf{x},\mathbf{y})$ to avoid complicated expressions.

$$L_i = \left\{\ell\delta_i(f) \mid f \in \mathbb{F}(\mathbf{t},\mathbf{x},\mathbf{y})^\times \right\}, \; i = 1,\dots,l,$$

$$M_i = \left\{\sum_{j=1}^m \ell\delta_i(g_j)\,x_j \mid g_j \in \mathbb{F}(\mathbf{t},\mathbf{y})^\times\right\}, \; i = 1,\dots,l.$$

For $i = 1,\dots,l$ and $j = 1,\dots,m$, $M_{i,j}$ denotes the group

$$\left\{\sum_{k=1}^{j-1} \ell\delta_i(g_k)\,x_k + \sum_{k=j+1}^m \ell\delta_i(g_k)\,x_k \mid g_k \in \mathbb{F}(\mathbf{t},x_j,\mathbf{y})^\times\right\}.$$

Moreover, we set

$$N_i = L_i + M_i + \mathbb{F}(\mathbf{t},\mathbf{y}) \quad \text{and} \quad N_{i,j} = L_i + M_{i,j} + \mathbb{F}(\mathbf{t},x_j,\mathbf{y}).$$

Let $Z = \{t_1,\dots,t_l,x_1,\dots,x_m,y_1,\dots,y_n\}$. We will use an evaluation trick in the sequel. Let $Z' = \{z_1,\dots,z_s\}$ be a subset of Z. For $f \in \mathbb{F}(\mathbf{t},\mathbf{x},\mathbf{y})^\times$, there exist $\xi_1,\dots,\xi_s$ in $\mathbb{F}$ s.t. f evaluated at $z_1 = \xi_1,\dots,z_s = \xi_s$ is a well-defined and nonzero rational function f'. We say that f' is a *proper evaluation* of f w.r.t. Z'. A proper evaluation can be carried out for finitely many rational functions as well. In addition, we say that a rational function f is free of Z' if it is free of every indeterminate in Z'.

REMARK 4.1. *If* $Z' \subset Z$, $f \in L_i$ *and* $t_i \notin Z'$, *then all proper evaluations of* f *w.r.t.* Z' *are also in* L_i.

In the next example, we illustrate two typical proper evaluations to be used later.

EXAMPLE 4.2. *Let* $f = \ell\delta_i(r)$ *for some* $f,r \in \mathbb{F}(\mathbf{t},\mathbf{x},\mathbf{y})^\times$. *Assume that both* $f(\mathbf{t},\boldsymbol{\xi},\mathbf{y})$ *and* $r(\mathbf{t},\boldsymbol{\xi},\mathbf{y})$ *are well-defined and nonzero, where* $\boldsymbol{\xi} \in \mathbb{F}^m$. *Then* $f(\mathbf{t},\boldsymbol{\xi},\mathbf{y})$ *is still in* L_i.

Let $g \in \mathbb{F}(\mathbf{t},\mathbf{y})^\times$. *Then* $\delta_i(z) = gz$ *has a rational solution in* $\mathbb{F}(\mathbf{t},\mathbf{y})^\times$ *if it has a rational solution in* $\mathbb{F}(\mathbf{t},\mathbf{x},\mathbf{y})^\times$. *This can also be shown by a proper evaluation.*

The following lemma helps us merge rational expressions involving logarithmic derivatives.

LEMMA 4.1. *Let* $i \in \{1,\dots,l\}$.

(i) *Let* $Z_1,Z_2 \subset Z$ *with* $Z_1 \cap Z_2 = \emptyset$. *If* $\mathbb{A}$ *is any subfield of* $\mathbb{F}(\mathbf{t},\mathbf{x},\mathbf{y})$ *whose elements are free of* t_i *and free of* $Z_1 \cup Z_2$, *then*

$$L_i + \mathbb{A}(t_i) = (L_i + \mathbb{A}(t_i,Z_1)) \cap (L_i + \mathbb{A}(t_i,Z_2)).$$

(ii) *If* $d,e \in \{1,\dots,m\}$ *with* $d \neq e$, *then* $N_i = N_{i,d} \cap N_{i,e}$.

PROOF. To prove the first assertion, note that $L_i + \mathbb{A}(t_i)$ is a subset of $(L_i + \mathbb{A}(t_i,Z_1)) \cap (L_i + \mathbb{A}(t_i,Z_2))$. Assume that a is in $(L_i + \mathbb{A}(t_i,Z_1)) \cap (L_i + \mathbb{A}(t_i,Z_2))$. Then there exist $a_1 \in \mathbb{A}(t_i,Z_1)$ and $a_2 \in \mathbb{A}(t_i,Z_2)$ s.t.

$$a \equiv a_1 \mod L_i \quad \text{and} \quad a \equiv a_2 \mod L_i.$$

Hence, $a_1 - a_2 \in L_i$. Let $Z_2' = Z_2 \setminus \{t_i\}$, and a_2' be a proper evaluation of a_2 w.r.t. Z_2'. Then $a_1 - a_2'$ is a proper evaluation of $a_1 - a_2$ w.r.t. Z_2', because a_1 is free of Z_2'. Thus, $a_1 - a_2'$ belongs to L_i by Remark 4.1. Since a_2' is in $\mathbb{A}(t_i)$, a_1 is in $L_i + \mathbb{A}(t_i)$, and so is a.

To prove the second assertion, assume $i = 1$, $d = 1$ and $e = m$. Note that $N_1 \subset N_{1,1} \cap N_{1,m}$, because M_1 is contained in $(M_{1,1} + \mathbb{F}(\mathbf{t},x_1,\mathbf{y})) \cap (M_{1,m} + \mathbb{F}(\mathbf{t},x_m,\mathbf{y}))$. It remains to show $N_{1,1} \cap N_{1,m} \subset N_1$. Let $a \in N_{1,1} \cap N_{1,m}$. Then

$$a = \ell\delta_1(f) + \left(\sum_{j=2}^{m-1} \ell\delta_1(g_j)\,x_j\right) + \ell\delta_1(g_m)\,x_m + r \quad (14)$$

$$= \ell\delta_1(\tilde{f}) + \ell\delta_1(\tilde{g}_1)\,x_1 + \left(\sum_{j=2}^{m-1} \ell\delta_1(\tilde{g}_j)\,x_j\right) + \tilde{r}, \quad (15)$$

where $f,\tilde{f} \in \mathbb{F}(\mathbf{t},\mathbf{x},\mathbf{y})$, $g_j,r \in \mathbb{F}(\mathbf{t},x_1,\mathbf{y})$, $\tilde{g}_j,\tilde{r} \in \mathbb{F}(\mathbf{t},x_m,\mathbf{y})$ and $f\tilde{f}g_j\tilde{g}_j \neq 0$. For all j with $1 \leq j \leq m$, let P_j be the polynomial part of a w.r.t. x_j. Then $\deg_{x_j} P_j \leq 1$ for all j with $1 \leq j \leq m-1$ by Remark 2.2 and (15), and $\deg_{x_m} P_m \leq 1$ by the same Remark and (14).

Claim. Let b_j denote the coefficient of x_j in P_j. Then there exists $s_j \in \mathbb{F}(\mathbf{t},\mathbf{y})$ s.t. $b_j = \ell\delta_1(s_j)$ for all j with $1 \leq j \leq m$.

Proof of Claim. By (14) and Remark 2.2, b_1 is the coefficient of x_1 in the polynomial part of r w.r.t. x_1. So b_1 is in $\mathbb{F}(\mathbf{t},\mathbf{y})$. By (15) and the same remark, $b_1 = \ell\delta_1(\tilde{g}_1)$. Let s_1 be a proper evaluation of $\tilde{g}_1$ w.r.t. x_m. Then $b_1 = \ell\delta_1(s_1)$ as b_1 is free of x_m. By the same argument, $b_m = \ell\delta_1(s_m)$ for some s_m in $\mathbb{F}(\mathbf{t},\mathbf{x})$. By (14) and (15), $b_j = \ell\delta_1(g_j) = \ell\delta_1(\tilde{g}_j)$ for all j with $2 \leq j \leq m-1$. Let s_j be a proper evaluation of $\tilde{g}_j$ w.r.t. x_m. Then $\ell\delta_j(g_j) = \ell\delta_j(s_j)$, because g_j is free of x_m. Hence, $b_j = \ell\delta_1(s_j)$. The claim holds.

Set $b = \sum_{j=1}^m b_j x_j$. Then $a - b$ is in $L_1 + \mathbb{F}(\mathbf{t},x_1,\mathbf{y})$ and $L_1 + \mathbb{F}(\mathbf{t},x_m,\mathbf{y})$ by (14), (15) and the claim. Thus, $a - b$ is in $L_1 + \mathbb{F}(\mathbf{t},\mathbf{y})$ by the first assertion (setting $Z_1 = \{x_1\}$, $Z_2 = \{x_m\}$, and $\mathbb{A} = \mathbb{F}(t_2,\dots,t_l,\mathbf{y})$). By the claim, b is in M_1. Thus, a is in $L_1 + M_1 + \mathbb{F}(\mathbf{t},\mathbf{y})$. $\square$

We define a few multiplicative subgroups in $\mathbb{F}(\mathbf{t},\mathbf{x},\mathbf{y})^\times$. Let $G_j = \{\ell\sigma_j(f) \mid f \in \mathbb{F}(\mathbf{t},\mathbf{x},\mathbf{y})^\times\}$ for $j = 1,\dots,m$. Similarly, let $H_k = \{\ell\tau_k(f) \mid f \in \mathbb{F}(\mathbf{t},\mathbf{x},\mathbf{y})^\times\}$ for $k = 1,\dots,n$.

REMARK 4.3. *If* $Z' \subset Z$, $f \in H_k$ *and* $y_k \notin Z'$, *then all proper evaluations of* f *w.r.t.* Z' *are in* H_k. *The same holds for* G_j.

The next lemma helps us merge rational expressions involving shift or q-shift quotients.

LEMMA 4.2. *Let* $j \in \{1,\dots,m\}$, $k \in \{1,\dots,n\}$. *Assume that* Z_1 *and* Z_2 *are disjoint subsets of* Z.

(i) *If $\mathbb{A}$ is any subfield of $\mathbb{F}(\mathbf{t},\mathbf{x},\mathbf{y})$ whose elements are free of x_j and free of $Z_1 \cup Z_2$, then*

$$G_j \mathbb{A}(x_j)^{\times} = \left(G_j \mathbb{A}(x_j, Z_1)^{\times} \right) \cap \left(G_j \mathbb{A}(x_j, Z_2)^{\times} \right).$$

(ii) *If $\mathbb{A}$ is any subfield of $\mathbb{F}(\mathbf{t},\mathbf{x},\mathbf{y})$ whose elements are free of y_k and free of $Z_1 \cup Z_2$, then*

$$H_k \mathbb{A}(y_k)^{\times} = \left(H_k \mathbb{A}(y_k, Z_1)^{\times} \right) \cap \left(H_k \mathbb{A}(y_k, Z_2)^{\times} \right).$$

(iii) *If $\mathbb{A} = \mathbb{F}(\mathbf{t},\mathbf{y})$ and $\mathbb{B} = \mathbb{F}(\mathbf{x},\mathbf{y})$, then*

$$G_j \mathbb{A}^{\times} \mathbb{B}^{\times} = \left(G_j \mathbb{A}^{\times} \mathbb{B}(Z_1)^{\times} \right) \cap \left(G_j \mathbb{A}^{\times} \mathbb{B}(Z_2)^{\times} \right).$$

PROOF. The proofs of the first two assertions are similar to that of Lemma 4.1 (i). So we only outline the proof of the second assertion. Clearly,

$$H_k \mathbb{A}(y_k)^{\times} \subset \left(H_k \mathbb{A}(y_k, Z_1)^{\times} \right) \cap \left(H_k \mathbb{A}(y_k, Z_2)^{\times} \right).$$

For an element $a \in \left(H_k \mathbb{A}(y_k, Z_1)^{\times} \right) \cap \left(H_k \mathbb{A}(y_k, Z_2)^{\times} \right)$, there exist $a_1 \in \mathbb{A}(y_k, Z_1)^{\times}$ and $a_2 \in \mathbb{A}(y_k, Z_2)^{\times}$ s.t.

$$a \equiv a_1 \mod H_k \quad \text{and} \quad a \equiv a_2 \mod H_k.$$

Using a proper evaluation, one sees that a is in $H_k \mathbb{A}(y_k)^{\times}$.

We present a detailed proof of the third assertion due to the presence of both $\mathbb{A}$ and $\mathbb{B}$, though the idea goes along the same line as before. It suffices to show that the intersection of $G_j \mathbb{A}^{\times} \mathbb{B}(Z_1)^{\times}$ and $G_j \mathbb{A}^{\times} \mathbb{B}(Z_2)^{\times}$ is a subset of $G_j \mathbb{A}^{\times} \mathbb{B}^{\times}$. Assume that a is in the intersection. Then

$$a \equiv a_1 b_1 \mod G_j \quad \text{and} \quad a \equiv a_2 b_2 \mod G_j \quad (16)$$

for some a_1, a_2 in $\mathbb{A}^{\times}$, b_1 in $\mathbb{B}(Z_1)^{\times}$, and b_2 in $\mathbb{B}(Z_2)^{\times}$. Let $Z_2' = Z_2 \setminus \mathbb{B}$, and c be a proper evaluation of $a_1/(a_2 b_2)$ w.r.t. Z_2'. Then $c b_1$ is a proper evaluation of $a_1 b_1/(a_2 b_2)$ w.r.t. Z_2', as b_1 is free of Z_2'. So $c b_1$ is in G_j by Remark 4.3. Since c is in $\mathbb{A}^{\times} \mathbb{B}^{\times}$, b_1 is in $G_j \mathbb{A}^{\times} \mathbb{B}^{\times}$, and so is a. $\square$

The next lemma says that some compatible rational functions belong to a common coset.

LEMMA 4.3. *Let $v_1, \ldots, v_m, w_1, \ldots, w_n \in \mathbb{F}(\mathbf{t},\mathbf{x},\mathbf{y})^{\times}$. Assume that the compatibility conditions in (4) and (5) hold.*

(i) *If v_j is in $G_j \mathbb{F}(\mathbf{t},\mathbf{y})^{\times} \mathbb{F}(\mathbf{x},\mathbf{y})^{\times}$ for all j with $1 \leq j \leq m$, then there exists $f \in \mathbb{F}(\mathbf{t},\mathbf{x},\mathbf{y})$ s.t. each v_j is in the coset $\ell\sigma_j(f)\mathbb{F}(\mathbf{t},\mathbf{y})^{\times}\mathbb{F}(\mathbf{x},\mathbf{y})^{\times}$.*

(ii) *Let $\mathbb{E}$ be a subfield of $\mathbb{F}(\mathbf{t},\mathbf{x})$. If $w_k \in H_k\mathbb{E}(\mathbf{y})^{\times}$ for all k with $1 \leq k \leq n$, then there exists $f \in \mathbb{F}(\mathbf{t},\mathbf{x},\mathbf{y})$ s.t. each w_k is in the coset $\ell\tau_k(f)\mathbb{E}(\mathbf{y})^{\times}$.*

PROOF. We are going to show the second assertion. The first one can be proved in the same fashion.

The second assertion clearly holds when $n = 1$. Assume that $n > 1$ and the lemma holds for $n - 1$. Then there exist $g \in \mathbb{F}(\mathbf{t},\mathbf{x},\mathbf{y})$ and $b_1, \ldots, b_{n-1} \in \mathbb{E}(\mathbf{y})$ s.t. $w_k = \ell\tau_k(g)b_k$ for all k with $1 \leq k \leq n-1$. Assume

$$w_n = \ell\tau_n(g)\, a \quad \text{for some } a \in \mathbb{F}(\mathbf{t},\mathbf{x},\mathbf{y}). \quad (17)$$

Then the compatibility conditions in (5) imply that the first-order system $\{\tau_k(z) = \ell\tau_n(b_k)\, z \mid k = 1, \ldots, n-1\}$ has a solution a in $\mathbb{F}(\mathbf{t},\mathbf{x},\mathbf{y})^{\times}$. It follows from the hypothesis $b_k \in \mathbb{E}(\mathbf{y})$ for all k with $1 \leq k \leq n-1$ that the above system has a solution a' in $\mathbb{E}(\mathbf{y})^{\times}$. Thus, $a = c\, a'$ for some constant c w.r.t. $\tau_1, \ldots, \tau_{n-1}$. Consequently, c belongs to $\mathbb{F}(\mathbf{t},\mathbf{x},y_n)$. On one hand, (17) leads to

$$w_n = \ell\tau_n(g)\, c a'. \quad (18)$$

On the other hand, $w_n \in H_n\mathbb{E}(\mathbf{y})^{\times}$ implies $c = \ell\tau_n(s)\, r$ for some r in $\mathbb{E}(\mathbf{y})$ and s in $\mathbb{F}(\mathbf{t},\mathbf{x},\mathbf{y})$. Let $Z' = \{y_1, \ldots, y_{n-1}\}$, and let s' and r' be two proper evaluations of s and r w.r.t. Z' at a point in $\mathbb{F}^{n-1}$, respectively. Then $c = \ell\tau_n(s')\, r'$ since c is free of Z'. By (18), $w_n = \ell\tau_n(s'g)\, r'a'$. Set $f = s'g$ and $b_n = r'a'$. Then $w_k = \ell\tau_k(f)\, b_k$ for all k with $1 \leq k \leq n$, as s' is a constant w.r.t. $\tau_1, \ldots, \tau_{n-1}$. $\square$

5. A STRUCTURE THEOREM

In this section, we extend Lemmas 3.1, 3.2 and 3.3, and then combine these results to a structure theorem on Δ-compatible rational functions.

The first proposition extends Lemma 3.1.

PROPOSITION 5.1. *Let $u_1, \ldots, u_l, v_1, \ldots, v_m$ be rational functions in $\mathbb{F}(\mathbf{t},\mathbf{x},\mathbf{y})$ with $v_1 \cdots v_m \neq 0$. If the compatibility conditions in (3), (4) and (6) hold, then there exist f in $\mathbb{F}(\mathbf{t},\mathbf{x},\mathbf{y})$, $a_1, \ldots, a_m, b_1, \ldots, b_l$ in $\mathbb{F}(\mathbf{t},\mathbf{y})$, and $c_1, \ldots, c_m$ in $\mathbb{F}(\mathbf{x},\mathbf{y})$ s.t., for all i with $1 \leq i \leq l$,*

$$u_i = \ell\delta_i(f) + \ell\delta_i(a_1)\, x_1 + \cdots + \ell\delta_i(a_m)\, x_m + b_i,$$

and, for all j with $1 \leq j \leq m$,

$$v_j = \ell\sigma_j(f)\, a_j\, c_j.$$

Moreover, the sequence $b_1, \ldots, b_l, c_1, \ldots, c_m$ is compatible w.r.t. $\{\delta_1, \ldots, \delta_l, \sigma_1, \ldots, \sigma_m\}$.

PROOF. First, we consider the case in which $l = 1$ and m arbitrary. The proposition holds when $m = 1$ by Lemma 3.1. Assume that $m > 1$ and the proposition holds for the values lower than m. Applying the induction hypothesis to $t_1, x_1, \ldots, x_{m-1}$ and to $t_1, x_2, \ldots, x_m$, respectively, we see that both $u_1 \in N_{1,m}$ and $u_1 \in N_{1,1}$. Since $m > 1$, $u_1 \in N_1$ by Lemma 4.1 (ii). Hence,

$$u_1 = \ell\delta_1(f) + \ell\delta_1(a_1)\, x_1 + \cdots + \ell\delta_1(a_m)x_m + b_1$$

for some $f \in \mathbb{F}(t_1,\mathbf{x},\mathbf{y})$ and $a_1, \ldots, a_m, b_1 \in \mathbb{F}(t_1,\mathbf{y})$. Assume that $v_j = \ell\sigma_j(f)\, a_j c_j$. Then $c_1, \ldots, c_m$ are in $\mathbb{F}(\mathbf{x},\mathbf{y})$ by the compatibility conditions in (6) (see Example 3.2). The proposition holds for $l = 1$ and m arbitrary.

Second, we show that the proposition holds for all l and m by induction on l. It holds if $l = 1$ by the preceding paragraph. Assume that $l > 1$ and that the proposition holds for the values lower than l. Applying the induction hypothesis to $t_1, \ldots, t_{l-1}, \mathbf{x}$ and to $t_2, \ldots, t_l, \mathbf{x}$, respectively, we have

$$v_j \in \left(G_j \mathbb{A}^{\times} \mathbb{B}(Z_1)^{\times} \right) \cap \left(G_j \mathbb{A}^{\times} \mathbb{B}(Z_2)^{\times} \right),$$

where $\mathbb{A} = \mathbb{F}(\mathbf{t},\mathbf{y})$, $\mathbb{B} = \mathbb{F}(\mathbf{x},\mathbf{y})$, $Z_1 = \{t_l\}$, and $Z_2 = \{t_1\}$. We see that $v_j \in G_j \mathbb{A}^{\times} \mathbb{B}^{\times}$ by Lemma 4.2 (iii). So $v_j \in \ell\sigma_j(f)\mathbb{A}^{\times}\mathbb{B}^{\times}$ for some f in $\mathbb{F}(\mathbf{t},\mathbf{x},\mathbf{y})$ by Lemma 4.3 (i). Thus,

$$v_j = \ell\sigma_j(f)\, a_j\, c_j,$$

where $a_j \in \mathbb{A}$, $c_j \in \mathbb{B}$ and $j = 1, \ldots, m$. Assume that, for all i with $1 \leq i \leq l$, $u_i = \ell\delta_i(f) + \sum_{j=1}^{m} \ell\delta_i(a_j)\, x_j + b_i$. All the b_i's belong to $\mathbb{F}(\mathbf{t},\mathbf{y})$ by the compatibility conditions in (6) (see Example 3.2). The sequence $b_1, \ldots, b_l, c_1, \ldots, c_m$ is compatible because of (3), (4) and (6). $\square$

The second proposition extends Lemma 3.2.

PROPOSITION 5.2. *Let $u_1, \ldots, u_l, w_1, \ldots, w_n$ be rational functions in $\mathbb{F}(\mathbf{t},\mathbf{x},\mathbf{y})$ with $w_1 \cdots w_n \neq 0$. Assume that the compatibility conditions (3), (5) and (7) hold. Then* there exist f in $\mathbb{F}(\mathbf{t}, \mathbf{x}, \mathbf{y})$, $a_1, \ldots, a_l$ in $\mathbb{F}(\mathbf{t}, \mathbf{x})$, and $b_1, \ldots, b_n$ in $\mathbb{F}(\mathbf{x}, \mathbf{y})$ s.t.

$$u_i = \ell\delta_i(f) + a_i \quad \text{and} \quad w_k = \ell\tau_k(f)\, b_k$$

for all i with $1 \leq i \leq l$ and k with $1 \leq k \leq n$. Moreover, the sequence $a_1, \ldots, a_l, b_1, \ldots, b_n$ is compatible w.r.t. the set $\{\delta_1, \ldots, \delta_l, \tau_1, \ldots, \tau_n\}$.

The proof of this proposition goes along the same line as in that of Proposition 5.1.

The last proposition extends Lemma 3.3.

PROPOSITION 5.3. *Let* $v_1, \ldots, v_m, w_1, \ldots, w_n$ *be rational functions in* $\mathbb{F}(\mathbf{t}, \mathbf{x}, \mathbf{y})^\times$. *Assume that the compatibility conditions in (4), (5) and (8) hold. Then there exist a rational function* f *in* $\mathbb{F}(\mathbf{t}, \mathbf{x}, \mathbf{y})$, $a_1, \ldots, a_m$ *in* $\mathbb{F}(\mathbf{t}, \mathbf{x})$, *and* $b_1, \ldots, b_n$ *in* $\mathbb{F}(\mathbf{t}, \mathbf{y})$ *s.t., for all* j *with* $1 \leq j \leq m$ *and* k *with* $1 \leq k \leq n$,

$$v_j = \ell\sigma_j(f)\, a_j \quad \text{and} \quad w_k = \ell\tau_k(f)\, b_k.$$

Furthermore, the sequence $a_1, \ldots, a_m, b_1, \ldots, b_n$ *is compatible w.r.t.* $\{\sigma_1, \ldots, \sigma_m, \tau_1, \ldots, \tau_n\}$.

PROOF. First, we consider the case, in which $m = 1$ and n arbitrary. We proceed by induction on n. The proposition holds when $n = 1$ by Lemma 3.3. Assume that $n > 1$, and the proposition holds for the values lower than n. Applying the induction hypothesis to $x_1, y_1, \ldots, y_{n-1}$ and to $x_1, y_2, \ldots, y_n$, respectively, we get $v_1 \in G_1\mathbb{F}(\mathbf{t}, x_1, y_n)^\times \cap G_1\mathbb{F}(\mathbf{t}, x_1, y_1)^\times$. Setting $\mathbb{A} = \mathbb{F}(\mathbf{t})$, $Z_1 = \{y_n\}$ and $Z_2 = \{y_1\}$ in Lemma 4.2 (i), we see that $v_1 \in G_1\mathbb{F}(\mathbf{t}, x_1)^\times$, which, together with the definition of $G_1\mathbb{F}(\mathbf{t}, x_1)^\times$, there exist f in $\mathbb{F}(\mathbf{t}, x_1, \mathbf{y})$ and a in $\mathbb{F}(\mathbf{t}, x_1)$ s.t. $v_1 = \ell\sigma_1(f)\, a$. Assume that $w_k = \ell\tau_k(f)\, b_k$ for some b_k in $\mathbb{F}(\mathbf{t}, x_1, \mathbf{y})$ and for all k with $1 \leq k \leq n$. By (8), $\sigma_1(b_k) = b_k$, i.e., $b_k \in \mathbb{F}(\mathbf{t}, \mathbf{y})$ (see Example 3.4). The proposition holds for $m = 1$ and n arbitrary.

Second, assume that $m > 1$ and the proposition holds for values lower than m and arbitrary n. Applying this induction hypothesis to $x_1, \ldots, x_{m-1}, \mathbf{y}$ and to $x_2, \ldots, x_m, \mathbf{y}$, respectively, we have

$$w_k \in \left(H_k\mathbb{A}(y_k, Z_1)^\times\right) \cap \left(H_k\mathbb{A}(y_k, Z_2)^\times\right),$$

where $\mathbb{A} = \mathbb{F}(\mathbf{t}, y_1, \ldots, y_{k-1}, y_{k+1}, \ldots, y_n)$, Z_1 and Z_2 are equal to $\{x_m\}$ and $\{x_1\}$, respectively. Thus, $w_k \in H_k\mathbb{A}(y_k)^\times$ by Lemma 4.2 (ii), and $w_k \in \ell\tau_k(f)\mathbb{A}(y_k)^\times$ for some f in $\mathbb{F}(\mathbf{t}, \mathbf{x}, \mathbf{y})$ by Lemma 4.3 (ii). Let $w_k = \ell\tau_k(f)\, b_k$, where b_k is in $\mathbb{A}(y_k)^\times$, and $k = 1, \ldots, n$. Let $a_j = v_j/\ell\sigma_j(f)$ for all j with $1 \leq j \leq m$. Then $\tau_k(a_j) = a_j$ for all k with $1 \leq k \leq n$ and j with $1 \leq j \leq m$ by the compatibility conditions in (8) (see Example 3.4). Hence, all the a_j's are in $\mathbb{F}(\mathbf{t}, \mathbf{x})$. The sequence $a_1, \ldots, a_m, b_1, \ldots, b_n$ is compatible because of (4), (5) and (8). $\square$

Now, we present a theorem describing the structure of compatible rational functions.

THEOREM 5.4. *Let*

$$u_1, \ldots, u_l, \ v_1, \ldots, v_m, \ w_1, \ldots, w_n \tag{19}$$

be a sequence of rational functions in $\mathbb{F}(\mathbf{t}, \mathbf{x}, \mathbf{y})$. *If the sequence is* Δ-*compatible, then there exist* f *in* $\mathbb{F}(\mathbf{t}, \mathbf{x}, \mathbf{y})$, $\alpha_1, \ldots, \alpha_m, \beta_1, \ldots, \beta_l$ *in* $\mathbb{F}(\mathbf{t})$, $\lambda_1, \ldots, \lambda_m$ *in* $\mathbb{F}(\mathbf{x})$, *and* $\mu_1, \ldots, \mu_n$ *in* $\mathbb{F}(\mathbf{y})$ *s.t., for all* i *with* $1 \leq i \leq l$,

$$u_i = \ell\delta_i(f) + \ell\delta_i(\alpha_1)\, x_1 + \cdots + \ell\delta_i(\alpha_m)\, x_m + \beta_i, \tag{20}$$

for all j *with* $1 \leq j \leq m$, *and, for all* k *with* $1 \leq k \leq n$,

$$v_j = \ell\sigma_j(f)\, \alpha_j\lambda_j \quad \text{and} \quad w_k = \ell\tau_k(f)\, \mu_k. \tag{21}$$

Moreover, the sequence $\beta_1, \ldots, \beta_l, \lambda_1, \ldots, \lambda_m, \mu_1, \ldots, \mu_n$ *is* Δ-*compatible.*

PROOF. By Propositions 5.2 and 5.3,

$$w_k = \ell\tau_k(g')\, a'_k = \ell\tau_k(\tilde{g})\, \tilde{a}_k$$

for some $g', \tilde{g} \in \mathbb{F}(\mathbf{t}, \mathbf{x}, \mathbf{y})$, $a'_k \in \mathbb{F}(\mathbf{x}, \mathbf{y})$, and $\tilde{a}_k \in \mathbb{F}(\mathbf{t}, \mathbf{y})$ with $1 \leq k \leq n$. Set $Z_1 = \{t_1, \ldots, t_l\}$, $Z_2 = \{x_1, \ldots, x_m\}$, and $\mathbb{A} = \mathbb{F}(y_1, \ldots, y_{k-1}, y_{k+1}, \ldots, y_n)$ in Lemma 4.2 (ii). Then the lemma implies that there exist μ_k in $\mathbb{F}(\mathbf{y})$ and g_k in $\mathbb{F}(\mathbf{t}, \mathbf{x}, \mathbf{y})$ s.t. $w_k = \ell\tau_k(g_k)\, \mu_k$. Setting $\mathbb{E} = \mathbb{F}$ in the second assertion of Lemma 4.3, we may further assume that all the g_k's are equal to a rational function, say g. Let

$$u_i = \ell\delta_i(g) + r_i \ (1 \leq i \leq l) \text{ and } v_j = \ell\sigma_j(g)\, s_j \ (1 \leq j \leq m).$$

Then the compatibility conditions in (7) imply that the r_i's are in $\mathbb{F}(\mathbf{t}, \mathbf{x})$ (see Example 3.3). Similarly, those conditions in (8) imply that the s_j's are in $\mathbb{F}(\mathbf{t}, \mathbf{x})$ (see Example 3.4). Furthermore, $r_1, \ldots, r_l, s_1, \ldots, s_m$ are compatible w.r.t. the set $\{\delta_1, \ldots, \delta_l, \sigma_1, \ldots, \sigma_m\}$. By Proposition 5.1, we get

$$r_i = \ell\delta_i(b) + \ell\delta_i(\alpha_1)\, x_1 + \cdots + \ell\delta_i(\alpha_m)\, x_m + \beta_i,$$

and $s_j = \ell\sigma_j(b)\, \alpha_j\lambda_j$ for some b in $\mathbb{F}(\mathbf{t}, \mathbf{x})$, α_j, β_i in $\mathbb{F}(\mathbf{t})$, λ_j in $\mathbb{F}(\mathbf{x})$, $1 \leq i \leq l$, and $1 \leq j \leq m$. Note that b belongs to $\mathbb{F}(\mathbf{t}, \mathbf{x})$. Setting $f = gb$, we get the desired form for u_i's, v_j's and w_k's. The compatibility of the sequence $\beta_1, \ldots, \beta_l$, $\lambda_1, \ldots, \lambda_m, \mu_1, \ldots, \mu_n$ follows from that of $u_1, \ldots, u_l, v_1, \ldots, v_m, w_1, \ldots, w_n$. $\square$

With the notation introduced in Theorem 5.4, we say that the sequence:

$$f, \alpha_1, \ldots, \alpha_m, \beta_1, \ldots, \beta_l, \lambda_1, \ldots, \lambda_m, \mu_1, \ldots, \mu_n \tag{22}$$

is a *representation* of Δ-compatible rational functions given in (19) if the equalities in (20) and (21) hold.

A rational function $\mathbb{F}(\mathbf{t}, \mathbf{x}, \mathbf{y})$ is said to be *nonsplit* w.r.t. $\mathbf{t}$ if its denominator and numerator have no irreducible factors in $\mathbb{F}[\mathbf{t}]$. Similarly, we define the notion of nonsplitness w.r.t. $\mathbf{x}$ or $\mathbf{y}$. Let $\prec$ be a fixed monomial ordering on $\mathbb{F}[\mathbf{t}, \mathbf{x}, \mathbf{y}]$. A nonzero rational function in $\mathbb{F}(\mathbf{t}, \mathbf{x}, \mathbf{y})$ is said to be *monic* w.r.t. $\prec$ if its denominator and numerator are both monic w.r.t. $\prec$. A representation (22) of Δ-compatible rational functions in (19) is said to be *standard* w.r.t. $\prec$ if

(i) f is nonsplit w.r.t. $\mathbf{t}$, $\mathbf{x}$, and $\mathbf{y}$, that is, the nontrivial irreducible factors of $\mathrm{den}(f)\mathrm{num}(f)$ are neither in $\mathbb{F}[\mathbf{t}]$, nor in $\mathbb{F}[\mathbf{x}]$, nor in $\mathbb{F}[\mathbf{y}]$;

(ii) both f and α_j are monic w.r.t. $\prec$, $j = 1, 2, \ldots, m$.

Assume that the sequence (22) is a representation of (19). Factor $f = f_1 f_2 f_3 f_4$, where f_1 is monic and nonsplit w.r.t. $\mathbf{t}$, $\mathbf{x}$ and $\mathbf{y}$, f_2 is in $\mathbb{F}(\mathbf{t})$, f_3 in $\mathbb{F}(\mathbf{x})$, and f_4 in $\mathbb{F}(\mathbf{y})$. Set $\alpha_j = c_j\alpha'_j$, where $c_j \in \mathbb{F}$, and α'_j is monic. Then

$$f_1, \alpha'_1, \ldots, \alpha'_m, \beta_1 + \ell\delta_1(f_2), \ldots, \beta_l + \ell\delta_l(f_2),$$

$$\ell\sigma_1(f_3)c_1\lambda_1, \ldots, \ell\sigma_m(f_3)c_m\lambda_m, \ell\tau_1(f_4)\mu_1, \ldots, \ell\tau_n(f_4)\mu_n$$

is also a representation of (19). This proves the existence of standard representations. Its uniqueness follows from the uniqueness of factorization of rational functions.

COROLLARY 5.5. *A* Δ-*compatible sequence has a unique standard representation w.r.t. a given monomial ordering.*

6. ALGORITHMS AND APPLICATIONS

In this section, we discuss how to compute a representation of compatible rational functions, and present two applications in analyzing H-solutions. Let us fix a monomial ordering on $\mathbb{F}[\mathbf{t},\mathbf{x},\mathbf{y}]$ for standard representations.

Let the sequence given in (19) be Δ-compatible. We compute a representation of the sequence in the form of (22).

First, we compute $\mu_1(\mathbf{y}),\ldots,\mu_n(\mathbf{y})$ in the sequence (22). By gcd-computation, we write $w_k = a_k b_k$, where a_k is nonsplit w.r.t. $\mathbf{y}$, b_k is in $\mathbb{F}(\mathbf{y})$, and $k = 1,\ldots,n$. By Theorem 5.4, $w_k = \ell\tau_k(f)\,\mu_k$, where f is nonsplit w.r.t. $\mathbf{y}$ and μ_k is in $\mathbb{F}(\mathbf{y})$. Thus, $b_k = c_k \mu_k$ for some $c_k \in \mathbb{F}^\times$.

To determine c_k, write $a_k = \ell\tau_k(g_k)\,r_k$, where g_k and r_k are in $\mathbb{F}(\mathbf{t},\mathbf{x},\mathbf{y})$ with r_k being τ_k-reduced. By the two expressions of w_k, $c_k r_k = \ell\tau_k(f/g_k)$. Since a_k is nonsplit w.r.t. $\mathbf{y}$ and r_k is τ_k-reduced, g_k can be chosen to be nonsplit w.r.t. $\mathbf{y}$, and so is f/g_k. Thus, f/g_k is free of y_k, because $c_k r_k$ is τ_k-reduced. Accordingly, $c_k r_k = 1$ and $\mu_k = r_k b_k$. As a byproduct, we obtain g_k with $\ell\tau_k(f) = \ell\tau_k(g_k)$.

Second, we compute $\alpha_1,\ldots,\alpha_m$ and $\lambda_1,\ldots,\lambda_m$. Assume that j is an integer with $1 \le j \le m$. By gcd-computation, we write $v_j = s_j a_j b_j$, where s_j is nonsplit w.r.t. $\mathbf{t}$ and $\mathbf{x}$, a_j is in $\mathbb{F}(\mathbf{t})$, and b_j in $\mathbb{F}(\mathbf{x})$. Moreover, set a_j to be monic. By Theorem 5.4, $v_j = \ell\sigma_j(f)\,\alpha_j \lambda_j$, where f is nonsplit w.r.t. $\mathbf{t}$ and $\mathbf{x}$, α_j is a monic element in $\mathbb{F}(\mathbf{t})$, and λ_j is in $\mathbb{F}(\mathbf{x})$. Hence, $a_j = \alpha_j$ and $b_j = c_j \lambda_j$ for some $c_j \in \mathbb{F}^\times$. As in the preceding paragraph, we write $s_j = \ell\sigma_j(g_j')\,r_j$ with r_j being σ_j-reduced. Then $c_j r_j = \ell\sigma_j(f/g_j')$. Since $c_j r_j$ is σ_j-reduced, $c_j r_j = 1$. Hence, $\lambda_j = r_j b_j$. As a byproduct, we find g_j' with $\ell\sigma_j(f) = \ell\sigma_j(g_j')$.

Third, we compute f. Note that f is a nonzero rational solution of the system $\{\sigma_j(z) = \ell\sigma_j(g_j')\,z, \tau_k(z) = \ell\tau_k(g_k)\,z\}$, where $1 \le j \le m$, $1 \le k \le n$, and g_j', g_k are obtained in the first two steps. So f can be computed by several methods, e.g., the method in the proof of [14, Proposition 3].

At last, we set $\beta_i = u_i - \ell\delta_i(f) - \sum_{j=1}^m \ell\delta_i(\alpha_j)\,x_j$, for all i with $1 \le i \le l$. Using $v_j = \ell\sigma_j(f)\,\alpha_j\lambda_j$ and $w_k = \ell\tau_k(f)\,\mu_k$ and the compatibility conditions in (6) and (7), we see that all the β_i's are in $\mathbb{F}(\mathbf{t})$, as required.

EXAMPLE 6.1. *Consider the case $l = m = n = 1$. Let u, v and w be compatible rational functions, where*

$$u = \frac{(4t + 2x + y^2)(t+1) + (t+x+1)(t+x)(2t+y^2)}{(t+1)(t+x)(2t+y^2)},$$

$$v = \frac{2(2x+3)(x+1)(t+1)(t+x+1)(5x+y)}{(5x+y+5)(t+x)},$$

$$w = \frac{(5x+y)(2t+q^2y^2)(1+qy)}{(5x+qy)(2t+y^2)}.$$

A representation of u,v,w is of the form

$$\left(\frac{(2t+y^2)(t+x)}{5x+y},\ t+1,\ 1,\ 2(2x+3)(x+1),\ qy+1 \right).$$

From now on, we assume that our ground field $\mathbb{F}$ is algebraically closed. In general, Δ-extensions of $\mathbb{F}(\mathbf{t},\mathbf{x},\mathbf{y})$ are rings. We recall that an H-solution over $\mathbb{F}(\mathbf{t},\mathbf{x},\mathbf{y})$ is a nonzero solution of system (1) and, given a finite number of H-solutions, there is a Δ-extension of $\mathbb{F}(\mathbf{t},\mathbf{x},\mathbf{y})$ containing these H-solutions and their inverses. The ring of constants of this Δ-extension is equal to $\mathbb{F}$ by Theorem 2 in [5]. We will only encounter finitely many pairwise dissimilar H-solutions. Hence, it makes sense to multiply and

invert them in some Δ-extension, which will not be specified explicitly if no ambiguity arises. All H-solutions we consider will be over $\mathbb{F}(\mathbf{t},\mathbf{x},\mathbf{y})$. Denote by $\mathbf{0}_s$ and $\mathbf{1}_s$ the sequences consisting of s 0's and of s 1's, respectively.

An H-solution is said to be a *symbolic power* if its certificates are of the form

$$\sum_{j=1}^m x_j \ell\delta_1(\alpha_j),\ \ldots,\ \sum_{j=1}^m x_i \ell\delta_l(\alpha_j),\ \alpha_1,\ \ldots,\ \alpha_m,\ \mathbf{1}_n, \quad (23)$$

where $\alpha_1,\ldots,\alpha_m$ are monic elements in $\mathbb{F}(\mathbf{t})^\times$. It is easy to verify that such a sequence is Δ-compatible. Such a symbolic power is denoted $\alpha_1^{x_1} \cdots \alpha_m^{x_m}$. The monicity of the α_i's excludes the case, in which some α_i is a constant different from one. By an E-solution, we mean an H-solution whose certificates are of the form $\beta_1,\ldots,\beta_l,\mathbf{1}_{m+n}$, where $\beta_1,\ldots,\beta_l$ are in $\mathbb{F}(\mathbf{t})$. An E-solution is a hyperexponential function w.r.t. the derivations, and a constant w.r.t. other operators. By a G-solution, we mean an H-solution whose certificates are of the form $\mathbf{0}_l,\lambda_1,\ldots,\lambda_m,\mathbf{1}_n$, where $\lambda_1,\ldots,\lambda_m$ are in $\mathbb{F}(\mathbf{x})^\times$. A G-solution is a hypergeometric term w.r.t. the shift operators, and a constant w.r.t. other operators. Similarly, by a Q-solution, we mean an H-solution whose certificates are of the form $\mathbf{0}_l,\mathbf{1}_m,\mu_1,\ldots,\mu_n$, where $\mu_1,\ldots,\mu_n$ are in $\mathbb{F}(\mathbf{y})^\times$. A Q-solution is a q-hypergeometric term w.r.t. the q-shift operators, and a constant w.r.t. other operators.

The next proposition describes a multiplicative decomposition of H-solutions.

PROPOSITION 6.1. *An H-solution is a product of an element in $\mathbb{F}^\times$, a rational function in $\mathbb{F}(\mathbf{t},\mathbf{x},\mathbf{y})$, a symbolic power, an E-solution, a G-solution, and a Q-solution.*

PROOF. Let h be an H-solution. Then its certificates are compatible. By Theorem 5.4, the certificates have a standard representation $f,\alpha_1,\ldots,\alpha_m,\beta_1,\ldots,\beta_l,\lambda_1,\ldots,\lambda_m,\mu_1,\ldots,\mu_n$. Moreover, the following three sequences:

$$\beta_1,\ldots,\beta_l,\mathbf{1}_{m+n}; \quad \mathbf{0}_l,\lambda_1,\ldots,\lambda_m,\mathbf{1}_n; \quad \mathbf{0}_l,\mathbf{1}_m,\mu_1,\ldots,\mu_n$$

are Δ-compatible, respectively. Hence, there exist an E-solution $\mathcal{E}$, a G-solution $\mathcal{G}$, and a Q-solution $\mathcal{Q}$ s.t. their certificates are given in the above three sequences, respectively. It follows from Theorem 5.4 that h and the product $f\alpha_1^{x_1}\cdots\alpha_m^{x_m}\mathcal{E}\mathcal{G}\mathcal{Q}$ have the same certificates. So they differ by a multiplicative constant, which is in $\mathbb{F}$. $\square$

The H-solution in Example 6.1 can be decomposed as

$$\frac{(2t+y^2)(t+x)}{5x+y}\,(t+1)^x\,\exp(t)\,(2x+1)!\,\Gamma_q(1+qy),$$

where $\Gamma_q(1+qy)$ is a Q-solution with certificates $0,1,1+qy$.

The next proposition characterizes rational H-solutions via their standard representations.

PROPOSITION 6.2. *Let $\mathcal{P}$ be a symbolic power, $\mathcal{E}$ an E-solution, $\mathcal{G}$ a G-solution and $\mathcal{Q}$ a Q-solution. Then $\mathcal{P}\mathcal{E}\mathcal{G}\mathcal{Q}$ is in $\mathbb{F}(\mathbf{t},\mathbf{x},\mathbf{y})$ iff $\mathcal{P} \in \mathbb{F}$, $\mathcal{E} \in \mathbb{F}(\mathbf{t})$, $\mathcal{G} \in \mathbb{F}(\mathbf{x})$ and $\mathcal{Q} \in \mathbb{F}(\mathbf{y})$.*

PROOF. ($\Leftarrow$) Clear.

($\Rightarrow$) Assume that f is rational and equal to $\mathcal{P}\mathcal{E}\mathcal{G}\mathcal{Q}$, where $\mathcal{P},\mathcal{E},\mathcal{G},\mathcal{Q}$ are a symbolic power, an E-, a G-, and a Q-solution, respectively. Suppose that the certificates of $\mathcal{P}$ are given in (23). Applying $\ell\delta_i$ to f, $i=1,\ldots,l$, we see that

$$\ell\delta_i(f) = \sum_{j=1}^m \ell\delta_i(\alpha_j)x_j + \ell\delta_i(\mathcal{E}).$$

Comparing the polynomial parts of the left and right hand-sides of the above equality w.r.t. x_j, we see that $\ell\delta_i(\alpha_j) = 0$ by Remark 2.2 and $\ell\delta_i(\mathcal{E}) \in \mathbb{F}(\mathbf{t})$ for all i and j. Hence, all the α_j's are in $\mathbb{F}$, and, consequently, all the α_j's are equal to one as they are monic. Hence, $\mathcal{P}$ is in $\mathbb{F}$. Moreover,

$$\ell\delta_i(f) = \ell\delta_i(\mathcal{E}) \quad \text{for all } i \text{ with } 1 \le i \le l.$$

Let g be a proper evaluation of f w.r.t. $\mathbf{x}$ and $\mathbf{y}$. Then

$$\ell\delta_i(g) = \ell\delta_i(\mathcal{E}) \quad \text{for all } i \text{ with } 1 \le i \le l,$$

since $\ell\delta_i(\mathcal{E})$ is in $\mathbb{F}(\mathbf{t})$. Hence, $\ell\delta_i(\mathcal{E}/g) = 0$, $\ell\sigma_j(\mathcal{E}/g) = 1$, and $\ell\tau_k(\mathcal{E}/g) = 1$, where $1 \le i \le l$, $1 \le j \le m$, and $1 \le k \le n$. We conclude that $\mathcal{E} = cg$ for some $c \in \mathbb{F}$. So $\mathcal{E}$ is in $\mathbb{F}(\mathbf{t})$.

Applying $\ell\sigma_j$ and $\ell\tau_k$ to f leads to $\ell\sigma_j(f) = \ell\sigma_j(\mathcal{G})$, and $\ell\tau_k(f) = \ell\tau_k(\mathcal{Q})$, respectively. One can show that $\mathcal{G}$ is in $\mathbb{F}(\mathbf{x})$ and $\mathcal{Q}$ is in $\mathbb{F}(\mathbf{y})$ by similar arguments. $\square$

Now, we consider how to determine whether a finite number of H-solutions are algebraically dependent over $\mathbb{F}(\mathbf{t}, \mathbf{x}, \mathbf{y})$. Let $h_1, \cdots, h_s$ be H-solutions. By Proposition 6.1,

$$h_i \equiv \mathcal{P}_i \mathcal{E}_i \mathcal{G}_i \mathcal{Q}_i \mod \mathbb{F}(\mathbf{t}, \mathbf{x}, \mathbf{y})^\times, \quad i = 1, \ldots, s, \quad (24)$$

where $\mathcal{P}_i, \mathcal{E}_i, \mathcal{G}_i, \mathcal{Q}_i$ are a symbolic power, an E-solution, a G-solution, and a Q-solution, respectively.

COROLLARY 6.3. *Let $h_1, \ldots, h_s$ be H-solutions s.t. all the congruences in (24) hold. Then they are algebraically dependent over $\mathbb{F}(\mathbf{t}, \mathbf{x}, \mathbf{y})$ iff there exist integers $\omega_1, \ldots \omega_s$, not all zero, s.t. $\mathcal{P}_1^{\omega_1} \cdots \mathcal{P}_s^{\omega_s}$ is in $\mathbb{F}$, $\mathcal{E}_1^{\omega_1} \cdots \mathcal{E}_s^{\omega_s}$ in $\mathbb{F}(\mathbf{t})$, $\mathcal{G}_1^{\omega_1} \cdots \mathcal{G}_s^{\omega_s}$ in $\mathbb{F}(\mathbf{x})$ and $\mathcal{Q}_1^{\omega_1} \cdots \mathcal{Q}_s^{\omega_s}$ in $\mathbb{F}(\mathbf{y})$.*

PROOF. It follows from [15, Corollary 4.2] that $h_1, \cdots, h_s$ are algebraically dependent over $\mathbb{F}(\mathbf{t}, \mathbf{x}, \mathbf{y})$ iff there exist integers $\omega_1, \ldots \omega_s$, not all zero, s.t. $h_1^{\omega_1} \cdots h_s^{\omega_s}$ is in $\mathbb{F}(\mathbf{t}, \mathbf{x}, \mathbf{y})$. The corollary follows from (24) and Proposition 6.2. $\square$

By the above corollary, one may determine the algebraic dependence of $h_1, \ldots, h_s$ using the decompositions in Proposition 6.1. By gcd-computation, one can find all nonzero integer vectors $(\omega_1, \ldots \omega_s)$ s.t. $\mathcal{P}_1^{\omega_1} \cdots \mathcal{P}_s^{\omega_s}$ is in $\mathbb{F}$. According to [19], one can find all nonzero integer vectors $(\omega_1, \ldots \omega_s)$ s.t. $\mathcal{E}_1^{\omega_1} \cdots \mathcal{E}_s^{\omega_s} \in \mathbb{F}(\mathbf{t})$ by seeking rational number solutions of a linear homogeneous system over $\mathbb{F}$. Computing all nonzero integer vectors $(\omega_1, \ldots \omega_s)$ s.t. $\mathcal{G}_1^{\omega_1} \cdots \mathcal{G}_s^{\omega_s} \in \mathbb{F}(\mathbf{x})$ reduces to the following subproblem: given $c_1, \ldots, c_s \in \mathbb{F}^\times$, compute integers $\omega_1, \ldots \omega_s$, not all zero, with $c_1^{\omega_1} \cdots c_s^{\omega_s} = 1$ (see [19]). Algorithms for tackling this subproblem and related discussions are contained in [13, §7.3] and the references given there. We are trying to develop an algorithm that finds integers $\omega_1, \ldots \omega_s$, not all zero, s.t. $\mathcal{Q}_1^{\omega_1} \cdots \mathcal{Q}_s^{\omega_s}$ belongs to $\mathbb{F}(\mathbf{y})$.

The reader is referred to [6] for an extended version of this paper, which contains a short proof of Fact 3.1 and a proof of Proposition 5.2. A Maple implementation is being written for decomposing H-solutions. We shall apply the structure theorem to study the existence of telescopers in the mixed cases in which any two of differential, shift and q-shift operators appear.

Acknowledgments. The authors thank Frédéric Chyzak, Bruno Salvy, Michael Singer and anonymous referees for helpful discussions and suggestions.

7. REFERENCES

[1] S. A. Abramov. When does Zeilberger's algorithm succeed? *Adv. in Appl. Math.*, 30(3):424–441, 2003.

[2] S. A. Abramov and M. Petkovšek. Proof of a conjecture of Wilf and Zeilberger. Preprints Series of the Inst. Math, Physics and Mechanics, 39(748), Ljubljana, 2001.

[3] S. A. Abramov and M. Petkovšek. Dimensions of solution spaces of H-systems. *J. Symbolic Comput.*, 43(5):377–394, 2008.

[4] S. A. Abramov and M. Petkovšek. On the structure of multivariate hypergeometric terms. *Adv. in Appl. Math.*, 29(3):386–411, 2002.

[5] M. Bronstein, Z. Li, and M. Wu. Picard–Vessiot extensions for linear functional systems. In *Proc. of ISSAC '05*, 68–75, New York, USA, 2005. ACM.

[6] S. Chen, R. Feng, G. Fu and Z. Li. On the structure of compatible rational functions. MM-Res. Preprints, 30: 20-38, 2011. (http://www.mmrc.iss.ac.cn/pub/mm30/02-Chen.pdf)

[7] S. Chen, F. Chyzak, R. Feng, and Z. Li. The existence of telescopers for hyperexponential-hypergeometric functions. MM-Res. Preprints, 29: 239-267, 2010. (http://www.mmrc.iss.ac.cn/pub/mm29/13-Chen.pdf)

[8] W. Y. C. Chen, Q.-H. Hou, and Y.-P. Mu. Applicability of the q-analogue of Zeilberger's algorithm. *J. Symbolic Comput.*, 39(2):155–170, 2005.

[9] C. Christopher. Liouvillian first integrals of second order polynomial differential equations. *Electron. J. Differential Equations*, 49: 1-7 (electronic), 1999.

[10] R. Feng, M. F. Singer, and M. Wu. An algorithm to compute Liouvillian solutions of prime order linear difference-differential equations. *J. Symbolic Comput.*, 45(3):306–323, 2010.

[11] I. Gel'fand, M. Graev, and V. Retakh. General hypergeometric systems of equations and series of hypergeometric type. *Uspekhi Mat. Nauk (Russian), Engl. transl. in Russia Math Surveys*, 47(4):3–82, 1992.

[12] C. Hardouin and M. F. Singer. Differential Galois theory of linear difference equations. *Math. Ann.*, 342(2):333–377, 2008.

[13] M. Kauers. *Algorithms for Nonlinear Higher Order Difference Equations.* PhD thesis, RISC-Linz, Linz, Austria, 2005.

[14] G. Labahn and Z. Li. Hyperexponential solutions of finite-rank ideals in orthogonal Ore rings. In *Proc. of ISSAC'04*, 213–220. ACM, New York, 2004.

[15] Z. Li, M. Wu, and D. Zheng. Testing linear dependence of hyperexponential elements. *ACM Commun. Comput. Algebra*, 41(1):3–11, 2007.

[16] O. Ore. Sur la forme des fonctions hypergéométriques de plusieurs variables. *J. Math. Pures Appl.*, 9(4):311–326, 1930.

[17] G. H. Payne. *Multivariate Hypergeometric Terms.* PhD thesis, Penn. State Univ., Pennsylvania, USA, 1997.

[18] M. Sato. Theory of prehomogeneous vector spaces (algebraic part)– the English translation of Sato's lecture from Shintani's note. *Nagoya Math. J.*, 120:1–34, 1990.

[19] M.F. Singer. A note on solutions of first-order linear functional equations. Manuscript for discussions at the Second NCSU-China Symbolic Computation Collaboration Workshop, Hangzhou, March, 2007.

[20] M. van der Put and M.F. Singer. *Galois Theory of Difference Equations*, volume 1666 of *Lecture Notes in Mathematics*. Springer-Verlag, Berlin, 1997.

[21] H. Zoladek. The extended monodromy group and Liouvillian first integrals. *J. Dynam. Control Systems*, 4(1):1–28, 1998.

Signature-based Algorithms to Compute Gröbner Bases

Christian Eder
c/o Department of Mathematics
TU Kaiserslautern
67653 Kaiserslautern, Germany
ederc@mathematik.uni-kl.de

John Perry
c/o Department of Mathematics
University of Southern Mississippi
Hattiesburg MS 39406-5045 USA
john.perry@usm.edu

ABSTRACT

This paper describes a Buchberger-style algorithm to compute a Gröbner basis of a polynomial ideal, allowing for a selection strategy based on "signatures". We explain how three recent algorithms can be viewed as different strategies for the new algorithm, and how other selection strategies can be formulated. We describe a fourth as an example. We analyze the strategies both theoretically and empirically, leading to some surprising results.

Categories and Subject Descriptors

I.1.2 [**Symbolic and Algebraic Manipulation**]: Algorithms—*Algebraic Algorithms*

General Terms

Algorithms

Keywords

Gröbner bases, F5 Algorithm, G^2V Algorithm

1. INTRODUCTION

A fundamental tool of symbolic and algebraic computation is the method of Gröbner bases. The first algorithm to compute a Gröbner basis was introduced by Buchberger in 1965 [5]; subsequently, the computer algebra community has developed a number of additional algorithms, such as [4, 9, 12, 14]. In recent years, a new genus of algorithm has emerged, exemplified by F5 and G^2V [10, 11].

While they are presented as different algorithms, both use a property called a "signature" to control the computation and reduction of S-polynomials. While studying the two, we realized that they could be viewed as variations in the selection strategy of a basic algorithm common to both. A third recent algorithm of Arri likewise fits this mold [2], so it seemed instructive to formulate explicitly both the underlying structure and the three algorithms as strategies for

implementation. This provides a common theoretical framework which allows a careful comparison, looking both at how the criteria employed by the strategies are related, and at experimental timings in a unified environment. For the latter, we employed both interpreted code (via Sage [15] and SINGULAR [7]) and compiled code (via SINGULAR). We examined both the original implementations and new implementations of the algorithms as "plugins" to the common algorithm. For consistency, the algorithms should all compute a reduced Gröbner basis incrementally, so when the reader sees "F5", s/he should understand "F5C" [8].

Section 2 reviews basic notation and concepts, adapting different sources which vary considerably in notation [2, 8, 10, 11, 16]. Theoretical contributions, which include the new "sig-redundant criterion", begin in Section 2.2 and continue into Section 3. Section 4 gets to the meat of comparing the strategies; both the analysis of Section 4.1 and the timings of Section 4.2 produce surprising and unexpected results.

2. BACKGROUND

Let $i \in \mathbb{N}$, $\mathbb{F}$ a field, and $R = \mathbb{F}[x_1, \ldots, x_n]$. Throughout this paper, $F_i = (f_1, \ldots, f_i)$ where each $f_j \in R$, and $I_i = \langle F_i \rangle$ is the ideal of R generated by the elements of F_i. Fix a degree-compatible ordering $<$ on the monoid $\mathbb{M}$ of monomials of $x_1, \ldots, x_n$; for any $p \in R$, we denote p's leading monomial by $\mathrm{lm}\,(p)$, its leading coefficient by $\mathrm{lc}\,(p)$, and write $\mathrm{lt}\,(p) = \mathrm{lc}\,(p)\,\mathrm{lm}\,(p)$. For brevity, we may denote $t_p = \mathrm{lm}\,(p)$, $c_p = \mathrm{lc}\,(p)$, and $\mathrm{lcm}\,(t_p, t_q) = t_{p,q}$.

Let $f_{i+1} \in R \backslash I_i$. We want an algorithm that, given a Gröbner basis G_i of I_i, computes a Gröbner basis of $I_{i+1} = \langle F_{i+1} \rangle$, where $F_{i+1} = (f_1, \ldots, f_{i+1})$.

2.1 The traditional approach

Given $p, q \in R$, the S-**polynomial** of p and q is

$$S_{p,q} = \frac{t_{p,q}}{t_p} \cdot p - \frac{c_p}{c_q} \cdot \frac{t_{p,q}}{t_q} \cdot q.$$

(It makes some things easier later if we multiply only q by a field element.) Further, given $p, r \in R$ and $G \subset R$, we say p **reduces to** r **modulo** G if there exist $\Lambda_1, \ldots, \Lambda_\ell \in \mathbb{N}$, $t_1, \ldots, t_\ell \in \mathbb{M}$, $c_1, \ldots, c_\ell \in \mathbb{F}$, and $r_0, \ldots, r_\ell \in R$ such that

- $r_0 = p$ and $r_\ell = r$; and

- for all $i = 1, \ldots, \ell$,

  - $r_i = r_{i-1} - c_i t_i g_{\Lambda_i}$, and
  - $\mathrm{lm}\,(r_i) < \mathrm{lm}\,(r_{i-1})$.

Buchberger's algorithm computes the Gröbner basis G of $\langle F_{i+1} \rangle$ by computing S-polynomials and reducing them modulo the current value of G: initially the S-polynomials of f_j, f_{i+1} where $j = 1, \ldots, i$; then, for any S-polynomial that reduces to nonzero r, also for the pairs r, g where $g \in G$, adding r to the basis after determining new pairs. Termination is guaranteed by Dickson's Lemma, since no polynomial is added to G_{i+1} unless it expands the $\mathbb{M}$-submodule $\langle \mathrm{lm}\,(G_{i+1}) \rangle$ of the Noetherian $\mathbb{M}$-monomodule $\mathbb{M}$ [13].

The following is fundamental to the traditional approach.

DEFINITION 1. *Let $s \in R$ and $G \subset R$, with $\#G = \ell$. We say that s has a **standard representation with respect to** G if there exist $h_1, \ldots, h_\ell \in R$ such that $s = h_1 g_1 + \cdots + h_\ell g_\ell$ and for each $k = 1, \ldots, \ell$ either $h_k = 0$ or $\mathrm{lm}\,(h_k)\,\mathrm{lm}\,(g_k) \leq \mathrm{lm}\,(s)$. We may also say that $(h_1, \ldots, h_\ell)$ is a standard representation of s with respect to G.*

If s reduces to r modulo G, then it has a standard representation modulo G; the converse, however, is often false.

2.2 Signature-based strategies

All algorithms to compute a Gröbner basis follow the basic blueprint of Buchberger's algorithm, but recent algorithms introduce a new point of view, a "signature-based strategy."

DEFINITION 2. *Let $\mathbf{F}_1, \ldots, \mathbf{F}_m$ be the canonical generators of the free R-module R^m. Let $p \in \langle F_{i+1} \rangle$, $j \in \mathbb{N}$ with $j \leq i + 1$, and $h_1, \ldots, h_j \in R$ such that $h_j \neq 0$ and*

$$p = h_1 f_1 + \cdots h_j f_j.$$

*If $c = \mathrm{lc}\,(h_j)$ and $\tau = \mathrm{lm}\,(h_j)$, we say that $c\tau \mathbf{F}_j$ is **a natural signature** of p. Let $\mathbb{S}$ be the set of all natural signatures:*

$$\mathbb{S} = \{c\tau \mathbf{F}_j : c \in \mathbb{F} \setminus \{0\}, \tau \in \mathbb{M}, j = 1, \ldots, m\}.$$

*We extend the ordering $<$ on $\mathbb{M}$ to a partial ordering $\prec$ on $\mathbb{S}$ in the following way: $c\sigma \mathbf{F}_j \prec d\tau \mathbf{F}_k$ iff $j < k$, or $j = k$ and $\sigma < \tau$. If $j = k$, $\sigma = \tau$, and $c = d$, we say that $c\sigma \mathbf{F}_j = d\tau \mathbf{F}_k$. If $j = k$ and $\sigma = \tau$, we say that $c\sigma \mathbf{F}_j$ and $d\tau \mathbf{F}_k$ are **level**. We do not otherwise compare them.*

PROPOSITION 3. *The ordering $\prec$ is a well-ordering on $\widehat{\mathbb{S}} = \{\tau \mathbf{F}_j : \tau \in \mathbb{M}, j = 1, \ldots, m\}$. Thus, for each $p \in R$, we can identify a unique, minimal, monic natural signature.*

(Our "Propositions" are either trivial or proved elsewhere.)

DEFINITION 4. *We call the unique minimal monic natural signature of $p \in R$ its **minimal signature**. We denote the set of all natural signatures of p by $\mathrm{sig}\,(p)$, and the minimal signature of p by $\mathcal{S}\,(p)$.*

PROPOSITION 5. *Let $p, q \in I_{i+1}$. Assume that $c\sigma \mathbf{F}_j \in \mathrm{sig}\,(p)$ and $d\tau \mathbf{F}_k \in \mathrm{sig}\,(q)$. Let $t \in \mathbb{M}$. We have*

(A) $c\sigma \mathbf{F}_j \in \mathrm{sig}\,(p \pm q)$ if $c\sigma \mathbf{F}_j \succ d\tau \mathbf{F}_k$;

(B) $(c \pm d)\sigma \mathbf{F}_j \in \mathrm{sig}\,(p \pm q)$ if $c\sigma \mathbf{F}_j$ and $d\tau \mathbf{F}_k$ are level and $c \pm d \neq 0$; and

(C) $ct\sigma \mathbf{F}_j \in \mathrm{sig}\,(tp)$.

COROLLARY 6. *Let $p, q \in I_{i+1}$. Assume that $c\sigma \mathbf{F}_j \in \mathrm{sig}\,(p)$ and $d\tau \mathbf{F}_k \in \mathrm{sig}\,(q)$. Suppose that there exist $a \in \mathbb{F}$ and $t \in \mathbb{M}$ such that $at\,\mathrm{lt}\,(q) = \mathrm{lt}\,(p)$.*

(A) If $t\tau \mathbf{F}_k \prec \sigma \mathbf{F}_j$, then $c\sigma \mathbf{F}_j \in \mathrm{sig}\,(p - atq)$.

(B) If $t\tau \mathbf{F}_k$, $\sigma \mathbf{F}_j$ are level and $ad \neq c$, then $(c - ad)\sigma \mathbf{F}_j \in \mathrm{sig}\,(p - atq)$.

DEFINITION 7. *If $(c\sigma \mathbf{F}_j, p), (d\tau \mathbf{F}_k, q) \in \mathbb{S} \times I_{i+1}$, $a \in \mathbb{F}$, and $t \in \mathbb{M}$ satisfy (A) or (B) of Corollary 6, we say that $p - atq$ is a **σ-reduction of p with respect to** q. Otherwise, $p - atq$ is **σ-unsafe**. When it is clear from context that we mean σ-reduction for appropriate σ, we refer simply to reduction.*

*We define a **σ-reduction of p modulo** G analogously, and say that it is **complete** when no reductions of the type described in Corollary 6 are possible. It is **semi-complete** when reductions of type (B) can be performed, but not reductions of type (A).*

We now adapt the notion of a standard representation to consider natural signatures.

DEFINITION 8. *Let $G \subset \mathbb{S} \times I_{i+1}$ with $\#G = \ell$, and suppose that for each $(d\tau \mathbf{F}_j, g) \in G$ we have $d\tau \mathbf{F}_j = \mathcal{S}\,(g)$. We say that any $(c\sigma \mathbf{F}_{i+1}, s) \in \mathbb{S} \times I_{i+1}$ has a **standard representation with respect to** G (or **sig-representation**, or **σ-representation** for short) if $c\sigma \mathbf{F}_{i+1} \in \mathrm{sig}\,(s)$ and there exist $h_1, \ldots, h_\ell \in R$ such that $(h_1, \ldots, h_\ell)$ is a standard representation of s and $\sigma \mathbf{F}_{i+1} \succeq \mathcal{S}\,(h_1 g_1 + \cdots + h_\ell g_\ell)$.*

Just as a reduction of p to zero modulo G corresponds to a $\mathrm{lm}\,(p)$-representation of p with respect to G in the traditional case, a σ-reduction to zero modulo G corresponds to a σ-representation with respect to G.

THEOREM 9. *Let $c_1, \ldots, c_\ell \in \mathbb{F}$, $\tau_1, \ldots, \tau_\ell \in \mathbb{M}$, and $p_1, \ldots, p_\ell \in I_{i+1} \setminus \{0\}$ such that*

$$G = \{(\mathbf{F}_1, f_1), \ldots, (\mathbf{F}_{i+1}, f_{i+1})\}$$
$$\cup \{(c_1 \tau_1 \mathbf{F}_{i+1}, p_1), \ldots, (c_\ell \tau_\ell \mathbf{F}_{i+1}, p_\ell)\},$$

$c\sigma \mathbf{F}_j = \mathcal{S}\,(g)$ for all $(c\sigma \mathbf{F}_j, g) \in G$, and for all $(c\sigma \mathbf{F}_{i+1}, p)$, $(d\tau \mathbf{F}_j, q) \in G$ one of the following holds:

- $\left(\frac{t_{p,q}}{t_p} \cdot \sigma\right) \mathbf{F}_{i+1} = \left(\frac{t_{p,q}}{t_q} \cdot \tau\right) \mathbf{F}_j$, or

- $\left(\frac{t_{p,q}}{t_p} \cdot \sigma\right) \mathbf{F}_{i+1} \succ \left(\frac{t_{p,q}}{t_q} \cdot \tau\right) \mathbf{F}_j$ and $\left(\frac{t_{p,q}}{t_p} \cdot \sigma \mathbf{F}_{i+1}, S_{p,q}\right)$ has a standard representation with respect to G.

Then $\widehat{G} = \{g : \exists\,(\sigma \mathbf{F}_j, g) \in G\}$ is a Gröbner basis of I_{i+1}.

PROOF. Recall from [3] that $\widehat{G}$ is a Gröbner basis of I_{i+1} iff $\langle \widehat{G} \rangle = I_{i+1}$ and $S_{p,q}$ has a standard representation with respect to $\widehat{G}$ for all distinct $p, q \in \widehat{G}$. Since F_i is a Gröbner basis of I_i, we know that $S_{p,q}$ has a standard representation for every $p, q \in F_i$, so it suffices to check only the pairs $p, q \in \widehat{G}$ such that at least $p \notin F_i$. For any such pair where $\left(\frac{t_{p,q}}{t_p} \cdot \sigma\right) \mathbf{F}_{i+1} \succ \left(\frac{t_{p,q}}{t_q} \cdot \tau\right) \mathbf{F}_j$, by hypothesis $\left(\frac{t_{p,q}}{t_p} \cdot \sigma \mathbf{F}_{i+1}, S_{p,q}\right)$ has a standard representation with respect to G; by definition, $S_{p,q}$ also has a standard representation with respect to $\widehat{G}$.

Order the remaining S-polynomials by ascending level signature, and choose one such S-polynomial $S_{p,q}$ such that $\mathcal{S}\,(p) = c\sigma \mathbf{F}_{i+1}$, $\mathcal{S}\,(q) = d\tau \mathbf{F}_{i+1}$, and $\left(\frac{t_{p,q}}{t_p} \cdot \sigma\right) \mathbf{F}_{i+1} = \left(\frac{t_{p,q}}{t_q} \cdot \tau\right) \mathbf{F}_{i+1}$ is minimally level. Now, $s = \frac{t_{p,q}}{t_p} \cdot p - \frac{c}{d} \cdot \frac{t_{p,q}}{t_q} \cdot q$ has signature less than $\left(\frac{t_{p,q}}{t_p} \cdot \sigma\right) \mathbf{F}_{i+1}$; let $h_1, \ldots, h_j \in R$

such that $s = \sum_{k=1}^{j} h_k f_k$ and $\mathrm{lm}\,(h_j)\,\mathbf{F}_j = \mathcal{S}(s)$. Each $\mathrm{lm}\,(h_k)\,\mathrm{lm}\,(f_k)\,\mathbf{F}_k$ is smaller than $\left(\frac{t_{p,q}}{t_p}\cdot\sigma\right)\mathbf{F}_{i+1}$, the minimal level signature. By hypothesis, S-polynomials corresponding to top-cancellations among these $\mathrm{lm}\,(h_k)\,\mathrm{lm}\,(f_k)$ have sig-representations with respect to G. Thus, there exist $H_1,\ldots,H_{\#G}$ such that $s = \sum H_k g_k$, $\mathcal{S}(s) \succeq \mathcal{S}(\sum H_k g_k)$, and for each k, $H_k = 0$ or $\mathrm{lm}\,(H_k)\,\mathrm{lm}\,(g_k) \le \mathrm{lm}\,(s)$. If $s = S_{p,q}$, we are done. Otherwise, $\mathrm{lm}\,(s) = t_{p,q}$, implying $\mathrm{lm}\,(H_\ell)\,\mathrm{lm}\,(g_\ell) = t_{p,q}$ for some ℓ. Thus, there exist $u \in \mathbb{M}$ and $(\mu\mathbf{F}_j, g) \in G$ such that $u\,\mathrm{lm}\,(g) = t_{p,q}$, and $(u\mu)\,\mathbf{F}_j \prec \left(\frac{t_{p,q}}{t_p}\cdot\sigma\right)\mathbf{F}_{i+1}$. Since $(u\mu)\,\mathbf{F}_j \prec \left(\frac{t_{p,q}}{t_p}\cdot\sigma\right)\mathbf{F}_{i+1}$, by hypothesis $S_{p,g}$ and $S_{g,q}$ have sig-representations with respect to G; since $S_{p,q} = \frac{t_{p,q}}{t_{p,g}}S_{p,g} + \frac{t_{p,q}}{t_{g,q}}S_{g,q}$, so does $S_{p,q}$.

For the remaining S-polynomials, proceed similarly by ascending level signature. Top-cancellations of level signature will be smaller than the working signature, and so will have been considered already. $\square$

We need one more concept. It looks innocent, but is quite powerful. We have not seen it elsewhere, but it is inspired by other work; see Lemma 15.

DEFINITION 10. *Let $G \subset \mathbb{S} \times R$ and $(\sigma\mathbf{F}_{i+1}, f) \in \mathbb{S} \times R$. If there exists $(\tau\mathbf{F}_{i+1}, g) \in G$ such that $\tau \mid \sigma$ and $\mathrm{lm}\,(g) \mid \mathrm{lm}\,(f)$, then $(\sigma\mathbf{F}_{i+1}, f)$ is **natural signature-redundant** to G, or **sig-redundant** for short.*

The proof of Theorem 9 uses a technique common to signature-based algorithms: proceed from smaller to larger signature, reusing previous work to rewrite S-polynomials. This suggests an algorithm to compute a Gröbner basis; see Algorithm 1. It follows the basic outline of Buchberger's algorithm, with several exceptions.

- As we will show in Lemma 12, Algorithm 1 prepends a natural signature to each critical "pair", and considers pairs by ascending natural signature (as in [1, 2, 11, 16]), rather than by ascending lcm (as in [6, 8]).

- Only σ-reductions of $(\sigma\mathbf{F}_{i+1}, r)$ are computed directly. We require semi-complete reduction, but complete reduction implies this. If we perform a complete reduction and conclude with $(c\sigma\mathbf{F}_{i+1}, r)$, we multiply r by c^{-1} to ensure $\sigma\mathbf{F}_{i+1} \in \mathrm{sig}\,(r)$ for line 18. Reductions that are σ-unsafe occur in line 28 via the generation of new critical pairs. Algorithm 1 adds these to S rather than P to preserve the strategy of ascending signature.

- The **if** statement of line 20 rejects not only zero polynomials, but sig-redundant polynomials as well. This has a double effect in Lemma 13 and Theorem 14.

- We adopted the following from F5, partly to illuminate the relationship with this algorithm better. Algorithm 1 is easily reformulated without them, in which case it begins to resemble $\mathrm{G}^2\mathrm{V}$ and Arri's algorithm.

  - Critical pairs are oriented: any $(\sigma\mathbf{F}_{i+1}, p, q) \in P$ corresponds to $S_{p,q} = up - cvq$ where $(\tau\mathbf{F}_{i+1}, p)$, $(\mu\mathbf{F}_j, q) \in G$ and $\sigma = u\tau \succ v\mu$.

  - Line 12 selects all pairs of minimal degree of natural signature. With homogeneous polynomials and a degree-compatible ordering, this selects all S-polynomials of minimal degree. An inner loop processes these by ascending signature.

Algorithm 1 Signature-based Gröbner basis computation

1: **inputs**
2:     $F_i \subset R$, such that F_i is a Gröbner basis of $\langle F_i \rangle$ and $f_j \notin \langle f_1, \ldots, f_{j-1}\rangle$
3:     $f_{i+1} \in R \setminus \langle F_i \rangle$
4: **outputs**
5:     $G \subset \mathbb{S} \times R$ satisfying the hypothesis of Theorem 9
6: **do**
7:     Let $G = ((\mathbf{F}_1, f_1), \ldots, (\mathbf{F}_i, f_i), (\mathbf{F}_{i+1}, f_{i+1}))$
8:     Let $P = \left\{ \left(\frac{t_{f_{i+1},f}}{t_{f_{i+1}}}\mathbf{F}_{i+1}, f_{i+1}, f \right) : f \in F_i \right\}$
9:     Initialize Syz — TBD
10:    **while** $P \ne \emptyset$ **do**
11:      Prune P using Syz — TBD
12:      Let $S = \{(\sigma\mathbf{F}_{i+1}, p, q) \in P : \deg\sigma \text{ minimal}\}$
13:      Let $P = P \setminus S$
14:      **while** $S \ne \emptyset$ **do**
15:       Prune S using Syz, G — TBD
16:       Let $(\sigma\mathbf{F}_{i+1}, p, q) \in S$ such that $\sigma\mathbf{F}_{i+1}$ is minimal
17:       Remove $(\sigma\mathbf{F}_{i+1}, p, q)$ from S
18:       Let $(\sigma\mathbf{F}_{i+1}, r)$ be a semi-complete σ-reduction of $S_{p,q} \bmod G$
19:       Update Syz using $(\sigma\mathbf{F}_{i+1}, r)$ — TBD
20:       **if** $r \ne 0$ and $(\sigma\mathbf{F}_{i+1}, r)$ not sig-redundant to G **then**
21:        **for** $(\tau\mathbf{F}_{i+1}, g) \in G$ such that $g \ne 0$ and g not sig-redundant **do**
22:         **if** $\frac{t_{r,g}}{t_r}\cdot\sigma \ne \frac{t_{r,g}}{t_g}\cdot\tau$ **then**
23:         **if** $\frac{t_{r,g}}{t_r}\cdot\sigma > \frac{t_{r,g}}{t_g}\cdot\tau$ **then**
24:          Let $(\mu\mathbf{F}_{i+1}, p, q) = \left(\frac{t_{r,g}}{t_r}\cdot\sigma\mathbf{F}_{i+1}, r, g\right)$
25:         **else**
26:          Let $(\mu\mathbf{F}_{i+1}, p, q) = \left(\frac{t_{r,g}}{t_g}\cdot\tau\mathbf{F}_{i+1}, g, r\right)$
27:         **if** $\deg\mu = d$ **then**
28:          Add $(\mu\mathbf{F}_{i+1}, p, q)$ to S
29:         **else**
30:          Add $(\mu\mathbf{F}_{i+1}, p, q)$ to P
31:       Append $(\sigma\mathbf{F}_{i+1}, r)$ to G
32:    **return** $\{(\sigma\mathbf{F}_{i+1}, g) \in G : g \ne 0, \text{ not sig-redundant}\}$

- Zero and sig-redundant polynomials are retained in the basis for reasons that become clear later; however, line 21 prevents them from being used to compute new critical pairs, and line 32 does not add them to the output.

REMARK 11. *For now, we define lines 9, 11, 15, and 19 to do nothing, and discuss them in Section 2.3.*

We prove the correctness of Algorithm 1 in several steps.

LEMMA 12. *Suppose that one of lines 8, 28, or 30 creates $(\sigma\mathbf{F}_{i+1}, p, q)$. Write $s = S_{p,q}$; not only is $\sigma\mathbf{F}_{i+1} \in \mathrm{sig}\,(s)$, but $\sigma\mathbf{F}_{i+1} = \mathcal{S}(s)$ unless s already has a sig-representation w.r.t. G when Algorithm 1 would generate it.*

PROOF. That $\sigma\mathbf{F}_{i+1} \in \mathrm{sig}\,(s)$ follows from Proposition 5, Corollary 6, and inspection of the algorithm. For the second assertion, suppose that $\sigma\mathbf{F}_{i+1} \ne \mathcal{S}(s)$. Let $\tau\mathbf{F}_j = \mathcal{S}(s)$; by definition, there exist $h_1, \ldots, h_j$ such that $j \le i+1$, $s = h_1 f_1 + \cdots + h_j f_j$, $h_j \ne 0$, and $\mathrm{lm}\,(h_j) = \tau$. Notice $\tau\mathbf{F}_j \prec \sigma\mathbf{F}_{i+1}$. Since the algorithm proceeds by ascending natural signature, top-cancellations of smaller signature have been considered already. Hence, all top-cancellations among the $h_k f_k$ would have sig-representations at the moment Algorithm 1 would generate s. We can therefore rewrite the top-cancellations repeatedly until we conclude with a sig-representation of s. $\square$

LEMMA 13. *Suppose that line 20 prevents the algorithm from creating critical pairs using* $(\sigma\mathbf{F}_{i+1}, r)$. *Then* $r = 0$, *the corresponding S-polynomials have sig-representations already, or will after consideration of pairs queued in* $P \cup S$.

PROOF. If $r = 0$, then we are done. Suppose $r \neq 0$; by line 20, there exist $(\tau\mathbf{F}_{i+1}, g) \in G$ such that $\tau \mid \sigma$ and $\operatorname{lm}(g) \mid \operatorname{lm}(r)$. Let $u \in \mathbb{M}$ such that $u\operatorname{lm}(g) = \operatorname{lm}(r)$. If $u\tau < \sigma$, then line 18 did not perform a semi-complete σ-reduction of $S_{p,q}$, a contradiction. Hence $u\tau \geq \sigma$.

Let $t \in \mathbb{M}$ such that $u\tau \geq \sigma = t\tau$, so $\operatorname{lm}(r) = u\operatorname{lm}(g) \geq t\operatorname{lm}(g)$. The signature $\mu\mathbf{F}_j$ of $s = r - tg$ is smaller than $\sigma\mathbf{F}_{i+1}$, so Algorithm 1 has considered top-cancellations of this and smaller natural signature. Hence, $(\mu\mathbf{F}_j, s)$ has a μ-representation. Critical pairs have been generated for g, so for any $(\zeta\mathbf{F}_{i+1}, q) \in G$, $S_{r,q} = ur - cvq = u(s + tg) - cvq$, whose top-cancellations already have a sig-representation or will after consideration of pairs queued in $P \cup S$. $\square$

THEOREM 14. *Algorithm 1 terminates correctly.*

PROOF. *Correctness:* If we show that the output of the algorithm satisfies the hypothesis of Theorem 9, then we are done. By Lemma 12 and the strategy of ascending signature, we know for any $(\sigma\mathbf{F}_j, g) \in G$ that $g = 0$ or $\sigma\mathbf{F}_j = \mathcal{S}(g)$. The only S-polynomials for which the algorithm does not explicitly compute sig-representations are those satisfying the criteria of the **if** statement of line 20 and the criterion of line 22. The criterion of line 20 is the hypothesis of Lemma 13; with it and the criterion of line 22, we complete the hypothesis of Theorem 9.

Termination: Let $\mathbb{M}'$ be the monoid of monomials in $x_1, \ldots, x_{2n}$; as with $\mathbb{M}$, we can consider it to be a Noetherian $\mathbb{M}'$-monomodule. Any $(\sigma\mathbf{F}_{i+1}, r)$ added to G with $r \neq 0$ corresponds to an element of $\mathbb{M}'$ via the bijection

$$(\sigma, \operatorname{lm}(r)) = \left(\prod x_i^{\alpha_i}, \prod x_i^{\beta_i} \right) \to \prod x_i^{\alpha_i} \prod x_{n+i}^{\beta_i}.$$

Let J be the $\mathbb{M}'$-submodule generated by these elements of G. Suppose the algorithm adds $(\sigma\mathbf{F}_{i+1}, r)$ to G and J does not expand; this implies that there exists $(\tau\mathbf{F}_{i+1}, g) \in G$ such that $\tau \mid \sigma$ and $\operatorname{lm}(g) \mid \operatorname{lm}(r)$. Since $(\sigma\mathbf{F}_{i+1}, r)$ is sig-redundant, line 20 prevents it from generating new pairs.

Hence, every time Algorithm 1 adds $(\sigma\mathbf{F}_{i+1}, r)$ to G, either the submodule J expands, or the algorithm abstains from computing pairs. A submodule of $\mathbb{M}'$ can expand only finitely many times, so the algorithm can compute only finitely many pairs. Hence, the algorithm terminates. $\square$

The following interesting result will prove useful; its criterion is used in [2, 11] to prevent the generation of new pairs.

LEMMA 15. *To see if* $(\sigma\mathbf{F}_{i+1}, r)$ *is sig-redundant in Algorithm 1, it suffices to check if there exist* $(\tau\mathbf{F}_{i+1}, g) \in G$ *and* $t \in \mathbb{M}$ *such that* $t\tau = \sigma$ *and* $t\operatorname{lm}(g) = \operatorname{lm}(r)$.

PROOF. Assume that there exists $(\tau\mathbf{F}_{i+1}, g) \in G$ such that $\tau \mid \sigma$ and $\operatorname{lm}(g) \mid \operatorname{lm}(r)$. Let $t, u \in \mathbb{M}$ such that $t\tau = \sigma$ and $u\operatorname{lm}(g) = \operatorname{lm}(r)$. If $u\tau < \sigma$, then line 18 did not compute a semi-complete σ-reduction of $S_{p,q}$, a contradiction.

If $u\tau > \sigma$, then $u > t$, so $\operatorname{lm}(r) = u\operatorname{lm}(g) > t\operatorname{lm}(g)$. The signature of $r - tg$ is smaller than σ, so $r - tg$ has a sig-representation with respect to G. In addition, $\operatorname{lm}(r - tg) = \operatorname{lm}(r)$; by the definition of a sig-representation, there exist $(\mu\mathbf{F}_j, h) \in G$ and $u \in \mathbb{M}$ such that $u\operatorname{lm}(h) = \operatorname{lm}(r - tg) = \operatorname{lm}(r)$ and $u \cdot \mu\mathbf{F}_j$ is no greater than the signature of $r - tg$; that is, $u \cdot \mu\mathbf{F}_j \prec \sigma\mathbf{F}_{i+1}$. But then line 18 did not compute a semi-complete σ-reduction of $S_{p,q}$, a contradiction. $\square$

2.3 Pruning P and S

This section does not propose any criteria that have not appeared elsewhere; rather, it lays the groundwork for showing how lines 9, 11, 15, and 19 can use such criteria to improve the efficiency of Algorithm 1. The general idea is:

- *Syz* will consist of a list of monomials corresponding to known syzygies; i.e., if $t \in Syz$, then $t\mathbf{F}_{i+1}$ is a natural signature of a known syzygy.

- Line 11 removes $(\sigma\mathbf{F}_{i+1}, p, q)$ from P if there exists $t \in Syz$ such that $t \mid \sigma$.

- Line 15 does the same, and ensures that if $(\sigma\mathbf{F}_{i+1}, p, q)$, $(\sigma\mathbf{F}_{i+1}, f, g) \in S$, then at most one of these is retained.

Already, Lemma 12 suggests:

(NM) Discard any $(\sigma\mathbf{F}_{i+1}, f, g) \in P \cup S$ if $\sigma\mathbf{F}_{i+1}$ is not the minimal signature of $S_{f,g}$.

PROPOSITION 16. *Line 9 can put* $Syz = \{\operatorname{lm}(g) : g \in F_i\}$.

For a proof, see Lemma 16 in [8] (Faugère's Criterion). It is similar to the proof of the following criterion [2, 11]:

LEMMA 17. *If the result of line 18 is* $(\sigma\mathbf{F}_{i+1}, r)$ *with* $r = 0$, *then line 19 can add* σ *to* Syz.

PROOF (SKETCH). Suppose that line 18 gives $(\sigma\mathbf{F}_{i+1}, r)$ with $r = 0$. Now, r is the σ-reduction of $s = S_{p,q}$ from line 18, and by Lemma 12 $\sigma\mathbf{F}_{i+1} \in \operatorname{sig}(s)$. By definition, $\exists h_1, \ldots, h_{i+1} \in R$ such that $s = \Sigma h_k f_k$ and $\operatorname{lm}(h_{i+1}) = \sigma$. Since $r = 0$, there exist $H_1, \ldots, H_{\#G}$ such that $s = \Sigma H_k g_k$, each $H_k = 0$ or $\operatorname{lm}(H_k)\operatorname{lm}(g_k) \leq \operatorname{lm}(s)$, and $\mathcal{S}(\Sigma H_k g_k) \prec \sigma\mathbf{F}_{i+1}$. Hence $\Sigma h_k f_k - \Sigma H_k g_k = 0$ and has natural signature $\sigma\mathbf{F}_{i+1}$. Suppose there exist $(\tau\mathbf{F}_{i+1}, p, q) \in P \cup S$ and $u \in \mathbb{M}$ such that $u\sigma = \tau$; then $S_{p,q} = S_{p,q} - u(\Sigma h_k f_k - \Sigma H_k g_k)$ has signature smaller than τ; now apply Lemma 12. $\square$

Another criterion is implied by the following lemma.

LEMMA 18. *Let* $\tau \in \mathbb{M}$, $B = \{(\sigma_j\mathbf{F}_{i+1}, f_j) \in G : \sigma_j \mid \tau\}$. *We can choose any* $(\sigma\mathbf{F}_{i+1}, f) \in B$ *and discard in line 15 any* $(\tau\mathbf{F}_{i+1}, p, q) \in P$ *if* $p \neq f$, *or if we compute* $(\tau\mathbf{F}_{i+1}, f, g)$ *where* $p = f$ *and* $g \neq q$.

PROOF (SKETCH). Choose any $(\sigma\mathbf{F}_{i+1}, f) \in B$, and let $(\mu\mathbf{F}_{i+1}, p), (\mu'\mathbf{F}_{i+1}, q) \in G$ such that $(\tau\mathbf{F}_{i+1}, p, q) \in P \cup S$. Let $t, u \in \mathbb{M}$ such that $t\sigma = u\mu = \tau$. The signature of $up - tf$ is smaller than τ, so it has a standard representation with respect to G; say $up - tf = \sum h_k g_k$. Then $S_{p,q} = up - vq = u(tf + \sum h_k g_k) - vq$. All top-cancellations in this representation of $S_{p,q}$ are of equal or smaller natural signature, so $S_{p,q}$ will have a standard representation with respect to G once line 16 chooses $\sigma\mathbf{F}_{i+1} \succ \tau\mathbf{F}_{i+1}$. $\square$

Notice that Lemma 18 requires only divisibility; if there are no $(\tau\mathbf{F}_{i+1}, p, q) \in S$ such that $p = f$, then we could discard all $(\tau\mathbf{F}_{i+1}, p, q) \in S$. We thus have a "rewritable" criterion:

(RW) For any $\tau\mathbf{F}_{i+1} \in \widehat{\mathbb{S}}$ select $(\sigma\mathbf{F}_{i+1}, f) \in G$ such that $\sigma \mid \tau$; discard any $(\tau\mathbf{F}_{i+1}, p, q)$ if $p \neq f$, or if $p = f$ and we retain another $(\tau\mathbf{F}_{i+1}, f, g) \in S$ where $q \neq g$.

For simplicity's sake, we assume that we apply (RW) only in line 15, but (NM) both there and in line 11.

3. KNOWN STRATEGIES

This section sketches briefly how Arri's algorithm, G^2V, and F5 can be viewed as strategies for Algorithm 1, distinguished by:

1. whether reduction is complete or semi-complete; and

2. how they prune P and S.

Space restrictions prevent us from going too far into each algorithm's workings, or proving in detail the characterization of each as a strategy for Algorithm 1. However, the reader can verify this by inspecting the relevant papers.

3.1 Arri's algorithm

Algorithm 1 is very close to Arri's algorithm, which uses semi-complete reduction. Although [2] presents this algorithm in non-incremental fashion, with a more general way to choose the signatures, we consider it incrementally, with the definition of signature as given here.

The algorithm maintains a list G similar to that of Algorithm 1, and discards $S_{f,g}$ if f, g do not satisfy a definition of a "normal pair". This differs from the definition in [10]:

DEFINITION 19. *Any $f, g \in I_{i+1}$ are a **normal pair** if $S_{f,g} = uf - cvg$ and*

- *for any $(\sigma\mathbf{F}_{i+1}, p) \in \{(\mathcal{S}(f), f), (\mathcal{S}(g), g)\}$ there does not exist $(\tau\mathbf{F}_{i+1}, q) \in G$ and $t \in \mathbb{M}$ such that $t\tau = \sigma$ and $t\mathrm{lm}(q) = \mathrm{lm}(p)$;*

- $\mathcal{S}(uf) = u \cdot \mathcal{S}(f)$ *and* $\mathcal{S}(vg) = v \cdot \mathcal{S}(g)$; *and*

- $\mathcal{S}(uf) \neq \mathcal{S}(vg)$.

In addition to G, Arri's algorithm maintains a list L of leading monomials used to prune P (there called B). These correspond to known syzygies; whenever s sig-reduces to zero, the monomial part of its natural signature is added to L.

We can characterize this as a strategy for Algorithm 1 in the following way. The first bullet of Definition 19 implies the sig-redundant property (Lemma 15). To implement the second bullet, [2] counsels initializing L to $\{\mathrm{lm}(f) : f \in F_i\}$ and adding σ to L if the σ-reduction of r concludes with 0. This implements Proposition 16 and Lemma 17. In addition, [2] points out that for any fixed natural signature one should keep a polynomial of minimal leading monomial; after all, σ-reduction occurs when the leading monomial decreases and the natural signature is preserved. Thus, the algorithm discards any S-polynomial if another polynomial of the same natural signature has lower leading monomial. This implements Lemma 18. So, Arri's algorithm discards $(\sigma\mathbf{F}_{i+1}, p, q)$ if either of the following holds:

(AM) for some $g \in F_i$, $\mathrm{lm}(g) \mid \sigma$, or for some $(\tau\mathbf{F}_{i+1}, r) \in G$, $\tau \mid \sigma$ and $r = 0$; or

(AR) there exist $(\tau\mathbf{F}_{i+1}, g) \in G$ and $t \in \mathbb{M}$ such that $t\tau = \sigma$ and $\mathrm{lm}(tg) < \mathrm{lm}(S_{p,q})$, or there exist $(\tau\mathbf{F}_{i+1}, f, g) \in S \cup P$ and $t \in \mathbb{M}$ such that $t\tau = \sigma$ and $\mathrm{lm}(tS_{f,g}) < \mathrm{lm}(S_{p,q})$.

Notice that (AR) checks divisibility of σ, not equality.

PROPOSITION 20. *Arri's algorithm implements Algorithm 1 with semi-complete reduction: (AM) implements (NM) and (AR) implements (RW).*

3.2 G^2V

Although G^2V can be used to compute the colon ideal, we consider it only in the context of computing a Gröbner basis. Thus, we are really looking at a special case of G^2V.

G^2V maintains two lists of polynomials, U and V. The polynomials of V are the elements of the basis. The polynomials of U are paired with those of V such that

- if $v_j \in F_i$, then $u_j = 0$;

- if $v_j = f_{i+1}$, then $u_j = 1$; and

- if $v_j = ct_k v_k \pm dt_\ell v_\ell$ for some $c, d \in \mathbb{F}$, $t_k, t_\ell \in \mathbb{M}$, and $v_k, v_\ell \in V$, then $u_j = ct_k u_k \pm dt_\ell u_\ell$.

In addition, S-polynomials and reductions are computed in such a way that $\mathrm{lm}(u_j)$ is invariant for all j: G^2V computes $v_j - ctv_k$ only if $\mathrm{lm}(u_j) > t\mathrm{lm}(u_k)$ or $\mathrm{lm}(u_j) = t\mathrm{lm}(u_k)$ but $\mathrm{lc}(u_j) \neq \mathrm{lc}(cu_k)$. Thus, if $u_j \neq 0$, then $u_j\mathbf{F}_{i+1} \in \mathrm{sig}(v_j)$.

The algorithm maintains another list H of monomials that is initialized with the leading monomials of all $f \in F_i$, and expanded during the course of the algorithm by adding $\mathrm{lm}(u_j)$ whenever v_j reduces to zero. It does not compute an S-polynomial for v_j and v_k if:

(GM) $\max\left(\frac{t_{v_j,v_k}}{t_{v_j}} \cdot u_j, \frac{t_{v_j,v_k}}{t_{v_k}} \cdot u_k\right)$ is divisible by a $t \in H$.

In addition, if every possible reduction of v_j is by some v_k such that $\mathrm{lt}(v_j) = d\mathrm{lt}(v_k)$ and $\mathrm{lt}(u_j) = d v\mathrm{lt}(u_k)$, then v_j is **super top-reducible**, and [11] abstains from generating critical pairs for $S_{p,q}$ if:

(GS) either p or q is super top-reducible.

Criterion (GM) implements Proposition 16 and Lemma 17, while (GS) implies the sig-redundant property (Lemma 15). G^2V offers no implementation of (RW) beyond, "store only one [pair] for each distinct [natural signature]". *Which* pair is left somewhat ambiguous, but we will see that the choice is important.

PROPOSITION 21. *G^2V implements Algorithm 1 with complete reduction: (GM) implements (NM).*

3.3 F5

As explained in the introduction, we use the F5C variant of F5 [8]. In fact, we actually use a simplified version of F5; we describe the differences below.

F5 maintains several lists $G_1, \ldots, G_{i+1} \subset \widehat{\mathbb{S}} \times R$; for $j = 1, \ldots, i$, each G_j is a Gröbner basis of $\langle f_1, \ldots, f_j \rangle$. Whenever a $(\sigma\mathbf{F}_{i+1}, r)$ concludes σ-reduction, (σ, r) is added to the $(i+1)$-st list in a list named *Rules*.

F5 discards $(\sigma\mathbf{F}_{i+1}, p, q)$ if:

(FM) for some $g \in F_i$, $\mathrm{lm}(g) \mid \sigma$, or

(FR) there exists $(\tau, g) \in \mathit{Rules}_{i+1}$, not sig-redundant, such that g was computed after p and $\tau \mid \sigma$.

Notice that (FR), like (AR), checks divisibility of σ, not equality.

103

PROPOSITION 22. *The simplified F5 described here implements Algorithm 1 with semi-complete reduction: (FM) implements (NM), and (FR) implements (RW).*

As noted, the F5 described here is simpler than [10], where:

- S-polynomials of minimal degree are not computed in any particular order (but the code of [8] proceeds by ascending lcm rather than ascending natural signature);

- if $S_{p,q} = up - cvq$, then Criteria (FM) and (FR) are applied not only to up but to vq; in addition, for any potential σ-reduction $r - tg$, the criteria are used to reject some tg.

Omitting these does not represent a significant difference from the original algorithm. In fact, descriptions of F5 by ascending signature have been around for some time ([1, 16]); the second bullet can be viewed an optimization that makes sense in an F4-style implementation, such as [1].

There is one significant difference: the original F5 would not check for sig-redundant polynomials. In view of this, when we view F5 as a strategy for Algorithm 1, we will include the sig-redundant criterion; but in Section 4.2 we will look at F5 with and without this criterion.

That said, in Section 4.2 we will look at both the simpler F5 described here, and an implementation of the original.

4. COMPARISON OF THE ALGORITHMS

The thrust of Section 3 was to show that Arri's algorithm, G^2V, and a simplified F5 can be viewed as implementations of Algorithm 1. Section 4.1, by contrast, compares the three algorithms as their authors originally defined them, using a strictly logical comparison of which critical pairs are discarded, without regard to timings. Nevertheless, we retain the notation of Algorithm 1.

Section 4.2 compares the three algorithms both ways: as implementations to, or "plugins" for, Algorithm 1, and for G^2V and F5 as standalone implementations. The results between the approaches (plugin vs. original) do not differ significantly, but provide both surprising results and additional insights.

4.1 Logical comparison of the algorithms

In this section we consider carefully how the criteria of Arri's algorithm, G^2V, and the simplified F5 overlap. We begin with complete vs. semi-complete reductions:

FACT 23. *G^2V reduces using some polynomials that F5 and Arri's algorithm do not.*

PROOF. This is because reductions are complete in G^2V, but only semi-complete in F5 and Arri's algorithm. □

On the other hand:

FACT 24. *In Algorithm 1, there cannot exist a reduction of type (B) in Corollary 6 without a reduction of type (A).*

PROOF. Let $(\tau\mathbf{F}_{i+1}, r), (\sigma\mathbf{F}_{i+1}, g) \in G$ such that $\mathrm{lc}(g) = d$, $\mathrm{lc}(r) = c \neq d$, and there exists $t \in \mathbb{M}$ such that $\mathrm{lm}(r) = t\mathrm{lm}(g)$ and $\tau = t\sigma$. Then $r - tg$ has a natural signature smaller than $\tau\mathbf{F}_{i+1}$; since the algorithm proceeds by ascending natural signature, $r - tg$ has a sig-representation. Since $\mathrm{lc}(g) \neq \mathrm{lc}(r)$, we have $\mathrm{lm}(r - tg) = \mathrm{lm}(r)$, so the sig-representation of $r - tg$ implies that there exist $u \in \mathbb{M}$, $(\mu\mathbf{F}_{i+1}, f) \in G$ such that $u\mathrm{lm}(f) = \mathrm{lm}(r)$ and $u\mu < \tau$. This is a reduction of type (A). □

Together, Facts 23 and 24 mean that while G^2V can reduce a polynomial using polynomials that F5 and Arri's algorithm cannot, they can still reduce it using other polynomials.

The next observation regards non-trivial syzygies.

FACT 25. *(GM) and (AM) are equivalent. In addition, some pairs $(\sigma\mathbf{F}_{i+1}, p, q)$ rejected by (GM) and (AM), but not by (FM), are also rejected (FR).*

PROOF. It is trivial that (GM) and (AM) are equivalent. Inspection shows that $(FM) \implies (GM)$, but not the converse. Assume therefore that (GM) rejects a critical pair $(\sigma\mathbf{F}_{i+1}, p, q)$ that (FM) does not; this implies that σ is divisible by some $\tau \in \mathbb{M}$, where $(\tau\mathbf{F}_{i+1}, r)$ was the result of a complete or semi-complete reduction, and $r = 0$.

Fact 24 implies that r σ-reduces to zero in F5 as well. This is recorded in *Rules* by appending (τ, r) to $Rules_{i+1}$. Since $r = 0$, F5 generates no more critical pairs for it. So $p, q \neq r$. If r was generated after p, then $\mathtt{Rewritten}(\sigma) \neq p$, so $\mathtt{Rewritten?}(\sigma\mathbf{F}_{i+1}, p)$ would return $\mathtt{True}$. In this case, (FR) rejects $(\tau\mathbf{F}_{i+1}, p, q)$. Hence at least some pairs $(\sigma\mathbf{F}_{i+1}, p, q)$ rejected by (GM) but not by (FM) are also rejected by (FR).

On the other hand, suppose that F5 computed p after r; then $\mathtt{Rewritten}(\sigma\mathbf{F}_{i+1}) \neq r$. In fact, it might return p, and $\mathtt{Rewritten?}(\sigma\mathbf{F}_{i+1}, p)$ would return $\mathtt{False}$, so that F5 would not reject $(\sigma\mathbf{F}_{i+1}, p, q)$, whereas (GM) would. □

On the other hand, Lemma 17 implies that one could modify (FM) to consider zero reductions as well as trivial syzygies, as the other algorithms do. We try this in the next section. Alternately, one could modify (FR) to scan $Rules_{i+1}$ for pointers to zero reductions, using them to discard pairs before performing the usual (FR) criterion. Either works, but the former would likely be more efficient in interpreted code; see a related discussion in the following section.

FACT 26. *Some critical pairs computed by F5 are not computed by G^2V and Arri's algorithm.*

PROOF. From Lemma 15, we know that G^2V and Arri's algorithm do not compute critical pairs for sig-redundant polynomials, whereas F5 does. □

FACT 27. *Some pairs $(\sigma\mathbf{F}_{i+1}, p, q)$ discarded by (FR) are not discarded by G^2V. Likewise, some pairs $(\sigma\mathbf{F}_{i+1}, p, q)$ discarded by (AR) are not discarded by G^2V.*

PROOF. As noted in Section 3.2, G^2V implements (RW) by checking for equal signatures only, whereas (FR) and (AR) check for divisibility. As a consequence, (FR) and (AR) can discard $(\sigma\mathbf{F}_{i+1}, p, q)$ because $(\tau\mathbf{F}_{i+1}, f) \in G$ and $\tau \mid \sigma$, even if f generates no pairs of natural signature σ. □

4.2 Experimental results

Although Facts 25 and 26 imply an advantage for G^2V and Arri's algorithm over F5, Fact 27 implies an advantage for F5 and Arri's algorithm over G^2V. We will see that the latter advantage is more significant than the former.

We first look at some timings of the algorithms as plugins for Algorithm 1. To do this, we implemented Algorithm 1 as a C++ class in the kernel of a developer version of SINGULAR 3-1-2, then created descendant classes corresponding to the other algorithms. This allowed us to implement complete reductions for G^2V and semi-complete reductions for F5 and Arri's algorithm without giving either an otherwise unfair advantage. Using compiled code allows us to avoid

Test case	F5	G²V	Arri	Arri+(MR)
Katsura-9	14.98	17.63	18.25	20.95
Katsura-10	153.35	192.20	185.76	220.01
Eco-8	2.24*	0.49	0.45	0.53
Eco-9	77.13*	13.15	5.20	14.59
Schrans-Troost	3.7	5.3	6.46	7.72
F744	19.35*	26.86	7.37	27.77
Cyclic-7	7.00	33.85	8.82	40.54
Cyclic-8	7310	26242	17672	>8h

*See the discussion in the text.

Table 1: Timings, in seconds, of compiled Singular implementations of the strategies, implemented as plugins for Algorithm 1. Computed on a workstation with a 2.66GHz Intel Core 2 Duo P8800 and 4 GB RAM, running 64-bit Ubuntu 10.10. Base field is $\mathbb{F}_{32003}$; ordering is degree reverse lexicographic.

Test case	F5	G²V	Arri
Katsura-9	886;0	886;0	886;0
Katsura-10	1781;0	1781;0	1781;0
Eco-8	830;322*	2012;57	694;57
Eco-9	2087;929*	5794;120	1852;120
Schrans-Troost	380;0	451;0	370;0
F744	1324;342*	2145;169	1282;169
Cyclic-7	1063;44	3108;36	781;36
Cyclic-8	7066;244	24600;244	5320;244

*See the discussion in the text.

Table 2: Number of critical pairs reduced by each strategy, followed by number of zero reductions. We omit Arri+(MR) for space; it is comparable to G²V.

the overhead of an interpreter, but the code was otherwise unoptimized, linking to Singular's polynomial arithmetic. Table 1 lists timings in seconds corresponding to this implementation. We do not include timings for a bare-bones Algorithm 1; having no criteria to prune P or S, it is unbearably slow. In Table 2, we count the number of critical pairs reduced, along with the number of zero reductions.

As an example, we considered a fourth strategy that is essentially Arri's algorithm, but we replace (AR) by

(MR) there exist $(\tau\mathbf{F}_{i+1}, g) \in G$ and $t \in \mathbb{M}$ such that $t\tau = \sigma$ and g has fewer monomials than $S_{p,q}$, in which case we consider tg in place of $S_{p,q}$; if $(\sigma, f, g) \in S$ then we may choose either (σ, p, q) or (σ, f, g) freely.

This implementation of (RW) causes *more* work than necessary. The first polynomials generated tend to have the fewest monomials, so (MR) selects these instead of later polynomials, and so repeats many earlier reductions. The algorithm still computes a Gröbner basis, but takes the scenic route.

In general, F5 terminated the most quickly, but there were exceptions where Arri's algorithm did. This is explained by the discussion in the proof of Fact 25: (FR) is sometimes too aggressive, and does not notice some zero reductions. We modified (FM) to check for these first, and this modified F5 terminates for Eco-8 (-9) in 0.38s (8.19s), and for F744 in 8.79s. Regarding critical pairs, it computes 565 (1278) critical pairs for Eco-8 (-9), of which 57 (120) reduce to zero; and 1151 critical pairs for F744, of which 169 reduce to zero. This suggests that computing $\mathrm{lm}(S_{p,q})$ in order to

Test case	F5	G²V	F5/G²V	F5/G²V in [11]
Katsura-6	1.2	0.53	2.26	6.32
Katsura-7	12.2	6.7	1.82	4.91
Katsura-8	134.28	50.1	2.68	5.95
Schrans-Troost	261.69	50.61	5.17	14.04
F633	16.19	2.72	5.95	14.50
Cyclic-6	7.1	7.3	0.97	3.90
Cyclic-7	693.3	962.5	0.72	3.12

Table 3: Timings, in seconds, of Singular libraries, *not* implemented as plugins to Algorithm 1. Computed on a MacBook Pro with a 2.4GHz Intel Core 2 Duo and 4 GB RAM, running OS X 10.6.5. Base field is $\mathbb{F}_{32003}$; ordering is degree reverse lexicographic.

check (AR) is usually too expensive for the benefit that we would expect, but in some cases it may be worthwhile.

The results of Table 1 surprised us, in that it contradicts the unequivocal assertion of [11] that G²V is "two to ten times faster" than F5. Apparently, this is because [11] compared *implementations* and not *algorithms*. Why is this problematic? Primarily it is due to the use in [11] of interpreted code. Some natural adjustments to the implementation of F5 used in [8, 11] are needed merely to start making the two comparable. We tried the following:

- Formerly, the F5 implementation checked (FM) using an interpreted `for` loop, but the implementation of G²V checked (GM) using Singular's `reduce()`, pushing the `for` loop into compiled code (line 173, for example). We changed the F5 code to check (FM) using `reduce()`.

- As specified in [10], `TopReduction` and `CritPair` return after each reduction or creation of a critical pair. This back-and-forth incurs a penalty; it is sensible to loop within these functions, returning only when reduction is semi-complete or all critical pairs have been considered. (The code for G²V did this already.)

- In the code accompanying [8], `Spol` computes S-polynomials by ascending lcm, but one could proceed by ascending natural signature instead [1, 16]. (The code for G²V did this already.)

Some other changes contributed a little; see Table 3 for timings, and Section 5 for source code. With this new implementation, G²V sometimes outperforms F5, but by a much smaller ratio than before. Tellingly, F5 outperforms G²V handily for Cyclic-n. This is despite the persistence of at least one major disadvantage: the code to check (FR) still uses an interpreted `for` loop. This imposes a penalty not only in `Spol` but also in `IsReducible` (called `find_reductor` in the implementation); the interpreted `for` loop checking (FR) is one reason `IsReducible` consumes about half the time required to compute a Gröbner basis in some systems.

For G²V, on the other hand, we observed a disadvantage inherent to the algorithm and not to the implementation: its implementation of (RW) checks only equality, not divisibility. Fact 27 is especially evident in Table 2! Most S-polynomials are subsequently discarded as super top-reducible. These discards are not reflected in Table 2 of [11], which mistakenly implies G^2V computes fewer polynomials than F5. *Time lost in reduction is unrecoverable.*

A final note. When we first implemented G^2V we obtained much worse timings than those of Table 1. When we inspected the source code accompanying [11], we found that the choice of which pair to store for a given signature is not arbitrary: the implementation prefers the most recently computed polynomial that can generate a given signature (lines 176–183). That is, it discards $(\sigma \mathbf{F}_{i+1}, p, q) \in S$ if

(GR') there exists $(\sigma \mathbf{F}_{i+1}, f, g) \in P$ such that $p \neq f$ and f was computed after p, or $p = f$ and q was computed after g.

Note the similarity with (FR).

5. CONCLUSION

This paper has described a common algorithm for which F5, G^2V, and Arri's algorithm can be considered strategies, implemented as "plugins". Algorithm 1 makes use of a new criterion to reject polynomials and to guarantee termination, not only for itself, but for G^2V and Arri's algorithm as well, through Lemma 15. The matter is not so clear for F5, which seems to terminate all the same; we have not yet determined if some mechanism in F5 implies the sig-redundant criterion.

Both timings and logical analysis imply that claims in [11] that G^2V is "two to ten times faster than F5" are based on a flawed comparison of implementations, rather than criteria. Indeed, the inherent advantages appear to lie with F5 and Arri's algorithm: in cases where F5 is not the most efficient, Arri's is, and modifying (FM) to check for non-trivial syzygies usually turns the scales back in F5's favor:

(FM') $\max \left(\frac{t_{p,q}}{t_p} \cdot \sigma, \frac{t_{p,q}}{t_q} \cdot \tau \right)$ is divisible by $\operatorname{lm}(g)$ for some $g \in F_i$, or by μ for some $(\mu \mathbf{F}_{i+1}, 0) \in G$.

Source code developed for Table 3, along with a demonstration version of the algorithms for the Sage computer algebra system [15], can be found at

`www.math.usm.edu/perry/Research/`

by appending to the above path one of the filenames

`f5_ex.lib`, `f5_library.lib`, `f5_library_new.lib`, or `basic_sigbased_gb.py` .

Acknowledgments

The authors wish to thank the Centre for Computer Algebra at Universität Kaiserslautern for their hospitality, encouragement, and assistance with the SINGULAR computer algebra system. Comments by Martin Albrecht, Roger Dellaca, and Lei Huang helped improve the paper immensely.

6. REFERENCES

[1] Martin Albrecht and John Perry. F4/5. Preprint, 2010. Available online at arxiv.org/abs/1006.4933.

[2] Alberto Arri and John Perry. The F5 Criterion revised. Submitted to the *Journal of Symbolic Computation*, 2009, preprint online at `arxiv.org/abs/1012.3664`.

[3] Thomas Becker, Volker Weispfenning, and Hans Kredel. *Gröbner Bases: a Computational Approach to Commutative Algebra*. Springer-Verlag New York, Inc., New York, 1993.

[4] Michael Brickenstein. Slimgb: Gröbner bases with slim polynomials. *Revista Matemática Complutense*, 23(2):453–466, 2009.

[5] Bruno Buchberger. *Ein Algorithmus zum Auffinden der Basiselemente des Restklassenringes nach einem nulldimensionalem Polynomideal (An Algorithm for Finding the Basis Elements in the Residue Class Ring Modulo a Zero Dimensional Polynomial Ideal)*. PhD thesis, Mathematical Institute, University of Innsbruck, Austria, 1965. English translation published in the Journal of Symbolic Computation (2006) 475–511.

[6] Bruno Buchberger. Gröbner-bases: An algorithmic method in polynomial ideal theory. In N. K. Bose, editor, *Multidimensional Systems Theory - Progress, Directions and Open Problems in Multidimensional Systems*, pages 184–232, Dotrecht – Boston – Lancaster, 1985. Reidel Publishing Company.

[7] W. Decker, G.-M. Greuel, G. Pfister, and H. Schönemann. SINGULAR 3-1-2. A Computer Algebra System for Polynomial Computations, Centre for Computer Algebra, University of Kaiserslautern, 2010. www.singular.uni-kl.de.

[8] Christian Eder and John Perry. F5C: A variant of Faugère's F5 algorithm with reduced Gröbner bases. *Journal of Symbolic Computation*, 45(12):1442–1458, 2010.

[9] Jean-Charles Faugère. A new efficient algorithm for computing Gröbner bases (F4). *Journal of Pure and Applied Algebra*, 139(1–3):61–88, June 1999.

[10] Jean-Charles Faugère. A new efficient algorithm for computing Gröbner bases without reduction to zero F5. In *International Symposium on Symbolic and Algebraic Computation Symposium - ISSAC 2002, Villeneuve d'Ascq, France*, pages 75–82, Jul 2002. Revised version downloaded from fgbrs.lip6.fr/jcf/Publications/index.html.

[11] Shuhong Gao, Yinhua Guan, and Frank Volny. A new incremental algorithm for computing Groebner bases. In *Proceedings of the 2010 International Symposium on Symbolic and Algebraic Computation*. ACM Press, 2010.

[12] Rudiger Gebauer and Hans Möller. On an installation of Buchberger's algorithm. *Journal of Symbolic Computation*, 6:275–286, 1988.

[13] Martin Kreuzer and Lorenzo Robbiano. *Computational Commutative Algebra I*. Springer-Verlag, Heidelberg, 2000.

[14] Hans Möller, Ferdinando Mora, and Carlo Traverso. Gröbner bases computation using syzygies. In P. S. Wang, editor, *Proceedings of the 1992 International Symposium on Symbolic and Algebraic Computation*, pages 320–328. Association for Computing Machinery, ACM Press, July 1992.

[15] William Stein. *Sage: Open Source Mathematical Software (Version 3.1.1)*. The Sage Group, 2008. www.sagemath.org.

[16] Alexey Zobnin. Generalization of the F5 algorithm for calculating Gröbner bases for polynomial ideals. *Programming and Computer Software*, 36(2):75–82, 2010.

2-descent for Second Order Linear Differential Equations

Tingting Fang
Department of Mathematics
Florida State University
Tallahassee, FL 32306-3027, USA
tfang@math.fsu.edu

Mark van Hoeij[*]
Department of Mathematics
Florida State University
Tallahassee, FL 32306-3027, USA
hoeij@math.fsu.edu

ABSTRACT

Let L be a second order linear ordinary differential equation with coefficients in $\mathbb{C}(x)$. The goal in this paper is to reduce L to an equation that is easier to solve. The starting point is an irreducible L, of order two, and the goal is to decide if L is projectively equivalent to another equation $\tilde{L}$ that is defined over a subfield $\mathbb{C}(f)$ of $\mathbb{C}(x)$.

This paper treats the case of 2-descent, which means reduction to a subfield with index $[\mathbb{C}(x) : \mathbb{C}(f)] = 2$. Although the mathematics has already been treated in other papers, a complete implementation could not be given because it involved a step for which we do not have a complete implementation. The contribution of this paper is to give an approach that is fully implementable [5]. Examples illustrate that this algorithm is very useful for finding closed form solutions (2-descent, if it exists, reduces the number of true singularities from n to at most $n/2 + 2$).

Categories and Subject Descriptors

G.4 [**Mathematical Software**]: Algorithm design and analysis; I.1.2 [**Symbolic and Algebraic Manipulation**]: Algorithms—*Algebraic algorithms*

General Terms

Algorithms

1. INTRODUCTION

Let $L = \sum_{i=0}^{n} a_i \partial^i$ be a differential operator with coefficients in a differential field $K = \mathbb{C}(x)$, where ∂ is the usual differentiation $\frac{d}{dx}$. The corresponding differential equation is $L(y) = 0$, i.e. $a_n y^{(n)} + \cdots + a_1 y' + a_0 y = 0$. The problem of finding closed form solutions of L becomes easier if we can factor L as a product of lower order operators [2, 7, 1] or apply some other approach to reduce the order [9, 14].

A different type of reduction is called *descent*. Here, the goal is to reduce L to an operator $\tilde{L}$ of the same order, but

this time defined over a proper subfield $k = \mathbb{C}(f)$ of K. Here $\tilde{L}$ must be *projectively equivalent* to L. Informally, this means that L can be solved in terms of the solutions of $\tilde{L}$ and vice versa (a precise definition will be given in Section 2.2).

In this paper, we treat the case of 2-descent, meaning that k is a subfield of K with index 2. For now, we treat only second order equations. After applying Kovacic' algorithm, we can assume that L is irreducible (i.e. not a product of lower order factors), and that it has no Liouvillian solutions.

Descent reduces the number of true singularities (Definition 5) from n to $\leq n/2 + 2$, which helps to solve differential equations as illustrated in Section 7. In particular, if the number of true singularities[1] drops to 3, and if these are regular singularities[2], then a $_2F_1$-type solution can be obtained quickly. We can also stop reducing when we reach an operator with four true singularities, because 4-singularity equations with $_2F_1$-type solutions are currently being classified [6] by van Hoeij and Vidunas. Classifying equations with closed form solutions and > 4 singularities would be hard to do, this is where 2-descent becomes crucial.

If $L \in \mathbb{C}(x)[\partial]$ then there is a finitely generated extension $\mathbb{Q} \subseteq C$ with $L \in C(x)[\partial]$, just take C to be the extension of $\mathbb{Q}$ given by the coefficients of L. The main design goal for our algorithm is to introduce as few algebraic extensions of C as possible. Without this design goal, Sections 3 and 5 would have been much shorter (if we simply compute the splitting field of the singularities then for Section 5 we can follow [3] and Section 3 becomes trivial. Sections 3 and 5 become non-trivial when we aim to minimize field extensions).

The main results in this paper are in Section 4. We know from [11] that if there is a gauge transformation G from L to $\sigma(L)$, then L will allow descent with respect to σ. The question is, given G, how to find the descent? Is it necessary (as in the terminology in [11]) to trivialize a 2-cocycle, or to perform some equivalent complicated operation such as finding a point on a conic over $C(x)$? The answer is no; we give a short and efficient algorithm in Section 4, and we even show (Theorem 1) that it produces a result over an optimal extension of C.

1.1 Relation to prior work

It is shown in [3, 11] that the problem of computing 2-descent can be reduced to another problem (trivializing a 2-cocycle) although no step by step algorithm is given in these papers. The paper [9] does give an algorithm, and im-

[*]Supported by NSF grant 1017880.

---

[1]the number of *removable* singularities (Def. 5) is irrelevant
[2]for the irregular singular case, finding closed form solutions if they exist can be done with [12, 4]

plementation, that can be used to find 2-descent, as follows. If σ is a Möbius transformation of order 2, and $\mathbb{C}(f)$ is the fixed field of σ, and if L is projectively equivalent to $\sigma(L)$, then we can compute the so-called symmetric product of $L, \sigma(L)$, then apply factorization (DFactorLCLM in Maple), take the 3'rd order factor found that way, and run the algorithm from [9] to find a second order operator. All of these steps are implemented, and the end result is a 2-descent.

The problem with the above methods is that they rely on an algorithm that can find a point on a conic defined over K (or an algorithm that solves an equivalent problem). Although such a point must exist when $K = \mathbb{C}(x)$, the proof does not show how to find such a point over a field of constants that is optimal or close to optimal (recall that we wish to minimize the extension of C that the algorithm introduces, where $C \subset \mathbb{C}$). There is only an implementation [10] for this step if C is $\mathbb{Q}$ or a transcendental extension of $\mathbb{Q}$. If L contains algebraic numbers, then there is no implementation for finding a point on a conic, and without that, it is not clear how to obtain from [11, 9, 3] a complete implementation for finding 2-descent.

In this paper we describe a step by step algorithm for finding 2-descent. The algorithm can be fully implemented [5] because it does not call a conic algorithm. Note: If $L \in C(x)[\partial]$ with $C \subset \mathbb{C}$, and if one allows unnecessary algebraic extensions of C (potentially exponentially large), then it is not hard to implement a conic algorithm, in which case one can consider 2-descent an already solved problem. But in practice our algorithm would be much preferable because it only extends C when necessary (i.e. when there is no 2-descent defined over C).

2. PRELIMINARIES

2.1 Differential Operators and Singularities

Let $K = \mathbb{C}(x)$ denote the differential field and let $\mathcal{D}=K[\partial]$ be the ring of differential operators with coefficients in the differential field K. Here ∂ denotes the usual differentiation $\frac{d}{dx}$. Then elements $L \in \mathcal{D}$ are of the form $L = a_n\partial^n + \cdots + a_1\partial + a_0$ with $a_i \in K$.

A point $p \in \mathbb{P}^1 = \mathbb{C} \cup \{\infty\}$ is called a *singularity* of a differential operator $L \in K[\partial]$, if p is a zero of the leading coefficient of L or p is a pole of one of the other coefficients of L. p is called a *regular* point if it is not a *singularity*.

We denote the solution space of a differential operator as $V(L) = \{y|L(y) = 0\}$ where the y are taken in some universal extension [15] of $\mathbb{C}(x)$. If p is a regular point of L, we can write all solutions of L at p as convergent power series $\sum_{i=0}^{\infty} a_i t_p^i$, where t_p denotes the local parameter which is $t_p = \frac{1}{x}$ if $p = \infty$ and $t_p = x - p$, otherwise.

2.2 Transformations

There are three known types of transformations that send, for any second order $L_1 \in K[\partial]$, the solution space of L_1 to the solution space of some $L_2 \in K[\partial]$, again of order 2. They are (notation as in [4]):

(i) change of variables: $y(x) \to y(f(x))$, $\quad f(x) \in K \setminus \mathbb{C}$.
(ii) exp-product: $y \to e^{\int r\,dx} \cdot y$, $\quad\quad\quad r \in K$.
(iii) gauge transformation: $y \to r_0 y + r_1 y'$, $\quad r_0, r_1 \in K$.

DEFINITION 1. *Let $L_1, L_2 \in K[\partial]$ with order 2. They are called* gauge equivalent *(notation: $L_1 \sim_g L_2$) if there exists a*

so-called gauge transformation from $V(L_1)$ to $V(L_2)$, which means a bijection of the form (iii).

REMARK 1. *Let $L_1, L_2 \in K[\partial]$. The $\mathcal{D}$-modules $\mathcal{D}/\mathcal{D}L_i$, $i = 1, 2$ are isomorphic if and only if $L_1 \sim_g L_2$. In particular, $\sim_g$ is an equivalence relation (see [1]).*

DEFINITION 2. *Let $L_1, L_2 \in K[\partial]$ with order 2. They are called* projectively equivalent *(notation: $L_1 \sim_p L_2$) if there exists a bijection $V(L_1) \to V(L_2)$ of the form*

$$y \longrightarrow e^{\int r} \cdot (r_0 y + r_1 y') \tag{1}$$

for some $r, r_0, r_1 \in K$.

Projective equivalence is also an equivalence relation, see [1]. An implementation (for order 2) is given in [8] to decide if $L_1 \sim_p L_2$, and if so, to find the projective equivalence (the r, r_0, r_1 in (1)). An algorithm for arbitrary order n was given in [1] (implemented in ISOLDE).

2.3 2-descent

DEFINITION 3. *Let $f = \frac{A}{B}$ with $A, B \in \mathbb{C}[x]$ coprime, then the degree of f is defined as*

$$\deg(f) = \max(\deg(A), \deg(B)) = [\mathbb{C}(x) : \mathbb{C}(f)].$$

REMARK 2. *If $\sigma \in \mathrm{Aut}(\mathbb{C}(x)/\mathbb{C})$ has order 2, then the fixed field of σ is a subfield of $\mathbb{C}(x)$ of index 2, and by Lüroth's theorem this subfield is of the form $\mathbb{C}(f)$, for some $f \in \mathbb{C}(x)$ of degree 2 (note: we can find such f in $\{x + \sigma(x), x\sigma(x)\} \setminus C$). Any subfield $\mathbb{C}(f) \subset \mathbb{C}(x)$ of index 2 is the fixed field of some $\sigma \in \mathrm{Aut}(\mathbb{C}(x)/\mathbb{C})$ of order 2 (after all, every extension of degree 2 is Galois). The automorphisms of $\mathbb{C}(x)$ over $\mathbb{C}$ are Möbius transformations:*

$$x \mapsto \frac{ax + b}{cx + d} \tag{2}$$

This paper treats 2-descent, so we only consider σ of order 2, which is equivalent to having $d = -a$ in (2).

REMARK 3. *Any $\sigma \in \mathrm{Aut}(\mathbb{C}(x)/\mathbb{C})$ extends to an automorphism of $\mathbb{C}(x)[\partial]$. If σ has finite order, and if $\mathbb{C}(f)$ is the fixed field of σ, and if $L \in \mathbb{C}(x)[\partial]$, then*

$$L = \sigma(L) \iff L \in \mathbb{C}(f)[\partial_f], \tag{3}$$

in other words, $\mathbb{C}(f)[\partial_f]$ is the fixed ring of σ. Here $\partial_f := \frac{d}{df} = \frac{1}{f'}\partial$, where $'$ is differentiation w.r.t. x.

DEFINITION 4. *Let $L \in \mathbb{C}(x)[\partial]$. We say that L has 2-descent if $\exists f \in \mathbb{C}(x)$ with $\deg(f) = 2$ and $\exists \tilde{L} \in \mathbb{C}(f)[\partial_f]$ such that $L \sim_p \tilde{L}$.*

One could instead use the term "projective 2-descent" for this (because we use projective equivalence $\sim_p$) but we opted to use the shorter term.

Main goal: Let $L \in K[\partial]$ be irreducible and of order 2. The goal of this paper is to give an explicit algorithm that can decide if L has 2-descent, and if so, find it (i.e. find $\tilde{L} \in \mathbb{C}(f)[\partial_f]$ with $L \sim_p \tilde{L}$ for some f of degree 2). Moreover, if L is defined over some field $C \subset \mathbb{C}$, we should only introduce algebraic extensions of C when necessary.

We will divide our algorithm into several steps. The first step is to find candidates for $\mathbb{C}(f)$ with $\deg(f) = 2$. Such a field is the fixed field of a Möbius transformation of order 2.

3. MÖBIUS TRANSFORMATIONS

PROPOSITION 1. *A Möbius transformation has order 2 if it is of the form $\sigma(x) = \frac{ax+b}{cx-a}$. Such σ has 2 fixed points in $\mathbb{C} \cup \{\infty\}$.*

One could apply a transformation that moves the fixed points of σ to $0, \infty$, which reduces σ to the notationally convenient $x \mapsto -x$. Our algorithm does not do this because it can introduce an unnecessary algebraic extension of the constants.

3.1 The singularity structure

DEFINITION 5. *Let $L \in \mathcal{D}$ have order n. Assume p is a singularity of L. If there exists a basis of $V(L)$ of the form $e^{\int r} f_1, \ldots, e^{\int r} f_n$ where $r \in \mathbb{C}(x)$ and $f_1, \ldots, f_n$ are analytic at $x = p$, then p is called a* removable *singularity (also called* false *singularity). Otherwise p is called a* true *singularity.*

Suppose p is a singularity of L. If there exists a projectively equivalent $\tilde{L}$ for which p is a regular point, then p is a removable singularity. The true singularities of L are precisely those p that stay singular when L is replaced by any projectively equivalent operator.

Denote (as in [12, 4]) the (generalized) exponent-difference as $\Delta(L, p)$.

DEFINITION 6. *For any true singularity p, denote*

$$\text{type}(L,p) := \begin{cases} ''\text{irreg}'' & \text{if} \quad \Delta(L,p) \notin \mathbb{C} \\ ''\text{irrat}'' & \text{if} \quad \Delta(L,p) \in \mathbb{C} \setminus \mathbb{Q} \\ e \in [0, \frac{1}{2}] & \text{if} \quad \Delta(L,p) \in \mathbb{Q} \end{cases}$$

Here, $e \in [0, \frac{1}{2}]$ such that $\Delta(L,p) \in (e + \mathbb{Z}) \cup (-e + \mathbb{Z})$. Then we write the *singularity structure* of L as

$$S^{\text{type}} := \{(p, \text{type}(L,p)) \mid p \text{ true sing}\}.$$

Let π_i project on the i'th entry of S^{type}, then $S := \pi_1(S^{\text{type}}) \subseteq \mathbb{P}^1(\mathbb{C})$ denotes the set of true singularities of L.

LEMMA 1. *[12, 4] If $L \sim_p \tilde{L} \in \mathcal{D}$ then L and $\tilde{L}$ have the same singularity structure S^{type}.*

If $L \in C(x)[\partial]$ for some field $C \subset \mathbb{C}$, we denote:

$$M_{\mathbb{C}} := \{\sigma = \frac{ax+b}{cx-a} \mid a,b,c \in \mathbb{C} \text{ and } \sigma(S) = S\}$$

$$M_C := \{\sigma = \frac{ax+b}{cx-a} \mid a,b,c \in C \text{ and } \sigma(S) = S\}$$

$$M_{\mathbb{C}}^{\text{type}} := \{\sigma \in M_{\mathbb{C}} \mid \sigma(S^{\text{type}}) = S^{\text{type}}\}$$

$$M_C^{\text{type}} := \{\sigma \in M_C \mid \sigma(S^{\text{type}}) = S^{\text{type}}\}$$

$\text{places}(C) := \{f \in C[x] \mid f \text{ is monic and irreducible}\} \bigcup \{\infty\}$.

REMARK 4. $\text{places}(\mathbb{C}) \cong \mathbb{P}^1(\mathbb{C}) = \mathbb{C} \bigcup \{\infty\}$

If $\sigma \in \text{Aut}(C(x)/C)$ then σ acts on $\text{places}(C)$ in a natural way, preserving degrees, which are defined as:

$$\deg(p) = \begin{cases} 1 & \text{if} \quad p = \infty; \\ \deg(p) & \text{if} \quad p \text{ is a polynomial}. \end{cases}$$

If $L = a_n \partial^n + \cdots + a_0 \partial^0$ with $a_0, \ldots, a_n \in C[x]$, then computing the singularities as a subset of $\mathbb{P}^1(\overline{C}) \subset \mathbb{P}^1(\mathbb{C})$ would mean computing all roots (the splitting field) of a_n.

The algorithm does not compute this splitting field because it could have exponentially high degree over C. Instead, it uses irreducible factors of a_n in $C[x]$ (and the point ∞) to represent the singularities, then we have the notation S_C^{type} and

$$M_C^{\text{type}} := \{\sigma \in M_C \mid \sigma(S_C^{\text{type}}) = S_C^{\text{type}}\}$$

To ensure that S is invariant under $\sim_p$ it is essential to discard all removable singularities.

EXAMPLE 1. *Let $C = \mathbb{Q}$, and*

$$L := \partial^2 + \frac{12x^4 + 1}{x(2x^2 - 1)(2x^2 + 1)} \partial - \frac{8}{(2x^2 - 1)^2}$$

For this example we find

$$S^{\text{type}} := \{(\infty, 0), (0, 0), (\frac{-1}{\sqrt{2}}, 0), (\frac{1}{\sqrt{2}}, 0), (\frac{-1}{\sqrt{-2}}, 0), (\frac{1}{\sqrt{-2}}, 0)\}.$$

The set of true singularities is

$$S = \pi_1(S^{\text{type}}) = \{\infty, 0, \frac{1}{\sqrt{2}}, \frac{-1}{\sqrt{2}}, \frac{1}{\sqrt{-2}}, \frac{-1}{\sqrt{-2}}\}$$

Written in terms of $\text{places}(\mathbb{Q})$ *it becomes*

$$S_C := \{\infty, x, x^2 + \frac{1}{2}, x^2 - \frac{1}{2}\} \subset \text{places}(\mathbb{Q}),$$

$$S_C^{\text{type}} := \{(\infty, 0), (x, 0), (x^2 + \frac{1}{2}, 0), (x^2 - \frac{1}{2}, 0)\}$$

and

$$M_C^{\text{type}} = \{-x, \frac{1}{2x}, \frac{-1}{2x}\}.$$

This example was quite easy because it has obvious 2-descent. Moreover, all singularities were true singularities with $\text{type}(L,p) = 0$. Removable singularities are common in larger examples, such as Example 3 in Section 7. Using S instead of S_C would have introduced an extension of $C = \mathbb{Q}$ of degree 4 in this example, however, such an extension could have been much larger (e.g. if $x^5 - x - 1$ had appeared in the denominator of L, which has a splitting field of degree 120).

3.2 Finding candidates for σ

For $i = 1, 2, \ldots$, let S_i denote the set of all $p \in S_C$ with $\deg(p) = i$.

Algorithm: Compute Möbius transformations.

Input: The singularity structure S_C^{type}.

Output: The set M_C^{type}, i.e., the set of all $\sigma \in \text{Aut}(C(x)/C)$ of order 2 that fix S_C^{type}. (In this paper we omit 2-descent for σ's that are not defined over C because in that case is better to compute a larger descent, of type $C_2 \times C_2$, D_n, A_4, S_4, or A_5).

Step 1: Compute S_i from S_C^{type} and let n_i denote the number of elements of S_i.

Step 2: Let $n_{sing} := \sum i \, n_i$ (the total number of true singularities when counted in $\mathbb{P}^1(\overline{C})$).

Step 3: If $n_{sing} < 3$ then return "With < 3 singularities, descent is not necessary nor implemented" and stop.

Step 4: Now $n_{sing} \geq 3$.

(i) If $n_1 \geq 3$, then call **Case1**
(ii) If $n_1 = 1, n_2 = 1$, then call **Case2**
(iii) If $n_1 = 2, n_2 = 1$, then call **Case3**
(iv) If $n_2 \geq 2$, then call **Case4**
(v) If $n_i \geq 1$ for some $i \geq 3$, then call **Case5**

Algorithm: Case1.

Input: S_C^{type} with S_1 having ≥ 3 elements.

Output: The set M_C^{type}.

Before describing Algorithm Case1, first some remarks. In general $\sigma = \frac{ax+b}{cx+d}$ is determined by the image of three points $\sigma(p_1), \sigma(p_2), \sigma(p_3)$. Since we assume $|\sigma| = 2$, we can write $\sigma = \frac{ax+b}{cx-a}$. In general, such σ is determined by two points $\sigma(p_1)$, $\sigma(p_2)$ except in one case: when $\sigma(p_1) = p_2$, $\sigma(p_2) = p_1$. In that case one more point is needed to determine $\sigma = \frac{ax+b}{cx-a}$.

Algorithm Case1 will choose a pair $p_1, p_2 \in S_1$ ($p_1 \neq p_2$) and loops over all $n(n-1)$ pairs $q_1, q_2 \in S_1$ ($q_1 \neq q_2$). If the types of q_1, q_2 match those of p_1, p_2, the algorithm will compute the σ that maps p_1, p_2 to q_1, q_2. In the one case that $q_1, q_2 = p_2, p_1$, a third point p_3 is used to determine σ. There are $n-2$ choices for $\sigma(p_3)$, namely from $S_1 - \{p_1, p_2\}$. The number of computed σ's is then $\leq n(n-1) - 1 + (n-2)$ (equality if they all have the same type). Then we remove those σ for which S_C^{type} is not σ-invariant (That means remove all σ's that send a true singularity to a non-singular point or to a false singularity (Definition 5), and, remove all σ's that send a singularity to a singularity of a different type).

Algorithm: Case2

Input: S_C^{type} with S_1 having 1 element and S_2 having 1 element.

Output: The set M_C^{type}.

Step 1: Let the polynomial in S_2 be $x^2 + c_1 x + c_0$.

Step 2: Write $\sigma_1 = -\frac{c_1 x + 2c_0}{2x + c_1}$ and $\sigma_2 = \frac{ax + c_0 \, c + c_1 \, a}{c \, x - a}$.

> REMARK 5. σ_1 *is the unique Möbius transformation of order 2 that fixes the roots of* $x^2 + c_1 x + c_0$; σ_2 *is the parameterized family of all* σ *of order 2 that swap the roots of* $x^2 + c_1 x + c_0$.

Step 3: Let p_1 be the one element of S_1. Equating $\sigma(p_1)$ to p_1 gives a linear equation that determines the values of the homogeneous parameters a, c in σ_2.

Step 4: Check which (if any) of σ_1, σ_2 fix S_C^{type} and return those.

Algorithm **Case3** is similar to Algorithm **Case2**.

Algorithm: Case4

Input: S_C^{type} with S_2 having ≥ 2 elements.

Output: The set M_C^{type}.

Step 1: Choose one polynomial from S_2. Denote it as $f_1 = x^2 + c_1 \, x + c_0$.

Step 2: Do the following substeps $1 - 4$ to get the set T_1:

1. Write $\sigma_1 = -\frac{c_1 x + 2c_0}{2x + c_1}$ and $\sigma_2 = \frac{a x + c_0 \, c + c_1 \, a}{c \, x - a}$ (See the Remark in Algorithm Case2).

2. Choose another polynomial in S_2, and denote it as $f_2 = x^2 + d_1 \, x + d_0$.

3. Write $\sigma_3 = -\frac{d_1 x + 2d_0}{2x + d_1}$ and $\sigma_4 = \frac{a x + d_0 \, c + d_1 \, a}{c \, x - a}$.

4. Let $a := d_0 - c_0$, $c := c_1 - d_1$, then $\sigma_2 = \sigma_4$ swaps the roots of f_1 as well as the roots of f_2.
   $T_1 := \{\sigma \in \{\sigma_1, \sigma_2, \sigma_3\} | \sigma$ fixes $S_C^{\text{type}}\}$.

Step 3: Denote the polynomials in S_2 as f_i, then $T_2 :=$
$$\bigcup_{i=2}^{n_2} \text{FindMaps}(f_1, f_i)$$
(See below for the subalgorithm **FindMaps**)

Step 4: $T_3 := \bigcup_{i=3}^{n_2} \text{FindMaps}(f_2, f_i)$.

Step 5: $T_1 \bigcup T_2 \bigcup T_3$.

> **Remark.** Taking a set union means removing duplicates. The duplicates are the elements of T_3 that do not swap the roots of f_1, and σ_3 might also be duplicate (it could be in T_2 if $n_2 > 2$).

Subalgorithm: FindMaps

Input: Two irreducible polynomials $f, g \in C[x]$ of degree 2.

Output: All $\sigma \in M_C^{\text{type}}$ that map roots of f to roots of g.

1. Compute the roots of g in $C(\alpha) \cong C[x]/(f)$. (**Note:** there are either 0 or 2 roots β_j)

2. For each root β_j, compute $a, b, c \in C$ (not all 0) with $\frac{a \, \alpha + b}{c \, \alpha - a} = \beta_j$.
   This is done by computing coefficients (w.r.t α) of $a \, \alpha + b - \beta_j(c \, \alpha - a)$ and equating them to 0.

3. For each $\frac{a \, x + b}{c \, x - a}$ found in step 2 check if it fixes S_C^{type}, if so, include it in the output.

Algorithm: Case5

Input: S_C^{type} with S_i having ≥ 1 elements and $i \geq 3$.

Output: The set M_C^{type}.

Step 1: Find S_i for an $i \geq 3$ with $n_i > 0$.

Step 2: Choose a polynomial f in S_i. Denote $C(\alpha) \cong C[x]/(f)$, with $f(\alpha) = 0$.

Step 3: For each polynomial $g \in S_i$, call FindMaps(f, g). Then M_C^{type} would be $\bigcup_{g \in S_i} \text{FindMaps}(f, g)$.

4. COMPUTING 2-DESCENT, CASE A

Notations: Let $L \in C(x)[\partial]$ have order 2, and be irreducible (even in $\mathbb{C}(x)[\partial]$). Let $\sigma \in \text{Aut}(C(x)/C)$ have order 2 and fixed field $C(f) \subset C(x)$.

LEMMA 2. *If* $\exists \tilde{L} \in \mathbb{C}(f)[\partial_f]$ *with* $L \sim_p \tilde{L}$, *then* $L \sim_p \sigma(L)$.

PROOF. $L \sim_p \tilde{L} = \sigma(\tilde{L}) \sim_p \sigma(L)$. $\square$

So if not $L \sim_p \sigma(L)$ then $L \in C(x)[\partial] \subset \mathbb{C}(x)[\partial]$ does not descend to $\mathbb{C}(f)$. If $L \sim_p \sigma(L)$ then we will consider two cases:

110

NOTATION 1. **_Case A_** *is when there exists* $G = r_0 + r_1 \partial \in \mathbb{C}(x)[\partial]$ *such that* $G(V(L)) = V(\sigma(L))$, *i.e.* $L \sim_g \sigma(L)$.

　　　　　Case B *is when there exists* $G = e^{\int r} \cdot (r_0 + r_1 \partial)$ *such that* $G(V(L)) = V(\sigma(L))$, *i.e.* $L \sim_p \sigma(L)$. *(**Note:** Case A $\Rightarrow$ Case B.)*

This section treats only Case A. Section 5 will reduce Case B to Case A.

In **Case A**, when $L \sim_g \sigma(L)$, it is known [11] that there exists $\tilde{L} \in \mathbb{C}(f)[\partial_f]$ with $\tilde{L} \sim_g L$. Then we have the following diagram:

Diagram 1

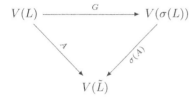

Here, A, $\sigma(A)$, and $\tilde{L}$ are unknown. Whether or not such a diagram commutes is studied in Theorem 1 below.

REMARK 6. *A gauge transformation is a bijective map* $A : V(L) \to V(\tilde{L})$ *that can be represented by a differential operator in* $\mathbb{C}(x)[\partial]$. *So we can define* $\sigma(A)$ *simply by applying* σ *to the operator that represents the map* A.

THEOREM 1. *Let* L *and* σ *be as before, and* $G : V(L) \to V(\sigma(L))$ *be a gauge transformation. Suppose* $\tilde{L}_1, \tilde{L}_2 \in \mathbb{C}(f)[\partial_f]$ *and* $A_i : V(L) \to V(\tilde{L}_i)$ *are gauge transformations. Then:*

1. *For each* $i = 1, 2$, *there is exactly one* $\lambda_i \in \mathbb{C}^*$ *such that the following diagram commutes.*

   Diagram 2

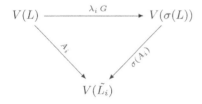

2. *If* $\tilde{L}_1 \sim_g \tilde{L}_2$ *over* $\mathbb{C}(f)$, *then* $\lambda_1 = \lambda_2$; *Otherwise*, $\lambda_1 = -\lambda_2$.

3. *In particular,* $\{\lambda_1, -\lambda_1\}$ *depends only on* (L, σ, G).

PROOF. First consider the diagram without λ_i in it. In it we find two gauge transformations $V(L) \to V(\tilde{L}_i)$, namely A_i and $\sigma(A_i)G$. After choosing bases of $V(L)$ and $V(\tilde{L}_i)$, we can view these gauge transformations as bijections: $\mathbb{C}^2 \to \mathbb{C}^2$. Then by linear algebra, there is a constant $\lambda_i \in \mathbb{C}^*$ such that the map:

$$A_i - \lambda_i \sigma(A_i)G : V(L) \to V(\tilde{L}_i). \qquad (4)$$

has a non-zero kernel. The kernel of (4) corresponds to a right hand factor of L, namely, the GCRD of L and the operator in (4). However, L is irreducible so this kernel must be $V(L)$ itself. That means Diagram 2 commutes. That λ_i is unique follows from linear algebra: there can be at most one λ_i for which (4) is the zero map. Item 1 follows.

For item 2, since $\tilde{L}_1 \sim_g L \sim_g \tilde{L}_2$, there exists a gauge transformation $B : V(\tilde{L}_1) \to V(\tilde{L}_2)$. This B is unique up to multiplying by a constant that we choose in such a way that the composition $BA_1 : V(L) \to V(\tilde{L}_2)$ coincides with A_2. Since $\sigma(\tilde{L}_1) = \tilde{L}_1$, $\sigma(\tilde{L}_2) = \tilde{L}_2$ one sees that $\sigma(B)$ maps $V(\tilde{L}_1)$ to $V(\tilde{L}_2)$ as well. So $\sigma(B)$ must be $c \cdot B$ for some $c \in \mathbb{C}^*$. Then $|\sigma| = 2$ implies that $c = \pm 1$. Now $c = 1$ iff $\sigma(B) = B$ iff $B \in \mathbb{C}(f)[\partial_f]$ iff $\tilde{L}_1, \tilde{L}_2$ are gauge-equivalent over $\mathbb{C}(f)$. Otherwise, if $c = -1$, then $B \notin \mathbb{C}(f)[\partial_f]$ and $\tilde{L}_1, \tilde{L}_2$ are gauge-equivalent over $\mathbb{C}(x)$ but not over $\mathbb{C}(f)$. To prove item 2 we now have to show that $\lambda_2 = c\lambda_1$.

If λ_i is such that Diagram 2 commutes (for $i = 1, 2$) then the following diagram commutes:

Diagram 3

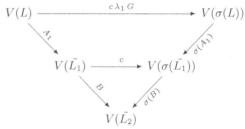

The composed map BA_1 at the left of Diagram 3 coincides with the map A_2 in Diagram 2 for $i = 2$. Applying σ to BA_1 and A_2, we see that the composed map at the right of Diagram 3 coincides with the map $\sigma(A_2)$ in Diagram 2 for $i = 2$. Then the maps at the top of Diagram 3 and Diagram 2 for $i = 2$ must coincide as well, i.e., $\lambda_2 G = c\lambda_1 G$. Hence $\lambda_2 = c\lambda_1$. Item 2 (and hence item 3) follow. $\square$

4.1 Algorithm for finding 2-descent in Case A

Notations L, C, G, σ, A are as in Section 4. Our goal is to compute 2-descent: $L \sim_p \tilde{L} \in \mathbb{C}(f)[\partial_f]$. Here f is determined from σ as in Remark 2. We will compute $A : V(L) \to V(\tilde{L})$ first, then use A to find $\tilde{L}$.

Algorithm: Case A for computing a 2-descent $\tilde{L}$ for L.

Input: L, G, σ and C.

Output: $\tilde{L}$ and A, defined over an optimal extension of C.

Step 1: Write $A = (a_{00} + a_{01}x)\partial + (a_{10} + a_{11}x)$, with a_{00}, a_{01}, a_{10}, a_{11} unknowns (which will take values in $\mathbb{C}(f)$).

Step 2: The operator $A - \lambda\sigma(A)G$ in (4) should vanish on $V(L)$, so the remainder of $A - \sigma(A)\lambda G$ right divided by L must be 0. This remainder is of the form $(R_{00} + R_{01}x)\partial^0 + (R_{10} + R_{11}x)\partial$, where the R_{ij} are $C(\lambda, f)$-linear combinations of a_{ij}. This produces a system of 4 equations $R_{ij} = 0$ in 4 unknowns a_{ij}.

Step 3: To have a nontrivial solution, the corresponding 4×4 matrix M must have determinant 0. Equating $\det(M)$ to 0 gives a degree 4 equation for λ. Solve for λ.

　　Remark. The equation for λ is of the form $(\lambda^2 - a)^2 = 0$, where $a = \lambda_1^2 = \lambda_2^2$ with λ_1, λ_2 as in Theorem 1. If L and σ are defined over a field $C \subseteq \mathbb{C}$ then $\tilde{L}$ and A are defined over $C(\sqrt{a})$.

　　If $\sqrt{a} \notin C$ then it follows from Theorem 1 that the extension by $\lambda_i = \pm\sqrt{a}$ is necessary.

Step 4: Plug in one value for λ in M, then solve M to find values for $a_{00}, a_{01}, a_{10}, a_{11}$ in $C(\sqrt{a}, f)$.

Step 5: Compute LCLM(A, L) to obtain $\tilde{L}A$. Right divide by A to find $\tilde{L} \in C(\sqrt{a}, f)[\partial_f]$.

Step 6: (optional) Introduce a new variable, say x_1, and compute an operator $L_{x_1} \in C(\sqrt{a}, x_1)[\partial_{x_1}]$ that corresponds to $\tilde{L}$ under the change of variables $x_1 \mapsto f$.

5. COMPUTING 2-DESCENT, CASE B

DEFINITION 7. *Let* $L_1, L_2 \in \mathcal{D} = K[\partial]$. *The symmetric product* $L_1 \text{\textcircled{S}} L_2$ *is defined as the monic differential operator in* $\mathcal{D}$ *with minimal order for which* $y_1 y_2 \in V(L_1 \text{\textcircled{S}} L_2)$ *for all* $y_1 \in V(L_1)$, $y_2 \in V(L_2)$.

LEMMA 3. *If* $L = \partial^2 + c_0 \in C(x)[\partial]$, *and* $G := e^{\int r} \cdot (r_0 + r_1 \partial)$ *is a bijection from* $V(L)$ *to* $V(\sigma(L))$, *then* $(e^{\int r})^2$ *is a rational function.*
If $L := \partial^2 + a_1 \partial + a_0 \in \mathbb{C}(x)[\partial]$, *then* $L_1 := L \text{\textcircled{S}} (\partial - \frac{1}{2} a_1)$ *is of the form* $\partial^2 + c_0$ *(with* $c_0 = a_0 - \frac{1}{4} a_1^2 - \frac{1}{2} a_1'$*).*

The proof of the lemma follows by computing the effect of G on the Wronskian, and the fact that the Wronskians of $\partial^2 + c_0$ and $\sigma(\partial^2 + c_0)$ are rational functions (1 and $\sigma(x)'$ respectively).

Let $L \in C(x)[\partial]$ irreducible (even over $\mathbb{C}(x)$) and of order 2, and $\sigma \in \mathrm{Aut}(C(x)/C)$ of order 2. The implementation equiv [8] can check if $L \sim_p \sigma(L)$, and if so, find $r, r_0, r_1 \in C(x)$ for which $G := e^{\int r} \cdot (r_0 + r_1 \partial)$ is a bijection from $V(L)$ to $V(\sigma(L))$. Assume that such σ and G are given. After the simple transformation in the lemma above, we may assume that $(e^{\int r})^2$ is a rational function.

If $e^{\int r}$ itself is a rational function, then we are in Case A. Otherwise, we can write $e^{\int r} = p(x)\sqrt{f(x)}$ for some square-free polynomial $f(x)$, and some $p(x) \in C(x)$.

DEFINITION 8. *The branch points of* G *are the roots of* $f(x)$, *and* ∞ *if* $f(x)$ *has odd degree.*

To reduce Case B to Case A, we have to eliminate the branch points. Our algorithm will first eliminate all branch points that can be eliminated without a field extension of C. It will only extend C if there is no descent w.r.t. σ defined over C.

5.1 Branch points

It is convenient to view the set of branch points as a subset of $\mathbb{P}^1(\overline{C})$. However, to avoid splitting fields, the algorithm represents the branch points with a set $B \subset \mathrm{places}(C)$ instead. This B is the set of irreducible factors of $f(x)$ in $C[x]$, as well as ∞ if $f(x)$ has odd degree. The goal is to eliminate branch points until we reach $B = \emptyset$, i.e., Case A.

DEFINITION 9. *If* $\sigma(\infty) = \infty$, *then denote* $\mathrm{Inf} := \{\infty\}$, *otherwise* $\mathrm{Inf} := \{\infty, x - \sigma(\infty)\}$. *Denote* $B_I = B \bigcap \mathrm{Inf}$ *and* $B_N = B \setminus B_I$.
Let $f_1(x), f_2(x) \in B_N$. *We say that* $f_1(x)$ *matches* $f_2(x)$ *when the roots of* $f_2(x)$ *are the same as the roots of* $f_1(\sigma(x))$ *(i.e. the numerator of* $f_1(\sigma(x))$ *is* f_2*).*
If $\sigma(\infty) \neq \infty$, *then we say that the polynomial* $x - \sigma(\infty)$ *matches* ∞.

LEMMA 4. *If* $f_1(x) \neq f_2(x) \in B_N$ *and* $f_1(x)$ *matches* $f_2(x)$, *then* B_N *turns into* $B_N \setminus \{f_1, f_2\}$ *when we replace* L *by* $L_{\mathrm{new}} := L \text{\textcircled{S}} (\partial - \frac{1}{2} \cdot \frac{f_1(x)'}{f_1(x)})$.

PROOF. The composed transformation

$$V(L_{\mathrm{new}}) \to V(L) \to V(\sigma(L)) \to V(\sigma(L_{\mathrm{new}}))$$

is

$$\sqrt{\sigma(f_1)} \cdot G \cdot \frac{1}{\sqrt{f_1}}.$$

The polynomial f equals $f_1 f_2 \cdots$ where the $\cdots$ refer to the other factors of f in $B \setminus \{\infty\}$. The transformation G is of the form $\sqrt{f_1 f_2 \cdots} (r_0 + r_1 \partial)$. Factors can be removed from the square-root in G either by division or by multiplication by a square-root (factors in $C(x)$ can be moved to r_0, r_1). So in the composed transformation, the factors f_1 and f_2 will disappear from the square-root in G (note: this uses the assumption $f_1 \neq f_2$ (which implies that their gcd is 1 since they are monic irreducible polynomials)).
A subtlety is that if $\sigma(\infty) \neq \infty$, then $\sigma(f_1)$ is not f_2 but $c f_2 / (x - \sigma(\infty))^d$, for some $c \in C$, where d is the degree of f_1 and f_2. This means that if $\sigma(\infty) \neq \infty$ and d is odd, then the set B_I will change when we replace L by L_{new} ($B_I = \emptyset$ will change to Inf, and $B_I = \mathrm{Inf}$ will change to $\emptyset$). $\square$

LEMMA 5. *If* $\sigma(\infty) \neq \infty$, *and* $B_I = \{\infty, f_1\}$ *(here* $f_1 = x - \sigma(\infty)$*) then the factor* f_1 *inside the square root in* G *will cancel out (i.e.* B_I *will become* $\emptyset$*) if we replace* L *by* $L_{\mathrm{new}} := L \text{\textcircled{S}} (\partial - \frac{1}{4} \cdot \frac{1}{f_1})$.

PROOF. The solutions of L_{new} differ a factor $\sqrt[4]{f_1}$ from the solutions of L. The lemma follows from a similar computation as the proof of Lemma 4, except that this time $\sigma(f_1)$ is of the form c/f_1 for some constant c. Thus, the composed map is of the form $\sqrt[4]{c/f_1} \cdot G \cdot 1/\sqrt[4]{f_1}$, and $\sqrt{f_1}$ is cancelled from the square root in G. $\square$

In the following algorithm, L and σ are as in Section 4, and $G = e^{\int r} \cdot (r_0 + r_1 \partial)$ with $r, r_0, r_1 \in C(x)$.

Algorithm: Case B for computing a 2-descent $\tilde{L}$ for L.

Input: L, G, σ and C.

Output: $\tilde{L}$ and A (defined over C whenever possible).

Step 1 Initialization: If $(e^{\int r})^2$ is not a rational function, then replace L by $L \text{\textcircled{S}} (\partial - \frac{1}{2} \cdot \frac{a_1}{a_2})$ as in Lemma 3 and update G accordingly.
Rewrite G as $\sqrt{f(x)}(r_0 + r_1 \partial)$ with $f(x)$ monic and square-free (updating $r_0, r_1 \in C(x)$ to move any rational factor from $e^{\int r}$ to r_0, r_1).
If $f(x) = 1$ then call **Case A** and stop.

Step 2: Factor $f(x)$ in $C[x]$ to find $B, B_I, B_N \subset \mathrm{places}(C)$.

Step 3: $g :=$**Findg**(B_N, σ, C).
(See below for the subalgorithm **Findg**)

Step 4: Let $h := \frac{1}{2} \cdot \frac{g'}{g}$. Replace L by $L \text{\textcircled{S}} (\partial - h)$ and update G, B, B_I, B_N accordingly. Now B_N should be $\emptyset$.

Step 5: If $B_I \neq \emptyset$ then let $h := \frac{1}{4} \cdot \frac{1}{f_1}$ with f_1 as in Lemma 5. Replace L by $L \text{\textcircled{S}} (\partial - h)$ and update G, B accordingly. Now B should be $\emptyset$.

Step 6: Call **Case A**.

Subalgorithm: Findg.

Input: B_N, σ, C.

Output: g.

Step 1: If $B_N = \emptyset$, return 1 and stop.

Step 2: Else, for each $P_i \in B_N$,

    1. Find its matched (Def. 9) element $P_j \in B_N$.

    2. If $P_i \neq P_j$ then $g := \mathbf{Findg}(B_N \setminus \{P_i, P_j\}, \sigma, C)$, return $g \cdot P_i$ and stop.

Step 3: Now each $P \in B_N$ matches itself, and hence has even degree. Choose $P \in B_N$ with minimal degree, and let $\alpha \in \overline{C}$ be one root of P, so $C(\alpha) \cong C[x]/(P)$. Let B_N^α be the set of all irreducible factors in $C(\alpha)[x]$ of all elements of B_N. Return $\mathbf{Findg}(B_N^\alpha, \sigma, C(\alpha))$.

6. MAIN ALGORITHM

Algorithm 2-descent.

Input: A second order irreducible differential operator $L \in C(x)[\partial]$ and the field C.

Output: descent, if it exists for some $\sigma \in \mathrm{Aut}(C(x)/C)$ of order 2.

Step 1: Compute the set of true singularities, and the singularity structure S_C^{type}.

Step 2: Call **Compute Möbius transformations** in Section 3.2 to compute the set M_C^{type}.

Step 3: For each $\sigma \in M_C^{\text{type}}$, call [8] to check if $L \sim_p \sigma(L)$, and if so, to find $G : V(L) \to V(\sigma(L))$.
If we find σ with $L \sim_p \sigma(L)$, then call algorithm Case B in Section 5.1 and stop.

7. EXAMPLES

We give two examples. The first example is easy (it has $G = r_0 + r_1 \partial$ with $r_1 = 0$). The second one is less trivial[3]. The first example is in **Case A** as in Section 4, the second example involves both **Case A** and **Case B**.

EXAMPLE 2. *Let*

$$L = \partial^2 + \frac{28x - 5}{x(4x - 1)}\partial + \frac{144x^2 + 20x - 3}{x^2(4x - 1)(4x + 1)}$$

Step 1: *Compute the singularity structure of L*

$$S_C^{\text{type}} := \{(x, 0), (\infty, 0), (x - \tfrac{1}{4}, 0), (x + \tfrac{1}{4}, 0)\}$$

Step 2: *Compute Möbius transformations. Since S_1 has $n_1 = 4$ elements, we end up in algorithm **Case1** of Section 3.2 which produces:*

$$\{-x, \frac{-1}{16x}, \frac{1}{16x}, \frac{-1}{4}\frac{4x-1}{4x+1}, \frac{1}{4}\frac{4x+1}{4x-1}\}$$

Step 3: *There are 5 choices for σ. The first one is $x \mapsto -x$ corresponding to the subfield $C(f) = C(x^2)$. The **equiv** [8] program finds $G = \frac{4x-1}{4x+1}$. Next we compute $A := -4x^2 + x$, and then $\tilde{L}$. After applying a change of variable $x \mapsto \sqrt{x_1}$ the result reads*

$$L_{x_1} := (16x_1 - 1)x_1 \partial^2 + (32x_1 - 2)\partial + 4$$

which has 3 true singularities and is easy to solve.

---

[3]it was e-mailed to one of us to find its closed form solutions. There have been many such requests, which motivates us to develop these algorithms.

EXAMPLE 3. *Consider the operator:*

$$L := \partial^2 + \frac{4(1296x^5 + 576x^4 - 144x^3 - 72x^2 + x + 1)}{x(6x-1)(2x+1)(6x+1)(12x^2-1)}\partial +$$
$$\frac{2(5184x^6 - 864x^5 - 1656x^4 + 48x^3 + 162x^2 + 6x - 1)}{(-1+2x)x^2(6x-1)(2x+1)(6x+1)(12x^2-1)}$$

Step 1: *Compute the singularity structure of L*

$$S_C^{\text{type}} := \{(x, 0), (\infty, 0), (x - \tfrac{1}{2}, 0), (x + \tfrac{1}{2}, 0), (x - \tfrac{1}{6}, 0), (x + \tfrac{1}{6}, 0)\}$$

($12x^2 - 1$ is a removable singularity, Definition 5).

Step 2: *Compute Möbius transformations. Since S_1 has $n_1 = 6$ elements, we are again in Case1, and find:*

$$\{-x, \frac{-1}{12x}, \frac{1}{12x}, \frac{-1}{2}\frac{2x-1}{6x+1}, \frac{1}{2}\frac{2x+1}{6x-1}, \frac{-1}{6}\frac{6x-1}{2x+1}, \frac{1}{6}\frac{6x+1}{2x-1}\}$$

Step 3: *The first σ we try is $x \mapsto -x$. The **equiv** program finds*

$$G := \frac{x(12x^2 + 4x - 1)}{12x^2 - 1}\partial + \frac{3}{2}\frac{(2x+1)(10x-1)}{12x^2 - 1}$$

so $G(V(L)) = V(\sigma(L))$. Then compute a 4 by 4 matrix from the linear equations for the a_{ij}, equate the determinant to 0 and find $\lambda = \pm 2$. We choose $\lambda = 2$ and find

$$A := (-36x^4 - \frac{1}{4} + 10x^2)\partial + 1 - \frac{1}{4}\frac{(288x^4 + 1 - 84x^2)}{x}.$$

We get

$$L_{x_1} := 4x_1^2(-1 + 36x_1)(4x_1 - 1)(12x_1 - 1)^2\partial^2 +$$
$$8x_1(12x_1 - 1)(4x_1 - 1)(216x_1^2 - 54x_1 + 1)\partial$$
$$- 3 - 2544x_1^2 + 10368x_1^3 + 48x_1$$

*which is $\tilde{L} \in C(x^2)[\partial_{x^2}]$ rewritten with $x \mapsto \sqrt{x_1}$. This L_{x_1} has 4 true singularities, and allows a further 2-descent. Applying steps (1)(2)(3) to L_{x_1} again, we are actually in **Case B** as in Section 5, applying the algorithm (details are given in a Maple worksheet [5]) we find a new operator $\tilde{L}_1 \sim_p L_{x_1}$ defined over the subfield $\mathbb{C}(f_1)$ where $f_1 := x_1 + \frac{1}{144x_1}$. Replacing f_1 by a new variable x_2 we get:*

$$L_{x_2} := 4(36x_2 + 11)(18x_2 - 5)(6x_2 + 1)(6x_2 - 1)^2\partial^2 +$$
$$36(6x_2 - 1)(1296x_2^3 + 1620x_2^2 + 20x_2 - 9)\partial$$
$$+ 34992x_2^3 - 207036x_2^2 - 2331 + 3456x_2$$

which has 3 true regular singularities (as well as a few removable singularities). That means that L_{x_2} (and hence L) has closed form solutions (see [5]) in terms of hypergeometric $_2F_1$ functions.

8. FUTURE WORK

At the moment, we only consider σ's that are defined over the same field of constants C over which L is defined. We can modify the Compute Möbius transformations algorithm to also find σ's defined over an extension of C. However, for such σ we do not plan to compute 2-descent because if there exists descent w.r.t. a σ that is not defined over C, then a larger descent should exist as well.

We plan to work on finding (if it exists) descent to subfields of index 3. Degree 3 extensions need not be Galois, and so in general, to find 3-descent it is not enough to try all Möbius transformations that fix the singularity structure.

9. REFERENCES

[1] BARKATOU, M. A., AND PFLÜGEL, E. On the Equivalence Problem of Linear Differential Systems and its Application for Factoring Completely Reducible Systems. In *ISSAC 1998*, 268–275.

[2] BRONSTEIN, M. An improved algorithm for factoring linear ordinary differential operators. In *ISSAC 1994*, 336–340.

[3] COMPOINT, E., VAN DER PUT, M., AND WEIL, J.A. Effective descent for differential operators. *J. Algebra. 324* (2010), 146–158.

[4] DEBEERST, R, VAN HOEIJ, M, AND KOEPF. W. Solving Differential Equations in Terms of Bessel Functions. In *ISSAC 2008*, 39–46.

[5] FANG, T. Implementation and examples for 2-descent www.math.fsu.edu/~tfang/2descentprogram/

[6] VAN HOEIJ, M., AND VIDUNAS, R. All non-Liouvillian $_2F_1$-solvable Heun equations with pullbacks in $\mathbb{C}(x)$. www.math.fsu.edu/~hoeij/files/Heun/TextFormat/

[7] VAN HOEIJ, M. *Factorization of Linear Differential Operators*. PhD thesis, Universiteit Nijmegen, 1996.

[8] VAN HOEIJ, M. Implementation for finding equivalence map. *www.math.fsu.edu/~hoeij/files/equiv.*

[9] VAN HOEIJ, M. Solving Third Order Linear Differential Equations in Terms of Second Order Equations. In *ISSAC 2007*, 355–360. Implementation at: *www.math.fsu.edu/~hoeij/files/ReduceOrder*

[10] VAN HOEIJ, M, AND CREMONA, J. Solving conics over function fields. *J. de Theories des Nombres de Bordeaux.18*(2006), 595–606.

[11] VAN HOEIJ, M, AND VAN DER PUT, M. Descent for differential modules and skew fields. *J. Algebra. 296*(2006), 18–55.

[12] VAN HOEIJ, M, AND YUAN, Q Finding all Bessel type solutions for Linear Differential Equations with Rational Function Coefficients. In *ISSAC 2010*, 37–44

[13] VAN DER HOEVEN, J. Around the Numeric-Symbolic Computation of Differential Galois Groups. *J. Symb. Comp. 42* (2007), 236–264.

[14] NGUYEN, A. K. A modern perspective on Fano's approach to linear differential equations. PhD thesis (2008).

[15] VAN DER PUT, M., AND SINGER, M. F. *Galois Theory of Linear Differential Equations*, vol. 328 of *A Series of Comprehensive Studies in Mathematics*. Springer, Berlin, 2003.

Fast Algorithm for Change of Ordering of Zero-dimensional Gröbner Bases with Sparse Multiplication Matrices[*]

Jean-Charles Faugère
INRIA Paris-Rocquencourt, SALSA Project
UPMC Univ Paris 06, UMR 7606, LIP6
CNRS, UMR 7606, LIP6
4 place Jussieu, 75005 Paris, France
Jean-Charles.Faugere@inria.fr

Chenqi Mou
LMIB, SMSS, Beihang University
Beijing 100191, PR China
and
INRIA Paris-Rocquencourt, SALSA Project
UPMC Univ Paris 06, UMR 7606, LIP6
CNRS, UMR 7606, LIP6
4 place Jussieu, 75005 Paris, France
Chenqi.Mou@lip6.fr

ABSTRACT

Let $I \subset \mathbb{K}[x_1, \ldots, x_n]$ be a 0-dimensional ideal of degree D where $\mathbb{K}$ is a field. It is well-known that obtaining efficient algorithms for change of ordering of Gröbner bases of I is crucial in polynomial system solving. Through the algorithm FGLM, this task is classically tackled by linear algebra operations in $\mathbb{K}[x_1, \ldots, x_n]/I$. With recent progress on Gröbner bases computations, this step turns out to be the bottleneck of the whole solving process.

Our contribution is an algorithm that takes advantage of the sparsity structure of multiplication matrices appearing during the change of ordering. This sparsity structure arises even when the input polynomial system defining I is dense. As a by-product, we obtain an implementation which is able to manipulate 0-dimensional ideals over a prime field of degree greater than 30000. It outperforms the Magma/Singular/FGb implementations of FGLM.

First, we investigate the particular but important shape position case. The obtained algorithm performs the change of ordering within a complexity $O(D(N_1 + n\log(D)))$, where N_1 is the number of nonzero entries of a multiplication matrix. This almost matches the complexity of computing the minimal polynomial of *one* multiplication matrix. Then, we address the general case and give corresponding complexity results. Our algorithm is dynamic in the sense that it selects automatically which strategy to use depending on the input. Its key ingredients are the Wiedemann algorithm to handle 1-dimensional linear recurrence (for the shape position case), and the Berlekamp–Massey–Sakata algorithm from Coding Theory to handle multi-dimensional linearly recurring sequences in the general case.

Categories and Subject Descriptors

I.1.2 [**Computing Methodologies**]: Symbolic and Algebraic Manipulation—*Algorithms*; F.2.2 [**Theory of Computation**]: Analy-

sis of Algorithms and Problem Complexity—*Nonnumerical algorithms and problems*

General Terms

Algorithms

Keywords

Gröbner bases, Change of ordering, Zero-dimensional ideals, Sparse matrix, FGLM algorithm, Wiedemann algorithm, BMS algorithm

1. INTRODUCTION

Gröbner basis is a major tool in computational ideal theory [5, 8, 3], in particular for polynomial system solving. It is well-known that the Gröbner basis of an ideal with respect to (w.r.t.) the lexicographical ordering (LEX) holds good algebraic structures, and hence is convenient to use for polynomial system solving. From the computational point of view, the common strategy to obtain such a Gröbner basis is to first compute a Gröbner basis w.r.t. the degree reverse lexicographical ordering (DRL), which is usually easier to compute, and then convert its ordering to LEX.

With recent progress on Gröbner basis computations [10, 11], the first step above has been greatly enhanced, leaving the second step, namely changing orderings of Gröbner bases, as the bottleneck of the whole solving process. Hence, currently, efficient algorithms to perform the change of ordering are of crucial significance in polynomial system solving. Furthermore, some practical problems can be modeled directly as a change of ordering [6, 15]. The purpose of this paper is precisely to provide a faster algorithm to perform the change of ordering of Gröbner bases of 0-dimensional ideals.

There already exist a few algorithms for the change of ordering of Gröbner bases, for example the FGLM algorithm [12] for 0-dimensional ideals and the Gröbner walk for generic cases [7]. The number of field operations needed by the FGLM algorithm is $O(nD^3)$, where n is the number of variables and D is degree of the given ideal $I \subset \mathbb{K}[x_1, \ldots, x_n]$. We would like to mention that other algorithms have been proposed to change the orderings of triangular sets [16, 9] or using the LLL algorithm [1] in the bivariate case. The connection between the change of ordering and linear algebra is done through the multiplication matrices T_i which represents the multiplication by x_i in the quotient ring $\mathbb{K}[x_1, \ldots, x_n]/I$ viewed as a vector space. According to our experiments (see table 2), these matrices are sparse, even when the input polynomial system is dense. The proposed algorithm takes advantage of this sparsity structure to obtain good complexity and performances.

First the particular but important case when the 0-dimensional ideal I is in shape position is studied. We consider the sequence

[*]This work is supported by the EXACTA grant of the French National Research Agency (ANR-09-BLAN-0371-01) and the National Science Foundation of China (NSFC 60911130369)

$[\langle r, T_1^i e \rangle : i = 0, \ldots, 2D-1]$, where r is a randomly chosen vector and $e = (1, 0, \ldots)^t$ is the canonical vector representing the term 1 in $\mathbb{K}[x_1, \ldots, x_n]/I$. It is easy to see that the minimal polynomial f_1 in $\mathbb{K}[x_1]$ of this linearly recurring sequence is indeed a polynomial in the Gröbner basis of I w.r.t LEX ($x_1 < \cdots < x_n$) when $\deg(f_1) = D$; moreover, it can be computed by applying the Berlekamp–Massey algorithm [20]. Furthermore, we show in section 3.1 how to recover efficiently the other polynomials in the Gröbner basis by solving structured (Hankel) linear systems. Hence, we are able to propose a complete method for the change of ordering to LEX for ideals in shape position. Its complexity is $O(D(N_1 + n\log(D)))$, where N_1 is the number of nonzero entries in T_1. When $n \ll D$ this almost matches the complexity of computing the minimal polynomial.

Next, for general ideals to which the method above may be no longer applicable, we generalize the linearly recurring sequence to a n-dimensional array $E : (s_1, \ldots, s_n) \longmapsto \langle r, T_1^{s_1} \cdots T_n^{s_n} e \rangle$. The minimal set of generating polynomials for the linearly recurring relation determined by E is essentially the Gröbner basis of the ideal defined by E, and this polynomial set can be obtained via the Berlekamp–Massey–Sakata (BMS for short hereafter) algorithm from Coding Theory [18, 19]. With some modifications of the BMS algorithm, we design a method to change the ordering in the general case. The algorithm is deterministic and the complexity with LEX as the target ordering is $O(nD^3)$ in the worst case and $O(nD(N + \hat{N}\bar{N}D))$ otherwise, where N is the maximal number of nonzero entries in matrices $T_1, \ldots, T_n$, while $\hat{N}$ and $\bar{N}$ are respectively the number of polynomials and the maximal term number of all polynomials in the resulting Gröbner basis.

Combining the two methods above, we propose a fast deterministic algorithm for the change of ordering for 0-dimensional ideals. This algorithm works for any term ordering, but we restrict the description to the case where LEX is the target ordering. It selects automatically which method to use depending on the input. The efficiency of the proposed algorithm has been verified by experiments. The current implementation outperforms the FGLM implementations in Magma/Singular/FGb. Take for example the Katsura12 instance over $\mathbb{F}_{65521}$, an ideal in shape position of degree 2^{12}, the change of ordering to LEX can be achieved in 26.3 seconds: this is 53.7 (resp 99.8) faster than the corresponding Magma (resp. Singular) function. As shown in table 2, 0-dimensional ideals over a prime field of degree greater than 30000 are now tractable.

The organization of this paper is as follows. Related algorithms used in this paper, together with some notations, are first reviewed in Section 2. Then Section 3 is devoted to our main algorithm. The complexity analysis of this algorithm is stated in Section 4 and experimental results are given in Section 5 respectively. The proof of one main theorem in the complexity analysis depends on properties of objects arising in the BMS algorithm applied in our context. The proof being technical, it is postponed in Section 6. This paper concludes with some remarks in Section 7.

2. FGLM AND BMS ALGORITHMS

2.1 FGLM

The FGLM algorithm is an efficient approach to convert the Gröbner basis of a 0-dimensional ideal w.r.t. a term ordering to another term ordering [12].

Let $\mathbb{K}$ be a field and $\mathbb{K}[x_1, \ldots, x_n]$ be the polynomial ring over $\mathbb{K}$. Suppose now the Gröbner basis G_1 of a 0-dimensional ideal I w.r.t. $<_1$ is known and one wants to compute its Gröbner basis G_2 w.r.t. $<_2$ with the FGLM algorithm. Let D be the degree of I and $B = [\varepsilon_1, \ldots, \varepsilon_D]$ be the canonical basis of $\mathbb{K}[x_1, \ldots, x_n]/\langle G_1 \rangle$ ordered according to $<_1$.

The algorithm first computes $(D \times D)$-matrices T_i, called the

multiplication matrix by x_i, to record the mapping ϕ_i on B:

$$\phi_i(b_j) = \text{NormalForm}(x_i b_j), \quad j = 1, \ldots, D$$

for $i = 1, \ldots, n$, where $\text{NormalForm}()$ is the normal form w.r.t. G_1. The jth column of T_i is the coordinate vector of $\text{NormalForm}(x_i b_j)$ w.r.t. B. Thus from the basis B, one can construct all the matrices $T_1, \ldots, T_n$ accordingly. As can be seen here, all T_i and T_j commute.

Then terms in $\mathbb{K}[x_1, \ldots, x_n]$ are handled one by one, following the term ordering $<_2$. For a term x^s with $s = (s_1, \ldots, s_n)$, its coordinate vector v_s w.r.t. B can be computed by

$$v_s = T_1^{s_1} \cdots T_n^{s_n} e, \tag{1}$$

where $e = (1, 0, \ldots, 0)^t$ is the coordinate vector of the term 1. Then a linear dependency like

$$\sum_s c_s v_s = 0 \tag{2}$$

will furnish an element in G_2:

$$f = x^l + \sum_{s \neq l} \frac{c_s}{c_l} x^s, \tag{3}$$

where x^l is the leading term of f w.r.t. $<_2$ (denoted by $\text{lt}(f)$) [12]. The test of linear dependency can be realized by maintaining an echelon form of the matrix whose columns are coordinate vectors of previously computed terms w.r.t. B.

As for its complexity, the FGLM algorithm needs $O(nD^3)$ field operations to finish the change of ordering.

2.2 BMS

The BMS algorithm is one that can be used to find the minimal set w.r.t. a term ordering $<$ of a linearly recurring relation generated by a given multi-dimensional array [18, 19, 17]. It is a generalization of Berlekamp–Massey algorithm, which determines the minimal polynomial of a linearly recurring sequence.

As a vector $u = (u_1, \ldots, u_n) \in \mathbb{Z}_{\geq 0}^n$ and a term $x^u = x_1^{u_1} \cdots x_n^{u_n} \in \mathbb{K}[x_1, \ldots, x_n]$ are 1–1 corresponding, usually we do not distinguish them. Besides the term ordering, we define the following partial ordering: for two terms $u = (u_1, \ldots, u_n)$ and $v = (v_1, \ldots, v_n)$, we say that $u \prec v$ if $u_i \leq v_i$ for $i = 1, \ldots, n$.

A mapping $E : \mathbb{Z}_{\geq 0}^n \longrightarrow \mathbb{K}$ is called a *n-dimensional array*. For a polynomial $f = \sum_s f_s x^s \in \mathbb{K}[x_1, \ldots, x_n]$, a n-dimensional array E is said to satisfy the n-dimensional linearly recurring relation with characteristic polynomial f if

$$\sum_s f_s E_{s+r} = 0, \quad \forall r \succ 0. \tag{4}$$

The set of all characteristic polynomials of n-dimensional linearly recurring relations for the array E forms an ideal, denoted by $I(E)$. And the minimal set of generating polynomials for $I(E)$, which the BMS algorithm computes, is actually the Gröbner basis of $I(E)$ w.r.t. $<$ [19, Lemma 5]. The canonical basis of $\mathbb{K}[x_1, \ldots, x_n]/I(E)$ is also called the *delta set* of E.

Instead of studying the infinite array E as a whole, the BMS algorithm deals with a truncated subarray of E up to some term u according to a given term ordering. A polynomial f with $\text{lt}(f) = s$ is said to be *valid for E up to* u if either $u \not\succ s$ or $\sum_t f_t E_{t+r} = 0, \forall r (0 \prec r \leq u - s)$. E may be omitted if no ambiguity occurs.

Similar to FGLM, the BMS algorithm also handles terms in $\mathbb{K}[x_1, \ldots, x_n]$ one by one according to $<$, so that the polynomial set it maintains is valid for E up to the new term. Let $F \subset \mathbb{K}[x_1, \ldots, x_n]$ be a set of polynomials whose elements are all valid up to some term u. When the next term of u w.r.t. the term ordering, denoted by $\text{Next}(u)$, is considered, the BMS algorithm will update F so that all the new polynomials in it are valid up to $\text{Next}(\boldsymbol{u})$. Meanwhile, another term determined by $\text{Next}(\boldsymbol{u})$ is also tested to see whether it is a member of the delta set of E. Therefore, more and more terms will be verified as members of the delta set of E while terms are handled by the BMS algorithm. The set of verified terms in the delta set of E after the term $\boldsymbol{u}$ is called the *delta set up to* $\boldsymbol{u}$. After a certain number of terms are considered, this polynomial set F grows to a minimal set of polynomials generating the linearly recurring relation, namely a Gröbner basis of $I(E)$, and all members in the delta set of E are verified.

Due to limited space, only outlines of the above update procedure (which is also the main part) in the BMS algorithm are summarized here so that this paper is self-contained. One may refer to [17] for details. The polynomial set G below, called the *witness set*, is auxiliary and will not be returned with F in the end.

Algorithm 1: $(F^+, G^+) := \text{BMSUpdate}(F, G, \text{Next}(\boldsymbol{u}), E)$

Input:

F, a minimal polynomial set valid up to $\boldsymbol{u}$;

G, a witness set up to $\boldsymbol{u}$;

$\text{Next}(\boldsymbol{u})$, a term;

E, a n-dimensional array up to $\text{Next}(\boldsymbol{u})$.

Output:

F^+, a minimal polynomial set valid up to $\text{Next}(\boldsymbol{u})$;

G^+, a witness set up to $\text{Next}(\boldsymbol{u})$.

1. Test whether every polynomial in F is valid up to $\text{Next}(\boldsymbol{u})$
2. Update G^+ and compute the new delta set up to $\text{Next}(\boldsymbol{u})$ accordingly
3. Construct new polynomials in F^+ such that they are valid up to $\text{Next}(\boldsymbol{u})$

Let k be the number of terms the BMS algorithm has handled before it stops at some term when F is the Gröbner basis and l be the number of polynomials it returns. Then the claimed complexity of the BMS algorithm is $O(lk^2)$ for graded term orderings [19].

3. MAIN ALGORITHM

3.1 Shape position

An ideal $I \subset \mathbb{K}[x_1, \ldots, x_n]$ is said to be *in shape position* if its Gröbner basis w.r.t. LEX ($x_1 < \cdots < x_n$) is of the form

$$[f_1(x_1), x_2 - f_2(x_1), \ldots, x_n - f_n(x_1)]. \quad (5)$$

For exact characterization of such ideals, one may refer to [2]. Ideals in shape position take a large proportion in all the consistent ideals. Thanks to their structures, we are able to design a specific and efficient method for the change of ordering with LEX as the target ordering.

Suppose the Gröbner basis of the deal I w.r.t. LEX is of form (5), $\deg(f_1) = D$ and $f_i = \sum_{k=0}^{D-1} c_{i,k} x_1^k$ $(i = 2, \ldots, n)$, where $c_{i,k}$ are unknown coefficients in $\mathbb{K}$. We consider now the linearly recurring sequence

$$[\langle \boldsymbol{r}, T_1^i \boldsymbol{e} \rangle : i = 0, \ldots, 2D - 1], \quad (6)$$

where $\boldsymbol{r} \in \mathbb{K}^{(D \times 1)}$ is a randomly chosen vector, T_1 is the matrix constructed in the FGLM algorithm, and $\boldsymbol{e}$ is the vector representing 1 w.r.t. the canonical basis of $\mathbb{K}[x_1, \ldots, x_n]/I$. We first recall some basic facts about linearly recurring sequences:

DEFINITION 3.1. *Let* $T = [t_0, t_1, t_2, \cdots]$ *be a sequence of elements of* $\mathbb{K}$ *and* d *an integer. We define the following* $d \times d$ *Hankel matrix:*

$$H_d(T) = \begin{bmatrix} t_0 & t_1 & t_2 & \cdots & t_{d-1} \\ t_1 & t_2 & t_3 & \cdots & t_d \\ \vdots & \vdots & \vdots & \ddots & \vdots \\ t_{d-1} & t_d & t_{d+1} & \cdots & t_{2d-2} \end{bmatrix}.$$

THEOREM 3.1. ([14]) *Let* $T = [t_0, t_1, t_2, \cdots]$ *be a linearly recurring sequence. Then, the minimal polynomial* $M^{(T)}(x) = \sum_{i=0}^d m_i x^i$ *of the sequence* T *is such that:*

(i) $d = \text{rank}(H_d(T)) = \text{rank}(H_i(T))$ *for all* $i > d$.

(ii) $\ker(H_{d+1}(T))$ *is a vector space of dimension* 1 *generated by* $(m_0, m_1, \ldots, m_d)^t$.

Moreover, since a bound on the size of the linearly recurring sequence is known (D is always a bound), the Berlekamp–Massey algorithm can compute the minimal polynomial $\tilde{f}_1$ of the sequence (6) (it is also possible to use the *deterministic variant* of the Wiedemenann algorithm [20] to compute directly f_1). Next we check whether $\deg(\tilde{f}_1) = D$, which implies that $\tilde{f}_1 = f_1$. If it holds, then computing the full Gröbner basis of I w.r.t. LEX reduces to determining all the unknown coefficients $c_{i,k}$.

For each $i = 2, \ldots, n$, from $\text{NormalForm}(x_i - \sum_{k=0}^{D-1} c_{i,k} x_1^k) = 0$ one can get $\boldsymbol{v}_i := T_i \boldsymbol{e} = \sum_{k=0}^{D-1} c_{i,k} \cdot T_1^k \boldsymbol{e}$. Then one can further construct D linear equations,

$$\langle \boldsymbol{r}, T_1^j \boldsymbol{v}_i \rangle = \sum_{k=0}^{D-1} c_{i,k} \cdot \langle \boldsymbol{r}, T_1^{k+j} \boldsymbol{e} \rangle, \quad j = 0, \ldots, D-1. \quad (7)$$

With $c_{i,k}$ considered as unknowns, the coefficient matrix H with entries $\langle \boldsymbol{r}, T_1^{k+j} \boldsymbol{e} \rangle$ is a Hankel one. From theorem 3.1 we know that H is invertible. Furthermore, the linear equation set (7) with the Hankel matrix H can be efficiently solved with complexity $O(D \log(D))$ if fast polynomial multiplication is used [4]. In the end, the solution of (7) will lead to the Gröbner basis we want to compute.

We explain now how the linear systems (7) can be generated for free. Note that for any $\boldsymbol{a}, \boldsymbol{b} \in \mathbb{K}^{(D \times 1)}$ and $T \in \mathbb{K}^{(D \times D)}$, we have $\langle \boldsymbol{a}, T \boldsymbol{b} \rangle = \langle T^t \boldsymbol{a}, \boldsymbol{b} \rangle$, where T^t denotes the transpose of T. Thus

$$\langle \boldsymbol{r}, T_1^i \boldsymbol{e} \rangle = \langle (T_1^t)^i \boldsymbol{r}, \boldsymbol{e} \rangle, \quad \langle \boldsymbol{r}, T_1^j \boldsymbol{v}_i \rangle = \langle (T_1^t)^j \boldsymbol{r}, \boldsymbol{v}_i \rangle$$

in (6) and (7). Therefore, when computing the sequence (6), we can record $(T_1^t)^i \boldsymbol{r}$ $(i = 0, \ldots, 2D - 1)$ and use them for construction of the linear equation set (7).

3.2 General case

Now we demonstrate the method for the change of ordering of a 0-dimensional Gröbner basis in the general case. In what follows, we always assume that $\mathbb{K}$ is field of characteristic 0 or a finite field of large cardinality. This is because otherwise "bad" random vectors would be frequently chosen so that BMS algorithm may not work.

Define a mapping $E : \mathbb{Z}_{\geq 0}^n \longrightarrow \mathbb{K}$ as

$$(s_1, \ldots, s_n) \longmapsto \langle \boldsymbol{r}, T_1^{s_1} \cdots T_n^{s_n} \boldsymbol{e} \rangle,$$

where $\boldsymbol{r} \in \mathbb{K}^{(D \times 1)}$ is a random vector. Combining (1) and (2), one can easily verify that the polynomial f in (3) is a characteristic polynomial for the n-dimensional linearly recurring relation defined by the array E. That is, f in (3) satisfies (4). This observation links FGLM and BMS algorithms: one can first construct the n-dimensional array E via matrices $T_1, \ldots, T_n$, and then compute the Gröbner basis of $I(E)$ with the BMS algorithm w.r.t. $<_2$.

This idea can actually be regarded as a generalization of the Wiedemann algorithm to the multivariate case, with the BMS algorithm to compute the minimal set of generating polynomials just as the role of Berlekamp–Massey algorithm. Unfortunately, similar to the Wiedemann algorithm, the strategy used here may also fail returning all the linear dependencies needed by the FGLM algorithm to form the Gröbner basis w.r.t. $<_2$. That is to say, the polynomial set returned by the BMS algorithm may only be a Gröbner basis of

$I(E)$ instead of I, where $I \subset I(E)$. However, one can easily check whether the set returned by the BMS algorithm is a Gröbner basis of I or not by testing the linear dependency in (2).

We remark that when the target ordering is LEX, computation of the first characteristic polynomial in the method above is essentially the same as that based on the Wiedemann algorithm described in section 3.1. This is true because for the LEX ordering ($x_1 < \cdots < x_n$), the terms are ordered as $[1, x_1, x_1^2, \ldots, x_2, x_1 x_2, x_1^2 x_2, \ldots]$, hence the first part of E is $E((p_1, 0, \ldots, 0)) = \langle r, T_1^{p_1} e \rangle$, and the BMS algorithm degenerates to the Berlekamp–Massey one now.

3.3 Algorithm description

Here the description of the main algorithm with the target ordering as LEX is given, together with some explanations and comments.

In algorithm 2 below, BerlekampMassey() is the Berlekamp–Massey algorithm, which takes a sequence over $\mathbb{K}$ as input and returns the minimal polynomial of this sequence [20]; Reduce(F) performs reduction on F so that every polynomial $f \in F$ is reduced w.r.t. $F \setminus \{f\}$; IsGB(F) returns true if F is the Gröbner basis of I w.r.t. LEX, and returns false otherwise; FGLM() is the FGLM algorithm.

Algorithm 2: Main algorithm

Input: G_1, the Gröbner basis of a 0-dimensional ideal
$\quad I \subset \mathbb{K}[x_1, \ldots, x_n]$ w.r.t. $<_1$
Output: the Gröbner basis of I w.r.t. LEX

1 Compute the canonical basis $[\varepsilon_1 = 1 <_1 \cdots <_1 \varepsilon_D]$ of
$\quad \mathbb{K}[x_1, \ldots, x_n]/\langle G_1 \rangle$
2 $e := (1, 0, \ldots, 0)^t \in \mathbb{K}^{(D \times 1)}$
3 Compute $T_1, \ldots, T_n$ the multiplication matrices
4 Choose $r_0 = r \in \mathbb{K}^{(D \times 1)}$ randomly
5 **for** $i := 1, \ldots, 2D-1$ **do** $\quad r_i := (T_1^t) r_{i-1}$
6 Generate the sequence $s := [\langle r_i, e \rangle : i = 0, \ldots, 2D-1]$
7 $f_1 := \text{BerlekampMassey}(s)$
8 **if** $\deg(f_1) = D$ **then**
9 $\quad H := H_D(s)$ $\qquad$ // Construct the Hankel matrix
10 $\quad$ **for** $i := 2, \ldots, n$ **do**
11 $\quad\quad b := \left(\langle r_j, T_i e \rangle : j = 0, \ldots, D-1 \right)^t$
12 $\quad\quad$ Compute $c = (c_1, \ldots, c_D)^t := H^{-1} b$
13 $\quad\quad f_i := \sum_{k=0}^{D-1} c_{k+1} x_1^k$
14 $\quad$ **end**
15 $\quad$ **return** $[f_1, x_2 - f_2, \ldots, x_n - f_n]$
16 **else**
17 $\quad u := 0; F := [1]; G := [\ ]; E := [\ ]$ $\qquad$ // General case
18 $\quad$ **repeat**
19 $\quad\quad e := \langle r, T_1^{u_1} \cdots T_n^{u_n} e \rangle$
20 $\quad\quad E := E \cup [e]$
21 $\quad\quad F, G := \text{BMSUpdate}(F, G, u, E)$
22 $\quad\quad u := \text{Next}(u)$ w.r.t. LEX
23 $\quad\quad F := \text{Reduce}(F)$
24 $\quad$ **until** *Termination Criteria* ;
25 $\quad$ **if** *not* IsGB(F) **then**
26 $\quad\quad F := \text{FGLM}(G_1, <_1)$
27 $\quad$ **end**
28 $\quad$ **return** F
29 **end**

With earlier computed values $T_1^{u_1} \cdots T_n^{u_n} e$ recorded, the computation of e at line 19 can be simplified. Suppose for $v = (v_1, \ldots, v_n)$, the vector $\tilde{e} = T_1^{v_1} \cdots T_i^{v_i - 1} \cdots T_n^{v_n} e$ has been recorded. Then $\langle r, T_1^{v_1} \cdots T_n^{v_n} e \rangle = \langle r, T_i \tilde{e} \rangle$, for all T_i and T_j commute.

Though the BMS algorithm from Coding Theory is mainly designed for graded term orderings, it works for all term orderings. However, for orderings that depend on lexicographical orderings (for instance LEX or block orderings which break ties with LEX), some other techniques not mentioned in the original presentation of BMS algorithm should be used. For example, the reduction step is introduced to control the size of intermediate polynomials. This is actually not a problem for orderings like DRL, for in that case the leading term of a polynomial itself will give a bound on the size of terms in that polynomial.

Unfortunately the termination criteria of the BMS algorithm are not well studied in the literature. There exist some general (necessary or sufficient) conditions on when the polynomial set F the BMS algorithm maintains will eventually become the Gröbner basis [19], but basically they are not very suitable to use as termination criteria. Hence here we mainly use the criterion that the main loop (lines 18–24) ends when F keeps unchanged for a certain number of passes.

REMARK 3.1. To change algorithm 2 to one suitable for all target orderings, one only needs to skip lines 5–15, that is, the method designed for ideals in shape position for LEX.

3.4 Correctness and termination

Now we are in a position of proving the correctness and termination of algorithm 2 proposed above.

Correctness. Lines 5–15 are for ideals in shape position, the correctness of this method is obvious from its description in section 3.1. After the termination criteria are reached, the main loop ends and whether the returned polynomial set F is the Gröbner basis of I w.r.t. LEX is tested. If IsGB(F) = true, F is already the Gröbner basis we want to compute and the algorithm naturally finishes. While IsGB(F) = false means that the BMS algorithm returns a polynomial set F which is only Gröbner basis of $I(E)$, but $I(E) \neq I$ (on the assumption that the termination criteria work). Then we have to return to the original FGLM algorithm to complete the change of ordering.

Termination. Once the main loop ends, the algorithm almost finishes. Hence we shall prove the termination of this main loop. Clearly when the polynomial set F the BMS algorithm maintains turns to a Gröbner basis of $I(E)$, the current termination criterion, namely F keeps unchanged for a certain number of passes, will be satisfied. And a sufficient condition for F being a Gröbner basis is given in [19, Theorem 6].

3.5 Illustrative examples

Shape position

A toy example Katsura2 is given here to illustrate how the method based on the Wiedemann algorithm works for ideals in shape position. Consider the ideal

$$I = \langle -x_3 + 2x_2^2 + 2x_1^2 + x_3^2, -x_2 + 2x_3 x_2 + 2x_2 x_1, x_3 + 2x_2 + 2x_1 - 1 \rangle$$

in $\mathbb{F}_{23}[x_1, x_2, x_3]$. Its Gröbner basis w.r.t. DRL is

$$\{x_1^3 + 12x_1^2 + 10x_2 + x_1, x_2^2 + 4x_1^2 + 9x_2 + 14x_1,$$
$$x_2 x_1 + 15x_1^2 + 16x_2 + 18x_1, x_3 + 2x_2 + 2x_1 + 22\},$$

from which we can compute the degree of I ($D = 4$) and the basis of $\mathbb{F}_{23}[x_1, x_2, x_3]/I$ ($B = [1, x_1, x_2, x_1^2]$), and further construct the matrices T_1, T_2 and T_3.

Now we aim at computing the Gröbner basis G w.r.t. LEX. A random vector $r = (16, 2, 18, 22)^t \in \mathbb{F}_{23}^{(4 \times 1)}$ is chosen first. With the sequence $[\langle \boldsymbol{r}, T_1^i \boldsymbol{e} \rangle : i = 0, \ldots, 2D - 1]$, one can obtain the first polynomial in G with the Berlekamp–Massey algorithm: $x_1^4 + 5x_1^3 + 20x_1^2 + 20x_1$. It verifies that this ideal is in shape position, hence the method is applicable. Next one can directly write the matrix H down as

$$\begin{bmatrix} 16 & 2 & 22 & 14 \\ 2 & 22 & 14 & 2 \\ 22 & 14 & 2 & 6 \\ 14 & 2 & 6 & 18 \end{bmatrix},$$

for actually all its entries have been computed in the earlier sequence. Take the polynomial $x_2 - f_2(x_1) \in G$ as in form (5) for example, the vector $\boldsymbol{b}$ can be computed as $(18, 13, 14, 0)^t$. Solving the linear equation set $H\boldsymbol{c} = \boldsymbol{b}$, one can obtain the coefficient vector of f_2 as $(0, 16, 8, 16)^t$, thus the corresponding polynomial in G is $x_2 + 7x_1 + 15x_1^2 + 7x_1^3$. The other polynomial $x_3 - f_3(x_1)$ can be obtained similarly. To summarize,

$$G = \{x_1^4 + 5x_1^3 + 20x_1^2 + 20x_1, \ x_2 + 7x_1^3 + 15x_1^2 + 7x_1,$$
$$x_3 + 9x_1^3 + 16x_1^2 + 11x_1 + 22\}.$$

General case

Consider the following Gröbner basis in $\mathbb{F}_{65521}[x_1, x_2]$ w.r.t. DRL $(x_1 < x_2)$

$$G_1 = \{x_2^4 + 2x_1^3 x_2 + 21x_2^3 + 11x_1 x_2^2 + 4x_1^2 x_2 + 22x_1^3 + 9x_2^2$$
$$+ 17x_1 x_2 + 19x_1^2 + 2x_2 + 19x_1 + 5, \ x_1^2 x_2^2 + 10x_2^3$$
$$+ 12x_1^2 x_2 + 20x_1^3 + 21, \ x_1^4 + 15x_1^2 + 19x_1 + 3\}.$$

Here $\mathbb{F}_{65521}[x_1, x_2]/\langle G_1 \rangle$ is of dimension 12. Its basis, and further the multiplication matrices T_1 and T_2, can be computed accordingly.

Now we want to get the Gröbner basis G_2 of $\langle G_1 \rangle$ w.r.t. LEX. With a vector

$$\boldsymbol{r} = (6757, 43420, 39830, 45356, 52762, 17712,$$
$$27676, 17194, 138, 48036, 12649, 11037)^t \in \mathbb{F}_{65521}^{(12 \times 1)}$$

chosen randomly, the 2-dimensional array E can be constructed. Then BMSUpdate() is applied term by term according to the LEX ordering, with the resulting Δ and F after each term shown in table 1. For example, at the term $(4, 0)$, the polynomial $x_1^2 + 62681x_1 + 41493 \in F$ is not valid up to $(4, 0)$. Then the delta set is updated as $\{(0, 0), (1, 0), (2, 0)\}$, and F is reconstructed such that the new polynomial $x_1^3 + 62681x_1^2 + 35812x_1 + 18557$ is valid up to $(4, 0)$.

The first polynomial in G_2

$$g_1 = x_1^4 + 15x_1^2 + 19x_1 + 3$$

is obtained at the term $(7, 0)$. Clearly the method for ideals in shape position is not applicable to this example. Next BMSUpdate() is executed to compute other members of $I(E)$ according to the remaining term sequence $[x_2, x_1 x_2, \ldots, x_2^2, x_1^2 x_2^2, \ldots,]$, until the other polynomial in $G_2 : g_2 = x_2^3 + 7x_1^2 x_2^2 + 15x_1^2 x_2 + 2x_1^3 + 9$ is obtained at $(3, 5)$. Now the main loop of algorithm 2 ends. Then one can easily verify that $\{g_1, g_2\} \subset G_2$ and $\dim(\mathbb{F}_{23}[x_2, x_1]/\langle g_1, g_2 \rangle) = 12$, thus $G_2 = \{g_1, g_2\}$.

Here is an example where this method fails. Let $G = \{x_1^3, x_1^2 x_2, x_1 x_2^2, x_2^3\} \subset \mathbb{F}_{65521}[x_1, x_2]$. Then the ideal $\langle G \rangle$ is 0-dimensional with degree $D = 6$. It is easy to see that G is Gröbner basis w.r.t. both DRL and LEX. Starting from G as a Gröbner basis w.r.t. DRL, the method based on the BMS algorithm to compute the Gröbner basis w.r.t. LEX will not be able to return the correct Gröbner basis, even the base field itself is quite large and different random vectors $\boldsymbol{r}$ are tried.

4. COMPLEXITY ANALYSIS

As the main usage of algorithms for the change of ordering is to change Gröbner basis w.r.t. DRL to that w.r.t. LEX, here we also restrict the complexity analysis to cases where the target term ordering is LEX. In this paper, we assume that the multiplication matrices T_i are already computed.

4.1 Shape position

We first deal with ideals in shape position. Suppose the number of nonzero entries in T_1 is N_1. In total the Wiedemann algorithm (lines 5–7) will take $O(D(N_1 + \log(D)))$ operations to obtain the first polynomial f_1 [20]. As all the entries in the matrix H are actually already computed during the Wiedemann algorithm, its construction is free of field operations. Then, for each $i = 2, \ldots, n$, as H is a Hankel matrix, solving the linear equation set $H\boldsymbol{c} = \boldsymbol{b}_i$ only needs $O(D \log(D))$ operations [4]. As explained in section 3.1, computing $\boldsymbol{b}_i$ is equivalent to computing $\langle (T_1^t)^j \boldsymbol{r}, \boldsymbol{v}_i \rangle$, where $(T_1^t)^j$ has already been computed and $\boldsymbol{v}_i = T_i \boldsymbol{e} = \text{NormalForm}(x_i)$. Without loss of generality, we can assume that $\text{NormalForm}(x_i) = x_i$ (this is not true only if there is a linear equation $x_i + \cdots$ in the Gröbner basis G_1, and in that case we can eliminate the variable x_i). Consequently $\boldsymbol{v}_i$ is a vector with all its components equal to 0 except for one component equal to 1. Hence computing $\langle (T_1^t)^j \boldsymbol{r}, \boldsymbol{v}_i \rangle$ is equivalent to extracting some component from the vector $(T_1^t)^j \boldsymbol{r}$ and there is not additional cost. To summarize:

THEOREM 4.1. *Assume that T_1 is constructed (note that $T_2, \ldots, T_n$ are not needed). When $\deg(f_1) = D$ in algorithm 2 (line 8), the complexity of algorithm 2 is bounded by*

$$O(D(N_1 + \log(D)) + (n-1)D \log(D)) = O(D(N_1 + n \log(D))).$$

4.2 General case

Next we analyze the complexity of the BMS-based method for the general case. For the detailed description of the BMS algorithm, which is not given in this paper, readers may refer to [17]. As already explained, the computation of one value e of E can be achieved within $O(N)$ operations, where N is the maximal number of nonzero entries in matrices $T_1, \ldots, T_n$. The three steps with their complexities in the subalgorithm BMSUpdate() are:

1. checking whether every polynomial in F is valid up to $\text{Next}(\boldsymbol{u})$, which needs $O(\hat{N}D)$ operations, where $\hat{N}$ is the number of polynomials in G_2 (Note that the number of terms in every polynomial is bounded by $D + 1$ because of the reduction step);

2. computing the new delta set up to $\text{Next}(\boldsymbol{u})$, which only involves integer computations and thus no field operation is needed;

3. constructing the new polynomial set F^+ such that every polynomial is valid up to $\text{Next}(\boldsymbol{u})$, which requires $O(\hat{N}D)$ operations at most.

In step 1 above, new values of E other than e may be needed for the verification. The complexity for computing them is still $O(N)$ and this is another difference from the original BMS algorithm for graded term orderings. After the update is complete, a polynomial reduction is applied to F control the size of every polynomial. This requires $O(\hat{N}\bar{N}D)$ operations, where $\bar{N}$ denotes the maximum term number of polynomials in G_2. To summarize, the total operations needed in each pass of the main loop in algorithm 2 is

$$O(N + \hat{N}D + \hat{N}\bar{N}D) = O(N + \hat{N}\bar{N}D).$$

Hence to estimate the whole complexity of the method, we only need an upper bound for the number of passes it takes in the main loop.

119

Table 1: Sakata

Term	Δ	F
$(0,0)$	$(0,0)$	x_1, x_2
$(1,0)$	——	$x_1 + 65437, x_2$
$(2,0)$	$(0,0),(1,0)$	$x_1^2 + 65437x_1 + 21672, x_2$
$(3,0)$	——	$x_1^2 + 62681x_1 + 41493, x_2$
$(4,0)$	$(0,0),(1,0),(2,0)$	$x_1^3 + 62681x_1^2 + 35812x_1 + 18557, x_2$
$(5,0)$	——	$x_1^3 + 30688x_1^2 + 45566x_1 + 54643, x_2$
$(6,0)$	$(0,0),(1,0),(2,0),(3,0)$	$x_1^4 + 30688x_1^3 + 20026x_1^2 + 45766x_1 + 5434, x_2$
$(7,0)$	——	g_1, x_2
$(0,1)$	——	$g_1, x_2 + 65034x_1^3 + 24330x_1^2 + 14876x_1 + 52361$
$\vdots$	$\vdots$	$\vdots$

THEOREM 4.2. *Suppose that the input ideal $I \subset \mathbb{K}[x_1,\ldots,x_n]$ is of degree D. Then the passes of the loop (lines 18–24) in algorithm 2 is bounded by $2nD$.*

PROOF. See Section 6. □

Thus the method based on the BMS algorithm for the general case requires at most $O(nD(N + \hat{N}\bar{N}D))$ field operations to finish.

5. EXPERIMENTS

The method for the shape position case has been implemented in C, while a preliminary implementation of the BMS-based method has been done in Magma. Several benchmarks are used to test the correctness and efficiency of these two methods. All the experiments were made under Scientific Linux OS release 5.5 on 8 Intel(R) Xeon(R) CPUs E5420 at 2.50 GHz with 20.55G RAM.

Table 2 illustrates performances of the implementation for the shape position case with benchmarks like Cyclic or Katsura instances, MinRank problems [13], randomly generated quadratic polynomial systems and examples coming from algebraic cryptanalysis of some curve-based cryptosystem. Instances with ideals not in shape position are marked with †, and the timings for such instances only indicate that of computing the minimal polynomial. In this table, D denotes the degree of the input ideal, and the column "Sparsity" means the percentage of nonzero entries in T_1. Timings for the computation of Gröbner bases w.r.t. DRL and the change of ordering to LEX are recorded (in seconds) for our implementation and corresponding implementations in Magma (version 2-17-1) and Singular (version 3-1-2), together with the speedup factors.

As shown by all the instances here, the multiplication matrix T_1 has a sparsity structure, even for random dense polynomial systems. Furthermore, in fact only last columns of this matrix are dense, with most of the other columns have only one nonzero component equal to 1. For matrices with such structures, we store them in a half-sparse way, that is, the sparse parts of these matrices are stored as a permutation and the others normally.

The current implementation of the algorithm for change of ordering outperforms the FGLM implementations in Magma/Singular/FGb. For example, changing the ordering to LEX for the Katsura12 instance, an ideal of degree 2^{12}, can be achieved in 26.3 seconds (1408.1 sec in Magma and 2623.5 sec in Singular respectively). It is important to note that with the new algorithm the time devoted to the change of ordering is of the same order of magnitude as the DRL Gröbner basis computation.

Table 3 illustrates the performances of the BMS-based method for the general case. As currently this method is only implemented preliminarily in Magma, only the number of field multiplications and other important parameters are recorded, instead of the timings.

Benchmarks derived from Cyclic 5 and 6 instances are used. Instances with ideals in shape position (marked with ‡) are also tested to demonstrate the generality of this method. Besides n and D denoting the number of variables and degree of the input ideal, the columns "Mat Density" and "Poly Density" denote the maximal percentage of nonzero entries in the matrices $T_1,\ldots,T_n$ and the density of resulting Gröbner bases respectively. The following 4 columns record the numbers of passes in the main loop of algorithm 2, matrix multiplications, reductions and field multiplications.

As shown in this table, the numbers of passes accord with theorem 4.2, and the number of operations is less than the original FGLM algorithm for Cyclic-like benchmarks. However, for instances with ideals in shape position, this method works but the complexity is not satisfactory. This is mainly because the resulting Gröbner bases in these cases are no longer sparse, and thus the reduction step becomes complex. The complexity may be reduced if the reduction step is handled more carefully.

6. PROOF OF THEOREM 4.2

The delta set in the BMS algorithm is determined in the following way. Given an array E, suppose F is a polynomial set valid for E up to $\boldsymbol{u}$ and the current delta set up to $\boldsymbol{u}$ is $\Delta_{\boldsymbol{u}}$. If there exists $f \in F$ such that f is not valid up to $\text{Next}(\boldsymbol{u})$ and $\text{Next}(\boldsymbol{u}) - \text{lt}(f) \notin \Delta_{\boldsymbol{u}}$, then $\text{Next}(\boldsymbol{u}) - \text{lt}(f)$ is confirmed as a new term in $\Delta_{\text{Next}(\boldsymbol{u})}$ [17].

This observation sheds light on which terms are indeed needed to handle in the BMS-based method on the assumption that the delta set Δ of E is known. On one hand, we have to handle the terms one of whose corresponding terms is in Δ (Criterion 1). For example, suppose $\boldsymbol{v} \in \Delta$, then the first term $\boldsymbol{u}$ such that $\boldsymbol{u} - \text{lt}(f) = \boldsymbol{v}$ for some $f \in F$ has to be handled. On the other hand, we can skip those terms whose corresponding terms are not in Δ (Criterion 2), for F will be valid up to those terms automatically, otherwise the final delta set will be a wrong one. Based on these two criteria, the terms needed at most in this method are determined by the following inductive procedure.

Let G be the Gröbner basis of $I(E)$ w.r.t LEX and Δ be the delta set of E. Denote $\Delta_i = \Delta \cap \mathbb{K}[x_1,\ldots,x_i]$, $i = 1,\ldots,n$. Suppose $f \in G \cap \mathbb{K}[x_1]$ and $\deg(f) = d_1$. Then the terms needed to compute f are $P_0 = \{(j,0,\ldots,0) \in \mathbb{Z}_{\geq 0}^n : j = 0,\ldots,2d_1 - 1\}$. Set $P = \hat{P}_0$ and $Q = \Delta_1$, where $\hat{P}_0$ is the set obtained by deleting the biggest term w.r.t. LEX from P_0. These two sets P and Q will be updated from time to time in the whole procedure.

Now suppose $G \cap \mathbb{K}[x_1,\ldots,x_k]$ has been computed with updated $P, Q \subseteq \mathbb{K}[x_1,\ldots,x_k]$. Next we show the terms needed at most to obtain $G \cap \mathbb{K}[x_1,\ldots,x_{k+1}]$. For convenience, we will omit the last $n-t$ zero components for a term $\boldsymbol{u} = (u_1,\ldots,u_t,0,\ldots,0) \in \mathbb{K}[x_1,\ldots,x_t]$ if no ambiguity occurs.

Suppose $\Delta_{k+1} = \bigcup_{j=0,\ldots,m} \Delta_{k+1,j}$ for some integer m, where

$$\Delta_{k+1,j} = \Delta_{k+1} \cap \{\boldsymbol{u} : \boldsymbol{u} = (u_1,\ldots,u_k,j)\}.$$

Then we have the following results.

Table 2: Timings of the method for the shape position case from DRL to LEX

Name	D	Sparsity	FGb		Magma		Singular		Speedup	
			$F_5(C)$	New Algorithm	F_4	FGLM	DRL	FGLM	Magma	Singular
Katsura11	2^{11}	21.53%	4.9	3.4	18.2	178.6	632.0	328.4	52.7	96.9
Katsura12	2^{12}	21.26%	31.9	26.3	147.9	1408.1	5061.8	2623.5	53.6	99.8
Katsura13	2^{13}	19.86%	186.3	189.1	1037.2	10895.4			57.6	
Katsura14	2^{14}	19.64%	1838.9	1487.4	9599.0	87131.9			58.5	
Katsura15	2^{15}	18.52%	11456.3	12109.2						
MinR(9,6,3)	980	26.82%	1.1	0.5	6.3	22.7	137.5	38.1	43.6	73.2
MinR(9,7,4)	4116	22.95%	28.4	28.5	208.1	1360.4	4985.8	2490.3	47.7	87.4
MinR(9,8,5)	14112	19.04%	543.6	1032.8						
MinR(9,9,6)	41580	16.91%	9048.2	22171.3						
Random 11	2^{11}	21.53%	4.7	3.4	18.1	169.3	623.9	328.6	49.2	95.5
Random 12	2^{12}	21.26%	26.6	26.9	134.9	1335.8	4867.4	2581.1	49.6	95.8
Random 13	2^{13}	19.98%	146.8	193.5	949.6	10757.4	36727.0	19820.23	55.6	102.4
Random 14	2^{14}	19.64%	1000.7	1489.5	7832.4	84374.6			56.6	
Random 15	2^{15}	18.52%	6882.5	10914.02						
Weierstrass	4096	7.54%	4.0	9.0	5.8	418.3	72.4	1823.6	46.7	203.7
Edwards †	4096	3.41%	0.1	2.4	0.2	176.7	1.0	839.9	72.7	345.6
Cyclic 10 †	34940	1.00%		3586.9	>16 hrs and >16 Gig					

Table 3: Performances of the BMS-based method from DRL to LEX

Name	n	D	Mat Density	Poly Density	N. Passes	N. Matrix	N. Reduction	N. Multiplication
Cyclic5-2	2	55	4.89%	17.86%	165	318	107	$nD^{2.544}$
Cyclic5-3	3	65	8.73%	19.7%	294	704	227	$nD^{2.674}$
Cyclic5-4	4	70	10.71%	21.13%	429	1205	355	$nD^{2.723}$
Cyclic5	5	70	12.02%	21.13%	499	1347	421	$nD^{2.702}$
Cyclic6	6	156	11.46%	17.2%	1363	4464	1187	$nD^{2.781}$
Uteshev Bikker ‡	4	36	60.65%	100%	179	199	105	$nD^{2.992}$
D1 ‡	12	48	34.2%	51.02%	624	780	517	$nD^{2.874}$
Dessin2-6 ‡	6	42	46.94%	100%	294	336	205	$nD^{2.968}$

1. For $j = 0$, the terms needed by the BMS-based method are $(Q,1)$, where $(Q,i) := \{(\boldsymbol{q},i) : \boldsymbol{q} \in Q\}$.

2. For each $j = 1,\ldots,m$, the terms needed are

$$\begin{cases} (Q,i) \cup P', & i = 2j; \\ (Q,i), & i = 2j+1, \end{cases}$$

where P' is defined as follows.

(a) If there does not exist $g \in G \cap \mathbb{K}[x_1,\ldots,x_{k+1}]$ such that $\deg(g,x_{k+1}) = j$, then $P' = (P,i)$.

(b) Else suppose $\mathrm{lt}(g) = \boldsymbol{v} = (v_1,\ldots,v_k,j)$. Then

$$P' := \{\boldsymbol{u}+(0,\ldots,0,j) : \boldsymbol{u} \in \Delta_{k+1,j}\} \cup \{\boldsymbol{u}+\boldsymbol{v} : \boldsymbol{u} \in \Delta_{k+1,j}\}.$$

Furthermore, P and Q are updated as

$$Q := \{\boldsymbol{q} : (\boldsymbol{q},j) \in \Delta_{k+1,j}\}, \quad P := \{\boldsymbol{p} : (\boldsymbol{p},j) \in \hat{P}'\},$$

where $\hat{P}'$ is the set obtained by deleting the biggest term from P', similar to $\hat{P}_0$.

3. Finally when $G \cap \mathbb{K}[x_1,\ldots,x_{k+1}]$ is obtained, P is updated as the set of all terms needed for $G \cap \mathbb{K}[x_1,\ldots,x_{k+1}]$ and Q as Δ_{k+1}.

For example, figure 1 illustrates the procedure described above for the instance Cyclic5-2.

Actually the sets P and Q represent the two criteria 1 and 2 mentioned above: P is the set of terms we have to handle so that all terms in Δ are correctly added, while Q stands for those we need to handle at most according to Criterion 2. Furthermore, P is totally determined by the current $\Delta_{k+1,j}$ we have to add to Δ, and Q is determined by the latest $\Delta_{k+1,j'}$ already handled. Hence when a polynomial in $G \cap \mathbb{K}[x_1,\ldots,x_{k+1}]$ is found, say at the term $(\ldots,2j)$,

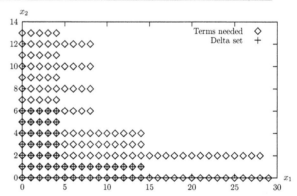

Figure 1: Delta set (+) and terms needed (◇) for Cyclic5-2

all the following $\Delta_{k+1,l}$ $(l \geq j)$ will be different from $\Delta_{k+1,j-1}$, and thus P and Q are updated accordingly.

The justification of the procedure follows naturally from the above remarks and how the terms in Δ are determined. First computation of the polynomial $f \in G \cap \mathbb{K}[x_1]$ is the same as what is done in the Berlekamp algorithm, thus at most P_0 are needed. Then P is set with one term less than P_0. This is because only $\deg(f) = d_1$, and for all the other $g \in G$, $\deg(g,x_1) < d_1$. Hence the terms needed here to get $\Delta \cap \mathbb{K}[x_1]$ have one term more than others at least. This difference can be seen from figure 1 for $x_2 = 0$ and 2. Moreover, Q is set as Δ_1.

Next for each $i = 1,\ldots,2m+1$, (Q,i) are the terms needed at most according to Criterion 2 and they are included every time. For odd $i = 2j+1$ $(j = 0,\ldots,m)$, no term is going to be added to Δ, therefore (Q,i) are all the terms needed. While for even $i = 2j$ $(j = 1, \ldots, m)$, new terms are added to Δ. In case (a), we have

$$\Delta_{k+1,j} = \Delta_{k+1,j-1} + (0, \ldots, 0, 1), \qquad (8)$$

thus P' here is just a translation of the previous P for $\Delta_{k+1,j-1}$. In case (b) however, the equality (8) does not hold, and P' is defined according to $\Delta_{k+1,j}$ based on both Criteria 1 and 2. Next P and Q are updated so that subsequent computation can follow correctly. Note for similar reasons to $P = \hat{P}_0$, P here is set with one term less than P'.

With the preparation above, now we are able to give the proof of Theorem 4.2.

PROOF OF THEOREM 4.2. Denote the number of terms needed to compute $G \cap \mathbb{K}[x_1, \ldots, x_i]$ by χ_i and $\Delta_i = \Delta \cap \mathbb{K}[x_1, \ldots, x_i]$ still. Clearly $\Delta = \Delta_n$. As $I \subset I(E)$, we know that Δ, the delta set of E, is a subset of the canonical basis of $\mathbb{K}[x_1, \ldots, x_n]/I$, and hence $|\Delta| \leq D$. To prove the theorem, we only need to prove $2n|\Delta|$ is an upper bound.

We induce on the number of variable i of $\mathbb{K}[x_1, \ldots, x_i]$. For $i = 1$, one can easily see $\chi_1 \leq 2|\Delta_1|$. Now suppose $\chi_k \leq 2k|\Delta_k|$ for $k(<n)$. Next we prove $\chi_{k+1} \leq 2(k+1)|\Delta_{k+1}|$.

First we ignore all the terms (Q,i) as in case (b) from all the terms needed to compute $G \cap \mathbb{K}[x_1, \ldots, x_{k+1}]$, with all the remaining terms denoted by T_{k+1}. We claim that $|T_{k+1}|$ is bounded by $(2k+1)|\Delta_{k+1}|$.

Suppose

$$\Delta_{k+1} = \bigcup_{j=0,\ldots,m} \Delta_{k+1,j}, \quad T_{k+1} = \bigcup_{l=0,\ldots,2m+1} T_{k+1,l}$$

for some integer m, where

$$\Delta_{k+1,j} = \Delta_{k+1} \cap \{u : u = (u_1, \ldots, u_k, j)\},$$
$$T_{k+1,l} = T_{k+1} \cap \{u : u = (u_1, \ldots, u_k, l)\}.$$

Then for each $\Delta_{k+1,j}$, one can see from the procedure above that $|T_{k+1,2j}|$ is bounded by either $2k|\Delta_k|$ (if $\Delta_{k+1,j}$ is before the first element in G is found, and in that case $|\Delta_{k+1,j}| = |\Delta_k|$), or $2|\Delta_{k+1,j}|$ ($\leq 2k|\Delta_{k+1,j}|$). Furthermore, $|T_{k+1,2j+1}|$ is bounded by $|\Delta_{k+1,j}|$. Hence we have

$$|T_{k+1,2j}| + |T_{k+1,2j+1}| \leq (2k+1)|\Delta_{k+1,j}|,$$

which leads to $|T_{k+1}| \leq (2k+1)|\Delta_{k+1}|$.

Now we only need to prove the number of all the terms (Q,i) in case (b) is bounded by $|\Delta_{k+1}|$. Suppose these cases occur at $(p_l, l), l = i_1, \ldots, i_{m'}$. Again from the procedure, one can see that the number of terms in (Q,i) for (p_1, i_1) is bounded by $|\Delta_k|$. And after it occurs at some term (p_{i_l}, i_l), the newly updated set Q_{i_l} will bound the terms occurring at $(p_{i_{l+1}}, i_{l+1})$. Then the conclusion can be proved if one notices $\Delta_k \cup (Q_{i_1}, i_1) \cup \cdots \cup (Q_{i_{m'-1}}, i_{m'-1}) \subseteq \Delta_{k+1}$. $\square$

7. CONCLUDING REMARKS

Both methods proposed in this paper follow the thought of Wiedemann algorithm. That is, we take advantage of the matrix sparsity by first constructing linearly recurring relations and then finding the generators for these relations with the (generalized) Berlekamp–Massey algorithm. Multiplication matrices in the FGLM algorithm serve as a bridge between the change of ordering and linearly recurring relations.

The BMS algorithm itself, as a multi-dimensional generalization of the Berlekamp–Massey algorithm, is worth studying. We hope that this paper is just a first step for the study of this algorithm. Several problems concerning it are still unsolved and left as future

works: the complete characterization of its termination criteria, the probability for $I(E) = I$, what to do when $I(E) \neq I$, and further improvement of the algorithm.

Moreover, the sparsity of multiplication matrices is now demonstrated by several benchmarks. Could we express the sparsity of the matrices as $O(D^\alpha)$ with $\alpha < 2$, it would give immediately a better complexity for the change of ordering.

8. REFERENCES

[1] A. Basiri and J.-C. Faugère. Changing the ordering of Gröbner bases with LLL: case of two variables. In *Proceedings of ISSAC 2003*, pages 23–29. ACM, 2003.

[2] E. Becker, T. Mora, M. Marinari, and C. Traverso. The shape of the Shape Lemma. In *Proceedings of ISSAC 1994*, pages 129–133. ACM, 1994.

[3] T. Becker, V. Weispfenning, and H. Kredel. *Gröbner Bases: a Computational Approach to Commutative Algebra*. Graduate Texts in Mathematics. Springer, New York, 1993.

[4] R. P. Brent, F. G. Gustavson, and D. Y. Y. Yun. Fast solution of toeplitz systems of equations and computation of Padé approximants. *Journal of Algorithms*, 1(3):259–295, 1980.

[5] B. Buchberger. Gröbner bases: An algorithmic method in polynomial ideal theory. In *Multidimensional Systems Theory*, pages 184–232. Reidel, Dordrecht, 1985.

[6] J. Buchmann, A. Pyshkin, and R.-P. Weinmann. A zero-dimensional Gröbner basis for AES-128. In M. Robshaw, editor, *Fast Software Encryption*, volume 4047 of *LNCS*, pages 78–88. Springer, Berlin / Heidelberg, 2006.

[7] S. Collart, M. Kalkbrener, and D. Mall. Converting bases with the Gröbner walk. *Journal of Symbolic Computation*, 24(3–4):465–469, 1997.

[8] D. A. Cox, J. B. Little, and D. O'Shea. *Ideals, Varieties, and Algorithms: an Introduction to Computational Algebraic Geometry and Commutative Algebra (2nd edn.)*. Undergraduate Texts in Mathematics. Springer, New York, 1997.

[9] X. Dahan, X. Jin, M. Moreno Maza, and E. Schost. Change of order for regular chains in positive dimension. *Theoretical Computer Science*, 392:37–65, 2008.

[10] J.-C. Faugère. A new efficient algorithm for computing Gröbner bases (F_4). *Journal of Pure and Applied Algebra*, 139(1–3):61–88, 1999.

[11] J.-C. Faugère. A new efficient algorithm for computing Gröbner bases without reduction to zero (F_5). In *Proceedings of ISSAC 2002*, pages 75–83. ACM, 2002.

[12] J.-C. Faugère, P. Gianni, D. Lazard, and T. Mora. Efficient computation of zero-dimensional Gröbner bases by change of ordering. *Journal of Symbolic Computation*, 16(4):329–344, 1993.

[13] J.-C. Faugère, M. Safey El Din, and P.-J. Spaenlehauer. Computing loci of rank defects of linear matrices using Gröbner bases and applications to cryptology. In *Proceedings of ISSAC 2010*, pages 257–264. ACM, 2010.

[14] E. Jonckheere and C. Ma. A simple Hankel interpretation of the Berlekamp–Massey algorithm. *Linear Algebra and its Applications*, 125:65–76, 1989.

[15] P. Loustaunau and E. York. On the decoding of cyclic codes using Gröbner bases. *Applicable Algebra in Engineering, Communication and Computing*, 8(6):469–483, 1997.

[16] C. Pascal and E. Schost. Change of order for bivariate triangular sets. In *Proceedings of ISSAC 2006*, pages 277–284. ACM, 2006.

[17] K. Saints and C. Heegard. Algebraic-geometric codes and multidimensional cyclic codes: a unified theory and algorithms for decoding using Gröbner bases. *IEEE Transactions on Information Theory*, 41(6):1733–1751, 2002.

[18] S. Sakata. Finding a minimal set of linear recurring relations capable of generating a given finite two-dimensional array. *Journal of Symbolic Computation*, 5(3):321–337, 1988.

[19] S. Sakata. Extension of the Berlekamp–Massey algorithm to N dimensions. *Information and Computation*, 84(2):207–239, 1990.

[20] D. Wiedemann. Solving sparse linear equations over finite fields. *IEEE Transactions on Information Theory*, 32(1):54–62, 1986.

Diversification Improves Interpolation

Mark Giesbrecht

Symbolic Computation Group
University of Waterloo
Waterloo, Ontario, Canada
mwg@cs.uwaterloo.ca

Daniel S. Roche

Symbolic Computation Group
University of Waterloo
Waterloo, Ontario, Canada
droche@cs.uwaterloo.ca

ABSTRACT

We consider the problem of interpolating an unknown multivariate polynomial with coefficients taken from a finite field or as numerical approximations of complex numbers. Building on the recent work of Garg and Schost, we improve on the best-known algorithm for interpolation over large finite fields by presenting a Las Vegas randomized algorithm that uses fewer black box evaluations. Using related techniques, we also address numerical interpolation of sparse polynomials with complex coefficients, and provide the first provably stable algorithm (in the sense of relative error) for this problem, at the cost of modestly more evaluations. A key new technique is a randomization which makes all coefficients of the unknown polynomial distinguishable, producing what we call a *diverse* polynomial. Another departure from most previous approaches is that our algorithms do not rely on root finding as a subroutine. We show how these improvements affect the practical performance with trial implementations.

Categories and Subject Descriptors

F.2.1 [**Analysis of Algorithms and Problem Complexity**]: Numerical Algorithms and Problems—*Computations on polynomials*; G.1.1 [**Numerical Analysis**]: Interpolation; G.4 [**Mathematical Software**]: Algorithm Design and Analysis

General Terms

Algorithms, Theory, Performance

Keywords

Sparse polynomials, symbolic-numeric, interpolation

1. INTRODUCTION

Polynomial interpolation is a long-studied and important problem in computer algebra and symbolic computation.

Given a way to evaluate an unknown polynomialand an upper bound on its degree, the interpolation problem is to determine a representation for the polynomial. In *sparse* interpolation, we are also given an upper bound on the number of nonzero terms in the unknown polynomial, and the output is returned in the sparse (also *lacunary* or *supersparse*) representation, wherein only nonzero terms are explicitly stored.

Applications of sparse interpolation include the manipulation and factorization of multivariate polynomials and system solving (see, e.g., Canny et al. (1989); Kaltofen and Trager (1990); Díaz and Kaltofen (1995, 1998); Javadi and Monagan (2007, 2009). With the advent of hybrid symbolic-numeric algorithms for (systems of) multivariate polynomials with approximate coefficients, we find applications of approximate sparse interpolation, in particular for solving nonlinear systems of equations (see, e.g., Sommese et al. (2001, 2004); Stetter (2004)) and factoring approximate multivariate polynomials (see, e.g., Kaltofen et al. (2008)).

Sparse interpolation is also a non-trivial generalization of the *polynomial identity testing* problem, determining if an unknown polynomial given by an algebraic circuit is identically zero. A relevant result in our setting is Bläser et al. (2009); see also the recent survey by Saxena (2009).

Here we examine the sparse interpolation problem in two settings which have received recent attention: when the coefficients are elements of finite fields (particularly large finite fields, over which we have no choice) and when they are approximations to complex numbers. We give improvements over the state of the art in both cases, and demonstrate our new algorithms in practice with an implementation in C++.

1.1 Problem definition

A multivariate polynomial $f \in \mathsf{F}[x_1, \ldots, x_n]$ with coefficients in a field F is t-sparse for some $t \in \mathbb{N}$ if f has at most t nonzero terms; that is, f can be written

$$f = \sum_{i=1}^{t} c_i x_1^{e_{i1}} x_2^{e_{i2}} \cdots x_n^{e_{in}}$$

for coefficients $c_i \in \mathsf{F}$ and exponent tuples $(e_{i1}, \ldots, e_{in}) \in \mathbb{N}^n$ for $1 \leq i \leq t$. If each $e_{ij} < d$, then the size of this representation is $O(t)$ field elements plus $O(tn \log d)$ bits. We seek algorithms which are polynomial-time in this size.

Let $f \in \mathsf{F}[x_1, \ldots, x_n]$. A *black box* for f is a function which takes as input a vector $(a_1, \ldots, a_n) \in \mathsf{F}^n$ and produces $f(a_1, \ldots, a_n) \in \mathsf{F}$. The cost of the black box is the number of operations in F required to evaluate it at a given input.

Clausen et al. (1991) showed that, if only evaluations over F are allowed, then for some instances at least $\Omega(n^{\log t})$ black box probes are required. Hence if we seek polynomial-time algorithms, we must extend the capabilities of the black box. To this end, Díaz and Kaltofen (1998) introduced the *extended domain black box* which is capable of evaluating $f(b_1, \ldots, b_n) \in \mathsf{E}$ for any $(b_1, \ldots, b_n) \in \mathsf{E}^n$ where E is any extension field of F. That is, we can change every black box operation to work over an extension field, usually paying an extra cost proportional to the size of the extension.

Motivated by the case of black boxes that are division-free algebraic circuits, we will use the following model which we believe to be fair and cover all previous relevant results. Here $\mathsf{M}(m)$ is the number of field operations required to multiply two univariate polynomials with degrees less than m, and $O\tilde{\ }(m)$ represents any function bounded by $m(\log m)^{O(1)}$.

DEFINITION 1.1. *Let $f \in \mathsf{F}[x_1, \ldots, x_n]$ and $\ell > 0$. A remainder black box for f with size ℓ is a procedure which, given any monic square-free polynomial $g \in \mathsf{F}[y]$ with $\deg g = m$, and any $h_1, \ldots, h_n \in \mathsf{F}[y]$ with each $\deg h_i < m$, produces $f(h_1, \ldots, h_n) \operatorname{rem} g$ using at most $\ell \cdot \mathsf{M}(m)$ operations in F.*

This definition is general enough to cover the algorithms we know of over finite fields, and we submit that the cost model is fair to the standard black box, extended domain black box, and algebraic circuit settings. The model also makes sense over complex numbers as well, as we will see.

1.2 Interpolation over finite fields

We first summarize previously known univariate interpolation algorithms when F is a finite field with q elements and identify our new contributions. For now, let $f \in \mathbb{F}_q[x]$ have degree less than d and sparsity t. We will assume we have a remainder black box for f with size ℓ. Since field elements can be represented with $O(\log q)$ bits, a polynomial-time algorithm will have cost polynomial in ℓ, t, $\log d$, and $\log q$.

For the dense output representation, one can use the classical method of Newton/Waring/Lagrange to interpolate in $O\tilde{\ }(\ell d)$ time (von zur Gathen and Gerhard, 2003, §10.2).

The algorithm of Ben-Or and Tiwari (1988) for sparse polynomial interpolation, with improvements by Kaltofen and Yagati (1989), can be adapted to arbitrary finite fields. Unfortunately, these algorithms require t discrete logarithm computations in $\mathbb{F}_q^*$, whose cost is small if the field size q is chosen carefully (as in Kaltofen (2010)), but not in general. The best approach for arbitrary q seems to be Pollard's "kangaroo" algorithm (1978), using the fact that the discrete logs must fall in the range $[0, \ldots, d-1]$. The total cost of this method is $O(t\ell + t^2 + t\sqrt{d})$.

The current study builds most directly on the work of Garg and Schost (2009), who gave the first polynomial-time algorithm for sparse interpolation over an arbitrary finite field. Their algorithm works roughly as follows. For very small primes p, use the black box to compute f modulo $x^p - 1$. A prime p is a "good prime" if and only if all terms of f are distinct modulo $x^p - 1$. We do this for p in the range of roughly $O(t^2 \log d)$ until there are sufficient good primes to recover the unique symmetric polynomial over $\mathbb{Z}[y]$ whose roots are the exponents of nonzero terms in f. We then factor this polynomial to find those exponents, and correlate with any good prime image to determine the coefficients. The total cost is $O\tilde{\ }(\ell t^4 \log^2 d)$ field operations. Using randomization, it is easy to reduce this to $O\tilde{\ }(\ell t^3 \log^2 d)$.

The coefficients of the symmetric integer polynomial in Garg & Schost's algorithm are bounded by $O(d^t)$, much

larger than the $O(d)$ size of the exponents ultimately recovered. Our new algorithm over finite fields of size at least $\Omega(t^2 d)$ avoids evaluating the symmetric polynomial and finding its roots entirely. As a result, we reduce the total number of required evaluations and develop a randomized algorithm with cost $O\tilde{\ }(\ell t^2 \log^2 d)$, which is roughly quadratic in the input and output sizes. Since this can be deterministically verified in the same time, our algorithm (as well as the randomized version of Garg & Schost) is of the Las Vegas type.

These results are summarized in Table 1, where we assume in all cases that the field size q is "large enough". In the table, the "probe degree" refers to the degree of g in each evaluation of the remainder black box as defined above.

Two techniques are available to adapt a univariate interpolation algorithm to the multivariate case. The first is Kronecker substitution: given a remainder black box for an unknown $f \in \mathsf{F}[x_1, \ldots, x_n]$ with max degree less than d, we can easily construct a remainder black box for the univariate polynomial $f(x, x^d, x^{d^2}, \ldots, x^{d^{n-1}}) \in \mathsf{F}[x]$, whose terms correspond one-to-one with terms of f. The cost is that of the univariate algorithm with sparsity t and degree d^n.

The other method for constructing a multivariate interpolation algorithm is due to Zippel (1990). The technique is inherently probabilistic of the Monte Carlo type and works variable-by-variable, at each step solving a number of transposed Vandermonde systems and making $O(t)$ calls to a univariate interpolation algorithm. Say this underlying algorithm uses $\rho(d, t)$ black box evaluations of degree $\Delta(d, t)$ and $\psi(d, t)$ other field operations to interpolate univariate polynomials with sparsity t and degrees less than d. Then the resulting algorithm using Zippel's method has total cost

$$O\tilde{\ }(nt\psi(d, t) + \ell nt\rho(d, t)\Delta(n, t))$$

to interpolate an n-variate t-sparse polynomial with max degree less than d. Zippel (1990) used the dense algorithm for univariate interpolation; using Ben-Or and Tiwari's algorithm instead was studied by Kaltofen and Lee (2003).

Grigoriev et al. (1990) give a parallel algorithm with small depth but which is not competitive in our model due to the large number of processors required. A practical parallel version of Ben-Or and Tiwari's algorithm has been developed by Javadi and Monagan (2010). Kaltofen et al. (1990) and Avendaño et al. (2006) present modular algorithms for interpolating polynomials with rational and integer coefficients, but their methods do not seem to apply to finite fields.

1.3 Approximate polynomial interpolation

Recently, a number of numerically-focussed sparse interpolation algorithms have been presented. The algorithm of Giesbrecht et al. (2009) is a numerical adaptation of Ben-Or and Tiwari (1988), which samples f at $O(t)$ randomly chosen roots of unity $\omega \in \mathbb{C}$ on the unit circle. In particular, ω is chosen to have (high) order at least the degree, and a randomization scheme is used to avoid clustering of nodes which will cause dramatic ill-conditioning. A relatively weak theoretical bound is proven there on the randomized conditioning scheme, though experimental and heuristic evidence suggests it is much better in practice. Cuyt and Lee (2008) adapt Rutishauser's qd algorithm to alleviate the need for bounds on the partial degrees and the sparsity, but still evaluate at high-order roots of unity. Approximate sparse rational function interpolation is considered by Kaltofen and Yang (2007) and Kaltofen et al. (2007), using the Structured

	Probes	Probe degree	Computation cost	Total cost	Type
Dense	d	1	$\tilde{O}(d)$	$\tilde{O}(\ell d)$	deterministic
Ben-Or & Tiwari	$O(t)$	1	$O(t^2 + t\sqrt{d})$	$\tilde{O}(\ell t + t^2 + t\sqrt{d})$	deterministic
Garg & Schost	$\tilde{O}(t^2 \log d)$	$\tilde{O}(t^2 \log d)$	$\tilde{O}(t^4 \log^2 d)$	$\tilde{O}(\ell t^4 \log^2 d)$	deterministic
Randomized G & S	$\tilde{O}(t \log d)$	$\tilde{O}(t^2 \log d)$	$\tilde{O}(t^3 \log^2 d)$	$\tilde{O}(\ell t^3 \log^2 d)$	Las Vegas
Ours	$O(\log d)$	$\tilde{O}(t^2 \log d)$	$\tilde{O}(t^2 \log^2 d)$	$\tilde{O}(\ell t^2 \log^2 d)$	Las Vegas

Table 1: Sparse univariate interpolation over large finite fields, with black box size ℓ, degree d, and t nonzero terms

Total Least Norm (STLN) method and, in the latter, randomization to improve conditioning. Approximate sparse interpolation is also considered for integer polynomials by Mansour (1995), where a polynomial-time algorithm is presented in quite a different model from ours. In particular the evaluation error is absolute (not relative) and the complexity is sensitive to the bit length of the integer coefficients.

Our new algorithm for approximate sparse interpolation is presented in Section 4. We provide the first algorithm which is provably numerically stable without heuristics or conjectures. We define an "ϵ-approximate black box" as one which evaluates an unknown t-sparse target polynomial $f \in \mathbb{C}[x]$, of degree d, with relative error at most $\epsilon > 0$. Our goal is to build a t-sparse polynomial g such that $\|f - g\|_2 \leq \epsilon \|f\|_2$. A bound on the degree and sparsity of the target polynomial, as well as ϵ, must also be provided. After demonstrating that the problem is well-posed, we adapt our variant of the Garg and Schost (2009) algorithm for the approximate case, prove it is numerically accurate in terms of the relative error of the output, and analyze its cost. Our algorithm typically requires $\tilde{O}(t^2 \log^2 d)$ evaluations at primitive roots of unity of order $\tilde{O}(t^2 \log d)$ (as opposed to order d in previous approaches). We guarantee that it finds a t-sparse polynomial g such that $\|g - f\|_2 \leq 2\epsilon \|f\|_2$. An experimental demonstration of the numerical robustness is given in Section 5.

Note that all these works evaluate the polynomial only on the unit circle. This is necessary because we allow and expect f to have very large degree, which would cause a catastrophic loss of precision at data points of non-unit magnitude. Similarly, we assume that the complex argument of evaluation points is exactly specified, which is again necessary because any error in the argument would be exponentially magnified by the degree.

2. SPARSE INTERPOLATION FOR GENERIC FIELDS

Here and for the remainder, we focus on interpolating an unknown t-sparse univariate polynomial $f \in \mathbb{F}[x]$ with degree less than d. As discussed above, these algorithms can be adapted to multivariate interpolation using Kronecker substitution or Zippel's method.

Assume a fixed, unknown $f \in \mathbb{F}[x]$ with sparsity at most t and degree at most d. We will use a remainder black box for f to evaluate $f \operatorname{rem}(x^p - 1)$ for small primes p. We say p is a "good prime" if the sparsity of $f \operatorname{rem}(x^p - 1)$ is the same as that of f itself — that is, none of the exponents are equivalent modulo p.

The following lemma shows the size of primes required to randomly choose good primes with high probability.

LEMMA 2.1. *Let $f \in \mathbb{F}[x]$ be a t-sparse polynomial with degree d, and let $\lambda = \max\left(21, \left\lceil \frac{5}{3} t(t-1) \ln d \right\rceil\right)$. A prime chosen at random in the range $\lambda, \ldots, 2\lambda$ is a good prime for f with probability at least $1/2$.*

PROOF. Let $e_1, \ldots, e_t$ be the exponents of nonzero terms in f. If p is a bad prime, then p divides $(e_j - e_i)$ for some $i < j$. Each $e_j - e_i \leq d$, so there can be at most $\log_\lambda d = \ln d / \ln \lambda$ primes that divide each $e_j - e_i$. There are exactly $\binom{t}{2}$ such pairs of exponents, so the total number of bad primes is at most $(t(t-1) \ln d)/(2 \ln \lambda)$.

From Rosser and Schoenfeld (1962, Corollary 3 to Theorem 2), the total number of primes in the range $\lambda, \ldots, 2\lambda$ is at least $3\lambda/(5 \ln \lambda)$ when $\lambda \geq 21$, which is at least $t(t-1) \ln d / \ln \lambda$, at least twice the number of bad primes. □

Now observe an easy case for the sparse interpolation problem. If a polynomial $f \in \mathbb{F}[x]$, has all coefficients distinct; that is, $f = \sum_{1 \leq i \leq t} c_i x^{e_i}$ and $c_i = c_j \Rightarrow i = j$, then we say f is *diverse*. To interpolate a diverse polynomial $f \in \mathbb{F}[x]$, we first follow the method of Garg and Schost (2009) by computing $f \operatorname{rem}(x^{p_i} - 1)$ for "good primes" p_i such that the sparsity of $f \operatorname{rem}(x^{p_i} - 1)$ is the same as that of f. Since f is diverse, $f \operatorname{rem}(x^{p_i} - 1)$ is also diverse and in fact each modular image has the same set of coefficients. Using this fact, we avoid the need to construct and subsequently factor the symmetric polynomial in the exponents. Instead, we correlate like terms based on the (unique) coefficients in each modular image, then use simple Chinese remaindering to construct each exponent e_i from its image modulo each p_i. This requires only $O(\log d)$ remainder black box evaluations at good primes, gaining a factor of t improvement over the randomized version of Garg and Schost (2009).

In the following sections, we will show how to choose an $\alpha \in \mathbb{F}$ so that $f(\alpha x)$ — which we can easily construct a remainder black box for — is diverse. With such a procedure, Algorithm 1 gives a Monte Carlo algorithm for interpolation over a general field.

THEOREM 2.2. *With inputs as specified, Algorithm 1 correctly computes the unknown polynomial f with probability at least $1 - \mu$. The total cost in field operations (except for step 8) is*

$$O\left(\ell \cdot \left(\frac{\log D}{\log T + \log\log D} + \log \frac{1}{\mu}\right) \cdot \mathsf{M}\left(T^2 \log D\right)\right).$$

PROOF. The for loop on line 3 searches for the true sparsity t and a single good prime ϱ. Since each prime p in the given range is good with probability at least $1/2$ by Lemma 2.1, the probability of failure at this stage is at most $\mu/3$.

The for loop on line 12 searches for and uses sufficiently many good primes to recover the exponents of f. The product of all the good primes must be at least D, and since each prime is at least λ, at least $(\ln D)/(\ln \lambda)$ good primes are required.

125

Algorithm 1: Generic interpolation

Input: $\mu \in \mathbb{R}_{>0}$, $T, D, q \in \mathbb{N}$, and a remainder black box for unknown T-sparse $f \in \mathsf{F}[x]$ with $\deg f < D$

Output: $t \in \mathbb{N}$, $e_1, \ldots, e_t \in \mathbb{N}$, and $c_1, \ldots, c_t \in \mathsf{F}$ such that $f = \sum_{1 \le i \le t} c_i x^{e_i}$

1 $t \leftarrow 0$
2 $\lambda \leftarrow \max\left(21, \left\lceil \frac{5}{3}T(T-1)\ln D \right\rceil \right)$
3 **for** $\lceil \log_2(3/\mu) \rceil$ *primes* $p \in \{\lambda, \ldots, 2\lambda\}$ **do**
4   Use black box to compute $f_p = f(x) \operatorname{rem} (x^p - 1)$
5   **if** f_p *has more than* t *terms* **then**
6         $t \leftarrow$ sparsity of f_p
7         $\varrho \leftarrow p$
8 $\alpha \leftarrow$ element of F s.t. $\Pr[f(\alpha x) \text{ not diverse}] < \mu/3$
9 $g_\varrho \leftarrow f(\alpha x) \operatorname{rem}(x^\varrho - 1)$
10 $c_1, \ldots, c_t \leftarrow$ nonzero coefficients of g_ϱ
11 $e_1, \ldots, e_t \leftarrow 0$
12 **for** $\lceil 2\ln(3/\mu) + 4(\ln D)/(\ln \lambda) \rceil$ *primes* $p \in \{\lambda, \ldots, 2\lambda\}$ **do**
13   Use black box to compute $g_p = f(\alpha x) \operatorname{rem}(x^p - 1)$
14   **if** g_p *has exactly* t *nonzero terms* **then**
15   **for** $i = 1, \ldots, t$ **do** Update e_i with exponent of c_i in g_p modulo p via Chinese remaindering
16 **for** $i = 1, \ldots, t$ **do** $c_i \leftarrow c_i \alpha^{-e_i}$
17 **return** $f(x) = \sum_{1 \le i \le t} c_i x^{e_i}$

Let $n = \lceil 2\ln(3/\mu) + 4(\ln D)/(\ln \lambda) \rceil$ be the number of primes sampled in this loop, and $k = \lceil (\ln D)/(\ln \lambda) \rceil$ the number of good primes required. We can derive that

$$\exp\left(\frac{-2(n/2 - k)^2}{n} \right) < \frac{\mu}{3}.$$

Then from Hoeffding's Inequality (1963), the probability of encountering fewer than k good primes is less than $\mu/3$.

Therefore the total probability of failure is at most μ. For the cost analysis, the dominating cost will be the modular black box evaluations in the last for loop. The number of evaluations in this loop is $O(\log(1/\mu) + (\log D)/(\log \lambda))$, and each evaluation has cost $O(\ell \cdot \mathsf{M}(\lambda))$. Since

$$(\log D)/(\log \lambda) \in \Theta((\log D)/(\log T + \log\log D)),$$

the complexity bound is correct as stated. □

In case the bound T on the number of nonzero terms is very bad, we could choose a smaller value of λ based on the true sparsity t before line 8, improving the cost of the remainder of the algorithm.

In addition, as our bound on possible number of "bad primes" seems to be quite loose, a more efficient approach in practice would be to replace the for loop on line 12 with one that starts with a prime much smaller than λ and incrementally searches for the next larger primes until the product of all good primes is at least D. We could choose the lower bound to start searching from based on lower bounds on the birthday problem. That is, assuming (falsely) that the exponents are randomly distributed modulo p, start with the least p that will have no exponents collide modulo p with high probability. This would yield an algorithm more sensitive to the true bound on bad primes, but unfortunately gives a worse formal cost analysis.

3. SPARSE INTERPOLATION OVER FINITE FIELDS

3.1 Diversification

For a prime power q, we use $\mathbb{F}_q$ to denote the finite field with q elements. In order to use Algorithm 1 over $\mathbb{F}_q[x]$, we must find an α so that $f(\alpha x)$ is diverse. A surprisingly simple trick works: evaluating $f(\alpha x)$ for a random nonzero $\alpha \in \mathbb{F}_q$.

THEOREM 3.1. *For* $q \ge T(T-1)D$ *and any* T-*sparse polynomial* $f \in \mathbb{F}_q[x]$ *with* $\deg f < D$, *if* α *is chosen uniformly at random from* $\mathbb{F}_q^*$, *the probability that* $f(\alpha x)$ *is diverse is at least* $1/2$.

PROOF. Let $t \le T$ be the exact number of nonzero terms in f, and write $f = \sum_{1 \le i \le t} c_i x^{e_i}$, with nonzero coefficients $c_i \in \mathbb{F}_q^*$ and $e_1 < e_2 < \cdots < e_t$. So the ith coefficient of $f(\alpha x)$ is $c_i \alpha^{e_i}$.

If $f(\alpha x)$ is *not* diverse, then we must have $c_i \alpha^{e_i} = c_j \alpha^{e_j}$ for some $i \ne j$. Therefore consider the polynomial $A \in \mathbb{F}_q[y]$ defined by

$$A = \prod_{1 \le i < j \le t} \left(c_i y^{e_i} - c_j y^{e_j} \right).$$

We see that $f(\alpha x)$ is diverse if and only if $A(\alpha) \ne 0$, hence the number of roots of A over $\mathbb{F}_q$ is exactly the number of unlucky choices for α.

The polynomial A is the product of exactly $\binom{t}{2}$ binomials, each of which has degree less than D. Therefore

$$\deg A < \frac{T(T-1)D}{2},$$

and this also gives an upper bound on the number of roots of A. Hence $q - 1 \ge 2 \deg A$, and at least half of the elements of $\mathbb{F}_q^*$ are not roots of A, yielding the stated result. □

Using this result, given a black box for f and the exact sparsity t of f, we can find an $\alpha \in \mathbb{F}_q$ such that $f(\alpha x)$ is diverse by sampling random values $\alpha \in \mathbb{F}_q$, evaluating $f(\alpha x) \operatorname{rem} x^p - 1$ for a single good prime p, and checking whether the polynomial is diverse. With probability at least $1 - \mu$, this will succeed in finding a diversifying α after at most $\lceil \log_2(1/\mu) \rceil$ iterations. Therefore we can use this approach in Algorithm 1 with no effect on the asymptotic complexity.

3.2 Verification

So far, Algorithm 1 over a finite field is probabilistic of the Monte Carlo type; that is, it may give the wrong answer with some controllably-small probability. To provide a more robust Las Vegas probabilistic algorithm, we require only a fast way to check that a candidate answer is in fact correct. To do this, observe that given a modular black box for an unknown T-sparse $f \in \mathbb{F}_q[x]$ and an explicit T-sparse polynomial $g \in \mathbb{F}_q[x]$, we can construct a modular black box for the $2T$-sparse polynomial $f - g$ of their difference. Verifying that $f = g$ thus reduces to the well-studied problem of deterministic polynomial identity testing.

The following algorithm is due to Bläser et al. (2009) and provides this check in essentially the same time as the interpolation algorithm; we restate it in Algorithm 2 for completeness and to use our notation.

Algorithm 2: Verification over finite fields

Input: $T, D, q \in \mathbb{N}$ and modular black box for unknown T-sparse $f \in \mathbb{F}_q[x]$ with $\deg f \leq D$

Output: ZERO iff f is identically zero

1 **for** *the least* $(T-1)\log_2 D$ *primes* p **do**

2 $\quad$ Use black box to compute $f_p = f \operatorname{rem}(x^p - 1)$

3 $\quad$ **if** $f_p \neq 0$ **then return NONZERO**

4 return ZERO

THEOREM 3.2. *Algorithm 2 works correctly as stated and uses at most*

$$O\left(\ell T \log D \cdot \mathsf{M}\left(T \log D \cdot (\log T + \log\log D)\right)\right)$$

field operations.

PROOF. See (Bläser et al., 2009, Theorem 14). $\square$

This provides all that we need to prove the main result of this section:

THEOREM 3.3. *Given* $q \geq T(T-1)D+1$, *any* $T, D \in \mathbb{N}$, *and a modular black box for unknown* T-sparse $f \in \mathbb{F}_q[x]$ *with* $\deg f \leq D$, *there is an algorithm that always produces the correct polynomial* f *and with high probability uses only* $O^\sim\left(\ell T^2 \log^2 D\right)$ *field operations.*

PROOF. Use Algorithms 1 and 2 with $\mu = 1/2$, looping as necessary until the verification step succeeds. With high probability, only a constant number of iterations will be necessary, and so the cost is as stated. $\square$

For the small field case, when $q \in O(T^2 D)$, the obvious approach would be to work in an extension E of size $O(\log T + \log D)$ over $\mathbb{F}_q$. Unfortunately, this would presumably increase the cost of each evaluation by a factor of $\log D$, potentially dominating our factor of T savings compared to the randomized version of Garg and Schost (2009) when the unknown polynomial has very few terms and extremely high degree.

In practice, it seems that a much smaller extension than this is sufficient in any case to make each $\gcd(e_j - e_i, q-1)$ small compared to $q-1$, but we do not yet know how to prove any tighter bound in the worst case.

4. ALGORITHMS FOR APPROXIMATE SPARSE INTERPOLATION

In this section we consider the problem of interpolating an approximate sparse polynomial $f \in \mathbb{C}[x]$ from evaluations on the unit circle. We will generally assume that f is t-sparse:

$$f = \sum_{1 \leq i \leq t} c_i x^{e_i} \text{ for } c_i \in \mathbb{C} \text{ and } e_1 < \cdots < e_t = d. \quad (4.1)$$

We require a notion of size for such polynomials, and define the coefficient 2-norm of $f = \sum_{0 \leq i \leq d} f_i x^i$ as

$$\|f\|_2 = \sqrt{\sum_{0 \leq i \leq d} |f_i|^2}.$$

The following identity relates the norm of evaluations on the unit circle and the norm of the coefficients. As in Section 2, for $f \in \mathbb{C}[x]$ is as in (4.1), we say that a prime p is a *good prime* for f if $p \nmid (e_i - e_j)$ for all $i \neq j$.

LEMMA 4.1. *Let* $f \in \mathbb{C}[x]$, p *a good prime for* f, *and* $\omega \in \mathbb{C}$ *a* pth *primitive root of unity. Then*

$$\|f\|_2^2 = \frac{1}{p} \sum_{0 \leq i < p} \left|f(\omega^i)\right|^2.$$

See Giesbrecht and Roche (2010, Theorem 2.9).

We can now formally define the approximate sparse univariate interpolation problem.

DEFINITION 4.2. *Let* $\epsilon > 0$ *and assume there exists an unknown* t-sparse $f \in \mathbb{C}[x]$ *of degree at most* D. *An* ϵ-*approximate black box for* f *takes an input* $\xi \in \mathbb{C}$ *and produces a* $\gamma \in \mathbb{C}$ *such that* $|\gamma - f(\xi)| \leq \epsilon |f(\xi)|$.

The *approximate sparse univariate interpolation problem* is then as follows: given $D, T \in \mathbb{N}$ and $\delta \geq \epsilon > 0$, and an ϵ-approximate black box for an unknown T-sparse polynomial $f \in \mathbb{C}[x]$ of degree at most D, find a T-sparse polynomial $g \in \mathbb{C}[x]$ such that $\|f - g\|_2 \leq \delta \|g\|_2$.

The following theorem shows that t-sparse polynomials are well-defined by good evaluations on the unit circle.

THEOREM 4.3. *Let* $\epsilon > 0$ *and* $f \in \mathbb{C}[x]$ *be a* t-sparse polynomial. *Suppose there exists a* t-sparse polynomial $g \in \mathbb{C}[x]$ *such that for a prime* p *which is good for* f *and* $f - g$, *and* pth *primitive root of unity* $\omega \in \mathbb{C}$, *we have*

$$|f(\omega^i) - g(\omega^i)| \leq \epsilon |f(\omega^i)| \quad \text{for } 0 \leq i < p.$$

Then $\|f - g\|_2 \leq \epsilon \|f\|_2$. *Moreover, if* $g_0 \in \mathbb{C}[x]$ *is formed from* g *by deleting all the terms not in the support of* f, *then* $\|f - g_0\|_2 \leq 2\epsilon \|f\|_2$.

PROOF. Summing over powers of ω we have

$$\sum_{0 \leq i < p} |f(\omega^i) - g(\omega^i)|^2 \leq \epsilon^2 \sum_{0 \leq i < p} |f(\omega^i)|^2.$$

Thus, since p is a good prime for both $f - g$ and f, and using Lemma 4.1, $p \cdot \|f - g\|_2^2 \leq \epsilon^2 \cdot p \cdot \|f\|_2^2$ and $\|f - g\|_2 \leq \epsilon \|f\|_2$.

Since $g - g_0$ has no support in common with f,

$$\|g - g_0\|_2 \leq \|f - g\|_2 \leq \epsilon \|f\|_2.$$

Thus

$$\|f - g_0\|_2 = \|f - g + (g - g_0)\|_2$$
$$\leq \|f - g\|_2 + \|g - g_0\|_2 \leq 2\epsilon \|f\|_2. \quad \square$$

In other words, any t-sparse polynomial whose values are very close to f must have the same support except possibly for some terms with very small coefficients.

4.1 Constructing an ϵ-approximate remainder black box

Assume that we have chosen a good prime p for a t-sparse $f \in \mathsf{F}[x]$. Our goal in this subsection is a simple algorithm and numerical analysis to accurately compute $f \operatorname{rem} x^p - 1$.

Assume that $f \operatorname{rem} x^p - 1 = \sum_{0 \leq i < p} b_i x^i$ exactly. For a primitive pth root of unity $\omega \in \mathbb{C}$, let $V(\omega) \in \mathbb{C}^{p \times p}$ be the Vandermonde matrix built from the points $1, \omega, \ldots, \omega^{p-1}$. Recall that $V(\omega) \cdot (b_0, \ldots, b_{p-1})^T = (f(\omega^0), \ldots, f(\omega^{p-1}))^T$ and $V(\omega^{-1}) = p \cdot V(\omega)^{-1}$. Matrix vector product by such Vandermonde matrices is computed very quickly and in a numerically stable manner by the Fast Fourier Transform (FFT).

Algorithm 3: Approximate Remainder

Input: An ϵ-approximate black box for the unknown t-sparse $f \in \mathbb{C}[x]$, and $p \in \mathbb{N}$, a good prime for f

Output: $h \in \mathbb{C}[x]$ such that
$$\|(f \text{ rem } x^p - 1) - h\|_2 \le \epsilon \|f\|_2.$$

1 $w \leftarrow (f(\omega^0), \ldots, f(\omega^{p-1})) \in \mathbb{C}^p$ computed using the ϵ-approximate black box for f

2 $u \leftarrow (1/p) \cdot V(\omega^{-1})w \in \mathbb{C}^p$ using the FFT algorithm

3 **return** $h = \sum_{0 \le i < p} u_i x^i \in \mathbb{C}[x]$

THEOREM 4.4. *Algorithm 3 works as stated, and produces an h such that $\|(f \text{ rem } x^p - 1) - h\|_2 \le \epsilon \|f\|_2$. It requires $O(p \log p)$ floating point operations and p evaluations of the black box.*

PROOF. Because f and $f \text{ rem } x^p - 1$ have exactly the same coefficients (p is a good prime for f), they have exactly the same norm. The FFT in Step 2 is accomplished in $O(p \log p)$ floating point operations. This algorithm is numerically stable since $(1/\sqrt{p}) \cdot V(\omega^{-1})$ is unitary. That is, assume $v = (f(\omega_0), \ldots, f(\omega^{p-1})) \in \mathbb{C}^p$ is the vector of *exact* evaluations of f, so $\|v - w\|_2 \le \epsilon \|v\|_2$ by the black box specification. Then, using the fact that $\|v\|_2 = \sqrt{p} \|f\|_2$,

$$\|(f \text{ rem } x^{p-1}) - h\|_2 = \left\| \frac{1}{p} V(\omega^{-1})v - \frac{1}{p} V(\omega^{-1})w \right\|_2$$
$$= \frac{1}{\sqrt{p}} \left\| \frac{1}{\sqrt{p}} V(\omega^{-1}) \cdot (v - w) \right\|_2 = \frac{1}{\sqrt{p}} \|v - w\|_2,$$

which is at most $(\epsilon/\sqrt{p}) \|v\|_2 = \epsilon \|f\|_2$. $\square$

4.2 Creating ϵ-diversity

First, we extend the notion of polynomial diversity to the approximate case.

DEFINITION 4.5. *Let $f \in \mathbb{C}[x]$ be a t-sparse polynomial as in (4.1) and $\delta \ge \epsilon > 0$ such that $|c_i| \ge \delta \|f\|_2$ for $1 \le i \le t$. The polynomial f is said to be ϵ-diverse if and only if every pair of distinct coefficients is at least $\epsilon \|f\|_2$ apart. That is, for every $1 \le i < j \le t$, $|c_i - c_j| \ge \epsilon \|f\|_2$.*

Intuitively, if $(\epsilon/2)$ corresponds to the machine precision, this means that an algorithm can reliably distinguish the coefficients of a ϵ-diverse polynomial. We now show how to choose a random α to guarantee ϵ-diversity.

THEOREM 4.6. *Let $\delta \ge \epsilon > 0$ and $f \in \mathbb{C}[x]$ a t-sparse polynomial whose non-zero coefficients are of magnitude at least $\delta \|f\|_2$. If s is a prime satisfying $s > 12$ and*

$$t(t-1) \le s \le 3.1 \frac{\delta}{\epsilon},$$

then for $\zeta = e^{2\pi i/s}$ an s-PRU and $k \in \mathbb{N}$ chosen uniformly at random from $\{0, 1, \ldots, s-1\}$, $f(\zeta^k x)$ is ϵ-diverse with probability at least $\frac{1}{2}$.

PROOF. For each $1 \le i \le t$, write the coefficient c_i in polar notation to base ζ as $c_i = r_i \zeta^{\theta_i}$, where each r_i and θ_i are nonnegative real numbers and $r_i \ge \delta \|f\|_2$.

Suppose $f(\zeta^k x)$ is *not* ϵ-diverse. Then there exist indices $1 \le i < j \le t$ such that

$$\left| r_i \zeta^{\theta_i} \zeta^{ke_i} - r_j \zeta^{\theta_j} \zeta^{ke_j} \right| \le \epsilon \|f\|_2.$$

Algorithm 4: Adaptive diversification

Input: ϵ-approximate black box for f, known good prime p, known sparsity t

Output: ζ, k such that $f(\zeta^k x)$ is ϵ-diverse, or FAIL

1 $s \leftarrow 1, \quad \delta \leftarrow \infty, \quad f_p \leftarrow 0$

2 **while** $s \le t^2$ and $\#\{\text{coeffs } c \text{ of } f_s \text{ s.t. } |c| \ge \delta\} < t$ **do**

3 $\quad$ $s \leftarrow$ least prime $\ge 2s$

4 $\quad$ $\zeta \leftarrow \exp(2\pi i/s)$

5 $\quad$ $k \leftarrow$ random integer in $\{0, 1, \ldots, s-1\}$

6 $\quad$ Compute $f_s = f(\zeta^k x) \text{ rem } x^p - 1$

7 $\quad$ $\delta \leftarrow$ least number s.t. all coefficients of f_s at least δ in absolute value are pairwise ϵ-distinct

8 **if** $\delta > 2\epsilon$ **then return** FAIL

9 **else return** ζ^k

Because $\min(r_i, r_j) \ge \delta \|f\|_2$, the left hand side is at least $\delta \|f\|_2 \cdot |\zeta^{\theta_i + ke_i} - \zeta^{\theta_j + ke_j}|$. Dividing out $\zeta^{\theta_j + ke_i}$, we get

$$\left| \zeta^{\theta_i - \theta_j} - \zeta^{k(e_j - e_i)} \right| \le \frac{\epsilon}{\delta}.$$

By way of contradiction, assume that there exist distinct choices of k that satisfy the above inequality, say $k_1, k_2 \in \{0, \ldots, s-1\}$. Since $\zeta^{\theta_i - \theta_j}$ and $\zeta^{e_j - e_i}$ are a fixed powers of ζ not depending on the choice of k, this means

$$\left| \zeta^{k_1(e_j - e_i)} - \zeta^{k_2(e_j - e_i)} \right| \le 2 \frac{\epsilon}{\delta}.$$

Because s is prime, $e_i \ne e_j$, and we assumed $k_1 \ne k_2$, the left hand side is at least $|\zeta - 1|$. Observe that $2\pi/s$, the distance on the unit circle from 1 to ζ, is a good approximation for this Euclidean distance when s is large. In particular, since $s > 12$,

$$\frac{|\zeta - 1|}{2\pi/s} > \frac{\sqrt{2}\left(\sqrt{3} - 1\right)/2}{\pi/6},$$

and therefore $|\zeta - 1| > 6\sqrt{2}(\sqrt{3} - 1)/s > 6.2/s$, which from the statement of the theorem is at least $2\epsilon/\delta$. This is a contradiction, and therefore the assumption was false; namely, there is at most one choice of k such that the i'th and j'th coefficients collide.

Then, since there are exactly $\binom{t}{2}$ distinct pairs of coefficients, and $s \ge t(t-1) = 2\binom{t}{2}$, $f(\zeta^k x)$ is diverse for at least half of the choices for k. $\square$

We note that the diversification which maps the polynomial $f(x)$ to $f(\zeta^k x)$ and back is numerically stable since ζ is on the unit circle.

In practice, the previous theorem will be far too pessimistic. We therefore propose the method of Algorithm 4 to adaptively choose s, δ, and ζ^k simultaneously, given a good prime p.

Suppose there exists a threshold $S \in \mathbb{N}$ such that for all primes $s > S$, a random sth primitive root of unity ζ^k makes $f(\zeta^k x)$ ϵ-diverse with high probability. Then Algorithm 4 will return a root of unity whose order is within a constant factor of S, with high probability. From the previous theorem, if such an S exists it must be $O(t^2)$, and hence the number of iterations required is $O(\log t)$.

Otherwise, if no such S exists, then we cannot diversify the polynomial. Roughly speaking, this corresponds to the situation that f has too many coefficients with absolute value close to the machine precision. In this case, we can simply use the algorithm of Garg and Schost (2009) numerically, achieving the same stability but using a greater number of evaluations and bit operations. It is possible to establish an adaptive hybrid between our algorithm and that of Garg and Schost (2009) by making f as ϵ-diverse *as possible* given our precision. The non-zero coefficients of f are clustered into groups which are not ϵ-diverse (i.e., are within $\epsilon \|f\|_2$ of each other). We can use the symmetric polynomial reconstruction of Garg and Schost (2009) to extract the exponents within each group.

4.3 Approximate interpolation algorithm

We now plug our ϵ-approximate remainder black box, and method for making f ϵ-diverse, into our generic Algorithm 1 to complete our algorithm for approximate interpolation.

THEOREM 4.7. *Let $\delta > 0$, $f \in \mathbb{C}[x]$ with degree at most D and sparsity at most T, and suppose all nonzero coefficients c of f satisfy $|c| > \delta \|f\|_2$. Suppose also that $\epsilon < 1.5\delta/(T(T-1))$, and we are given an ϵ-approximate black box for f. Then, for any $\mu < 1/2$ we have an algorithm to produce a $g \in \mathbb{C}[x]$ satisfying the conditions of Theorem 4.3. The algorithm succeeds with probability at least $1-\mu$ and uses $O^\sim(T^2 \cdot \log(1/\mu) \cdot \log^2 D)$ black box evaluations and floating point operations.*

PROOF. Construct an approximate remainder black box for f using Algorithm 3. Then run Algorithm 1 using this black box as input. On step 8 of Algorithm 1, run Algorithm 4, iterating steps 5–7 $\lceil \log_2(3/\mu) \rceil$ times on each iteration through the while loop to choose a diversifying $\alpha = \zeta^k$ with probability at least $1 - \mu/3$.

The cost comes from Theorems 2.2 and 4.4 along with the previous discussion and Theorem 4.6. □

Observe that the resulting algorithm is Monte Carlo, but could be made Las Vegas by combining the finite fields zero testing algorithm discussed in Section 3.2 with the guarantees of Theorem 4.3.

5. IMPLEMENTATION RESULTS

We implemented our algorithms in C++ using GMP (gmplib.org) and NTL (www.shoup.net/ntl) for the exponent arithmetic.

In our timing results, "Determ" refers to the deterministic algorithm as stated in Garg and Schost (2009) and "Alg 1" is the algorithm we have presented here over finite fields, without the verification step. We also developed and implemented a more adaptive, Monte Carlo version of these algorithms, as briefly described at the end of Section 2. The basic idea is to sample modulo $x^p - 1$ for just one prime $p \in \Theta(t^2 \log d)$ that is good with high probability, then to search for much smaller good primes. This good prime search starts at a lower bound of order $\Theta(t^2)$ based on the birthday problem, and finds consecutively larger primes until enough primes have been found to recover the symmetric polynomial in the exponents (for Garg & Schost) or just the exponents (for our method). The corresponding improved algorithms are referred to as "G&S MC" and "Alg 1++" below, respectively.

Table 2 summarizes some timings for these four algorithms over the finite field $\mathbb{Z}/65521\mathbb{Z}$. This modulus was chosen for convenience of implementation, although of course other

$\log_2 D$	T	Determ	G&S MC	Alg 1	Alg 1++
12	10	3.77	0.03	0.03	0.01
16	10	46.82	0.11	0.11	0.08
20	10	—	0.38	0.52	0.33
24	10	—	0.68	0.85	0.38
28	10	—	1.12	2.35	0.53
32	10	—	1.58	2.11	0.66
12	20	37.32	0.15	0.02	0.02
16	20	—	0.91	0.52	0.28
20	20	—	3.5	3.37	1.94
24	20	—	6.59	5.94	2.99
28	20	—	10.91	10.22	3.71
32	20	—	14.83	16.22	4.24
12	30	—	0.31	0.01	0.01
16	30	—	3.66	1.06	0.65
20	30	—	10.95	6.7	3.56
24	30	—	25.04	12.42	9.32
28	30	—	38.86	19.36	13.8
32	30	—	62.53	68.1	14.66
12	40	—	0.58	0.01	0.02
16	40	—	8.98	3.7	1.54
20	40	—	30.1	12.9	8.42
24	40	—	67.97	38.34	16.57
28	40	—	—	73.69	36.24
32	40	—	—	—	40.79

Table 2: Finite Fields Algorithm Timings

Noise	Mean Error	Median Error	Max Error
0	4.440 e−16	4.402 e−16	8.003 e−16
$\pm 10^{-12}$	1.113 e−14	1.119 e−14	1.179 e−14
$\pm 10^{-9}$	1.149 e−11	1.191 e−11	1.248 e−11
$\pm 10^{-6}$	1.145 e−8	1.149 e−8	1.281 e−8

Table 3: Approximate Algorithm Stability

algorithms might be more efficient over this particularly small finite field. The timings are given in seconds of CPU time on a 64-bit AMD Phenom II 3.2GHz processor with 512K/2M/6M cache. Note that the numbers listed reflect the *base-2 logarithm* of the degree bound and the sparsity bound for the randomly-generated test cases.

The timings are mostly as expected based on our complexity estimates, and also confirm our suspicion that primes of size $O(t^2)$ are sufficient to avoid exponent collisions. It is satisfying but not particularly surprising to see that our "Alg 1++" is the fastest on all inputs, as all the algorithms have a similar basic structure. Had we compared to the Ben-Or and Tiwari or Zippel's method, they would probably be more efficient for small sizes, but would be easily beaten for large degree and arbitrary finite fields as their costs are super-polynomial.

The implementation of the approximate algorithm uses machine `double` precision (IEEE), the C++ standard template library `complex<double>` type, and the popular FFTW package (www.fftw.org) for FFTs. Our stability results are summarized in Table 3. Each test case was randomly generated with degree at most 2^{20} and at most 50 nonzero terms. We varied the precision as specified in the table and ran 10 tests in each range. Observe that the error in our results was often *less* than the ϵ error on the evaluations themselves.

Both implementations are freely available for download at http://www.cs.uwaterloo.ca/~droche/diverse/.

6. CONCLUSIONS

We have shown how to use the idea of diversification to improve the complexity of sparse interpolation over large finite fields by a factor of t, the number of nonzero terms. We achieve a similar complexity for approximate sparse interpolation, and provide the first provably numerically stable algorithm for this purpose. Our experiments confirm these theoretical results.

Numerous open problems remain. A primary shortcoming of our algorithms is the quadratic dependence on t, as opposed to linear in the case of dense interpolation or even sparse interpolation in smaller or chosen finite fields using the Ben-Or and Tiwari algorithm. It seems that reducing this quadratic dependency will not be possible without a different approach, because of the birthday problem embedded in the diversification step. In the approximate case, a provably numerically stable algorithm for sparse interpolation with only $O(t)$ probes is still an open question. And, while general backward error stability is not possible in the high degree case, it would be interesting in the case of low degree and many variables.

Acknowledgements

We thank Reinhold Burger and Éric Schost for pointing out an error in an earlier draft. The comments and suggestions of the anonymous referees were also very helpful, in particular regarding connections to previous results and the proof of Theorem 3.1.

References

M. Avendaño, T. Krick, and A. Pacetti. Newton-Hensel interpolation lifting. *Found. Comput. Math.*, 6(1):81–120, 2006.

M. Ben-Or and P. Tiwari. A deterministic algorithm for sparse multivariate polynomial interpolation. In *Proc. STOC'88*, pages 301–309, New York, NY, USA, 1988. ACM.

M. Bläser, M. Hardt, R. J. Lipton, and N. K. Vishnoi. Deterministically testing sparse polynomial identities of unbounded degree. *Information Processing Letters*, 109(3):187 – 192, 2009.

J. Canny, E. Kaltofen, and L. Yagati. Solving systems of nonlinear polynomial equations faster. In *Proc. ISSAC'89*, pages 121–128, 1989.

M. Clausen, A. Dress, J. Grabmeier, and M. Karpinski. On zero-testing and interpolation of k-sparse multivariate polynomials over finite fields. *Theor. Comput. Sci.*, 84(2):151 – 164, 1991.

A. Cuyt and W. Lee. A new algorithm for sparse interpolation of multivariate polynomials. *Theoretical Computer Science*, 409(2):180–185, 2008.

A. Díaz and E. Kaltofen. On computing greatest common divisors with polynomials given by black boxes for their evaluations. In *Proc. ISSAC'95*, pages 232–239, 1995.

A. Díaz and E. Kaltofen. FOXBOX: a system for manipulating symbolic objects in black box representation. In *Proc. ISSAC'98*, pages 30–37, 1998.

S. Garg and É. Schost. Interpolation of polynomials given by straight-line programs. *Theoretical Computer Science*, 410(27-29):2659 – 2662, 2009.

J. von zur Gathen and J. Gerhard. *Modern Computer Algebra*. Cambridge University Press, Cambridge, second edition, 2003.

M. Giesbrecht and D. S. Roche. Detecting lacunary perfect powers and computing their roots. *Journal of Symbolic Computation*, 2010. To appear; preprint at arXiv:1901.1848.

M. Giesbrecht, G. Labahn, and W. Lee. Symbolic-numeric sparse interpolation of multivariate polynomials. *Journal of Symbolic Computation*, 44(8):943 – 959, 2009.

D. Y. Grigoriev, M. Karpinski, and M. F. Singer. Fast parallel algorithms for sparse multivariate polynomial interpolation over finite fields. *SIAM J. Comput.*, 19(6):1059–1063, 1990.

W. Hoeffding. Probability inequalities for sums of bounded random variables. *J. Amer. Statist. Assoc.*, 58:13–30, 1963.

S. Javadi and M. Monagan. Parallel sparse polynomial interpolation over finite fields. In *Proc. Intl. Wkshp. Parallel and Symbolic Computation (PASCO)*, pages 160–168, 2010.

S. M. M. Javadi and M. Monagan. A sparse modular GCD algorithm for polynomials over algebraic function fields. In *Proc. ISSAC'07*, pages 187–194, 2007.

S. M. M. Javadi and M. Monagan. On factorization of multivariate polynomials over algebraic number and function fields. In *Proc. ISSAC'09*, pages 199–206, 2009.

E. Kaltofen and W. Lee. Early termination in sparse interpolation algorithms. *J. Symbolic Comput.*, 36(3-4):365–400, 2003.

E. Kaltofen and B. M. Trager. Computing with polynomials given by black boxes for their evaluations: Greatest common divisors, factorization, separation of numerators and denominators. *Journal of Symbolic Computation*, 9:301–320, 1990.

E. Kaltofen and L. Yagati. Improved sparse multivariate polynomial interpolation algorithms. In *Proc. ISSAC'88*, pages 467–474, 1989.

E. Kaltofen and Z. Yang. On exact and approximate interpolation of sparse rational functions. In *Proc. ISSAC'07*, pages 11–18, 2007.

E. Kaltofen, Y. N. Lakshman, and J.-M. Wiley. Modular rational sparse multivariate polynomial interpolation. In *Proc. ISSAC'90*, pages 135–139, New York, NY, USA, 1990. ACM.

E. Kaltofen, Z. Yang, and L. Zhi. On probabilistic analysis of randomization in hybrid symbolic-numeric algorithms. In *Proc. Workshop on Symbolic-Numeric Computation (SNC 2007)*, pages 203–210, 2007.

E. Kaltofen, J. P. May, Z. Yang, and L. Zhi. Approximate factorization of multivariate polynomials using singular value decomposition. *Journal of Symbolic Computation*, 2008.

E. L. Kaltofen. Fifteen years after DSC and WLSS2: What parallel computations I do today. In *Proc. Intl. Wkshp. Parallel and Symbolic Computation (PASCO)*, pages 10–17, 2010.

Y. Mansour. Randomized approximation and interpolation of sparse polynomials. *SIAM J. Comput.*, 24(2):357–368, 1995.

J. M. Pollard. Monte Carlo methods for index computation (mod p). *Math. Comp.*, 32(143):918–924, 1978.

J. B. Rosser and L. Schoenfeld. Approximate formulas for some functions of prime numbers. *Ill. J. Math.*, 6:64–94, 1962.

N. Saxena. Progress on polynomial identity testing. *Bull. EATCS*, 99:49–79, 2009.

A. J. Sommese, J. Verschelde, and C. W. Wampler. Numerical decomposition of the solution sets of polynomial systems into irreducible components. *SIAM Journal on Numerical Analysis*, 38(6):2022–2046, 2001.

A. J. Sommese, J. Verschelde, and C. W. Wampler. Numerical factorization of multivariate complex polynomials. *Theoretical Computer Science*, pages 651–669, 2004.

H. J. Stetter. *Numerical Polynomial Algebra*. SIAM, 2004.

R. Zippel. Interpolating polynomials from their values. *Journal of Symbolic Computation*, 9(3):375 – 403, 1990.

Deciding Reachability of the Infimum
of a Multivariate Polynomial [*]

Aurélien Greuet
Laboratoire de Mathématiques (LMV-UMR8100)
Université de Versailles-Saint-Quentin
45 avenue des États-unis
78035 Versailles Cedex, France
greuet@math.uvsq.fr

Mohab Safey El Din
UPMC, Université Paris 06
INRIA, Paris Rocquencourt Center
SALSA Project, LIP6/CNRS
UMR 7606, France
Mohab.Safey@lip6.fr

ABSTRACT

Let $f \in \mathbb{Q}[X_1, \ldots, X_n]$ be of degree D. Algorithms for solving the unconstrained global optimization problem $f^\star = \inf_{\mathbf{x} \in \mathbb{R}^n} f(\mathbf{x})$ are of first importance since this problem appears frequently in numerous applications in engineering sciences. This can be tackled by either designing appropriate quantifier elimination algorithms or by certifying lower bounds on $f^\star$ by means of sums of squares decompositions but there is no efficient algorithm for deciding if $f^\star$ is a minimum.

This paper is dedicated to this important problem. We design a probabilistic algorithm that decides, for a given f and the corresponding $f^\star$, if $f^\star$ is reached over $\mathbb{R}^n$ and computes a point $\mathbf{x}^\star \in \mathbb{R}^n$ such that $f(\mathbf{x}^\star) = f^\star$ if such a point exists. This algorithm makes use of algebraic elimination algorithms and real root isolation. If L is the length of a straight-line program evaluating f, algebraic elimination steps run in $O\left(\log(D-1)n^6(nL + n^4)\mathcal{U}\left((D-1)^{n+1}\right)^3\right)$ arithmetic operations in $\mathbb{Q}$ where $D = \deg(f)$ and $\mathcal{U}(x) = x\left(\log(x)\right)^2 \log\log(x)$. Experiments show its practical efficiency.

Categories and Subject Descriptors

I.1.2 [**Computing Methodologies**]: Symbolic and Algebraic Manipulation—*Algorithms*; G.1.6 [**Mathematics of computing**]: Numerical Analysis—*Optimization*

General Terms

Theory, algorithms

Keywords

Global optimization, polynomials

[*]Mohab Safey El Din and Aurélien Greuet are supported by the EXACTA grant of the National Science Foundation of China (NSFC 60911130369) and the French National Research Agency (ANR-09-BLAN-0371-01).

1. INTRODUCTION

Motivations and problem statement. Consider the global optimization problem $f^\star = \inf_{\mathbf{x} \in \mathbb{R}^n} f(\mathbf{x})$ with $f \in \mathbb{Q}[X_1, \ldots, X_n]$. Solving these problems is of first importance since they occur frequently in engineering sciences (e.g. in systems theory or system identification [15]) or in the proof of some theorems (see [10, 18]). However, this infimum can be unreached: consider the polynomial $f(x, y) = (xy - 1)^2 + x^2$. As a sum of squares, $f \geq 0$. But f has only one critical value, $f(0, 0) = 1$, whereas $f(1/\ell, \ell)$ tends to 0 when ℓ tends to ∞. Thus, $f^\star = 0$, which is not a value taken by f.

Lower bounds on $f^\star$ can be computed via sums of squares decompositions which provide algebraic certificates of positivity [17, 22]. Following [21], this solving process can be improved when it is already known that $f^\star$ is a minimum but, in this framework, there is no given algorithm to test if $f^\star$ is a minimum. Global optimization problems can also be tackled via quantifier elimination (see [7, Chap. 14] or a dedicated algorithm in [25]). The algorithm given in [7, Chap. 14] allows to decide if $f^\star$ is a minimum within a complexity $D^{O(n)}$ but the complexity constant in the exponent is so large that it can't be used in practice. The algorithm given in [25] is much more efficient in practice but does not decide if $f^\star$ is a minimum. Our goal is to tackle this important problem.

To decide if $f^\star$ is a minimum, it is sufficient to decide if $f - f^\star = 0$ has real solutions. Recall that $f^\star$ is a real algebraic number whose degree may be large. Thus, one would prefer to decide if the real algebraic set defined by $\frac{\partial f}{\partial X_1} = \cdots = \frac{\partial f}{\partial X_n} = 0$ contains a point $\mathbf{x}$ such that $f(\mathbf{x}) = f^\star$. Difficulties arise when the aforementioned system generates an ideal which is not equidimensional and/or not radical and/or defines a non-smooth real algebraic set. This task could be tackled by using algorithms in [7, Chap. 14] running in time $D^{O(n)}$ (where $D = \deg(f)$) but, again, the complexity constants (in the exponent) are so large that these algorithms can't be used in practice. Other algorithms based on the so-called critical point method whose complexities are not known are described in [1, 27]. Another alternative consists in using Collins'Cylindrical Algebraic Decomposition [8].

We provide a probabilistic algorithm that decides if $f^\star$ is a minimum. When $f^\star$ is reached, it computes also a minimizer. It runs within $\widetilde{O}\left(n^6(nL + n^4)\mathcal{U}\left((D-1)^{n+1}\right)^3\right)$ arithmetic operations in $\mathbb{Q}$, where $D = \deg(f)$ and $\mathcal{U}(x) = x\left(\log(x)\right)^2 \log\log(x)$. Experiments show that it is practically more efficient of several orders of magnitude than other algorithms that can be used for a similar task.

Related works. Using computer algebra techniques to solve global optimization problems is an emerging trend. These problems are tackled using sums-of-squares decomposition to produce certificates of positivity [17, 22, 21, 14, 28] or quantifier elimination [7, 25]. The objects used in this paper are similar to those used in [14] where the existence of new algebraic certificates based on sums of squares are proved. Such objects are also used in [25] to design an efficient algorithm computing the global infimum of a multivariate polynomial over the reals.

Polar varieties are introduced in computer algebra in [2] to grab sample points in smooth equidimensional real algebraic sets (see also [3, 4, 26, 27, 5] and references therein). The interplay between properness properties of polar varieties to answer algorithmic questions in effective real algebraic geometry is introduced in [26]. An algorithm computing real regular points in singular real hypersurfaces is given in [6]. An algorithm for computing real points in each connected component of the real counterpart of a singular hypersurface is given in [24].

The paper is organized as follows. The algorithm is described in Section 2. Then in Section 3 we present the practical performances. A complexity analysis is done in Section 4. Finally, we give the correctness proof in Section 5.

2. DESCRIPTION OF THE ALGORITHM

We present now the algorithm. It takes as input a polynomial $f \in \mathbb{Q}[\mathbf{X}]$ bounded from below, P a univariate polynomial in $\mathbb{Q}[T]$ and I a real interval such that $f^\star = \inf_{\mathbf{x} \in \mathbb{R}^n} f(\mathbf{x})$ is the *unique root of P in I*. Such a polynomial can be obtained with the algorithm given in [25].

Given a matrix $\mathbf{A} \in GL_n(\mathbb{Q})$ and a polynomial f, we denote by $f^{\mathbf{A}}$ the polynomial $f^{\mathbf{A}}(\mathbf{X}) = f(\mathbf{A}\mathbf{X})$.

Our algorithm is probabilistic: the correctness of the output depends on the choice of a random matrix $\mathbf{A}$. We prove in Section 5 that the bad choices of $\mathbf{A}$ (that is the choices of $\mathbf{A}$ such that the algorithm fails or returns a wrong result) are contained in a strict Zariski-closed subset of $GL_n(\mathbb{Q})$. Practically, this means that for a generic choice of $\mathbf{A}$, the algorithm returns a correct result.

To describe the algorithm, we need to introduce some classical subroutines in polynomial system solving solvers. A representation of an algebraic variety V means a finite set of polynomials generating V or a geometric resolution of V (see [13, 20]).

- DescribeCurve: takes as input a finite set of polynomials $\mathbf{F} \subset \mathbb{Q}[\mathbf{X}]$ and a polynomial $g \in \mathbb{Q}[\mathbf{X}]$ and returns a representation of $\overline{V(\mathbf{F}) - V(g)}^Z$ if its dimension is at most 1, else it returns an error.
- Intersect: takes as input a representation of a variety V whose dimension is at most one and polynomials $g_1, \ldots, g_s$ and returns a representation of $V \cap V(g_1, \ldots, g_s)$.
- RealSolve: takes as input a rational parametrization of a 0-dimensional system V, f, the univariate polynomial P and an interval I isolating one real root $f^\star$ of P; it decides if there exists a real point $\mathbf{x} \in V$ such that $f(\mathbf{x}) = f^\star$ by returning a polynomial R for which $\mathbf{x}$ is a root and a box isolating $\mathbf{x}$ if such a point exists, else it returns false.

Note that DescribeCurve and Intersect can be implemented

using any algebraic elimination technique (e.g. Gröbner basis, triangular sets, geometric resolution). The routine RealSolve relies exclusively on univariate evaluation and real root isolation.

_____ IsReached _____
Input: $f \in \mathbb{Q}[X_1, \ldots, X_n]$ bounded below. A real interval I and $P \in \mathbb{Q}(T)$ encoding $f^\star = \inf_{\mathbf{x} \in \mathbb{R}^n} f(\mathbf{x})$.
Output: a boolean which equals false if $f^\star$ is not reached, a list L containing a polynomial and an interval encoding a point $\mathbf{x}$ such that $f(\mathbf{x}) = f^\star$ if $f^\star$ is reached.

1. choose randomly $\mathbf{A} \in GL_n(\mathbb{Q})$.
2. For $1 \leq i \leq n - 1$ do

   a. $\mathbf{C}_{n-i+1} \leftarrow \mathsf{DescribeCurve}([\mathbf{X}_{\leq i-1}, \frac{\partial f^{\mathbf{A}}}{\partial X_{i+1}}, \ldots, \frac{\partial f^{\mathbf{A}}}{\partial X_n}], \frac{\partial f^{\mathbf{A}}}{\partial X_1})$

   b. $\mathbf{F}_{n-i+1} \leftarrow \mathsf{Intersect}(\mathbf{C}_{n-i+1}, \frac{\partial f^{\mathbf{A}}}{\partial X_1}, \ldots, \frac{\partial f^{\mathbf{A}}}{\partial X_i})$;

   c. If $L \leftarrow \mathsf{RealSolve}(\mathbf{F}_{n-i+1}, f, P, I)$ is not empty return L.

3. a. $\mathbf{F}_1 \leftarrow [\mathbf{X}_{\leq n-1}, \frac{\partial f^{\mathbf{A}}}{\partial X_1}, \ldots, \frac{\partial f^{\mathbf{A}}}{\partial X_n}]$;

   b. If $L \rightarrow \mathsf{RealSolve}(\mathbf{F}_1, f, P, I)$ is not empty return L.

4. return false.

---

3. PRACTICAL PERFORMANCES

We have implemented our algorithm using Gröbner basis engine FGb implemented in C by J.-C. Faugère [11]. We also used some results in [27] for computing the set of non-properness of a polynomial map to check properness assumptions required to apply Theorem 1.

Examples named **K1, K2, K3, K4, Vor1,** and **Vor2** are coming from applications and extracted from [18, 10]. We also consider a polynomial available at
http://www.expmath.org/extra/9.2/sottile/SectIII.7.html.

Computations have been performed on a PC under Scientific Linux OS release 5.5 on Intel(R) Xeon(R) CPUs E5420 at 2.50 GHz with 20.55G RAM. All these examples are global optimization problems arising in computer proofs of Theorems in computational geometry or related areas. In this context, exhibiting a minimizer is sometimes meaningful for the geometric phenomenon under study. None of these examples can be solved using the implementations QEPCAD, and REDLOG of Collins' Cylindrical Algebraic Decomposition within one week of computation, even when providing to CAD solvers the fact that $f^\star$ is an infimum. Also, our implementations of [1, 27] fail on these problems in less than one week.

The columns **D**, **n** and ♯**Terms** contain respectively the degree, the number of variables and the number of terms of the considered polynomial. As one can see, the implementation of our algorithm outperforms other implementations since one can solve previously unreachable problems.

	D	**n**	♯Terms	Time
Sot1	24	4	677	3 h.
Vor1	6	8	63	< 1 min.
Vor2	5	18	253	5 h.
K1	4	8	77	< 1 min.
K2	4	8	53	< 1 min.
K3	4	8	67	< 1 min.
K4	4	8	45	< 1 min.

4. COMPLEXITY RESULTS

Let $\mathbf{F} = (f_1, \ldots, f_s)$ and g in $\mathbb{Q}[X_1, \ldots, X_n]$ of degree bounded by d given by a straight-line program of size $\leq L$.

We denote by δ_i^a the algebraic degree of $V(f_1, \ldots, f_i)$, δ^a the maximum of the previous δ_i^a and $\mathcal{U}(x) = x(\log x)^2 \log \log x$ (see [20]). We only estimate the complexities of steps relying on algebraic elimination algorithms (DescribeCurve and Intersect) using the following subroutines:

- GeometricSolve ([20]): given $\mathbf{F}$ and g as above, returns an equidimensional decomposition of $\overline{V(\mathbf{F}) \setminus V(g)}^{\mathcal{Z}}$, encoded by a set of irreducible lifting fibers, in time

$$O\left(s \log(d) n^4 (nL + n^4) \mathcal{U}(d\delta^a)^3\right).$$

- LiftCurve ([20]): given an irreducible lifting fiber F of the above output, returns a rational parametrization of the lifted curve of F in time

$$O\left(s \log(d) n^4 (nL + n^4) \mathcal{U}(d\delta^a)^2\right).$$

- OneDimensionalIntersect ([13] removing the Clean step): if $\langle \mathbf{F} \rangle$ is 1-dimensional, $\mathfrak{I}$ a geometric resolution of $\langle \mathbf{F} \rangle$ and a polynomial g, it returns a rational parametrization of $V(\mathfrak{I} + g)$ in time $O\left(n(L + n^2)\mathcal{U}(\delta^a)\mathcal{U}(d\delta^a)\right)$.

We deduce the complexity of the algebraic steps of our algorithm:

PROPOSITION 1. *Let D be the degree of a polynomial $f \in \mathbb{Q}[X_1, \ldots, X_n]$ bounded below. There exists a probabilistic algorithm deciding whether the infimum of f is reached over the reals or not with a complexity within*

$$O\left(\log(D-1) n^6 (nL + n^4) \mathcal{U}\big((D-1)^{n+1}\big)^3\right)$$

arithmetic operations in $\mathbb{Q}$.

PROOF. We use LiftCurve with the output of GeometricSolve to obtain our DescribeCurve. Then we compute n geometric resolutions for n polynomials of degree at most $D-1$ using OneDimensionalIntersect as our Intersect routine. Using the Refined Bézout Theorem (see Theorem 12.3 and Example 12.3.1 page 223 in [12]) we can bound δ^a by $(D-1)^n$. Replacing s with n and δ^a with $(D-1)^n$ in the above complexity results and remarking that the costs of other steps are negligible ends the proof. $\square$

5. PROOF OF CORRECTNESS

Notations and basic definitions. For any set Y in a euclidean space, we denote by $\overline{Y}$ the closure of Y for the euclidean topology and by $\overline{Y}^{\mathcal{Z}}$ the Zariski closure of Y. Without more precision, a closed set means a closed set for the euclidean topology.

For $\mathbf{A} \in \mathrm{GL}_n(\mathbb{R})$ and $g \in \mathbb{Q}[X_1, \ldots, X_n]$, we write $g^{\mathbf{A}}(X) = g(\mathbf{A}X)$. Similarly, if $\mathbf{G} = (g_1, \ldots, g_s)$ is a finite subset of $\mathbb{Q}[X_1, \ldots, X_n]$, $\mathbf{G}^{\mathbf{A}} = (g_1^{\mathbf{A}}, \ldots, g_s^{\mathbf{A}})$. If I is an ideal of $\mathbb{Q}[X_1, \ldots, X_n]$, $I^{\mathbf{A}}$ is the ideal $\{g^{\mathbf{A}} \mid g \in I\}$.

We will consider objects, called *polar varieties* which are close to the ones already used in [2, 26] in the framework of non-singular algebraic sets. These objects are related to some projections. For $1 \le i \le n-1$, we will denote by Π_i the canonical projection $(x_1, \ldots, x_n) \to (x_1, \ldots, x_i)$ and by φ_i the canonical projection $(x_1, \ldots, x_n) \to x_i$.

For $g \in \mathbb{Q}[X_1, \ldots, X_n]$, $1 \le i \le n$ and $\mathbf{A} \in \mathrm{GL}_n(\mathbb{Q})$, we define

- $\mathbf{0}_{i-1}$ denotes the hyperplane in $\mathbb{C}^n$ defined by $X_1 = \cdots = X_{i-1} = 0$; by convention $\mathbf{0}_0$ denotes $\mathbb{C}^n$;
- $W_{n-i+1}^{\mathbf{A},g} = V\left(g^{\mathbf{A}}, \frac{\partial g^{\mathbf{A}}}{\partial X_{i+1}}, \ldots, \frac{\partial g^{\mathbf{A}}}{\partial X_n}\right)$;

- $\mathfrak{C}_{n-i+1}^{\mathbf{A},g} = \overline{\left(V\left(\frac{\partial g^{\mathbf{A}}}{\partial X_{i+1}}, \ldots, \frac{\partial g^{\mathbf{A}}}{\partial X_n}\right) \cap \mathbf{0}_{i-1}\right) \setminus V\left(\frac{\partial g^{\mathbf{A}}}{\partial X_1}\right)}^{\mathcal{Z}}$;
- $\mathscr{F}_{n-i+1}^{\mathbf{A},g} = \mathfrak{C}_{n-i+1}^{\mathbf{A},g} \cap V\left(\frac{\partial g^{\mathbf{A}}}{\partial X_1}, \ldots, \frac{\partial g^{\mathbf{A}}}{\partial X_i}\right)$.

When $i = n$, $W_{n-i+1}^{\mathbf{A},g} = V(g^{\mathbf{A}})$ and $\mathfrak{C}_1^{\mathbf{A},g} = \mathbf{0}_{n-1}$ by convention. The superscript g will be omitted when there is no ambiguity.

We will also make use of the notion of properness of a polynomial map. Given a polynomial map $\varphi : Y \to Z$ where Y and Z are euclidean spaces, we will say that φ is proper at $z \in Z$ if there exists a closed ball $\overline{B} \subset Z$ containing z such that $\varphi^{-1}(\overline{B})$ is closed and bounded. The map φ will be said to be proper if it is proper at any point in Z.

For $i = 0$, we denote by $W_0^{\mathbf{A}}$ the algebraic set

$$W_0^{\mathbf{A}} = \overline{\mathbb{V}\left(\frac{\partial f^{\mathbf{A}}}{\partial X_2}, \ldots, \frac{\partial f^{\mathbf{A}}}{\partial X_n}\right) \setminus \mathbb{V}\left(\frac{\partial f^{\mathbf{A}}}{\partial X_1}\right)}^{\mathcal{Z}}.$$

For $1 \le i \le n-2$, we denote by $W_i^{\mathbf{A}}$ the algebraic set

$$W_i^{\mathbf{A}} = \overline{\mathbb{V}\left(X_1, \ldots, X_i, \frac{\partial f^{\mathbf{A}}}{\partial X_{i+2}}, \ldots, \frac{\partial f^{\mathbf{A}}}{\partial X_n}\right) \setminus \mathbb{V}\left(\frac{\partial f^{\mathbf{A}}}{\partial X_{i+1}}\right)}^{\mathcal{Z}}.$$

At last for $i = n-1$, $W_{n-1}^{\mathbf{A}}$ stands for the algebraic set $\mathbb{V}(X_1, \ldots, X_{n-1})$.

Let $C^{\mathbf{A}}$ be a connected component of $\mathbb{V}(f^{\mathbf{A}}) \cap \mathbb{R}^n$. For $0 \le k \le n-2$, we denote by $C_k^{\mathbf{A}} = \mathbb{V}(X_1, \ldots, X_k) \cap C^{\mathbf{A}} \subset \mathbb{R}^n$ and by π_{k+1} the canonical projection

$$\pi_{k+1}: \qquad \mathbb{R}^{n-k} \longrightarrow \mathbb{R}$$
$$(x_{k+1}, \ldots, x_n) \longmapsto x_{k+1}$$

We will say that, given $\mathbf{A} \in \mathrm{GL}_n(\mathbb{C})$, property $\mathcal{P}(\mathbf{A})$ holds if, for $1 \le i \le n$, there exists algebraic sets $V_{n-i+1}^{\mathbf{A}} \subset V(f^{\mathbf{A}} - f^\star)$ such that for all connected component $C^{\mathbf{A}}$ of $V(f^{\mathbf{A}} - f^\star) \cap \mathbb{R}^n$

- the restriction of Π_{i-1} to $V_{n-i+1}^{\mathbf{A}}$ is proper;
- the boundary of $\Pi_i(C^{\mathbf{A}})$ is contained in $\Pi_i(C^{\mathbf{A}} \cap V_{n-i+1}^{\mathbf{A}})$.
- for $1 \le i \le n-1$, for all point $\mathbf{x}$ in a connected component $C^{\mathbf{A}} \subset V(f^{\mathbf{A}} - f^\star) \cap \mathbb{R}^n$ not belonging to $V_{n-i+1}^{\mathbf{A}}$, there exists a ball $\mathcal{B}$ containing $\mathbf{x}$ such that $\dim(\Pi_i(\mathcal{B} \cap C^{\mathbf{A}})) = i$.

Following [26], the properness property of Π_{i-1} implies that $\dim(V_{n-i+1}^{\mathbf{A}}) \le i-1$. We will prove in the sequel that $\mathcal{P}(\mathbf{A})$ holds for a generic choice of $\mathbf{A}$ by considering more general algebraic sets than polar varieties.

We will also say that property $\mathcal{Q}(\mathbf{A})$ holds if for all $1 \le i \le n$, $W_{n-i+1}^{\mathbf{A}, f-\varepsilon} \cap \mathbf{0}_{i-1} \cap V\left(\frac{\partial f^{\mathbf{A}}}{\partial X_1}\right)$ (where ε is an infinitesimal) is empty.

Sketch of proof. Let $f \in \mathbb{Q}[X_1, \ldots, X_n]$ and $f^\star = \inf_{\mathbf{x} \in \mathbb{R}^n} f(\mathbf{x})$.

THEOREM 1. *Suppose that $f^\star > -\infty$. Let $\mathbf{A} \in \mathrm{GL}_n(\mathbb{Q})$ be such that $\mathcal{P}(\mathbf{A})$ and $\mathcal{Q}(\mathbf{A})$ hold. Then, the union of the sets $\cup_{i=1}^n \mathscr{F}_{n-i+1}^{\mathbf{A}}$ meets every connected component of $V(f^{\mathbf{A}} - f^\star) \cap \mathbb{R}^n$.*

Under the assumption that $\mathcal{P}(\mathbf{A})$ and $\mathcal{Q}(\mathbf{A})$ hold, the above result allows us to reduce the problem of deciding the emptiness of $V(f^{\mathbf{A}} - f^\star) \cap \mathbb{R}^n$ to the one of deciding the emptiness of $(\cup_{i=1}^n \mathscr{F}_{n-i+1}^{\mathbf{A}}) \cap V(f^{\mathbf{A}} - f^\star) \cap \mathbb{R}^n$. Supposing that $\cup_{i=1}^n \mathscr{F}_{n-i+1}^{\mathbf{A}}$ has dimension 0, any solver for 0-dimensional polynomial system can be used to decide the emptiness of $V(f^{\mathbf{A}} - f^\star) \cap \mathbb{R}^n$.

Thus, Theorem 1 is algorithmically useful if it is easy to ensure that $\mathcal{P}(\mathbf{A})$ and $\mathcal{Q}(\mathbf{A})$ hold and if the set $\cup_{i=1}^n \mathscr{F}_{n-i+1}^{\mathbf{A}}$

have dimension 0. The result below ensures that $\mathcal{Q}(\mathbf{A})$ holds for a generic choice of $\mathbf{A}$ and that the set $\cup_{i=1}^{n} \mathscr{F}_{n-i+1}^{\mathbf{A}}$ has dimension at most 0.

THEOREM 2. *There exists a non-empty Zariski-open set $\mathscr{O} \subset \mathrm{GL}_n(\mathbb{C})$ s.t. for all $\mathbf{A} \in \mathrm{GL}_n(\mathbb{Q}) \cap \mathscr{O}$ and $1 \leq i \leq n$,*

- *the sets $\mathfrak{C}_{n-i+1}^{\mathbf{A}}$ have dimension at most 1*
- *the sets $\mathscr{F}_{n-i+1}^{\mathbf{A}}$ have dimension at most 0;*
- *the sets $W_{n-i+1}^{\mathbf{A}, f-\varepsilon} \cap \mathbf{0}_{i-1} \cap V\left(\frac{\partial f^{\mathbf{A}}}{\partial X_1}\right)$ are empty*

Finally, it remains to show how to ensure $\mathcal{P}(\mathbf{A})$ in order to apply algorithmically Theorem 1. Again, the result below ensures $\mathcal{P}(\mathbf{A})$ holds if $\mathbf{A}$ is chosen generically.

THEOREM 3. *Let $V \subset \mathbb{C}^n$ be an algebraic variety of dimension d. There exists a non-empty Zariski-open set $\mathscr{O} \subset \mathrm{GL}_n(\mathbb{C})$ such that for all $\mathbf{A} \in \mathrm{GL}_n(\mathbb{Q}) \cap \mathscr{O}$, and $1 \leq i \leq d+1$, there exist algebraic sets $V_{n-i+1}^{\mathbf{A}} \subset V^{\mathbf{A}}$ such that for all connected component $C^{\mathbf{A}}$ of $V^{\mathbf{A}} \cap \mathbb{R}^n$*

(i) *the restriction of Π_{i-1} to $V_{n-i+1}^{\mathbf{A}}$ is proper;*
(ii) *the boundary of $\Pi_i(C^{\mathbf{A}})$ is contained in $\Pi_i(C^{\mathbf{A}} \cap V_{n-i+1}^{\mathbf{A}})$.*
(iii) *for all point $\mathbf{x}$ in a connected component $C^{\mathbf{A}} \subset V(f^{\mathbf{A}} - f^\star) \cap \mathbb{R}^n$ not belonging to $V_{n-i+1}^{\mathbf{A}}$, there exists a ball $\mathcal{B}$ containing $\mathbf{x}$ such that $\dim(\Pi_i(\mathcal{B} \cap C^{\mathbf{A}})) = i$.*

The proof of Theorem 2 is widely inspired by [2]; the proof of Theorem 3 is inspired by [26] and a construction introduced in [27].

Proof of Theorem 1. We start with a Lemma which is a consequence of $\mathcal{P}(\mathbf{A})$.

LEMMA 1. *Suppose that $\mathcal{P}(\mathbf{A})$ holds and let $C^{\mathbf{A}}$ be a connected component of $V(f^{\mathbf{A}} - f^\star) \cap \mathbb{R}^n$. There exists $i_0 \in \{1, \dots, n-1\}$ and a connected component $Z_{i_0}^{\mathbf{A}}$ of $C^{\mathbf{A}} \cap \mathbf{0}_{i_0-1} \cap \mathbb{R}^n$ such that $\varphi_{i_0}(Z_{i_0}^{\mathbf{A}}) \neq \mathbb{R}$ and there exists $\mathbf{x} \in Z_{i_0}^{\mathbf{A}}$ such that $a = \varphi_{i_0}(\mathbf{x})$ lies in the boundary of $\varphi_{i_0}(Z_{i_0}^{\mathbf{A}})$. Moreover, there exists $r > 0$ such that $B(\mathbf{x}, r) \cap Z_{i_0}^{\mathbf{A}} \cap \varphi_{i_0}^{-1}(a) = \{\mathbf{x}\}$.*

PROOF. Since $\mathcal{P}(\mathbf{A})$ holds, the boundary of $\Pi_i(C^{\mathbf{A}})$ is contained in $\Pi_i(C^{\mathbf{A}} \cap V_{n-i+1}^{\mathbf{A}})$ for $1 \leq i \leq n-1$. In particular, this implies that $\Pi_i(C^{\mathbf{A}})$ is closed.

Consider the largest $i_0 \in \{1, \dots, n-1\}$ such that $C^{\mathbf{A}} \cap \mathbf{0}_{i_0-1} \neq \emptyset$ and $C^{\mathbf{A}} \cap \mathbf{0}_{i_0} = \emptyset$; whence $\varphi_{i_0}(C^{\mathbf{A}} \cap \mathbf{0}_{i_0-1})$ is a union of segments in the X_{i_0}-axis. This implies that there exists $\mathbf{y}$ in the intersection of $\Pi_{i_0}(C^{\mathbf{A}} \cap \mathbf{0}_{i_0-1})$ with the boundary of $\Pi_{i_0}(C^{\mathbf{A}})$. Note also that since $\Pi_{i_0}(C^{\mathbf{A}} \cap \mathbf{0}_{i_0-1})$ is a union of segments in the X_{i_0}-axis not containing the origin of this axis, one can choose $\mathbf{y}$ such that its X_{i_0}-coordinate belongs to the boundary of $\varphi_{i_0}(C^{\mathbf{A}} \cap \mathbf{0}_{i_0-1})$.

Since $\mathcal{P}(\mathbf{A})$ holds, the boundary of $\Pi_{i_0}(C^{\mathbf{A}})$ is itself contained in $\Pi_{i_0}(C^{\mathbf{A}} \cap V_{n-i_0+1}^{\mathbf{A}})$. Consequently, there exists $\mathbf{x} \in C^{\mathbf{A}} \cap V_{n-i_0+1}^{\mathbf{A}}$ such that $\Pi_{i_0}(\mathbf{x}) = \mathbf{y}$. Moreover, since $\mathbf{y} \in \Pi_{i_0}(C^{\mathbf{A}} \cap \mathbf{0}_{i_0-1})$, $\mathbf{x} \in \mathbf{0}_{i_0-1}$. Let now $Z_{i_0}^{\mathbf{A}}$ be the connected component of $C^{\mathbf{A}} \cap \mathbf{0}_{i_0-1} \subset V(f^{\mathbf{A}} - f^\star) \cap \mathbf{0}_{i_0-1} \cap \mathbb{R}^n$ containing $\mathbf{x}$. Obviously, $Z_{i_0}^{\mathbf{A}} \subset C^{\mathbf{A}}$ is also a connected component of $V(f^{\mathbf{A}} - f^\star) \cap \mathbf{0}_{i_0-1} \cap \mathbb{R}^n$ and, by construction $\mathbf{x} \in Z_{i_0}^{\mathbf{A}}$ lies in $C^{\mathbf{A}} \cap \mathbf{0}_{i_0-1} \cap V_{n-i_0+1}^{\mathbf{A}}$. Since we have chosen $\mathbf{y}$ such that its X_{i_0}-coordinate lies in the boundary of $\varphi_{i_0}(C^{\mathbf{A}} \cap \mathbf{0}_{i_0-1})$, this implies that $\varphi_{i_0}(\mathbf{x})$ lies in the boundary of $\varphi_{i_0}(Z_{i_0}^{\mathbf{A}})$.

Let $a = \varphi_{i_0}(\mathbf{x})$. It remains to prove that there exists $r > 0$ such that $\varphi_{i_0}^{-1}(a) \cap Z_{i_0}^{\mathbf{A}} \cap B(\mathbf{x}, r) = \{\mathbf{x}\}$. To do that, we prove that it has dimension 0.

Suppose on the contrary that there exists a connected semi-algebraic set $\gamma \subset \varphi_{i_0}^{-1}(a) \cap Z_{i_0}^{\mathbf{A}}$ containing $\mathbf{x}$ such that $\gamma \neq \{\mathbf{x}\}$. Then, by construction, $\Pi_{i_0}(\gamma) = \Pi_{i_0}(\mathbf{x})$. Recall that $\Pi_{i_0}(\mathbf{x})$ lies in the boundary of $\Pi_{i_0}(C^{\mathbf{A}})$. Since $\mathcal{P}(\mathbf{A})$ holds $\Pi_{i_0}(\gamma) \in \Pi_{i_0}(V_{n-i_0+1}^{\mathbf{A}})$ and the restriction of Π_{i_0-1} to $V_{n-i_0+1}^{\mathbf{A}}$ is proper. This latter property implies that the restriction of Π_{i_0-1} to $V_{n-i_0+1}^{\mathbf{A}}$ is finite. Recall that $\mathbf{x} \in \mathbf{0}_{i_0-1}$, thus there exists $r > 0$ small enough for which $\gamma \cap V_{n-i_0+1}^{\mathbf{A}} \cap B(\mathbf{x}, r) = \{\mathbf{x}\}$. Since we have supposed that $\gamma \neq \{\mathbf{x}\}$, there exists $\mathbf{x}' \in \gamma \cap B(\mathbf{x}, r) \setminus \{\mathbf{x}\}$; consequently $\mathbf{x}' \notin V_{n-i_0+1}^{\mathbf{A}}$. Since $\mathcal{P}(\mathbf{A})$ holds, there exists a ball $\mathcal{B}$ containing $\mathbf{x}'$ such that $\dim(\pi_{i_0}(\mathcal{B} \cap C^{\mathbf{A}})) = i_0$. This implies that $\pi_{i_0}(\mathbf{x}') = \pi_{i_0}(\mathbf{x})$ is not in the boundary of $\pi_{i_0}(C^{\mathbf{A}})$, a contradiction. $\square$

Now, let $C^{\mathbf{A}}$ be a connected component of $V(f^{\mathbf{A}} - f^\star) \cap \mathbb{R}^n$. Remark that at all points of $C^{\mathbf{A}}$, all the partial derivatives of $f^{\mathbf{A}}$ vanish. By the above Lemma, there exists a connected component $Z_{i_0}^{\mathbf{A}}$ of $V(f^{\mathbf{A}} - f^\star) \cap \mathbf{0}_{i_0-1} \cap \mathbb{R}^n$ such that $Z_{i_0}^{\mathbf{A}} \subset C^{\mathbf{A}}$ and $\varphi_{i_0}(Z_{i_0}^{\mathbf{A}}) \neq \mathbb{R}$ but is closed since $\mathcal{P}(\mathbf{A})$ holds. Note that this implies that all partial derivatives of $f^{\mathbf{A}}$ vanish at all points of $Z_{i_0}^{\mathbf{A}}$.

We prove below that $Z_{i_0}^{\mathbf{A}}$ has a non-empty intersection with $\mathfrak{C}_{n-i_0+1}^{\mathbf{A}}$. Since $Z_{i_0}^{\mathbf{A}} \subset C^{\mathbf{A}}$ and all the partial derivatives of $f^{\mathbf{A}}$ vanish at any point of $C^{\mathbf{A}}$, this will conclude the proof.

Let H be a real hyperplane orthogonal to the X_{i_0}-axis which does not meet $\varphi_{i_0}(Z_{i_0}^{\mathbf{A}})$. Because $\varphi_{i_0}(Z_{i_0}^{\mathbf{A}})$ is a closed and strict subset of $\mathbb{R}$, $\mathrm{dist}(Z_{i_0}^{\mathbf{A}}, H)$ between $\varphi_{i_0}(Z_{i_0}^{\mathbf{A}})$ and H is reached at a point $\mathbf{x}^\star$ in $Z_{i_0}^{\mathbf{A}}$. By Lemma 1, one can also assume that there exists $r > 0$ such that $\mathbf{x}^\star$ is the unique minimizer of $\mathrm{dist}(Z_{i_0}^{\mathbf{A}}, H)$ in the ball $B(\mathbf{x}^\star, r)$. To finish the proof of Theorem 1, it is sufficient to prove the lemma below.

LEMMA 2. *The point $\mathbf{x}^\star \in C^{\mathbf{A}}$ belongs to $\mathfrak{C}_{n-i_0+1}$.*

Additionally, up to choosing a small $r > 0$, one can suppose that $B(\mathbf{x}^\star, r) \cap ((V(f^{\mathbf{A}} - f^\star) \cap \mathbf{0}_{i_0-1}) \setminus Z_{i_0}^{\mathbf{A}}) = \emptyset$.

Roughly speaking, the idea of the proof is to consider algebraic sets $V(f^{\mathbf{A}} - (f^\star + e)) \cap \mathbf{0}_{i_0-1}$ for small enough $e > 0$ which are "deformations" of $V(f^{\mathbf{A}} - f^\star) \cap \mathbf{0}_{i_0-1}$, and exhibit a sequence of points $(\mathbf{x}_e)_e$ lying in $\mathfrak{C}_{n-i_0+1} \cap B(\mathbf{x}^\star, r)$ which converge to $\mathbf{x}^\star$ when $e \to 0$. To do that rigorously, we need to use materials about infinitesimals and Puiseux series that we introduce now.

Preliminaries on infinitesimals and Puiseux series. We denote by $\mathbb{R}\langle \varepsilon \rangle$ (resp. $\mathbb{C}\langle \varepsilon \rangle$) the real closed field (resp. algebraically closed field) of algebraic Puiseux series with coefficients in $\mathbb{R}$ (resp. $\mathbb{C}$), where ε is an infinitesimal. We will use the classical notions of bounded elements in $\mathbb{R}\langle \varepsilon \rangle^n$ (resp. $\mathbb{C}\langle \varepsilon \rangle^n$) over $\mathbb{R}^n$ (resp. $\mathbb{C}^n$) and their limits. The limit of a bounded element $z \in \mathbb{R}\langle \varepsilon \rangle^n$ (resp. $z \in \mathbb{R}\langle \varepsilon \rangle^n$) will be denoted by $\lim_0(z)$. The ring homomorphism $\lim_0$ will also be used on sets of $\mathbb{R}\langle \varepsilon \rangle^n$ and $\mathbb{C}\langle \varepsilon \rangle^n$

Also for semi-algebraic sets $S \subset \mathbb{R}^n$ defined by a system of polynomial equations and inequalities, we will denote by $\mathrm{ext}(S, \mathbb{R}\langle \varepsilon \rangle)$ the solution set of the considered system in $\mathbb{R}\langle \varepsilon \rangle^n$. We refer to [7, Chap. 2.6] for precise statements of these notions.

Proof of Lemma 2. We simplify the notations by letting $f^{\mathbf{A}} = f^{\mathbf{A}} - f^\star$ and $V(f^{\mathbf{A}})_{i_0-1} = V(f^{\mathbf{A}}) \cap \mathbf{0}_{i_0-1}$. By [23, Lemma 3.6], $V(f^{\mathbf{A}})_{i_0-1} \cap \mathbb{R}^n = \lim_0(V(f^{\mathbf{A}} - \varepsilon) \cup V(f^{\mathbf{A}} + \varepsilon)) \cap \mathbf{0}_{i_0-1} \cap \mathbb{R}^n = \lim_0(V(f^{\mathbf{A}} - \varepsilon) \cap \mathbf{0}_{i_0-1}) \cap \mathbb{R}^n$. Then, there exists a connected component $C_\varepsilon^{\mathbf{A}} \subset \mathbb{R}\langle \varepsilon \rangle^n$ of $V(f^{\mathbf{A}} - \varepsilon) \cap \mathbf{0}_{i_0-1} \cap \mathbb{R}\langle \varepsilon \rangle^n$ such that $C_\varepsilon^{\mathbf{A}}$ contains a $\mathbf{x}_\varepsilon$ such that $\lim_0(\mathbf{x}_\varepsilon) = \mathbf{x}^\star$.

Thus $\text{ext}(B(\mathbf{x}^\star, r), \mathbb{R}\langle\varepsilon\rangle) \cap C_\varepsilon^\mathbf{A} \neq \emptyset$. Since $\text{ext}(B(\mathbf{x}^\star, r), \mathbb{R}\langle\varepsilon\rangle)$ is bounded over $\mathbb{R}$, $\text{dist}\big(C_\varepsilon^\mathbf{A} \cap \text{ext}(B(\mathbf{x}^\star, r), \mathbb{R}\langle\varepsilon\rangle), \text{ext}(H, \mathbb{R}\langle\varepsilon\rangle)\big)$ is also bounded over $\mathbb{R}$; let $\mathfrak{d}_0$ be its image by $\lim_0$. Since r has been chosen such that $B(\mathbf{x}^\star, r)$ has an empty intersection with all connected components of $V(\mathfrak{f}^\mathbf{A})_{i_0-1} \cap \mathbb{R}^n$ which are not $C^\mathbf{A}$, all points in $C_\varepsilon^\mathbf{A} \cap \text{ext}(B(\mathbf{x}^\star, r))$ have their image by $\lim_0$ in $Z_{i_0}^\mathbf{A}$. This implies that $\mathfrak{d}_0 = \text{dist}(Z_{i_0}^\mathbf{A}, H)$.

Let $S(\mathbf{x}^\star, r) \subset \mathbb{R}^n$ be the sphere centered at $\mathbf{x}^\star$ of radius r. Suppose for the moment that all points in

$$\text{ext}(S(\mathbf{x}^\star, r), \mathbb{R}\langle\varepsilon\rangle) \cap C_\varepsilon^\mathbf{A}$$

don't minimize $\text{dist}\big(C_\varepsilon^\mathbf{A} \cap \text{ext}(B(\mathbf{x}^\star, r), \mathbb{R}\langle\varepsilon\rangle), \text{ext}(H, \mathbb{R}\langle\varepsilon\rangle)\big)$. Thus $\text{dist}\big(C_\varepsilon^\mathbf{A} \cap \text{ext}(B(\mathbf{x}^\star, r), \mathbb{R}\langle\varepsilon\rangle), \text{ext}(H, \mathbb{R}\langle\varepsilon\rangle)\big)$ is realized at a point $\mathbf{x}_\varepsilon^\star \in C_\varepsilon^\mathbf{A}$ lying in the interior of $\text{ext}(B(\mathbf{x}^\star, r), \mathbb{R}\langle\varepsilon\rangle)$. Remark that this also implies that $\mathbf{x}_\varepsilon^\star$ is bounded over $\mathbb{R}$. Since $\mathfrak{d}_0 = \text{dist}(C^\mathbf{A}, H)$ and $\mathbf{x}^\star$ is the unique point of $B(\mathbf{x}^\star, r) \cap C^\mathbf{A}$ realizing $\text{dist}(C^\mathbf{A}, H)$, $\mathbf{x}^\star = \lim_0(\mathbf{x}_\varepsilon^\star)$. Since $\mathfrak{C}_{n-i_0+1}^\mathbf{A}$ is defined by polynomials with coefficients in $\mathbb{Q}$, in order to conclude it remains to prove that $\mathbf{x}_\varepsilon^\star$ lies in $\text{ext}(\mathfrak{C}_{n-i_0+1}^\mathbf{A}, \mathbb{R}\langle\varepsilon\rangle)$.

Moreover, by the implicit function theorem [7, Chap. 3.5], $\frac{\partial f^\mathbf{A}}{\partial X_{i_0+1}}, \ldots, \frac{\partial f^\mathbf{A}}{\partial X_n}$ vanish at $\mathbf{x}_\varepsilon^\star \in V(\mathfrak{f}^\mathbf{A} - \varepsilon) \cap \mathbf{0}_{i_0-1}$. By $\mathcal{Q}(\mathbf{A})$, this implies that $\frac{\partial f^\mathbf{A}}{\partial X_1}$ doesn't vanish at $\mathbf{x}_\varepsilon^\star$. Consequently, $\mathbf{x}_\varepsilon^\star$ lies in $\text{ext}(\mathfrak{C}_{n-i_0+1}^\mathbf{A}, \mathbb{R}\langle\varepsilon\rangle)$.

Now, we prove the claim announced above, that is that $\text{dist}\big(C_\varepsilon^\mathbf{A} \cap \text{ext}(B(\mathbf{x}^\star, r), \mathbb{R}\langle\varepsilon\rangle), \text{ext}(H, \mathbb{R}\langle\varepsilon\rangle)\big)$ is not reached at $\text{ext}(S(\mathbf{x}^\star, r), \mathbb{R}\langle\varepsilon\rangle) \cap C_\varepsilon^\mathbf{A}$. Suppose on the contrary that there exists $\mathbf{x}_\varepsilon \in \text{ext}(S(\mathbf{x}^\star, r), \mathbb{R}\langle\varepsilon\rangle) \cap C_\varepsilon^\mathbf{A}$ which realizes this distance. Since $\mathbf{x}_\varepsilon \in \text{ext}(S(\mathbf{x}^\star, r), \mathbb{R}\langle\varepsilon\rangle)$, $\mathbf{x}_\varepsilon$ is bounded over $\mathbb{R}$ and its image by $\lim_0$, that we will denote by $\mathbf{x}_0$, lies in $S(\mathbf{x}^\star, r)$ since $S(\mathbf{x}^\star, r)$ is defined by polynomials with coefficients in $\mathbb{R}$. Note also that $\mathbf{x}_0$ lies in $Z_{i_0}^\mathbf{A}$ since r has been chosen such that $B(\mathbf{x}^\star, r) \cap Z_{i_0}^\mathbf{A}$ has an empty intersection with all connected components of $V(\mathfrak{f}^\mathbf{A})_{i_0-1} \cap \mathbb{R}^n$ distinct from $Z_{i_0}^\mathbf{A}$. This is a contradiction since r has been also chosen small enough such that $\mathbf{x}^\star$ is the unique point $B(\mathbf{x}^\star, r) \cap Z_{i_0}^\mathbf{A}$ which realizes $\text{dist}(Z_{i_0}^\mathbf{A}, H)$. $\qquad\square$

Proof of Theorem 2. We prove this result in three steps:

(i) there exists a non-empty Zariski open set $\mathscr{O}_1 \subset \text{GL}_n(\mathbb{C})$ such that for all $\mathbf{A} \in \text{GL}_n(\mathbb{Q}) \cap \mathscr{O}_1$, the Zariski-closure $\mathfrak{C}_{n-i+1}$ of $V\left(X_1, \ldots, X_{i-1}, \frac{\partial f^\mathbf{A}}{\partial X_{i+1}}, \ldots, \frac{\partial f^\mathbf{A}}{\partial X_n}\right) \setminus V\left(\frac{\partial f^\mathbf{A}}{\partial X_1}\right)$ has dimension at most 1;

(ii) $\forall \mathbf{A} \in \mathscr{O}_1$, $\mathfrak{C}_{n-i+1}^\mathbf{A} \cap V\left(\frac{\partial f^\mathbf{A}}{\partial X_1}\right)$ has dimension at most 0;

(iii) there exists a non-empty Zariski open set $\mathscr{O}_2 \subset \text{GL}_n(\mathbb{C})$ such that for all $\mathbf{A} \in \text{GL}_n(\mathbb{Q}) \cap \mathscr{O}_2$, the n equations $X_1, \ldots, X_{i-1}, \frac{\partial f^\mathbf{A}}{\partial X_1}, \frac{\partial f^\mathbf{A}}{\partial X_{i+1}}, \ldots, \frac{\partial f^\mathbf{A}}{\partial X_n}$ intersect transversely.

Then, writing $\mathscr{O} = \mathscr{O}_1 \cap \mathscr{O}_2$ will give a non-empty Zariski open set satisfying the announced properties.

The most difficult step is step *(i)*. Its proof is widely inspired by [2, Proposition 3].

Proof of step (i). First, since $\mathfrak{C}_1^\mathbf{A} = \mathbf{0}_{n-1}$ is the line $\{X_1 = \cdots = X_{n-1} = 0\}$, the first point of the statement is obvious for $i = n$.

Let $1 \leq i \leq n-1$. Remark that the differential $d_\mathbf{x} f^\mathbf{A}$ is the matrix product $\begin{bmatrix} \frac{\partial f}{\partial X_1}(\mathbf{Ax}) & \cdots & \frac{\partial f}{\partial X_n}(\mathbf{Ax}) \end{bmatrix} \mathbf{A}$. If we denote by a_{ij} the coefficients of the matrix $\mathbf{A}$ then this product equals $\begin{bmatrix} \sum_{k=1}^n a_{k1} \frac{\partial f}{\partial X_k}(\mathbf{Ax}) & \cdots & \sum_{k=1}^n a_{k,n} \frac{\partial f}{\partial X_k}(\mathbf{Ax}) \end{bmatrix}$ which

means that for $1 \leq i \leq n$, $\frac{\partial f^\mathbf{A}}{\partial X_i}(\mathbf{x}) = \sum_{k=1}^n a_{ki} \frac{\partial f}{\partial X_k}(\mathbf{Ax})$. For $1 \leq i \leq n-1$, consider the mapping $\Phi_i : \mathbb{C}^n \times \mathbb{C}^{n(n-i)} \to \mathbb{C}^{n-1}$ which maps a point $(\mathbf{x}, a_{1,i+1}, a_{2,i+1}, \ldots, a_{n,i+1}, a_{1,i+2}, \ldots, a_{n,n})$, where $\mathbf{x} = (x_1, \ldots, x_n)$, to

$$\left(x_1, \ldots, x_{i-1}, \sum_{k=1}^n a_{k,i+1} \frac{\partial f}{\partial X_k}(\mathbf{Ax}), \ldots, \sum_{k=1}^n a_{k,n} \frac{\partial f}{\partial X_k}(\mathbf{Ax})\right).$$

Thus the Jacobian matrix at a point $\alpha = (\mathbf{x}, a_{1,i+1}, \ldots) \in \mathbb{C}^n \times \mathbb{C}^{n(n-i)}$ is the evaluation at $\mathbf{Ax}$ of the matrix

$$\begin{bmatrix}
\mathbf{I}_{i-1} & 0 & \cdots & & \cdots & & \cdots & & \\
* & \cdots & * & \frac{\partial f}{\partial X_1} \cdots \frac{\partial f}{\partial X_n} & 0 & & \cdots & & \\
\vdots & \cdots & \vdots & 0 & \cdots & 0 & \frac{\partial f}{\partial X_1} \cdots \frac{\partial f}{\partial X_n} & 0 & \cdots & 0 \\
\vdots & \cdots & \vdots & 0 & \cdots & 0 & \cdots & 0 & \ddots & 0 \\
* & \cdots & * & 0 & \cdots & 0 & 0 & \cdots & 0 & \frac{\partial f}{\partial X_1} \cdots \frac{\partial f}{\partial X_n}
\end{bmatrix},$$

where $\mathbf{I}_{i-1}$ is the identity matrix of size $i-1$.

Consider the Zariski-open set $\mathcal{V}^\mathbf{A}$ of all points in $\mathbb{C}^n$ such that at least one partial derivative of $f^\mathbf{A}$ does not vanish. Then we prove that the restriction of Φ_i to $\mathcal{V}^\mathbf{A} \times \mathbb{C}^{n(n-i)}$ is transverse to $(0, \ldots, 0) \in \mathbb{C}^{n-1}$. Indeed, we consider a point $\alpha = (\mathbf{x}, a_{1,i+1}, \ldots, a_{nn}) \in \mathcal{V}^\mathbf{A} \times \mathbb{C}^{n(n-i)}$ with $\Phi_i(\alpha) = 0$.

Suppose that the Jacobian matrix Φ_i has not maximal rank at α. Then all the partial derivative in the matrix have to vanish. This implies that all the partial derivatives of $f^\mathbf{A}$ vanish too, which is impossible if $\alpha \in \mathcal{V}^\mathbf{A} \times \mathbb{C}^{n(n-i)}$. Thus the Jacobian matrix has maximal rank at α, which means that α is a regular point of Φ_i. This is true for all $\alpha \in \Phi_i^{-1}(0) \cap \left(\mathcal{V}^\mathbf{A} \times \mathbb{C}^{n(n-i)}\right)$ therefore the restriction of Φ_i is transverse to $(0, \ldots, 0)$ as announced. Then by the Weak Transversality Theorem of Thom-Sard (see [9, Theorem 3.7.4 p. 79]), there exists a Zariski-open set $\mathscr{O}_1 \subset \text{GL}_n(\mathbb{C})$ such that for all $\mathbf{A} \in \text{GL}_n(\mathbb{Q}) \cap \mathscr{O}_1$, the restriction of Φ_i to $\mathcal{V}^\mathbf{A} \times \mathbb{C}^{n(n-i)}$ is transverse to $(0, \ldots, 0)$. This means that for all $\mathbf{A} \in \text{GL}_n(\mathbb{Q}) \cap \mathscr{O}_1$, the equations $\frac{\partial f^\mathbf{A}}{\partial X_{i+1}} = 0, \ldots, \frac{\partial f^\mathbf{A}}{\partial X_n} = 0, X_1 = 0, \ldots, X_{i-1} = 0$ intersect transversely at any of their common solutions which are in $\mathcal{V}^\mathbf{A}$. In particular this is true for the solutions in $\left\{\frac{\partial f^\mathbf{A}}{\partial X_1} \neq 0\right\} \subset \mathcal{V}^\mathbf{A}$. Finally, this means that if the algebraic variety

$$\overline{V\left(X_1, \ldots, X_{i-1}, \frac{\partial f^\mathbf{A}}{\partial X_{i+1}}, \ldots, \frac{\partial f^\mathbf{A}}{\partial X_n}\right) \setminus V\left(\frac{\partial f^\mathbf{A}}{\partial X_1}\right)}^z,$$

which is precisely $\mathfrak{C}_{n-i+1}^\mathbf{A}$, has dimension one or is empty. $\qquad\square$

Proof of step (ii). Let $\mathscr{O}_1$ be the Zariski-closed open set given in the previous proof. Let $\mathbf{A} \in \text{GL}_n(\mathbb{Q}) \cap \mathscr{O}_1$ and let $i \in \{1, \ldots, n-1\}$. Then according to step *(i)*, $\mathfrak{C}_{n-i+1}^\mathbf{A}$ has dimension at most one. Assume that $\mathfrak{C}_{n-i+1}^\mathbf{A} \cap V\left(\frac{\partial f^\mathbf{A}}{\partial X_1}\right)$ is nonempty. Then by definition, $\mathfrak{C}_{n-i+1}^\mathbf{A}$ is not included in $V\left(\frac{\partial f^\mathbf{A}}{\partial X_1}\right)$. By Krull's Principal Ideal Theorem [19, Cor. 3.2 p. 131], we deduce that $\dim\left(\mathfrak{C}_{n-i+1}^\mathbf{A} \cap V\left(\frac{\partial f^\mathbf{A}}{\partial X_1}\right)\right) = \dim(\mathfrak{C}_{n-i+1}^\mathbf{A}) - 1 \leq 0$. Then, $\mathscr{F}_{n-i+1}^\mathbf{A} = \mathfrak{C}_{n-i+1}^\mathbf{A} \cap V\left(\frac{\partial f^\mathbf{A}}{\partial X_1}\right) \cap V\left(\frac{\partial f^\mathbf{A}}{\partial X_2}, \ldots, \frac{\partial f^\mathbf{A}}{\partial X_n}\right)$ has also dimension less than 0.

Let $i = n$ and assume that $\mathscr{F}_1 \neq \varnothing$. Then if $\mathbf{A}$ is generic enough, it is clear that there exists $k \in \{1, \ldots, n\}$ such that $\mathfrak{C}_1^\mathbf{A} = \mathbf{0}_{n-1}$ in not contained in $V\left(\frac{\partial f^\mathbf{A}}{\partial X_k}\right)$. As above, by Krull's Principal Ideal Theorem we deduce that $\dim\left(\mathfrak{C}_1^{\mathbf{A}} \cap V\left(\frac{\partial f^{\mathbf{A}}}{\partial X_k}\right)\right) = \dim(\mathfrak{C}_1^{\mathbf{A}}) - 1 \leq 0$, which implies that $\mathscr{F}_1 = \mathfrak{C}_1 \cap V\left(\frac{\partial f^{\mathbf{A}}}{\partial X_1}, \ldots, \frac{\partial f^{\mathbf{A}}}{\partial X_n}\right)$ has dimension ≤ 0. $\qquad\square$

Proof of step (iii). For $1 \leq i \leq n$, consider the mapping $\Psi_i \colon \mathbb{C}^n \times \mathbb{C}^{n(n-i+1)} \to \mathbb{C}^{n+1}$ which maps a point

$$(\mathbf{x}, a_{1,1}, \ldots, a_{n,1}, a_{1,i+1}, a_{2,i+1}, \ldots, a_{n,i+1}, a_{1,i+2}, \ldots, a_{n,n}),$$

where $\mathbf{x} \in \mathbb{C}^n$ to $\left(x_1, \ldots, x_{i-1}, \frac{\partial f^{\mathbf{A}}}{\partial X_1}, \frac{\partial f^{\mathbf{A}}}{\partial X_{i+1}}, \ldots, \frac{\partial f^{\mathbf{A}}}{\partial X_n}\right)$.

Consider the Zariski-open set $\mathcal{V}^{\mathbf{A}}$ of all points in $\mathbb{C}^n$ such that at least one partial derivative of $f^{\mathbf{A}}$ does not vanish. As above, we prove that the restriction of Ψ_i to $\mathcal{V}^{\mathbf{A}} \times \mathbb{C}^{n(n-i+1)}$ is transverse to $(0, \ldots, 0) \in \mathbb{C}^n$: we consider a point $\beta = (\mathbf{x}, a_{1,i+1}, \ldots, a_{nn}) \in \mathcal{V}^{\mathbf{A}} \times \mathbb{C}^{n(n-i+1)}$ with $\Phi_i(\beta) = 0$. Because $\mathbf{x} \in \mathcal{V}^{\mathbf{A}}$, at least one partial derivative of $f^{\mathbf{A}}$ does not vanish at $\mathbf{x}$, which means that at least one partial derivative of f does not vanish at $\mathbf{Ax}$. Thus the shape of the Jacobian matrix of Ψ_i is such that it has maximal rank at β and β is a regular point of Ψ_i. Therefore the restriction of Ψ_i is transverse to $(0, \ldots, 0)$. Then by the Weak Transversality Theorem of Thom-Sard, there exists a Zariski-open set $\mathscr{O}_2 \subset GL_n(\mathbb{C})$ such that for all $\mathbf{A} \in GL_n(\mathbb{Q}) \cap \mathscr{O}_2$, the restriction of Ψ_i to $\mathcal{V}^{\mathbf{A}} \times \mathbb{C}^{n(n-i+1)}$ is transverse to $(0, \ldots, 0)$. This means that for all $\mathbf{A} \in GL_n(\mathbb{Q}) \cap \mathscr{O}_2$, the equations $\frac{\partial f^{\mathbf{A}}}{\partial X_1} = 0$, $\frac{\partial f^{\mathbf{A}}}{\partial X_{i+1}} = 0$, ..., $\frac{\partial f^{\mathbf{A}}}{\partial X_n} = 0$, $X_1 = 0$, ..., $X_{i-1} = 0$ intersect transversely at any of their common solutions which are in $\mathcal{V}^{\mathbf{A}}$. Because ε is an infinitesimal, the variety $V\left(f^{\mathbf{A}} - \varepsilon\right)$ is smooth, thus is a subset of $\mathcal{V}^{\mathbf{A}}$. Then $W_{n-i+1}^{\mathbf{A}, f-\varepsilon} \cap \mathbf{0}_{i-1} \cap V\left(\frac{\partial f^{\mathbf{A}}}{\partial X_1}\right)$, that is the intersection of $V\left(X_1, \ldots, X_{i-1}, \frac{\partial f^{\mathbf{A}}}{\partial X_1}, \frac{\partial f^{\mathbf{A}}}{\partial X_{i+1}}, \ldots, \frac{\partial f^{\mathbf{A}}}{\partial X_n}\right)$ with the hypersurface $V(f^{\mathbf{A}} - \varepsilon)$, is empty. $\qquad\square$

Proof of Theorem 3.

We start with the third point.

LEMMA 3. *Let $C^{\mathbf{A}}$ be a connected component of $V(f^{\mathbf{A}} - f^{\star})$. For all $i \in \{1, \ldots, n-1\}$, for all $\mathbf{x} \in C^{\mathbf{A}}$ such that $\mathbf{x} \notin V_{n-i+1}^{\mathbf{A}}$, there exists a ball $\mathcal{B}_i$ containing $\mathbf{x}$ such that $\dim\left(\pi_i(\mathcal{B}_i \cap C^{\mathbf{A}})\right) = i$.*

PROOF. For $i = n-1$, let $\mathbf{x} = (x_1, \ldots, x_n) \notin V_2$. By definition of V_2, $\mathbf{x}$ is in the $n-1$-equidimensional component of $V(f - f^{\star})$ and is not a critical point of the restriction to C of π_{n-1}. Then using the implicit functions theorem, there exists a ball $\mathcal{B}_{n-1}$ centered on $\mathbf{x}$ and a continuously differentiable function ϕ such that for every $\mathbf{y} \in \mathcal{B}_{n-1}$, $\mathbf{y} \in C$ iff $\mathbf{y} = (y_1, \ldots, y_{n-1}, \phi(y_1, \ldots, y_{n-1}))$. Then the image of $\mathcal{B}_{n-1} \cap C$ by π_{n-1} has dimension $n-1$.

Let $i \in \{1, \ldots, n-1\}$ and assume that for all $\mathbf{x} \notin V_{n-i}$, there exists a ball $\mathcal{B}_{n-i}$ centered on $\mathbf{x}$ such that the projection $\pi_{i+1}(\mathcal{B}_{n-i} \cap C)$ has dimension $i+1$. Let us show that this implies that for all $\mathbf{x} \notin V_{n-i+1}$, there exists a ball $\mathcal{B}_{n-i+1}$ centered on $\mathbf{x}$ such that $\dim(\pi_i(\mathcal{B}_{n-i+1} \cap C)) = i$.

Let $\mathbf{x} \notin V_{n-i+1}$. If $\mathbf{x} \notin V_{n-i}$ then by assumption, there exists a ball $\mathcal{B}_{n-i}$ centered on $\mathbf{x}$ such that the projection $\pi_{i+1}(\mathcal{B}_{n-i} \cap C)$ has dimension $i+1$. It is clear that for all $j \leq i+1$, $\pi_j(\mathcal{B}_{n-i} \cap C)$ has dimension j. In particular for $j = i$, the result is proved.

Else, $\mathbf{x} \in V_{n-i}$ and $\mathbf{x} \notin V_{n-i+1}$. By definition of V_{n-i+1} and V_{n-i}, $\mathbf{x}$ belongs to the i-equidimensional component of V_{n-i}. Then this component is locally defined by $n-i$ equations. Moreover, $\mathbf{x}$ is not in singular locus of $\mathbb{V}_{n-i}$ and not in the critical locus of the projection π_i. This means

that the Jacobian of the $n-i$ equations defining locally the i-equidimensional component of V_{n-i} with respect to the variables $x_{i+1}, \ldots, x_n$ is invertible. Then the implicit functions theorem applies and ensures that there exists a ball $\mathcal{B}_{n-i+1}$ centered on $\mathbf{x}$ and a continuously differentiable function ϕ such that for every $\mathbf{y} \in \mathcal{B}_{n-i+1}$, $\mathbf{y} \in C$ iff $\mathbf{y} = (y_1, \ldots, y_i, \phi(y_1, \ldots, y_i))$. Then the image of $\mathcal{B}_{n-i+1} \cap C$ by π_{n-i+1} has dimension i. $\qquad\square$

Then we give the intuition of the proof of the first two points. It consists by constructing recursively $V_{n-i+1}^{\mathbf{A}}$ from $V_{n-i}^{\mathbf{A}}$ with $V_{n-d}^{\mathbf{A}} = V^{\mathbf{A}}$. Suppose that we have found $\mathbf{A}$ such that properties *(i)* and *(ii)* are satisfied by $V_{n-i}^{\mathbf{A}}$. Then, we need to construct $V_{n-i+1}^{\mathbf{A}}$ in such a way that the boundary of $\Pi_i(C^{\mathbf{A}})$ is contained in $\Pi_i(C^{\mathbf{A}} \cap V_{n-i+1}^{\mathbf{A}})$. We will see that the implicit function theorem and the properness property of the restriction of Π_i to $V_{n-i}^{\mathbf{A}}$ enables us to choose $V_{n-i+1}^{\mathbf{A}}$ as the union of

- the j-equidimensional components of $V_{n-i}^{\mathbf{A}}$ for $1 \leq j \leq i-1$
- the singular locus of the i-equidimensional component of $V_{n-i}^{\mathbf{A}}$.
- the critical locus of the restriction of Π_i to the i-equidimensional component of $V_{n-i}^{\mathbf{A}}$;

Nevertheless, for this matrix $\mathbf{A}$, the restriction of Π_{i-1} to $V_{n-i+1}^{\mathbf{A}}$ may not be proper. Then, a generic change of variables on the coordinates $X_1, \ldots, X_i$ will not alter $V_{n-i+1}^{\mathbf{A}}$ but will restore the properness property of Π_{i-1}.

Our proof is widely inspired by the one of [26, Theorem 1 and Proposition 2] which state a similar result when V is smooth and equidimensional.

As in [26], to obtain the existence of the Zariski-open set $\mathscr{O}$, we need to adopt an algebraic viewpoint.

Strategy of proof. To adopt this algebraic viewpoint, we consider a finite family $\mathbf{F} \subset \mathbb{Q}[X_1, \ldots, X_n]$ generating the ideal associated to V which has dimension d. As in Section 2, $\mathbf{X}_{\leq i}$ denotes $X_1, \ldots, X_i$ for $1 \leq i \leq n$ and $\mathbf{X}_{\geq i}$ denotes $X_i, \ldots, X_n$.

Let $\mathfrak{A}$ be a $n \times n$ matrix whose entries are new indeterminates $(\mathfrak{A}_{i,j})_{1 \leq i,j \leq n}$. Define $f^{\mathfrak{A}} \in \mathbb{Q}(\mathfrak{A}_{i,j})[\mathbf{X}]$ as $f^{\mathfrak{A}} = f(\mathfrak{A}\mathbf{X})$. Thus, $\mathbf{F}^{\mathfrak{A}}$ denotes the set obtained by performing the change of variables $\mathfrak{A}$ on all polynomials in $\mathbf{F}$. This notation is also used for polynomial ideals. We will also denote by $\mathfrak{k}$ an algebraic closure of $\mathbb{Q}(\mathfrak{A}_{i,j})$. Finally, given an ideal I in $k[X_1, \ldots, X_n]$ where k is a field, we denote by $\mathbf{G}(I)$ a finite set of generators (e.g. a Gröbner basis) of I.

Our construction is recursive. We start by defining $\Delta_{n-d}^{\mathfrak{A}} = \langle \mathbf{F}^{\mathfrak{A}} \rangle \subset \mathbb{Q}(\mathfrak{A}_{i,j})[\mathbf{X}]$. Remark that $\dim(\Delta_{n-d}^{\mathfrak{A}}) = d$ and $\Delta_{n-d}^{\mathfrak{A}}$ is radical (since $\langle \mathbf{F} \rangle$ is so). Then, for $1 \leq i \leq d$, we denote by $\Delta_{n-d,n-i}^{\mathfrak{A}}$ the intersection of the prime ideals of co-dimension $n-i$ associated to $\Delta_{n-d}^{\mathfrak{A}}$ if such prime ideals exist, else we fix $\Delta_{n-d,n-i}^{\mathfrak{A}} = \langle 1 \rangle$; we will also denote $\cap_{0 \leq i \leq k} \Delta_{n-d,n-i}^{\mathfrak{A}}$ by $\Delta_{n-d, \geq n-k}^{\mathfrak{A}}$.

Now, we describe how we define recursively $\Delta_{n-i+1}^{\mathfrak{A}}$ from $\Delta_{n-i}^{\mathfrak{A}}$ for $1 \leq i \leq d$. In the sequel, $\Delta_{n-i,n-j}$ denotes the intersection of prime ideals of co-dimension $n-j$ if such prime ideals exist else we fix $\Delta_{n-i,n-j} = \langle 1 \rangle$.

Our construction works as follows. We consider the algebraic set defined by $\Delta_{n-i,n-i}^{\mathfrak{A}}$ in $\mathfrak{k}^n$ and its equidimensional component of dimension i that we denote by $\mathfrak{V}_{n-i,n-i}$ here after.

We start by constructing the ideal associated to the union

of the singular locus of $\mathfrak{V}_{n-i,n-i}$ and the critical locus of Π_i restricted to $\mathfrak{V}_{n-i,n-i}$. If $\Delta^{\mathfrak{A}}_{n-i,n-i} = \langle 1 \rangle$ then we let $\mathsf{M}^{\mathfrak{A}}_{n-i} = \langle 1 \rangle$ else $\mathsf{M}^{\mathfrak{A}}_{n-i}$ is the ideal generated by the $(n-i)$-minors of $\mathsf{jac}(\mathbf{G}(\Delta^{\mathfrak{A}}_{n-i,n-i}), \mathbf{X}_{\geq i+1})$ and $\Sigma^{\mathfrak{A}}_{n-i+1}$ be the radical ideal $\sqrt{\Delta^{\mathfrak{A}}_{n-i,n-i} + \mathsf{M}^{\mathfrak{A}}_{n-i}}$. By construction, the ideal $\Sigma^{\mathfrak{A}}_{n-i+1}$ is the ideal associated to the union of the singular locus of $\mathfrak{V}_{n-i,n-i}$ and the critical locus of the restriction of Π_i to $\mathfrak{V}_{n-i,n-i}$. Thus, the definition of $\Sigma^{\mathfrak{A}}_{n-i+1}$ does not depend on $\mathbf{G}(\Delta^{\mathfrak{A}}_{n-i+1})$.

Then, we define $\Delta^{\mathfrak{A}}_{n-i+1}$ as $\Sigma^{\mathfrak{A}}_{n-i+1} \cap \Delta^{\mathfrak{A}}_{n-i,\geq n-i+1}$.

As said above, we will consider linear change of variables. Consider a matrix $\mathbf{B}_r = \mathrm{GL}_n(\mathbb{Q})$ of the form $\mathbf{B}_r = \begin{bmatrix} \mathbf{B}' & 0 \\ 0 & \mathbf{I}_{n-r} \end{bmatrix}$, where $\mathbf{B}'$ is square of size r, $\mathbf{I}_{n-r}$ is the identity matrix of size $n-r$. We let $\mathfrak{B} = \mathfrak{A}\mathbf{B}_r$ whose entries are linear forms in the entries of $\mathfrak{A}$; then for $f \in \mathbb{Q}(\mathfrak{A}_{i,j})[\mathbf{X}]$, $\mathsf{Subs}_{\mathfrak{B}}(f)$ denotes the polynomial obtained by substituting in f the entries of $\mathfrak{A}$ by those of $\mathfrak{B}$. If I is an ideal in $\mathbb{Q}(\mathfrak{A}_{i,j})[\mathbf{X}]$, then $I^{\mathbf{B}_r}$ denotes the ideal $\{f(\mathbf{B}_r\mathbf{X}) \mid f \in I\}$ and $\mathsf{Subs}_{\mathfrak{B}}(I)$ denotes the ideal $\{\mathsf{Subs}_{\mathfrak{B}}(f) \mid f \in I\}$.

LEMMA 4. *Let $r \leq i$. If $\Delta^{\mathfrak{A}\mathbf{B}_r}_{n-i} = \mathsf{Subs}_{\mathfrak{B}}(\Delta^{\mathfrak{A}}_{n-i})$, then $\Delta^{\mathfrak{A}\mathbf{B}_r}_{n-i+1} = \mathsf{Subs}_{\mathfrak{B}}(\Delta^{\mathfrak{A}}_{n-i+1})$.*

PROOF. The proof is done by induction. We detail below the induction; the initialization step being obtained by substituting i by $d+1$ in the sequel.

By assumption $\Delta^{\mathfrak{A}\mathbf{B}_r}_{n-i} = \mathsf{Subs}_{\mathfrak{B}}(\Delta^{\mathfrak{A}}_{n-i})$. Recall that these ideals are radical. Consequently, the uniqueness of prime decomposition implies that $\Delta^{\mathfrak{A}\mathbf{B}_r}_{n-i,n-i} = \mathsf{Subs}_{\mathfrak{B}}(\Delta^{\mathfrak{A}}_{n-i,n-i})$ and $\Delta^{\mathfrak{A}\mathbf{B}_r}_{n-i,\geq n-i+1} = \mathsf{Subs}_{\mathfrak{B}}(\Delta^{\mathfrak{A}}_{n-i,\geq n-i+1})$. Thus, to conclude it is sufficient to prove that $\Sigma^{\mathfrak{A}\mathbf{B}_r}_{n-i+1} = \mathsf{Subs}_{\mathfrak{B}}(\Sigma^{\mathfrak{A}}_{n-i+1})$. Let $\mathbf{G} = \mathbf{G}(\Delta^{\mathfrak{A}}_{n-i,n-i})$. Since $\Delta^{\mathfrak{A}\mathbf{B}_r}_{n-i,n-i} = \mathsf{Subs}_{\mathfrak{B}}(\Delta^{\mathfrak{A}}_{n-i,n-i})$, we get $\langle \mathbf{G}^{\mathbf{B}_r} \rangle = \langle \mathsf{Subs}_{\mathfrak{B}}(\mathbf{G}) \rangle$. Equality $\langle \mathbf{G}^{\mathbf{B}_r} \rangle = \langle \mathsf{Subs}_{\mathfrak{B}}(\mathbf{G}) \rangle$ implies that both ideals define the same algebraic variety $\mathfrak{V}$ in $\mathfrak{k}^n$. By construction, the ideal $\Sigma^{\mathfrak{A}\mathbf{B}_r}_{n-i+1}$ is the ideal associated to the union of the singular locus of $\mathfrak{V}$ and the critical locus of the restriction of Π_i to $\mathfrak{V}$. The same statement occurs for $\mathsf{Subs}_{\mathfrak{B}}(\Sigma^{\mathfrak{A}}_{n-i+1})$ so these ideals coincide. $\square$

Let k be a field; given an ideal $I \subset k[\mathbf{X}]$, we denote by $\mathcal{R}(I)$ the following property: *Let P be a prime ideal appearing in the prime decomposition of $\sqrt{I}$, and r its dimension. Then $k[\mathbf{X}_{\leq r}] \to k[\mathbf{X}]/P$ is integral.*

PROPOSITION 2. *Let $i \in \{1, \ldots, d+1\}$, the ideal $\Delta^{\mathfrak{A}}_{n-i+1}$ satisfies property $\mathcal{R}$, and has dimension at most $i-1$.*

PROOF. We prove the property by decreasing induction on $i = d+1, \ldots, 1$. The case $i = d+1$ is obtained following the Noether Normalization Theorem.

Let us now assume that the property holds for index $i+1$, and prove it for index i. We first establish property $\mathcal{R}(\Delta^{\mathfrak{A}}_{n-i+1})$. The dimension property will follow from it since it implies that Π_i restricted the variety defined by $\Delta^{\mathfrak{A}}_{n-i+1}$ is a finite map. Then, the algebraic Bertini-Sard theorem allows us to conclude.

Preliminaries. Recall that $\Delta^{\mathfrak{A}}_{n-i+1} = \Sigma^{\mathfrak{A}}_{n-i+1} \cap \Delta^{\mathfrak{A}}_{n-i,\geq n-i+1}$. Since $\mathcal{R}(\Delta^{\mathfrak{A}}_{n-i})$ holds by assumption, $\mathcal{R}(\Delta^{\mathfrak{A}}_{n-i,\geq n-i+1})$ holds trivially. Thus, it is sufficient to prove that $\mathcal{R}(\Sigma^{\mathfrak{A}}_{n-i+1})$ holds. Recall also that $\Sigma^{\mathfrak{A}}_{n-i+1}$ is the radical of $\Delta^{\mathfrak{A}}_{n-i,n-i} + \mathsf{M}^{\mathfrak{A}}_{n-i}$ where $\mathsf{M}^{\mathfrak{A}}_{n-i}$ is the ideal generated by the $(n-i)$-minors $M_1, \ldots, M_N$ of $\mathsf{jac}(\mathbf{G}(\Delta^{\mathfrak{A}}_{n-i,n-i}), \mathbf{X}_{\geq i+1})$. We will consider

this intersection process incrementally since for proving that $\mathcal{R}(\Delta^{\mathfrak{A}}_{n-i,n-i} + \mathsf{M}^{\mathfrak{A}}_{n-i})$ holds, it is enough to prove that property $\mathcal{R}(\Delta^{\mathfrak{A}}_{n-i,n-i} + \langle M_1, \ldots, M_j \rangle)$ holds for $1 \leq j \leq N$. Note that by assumption $\mathcal{R}(\Delta^{\mathfrak{A}}_{n-i+1})$ holds and we prove below by increasing induction that if $\mathcal{R}(\Delta^{\mathfrak{A}}_{n-i,n-i} + \langle M_1, \ldots, M_j \rangle)$ holds then $\mathcal{R}(\Delta^{\mathfrak{A}}_{n-i,n-i} + \langle M_1, \ldots, M_{j+1} \rangle)$ holds. To simplify notations, we fix $\Delta = \Delta^{\mathfrak{A}}_{n-i,n-i} + \langle M_1, \ldots, M_j \rangle$, $M = M_{j+1}$ and $\Delta' = \Delta + \langle M \rangle$ for $0 \leq j \leq N-1$.

Consider now the prime decomposition $\cap_\ell P_{\ell \leq L}$ of $\sqrt{\Delta}$ for some L and remark that the set of prime components of $\sqrt{\Delta'}$ is the union of the prime components of $\sqrt{P_\ell + \langle M \rangle}$ for $1 \leq \ell \leq L$. Consequently, it is enough to prove that $P_\ell + \langle M \rangle$ satisfies property $\mathcal{R}$ for those ℓ such that $P_\ell + \langle M \rangle \neq \langle 1 \rangle$. Thus, as in [26], we partition $\{1, \ldots, L\}$ in four subsets:

- $\ell \in L^+$ if $\dim(P_\ell) = r$ and $M \in P_\ell$;
- $\ell \in L^-$ if $\dim(P_\ell) = r$, $M \notin P_\ell$ and $P_\ell + \langle M \rangle \neq \langle 1 \rangle$;
- $\ell \in S$ if $\dim(P_\ell) = r$, $M \notin P_\ell$ and $P_\ell + \langle M \rangle = \langle 1 \rangle$;
- $\ell \in R$ if $\dim(P_\ell) \neq r$.

We will prove that $\mathcal{R}(P_\ell + \langle M \rangle)$ holds for $\ell \in L^+ \cup L^-$ while letting $r \leq i$ vary will conclude the proof.

For $\ell \in L^+$, $M \in P_\ell$, $P_\ell + \langle M \rangle = P_\ell$ while $\mathcal{R}(P_\ell)$ holds by assumption; the conclusion follows. Suppose now that $\ell \in L^-$. Since P_ℓ is prime, by Krull's Principal Ideal Theorem, $P_\ell + \langle M \rangle$ has dimension $r-1$ and is equidimensional. By [26, Lemma 1], it is sufficient to prove that the extension $\mathbb{Q}(\mathfrak{A}_{i,j})[\mathbf{X}_{\leq r-1}] \to \mathbb{Q}(\mathfrak{A}_{i,j})[\mathbf{X}_{\leq r-1}]/(P_\ell + \langle M \rangle)$ is integral which is what we do below.

Proving the integral extension. This step of the proof is common with the one of [26, Proposition 1]; we summarize it. By assumption, the extension $\mathbb{Q}(\mathfrak{A}_{i,j})[\mathbf{X}_{\leq r}] \to A_\ell = \mathbb{Q}(\mathfrak{A}_{i,j})[\mathbf{X}_{\leq r}]/P_\ell$ is integral, it is only needed to prove that $P_\ell + \langle M \rangle$ contains a monic polynomial in $\mathbb{Q}(\mathfrak{A}_{i,j})[\mathbf{X}_{\leq r-1}][\mathbf{X}_r]$. To this end, the characteristic polynomial of the multiplication by M in A_ℓ is naturally considered and more particularly, we consider its constant term α_ℓ. Since $\ell \in L^-$, M does not divide zero in A_ℓ and α_ℓ is not a constant (and hence it is not zero). Moreover, by Cayley-Hamilton's Theorem, $\alpha_\ell \in P_\ell + \langle M \rangle$. This polynomial α_ℓ is proved to be monic in X_r hereafter.

Consider a matrix $\mathbf{B} = \mathrm{GL}_n(\mathbb{Q})$ which lets invariant the last $n-r$ variables and such that $\alpha_\ell(\mathbf{BX})$ is monic in X_r (recall that $r \leq i$). Following *mutatis mutandis* the reasoning of [26, Sect 2.3] (paragraph entitled *Introduction of a change of variables*), we get that

- the constant term of the multiplication by $M(\mathbf{BX})$ modulo $P_\ell^{\mathbf{B}}$ is $\alpha_\ell(\mathbf{BX})$;
- the constant term of the multiplication by $\mathsf{Subs}_{\mathfrak{B}}(M)$ modulo $\mathsf{Subs}_{\mathfrak{B}}(P_\ell)$ is $\mathsf{Subs}_{\mathfrak{B}}(\alpha_\ell)$;

Note that we have chosen $\mathbf{B}$ such that $\alpha_\ell(\mathbf{BX})$ is monic in X_r. Thus, if we prove that $\alpha_\ell(\mathbf{BX}) = \mathsf{Subs}_{\mathfrak{B}}(\alpha_\ell)$, we are done (recall that $\mathsf{Subs}_{\mathfrak{B}}$ only consists in substituting the entries of $\mathfrak{A}_{i,j}$ with those of $\mathfrak{A}\mathbf{B}$ which do not depend on $X_1, \ldots, X_n$).

Since $\mathbf{B}$ lets invariant the last $n-r$ variables $X_{r+1}, \ldots, X_n$, we get from Lemma 4 that $\Delta^{\mathbf{B}} = \mathsf{Subs}_{\mathfrak{B}}(\Delta)$ and $M^{\mathbf{B}} = \mathsf{Subs}_{\mathfrak{B}}(M)$. The uniqueness of prime decomposition implies that $\{P_\ell^{\mathbf{B}}, \ell \in L\} = \{\mathsf{Subs}_{\mathfrak{B}}(P_\ell), \ell \in L\}$. Moreover, since $\dim(\mathsf{Subs}_{\mathfrak{B}}(P_\ell)) = \dim(P_\ell^{\mathbf{B}}) = \dim(P_\ell)$, we also have

$$\{P_\ell^{\mathbf{B}}, \ell \in L^+ \cup L^- \cup S\} = \{\mathsf{Subs}_{\mathfrak{B}}(P_\ell), \ell \in L^+ \cup L^- \cup S\}$$

The rest of the reasoning is the same as the one of [26]. Indeed, the above equality implies that for $\ell \in L^-$, there exists $\ell' \in L^+ \cup L^- \cup S$ such that $\mathsf{Subs}_{\mathfrak{B}}(P_\ell) = P_{\ell'}^{\mathbf{B}}$. Since $M^{\mathbf{B}} = \mathsf{Subs}_{\mathfrak{B}}(M)$, the characteristic polynomials of $M^{\mathbf{B}}$ modulo $P_{\ell'}^{\mathbf{B}}$ coincides with the characteristic polynomial of $\mathsf{Subs}_{\mathfrak{B}}(M)$ modulo $\mathsf{Subs}_{\mathfrak{B}}(P_\ell)$, so $\mathsf{Subs}_{\mathfrak{B}}(\alpha_\ell) = \alpha_{\ell'}(\mathbf{BX})$. Recall now that α_ℓ is neither 0 nor a constant, then $\ell' \in L^-$. Thus, $\mathsf{Subs}_{\mathfrak{B}}(\alpha_\ell) = \alpha_{\ell'}(\mathbf{BX})$ is monic in X_r as requested.$\square$

As in [26, Subsection 6.4], this property specializes. For $\mathbf{A} \in \mathrm{GL}_n(\mathbb{Q})$, we denote by $\Delta_{n-i+1}^{\mathbf{A}}$ the ideal obtained by substituting the entries of $\mathfrak{A}$ by those of $\mathbf{A}$. The proof of the result below is skipped but follows *mutatis mutandis* the one of [26, Proposition 2].

PROPOSITION 3. *There exists a non-empty Zariski open set $\mathscr{O} \subset \mathrm{GL}_n(\mathbb{C})$ such that for $\mathbf{A}$ in $\mathscr{O}$, the following holds. Let $1 \le i \le d+1$, $P^{\mathbf{A}}$ be one of the prime components of $\Delta_{n-i+1}^{\mathbf{A}}$, and r its dimension. Then $\mathbb{C}[\mathbf{X}_{\le r}] \to \mathbb{C}[\mathbf{X}]/P^{\mathbf{A}}$ is integral.*

Once the above result is proved, one can conclude the proof of properness properties by using a result of [16] relating the properness property and the above normalization result. More precisely, we use [26, Proposition 3] that we restate below in a form that fits with our construction:

PROPOSITION 4. *[26] Let $\mathbf{A}$ be in $\mathrm{GL}_n(\mathbb{C})$ and $1 \le i \le d+1$. The following assertions are equivalent.*

- *For every prime component $P^{\mathbf{A}}$ of $\Delta_{n-i+1}^{\mathbf{A}}$, the following holds. Let r be the dimension of $P^{\mathbf{A}}$; then $\mathbb{C}[\mathbf{X}_{\le r}] \to \mathbb{C}[\mathbf{X}]/P^{\mathbf{A}}$ is integral.*
- *The restriction of Π_r to $V(P^{\mathbf{A}})$ is proper.*

Finally, we define $V_{n-i}^{\mathbf{A}} \subset \mathbb{C}^n$ as the algebraic variety associated to $\Delta_{n-i}^{\mathbf{A}}$ for $0 \le i \le d$. For $j \le i$, we denote by $V_{n-i,n-j}^{\mathbf{A}} \subset \mathbb{C}^n$ (resp. $V_{n-i,\ge n-j}^{\mathbf{A}} \subset \mathbb{C}^n$) the algebraic variety associated to $\Delta_{n-i,n-j}^{\mathbf{A}}$ (resp. $\Delta_{n-i,\ge n-j}^{\mathbf{A}}$). Consider now a connected component C of $V_{n-i}^{\mathbf{A}} \cap \mathbb{R}^n$. It is the union of some connected components $C_1, \ldots, C_k$ of the real algebraic sets $V_{n-i,n-j_1}^{\mathbf{A}} \cap \mathbb{R}^n, \ldots, V_{n-i,n-j_k}^{\mathbf{A}} \cap \mathbb{R}^n$. Consequently, the boundary of $\Pi_i(C)$ is contained in the boundary of $\cup_{1 \le \ell \le k} \Pi_i(C_\ell)$. By construction of $V_{n-i+1}^{\mathbf{A}}$, if $j_\ell > i$ then the boundary of $\Pi_i(C_\ell)$ is contained in $\Pi_i(V_{n-i+1}^{\mathbf{A}})$. By construction of $V_{n-i+1}^{\mathbf{A}}$, $V_{n-i+1,n-i+1}^{\mathbf{A}}$ is the union of the singular points of $V_{n-i,n-i}^{\mathbf{A}}$ and the critical locus of Π_i restricted to $V_{n-i,n-i}^{\mathbf{A}}$. Thus, if $j_\ell = i$, the properness of Π_i restricted to $V_{n-i,n-i}^{\mathbf{A}}$ implies that the boundary of $\Pi_i(C_i)$ is contained in the image by Π_i of $C \cap V_{n-i+1,n-i+1}^{\mathbf{A}}$. This leads to the following lemma which concludes the proof.

LEMMA 5. *Let $\mathbf{A} \in \mathscr{O} \cap \mathrm{GL}_n(\mathbb{Q})$ be such that for $1 \le i \le d+1$ and all prime components $P^{\mathbf{A}}$ of $\Delta_{n-i+1}^{\mathbf{A}}$ the restriction of Π_r to $V(P^{\mathbf{A}})$ is proper and $C^{\mathbf{A}}$ be a connected component of $V_{n-d}^{\mathbf{A}} \cap \mathbb{R}^n$. Then the boundary of $\Pi_i(C^{\mathbf{A}})$ is contained in $\Pi_i(V_{n-i+1}^{\mathbf{A}})$.*

6. REFERENCES

[1] P. Aubry, F. Rouillier, and M. Safey El Din. Real solving for positive dimensional systems. *J. Symbolic Comput.*, 34(6):543–560, 2002.

[2] B. Bank, M. Giusti, J. Heintz, and G. M. Mbakop. Polar varieties, real equation solving, and data structures: the hypersurface case. *J. Complexity*, 13(1):5–27, 1997.

[3] B. Bank, M. Giusti, J. Heintz, and L. M. Pardo. Generalized polar varieties and an efficient real elimination procedure. *Kybernetika (Prague)*, 40(5):519–550, 2004.

[4] B. Bank, M. Giusti, J. Heintz, and L. M. Pardo. On the intrinsic complexity of point finding in real singular hypersurfaces. *Inform. Process. Lett.*, 109(19):1141–1144, 2009.

[5] B. Bank, M. Giusti, J. Heintz, M. Safey El Din, and E. Schost. On the geometry of polar varieties. *Appl. Algebra Engrg. Comm. Comput.*, 21(1):33–83, 2010.

[6] B. Bank, M. Giusti, J. Heintz, M. Safey El Din, and E. Schost. On the geometry of polar varieties. *Appl. Algebra Engrg. Comm. Comput.*, 21(1):33–83, 2010.

[7] S. Basu, R. Pollack, and M.-F. Roy. *Algorithms in real algebraic geometry*, volume 10 of *Algorithms and Computation in Mathematics*. Springer-Verlag, second edition, 2006.

[8] G. E. Collins. Quantifier elimination for real closed fields by cylindrical algebraic decomposition. *Lecture Notes in Comput. Sci.*, 33:515–532, 1975.

[9] M. Demazure. *Bifurcations and catastrophes. Geometry of solutions to non-linear problems*. Springer, 2000.

[10] H. Everett, D. Lazard, S. Lazard, and M. Safey El Din. The Voronoi diagram of three lines. *Discrete Comput. Geom.*, 42(1):94–130, 2009.

[11] J.-C. Faugère. Fgb, gröbner basis engine. available at http://www-salsa.lip6.fr/~jcf/Software/index.html.

[12] W. Fulton. *Intersection Theory*. Springer-Verlag, second edition, 1998.

[13] M. Giusti, G. Lecerf, and B. Salvy. A Gröbner free alternative for polynomial system solving. *J. Complexity*, 17(1):154–211, 2001.

[14] F. Guo, M. Safey El Din, and L. Zhi. Global optimization of polynomials using generalized critical values and sums of squares. In *Proceedings of ISSAC 2010*, pages 107–114, New York, NY, USA, 2010. ACM.

[15] D. Henrion. *Polynômes et optimisation convexe en commande robuste*. PhD thesis, LAAS, Toulouse, 2007. Habilitation à diriger des recherches.

[16] Z. Jelonek. Testing sets for properness of polynomial mappings. *Math. Ann.*, 315(1):1–35, 1999.

[17] E. Kaltofen, B. Li, Z. Yang, and L. Zhi. Exact certification in global polynomial optimization via sums-of-squares of rational functions with rational coefficients, 2010. Journal of Symbolic Computation.

[18] E. Kaltofen, Z. Yang, and L. Zhi. A proof of the monotone column permanent (MCP) conjecture for dimension 4 via sums-of-squares of rational functions. In *Proceedings of SNC 2009*, pages 65–70. ACM, 2009.

[19] E. Kunz. *Introduction to commutative algebra and algebraic geometry*. Birkhäuser Boston, 1984.

[20] G. Lecerf. Computing the equidimensional decomposition of an algebraic closed set by means of lifting fibers. *J. Complexity*, 19(4):564–596, 2003.

[21] J. Nie, J. Demmel, and B. Sturmfels. Minimizing polynomials via sum of squares over the gradient ideal. *Math. Program.*, 106(3):587–606, 2006.

[22] H. Peyrl and P. A. Parrilo. Computing sum of squares decompositions with rational coefficients. *Theoret. Comput. Sci.*, 409(2):269–281, 2008.

[23] F. Rouillier, M.-F. Roy, and M. Safey El Din. Finding at least one point in each connected component of a real algebraic set defined by a single equation. *J. Complexity*, 16(4):716–750, 2000.

[24] M. Safey El Din. Finding sampling points on real hypersurfaces in easier in singular situations. In *MEGA*, 2005.

[25] M. Safey El Din. Computing the global optimum of a multivariate polynomial over the reals. In *ISSAC 2008*, pages 71–78. ACM, New York, 2008.

[26] M. Safey El Din and É. Schost. Polar varieties and computation of one point in each connected component of a smooth algebraic set. In *Proceedings of ISSAC 2003*, pages 224–231 (electronic), New York, 2003. ACM.

[27] M. Safey El Din and É. Schost. Properness defects of projections and computation of at least one point in each connected component of a real algebraic set. *Discrete Comput. Geom.*, 32(3):417–430, 2004.

[28] M. Safey El Din and L. Zhi. Computing rational points in convex semialgebraic sets and sum of squares decompositions. *SIAM J. Optim.*, 20(6):2876–2889, 2010.

An Algorithm for Computing Set-Theoretic Generators of an Algebraic Variety

Leilei Guo
KLMM,Institute of Systems Science
AMSS,Academia Sinica
Beijing, China
leiguo@mmrc.iss.ac.cn

Feng Liu
Department of Mathematics
Suzhou University
Suzhou, China

ABSTRACT

Based on Eisenbud's idea (see [Eisenbud, D., Evans, G., 1973. Every algebraic set in n-space is the intersection of n hypersurfaces. Invent. Math. 19, 107-112]), we present an algorithm for computing set-theoretic generators for any algebraic variety in the affine n-space, which consists of at most n polynomials. With minor modifications, this algorithm is also valid for projective algebraic variety in projective n-space.

Categories and Subject Descriptors: I.1.2 [Computing Methodologies]: Symbolic and Algebraic Manipulation-Algebraic Algorithms

General Terms: Algorithms, Theory.

Keywords: Set-theoretic generators, Regular sequence, Gröbner basis, Triangular decomposition.

1. INTRODUCTION

The set-theoretic generators for an algebraic variety are a set of hypersurfaces whose intersection is exactly equal to the algebraic variety. The minimal number of set-theoretic generators for an algebraic variety may vary with the number and the type of the singularities of the algebraic variety. Thus computing minimal set-theoretic generators for an algebraic variety can be a difficult task.

In algebraic geometry, finding the minimal number of set-theoretic generators for an algebraic variety is a classical problem. There is a long history for this. Kronecker [14] announced the classical result that any radical ideal in a polynomial ring in n variables over the field $\mathbb{K}$ is the radical of an ideal generated by at most $n + 1$ polynomials. Van der Waerden [21] gave the first modern proof of Kronecher's theorem. For the special case of space curves, Kneser [12] proved that every algebraic curve in 3-space is the intersection of three surfaces. Based on Kneser's idea, Eisenbud and Evans [5] made a breakthrough by proving that every algebraic variety in n-dimension space is the intersection of n hypersurfaces. This result is optimal in the sense that a zero

dimensional variety does need n generators. There is an unsolved problem whether every irreducible curve in 3-space is a set-theoretic complete intersection of two surfaces or not. The research in the field of Algebraic Geometry focuses on the theory of set-theoretic generators, but few algorithms are provided.

To our knowledge, there has been only some very preliminary work on constructing set-theoretic (ideal-theoretic) generators for algebraic variety until recently. In the recent paper [11], the authors show how to calculate three set-theoretic generators for some special rational space curves in the $\mathbb{P}^3(\mathbb{K})$. In the recent paper [8], E. Fortuna et.al show that if $\mathcal{I}$ is an unmixed one-dimensional radical ideal of $\mathbb{K}[x, y, z]$ defining a curve $\mathcal{C} = \mathbb{V}(\mathcal{I}) \subseteq \mathbb{K}^3$ such that the Jacobian matrix $Jac(\mathcal{I}, p)$ of $\mathcal{I}$ at p has rank ≥ 1 for each $p \in \mathcal{C}$, then $\mathcal{I}$ is generated by three polynomials that can be computed. The aim of this paper is to present an algorithm for computing set-theoretic generators for any algebraic variety in n-space, which consists of at most n polynomials. Although the idea about this algorithm is essentially due to Eisenbud and Evans [5], it seems to have escaped the attention of the community of symbolic computation.

As far as I know, this is the first algorithm for computing set-theoretic generators consisting of at most n polynomials for any algebraic variety in n-space. This can be regarded as our main contribution. Our algorithm relies on many operations about Gröbner bases and Triangular decomposition.

The paper is organized as follows. In Section 2.1 and 2.2, we begin with a brief review of basic definitions such as the concepts of set-theoretic generators and some properties of Gröbner basis and regular chain. In section 2.3, we recall some operations using Gröbner bases and Triangular decomposition. In Section 3.1-3.3, we provide an algorithm for computing set-theoretic generators consisting of at most n polynomials for any algebraic variety in n-space, and we prove the validity of our algorithm. In section 3.4, We illustrate our methods with two examples. The paper is concluded with a few remarks.

2. PRELIMINARIES

2.1 Set-theoretic generators

Throughout this paper, let $\mathbb{K}$ be a field and $\mathbb{K}[X] = \mathbb{K}[x_1, \ldots, x_n]$ denotes the ring of polynomials in n variables over $\mathbb{K}$. Let F be a subset of $\mathbb{K}[X]$. The ideal generated by F is denoted by (F) and the radical of (F) by $\sqrt{(F)}$. Let $\mathbb{A}^n(\mathbb{K})$ denote the n dimension affine space over $\mathbb{K}$. We denote by $\mathbb{V}(F)$ the zero set (or algebraic variety) of F in $\mathbb{A}^n(\mathbb{K})$.

For a polynomial G, we define $\mathbb{V}(F/G) = \mathbb{V}(F)\backslash\mathbb{V}(G)$. The (vanishing) ideal $\mathbb{I}(\mathcal{V})$ of an affine variety $\mathcal{V}$ is defined as $\mathbb{I}(\mathcal{V}) := \{f \in \mathbb{K}[X] \mid f(X) = 0 \text{ for } \forall X \in \mathcal{V}\}$.

Before we investigate set-theoretic generators for algebraic varieties, we recall some basic terminologies to be used throughout this paper.

DEFINITION 2.1. *Let $\mathcal{I}$ be the ideal of an algebraic variety $\mathcal{V}$. A set of polynomials $f_1, \ldots, f_s \in \mathbb{K}[X]$ are called set-theoretic generators of the algebraic variety $\mathcal{V}$ if $\mathbb{V}(f_1, \ldots, f_s) = \mathbb{V}(\mathcal{I})$.*

REMARK 2.2. *If the zeros are not taken in an algebraically closed field, then every algebraic variety could be defined by just one equation. In fact, if $\mathbb{K}$ is not an algebraically closed field, we easily know that there exists $f \in \mathbb{K}[X]$ such that the algebraic variety defined $f = 0$ consists of just the origin $(0, \cdots, 0) \in \mathbb{A}^n(\mathbb{K})$. If $\mathcal{V} = \mathbb{V}(f_1, \ldots, f_r)$, consider the polynomial $f(f_1, \ldots, f_r)$, then we have $\mathcal{V} = \mathbb{V}(f(f_1, \ldots, f_r))$. For example, if $\mathbb{K}$ denotes real field $\mathbb{R}$, then $\mathcal{V} = \mathbb{V}(f_1, \ldots, f_r) = \mathbb{V}(f_1^2 + \ldots + f_r^2)$.*

DEFINITION 2.3. *Let $\mathcal{I}$ be the ideal of an algebraic variety $\mathcal{V}$. A set of polynomials $f_1, \ldots, f_s \in \mathbb{K}[X]$ are ideal-theoretic generators of the algebraic variety $\mathcal{V}$ if $(f_1, \ldots, f_s) = \mathcal{I}$.*

EXAMPLE 2.4. *Consider the space curve $\mathcal{C}$ defined parametrically by*

$$x = t^3, \ y = t^4, \ z = t^5$$

The ideal of the above curve is given by $\mathbb{I}(\mathcal{C}) = (x^3 - yz, y^2 - xz, z^2 - x^2 y)$. Let $f = z^2 - x^2 y$, $g = x^4 - 2xyz + y^3$. One can easily check that $\sqrt{(f,g)} = \sqrt{\mathbb{I}(\mathcal{C})}$ and $(f,g) \neq \mathbb{I}(\mathcal{C})$ by the Gröbner basis method. Therefore, f and g form set-theoretic generators for the space curve $\mathcal{C}$, but not ideal-theoretic generators for the space curve $\mathcal{C}$.

2.2 Grobner basis

We fix some notation, which will be used throughout this paper. We denote by $X = \{x_1, \cdots, x_n\}$ and by $[X]$ the set of monomials in these variables. Let $Y = \{x_1, \cdots, x_{n-1}\}$ be a subset of $n-1$ variables and $z = x_n$, we can consider $\mathbb{K}[X] = R[z]$ as a polynomial ring with base ring $R = \mathbb{K}[Y]$. A block order eliminating the z-variables is a monomial order on $[X]$ such that $mn < m'n'$ whenever $m < m'$ for $m, m' \in [z]$ and $n, n' \in [Y]$. For example, the lex order where $x_1 < \cdots < x_n$ is a block order eliminating the x_n-variables. In particular, a Gröbner basis G in $\mathbb{K}[X]$ is also a Gröbner basis in $R[z]$ w.r.t a block order eliminating the z-variables. The following theorem comes from [20].

THEOREM 2.5. *Let G be a Gröbner basis for the ideal $\mathcal{I} \subset R[x]$, $R[x]$ a polynomial ring in one variable over R and $\sigma : R \to \mathbb{K}$ a ring homomorphism to a field $\mathbb{K}$. Suppose that G contains a polynomial whose leading coefficient is not annihilated by σ. Then $\sigma(\mathcal{I}) = \sigma((g))$, where $g \in G$ is of least degree with the property $\sigma(lc(g)) \neq 0$.*

Let R be a Noetherian commutative ring with identity and $\mathcal{I}$ be an ideal in R. An element p of R is said to be a zero divisor modulo $\mathcal{I}$ if its canonical image in $R/\mathcal{I}$ is a zero divisor. An element p of R is regular modulo $\mathcal{I}$ if it is neither zero, nor a zero divisor modulo $\mathcal{I}$. The following corollary is a direct consequence of Theorem 2.5.

COROLLARY 2.6. *Let G be a Gröbner basis for the ideal $\mathcal{I} \subset R[x]$, $R[x]$ a polynomial ring in one variable over R and $\sigma : R \to L$ a ring homomorphism to a product of fields L. Suppose that $g \in G$ is of least degree and $\sigma(lc(g))$ is regular modulo (0) in L. Then $\sigma(\mathcal{I}) = \sigma((g))$.*

2.3 Triangular set

For a non-constant polynomial $f \in \mathbb{K}[X]$, the greatest variable appearing in f is called main variable, denoted by $mvar(f)$. We regard f as a univariate polynomial in its main variable. The leading coefficient of f as a univariate polynomial in $mvar(f)$ is called initial of f, denoted by $init(f)$. A subset T of non-constant polynomials of $\mathbb{K}[X]$ is a triangular set if the polynomials in T have pairwise distinct main variables. For a nonempty triangular set T, we define the saturated ideal $sat(T)$ of T to be the ideal $(T) : h^\infty = \{f \in \mathbb{K}[X] \mid \exists e \in \mathbb{Z} \text{ s.t. } h^e f \in (T)\}$ where h is the product of the initials of the polynomials in T. The notion of a regular chain was introduced independently in [13] and [23].

DEFINITION 2.7. *Let T be a nonempty triangular set in $\mathbb{K}[X]$, p the polynomial of T with the greatest main variable and C the set of other polynomials in T. We say that T is a regular chain, if C is a regular chain and $init(p)$ is regular modulo $sat(C)$.*

In commutative algebra, there is a closely related concept called regular sequence.

DEFINITION 2.8. *A sequence $r_1, \ldots, r_s$ of nonzero elements in $\mathcal{R}$ is called a regular sequence (see [7]) in $\mathcal{R}$ if the following conditions are satisfied:*
(1) $(r_1, \ldots, r_s)$ is a proper ideal of $\mathcal{R}$;
(2) r_i is not a zero divisor modulo $(r_1, \ldots, r_{i-1})$, for each $2 \leq i \leq s$.

We recall several important results on regular chains and saturated ideals, which will be used throughout this paper. Pseudo division and iterated resultant are fundamental tools in this context. Let p and q be polynomials of $\mathbb{K}[X]$, with $q \notin \mathbb{K}$. Denote by $prem(p,q)$ and $pquo(p,q)$ the pseudo-remainder and the pseudo quotient of p by q, regarding p and q as univariate polynomials in $mvar(q)$.

We denote by $res(p,q)$ the resultant of p and q regarding them as univariate polynomials in $mvar(q)$. For a polynomial p and a regular chain T, we define the iterated resultant of p w.r.t. T, denoted by $ires(p,T)$, as follows:

$$ires(p,T) = \begin{cases} p & \text{if } T = \varnothing, \\ ires(res(p,t), T') & \text{if } T = T' \bigcup \{t\}. \end{cases}$$

where t is the polynomial in T with greatest main variable.

THEOREM 2.9. *Let T be a regular chain and f be a polynomial, f is regular modulo $sat(T)$ if and only if $ires(f,T) \neq 0$.*

For the proof, we refer to [15].

An ideal in $\mathbb{K}[X]$ is unmixed, if all its associated primes have the same dimension.

THEOREM 2.10. *Let $T = C \bigcup \{t\}$ be a regular chain in $\mathbb{K}[X]$ with t having greatest main variable in T. Then $sat(T)$ is an unmixed ideal with dimension $n - |T|$.*

For the proof, we refer to [3].

REMARK 2.11. *Attention the following subtle fact: a polynomial f regular modulo $\sqrt{\mathcal{I}}$ may not be regular modulo $\mathcal{I}$. For example, consider $f = x$ and $\mathcal{I} = (y^2, xy)$. Then f is a zero divisor modulo $\mathcal{I}$ but f is regular modulo $\sqrt{\mathcal{I}} = (y)$. However, if $\mathcal{I}$ is unmixed, then f is regular modulo $\mathcal{I}$ if and only if f is regular modulo $\sqrt{\mathcal{I}}$.*

2.4 Some basic operations

We list below the specifications of some basic operations used in this paper. We need to point out the following operations are factorization-free. For the below five operations, we refer to [9] and [4].

GröbnerBasis: The operation **GröbnerBasis**$(F, >)$ inputs a set of polynomials F, an monomial order $>$ and outputs a Gröbner basis of (F) w.r.t. the monomial order.

GOI: The operation **GOI**(F,G) inputs two sets of polynomials F and G and outputs a set of generators for $(F) \bigcap (G)$.

GOS: The operation **GOS**(F,f) inputs a set of polynomials F and a polynomial f and outputs a set of generators for $(F) : f^\infty$.

Radical: The operation **Radical**(F) inputs a set of polynomials F and outputs a set of generators for $\sqrt{(F)}$.

NormalForm: The operation **NormalForm**$(f, G, >)$ inputs a Gröbner basis G of some ideal $\mathcal{I}$ w.r.t. a monomial order $>$, a polynomial f and outputs the normal form of f w.r.t. G.

For the below two operations, we refer to [13] and [10].

Triangularize: The operation **Triangularize**(F) inputs a polynomial system F and outputs a finite set of regular chains A_i such that $\sqrt{(F)} = \bigcap_{i=1}^{m} \sqrt{sat(A_i)}$ is an irredundant decomposition where the irredundant means the sets of minimal prime ideals of the $sat(A_i)$ for $i = 1, \cdots, m$ gives a partition of the set of minimal prime ideals of (F). In other words, if P is a minimal prime of $\sqrt{(F)}$, there exists a unique i such that $\sqrt{sat(A_i)} \subseteq P$.

Split: The operation **Split**(C, f) inputs a regular chain C and a polynomial f and outputs a pair of regular chain set $(\mathcal{W}, \mathcal{U})$ such that $\sqrt{sat(C)} = \bigcap_{A \in \mathcal{W} \bigcup \mathcal{U}} \sqrt{sat(A)}$ is an irredundant decomposition and $f \in sat(A), \forall A \in \mathcal{W}$ while f is regular modulo $sat(A), \forall A \in \mathcal{U}$.

Let $\mathcal{I}$ be an ideal in $\mathbb{K}[X]$ and F be a subset of $\mathcal{I}$. The subset F is said to be a maximal system of parameters in $\mathcal{I}$ if $dim((F)) = dim(\mathcal{I})$ and $\sharp F = n - dim(\mathcal{I})$.

MSP: The operation **MSP**(F) inputs a set of polynomials F and outputs a maximal system of parameters in (F). The details about **MSP** can be seen from the algorithm 1.3. in the paper [6].

When our input is an ideal in the below, this means our input is a set of generators for the ideal.

3. SET-THEORETIC GENERATORS OF AN ALGEBRAIC VARIETY

3.1 The main algorithm

In this section, we present an algorithm to compute set-theoretic generators consisting of at most n polynomials for any algebraic variety in affine n-space.

We first introduce the key concept of gcd in a ring. Let $\mathcal{R}$ be a ring, $\mathcal{Z}(\mathcal{R})$ the set of zero divisors of $\mathcal{R}$. The total

quotient ring of $\mathcal{R}$, that is, the localization of $\mathcal{R}$ at $\mathcal{R} \setminus \mathcal{Z}(\mathcal{R})$ will be written as $\mathcal{Q}(\mathcal{R})$. The following gcd definition comes from [17].

DEFINITION 3.1. *Let $\mathcal{R}$ be a ring, F a set of polynomials in $\mathcal{R}[x]$, $g \in \mathcal{R}[x]$. We say that g is a gcd of the polynomials in F if $(F) = (g)$ in the total quotient ring $\mathcal{Q}(\mathcal{R})[x]$.*

The key step of the algorithm is to compute a gcd in certain rings. We will give its definition below and give the algorithm in section 3.2.

Let F and Φ be finite sets of polynomials in $\mathbb{K}[Y][z]$, $\mathcal{R} = \mathbb{K}[Y]/\sqrt{(\Phi)}$. The algorithm **RGCD** (Algorithm 3.18) will take F and Φ as input and output two polynomials f, u such that $f \in (F)$, $(F) = (f)$ in $\mathcal{Q}(\mathbb{K}[Y]/\sqrt{(\Phi)})[z]$ and $u \in S$, $u(F) \subseteq (f)$ in $\mathbb{K}[Y][z]$ where $S = \mathbb{K}[Y] \setminus \bigcup_{i=1}^{r} \mathcal{P}_i$ and $\sqrt{(\Phi)} = \bigcap_{i=1}^{r} \mathcal{P}_i$ is an irredundant prime decomposition in $\mathbb{K}[Y]$.

We now give the following algorithm to compute set-theoretic generators consisting of at most n polynomials for any algebraic variety in affine n-space.

ALGORITHM 3.2. **SETG**
Input: *A set of polynomials $F = \{f_1, \cdots, f_m\} \in \mathbb{K}[Y][z]$*
Output: *A set Ω such that $\sqrt{(F)} = \sqrt{(\Omega)}$ in $\mathbb{K}[Y][z]$ and $\sharp \Omega \leq n$.*

 $\mathcal{J}_1 := (F) \bigcap \mathbb{K}[Y]$;
 $\Phi := MSP(\mathcal{J}_1)$;
 $\Omega := MSP(\mathcal{J}_1)$;
 while $\sharp(\Omega) < n$ *repeat*
  $(g, u) := $**RGCD**$(F, \Phi)$; *(Algorithm **RGCD**)*
  if $(u, \Phi) = (1)$, *then*
   return $\Omega = \Omega \bigcup \{g\}$;
  else
   $\Phi = \Phi \bigcup \{u\}$ *and* $\Omega = \Omega \bigcup \{g\}$;
  end if
 end while
 return Ω.

To prove the correctness of the above algorithm, we first give some lemmas. Some results may have been known in the below, but we have not always found the original sources. For this reason and for an easier reading, we give self-contained proofs.

LEMMA 3.3. *Let $\mathcal{I} = (f_1, \cdots, f_s)$ and $\mathcal{J} = (g_1, \cdots, g_t)$ be ideals in the $\mathbb{K}[X]$. If we have $\mathcal{J} \subseteq \mathcal{I}$ and $u\mathcal{I} \subseteq \mathcal{J}$ where $u \in \mathbb{K}[X]$ is a polynimial, then $\mathbb{V}(\mathcal{I}) = \mathbb{V}(\mathcal{J}/u) \bigcup \mathbb{V}(\mathcal{I}, u)$.*

Proof: We easily have $\mathbb{V}(\mathcal{I}) = \mathbb{V}(\mathcal{I}/u) \bigcup \mathbb{V}(\mathcal{I}, u)$. It suffices to show that $\mathbb{V}(\mathcal{I}/u) = \mathbb{V}(\mathcal{J}/u)$.

On one hand, since $\mathcal{J} \subseteq \mathcal{I}$, we have $\mathbb{V}(\mathcal{I}/u) \subseteq \mathbb{V}(\mathcal{J}/u)$. On the other hand, for any $x \in \mathbb{V}(\mathcal{J}/u)$, we have $\forall g \in \mathcal{J}, g(x) = 0$ and $u(x) \neq 0$. Since $u\mathcal{I} \subseteq \mathcal{J}$ and $\forall f \in \mathcal{I}$, there exist $a_1, a_2, \cdots, a_t$ such that $uf = a_1 g_1 + \cdots + a_t g_t$. Furthermore $u(x)f(x) = 0$, we have $\mathbb{V}(\mathcal{J}/u) \subseteq \mathbb{V}(\mathcal{I}/u)$. Then $\mathbb{V}(\mathcal{I}/u) = \mathbb{V}(\mathcal{J}/u)$. $\square$

LEMMA 3.4. *Let $\mathcal{J} \subset \mathbb{K}[Y]$ be a zero dimension ideal and $\mathcal{I} \subset \mathbb{K}[Y][z]$ an ideal satisfying $\mathcal{J} \subseteq \mathcal{I}$. Let $(f, u) = $ **RGCD**(**Radical**$(\mathcal{I})$, **Radical**$(\mathcal{J})$). Then $\sqrt{\mathcal{I}} = \sqrt{(\mathcal{J}, f)}$.*

Proof: Let $\sqrt{\mathcal{J}} = \bigcap_{i=1}^{m} P_i$ be an irredundant prime decomposition where P_i is a maximal ideal for $i = 1, 2, \cdots, m$. Since $\sqrt{\mathcal{J}}$ is a zero dimension radical ideal, $\mathcal{Q}(\mathbb{K}[Y]/\sqrt{(\mathcal{J})}) = \mathbb{K}[Y]/\sqrt{\mathcal{J}}$. From the specifications of algorithm **RGCD**, we know $f \in \sqrt{\mathcal{I}}$ abd $\sqrt{\mathcal{I}} = (f)$ in $(\mathbb{K}[Y]/\sqrt{\mathcal{J}})[z]$.

On one hand, since $\sqrt{\mathcal{J}} \subseteq \sqrt{\mathcal{I}}$ and $f \in \sqrt{\mathcal{I}}$, we have $\sqrt{(\mathcal{I})} \supseteq \sqrt{(\mathcal{J}, f)}$. On the other hand, for any $g \in \sqrt{\mathcal{I}}$ and $\sqrt{\mathcal{I}} = (f)$ in $(\mathbb{K}[Y]/\sqrt{\mathcal{J}})[z]$, we have $h_1 g - h_2 f \in \sqrt{\mathcal{J}}$ and $h_1 \notin \bigcup_{i=1}^{m} P_i$. Furthermore we have $h_1 g \in \sqrt{(\mathcal{J}, f)}$ and $g \in \sqrt{(\mathcal{J}, f)}$. So we have $\sqrt{(\mathcal{I})} \subseteq \sqrt{(\mathcal{J}, f)}$. Then $\sqrt{\mathcal{I}} = \sqrt{(\mathcal{J}, f)}$. $\square$

PROPOSITION 3.5. *Let $\mathcal{I} = (f_1, \ldots, f_s)$ be an ideal in $\mathbb{K}[X]$ and $dim(\mathcal{I}) = n - s$. Let g be a regular sequence in $\mathbb{K}[X]/\mathcal{I}$. Then $(\mathcal{I}, g)$ is an unmixed ideal with dimension $n - s - 1$.*

Proof: Let $\sqrt{\mathcal{I}} = \bigcap_{i=1}^{r} \mathcal{P}_i$ be an irredundant prime decomposition in $\mathbb{K}[X]$. By the Macaulay Unmixedness Theorem (Theorem 5.7 in [19]), we have $dim\mathcal{P}_i = n - s$ for $1 \le j \le r$. We have $\sqrt{(\mathcal{I}, g)} = \bigcap_{i=1}^{r} \sqrt{(\mathcal{P}_i, g)}$. If $(\mathcal{P}_i, g) = \mathbb{K}[X]$, we delete $\sqrt{(\mathcal{P}_i, g)}$ and get $\sqrt{(\mathcal{I}, g)} = \bigcap_{i=1}^{r_1} \sqrt{(\mathcal{P}_i, g)}$ (This decomposition may not be prime decomposition). By the definition of regular sequence, there exists some j such that $(\mathcal{P}_j, g) \neq \mathbb{K}[X]$, so $r_1 \neq 0$. Since $g \notin \mathcal{P}_j$, we have $\dim(P_j, g) = n - s - 1$ for $j = 1, 2, \cdots, r_1$. Then $(\mathcal{I}, g)$ is an unmixed ideal with dimension $n - s - 1$. $\square$

The following corollary is a direct consequence of Proposition 3.5.

COROLLARY 3.6. *Let $\mathcal{I} = (f_1, \ldots, f_s)$ be an ideal in $\mathbb{K}[X]$ and $dim(\mathcal{I}) = n - s$. Let $g_1, \cdots, g_t$ be a regular sequence in $\mathbb{K}[X]/\mathcal{I}$. Then $(\mathcal{I}, g_1, \cdots, g_t)$ is an unmixed ideal with dimension $n - s - t$.*

Before proving the main algorithm, we need to point out that some important ideas about this algorithm are essentially contained in Eisenbud [5].

Proof of Algorithm **SETG**. The termination of the algorithm follows from the fact that in each recursive procedure the number of polynomials in the Ω increases by 1.

In the following, we will show the correctness of the above algorithm. First, we assume the algorithm **RGCD** is correct. Without loss of generality, we assume that $\mathbb{K}$ is an algebraically closed field. In each recursive procedure the above algorithm will divide a variety into a quasi variety and a smaller variety. Let $\Phi_0 = \mathbf{MSP}(\mathcal{J}_1)$ and $\mathcal{I} = (F)$. Let $\Phi_i = \{\Phi_0, u_1, \cdots, u_i\}$ denote Φ after i times recursive procedure and g_i denote g after i times recursive procedure, $\mathcal{I}_0 = \mathcal{I}$ and $\mathcal{I}_i = (\mathcal{I}, u_1, \cdots, u_i)$ for $i = 1, \cdots, n - dim(\mathcal{J}_1)$.

There are two cases. One case, there exists some $t \le n - dim(\mathcal{J}_1)$ such that $(\Phi_{t-1}) \neq (1)$ and $(\Phi_t) = (1)$. Since $u_{i+1}\mathcal{I} \subseteq (g_{i+1})$, we have $u_{i+1}\mathcal{I}_i \subseteq (g_{i+1}, \Phi_i)$ for $i = 0, 1 \cdots, t - 1$. From the proof in the Lemma 3.3 and $(g_{i+1}, \Phi_i) \subseteq \mathcal{I}_i$, we have $\mathbb{V}(\mathcal{I}_i/u_{i+1}) = \mathbb{V}((g_{i+1}, \Phi_i)/u_{i+1})$ for $i = 0, 1 \cdots, t - 1$. Thus we have the following decomposition:

$$\mathbb{V}(\mathcal{I}) = \mathbb{V}(\mathcal{I}/u_1) \bigcup \mathbb{V}(\mathcal{I}, u_1) \bigcup \cdots \bigcup \mathbb{V}((\mathcal{I}, u_1, \cdots, u_{t-1})/u_t)$$
$$= \mathbb{V}((g_1, \Phi_0)/u_1) \bigcup \mathbb{V}((g_2, \Phi_1)/u_2) \bigcup \cdots \bigcup \mathbb{V}((g_t, \Phi_{t-1})/u_t)$$

On one hand, we have $(\Phi_0, g_1, \cdots, g_t) \subseteq \mathcal{I}$, thus $\mathbb{V}(\mathcal{I}) \subseteq \mathbb{V}(\Phi_0, g_1, \cdots, g_t)$. One the other hand, $\forall x \in \mathbb{V}(\Phi_0, g_1, \cdots, g_t)$, if $x \in \mathbb{V}(\Phi_j)$ and $u_{j+1}(x) \neq 0$ for any $j \in \{0, 1, \cdots, t-1\}$, then we have $x \in \mathbb{V}((g_{j+1}, \Phi_j)/u_{j+1})$. Otherwise $x \in \mathbb{V}(\Phi_t)$, this is impossible because $\mathbb{V}(\Phi_t) = \emptyset$. From the above zero decomposition formula, we have $\mathbb{V}(\Phi_0, g_1, \cdots, g_t) \subseteq \mathbb{V}(\mathcal{I})$. Thus $\mathbb{V}(\Phi_0, g_1, \cdots, g_t) = \mathbb{V}(\mathcal{I})$.

Another case, we have $t = n - dim(\mathcal{J}_1)$ and $(\Phi_t) \neq (1)$. In this case, we have $u_1, \cdots, u_i$ is a regular sequence in $(\mathbb{K}[Y]/\sqrt{(\Phi_0)})[z]$ for any $i \in \{1, 2, \cdots, t-1\}$. By the Corollary 3.6, we have $\dim(\Phi_{t-1}) = 0$ in $\mathbb{K}[Y]$. By the Lemma 3.4, we have $\mathbb{V}(\mathcal{I}, \Phi_{t-1}) = \mathbb{V}(g_t, \Phi_{t-1})$ for some g_t. Thus we also have the following decomposition:

$$\mathbb{V}(\mathcal{I}) = \mathbb{V}(\mathcal{I}/u_1) \bigcup \mathbb{V}(\mathcal{I}, u_1) \bigcup \cdots \bigcup \mathbb{V}(\mathcal{I}, \Phi_{t-1})$$
$$= \mathbb{V}((g_1, \Phi_0)/u_1) \bigcup \mathbb{V}((g_2, \Phi_1)/u_2) \bigcup \cdots \bigcup \mathbb{V}(g_t, \Phi_{t-1})$$

It suffices to show that $\mathbb{V}(\Phi_0, g_1, \cdots, g_t) \subseteq \mathbb{V}(\mathcal{I})$. The correct easily follows from the above decomposition. $\square$

REMARK 3.7. *1. Though the number of set-theoretic generators of algebraic variety in affine n-space is finite, the number of ideal-theoretic generators of algebraic variety in affine n-space can not be bounded by a finite number. Macaulay [1] has shown that there exist singular space curves whose ideals require an arbitrary number of generators. In [18], T.T.Moh even proved a stronger result: Let $\mathbb{K}$ be a field of characteristic zero and $\mathcal{R} = \mathbb{K}[[x, y, z]]$, the power series ring in 3 variables over $\mathbb{K}$. Then for each $n \ge 1$, there exists a prime ideal $P_n \subset \mathbb{K}[[x, y, z]]$ such that P_n needs at least n generators.*

2. In the projective case we denote $\mathbb{K}[X] = \mathbb{K}[Y][z] = \mathbb{K}[x_0, \ldots, x_n]$ and $I = (F) \subset \mathbb{K}[X]$. Without loss of generality, we assume there exists a polynomial $f \in \mathcal{I}$ and $f \in \mathbb{K}[X]\backslash\mathbb{K}[Y]$ such that $init(f) = 1$. We assume the output of algorithm **SGCD** *is homogeneous. Let Ω be the output of algorithm* **SETG**(F). *We will show $\sharp\Omega \le n$. It suffices to prove the second case. In this case, we have $t = n+1-dim(\mathcal{J}_1)$ and $(\Phi_t) \neq (1)$. By the Corollary 3.6, we have $\dim(\Phi_{t-1}) = 0$ in $\mathbb{K}[Y]$. So we have $\mathbb{V}(\mathcal{I}, \Phi_{t-1}) = \emptyset$.*

3.2 Compute the gcd in some ring

This section will mainly present the algorithm **RGCD** (Algorithm 3.18). We first give several lemmas and sub-algorithms. In this section, when we say an ideal, we mean a finite set of generators of the ideal is given.

LEMMA 3.8. *Let $\mathcal{I}, \mathcal{I}_i$ be ideals in the $\mathbb{K}[X]$ and $\mathcal{I}\backslash\mathcal{I}_i \neq \{0\}$ for $i = 1, 2, \cdots, t$. Then we can compute a non-zero polynomial f such that $f \in \mathcal{I}\backslash \bigcup_{i=1}^{t} \mathcal{I}_i$.*

Proof: We proceed by induction on the number of $\{\mathcal{I}_i \mid i = 1, 2, \cdots, t\}$. When $t = 1$, the proof follows obviously using Gröbner bases method.

Suppose $t = s$, the Lemma is ture. While $t = s + 1$, by inductive hypothesis we have $g \in \mathcal{I}\backslash \bigcup_{i=1}^{s} \mathcal{I}_i$ and $h \in \mathcal{I}\backslash\mathcal{I}_{s+1}$, then in the $s+2$ elements $h, h+g, \cdots, h+(s+1)g$, there must be one element which is not in $\bigcup_{i=1}^{s+1} \mathcal{I}_i$. Otherwise there must exist two different elements $h+k_1g, h+k_2g$ which are in $\mathcal{I}_i$ for some $i \in \{1, 2, \cdots, s+1\}$ and $k_1 \neq k_2 \in \{0, 1, 2, \cdots, s+1\}$. Furthermore, we have $(k_1 - k_2)g \in \mathcal{I}_i$ for the above i, $g \in \mathcal{I}_i$.

If $1 \leq i \leq s$, this will contradict the fact that $g \notin \bigcup_{i=1}^{s} \mathcal{I}_i$. If $i = s+1$, we have $h \in \mathcal{I}_{s+1}$, this will contradict the fact that $h \notin \mathcal{I}_{s+1}$. From the above analysis, we can compute a non-zero polynomial f such that $f \in \mathcal{I} \backslash \bigcup_{i=1}^{t} \mathcal{I}_i$ using the Gröbner basis method. □

LEMMA 3.9. *Let $\mathcal{I}$, $\mathcal{I}_i$ be ideals in the $\mathbb{K}[X]$ and $f \notin \mathcal{I}$, $\mathcal{I} \backslash \mathcal{I}_i \neq \{0\}$ for $i = 1, 2, \cdots, t$. Then we can compute a non-zero polynomial g such that $g \in \mathcal{I}$ and $f + g \notin \mathcal{I} \bigcup \{\bigcup_{i=1}^{t} \mathcal{I}_i\}$.*

Proof: By Lemma 3.8, we can compute a non-zero polynomial h such that $h \in \mathcal{I} \backslash \bigcup_{i=1}^{t} \mathcal{I}_i$. In the $t + 1$ elements $f, f+h, \cdots, f+th$, there must be one element which is not in $\bigcup_{i=1}^{t} \mathcal{I}_i$. Otherwise there must be two different elements which are in $\mathcal{I}_i$ for some i. We have $f + k_1 h, f + k_2 h \in \mathcal{I}_i$, $(k_1 - k_2)h \in \mathcal{I}_i$, $h \in \mathcal{I}_i$, we get a contradiction. Thus there exists $f + sh \notin \bigcup_{i=1}^{t} \mathcal{I}_i$ for some s. So we have $f + sh \notin \mathcal{I} \bigcup \{\bigcup_{i=1}^{t} \mathcal{I}_i\}$. We can take $g = sh$. □

REMARK 3.10. *From the proof of Lemma 3.8 and 3.9, we easily know if the above ideals are homogeneous, then the result polynomial can be chosen homogeneous as well.*

By the above lemmas, we have the following algorithm.

ALGORITHM 3.11. **$TAP(\mathcal{I}, \mathcal{I}_1, \cdots, \mathcal{I}_m, f)$** *(take a polynomial)*
Input: *$\mathcal{I} = (f_1, \cdots, f_s)$, $\mathcal{I}_1 = (f_{11}, \cdots, f_{1s_1})$, $\cdots$, $\mathcal{I}_m = (f_{m1}, \cdots, f_{ms_m})$ are ideals in $\mathbb{K}[X]$ such that $\mathcal{I} \backslash \mathcal{I}_1 \neq \{0\}, \cdots, \mathcal{I} \backslash \mathcal{I}_m \neq \{0\}$ and $f \notin \mathcal{I}$.*

Output: *a polynomial $g \in \mathcal{I}$ such that $f + g \notin \mathcal{I} \bigcup (\bigcup_{i=1}^{m} \mathcal{I}_i)$*

$i := 0$;
$g := \textbf{\textit{TAP2}}(\mathcal{I}, \mathcal{I}_1, \cdots, \mathcal{I}_m)$;
while $i \leq m$
  for $k = 1$ *to* m
    $g_{ik} := \textbf{\textit{NormalForm}}(f + ig, \textbf{\textit{GröbnerBasis}}(\mathcal{I}_k))$;
  end for
  $g_i := \prod_{k=1}^{m} g_{ik}$;
  if $g_i \neq 0$, *then*
    $g := ig$;
    return g;
  else
    $i := i + 1$;
  end if
end while
return g.

ALGORITHM 3.12. **$TAP2(\mathcal{I}, \mathcal{I}_1, \cdots, \mathcal{I}_m)$**
Input: *$\mathcal{I} = (f_1, \cdots, f_s)$, $\mathcal{I}_1 = (f_{11}, \cdots, f_{1s_1})$, $\cdots$, $\mathcal{I}_m = (f_{m1}, \cdots, f_{ms_m})$ are ideals in $\mathbb{K}[X]$ such that $\mathcal{I} \backslash \mathcal{I}_1 \neq \{0\}, \cdots, \mathcal{I} \backslash \mathcal{I}_m \neq \{0\}$*

Output: *a polynomial $g \in \mathcal{I} \backslash (\bigcup_{i=1}^{m} \mathcal{I}_i)$*

$i := 2$;
$g := \textbf{\textit{TAP1}}(\mathcal{I}, \mathcal{I}_1)$;

if $i \leq m$, *then*
  $j := 0$;
  $h := \textbf{\textit{TAP1}}(\mathcal{I}, \mathcal{I}_i)$;
    while $j \leq i$ *repeat*
      for $k = 1$ *to* i
      $g_{jk} := \textbf{\textit{NormalForm}}(h + jg, \textbf{\textit{GröbnerBasis}}(\mathcal{I}_k))$;
      end for
      $g_j := \prod_{k=1}^{i} g_{jk}$;
      if $g_j \neq 0$, *then*
        $g := h + jg$;
      else
        $j := j + 1$;
      end if
    end while
  $i := i + 1$;
end if
return g.

ALGORITHM 3.13. **$TAP1(\mathcal{I}, \mathcal{J})$**
Input: *$\mathcal{I} = (f_1, \cdots, f_t)$ and $\mathcal{J} = (g_1, \cdots, g_s)$ such that $\mathcal{I} \backslash \mathcal{J} \neq \{0\}$*
Output: *a polynomial $g \in \mathcal{I} \backslash \mathcal{J}$*
$i := 1$;
while $i \leq t$
  $h_i := \textbf{\textit{NormalForm}}(f_i, \textbf{\textit{GröbnerBasis}}(\mathcal{J}))$;
    if $h_i \neq 0$, *then*
      $g := f_i$;
      return g;
    else
      $i := i + 1$;
return g.

Let $\mathcal{J} = \bigcap_{i=1}^{r} \mathcal{J}_i$ be an irredundant decomposition. Suppose that there are polynomials $s_1, \cdots, s_r$ in $\mathbb{K}[X]$ which satisfy the following conditions:

$$s_i \notin \mathcal{J}_i \quad and \quad s_i \in \mathcal{J}_j \quad for \quad i \neq j \qquad (1)$$

DEFINITION 3.14. *For a radical ideal $\mathcal{J}$, each s_i which satisfies condition (1) is called a separator of $\mathcal{J}$ with respect to $\mathcal{J}_i$, and the set $\{s_1, \cdots, s_r\}$ is called a system of separators of $\mathcal{J}$.*

ALGORITHM 3.15. **$Separators(\mathcal{I}_1, \cdots, \mathcal{I}_m)$**
Input: *$\mathcal{I}_1, \cdots, \mathcal{I}_m$ are ideals in $\mathbb{K}[Y]$ such that $\mathcal{J}_i = \mathcal{I}_1 \bigcap \cdots \bigcap \widehat{\mathcal{I}_i} \bigcap \cdots \bigcap \mathcal{I}_m$ and $\mathcal{J}_i \backslash \mathcal{I}_i \neq \{0\}$ for $i = 1, \cdots, m$*
Output: *a set of polynomials $s_1, \cdots, s_m$ such that $s_i \notin \mathcal{I}_i$ and $s_i \in \mathcal{I}_j$ for $i \neq j$ and $i, j = 1, \cdots, m$*
for $k = 1$ *to* m
  $\mathcal{J}_k := \emptyset$;
    while $i \in \{1, \cdots, \widehat{k}, \cdots, m\}$ *repeat*
      $\mathcal{J}_k := \textbf{\textit{GOI}}(\mathcal{J}_k, \mathcal{I}_i)$;
    end while
end for
for $i = 1$ *to* m
  $s_i := \textbf{\textit{TAP1}}(\mathcal{J}_i, \mathcal{I}_i)$;
end for
return $(s_1, \cdots, s_r)$

We have the following important result.

PROPOSITION 3.16. *Let* $\mathcal{R} = \mathbb{K}[Y]/\sqrt{(\Phi)}$, $S = \mathbb{K}[Y]\backslash \bigcup_{i=1}^{r} \mathcal{P}_i$ *and* $\sqrt{(\Phi)} = \bigcap_{i=1}^{r} \mathcal{P}_i$ *be an irredundant prime decomposition in* $\mathbb{K}[Y]$. *Then*

- $S^{-1}\mathbb{K}[Y]/\mathcal{P}_i$ *is a field for* $i = 1, \cdots, r$

- $\mathcal{Q}(\mathcal{R}) = S^{-1}\mathbb{K}[Y]/\bigcap_{i=1}^{r} \mathcal{P}_i \cong \bigoplus_{i=1}^{r} S^{-1}\mathbb{K}[Y]/\mathcal{P}_i$

Proof: For the first fact, it suffices to show that $\mathcal{P}_i$ is a maximal ideal in $S^{-1}\mathbb{K}[Y]$ for $i = 1, \cdots, r$. In fact, if $\mathcal{P}_i$ is not a maximal ideals in $S^{-1}\mathbb{K}[Y]$ for $i = 1, \cdots, r$, then there exists a maximal $\mathcal{J}$ such that $\mathcal{P}_i \subset \mathcal{J} \subset \bigcup_{i=1}^{r} \mathcal{P}_i$. By proposition 1.11 (page 8 in [2]), $\mathcal{P}_i \subset \mathcal{J} \subset \mathcal{P}_k$ for some k, we have $i = k$. Furthermore, $\mathcal{P}_i = \mathcal{J}$, we get a contradiction.

We show the correctness of the second fact. Let $\overline{S} = \mathcal{R} \setminus \mathcal{Z}(\mathcal{R})$ be the image of $S = \mathbb{K}[Y]\backslash \bigcup_{i=1}^{r} \mathcal{P}_i$ in $\mathcal{R}$. We have $\mathcal{Q}(\mathcal{R}) = \overline{S}^{-1}\mathcal{R} = S^{-1}\mathbb{K}[Y]/\sqrt{(\Phi)}$. In $S^{-1}\mathbb{K}[Y]$, we claim that $\mathcal{P}_i + \mathcal{P}_j = S^{-1}\mathbb{K}[Y]$. This claim follows from the fact $\mathcal{P}_i$ is a maximal ideal in $S^{-1}\mathbb{K}[Y]$ for $i = 1, \cdots, r$. By the Chinese Remainder Theorem (Exercise 2.6 in [7]), the second fact is true. $\square$

PROPOSITION 3.17. *Let* $\mathcal{R} = \mathbb{K}[Y]/\sqrt{(\Phi)}$, $S = \mathbb{K}[Y]\backslash \bigcup_{i=1}^{r} \mathcal{P}_i$ *and* $\sqrt{(\Phi)} = \bigcap_{i=1}^{m} \sqrt{sat(A_i)}$ *be an irredundant decomposition. Then*

- $S^{-1}\mathbb{K}[Y]/\sqrt{sat(A_i)}$ *is a product of fields for* $i = 1, \cdots, r$

- $\mathcal{Q}(\mathcal{R}) = S^{-1}\mathbb{K}[Y]/\bigcap_{i=1}^{r} \sqrt{sat(A_i)} \cong \bigoplus_{i=1}^{r} S^{-1}\mathbb{K}[Y]/\sqrt{sat(A_i)}$

Proof: It suffices to show that $\sqrt{sat(A_i)} + \sqrt{sat(A_j)} = S^{-1}\mathbb{K}[Y]$ for $i \neq j$ and $i, j = 1, \cdots, m$. Otherwise, we have $\sqrt{sat(A_i)} + \sqrt{sat(A_j)} \subset \bigcup_{i=1}^{r} \mathcal{P}_i$. By proposition 1.11 (page 8 in [2]), $\sqrt{sat(A_i)} + \sqrt{sat(A_j)} \subset \mathcal{P}_k$ for some k. We have $\sqrt{sat(A_i)} \subset \mathcal{P}_k$ and $\sqrt{sat(A_i)} \subset \mathcal{P}_k$. Since $\sqrt{sat(A_i)}$ and $\sqrt{sat(A_i)}$ are the intersection of some prime ideals and $\sqrt{(\Phi)} = \bigcap_{i=1}^{m} \sqrt{sat(A_i)}$ is an irredundant decomposition, we have $\mathcal{P}_{i_1} \subset \mathcal{P}_k$ and $\mathcal{P}_{i_2} \subset \mathcal{P}_k$ where $i_1 \neq i_2$. This will contradict the fact that $\sqrt{(\Phi)} = \bigcap_{i=1}^{r} \mathcal{P}_i$ is the irredundant prime decomposition in $\mathbb{K}[Y]$. $\square$

Let $\sqrt{(\Phi)} = \bigcap_{i=1}^{r} \mathcal{P}_i$ be an irredundant prime decomposition in $\mathbb{K}[Y]$, $\mathcal{R} = \mathbb{K}[Y]/\sqrt{(\Phi)}$ and $S = \mathbb{K}[Y]\backslash \bigcup_{i=1}^{r} \mathcal{P}_i$. We have the following algorithm **RGCD**.

ALGORITHM 3.18. **RGCD**(F, Φ)
Input: $F = \{f_1, \cdots, f_t\} \subseteq \mathbb{K}[X]$ and $\Phi \subseteq \mathbb{K}[Y]$
Output: *two polynomials* f, u *such that* $f \in (F)$, $(F) = (f)$ *in* $\mathcal{Q}(\mathbb{K}[Y]/\sqrt{(\Phi)})[z]$ *and* $u \in S$, $u(F) \subseteq (f)$ *in* $\mathbb{K}[Y][z]$
$\mathcal{U} := \varnothing$;

$\{A_1, \cdots, A_r\} := \textbf{\textit{Triangularize}}(\Phi)$;
for $i = 1$ *to* r
$\quad \mathcal{U} := \mathcal{U} \bigcup \textbf{SGCD}(A_i, F)$;
end for
$P_i := \textbf{\textit{Radical}}(\textbf{\textit{GOS}}(B_i, I_i))$ *for* $i = 1, \cdots, d$ *where* I_i *is the product of the initials of the polynomials in* B_i *and* $\mathcal{U} = \{(B_1, h_1), \cdots, (B_d, h_d)\}$;
$\{s_1, \cdots, s_d\} := \textbf{\textit{Separators}}(P_1, \cdots, P_d)$;
$s_i' := s_i + \textbf{\textit{TAP}}(P_i, P_1, \cdots, P_{i-1}, P_{i+1}, \cdots, P_d, s_i)$ *for* $i = 1, \cdots, d$;
for $i = 1$ *to* d
$\quad$ **if** $h_i \in \mathbb{K}[Y]$, **then**
$\quad\quad f_j = h_i m_{ij}$ *in* $(S^{-1}\mathbb{K}[Y]/\sqrt{sat(B_i)})[z]$ *where* $m_{ij} = f_j/h_i$ *for* $j = 1, \cdots, t$;
$\quad\quad h_{ij} := f_j$ *for* $j = 1, \cdots, t$;
$\quad\quad s_{ij} := h_i$ *for* $j = 1, \cdots, t$;
$\quad$ **else**
$\quad\quad f_j = h_i m_{ij}$ *in* $(S^{-1}\mathbb{K}[Y]/\sqrt{sat(B_i)})[z]$ *where* $m_{ij} = h_{ij}/init(h_i)^{e_i}$ *and* $e_i = max\{deg_z(f_k) - deg_z(h_i) + 1 \mid k = 1, \cdots, t\}$ *for* $j = 1, \cdots, t$;
$\quad\quad init(h_i)^{e_i'} := init(h_i)^{e_i} + \textbf{\textit{TAP}}(P_i, P_1, \cdots, P_{i-1}, P_{i+1}, \cdots, P_r, init(h_i)^{e_i})$;
$\quad\quad h_{ij} := h_{ij}$ *for* $j = 1, \cdots, t$;
$\quad\quad s_{ij} := init(h_i)^{e_i}$ *for* $j = 1, \cdots, t$;
$\quad$ **end if**
end for
$s_{ij}' := s_{ij} + \textbf{\textit{TAP}}(P_i, P_1, \cdots, P_{i-1}, P_{i+1}, \cdots, P_r, s_{ij})$; *for* $i = 1, \cdots, d$ *and* $j = 1, \cdots, t$;
$m_i := \sum_{j=1}^{d} h_{ji} s_j/(s_{ji}' s_j')$ *for* $i = 1, \cdots, d$;
$f' := \sum_{j=1}^{d} h_j s_j/s_j'$;
$s := lcm(s_1', \cdots, s_d')$ *where* lcm *denotes the least common multiple*;
$u_i := lcm(s_{1i}' s_i', \cdots, s_{di}' s_i')$;
$f := sf'$;
$u := lcm(su_1, \cdots, su_d)$;
return u, f

Proof: Termination of the algorithm is obvious. In the following, we will show the correctness of algorithm. First, we assume algorithms **SGCD**, **Separators** and **TAP** are correct.

From algorithm **RGCD** and the the specifications of algorithm **SGCD**, we know $\sqrt{(\Phi)} = \bigcap_{i=1}^{d} \sqrt{sat(B_i)}$ is an irredundant decomposition in $\mathbb{K}[Y]$ and $h_i \in (F)$, $(F) = (h_i)$ in $(S^{-1}\mathbb{K}[Y]/\sqrt{sat(B_i)})[z]$ for $i = 1, \cdots, d$. Let δ be an isomorphism from $\mathcal{Q}(\mathcal{R})[z]$ to $\bigoplus_{i=1}^{d} (S^{-1}\mathbb{K}[Y]/\sqrt{sat(B_i)})[z]$ and f', m_i be the unique element such that $\delta(f') = (h_1, \cdots, h_d)$, $\delta(m_i) = (m_{1i}, \cdots, m_{di})$ where $f_j = h_i m_{ij}$, $m_{ij} = h_{ij}/s_{ij}$, $s_{ij} \notin P_i$ for $i = 1, \cdots, d$ and $j = 1, \cdots, t$.

In the Algorithm **RGCD**, if $h_i \in \mathbb{K}[Y]$, then $m_{ij} = f_j/h_i$ for $j = 1, \cdots, t$ is obvious. If $h_i \in \mathbb{K}[X] \setminus \mathbb{K}[Y]$, we know $(S^{-1}\mathbb{K}[Y]/\sqrt{sat(B_i)})[z]$ is a direct product of fields. We have $S^{-1}\mathbb{K}[Y]/\sqrt{sat(B_i)} \cong \bigoplus_{i=1}^{l} S^{-1}\mathbb{K}[Y]/Q_i$ where $\sqrt{sat(B_i)} = \bigcap_{i=1}^{l} Q_i$ is an irredundant prime decomposition in $\mathbb{K}[Y]$. For each $S^{-1}\mathbb{K}[Y]/Q_i$, $prem(f_j, h_i) \in Q_i$ for $j = 1, \cdots, t$. So we have $prem(f_j, h_i) \in \sqrt{sat(B_i)}$ and $s_{ij} = init(h_i)^{e_i}$.

144

By Algorithm **TAP**, we know $s'_{ij} \notin P_1 \bigcup \cdots \bigcup P_d$ and $s'_{ij} - s_{ij} \in P_i$ for $i = 1, \cdots, d$ and $j = 1, \cdots, t$. By Algorithm **TAP**, we also know $s'_i \notin P_1 \bigcup \cdots \bigcup P_d$ and $s'_i - s_i \in P_i$ for $i = 1, \cdots, d$. Since the set $\{s_1, \cdots, s_d\}$ is a system of separators of $\sqrt{(\Phi)}$, we have

$$m_i = \sum_{j=1}^d h_{ji} s_j/(s'_{ji} s'_j) \qquad f' = \sum_{j=1}^d h_j s_j/s'_j \qquad f_i = f' m_i$$

We remove the denominator to get a polynomial f. Since $h_i \in (F)$ for $i = 1, \cdots, d$, we have $f \in (F)$. $(F) = (f)$ in $\mathcal{Q}(\mathbb{K}[Y]/\sqrt{(\Phi)})[z]$ is also obvious. Let $s = lcm(s'_1, \cdots, s'_d)$, $u_i = lcm(s'_{1i} s'_i, \cdots, s'_{di} s'_i)$ and $u = lcm(su_1, \cdots, su_d)$. So we have $u f_i \subseteq (f)$ in $\mathbb{K}[X]$ for $i = 1, \cdots, t$. Furthermore, we have $u(F) \subseteq (f)$ in $\mathbb{K}[X]$ where $u \in S$ is obvious. $\square$

REMARK 3.19. *If F and Φ are homogeneous , then the output of algorithm 3.18 can be homogeneous with minor modifications. In fact, let $S^{(1)} = \{f \in \mathbb{K}[X] \mid f$ is homogeneous with $deg(f) = 1\}$. The key point is that we can choose $s \in S^{(1)}$ such that $s \notin \bigcup_{i=1}^r \mathcal{P}_i$ where $\sqrt{(\Phi)} = \bigcap_{i=1}^m \mathcal{P}_i$ is an irredundant prime decomposition. In order to the output is homogeneous, we can multiply some polynomials in the algorithm 3.18 by a power of s (for more details, see Theorem 2 in [5]).*

ALGORITHM 3.20. **SGCD**(C, F)
Input: *C a regular chain in $\mathbb{K}[Y]$ and $F = \{f_1, \cdots, f_t\} \subseteq \mathbb{K}[X]$ where $init(f_i) \in \mathbb{K}$ for some i and $f_i \in \mathbb{K}[X] \setminus \mathbb{K}[Y]$ (otherwise we make a invertible linear transformation)*
Output: *A set of pairs $(A_1, g_1), \cdots, (A_r, g_r)$ such that $\sqrt{sat(C)} = \bigcap_{i=1}^r \sqrt{sat(A_i)}$ is an irredundant decomposition and $g_i \in (F)$, $(F) = (g_i)$ in $(S^{-1} \mathbb{K}[Y]/\sqrt{sat(A_i)})[z]$.*

$G := \{m_1, \cdots, m_{r_1}, h_1, \cdots, h_{r_2}\} = \boldsymbol{GröbnerBasis}(F, >)$ where $<$ is any block order eliminating z and $m_1, \cdots, m_{r_1} \in \mathbb{K}[Y], h_1, \cdots, h_{r_2} \in \mathbb{K}[X] \setminus \mathbb{K}[Y]$, $m_1 < \cdots < m_{r_1} < h_1 < \cdots < h_{r_2}$;
$W := \{w_1, \cdots, w_{r_1+r_2}\} := \{m_1, \cdots, m_{r_1}, init(h_1), \cdots, init(h_{r_2})\}$ where $w_i = m_i$, $w_{r_1+j} = init(h_j)$ for $i = 1, \cdots, r_1$ and $j = 1, \cdots, r_2$;
$\mathcal{C} := \emptyset$;
$i := 1$;
while $i \leq r_1 + r_2$
  if $ires(w_i, C) \neq 0$, **then**
    $\mathcal{C} := \mathcal{C} \bigcup (C, w_i)$;
    return$(\mathcal{C})$
  else
    if $w_i \notin \sqrt{sat(C)}$, **then**
      $(\mathcal{W}, \mathcal{U}) := \boldsymbol{Split}(C, w_i)$;
      $\mathcal{C} := \mathcal{C} \bigcup \{(A, w_i) \mid A \in \mathcal{U}\} \bigcup \{\boldsymbol{SGCD}(A, F) \mid A \in \mathcal{W}\}$;
    else
      $i := i + 1$;
return$(\mathcal{C})$

Proof: We first show that the termination of algorithm. If the algorithm does not terminates for some input (C, F) where C a regular chain in $\mathbb{K}[Y]$, then there must exist a infinite ascending chain of ideal $\sqrt{sat(C)} \subset \sqrt{sat(C_1)} \subset \cdots \subset \sqrt{sat(C_r)} \subset \cdots$ in $\mathbb{K}[Y]$. The claim follows from the

specifications of **Split**. This would contradict the fact that $\mathbb{K}[Y]$ is a Noetherian ring.

In the following, we will show the correctness of algorithm. Because we assume that $init(f_i) \in \mathbb{K}$ for some i and $f_i \in \mathbb{K}[X] \setminus \mathbb{K}[Y]$, the termination of algorithm must be in the first if. By Theorem 2.9, we know f is regular modulo $sat(T)$ if and only if $ires(f, T) \neq 0$ where T is a regular chain. By Theorem 2.10, $sat(T)$ is an unmixed ideal. We need to distinguish two cases. For the first if, the correctness of Algorithm follows from Remark 2.11 and Corollary 2.6. For the second if, the correctness of Algorithm follows from Corollary 2.6 and the specifications of **Split**. $\square$

3.3 Projective case

Because the space is limited, we briefly discuss this case. Since $prem(f, g)$ and $S(f, g)$ are homogeneous for two homogeneous polynomial f, g where $S(f, g)$ is S-polynomial of f and g, these operation in the section 2.3 output homogeneous polynomials if the input is homogeneous polynomials. By Remark 3.7, 3.10 and 3.19, we know algorithm **SETG** with minor modifications is also valid for projective algebraic variety in projective n-space .

3.4 Examples

EXAMPLE 3.21. *The following example comes from [18]. Let n be an odd positive integer, and $m = (n+1)/2$. Let λ be an integer $> n(n+1)m$ with $Gcd(\lambda, m) = 1$. Let $\mathbb{K}[x, y, z]$ be a polynomial ring over a field $\mathbb{K}$. The homomorphism $\theta : \mathbb{K}[x, y, z] \to \mathbb{K}[t]$*

$$(\theta x, \theta y, \theta z) = (t^{nm} + t^{nm+\lambda}, t^{(n+1)m}, t^{(n+2)m})$$

Its kernel is denoted by $\mathcal{I}$. The minimal number of ideal-theoretic generators for $\mathcal{I}$ is bigger than n. The fact has been proved in the paper [18].

If $n = 5$, $m = 3$, $\lambda = 91$, then $\mathcal{I} = (f_1, \cdots, f_{11})$ where $f_1, \cdots, f_{11}$ is a Gröbner basis with respect to lex order $x > y > z$ and $f_1 < \cdots < f_{11}$.

$f_1 = y^7 - z^6$, $f_2 = 3zy^4x - 3z^2y^2x^2 + z^3x^3 - y^6z^{13} - y^6$
$f_3 = -z^5 + z^2yx^3 - z^{18} - 3zy^3x^2 + 3xy^5$
$f_4 = -3y^5x^2 - z^{17}y^2 - z^4y^2 + 3z^5x + y^3x^3z$
$f_5 = -z^3y^4 - 3x^2z^5 + 3xy^2z^4 - z^{16}y^4 + y^5x^3$
$f_6 = -z^4y - 8zy^2x^3 - yz^{17} + 3z^2x^4 - 3y^6z^{12}x + 6y^4x^2$
$f_7 = -z^3y^2 - 2y^3x^3 - z^{16}y^2 + 2z^4x + zx^4y - z^{17}x$
$f_8 = -3z^2y^4 + y^3x^4 - 3y^4z^{15} - 6z^4x^2 + 8xz^3y^2 - z^{16}xy^2$
$f_9 = 5z^3yx + 3zx^5 - 5y^2x^4 - 3z^2y^3 - 4xyz^{16} - 3y^6z^{11}x^2 - 3y^3z^{15}$
$f_{10} = 15z^2y^2x - 6zy^4 - 10x^2z^3 - 6z^{14}y^4 + x^5y - z^{16}x^2 - 3xz^{15}y^2$
$f_{11} = -10y^5 - 3xz^{14}y^3 - 6x^2yz^{15} + 24zy^3x + x^6 - 15z^2yx^2 - z^{26}y^5 - 11z^{13}y^5$

We can compute the 3 set-theoretic generators for $\mathbb{V}(\mathcal{I})$ using the Algorithm 3.2 in $\mathbb{K}[y, z][x]$.

1. At the beginning, we have $\mathcal{J}_1 = \mathcal{I} \bigcap \mathbb{K}[y, z] = (f_1)$ and $\Omega = \Phi = \{f_1\}$. $z^3 = init(f_2)$ is regular modulo (f_1) in $\mathbb{K}[x, y, z]$, so $(f_2, z^{12}) = \boldsymbol{RGCD}(\mathcal{I}, \Phi)$. We get $u_1 = z^{12}$ and $g_1 = f_2$.

2. In the second proceed, we have $\Phi = \{f_1, u_1\}$, $\Omega = \{f_1, f_2\}$ and $\mathcal{I} = (f_{11})$ in $\mathcal{R} = \mathbb{K}[y, z]/\sqrt{(\Phi)} = \mathbb{K}[y, z]/(y, z)$. $(f_{11}, u_2) = \boldsymbol{RGCD}(\mathcal{I}, \Phi)$. We get $g_2 = f_{11}$. So we have $\mathbb{V}(\mathcal{I}) = \mathbb{V}(f_1, f_2, f_{11})$.

EXAMPLE 3.22. *The following example comes from [11]. Let the projective rational sextic space curve $\mathcal{C}$ defined parametrically by*

$$x = 3s^4t^2 - 9s^3t^3 - 3s^2t^4 + 12st^5 + 6t^6$$
$$y = -3s^6 + 18s^5t - 27s^4t^2 - 12s^3t^3 + 33s^2t^4 + 6st^5 - 6t^6$$
$$z = s^6 - 6s^5t + 13s^4t^2 - 16s^3t^3 + 9s^2t^4 + 14st^5 - 6t^6$$
$$w = -2s^4t^2 + 8s^3t^3 - 14s^2t^4 + 20st^5 - 6t^6$$

In the paper [11], The authors can not show the above curve $\mathcal{C}$ is the intersection of three surfaces.

$\mathcal{I} = \mathbb{I}(\mathcal{C}) = (f_1, \cdots, f_5)$ where $f_1, \cdots, f_5$ is a Gröbner basis with respect to lex order $x > y > z > w$ and $f_1 < \cdots < f_5$.

$f_1 = -84yz^2w + 9z^2w^2 + 54yzw^2 + 36z^4 + 4y^2z^2 + 33y^2w^2 - 22y^2wz + 24yz^3 - 54z^3w$

$f_2 = 4yz^2 + 12z^3 - 22yzw - 18z^2w + 17yw^2 + 3zw^2 + 16z^2x - 24zwx + 4w^2x$

$f_3 = 51yw^2 + 24yz^2 + 36z^3 - 60yzw - 54z^2w + 9zw^2 - 36zwx + 12w^2x + 20ywx + 4y^2z - 14y^2w$

$f_4 = 153yw^2 + 80yzx + 132yz^2 + 108z^3 - 210yzw - 162z^2w + 27zw^2 - 168zwx + 36w^2x + 32y^2z - 132y^2w$

$f_5 = -2601yw^2 - 324yz^2 - 1836z^3 + 2610yzw + 2754z^2w - 459zw^2 + 936zwx - 612w^2x + 216y^2z - 156y^2w - 1440zx^2 + 480wx^2 + 40y^3 - 240y^2x + 800yx^2$

We can compute the 3 set-theoretic generators for $\mathcal{C}$ using the Algorithm 3.2 in $\mathbb{K}[y, z, w][x]$.

1. At the beginning, we have $\mathcal{J}_1 = \mathcal{I} \bigcap \mathbb{K}[y, z, w] = (f_1)$ and $\Omega = \Phi = \{f_1\}$. $16z^2 - 24zw + 4w^2 = init(f_2)$ is regular modulo (f_1), so $(f_2, (4z^2 - 6zw + w^2)^2) = RGCD(\mathcal{I}, \Phi)$. We get $u_1 = (4z^2 - 6zw + w^2)^2$ and $g_1 = f_2$.

2. In the second proceed, we have $\Phi = \{f_1, u_1\}$ and $\Omega = \{f_1, f_2\}$, $\mathcal{R} = \mathbb{K}[y, z, w]/\sqrt{(\Phi)}$ where $\sqrt{(\Phi)} = (4z^2 - 6zw + w^2, 5y^2w + 9yzw - 12yz^2, 5y^2z + 3yzw - 9yz^2)$. $(wf_3 + yf_5, u_2) = \mathbf{RGCD}(\mathcal{I}, \Phi)$. We get $g_2 = wf_3 + yf_5$. So we have $\mathcal{C} = \mathbb{V}(f_1, f_2, wf_3 + yf_5)$.

4. CONCLUSION

In this paper, we give an algorithm to compute set-theoretic generators consisting of at most n polynomials for any algebraic variety in the n-space. The algorithm depends on the computation of Gröbner bases and Ritt-Wu's characteristic sets and thus is computationally challenging. To give more efficient algorithms for this problem is of both theoretical and practical importance.

Since many examples are given by Parameter equation, giving an algorithm to compute such set-theoretic generators from the Parameter equation directly is an interesting problem.

5. REFERENCES

[1] Abhyankar, S.S., 1973. On Macaulay's example. In: Conf. Comm. Algebra, Lawrence 1972, Springer LNM, vol311, 1-16.

[2] Atiyah, M.F., Macdonald, I.G., 1969. Introduction to Commutative Algebra, Addison-Wesley Publishing Company.

[3] Chou , S.C. and Gao, X.S., 1991. On the dimension of an arbitrary ascending chain. Chinese Bull. of Sci. 38, 799-804.

[4] Cox, D., Little, J., O'Shea, D., 1996. Ideals, Varieties, and Algorithms, Second Edition. Springer.

[5] Eisenbud, D., Evans, G., 1973. Every algebraic set in n-space is the intersection of n hypersurfaces. Invent. Math. 19, 107-112.

[6] Eisenbud, D., Sturmfels, B., 1994. Finding sparse systems of parameters. Journal of Pure and Applied Algebra, 143-157.

[7] Eisenbud, D., 1994. Commutative Algebra with a View toward Algebraic Geometry. Graduate Texts in Mathematics. Springer-Verlag New York.

[8] Fortuna, E., Gianni, P., Trager, B., 2009. Generators of the ideal of an algebraic space curve. Journal of Symbolic Computation 44, 1234-1254.

[9] Gianni, P., Trager, B., Zacharias, G., 1988. Gröbner bases and primary decomposition of polynomial ideals. Journal of Symbolic Computation 6, 149-167.

[10] Hubert, E., 2003. Notes on triangular sets and triangulation-decomposition algorithms I: Polynomial systems. In Symbolic and Numerical Scientific Computing 2001, pages 1-39.

[11] Jia, X., Wang, H., Goldmand, R., 2010. Set-theoretic generators of rational space curves. Journal of Symbolic Computation 45, 414-433.

[12] Kneser, M., 1960. Über die Darstellung algebraischer Raumkurven als Durchschnitte von Flächen. Arch. Math. 11, 157-158.

[13] Kalkbrener, M., 1993. A generalized euclidean algorithm for computing triangular representations of algebraic varieties. J. Symb. Comp.15, 143-167.

[14] Kronecher, L., 1882. Grundzüge einer arithmetischen Theorie der algebraischen Größen. J. Reine Angew. Math. 92, 1-123.

[15] Lemaire, F., Moreno Maza, M., Pan, W., and Xie, Y., 2008. When does (T) equal Sat(T)?. In Proc. ISSAC'2008, 207-214. ACM Press.

[16] Laplagne, S., 2006. An algorithm for the computation of the radical of an ideal. ISSAC'2006, July 09-12, Genoa, Italy.

[17] Maza, M.M., Rioboo, R., 1995. Polynomial gcd computations over towers of algebraic extensions. In Applied algebra, algebraic algorithms and errorcorrecting codes, 365-382. Springer, Berlin.

[18] Moh, T.T., 1974. On the unboundedness of generators of prime ideals in power series rings of three variables, J.Math.Soc.Japan 26, 722-734.

[19] Sturmfels, B., 2002. Solving Systems of Polynomial Equations. Amer.Math.Soc.

[20] Schauenburg, P., 2007. A Gröbner-based treatment of elimination theory for affine varieties. Journal of Symbolic Computation 42, 859-870.

[21] Van der Waerden, B.L., 1941. Review. Zentralblatt für Math. 24, 276.

[22] Wu, W.T., 2003. Mathematics Machenization. Science Press/Kluwer, Beijing.

[23] Yang, L. and Zhang, J., 1991. Searching dependency between algebraic equations: an algorithm applied to automated reasoning. Technical report ic/91/6, International Atomic Engery Angency, Miramare, Trieste, Italy.

On Rota's Problem for Linear Operators in Associative Algebras

Li Guo[*]
Department of Mathematics
and Computer Science
Rutgers University
Newark, NJ 07102
liguo@rutgers.edu

William Y. Sit[†]
Department of Mathematics
City College of New York
City University of New York
New York, NY 10031
wsit@ccny.cuny.edu

Ronghua Zhang[‡]
Research Institute of Natural
Sciences
Yunnan University
Kunming 650091, P. R. China
rhzhang@ynu.edu.cn

ABSTRACT

A long standing problem of Gian-Carlo Rota for associative algebras is the classification of all linear operators that can be defined on them. In the 1970s, there were only a few known operators, for example, the derivative operator, the difference operator, the average operator and the Rota-Baxter operator. A few more appeared after Rota posed his problem. However, little progress was made to solve this problem in general. In part, this is because the precise meaning of the problem is not so well understood. In this paper, we propose a formulation of the problem using the framework of operated algebras and viewing an associative algebra with a linear operator as one that satisfies a certain operated polynomial identity. To narrow our focus more on the operators that Rota was interested in, we further consider two particular classes of operators, namely, those that generalize differential or Rota-Baxter operators. With the aid of computer algebra, we are able to come up with a list of these two classes of operators, and provide some evidence that these lists may be complete. Our search have revealed quite a few new operators of these types whose properties are expected to be similar to the differential operator and Rota-Baxter operator respectively.

Recently, a more unified approach has emerged in related areas, such as difference algebra and differential algebra, and Rota-Baxter algebra and Nijenhuis algebra. The similarities in these theories can be more efficiently explored by advances on Rota's problem.

Categories and Subject Descriptors

G.0 [Mathematics of Computing]:General

General Terms

Algorithms, Theory

Keywords

Rota's Problem; operators; classification; differential type operators, Rota-Baxter type operators

[*]L. Guo thanks NSF for its support through grant number DMS-1001855.

[†]Corresponding author

[‡]R. Zhang thanks the hospitality of Rutgers University at Newark during his visit in 2008-2009.

1. INTRODUCTION

Throughout the history of mathematics, objects are often understood by studying operators defined on them. Well-known examples are found in Galois theory, where a field is studied by its automorphisms, and in analysis and geometry, where functions and manifolds are studied through derivatives and vector fields. These operators abstract to the following linear operators on associative algebras.

$$\text{automorphism} \quad P(xy) = P(x)P(y), \tag{1}$$
$$\text{derivation} \quad \delta(xy) = \delta(x)y + x\delta(y). \tag{2}$$

By the 1970s, several more special operators, denoted by P below with corresponding name and defining property, had been studied in analysis, probability and combinatorics, including

$$\text{average} \quad P(x)P(y) = P(xP(y)), \tag{3}$$
$$\text{inverse average} \quad P(x)P(y) = P(P(x)y), \tag{4}$$
$$\text{(Rota-)Baxter} \quad P(x)P(y) = P(xP(y) + P(x)y + \lambda xy), \tag{5}$$
$$\text{where } \lambda \text{ is a fixed constant,}$$
$$\text{Reynolds} \quad P(x)P(y) = P(xP(y) + P(x)y - P(x)P(y)). \tag{6}$$

Rota [24] posed the question of finding all the identities that could be satisfied by a linear operator defined on associative algebras. He also suggested that there should not be many such operators other than these previously known ones. Even though there were some work on relating these different operators [14], little progress was made on finding *all* such operators. In the meantime, new operators have emerged from physics, algebra and combinatorial studies, such as

$$P(x)P(y) = P(xP(y) + P(x)y - P(xy)), \tag{7}$$
$$P(x)P(y) = P(xP(y) + P(x)y - xP(1)y), \tag{8}$$
$$\delta(xy) = \delta(x)y + x\delta(y) + \lambda\delta(x)\delta(y). \tag{9}$$

which are known, respectively, as the Nijenhuis operator, the Leroux's TD operator, and the differential operator of weight λ. The previously known operators continue to find remarkable applications in pure and applied mathematics. For differential operators, we have the development of differential algebra [22], difference algebra [7], and quantum differential operators [20, 21]. For Rota-Baxter algebras, we note their relationship with the classical Yang-Baxter equation, operads, combinatorics, and most prominently, the renormalization of quantum field theory through the Hopf algebra framework of Connes and Kreimer [1, 2, 4, 9, 11, 12, 13, 16, 17, 18, 19].

1.1 Our approach

These interesting developments motivate us to return to Rota's question and try to understand the problem better.[1] In doing so, we found that two key points in Rota's question deserve further thoughts. First, we need a suitable framework to formulate precisely what is an "operator identity," and second, we need to determine a suitable scope for the operator identities that are "computationally feasible."

For the first point, we note that a simplified but analogous framework has already been formulated in the 1970s and subsequently explored with great success. This is the study of PI-rings and PI-algebras, whose elements a set of satisfy polynomial identities (PI) [10, 23, 25].

Let **k** be a commutative unitary ring. In this paper, all algebras are unitary, associative but generally non-commutative **k**-algebras, and all algebra homomorphisms will be over **k**, unless the contrary is noted or obvious. Recall that an algebra R *satisfies a polynomial identity* if there is a non-zero (non-commutative) polynomial $\phi(X)$ in a finite set X of indeterminates over **k** (that is, $\phi(X) \in \mathbf{k}\langle X \rangle$, the free algebra on X such that $\phi(X)$ is sent to zero under any algebra homomorphism $f : \mathbf{k}\langle X \rangle \to R$. To generalize this framework to the operator case, we introduce operated algebras and the operated polynomial algebra $\mathbf{k}\lfloor X \rfloor$ as the free operated algebra on X. An operator identity corresponds to a particular element $\phi(X)$ in $\mathbf{k}\lfloor X \rfloor$. Analogous to PI-algebras, an OPI-algebra[2] R is an algebra with a **k**-linear operator P, a finite set X, and an operated polynomial $\phi(X) \in \mathbf{k}\lfloor X \rfloor$ such that $\phi(X)$ is sent to zero under any morphism $f : \mathbf{k}\lfloor X \rfloor \to R$ of operated algebras. The operated polynomial ϕ, or the equation $\phi(X) = 0$, is called an operated polynomial identity (OPI) on R and we say P (as well as R) *satisfies the OPI* ϕ (or $\phi(X) = 0$). For example, a differential algebra[3] is an OPI-algebra R with operator δ, where the OPI is defined using $X = \{x, y\}$ and $\phi(x, y) := \lfloor xy \rfloor - \lfloor x \rfloor y - x \lfloor y \rfloor$, where $\lfloor\ \rfloor$ denotes the operator in $\mathbf{k}\lfloor X \rfloor = \mathbf{k}\lfloor x, y \rfloor$. As another example, a difference algebra S is an OPI-algebra where the **k**-linear operator P is an endomorphism, that is, S satisfies $P(r)P(s) = P(rs)$ for all $r, s \in S$.

Next, we address the second point mentioned above, namely, what is the class of OPIs that are computationally feasible. This is an essential restriction since we derive our list of OPIs by symbolic computation. An OPI ϕ can be applied recursively and such applications may or may not lead to infinite recursion. If it does, it is not computationally feasible to derive meaningful consequences on the associative algebra due to ϕ. An example is the Reynolds operator identity in Eq. (6), where the right hand side contains the expression $P(x)P(y)$ that is the left-hand-side, leading to more and more complicated expressions as the identity is applied repeatedly *ad infinitum*. The other operators do not share this problem.

By avoiding OPIs like the Reynolds identity, we in effect cut down the class of OPIs under investigation and this allows us to apply symbolic computation to search for a list of identities for two broad families that include all the previously mentioned OPIs except the Reynolds identity. One family of operators consists

of the OPIs of differential type, which include derivations, endomorphisms, differential operators of weight λ, and more generally operators δ satisfying an OPI of the form $\phi := \lfloor xy \rfloor - N(x, y)$, where $N(x, y)$ is a formal expression in $\mathbf{k}\lfloor x, y \rfloor$ that does not contain any subexpression of the form $\lfloor uv \rfloor$ for any $u, v \in \mathbf{k}\lfloor x, y \rfloor$. The other family consists of the OPIs of Rota-Baxter type, which include those defining the average, Rota-Baxter, Nijenhuis, Leroux's TD operators, and more generally OPIs of the form $\phi := \lfloor x \rfloor \lfloor y \rfloor - \lfloor M(x, y) \rfloor$ where $M(x, y)$ is an expression in $\mathbf{k}\lfloor x, y \rfloor$ not involving any subexpression of the form $\lfloor u \rfloor \lfloor v \rfloor$ for any $u, v \in \mathbf{k}\lfloor x, y \rfloor$.

These two families share a common feature: each OPI involves a product: xy for differential type, and $\lfloor x \rfloor \lfloor y \rfloor$ for Rota-Baxter type. These families of OPIs thus provide properties arising from associativity of multiplication, which we can explore in our computational experiments.

For the rest of the paper, we will explain the differential type and Rota-Baxter type OPIs, beginning with the construction of the free operated monoid using bracketed words, and formulate Rota's problem precisely by casting it as one for determining a complete list of these types of OPIs. We then propose a conjectural answer to the problem with a list of differential type OPIs. As evidence of our conjecture, we verify in Section 3.2 that the operators in the list all satisfy the properties prescribed for a differential type operator. We will also give a conjecture for the complete list of Rota-Baxter type OPIs. To support our conjectures, we give a description of the computational approach, and post the full program and computed data on-line. In the final section, we explain our approach in the context of varieties of algebras, providing research directions towards a further understanding of Rota's Problem and possibly tools toward theoretical proofs of our conjectures.

2. OPERATOR IDENTITIES

In this section we give a precise definition of an OPI in the framework of operated algebras.[4] We review the concept of operated monoids, operated algebras, and bracketed words, followed by a construction for the free operated monoids and algebras using bracketed words. Bracketed words are related to Motzkin words and decorated rooted trees [15].

2.1 Operated monoids and algebras

DEFINITION 2.1. *An **operated monoid** is a monoid U together with a map $P : U \to U$. A morphism from an operated monoid[5] U to an operated monoid V is a monoid homomorphism $f : U \to V$ such that $f \circ P = P \circ f$, that is, the diagram below is commutative:*

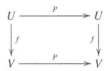

Let **k** be a commutative unitary ring. In Def. 2.1, we may replace "monoid" by "semigroup," "**k**-algebra," or "nonunitary **k**-algebra" to define[6] **operated semigroup**, **operated k-algebra** and **operated**

---

[1]Disclaimer: We are still exploring the best way to formulate Rota's problem and nothing in this paper is meant to provide a definitive forumlation.

[2]More precise definitions will be given in Section 2.

[3]We illustrate only with an ordinary differential algebra, where the common notation for the derivation is δ. In this paper, we have three symbols for the operator: $\lfloor\ \rfloor$, P, and δ, to be used respectively for a general (or bracketed word) setting, the Rota-Baxter setting, and the differential/difference setting; often, they are interchangeable. We use $\lfloor\ \rfloor$ for $\mathbf{k}\lfloor X \rfloor$ to emphasize that $\mathbf{k}\lfloor X \rfloor$ is *not* the differential polynomial ring. Any dependence of the operator on parameters is suppressed, unless clarity requires otherwise.

[4]The concepts, construction of free objects and results in this section are covered in more generality in texts on universal algebra [3, 5, 6]. Our review makes this paper more accessible and allows us to establish our own notations.

[5]As remarked in Footnote 3, we use the same symbol P for all distinguished maps and hence we shall simply use U for an operated monoid.

[6]For operated **k**-algebra categories, P is assumed to be a **k**-linear map in Definition 2.1.

nonunitary k-algebra, respectively. For example, the semigroup $\mathfrak{F}$ of rooted forests with the grafting map $\lfloor \ \rfloor$ and the concatenation product is an operated semigroup [15]. The **k**-module $\mathbf{k}\mathfrak{F}$ generated by $\mathfrak{F}$ is an operated nonunitary **k**-algebra. The unitarization of this algebra has appeared in the work [8] of Connes and Kreimer on renormalization of quantum field theory.

The adjoint functor of the forgetful functor from the category of operated monoids to the category of sets gives the free operated monoids in the usual way. More precisely, a **free operated monoid** on a set X is an operated monoid U together with a map $j : X \to U$ with the property that, for any operated monoid V together with a map $f : X \to V$, there is a unique morphism $\overline{f} : U \to V$ of operated monoids such that $f = \overline{f} \circ j$. Any two free operated monoid on the same set X are isomorphic via a unique isomorphism.

We similarly define the notion of a free operated (nonunitary) **k**-algebra on a set X. As shown in [15], the operated non-unitary **k**-algebra of rooted forests mentioned above is the free operated non-unitary **k**-algebra on one generator.

An **operated ideal** in an operated **k**-algebra R is an ideal closed under the operator. The operated ideal **generated by a set** $\Phi \subseteq R$ is the smallest operated ideal in R containing Φ.

2.2 Free operated monoids

For any set Y, let $M(Y)$ be the free monoid generated by Y and let $\lfloor Y \rfloor$ be the set $\{\lfloor y \rfloor \mid y \in Y\}$, which is just another copy of Y whose elements are denoted by $\lfloor y \rfloor$ for distinction.

We now construct the free operated monoid over a given set X recursively using a directed system

$$\{\iota_n : \mathfrak{M}_n \to \mathfrak{M}_{n+1}\}_{n=0}^{\infty}$$

of free monoids $\mathfrak{M}_n$, where the transition morphisms ι_n are natural embeddings. For this purpose, let $\mathfrak{M}_0 = M(X)$, let

$$\mathfrak{M}_1 := M(X \cup \lfloor \mathfrak{M}_0 \rfloor),$$

and let ι_0 be the natural embedding $\iota : \mathfrak{M}_0 \hookrightarrow \mathfrak{M}_1$, by which we identify $\mathfrak{M}_0$ with its image in $\mathfrak{M}_1$. Note that elements in $\lfloor M(X) \rfloor$ are only symbols indexed by elements in $M(X)$. Thus, while $\mathbf{1} \in \mathfrak{M}_0$ is identified with $\iota_0(\mathbf{1}) = \mathbf{1} \in \mathfrak{M}_1$, $\lfloor \mathbf{1} \rfloor \in \mathfrak{M}_1$ is not the identity.

Assuming by induction that for $n \geq 2$, the free monoids $\mathfrak{M}_{n-1}$ and the embeddings $\iota_{n-2} : \mathfrak{M}_{n-2} \to \mathfrak{M}_{n-1}$ have been defined, we let

$$\mathfrak{M}_n := M(X \cup \lfloor \mathfrak{M}_{n-1} \rfloor). \quad (10)$$

The identity map on X and embedding ι_{n-2} induce an injection

$$X \cup \lfloor \mathfrak{M}_{n-2} \rfloor \hookrightarrow X \cup \lfloor \mathfrak{M}_{n-1} \rfloor, \quad (11)$$

which yields an embedding of free monoids

$$\iota_{n-1} : M(X \cup \lfloor \mathfrak{M}_{n-2} \rfloor) \hookrightarrow M(X \cup \lfloor \mathfrak{M}_{n-1} \rfloor). \quad (12)$$

by functoriality of M, completing the induction. Finally we define the monoid $\mathfrak{M}(X)$ by

$$\mathfrak{M}(X) := \varinjlim \mathfrak{M}_n = \bigcup_{n \geq 0} \mathfrak{M}_n$$

where the identity of $\mathfrak{M}(X)$ is (the directed limit of) $\mathbf{1}$.

THEOREM 2.2. ([15, Corollary 3.6, Corollary 3.7])

1. *The monoid $\mathfrak{M}(X)$, with operator $P := \lfloor \ \rfloor$ and natural embedding $j : X \to \mathfrak{M}(X)$, is the free operated monoid on X.*

2. *The unitary **k**-algebra $\mathbf{k}\,\mathfrak{M}(X)$, with the **k**-linear operator P induced by $\lfloor \ \rfloor$ and the natural embedding $j : X \to \mathbf{k}\,\mathfrak{M}(X)$, is the free operated unitary algebra on X.*

Elements in $\mathfrak{M}(X)$ may be interpreted in terms of rooted trees or Motzkin paths. For symbolic computation, it is best to view them simply as strings or words. Indeed, $\mathfrak{M}(X)$ is the set of **bracketed words** w of the free monoid $M(X \cup \{\lfloor, \rfloor\})$ generated by $X \cup \{\lfloor, \rfloor\}$, in which the brackets $\lfloor \ \rfloor$ form balanced pairs, or more explicitly,

1. the total number of $\lfloor$ in the word w equals to the total number of $\rfloor$ in w; and

2. counting from the left to the right of w, the number of $\lfloor$ is always greater or equal to the number of $\rfloor$.

For example, for the set $X = \{x\}$, the element $\lfloor x \rfloor x \lfloor x \lfloor x \rfloor \rfloor$ is a bracketed word in $M(\{x, \lfloor, \rfloor\})$, while neither $\lfloor \lfloor x \rfloor$ (failing the first condition) nor $\rfloor x \lfloor$ (failing the second condition) is.

For this reason, we call elements in $\mathfrak{M}(X)$ **bracketed words on the generator set** X and we denote the free operated unitary algebra $\mathbf{k}\mathfrak{M}(X)$ on X by $\mathbf{k}\lfloor X \rfloor\!\!\rfloor$, with operator $\lfloor \ \rfloor$. If $X = \{x_1, \ldots, x_k\}$, we also write $\mathbf{k}\lfloor X \rfloor\!\!\rfloor$ simply as $\mathbf{k}\lfloor x_1, \ldots, x_k \rfloor\!\!\rfloor$.

2.3 Operated polynomial identity algebras

We recall the concept of a polynomial identity algebra. Let $\mathbf{k}\langle X \rangle$ denote the free non-commutative **k**-algebra on a finite set $X = \{x_1, \ldots, x_k\}$. A given $\phi \in \mathbf{k}\langle X \rangle$, $\phi \neq 0$, defines a category $\mathbf{Alg}_\phi$ of algebras, whose objects are **k**-algebras R satisfying $\phi(r_1, \ldots, r_k) = 0$ for all $r_1, \ldots, r_k \in R$. The non-commutative polynomial ϕ (formally, the equation $\phi(x_1, \ldots, x_k) = 0$, or its equivalent $\phi_1(x_1, \ldots, x_.) = \phi_2(x_1, \ldots, x_k)$ if $\phi := \phi_1 - \phi_2$) is classically called a **polynomial identity** (PI) and we say R is a **PI-algebra** if R satisfies ϕ for some ϕ. For any set Z, we may define the free PI-algebra on Z in $\mathbf{Alg}_\phi$ by the obvious universal property.

We extend this notion to operated algebras. Let R be an operated algebra, let $r = (r_1, \ldots, r_k) \in R^k$, and let $\phi \in \mathbf{k}\lfloor X \rfloor\!\!\rfloor$. The substitution map $f_r : \{x_1, \ldots, x_k\} \to R$ that maps x_i to r_i induces a unique morphism $\overline{f_r} : \mathbf{k}\lfloor x_1, \ldots, x_k \rfloor\!\!\rfloor \to R$ of operated algebras that extends f_r. Let $\phi_R : R^k \to R$ be defined by

$$\phi_R(r_1, \ldots, r_k) := \overline{f_r}(\phi(x_1, \ldots, x_k)). \quad (13)$$

DEFINITION 2.3. *Let R be an operated algebra. If*

$$\phi_R(r_1, \ldots, r_k) = 0, \quad \forall \ r_1, \ldots, r_k \in R,$$

*then R is called a ϕ-**algebra**, the operator P defining R is called a ϕ-**operator**, and ϕ (or $\phi = 0$) is called an **operated polynomial identity** (OPI). An **operated polynomial identity algebra** or an **OPI-algebra** is a ϕ-algebra for some $\phi \in \mathbf{k}\lfloor x_1, \ldots, x_k \rfloor\!\!\rfloor$ for some positive integer k.*

EXAMPLE 2.4. *When $\phi := \lfloor xy \rfloor - x\lfloor y \rfloor - \lfloor x \rfloor y$, then a ϕ-operator on a **k**-algebra R is a derivation on R, usually denoted by δ, and R is an ordinary, possibly non-commutative, differential algebra.*

EXAMPLE 2.5. *When $\phi := \lfloor x \rfloor \lfloor y \rfloor - \lfloor x\lfloor y \rfloor \rfloor - \lfloor \lfloor x \rfloor y \rfloor - \lambda \lfloor xy \rfloor$, where $\lambda \in \mathbf{k}$, then a ϕ-operator (resp. ϕ-algebra) is a Rota-Baxter operator (resp. Rota-Baxter algebra) of weight λ. We denote such operators by P.*

EXAMPLE 2.6. *When ϕ is from the noncommutative polynomial algebra $\mathbf{k}\langle X \rangle$, then a ϕ-algebra is an algebra with polynomial identity, which we may regard as an operated algebra where the operator is the identity map.*

The next proposition is a consequence of the universal property of free operated algebras and can be regarded as a special case of a very general result on Ω-algebras, where Ω is a set called the signature and represents a family of operations on the algebra (see, for example, [6, Chap. I, Prop. 3.6]). For the sake of accessibility, we include the proof. We caution the reader that there are two sets involved: the set X in terms of which an OPI is expressed, and the set Z on which the free ϕ-algebra is constructed.

PROPOSITION 2.7. *Let $X = \{x_1, \ldots, x_k\}$ and $\phi \in \mathbf{k}\lfloor\!\lfloor X \rfloor\!\rfloor$. Let Z be a set, let $R = \mathbf{k}\lfloor\!\lfloor Z \rfloor\!\rfloor$, and let $j_Z : Z \to R$ be the natural embedding. Let $\phi_R : R^k \to R$ be as defined in Eq. (13), let $I_\phi(Z)$ be the operated ideal of R generated by the set*

$$\{\,\phi_R(r_1, \ldots, r_k) \mid r_1, \ldots, r_k \in R = \mathbf{k}\lfloor\!\lfloor Z \rfloor\!\rfloor\,\},$$

and let $\pi_\phi : R \to R/I_\phi(Z)$ be the quotient morphism. Let

$$i_Z := \pi_\phi \circ j_Z : Z \to R/I_\phi(Z).$$

Then the quotient operated algebra $R/I_\phi(Z)$, together with i_Z and the operator P induced by $\lfloor\ \rfloor$, is the free ϕ-algebra on Z.

PROOF. Clearly $R/I_\phi(Z)$ with operator P is a ϕ-algebra. We claim it satisfies the universal property for being free on Z:
For any ϕ-algebra S and any map $g : Z \to S$, there exists a unique ϕ-algebra homomorphism $g_\phi : R/I_\phi(Z) \to S$ such that $g_\phi \circ i_Z = g$.

Let S and $g : Z \to S$ be given. By the universal property of $R = \mathbf{k}\lfloor\!\lfloor Z \rfloor\!\rfloor$, there is a unique homomorphism $\bar{g} : R \to S$ of operated algebras such that $\bar{g} \circ j_Z = g$. We claim that $I_\phi(Z) \subseteq \ker \bar{g}$.

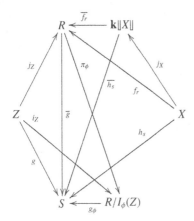

Let $r = (r_1, \ldots, r_k) \in R^k$ and consider the map $f_r : X \to R$ defined by $f_r(x_i) := r_i$, $1 \leq i \leq k$. By the universal property of $\mathbf{k}\lfloor\!\lfloor X \rfloor\!\rfloor$, there is a unique morphism $\overline{f_r} : \mathbf{k}\lfloor\!\lfloor X \rfloor\!\rfloor \to R$ of operated algebras such that $\overline{f_r} \circ j_X = f_r$. Similarly, letting $s = (s_1, \ldots, s_k)$, where $s_i := \bar{g}(r_i) \in S$ for $1 \leq i \leq k$, the map $h_s : X \to S$ defined by $h_s(x_i) := s_i$ for $1 \leq i \leq k$, induces a unique morphism $\overline{h_s} : \mathbf{k}\lfloor\!\lfloor X \rfloor\!\rfloor \to S$ of operated algebras such that $\overline{h_s} \circ j_X = h_s$. Since by definition $\bar{g} \circ f_r = h_s$, we obtain

$$\bar{g} \circ \overline{f_r} \circ j_X = \bar{g} \circ f_r = h_s = \overline{h_s} \circ j_X,$$

leading to $\bar{g} \circ \overline{f_r} = \overline{h_s}$ by uniqueness of $\overline{h_s}$. Now for any generator $\phi_R(r)$ of $I_\phi(Z)$, we have

$$\bar{g}(\phi_R(r)) = \bar{g}(\overline{f_r}(\phi(X)) = \overline{h_s}(\phi(X)) = \phi_S(s) = 0$$

since S is a ϕ-algebra. Thus $I_\phi(Z) \subseteq \ker \bar{g}$, which induces an operated algebra homomorphism $g_\phi : R/I_\phi(Z) \to S$ such that $g_\phi \circ \pi_\phi = \bar{g}$. Then we have

$$g_\phi \circ i_Z = \bar{g}_\phi \circ \pi_\phi \circ j_Z = \bar{g} \circ j_Z = g. \quad (14)$$

So g_ϕ is what we need for the existence part of the universal property of $R/I_\phi(Z)$ as a free ϕ-algebra.

To show uniqueness of g_ϕ, suppose there is another homomorphism $p : R/I_\phi(Z) \to S$ such that $p \circ i_Z = g$. Then

$$p \circ \pi_\phi \circ j_Z = g = \bar{g} \circ j_Z = g_\phi \circ \pi_\phi \circ j_Z.$$

By the uniqueness of $\bar{g}$, we have

$$p \circ \pi_\phi = \bar{g} = g_\phi \circ \pi_\phi.$$

Since π_ϕ is surjective, we must have $p = g_\phi$, as needed. $\quad\square$

Proposition 2.7 shows that for any non-zero $\phi \in \mathbf{k}\lfloor\!\lfloor X \rfloor\!\rfloor$, there is always a (free) ϕ-algebra. Thus the "formulation" below of Rota's Problem would not be helpful.

> Find all non-zero $\phi \in \mathbf{k}\lfloor\!\lfloor X \rfloor\!\rfloor$ such that the OPI $\phi = 0$ can be satisfied by some linear operator on some associative algebra.

While the construction in Proposition 2.7 is general, we note that the free ϕ-algebra may have hidden consequences.

EXAMPLE 2.8. *Let $\phi(x, y) := \lfloor xy \rfloor - y \lfloor x \rfloor$. Let Z be a set and let $Q = \mathbf{k}\lfloor\!\lfloor Z \rfloor\!\rfloor / I_\phi(Z)$ be the free ϕ-algebra with the operator P induced by $\lfloor\ \rfloor$ on $R = \mathbf{k}\lfloor\!\lfloor Z \rfloor\!\rfloor$. Let $a, b, c \in Q$ be arbitrary. We must have $P((ab)c) = P(a(bc))$. Applying the identity $\phi = 0$ on Q to both sides, we find that $(bc - cb)P(a) = 0$. Thus, the commutator $[b, c]$ and $P(a)$ are zero divisors for all $a, b, c \in Q$. We do not know if $I_\phi(Z)$ is prime or not, but if it is, then we would have two possibilities: Q is commutative, or Q is not commutative but $P[a] = 0$ for all $a \in Q$. We also note that any commutative algebra with the identity as operator would be a ϕ-algebra.*

3. TWO TYPES OF OPIs

As remarked in the Introduction, we restrict our attention to those OPIs that are computationally feasible, in particular, to two families that are broad enough to include all the operators in Rota's list, except the Reynolds operator. These families are identified by how they behave with respect to multiplication for which associativity is assumed. As differentiation is easier than integration, we progress more on differential type OPIs than on Rota-Baxter type ones.

3.1 Differential type operators

Our model is the free differential algebra and its weighted generalization as considered in [17]. We refer the reader there for further details on construction of free (noncommutative) differential algebras of weight λ.

The known OPIs that define an endomorphism operator, a differential operator, or a differential operator of weight λ share a common pattern, based on which we will define OPIs of differential type. For this family of operators, we shall use the prefix notation $\delta(r)$ (or δr) for the image of r in such an algebra, which is more traditional, but we shall continue to use the infix notation $\lfloor r \rfloor$ in $\mathbf{k}\lfloor\!\lfloor X \rfloor\!\rfloor$ to emphasize the string attribute of bracketed expressions.

DEFINITION 3.1. *We say an expression $E(X) \in \mathbf{k}\lfloor\!\lfloor X \rfloor\!\rfloor$ is **in differentially reduced form** (DRF) if it does not contain any subexpression of the form $\lfloor uv \rfloor$ for any non-units $u, v \in \mathbf{k}\lfloor\!\lfloor X \rfloor\!\rfloor$. Let Σ be a rewriting system [3] in $\mathbf{k}\lfloor\!\lfloor X \rfloor\!\rfloor$. We say $E(X)$ is Σ-reducible if $E(X)$ can be reduced to zero under Σ.*

DEFINITION 3.2. *Let $\phi(x, y) := \lfloor xy \rfloor - N(x, y) \in \mathbf{k}\lfloor\!\lfloor x, y \rfloor\!\rfloor$ and define an associated rewriting system*

$$\Sigma_\phi := \{\lfloor ab \rfloor \mapsto N(a, b) \mid a, b \text{ are non units } \in \mathbf{k}\lfloor\!\lfloor x, y \rfloor\!\rfloor\}.$$

*An expression $E(x, y) \in \mathbf{k}\lfloor\!\lfloor x, y \rfloor\!\rfloor$ is **differentially ϕ-reducible** if it is Σ_ϕ-reducible.*

DEFINITION 3.3. *We say an OPI $\phi \in \mathbf{k}\lfloor\!\lfloor x, y\rfloor\!\rfloor$ or $\phi = 0$ is of differential type (OPIDT) if ϕ has the form $\lfloor xy\rfloor - N(x, y)$, where $N(x, y)$ satisfies the two conditions:*

1. $N(x, y)$ is in DRF;

2. $N(uv, w) - N(u, vw)$ is differentially ϕ-reducible $\forall\ u, v, w \in \mathbf{k}\lfloor\!\lfloor x, y\rfloor\!\rfloor$.

If $\phi := \lfloor xy\rfloor - N(x, y)$ is an OPIDT, we also say the expression $N(x, y)$ and the defining operator P of a ϕ-algebra S are of differential type.

REMARK 3.1. *Condition 1 is needed to avoid infinite rewriting under Σ_ϕ. Condition 2 is not equivalent to*

$$\phi_{\mathbf{k}\lfloor\!\lfloor x, y\rfloor\!\rfloor}(uv, w) - \phi_{\mathbf{k}\lfloor\!\lfloor x, y\rfloor\!\rfloor}(u, vw) \in I_\phi(\{x, y\})\ \forall\ u, v, w \in \mathbf{k}\lfloor\!\lfloor x, y\rfloor\!\rfloor,$$

which is always true. The non-unit requirement is to avoid infinite rewriting of the form such as $\lfloor u\rfloor = \lfloor u \cdot \mathbf{1}\rfloor \mapsto N(u, \mathbf{1})$, when $N(u, \mathbf{1})$ may involve $\lfloor u\rfloor$.

EXAMPLE 3.4. *For any $\lambda \in \mathbf{k}$, the expressions λxy, $\lambda\lfloor x\rfloor\lfloor y\rfloor$ (operators are semi-endomorphisms), and $\lambda\lfloor y\rfloor\lfloor x\rfloor$ (operators are semi-antimorphisms) are of differential type. A differential operator of weight λ satisfy an OPI of differential type (Eq. (9)). This can be easily verified.*

We can now state the classification problem of differential type OPIs and operators

PROBLEM 3.5. **(Rota's Problem: the Differential Case)** *Find all operated polynomial identities of differential type by finding all expressions $N(x, y) \in \mathbf{k}\lfloor\!\lfloor x, y\rfloor\!\rfloor$ of differential type.*

We propose the following answer to this problem.

CONJECTURE 3.6. **(OPIs of Differential Type)** *Let $\mathbf{k}$ be a field of characteristic zero. Every expression $N(x, y) \in \mathbf{k}\lfloor\!\lfloor x, y\rfloor\!\rfloor$ of differential type takes one (or more) of the forms below for some $a, b, c, e \in \mathbf{k}$:*

1. $b(x\lfloor y\rfloor + \lfloor x\rfloor y) + c\lfloor x\rfloor\lfloor y\rfloor + exy$ where $b^2 = b + ce$,

2. $ce^2 yx + exy + c\lfloor y\rfloor\lfloor x\rfloor - ce(y\lfloor x\rfloor + \lfloor y\rfloor x)$,

3. $axy\lfloor 1\rfloor + b\lfloor 1\rfloor xy + cxy$,

4. $x\lfloor y\rfloor + \lfloor x\rfloor y + ax\lfloor 1\rfloor y + bxy$,

5. $\lfloor x\rfloor y + a(x\lfloor 1\rfloor y - xy\lfloor 1\rfloor)$,

6. $x\lfloor y\rfloor + a(x\lfloor 1\rfloor y - \lfloor 1\rfloor xy)$.

Note that the list is not symmetric in x and y. One might think that if $N(x, y)$ is of differential type, then so is $N(y, x)$. But this is not true.

EXAMPLE 3.7. *$N_1(x, y) := x\lfloor y\rfloor$ is of differential type since*

$$\begin{aligned} N_1(uv, w) - N_1(u, vw) &= uv\lfloor w\rfloor - u\lfloor vw\rfloor \\ &\mapsto uv\lfloor w\rfloor - uv\lfloor w\rfloor = 0 \end{aligned}$$

for all $u, v, w \in \mathbf{k}\lfloor\!\lfloor x, y\rfloor\!\rfloor$. However, $N_2(x, y) := y\lfloor x\rfloor$ is not, since

$$\begin{aligned} N_2(xy, x) - N_2(x, yx) &= x\lfloor xy\rfloor - yx\lfloor x\rfloor \\ &\mapsto xy\lfloor x\rfloor - yx\lfloor x\rfloor = (xy - yx)\lfloor x\rfloor, \end{aligned}$$

which is in DRF (no further reduction using Σ_ϕ is possible, where $\phi := \lfloor xy\rfloor - N_2(x, y)$) but non-zero. See also Example 2.8.

3.2 Evidence for the conjecture

We provide evidence, both computational and theoretical, for Conjecture 3.6.

3.2.1 Verification of the operators

THEOREM 3.8. *The OPI $\phi := \lfloor xy\rfloor - N(x, y)$, where $N(x, y)$ is any expression listed in Conjecture 3.6 is of differential type.*

PROOF. Clearly, all six expressions are in DRF. We check ϕ-reducibility for the first two cases.

Case 1. Here $N(x, y) := b(x\lfloor y\rfloor + \lfloor x\rfloor y) + c\lfloor x\rfloor\lfloor y\rfloor + exy$, where $b^2 = b + ce$. We have

$$cN(x, y) + bxy = (c\lfloor x\rfloor + bx)(c\lfloor y\rfloor + by). \tag{15}$$

Let α be the operator defined by $\alpha(u) := c\lfloor u\rfloor + bu$ for $u \in \mathbf{k}\lfloor\!\lfloor x, y\rfloor\!\rfloor$. Then for any non-units $u, v \in \mathbf{k}\lfloor\!\lfloor x, y\rfloor\!\rfloor$, the rewriting rule $\lfloor uv\rfloor \mapsto N(u, v)$ gives the rewriting rules

$$\alpha(uv) = c\lfloor uv\rfloor + buv \mapsto cN(u, v) + buv = \alpha(u)\alpha(v)$$

by Eq. (15). Again, by Eq. (15), for a non-unit w, we have

$$\begin{aligned} cN(uv, w) + b(uv)w &= \alpha(uv)\alpha(w) \mapsto (\alpha(u)\alpha(v))\alpha(w), \\ cN(u, vw) + bu(vw) &= \alpha(u)\alpha(vw) \mapsto \alpha(u)(\alpha(v)\alpha(w)). \end{aligned}$$

Then $c(N(uv, w) - N(u, vw))$ is differentially ϕ-reducible by associativity. If $c \neq 0$, then $N(x, y)$ is of differential type. Suppose $c = 0$. The constraint $b^2 = b + ce$ becomes $b^2 = b$ and either $b = 0$ or $b = 1$. When $b = 0$, $\phi = \lfloor xy\rfloor - exy$ (semi-endomorphism case), and when $b = 1$, $\phi = \lfloor xy\rfloor - (x\lfloor y\rfloor + \lfloor x\rfloor y + exy)$. These are easily verified directly to be OPIs of differential type.

Case 2. Here $N(x, y) := ce^2 yx + exy + c\lfloor y\rfloor\lfloor x\rfloor - ce(y\lfloor x\rfloor + \lfloor y\rfloor x)$ and we have $N(x, y) - exy = c(\lfloor y\rfloor - ey)(\lfloor x\rfloor - ex)$. Let $\alpha(u) = \lfloor u\rfloor - eu$ and the rest of the proof is similar to Case 1.

For the remaining cases, it is routine to check that $N(uv, w) - N(u, vw)$ is differentially ϕ-reducible for $\phi := \lfloor xy\rfloor - N(x, y)$. For example, for Case 5, we have, using associativity,

$$\begin{aligned} N(uv, w) &= \lfloor uv\rfloor w + a(uv\lfloor 1\rfloor w - uvw\lfloor 1\rfloor) \\ &\mapsto (\lfloor u\rfloor v + a(u\lfloor 1\rfloor v - uv\lfloor 1\rfloor))w + a(uv\lfloor 1\rfloor w - uvw\lfloor 1\rfloor) \\ &= \lfloor u\rfloor vw + a(u\lfloor 1\rfloor vw - uvw\lfloor 1\rfloor) \\ &= N(u, vw). \quad \square \end{aligned}$$

3.2.2 Computational evidence

DEFINITION 3.9. *The **operator degree** of a monomial in $\mathbf{k}\lfloor\!\lfloor X\rfloor\!\rfloor$ is the total number the operator $\lfloor\ \rfloor$ appearing in the monomial. The **operator degree** of a polynomial ϕ in $\mathbf{k}\lfloor\!\lfloor X\rfloor\!\rfloor$ is the maximum of the operator degrees of the monomials appearing in ϕ.*

THEOREM 3.10. *Let $\mathbf{k}$ be a field. The only expressions $N(x, y)$ of differential type for which the total operator degrees $\leqslant 2$ are the ones listed in Conjecture 3.6. Moreover, the only expressions of differential type in the form*

$$\begin{aligned} N(x, y) := &\ a_{0,1} x\lfloor y\rfloor + a_{0,2} x\lfloor\lfloor y\rfloor\rfloor + a_{1,0}\lfloor x\rfloor y + a_{1,1}\lfloor x\rfloor\lfloor y\rfloor \\ &+ a_{1,2}\lfloor x\rfloor\lfloor\lfloor y\rfloor\rfloor + a_{2,0}\lfloor\lfloor x\rfloor\rfloor y + a_{2,1}\lfloor\lfloor x\rfloor\rfloor\lfloor y\rfloor + a_{2,2}\lfloor\lfloor x\rfloor\rfloor\lfloor\lfloor y\rfloor\rfloor \\ &+ b_{0,1} y\lfloor x\rfloor + b_{0,2} y\lfloor\lfloor x\rfloor\rfloor + b_{1,0}\lfloor y\rfloor x + b_{1,1}\lfloor y\rfloor\lfloor x\rfloor \\ &+ b_{1,2}\lfloor y\rfloor\lfloor\lfloor x\rfloor\rfloor + b_{2,0}\lfloor\lfloor y\rfloor\rfloor\lfloor x\rfloor + b_{2,2}\lfloor\lfloor y\rfloor\rfloor\lfloor\lfloor x\rfloor\rfloor \\ &+ a_{0,0} xy + b_{0,0} yx \end{aligned}$$

where $a_{i,j}, b_{i,j} \in \mathbf{k}\ (0 \leqslant i, j \leqslant 2)$, are the ones listed.

PROOF. This is obtained and verified by computations in *Mathematica* [27]. See Section 4 for a brief description and [26] for details and results. $\square$

3.2.3 Theoretical evidence

We now give some result to show that the condition of operator degree $\leqslant 2$ in our computational evidence is not too restrictive. For ease of notation, we use δ for $\lfloor\ \rfloor$ in $\mathbf{k}\|x,y\|$.

Proposition 3.11. *Let $\phi := \delta(xy) - N(x,y)$ be an OPI of differential type where $N(x,y)$ has the form*

$$N(x,y) := \sum_{m,n \geqslant 0} c_{m,n}\delta^m(x)\delta^n(y), \quad c_{m,n} \in \mathbf{k}. \tag{16}$$

Then ϕ has operator degree $\leqslant 2$.

Proof. Let $u,v,w \in \mathbf{k}\|x,y\|$ be non-units. Apply Σ_ϕ-reductions of the form $\delta(ab) \mapsto N(a,b)$ repeatedly, and obtain

$$N(uv,w) = \sum_{m,n \geqslant 0} c_{m,n}\delta^m(uv)\delta^n(w) \tag{17}$$

$$\mapsto \sum_{m,n \geqslant 0} c_{m,n} \sum_{i_1,\ldots,i_m,j_1,\ldots,j_m \geqslant 0} c_{i_1,j_1}\cdots c_{i_m,j_m}\delta^{i_1+\cdots+i_m}(u)\delta^{j_1+\cdots+j_m}(v)\delta^n(w).$$

Similarly, we have

$$N(u,vw) = \sum_{m,n \geqslant 0} c_{m,n}\delta^m(u)\delta^n(vw) \tag{18}$$

$$\mapsto \sum_{m,n \geqslant 0} c_{m,n} \sum_{i_1,\ldots,i_n,j_1,\ldots,j_n \geqslant 0} c_{i_1,j_1}\cdots c_{i_n,j_n}\delta^m(u)\delta^{i_1+\cdots+i_n}(v)\delta^{j_1+\cdots+j_n}(w).$$

Taking $u = w = x$ and $v = y$, for example, all monomials appearing in the expressions after reduction are of the form $\delta^i(x)\delta^j(y)\delta^k(x)$, which are monomials in DRF, and are distinct for distinct triplets (i,j,k). The totality B of these monomials are linearly independent over $\mathbf{k}$. We now show that we may take $n \leqslant 1$ in $N(x,y)$. A similar argument will show that we may also take $m \leqslant 1$ in $N(x,y)$.

We order these monomials lexicographically by operator orders from right to left. More precisely, define

$$\delta^{i_1}(u)\delta^{j_1}(v)\delta^{k_1}(w) \leqslant \delta^{i_2}(u)\delta^{j_2}(v)\delta^{k_2}(w)$$

if $k_1 < k_2$, or if $k_1 = k_2$ and $j_1 < j_2$, or if $k_1 = k_2$, $j_1 = j_2$ and $i_1 < i_2$. We write $N(x,y) = c_{\overline{m},\overline{n}}\delta^{\overline{m}}(x)\delta^{\overline{n}}(y) + N'(x,y)$, where

$$\overline{n} := \max\{n \mid c_{m,n} \neq 0 \text{ for some } m\},$$
$$\overline{m} := \max\{m \mid c_{m,\overline{n}} \neq 0\},$$

$c_{\overline{m},\overline{n}} \neq 0$, and $N'(x,y)$ has order $n < \overline{n}$ in y. We claim that the highest monomial M (with a non-zero coefficient) in Eq. (18) is unique and is $\delta^{\overline{m}}(u)\delta^{\overline{m}\,\overline{n}}(v)\delta^{\overline{n}^2}(w)$. Consider all $M = \delta^m(u)\delta^{i_1+\cdots+i_n}(v)\delta^{j_1+\cdots+j_n}(w)$. The order of $\delta^{j_1+\cdots+j_n}(w)$ is highest when every j_r, $1 \leqslant r \leqslant n$, is $\overline{n}$, and this order is $n\overline{n}$ and hence the highest order in w in Eq. (18) is $\overline{n}^2$. Fixing this order in w, the order $i_1 + \cdots + i_n = i_1 + \cdots + i_{\overline{n}}$ in v will be the largest only when every i_r, $1 \leqslant r \leqslant \overline{n}$, is $\overline{m}$ and this order is thus $\overline{m}\,\overline{n}$. It is clear the order in u is $\overline{m}$, proving the claim.

Consider all monomials $M = \delta^{i_1+\cdots+i_m}(u)\delta^{j_1+\cdots+j_m}(v)\delta^n(w)$ (with a non-zero coefficient) in Eq. (17). The highest order in w is $\leqslant \overline{n}$. Therefore since $N(uv,w) - N(u,vw)$ is differentially ϕ-reducible, we must have $\overline{n}^2 \leqslant \overline{n}$ (by linear independence of B). Since $\overline{n} \geqslant 0$, all non-zero coefficients $c_{m,n}$ in $N(x,y)$ must have $n \leqslant \overline{n} \leqslant 1$. $\square$

For a special case, we can verify the conjecture directly.

Proposition 3.12. *Suppose $\phi := \delta(xy) - N(x,y)$ is of differential type, where $N(x,y)$ has the form*

$$N(x,y) := a\,\delta^n(x)\delta^n(y) + b\,\delta^n(y)\delta^n(x),$$

for some natural number n and $a,b \in \mathbf{k}$ with at least one of a, or b is non-zero. Then $n = 0$ or 1, $ab = 0$, and $N(x,y)$ is in the list in Conjecture 3.6

Proof. By induction we verify, for non-units $u,v \in \mathbf{k}\|x,y\|$, that

$$\delta^k(uv) \mapsto A_k(a,b)\delta^{kn}(u)\delta^{kn}(v) + B_k(a,b)\delta^{kn}(u)\delta^{kn}(v), \tag{19}$$

where

$$A_k(a,b) = \sum_{\substack{0 \leqslant i \leqslant k, \\ i \equiv k \,(\text{mod }2)}} \binom{k}{i}a^i b^{k-i}$$

$$B_k(a,b) = \sum_{\substack{0 \leqslant i \leqslant k, \\ i \equiv k-1 \,(\text{mod }2)}} \binom{k}{i}a^i b^{k-i}.$$

We then have

$$N(xy,x) = a\delta^n(xy)\delta^n(x) + b\delta^n(x)\delta^n(xy)$$

$$\mapsto a\big(A_n(a,b)\delta^{n^2}(x)\delta^{n^2}(y) + B_n(a,b)\delta^{n^2}(y)\delta^{n^2}(x)\big)\delta^n(x)$$

$$+b\delta^n(x)\big(A_n(a,b)\delta^{n^2}(x)\delta^{n^2}(y) + B_n(a,b)\delta^{n^2}(y)\delta^{n^2}(x)\big).$$

Similarly,

$$N(x,yx) = a\delta^n(x)\delta^n(yx) + b\delta^n(yx)\delta^n(x)$$

$$\mapsto a\delta^n(x)\big(A_n(a,b)\delta^{n^2}(y)\delta^{n^2}(x) + B_n(a,b)\delta^{n^2}(x)\delta^{n^2}(y)\big)$$

$$+b\big(A_n(a,b)\delta^{n^2}(y)\delta^{n^2}(x) + B_n(a,b)\delta^{n^2}(x)\delta^{n^2}(y)\big)\delta^n(x).$$

Suppose $n \geqslant 2$. Then all the monomials on the right-hand-sides of the Σ_ϕ-reductions for $N(xy,x)$ and $N(x,yx)$ are unlike terms in $\mathbf{k}\|x,y\|$ and are in DRF. Thus since $N(xy,x) - N(x,yx)$ is differentially ϕ-reducible, all the coefficients must be zero. So we have

$$aA_n(a,b) = aB_n(a,b) = bA_n(a,b) = bB_n(a,b) = 0.$$

Noting that $A_n(a,b) + B_n(a,b) = (a+b)^n$, we have

$$a(a+b)^n + b(a+b)^n = 0.$$

Then $(a+b)^{n+1} = 0$ and thus $a + b = 0$ and $b = -a$. Plugging this in $aA_n(a,b) = 0$, we obtain

$$aA_n(a,b) = a \sum_{\substack{0 \leqslant i \leqslant n, \\ i \equiv n \,(\text{mod }2)}} \binom{n}{i}a^n = 0$$

since $(-1)^{n-i} = 1$ for $i \equiv n \pmod 2$. Thus $a = 0$. By a similar argument, we have $b = 0$, contradicting the hypothesis.

Thus we must have $n \leqslant 1$. When $n \leqslant 1$, it is directly verified that $a = 0$ or $b = 0$ and $N(x,y)$ is in the list in onjecture 3.6. $\square$

3.3 Rota-Baxter type operators

Definition 3.13. *We say an expression $E(X) \in \mathbf{k}\|X\|$ is in Rota-Baxter reduced form (RBRF) if it does not contain any subexpression of the form $\lfloor u\rfloor\lfloor v\rfloor$ for any $u,v \in \mathbf{k}\|X\|$.*

Definition 3.14. *An OPI $\phi \in \mathbf{k}\|x,y\|$ is of Rota-Baxter type if it has the form $\lfloor x\rfloor\lfloor y\rfloor - \lfloor M(x,y)\rfloor$ for some $M(x,y) \in \mathbf{k}\|x,y\|$ that satisfies the two conditions:*

1. *$M(x,y)$ is in RBRF;*

2. *$M(M(u,v),w) - M(u,M(v,w))$ is Π_ϕ-reducible for all $u,v,w \in \mathbf{k}\|x,y\|$, where Π_ϕ is the rewriting system*

$$\Pi_\phi := \{\lfloor a\rfloor\lfloor b\rfloor \mapsto \lfloor M(a,b)\rfloor \mid a,b \in \mathbf{k}\|x,y\|\}.$$

If $\phi := \lfloor x\rfloor\lfloor y\rfloor - \lfloor M(x,y)\rfloor$ is of Rota-Baxter type, we also say the expression $M(x,y)$, and the defining operator P of a ϕ-algebra S are of Rota-Baxter type.

EXAMPLE 3.15. *The expression $M(x, y) := x\lfloor y \rfloor$ that defines the average operator is of Rota-Baxter type since*

$$
\begin{aligned}
M(M(u, v), w) - M(u, M(v, w)) &= M(u, v)\lfloor w \rfloor - u\lfloor M(v, w) \rfloor \\
&= u\lfloor v \rfloor\lfloor w \rfloor - u\lfloor v\lfloor w \rfloor\rfloor \\
&\mapsto u\lfloor v\lfloor w \rfloor\rfloor - u\lfloor v\lfloor w \rfloor\rfloor = 0.
\end{aligned}
$$

Other examples are OPIs corresponding to a Rota-Baxter operator or a Nijenhuis operator.

PROBLEM 3.16. (**Rota's Classification Problem: Rota-Baxter Case**) *Find all Rota-Baxter type operators. In other words, find all Rota-Baxter type expressions $M(x, y) \in \mathbf{k}\lfloor\!\lfloor x, y\rfloor\!\rfloor$.*

We propose the following answer to this problem.

CONJECTURE 3.17. (**OPIs of Rota-Baxter Type**) *For any $d, \lambda \in \mathbf{k}$, the expressions $M(x, y)$ in the list below are of Rota-Baxter type (new types are underlined). Moreover, any OPI of Rota-Baxter type is necessarily of the form*

$$
\phi := \lfloor x \rfloor\lfloor y \rfloor - \lfloor M(x, y)\rfloor,
$$

for some $M(x, y)$ in the list.

1. $x\lfloor y \rfloor$ (*average operator*),

2. $\lfloor x \rfloor y$ (*inverse average operator*),

3. $x\lfloor y \rfloor + y\lfloor x \rfloor$,

4. $\underline{\lfloor x \rfloor y + \lfloor y \rfloor x}$,

5. $x\lfloor y \rfloor + \lfloor x \rfloor y - \lfloor xy \rfloor$ (*Nijenhuis operator*),

6. $x\lfloor y \rfloor + \lfloor x \rfloor y + \lambda xy$ (*Rota-Baxter operator of weight λ*),

7. $\underline{x\lfloor y \rfloor - x\lfloor 1 \rfloor y + \lambda xy}$,

8. $\underline{\lfloor x \rfloor y - x\lfloor 1 \rfloor y + \lambda xy}$,

9. $\underline{x\lfloor y \rfloor + \lfloor x \rfloor y - x\lfloor 1 \rfloor y + \lambda xy}$ (*generalized Leroux TD operator with weight λ*),

10. $\underline{x\lfloor y \rfloor + \lfloor x \rfloor y - xy\lfloor 1 \rfloor - x\lfloor 1 \rfloor y + \lambda xy}$,

11. $\underline{x\lfloor y \rfloor + \lfloor x \rfloor y - x\lfloor 1 \rfloor y - \lfloor xy \rfloor + \lambda xy}$,

12. $\underline{x\lfloor y \rfloor + \lfloor x \rfloor y - x\lfloor 1 \rfloor y - \lfloor 1 \rfloor xy + \lambda xy}$,

13. $\underline{dx\lfloor 1 \rfloor y + \lambda xy}$ (*generalized endomorphisms*),

14. $\underline{dy\lfloor 1 \rfloor x + \lambda yx}$ (*generalized antimorphisms*).

REMARK 3.2. *Let Z be any set. Recall that the bracketed words in Z that are in RBRF when viewed as elements of $\mathbf{k}\lfloor\!\lfloor Z\rfloor\!\rfloor$ are called* **Rota-Baxter words** *and that they form a $\mathbf{k}$-basis of the free Rota-Baxter $\mathbf{k}$-algebra on Z [18]. Every expression in RBRF is a $\mathbf{k}$-linear combination of Rota-Baxter words in $\mathbf{k}\lfloor\!\lfloor x, y\rfloor\!\rfloor$.*

More generally, if $\phi(x, y)$ is of Rota-Baxter type, then the free ϕ-algebras on a set Z in the corresponding categories of Rota-Baxter type ϕ-algebras have special bases that can be constructed uniformly. Indeed, if $\mathbf{k}\{Z\}'$ denotes the set of Rota-Baxter words in $\mathbf{k}\lfloor\!\lfloor Z\rfloor\!\rfloor$, then the map

$$
\mathbf{k}\{Z\}' \to \mathbf{k}\lfloor\!\lfloor Z\rfloor\!\rfloor \to \mathbf{k}\lfloor\!\lfloor Z\rfloor\!\rfloor/I_\phi(Z)
$$

is bijective. Thus a suitable multiplication on $\mathbf{k}\{Z\}'$ makes it the free ϕ-algebra on Z. This is in fact how the free Rota-Baxter $\mathbf{k}$-algebra on Z is constructed when $\phi(x, y)$ is the OPI corresponding to the Rota-Baxter operator.

4. COMPUTATIONAL EXPERIMENTS

In this section, we give a brief description of the computational experiments in *Mathematica* that results in Conjectures 3.6 and 3.17. The programs consist of several Notebooks, available at [26] in a zipped file.

Basically, the non-commutative arithmetic for an operated algebra was implemented *ad hoc*, using bracketed words and relying as much as possible on the built-in facilities in *Mathematica* for non-commutative multiplication, list operations, rewriting, and equation simplification. Care was taken to avoid infinite recursions during rewriting of expressions. An elaborate ansatz with indeterminate coefficients (like the expression $N(x, y)$ in Theorem 3.10) is given as input, and to obtain differential type OPIs, the difference $N(uv, w) - N(u, vw)$ is differentially ϕ-reduced using the rewrite rule system Σ_ϕ. The Rota-Baxter type OPIs are obtained similarly using an ansatz $M(x, y)$ and reducing the difference $M(M(u, v), w) - M(u, M(v, w))$ with the rewrite rule system Π_ϕ. The resulting reduced form is equated to zero, yielding a system of equations in the indeterminate coefficients. This system is simplified using Gröber basis method (a heuristic application of Divide and Conquer has been automated). Once the ansatz is entered, the "algebras" can either be obtained in one command `getAlgebras`, or the computation can be stepped through.

The programs provided 10 classes of differential type based on an ansatz of 14 terms, which is then manually merged into the 6 classes in Conjecture 3.6. We obtain no new ones after expanding the ansatz to 20 terms, including terms such as $\lfloor\lfloor x \rfloor\rfloor\lfloor\lfloor y \rfloor\rfloor$. This is explained by Proposition 3.11. The list for Rota-Baxter type OPIs are obtained from an ansatz with 14 terms, some involving $P(1)$ (or $\lfloor 1 \rfloor$, in bracket notation) in a triple product.

We are quite confident that our list of differential type operators is complete. For Rota-Baxter type operators, our list may not be complete, since in our computations, we have restricted our rewriting system Π_ϕ to disallow units in order to get around the possibly non-terminating reduction sequences modulo the identities. This is especially the case when the OPIs involve $\lfloor 1 \rfloor$. Typically, for Rota-Baxter type OPIs, we don't know how to handle the appearance of $\lfloor\lfloor 1 \rfloor\lfloor 1 \rfloor\rfloor$ computationally (they may cancel, or not, if our rewriting system Π_ϕ is expanded to include units as in Definition 3.14). While expressions involving $\lfloor 1 \rfloor$ alone may be reduced to zero using an expanded rewriting system, monomials involving a mix of bracketed words and $\lfloor 1 \rfloor$ are often linearly independent over $\mathbf{k}$.

The *Mathematica* Notebook `DTOrderTwoExamples.nb` shows the computations for differential type operators and the Notebook `VariationRotaBaxterOperators.nb` does the same for Rota-Baxter type ones. Non-commutative multiplication is printed using the symbol $\otimes$ instead of $**$. It is known that the output routines fail to be compatible with *Mathematica*, Version 8, and we will try to fix this incompatibility and post updated versions on-line.

5. SUMMARY AND OUTLOOK

We study Rota's classification problem by considering algebras with a unary operator that satisfies operated polynomial identities. For this, we review the construction of the operated polynomial algebra.

A far more general theory called variety of algebras exists, of which the theories of PI-rings, PI-algebras, and OPI-algebras are special cases [10]. An "algebra" is any set with a set of functions (operations), together with some identities perhaps. A Galois connection between identities and "variety of algebras" is set up similar to the correspondence between polynomial ideals and algebraic varieties. Thus, differential algebra is one variety of algebra, Rota-Baxter algebra is another, and so on.

In mathematics, specifically universal algebra [5, 6], a *variety of algebras* [or a *finitary algebraic category*] is the class of all algebraic structures of a given signature satisfying a given set of identities. Equivalently, a variety is a class of algebraic structures of the same signature which satisfies the HSP properties: closed under the taking of homomorphic images, subalgebras and (direct) products.

This equivalence, known as the HSP Theorem, is a result of G. Birkhoff, which is of fundamental importance in universal algebra. We refer interested readers to [6, Chap. I, Theorem 3.7], [5, Theorem 9.5] and, for computer scientists with a model theory background, [3, Theorem 3.5.14]. It is simple to see that the class of algebras satisfying some set of equations will be closed under the HSP operations. Proving the converse—classes of algebras closed under the HSP operations must be equational—is much harder.

By restricting ourselves to those special cases of Rota's Problem that Rota was interested in, and by exploiting the structures of operated algebra and compatibility of associativity on one hand, and symbolic computation (*Mathematica*) on the other, we are able to give two conjectured lists of OPI-algebras.

The project arose from our belief that the construction of free objects in each class of the varieties should be uniformly done. Currently, similar results for the known classes are proved individually.

We also believe that there is a Poincaré-Birkhoff-Witt type theorem, similar to the enveloping algebra of a Lie algebra, where a canonical basis of the enveloping algebra is constructed from a basis of the Lie algebra. Here, the free algebra of the variety is constructed from the generating set Z with Rota-Baxter words or terms (see Remark 3.2).

The theory of OPI-rings need to be studied further and there are many open problems. We end this discussion by providing just one. A variety is **Schreier** if every subalgebra of a free algebra in the variety is free. For example, the variety of all groups (resp. abelian groups) is Schreier. A central problem in the theory of varieties is whether a particular variety of algebras is Schreier. Which of the varieties of differential type algebras or Rota-Baxter type algebras are Schreier?

6. REFERENCES

[1] M. Aguiar, On the associative analog of Lie bialgebras, *J. Algebra* **244** (2001), 492–532.

[2] G. E. Andrews, L. Guo, W. Keigher and K. Ono, Baxter algebras and Hopf algebras, *Trans. Amer. Math. Soc.* **355** (2003), 4639–4656.

[3] F. Baader and T. Nipkow, *Term Rewriting and All That*. Cambridge Univ. Press, Cambridge, 1998.

[4] C. Bai, A unified algebraic approach to classical Yang-Baxter equation, *Jour. Phys. A: Math. Theor.* **40** (36) (2007), 11073–11082.

[5] S. Burris and H. P. Sankappanavar, *A Course in Universal Algebra*, Springer, 1981. The Millennium Ed. available at http://www.math.uwaterloo.ca/~snburris/htdocs/ualg.html

[6] P. M. Cohn, *Algebra*, Vol. 3, 2nd ed., J. Wiley & Sons, Chichester 1991.

[7] R. Cohn, *Difference Algebra*, Interscience Publishers John Wiley & Sons, New York-London-Sydeny 1965.

[8] A. Connes, D. Kreimer, Hopf algebras, renormalization and noncommutative geometry, *Comm. Math. Phys.* **199** (1998), 203–242.

[9] A. Connes and D. Kreimer, Renormalization in quantum field theory and the Riemann-Hilbert problem. I. The Hopf algebra structure of graphs and the main theorem, *Comm. Math. Phys.* **210** (2000), 249–273.

[10] V. Drersky and E. Fromanek, *Polynomial Identity Rings*, Birkhäuser, 2004.

[11] K. Ebrahimi-Fard and L. Guo, Free Rota-Baxter algebras and dendriform algebras, *J. Pure Appl. Algebra* **212** (2008), 320–339.

[12] K. Ebrahimi-Fard, L. Guo and D. Kreimer, Spitzer's Identity and the Algebraic Birkhoff Decomposition in pQFT, *J. Phys. A: Math. Gen.* **37** (2004), 11037–11052.

[13] K. Ebrahimi-Fard, L. Guo and D. Manchon, Birkhoff type decompositions and the Baker-Campbell-Hausdorff recursion, *Comm. in Math. Phys.* **267** (2006), 821–845.

[14] J. M. Freeman, On the classification of operator identities, *Studies in Appl. Math.* **51** (1972), 73–84.

[15] L. Guo, Operated semigroups, Motzkin paths and rooted trees, *J. Alg. Comb.* **29** (2009), 35–62.

[16] L. Guo, W. Keigher, Baxter algebras and shuffle products, *Adv. Math.* **150** (2000), 117–149.

[17] L. Guo and W. Keigher, On differential Rota-Baxter algebras, *J. Pure Appl. Algebra* **212** (2008), 522–540.

[18] L. Guo and W. Y. Sit, Enumeration of Rota-Baxter words, *Proc. ISSAC 2006*, Genoa, Italy, ACM Press, 124–131.

[19] L. Guo and B. Zhang, Renormalization of multiple zeta values, *J. Algebra* **319** (2008), 3770–3809.

[20] V. A. Lunts and A. K. Rosenberg, Differential operators on noncommutative rings, Selecta Math. (N.S.) **3** (1997), 335–359.

[21] V. A. Lunts and A. K. Rosenberg, Localization for quantum groups. Selecta Math. (N.S.) **5** (1999), 123–159.

[22] E. Kolchin, *Differential Algebraic Groups*, Academic Press, Inc., Orlando, FL, 1985.

[23] C. Procesi, *Rings with Polynomial Identities*, Pure Appl. Math. **17**, Marcel Dekker, Inc., New York, 1973.

[24] G.-C. Rota, Baxter operators, an introduction, In: *Gian-Carlo Rota on Combinatorics, Introductory Papers and Commentaries*, Joseph P. S. Kung, Editor, Birkhäuser, Boston, 1995.

[25] L. H. Rowen, *Polynomial Identities in Ring Theory*, Pure Appl. Math. **84**, Academic Press, Inc, 1980.

[26] W. Y. Sit, *Mathematica* Notebooks, http://scisun.sci.ccny.cuny.edu/~wyscc/research.html, 2006–2010.

[27] *Mathematica*, Version 7, Wolfram Research, Inc., 2008.

Computing Hermite Forms of Polynomial Matrices

Somit Gupta
somit.gupta@gmail.com

Arne Storjohann
astorjoh@uwaterloo.ca

David R. Cheriton School of Computer Science
University of Waterloo, Ontario, Canada N2L 3G1

ABSTRACT

This paper presents a new algorithm for computing the Hermite form of a polynomial matrix. Given a nonsingular $n \times n$ matrix A filled with degree d polynomials with coefficients from a field, the algorithm computes the Hermite form of A using an expected number of $(n^3 d)^{1+o(1)}$ field operations. This is the first algorithm that is both softly linear in the degree d and softly cubic in the dimension n. The algorithm is randomized of the Las Vegas type.

Categories and Subject Descriptors

G.4 [**Mathematical Software**]: Algorithm Design and Analysis; I.1.2 [**Symbolic and Algebraic Manipulation**]: Algorithms; F.2.1 [**Analysis of Algorithms and Problem Complexity**]: Numerical Algorithms and Problems

General Terms

Algorithms

Keywords

Hermite form, Polynomial matrices

1. INTRODUCTION

Among the classical normal forms for matrices over a principal ideal domain, the Hermite form is the best known. Recall the definition of the form over the ring $\mathsf{K}[x]$ of univariate polynomials over a field K. Corresponding to any nonsingular $A \in \mathsf{K}[x]^{n \times n}$ is a unimodular matrix $U \in \mathsf{K}[x]^{n \times n}$ such that

$$H = UA = \begin{bmatrix} h_1 & \bar{h}_{12} & \cdots & \bar{h}_{1n} \\ & h_2 & \cdots & \bar{h}_{2n} \\ & & \ddots & \vdots \\ & & & h_n \end{bmatrix}$$

is upper triangular, h_j is monic for $1 \leq j \leq n$, and $\deg \bar{h}_{ij} < \deg h_j$ for $1 \leq i < j \leq n$. The problem of computing the

Hermite form has received a lot of attention. For example, the thesis [5, 18, 15, 27, 6, 19] and ISSAC papers [25, 24, 26, 16] have addressed this topic.

Modulo determinant algorithms [11, 12, 7], see also [4], compute the Hermite form of A working modulo the determinant and require $O\tilde{\ }(n^4 d)$ field operations from K. Matrix multiplication can be introduced [11, 24] to reduce the cost to $O\tilde{\ }(n^{\omega+1} d)$, where $2 < \omega \leq 3$ is the exponent of matrix multiplication. The iterative approach in [17] gives a deterministic $O(n^3 d^2)$ algorithm, achieving a running time that is cubic in n but at the cost of increasing the exponent of d to two. In this paper we give a Las Vegas algorithm to compute H using an expected number of $O\tilde{\ }(n^3 d)$ field operations from K. To the best of our knowledge, this is the first algorithm that achieves a running time that is both softly cubic in the matrix dimension n and softly linear in the dimension d.

To put the problem of computing the Hermite form into context, we note that many problems on polynomial matrices now have algorithm that complete in $O\tilde{\ }(n^\omega d)$ field operations. Examples include the high-order lifting based linear solving, determinant and Smith form algorithms in [20, 21], the fast row reduction algorithm of [9] and minimal approximant basis algorithms in [9, 28]. The techniques in [14] can be adapted to the case of polynomial matrices and achieve algorithms that are subcubic in n for many problems. It is even known that the explicit inverse of A, which has total size $\Omega(n^3 d)$, can be computed in nearly optimal time $O\tilde{\ }(n^3 d)$ [13, 23].

The main difficulty to obtain fast algorithms for the Hermite form seems to be the unpredictability and nonuniformity of the degrees of the diagonal entries. The best *a priori* bound for $\deg h_j$ is jd, $1 \leq j \leq n$. Summing these a priori bounds gives $\sum_{j=1}^{n} jd \in \Theta(n^2 d)$, which overshoots by a factor of n the *a priori* bound $\sum_{j=1}^{n} \deg h_j = \det A \leq nd$. For comparison, for the diagonal Smith form $S := \bar{U} A \bar{V} = \mathrm{Diag}(s_1, \ldots, s_n)$ of A, a canonical form under left and right unimodular multiplication, we have the *a priori* bounds $\deg s_j \leq (n/(n-j+1))d$; summing these yields $\Theta(nd \log n)$. These good *a priori* bounds for the invariant factors s_j are exploited, for example, in [20, 8] to get improved algorithms for computing the Smith form.

The key to our approach in this paper is to use the Smith form S of A, together with partial information of a right unimodular transform $\bar{V}$, in order to obtain the Hermite form H of A. Our algorithm has two main phases.

The first phase is to compute the degrees of the diagonal entries of H. We show that this can be accomplished via a unimodular matrix triangularization:

$$\left[\begin{array}{c|c} S & \\ \hline V & I_n \end{array}\right] \longrightarrow \left[\begin{array}{c|c} I_n & * \\ \hline & T \end{array}\right] \in \mathsf{K}[x]^{2n \times 2n}. \qquad (1)$$

The matrix V is obtained from $\bar{V}$ by reducing entries in column j modulo s_j, $1 \leq j \leq n$. We show that the submatrix T in (1) will be left equivalent to A and thus, up to associates, has the same diagonal entries as H. When performing the triangularization in (1), we exploit the fact that S is diagonal by keeping offdiagonal entries in the first n columns of the work work matrix reduced modulo the diagonal entry in the same column. Using the upper bound $\sum_{j=1}^{n} \deg s_j \leq nd$, and by avoiding explicit computation of the offdiagonal entries of T and the block above T, we can compute the diagonal entries of T in $O^{\tilde{}}(n^3 d)$ operations from K.

The second phase of our algorithm uses the knowledge of the degrees of the diagonal entries of H to set up a minimal approximant basis problem for recovering H. In particular, the Hermite form H can recovered by computing a left kernel basis in canonical form for the first n columns of the matrix in (1):

$$\left[\begin{array}{c|c} -HVS^{-1} & H \end{array}\right] \left[\begin{array}{c} S \\ \hline V \end{array}\right] = 0.$$

Our main contribution is to show how to transform the kernel computation shown above to an equivalent problem that can be solved in time $O(n^\omega \mathsf{B}(d))$ using the fast minimal approximant basis algorithm of [9]. Our problem transformation makes use of the partial linearization and reduction of order techniques in [22].

The rest of this paper is organised as follows. Section 2 gives our algorithm for computing the diagonal entries of H. Section 3 gives the algorithm to compute the entire Hermite form given knowledge of the degrees of the diagonal entries. Section 4 makes some concluding remarks. Our cost model is defined below.

Cost model

Algorithms are analysed by bounding the number of required field operations from a field K on an algebraic random access machine; the operations $+$, $-$, $\times$ and "divide by a nonzero" involving two field elements have unit cost.

We use M for polynomial multiplication: let $\mathsf{M}: \mathbb{Z}_{\geq 0} \to \mathbb{R}_{>0}$ be such that polynomials in $\mathsf{K}[x]$ of degree bounded by d can be multiplied using at most $\mathsf{M}(d)$ field operations from K. Given two polynomials $a, b \in \mathsf{K}[x]$ with b nonzero, we denote by $\text{Rem}(a, b)$ and $\text{Quo}(a, b)$ the unique polynomials such that $a = \text{Quo}(a, b) b + \text{Rem}(a, b)$ with $\deg \text{Rem}(a, b) < \deg b$. If a and b have degree bounded by d then both of these operations have cost $O(\mathsf{M}(d))$. M is superlinear: $\mathsf{M}(ab) \leq \mathsf{M}(a)\mathsf{M}(b)$ for $a, b \in \mathbb{Z}_{>1}$.

The Gcdex operation takes as input two polynomials $a, b \in \mathsf{K}[x]$, and returns as output the polynomials $g, s, t, u, v \in \mathsf{K}[x]$ such that

$$\left[\begin{array}{cc} s & t \\ u & v \end{array}\right] \left[\begin{array}{c} a \\ b \end{array}\right] = \left[\begin{array}{c} g \\ \end{array}\right], \qquad (2)$$

with g a greatest common divisor of a and b, and $sv - tu$ a nonzero constant polynomial. It will be useful to define an additional function B to bound the cost of the extended gcd operation, as well as other gcd–related computations. We assume that $\mathsf{B}(d) = \mathsf{M}(d) \log d$.

2. THE DIAGONAL ENTRIES

Throughout this section let $A \in \mathsf{K}[x]^{n \times n}$ be nonsingular with degree d.

In this section we show how to pass over the Smith form of A in order to recover the degrees of the diagonal entries of the Hermite form of A. The algorithm actually recovers the diagonal entries and not just the degrees, but it is the degrees that will be required by our Hermite form algorithm in the next section. Some mathematical background and previous results are developed and recalled in Subsection 2.1. The algorithm for computing the diagonal entries is given in Subsection 2.2.

2.1 Hermite form via kernel basis

The Hermite form is a canonical form for left equivalence over $\mathsf{K}[x]$. A Hermite form H is *the Hermite form of A* if H is left equivalent to A: $H = UA$ for a unimodular transformation U. Solving for U gives $U = HA^{-1}$. The following lemma gives an alternative, equivalent criteria for a Hermite form H to be left equivalent to A that does not explicitly involve U.

LEMMA 1. *A Hermite form H is the Hermite form of A if $\deg \det H \leq \deg \det A$ and HA^{-1} is over $\mathsf{K}[x]$.*

To obtain a more compact representation of the matrix A^{-1} in Lemma 1 we will pass over the Smith form. Recall the definition: corresponding to A are unimodular matrices $\bar{U}, \bar{V} \in \mathsf{K}[x]^{n \times n}$ such that $S := \bar{U}A\bar{V} = \text{Diag}(s_1, \ldots, s_n)$ is the Smith canonical form of A, that is, each s_i is monic and $s_i \mid s_{i+1}$ for $1 \leq i \leq n-1$. Solving for A^{-1} gives $A^{-1} = \bar{V}S^{-1}\bar{U}$. Considering Lemma 1, and noting that $\bar{U}$ is unimodular, we may conclude that, for any matrix $H \in \mathsf{K}[x]^{n \times n}$, HA^{-1} is over $\mathsf{K}[x]$ if and only if $H\bar{V}S^{-1}$ is over $\mathsf{K}[x]$. Multiplying S^{-1} by s_n, the largest invariant factor, gives $s_n S^{-1} = \text{Diag}(s_n/s_1, \ldots, s_n/s_n) \in \mathsf{K}[x]^{n \times n}$. We conclude that $H\bar{V}S^{-1}$ is over $\mathsf{K}[x]$ if and only if $H\bar{V}(s_n S^{-1}) \equiv 0 \bmod s_n$. We obtain the following result.

LEMMA 2. *Suppose $S = \bar{U}A\bar{V} = \text{Diag}(s_1, \ldots, s_n)$ is the Smith form of A, where $\bar{U}$ and $\bar{V}$ are unimodular, and let $V \in \mathsf{K}[x]^{n \times n}$ be the matrix obtained from $\bar{V}$ by reducing column j of $\bar{V}$ modulo s_j, $1 \leq j \leq n$. Then a Hermite form H is the Hermite form of A if $\deg \det H \leq \deg \det A$ and $H\bar{V}(s_n S^{-1}) \equiv 0 \bmod s_n$.*

The following corollary of Lemma 2 is the basis for our approach to compute the diagonal entries of the Hermite form of A.

COROLLARY 3. *Let V and S be as in Lemma 2. The Hermite form of*

$$\left[\begin{array}{c|c} S & \\ \hline V & I_n \end{array}\right] \in \mathsf{K}[x]^{2n \times 2n} \qquad (3)$$

has the shape

$$\left[\begin{array}{c|c} I_n & * \\ \hline & H \end{array}\right] \in \mathsf{K}[x]^{2n \times 2n}, \qquad (4)$$

where H is the Hermite form of A.

PROOF. First note that $\left[\begin{array}{c|c} S & V^T \end{array}\right]^T$ is left equivalent to $\left[\begin{array}{c|c} S & \bar{V}^T \end{array}\right]^T$ where V is a unimodular matrix. It follows that the principal $n \times n$ submatrix of the Hermite form of

156

the matrix in (3) must be I_n. It remains to prove that H is the Hermite form of A. The unimodular transformation that transforms the matrix in (3) to its Hermite form in (4) must have the following shape:

$$\left[\begin{array}{c|c} & * \\ \hline -HVS^{-1} & H \end{array}\right]\left[\begin{array}{c|c} S & \\ \hline V & I_n \end{array}\right] = \left[\begin{array}{c|c} I_n & * \\ \hline & H \end{array}\right].$$

The result follows as the last n rows $[\,-HVS^{-1}\,|\,H\,]$ of the transformation matrix are a left kernel basis for $[\,S\,|\,V^T\,]^T$. $\square$

THEOREM 4. *Let $A \in \mathsf{K}[x]^{n \times n}$ be nonsingular of degree d. If $\#\mathsf{K} \geq 8nd$, matrices S and V as in Lemma 2 can be computed in a Las Vegas fashion with an expected number of $O(n^2\,\mathsf{B}(nd))$ operations from K.*

PROOF. First compute a row reduced form R of A using the algorithm of [9], or the deterministic variant in [10]. The Las Vegas algorithm supporting [23, Theorem 28] can now be used to compute V and S from R in the allotted time. $\square$

2.2 The algorithm for diagonal entries

Corresponding to a nonsingular input matrix $A \in \mathsf{K}[x]^{n \times n}$ of degree d, let S and V be as in Lemma 2. Instead of working with the matrix in (3) it will be useful to reverse the columns of V. To this end, let P be the $n \times n$ permutation matrix with ones on the antidiagonal. Note that postmultiplying a matrix by P reverses the order of the columns. Our input matrix has the shape

$$G = \left[\begin{array}{c|c} P & \\ \hline & I \end{array}\right]\left[\begin{array}{c|c} S & \\ \hline V & I \end{array}\right]\left[\begin{array}{c|c} P & \\ \hline & I \end{array}\right]$$

$$= \left[\begin{array}{cccc|cccc} s_n & & & & & & & \\ & s_{n-1} & & & & & & \\ & & \ddots & & & & & \\ & & & s_1 & & & & \\ \hline * & * & \cdots & * & 1 & & & \\ * & * & \cdots & * & & 1 & & \\ \vdots & \vdots & & \vdots & & & \ddots & \\ * & * & \cdots & * & & & & 1 \end{array}\right] \in \mathsf{K}[x]^{2n \times 2n},$$

and satisfies the following properties:

1. $\mathrm{Diag}(s_1, \ldots, s_n)$ is the Smith form of A and hence satisfies $\sum_{j=1}^n \deg s_j = \deg \det A \leq nd$, where $d = \deg A$.

2. Off diagonal entries in column j of G have degree less than the diagonal entry in the same column, $1 \leq j \leq n$.

Our goal is to recover the last n diagonal entries of the Hermite form of G. The standard approach to triangularize G, without any regard to cost or concern for growth of degrees, is to use extended gcd computations and unimodular row operations to zero out entries below the pivot entry in each column.

for j **from** 1 **to** $2n-1$ **do**
    for i **from** $j+1$ **to** $2n$ **do**
        $(g,s,t,u,v) := \mathrm{Gcdex}(G[j,j], G[i,j]);$
        $\left[\begin{array}{c} G[j,*] \\ G[i,*] \end{array}\right] := \left[\begin{array}{cc} s & t \\ u & v \end{array}\right]\left[\begin{array}{c} G[j,*] \\ G[i,*] \end{array}\right]$
    od
od

Note that, for $j = 1, 2 \ldots, n-1$, the first $n-j$ iterations of the inner loop do nothing since the principal $n \times n$ block of

G remains upper triangular during the elimination; omitting these vacuous iterations, the following example shows how the shape of the work matrix changes as in the case $n = 3$:

$$\left[\begin{array}{ccc|ccc} s_3 & & & & & \\ & s_2 & & & & \\ & & s_1 & & & \\ \hline * & * & * & 1 & & \\ * & * & * & & 1 & \\ * & * & * & & & 1 \end{array}\right] \rightarrow \left[\begin{array}{ccc|ccc} * & * & * & * & & \\ & s_2 & & & & \\ & & s_1 & & & \\ \hline * & * & * & * & & \\ * & * & * & & 1 & \\ * & * & * & & & 1 \end{array}\right] \rightarrow \left[\begin{array}{ccc|ccc} * & * & * & * & * & \\ & s_2 & & & & \\ & & s_1 & & & \\ \hline * & * & * & * & * & \\ * & * & * & * & * & \\ * & * & * & & & 1 \end{array}\right]$$

$$\rightarrow \left[\begin{array}{ccc|ccc} * & * & * & * & * & * \\ & s_2 & & & & \\ & & s_1 & & & \\ \hline * & * & * & * & * & * \\ * & * & * & * & * & * \\ * & * & * & * & * & * \end{array}\right] \rightarrow \left[\begin{array}{ccc|ccc} * & * & * & * & * & * \\ & & * & * & * & * \\ & & s_1 & & & \\ \hline * & * & * & * & * & * \\ * & * & * & * & * & * \\ * & * & * & * & * & * \end{array}\right] \rightarrow \cdots$$

Note that even after only the first column has been eliminated, the upper triangular structure of the trailing $n \times n$ block has been lost, thus necessitating that j range up to $2n$. Our first refinement of the algorithm is to reverse the order of elimination of entries in the southwest block of G, thus preserving the upper triangularity of the southeast block.

for j **from** 1 **to** n **do**
    for i **from** $2n$ **by** -1 **to** $n+1$ **do**
        $(g,s,t,u,v) := \mathrm{Gcdex}(G[j,j], G[i,j]);$
        $\left[\begin{array}{c} G[j,*] \\ G[i,*] \end{array}\right] := \left[\begin{array}{cc} s & t \\ u & v \end{array}\right]\left[\begin{array}{c} G[j,*] \\ G[i,*] \end{array}\right]$
    od
od

The following example for $n = 3$ shows how the shape of the shape of the work matrix changes during the first few iterations:

$$\left[\begin{array}{ccc|ccc} s_3 & & & & & \\ & s_2 & & & & \\ & & s_1 & & & \\ \hline * & * & * & 1 & & \\ * & * & * & & 1 & \\ * & * & * & & & 1 \end{array}\right] \rightarrow \left[\begin{array}{ccc|ccc} * & * & * & & * & \\ & s_2 & & & & \\ & & s_1 & & & \\ \hline * & * & * & 1 & & \\ * & * & * & & 1 & \\ * & * & * & & & * \end{array}\right] \rightarrow \left[\begin{array}{ccc|ccc} * & * & * & & * & * \\ & s_2 & & & & \\ & & s_1 & & & \\ \hline * & * & * & 1 & & \\ * & * & * & & * & * \\ * & * & * & & & * \end{array}\right]$$

$$\rightarrow \left[\begin{array}{ccc|ccc} * & * & * & * & * & * \\ & s_2 & & & & \\ & & s_1 & & & \\ \hline * & * & * & * & * & * \\ * & * & * & & * & * \\ * & * & * & & & * \end{array}\right] \rightarrow \left[\begin{array}{ccc|ccc} * & * & * & * & * & * \\ & & * & * & * & * \\ & & s_1 & & & \\ \hline * & * & * & * & * & * \\ * & * & * & & * & * \\ * & * & * & & & * \end{array}\right] \rightarrow \cdots$$

Our next two refinements of the triangularization algorithm concern the cost.

Initially, we assume that the offdiagonal entries in G are reduced modulo the diagonal entry in the same column. As the algorithm eliminates entries in column j, we can implicitly perform unimodular row operations to reduce entries in column $j+1, \ldots, n$ modulo the diagonal entry in the same column. In the following example, entries that are kept reduced modulo the diagonal entry in the same column are represented by $\bar{*}$.

$$\left[\begin{array}{ccc|ccc} s_3 & & & & & \\ & s_2 & & & & \\ & & s_1 & & & \\ \hline * & * & * & 1 & & \\ \bar{*} & \bar{*} & \bar{*} & & 1 & \\ \bar{*} & \bar{*} & \bar{*} & & & 1 \end{array}\right] \rightarrow \left[\begin{array}{ccc|ccc} * & \bar{*} & \bar{*} & & * & \\ & s_2 & & & & \\ & & s_1 & & & \\ \hline * & * & * & 1 & & \\ \bar{*} & \bar{*} & \bar{*} & & 1 & \\ \bar{*} & \bar{*} & \bar{*} & & & * \end{array}\right] \rightarrow \left[\begin{array}{ccc|ccc} * & \bar{*} & \bar{*} & & * & * \\ & s_2 & & & & \\ & & s_1 & & & \\ \hline * & * & * & 1 & & \\ \bar{*} & \bar{*} & \bar{*} & & * & * \\ \bar{*} & \bar{*} & \bar{*} & & & * \end{array}\right]$$

$$\rightarrow \left[\begin{array}{ccc|ccc} * & \bar{*} & \bar{*} & * & * & * \\ & s_2 & & & & \\ & & s_1 & & & \\ \hline * & * & * & * & * & * \\ \bar{*} & \bar{*} & \bar{*} & & * & * \\ \bar{*} & \bar{*} & \bar{*} & & & * \end{array}\right] \rightarrow \left[\begin{array}{ccc|ccc} * & * & \bar{*} & * & * & * \\ & * & \bar{*} & & * & \\ & & s_1 & & & \\ \hline * & * & * & * & * & * \\ \bar{*} & \bar{*} & \bar{*} & & * & * \\ \bar{*} & \bar{*} & \bar{*} & & & * \end{array}\right] \rightarrow \cdots \quad (5)$$

The second refinement of the algorithm is to keep the $\bar{*}$ entries reduced modulo the diagonal entry in the same column during the elimination.

157

```
for j from 1 to n do
    for i from 2n by −1 to n + 1 do
        (g, s, t, u, v) := Gcdex(G[j, j], G[i, j]);
        G[j, j], G[i, j] := g, 0;
        U := [ s  t ]
             [ u  v ];
        for k from j + 1 to n do
            [ G[j, k] ]        [ G[j, k] ]
            [ G[i, k] ] := Rem ( U [ G[i, k] ] , s_{n-k+1} )
        od;
        for k from n + 1 to 2n do
            [ G[j, k] ]      [ G[j, k] ]
            [ G[i, k] ] := U  [ G[i, k] ]
        od
    od
od
```

Notice in (5) that entries in the last n columns of the work matrix G are not kept reduced and can suffer from expression swell. However, our goal is to recover only the trailing n diagonal entries of the last n columns of the triangularization of G. To avoid the cost associated with performing the unimodular row operations on the last n columns of the work matrix, we can exploit the special structure of the work matrix and modify the elimination procedure to only keep track of the the last n diagonals. The following illustrates our point with an example for $n = 3$. Let

$$G = \begin{bmatrix} & & s_3 & & & \\ & s_2 & & & & \\ & & s_1 & & & \\ \hline * & * & * & 1 & & \\ * & * & * & & 1 & \\ a_1 & * & * & & & 1 \end{bmatrix}.$$

The first elimination step computes the extended gcd of s_3 and a_1, $(g, s, t_1, u, v_1) = \mathrm{Gcdex}(s_3, a_1)$, and updates the work matrix to have the following shape:

$$\begin{bmatrix} s & & & & & t_1 \\ & 1 & & & & \\ & & 1 & & & \\ \hline & & & 1 & & \\ & & & & 1 & \\ u & & & & & v_1 \end{bmatrix} \begin{bmatrix} & & s_3 & & & 0 \\ & s_2 & & & & \\ & & s_1 & & & \\ \hline * & * & * & 1 & & \\ * & * & * & & 1 & \\ a_1 & * & * & & & 1 \end{bmatrix} = \begin{bmatrix} & & g & * & * & t_1 \\ & s_2 & & & & \\ & & s_1 & & & \\ \hline * & * & * & 1 & & \\ a_2 & * & * & & 1 & \\ & & * & & & v_1 \end{bmatrix}.$$

Continuing the elimination gives

$$\begin{bmatrix} * & * & * & & & t_1 \\ & s_2 & & & & \\ & & s_1 & & & \\ \hline * & * & * & 1 & & \\ a_2 & * & * & & 1 & \\ & & * & & & v_1 \end{bmatrix} \rightarrow \begin{bmatrix} * & * & * & & t_2 & * \\ & s_2 & & & & \\ & & s_1 & & & \\ \hline a_3 & * & * & 1 & & \\ & & * & & v_2 & * \\ & & * & & & v_1 \end{bmatrix}$$

$$\rightarrow \begin{bmatrix} * & * & * & t_3 & * & * \\ & s_2 & & & & \\ & & s_1 & & & \\ \hline & & * & v_3 & * & * \\ & & * & & v_2 & * \\ a_4 & * & * & & & v_1 \end{bmatrix} \rightarrow \begin{bmatrix} * & * & * & * & * & * \\ & * & * & & & \\ & & s_1 & & & \\ \hline & & * & v_3 & * & * \\ & & * & & v_2 & * \\ & & * & & & v_1 v_4 \end{bmatrix} \cdots$$

The key observation is that, although the offdiagonal entries in the last n columns are modified during the elimination, they never affect the last n diagonal entries entries which will depend only on the v_i computed by the calls to Gcdex. Our third refinement of the algorithm is to avoid storing and updating any of the offdiagonal entries in the last n columns of the matrix. Instead, we can keep track of the last n diagonal entries using a vector $D \in \mathsf{K}[x]^{1 \times n}$.

For $n = 3$, the following shows the state of G and D during the execution of Algorithm DiagonalHermite. Here v_i is the

```
DiagonalHermite(S, V)
Input:  • S ∈ K[x]^{n×n}, the Smith form of a
          nonsingular A ∈ K[x]^{n×n} of degree d.
        • V ∈ K[x]^{n×n}, deg Col(V, j) < deg s_j, 1 ≤ j ≤ n.
Output: D ∈ ℤ^{1×n}, the degrees of the last n diagonals
                    ⎡ S ⎤
          in the Hermite form of ⎢───⎥.
                    ⎣ V │ I ⎦

Let P be equal to I_n with columns reversed.

               ⎡ P │   ⎤ ⎡ S ⎤
Intialize G =  ⎢───────⎥ ⎢───⎥ P.
               ⎣   │ I ⎦ ⎣ V ⎦

Initialize D = [1, . . . , 1].
for j from 1 to n do
    for i from 2n by −1 to n + 1 do

        (g, s, t, u, v) := Gcdex(G[j, j], G[i, j]);
        G[j, j], G[i, j] := g, 0;

        U := [ s  t ]
             [ u  v ];
        for k from j + 1 to n do
            U := Rem(U, s_{n-k+1});
            [ G[j, k] ]        [ G[j, k] ]
            [ G[i, k] ] := Rem ( U [ G[i, k] ] , s_{n-k+1} )
        od;
        D[i − n] := D[i − n] × v
    od
od;
return [deg D[1], . . . , deg D[n]]
```

Figure 1: Algorithm DiagonalHermite

value of v on the i'th call to Gcdex in the above algorithm.

$$G = \begin{bmatrix} & & s_3 & & & \\ & s_2 & & & & \\ & & s_1 & & & \\ \hline * & * & * & & & \\ * & * & * & & & \\ * & * & * & & & \end{bmatrix} \rightarrow \begin{bmatrix} * & * & * & & & \\ & s_2 & & & & \\ & & s_1 & & & \\ \hline * & * & * & & & \\ * & * & * & & & \\ * & * & * & & & \end{bmatrix} \cdots \rightarrow \begin{bmatrix} * & * & * & & & \\ & s_2 & & & & \\ & & s_1 & & & \\ \hline * & * & * & & & \\ & * & * & & & \\ & * & * & & & \end{bmatrix} \rightarrow \begin{bmatrix} * & * & * & & & \\ & * & * & & & \\ & & s_1 & & & \\ \hline & * & * & & & \\ & * & * & & & \\ & * & * & & & \end{bmatrix} \cdots$$

$$D = \begin{matrix} [1, 1, 1] & \quad [1, 1, v_1] & \quad [v_3, v_2, v_1] & \quad [v_3, v_2, v_1 v_4] \end{matrix}$$

We now bound the running time of Algorithm **Diagonal-Hermite**. During the elimination of column j, entries in column j remain bounded in degree by the diagonal entry, a divisor of s_{n-j+1}. Thus, each call to Gcdex is bounded by $\mathsf{B}(\deg s_{n-j+1})$ operations from K. The cost of all n^2 calls to Gcdex is thus bounded by $n \sum_{j=1}^{n} \mathsf{B}(\deg s_j) \leq n\mathsf{B}(nd)$, using $\sum_{j=1}^{n} \deg s_j \leq nd$.

The cost of applying the transformation U, in each iteration of i, is bounded by $c_1 \sum_{k=1}^{n-j+1} \mathsf{M}(\deg s_k)$ for some constant $c_1 > 0$. For every column j, the total cost of applying transformations is bounded by $nc_1 \sum_{k=1}^{n-j+1} \mathsf{M}(\deg s_k)$. Thus the cost of applying the transformation U, in all iterations, is bounded by

$$nc_1 \sum_{j=1}^{n} \sum_{k=1}^{n-j+1} \mathsf{M}(\deg s_k) \leq c_1 n^2 \mathsf{M}(nd),$$

using the superlinearity of M and that fact that $\sum_{j=1}^{n} \deg s_j \leq nd$.

Each entry in D is updated n times and also at any time during the execution of the algorithm $\sum_{i=1}^{n} \deg D[i] \leq nd$. This provides a bound for the cost of all updates to D as $O(n\mathsf{M}(nd))$.

We obtain the following result.

THEOREM 5. *Algorithm* `DiagonalHermite` *is correct. The cost of the algorithm is $O(n^2 \, \mathsf{M}(nd) + n \, \mathsf{B}(nd))$ operations from* K.

3. FROM DIAGONAL TO HERMITE

We begin by defining some notation. Let $\mathbf{e} = (e_1, \ldots, e_n)$ be a tuple of integers and $u = \begin{bmatrix} u_1 & \cdots & u_n \end{bmatrix} \in \mathsf{K}[x]^{1 \times n}$. Following [2], the $\mathbf{e}$-degree of u is equal to $\min_i \deg u_i - e_i$. We define $\mathcal{L}_{\mathbf{e}}(A)$ to be the set of row vectors of $\mathcal{L}(A)$ that have nonpositive $\mathbf{e}$-degree, that is, those vectors u that satisfy $\deg u_i \leq e_i$, $1 \leq i \leq n$.

DEFINITION 6. *Let* $L \in \mathsf{K}[x]^{* \times n}$ *and* $\mathbf{e} = (e_1, \ldots, e_n)$ *be a tuple of degree constraints. A matrix* $G \in \mathsf{K}[x]^{* \times n}$ *is a genset of type* $\mathbf{e} = (e_1, \ldots, e_n)$ *for* $\mathcal{L}_{\mathbf{e}}(L)$ *if*

- *every row of* G *has nonpositive* $\mathbf{e}$-*degree,*

- $\mathcal{L}_{\mathbf{e}}(G) = \mathcal{L}_{\mathbf{e}}(L)$.

Note that for some tuples $\mathbf{e}$ we may have $\mathcal{L}(\mathcal{L}_{\mathbf{e}}(A)) \subset \mathcal{L}(A)$. In other words, there may not exist a basis for the lattice $\mathcal{L}(A)$ for which every row in the a basis has degree bounded by $\mathbf{e}$. An obvious example is when $\mathbf{e} = (-1, \ldots, -1)$, in which case $\mathcal{L}(\mathcal{L}_{\mathbf{e}}(A))$ has dimension zero.

3.1 From genset to Hermite form

Let $\mathbf{d} = (d_1, \ldots, d_n)$ be the degrees of the diagonal entries of the Hermite form H of a nonsingular $A \in \mathsf{K}[x]^{n \times n}$. Because H is a basis for $\mathcal{L}(A)$, and each row of H has nonpositive $\mathbf{d}$-degree, we have the following result.

LEMMA 7. $\mathcal{L}(\mathcal{L}_{\mathbf{d}}(A)) = \mathcal{L}(A)$.

The following lemma shows how to recover H from a genset $\bar{H}$ of type $\mathbf{d}$ for $\mathcal{L}_{\mathbf{d}}(A)$. The lemma follows as a corollary of Lemma 7 and the following fact regarding H: From among all rows of $\mathcal{L}(A)$ which have first $i-1$ entries zero and entry i nonzero, the i'th row of the Hermite form has i'th entry of minimal degree, $1 \leq i \leq n$.

LEMMA 8. *Suppose* $\bar{H} \in \mathsf{K}[x]^{m \times n}$ *is a genset of type* $\mathbf{d}$ *for* $\mathcal{L}_{\mathbf{d}}(A)$. *Let* $L \in \mathsf{K}^{m \times n} : \mathrm{Col}(L, j) = \mathrm{Coeff}(\mathrm{Col}(\bar{H}, j), x^{d_j})$, $1 \leq j \leq n$. *If* $U \in \mathsf{K}^{m \times m}$ *is a nonsingular matrix such that* UL *is in reduced row echelon form, then* $U\bar{H}$ *will have principal* $n \times n$ *submatrix equal to* H, *and last* $m - n$ *rows zero.*

EXAMPLE 9. *Let* $\mathsf{K} = \mathbb{Z}/(7)$, *and consider the following Hermite form* $H \in \mathsf{K}[x]^{3 \times 3}$, *together with a genset* $\bar{H} \in \mathsf{K}[x]^{5 \times 3}$ *of type* $(1, 3, 2)$ *for* $\mathcal{L}(H)$.

$$H = \begin{bmatrix} x & x^2 + 1 & x + 2 \\ & x^3 + 2x^2 & x + 3 \\ & & x^2 + 2 \end{bmatrix}$$

$$\bar{H} = \begin{bmatrix} 4x & 6x^3 + 2x^2 + 4 & 6x^2 + 3x + 3 \\ x & 4x^3 + 2x^2 + 1 & 5x^2 + 5x + 3 \\ x & 2x^3 + 5x^2 + 1 & 3x^2 + 3x \\ 3x & 5x^3 + 6x^2 + 3 & 4x^2 + x + 1 \\ 2x & 2x^2 + 2 & 4x^2 + 2x + 5 \end{bmatrix}$$

The following shows the leading coefficient matrix L of $\bar{H}$, together with a nonsingular matrix $U \in \mathsf{K}^{5 \times 5}$ that transforms L to reduced row echelon form, which due to Lemma 8 will necessarily have principle 3×3 submatrix equal to I_3.

$$\overset{U}{\begin{bmatrix} 2 & 1 & 6 & 0 & 0 \\ 2 & 6 & 0 & 0 & 0 \\ 5 & 5 & 3 & 0 & 0 \\ 6 & 3 & 5 & 1 & 0 \\ 2 & 3 & 2 & 0 & 4 \end{bmatrix}} \overset{L}{\begin{bmatrix} 4 & 6 & 6 \\ 1 & 4 & 5 \\ 1 & 2 & 3 \\ 3 & 5 & 4 \\ 2 & 0 & 4 \end{bmatrix}} = \begin{bmatrix} 1 & & \\ & 1 & \\ & & 1 \\ & & \\ & & \end{bmatrix}$$

$U\bar{H}$ *is equal to the Hermite form* H *augmented with two zero rows.*

3.2 Hermite form via kernel basis

The quantities defined in this subsection will be used in the remaining subsections. Let $A \in \mathsf{K}[x]^{n \times n}$ be nonsingular, with the following quantities precomputed:

- The Smith form $S = \mathrm{Diag}(s_1, \ldots, s_n) \in \mathsf{K}[x]^{n \times n}$ of A.

- A matrix $V \in \mathsf{K}[x]^{n \times n}$ such that $u \in \mathcal{L}(A)$ if and only if uVS^{-1} is over $\mathsf{K}[x]$. The i'th column of V has entries of degree less than $\deg s_i$.

- The degrees $\mathbf{d} = (d_1, \ldots, d_n)$ of the diagonal entries of the Hermite form H of A.

Let $R := -HVS^{-1} \in \mathsf{K}[x]^{n \times n}$. Then

$$\begin{bmatrix} R \mid H \end{bmatrix} \begin{bmatrix} \dfrac{S}{V} \end{bmatrix} = 0. \tag{6}$$

Since column i of V has degree strictly less than $\deg s_i$, we have $\deg R \leq D$ where $D = \max_i d_i - 1$. Let $\mathbf{D} = (D, \ldots, D)$, of length n. The matrix $\begin{bmatrix} R \mid H \end{bmatrix}$ is a basis (with all rows of nonpositive $(\mathbf{D}, \mathbf{d})$-degree) for the left kernel of $\begin{bmatrix} S \mid V^T \end{bmatrix}^T$. In fact, by Lemma 8, to recover H it will be sufficient to compute a genset $\begin{bmatrix} \bar{R} \mid \bar{H} \end{bmatrix}$ of type $(\mathbf{D}, \mathbf{d})$ for $\mathcal{L}_{(\mathbf{D}, \mathbf{d})}(\begin{bmatrix} R \mid H \end{bmatrix})$. The next subsection computes such a genset using fast minimal approximant basis computation.

We remark that the transformation of a canonical form computation to that of a kernel computation is used in [2, 3]. In particular, note that

$$\begin{bmatrix} U \mid H \end{bmatrix} \begin{bmatrix} \dfrac{A}{I_n} \end{bmatrix} = 0. \tag{7}$$

The setup in (7) requires no precomputation, and is useful if the unimodular transformation U to achieve the Hermite form is also required. What is important in our approach shown in (6) is the shape of the input problem: we will exploit the fact that S is diagonal, with sum of column degrees in both S and V bounded by nd.

3.3 Hermite via minimal approximant basis

Let $G \in \mathsf{K}[x]^{n \times m}$ and $\mathbf{e}$ be a tuple of nonnegative integers. The entries of $\mathbf{e}$ may be considered to be degree constraints. Recall that an order N minimal approximant basis (or σ-basis [1]) of type $\mathbf{e}$ for G is a nonsingular and row reduced matrix $M \in \mathsf{K}[x]^{n \times n}$ such that $MG \equiv 0 \bmod x^N$. The minimality condition means that the rows of M have $\mathbf{e}$-degrees as small as possible.

LEMMA 10. *Let* $M \in \mathsf{K}[x]^{2n \times 2n}$ *be an order* $N = D + \deg s_n + 1$ *minimal approximant basis of type* $(\mathbf{D}, \mathbf{d})$ *for* $\begin{bmatrix} S \mid V^T \end{bmatrix}^T$. *The submatrix of rows of* M *that have nonpositive* $(\mathbf{D}, \mathbf{d})$-*degree comprise a basis for* $\mathcal{L}(\begin{bmatrix} R \mid H \end{bmatrix})$.

PROOF. Let $v \in K[x]^{1 \times 2n}$ have nonpositive $(\mathbf{D}, \mathbf{d})$-degree. The order N is high enough that $v \left[\left. S \right| V^T \right]^T = 0$ if and only if $v \left[\left. S \right| V^T \right]^T \equiv 0 \bmod x^N$. □

EXAMPLE 11. *Consider the matrix H from Example 9. The degrees of the diagonal entries of H are $(1, 3, 2)$ and thus $D = 2$. The Smith form of H is $\mathrm{diag}(1, 1, x^6 + 2x^5 + 2x^4 + 4x^3)$. Since the first two invariant factors are trivial, we can restrict S to its last entry and V to its last column as the input:*

$$\left[\frac{S}{V} \right] = \begin{bmatrix} x^6 + 2x^5 + 2x^4 + 4x^3 \\ \hline 5x^5 + x^3 + 6x^2 + 6 \\ 6x^5 + 3x^4 + 3x^3 + x \\ 4x^5 + 2x^4 + 2x^3 \end{bmatrix}. \qquad (8)$$

The following shows an order 9 minimal approximant basis M of type $(2, 1, 3, 2)$ for $\left[\left. S \right| V^T \right]^T$, rows permuted to be in nondecreasing $(\mathbf{D}, \mathbf{d})$-degree.

$$M = \begin{bmatrix} 3x + 6 & & & x^2 + 2 \\ x & x & x^2 + 1 & x + 2 \\ x^2 + 4x + 5 & x^3 + 2x^2 & x + 3 \\ \hline x^4 + 5x^3 + 2x^2 + x + 4 & 0 & 5x^2 & x \end{bmatrix}$$

Exactly the first $n = 3$ rows have nonpositive $(\mathbf{D}, \mathbf{d})$-degree. For this example, the northeast block of M is the Hermite form of A up to a row permutation. In general, the northeast block will be a genset of full row rank for $\mathcal{L}_\mathbf{d}(H)$.

Using directly the approach of Lemma 10 to recover H is too expensive because the required order $N = D + \deg s_n + 1$ of the minimal approximant basis computation is too high. Indeed, we may have $N \in \Omega(nd)$. The reduction of order technique in [22, Section 2] can be used to reduce the order down to one more than times the maximum of the degree constraints in $(\mathbf{D}, \mathbf{d})$. Unfortunately, the largest entry in $\mathbf{d}$ and $\mathbf{D}$ may be $\Omega(nd)$. Before applying the reduction of order technique we apply the partial linearization technique from [22, Section 3] to transform to a new minimal approximant basis problem of type $(\mathbf{D}, \mathbf{d}_1)$, with all entries of $\mathbf{d}_1$ bounded by d.

We need to recall some notation from [22]. The norm of a tuple of degree constraints $\mathbf{d}$ is defined to be $\|\mathbf{d}\| = (d_1 + 1) + \cdots + (d_n + 1)$. For $b \geq 0$, let ϕ_b be the function which maps a single degree bound d_i to a sequence of degree bounds, all element of the sequence equal to b except for possibly the last, and such that $\|(d_i)\| = d_i + 1 = \|(\phi_b(d_i))\|$. Let $\mathrm{len}(\phi_b(d_i))$ denote the length of the sequence. For example, we have $\phi_3(10) = 3, 3, 2$ with $\mathrm{len}(\phi_3(10)) = 3$, while $\phi_2(11) = 2, 2, 2, 2$ and $\mathrm{len}(\phi_2(11)) = 4$. Computing a genset of type $(\mathbf{D}, \mathbf{d})$ for $\mathcal{L}_{(\mathbf{D}, \mathbf{d})}(\left[\left. R \right| H \right])$ can be reduced to computing an order N genset of type $\mathbf{d}_1 = (\phi_b(d_1), \ldots, \phi_b(d_n))$. Corresponding to $\mathbf{d}_1$ define the following $\bar{n} \times n$ expansion / compression matrix

$$B := \begin{bmatrix} \begin{array}{c} 1 \\ x^{b+1} \\ \vdots \\ x^{(b+1)\mathrm{len}(\phi_b(d_1))-1} \end{array} & & & \\ & \begin{array}{c} 1 \\ x^{b+1} \\ \vdots \\ x^{(b+1)(\mathrm{len}(\phi_b(d_2))-1)} \end{array} & \\ & & \ddots \end{bmatrix},$$

where $\bar{n} = \sum_i^n \mathrm{len}(\phi_b(d_i)) = \sum_i^n \lceil (d_i + 1)/(b + 1) \rceil$.

LEMMA 12. *Let $b \geq 0$ and define $e_i = \lceil (d_i + 1)/(b + 1) \rceil$, $1 \leq i \leq n$. Let M_1 be an order $N = D + \deg s_n + 1$ minimal approximant basis of type $(\mathbf{D}, \mathbf{d}_1)$ for $\left[\left. S \right| (BV)^T \right]^T$, where $\mathbf{d}_1 = (\phi_b(d_1), \ldots, \phi_b(d_n))$. If $\left[\left. \bar{R}_1 \right| \bar{H}_1 \right]$ is the subset of rows of M_1 which have degree bounded by $(\mathbf{D}, \mathbf{d}_1)$, then $\left[\left. \bar{R}_1 \right| \bar{H}_1 B \right]$ is a genset of type $(\mathbf{D}, \mathbf{d})$ for $\mathcal{L}_{(\mathbf{D}, \mathbf{d})}(H)$.*

Furthermore, with the choice $b = d$ the row dimension $\bar{n}$ of BV will satisfy $\bar{n} \in O(n)$.

EXAMPLE 13. *The problem in Example 11 was to compute a minimal approximant of type $(\mathbf{D}, \mathbf{d}) = (2, 1, 3, 2)$ for the 4×1 input matrix shown in (8). Consider setting the linearization parameter b in Lemma 12 as $b = 1$. The expanded problem BV is*

$$\begin{matrix} B \\ \begin{bmatrix} 1 & & & \\ x^2 & & & \\ & 1 & & \\ & & x^2 & \\ & & & x^2 \end{bmatrix} \end{matrix} V = \begin{matrix} BV \\ \begin{bmatrix} 5x^5 + x^3 + 6x^2 + 6 \\ 6x^5 + 3x^4 + 3x^3 + x \\ 6x^7 + 3x^6 + 3x^5 + x^3 \\ 4x^5 + 2x^4 + 2x^3 \\ 4x^7 + 2x^6 + 2x^5 \end{bmatrix} \end{matrix}. \qquad (9)$$

The degree constraints for the expanded problem are

$$\begin{aligned} (\mathbf{D}, \mathbf{d}_1) &= (2, \phi_1(1), \phi_1(3), \phi_1(2)) \\ &= (2, 1, 1, 1, 1, 0). \end{aligned}$$

The following shows an order 9 minimal approximant basis of type $(2, 1, 1, 1, 1, 0)$ for $\left[\left. S \right| (BV)^T \right]^T$.

$$M = \begin{bmatrix} 3x + 6 & 0 & 0 & 0 & 2 & 1 \\ x^2 + 4x + 5 & 0 & 0 & x + 2 & x + 3 & 0 \\ x & x & 1 & 1 & x + 2 & 0 \\ \hline 3x + 6 & 0 & 0 & 0 & x^2 + 2 & 0 \\ 0 & 0 & x^2 & 6 & 0 & 0 \\ x^4 + 5x^3 + 2x^2 + x + 4 & 0 & 0 & 5 & x & 0 \end{bmatrix}$$

The first 3 rows of M have nonpositive $(\mathbf{D}, \mathbf{d}_1)$-degree. Applying the compression matrix to the northwest block of M gives a genset $\bar{H}$ of type $\mathbf{d}$ for $\mathcal{L}_\mathbf{d}(H)$:

$$\begin{bmatrix} 0 & 0 & 0 & 2 & 1 \\ 0 & 0 & x + 2 & x + 3 & 0 \\ x & 1 & 1 & x + 2 & 0 \end{bmatrix} B = \begin{matrix} \bar{H} \\ \begin{bmatrix} 0 & 0 & x^2 + 2 \\ 0 & x^3 + 2x^2 & x + 3 \\ x & x^2 + 1 & x + 2 \end{bmatrix} \end{matrix}.$$

Note that in this example $\bar{H}$ has full row rank. We remark that, in general, the genset produced using this expansion/compression technique may have linearly dependent rows.

At this point, we have reduced the problem of computing H to that of computing the rows $\left[\left. \bar{R}_1 \right| \bar{H}_1 \right]$ of nonpositive $(\mathbf{D}, \mathbf{d}_1)$-degree in an order $N = D + \deg s_1 + 1$ minimal approximant basis of type $(\mathbf{D}, \mathbf{d}_1)$, namely

$$\left[\left. \bar{R}_1 \right| \bar{H}_1 \right] \left[\frac{S}{BV} \right] = 0 \bmod x^N.$$

The degree constraints $\mathbf{D} = (D, \ldots, D)$ corresponding the columns of $\bar{R}_1$ may still be too large in general, since $D = \max_i d_i - 1 \in \Omega(nd)$ in the worst case. The key idea now is that $\bar{R}_1$ is not required. Let C be a matrix such that $BV - CS$ has each column of degree bounded by s_i, and consider the transformed input:

$$\left[\frac{I_n}{-C} \bigg| I \right] \left[\frac{S}{BV} \right] = \left[\frac{S}{E} \right]. \qquad (10)$$

160

Note that each column in E has degree strictly less than the corresponding diagonal entry in S.

LEMMA 14. *Let* $\mathbf{D}_1 = (d-1, \ldots, d-1)$, *of length n. Let M_2 be an order $N = D + \deg s_n + 1$ minimal approximant basis of type* $(\mathbf{D}_1, \mathbf{d}_1)$ *for* $\left[\ S \mid E^T\ \right]^T$. *Let* $\left[\ \bar{R}_2 \mid \bar{H}_2\ \right]$ *be the submatrix of M_2 comprised of rows that have nonpositive* $(\mathbf{D}_1, \mathbf{d}_1)$-*degree. Then $\bar{H}_2 B$ is a genset of type $\mathbf{d}$ for $\mathcal{L}_\mathbf{d}(H)$.*

PROOF. The order N is large enough to ensure that

$$\left[\ \bar{R}_2 \mid \bar{H}_2\ \right] \left[\ S \mid E^T\ \right]^T = 0,$$

and (10) gives that $\left[\ \bar{R}_2 - \bar{H}_2 C \mid \bar{H}_2\ \right] \left[\ S \mid (BV)^T\ \right]^T = 0$, which implies that

$$\left[\ \bar{R}_2 - \bar{H}_2 C \mid \bar{H}_2 B\ \right] \left[\frac{S}{V} \right]^T = 0,$$

with all rows in $\bar{H}_2 B$ of nonpositive $\mathbf{d}$-degree. But since V has degrees of entries bounded by the corresponding diagonal entry of S, each row of $\bar{R}_2 - \bar{H}_2$ has nonpositive $\mathbf{D}$ degree. We conclude that $\left[\ \bar{R}_2 - \bar{H}_2 C \mid \bar{H}_2\ \right] \subseteq \mathcal{L}_{(\mathbf{D}, \mathbf{d})}(\left[\ R \mid H\ \right])$. The other direction is similar. $\square$

Provided we have chosen the linearization parameter b in Lemma 12 to satisfy $b \in \Theta(d)$ (e.g., $b = d$ will suffice), the final minimal approximant problem in Lemma 14 will have dimension $O(n) \times n$. Note that entries of the compression/expansion matrix B are all powers of x. Thus, the only computation (in terms of field operations) required to construct the input problem in Lemma 14 is to construct E from BV by reducing entries in each column i modulo the diagonal entry in the same column of S, $1 \le i \le n$.

EXAMPLE 15. *The problem in Example 13 was to compute a minimal approximant of type* $(\mathbf{D}, \mathbf{d}_1) = (2, 1, 1, 1, 1, 0)$ *for the partially linearized 6×1 input matrix B shown in (9). Reducing the last 5 entries modulo the the principal entry we obtain the new input*

$$\left[\frac{S}{E} \right] = \left[\begin{array}{c} x^6 + 2x^5 + 2x^4 + 4x^3 \\ \hline 5x^5 + x^3 + 6x^2 + 6 \\ 6x^5 + 3x^4 + 3x^3 + x \\ 2x^5 + x^4 + 2x^3 \\ \hline 4x^5 + 2x^4 + 2x^3 \\ 6x^5 + 3x^4 + 3x^3 \end{array} \right]. \qquad (11)$$

The following shows the submatrix of an order $N = D + \deg s_n + 1 = 9$ minimal approximant basis of type $(\mathbf{D}_1, \mathbf{d}_1) = (0, 1, 1, 1, 1, 0)$ *for* $\left[\ S \mid E^T\ \right]^T$ *comprised of rows that have nonpositive* $(\mathbf{D}_1, \mathbf{d}_1)$-*degree:*

$$\left[\ \bar{R}_2 \mid \bar{H}_2\ \right] = \left[\begin{array}{c|ccccc} 0 & 0 & 0 & 0 & 2 & 1 \\ 0 & x & 1 & 2x+5 & 3x+1 & 0 \\ 1 & 0 & 0 & x+2 & x+3 & 0 \end{array} \right].$$

Applying the compression matrix B to $\bar{H}_2$ yields a genset $\bar{H}_2 B$ of type $\mathbf{d}$ for $\mathcal{L}_\mathbf{d}(H)$.

At this point (Lemma 14) we have reduced the problem of computing H to that of computing the rows $\left[\ \bar{R}_2 \mid \bar{H}_2\ \right]$ of nonpositive $(\mathbf{D}_1, \mathbf{d}_1)$-degree of a minimal approximant basis of order $N = D + \deg s_n + 1$ for an input $\left[\ S \mid E^T\ \right]^T$. If the partial linearization parameter in Lemma 12 was chosen as $b = d$, then E has dimension $O(n) \times n$, and all degree

constrains in $(\mathbf{D}_1, \mathbf{d}_1)$ are bounded by d. Since the sum of the column degrees in $\left[\ S \mid E^T\ \right]^T$ is bounded by nd, the reduction of order technique in [22, Section 2] can be used to transform to an equivalent problem of dimension $O(n) \times O(n)$ and order only $2d+1$. We refer to [22] for details of the reduction of order technique, and only illustrate the technique here on our running example.

EXAMPLE 16. *In Example 15 we computed an order 9 minimal approximant basis of type* $(\mathbf{D}_1, \mathbf{d}_1) = (0, 1, 1, 1, 1, 0)$ *for the 6×1 input $F := \left[\ S \mid E^T\ \right]^T$ shown in (11). Since the maximum degree constraint is 1, we can instead compute an order $2 \cdot 1 + 1 = 3$ minimal approximant basis $\bar{M}$ of type* $(\mathbf{D}_1, \mathbf{d}_1, d-1, d-1) = (0, 1, 1, 1, 1, 0, 0, 0)$ *for the following input:*

$$\bar{F} = \left[\begin{array}{c|c|c} F & \text{Quo}(F, x^2) & \text{Quo}(F, x^4) \\ \hline & 1 & \\ \hline & & 1 \end{array} \right] \in \mathsf{K}[x]^{8 \times 3}.$$

Indeed, the submatrix of $\bar{M}$ comprised of rows that have nonpositive $(\mathbf{D}_1, \mathbf{d}_1, 0, 0)$-*degree can be written as* $\left[\ W \mid *\ \right]$, *where W is the submatrix of an order 9 minimal approximant basis of type* $(\mathbf{D}_1, \mathbf{d}_1)$ *for F.*

We obtain the following theorem.

THEOREM 17. *Let $A \in \mathsf{K}[x]^{n \times n}$ be nonsingular of degree d. Assuming $\#\mathsf{K} \ge 8nd$, there exists a Las Vegas probabilistic algorithm that computes the Hermite form H of A using an expected number of $O(n^2 \mathsf{B}(nd))$ field operations from K.*

PROOF. By Theorem 4, the Smith form S of A and corresponding V as described in Subsection 3.2 can be computed in a Las Vegas fashion in the allotted time. By Theorem 5, the degrees of the diagonal entries of H can be computed in the allotted time using Algorithm DiagonalHermite. Construct column i of the block E of the input $\left[\ S \mid E^T\ \right]^T$ to the minimal approximant problem of Lemma 14 by reducing modulo s_i the entries in column i of BV, $1 \le i \le n$. Compute the rows of nonpositive degree in the minimal approximant indicate in Lemma 14 by first applying the reduction of order technique from [22, Section 2] to obtain a new problem of dimension $O(n) \times O(n)$ and order $2d + 1$, and then apply algorithm PM-Basis from [9] in time $O(n^\omega \mathsf{B}(d))$ operations from K. Finally, use the approach of Lemma 8 to recover the Hermite form from the genset for $\mathcal{L}_\mathbf{d}(H)$. $\square$

4. CONCLUSIONS

We have given a Las Vegas algorithm for computing the Hermite form of a nonsingular $A \in \mathsf{K}[x]^{n \times n}$ using $O^{\sim}(n^3 d)$ field operations form K. The algorithm has four phases:

1. Compute a row reduced form of A.

2. Compute the Smith form S and the image V of a Smith post-multiplier for A.

3. Compute the diagonal entries of H from S and V.

4. Compute H from S and V and the knowledge of the degrees of the diagonal entries of H

We remark that row reduction algorithm of [9] can accomplish phase 1 using an expected number of $O^{\sim}(n^\omega d)$ field operations, and we have shown how to apply the fast minimal approximant basis algorithm of [9] to accomplish phase 4 in the same time. $O^{\tilde{}}(n^\omega d)$ algorithms for phases 2 and 3 may be possible by incorporating blocking into the iterative algorithms currently used, although some additional novel ideas seem to be required for phase 2.

5. REFERENCES

[1] B. Beckermann and G. Labahn. A uniform approach for the fast computation of matrix–type Padé approximants. *SIAM Journal on Matrix Analysis and Applications*, 15(3):804–823, 1994.

[2] B. Beckermann, G. Labahn, and G. Villard. Shifted normal forms of polynomial matrices. In S. Dooley, editor, *Proc. Int'l. Symp. on Symbolic and Algebraic Computation: ISSAC '99*, pages 189—196. ACM Press, New York, 1999.

[3] B. Beckermann, G. Labahn, and G. Villard. Normal forms for general polynomial matrices. *Journal of Symbolic Computation*, 41(6):708–737, 2006.

[4] H. Cohen. *A Course in Computational Algebraic Number Theory*. Springer-Verlag, 1996.

[5] P. D. Domich. Three new polynomially-time bounded Hermite normal form algorithms. Master's thesis, School of Operations Research and Industrial Engineering, Cornell University, Ithaca, NY, 1983.

[6] P. D. Domich. *Residual Methods for Computing Hermite and Smith Normal Forms*. PhD thesis, School of Operations Research and Industrial Engineering, Cornell University, Ithaca, NY, 1985.

[7] P. D. Domich, R. Kannan, and L. E. Trotter, Jr. Hermite normal form computation using modulo determinant arithmetic. *Mathematics of Operations Research*, 12(1):50–59, 1987.

[8] W. Eberly, M. Giesbrecht, and G. Villard. Computing the determinant and Smith form of an integer matrix. In *Proc. 31st Ann. IEEE Symp. Foundations of Computer Science*, pages 675–685, 2000.

[9] P. Giorgi, C.-P. Jeannerod, and G. Villard. On the complexity of polynomial matrix computations. In R. Sendra, editor, *Proc. Int'l. Symp. on Symbolic and Algebraic Computation: ISSAC '03*, pages 135–142. ACM Press, New York, 2003.

[10] S. Gupta, S. Sarkar, A. Storjohann, and J. Valeriote. Triangular x-basis decompositions and derandomization of linear algebra algorithms over k[x]. 10 2010. Submitted for publication.

[11] J. L. Hafner and K. S. McCurley. Asymptotically fast triangularization of matrices over rings. *SIAM Journal of Computing*, 20(6):1068–1083, Dec. 1991.

[12] C. S. Iliopoulos. Worst-case complexity bounds on algorithms for computing the canonical structure of finite abelian groups and the Hermite and Smith normal forms of an integer matrix. *SIAM Journal of Computing*, 18(4):658–669, 1989.

[13] C. P. Jeannerod and G. Villard. Essentially optimal computation of the inverse of generic polynomial matrices. *Journal of Complexity*, 21:72–86, 2005.

[14] E. Kaltofen and G. Villard. On the complexity of computing determinants. *Computational Complexity*, 13(3–4):91–130, 2004.

[15] S. E. Labhalla. *Complexité en temps polynomial : calcul d'une réduite d'Hermite, les différentes représentations des nombres réels*. Doctorat d'Etat, Université Cadi Ayyad, Faculté des Sciences Semlalia, Marrakech, 1991.

[16] D. Micciancio and B. Warinschi. A linear space algorithm for computing the Hermite normal form. In B. Mourrain, editor, *Proc. Int'l. Symp. on Symbolic and Algebraic Computation: ISSAC '01*, pages 231—236. ACM Press, New York, 2001.

[17] T. Mulders and A. Storjohann. On lattice reduction for polynomial matrices. *Journal of Symbolic Computation*, 35(4):377–401, 2003.

[18] A. Storjohann. Computation of Hermite and Smith normal forms of matrices. Master's thesis, Dept. of Computer Science, University of Waterloo, 1994.

[19] A. Storjohann. *Algorithms for Matrix Canonical Forms*. PhD thesis, Swiss Federal Institute of Technology, ETH–Zurich, 2000.

[20] A. Storjohann. High–order lifting. Extended Abstract. In T. Mora, editor, *Proc. Int'l. Symp. on Symbolic and Algebraic Computation: ISSAC '02*, pages 246–254. ACM Press, New York, 2002.

[21] A. Storjohann. High–order lifting and integrality certification. *Journal of Symbolic Computation*, 36(3–4):613–648, 2003.

[22] A. Storjohann. Notes on computing minimal approximant bases. In W. Decker, M. Dewar, E. Kaltofen, and S. Watt, editors, *Challenges in Symbolic Computation Software*, number 06271 in Dagstuhl Seminar Proceedings. Internationales Begegnungs- und Forschungszentrum fuer Informatik (IBFI), Schloss Dagstuhl, Germany, 2006. http://drops.dagstuhl.de/opus/volltexte/2006/776 [date of citation: 2006-01-01].

[23] A. Storjohann. On the complexity of inverting integer and polynomial matrices. *Computational Complexity*, 2010. Accepted for publication.

[24] A. Storjohann and G. Labahn. Asymptotically fast computation of Hermite normal forms of integer matrices. In Y. N. Lakshman, editor, *Proc. Int'l. Symp. on Symbolic and Algebraic Computation: ISSAC '96*, pages 259–266. ACM Press, New York, 1996.

[25] G. Villard. Computing Popov and Hermite forms of polynomial matrices. In Y. N. Lakshman, editor, *Proc. Int'l. Symp. on Symbolic and Algebraic Computation: ISSAC '96*, pages 251–258. ACM Press, New York, 1996.

[26] U. Vollmer. A note on the Hermite basis computation of large integer matrices. In R. Sendra, editor, *Proc. Int'l. Symp. on Symbolic and Algebraic Computation: ISSAC '03*, pages 255–257. ACM Press, New York, 2003.

[27] C. Wagner. *Normalformberechnung von Matrizen über euklidischen Ringen*. PhD thesis, Universität Karlsruhe, 1998.

[28] W. Zhou and G. Labahn. Efficient computation of order basis. In J. P. May, editor, *Proc. Int'l. Symp. on Symbolic and Algebraic Computation: ISSAC '09*. ACM Press, New York, 2009.

Practical Polynomial Factoring in Polynomial Time

William Hart[*]
University of Warwick
Mathematics Institute
Coventry CV4 7AL, UK
W.B.Hart@warwick.ac.uk

Mark van Hoeij[†]
Florida State University
Tallahassee, FL 32306
hoeij@math.fsu.edu

Andrew Novocin
CNRS-INRIA-ENSL
46 Allée d'Italie
69364 Lyon Cedex 07, France
andy@novocin.com

ABSTRACT

State of the art factoring in $\mathbb{Q}[x]$ is dominated in theory by a combinatorial reconstruction problem while, excluding some rare polynomials, performance tends to be dominated by Hensel lifting. We present an algorithm which gives a practical improvement (less Hensel lifting) for these more common polynomials. In addition, factoring has suffered from a 25 year complexity gap because the best implementations are much faster in practice than their complexity bounds. We illustrate that this complexity gap can be closed by providing an implementation which is comparable to the best current implementations and for which competitive complexity results can be proved.

Categories and Subject Descriptors

I.1.2 [**Symbolic and Algebraic Manipulation**]: Algorithms; G.4 [**Mathematics of Computing**]: Mathematical Software

General Terms

Algorithms

Keywords

Symbolic Computation, Factoring Polynomials, Lattice Reduction

1. INTRODUCTION

Most practical factoring algorithms in $\mathbb{Q}[x]$ use a structure similar to [22]: factor modulo a small prime, Hensel lift this factorization, and use some method of recombining these local factors into integer factors. Zassenhaus performed the recombination step by an exhaustive search which can be

---

[*]Author was supported by EPSRC Grant number EP/G004870/1

[†]Supported by NSF Grant numbers 0728853 and 1017880

made effective for as many as 40 local factors as is shown in [2]. While quite fast for many cases, the exponential complexity of this exhaustive technique is realized on many polynomials.

Polynomial time algorithms, based on lattice reduction, were given in [4, 12, 19]. For a polynomial f of degree N, and entries bounded in absolute value by 2^h, these algorithms perform $\mathcal{O}(N^2(N + h))$ LLL switches. These algorithms are slow in practice, because the size of the combinatorial problem depends only on r, where r is the number of local factors, while the LLL cost depends on N and h, which can be much larger than r. This problem was the motivation for van Hoeij's algorithm [8], but no complexity bound was given. There are several variations on van Hoeij's algorithm, as well as implementations. The most interesting is that of Belabas [3]. His version is designed in such a way that the vectors during LLL have entries with $\mathcal{O}(r)$ bits. In experiments, the number of LLL switches appears to be bounded by $\mathcal{O}(r^3)$. Other implementations, such as NTL and Magma, have a comparable performance in practice.

For a number of years, the practical behavior of these implementations was a complete mystery; there was no complexity bound that came anywhere near the running times observed in practice. There are two ways to reduce the gap between practical performance and theoretical complexity: (a) make the algorithm slower in practice (this was done in [4] because it makes it easier to prove a polynomial time bound), or (b) keep the algorithm at least equally fast in practice and do a more precise analysis.

Note that this $\mathcal{O}(r^3)$ in Belabas' version (and other well tuned implementations) is an observation only, we can not prove it, and suspect that it might be possible to construct counter examples. However, we can prove $\mathcal{O}(r^3)$ after making some modifications to Belabas' version. This was done in [17]. The phrase 'r^3 algorithm' in [17] refers to an algorithm for which we can prove an $\mathcal{O}(r^3)$ bound on the number of LLL switches. The paper [21] explains the lattice reduction techniques in an easier and more general way (more applications) than [17], however, for the application of factoring, the bound in [21] is $\mathcal{O}(Nr^2)$ LLL switches, which is not optimal. So in order to accomplish (b) in the previous paragraph, it remains to show the part "at least equally fast in practice", and this can only be done with an actual implementation.

The goals in this paper are: (1) Implement an algorithm that works well in practice (at least comparable to the best current implementations), that (2) is simpler than the algorithm in [17], and (3) for which the $\mathcal{O}(r^3)$ analysis from [17] still works. In addition, (4) verify the claim in [17] that the so-called early termination strategy can make the implementation faster on common classes of polynomials by doing less Hensel lifting, without hurting the practical performance on the remaining polynomials.

In [17] the metric termed Progress (see Section 2.3) is introduced. The main result of that work is that in order to guarantee $\mathcal{O}(r^3)$ total LLL-switches it is enough to ensure that LLL is only called when a sufficient increase in progress can be made, and that moreover, this is always possible.

At every step in our algorithm it is necessary to check that the properties which make the analysis in [17] go through, also hold for the decisions made by our algorithm.

The verification is routine, but it is *not* the aim of this paper to re-cast or simplify the analysis of [17]. Similarly it is not the aim of this paper to report on a highly optimised implementation of the new algorithm. Rather, our goal is to show, with an implementation, that it is possible to have the best theoretical complexity without sacrificing practical performance. A complete complexity analysis of the algorithm we present exists in pre-print format and can be found here [7].

Roadmap Necessary background information will be included in section 2. The algorithm is laid out in an implementable fashion in section 3. Practical notes, including running time and analysis are included in section 4.

2. BACKGROUND

In this section we will outline necessary information from the literature. The primary methods for factoring polynomials which we address can all be said to share a basic structure with the Zassenhaus algorithm of 1969 [22].

2.1 The Zassenhaus algorithm

In some ways this is the first algorithm for factoring polynomials over $\mathbb{Z}$ which properly uses the power of a computer. For background on the evolution of factoring algorithms see the fine treatment in [9].

The algorithm utilizes the fact that the irreducible factors of f over $\mathbb{Z}$ are also factors of f over the p-adic numbers $\mathbb{Z}_p$. So if one has both a bound on the size of the coefficients of any integral factors of f and an irreducible factorization in $\mathbb{Z}_p[x]$ of sufficient precision then one can find the integral factors via simple tests (e.g. trial division). To bound coefficients of integer factors of f we can use the Landau-Mignotte bound (see [5, Bnd 6.33] or [1] for other options). For the p-adic factorization it is common to choose a small prime p to quickly find a factorization over $\mathbb{F}_p$ then use the Hensel lifting method to increase the p-adic precision of this factorization. Due to a comprehensive search of all combinations of local factors the algorithm has an exponential complexity bound which is actually reached by application to the Swinnerton-Dyer polynomials [11].

ALGORITHM 2.1. *Description of Zassenhaus algorithm*
Input: *Square-free[1] polynomial $f \in \mathbb{Z}[x]$ of degree N*
Output: *The irreducible factors of f over $\mathbb{Z}$*

1. Choose a prime, p, such that $\gcd(f, f') \equiv 1$ modulo p.
2. **Modular Factorization:** Factor $f \mod p \equiv lc \cdot f_1 \cdots f_r$.

---
[1] Assumed square-free for simplicity. A standard $\gcd$-based technique can be used to obtain a square-free factorization (see [5, sct 14.6])

3. Compute the Landau-Mignotte bound $L = \sqrt{(N+1)} \cdot 2^N \cdot \| f \|_\infty$ and $a \in \mathbb{N}$ such that $p^a > 2L$.
4. **Hensel Lifting:** Hensel lift $f_1 \cdots f_r$ to precision p^a.
5. **Recombination:** For each $v \in \{0,1\}^r$ (and in an appropriate order) decide if $g_v := \text{pp}(lc \cdot \prod f_i^{v[i]} \bmod s \ p^a)$ divides f over $\mathbb{Z}$, where $\text{pp}(h) = h/\text{content}(h)$.

It is common to perform steps 1 and 2 several times to attempt to minimize, r, the number of local factors. Information from these attempts can also be used in clever ways to prove irreducibility or make the recombination in step 5 more efficient, see [2] for more details on these methods. Algorithms for steps 2, 3, and 4 have been well studied and we refer interested readers to a general treatment in [5, Chapters 14,15]. Our primary interests in this paper lie in the selection of a and the recombination of the local factors in step 5.

2.2 Overview of the LLL algorithm

In 1982 [12] Lenstra, Lenstra, and Lovász devised an algorithm, of a completely different nature, for factoring polynomials. Their algorithm for factoring had a polynomial time complexity bound but was not the algorithm of choice for most computer algebra systems as Zassenhaus was more practical for the majority of everyday tasks. At the heart of their algorithm for factoring polynomials was a method for finding 'nice' bases of lattices now known as the LLL algorithm. The LLL algorithm for lattice reduction is widely applied in many areas of computational number theory and cryptography, as it (amongst other things) gives an approximate solution to the shortest vector problem, which is NP-hard [14], in polynomial time. In fact, the van Hoeij algorithm for factoring polynomials [8] can be thought of as the application of the LLL lattice reduction algorithm to the Zassenhaus recombination step. The purpose of this section is to present some facts from [12] that will be needed throughout the paper. For a more general treatment of lattice reduction see [13].

A lattice, L, is a discrete subset of $\mathbb{R}^n$ that is also a $\mathbb{Z}$-module. Let $\mathbf{b}_1, \ldots, \mathbf{b}_d \in L$ be a basis of L and denote $\mathbf{b}_1^*, \ldots, \mathbf{b}_d^* \in \mathbb{R}^n$ as the Gram-Schmidt orthogonalization over $\mathbb{R}$ of $\mathbf{b}_1, \ldots, \mathbf{b}_d$. Let $\delta \in (1/4, 1]$ and $\eta \in [1/2, \sqrt{\delta})$. Let $l_i = \log_{1/\delta} \| \mathbf{b}_i^* \|^2$, and denote $\mu_{i,j} = \frac{\mathbf{b}_i \cdot \mathbf{b}_j^*}{\mathbf{b}_j^* \cdot \mathbf{b}_j^*}$. Note that $\mathbf{b}_i, \mathbf{b}_i^*, l_i, \mu_{i,j}$ will change throughout the algorithm sketched below.

DEFINITION 2.2. $\mathbf{b}_1, \ldots, \mathbf{b}_d$ *is LLL-reduced if* $\| \mathbf{b}_i^* \|^2 \leq \frac{1}{\delta - \mu_{i+1,i}^2} \| \mathbf{b}_{i+1}^* \|^2$ *for* $1 \leq i < d$ *and* $|\mu_{i,j}| \leq \eta$ *for* $1 \leq j < i \leq d$.

In the original algorithm the values for (δ, η) were chosen as $(3/4, 1/2)$ so that $\frac{1}{\delta - \eta^2}$ would simply be 2.

ALGORITHM 2.3. *Rough sketch of LLL-type algorithms*
Input: *A basis $\mathbf{b}_1, \ldots, \mathbf{b}_d$ of a lattice L.*
Output: *An LLL-reduced basis of L.*

1. $\kappa := 2$
2. **while** $\kappa \leq d$ **do:**
   (a) *(Gram-Schmidt over $\mathbb{Z}$).* By subtracting suitable $\mathbb{Z}$-linear combinations of $\mathbf{b}_1, \ldots, \mathbf{b}_{\kappa-1}$ from $\mathbf{b}_\kappa$ make sure that $|\mu_{i,\kappa}| \leq \eta$ for $i < \kappa$.
   (b) *(LLL Switch).* If interchanging $\mathbf{b}_{\kappa-1}$ and $\mathbf{b}_\kappa$ will decrease $l_{\kappa-1}$ by at least 1 then do so.

(c) *(Repeat)*. If not switched $\kappa := \kappa + 1$, if switched $\kappa = \max(\kappa - 1, 2)$.

That the above algorithm terminates, and that the output is LLL-reduced was shown in [12]. There are many variations of this algorithm (such as [10, 15, 18, 19, 20]) and we make every effort to use it as a black box for ease of implementation. What we do require is an algorithm which returns an LLL-reduced basis and whose complexity is measured in the number of switches (times step 2b is called). In fact the central complexity result of [17] is that the r^3 algorithm has $\mathcal{O}(r^3)$ switches throughout the entire algorithm, in spite of many calls to LLL.

Intuitively the Gram-Schmidt lengths of an LLL-reduced basis do not drop as fast as a generic basis (for more on generic bases and LLL see [16]). In practice this property is used in factoring algorithms to separate vectors of small norm from the rest.

2.3 Lattice-based Recombination

Each of [3, 4, 8, 17] use lattice reduction to directly attack the recombination phase of Zassenhaus' algorithm (step 5 in Algorithm 2.1). The goal of these algorithms is to find **target 0–1 vectors**, $\mathbf{w}_i \in \{0,1\}^r$, which correspond with the true irreducible factors of f over $\mathbb{Z}$, namely $g_i \equiv \prod_{j=1}^r f_j^{w_i[j]}$. Each of these algorithms begins with an $r \times r$ identity matrix where each row corresponds with one of the local factors $f_1, \ldots, f_r \in \mathbb{Z}_p[x]$. Then they augment columns and/or rows of data extracted from the corresponding local factors such that:

- The augmented target vectors have boundable norm

- The vectors which do not correspond with factors in $\mathbb{Z}[x]$ can be made arbitrarily large

- This augmented data respects the additive nature of the lattice.

So far, to the best of our knowledge, only traces of the f_i (sums of powers of roots) or so-called CLDs (Coefficients of Logarithmic Derivatives, i.e. $f \cdot f_i'/f_i$) have been used for this purpose. The CLD is important enough that we give a formal definition:

DEFINITION 2.4. *For a p-adic polynomial $g \in \mathbb{Z}_p[x]$ which divides a polynomial $f \in \mathbb{Z}[x]$ in $\mathbb{Z}_p$, we call the coefficient of x^j in the p-adic polynomial $g' \cdot f/g$ the jth **CLD** of g. This quantity is typically known to some p-adic precision, p^a.*

For example, the rows of the following matrix form the basis of a lattice which could be used:

$$\begin{pmatrix} & & & & & p^{a-b_N} \\ & & & & \cdot^{\cdot^{\cdot}} & \\ & & & p^{a-b_1} & & \\ 1 & & & c_{1,1} & \cdots & c_{1,N} \\ & \ddots & & \vdots & \ddots & \vdots \\ & & 1 & c_{r,1} & \cdots & c_{r,N} \end{pmatrix}$$

Where $c_{i,j}$ represents the jth CLD of f_i divided by p^{b_j} and p^{b_j} represents $\sqrt{N}$ times a bound of the jth CLD for any factor $g \in \mathbb{Z}[x]$ of f. In this lattice all target vectors have this format: $(\{0,1\}, \ldots, \{0,1\}, \epsilon_1, \ldots, \epsilon_N)$ where ϵ_j is a rational number of absolute value $\leq 1/\sqrt{N}$. These target vectors have a Euclidean-norm $\leq \sqrt{r+1}$, whereas a vector corresponding with a factor in $\mathbb{Z}_p[x] \setminus \mathbb{Z}[x]$ could have an arbitrarily large Euclidean-norm for arbitrarily precise p-adic data.

Brief differences of the algorithms. In [8] the first factoring algorithm to use LLL for the recombination phase was designed and in this case traces were used for the p-adic data. Belabas [3] also used traces, but fine tuned the idea by gradually using this data starting with the most significant bits; this led to more calls to LLL which cost less overall by working on smaller entries. In [4] the idea of using CLDs was introduced, for which we have tighter theoretical bounds than traces. This allowed for an upper bound on the amount of Hensel lifting needed before the problem is solved. Also lattices using CLDs instead of traces tend to have a greater degree of separation between the target vectors and non-targeted vectors at the same level of p-adic precision.

In [17] an approach is outlined which mimics the practical aspects of Belabas while making measures to ensure that the behavior is not harmed when attempting to solve the recombination phase 'too early'. The primary complexity result in [17] is a method of bounding and amortizing the cost of LLL throughout the entire algorithm. This was done by introducing a metric called **Progress** which was to never decrease and which was increased by at least 1 every time any call to LLL made a switch (step 2b of Algorithm 2.3).

The Progress metric mimicked an energy-function with an additional term to deal with 'removed' vectors, namely:

$$P := 0 \cdot l_1 + 1 \cdot l_2 + \cdots + (s-1) \cdot l_s + (r+1) \cdot n_{\text{rv}} \cdot \log\left(2^{3r}(r+1)\right)$$

Where l_i is the log of the norm of the ith Gram-Schmidt (from here on G-S) vector, s is the number of vectors at the moment, 2^{3r} was the bound on the norm of any vector throughout the process, and n_{rv} is the number of vectors which have been removed from the basis so far.

The factoring algorithm in [17] is then shown to terminate before the progress can cross some threshold of $\mathcal{O}(r^3)$, where r is the number of p-adic factors of f. The Progress metric gives us a method for determining that a call to LLL will be guaranteed to move the algorithm forward. Every decision made by the r^3 algorithm and the algorithm we present here is tied to ensuring that Progress is never decreased by too much and is increased every time LLL is called.

3. THE MAIN ALGORITHM

In this section we present a modified version of the algorithm presented in Novocin's thesis, [17], but for which the same complexity analysis holds. We divide the algorithm into several sub-algorithms to give a top-down presentation. The sub-algorithms are as follows:

- Algorithm 3.1 is the top layer of the algorithm. We choose a suitable prime, perform local factorization, decide if the Zassenhaus algorithm is sufficient, perform Hensel lifting, and call the recombination process.

- Algorithm 3.2 creates a knapsack lattice, processes the local factors (extracts information from CLDs) and tests how much impact on progress they will have. If the progress will be sufficient according to the results of [17] then the CLD information is added to a lattice and LLL is called. We test to see if the algorithm has solved the problem and decide if more Hensel lifting will be needed.

- Algorithm 3.3 takes CLD data and decides whether or not a call to LLL will make enough progress to justify the cost of the call to LLL. This step guarantees that the complexity analysis of [17] holds.

- Algorithm 3.4 is a practical method for bounding the size of CLDs arising from 'true factors'. This bound is the analogue of the trace bounds from [8] and gives us some idea of how much Hensel lifting will be needed before a call to LLL can be justified (via the Progress metric).

- Algorithm 3.5 gives a heuristic 'first' Hensel bound.

- Algorithm 3.6 decides whether or not we have found a true factorization of f.

3.1 Main Wrapper

The input to the algorithm is a square-free primitive polynomial, $f \in \mathbb{Z}[x]$. The output is the irreducible factorization of f. The strategy at this level is the same as that of van Hoeij's algorithm and indeed that of Zassenhaus and its variants.

We select a prime, p, for which f is square-free in $\mathbb{F}_p[x]$ and find the factorization of f modulo p. This step is well understood (see for example [5, Chpts.14,15]). Standard heuristics are used for selecting a 'good' prime.

Next, we perform Hensel lifting of the factors to increase their p-adic precision. We then call a recombination procedure to attempt a complete factorization at the current level of p-adic precision. If this process fails then we Hensel lift again and re-attempt recombination, etc.

ALGORITHM 3.1. *The main algorithm*
Input: *Square-free polynomial $f \in \mathbb{Z}[x]$ of degree N*
Output: *The irreducible factors of f over $\mathbb{Z}$*

1. Choose a prime, p, such that $\mathbf{gcd}(f, f') \equiv 1$ modulo p.
2. **Modular Factorization:** Factor f modulo $p \equiv lc \cdot f_1 \cdots f_r$.
3. **if** $r \leq 10$ **return** Zassenhaus(f)
4. Compute first target precision a with **Algorithm 3.5**
5. **until solved:**
   (a) **Hensel Lifting:** Hensel lift $f_1 \cdots f_r$ to precision p^a.
   (b) **Recombination:** Algorithm 3.2($f, f_1, \ldots, f_r, p^a$)
   (c) **if** not solved: $a := 2a$

3.1.1 Choosing an initial Hensel precision

Step 4 provides a starting p-adic precision, p^a, by calling Algorithm 3.5. Other standard algorithms choose this value such that $p^a \geq 2L$ where L is the Landau-Mignotte bound (see [5, sct 14.6]). This is an upper-bound precision for which the true factors can be provably reconstructed for every possible input.

Our algorithm attempts recombination at a lower level of p-adic precision, noting that the Landau-Mignotte bound is designed for the worst-case inputs. As section 4 shows our reduced precision is often sufficient, and is substantially lower than other methods.

An example of where this strategy pays dividends is when f can be proven irreducible in the recombination phase at

our reduced precision. In this case there is no need to Hensel lift to a higher precision. Another case is when we can reconstruct low-degree factors of f at the current precision and prove the irreducibility of the quotient when f is divided by these small factors. The precision needed to solve the recombination problem and the precision needed to reconstruct integer factors once the recombination is solved are unrelated. Further the precision needed to solve the recombination is not well understood, there is a theoretical worst-case in [4] which has never been reached in practice.

The worst-case for our algorithm is when either the recombination requires the same or more p-adic precision than the Landau-Mignotte bound or when the true factorization has two or more factors of large degree with large coefficients (in which case they each require precision near the Landau-Mignotte bound and they cannot all be discovered by division). We do not know, a priori, which case we will be in, so we design the algorithm to ensure that in the worst case we do no worse than other algorithms and in the best case we minimize Hensel lifting.

We designed our Hensel lifting procedure for the case that we need to increase the precision frequently. Our implementation uses a balanced factor tree approach as presented in [5, Sect. 15.5]. To minimize overhead in Hensel lifting multiple times our implementation caches the lifting tree, intermediate modular inverses computed by the extended gcd, and the intermediate products of the lifting tree itself. This way there is little difference between Hensel lifting directly to the end precision or lifting in several separate stages.

3.2 Recombination

The next several sub-algorithms form the core the new approach. In Algorithm 3.2 we are given a local factorization at a new p-adic precision and (except for the first call to this sub-algorithm) we are also given an LLL-reduced lattice. This is the layer of the algorithm which organizes all of the lattice decisions, including the creation of new columns and/or rows from the p-adic factorization, the decision as to when lattice reduction is justified, the lattice reduction itself, and the extracting of factors from the information in the reduced lattice.

ALGORITHM 3.2. *Attempt Reconstruction*
Input: *f, $f_1, \ldots, f_r$ the lifted factors, their precision p^a, and possibly $M \in \mathbb{Z}_{s \times (r+c)}$.*
Output: *If solved then the irreducible factors of f over $\mathbb{Z}$ otherwise an updated M.*

1. If this is the first call let $M := I_{r \times r}$
2. Choose a k heuristically (see below for details)
3. For $j \in \{0, \ldots, k-1, N-k-1, \ldots, N-1\}$ do:
   (a) Compute CLD bound, X_j, for x^j using Algorithm 3.4
   (b) If $\sqrt{N} \cdot X_j \leq p^a / 2^{1.5r}$ then compute new column vector $\mathbf{x}_j := (x_{1,j}, \ldots, x_{r,j})^T$ where $x_{i,j}$ is the coefficient of x^j in $f \cdot f_i'/f_i$
4. For each computed $\mathbf{x}_j$ do:
   (a) **justified**:= True; While **justified** is True do:
      i. Decide if LLL is justified using Algorithm 3.3 which augments M
      ii. If so then run LLL(M)
      iii. If not then **justified** := False
      iv. Compute G-S lengths of rows of M

v. Decrease the number of rows of M until the final Gram-Schmidt norm $\leq \sqrt{r+1}$

vi. Use Algorithm 3.6 to test if solved

This algorithm provides the basic framework of our attack. The rows of the matrix M provide the basis of our lattice-based recombination (see section 2.3). We compute bounds for the $2k$ CLDs, $\{0, \ldots, k-1, N-k-1, \ldots, N-1\}$, from these bounds we can determine if p^a is a sufficient level of p-adic precision to justify computing any of the $2k$ actual CLDs.

For each CLD which is actually computed we call Algorithm 3.3 to decide what to do. Details are given in the next section. Steps 4(a)iv and 4(a)v are the same as both [8] and [17], but we note that step 4(a)iv can be done with a well-chosen floating-point algorithm since M is LLL-reduced.

The heuristic k. In practice we need not compute all of the coefficients of the r p-adic polynomials $f_i' \cdot f/f_i$. Often only a few coefficients are needed to either solve the problem or decide that more precision will be needed. The value of k provides a guess at the number of coefficients which will be needed and can be determined experimentally. In our implementation we found that a value of $5 \leq k \leq 20$ was usually sufficient. A fail-safe value of $k = N/2$ can be used for the cases when the p-adic precision is close to the theoretical bound and where the problem is yet to be solved (which did not occur for us in practice).

It is best to compute the highest k coefficients and/or the lowest k coefficients of each logarithmic derivative. There are two reasons for this:

- To compute the bottom k coefficients of $f_i' \cdot f/f_i$ mod p^a, power series techniques can be used. Thus only the bottom k coefficients of f_i and f are needed (same for the top k coefficients) rather than all coefficients.

- The heuristic we use in Algorithm 3.5, for initial p-adic precision, only Hensel lifts far enough to guarantee that either the leading CLD or trailing CLD can justify a call to LLL.

The soundness of these heuristics is checked by examining the CLD bounds for true factors and comparing them with p^a. If our heuristics are well-adjusted then some of the computed $2k$ CLD bounds will be smaller than p^a. These CLD bounds are cheap to compute and a method is provided in Algorithm 3.4. Of course other choices are possible for each of our heuristics, and a more sophisticated heuristic could be designed.

3.3 Determining if a potential column justifies LLL

The following algorithm is given both a column vector whose i^{th} entry is the jth CLD i.e. the coefficient of x^j in the p-adic polynomial $f_i' \cdot f/f_i$ (which is known to a precision p^a) and a matrix M. The rows of M form a reduced basis of a lattice which must contain the small target vectors corresponding to irreducible factors of f over $\mathbb{Z}$.

The algorithm decides if augmenting M by an appropriate transformation of the given column vector would increase the norm of the rows of M by enough to justify a call to LLL on the augmented M. The metric used is the Progress metric of [17]. This algorithm also performs scaling in the style of [3], to prevent entries of more than $\mathcal{O}(r)$ bits in M.

This sub-algorithm is important to the proven bit-complexity of the algorithm and not to the practical complexity. The purpose of this sub-algorithm is to bound the timings of all potential worst-cases via the theoretical analysis of [17]. One of the important contributions of this paper is to show, via implementation, that this sub-algorithm does not harmfully impact the performance of our algorithm.

ALGORITHM 3.3. *Decide if column is worth calling LLL*
  Input: $M \in \mathbb{Z}_{s \times (r+c)}$, *data vector* $\mathbf{x}_j$, p^a, X_j *the CLD bound for* x^j
  Output: *A potentially updated* M *and a boolean* `justified`

1. Let $B := r+1$ and s be the number of rows of M
2. If $p^a < X_j \cdot B \cdot \sqrt{N} \cdot 2^{(1.5)r}$ `justified` $:= False$ and exit
3. Find U the first r columns of M
4. Compute $\mathbf{y}_j := U \cdot \mathbf{x}_j$
5. If $\| \mathbf{y}_j \|_\infty < X_j \cdot B \cdot \sqrt{N} \cdot 2^{(1.5)r}$ then `justified` := $False$ and exit
6. If $p^a - Bp^a/2^{(1.5)r} > \| \mathbf{y}_j \|_\infty \cdot (2(3/2)^{s-1} - 2)$ then no_vec :=True otherwise False
7. New column scaling 2^k, closest power of 2 to $\frac{\|\mathbf{y}_j\|_\infty}{X_j \cdot B \cdot \sqrt{N} \cdot 2^{(1.5)r}}$ if no_vec is True or to $\frac{p^a}{X_j \cdot B \cdot \sqrt{N} \cdot 2^{(1.5)r}}$ if False
8. Embed $\mathbf{x}_j$ and $p^a/2^k$ into $\mathbb{Z}/2^r$ by rounding and denote results as $\tilde{\mathbf{x}}_j$ and $\tilde{P}$
9. If no_vec is True then augment M with new column $\tilde{\mathbf{y}}_j = U \cdot \tilde{\mathbf{x}}_j$
   If no_vec False then also adjoin a new row so
   $$M := \left[\begin{array}{c|c} \mathbf{0} & \tilde{P} \\ \hline M & \tilde{\mathbf{y}}_j \end{array} \right]$$
10. Justified :=True; return M

The most significant change of this algorithm from the algorithm in [17] is that we round the new column after scaling. We keep $\log r$ bits after the decimal for the sake of numerical stability. Consider this change a practical heuristic which we can prove does not impact the $\mathcal{O}(r^3)$ bound for the number of LLL switches (see [7]). This proof uses the bounds we have on the size of unimodular transforms encountered throughout the algorithm.

As some implementations of LLL prefer to work on matrices with integer entries we note that a virtual decimal place can be accomplished using integers by scaling up the entries in U (the first r columns) by 2^r. Such a scaling requires replacing $\sqrt{r+1}$ with $\sqrt{2^{2r}(r+1)}$ in step 4(a)v of Algorithm 3.2.

3.4 Obtaining practical CLD bounds

The goal of this sub-algorithm is to quickly find a bound for the absolute value of the coefficient of x^j in any integer polynomial of the form $g' \cdot f/g$ where $g \in \mathbb{Z}[x]$ divides $f \in \mathbb{Z}[x]$. This bound, which we will frequently call the jth **CLD bound**, is the CLD equivalent of the Landau-Mignotte bound.

The following method (an analogous bound for the bivariate case is given in [4, Lemma 5.8]) quickly gives fairly tight bounds in practice. The method is based on the fact that $g'f/g = \sum_{\alpha | g(\alpha)=0} \frac{f}{x - \alpha}$ summed over all roots of the potential factor.

ALGORITHM 3.4. *CLD bound*

Input: $f = a_0 + \cdots + a_N x^N$ and $c \in \{0, \ldots, N-1\}$

Output: X_c, a bound for the absolute value of the coefficient of x^c in the polynomial $f g' / g$ for any $g \in \mathbb{Z}[x]$ dividing f.

1. Let $B_1(r) := \frac{1}{r^{c+1}}(|a_0| + \cdots + |a_c| r^c)$
2. Let $B_2(r) := \frac{1}{r^{c+1}}(|a_{c+1}| r^{c+1} + \cdots + |a_N| r^N)$
3. Find $r \in \mathbb{R}^+$ such that $\text{MAX}\{B_1(r), B_2(r)\}$ is minimized to within a constant.
4. return $X_c := N \cdot \text{MAX}\{B_1(r), B_2(r)\}$

In this method, for any positive real number r, either $B_1(r)$ or $B_2(r)$ is an upper bound for the coefficient of x^c in $\frac{f}{x-\alpha}$ for any possible complex root α (because of the monotonicity of B_1 and B_2, if $r \le |\alpha|$ then $B_1(r)$ is the upper bound and if $r \ge |\alpha|$ then $B_2(r)$ will be). Thus for every positive real number r the quantity $\text{MAX}\{B_1(r), B_2(r)\}$ is an upper bound for the coefficient of x^c in $\frac{f}{x-\alpha}$. The task is then to find an r for which $\text{MAX}\{B_1(r), B_2(r)\}$ is minimized. Since the CLD is summed over every root of g we use N as a bound for the number of roots of g to give a CLD bound of $N \cdot \text{MAX}\{B_1(r), B_2(r)\}$.

For finding an r which minimizes $\text{MAX}\{B_1(r), B_2(r)\}$ our floating-point method is as follows (where $\text{sign}(x)$ is 1 if x positive, -1 if x negative, and 0 otherwise).

1. Let $r := 1$, `scaling` $:= 2$, `cur_sign` $:= \text{sign}(B1(r) - B2(r))$, and `pos_ratio` $:= \left(\frac{B1(r)}{B2(r)}\right)^{\texttt{cur\_sign}}$
2. Until `cur_sign` changes or `pos_ratio` ≤ 2 do:
   (a) $r := r \cdot \texttt{scaling}^{\texttt{cur\_sign}}$
   (b) `cur_sign` $:= \text{sign}(B1(r) - B2(r))$
   (c) `pos_ratio` $:= \left(\frac{B1(r)}{B2(r)}\right)^{\texttt{cur\_sign}}$
3. If `pos_ratio` > 2 then `scaling` $:= \sqrt{\texttt{scaling}}$ and Go to step 2 Otherwise Return r.

Another method of finding r is simply solving $B_1(r) - B_2(r) = 0$ for which many Computer Algebra Systems have efficient implementations. Our method is a quick-and-dirty method which is good enough in practice.

3.5 The new starting precision heuristic

We now outline our suggested heuristic for selecting an initial p-adic precision, a. This heuristic is designed so that we lift just far enough to warrant at least one call to LLL from either the 0th CLD or the $(N-2)^{\text{nd}}$ CLD, which can be enough to solve the problem.

ALGORITHM 3.5. *Heuristic for initial precision*
Input: $f \in \mathbb{Z}[x]$, p
Output: Suggested target precision a

1. Use Algorithm 3.4 to compute b, the minimum of (CLD bound for x^0) and (CLD bound for x^{N-1}).
2. return $a := \left\lceil \frac{2.5r + \log_2 b + (\log_2 N)/2}{\log_2 p} \right\rceil$

This heuristic is focused on either the trailing coefficient or the leading coefficient of f and guarantees that at least one CLD is computed in step 3b of Algorithm 3.2 and will be used by Algorithm 3.3.

3.6 Checking if problem solved

Finally we briefly mention the new method in which we check for true factors. One of the central novelties to the algorithm is a reduced level of Hensel lifting when attempting to solve the problem. It has been observed that the Landau-Mignotte bound is often too pessimistic and that even Zassenhaus' algorithm could potentially terminate at a lower level of Hensel lifting. This is also true of our lattice based attack, as we can often prove the irreducibility of a potential factor before we can fully reconstruct each of its coefficients. This is seen most frequently in polynomials which turn out to have one large degree factor and zero or more smaller degree factors. In these cases we must check for true factors in a way that will recover the large factor by dividing away any small irreducible factors.

We will begin by using a short-cut for detecting a 0-1 basis of our lattice. Such a basis, if it exists, could potentially solve the recombination problem.

ALGORITHM 3.6. *Check if solved*
Input: M, f, $f_1, \ldots, f_r$ to precision p^a
Output: A Boolean, `solved`, and possibly the irreducible factors of f in $\mathbb{Z}[x]$

1. Sort the first r columns of M into classes of columns which are identical
2. If there are not more classes than there are rows of M then we have a potential solution otherwise `solved` $:= False$ and exit
3. For each class multiply[2] the p-adic polynomials corresponding with the columns in that class and reduce with symmetric remainder modulo p^a to find the potential factors
4. In order, from the lowest degree to the highest degree, perform trial divisions of f
5. If any two polynomials fail to divide f then `solved` $:= False$ and exit
6. `solved` $:= True$ if there is one failed polynomial then recover it by division of f by the successful factors

The goal of lattice-based recombination is to find the target 0–1 vectors shown in section 2.3. It is possible that we have a basis whose echelon form gives these 0–1 vectors. Since we know that a solution can only use each local factor once then any echelon form solution will have a unique 1 in each of the first r columns. We detect this by examining which columns are identical. The symmetric remainder of step 3 is required to capture polynomials with negative coefficients. By moving from the lowest degree to the highest degree we maximize the chances of solving the problem with less Hensel lifting than the Landau-Mignotte bound used in Zassenhaus. Specifically when there is only one large factor of f the small factors can be reconstructed and the large factor can be found by division.

4. RUNNING TIMES AND PRACTICAL OBSERVATIONS

In this section we illustrate that our algorithm is useful in practice and give direct evidence that our approach can factor successfully at a lower level of p-adic precision than the previous standard based on the Landau-Mignotte bound. Here we make progress on the complexity gap by illustrating that an algorithm for which a good complexity result exists (see [7]) can match (and sometimes exceed) the performance of the best current implementations for polynomial

---

[2] As in Zassenhaus' algorithm, if f is not monic then this product should also be multiplied by the leading coefficient of f. If the symmetric remainder mod p^a of this product is not primitive, then it needs to be divided by its content.

factoring. We do this by providing running times of our implementation side by side with highly polished implementations in NTL version 5.5.2 as well as the implementation in MAGMA version 2.16-7. We also provide the level of p-adic precision at which the routines completed the factorization. This is done for a collection of benchmark polynomials from the literature [3] which was collected by Paul Zimmerman and Mark van Hoeij. It is tempting to judge a new algorithm on its performance on the diabolical Swinnerton-Dyer polynomials (which are amongst our benchmarks), however the practical bottleneck for standard polynomials tends to be the cost of Hensel lifting (see [3, pg.11]). Because of this we wish to emphasize that our algorithm successfully terminates with far less Hensel lifting than the others.

Poly	MAG	NTL	Z-bnd	FLINT	N-bnd
P1	.03	.068	29^{311}	.096	89^{33}
P2	.08	.204	11^{437}	.104	11^{44*}
P3	.16	.312	11^{629}	.164	11^{62*}
P4	1.87	1.956	13^{745}	.940	7^{160*}
P5	.11	.088	19^{51}	.044	23^{26}
P6	.11	.12	19^{152}	.108	23^{76*}
P7	1.07	1.136	37^{78}	.524	19^{74}
P8	2.18	3.428	13^{324}	1.532	11^{84}
M12_5	9.54	12.429	13^{1171}	2.88	11^{180}
M12_6	21.49	21.697	13^{1555}	5.18	13^{380*}
S7	.42	.340	29^{78}	.20	47^{41}
S8	4.62	3.752	47^{140}	2.06	53^{79}
S9	165.2	71	137^{228}	20.7	149^{125}
T1	2.54	3.848	7^{495}	1.23	7^{40}
T2	2.06	3.18	7^{200}	1.25	7^{43}
T3	19.7	24.27	7^{984}	7.35	7^{82}
P7*M12_6	240m	–	19^{1438}	53m	29^{265}
M12_5*P7	145m	–	19^{1114}	78m	29^{236}

These timings are measured in seconds (unless otherwise stated) and were made on a 2400MHz AMD Quad-core Opteron processor, using gcc version 4.4.1 with the -O2 optimization flag, although the processes did not utilize all four cores.

These timings show that our algorithm, a simplification of the r-cubed algorithm of [17], can be comparable in practice to [8] on benchmark polynomials (and in most of the cases a bit faster). Also of interest are the columns labeled 'Z-bnd' (for Zassenhaus bound) compared with 'N-bnd' (for New bound) which give the p-adic precision at which the algorithms solved the factoring problem (MAGMA and NTL chose the same primes and precisions). In the case of the five polynomials which include a *, the level of Hensel lifting shown was sufficient to reconstruct all of the factors but the combinatorial problem was actually solved at half of the shown precision. In every case we were able to solve the factorization with significantly less Hensel lifting than the Landau-Mignotte bound used in NTL and MAGMA. We stopped the NTL factorizations of P7*M12_6 and P7*M12_5 after some time.

We designed the degree 900 polynomials T1 and T2 and degree 2401 polynomial T3 to illustrate 'everyday' factoring problems which a user of a number theory library might naturally face. They are taken from factorizations inside of Trager's Algorithm, and the Hensel lifting dominates the running times. Such examples are plentiful (see the discussion in section 3.1.1) and arise naturally in many applications. Observe the large gap in p-adic precisions between

our method and the others. Our implementation is open source and publicly available as of FLINT version 1.6 [6].

4.1 A new floating point LLL trick

We implemented a floating-point based LLL, in FLINT, using the template of [15]. In the process we noted that the performance of our algorithm was devastated when multi-limb floating-point computations were needed. In order to avoid this we implemented a new wrapper of floating-point LLL which avoids needing multi-precision floating points, we call it U-LLL. We present it here as this was the application it was developed for.

ALGORITHM 4.1. U-LLL
Input: M whose rows form a lattice in $\mathbb{R}^n$, step_size
Output: An updated M which is LLL-reduced in place

1. **loop:**
   (a) max_size $:= \| M \|_\infty$
   (b) Find smallest integer $k \geq 0$ such that $\| M/2^k \|_\infty \leq 2^{\text{step\_size}}$
   (c) if ($k == 0$) then **break**
   (d) Let $M_{\text{temp}} := \lfloor M/2^k \rceil$ rounded
   (e) $B := [M_{\text{temp}}|I]$ augment an identity matrix
   (f) LLL(B) $=: [UM_{\text{temp}}|U]$
   (g) $M := UM$
   (h) if $\| M \|_\infty > $ max_size$/2^{\text{step\_size}/4}$ then **break**
2. $M :=$ LLL(M)

The algorithm will always output an LLL-reduced M and if each iteration of truncation continues to decrease the bit-length of M then this algorithm will loop until the bit-size of M is small. The advantage of this approach is that the augmented identity on a lattice of small bit-size tends to be numerically stable as the matrix is well conditioned. This allowed us to avoid needing expensive multi-precision floating point computations in our lattice reductions by choosing a sensible step_size.

5. REFERENCES

[1] J. Abbott. Bounds on factors in Z[x]. arXiv:0904.3057, 2009.
[2] John Abbott, Victor Shoup, and Paul Zimmermann. Factorization in Z[x]: the searching phase. In *Proceedings of the 2000 International Symposium on Symbolic and Algebraic Computation*, ISSAC '00, pages 1–7, New York, NY, USA, 2000. ACM.
[3] Karim Belabas. A relative van Hoeij algorithm over number fields. *Journal of Symbolic Computation*, 37(5):641–668, 2004.
[4] Karim Belabas, Mark van Hoeij, Jürgen Klüners, and Allan Steel. Factoring polynomials over global fields. *Journal de Théorie des Nombres de Bordeaux*, 21:15–39, 2009.
[5] J. von zur Gathen and J. Gerhardt. *Modern Computer Algebra, 2nd edition*. Cambridge University Press, 2003. pages 235–242, 432–437.
[6] W. Hart. FLINT. open-source C-library http://www.flintlib.org.
[7] W. Hart, M. v. Hoeij, and A. Novocin. Complexity analysis of factoring polynomials. http://andy.novocin.com/pro/complexity.pdf, 2010.

[8] Mark Van Hoeij. Factoring polynomials and the knapsack problem. *Journal of Number Theory*, 95:167–189, 2002.

[9] E. Kaltofen. Factorization of polynomials. In *Computing, Suppl. 4*, pages 95–113. Springer-Verlag, 1982.

[10] E. Kaltofen. On the complexity of finding short vectors in integer lattices. In *Proceedings of European Conference on Computer Algebra 1983 EUROCAL'83*, volume 162 of *Lecture Notes in Computer Science*, pages 236–244. Springer-Verlag, 1983.

[11] Erich Kaltofen, David R. Musser, and B. David Saunders. A generalized class of polynomials that are hard to factor. *SIAM J. Comput.*, 12(3):473–483, 1983.

[12] A. K. Lenstra, H. W. Lenstra, Jr., and L. Lovász. Factoring polynomials with rational coefficients. *Mathematische Annalen*, 261:515–534, 1982.

[13] L. Lovász. *An Algorithmic Theory of Numbers, Graphs and Convexity*. Society for Industrial and Applied Mathematics (SIAM), 1986. (Conference Board of the Mathematical Sciences and National Science Foundarion) CBMS-NSF Regional Conference Series in Applied Mathematics.

[14] D. Micciancio. The shortest vector problem is NP-hard to approximate to within some constant. *Society for Industrial and Applied Mathematics (SIAM) Journal on Computing*, 30(6):2008–2035, 2001.

[15] P. Q. Nguyen and D. Stehlé. Floating-point LLL revisited. In *Proceedings of Eurocrypt 2005*, volume 3494 of *Lecture Notes in Computer Science*, pages 215–233. Springer-Verlag, 2005.

[16] Phong Q. Nguyen and Damien Stehlé. LLL on the average. In Florian Hess, Sebastian Pauli, and Michael E. Pohst, editors, *ANTS*, volume 4076 of *Lecture Notes in Computer Science*, pages 238–256. Springer, 2006.

[17] A. Novocin. *Factoring Univariate Polynomials over the Rationals*. PhD thesis, Florida State University, 2008.

[18] C. P. Schnorr. A more efficient algorithm for lattice basis reduction. *Journal of Algorithms*, 9(1):47–62, 1988.

[19] A. Schönhage. Factorization of univariate integer polynomials by Diophantine approximation and improved basis reduction algorithm. In *Proceedings of the 1984 International Colloquium on Automata, Languages and Programming (ICALP 1984)*, volume 172 of *Lecture Notes in Computer Science*, pages 436–447. Springer-Verlag, 1984.

[20] A. Storjohann. Faster Algorithms for Integer Lattice Basis Reduction. Technical Report TR249, Swiss Federal Institute of Technology Zürich, Department of Computer Science, 1996.

[21] Mark van Hoeij and Andrew Novocin. Gradual sub-lattice reduction and a new complexity for factoring polynomials. In *LATIN*, pages 539–553, 2010.

[22] H. Zassenhaus. On Hensel Factorization I. In *J. Number Theory*, number 1, pages 291–311, 1969.

Quadratic-Time Certificates in Linear Algebra*

Erich L. Kaltofen
Dept. of Mathematics, NCSU
Raleigh, North Carolina 27695-8205,USA
kaltofen@math.ncsu.edu www.kaltofen.us

Michael Nehring
Dept. of Mathematics, NCSU
Raleigh, North Carolina 27695-8205,USA
michaelnehring@yahoo.com

B. David Saunders
Dept. Comput. Inform. Sci., University of Delaware
Newark, Delaware 19716, USA
saunders@udel.edu www.cis.udel.edu/~saunders/

ABSTRACT

We present certificates for the positive semidefiniteness of an $n \times n$ matrix A, whose entries are integers of binary length $\log \|A\|$, that can be verified in $O(n^{2+\epsilon}(\log \|A\|)^{1+\epsilon})$ binary operations for any $\epsilon > 0$. The question arises in Hilbert/Artin-based rational sum-of-squares certificates, i.e., proofs, for polynomial inequalities with rational coefficients. We allow certificates that are validated by Monte Carlo randomized algorithms, as in Rusins M. Freivalds's famous 1979 quadratic time certification for the matrix product. Our certificates occupy $O(n^{3+\epsilon}(\log \|A\|)^{1+\epsilon})$ bits, from which the verification algorithm randomly samples a quadratic amount.

In addition, we give certificates of the same space and randomized validation time complexity for the Frobenius form and the characteristic and minimal polynomials. For determinant and rank we have certificates of essentially-quadratic binary space and time complexity via Storjohann's algorithms.

Categories and Subject Descriptors

I.1.2 [**Computing Methodologies**]: Symbolic and Algebraic Manipulation—*Algorithms*

General Terms: theory, algorithms, verification

Keywords: randomization, probabilistic proof, matrix determinant, matrix rank, Frobenius form, output validation

1. INTRODUCTION

For many unstructured and dense linear algebra problems concerning an $n \times n$ matrix, it is not known whether there is an algorithm running in $n^{2+o(1)}$ time, in other words essentially-linearly in the input size. Motivated by the arising theme of certified ("trustworthy," "reliable") computa-

*This research was supported in part by the National Science Foundation under Grants CCF-0830347, CCF-0514585 and DMS-0532140 (Kaltofen and Nehring) and under Grants CCF-1018063 (Saunders).

tion, in particular in numerical and hybrid symbolic numeric computation and global optimization, it is worthwhile to provide a-posteriori certificates that can be verified in time $n^{2+\epsilon}$ for any $\epsilon > 0$; see [7, 9] and the references therein. In particular the definition of what constitutes a certificate is given at the end of [9]:

> "A certificate for a problem that is given by input/output specifications is an input-dependent data structure and an algorithm that computes from that input and its certificate the specified output, and that has lower computational complexity than any known algorithm that does the same when only receiving the input. Correctness of the data structure is not assumed but validated by the algorithm (adversary-verifier model)."

Certification itself is a challenging problem for integer and rational matrices. Even the apparently straightforward thought of certifying, for $A \in \mathbb{Z}^{n \times n}$, the LU decomposition $A = LU$, by presenting the factors L and U, is problematic. Forming the product costs matrix multiplication time, $O(n^\omega)$ with $\omega > 2.37$. We accept probabilistic verification, so one could consider forming the product $(A - LU)v$ for a random vector $v \in \mathbb{Z}^n$ [2, 10]. In the algebraic model this can be done in $O(n^2)$ time, linear in input size. However, this is not at all the case in the bit model of computation given a rational or integer matrix. For instance consider the case of $A \in \mathbb{Q}^{n \times n}$. The entries of L and U are ratios of minors of A. Even when entries are integers having lengths bounded by a constant and A has determinant 1, the size of the LU decomposition is in general $n^{3+o(1)}$ and we know of no certificate to verify it in $n^{2+o(1)}$ time, deterministically or probabilistically. Here and in the following the "$n^{o(1)}$" corresponds to factors that are asymptotically bounded by a power of $\log(n)$, i.e., "$n^{\eta+o(1)}$" corresponds to a "soft big-Oh" of n^η. We shall refer to the complexity $(\log \|A\|)^{1+o(1)}$ as *essentially-linear* (in $\log \|A\|$), the complexity $n^{2+o(1)}$ as *essentially-quadratic* (in n), etc.

However, LU decomposition is primarily a means to an end, and one can in fact use LU decomposition in $n^{3+o(1)}$ space, $n^{2+o(1)}$ time, probabilistic certification, as we will show.

By *probabilistic certification* we mean a Monte Carlo randomized verification process (an algorithm whose input consists of the problem instance, the solution, and a certificate data structure). The result is "true" if the solution is verified correct with the aid of the certificate. The probability of "true" output when the solution and/or certificate are incorrect must be at most 50 percent. The probability of incorrect verification can then be made arbitrarily small through repetition. For instance, twenty independent repetitions of a 1/2 probability verification makes the probability of error less than one part in a million.

In the next section we discuss the certification framework and give some problems that can be probabilistically certified in essentially-quadratic time and space. Section 3 concerns LU decomposition based certifications of rank and determinant which require essentially-quadratic time and essentially-cubic space. Then Section 4 presents certificates in that same time/space complexity for the invariants of matrix similarity: minimal polynomial, characteristic polynomial, and Frobenius form. This leads to certification of our original motivating problem: positive definiteness and semidefiniteness. Finally Section 5 discusses certifications based on algorithms by Kaltofen and Villard [8] and by Storjohann [15, 16]. These certificates require smaller space asymptotically than the essentially-cubic space certificates of Section 4, but the "o(1)" hides larger factors.

2. PRELIMINARIES AND $n^{2+o(1)}$ SPACE AND TIME CERTIFICATES

The sizes of entries, of the determinant, and indeed of all the minor determinants arise in in the analysis of our certificates. Let $\|A\| = \|A\|_{\infty,1} = \max_{i,j} |a_{i,j}|$, and let $H_A = \max\{|M|$ such that M is a minor of $A\}$.

Results in this paper are a function of the matrix dimension and of the minors bound H_A. The next lemma bounds H_A in terms of the entry size.

Lemma 1. *If A is an $m \times n$ integer matrix, and $k = \min(m, n)$, Then $H_A \leq (k^{1/2}\|A\|)^k$.*

Note that $\log H_A$ is essentially-linear in k when $\|A\|$ is polynomial in k.

PROOF. One form of Hadamard determinant bound of an $i \times i$ minor is $(i^{1/2}\|A\|)^i$, with equality when the matrix rows or columns are pairwise orthogonal and each entry has absolute value $\|A\|$. Our bound expression is an increasing function of i, so bounds all minors when $k = \min(m, n)$. □

The magnitudes of the scalars used in our certificates are essentially-linear in $\log H_A$ and the time to do basic arithmetic operations on values bounded by $\log H_A$ is essentially-linear in $\log\log H_A$, using fast integer arithmetic. In the remainder of the paper, for simplicity, we will state results in terms of matrix dimension and $\log\|A\|$, making use of Lemma 1. Unless subscripted by the base, all log's are to base 2.

Lemma 2. *Zero equivalence of a matrix expression over $\mathbb{Z}_p^{n \times n}$ may be verified probabilistically in time proportional to the cost of multiplying the expression times a vector and with probability of error $1/p$ [2, Freivalds].*

If the matrix expression involves matrix multiplications then expanding the expression may well cost more than matrix-times-vector product. For example when the matrix order is n and the expression is $A - LU$, expanding $E = A - LU$ would cost $O(n^\omega)$ with $\omega > 2.37$, matrix multiplication time, but the matrix-vector product $Ev = Av - L(Uv)$

costs 3 matrix-times-vector products and a vector subtraction, so is $O(n^2)$ arithmetic operations.

PROOF. The verification is to apply the expression E to a random vector in $\mathbb{Z}_p^n$. If E is nonzero, its nullspace is at most an $n - 1$ dimensional subspace of $\mathbb{Z}_p^n$, containing p^{n-1} of the p^n possible vectors. Hence the probability of error is bounded by $1/p$. □

Kimbrel and Sinha [10] suggest for $p \geq 2n$ to use the vector $v = [1, r, r^2, \ldots, r^{n-1}]^T$ for a random residue r with $0 \leq r \leq 2n - 1$. At least half of the vectors must lead to a non-zero result, since otherwise E times a non-singular Vandermonde matrix would be the zero matrix. Their approach requires only $\log(n)$ random bits.

Theorem 1. *Let $A \in \mathbb{Z}^{n \times n}$ and $b \in \mathbb{Z}^n$. The following problems have $n^{2+o(1)}(\log \|[A, b]\|)^{o(1)}$ space and $n^{2+o(1)} \times (\log \|[A, b]\|)^{o(1)}$ time probabilistic certificates.*

1. *Nonsingularity of A,*

2. *Singularity of A,*

3. *Consistency of rational linear system $Ax = b$ (and the certificate is a solution to the system),*

4. *Inconsistency of rational linear system $Ax = b$.*

PROOF. For nonsingularity the certificate is (p, B), for a prime p and matrix $B = A^{-1} \mod p$. If A is singular it is not invertible modulo any prime, so one prime's testimony suffices. Verification is zero equivalence of $AB - I \mod p$. Because at most $n((\log n)/2 + \log \|A\|)$ primes divide $\det(A)$, a prime of length

$$\log \left(n((\log n)/2 + \log \|A\|) \right)$$

may be chosen, ensuring that the size of the certificate p, B is $n^{2+o(1)}(\log \|A\|)^{o(1)}$ and the cost of the zero equivalence check is $n^{2+o(1)}(\log \|A\|)^{o(1)}$ time.

For singularity the certificate is a sequence of

$$2n((\log n)/2 + \log \|A\|)$$

primes p_i and nonzero vectors v_i such that $Av_i = 0 \mod p_i$. The certificate verification is to choose index i at random and check that $Av_i = 0 \mod p_i$. At most $n((\log n)/2 + \log \|A\|)$ primes divide the determinant of A and could provide a misleading nullspace vector. So at least half of the primes can provide a nullspace vector only if A is singular. Thus with probability $1/2$ the certificate is verified. The first $2n((\log n)/2 + \log \|A\|)$ primes can be used, These primes are all of bit length essentially-constant in $\log n$ and $\log \|A\|$, since the k-th prime is $\leq k(\log_e(k) + \log\log_e(k) - 1/2)$ for $k \geq 20$ [13].

For consistency the certificate is an integer vector x and integer $\delta \neq 0$ such that $Ax = \delta b$ and δ and the numerators in x are bounded in absolute value by $n^{n/2}\|(A, b)\|^n$. Verification is zero equivalence of $Ax - \delta b$ modulo a randomly chosen prime. It is easy to see, by Cramer's rule, that a suitably small rational solution exists when A is square and nonsingular, the entries of x are minors of (A, b) and $\delta = \det(A)$. Otherwise, for $r = \text{rank}(A)$, rows and columns of A may be permuted so that the leading principal $r \times r$ minor is nonsingular. Thus without loss of generality, A and b have conformally the forms

$$A = \begin{bmatrix} B & C \\ D & DB^{-1}C \end{bmatrix}, \quad b = \begin{bmatrix} b_1 \\ b_2 \end{bmatrix},$$

where B is $r \times r$ nonsingular. Consistency requires $b_2 = DB^{-1}b_1$. Let x_1 be solution to $Bx_1 = \delta b_1$, where $\delta = \det(B)$. Then $x = x_1$ padded with zeroes is a solution to $Ax = \delta b$. The bit lengths of x is as required since those of x_1 and δ are. so that again the bit lengths are as required.

How many primes can testify that $Ax = \delta b$ for a incorrect solution x, δ? Let $\hat{x}, \hat{\delta}$ be a true solution. Because $n^{n/2} \|(A, b)\|^n$ bounds the entries of the true and purported solutions, $k = 1 + n((\log n)/2 + \log \|[A, b]\|)$ is a bound for bit lengths of the differences $x - \hat{x}, \delta - \hat{\delta}$ and at most k primes can falsely testify by being divisors of all $n + 1$ differences. For verification we choose a prime p uniformly at random from among the first $3k + 3$ primes so that the probability of a bad prime is at most $1/3$. Then we reduce x and δ modulo p in $n^{2+o(1)}(\log \|[A, b]\|)^{o(1)}$ time and do two trials of zero equivalence of $Ax - \delta b$ mod p so that zero equivalence is assured with probability of error $1/4$ and overall error probability bounded by $1/3 + 2/3 \times 1/4 = 1/2$.

For inconsistency the certificate, based on [3], is a sequence of $2n((\log n)/2 + \log \|[A, b]\|)$ primes p_i and vectors v_i, such that $v_i^T A = 0 \mod p_i$, but $v_i^T b \neq 0 \mod p_i$, which contradicts $v_i^T Ax = v_i^T b$ (over the integers) for any x. Verification consists in randomly choosing one pair p_i, v_i and checking the two conditions modulo p_i. The system is inconsistent if and only if the rank of $[A, b]$ is greater than $r = \text{rank}(A)$. The only way a consistent system can be made to look inconsistent in a modular image is to have a reduced rank of A in the modular image. Let M be a nonsingular $r \times r$ minor of A. If p does not divide $\det(M) \leq H$ then p cannot falsely testify to inconsistency. Thus at most $n((\log n)/2 + \log \|[A, b]\|)$ primes must be avoided and the primes in the certificate can be taken small (among the first $3n((\log n)/2 + \log \|[A, b]\|)$ primes) to achieve the stated space and time bounds. $\square$

3. CERTIFICATES BASED ON LU DECOMPOSITION

Definition 1. *An $m \times n$ matrix A has an LU decomposition of rank r if $A = LU$, L is a $m \times r$ unit lower triangular matrix, and U is a $r \times n$ upper triangular matrix with nonzero diagonal entries.*

LU decomposition is a common tool used in the solution of several matrix problems including rank, determinant, and system solving. The entries in the LU decomposition are ratios of minors of A. Thus if A is an $n \times n$ matrix with a minors bound of bit length $h = n^{1+o(1)}$, then the size of the LU decomposition is $n^{3+o(1)}$ (n^2 nonzero entries of length $n^{1+o(1)}$). This cubic size makes it difficult to certify LU decompositions over the integers.

Despite the fact that we do not know, for integer matrix A, how to certify $A = LU$ in $n^{2+o(1)}$ time, the LU decomposition modulo a prime is useful for several certificates. This leads us to the definition of an LU residue system.

For given $m \times n$ matrix A, a *LU residue system* of rank r and length k is a nonempty sequence of k distinct triples

$(p_1, L_1, U_1), \dots, (p_k, L_k, U_k)$ where (1) p_i is a prime, and $p_i > p_{i-1}$ for $i > 1$, (2) L_i, U_i is a LU decomposition of rank r for A modulo p_i, and (3) the entries of U_i and L_i are normalized modulo p_i ($0 \leq x < p_i$ for each entry). The primary property of a LU residue system is that $A = L_i U_i$ mod p_i. The rest of the conditions are secondary properties (that the p_i are prime and distinct, that each decomposition is of rank r and that U_i, L_i of the stated triangular and full rank forms). The secondary properties are either inherent in the presentation of the LU residue system or may be checked in $rk (\max \log p_i)^{1+o(1)}$ time, which is $n^{2+o(1)}$, when $k = n^{1+o(1)}$ and the primes are bounded in length by $(\log\log \|A\|)^{1+o(1)}$. In the sequel we will implicitly assume any verification includes checking the secondary properties.

The next lemma states that LU residue systems cannot overstate matrix rank and can understate it only if the residue system is short.

Lemma 3. *Let A have rank r and a LU residue system of rank s and let $h = n((\log n)/2 + \log \|A\|)$, which bounds the bit length of any minor of A in absolute value. Then*

1. *$s \leq r$, and*

2. *if $s < r$, then the length of the LU residue system is bounded by h.*

PROOF. First observe that the leading principal $s \times s$ minor of A is the product of the leading $s \times s$ minors of L and U. By construction of the residue system, this minor is nonzero modulo a prime, hence nonzero over the integers. Thus $s \leq \text{rank}(A)$.

Second if A has rank $r > s$ then some $r \times r$ minor of A is nonzero. Only for primes p which divide this minor can A have a rank s LU decomposition modulo p. The number of such primes, thus the length of a rank s LU residue system, is bounded by the bit length of the minor which is at most h. $\square$

A matrix A has an LU decomposition of rank r if and only if A is of rank r and has *generic rank profile* (leading principal minors are nonzero up to the rank). If A does not have generic rank profile, then there are permutation matrices P and Q such that PAQ does have generic rank profile. Define a *general* LU residue system for A to be a pair of permutations P, Q together with a LU residue system for PAQ. We use this first as a certificate for matrix rank.

Theorem 2. *Let $A \in \mathbb{Z}^{n \times n}$ and let $h = n((\log n)/2 + \log \|A\|)$, which bounds the bit length of any minor of A in absolute value. There exists a general LU residue system of length $3h$ and with primes of bit length $(\log h)^{1+o(1)}$ which is a certificate for rank(A). The certificate occupies $n^{3+o(1)}(\log \|A\|)^{1+o(1)}$ space and can be verified in $n^{2+o(1)} \times (\log \|A\|)^{1+o(1)}$ time.*

PROOF. Certificate verification consists in picking one of the triples (p, L, U) and validating the decomposition $PAQ = LU$ mod p. By Lemma 3, a false certificate (wrong rank of the residue system) can have at most h triples for which the LU decomposition modulo p is valid. The probability of that is thus bounded by $1/3$. In the remaining cases, the probability of an erroneous verification of a bad LU decomposition is $1/p$ by Lemma 2. Then the probability of incorrectly accepting a bad certificate is less than $1/3 + (2/3)(1/p) \leq 1/2$ when $p > 5$.

The $3h$ primes in a good certificate may be chosen among the first $4h + 3$ primes (Just excluding 2,3,5, and those that divide the largest determinantal divisor, i.e., the greatest common divisor of the $r \times r$ minors, for matrix of rank r). These primes are all of bit length $(\log h)^{1+o(1)}$ since the m-th prime is $\leq m(\log_e(m) + \log\log_e(m) - 1/2)$ for $m \geq 20$ [13]. $\square$

Next we address determinant certification.

Theorem 3. *Let $A \in \mathbb{Z}^{n \times n}$ and let $h = n((\log n)/2 + \log \|A\|)$, which bounds the bit length of any minor of A in absolute value. There exists a certificate for the determinant of A of form $(\det(A), C)$, where C is a general LU residue system for A of length $3h + 3$ with the primes in C of length at most $(\log h)^{1+o(1)}$. The certificate occupies $n^{3+o(1)}(\log \|A\|)^{1+o(1)}$ space and can be verified in $n^{2+o(1)} \times (\log \|A\|)^{1+o(1)}$ time.*

PROOF. Let d denote the purported determinant in the certificate (d, C). If the rank of the residue system is less than n, then d must be 0 and validation consists in checking the rank as in the previous theorem. If the rank of the residue system is n, chose a triple (p, L, U) and verify the LU decomposition (zero equivalence of $PAQ - LU$) and also verify that $d = \prod_{i=1}^{n} U_{i,i} \mod p$. The probability of a bad zero equivalence is $1/p$.

Since d and the true determinant have bit length h, their difference has bit length at most $h + 1$. Only primes that divide this difference can pass the $d = \prod_{i=1}^{n} U_{i,i} \mod p$ for a false d. Since at most $h+1$ such primes are in the certificate, the probability of this is bounded by $1/3$. Thus the overall validation error probability is $1/p + ((p-1)/p)(1/3) \leq 1/2$ for $p \geq 5$.

The $3h + 3$ primes in a good certificate may be chosen among the first $4h + 5$ primes. We exclude 2, 3 and those that divide the determinant, so as to present a residue system of full rank n. The selected primes are thus of bit length $(\log h)^{1+o(1)}$. For the certificate size and the verification runtime, observe that reducing d modulo p and computing the mod p determinant of U may be done in $n^{1+o(1)}(\log h)^{1+o(1)}$, so the costs are dominated by the LU residue system and are as in Theorem 2. $\square$

We remark that if H is any bound for the minors of A with a fast verification, then $\log H$ may substitute for the bit length bound

$$h = n((\log n)/2 + \log \|A\|)$$

that we have used. Then $\log H$ substitutes for a factor of $n^{1+o(1)}(\log \|A\|)^{1+o(1)}$ in our resource bounds. The bound does have to be verified to ensure that the LU residue systems are long enough to defeat bad primes. An example of a class of matrices with non-Hadamard minors bounds verifiable in $n^{2+o(1)}$ time is the family of matrices with a constant number of rows of entries having bit length essentially n and with the remaining rows having entry lengths essentially constant.

4. CERTIFICATES BASED ON SIMILARITY

Definition 2. *A square matrix is in Frobenius normal form (rational canonical form) if it is the direct sum (block diagonal composition) of companion matrices companion(f_1), ..., companion(f_k) for monic polynomials $f_1(x), \ldots, f_k(x)$ such that f_i divides f_{i+1}, for all i with $1 \leq i \leq k - 1$.*

Fact 1. *A square matrix over a field is similar to one and only one matrix in Frobenius normal form [11, Corollary 2, p391, for example].*

We use similarity to Frobenius form modulo primes in the following certificates. For a matrix pair $A, B \in \mathbb{Z}^{n \times n}$, define a *similarity residue system* for B with respect to A of length k to be a sequence of k tuples $(p, S, T, \bar{B})$ with distinct primes p, and matrices $S, T, \bar{B} \in \mathbb{Z}_p^{n \times n}$ such that S is invertible with $T \equiv S^{-1}$, $B \equiv \bar{B}$, and $A \equiv S\bar{B}T$ (all modulo p).

Theorem 4. *Let $A \in \mathbb{Z}^{n \times n}$. There exists a certificate for the characteristic polynomial of A of the form (f, C), in which $f(x)$ is the characteristic polynomial of A and C is a similarity residue system for the Frobenius normal form of A of length $6h_A + 6$, where $h_A = n(1 + (\log n)/2 + \log \|A\|)$ bounds the coefficient lengths in the characteristic polynomial of A, and with the primes in C of bit length $n^{o(1)} \times (\log \|A\|)^{o(1)}$. The residue system occupies*

$$n^{3+o(1)}(\log \|A\|)^{o(1)} + n^{1+o(1)}(\log \|A\|)^{1+o(1)}$$

space and can be verified in $n^{2+o(1)}(\log \|A\|)^{1+o(1)}$ time.

PROOF. Let $c^A(x)$ denote the characteristic polynomial of A and let $h_A = n(1 + (\log n)/2 + \log \|A\|)$. First we bound the size of $c^A(x)$. The i-th coefficient is a sum of the principal $i \times i$ minors of A. There are $\binom{n}{i}$ such minors. Thus, as the sum of less than 2^n numbers of bit length at most $h = n((\log n)/2 + \log \|A\|)$, the coefficient bit length is bounded by $n + h$ and the n coefficients of $c^A(x)$ occupy at most $n^2 + nh$ space. Better bounds are possible, see, e.g., [5]. If a polynomial f is offered that is not the characteristic polynomial but has coefficients bounded in absolute value by h_A, then $g(x) = f(x) - c^A(x)$ has coefficients of bit length $1 + h_A$. For a prime p to lie will require that g is mapped to zero modulo p.

To verify that $f(x) = c^A(x)$, do the following.

1. Choose at random a tuple $(p, S, T, \bar{B})$ in the similarity residue system C. Verify the zero equivalence (Lemma 2) of $ST - I$ and $A - S\bar{B}T$ (both modulo p) in $O(n^2)$ time and with error probability bounded by $2/p$ (which is less than $1/6$ for $p \geq 13$).

2. Verify (deterministically) that each f_i divides the next. Multiply together the polynomials of the companion matrices comprising B, obtaining $f_p(x) = \prod f_i(x) \mod p$, Since the Frobenius form is unique, the product is necessarily the modulo p residue of $c^A(x)$. The product can be computed using $O(n^2)$ arithmetic operations modulo p, and each division is degree$(f_{i+1})^{1+o(1)}$ arithmetic operations, so the divisibility checks in total are in $n^{2+o(1)}(\log p)^{1+o(1)}$ as well.

3. Verify (deterministically) that $f(x) = f_p(x) \mod p$. Since the size of f is $n^{2+o(1)}(\log\|A\|)^{1+o(1)}$, f can be reduced modulo p in $n^{2+o(1)}(\log\|A\|)^{1+o(1)}$ time.

Since each $f_p(x)$ is a modular residue of $c^A(x)$ the certificate must have $f(x) = c^A(x) \mod p$ for each p in the residue system. Also $f(x)$ and $c^A(x)$ have coefficients of bit length at most h_A, so the bit length of the coefficients of $f(x) - c^A(x)$ is bounded by $k = 1 + h_A$. Thus this polynomial is zero modulo at most k primes. The certificate can successfully pass the verification with an incorrect purported characteristic polynomial only with probability at most $k/(6h_A + 6) = 1/6$.

Thus we may fail to detect a bad similarity with probability $1/6$. In the remaining $5/6$ cases we could fail to detect a bad determinant with probability $1/3$, for overall probability of failure bounded by $1/2$.

The first $6h_A$ primes larger than 11 can be used in the certificate, ensuring that they have bit length essentially-constant in n and $(\log\|A\|)$. $\square$

The *signature* of matrix is the triple (n_+, n_0, n_-) indicating the number of positive, zero, and negative eigenvalues, respectively.

Corollary 1. *Let A be an $n \times n$ symmetric matrix having minors bound H of bit length $\log H_A = n^{1+o(1)}$. The signature of A can be verified in $n^{2+o(1)}$ binary operations with a $n^{3+o(1)}$ bit space characteristic polynomial certificate. Thus the same certificate serves for positive or negative definiteness or semidefiniteness.*

PROOF. Verify the characteristic polynomial $c^A(x)$ with the certificate of Theorem 4. Since the matrix is symmetric, all eigenvalues are real. The number of zero eigenvalues is the largest n_0 such that x^{n_0} divides $c^A(x)$. For instance, if A has all its eigenvalues $\alpha \geq 0$, i.e., if A is positive semidefinite, then the polynomial

$$\prod_{\alpha > 0}(x + \alpha) = (-1)^{n-n_0}\frac{c^A(-x)}{(-x)^{n_0}} \qquad (1)$$

has all positive coefficients. The condition is obviously sufficient, since a polynomial (1) with all positive coefficients cannot have a positive root, so all roots $x = -\alpha$ are negative. $\square$

We finally turn to certificates for the Frobenius form.

Fact 2. *Let $A \in \mathbb{Z}^{n \times n}$ and let $G \in \mathbb{Z}^{n \times n}$ be in Frobenius form with $\|G\| \leq 2^n e^{n/2} n^{n/2}\|A\|^n$. If the Frobenius forms for $(A \mod p_i)$ are equal to $(G \mod p_i)$ for distinct primes $p_1, \ldots, p_t$ with $\prod_{i=1}^{t} p_i \geq 8^n e^n n^{2n}\|A\|^{3n}$, then G is the Frobenius form of A [4, Theorem 2.1].*

There are at most $n^{3+o(1)} \log\|A\|$ unlucky primes q for which the Frobenius forms of $(A \mod q)$ are not equal to the (Frobenius form of A) mod q [6]. The Frobenius form of A can be represented in $n^{2+o(1)} \log\|A\|$ binary space. The bound given in Fact 2 for $\|G\|$ is a valid bound for the Frobenius form of A [4, Lemma 2.1]. Note that any factor coefficient bound for the characteristic polynomial will work. The certificate for the Frobenius form of A has, as in the proof of Theorem 4, a matrix G in Frobenius form and similarity

residues system for it. One selects a random system and verifies the modular property of Fact 2 for that prime. If we choose $2s$ prime moduli p_i in such a way that the product of any subset of s of the moduli is $\geq 8^n e^n n^{2n}\|A\|^{3n}$, then for a false G of the required entry size bound, the Frobenius form of $(A \mod p_i)$ cannot be equal to $(G \mod p_i)$ for more than half of the moduli. Hence a false certificate will be rejected with probability $\geq 1/2$. From $2^s \geq 8^n e^n n^{2n}\|A\|^{3n}$ we deduce that an $s = n^{1+o(1)} \log\|A\|$ suffices.

Corollary 2. *Let $A \in \mathbb{Z}^{n \times n}$. The Frobenius form of A can be verified in $n^{2+o(1)}(\log\|A\|)^{1+o(1)}$ binary operations with an $n^{3+o(1)}(\log\|A\|)^{1+o(1)}$ bit space certificate.*

5. ALGORITHM-BASED CERTIFICATES OF SPACE $n^{e+o(1)}$ WITH e < 3

Integer matrix algorithms that have bit complexity $n^{\eta+o(1)}$ with $\eta < 3$, where η depends on the matrix multiplication complexity exponent $\omega > 2.37$ [1, 8, 15, 16], automatically lead to faster certificates. The algorithms can be randomized of the Las Vegas kind, always correct and probably fast. For example, consider Storjohann's integer matrix determinant [15] and rank [16] algorithms of Las Vegas bit complexity $n^{\omega+o(1)}(\log\|A\|)^{1+o(1)}$. A certificate records a successful (lucky) choice of the used random bits and all occurring integer matrix multiplications and their results. Since for a hypothetical matrix multiplication algorithm with $\omega = 2$, the algorithm requires $n^{2+o(1)}(\log\|A\|)^{1+o(1)}$ bit operations, the certificate bit space is no more than that. The validation procedure simply reruns the algorithm and verifies each matrix product by Freivalds's method in $n^{2+o(1)}l^{1+o(1)}$ bit operations, where l is the bit length of the occurring entries.

Note that if the rank r of A is $r = n^{2/\omega+o(1)}$, it can be computed by a Monte Carlo algorithm without the help of any certificate in $n^{2+o(1)}(\log\|A\|)^{1+o(1)}$ bit steps [14].

The situation for the characteristic polynomial and the Frobenius form is somewhat different. The fastest known algorithms, assuming $\omega = 2$, have to our knowledge complexity $n^{2+1/2+o(1)}(\log\|A\|)^{1+o(1)}$ [8, Table 6.1, Line 7], and indeed need that much storage: the algorithm computes $A^{\lceil\sqrt{n}\rceil}$ which occupies $n^{2+1/2+o(1)}(\log\|A\|)^{1+o(1)}$ bit space. However, they are Monte Carlo randomized algorithms ("always fast, probably correct") which makes independent certification difficult.

We have the following theorem.

Theorem 5. *We have certificates of binary space $n^{2+o(1)} \times (\log\|A\|)^{1+o(1)}$ for the rank and determinant of an integer matrix $A \in \mathbb{Z}^{n \times n}$ that can be validated by a Monte Carlo algorithm in $n^{2+o(1)}(\log\|A\|)^{1+o(1)}$ binary operations.*

Acknowledgments: The certificate for nonsingularity in Theorem 1 was told to us by Jürgen Gerhard when discussing with him our singularity certificate at ACA 2008 in Montreal. The referees have provided comments which have improved the presentation of the paper.

175

6. REFERENCES

[1] EBERLY, W., GIESBRECHT, M., AND VILLARD, G. On computing the determinant and Smith form of an integer matrix. In *Proc. 41stAnnual Symp. Foundations of Comp. Sci.* (Los Alamitos, California, 2000), IEEE Computer Society Press, pp. 675–685.

[2] FREIVALDS, R. Fast probabilistic algorithms. In *Mathematical Foundations of Computer Science 1979, Proceedings, 8th Symposium, Olomouc, Czechoslovakia, September 3-7, 1979* (1979), J. Becvár, Ed., Springer, pp. 57–69. Lecture Notes in Computer Science, vol. 74.

[3] GIESBRECHT, M., LOBO, A., AND SAUNDERS, B. D. Certifying inconsistency of sparse linear systems. In *ISSAC 98 Proc. 1998 Internat. Symp. Symbolic Algebraic Comput.* (New York, N. Y., 1998), O. Gloor, Ed., ACM Press, pp. 113–119.

[4] GIESBRECHT, M., AND STORJOHANN, A. Computing rational forms of integer matrices. *J. Symbolic Comput. 34*, 3 (Sept. 2002), 157–172.

[5] GOLDSTEIN, A. J., AND GRAHAM, R. L. A Hadamard-type bound on the coefficients of a determinant of polynomials. *SIAM Rev. 16* (1974), 394–395.

[6] KALTOFEN, E., KRISHNAMOORTHY, M. S., AND SAUNDERS, B. D. Fast parallel computation of Hermite and Smith forms of polynomial matrices. *SIAM J. Alg. Discrete Math. 8* (1987), 683–690. URL: http://www.math.ncsu.edu/~kaltofen/bibliography/87/KKS87.pdf

[7] KALTOFEN, E., LI, B., YANG, Z., AND ZHI, L. Exact certification of global optimality of approximate factorizations via rationalizing sums-of-squares with floating point scalars. In *ISSAC 2008* (New York, N. Y., 2008), D. Jeffrey, Ed., ACM Press, pp. 155–163. URL: http://www.math.ncsu.edu/~kaltofen/bibliography/08/KLYZ08.pdf

[8] KALTOFEN, E., AND VILLARD, G. On the complexity of computing determinants. *Computational Complexity 13*, 3-4 (2004), 91–130. URL: ttp://www.math.ncsu.edu/~kaltofen/bibliography/04/KaVi04_2697263.pdf

[9] KALTOFEN, E. L., LI, B., YANG, Z., AND ZHI, L. Exact certification in global polynomial optimization via sums-of-squares of rational functions with rational coefficients, Jan. 2009. Accepted for publication in J. Symbolic Comput. URL: http://www.math.ncsu.edu/~kaltofen/bibliography/09/KLYZ09.pdf

[10] KIMBREL, T., AND SINHA, R. K. A probabilistic algorithm for verifying matrix products using $O(n^2)$ time and $\log_2 n + O(1)$ random bits. *Inf. Process. Lett. 45*, 2 (1993), 107–110.

[11] MACLANE, S., AND BIRKHOFF, G. *Algebra, second edition*. Macmillan, 1979.

[12] MAY, J. P., Ed. *ISSAC 2009 Proc. 2009 Internat. Symp. Symbolic Algebraic Comput.* (New York, N. Y., 2009), ACM.

[13] ROSSER, J. B., AND SCHOENFELD, L. Approximate formulas of some functions of prime numbers. *Illinois J. Math. 6* (1962), 64–94.

[14] SAUNDERS, B. D., AND YOUSE, B. S. Large matrix, small rank. In May [12], pp. 317–324.

[15] STORJOHANN, A. The shifted number system for fast linear algebra on integer matrices. *J. Complexity 21*, 5 (2005), 609–650.

[16] STORJOHANN, A. Integer matrix rank certification. In May [12], pp. 333–340.

Supersparse Black Box Rational Function Interpolation*

Erich L. Kaltofen
Dept. of Mathematics, NCSU
Raleigh, North Carolina 27695-8205,USA
kaltofen@math.ncsu.edu www.kaltofen.us

Michael Nehring
Dept. of Mathematics, NCSU
Raleigh, North Carolina 27695-8205,USA
michaelnehring@yahoo.com

ABSTRACT

We present a method for interpolating a supersparse black-box rational function with rational coefficients, for example, a ratio of binomials or trinomials with very high degree. We input a blackbox rational function, as well as an upper bound on the number of non-zero terms and an upper bound on the degree. The result is found by interpolating the rational function modulo a small prime p, and then applying an effective version of Dirichlet's Theorem on primes in an arithmetic progression progressively lift the result to larger primes. Eventually we reach a prime number that is larger than the inputted degree bound and we can recover the original function exactly. In a variant, the initial prime p is large, but the exponents of the terms are known modulo larger and larger factors of $p - 1$.

The algorithm, as presented, is conjectured to be polylogarithmic in the degree, but exponential in the number of terms. Therefore, it is very effective for rational functions with a small number of non-zero terms, such as the ratio of binomials, but it quickly becomes ineffective for a high number of terms.

The algorithm is oblivious to whether the numerator and denominator have a common factor. The algorithm will recover the sparse form of the rational function, rather than the reduced form, which could be dense. We have experimentally tested the algorithm in the case of under 10 terms in numerator and denominator combined and observed its conjectured high efficiency.

Categories and Subject Descriptors

I.1.2 [**Computing Methodologies**]: Symbolic and Algebraic Manipulation—*Algorithms*

General Terms: algorithms, experimentation

Keywords: lacunary polynomials, Cauchy interpolation, sparse solution vectors

---

*This research was supported in part by the National Science Foundation under Grants CCF-0830347, CCF-0514585 and DMS-0532140.

1. INTRODUCTION

A supersparse (lacunary) polynomial g over the integers $\mathbb{Z}$ in n variables with τ terms is represented as a sum (list) of monomials $g(x_1, \ldots, x_n) = \sum_{i=1}^{\tau} c_i \prod_{j=1}^{n} x_j^{e_{i,j}}$ where each monomial is represented as a coefficient $c_i \neq 0$ and the term degree vector $[\ldots, e_{i,j}, \ldots]$. The bit storage size, using "dense" binary numbers for the $e_{i,j}$, is $O(\sum_i \log(|c_i| + 2) + \sum_{i,j} \log(e_{i,j} + 2))$, hence proportional to the *logarithm* of the total degree $\deg(g) = \max_i \sum_j e_{i,j}$. Although several problems in polynomial algebra, such as greatest common divisor and root finding in a finite field, are NP-hard with respect to this compact size measure [26, 22], important other problems such as computing low degree factors and sparse roots have polynomial time algorithms [3, 23, 16, 4, 8, 9].

Here we consider the problem of interpolating a fraction of two supersparse polynomials $f = g/h$ over $\mathbb{Z}$. Again we seek algorithms that have polynomial running time in the supersparse size of the interpolant polynomials g and h. Since the values of a supersparse polynomial at integer points may have exponentially many bits in the size of the polynomial, we shall assume that the values can be obtained modulo any large prime p. That is, we have an algorithm ("black box") for evaluating f at *any* point modulo p. If the denominator h evaluates to 0, the black box returns ∞. This idea is illustrated below:

$$\gamma \in \mathbb{Z}_p^n, \ p \longrightarrow \boxed{} \xrightarrow{\quad f(\gamma) = \left(\frac{g}{h}(\gamma) \bmod p\right) \in \mathbb{Z}_p \cup \{\infty\} \quad}$$

$$g, h \in \mathbb{Z}[x_1, \ldots, x_n]$$

Note that a straight-line program representation for g/h [13] provides such a black box. We further assume that we have accurate (but not necessarily tight) bounds on the number of terms, the degree, and the coefficients.

Dense rational function interpolation goes back to Cauchy. Multivariate sparse rational function interpolation with algorithms that are polynomial in the degrees and number of variables and terms in g and h are presented in [13, 18, 21]. An important ingredient are Zippel's or Ben-Or and Tiwari's sparse multivariate *polynomial* interpolation algorithms (see, e.g., [17] and the references there). A variant of Ben-Or and Tiwari's polynomial interpolation modulo large primes p, where $p - 1$ have only small prime factors and hence one has a fast discrete logarithm [27], was given by Kaltofen in 1988 (see [14, 15]). Already there we observed that by Kronecker's substitution the multivariate problem reduces to the univariate problem (see Section 7.1 below). In [5] the supersparse polynomial interpolation problem is solved by Chinese remaindering the symmetric functions of the term exponents modulo small primes without the need of special primes.

Our algorithm consists of two major steps. The first step is to recover the rational function modulo a small prime. The second step is then to lift that rational function to progressively larger primes. The first step constitutes computing a sparse null space vector modulo a small prime of a Vandermonde-like matrix. At this time, we can execute this step efficiently only if there are a few terms. Unlike Cauchy interpolation, the critical input of this algorithm is a bound on the number of terms, not a bound on the degrees. If the bound is sufficiently tight, then the algorithm will recover a sparse form of the rational function (see Section 7.2).

A surprising property is that our algorithm recovers the sparse form of the function f even if $\mathrm{GCD}(g, h)$ is non-trivial. For instance, our algorithm can reconstruct the sparse fraction representation $(x^{2^\delta} - 1)/(x - 1)$ from a black box of the polynomial $\sum_{0 \le i < 2^\delta} x^i$ in polynomial time in δ. After learning about our result, [10] considered the problem of the sparsest polynomial multiple when the denominator of the fractional representation *of a polynomial* can be dense.

Our methods are adaptable to supersparse vector rational function recovery in the sense of [25], or computing a sparsest shift for the supersparse rational function in the sense of [6, 7], but we do not discuss those generalization here. We will focus on the univariate case, as the multivariate case is handled via Kronecker substitution.

Notation: For a prime p we have

$$x^e \equiv x \cdot x^{(e-1) \bmod (p-1)} \pmod{x^p - x}, \quad \text{for} \quad e \ge 1, \quad (1)$$

which preserves the sparsity of a polynomial. For our evaluations $\gamma \in \mathbb{Z}_p$ we have $\gamma^p = \gamma$ and we shall take the liberty to omit $x^p - x$ from our polynomial congruences such as $x^p \equiv x \pmod{p}$. Note that in (1) the exponent $e \bmod (p-1)$ is represented in a residue system $\{1, \ldots, p-1\}$.

Outline of approach: Suppose $f(x) = g(x)/h(x)$ is the supersparse fraction. Our algorithm chooses a relatively small random prime p and constructs a sparse fraction modulo $x^p - x$ by evaluating at $\gamma \in \mathbb{Z}_p$ and computing a sparse null space vector in the arising linear system

$$\left(g(x) \bmod (x^p - x) \right)(\gamma) \equiv f(\gamma) \left(h(x) \bmod (x^p - x) \right)(\gamma),$$

(see Section 2). We then lift the exponents from one prime p to the next prime p' by ensuring that $p' - 1$ is divisible by $p - 1$ so that the new exponent candidates in (1) are restricted to

$$1 + ((e-1) \bmod (p-1)) + i(p-1), \ 0 \le i < (p'-1)/(p-1). \quad (2)$$

(see Section 3). Such prime sequences exist due to effective versions of Dirichlet's Theorem on primes in an arithmetic progression (see Section 3.1). Once the term exponents are known, the rational coefficients are recovered by rational vector recovery. Alternatively, we may reduce the range of (2) to 2 choices by evaluating at powers of γ in the manner of the Silver-Pohlig/Hellman discrete logarithm algorithm (see Section 4).

2. COMPUTING A MODULAR IMAGE OF THE SUPERSPARSE FRACTION

First, we compute the fraction modulo a small prime. In Section 3 we enlarge that modulus.

2.1 A System of Linear Equations

Since f has a representation as a rational function, $f(x) = g(x)/h(x)$ let f be represented as follows:

$$f(x) = \left(\sum_{i=0}^d a_i x^{i+1} \right) \Big/ \left(\sum_{i=0}^d b_i x^{i+1} \right).$$

Note that the numerator and denominator are divisible by x, which does not affect the sparsity. There may be further common factors. The black box allows us to evaluate f at any point and get the value modulo p. Modulo p, $\gamma^p = \gamma$, so one only needs to concern one's self with the exponents from 1 to $p-1$ in the numerator and denominator before any wrap-around occurs. Note that there is no constant term in the numerator or denominator because we multiplied numerator and denominator by x to remove the constant term, and no other exponent maps to the constant term. This gives us the following:

$$f(x) \equiv \left(\sum_{i=1}^{p-1} \alpha_i x^i \right) \Big/ \left(\sum_{i=1}^{p-1} \beta_i x^i \right) \pmod{x^p - x, p}.$$

Clearing the denominators and subtracting the left side from the right yields the following.

$$\sum_{i=1}^{p-1} \alpha_i x^i - f(x) \times \left(\sum_{i=1}^{p-1} \beta_i x^i \right) \equiv 0 \pmod{x^p - x, p}$$

As in [21], for each evaluation of $x = \gamma$, $\gamma \in 1, 2, \ldots, p-1$, this produces a linear equation. Indeed, even for values for which the function is undefined there is a linear equation for the denominator. The resulting system of equations has the form $A = [V \mid DW]$, where V and W are Vandermonde matrices and D is a diagonal matrix. The matrix V will have a row of zeros whenever the residue of evaluation causes the function to be undefined. The matrix D has the values of the function f along the diagonal, and a 1 where for rows that correspond to a residue γ that makes $f(\gamma)$ undefined. The coefficient list of the rational function is a vector in the null space of that matrix. Unfortunately, for any prime p there are only $p - 1$ residues to work with and $2p - 2$ unknowns. There are only $p - 1$ useful residues, since 0 provides no useful information because we know in advance that the function will be undefined at 0. It is easy to see that the resulting matrix has full rank and therefore the null space has dimension $p - 1$. We wish to find a sparse vector in that null space. Finding the sparsest vector in a linear subspace is in general NP-hard [2], and we have observed no obvious property in the resulting null space that would make it much easier to find a sparse null space vector. It should be noted however if $g(x)/h(x)$ is a rational representation of the given function, then so is $x \times g(x)/(x \times h(x))$, $x^2 \times g(x)/(x^2 \times h(x))$, and so forth. This means, assuming that no unexpected wrap-around occurs, there will be $p-1$ sparse null space vectors, where one vector is the same as the other, except that the coefficients are shifted to the right and then wrapped around appropriately. That means that the null space contains many very sparse vectors and thus one can hope that they will not be too difficult to find.

2.2 Finding a Sparse Vector

The problem of finding the sparsest null space vector for any given matrix has been shown to be NP-hard. Due to the nature of the matrix being investigated, it may be possible to create an algorithm to find sparse vectors in the null space by exploiting the structure of the matrix and null space. However, we have not yet found such an algorithm.

The simplest exhaustive search technique is pick τ many columns and guess that those columns correspond to the non-zero coefficients. Then, we look in the null space to see if there is a vector where all other entries are zero. If so, then we have found a vector with the desired sparsity. If not, then we have to pick a different set of τ columns. We do this until we have searched all possible combinations. However, in practice, this technique is not as fast the following technique.

The current strategy, which is effective for a small number of non-zero terms, is to guess new linear equations. We currently have $p-1$ equations and $2p-2$ unknowns. However, we are told that most of the coefficients are zero. A coefficient being zero represents an additional linear equation. We are not told, however, which specific coefficients are zero. Therefore, the strategy is to pick at least $p-1$ coefficients at random and set them equal to zero. One may have to pick more if any unexpected equation dependencies occur. We pick enough coefficients that the dimension of the resulting null space is precisely 1. If we only picked only correct coefficients, then the null space vector will indeed be our desired sparse null space vector. If, however, we set coefficients equal to zero that are in fact non-zero, then the resulting null space vector will be an incorrect dense vector. We repeat this process until we find a vector whose density is no higher than the inputted bound. If we exhaust all combinations, then we conclude the bound is incorrect and return FAIL.

This process is exponential in the number of non-zero terms. We can note that one can decrease the chances of setting a non-zero coefficient to zero by picking a large p, because the pool of zero coefficients will increase, but the number of non-zero coefficients remains the same, thus decreasing the chances that we mistaken try to set a non-zero coefficient to zero. However, increasing p will also increase the computational cost of the algorithm.

At this point it should be noted that this process is more likely to find the sparsest vector, as opposed to a less sparse vector. The process forces certain coefficients to be zero, and determines the remaining coefficients. If there is a very sparse form, and a somewhat less sparse form, the process is more likely to hit a non-zero coefficient of the less sparse form, because it has more non-zero coefficients to hit.

Take for example the following function, mod 11, in the following two forms:

$$\frac{x^9 - 1}{x - 1} = \frac{x^8 + x^7 + x^6 + x^5 + x^4 + x^3 + x^2 + x + 1}{1}.$$

The first sparse form has only 4 non-zero terms, and the second model has 10 non-zero terms. So, in randomly setting coefficients to zero, the process is more likely to eliminate a coefficient corresponding to one of the 10 non-zero terms in the dense form than it is to eliminate a coefficient corresponding to one of the 4 non-zero terms in the sparse form. Therefore, this algorithm is unaware of whether the numerator and denominator have a common factor, and it will generally find the sparsest form before it finds other forms.

2.3 Uniqueness of the Sparsest Vector

One concern that this algorithm brings up is whether the sparsest vector in the null space is the vector we desire. In fact, this is not always the case. If $g(x)/h(x)$ and $\bar{g}(x)/\bar{h}(x)$ are both rational functions in the null space of the given matrix, then so is the following:

$$\left(\lambda g(x) + \bar{\lambda}\bar{g}(x)\right) \Big/ \left(\lambda h(x) + \bar{\lambda}\bar{h}(x)\right), \quad \lambda, \bar{\lambda} \in \mathbb{Z}.$$

So, if there are two rational functions in the null space that have the same monomials as support, then it would

be possible to eliminate one of those monomials by taking a linear combination of the two rational functions, thus resulting in a sparser function. Every rational function has a sparsest representation over the rational numbers, and that sparsest representation corresponds to a sparse representation modulo any given prime. If there is another vector in the null space with the same support, then a linear combination would result in a sparser vector for that prime. Also, for a finite number of primes, there is also the possibility that two non-zero monomials will collide, either to a single monomial, which is easy to deal with, or they may destructively collide to zero, which we have to deal with probabilistically later.

It is possible to construct examples where a given rational function has a sparser representation modulo a given prime. Here is one example to illustrate what happens. Take the rational function $(x^{34} + 4x)/(2x - 3x^{40})$ If we multiply the numerator and denominator by x^3, we get the same rational function in another form, $(x^{37} + 4x^4)/(2x^4 - 3x^{43})$. Now, we can look at both those rational functions modulo 7. Recall that modulo 7, the exponents wrap around modulo 6, so the functions are the following two functions, respectively: $(x^4 + 4x)/(2x - 3x^4)$ and $(4x^4 + x)/(2x^4 - 3x)$. We can now take the same linear combination of the numerator and denominator and get another equivalent rational function

$$\frac{(x^4 + 4x) - 4(4x^4 + x)}{(2x - 3x^4) - 4(2x^4 - 3x)} = \frac{-15x^4}{14x - 11x^4} \equiv \frac{-x^4}{3x^4} \bmod 7.$$

So, for certain rational functions, the sparsest representation over the integers may not be the sparsest modulo a certain prime. While we do not currently have a proof of this, it seems unlikely that there are many, if any, rational functions that have a sparser representation modulo many prime numbers. In any case, the valid sparse solution will be among the sparse candidate vectors.

2.4 An Example

Let $f(x)$ be a blackbox of the function
$$f(x) = (8x^{882704} - 3x^{6098})/(5x^{1048576} + 1).$$
We want there to be no constant terms, so $f(x)$ is the same as the following rational function, except at the point $x = 0$,
$$(8x^{882705} - 3x^{6099})/(5x^{1048577} + x).$$
We choose the prime $p = 13$, so all exponent wrap-around will occur modulo 12. We now evaluate this box black at all the residues modulo 13, except for 0.

x	1	2	3	4	5	6	7	8	9	10	11	12
$f(x)$	3	7	2	4	4	1	1	4	4	2	7	3

This data allows us to set up a system of linear equations, which is represented by the null space of the following matrix. The matrix

$$\begin{bmatrix}
1 & 1 & 1 & 1 & 1 & 1 & 1 & 1 & 1 & 1 & 1 & 1 & 10 & 10 & 10 & 10 & 10 & 10 & 10 & 10 & 10 & 10 & 10 & 10 \\
2 & 4 & 8 & 3 & 6 & 12 & 11 & 9 & 5 & 10 & 7 & 1 & 12 & 11 & 9 & 5 & 10 & 7 & 1 & 2 & 4 & 8 & 3 & 6 \\
3 & 9 & 1 & 3 & 9 & 1 & 3 & 9 & 1 & 3 & 9 & 1 & 7 & 8 & 11 & 7 & 8 & 11 & 7 & 8 & 11 & 7 & 8 & 11 \\
4 & 3 & 12 & 9 & 10 & 1 & 4 & 3 & 12 & 9 & 10 & 1 & 10 & 1 & 4 & 3 & 12 & 9 & 10 & 1 & 4 & 3 & 12 & 9 \\
5 & 12 & 8 & 1 & 5 & 12 & 8 & 1 & 5 & 12 & 8 & 1 & 6 & 4 & 7 & 9 & 6 & 4 & 7 & 9 & 6 & 4 & 7 & 9 \\
6 & 10 & 8 & 9 & 2 & 12 & 7 & 3 & 5 & 4 & 11 & 1 & 7 & 3 & 5 & 4 & 11 & 1 & 6 & 10 & 8 & 9 & 2 & 12 \\
7 & 10 & 5 & 9 & 11 & 12 & 6 & 3 & 8 & 4 & 2 & 1 & 6 & 3 & 8 & 4 & 2 & 1 & 7 & 10 & 5 & 9 & 11 & 12 \\
8 & 12 & 5 & 1 & 8 & 12 & 5 & 1 & 8 & 12 & 5 & 1 & 7 & 4 & 6 & 9 & 7 & 4 & 6 & 9 & 7 & 4 & 6 & 9 \\
9 & 3 & 1 & 9 & 3 & 1 & 9 & 3 & 1 & 9 & 3 & 1 & 3 & 1 & 9 & 3 & 1 & 9 & 3 & 1 & 9 & 3 & 1 & 9 \\
10 & 9 & 12 & 3 & 4 & 1 & 10 & 9 & 12 & 3 & 4 & 1 & 6 & 8 & 2 & 7 & 5 & 11 & 6 & 8 & 2 & 7 & 5 & 11 \\
11 & 4 & 5 & 3 & 7 & 12 & 2 & 9 & 8 & 10 & 6 & 1 & 1 & 11 & 4 & 5 & 3 & 7 & 12 & 2 & 9 & 8 & 10 & 6 \\
12 & 1 & 12 & 1 & 12 & 1 & 12 & 1 & 12 & 1 & 12 & 1 & 3 & 10 & 3 & 10 & 3 & 10 & 3 & 10 & 3 & 10 & 3 & 10
\end{bmatrix}$$

has the form $[V\,D\,W]$, where V and W are Vandermonde and D is a diagonal matrix whose values are the negative of the function values.

We wish to find a sparse vector in the null space of that matrix. The matrix has currently column dimension 24 and a 12 dimensional null space. The current strategy is to randomly add equations where we set one coefficient equal to zero. Since the rational function is sparse, we know that we have a reasonable chance of only adding correct equations. For visual illustrative purposes, rather than adding new rows to the matrix, we set the values in the corresponding columns to zero in

$$\begin{bmatrix}
0 & 1 & 0 & 0 & 0 & 1 & 1 & 0 & 1 & 1 & 1 & 0 & 0 & 0 & 10 & 0 & 10 & 0 & 10 & 10 & 10 & 0 & 0 & 10 \\
0 & 4 & 0 & 0 & 0 & 12 & 11 & 0 & 5 & 10 & 7 & 0 & 0 & 0 & 9 & 0 & 10 & 0 & 1 & 2 & 4 & 0 & 0 & 6 \\
0 & 9 & 0 & 0 & 0 & 1 & 3 & 0 & 1 & 3 & 9 & 0 & 0 & 0 & 11 & 0 & 8 & 0 & 7 & 8 & 11 & 0 & 0 & 11 \\
0 & 3 & 0 & 0 & 0 & 1 & 4 & 0 & 12 & 9 & 10 & 0 & 0 & 0 & 4 & 0 & 12 & 0 & 10 & 1 & 4 & 0 & 0 & 9 \\
0 & 12 & 0 & 0 & 0 & 12 & 8 & 0 & 5 & 12 & 8 & 0 & 0 & 0 & 7 & 0 & 6 & 0 & 7 & 9 & 6 & 0 & 0 & 9 \\
0 & 10 & 0 & 0 & 0 & 12 & 7 & 0 & 5 & 4 & 11 & 0 & 0 & 0 & 5 & 0 & 11 & 0 & 6 & 10 & 8 & 0 & 0 & 12 \\
0 & 10 & 0 & 0 & 0 & 12 & 6 & 0 & 8 & 4 & 2 & 0 & 0 & 0 & 8 & 0 & 2 & 0 & 7 & 10 & 5 & 0 & 0 & 12 \\
0 & 12 & 0 & 0 & 0 & 12 & 5 & 0 & 8 & 12 & 5 & 0 & 0 & 0 & 6 & 0 & 7 & 0 & 6 & 9 & 7 & 0 & 0 & 9 \\
0 & 3 & 0 & 0 & 0 & 1 & 9 & 0 & 1 & 9 & 3 & 0 & 0 & 0 & 9 & 0 & 10 & 0 & 3 & 1 & 9 & 0 & 0 & 9 \\
0 & 9 & 0 & 0 & 0 & 1 & 10 & 0 & 12 & 3 & 4 & 0 & 0 & 0 & 2 & 0 & 5 & 0 & 6 & 8 & 2 & 0 & 0 & 11 \\
0 & 4 & 0 & 0 & 0 & 12 & 2 & 0 & 8 & 10 & 6 & 0 & 0 & 0 & 4 & 0 & 3 & 0 & 12 & 2 & 9 & 0 & 0 & 6 \\
0 & 1 & 0 & 0 & 0 & 1 & 12 & 0 & 12 & 1 & 12 & 0 & 0 & 0 & 3 & 0 & 3 & 0 & 3 & 10 & 3 & 0 & 0 & 10
\end{bmatrix}$$

Now the null space of that matrix, ignoring the trivial null space vectors is the following:

$$[0\ 0\ 0\ 0\ 0\ 0\ 5\ 0\ 6\ 0\ 2\ 0\ \mathbf{0}\ 0\ 7\ 0\ 7\ 0\ 11\ 0\ 1\ 0\ 0\ 0]^T.$$

The bold entries correspond to the entries that we forced to be zero with our random equations. The vector has seven non-zero entries, instead of the required four non-zero entries. So we must try again with different columns, illustrated in the matrix below. Again, we look at the non-trivial null space vector of the matrix. Now it is the following:

$$[0\ 0\ 0\ 0\ 0\ 8\ 0\ 0\ 0\ 0\ 0\ 10\ \mathbf{0}\ 5\ 0\ 0\ 0\ 0\ 0\ 0\ 0\ 1\ 0\ 0]^T.$$

There are four non-zero entries in the new null space. That is the desired sparsity, so we selected correct columns and found a sparse vector. This vector corresponds to the rational function $\hat{f}(x) = (8x^6 + 10x^{12}) / (5x^2 + x^{10})$. The following relationship holds, where the exponents on the right are mapped according to $x^{13} \equiv x$, and the coefficients are taken modulo 13: $\hat{f}(x) \equiv f(x) \times x^{10}/x^{10} \bmod (x^{1}3 - x, 13)$.

$$\begin{bmatrix}
0 & 0 & 1 & 0 & 1 & 1 & 0 & 1 & 0 & 0 & 1 & 1 & 0 & 10 & 0 & 0 & 10 & 0 & 10 & 0 & 10 & 10 & 0 & 0 \\
0 & 0 & 8 & 0 & 6 & 12 & 0 & 9 & 0 & 0 & 7 & 1 & 0 & 11 & 0 & 0 & 10 & 0 & 1 & 0 & 4 & 8 & 0 & 0 \\
0 & 0 & 1 & 0 & 9 & 1 & 0 & 9 & 0 & 0 & 9 & 1 & 0 & 8 & 0 & 0 & 8 & 0 & 7 & 0 & 11 & 7 & 0 & 0 \\
0 & 0 & 12 & 0 & 10 & 1 & 0 & 3 & 0 & 0 & 10 & 1 & 0 & 1 & 0 & 0 & 12 & 0 & 10 & 0 & 4 & 3 & 0 & 0 \\
0 & 0 & 8 & 0 & 5 & 12 & 0 & 1 & 0 & 0 & 8 & 1 & 0 & 4 & 0 & 0 & 6 & 0 & 7 & 0 & 6 & 4 & 0 & 0 \\
0 & 0 & 8 & 0 & 2 & 12 & 0 & 3 & 0 & 0 & 11 & 1 & 0 & 3 & 0 & 0 & 11 & 0 & 6 & 0 & 8 & 9 & 0 & 0 \\
0 & 0 & 5 & 0 & 11 & 12 & 0 & 3 & 0 & 0 & 2 & 1 & 0 & 3 & 0 & 0 & 2 & 0 & 7 & 0 & 5 & 9 & 0 & 0 \\
0 & 0 & 5 & 0 & 8 & 12 & 0 & 1 & 0 & 0 & 5 & 1 & 0 & 4 & 0 & 0 & 7 & 0 & 6 & 0 & 7 & 4 & 0 & 0 \\
0 & 0 & 1 & 0 & 3 & 1 & 0 & 3 & 0 & 0 & 3 & 1 & 0 & 1 & 0 & 0 & 1 & 0 & 3 & 0 & 9 & 3 & 0 & 0 \\
0 & 0 & 12 & 0 & 4 & 1 & 0 & 9 & 0 & 0 & 4 & 1 & 0 & 8 & 0 & 0 & 5 & 0 & 6 & 0 & 2 & 7 & 0 & 0 \\
0 & 0 & 5 & 0 & 7 & 12 & 0 & 9 & 0 & 0 & 6 & 1 & 0 & 11 & 0 & 0 & 3 & 0 & 12 & 0 & 9 & 8 & 0 & 0 \\
0 & 0 & 12 & 0 & 12 & 1 & 0 & 1 & 0 & 0 & 12 & 1 & 0 & 10 & 0 & 0 & 3 & 0 & 3 & 0 & 3 & 10 & 0 & 0
\end{bmatrix}$$

3. LIFTING THE MODULAR IMAGE

3.1 Dirichlet's Theorem

Dirichlet's Theorem on Arithmetic Progressions states that for relatively prime numbers a and n, there are infinitely many prime numbers in the Arithmetic Progression $a + \lambda n$, $\lambda \in \mathbb{Z}_{\geq 0}$. In the lifting step that follows, we will need a sequence of primes of the form $p_1, p_2, p_3, \ldots, p_k$, where $p_i - 1$ divides $p_{i+1} - 1$. That is, $p_{i+1} = r_i(p_i - 1) + 1$. Such a prime is guaranteed to exist by Dirichlet's theorem, since $p_i - 1$ and 1 have no common factors. Since this particular sequence of primes will prove to be inconsequential in the final version of the algorithm, we will not discuss the distribution of such primes (see Section 4.1 instead). However, we will present a quick example, starting with 13, the prime we used in our example rational function.

i	1	2	3	4	5	6	7
p_i	13	37	73	433	1297	2593	10369
p_{i+1}	37	73	433	1297	2593	10369	72577
r_i	3	2	6	3	2	4	7

Digression: Our sequence construction above leads to the following, possibly new, number theoretic function: define $\kappa_p(n)$ as the minimum over all prime sequences starting at p and ending above n of the maximum of all multipliers in each sequence. For instance, we have the following minimal multipliers.

n	2^{10}	2^{20}	2^{40}	2^{80}	2^{160}	2^{320}	2^{640}	2^{1280}
$\kappa_2(n)$	4	5	15	16	49	53	132	224

3.2 Lifting to Larger Primes – The Easy Way

Assume that we know the rational function modulo a small prime p_1. We construct a sequence of primes $\{p_1, p_2, p_3, \ldots, p_k\}$ such that $(p_i - 1)$ divides $(p_{i+1} - 1)$ for $1 \leq i \leq k-1$ and p_k is larger than the upper bound on the degree. Furthermore, define $r_i = (p_{i+1} - 1)/(p_i - 1)$. Such a sequence can be constructed according to Dirichlet's Theorem.

As above, we remember that $x^p \equiv x \bmod x^p - x$. Specifically, if we know the rational function mod p_i, we know the exponents of the terms modulo $p_i - 1$. Suppose, for example, that one exponent is congruent to $m \bmod (p_i - 1)$. Since $p_i - 1$ divides $p_{i+1} - 1$, that is $p_{i+1} - 1 = r_i(p_i - 1)$, we know that there are precisely r_i possibilities for each exponent modulo $p_{i+1} - 1$. In our case, those possibilities are

$$m, m + (p_i - 1), m + 2(p_i - 1), \ldots, m + (r_i - 1)(p_i - 1). \quad (3)$$

This means if there are τ_i known exponents modulo $x^{p_i} - x$, then there are $\tau_i \cdot r_i$ unknown exponents modulo $x^{p_{i+1}} - x$. At this point we know that the coefficients of all other terms must be zero. Therefore, as above, we can construct a system of linear equations, but this time we have only $\tau_i \cdot r_i$ many unknowns, but up to p_{i+1} equations. Let $\{\alpha_1, \ldots, \alpha_{d_1}\}$ be the computed list of possible numerator exponents modulo $x^{p_{i+1}} - x$ and $\{\beta_1, \ldots, \beta_{d_2}\}$ be the list of computed exponents of possible denominator exponents modulo $x^{p_{i+1}} - x$. Then, the following equation holds:

$$a_1 x^{\alpha_1} + a_2 x^{\alpha_2} + \cdots + a_{d_1} x^{\alpha_{d_1}}$$
$$- f(x)(b_1 x^{\beta_1} + b_2 x^{\beta_2} + \cdots + b_{d_2} x^{\beta_{d_2}}) \equiv 0 \pmod{p_{i+1}}.$$

For every value of $\gamma \in \mathbb{Z}_{p_{i+1}}$ this yields of a linear equation with unknowns $\{a_1, \ldots, a_{d_1}, b_1, \ldots, b_{d_2}\}$. It should be noted at this point that not all p_{i+1} equations are needed to find the null space vector.

We can bound the number of new equations by proceeding as in [21, Section 4.1]. Assume that $g(x)/h(x)$ and $\overline{g}(x)/\overline{h}(x)$ are two different rational functions whose coefficient vectors lie in the null space of the matrix. Then $g(x)\overline{h}(x) - \overline{g}(x)h(x)$ evaluates to zero for every residue that we used in building the null space. That is to say that vector representing $g(x)\overline{h}(x) - \overline{g}(x)h(x)$ is in the null space of a Vandermonde-like matrix, with the difference being that we only consider a limited number of powers of x, specifically, those that could occur in $g(x)\overline{h}(x)$, of which there are at most $d_1 d_2$ many. Therefore, it is possible that picking two separate residues will not generate a unique row in the Vandermonde-like matrix. For example, if the only powers we are considering are x^2 and x^{10} modulo 13, then the residues 4 and 9 would both generate the row $[3, 9]$. However, this Vandermonde-like matrix is a submatrix of the full Vandermonde matrix, which is non-singular, and thus by adding sufficient rows (corresponding to residues), we can also insure that our

Vandermonde-like matrix is non-singular. If γ is a primitive root of unity modulo p_{i+1}, then picking the residues γ, γ^2, γ^3, ... will ensure that no row is repeated until all possible rows have been exhausted. Once we have $d_1 d_2$ many unique rows, then the Vandermonde-like matrix will have as many rows as columns, and will be non-singular. Since $g(x)\overline{h}(x) - \overline{g}(x)h(x)$ will lie in the null space of a non-singular matrix, that indicates that $g(x)\overline{h}(x) - \overline{g}(x)h(x) = 0$, and therefore $g(x)/h(x) = \overline{g}(x)/\overline{h}(x)$ up to a common factor in the numerator and denominator. As we see in the following example, having a common factor in the numerator and denominator is not bad, and in fact is expected and can be dealt with.

3.3 An Example For the Lifting Step

We will return to our previous example. Recall, we have a blackbox for the function

$$f(x) = (8x^{882704} - 3x^{6098})/(5x^{1048576} + 1).$$

In the initial step, we recovered this function as

$$\hat{f}(x) = (8x^6 + 10x^{12})/(5x^2 + x^{10}).$$

And we noted the following equality, where the exponents on the right are mapped according to $x^{13} = x$, and the coefficients are taken mod 13, $\hat{f}(x) \equiv f(x) \times x^{10}/x^{10} \bmod 13$. Note that $13-1$ divides $37-1$ and that $(37-1)/(13-1) = 3$. The exponent wrap-around occurs modulo 12. In our desired representation modulo 37, the exponent wrap-around will be modulo 36. The numerator exponents recovered from the first step are 6 and 12, and the denominator exponents are 2 and 10.

Numerator exponent pool: $\{6, 6+12, 6+24, 12, 12+12, 12+24\} = \{6, 18, 30, 12, 24, 36\}$.
Denominator exponent pool: $\{2, 2+12, 2+24, 10, 10+12, 10+24\} = \{2, 14, 26, 10, 22, 34\}$.
The remaining $36 - 6 = 30$ coefficients corresponding to other powers are known to be zero. Therefore, we essentially already have 60 linear equations, since we know that 60 coefficients are zero. Furthermore, we can garner 36 additional linear equations by evaluating the black box. Since there are only 72 unknowns, we will be able to determine the desired null space vector. For simplicity we will set up a system with only 12 unknowns corresponding to the 12 possible non-zero coefficients listed above. We now sample our blackbox to get some linear equations, as represented by the matrix below:

$$
\begin{bmatrix}
1 & 1 & 1 & 1 & 1 & 1 & 30 & 30 & 30 & 30 & 30 & 30 \\
27 & 26 & 36 & 10 & 11 & 1 & 1 & 34 & 26 & 33 & 10 & 7 \\
26 & 10 & 1 & 26 & 10 & 1 & 31 & 2 & 14 & 20 & 29 & 15 \\
26 & 10 & 1 & 26 & 10 & 1 & 10 & 16 & 26 & 12 & 1 & 9 \\
11 & 10 & 36 & 26 & 27 & 1 & 8 & 17 & 6 & 22 & 23 & 35 \\
36 & 1 & 36 & 1 & 36 & 1 & 8 & 8 & 8 & 8 & 8 & 8 \\
26 & 10 & 1 & 26 & 10 & 1 & 28 & 4 & 21 & 3 & 25 & 30 \\
36 & 1 & 36 & 1 & 36 & 1 & 18 & 32 & 18 & 32 & 18 & 32 \\
10 & 26 & 1 & 10 & 26 & 1 & 35 & 8 & 22 & 23 & 17 & 6 \\
1 & 1 & 1 & 1 & 1 & 1 & 7 & 34 & 7 & 34 & 7 & 34 \\
1 & 1 & 1 & 1 & 1 & 1 & 12 & 9 & 12 & 9 & 12 & 9 \\
10 & 26 & 1 & 10 & 26 & 1 & 12 & 1 & 16 & 26 & 9 & 10 \\
x^6 & x^{12} & x^{18} & x^{24} & x^{30} & x^{36} & x^2 & x^{10} & x^{14} & x^{22} & x^{26} & x^{34}
\end{bmatrix}
$$

(The final row labels the columns.)
We now look at the null space of that matrix:

$$[0\ 29\ 9\ 0\ 0\ 0\ 1\ 0\ 0\ 0\ 0\ 15]^T,$$
$$[9\ 0\ 0\ 0\ 0\ 29\ 0\ 0\ 0\ 15\ 1\ 0]^T,$$
$$[0\ 0\ 0\ 29\ 9\ 0\ 0\ 15\ 1\ 0\ 0\ 0]^T.$$

There are 3 vectors, and each vector is the same as the

other, up to wrap-around. This is expected, since the vectors correspond to the following rational functions modulo 37 (with exponents modulo 36).

$$\frac{29x^{12} + 9x^{18}}{x^2 + 15x^{34}}, \frac{9x^6 + 29x^{36}}{15x^{22} + x^{26}}, \frac{29x^{24} + 9x^{30}}{15x^{10} + x^{14}}$$

Note that each rational function is equal to each other rational function up to being multiplied by $\frac{x^{12}}{x^{12}}$ or $\frac{x^{24}}{x^{24}}$, with exponents wrapped around modulo 36. Any of those 3 vectors can be lifted.

3.4 Controlling Wrap-Around

Up to this point we have taken the direct approach to interpolating rational functions modulo a prime. However, this gives us little control of how the exponent wrap-around occurs. Indeed, it must always occur modulo one less than a prime. This can make complexity analysis on the lifting step difficult, because it is uncertain where the next prime will land. Also, it leaves us more vulnerable to destructive wrap-around. For example, the rational function $(x^N - x)/(x - 1)$ evaluates to zero at every point modulo the first 50 primes. Here $N = 1 + \mathrm{lcm}(2-1, 3-1, 5-1, 7-1, 11-1, \ldots, 223-1, 227-1, 229-1)$. Therefore, since each $p-1$ divides N for the first 50 primes, x^N will map to x for the first 50 primes and cancel with the $-x$ term, giving us the false impression that the rational function is zero. The chance of such destructive wrap-around is lowered if we do not limit ourselves to wrap-around modulo a prime minus one. Indeed, N is a 27 decimal digit number and has destructive wrap-around for all wrap-around modulo $p-1$ for $p-1 \leq 228$. If we could make our wrap-around occur modulo any n, where n is an integer, the same N would have to be 97 digits long to have destructive wrap-around modulo all $n \leq 228$.

Suppose we wish the wrap-around to occur modulo n, where n is any integer. The first step is to compute a prime of the form $p = kn + 1$, which always exists due to Dirichlet's Theorem. Now, instead of interpolating $f(x) \bmod p$, we interpolate $f(x^k) \bmod p$. Since k divides $p-1$, $f(x^k) \bmod x^p - x$ will map every exponent to a multiple of k, and have wrap-around modulo kn. We recover $f(x^k)$ as outlined earlier and divide each exponent by k and have the original function, but with the wrap-around occurring modulo n.

This can be briefly illustrated using our previous example function, $(8x^{882705} - 3x^{6099})/(5x^{1048577} + x)$. Suppose we want to know the exponents of rational function modulo 10. We first find a prime of the form $p = 10k+1$. One such prime is $31 = 3 \cdot 10 + 1$. Now, we know the following must be true: $f(x^3) = (8x^{3 \times 882705} - 3x^{3 \times 6099})/(5x^{3 \times 1048577} + x^{3 \times 1})$. We have a black box of $f(x^3)$. We simply evaluate at the cube of each residue. Thus, we see that $f(x^3)$ is equivalent to the following, modulo 31: $f(x^3) \equiv (8x^{15} + 28x^{27})/(5x^{21} + x^3)$. Note that the coefficients are taken modulo 31 and the exponent wrap-around occurs modulo 30. We divide each of the exponents by 3 to get back $f(x)$: $f(x) \equiv (8x^5 + 28x^9)/(5x^7 + x)$. And indeed we see that the exponents match modulo 10. This technique can be used both in the initial step, as illustrated by example here, or in the lifting step, as we will illustrate next.

4. SILVER-POHLIG/HELLMAN LIFTING

We now discuss how to reduce the number of candidate exponents in each lifting step (3) by adapting the powering technique of the Pohlig and Hellman [27] discrete logarithm algorithm, whose independent discovery they also attribute to Roland Silver (and Richard Schroeppel and H. Block).

4.1 Dirichlet's Theorem Revisited

Dirichlet's Theorem on Arithmetic Progressions states that for relatively prime numbers a and n, there are infinitely many prime numbers in the Arithmetic Progression $a + \lambda n$, $\lambda = 1, 2, \ldots$. In our algorithm we are interested in prime numbers p_j such that $2^j(p_0 - 1)$ divides $p_j - 1$, where p_0 is the initial prime that we picked. That is, we want primes of the form $p_j = m_j 2^j(p_0 - 1) + 1$. Since 1 and $n = 2^j(p_0 - 1)$ are relatively prime, Dirichlet's Theorem guarantees the existence of such prime numbers. Furthermore, we know there is a polynomial bound on the first such prime. Specifically, $p_j = O(n^L)$ for some Linnik's constant L $(= 5.5)$ (smaller bounds [24] exclude a zero-density set of multipliers n) or, assuming the Generalized Riemann Hypothesis holds, $p_j = O(\varphi(n)^2(\ln n)^2)$ where φ is Euler's totient function [12]. Heath-Brown [11] had stated earlier that the conjecture $L = 2$ "may presumably be reduced to $\ll n(\log n)^2$." Note that the later conjecture, as well as similar others, are asymptotic and do not provide effective estimates for the big-O constant implied by $\ll$. Since primality testing is computationally inexpensive, and because *in practice* the first prime generally occurs early in the sequence, finding such sequences of primes is feasible.

For $p_0 - 1 = 12$ we can have the following sequence:

j	0	1	2	3	4	5	6	7
$p_j - 1$ is div. by	12	24	48	96	192	384	768	1536
p_j	13	73	97	97	193	769	769	7681
m_j	1	3	2	1	1	2	1	5

The reader may have also already observed that one can pick a single prime number, the last prime in the sequence, and simply change the multipliers, as shown below:

j	0	1	2	3	4	5	6	7
$p_j - 1$ is div. by	12	24	48	96	192	384	768	1536
p_j	7681	7681	7681	7681	7681	7681	7681	7681
m_j	640	320	160	80	40	20	10	5

The latter is useful when a large number of evaluation points γ or a large modulus are needed at the start. In the single prime case, p_0 need not be a prime number.

4.2 SPH-Lifting to Larger Primes

Assume that we know the rational function modulo a small prime p_0. We construct a sequence of primes $\{p_0, p_1, p_2, \ldots, p_k\}$ such that $2^j(p_0 - 1)$ divides $p_j - 1$ for $1 \leq j \leq k$ and $2^k(p_0 - 1)$ is larger than the upper bound on the degree. Such a sequence can be constructed and will likely not have excessively large primes (see the above Section 4.1). We write $p_j = m_j 2^j(p_0 - 1) + 1$. Note $m_0 = 1$.

In the first step of the algorithm, we find the supersparse representation of the function modulo $x^{p_0} - x, p_0$. This means we know the exponents modulo $p_0 - 1$ since x^{p_0} evaluates the same as x modulo p_0. In this section, we will compute the exponents modulo $2(p_0 - 1)$, $2^2(p_0 - 1), \ldots$, $2^k(p_0 - 1)$. Since $2^k(p_0 - 1)$ is then larger than degree bound, we will actually know the exponents.

Suppose, at this point, that we know the exponents of the non-zero terms modulo $2^{j-1}(p_0 - 1)$ where j is between 1 and k. The case $j = 1$ is the initial step of the algorithm. We now wish to determine the exponents of the non-zero terms modulo $2^j(p_0 - 1)$.

Recall that f was represented as $f(x) = \sum_{\eta=1}^{d+1} a_\eta x^\eta$ /

$\sum_{\eta=1}^{d+1} b_\eta x^\eta$. Now, consider evaluating f at x^{m_j}. Then we get $f(x^{m_j}) = \sum_{\eta=1}^{d+1} a_\eta x^{m_j\eta} / \sum_{\eta=1}^{d+1} b_\eta x^{m_j\eta}$. Let $\eta_{j-1} = \eta \bmod (2^{j-1}(p_0 - 1))$ in the residue system $\{1, \ldots, (p_{j-1} - 1)/m_{j-1}\}$, where $(p_{j-1} - 1)/m_{j-1} = 2^{j-1}(p_0 - 1)$, and let $\zeta_j = (m_j\eta) \bmod (p_j - 1)$ in the residue system $\{1, \ldots, p_j - 1\}$ (see (1)). Since m_j divides $p_j - 1$, all ζ_j are divisible by m_j. Furthermore $\eta_j = \zeta_j/m_j = \eta \bmod (2^j(p_0 - 1))$, where $(p_j - 1)/m_j = 2^j(p_0 - 1)$, and either $\eta_j = \eta_{j-1}$ or $\eta_j = \eta_{j-1} + 2^{j-1}(p_0 - 1)$.

Now, we wish to exploit our knowledge of the term exponents modulo $2^{j-1}(p_0 - 1)$ to help us compute the exponents modulo $2^j(p_0 - 1)$. If x^e, $e \in \{1, 2, \ldots, 2^{j-1}(p_0 - 1) - 1\}$ has coefficient zero modulo $2^{j-1}(p_0 - 1)$, then we know both x^e and $x^{e+2^{j-1}(p_0-1)}$ have coefficient zero modulo $2^j(p_0 - 1)$. We are temporally ignoring the case where those two terms have coefficients that sum to zero. Similarly, suppose we have a complete set of residues of the exponents for the non-zero terms modulo $2^{j-1}(p_0 - 1)$, say $\{e_1, e_2, \ldots, e_\tau\}$, then we know the only possible terms with non-zero coefficients will have exponents $\{e_1, e_2, \ldots, e_\tau\} \cup \{e_1 + 2^{j-1}(p_0 - 1), e_2 + 2^{j-1}(p_0 - 1), \ldots, e_\tau + 2^{j-1}(p_0 - 1)\}$ modulo $2^j(p_0 - 1)$.

When we set up our new linear equation modulo p_j, we know in advance that most of the coefficients are going to be zero. We have at most 2τ possible terms that are going to be non-zero, but up to $(p_j - 1)/m_j = 2^j(p_0 - 1)$ equations. Therefore, the number of equations will far exceed the number of unknowns, and our system will likely have fullest possible rank.

With all that said, we can now formalize what we said into a system of linear equations. Let $\{e_1^{[num]}, e_2^{[num]}, \ldots, e_{\tau^{[num]}}^{[num]}\}$ be the exponents of the non-zero terms of the numerator modulo $2^{j-1}(p_0 - 1)$. Similarly, let $\{e_1^{[den]}, e_2^{[den]}, \ldots, e_{\tau^{[den]}}^{[den]}\}$ be the denominator. That simply says the following.

$$f(x^{m_{j-1}}) \equiv \frac{\sum_{i=1}^{\tau^{[num]}} \alpha_i x^{m_{j-1} e_i^{[num]}}}{\sum_{i=1}^{\tau^{[den]}} \beta_i x^{m_{j-1} e_i^{[den]}}} \bmod (x^{p_{j-1}} - x, p_{j-1}).$$

Lifting the prime to p_j and the exponents to $2^j(p_0 - 1)$ yields the following $\bmod (x^{p_j} - x, p_j)$:

$$f(x^{m_j}) \equiv \frac{\sum_{i=1}^{\tau^{[num]}} \hat{\alpha}_i x^{m_j e_i^{[num]}} + \tilde{\alpha}_i x^{m_j(e_i^{[num]} + 2^{j-1}(p_0-1))}}{\sum_{i=1}^{\tau^{[den]}} \hat{\beta}_i x^{m_j e_i^{[den]}} + \tilde{\beta}_i x^{m_j(e_i^{[den]} + 2^{j-1}(p_0-1))}} \quad (4)$$

We also note $\hat{\alpha}_i + \tilde{\alpha}_i = \alpha_i$ and $\hat{\beta}_i + \tilde{\beta}_i = \beta_i$ if the α_i's and β_i's are known as integers or if we use a single larger modulus (see Section 6). Clearing the denominators and evaluating at various residues will create linear equations in $\hat{\alpha}_i, \tilde{\alpha}_i, \hat{\beta}_i$, and $\tilde{\beta}_i$. Note that multiplying both numerator and denominator with $x^{m_j 2^{j-1}(p_0-1)} = x^{(p_j-1)/2}$ gives a second, possibly linearly independent solution coefficient vector to (4).

We will now briefly address that possibility of destructive wrap-around. For example, consider the polynomial $x^{80} - 3x^4 - x^2$. If this polynomial is looked at modulo 7, we observe that the exponent wrap-around occurs modulo 6, so the polynomial evaluates like $x^{80 \bmod 6} - 3x^{4 \bmod 6} - x^{2 \bmod 6} = x^2 - 3x^4 - x^2 = -3x^4$. So, it is possible for destructive wrap-around to occur, and that would make our rational function appear even sparser than it is. Furthermore, when we attempt to lift, we will fail, because we assume that the coefficients corresponding to x^{80} and x^2 are both zero, because the two coefficients canceled each other out modulo 6. The bad news is that we know of no elegant solution to fix this. The good news is that this can happen for only a small finite number of primes, so if destructive wrap-around causes the lifting step to fail, we can give up and try with a different initial prime and it will not take long until we have exhausted all primes for which destructive wrap-around occurs.

5. THE ALGORITHM

The reader may note at this point that we likely will never, by lifting alone, recover the actual original function, but rather an alternative representation thereof. That is because the lifting step cannot tell whether the numerator and denominator were both multiplied by a power of x. Also, the coefficients are taken modulo a prime, and may be multiplied by a constant. Furthermore, nothing will cause the exponents to match up exactly, but rather modulo the final wrap-around. However, once we have reached the degree bound and know we can stop lifting. The coefficients can easily be recovered using rational vector reconstruction [20, Section 4]. If we lift to a wrap-around that is at least twice the degree bound, which is computationally inexpensive since it is only one further lifting step, then we can easily compute an exponent shift such that all the exponents after shifting fall below the degree bound. If there are multiple such shifts, then one can sample the trial function and the blackbox at random points and compare. The function that corresponds to the blackbox is correct.

Outline of Algorithm

Input A blackbox of a supersparse rational function $f \in \mathbb{Q}(x)$, an upper bound on the number of non-zero coefficients τ, and an upper bound on the degree d, and an upper bound on the integer coefficient lengths.

Output A supersparse representation of the rational function or FAIL. The algorithm can fail in several ways. The moduli choices may be unlucky, say they cause destructive wrap-around or sparser image fractions. Or the input bounds for degree and sparsity may be too low. Those causes are not distinguishable.

SSRI1 Compute a prime p_0 such that $p_0 > 3\tau$.

SSRI2 Compute a list of primes $p_0, p_1, \ldots, p_k$ such that $p_j = m_j 2^j (p_0 - 1) + 1$ and $2^k (p_0 - 1) > 2d$.

SSRI3 Construct a $(p_0 - 1) \times 2(p_0 - 1)$ matrix A, where the ith row is $[1, i, i^2, \ldots, i^{p_0 - 1}, -f(i), -if(i), -i^2 f(i), \ldots, -i^{p_0 - 1} f(i)] \bmod p_0$.

Do until break

SSRI4 Select at least p_0 coefficients and set them to zero. That is, add a row of the form $[0, 0, \ldots, 0, 1, 0, \ldots, 0]$, where the 1 corresponds to the coefficient we wish to set to zero.

SSRI5 Compute the nullspace of the above matrix mod p_0.

SSRI6 If the number of non-zero entries in a null space vector is no more than τ, record the vector and break from do loop.

SSRI7 Else if there is more than one null space vector, remove at least one more column and go to SSRI5.

SSRI8 Else if all possible combination of columns have been attempted, return FAIL.

End do

For j from 1 to $k-1$ do

Let $v^{[num]} = \{e_1^{[num]}, e_2^{[num]}, \ldots, e_{\tau_{[num]}}^{[num]}\}$ and $v^{[den]} = \{e_1^{[den]}, e_2^{[den]}, \ldots, e_{\tau_{[den]}}^{[den]}\}$ be lists containing the exponents of the non-zero terms of the null space vector

modulo $2^{j-1}(p_0 - 1)$ of the numerator and denominator, respectively, that were computed in the previous step.

SSRI9 Let $V^{[num]} = \{e, e + 2^{j-1}(p_0 - 1) | e \in v^{[num]}\}$. Let $V^{[den]}$ be computed similarly. (Note that $V^{[num]}$ and $V^{[den]}$ represent the list of possible exponents mod $2^j(p_0 - 1)$.)

SSRI10 Select a list of at least $|V^{[num]}| + |V^{[den]}|$ random residues $i \bmod p_{j+1}$ and store in M, where $|V^{[num]}|$ represents the number of elements in the list $V^{[num]}$.

Do until break

SSRI11 Construct the $|M| \times (|V^{[num]}| + |V^{[den]}|)$ matrix A where the row for residue i in M is given by $[i^{m_j V_1^{[n]}}, i^{m_j V_2^{[n]}}, \ldots, -f(i^{m_j})i^{m_j V_1^{[d]}}, -f(i^{m_j})i^{m_j V_2^{[d]}}, \ldots] \bmod p_j$.

SSRI12 Compute the null space of $A \bmod p$ in reduced column echelon form.

SSRI13 If the null space has dimensions greater than 2, add more residues to M and thus more rows to A and go to SSRI12.

SSRI14 If the null space has dimension 2, select a null space vector at random and break.

SSRI15 If the null space has dimension less than 2, restart algorithm with new initial vector or prime. If all possible starting vectors have been exhausted, return FAIL.

End do until

SSRI16 Record the exponents from the null space vector in $v^{[num]}$ and $v^{[den]}$. These will be the exponents of the function mod p_{j+1}.

End do

SSRI17 Use rational vector recovery to recover the coefficients of the rational function. Multiply the numerator and denominator by the same power of x so that all exponents are less than the degree bound. (Recall that $2^k(p_0 - 1) > 2d$.) If no such power exists, return DEGREE BOUND TOO SMALL. Otherwise, return the rational function. **End of Algorithm.**

The algorithm inputs bounds on both the number of non-zero terms and the degree. Due to the nature of the linear system, it is of only moderate advantage to have separate degree bounds on the numerator and denominator, because both the numerator and denominator are lifted at every step. However, having separate bounds for the number of non-zero terms in the numerator and denominator can lead to better column elimination strategies in the initial step.

6. COMPLEXITY ANALYSIS

We now attempt to give some plausible reasons that the algorithm can be implemented to work in random polynomial time for a fixed τ, the bound for the sum of the number of terms in a ***sparsest*** solution $g/h \in \mathbb{Q}(x)$, $g, h \in \mathbb{Z}[x]$. We may assume, as before, that both g and h have a factor x.

We do not take into consideration several of the heuristic improvements discussed before, but wish to show that the algorithm can be modified to produce a correct result for ***fixed*** τ. We will work modulo a single large prime $p = \mu q 2^l + 1$, where q is a randomly chosen small prime that needs to have certain properties for the analysis to work, l is sufficiently large to cover the degree bounds, and μ is the smallest multiplier for the arithmetic progression $1 + \lambda q 2^l$,

$\lambda = 1, 2, \ldots$ We shall assume that a μ can be found (see Section 4.1). It needs not be small.

The algorithm, once q and l are chosen, computes the coefficients of a sparsest pair $\bar{g}_j, \bar{h}_j \in \mathbb{Z}_p[x]$ in terms of the number of nonzero coefficients of the linear system

$$(g\bar{h}_j - h\bar{g}_j)(x^{m_j}) \equiv 0 \bmod (x^p - x, p), \, m_j = \mu 2^{l-j}, \quad (5)$$

for $j = 0, \ldots, l$. Again, we may assume that $\bar{g}_j$ and $\bar{h}_j$ have a factor x. The terms x^{e+1} in g and h (5) map to $x\, x^{m_j e \bmod (p-1)} = x\, x^{(e \bmod q)\mu 2^{l-j}}$. We shall make the following two sparsity assumptions:

Sp1 q has been sampled so that the term exponents in g and the term exponents in h map to distinct residues modulo q with high probability. For that a random q with $O(\tau^2 \log(\deg g + \deg h))$ suffices: q must not divide the products of differences of the term degrees of the numerator and denominator (cf. [19, Lemma 4.3]).

Sp2 the image of g and h forms a sparsest solution to (5) for all j. At this moment we have no proof that the latter is true with high probability (see Section 2.3).

We shall perform the interpolation in Steps SSRI3 and SSRI-13 above at points γ^η where γ is a primitive root modulo p and η ranges $0 \le \eta < 2\tau^2$. Primitive roots are abundant as $\varphi(n) = \Omega(n / \ln \ln n)$ and if μ is small can be computed effectively as $p - 1$ is smooth. Since $(g\bar{h}_j - h\bar{g}_j)(x^{m_j}) \bmod (x^p - x)$ has no more than $2\tau^2$ terms, $(g\bar{h}_j - h\bar{g}_j)(\gamma^{m_j}) = 0$ for all η must imply (5) for $\bar{g}_j, \bar{h}_j$ by the argument in [21, Section 4.1], as the term evaluations in (5) remain distinct for the primitive root and the corresponding Vandermonde coefficient matrix is of full rank.

In Step SSRI3 our algorithm tests all sparse exponent vectors (modulo q times m_0) for $\bar{g}_0(x^{m_0})$ and $\bar{h}_0(x^{m_0})$. For a sparsest solution, the vector is unique (up to a scalar multiple) by the argument in Section 2.3. Two linearly independent solutions for the same exponent choice can produce a sparser solution via linear combination.

A similar argument works (for some f) for all $j > 0$ in Step SSRI13 above. There are two, possibly linearly independent, sparsest solutions, $\bar{g}_j, \bar{h}_j$ and $x^{(p-1)/(2m_j)}\bar{g}_j$, $x^{(p-1)/(2m_j)}\bar{h}_j$ for (5). Note that shifting the second solution by multiplying again by $x^{(p-1)/(2m_j)}$ results in the first since $x\, x^{p-1} \equiv x$. If our assumptions (Sp1) and (Sp2) hold, there is no sparser solution and lifting the sparsest solution corresponding to g and h will lead the sparsest solutions with exactly one of $\hat{\alpha}_i$ and $\tilde{\alpha}_i$ and exactly one of $\hat{\beta}_i$ and $\tilde{\beta}_i$ in (4) equal to 0 for all i. There are still $2^{\tau^{[num]} + \tau^{[den]}}$ many candidate interpolants, each of which we will test. Assume now that there is a third such sparsest interpolant $\bar{\bar{g}}_j, \bar{\bar{h}}_j$ at all γ^η. If the coefficient vector of $\bar{\bar{g}}_j(x^{m_j 2^j}), \bar{\bar{h}}_j(x^{m_j 2^j})$ is not the coefficient vector (or a scalar multiple) of $\bar{g}_0, \bar{h}_0$ then a sparser vector can be constructed for $j = 0$. Otherwise, in the two solutions

$$(\bar{g}_j - \bar{\bar{g}}_j)(x^{m_j 2^j}), (\bar{h}_j - \bar{\bar{h}}_j)(x^{m_j 2^j})$$
$$(x^{(p-1)/(2m_j)}\bar{g}_j - \bar{\bar{g}}_j)(x^{m_j 2^j}), (x^{(p-1)/(2m_j)}\bar{h}_j - \bar{\bar{h}}_j)(x^{m_j 2^j})$$

certain coefficients cancel to 0. In fact, if $\tau^{[num]} + \tau^{[den]}$ is an odd integer, one of the two solutions must have fewer non-zero terms, in contradiction to assumption (Sp2) above.

We add that the exact integer coefficients can be recovered for each j from their residues modulo p and false interpolants may be eliminated by virtue of having large recovered integer coefficients.

7. OBSERVATIONS AND EXPERIMENTS

7.1 Multiple Variables

The algorithm as presented works only for the single variable case. However, a simple variable substitution due to Kronecker can be applied to make this algorithm work in multiple variables. Suppose there are n variables, $x_1, \ldots, x_n$ and d is a bound on the degree of all individual variables. Then we can apply the substitutions $x_i = x^{(d+1)^{i-1}}$, $i = 1, \ldots, n$. This means that a general monomial is mapped as follows: $x_1^{e_1} \cdots x_n^{e_n} = x^E$ with $E = e_1 + (d+1)e_2 + \cdots + e_n(d+1)^{n-1}$. Because d is an upper bound on the degree, there is no chance that two multivariate monomials get mapped to the same single variable monomial. Furthermore, since the algorithm is conjectured to be polylogarithmic in the degree, then it would become polynomial in the number of variables.

7.2 Some Experiments

Both algorithms were implemented in Maple 12 and tested on a MacPro with 16 cores (Intel Xeon 2.67GHz) with 32GB of real memory on a Nehalem memory bus running Linux version Ubuntu 2.6.31-22.70 (Ubuntu). The times given in the table are in seconds. The first column is the number of non-zero terms in the numerator and in the denominator, and the first row is the degree of the numerator and denominator. The table below shows the time it took to recover the random rational function with random integer coefficients in the range $-5, \ldots, 5$ and includes the garbage collection cost.

	2^{10}	2^{20}	2^{30}	2^{40}	2^{50}	2^{60}	2^{70}	2^{100}
3	3.6	4.4	3.9	2.5	7.1	13.5	20.2	729.9
4	3.7	4.2	7.8	6.0	15.0	23.2	51.2	1109.2
5	4.4	5.2	8.2	22.4	30.9	65.9	77.2	809.3
6	5.0	7.5	9.9	27.0	51.6	121.9	278.1	3258.6
7	50.2	38.9	9.8	66.0	193.5	308.4	637.8	2926.5
8	144.7	75.8	339.2	554.4	2247.6	1703.2	8205.8	18092.0
9	1673.8	307.2	289.9	4126.5	2887.2	2011.4	1963.1	45148.1
10	440.9	1951.7	462.3	4453.91	14613.2	6262.2	29445.3	39455.0

The degrees of numerators and denominators given in the first row. The number of non-zero terms in both the numerators and denominators are given in the first column. The second table below shows the number of blackbox calls.

	2^{10}	2^{20}	2^{30}	2^{40}	2^{50}	2^{60}	2^{70}	2^{100}
3	347	527	707	729	1065	1422	1681	5090
4	377	617	1307	906	1295	1646	2240	5696
5	377	707	1007	1395	1736	2317	2592	5267
6	434	797	1157	1428	1818	2675	3651	7304
7	467	887	1307	1814	2654	3644	4319	7619
8	497	962	1457	2639	4118	5087	9116	12584
9	527	962	2543	3158	4222	5229	6502	11689
10	554	1151	1748	2353	5981	6817	8591	11941

Note that the performance is not uniform due to the sparse vector construction. The first three columns and the 10 terms problem for degree 2^{40} are runs with Silver-Pohlig/Hellman lifting (Section 4), and the others runs with "easy" lifting (Section 3.2).

Additionally, the algorithm with Kronecker's substitution was used on the rational function $f(x, y) = (x^{2^{100}} - 1) \times (y^{2^{50}} - 1) / ((x-1)(y-1))$. The given sparse form of the function, rather than the very dense reduced form, was recovered with easy lifting in 2771.9 seconds with 8600 black box calls.

7.3 Drawbacks

The algorithm, as presented, has a number of drawbacks. At the moment, there is no proven way of certifying that a null space vector is indeed the correct null space vector. Therefore, it would be possible to lift an incorrect vector, perhaps multiple times, before discovering that the vector does not represent the actual function.

In the lifting step, it is also not known what the dimension of the null space will be. Even if we did know that the matrix has the fullest possible rank given all possible equations, we do not know how many equations are needed to get that rank; however, see Section 6 for a possible solution.

The most significant shortcoming, however, is that the initial guess of the vector appears to be exponential in the number of non-zero terms, since one may have to traverse all possible combinations before the correct vector is found.

8. FURTHER WORK

Again, the obvious weak point of the algorithm is the fact that exponentially many combinations may have to be processed. Although finding the sparsest vector in a null space is NP-hard in general, it is certainly possible that the particular null spaces that are generated have special properties that allow one to find (at least with high probability) a sparse vector in polynomial time. Indeed, in general if one knows one vector in the null space generated in the initial step of the algorithm, one generally knows $p-2$ more vectors in the null space (except for finitely many degenerate p), since if $\frac{f}{g}$ is the rational function that generated the system of equations, then so is $x^i f(x)/(x^i g(x))$ for $i = 1, \ldots, p-2$. After $p-2$, everything wraps around mod $p-1$. This banded nature of the null space could possibly be exploitable to find sparse vectors in that null space.

If we change the model to one where the black box can be evaluated at complex roots of unity, say modulo cyclotomic polynomials of small degree over the rational numbers, as would be the case if the black box is a straight-line program [5], then the recovery of an initial sparse null space vector with rational entries could be attempted using techniques from compressed sensing, which started with [1]. There are many approaches known today that would recover a sparse vector. The lifting could then still be done modulo larger and larger primes.

Acknowledgments: We thank Éric Schost for many discussions on the supersparse rational function recovery problem, and Carl Pomerance for his references on conjectures related to the effective Dirichlet theorem. The referees have provided many useful comments which we would like to acknowledge.

9. REFERENCES

[1] CANDES, E., AND TAO, T. Decoding by linear programming. *IEEE Trans. Inf. Theory* IT-51, 12 (2005), 4203–4215.

[2] COLEMAN, T., AND POTHEN, A. The null space problem I. complexity. *SIAM. J. on Algebraic and Discrete Methods 7* (1986), 527–537.

[3] CUCKER, F., KOIRAN, P., AND SMALE, S. A polynomial time algorithm for diophantine equations in one variable. *J. Symbolic Comput. 27*, 1 (1999), 21–29.

[4] FILASETA, M., GRANVILLE, A., AND SCHINZEL, A. Irreducibility and greatest common divisor algorithms for sparse polynomials, 2007. Manuscript submitted.

[5] GARG, S., AND SCHOST, ÉRIC. Interpolation of polynomials given by straight-line programs. *Theoretical Computer Science 410*, 27-29 (2009), 2659 – 2662.

[6] GIESBRECHT, M., KALTOFEN, E., AND LEE, W. Algorithms for computing sparsest shifts of polynomials in power, Chebychev, and Pochhammer bases. *J. Symbolic Comput. 36*, 3–4 (2003), 401–424.

[7] GIESBRECHT. M., AND ROCHE, D. S. Interpolation of shifted-lacunary polynomials. *Computing Research Repository abs/0810.5685* (2008). URL: http://arxiv.org/abs/0810.5685.

[8] GIESBRECHT, M.. AND ROCHE. D. S. On lacunary polynomial perfect powers. In *ISSAC 2008* (New York, N. Y., 2008), D. Jeffrey, Ed., ACM Press, pp. 103–110.

[9] GIESBRECHT, M., AND ROCHE. D. S. Detecting lacunary perfect powers and computing their roots. *Computing Research Repository abs/0901.1848* (2009).

[10] GIESBRECHT, M., ROCHE. D. S., AND TILAK, H. Computing sparse multiples of polynomials. In *Proc. Internat. Symp. on Algorithms and Computation (ISAAC 2010)* (2010), p. to appear.

[11] HEATH-BROWN, D. R. Almost-primes in arithmetic progressions and short intervals. *Math. Proc. Camb. Phil. Soc. 83* (1978), 357–375.

[12] HEATH-BROWN, D. R. Zero-free regions for Dirichlet L-functions, and the least prime in an arithmetic progression. *Proc. London Math. Soc 3* (1992), 265–338.

[13] KALTOFEN, E. Greatest common divisors of polynomials given by straight-line programs. *J. ACM 35*, 1 (1988), 231–264.

[14] KALTOFEN, E. Unpublished article fragment, 1988. URL http://www.math.ncsu.edu/~kaltofen/bibliography/88/Ka88_ratint.pdf.

[15] KALTOFEN, E. Fifteen years after DSC and WLSS2 What parallel computations I do today [Invited lecture at PASCO 2010]. In *PASCO'10 Proc. 2010 Internat. Workshop on Parallel Symbolic Comput.* (New York, N. Y., July 2010), M. Moreno Maza and J.-L. Roch, Eds., ACM, pp. 10–17.

[16] KALTOFEN, E., AND KOIRAN, P. Finding small degree factors of multivariate supersparse (lacunary) polynomials over algebraic number fields. In *ISSAC MMVI Proc. 2006 Internat. Symp. Symbolic Algebraic Comput.* (New York, N. Y., 2006), J.-G. Dumas, Ed., ACM Press, pp. 162–168.

[17] KALTOFEN, E., AND LEE. W. Early termination in sparse interpolation algorithms. *J. Symbolic Comput. 36*, 3–4 (2003), 365–400. Special issue Internat. Symp. Symbolic Algebraic Comput. (ISSAC 2002). Guest editors: M. Giusti & L. M. Pardo.

[18] KALTOFEN, E., AND TRAGER. B. Computing with polynomials given by black boxes for their evaluations: Greatest common divisors, factorization, separation of numerators and denominators. *J. Symbolic Comput. 9*, 3 (1990), 301–320.

[19] KALTOFEN, E., AND VILLARD, G. On the complexity of computing determinants. *Computational Complexity 13*, 3-4 (2004), 91–130.

[20] KALTOFEN, E., AND YANG, Z. On exact and approximate interpolation of sparse rational functions. In *ISSAC 2007 Proc. 2007 Internat. Symp. Symbolic Algebraic Comput.* (New York, N. Y., 2007), C. W. Brown, Ed., ACM Press, pp. 203–210.

[21] KALTOFEN, E., YANG, Z., AND ZHI, L. On probabilistic analysis of randomization in hybrid symbolic-numeric algorithms. In *SNC'07 Proc. 2007 Internat. Workshop on Symbolic-Numeric Comput.* (New York, N. Y., 2007), J. Verschelde and S. M. Watt, Eds., ACM Press, pp. 11–17.

[22] KIPNIS, A., AND SHAMIR. A. Cryptanalysis of the HFE public key cryptosystem by relinearization. In *Proc. CRYPTO '99* (1999), M. J. Wiener, Ed., vol. 1666 of *Lecture Notes in Computer Science*, Springer, pp. 19–30.

[23] LENSTRA, JR., H. W. Finding small degree factors of lacunary polynomials. In *Number Theory in Progress* (1999), K. Győry, H. Iwaniec, and J. Urbanowicz, Eds., vol. 1 Diophantine Problems and Polynomials, Stefan Banach Internat. Center, Walter de Gruyter Berlin/New York, pp. 267–276.

[24] MIKAWA. H. On primes in arithmetic progressions. *Tsukuba J. Mathematics 25*, 1 (2001), 121–153.

[25] OLESH, Z., AND STORJOHANN, A. The vector rational function reconstruction problems. In *Proc. Waterloo Workshop on Computer Algebra: devoted to the 60th birthday of Sergei Abramov (WWCA)* (2007), pp. 137–149.

[26] PLAISTED, D. A. New NP-hard and NP-complete polynomial and integer divisibility problems. *Theoretical Comput. Sci. 13* (1984), 125–138.

[27] POHLIG, C. P., AND HELLMAN, M. E. An improved algorithm for computing logarithms over GF(p) and its cryptographic significance. *IEEE Trans. Inf. Theory* IT-24 (1978), 106–110.

Using Discriminant Curves To Recover A Surface Of $\mathbb{P}^4$ From Two Generic Linear Projections

Jeremy-Yrmeyahu Kaminski
Depart. of Computer Science
Holon Institute of Technology
Holon, Israel
jeremy.kaminski@gmail.com

Yann Sepulcre
Shamoon College of Engineering
Ashdod, Israel
yanns68@gmail.com

ABSTRACT

We study how an irreducible smooth and closed algebraic surface X embedded in $\mathbb{CP}^4$, can be recovered using its projections from two points onto embedded projective hyperplanes. The different embeddings are unknown. The only input is the defining equation of each projected surface. We show how both the embeddings and the surface in $\mathbb{CP}^4$ can be recovered modulo some action of the group of projective transformations of $\mathbb{CP}^4$.

We show how in a generic situation, a characteristic matrix of the pair of embeddings can be recovered. Then we use this matrix to recover the class of the couple of maps and as a consequence to recover the surface.

For a generic situation, two projections define a surface with two irreducible components. One component has degree $d(d-1)$ and the other has degree d, being the original surface.

Categories and Subject Descriptors

I.1.2 [**Computing Methodologies**]: Symbolic and Algebraic Manipulation—*Algebraic Algorithms*

General Terms

Algorithms

Keywords

Algebraic Surfaces, Discriminant Curves, Linear Projections, Computational Algebraic Geometry

1. INTRODUCTION

The study of varieties and their projections has old roots in algebraic geometry [7]. In the past three decades, an application of this subject, in computer vision, became of major importance. See for further details [8, 3]. However these applications mainly concerns the case of configurations of points or lines in $\mathbb{P}^3$ projected over embedded projective planes (or

mere camera images). More recently the case of curves received some attention [10]. Due to the similarity of our setting, we borrow from computer vision some of its classical terminology.

We consider hereafter the case of an irreducible surface embedded in $\mathbb{P}^4$. The surface is linearly projected into two generic hyperplanes. Neither the hyperplanes nor the centers of projection are known. The only input is the defining equation of each projected surface. From this input we recover the two linear projections modulo a projective automorphism of $\mathbb{P}^4$ and we show how the original surface can be computed. Our approach is based on Kulikov theorem [11], which is a particular case of Chisini's conjecture.

2. NOTATIONS AND PRELIMINARIES

We denote by $\mathbb{P}^n$ the projective space, defined as the quotient of $\mathbb{C}^{n+1} \setminus \{0\}$ by scalar mutiplication. The notation $\mathbb{L}\,\mathbb{P}^n$ designates the Grassmannian variety parameterizing lines in $\mathbb{P}^n$. If p, q are two points in $\mathbb{P}^n$ we shall denote the line joining p and q by $p \vee q$. If some point $e \in \mathbb{P}^n$ is given, we denote by $\mathbb{L}_e\mathbb{P}^n$ the closed subset of lines in $\mathbb{P}^n$ containing e. It is isomorphic to $\mathbb{P}^{n-1}$ in a non canonical way: once a hyperplane $H \subset \mathbb{P}^n$ missing e has been fixed, one obtains an isomorphism $H \xrightarrow{\sim} \mathbb{L}_e$ by mapping a point $p \in H$ to the line $p \vee e$. By a linear projection we mean a rational onto map $p : \mathbb{P}^n \longrightarrow \mathbb{P}^{n-1}$ induced by a linear map $\widehat{p} : \mathbb{C}^{n+1} \to \mathbb{C}^n$, represented by a full rank $n \times (n+1)$ matrix once two coordinates systems have been fixed on the source and target spaces. Since $\widehat{p}$ has a one-dimensional kernel such a map p is undefined at a point $c \in \mathbb{P}^n$ called its *center*.

The set $Pr(\mathbb{P}^n, \mathbb{P}^{n-1})$ of linear projections comes naturally with a right action of the linear group PGL_{n+1}: $p \cdot g(x) = p(g^{-1} \cdot x)$. In a similar manner PGL_{n+1} operates on pairs of projections: $(p_1, p_2) \cdot g = (p_1 \cdot g, p_2 \cdot g)$. Given now two projections $p_1, p_2 \in Pr(\mathbb{P}^n, \mathbb{P}^{n-1})$, which centers are $\mathfrak{c}_1$ and $\mathfrak{c}_2$, we shall refer to the points $\epsilon_1 := p_1(\mathfrak{c}_2)$ and $\epsilon_2 := p_2(\mathfrak{c}_1)$ in $\mathbb{P}^{n-1}$ as the **epipoles**. With the data pair (p_1, p_2) in hand one defines the following *fundamental* map:

$$F : \quad \mathbb{L}_{\epsilon_1} \to \mathbb{L}_{\epsilon_2}$$
$$L \longmapsto p_2\, p_1^{-1}(L) \ .$$

In the previous definition we first take the inverse image $\widetilde{L}$ of L by p_1, which is a 2−plane in $\mathbb{P}^n$ containing both centers, then $\widetilde{L}$ is projected by p_2 onto a line in $\mathbb{P}^{n-1}$ containing ϵ_2. It should be noted that F is actually an isomorphism: indeed its inverse map is expressed similarly as $F^{-1}(L) = p_1 p_2^{-1}(L)$. Moreover, by the previous observations, once two hyperplanes H_1 and H_2 in $\mathbb{P}^{n-1}$ are fixed with the constraint $\epsilon_i \notin H_i$ for $i = 1, 2$, the map F induces a linear isomorphism $\widetilde{F} : H_1 \to H_2$ making the following diagram commutative:

$$
\begin{array}{ccc}
\mathbb{L}_{\epsilon_1} & \xrightarrow{\ F\ } & \mathbb{L}_{\epsilon_2} \\
\sim \uparrow & & \uparrow \sim \\
H_1 & \xrightarrow[\widetilde{F}]{} & H_2
\end{array}
$$

The data $(\epsilon_1, \widetilde{F}, \epsilon_2)$ determines explicitly F. The following proposition is nothing new (see [10]), but we present here another proof.

PROPOSITION— 1. *The triplet $(\epsilon_1, \epsilon_2, \widetilde{F})$ introduced above determines the pair of projections $(p_1, p_2) \in Pr(\mathbb{P}^n, \mathbb{P}^{n-1})^2$ up to the right action of PGL_{n+1}. Indeed let $\{\alpha_1 \cdots \alpha_{n+1}\}$ be any generator set of $\mathbb{P}^n$ and $\{u_1, \cdots, u_{n-1}\}$ be any generator set of H_1. Then the pair (p_1, p_2) is PGL_{n+1}−equivalent to the pair (q_1, q_2) such that: α_j center of q_j, $q_j(\alpha_{3-j}) = \epsilon_j$ for $j = 1, 2$, and $q_1(\alpha_j) = u_{j-2}$, $q_2(\alpha_j) = \widetilde{F}(u_{j-2})$ for $j = 3, \cdots, n+1$.*

Proof: Let $v_1, \cdots, v_{n-1}$ be points of $\mathbb{P}^n$ such that $p_1(v_i) = u_i$ for each i; then $\{c_1, c_2, v_1, \cdots, v_{n-1}\}$ generates $\mathbb{P}^n$. Take the transformed points $w_i = \widetilde{F}(u_i) \in H_2$ for $i = 1, 2, \cdots, n-1$, which generate H_2; for all i we have

$$p_2(v_i) \in \epsilon_2 \vee w_i \quad i = 1, 2, \cdots n-1 \tag{1}$$

Now choose vectors $\widehat{c_1}, \widehat{c_2} \in \mathbb{C}^{n+1}$, $\widehat{\epsilon_1}, \widehat{\epsilon_2} \in \mathbb{C}^n$ and for $i = 1, 2, \cdots, n-1$ $\widehat{v_i} \in \mathbb{C}^{n+1}$, $\widehat{u_i} \in \mathbb{C}^n$ and $\widehat{w_i} \in \mathbb{C}^n$, representing the classes of $c_1, c_2, \epsilon_1, \epsilon_2, v_i, u_i, w_i$, and let also $\widehat{p_1}, \widehat{p_2} : \mathbb{C}^{n+1} \to \mathbb{C}^n$ be two linear maps representing p_1 and p_2. By multiplying the previous vectors by scalars, one can assume the identities:

$$
\begin{aligned}
\widehat{p_1}(\widehat{c_2}) &= \widehat{\epsilon_1}, \quad \widehat{p_2}(\widehat{c_1}) = \widehat{\epsilon_2}, \\
\widehat{p_2}(\widehat{v_i}) &= \widehat{w_i} + \lambda_i \widehat{\epsilon_2} \quad i = 1, 2, \cdots n-1, \lambda_i \in \mathbb{C}
\end{aligned} \tag{2}
$$

Hence for each $1 \leq i \leq n-1$ one has: $\widehat{p_1}(\widehat{v_i} - \lambda_i \widehat{c_1}) = \widehat{u_i}$ and $\widehat{p_2}(\widehat{v_i} - \lambda_i \widehat{c_1}) = \widehat{w_i}$. Given a generator set $\{\alpha_1, \cdots, \alpha_{n+1}\}$ of $\mathbb{P}^n$, define the automorphism $g \in PGL_{n+1}$ such that $g(\alpha_j) = c_j$ for $j = 1, 2$, and for $3 \leq j \leq n+1$ $g(\alpha_j)$ equal to the class of $\widehat{v_{j-2}} - \lambda_{j-2}\widehat{c_1}$ in $\mathbb{P}^n$. We have clearly $(p_1, p_2) \cdot g = (q_1, q_2)$ where (q_1, q_2) is the pair defined in the statement of the proposition. ∎

3. PROBLEM PRESENTATION

3.1 General statement

The problem we have in mind is the following. Let $X \subset \mathbb{P}^4$ be an irreducible smooth closed surface. Given two images X_1 and X_2 of X by two different generic projections $(p_1, p_2) \in Pr(\mathbb{P}^4, \mathbb{P}^3)^2$, how could we recover these two projections and X itself up to projective equivalence, and at most up to finite ambiguity ? More precisely let c_1 and c_2 be the (unknown) projection centers, and the epipoles defined by $\epsilon_1 := p_1(c_2)$, $\epsilon_2 := p_2(c_1)$. Given two equations $f_1 = 0$ and $f_2 = 0$ of X_1 and X_2 respectively, by prop.1 we wish to recover the 3−tuple $(\epsilon_1, \widetilde{F}, \epsilon_2)$ up to finite ambiguity. Let (q_1, q_2) be a known pair of projections in the same PGL_{n+1}−orbit of (p_1, p_2): then we have to recover X as a component of the cones intersection $p_1^{-1}(X_1) \cap p_2^{-1}(X_2)$.

Several comments are in order. First X_1 and X_2 do not in general correspond through some linear transformation of $\mathbb{P}^3$. We have also to suppose that each ϵ_i does not lie on some *already fixed* hyperplane H_i of $\mathbb{P}^3$; we suppose moreover that the restricted projections $p_i|_X : X \to X_i$ are birational. Moreover each projected surface X_i has a codimension 1 singular locus which is the image of the curve in X where the projection from the center c_i is not a local isomorphism; equivalently, it is the locus in X_i of points where the fibre of p_i contains more than one point (incuding multiplicities).

The reader may refer to [5] and [12] for much more detailed and general account of the topics presented now.

DEFINITION— 1. *For any closed projective subvariety $X \subset \mathbb{P}^n$, a line $L \subset \mathbb{P}^n$ is said to be tangent to X if there is a smooth point $x \in X$ such that projective closure $\overline{T_x X}$ of the tangent space $T_x X$ in $\mathbb{P}^N$ contains L; The closed subvariety $\widehat{X} \subset \mathbb{L}\mathbb{P}^n$ is defined as the closure of the subset of lines tangent to X in the above sense.*

Let $X^0 \subseteq X$ be the open subset of smooth points, and denote by $TX^0 \to X^0$ the tangent bundle over X^0, there exists a natural dominant map: $\Psi : \mathbb{P}(TX^0) \to \widehat{X}$, showing that $\widehat{X}$ is irreducible of dimension $\dim \widehat{X} \leq 2\dim X - 1$. This inequality is strict as soon as the generic fibre of Ψ is non-finite, i.e. when X is ruled.

Suppose now $X \subset \mathbb{P}^n$ is a projective surface. For every codimension 3 subspace $L \subset \mathbb{P}^n$ avoiding X we define the locally closed subset $R^0 \subset X$ of smooth points $x \in X$ such that the span $\langle L, x \rangle$ is tangent to X in the meaning that $\langle L, x \rangle \cap \overline{T_x X}$ contains at least a line. Denote also by R the closure of R^0 in X.

DEFINITION— 2. *Under the notations stated above, if $p_L : X \longrightarrow \mathbb{P}^2$ is the restriction of the linear projection from center L (it is a finite covering as soon as L does not intersect any line contained in X), the discriminant curve of p_L is defined as the curve $B = p_L(R)$. The curve R is referred as the ramification divisor of p_L.*

Definition 2 is a particular case of a more general one defining the discriminant curve of a finite covering as the image of the locus where the differential of the covering is not into. If $G_3(\mathbb{P}^n)$ is the Grassmanian of codimension 3 subspaces, there is a Zariski open subset $U \subset G_3(\mathbb{P}^n)$ such that for every $L \in U$ (avoiding X) the projection p_L is a *generic morphism* (see [11]): in other words p_L is finite, its discriminant curve $B \subset \mathbb{P}^2$ is irreducible with ordinary cusps and nodes as only singularities, and $p_L^*(B) = 2R + C$, where C reduced and $p_{L|R} : R \longrightarrow B$ is the normalization of B. Moreover for all $L \in U$ the curve B has fixed (even) degree, genus, and numbers of cusps and nodes.

Going back now to our surface X embedded in $\mathbb{P}^4$ consider the projection $p_L : X \longrightarrow \mathbb{P}^2$ from the line $L = c_1 \vee c_2$ joining c_1 and c_2, then there exists a Zariski open subset $U \subset \mathbb{P}^4 \times \mathbb{P}^4$ such that if $(c_1, c_2) \in U$ then p_L is a generic projection with discriminant curve B of fixed degree 2δ, genus g, and numbers c and n of cusps and nodes. From now on we shall suppose that c_1 and c_2 lie in such subset U. For $i = 1, 2$ let $\pi_i \in Pr(\mathbb{P}^3, \mathbb{P}^2)$ be the projection from the epipole ϵ_i, hence $p_L = \pi_1 p_1 = \pi_2 p_2$. Let $S_i \subset X$ be the closed subset of points lying on a secant to X passing through c_i: its image by p_i is the curve $D_i \subset X_i$ of singular points. We shall always assume that $S_1 \cup S_2$ does intersect properly the ramification divisor of p_L: this ensures that $\pi_i^{-1}(B)$ and D_i are distinct curves, and the ramification divisor R_i of π_i is non empty. The two discriminant curves of π_1 and π_2 are isomorphic to B, and we have $\pi_i(R_i) \simeq B$.

We end with few words about the numerics: let d be the degree of X, and $\bar{d}_i$ be the degree of the curve of singular points of X_i. Next lemma, proved in [11] (lemma 1), gives a relation between 2δ and $\bar{d}_i$.

LEMMA– 1. *We have*

$$\bar{d}_i \leq \frac{(d-1)(d-2)}{2} \ , \quad 2\delta = d(d-1) - 2\bar{d}_i.$$

Somewhat harder relations between the two curves, involving not only their degrees but also the genuses and their numbers of singularities, can be derived from Riemann-Roch and Noether formulas (see [6]).

3.2 Unicity result: Kulikov's theorem

The following main result of [11] solves the famous Chisini's conjecture (see [2]) in the particular case of coverings which are restrictions of linear projections.

THEOREM– 1. *Let* $X \subset \mathbb{P}^n$ *be a smooth projective surface and let* $f = p_{|X}$ *be the restriction to* X *of a generic linear projection* $p \in Pr\left(\mathbb{P}^n, \mathbb{P}^2\right)$ *in the meaning above. Denote by* $B \subset \mathbb{P}^2$ *the discriminant curve of* f. *Then provided* X *is not the image of the Veronese embedding* $\mathbb{P}^2 \hookrightarrow \mathbb{P}^5$, *the covering* (X, f) *is uniquely determined up to isomorphism by its discriminant curve* $B \subset \mathbb{P}^2$ *in the following meaning: if* $g : X' \longrightarrow \mathbb{P}^2$ *is another generic covering which discriminant curve* B' *is projectively isomorphic to* B *by* $\tau : \mathbb{P}^2 \to \mathbb{P}^2$, *there exists an isomorphism* $\sigma : X \longrightarrow X'$ *making the following diagram commutative:*

Note that in Th.1 the morphism f is unique as a covering, not only as the restriction of a projection, though we shall just need this weaker consequence. We shall now specialize to the only case of interest for us, namely when X is embedded in $\mathbb{P}^4$. The following result follows readily from Th.1 above. When x is a point of $\mathbb{P}^3$ we denote by π_x the projection onto $\mathbb{P}^2$ from center x.

COROLLARY– 1. *Suppose the surface* $X \subset \mathbb{P}^4$ *is embedded by its complete linear series* $|\mathcal{O}_X(1)|$, *and has moreover no non-trivial automorphism induced by some linear automorphism of* $\mathbb{P}^4$; *there are two non-empty Zariski open subsets* $U_1 \subset \mathbb{P}^3$ *and* $U_2 \subset \mathbb{P}^3$ *containing respectively* ϵ_1 *and* ϵ_2 *such that if* $(e_1, e_2) \in U_1 \times U_2$ *is a pair of points such that if* $\pi_{e_i}(\widetilde{R}_i)$ *for* $i = 1, 2$ *are projectively equivalent curves, where* $\widetilde{R}_i \subset X_i$ *is the ramification divisor of* π_{e_i}, *then* $(e_1, e_2) = (\epsilon_1, \epsilon_2)$.

Proof: Indeed one can find some neighbourhood Ω_1 of $\mathfrak{c}_1$, keeping $\mathfrak{c}_2$ otherwise fixed, such that the open subset of lines joining $\mathfrak{c}_2$ to some point of Ω_1 do define generic projections in the meaning explained above, because this is verified already for $L = \mathfrak{c}_1 \vee \mathfrak{c}_2$ (in other words, this is an "open"

property). Similarly one can find some neighbourhood Ω_2 of $\mathfrak{c}_2$ verifying the same property with the roles of $\mathfrak{c}_1$ and $\mathfrak{c}_2$ swapped. Therefore there exist two open subsets U_1 and U_2 in $\mathbb{P}^3$ containing respectively ϵ_1 and ϵ_2, such that for any $e_i \in U_i$ the line $L_i = p_i^{-1}(e_i)$ induces a generic projection $p_{L_i} : X \longrightarrow \mathbb{P}^2$. If such a pair $(e_1, e_2) \in U_1 \times U_2$ is distinct from (ϵ_1, ϵ_2), the two lines $l_i = p_i^{-1}(e_i)$ for $i = 1, 2$ in $\mathbb{P}^4$ are also distinct; if the discriminant curves $\pi_{e_i}(\widetilde{R}_i)$ for $i = 1, 2$ are projectively equivalent, the previous theorem asserts the existence of an automorphism σ of X compatible with the two coverings, in other words for some automorphism τ of $\mathbb{P}^2$ we have the commutative diagram

$$
\begin{array}{ccc}
X & \xrightarrow{\sigma} & X \\
\downarrow{\scriptstyle p_{L_1}} & & \downarrow{\scriptstyle p_{L_2}} \\
\mathbb{P}^2 & \xrightarrow{\tau} & \mathbb{P}^2
\end{array}
$$

We woud have necessarily

$$
\begin{aligned}
\sigma^*(\mathcal{O}_X(1)) &\simeq \sigma^*(p_{L_2}^*\mathcal{O}_{\mathbb{P}_2}(1)) \\
&\simeq p_{L_2}^*\tau^*\mathcal{O}_{\mathbb{P}_2}(1) \simeq \mathcal{O}_X(1)
\end{aligned}
$$

We suppose that X is embedded in $\mathbb{P}^4$ by the complete linear series $|\mathcal{O}_X(1)|$, or in other words that $\mathrm{H}^0(\mathcal{O}_X(1)) \simeq \mathrm{H}^0(\mathcal{O}_{\mathbb{P}^4}(1))$ so the isomorphism $\sigma : X \simeq X$ would be necessarily induced by some linear automorphism in PGL_5. By assumption this last one could be only the identity, hence the linear projections τp_{L_1} and p_{L_2} would coincide on X and therefore would have equal centers, since X is not contained in any hyperplane. The equalities $L_1 = L_2$ and hence $e_1 = \epsilon_1$, $e_2 = \epsilon_2$ follow at once. ∎

In the next section we seek for the pair of epipoles (ϵ_1, ϵ_2). We shall use the previous corollary to assert that this pair is an isolated point in a family of potential candidates.

4. EPIPOLAR RECOVERY BY DISCRIMINANT CURVES

4.1 The basic principle

We keep the notations and assumptions introduced in sections 2 and 3. For any point $e_i \in \mathbb{P}^3$ not in X_i let $\widehat{X}_{i, e_i} \subset \widehat{X}_i \subset \mathbb{L}_{e_i}\mathbb{P}^3$ be the closure of the locally closed subset of lines in $\mathbb{P}^3$ containing e_i and tangent to X_i. As such $\widehat{X}_{i, e_i}$ is isomorphic to the discriminant curve of π_{e_i}; suppose a hyperplane $H_i \subset \mathbb{P}^3$ was chosen with $e_i \notin H_i$, we can consider $\widehat{X}_{i, e_i}$ as a curve in H_i (every point is simply mapped to the line joining it to e_i). Again it is isomorphic to the discriminant curve of the projection $p_{p_i^{-1}(e_i)} : X \longrightarrow \mathbb{P}^2$ from the line $p_i^{-1}(e_i)$, which contains the center $\mathfrak{c}_{3-i}$.

PROPOSITION– 2. *For generic projections centers* $\mathfrak{c}_1$ *and* $\mathfrak{c}_2$ *in* $\mathbb{P}^4$, *the map* $\widetilde{F} : H_1 \to H_2$ *induces an isomorphism* $\widehat{X}_{1, \epsilon_1} \simeq \widehat{X}_{2, \epsilon_2}$. *Finally the point* (ϵ_1, ϵ_2) *is isolated in the subset* $\widehat{Z}$ *of all points* $(e_1, e_2) \in (\mathbb{P}^3 \setminus H_1) \times (\mathbb{P}^3 \setminus H_2)$ *such that* $\widehat{X}_{i, e_i}$ *for* $i = 1, 2$ *are projectively isomorphic plane curves.*

Proof: Let again $S = S_1 \cup S_2$ be the curve of X of points where p_1 or p_2 is not a local isomorphism. Let i be 1 or 2, and define $j = 3 - i$. Any point $x \in p_i(X \setminus S) \subset X_i$, necessarily smooth, lies on the divisor R_i as soon as the line $\epsilon_i \vee x$ is tangent to X_i at x. Necessarily the 2–plane $p_i^{-1}(\epsilon_i \vee x)$ in $\mathbb{P}^4$ is tangent to X, hence the projected line $p_j\left(p_i^{-1}(\epsilon_i \vee x)\right)$ is tangent to X_j at some *smooth* point y. Since the line $\epsilon_j \vee y$ is the image of $\epsilon_i \vee x$ by F, we obtain two rational maps between the two curves $\widehat{X}_{i,\epsilon_i}$ for $i = 1, 2$ which are inverse to each other. Since F is linear, hence is globally defined these birational maps can be extended to isomorphisms on the whole curves (this point is crucial since a birational map between possibly singular curves may not be extended to a global isomorphism).

Last assertion follows readily from corollary 1: inside an open subset $U_1 \times U_2$ containing (ϵ_1, ϵ_2) the pair $(e_1, e_2) = (\epsilon_1, \epsilon_2)$ is the sole point such that the curves $\widehat{X}_{i,e_i}$ are projectively equivalent. ■

In the next paragraph we shall explain the algorithm.

4.2 The algorithm

We keep the notations of the previous sections. The idea is to look for the subset of all 3-tuples $(e_1, \widetilde{F}, e_2)$ where e_1 and e_2 are two points in $\mathbb{P}^3 \setminus H_1$ and $\mathbb{P}^3 \setminus H_2$ respectively, and $\widetilde{F} \in PGL(H_1, H_2)$ inducing an isomorphism $\widehat{X}_{1,e_1} \simeq \widehat{X}_{2,e_2}$. Let us introduce homogeneous coordinates on $\mathbb{P}^3$: the point $e_i = \left[e_i^0 : \cdots : e_i^3\right]$ is the unknown, for $i = 1, 2$. We shall suppose that each H_i is the hyperplane at infinity defined by the vanishing of the last coordinate. So we assume $e_i^3 \neq 0$, and for such e_i we shall make use of the isomorphism between $\mathbb{L}_{e_i}\mathbb{P}^3$ and H_i mapping each point $p = [x_0; x_1; x_2; 0] \in H_i$ to the line $L_p = p \vee e_i$. For each such p the intersection $L_p \cap X_i$ is given by the (potentially multiple) roots of the polynomial

$$f_i(s\,e_i^0 + t\,x_0; \cdots; s\,e_i^2 + t\,x_2; s\,e_i^3) = \sum_{j=0}^{d} A_j(e_i; x_0, x_1, x_2)\, s^{d-j}\, t^j \tag{3}$$

We shall denote the polynomial in (3) by $g_{e_i,p}(s,t)$: its coefficients A_j are bihomogeneous forms of degree $d - j$ in the coordinates of e_i, and of degree j in x_0, x_1, x_2. If L_p is tangent to X_i at some smooth point, or if L_p meets the double points curve D_i, then $g_{e_i,p}(s,t)$ has at least one multiple root. This property is characterized by the vanishing of the following discriminant (see appendix 7), taking entries of e_i and p as parameters:

$$G_i^{e_i}(x_0, x_1, x_2) = \mathrm{Disc}_{[s,t]}\left(g_{e_i,p}(s,t)\right). \tag{4}$$

The projective curve $G_i^{e_i}(x_0, x_1, x_2) = 0$ is of degree $d(d-1)$ in the coordinates $[x_0; x_1; x_2]$. It is the union of the generators of the cone of vertex e_i over D_i and $\widehat{X}_{i,e_i}$, hence contains at least two irreducible components. We have the following factorization in the ring $\mathbb{C}\left(e_i^0; \cdots; e_i^3\right)[x_0; x_1; x_2]$:

$$G_i^{e_i}(x_0, x_1, x_2) = \mathfrak{D}_i^{e_i}(x_0, x_1, x_2) \cdot \mathfrak{R}_i^{e_i}(x_0, x_1, x_2) \tag{5}$$

In (5), the polynomial $\mathfrak{D}_i^{e_i}(x_0, x_1, x_2)$ generates the ideal of $\pi_{e_i}(D_i)$, and $\mathfrak{R}_i^{e_i}(x_0, x_1, x_2)$ generates the ideal of $\pi_{e_i}(R_i)$. If e_i is generic the polynomial $\mathfrak{R}_i^{e_i}(x_0, x_1, x_2)$ is irreducible, because $p_{p_i^{-1}(e_i)} : X \longrightarrow \mathbb{P}^2$ is a generic covering and therefore R_i is the image by p_i of the normalization of an irreducible curve, hence the set $\mathfrak{R}_i^{e_i}(x_0, x_1, x_2) = 0$ must be also irreducible. Beside, $\mathfrak{D}_i^{e_i}(x_0, x_1, x_2)$ might be reducible.

We are looking for all pairs $(e_1, e_2) \in (\mathbb{P}^3 \setminus H_1) \times (\mathbb{P}^3 \setminus H_2)$ together with the class of a linear automorphism, which can

be concretely written as:

$$\widetilde{F}[x_0 : x_1 : x_2] = [l_0(x_0, x_1, x_2) : l_1(x_0, x_1, x_2) : l_2(x_0, x_1, x_2)]$$

verifying:

$$\mathfrak{R}_1^{e_1}(x_0, x_1, x_2) = \mathfrak{R}_2^{e_2}(F(x_0, x_1, x_2)) \tag{6}$$

We need to identify the factors $\mathfrak{D}_i^{e_i}(x_0, x_1, x_2)$ for $i = 1, 2$, which we do by using elimination: consider the closed subset of points $([e_i^0 : \cdots : e_i^3], [x_0 : x_1 : x_2], [s : t])$ satisfying:

$$\nabla f_i(s\,e_i^0 + t\,x_0; s\,e_i^1 + t\,x_1; s\,e_i^2 + t\,x_2; s\,e_i^3) = 0. \tag{7}$$

This gives a system of 4 equations, from which we eliminate the variables s, t, in other words we obtain the ideal of the image of the closed subset (7) by the projection on the variables of e_i and p. It is generated by a polynomial in x_0, x_1, x_2 of degree $\overline{d}_i$, with coefficients depending on e_i ones. This is the factor $\mathfrak{D}_i^{e_i}(x_0, x_1, x_2)$. We can summarize up our algorithm now.

ALGORITHM– 1. *Given two equations $f_i = 0$ of the two projected surfaces X_i in $\mathbb{P}^3$:*

- *For $i = 1, 2$ eliminate the variables s, t in (7) to get $\mathfrak{D}_i^{e_i}(x_0, x_1, x_2)$;*

- *compute $G_i^{e_i}(x_0, x_1, x_2)$ by (4); form $\mathfrak{R}_i^{e_i}(x_0, x_1, x_2) = \dfrac{G_i^{e_i}(x_0, x_1, x_2)}{\mathfrak{D}_i^{e_i}(x_0, x_1, x_2)}$;*

- *introduce the unknown plane transformation $\widetilde{F}[x_0 : x_1 : x_2] = [l_0(x_0, x_1, x_2) : l_1(x_0, x_1, x_2) : l_2(x_0, x_1, x_2)]$ and write down the ideal generated by equality (6), which amounts to equalize $\binom{2\delta+2}{2} + 1$ coefficients of two degree 2δ homogeneous polynomials in 3 variables;*

- *then fix $e_i^3 = 1$ for $i = 1, 2$ and find zero-dimensional components of the image of this ideal by the projection*

$$\left(e_1, \widetilde{F}, e_2\right) \mapsto (e_1, e_2)$$

After the last step of the previous algorithm is completed, we have recovered the pair of epipoles up to a finite ambiguity. In the next section we work out an example.

4.3 An example

We worked out an example of the algorithm. We considered a surface of $\mathbb{P}^4$, being a complete intersection of two quadrics:

$$\begin{cases} f_1 = X_1{}^2 - X_3{}^2 + 2X_2X_4 + X_4{}^2 - X_1X_2 + X_2{}^2 + X_3X_0 \\ f_2 = X_2X_3 - X_0{}^2 + X_2{}^2 + X_1X_3 + X_4X_3 \end{cases}$$

The computation was performed using Maple 13, with includes the FastGB library [4], known as being one of the best available Groebner bases implementations. The surface is irreducible and smooth.

The projection maps were defined as follows:

$$M_1 = \begin{bmatrix} 1 & 0 & 0 & 0 & 0 \\ 0 & 0 & 1 & 0 & 0 \\ 0 & 0 & 0 & 1 & 0 \\ 0 & 1 & -1 & 0 & 0 \end{bmatrix} \quad M_2 = \begin{bmatrix} 1 & 0 & 0 & 0 & 0 \\ 0 & 1 & 0 & 0 & 0 \\ 0 & 0 & 0 & 1 & 0 \\ 0 & -1 & 1 & 0 & 1 \end{bmatrix}$$

In this setting the centers of projection in $\mathbb{P}^4$ are quite simple: $c_1 = \begin{bmatrix} 0 \\ 0 \\ 0 \\ 0 \\ 1 \end{bmatrix}$ and $c_2 = \begin{bmatrix} 0 \\ 0 \\ -1 \\ 0 \\ 1 \end{bmatrix} \in \mathbb{P}^4$. The epipoles are: $\epsilon_1 = \begin{bmatrix} 0 \\ -1 \\ 0 \\ 1 \end{bmatrix}, \epsilon_2 = \begin{bmatrix} 0 \\ 0 \\ 0 \\ 1 \end{bmatrix} \in \mathbb{P}^3$, while the map $\widetilde{F}$ is the class of the unit matrix I_3.

The equation $\mathfrak{R}_1^{e_1}$ obtained from the first projection for the set of lines passing through a symbolic epipole $e_1 = [e_1^1, e_1^2, e_1^3, 1]$ not lying on the plane at infinity and tangent to the surface at smooth points is far too long to be incorporated hereby. However the realization for the actual epipole $\epsilon_1 = [0, -1, 0, 1]^t$ is given by:

$$-\frac{9}{64}x_2^6 x_1^2 + \frac{1667}{8192}x_2^4 x_1^4 - \frac{177}{2048}x_1^6 x_2^2 - \frac{1}{256}x_1^8 -$$
$$\frac{1}{32}x_2^2 x_0^6 + \frac{1}{32}x_2^8 - \frac{3}{64}x_0 x_1^4 - \frac{15}{512}x_2 x_1^6 + \frac{17}{256}x_1^2 x_2^3 x_0^3 +$$
$$\frac{1}{32}x_1^2 x_0^6 - \frac{1}{32}x_2^5 x_0^3 - \frac{3}{32}x_0 x_2^7 - \frac{1}{32}x_0^4 x_2^4 +$$
$$\frac{3}{32}x_2^6 x_0^2 + \frac{1}{16}x_2^3 x_0^5 - \frac{3}{32}x_0^5 x_1^2 x_2 - \frac{49}{256}x_0^2 x_1^2 x_2^4 +$$
$$\frac{5}{64}x_0^4 x_1^2 x_2^2 - \frac{3}{64}x_0^3 x_1^4 x_2 - \frac{3}{512}x_0 x_1^6 x_2 - \frac{203}{1024}x_0 x_1^4 x_2^3 +$$
$$\frac{9}{32}x_0 x_1^2 x_2^5 + \frac{25}{256}x_0^2 x_1^4 x_2^2$$

Eliminating the variables s, t from (7) is done by projective elimination and performed through Groebner basis. It results in a ideal, which is not necessarily reduced. Since multiplicities are not used hereby, we take the radical of this ideal and find a unique generator: $\mathfrak{D}_i^{e_i}(x_0, x_1, x_2)$. A similar step is performed after the elimination of s and t from (4): we discard the multiplicities, which outputs the polynomial: $G_i^{e_i}(x_0, x_1, x_2)$. Then the division $\frac{G_i^{e_i}(x_0, x_1, x_2)}{\mathfrak{D}_i^{e_i}(x_0, x_1, x_2)}$ is straight forward.

As expected the singularities of the resulting curve are cusps and ordinary double points. More precisely, a Maple computation provides the following singular points:

$$[[1, 0, 0], 2, 1, 2]$$
$$\left[\left[RootOf(1 + 4Z^2), 1, 0\right], 2, 1, 2\right]$$
$$\begin{bmatrix} \begin{bmatrix} RootOf(3456Z^6 - 1728Z^5 + 3204Z^4 - 376Z^3 \\ +48Z^2 + 987Z - 947), \\ RootOf(3534051Z^2 - 2709968 + \\ \quad 2615728RootOf(3456Z^6 - 1728Z^5 + \\ \quad\quad 3763204Z^4 - Z^3 + 48Z^2 + 987Z - 947) + \\ \quad 1293232RootOf(3456Z^6 - 1728Z^5 + \\ \quad\quad 3204Z^4 - 376Z^3 + 48Z^2 + 987Z - 947)^2 - \\ \quad 1203408RootOf(3456Z^6 - 1728Z^5 + 3204Z^4 - \\ \quad\quad 48376Z^3 + Z^2 + 987Z - 947)^3 + \\ \quad 3756672RootOf(3456Z^6 - 1728Z^5 + 3204Z^4 - \\ \quad\quad 48376Z^3 + Z^2 + 987Z - 947)^4 - \\ \quad 13824RootOf(3456Z^6 - 1728Z^5 + 3204Z^4 - \\ \quad\quad 376Z^3 + 48Z^2 + 987Z - 947)^5), \\ 1 \end{bmatrix}, 2, 1, 1 \end{bmatrix}$$

Each singular point is given by its projective coordinates, followed by a list of three invariants: its multiplicity, its delta invariant and the number of local branches passing through the point. Thus the three first singularities are ordinary double points, while the last one is a cusp.

Once the reduced corresponding discriminant curves $\mathfrak{R}_1^{e_1}(x_0, x_1, x_2)$ and $\mathfrak{R}_2^{e_2}(x_0, x_1, x_2)$ have been computed, the remaining steps of the algorithm can be performed as follows: (i) from equation (6), we get a system of equation in the epipoles and the fundamental matrix, say $S(e_1, e_2, \widetilde{F})$.

In our example, this systems contained 45 equations. One can perform a projection to get a system over the epipoles only. Let $S(e_1, s_e)$ be this final system. The extraction of the zero dimensional component can be performed by first computing the radical of the ideal defined by $S(e_1, e_2)$ (we denote $K(e_1, e_2)$ this radical ideal), and then by looking for the points where the Jacobian matrix of the generators of $K(e_1, e_2)$ has full rank. We did not perform these last two steps, because they were computationally too heavy for our machine (Intel core 2 with 3GB RAM). However, we checked that when pluging the actual values of the epipoles and the fundamental matrix, the system $S(e_1, e_2, \widetilde{F})$ does vanish and that the Jacobian matrix at this point has full rank, showing that the point is isolated, which means that there is a single fundamental matrix in the fiber over the actual pair of epipoles. Therefore as proven earlier, this pair is an isolated point of the variety defined by $K(e_1, e_2)$.

5. SURFACE RECOVERY

Once the epipolar geometry is computed, one can recover the pair of projections up to projective equivalence as shown in section 2. Then the surface itself lies in the intersection of the cones defined by the projected surfaces and the centers of projections. Let us write $\Delta_1 = p_1^{-1}(X_1)$ and $\Delta_2 = p_2^{-1}(X_2)$ for these two cones. In the case the surface is irreducible, the intersection of the cones contains for generic projections two irreducible components. More precisely we have the following theorem.

THEOREM— 2. *Let X be an irreducible and smooth closed surface embedded in $\mathbb{P}^4$ of degree d. For a generic position of the centers of projection, namely when no epipolar hyperplane (hyperplane containing the two centers) is tangent twice to the surface X, the surface defined by $\{\Delta_1 = 0, \Delta_2 = 0\}$ has two irreducible components. One has degree d and is the actual solution of the reconstruction. The other one has degree $d(d - 1)$.*

PROOF. The proof relies on a similar theorem previously introduced for curves in $\mathbb{P}^3$ projected over planes. See [10] for more details. Thus we consider a section by a generic epipolar hyperplane. Since the center of projections are generic, by Bertini's theorem [9], the curve in this section is smooth and irreducible. This reduces the configuration to the case of curves, for which the theorem has already been proven. □

6. CONCLUSION

We have presented a solution for recovering a smooth surface embedded in $\mathbb{P}^4$ from two generic linear projections. Our algorithm is based on the discriminant curves and relies on Kulikov's theorem on the Chisini conjecture. We have also showed that when the surface is irreducible, it can be finally recovered as the single component of the right degree in the intersections of the two cones defined by the projections. Future work will consider other methods and algorithms for the recovery of the surface, as well as generalizations to general co-dimension 2 varieties.

7. APPENDIX: DISCRIMINANT OF A HOMOGENEOUS POLYNOMIAL

Suppose $P(s, t) = a_n s^n + a_{n-1} s^{n-1} t + \cdots + a_1 s t^{n-1} + a_0 t^n$ is a homogeneous polynomial of degree n. We define the discriminant of P respectively to the variables $[s,t]$ by the following expression:

$$Disc_{[s,t]}(P) = \frac{(-1)^{\frac{n(n-1)}{2}}}{a_n} \mathrm{Res}_s(P(s,1), \frac{\partial P}{\partial s}(s,1)), \quad (8)$$

where $\mathrm{Res}_X(F,G)$ denotes the resultant between two polynomials $F, G \in R[X]$ with R being some commutative ring. It is proved (see for instance [1]) that $Disc_{[s,t]}(P) = 0$ if and only if P contains a factor of the form $(t_0 s - s_0 t)^2$, i.e. P vanishes at order ≥ 2 along a direction in $[s,t]$.

8. REFERENCES

[1] F. Apery and J. Jouanolou. *Elimination: le cas d'une variable*. Herman, 2006.

[2] F. Catanese. On a problem of chisini. *Duke Math. J.*, 53(1):33–42, 1986.

[3] O. Faugeras and Q. Luong. *The Geometry of Multiple Images*. MIT Press, 2001.

[4] J.-C. Faugère. *FGb: A Library for Computing Gröbner Bases*, volume 6327 of *Lecture Notes in Computer Science*, pages 84–87. Springer., 2010. Mathematical Software ICMS 2010.

[5] W. Fulton. *Intersection Theory*. Springer, second edition, 1998.

[6] P. Griffiths and J. Harris. *Principles of Algebraic Geometry*. Wiley Classics Library, 1978.

[7] J. Harris. *Algebraic Geometry: a first course*. Springer, 1992.

[8] R. Hartley and A. Zisserman. *Multiple-View Geometry*. Cambridge University Press, 2sd edition, 2004.

[9] R. Hartshorne. *Algebraic Geometry*. Springer, 1977.

[10] J. Kaminski, M. Fryers, and M. Teicher. Recovering an algebraic curve from its projections onto different planes. *Journal of the European Mathematical Society*, 7(2):145–282, 2005.

[11] V. Kulikov. On chisini's conjecture ii. *Izv. Mat*, 72:5:901–913, 2008.

[12] R. Lazarsfeld. *Positivity in Algebraic Geometry*. Springer, 2004.

Computing Comprehensive Gröbner Systems and Comprehensive Gröbner Bases Simultaneously *

Deepak Kapur
Dept. of Computer Science
University of New Mexico
Albuquerque, NM, USA
kapur@cs.unm.edu

Yao Sun
KLMM
Academy of Mathematics and
Systems Science,CAS
Beijing 100190, China
sunyao@amss.ac.cn

Dingkang Wang
KLMM
Academy of Mathematics and
Systems Science,CAS
Beijing 100190, China
dwang@mmrc.iss.ac.cn

ABSTRACT

In Kapur et al (ISSAC, 2010), a new method for computing a comprehensive Gröbner system of a parameterized polynomial system was proposed and its efficiency over other known methods was effectively demonstrated. Based on those insights, a new approach is proposed for computing a comprehensive Gröbner basis of a parameterized polynomial system. The key new idea is not to simplify a polynomial under various specialization of its parameters, but rather keep track in the polynomial, of the power products whose coefficients vanish; this is achieved by partitioning the polynomial into two parts–*nonzero* part and *zero* part for the specialization under consideration. During the computation of a comprehensive Gröbner system, for a particular branch corresponding to a specialization of parameter values, nonzero parts of the polynomials dictate the computation, i.e., computing S-polynomials as well as for simplifying a polynomial with respect to other polynomials; but the manipulations on the whole polynomials (including their zero parts) are also performed. Gröbner basis computations on such pairs of polynomials can also be viewed as Gröbner basis computations on a module. Once a comprehensive Gröbner system is generated, both nonzero and zero parts of the polynomials are collected from every branch and the result is a *faithful* comprehensive Gröbner basis, to mean that every polynomial in a comprehensive Gröbner basis belongs to the ideal of the original parameterized polynomial system. This technique should be applicable to other algorithms for computing a comprehensive Gröbner system as well, thus producing both a comprehensive Gröbner system as well as a faithful comprehensive Gröbner basis of a parameterized polynomial system simultaneously. The approach is exhibited by adapting the recently proposed method for computing a compre-
hensive Gröbner system in (ISSAC, 2010) for computing a comprehensive Gröbner basis. The timings on a collection of examples demonstrate that this new algorithm for computing comprehensive Gröbner bases has better performance than other existing algorithms.

Categories and Subject Descriptors

I.1.2 [**Symbolic and Algebraic Manipulation**]: Algorithms

General Terms

Algorithms

Keywords

Gröbner basis, comprehensive Gröbner basis, comprehensive Gröbner system.

1. INTRODUCTION

The concept of a comprehensive Gröbner basis was introduced by Weispfenning [16] as a special basis of a parametric polynomial system such that for every possible specialization of its parameters, the basis obtained from the comprehensive Gröbner basis serves as a Gröbner basis of the ideal generated by the specialization of the parametric polynomial system (see also [7] where a related concept of a parametric Gröbner basis is introduced). In that paper, Weispfenning gave an algorithm for computing a comprehensive Gröbner basis from a comprehensive Gröbner system, consisting of Gröbner bases for various specializations of the parameters. In this paper, we show how both comprehensive Gröbner system and comprehensive Gröbner basis of a parametric polynomial system can be constructed together. The key idea is to retain terms in polynomials even when parameters are specialized, resulting in vanishing of the coefficients of these terms.

To illustrate the key idea, let us consider Example 8.4 from [17] where Weispfenning defined the concept of a canonical comprehensive Gröbner basis of a parametric polynomial system to mimic the concept of a reduced Gröbner basis of a polynomial system determined by the associated ideal and term order. Suppose there are two polynomials $f, g \in k[u, v][x, y]$:

$$f = y + ux + v, \quad g = uy + x + v.$$

---

*The first author is supported by the National Science Foundation award CCF-0729097 and the last two authors are supported by NKBRPC 2011CB302400, NSFC 10971217 and 60821002/F02.

Further, suppose we are interested in computing Gröbner basis with the lexicographic order induced by y > x.

Clearly, f can be used to simplify g, resulting in

$$h = g - uf = (1 - u^2)x - uv + v.$$

In fact, g can be deleted without any loss of generality. Based on the specialization of u and v, the leading power product of h is either x or 1.

For the branch where $(1 - u^2) \neq 0$, the nonzero part of h is $(1 - u^2)x + (-uv + v)$. Since both f and h have noncomparable leading power products, $\{f, h\}$ constitutes a Gröbner basis for this branch for those specializations satisfying $(1 - u^2) \neq 0$.

For the branch, where $(1 - u^2) = 0$ and $(-uv + v) \neq 0$ for all those specializations of u and v, the nonzero part of h is $(-uv + v)$ and the zero part of h is $(1 - u^2)x$. For this branch, a Gröbner basis is $\{h\}$, since the leading power product of the nonzero part of h is 1, which reduces every other power product. If h is simplified using the specializations of u and v, the Gröbner basis would have been $\{1\}$. However, such a Gröbner basis is not *faithful*, since 1 is not in $\langle f, g \rangle$. But to maintain faithfulness, we keep h instead.

Finally, for the branch where $(1 - u^2) = 0$ and $(-uv + v) = 0$, h vanishes completely. And, the nonzero part of f is itself, since the leading coefficient of f is 1. A Gröbner basis for this branch is $\{f\}$; if the specialization of u and v had been used to simplify f, we have $\{y + x + v\}$ as a Gröbner basis.

Using the proposed algorithm, a comprehensive Gröbner system consists of three branches: a branch corresponding to specializations satisfying $(1 - u^2) \neq 0$, for which $\{f, h\}$ is a Gröbner basis for a 0-dimensional specialization; another branch, corresponding to the specialization satisfying $(1 - u^2) = 0, (-uv + v) \neq 0$ (which can be further simplified to $u + 1 = 0, v \neq 0$), for which $\{h\}$ is a Gröbner basis for the ideal generated by 1; the last branch corresponds to the specialization $(1 - u^2) = 0, (-uv + v) = 0$, for which $\{f\}$ is a Gröbner basis for the one dimensional ideal.

The key difference between the output of this algorithm and other algorithms including our algorithm in [9], is that a Gröbner basis in every branch in a comprehensive Gröbner system is a subset of the original ideal, and hence contributes to a comprehensive Gröbner basis.

A *faithful* comprehensive Gröbner basis for the above system can be easily constructed by taking the union of Gröbner bases along all the branches; for every possible specialization, there is exactly one branch generating a Gröbner basis for the specialized ideal; furthermore, by construction, all the polynomials are in the ideal of the original system. For the above example, a comprehensive Gröbner basis is $\{f, h\}$.[1]

Based on the ideas illustrated for the above example, we propose in this paper, an algorithm for simultaneously computing a comprehensive Gröbner system as well as the associated comprehensive Gröbner basis that is faithful. This algorithm builds on our recently proposed algorithm [9] for computing a comprehensive Gröbner system as its foundation. The key difference between the new algorithm and the previous algorithm is that unlike in the old algorithm,

during computations, the zero part of a polynomial under a specialization is also kept in a tuple representation so as to recover the original polynomial when needed. Specifically, when computing a comprehensive Gröbner system of the set $F \subset k[U][X]$, we use a tuple $(q, \bar{q}) \in (k[U][X])^2$ to replace each polynomial $p = q + \bar{q}$ in the computation, with the following properties: (i) $p \in \langle F \rangle$, and (ii) $\bar{q}$ is 0 under the specialization of parameters being considered. When a comprehensive Gröbner system of F is obtained, then for each 2-tuple $(g, \bar{g})$ in this comprehensive Gröbner system, we recover the faithful polynomial $g + \bar{g}$; this way, a comprehensive Gröbner basis of F is obtained simultaneously with the comprehensive Gröbner system.

Generally, a comprehensive Gröbner basis for a given polynomial set F is harder to compute than a comprehensive Gröbner system of F. The difficulty of computing a comprehensive Gröbner basis of F is that, all the polynomials in this comprehensive Gröbner basis should be faithful polynomials, i.e., these polynomials should belong to the ideal $\langle F \rangle$, while the polynomials in a comprehensive Gröbner system of F are not necessarily faithful polynomials. Therefore, the algorithms for computing comprehensive Gröbner systems usually have better performance than those for comprehensive Gröbner bases. Consequently, a feasible method for computing comprehensive Gröbner bases is to compute comprehensive Gröbner systems first, and then transform all polynomials in the comprehensive Gröbner systems to faithful polynomials. Unfortunately, this transformation is usually expensive when the computation of comprehensive Gröbner systems is finished. So the goal of the new technique is to make this transformation easier. The proposed idea of retaining polynomials from the ideal of the original polynomial system while computing Gröbner bases along different branches can be used in all algorithms for computing comprehensive Gröbner systems, including Weispfenning's [16], Kapur's [7], Montes' [11, 10, 13], Wang's [2], Suzuki-Sato's [15], Nabeshima's [14] as well as our recently proposed algorithm [9].

Comprehensive Gröbner basis and Gröbner system constructions have been found useful in many engineering applications which can be modeled using parameterized polynomial systems; see [4, 6, 11] for examples of some applications. These constructions have also been found useful for automated geometry theorem proving [2] and automated geometry theorem discovery [12], as well as more recently, for computing loop invariants in program analysis [8]. Solving parametric polynomial systems has also been investigated by Chou and Gao [5] and Chen et al. [1] using the characteristic set construction, as well as by Wibmer [18] using Gröbner cover.

The paper is organized as follows. We give some notations and definitions in Section 2. The new technique mentioned above is described in Section 3. We propose a new algorithm for computing comprehensive Gröbner bases in Section 4. A simple example illustrates the proposed algorithm in Section 5. Empirical data and comparison with other existing algorithms are presented in Section 6. Concluding remarks follow in Section 7.

2. NOTATIONS AND DEFINITIONS

Let k be a field, R be the polynomial ring $k[U]$ in the parameters $U = \{u_1, \cdots, u_m\}$, and $R[X]$ be the polynomial ring over the parameter ring R in the variables $X =$

---

[1] An interested reader would notice that this result is different from the one reported in [17]. In fact, the canonical comprehensive Gröbner basis reported there for the same order is a proper superset of the above result, suggesting that after all, the definition in [17] does not quite capture the notion of minimality and hence, canonicity.

$\{x_1, \cdots, x_n\}$ where $X \cap U = \emptyset$, i.e. X and U are disjoint sets.

Let $PP(X)$, $PP(U)$ and $PP(U,X)$ be the sets of power products of X, U and $X \cup U$ respectively. $\prec_{X,U}$ is an admissible block term order on $PP(U,X)$ where $U \ll X$. The orders $\prec_X$ and $\prec_U$ are the restrictions of $\prec_{X,U}$ on $PP(X)$ and $PP(U)$ respectively.

For a polynomial $f \in R[X] = k[U][X]$, the leading power product, leading coefficient and leading monomial of f w.r.t. the order $\prec_X$ are denoted by $\mathrm{lpp}_X(f)$, $\mathrm{lc}_X(f)$ and $\mathrm{lm}_X(f)$ respectively. Since f can also be regarded as an element of $k[U, X]$, in this case, the leading power product, leading coefficient and leading monomial of f w.r.t. the order $\prec_{X,U}$ are denoted by $\mathrm{lpp}_{X,U}(f)$, $\mathrm{lc}_{X,U}(f)$ and $\mathrm{lm}_{X,U}(f)$ respectively. For f, we always have $\mathrm{lm}_X(f) = \mathrm{lc}_X(f)\mathrm{lpp}_X(f)$ and $\mathrm{lm}_{X,U}(f) = \mathrm{lc}_{X,U}(f)\mathrm{lpp}_{X,U}(f)$.

Given a field L, a specialization of R is a homomorphism $\sigma : R \longrightarrow L$. In this paper, we always assume L to be an algebraically closed field containing k and we only consider the specializations induced by the elements in L^m. That is, for $\bar{a} \in L^m$, the induced specialization $\sigma_{\bar{a}}$ is defined as follows.

$$\sigma_{\bar{a}} : f \longrightarrow f(\bar{a})$$

where $f \in R$. Every specialization $\sigma : R \longrightarrow L$ extends canonically to a specialization $\sigma : R[X] \longrightarrow L[X]$ by applying σ coefficient-wise.

For a parametric polynomial system, the comprehensive Gröbner system and comprehensive Gröbner basis are given below.

Definition 2.1 (CGS) *Let F be a subset of $R[X]$, $A_1, \cdots, A_l$ be algebraically constructible subsets of L^m, $G_1, \cdots, G_l$ be subsets of $R[X]$, and S be a subset of L^m such that $S \subseteq A_1 \cup \cdots \cup A_l$. A finite set $\mathcal{G} = \{(A_1, G_1), \cdots, (A_l, G_l)\}$ is called a* **comprehensive Gröbner system** *on S for F, if $\sigma_{\bar{a}}(G_i)$ is a Gröbner basis of the ideal $\langle \sigma_{\bar{a}}(F) \rangle$ in $L[X]$ for $\bar{a} \in A_i$ and $i = 1, \cdots, l$. Each (A_i, G_i) is called a branch of $\mathcal{G}$. If $S = L^m$, then $\mathcal{G}$ is simply called a comprehensive Gröbner system for F.*

For an $F \subset R = k[U]$, the variety defined by F in L^m is denoted by $V(F)$. In this paper, the constructible set A_i always has the form: $A_i = V(E_i) \setminus V(N_i)$ where E_i, N_i are subsets of $k[U]$. Particularly, we call E_i and N_i equality constraints and disequality constraints respectively. Clearly, if the set $A_i = V(E_i) \setminus V(N_i)$ is empty, the branch (A_i, G_i) is redundant.

Definition 2.2 (CGB) *Let F be a subset of $R[X]$ and S be a subset of L^m. A finite subset G in $R[X]$ is called a* **comprehensive Gröbner basis** *on S for F, if $\sigma_{\bar{a}}(G)$ is a Gröbner basis of the ideal $\langle \sigma_{\bar{a}}(F) \rangle$ in $L[X]$ for each $\bar{a}$ in S. If $S = L^m$, then G is simply called a comprehensive Gröbner basis for F.*
A comprehensive Gröbner basis G of F is called **faithful** *if in addition, every element of G is also in $\langle F \rangle$.*

A typical approach to compute a comprehensive Gröbner basis of F is to first compute a comprehensive Gröbner system of F and then further process it to generate a comprehensive Gröbner basis. It follows from the above definitions of a comprehensive Gröbner system and a comprehensive Gröbner basis that given a comprehensive Gröbner

system $\mathcal{G} = \{(A_1, G_1), \cdots, (A_l, G_l)\}$ on S for $F \subset R[X]$, if $G_i \subset \langle F \rangle$ for $i = 1, \cdots, l$, then the set $G_1 \cup \cdots \cup G_l$ is a comprehensive Gröbner basis on S for F. However, in almost all the known algorithms for computing a comprehensive Gröbner system, G_i is typically never a subset of the ideal $\langle F \rangle$, since polynomials get simplified based on parameter specialization. The main challenge is thus to recover $G_i' \subset \langle F \rangle$ such that $\sigma_{\bar{a}}(G_i) = \sigma_{\bar{a}}(G_i')$ for $\bar{a} \in A_i$. In the next section, we propose a new technique to obtain the G_i''s efficiently during the computation of a comprehensive Gröbner system.

3. A POLYNOMIAL AS A TUPLE UNDER PARAMETER SPECIALIZATION

As mentioned in the introduction and illustrated using an example, the key new idea in our approach is to keep track of polynomials in $\langle F \rangle$ while computing various Gröbner bases under different parameter specializations. If some terms in these polynomials vanish due to specialization of parameters during the computation of a comprehensive Gröbner system, this information can be kept by splitting the polynomial into the nonzero part and the zero part under the specialization.

A polynomial $p \in \langle F \rangle$ is replaced along a branch of a comprehensive Gröbner system computation for a specialization of parameters from a constructible set A_i, by a tuple $(q, \bar{q})$ such that (i) $p = q + \bar{q}$, and further, (ii) for every parameter specialization σ from A_i, $\sigma(\bar{q})$ is 0. We call $(q, \bar{q})$ an **admissible tuple representation** of p in the ideal $\langle F \rangle$ w.r.t. constructible set A_i.[2]

Let us observe some properties of admissible tuple representation of polynomials from an ideal. Given admissible tuple representations $(p, \bar{p})$ and $(q, \bar{q})$ of $p + \bar{p}$ and $q + \bar{q}$ in $\langle F \rangle$, w.r.t. A_i, $(p + q, \bar{p} + \bar{q})$ is an admissible tuple representation of $p + q + \bar{p} + \bar{q}$ in the ideal generated by $p + \bar{p}$ and $q + \bar{q}$ w.r.t. A_i. Furthermore, given a polynomial r, $(r \cdot p, r \cdot \bar{p})$ is an admissible tuple representation of $r \cdot p + r \cdot \bar{p}$ in the ideal generated by $p + \bar{p}$ w.r.t. A_i.

Let us now consider operations on polynomials and parameter specializations performed while computing a comprehensive Gröbner system. In Gröbner basis computations, there are two key steps – simplification of a polynomial by another polynomial and S-polynomial construction from a pair of distinct polynomials. In addition, we modify parametric constraints by adding disequalities and equalities on parameters, and modify the tuple representation of polynomials under consideration.

Particularly, if a parametric constraint h is added to a constructible set $A_i = V(E_i) \setminus V(N_i)$, with $E_i, N_i \subset k[U]$, the new constructible set A_i' should be nonempty, i.e., $A_i' = V(E_i') \setminus V(N_i') \neq \emptyset$ where either $E_i' = E_i \cup \{h\}, N_i' = N_i$ if the constraint is $h = 0$ or $E_i' = E_i, N_i' = \{n \cdot h \mid n \in N_i\}$ if the constraint is $h \neq 0$. Typically, h is the leading coefficient of the polynomial q in a tuple $(q, \bar{q})$ in a computation. If A_i is extended by adding $h \neq 0$, then the tuple is not changed; otherwise, if $h = 0$ is added as a new parameter constraint to E_i of A_i, then the above tuple is replaced by $(q', \bar{q}')$ by moving all terms in q that vanish to $\bar{q}'$ such that $q + \bar{q} = q' + \bar{q}'$ and the leading coefficient of q' is not always zero for the specializations from A_i' and $\bar{q}'$ is 0 w.r.t.

---

[2] We decided not to include an additional condition on an admissible tuple representation that $\mathrm{lc}_X(q) \neq 0$ wrt A_i, because this property is not preserved under addition. However, as the reader would observe later, this third condition is satisfied by tuples generated in the algorithms below.

A_i'. These are admissible tuple representations. We can make the leading coefficients of first components of tuples always nonzero w.r.t. some parametric constraints by using the method in [7, 11, 2].

For a constructible set A_i and two admissible tuple representations $\mathbf{p} = (p, \bar{p}), \mathbf{q} = (q, \bar{q})$ of $p + \bar{p}$ and $q + \bar{q}$, respectively, assuming both $\mathrm{lc}_X(p)$ and $\mathrm{lc}_X(q)$ are nonzero w.r.t. A_i, their **S-polynomial** is defined to be

$$\frac{\mathrm{lc}_X(q)L_{pq}}{\mathrm{lpp}_X(p)} \cdot (p, \bar{p}) - \frac{\mathrm{lc}_X(p)L_{pq}}{\mathrm{lpp}_X(q)} \cdot (q, \bar{q}),$$

where $L_{pq} = \mathrm{lcm}(\mathrm{lpp}_X(p), \mathrm{lpp}_X(q))$. Clearly, the S-polynomial of $\mathbf{p}$ and $\mathbf{q}$ is also an admissible tuple representation. And the polynomial corresponding to the above tuple is in the ideal of $\{p + \bar{p}, q + \bar{q}\}$.

Similarly, along a branch corresponding to a constructible set A_i, assuming $\mathrm{lpp}_X(g)$ divides $\mathrm{lpp}_X(f)$ and $\mathrm{lc}_X(g)$ is nonzero w.r.t. A_i, the result of reducing (simplifying) $\mathbf{f} = (f, \bar{f})$ by $\mathbf{g} = (g, \bar{g})$ is:

$$\begin{aligned} &\mathrm{lc}_X(g)\mathbf{f} - \frac{\mathrm{lm}_X(f)}{\mathrm{lpp}_X(g)} \cdot \mathbf{g} \\ = \;&(\mathrm{lc}_X(g)f - \frac{\mathrm{lm}_X(f)}{\mathrm{lpp}_X(g)}g, \mathrm{lc}_X(g)\bar{f} - \frac{\mathrm{lm}_X(f)}{\mathrm{lpp}_X(g)}\bar{g}), \end{aligned}$$

which is an admissible tuple representation of the simplified polynomial in the ideal of $\{f + \bar{f}, g + \bar{g}\}$.

In algorithms for computing a comprehensive Gröbner system from F, if we use the above admissible tuple representation of polynomials in F and perform the above S-polynomial and reduction as defined above on tuples, then, for each branch, we get a finite set of admissible tuples such that their first components constitute a Gröbner basis of F under the parameter specialization belonging to A_i. Furthermore, these constructions produce tuples such that the polynomials corresponding to them, obtained by adding the two components of the tuple, are in the ideal $\langle F \rangle$. In this way, a faithful Gröbner basis is generated for every branch corresponding to A_i.

3.1 Manipulating Tuple Representations of Polynomials using Module Operations

As the reader might have noticed, it suffices to perform various Gröbner basis operations only on the first component of the tuple representation of a polynomial from the input ideal to generate a comprehensive Gröbner system. However, to compute a comprehensive Gröbner basis consisting of faithful polynomials from the input ideal, the same operations have to be recorded on the second component also, even though computations on the second components do not affect the overall computation of a Gröbner basis along a branch under a specialization. A Gröbner basis implementation that also provides information about how the elements of a Gröbner basis can be obtained from the input basis (i.e., the representation of each element of a Gröbner basis in terms of the input basis), can be used to derive the required information about the second components; hence, in this way, the faithful polynomial corresponding to the first component in a Gröbner basis along a particular branch can be generated.

In the absence of such information available about Gröbner basis elements in terms of the input basis, existing implementations of Gröbner basis algorithms on modules can be used instead, since all the operations on admissible tuple representations can be converted to basic module operations.

Most of the terminologies on "module" in this section can be found in Chapter 5 of [3].

Let F be a subset of $R[X]$ and A_i be a constructible set. Then

$$\mathbf{M}(F, A_i) = \{(p, \bar{p}) \mid p + \bar{p} \in \langle F \rangle \text{ and } \sigma_{\bar{a}}(\bar{p}) = 0 \text{ for all } \bar{a} \in A_i\}$$

is the set of all admissible tuple representations of polynomials from $\langle F \rangle$ w.r.t. A_i. Clearly, $\mathbf{M}(F, A_i) \subset (R[X])^2$ is an $R[X]$-module with the following basic operations:

1. for $\mathbf{p} = (p, \bar{p}), \mathbf{q} = (q, \bar{q}) \in \mathbf{M}(F, A_i)$, $\mathbf{p} + \mathbf{q} = (p + q, \bar{p} + \bar{q}) \in \mathbf{M}(F, A_i)$, and

2. for $\mathbf{p} = (p, \bar{p}) \in \mathbf{M}(F, A_i)$ and $r \in R[X]$, $r \cdot \mathbf{p} = (r \cdot p, r \cdot \bar{p}) \in \mathbf{M}(F, A_i)$.

Since $\mathbf{M}(F, A_i)$ is a module, we can use general definitions of the S-polynomial and reduction in a module. To make these definitions consistent with those defined on tuples in last subsection, it suffices to extend the term order defined on $R[X]$ to the free $R[X]$-module $(R[X])^2$ in a POT (position over term) fashion with $(1, 0) \succ (0, 1)$.

An important operation for computing a comprehensive Gröbner system is simplifying $(p, \bar{p}) \in \mathbf{M}(F, A_i)$ w.r.t. A_i. As mentioned earlier, we can simplify $(p, \bar{p})$ to $(p', \bar{p}')$ by moving all terms in p that vanish to $\bar{p}$ such that $p + \bar{p} = p' + \bar{p}'$ and the leading coefficient of p' is not always zero for the specializations from A_i and $\bar{p}'$ is 0 w.r.t. A_i. This simplification can also be expressed using module operations. Assume $A_i = V(E) \setminus V(N)$ where $E, N \subset R$ and $\langle E \rangle$ is radical. Then simplifying $(p, \bar{p})$ w.r.t. A_i is equivalent to reducing $(p, \bar{p})$ by the set $\{(e, -e) \mid e \in E\} \subset \mathbf{M}(F, A_i)$. For example, let $F = \{ax^2 + bx + a + 1\} \subset \mathbb{Q}[a, b][x]$, $A_i = V(E) = V(\{a, b - 1\})$ and $\mathbf{p} = (ax^2 + bx + a + 1, 0) \in \mathbf{M}(F, A_i)$. Then $\mathbf{p} = (ax^2 + bx + a + 1, 0)$ can be reduced to $(x + 1, ax^2 + bx - x + a)$ as follows:

$$(ax^2 + bx + a + 1, 0) - (x^2 + 1) \cdot (a, -a) - x \cdot (b - 1, 1 - b)$$

$$= (x + 1, ax^2 + bx - x + a).$$

Notice that the result is also an element in $\mathbf{M}(F, A_i)$, since $(a, -a), (b - 1, 1 - b) \in \mathbf{M}(F, A_i)$.

4. A NEW ALGORITHM FOR COMPUTING A COMPREHENSIVE GRÖBNER BASIS

The algorithm proposed in [9] for computing a comprehensive Gröbner system is adapted so as to work on the tuple representation of polynomials. The output of the new algorithm is a comprehensive Gröbner system with the property that every branch is disjoint vis a vis specializations, and the output along each branch is a Gröbner basis for $\langle F \rangle$ under the specialization. Tuple representation of the output is used to extract polynomials from $\langle F \rangle$. Hence a faithful comprehensive Gröbner basis can be found by taking the union of the outputs along all branches. The correctness and termination of the new algorithm that outputs a comprehensive Gröbner system as well as a comprehensive Gröbner basis follow from the correctness and termination of the algorithm proposed in [9] for computing a comprehensive Gröbner system.

The algorithm for computing a comprehensive Gröbner system in [9] uses the following theorem; the definition below is used in this theorem.

Definition 4.1 (Minimal Dickson Basis) *For a polynomial set G in $k[U, X]$ and an admissible block order with $U \ll X$, we say $F \subset k[U, X]$, denoted by $\mathrm{MDBasis}(G)$, is a minimal Dickson basis of G, if*

1. *F is a subset of G,*

2. *for every polynomial $g \in G$, there is some polynomial $f \in F$ such that $\mathrm{lpp}_X(g)$ is a multiple of $\mathrm{lpp}_X(f)$, i.e. $\langle \mathrm{lpp}_X(F) \rangle = \langle \mathrm{lpp}_X(G) \rangle$, and*

3. *for any two distinct $f_1, f_2 \in F$, neither $\mathrm{lpp}_X(f_1)$ is a multiple of $\mathrm{lpp}_X(f_2)$ nor $\mathrm{lpp}_X(f_2)$ is a multiple of $\mathrm{lpp}_X(f_1)$.*

A minimal Dickson basis of a set may not be unique.

Theorem 4.2 (Kapur-Sun-Wang, 2010) *Let G be a Gröbner basis of the ideal $\langle F \rangle \subset k[U, X]$ w.r.t. an admissible block order with $U \ll X$. Let $G_r = G \cap k[U]$ and $G_m = \mathrm{MDBasis}(G \setminus G_r)$. If σ is a specialization from $k[U]$ to L such that*

1. *$\sigma(g) = 0$ for $g \in G_r$, and*

2. *$\sigma(h) \neq 0$, where $h = \prod_{g \in G_m} \mathrm{lc}_X(g) \in k[U]$,*

then $\sigma(G_m)$ is a (minimal) Gröbner basis of $\langle \sigma(F) \rangle$ in $L[X]$ w.r.t. $\prec_X$.

The theorem below serves as a basis of the proposed algorithm for computing a comprehensive Gröbner basis. The set E below refers to the set of equality constraints. It establishes that along a branch, for a specialization satisfying E, the first components of the tuple representation of polynomials constitute a comprehensive Gröbner basis of $\langle F \rangle$ and furthermore, every polynomial obtained by adding the two components in the tuple representation is in $\langle F \rangle$ ensuring faithfulness.

Theorem 4.3 *Let F be a set of polynomials in $k[U, X]$, E be a subset of $k[U]$, and $\mathbf{M}$ be a $k[U, X]$-module generated by $\{(f, 0) \mid f \in F\} \cup \{(e, -e) \mid e \in E\}$. Suppose $\mathbf{G}$ is a Gröbner basis of the module $\mathbf{M}$ w.r.t. an order extended from $\prec_{X,U}$ in a position over term fashion with $(0, 1) \prec (1, 0)$, where $\prec_{X,U}$ is an admissible block order with $U \ll X$.*

Denote $G^{1st} = \{g \mid (g, \bar{g}) \in \mathbf{G}\}$, $G_r = G^{1st} \cap k[U]$ and $G_m = \mathrm{MDBasis}(G^{1st} \setminus G_r)$. $\mathbf{G}_m$ is a subset of $\mathbf{G}$ such that $\{(g, \bar{g}) \in \mathbf{G}_m \mid g \in G_m\}$. If σ is a specialization from $k[U]$ to L such that

1. *$\sigma(g) = 0$ for $g \in G_r$, and*

2. *$\sigma(h) \neq 0$, where $h = \prod_{g \in G_m} \mathrm{lc}_X(g) \in k[U]$,*

then

(1). for each $(g, \bar{g}) \in \mathbf{G}_m$, $g + \bar{g} \in \langle F \rangle$ and $\sigma(\bar{g}) = 0$, and

(2). $\{\sigma(g + \bar{g}) \mid (g, \bar{g}) \in \mathbf{G}_m\}$ is a minimal Gröbner basis of $\langle \sigma(F) \rangle$ in $L[X]$ w.r.t. $\prec_X$.

That is, $\{(V(G_r) \setminus V(h), G_m)\}$ is comprehensive Gröbner system on $V(G_r) \setminus V(h)$ for F, and $\{g + \bar{g} \mid (g, \bar{g}) \in \mathbf{G}_m\}$ is a comprehensive Gröbner basis on $V(G_r) \setminus V(h)$ for F.

PROOF. For (1), we first show $E \subset \langle G_r \rangle$. Since $\mathbf{G}$ is a Gröbner basis of the module $\mathbf{M}$ generated by $\{(f, 0) \mid f \in F\} \cup \{(e, -e) \mid e \in E\}$ w.r.t. an order extended from $\prec_{X,U}$ in a POT fashion with $(0, 1) \prec (1, 0)$, we next show G^{1st} is a Gröbner basis for the ideal $\langle F \cup E \rangle$ w.r.t. $\prec_{X,U}$. For any $h \in \langle F \cup E \rangle$, we have $h = \sum_{f \in F} p_f f + \sum_{e \in E} q_e e$ where $p_f, q_e \in k[U, X]$, so $(h, -(\sum_{e \in E} q_e e)) = \sum_{f \in F} p_f (f, 0) + \sum_{e \in E} q_e (e, -e) \in \mathbf{M}$. As $\mathbf{G}$ is a Gröbner basis for $\mathbf{M}$, there exists $(g, \bar{g}) \in \mathbf{G}$ such that $\mathrm{lpp}(g)$ divides $\mathrm{lpp}(h)$, which means G^{1st} is a Gröbner basis for the ideal $\langle F \cup E \rangle$. Besides, $G_r = G^{1st} \cap k[U] \subset \langle F \cup E \rangle$, so we have $E \subset \langle G_r \rangle \subset k[U]$ since $\prec_{X,U}$ is a block order with $U \ll X$.

Notice that $\mathbf{G}_m$ is a subset of the module $\mathbf{M}$; for each $(g, \bar{g}) \in \mathbf{G}_m$, we have

$$\begin{pmatrix} g \\ \bar{g} \end{pmatrix} = \sum_{f \in F} p_f \begin{pmatrix} f \\ 0 \end{pmatrix} + \sum_{e \in E} q_e \begin{pmatrix} e \\ -e \end{pmatrix},$$

where $p_f, q_e \in k[U, X]$. So $g + \bar{g} = (\sum_{f \in F} p_f f + \sum_{e \in E} q_e e) + \sum_{e \in E} q_e(-e) = \sum_{f \in F} p_f f \in \langle F \rangle$, and $\bar{g} = \sum_{e \in E} q_e(-e)$. Since $E \subset \langle G_r \rangle$, then $\sigma(\bar{g}) = 0$.

For (2), G^{1st} is a Gröbner basis for the ideal $\langle F \cup E \rangle$ w.r.t. $\prec_{X,U}$ as shown above, $G_r = G^{1st} \cap k[U]$ and $G_m = \mathrm{MDBasis}(G^{1st} \setminus G_r)$, so $\sigma(G_m) = \{\sigma(g + \bar{g}) \mid (g, \bar{g}) \in \mathbf{G}_m\}$ is a minimal Gröbner basis of $\langle \sigma(F) \rangle$ by Theorem 4.2.

Therefore, combined with (1) and (2), $\{(V(G_r) \setminus V(h), G_m)\}$ is comprehensive Gröbner system on $V(G_r) \setminus V(h)$ for F, and $\{g + \bar{g} \mid (g, \bar{g}) \in \mathbf{G}_m\}$ is a comprehensive Gröbner basis on $V(G_r) \setminus V(h)$ for F. ∎

We emphasize that, in the above theorem, we do not necessarily need to compute a whole Gröbner basis for the module $\mathbf{M}$, what we really need is a $\mathbf{G} \subset \mathbf{M}$ such that $G^{1st} = \{g \mid (g, \bar{g}) \in \mathbf{G}\}$ is a Gröbner basis for the ideal $\langle F \cup E \rangle$.

4.1 Algorithm

Now, we give an algorithm for computing comprehensive Gröbner bases. The correctness of the algorithm is a direct result of the above theorem. Its termination also can be proved in a same way as in [9].

In order to keep the presentation simple, we have deliberately avoided tricks and optimizations such as factoring h below. All the tricks suggested in [9] can be used here as well. In fact, our implementation incorporates fully these optimizations.

The following algorithm computes a comprehensive Gröbner basis on $V(E) \setminus V(N)$ for $F \subset k[U, X]$.

Algorithm CGB(E, N, F)
Input: (E, N, F): E, N, finite subsets of $k[U]$; F, a finite subset of $k[U, X]$.
Output: a comprehensive Gröbner basis of the set F on $V(E) \setminus V(N)$.

1. $\mathcal{CGS} := \mathrm{CGSMain}(E, N, F)$, where $\mathcal{CGS}$ is a finite set of 3-tuples $(E_i, N_i, \mathbf{G}_i)$ such that $\{(V(E_i) \setminus V(N_i), G_i^{1st})\}$, where $G_i^{1st} = \{g \mid (g, \bar{g}) \in \mathbf{G}_i\}$, constitutes a comprehensive Gröbner system on $V(E) \setminus V(N)$ for F, and for each $(g, \bar{g}) \in \mathbf{G}_i$, $g + \bar{g} \in \langle F \rangle$ and $\sigma(\bar{g})$ is 0 for every parameter specialization σ from $V(E_i) \setminus V(N_i)$.

2. Return $\{g + \bar{g} \mid (g, \bar{g}) \in \mathbf{G}_i \text{ for all } i\}$.

Below we assume that all Gröbner basis computations are done in $(k[U, X])^2$ using the order extended by $\prec_{X,U}$ in a POT fashion with $(1, 0) \succ (0, 1)$.

Algorithm CGSMain(E, N, F)
Input: (E, N, F): E, N, finite subsets of $k[U]$; F, a finite subset of $(k[U, X])^2$.
Output: $\mathcal{CGS}$: a finite set of 3-tuples $(E_i, N_i, \mathbf{G}_i)$ such that $\{(V(E_i) \backslash V(N_i), G_i^{1st})\}$, where $G_i^{1st} = \{g \mid (g, \bar{g}) \in \mathbf{G}_i\}$, constitutes a comprehensive Gröbner system on $V(E) \backslash V(N)$ for F, and for each $(g, \bar{g}) \in \mathbf{G}_i$, $g + \bar{g} \in \langle F \rangle$ and $\sigma(\bar{g})$ is 0 for every parameter specialization σ from $V(E_i) \backslash V(N_i)$.

1. If inconsistent(E, N), then return $\emptyset$.

2. Otherwise, $\mathbf{G}_0 :=$ ReducedGröbnerBasis $(\{(f, 0) \mid f \in F\} \cup \{(e, -e) \mid e \in E\})$.

3. $\mathbf{G} := \mathbf{G}_0 \backslash \{(g, \bar{g}) \in \mathbf{G}_0 \mid g = 0\}$ and $G^{1st} := \{g \mid (g, \bar{g}) \in \mathbf{G}\}$.

4. If there exists $(1, \bar{g}) \in \mathbf{G}$, then return $\{(E, N, \{(1, \bar{g})\})\}$.

5. Let $\mathbf{G}_r := \{(g, \bar{g}) \in \mathbf{G} \mid g \in k[U]\}$ and $G_r := \{g \mid (g, \bar{g}) \in \mathbf{G}_r\}$.

6. If inconsistent(E, $G_r \times$ N), then $\mathcal{CGS} := \emptyset$, else $\mathcal{CGS} := \{(E, G_r \times N, \mathbf{G}_r)\}$.

7. If inconsistent(G_r, N), then return $\mathcal{CGS}$.

8. Otherwise, let $G_m :=$ MDBasis($G^{1st} \backslash G_r$) and $\mathbf{G}_m := \{(g, \bar{g}) \in \mathbf{G} \backslash \mathbf{G}_r \mid g \in G_m\}$.

9. if consistent(G_r, N$\times\{h\}$), then $\mathcal{CGS} := \mathcal{CGS} \cup \{(G_r, N \times \{h\}, \mathbf{G}_m)\}$, where $h = \text{lcm}\{h_1, \cdots, h_k\}$ and $\{h_1, \cdots, h_k\} = \{\text{lc}_X(g) \mid g \in G_m\}$.

10. Return $\mathcal{CGS} \cup \bigcup_{h \in [h_1, \cdots, h_k]}$ CGSMain($G_r \cup \{h_i\}, N \times \{h_1 h_2 \cdots h_{i-1}\}, \{g + \bar{g} \mid (g, \bar{g}) \in \mathbf{G} \backslash \mathbf{G}_r\}$).

In the above algorithm, $A \times B = \{fg \mid f \in A, g \in B\}$. Also, for the case $i = 1$, $N \times \{h_1 h_2 \cdots h_{i-1}\} = N$. inconsistent(E, N) returns true if $V(E) \backslash V(N)$ is empty, false otherwise. The above steps 2 and 3 present a method to get $\mathbf{G}$ such that G^{1st} is a Gröbner basis for $\langle F \cup E \rangle$. We can also get such $\mathbf{G}$ by using Suzuki-Sato's trick in [15]. The inconsistency check is performed using techniques discussed in detail in [9]; their discussion is omitted here because of lack of space.

Compared with Suzuki-Sato's algorithm for computing a comprehensive Gröbner basis [15], the new algorithm has three advantages, most of which are inherited from our algorithm for computing a comprehensive Gröbner system [9]. First, as should be evident from the description, polynomials are never generated for the case when $V(E) \backslash V(N)$ is empty; so many useless computations are avoided. Second, recursive calls on the CGSMain are made only for the cases when the leading coefficients of G_m are nonzero instead of having to consider the leading coefficients of the whole $G^{1st} \backslash G_r$; thus many unnecessary branches are avoided, because typically, the size of G_m is smaller than the size of $G^{1st} \backslash G_r$. Finally, while recursively calling the CGSMain function, the intermediate result $\{g + \bar{g} \mid (g, \bar{g}) \in \mathbf{G} \backslash \mathbf{G}_r\}$ is used in the new algorithm, instead of using the original F as input as in the Suzuki-Sato's algorithm, which should also contribute to the speedup of the proposed algorithm. Because of these

advantages, the proposed algorithm has a much better performance than the Suzuki-Sato algorithm as well as other existing algorithms, as shown in the experimental results in section 6.

5. A SIMPLE EXAMPLE

The proposed algorithm is illustrated using the same example discussed in [9] primarily to help an interested reader to see the differences between the algorithm in [9] and the new algorithm of this paper. The discussion here is however self-contained.

Example 5.1 *Let* $F = \{ax - b, by - a, cx^2 - y, cy^2 - x\} \subset \mathbb{Q}[a, b, c][x, y]$, *with the block order* $\prec_{X,U}$, $\{a, b, c\} \ll \{x, y\}$; *within each block*, $\prec_X$ *and* $\prec_U$ *are graded reverse lexicographic orders with* $y < x$ *and* $c < b < a$, *respectively.*

At the beginning, $F = \{ax - b, by - a, cx^2 - y, cy^2 - x\}$, $E = \emptyset$ and $N = \{1\}$. We compute a comprehensive Gröbner system for $\{(f, 0) \mid f \in F\} \in (\mathbb{Q}[a, b, c][x, y])^2$ using the tuple representation, so that along every branch, for every polynomial in a Gröbner basis, we can also extract the original polynomial from the input ideal generated by F to maintain faithfulness of the output.

(1) The set $V(E) \backslash V(N)$ is not empty. The reduced Gröbner basis of the $\mathbb{Q}[a, b, c][x, y]$-module $\langle (f, 0) \mid f \in F \rangle \subset (\mathbb{Q}[a, b, c][x, y])^2$ w.r.t. the order extended by $\prec_{X,U}$ in POT fashion, is

$$\mathbf{G}_0 = \mathbf{G} = \{(x^3 - y^3, 0), (cx^2 - y, 0), (ay^2 - bc, 0), (cy^2 - x, 0),$$

$$(ax - b, 0), (bx - acy, 0), (a^2 y - b^2 c, 0), (by - a, 0), (a^6 - b^6, 0),$$

$$(a^3 c - b^3, 0), (b^3 c - a^3, 0), (ac^2 - a, 0), (bc^2 - b, 0)\},$$

with $\mathbf{G}_r = \{(g, \bar{g}) \in \mathbf{G} \mid g \in \mathbb{Q}[a, b, c]\} = \{(a^6 - b^6, 0), (a^3 c - b^3, 0), (b^3 c - a^3, 0), (ac^2 - a, 0), (bc^2 - b, 0)\}$. Denote $G^{1st} = \{g \mid (g, \bar{g}) \in \mathbf{G}\}$ and $G_r = \{g \mid (g, \bar{g}) \in \mathbf{G}_r\}$.

It is easy to see that $(V(E) \backslash V(G_r)) \backslash V(N)$ is not empty. This implies that $\{\emptyset, G_r, \mathbf{G}_r\}$ is a trivial branch of the comprehensive Gröbner system for F.

(2) $G^{1st} \backslash G_r = \{x^3 - y^3, cx^2 - y, ay^2 - bc, cy^2 - x, ax - b, bx - acy, a^2 y - b^2 c, by - a\}$; $G_m =$ MDBasis($G^{1st} \backslash G_r$) $= \{bx - acy, by - a\}$ and $\mathbf{G}_m = \{(bx - acy, 0), (by - a, 0)\}$. Further, $h = \text{lcm}\{\text{lc}_X(bx - acy), \text{lc}_X(by - a)\} = b$. This gives us another branch of comprehensive system for F corresponding to the case when all polynomials in G_r are 0 and $b \neq 0$: $(G_r, \{b\}, \mathbf{G}_m)$. Notice that $V(G_r) \backslash V(b)$ is not empty.

(3) The next branch to consider is when $b = 0$. The Gröbner basis of $G_r \cup \{b\}$ is $\{a^3, ac^2 - a, b\}$, which is the input E' in the recursive call of CGSMain, with the other input being $N' = \{1\}$ and $F' = \{g + \bar{g} \mid (g, \bar{g}) \in \mathbf{G} \backslash \mathbf{G}_r\}$.

Since $V(E') \backslash V(N')$ is not empty, we can compute the reduced Gröbner basis for $\{(f, 0) \mid f \in F'\} \cup \{(a^3, -a^3), (ac^2 - a, -ac^2 + a), (b, -b)\}$. By removing the tuples whose first component is 0, we get $\mathbf{G}' = \{(x^3 - y^3, 0), (cx^2 - y, 0), (cy^2 - x, 0), (a, -by), (b, -b)\}$ of which $\mathbf{G}'_r = \{(a, -by), (b, -b)\}$. Similarly, denote $G'^{1st} = \{g \mid (g, \bar{g}) \in \mathbf{G}'\}$ and $G'_r = \{g \mid (g, \bar{g}) \in \mathbf{G}'_r\}$. It is easy to check the set $V(E') \backslash V(G'_r)$ is empty, so no element in $\mathbf{G}'_r$ contributes to the comprehensive Gröbner system.

Next, $G'_m = \{cx^2 - y, cy^2 - x\}$, $\mathbf{G}'_m = \{(cx^2 - y, 0), (cy^2 - x, 0)\}$ and $h' = \text{lcm}(\text{lc}_X(cx^2 - y), \text{lc}_X(cy^2 - x)) = c$. This results in another branch: $(G'_r, \{c\}, \mathbf{G}'_m)$.

(4) For the case when $h' = c = 0$, the set $E'' = \{a, b, c\}$ which is the Gröbner basis of $G'_r \cup \{c\}$. $N'' = \{1\}$ and $F'' = \{x^3 - y^3, cx^2 - y, cy^2 - x\}$. Computing the reduced Gröbner basis for $\{(f, 0) \mid f \in F''\} \cup \{(a, -a), (b, -b), (c, -c)\}$ and removing the tuples whose first component is 0, we get $\mathbf{G}'' = \{(x, -cy^2), (y, -cx^2), (a, -a), (b, -b), (c, -c)\}$. Then, $\mathbf{G}''_r = \{(a, -a), (b, -b), (c, -c)\}$, $G_m = \{x, y\}$ and $\mathbf{G}''_m = \{(x, -cy^2), (y, -cx^2)\}$. Further, $h'' = \text{lcm}(\text{lc}_X(x), \text{lc}_X(y)) = 1$. Similarly, denote G'' and G''_r as before. This gives the last branch: $(G''_r, \{1\}, \mathbf{G}''_m)$.

Since $h'' = 1$, no more branches are generated and the algorithm terminates. Thus, we obtain a comprehensive Gröbner system for F:

$$\begin{cases} \{(a^6 - b^6, 0), (a^3c - b^3, 0), & \text{if } a^6 - b^6 \neq 0 \text{ or } a^3c - b^3 \neq 0 \\ (b^3c - a^3, 0), (ac^2 - a, 0), & \text{or } b^3c - a^3 \neq 0 \text{ or } ac^2 - a \neq 0 \\ (bc^2 - b, 0)\}, & \text{or } bc^2 - b \neq 0, \\ \{(bx - acy, 0), (by - a, 0)\}, & \text{if } a^6 - b^6 = a^3c - b^3 \\ & = b^3c - a^3 = ac^2 - a \\ & = bc^2 - b = 0 \text{ and } b \neq 0, \\ \{(cx^2 - y, 0), (cy^2 - x, 0)\} & \text{if } a = b = 0 \text{ and } c \neq 0, \\ \{(x, -cy^2), (y, -cx^2)\} & \text{if } a = b = c = 0. \end{cases}$$

An interested reader would observe comparing the above output with the output from [9] that except for the last branch, the outputs are the same. In [9], the last branch for the case when $a = b = c = 0$, the Gröbner basis is: $\{x, y\}$, whereas in the above the Gröbner basis is: $\{x - cy^2, y - cx^2\}$, when the tuple representation is replaced by the corresponding polynomials from the ideal of F. $x - cy^2$ is the faithful polynomial from the ideal of F corresponding to the output element x in [9]; similarly, $y - cx^2$ is the faithful polynomial corresponding to y.

A comprehensive Gröbner basis of F, after removing the duplicate ones, can be obtained directly from the above comprehensive Gröbner system. That is $\{a^6 - b^6, a^3c - b^3, b^3c - a^3, ac^2 - a, bc^2 - b, bx - acy, by - a, cx^2 - y, cy^2 - x\}$.

6. IMPLEMENTATION AND COMPARATIVE PERFORMANCE

The proposed algorithm has been implemented on the computer algebra system *Singular*. The implementation has been experimented on a number of examples from different application domains including geometry theorem proving and computer vision, and it has been compared with implementations of other algorithms. Since the proposed algorithm uses the new technique and basic module operations, it is efficient and can compute comprehensive Gröbner basis for most problems in a few seconds. In particular, we have been successful in solving the famous P3P problem for pose-estimation from computer vision, which is investigated by Gao et al [6] using the characteristic set method; see the polynomial system below.

The following table shows a comparison of our implementation on Singular with other existing algorithms for computing comprehensive Gröbner bases, including: Suzuki-Sato algorithm implemented by Nabeshima in Risa/Asir (package PGB, ver20090915) and the function "cgb" for computing comprehensive Gröbner bases in Reduce (package RedLog). The versions of Singular, Risa/Asir and Reduce are ver3-1-2, ver20090715 and free CSL version, respectively.

The implementation has been tried on many examples including Examples F6 and F8 from [14]. Many of these ex-

amples could be solved very quickly. To generate complex examples, we modified problems F2, F3, F4, F5 and F8 in [14], and labeled them as S1, S2, S3, S4 and S5. As stated above, we also tried the famous P3P problem from computer vision. The polynomials for these problems are given below:

F6: $F = \{x^4 + ax^3 + bx^2 + cx + d, 4x^3 + 3ax^2 + 2bx + c\}, X = \{x\}, U = \{a, b, c, d\}$;

F8: $F = \{ax^2 + by, cw^2 + z, (x - z)^2 + (y - w)^2, 2dxw - 2by\}, X = \{x, y, z, w\}, U = \{a, b, c, d\}$;

S1: $F = \{ax^2y^3 + by + y, x^2y^2 + xy + 2x, ax^2 + by + 2\}, X = \{x, y\}, U = \{a, b, c\}$;

S2: $F = \{ax^4 + cx^2 + y, bx^3 + x^2 + 2, cx^2 + dx + y\}, X = \{x, y\}, U = \{a, b, c, d\}$;

S3: $F = \{ax^3y + cxz^2, x^4y + 3dy + z, cx^2 + bxy, x^2y^2 + ax^2, x^5 + y^5\}, X = \{x, y, z\}, U = \{a, b, c, d\}$;

S4: $F = \{ax^2y + bx + y^3, ax^2y + bxy + cx, y^2 + bx^2y + cxy\}, X = \{x, y\}, U = \{a, b, c\}$;

S5: $F = \{ax^2 + byz + c, cw^2 + by + z, (x - z)^2 + (y - w)^2, 2dxw - 2byz\}, X = \{x, y, z, w\}, U = \{a, b, c, d\}$;

P3P: $F = \{(1 - a)y^2 - ax^2 - py + arxy + 1, (1 - b)x^2 - by^2 - qx + brxy + 1\}, X = \{x, y\}, U = \{p, q, r, a, b\}$.

For all these examples, the term orders used on X are graded reverse lexicographic orders.

Table 1: Timings

Exa.	Algorithm	time(sec.)	#polys
F6	New(S)	0.310	7
	cgb(R)	0.590	6
	SuzukiSato(A)	*error*	–
F8	New(S)	0.650	28
	cgb(R)	> 1h	–
	SuzukiSato(A)	0.6708	284
S1	New(S)	0.120	8
	cgb(R)	> 1h	–
	SuzukiSato(A)	*error*	–
S2	New(S)	0.165	9
	cgb(R)	10.520	38
	SuzukiSato(A)	*error*	–
S3	New(S)	4.515	62
	cgb(R)	28.845	84
	SuzukiSato(A)	> 1h	–
S4	New(S)	5.410	27
	cgb(R)	50.180	39
	SuzukiSato(A)	> 1h	–
S5	New(S)	18.034	58
	cgb(R)	329.169	59
	SuzukiSato(A)	> 1h	–
P3P	New(S)	14.440	50
	cgb(R)	> 1h	–
	SuzukiSato(A)	> 1h	–

In Table 1, entries labelled with New(S) is the proposed algorithm implemented in Singular; (R) and (A) stand for Reduce and Risa/Asir, respectively. The column "#polys" is the number of polynomials in the comprehensive Gröbner basis output by the implementations. The label "*error*" is included if an implementation ran out of memory or broke down. The timings were obtained by running the implementations on Core i5 4×2.8GHz with 4GB memory running Windows 7.

As is evident from Table 1, the proposed algorithm has better performance in contrast to other algorithms.

7. CONCLUDING REMARKS

In this paper, we have adapted the algorithm proposed in [9] for computing a comprehensive Gröbner system of a parameterized polynomial system F such that the new algorithm not only produces a comprehensive Gröbner system of F but it also generates a comprehensive Gröbner basis of F. The main idea is to use polynomials from the ideal generated by F during the computation along various branches corresponding to constructible sets specializing parameters in the algorithm in [9]. Polynomials from $\langle F \rangle$ are represented as tuples, with the first component corresponding to its nonzero part under the specialization and the second component being zero under the specialization. The key steps of a Gröbner basis computation including reduction of a polynomial by another polynomial and S-polynomial construction, are performed on these tuple representations; these steps can also be viewed as computing Gröbner basis of a submodule over $R[X]^2$.

The new algorithm produces a comprehensive Gröbner system, in which each branch is a finite set of tuples along a constructible set (which is specified by a finite set of equalities over parameters and a finite set of disequalities over parameters), with the properties (i) the constructible sets constitute a partition over the set of parameter specializations under consideration, and (ii) for every parameter specialization in the constructible set of the branch, the second component of every tuple is 0 under the specialization and the leading coefficient of the first component in every tuple is nonzero under the specialization, and most importantly, (iii) the sum of the first component and the second component in the tuple is in the ideal generated by the input F. For generating a comprehensive Gröbner system, the second component of these tuples do not give any useful information and can hence be discarded. Using these second components however, a comprehensive Gröbner basis is the union over every branch of the set of polynomials obtained by adding the two components of each tuple. Further, such a comprehensive Gröbner basis is faithful since all the polynomials in the basis are also in the ideal.

The above construction can be used to adapt all known algorithms for computing a comprehensive Gröbner system. We believe that various optimization criteria to discard redundant computations can also be integrated in the proposed algorithm.

Using insights discussed above, we are investigating the design of a new algorithm for computing a minimal comprehensive Gröbner basis of a parametric polynomial systems, which will be reported in a forthcoming paper. Using this notion, we are able to define a canonical minimal comprehensive Gröbner basis, unlike the notion in Weispfenning [17], where a canonical comprehensive Gröbner basis is defined but it does not have the property of being minimal.

8. REFERENCES

[1] C. Chen, O. Golubitsky, F. Lemaire, M. Moreno Maza, and W. Pan. Comprehensive triangular decomposition. In Proceedings of CASC'07, Lect. Notes in Comp. Sci., Springer, Berlin, vol. 4770, 73-101, 2007.

[2] X.F. Chen, P. Li, L. Lin, and D.K. Wang. Proving geometric theorems by partitioned-parametric Gröbner bases. In Proceeding of Automated Deduction in Geometry (ADG) 2004, Lect. Notes in Comp. Sci., Springer, Berlin, vol. 3763, 34-43, 2005.

[3] D. Cox, J. Little, and D. O'Shea. Using algebraic geometry. Springer, New York, second edition, 2005.

[4] B. Donald, D. Kapur, and J.L. Mundy(eds.). Symbolic and numerical computation for artificial intelligence. Computational Mathematics and Applications, Academic Press Ltd., London, 1992.

[5] X.S. Gao and S.C. Chou. Solving parametric algebraic systems. In Proceedings of ISSAC'1992, ACM Press, New York, 335–341, 1992.

[6] X.S. Gao, X.R. Hou, J.L. Tang, and H.F. Chen. Complete solution classification for the Perspective-Three-Point problem. IEEE Tran. on PAMI, vol. 25, no. 8, 930-943, 2003.

[7] D. Kapur. An approach for solving systems of parametric polynomial equations. Principles and Practice of Constraint Programming (eds. Saraswat and Van Hentenryck). MIT Press, Cambridge, 1995.

[8] D. Kapur. A quantifier-elimination based heuristic for automatically generating inductive assertions for programs. J. Syst. Sci. Complex., Vol. 19, No. 3, 307-330, 2006.

[9] D. Kapur, Y. Sun, and D.K. Wang. A new algorithm for computing comprehensive Gröbner systems. In Proceedings of ISSAC'2010, ACM Press, New York, 29-36, 2010.

[10] M. Manubens and A. Montes. Improving DISPGB algorithm using the discriminant ideal. J. Symb. Comp., 41, no. 11, 1245-1263. 2006.

[11] A. Montes. A new algorithm for discussing Gröbner basis with parameters. J. Symb. Comp., vol. 33, 1-2, 183-208, 2002.

[12] A. Montes and T. Recio. Automatic discovery of geometry theorems using minimal canonical comprehensive Gröbner systems. In Proceeding of Automated Deduction in Geometry (ADG) 2006, Lecture Notes in Artificial Intelligence, Springer, Berlin, Heidelberg, vol. 4869, 113-138, 2007.

[13] A. Montes and M. Wibmer. Gröbner bases for polynomial systems with parameters. J. Symb. Comp., vol. 45, no. 12, 1391-1425, 2010.

[14] K. Nabeshima. A speed-up of the algorithm for computing comprehensive Gröbner systems. In Proceedings of ISSAC'2007, ACM Press, New York, 299-306, 2007.

[15] A. Suzuki and Y. Sato. A simple algorithm to compute comprehensive Gröbner bases using Gröbner bases. In Proceedings of ISSAC'2006, ACM Press, New York, 326-331, 2006.

[16] V. Weispfenning. Comprehensive Gröbner bases. J. Symb. Comp., vol. 14, no. 1, 1-29, 1992.

[17] V. Weispfenning. Canonical comprehensive Gröbner bases. J. Symb. Comp., vol. 36, no. 3-4, 669-683, 2003.

[18] M. Wibmer. Gröbner bases for families of affine or projective schemes. J. Symb. Comp., vol. 42, no. 8, 803-834, 2007.

A Refined Denominator Bounding Algorithm for Multivariate Linear Difference Equations

Manuel Kauers[*]

RISC
Johannes Kepler University
4040 Linz (Austria)
mkauers@risc.jku.at

Carsten Schneider[†]

RISC
Johannes Kepler University
4040 Linz (Austria)
cschneid@risc.jku.at

ABSTRACT

We continue to investigate which polynomials can possibly occur as factors in the denominators of rational solutions of a given partial linear difference equation. In an earlier article we have introduced the distinction between periodic and aperiodic factors in the denominator, and we have given an algorithm for predicting the aperiodic ones. Now we extend this technique towards the periodic case and present a refined algorithm which also finds most of the periodic factors.

Categories and Subject Descriptors

I.1.2 [**Computing Methodologies**]: Symbolic and Algebraic Manipulation—*Algorithms*

General Terms

Algorithms

Keywords

Difference Equations, Rational Solutions

1. INTRODUCTION

The usual approach for finding rational solutions of linear difference equations with polynomial coefficients is as follows. First one constructs a nonzero polynomial Q such that for any solution $y = p/q$ of the given equation (p, q coprime) we must have $q \mid Q$. Such a polynomial Q is called a denominator bound for the equation. Next, the denominator bound is used to transform the given equation into a new equation with the property that a polynomial P solves the new equation if and only if the rational function $y = P/Q$ solves the

[*]Supported by the Austrian FWF grant Y464-N18 and the EU grant PITN-GA-2010-264564.

[†]Supported by the Austrian FWF grant P20347-N18 and the EU grant PITN-GA-2010-264564.

original equation. Thus the knowledge of a denominator bound reduces rational solving to polynomial solving.

The first algorithm for finding a denominator bound Q was given by Abramov in 1971 [1, 2, 5]. During the past forty years, other algorithms were found [14, 11, 7, 9, 4] and the technique was generalized to matrix equations [3, 6] as well as to equation over function fields [15, 8, 16]. Last year [12] we made a first step towards a denominator bounding algorithm for equations in several variables (PLDEs). We found that some factors of the denominator are easier to predict than others. We called a polynomial periodic if it has a nontrivial gcd with one of its shifts, and aperiodic otherwise. For example, the polynomial $2n - 3k$ is periodic because shifting it twice in k and three times in n leaves it fixed. We say that it is periodic in direction $(3, 2)$. An example for an aperiodic polynomial is $nk + 1$. The main result of last year's paper was an algorithm for determining aperiodic denominator bounds for PLDEs, i.e., we can find Q such that whenever $y = \frac{p}{uq}$ solves the given equation, p and q are coprime, and q is aperiodic, then $q \mid Q$.

The present paper is a continuation of this work. We now turn to periodic factors and study under which circumstances a slightly adapted version of last year's algorithm can also predict periodic factors of the denominator. We propose an algorithm which finds the periodic factors for almost all directions. Every equation has however some directions which our algorithm does not cover. But if, for instance, we have a system of two equations and apply our algorithm to each of them, then the two bounds can under favorable circumstances (which can be detected algorithmically) be combined to a denominator bound which provably contains all the factors that can possibly occur in the denominator of any solution of the system. This was not possible before. So while until now we were just able to compute in all situations some factors, we can now also find in some situations all factors.

Despite this progress, we must confess that our results are still of a somewhat academic nature because denominator bounds in which some factors are missing are not really enough for solving equations. And even when a full denominator bound is known, it still remains to find the polynomial solutions of a PLDE, and nobody knows how to do this—the corresponding problem for differential equations is undecidable. But in practice, we can heuristically choose a degree bound for finding polynomial solutions, and knowing parts of the possible denominators is certainly better than knowing nothing, and the more factors we know, the better. Apart from this, we find it interesting to see how far the classical univariate techniques carry in the multivariate setting, and we would be curious to see new ideas leading towards algorithms which also find the factors that we still miss.

2. PREPARATIONS

Let $\mathbb{K}$ be a field of characteristic zero. We consider polynomials and rational functions in the r variables $n_1, \ldots, n_r$ with coefficients in $\mathbb{K}$. For each variable n_i, let N_i denote the shift operator mapping n_i to $n_i + 1$ and leaving all other variables fixed, so that

$$N_i q(n_1, \ldots, n_r)$$
$$= q(n_1, \ldots, n_{i-1}, n_i + 1, n_{i+1}, \ldots, n_r)$$

for every rational function q. Whenever it seems appropriate, we will use multiindex notation, writing for instance $\mathbf{n}$ instead of $n_1, \ldots, n_r$ or $N^{\mathbf{i}}$ for $N_1^{i_1} N_2^{i_2} \cdots N_r^{i_r}$.

We consider equations of the form

$$\sum_{\mathbf{s} \in S} a_{\mathbf{s}} N^{\mathbf{s}} y = f \tag{1}$$

where $S \subseteq \mathbb{Z}^r$ is finite and nonempty, $f \in \mathbb{K}[\mathbf{n}]$ and $a_{\mathbf{s}} \in \mathbb{K}[\mathbf{n}] \setminus \{0\}$ ($\mathbf{s} \in S$) are given, and y is an unknown rational function. The set S is called the *support* of the equation. Our goal is to determine the polynomials $p \in \mathbb{K}[\mathbf{n}]$ which may possibly occur in the denominator of a solution y, or at least to find many factors of p.

We recall the following definitions and results from our previous paper [12]. By convention, we understand that gcds are monic, so that saying "$\gcd(u, v) = 1$" is the same as saying "u and v are coprime". Also by convention, when writing a rational function $y \in \mathbb{K}(\mathbf{n})$ as a quotient $y = p/q$, we mean to say that p and q are in $\mathbb{K}[\mathbf{n}]$ and $\gcd(p, q) = 1$.

DEFINITION 1. *Let $p, q, d \in \mathbb{K}[\mathbf{n}]$.*

1. *The set $\mathrm{Spread}(p, q) := \{\, \mathbf{i} \in \mathbb{Z}^r : \gcd(p, N^{\mathbf{i}} q) \neq 1 \,\}$ is called the* spread *of p and q. For short, we write $\mathrm{Spread}(p) := \mathrm{Spread}(p, p)$.*

2. *The number $\mathrm{Disp}_k(p, q) := \max\{\, |i_k| : (i_1, \ldots, i_r) \in \mathrm{Spread}(p, q) \,\}$ is called the* dispersion *of p and q with respect to $k \in \{1, \ldots, r\}$. (We set $\max A := -\infty$ if A is empty and $\max A := \infty$ if A is unbounded.)*

3. *The polynomial p is called* aperiodic *if $\mathrm{Spread}(p)$ is finite, and* periodic *otherwise.*

4. *The polynomial d is called an* aperiodic denominator bound *for equation (1) if $d \neq 0$ and every solution y can be written as $\frac{a}{ub}$ for some $a, b, u \in \mathbb{K}[\mathbf{n}]$ where u is periodic and $b \mid d$.*

5. *A point $\mathbf{p} \in S \subseteq \mathbb{Z}^r \subseteq \mathbb{R}^r$ is called a* corner point *of S if there exists a vector $\mathbf{v} \in \mathbb{R}^r$ such that $(\mathbf{s} - \mathbf{p}) \cdot \mathbf{v} > 0$ for all $\mathbf{s} \in S \setminus \{\mathbf{p}\}$. Such a vector $\mathbf{v}$ is then called an* inner vector, *and the affine hyperplane $H := \{\mathbf{x} \in \mathbb{R}^r : (\mathbf{x} - \mathbf{p}) \cdot \mathbf{v} = 0\}$ is called a* border plane *for S.*

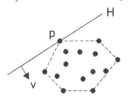

In the univariate case ($r = 1$), slightly different definitions are circulating in the literature. Our "denominator bound" corresponds most closely to what Abramov [1] calls "universal denominator" and to the reciprocal of what van Hoeij [11] calls a rational function which "bounds the denominator".

THEOREM 1. *Let $p, q \in \mathbb{K}[\mathbf{n}]$.*

1. *If p is irreducible, then $\mathrm{Spread}(p)$ is a submodule of $\mathbb{Z}^r$ and p is aperiodic if and only if $\mathrm{Spread}(p) = \{0\}$.*

2. *If p and q are irreducible, then there exists $\mathbf{s} \in \mathbb{Z}^r$ such that $\mathbf{s} + \mathrm{Spread}(p, q)$ is a submodule of $\mathbb{Z}^r$. This submodule has the property that whenever $m \in \mathbb{Z} \setminus \{0\}$ and $\mathbf{y} \in \mathbb{Z}^r$ are such that the module contains $m\mathbf{y}$, then it also contains $\mathbf{y}$.*

3. *$\mathrm{Spread}(p, q) = \bigcup_{u, v} \mathrm{Spread}(u, v)$, where the union is taken over all pairs (u, v) where u is a monic irreducible factor of p and v is a monic irreducible factor of q.*

4. *There is an algorithm for computing $\mathrm{Spread}(p, q)$.*

5. *There is an algorithm for computing an aperiodic denominator bound for (1) given the support S and the coefficients $a_{\mathbf{s}}$ ($\mathbf{s} \in S$).*

Throughout the rest of this paper, we will only consider submodules $M \subseteq \mathbb{Z}^r$ with the property quoted in Thm. 1.2: if $m \in \mathbb{Z} \setminus \{0\}$ and $\mathbf{y} \in \mathbb{Z}^r$ are such that $m\mathbf{y} \in M$, then also $\mathbf{y} \in M$. For lack of better names, let us call these submodules *good*. Note that a submodule $M \subseteq \mathbb{Z}^r$ is good if and only if $\mathbb{Z}^r / M$ is torsion free.

3. DENOMINATOR BOUNDS MODULO A PRESCRIBED MODULE

Our goal in this section is to determine the factors whose spread is contained in some prescribed set $W \subseteq \mathbb{Z}^r$. Under suitable assumptions about W such factors must pop up in the coefficients of the equation (cf. Lemma 2 below) and under stronger assumptions we can also give a bound on the dispersion between them (cf. Theorem 2 below). Using these two results we obtain a denominator bound relative to W (cf. Theorem 3 and Algorithm 1) below. In the next section, we then propose an algorithm which combines the denominator bounds with respect to several sets W. It turns out that by considering only finitely many sets W one can obtain a denominator bound with respect to infinitely many sets W.

DEFINITION 2. *Let $W \subseteq \mathbb{Z}^r$ with $0 \in W$. A polynomial $d \in \mathbb{K}[\mathbf{n}] \setminus \{0\}$ is called a* denominator bound *of (1) with respect to W if for every solution $y = p/q \in \mathbb{K}(\mathbf{n})$ of (1) and every irreducible factor u of q with multiplicity $m \in \mathbb{N}$ such that $\mathrm{Spread}(u) \subseteq W$ we have $u^m \mid d$.*

Typically, W will be a good submodule of $\mathbb{Z}^r$ or a finite union of such modules. The definition reduces to the notion of aperiodic denominator bound when $W = \{0\}$. In the other extreme, when $W = \mathbb{Z}^r$ then d is a "complete" denominator bound: it contains all the factors, periodic or not, that can possibly occur in the denominator of a solution y of (1). In general, d predicts all aperiodic factors in the denominator of a solution as well as the periodic factors whose spread is contained in W.

Denominator bounds with respect to different submodules can be combined as follows.

LEMMA 1. *Let $W_1, \ldots, W_m$ be good submodules of $\mathbb{Z}^r$, and let $d_1, \ldots, d_m$ be denominator bounds of (1) with respect to $W_1, \ldots, W_m$, respectively. Then $d := \operatorname{lcm}(d_1, \ldots, d_m)$ is a denominator bound with respect to $W := W_1 \cup \cdots \cup W_m$.*

PROOF. Let u be an irreducible factor of the denominator of some solution of (1) and suppose that $U := \operatorname{Spread}(u) \subseteq W$. It suffices to show that then $U \subseteq W_k$ for some k, because then it follows that $u \mid d_k \mid d$, as desired.

We show that if U contains some vector $\mathbf{x} \notin W_1$, then $U \subseteq W_2 \cup \cdots \cup W_m$. Applying the argument repeatedly proves that $U \subseteq W_k$ for some k.

If $U \cap W_1 = \{0\}$, then $U \subseteq W_2 \cup \cdots \cup W_m$ is obvious. If not, let $\mathbf{y} \in U \cap W_1$ be a nonzero vector. We show that $\mathbf{y} \in W_2 \cup \cdots \cup W_m$. Since U is a submodule of $\mathbb{Z}^r$, we have $\mathbf{x} + \alpha \mathbf{y} \in U$ for all $\alpha \in \mathbb{Z}$. By assumption $U \subseteq W_1 \cup \cdots \cup W_m$, so each such $\mathbf{x} + \alpha \mathbf{y}$ must belong to at least one module W_ℓ ($\ell = 1, \ldots, m$). It cannot belong to W_1 though, because together with $\mathbf{y} \in W_1$ this would imply $\mathbf{x} \in W_1$, which is not the case. Therefore: For every $\alpha \in \mathbb{Z}$ there exists $\ell \in \{2, \ldots, m\}$ such that $\mathbf{x} + \alpha \mathbf{y} \in W_\ell$.

Since $\mathbb{Z}$ is infinite and m is finite, there must be some index $\ell \in \{2, \ldots, m\}$ for which there are two different $\alpha_1, \alpha_2 \in \mathbb{Z}$ with $\mathbf{x} + \alpha_1 \mathbf{y} \in W_\ell$ and $\mathbf{x} + \alpha_2 \mathbf{y} \in W_\ell$. Since W_ℓ is also a submodule of $\mathbb{Z}^r$, it follows that $(\alpha_1 - \alpha_2)\mathbf{y} \in W_\ell$, and finally, because W_ℓ is good, $\mathbf{y} \in W_\ell \subseteq W_2 \cup \cdots \cup W_m$, as claimed. $\square$

The next result says that factors of denominators tend to leave traces in the coefficients of corner points of S.

LEMMA 2. *Let $y = p/q$ be a solution of (1), and let u be a monic irreducible factor of q. Let $\mathbf{p} \in S$ be a corner point of S with an inner vector $\mathbf{v} \in \mathbb{R}^r$ orthogonal to $\operatorname{Spread}(u)$ (meaning $\mathbf{w} \cdot \mathbf{v} = 0$ for all $\mathbf{w}$ in $\operatorname{Spread}(u)$). Then there exists $\mathbf{i} \in \mathbb{Z}^r$ such that $N^{\mathbf{i}} u \mid a_{\mathbf{p}}$.*

PROOF. Let $u_1, \ldots, u_m$ be all the distinct monic irreducible factors of q with $\operatorname{Spread}(u, u_k) \neq 0$. Let $\mathbf{c}_k \in \operatorname{Spread}(u, u_k)$ for $k = 1, \ldots, m$. Then $\gcd(u, N^{\mathbf{c}_k} u_k) \neq 1$, and therefore, since u and u_k are monic and irreducible, $u = N^{\mathbf{c}_k} u_k$ and $u_k = N^{-\mathbf{c}_k} u$.

For every $\mathbf{i} \in \mathbb{Z}^r$ we have

$$
\begin{aligned}
\mathbf{i} \in \operatorname{Spread}(u, u_k) &\iff \gcd(u, N^{\mathbf{i}} u_k) \neq 1 \\
&\iff u = N^{\mathbf{i}} u_k \\
&\iff N^{\mathbf{i}-\mathbf{c}_k} u = u \\
&\iff \mathbf{i} - \mathbf{c}_k \in \operatorname{Spread}(u) \\
&\iff \mathbf{i} \in \mathbf{c}_k + \operatorname{Spread}(u).
\end{aligned}
$$

It follows that $\operatorname{Spread}(u, u_k) = \mathbf{c}_k + \operatorname{Spread}(u)$, and with Thm. 1.3 that

$$
\operatorname{Spread}(u, q) = \bigcup_{k=1}^{m} (\mathbf{c}_k + \operatorname{Spread}(u)) = C + \operatorname{Spread}(u)
$$

where $C = \{\mathbf{c}_1, \ldots, \mathbf{c}_m\} \subseteq \operatorname{Spread}(u, q)$.

Let $k \in \{1, \ldots, m\}$ be such that $\mathbf{v} \cdot \mathbf{c}_k$ is maximal. Rewrite (1) as

$$
a_{\mathbf{p}} N^{\mathbf{p}} y = f - \sum_{\mathbf{s} \in S \setminus \{\mathbf{p}\}} a_{\mathbf{s}} N^{\mathbf{s}} y.
$$

Because of $N^{-\mathbf{c}_k} u = u_k$, the factor $N^{\mathbf{p}-\mathbf{c}_k} u = N^{\mathbf{p}} u_k$ appears in the denominator of $N^{\mathbf{p}} y$. Suppose that it also appears in the denominator of some $N^{\mathbf{s}} y$ on the right hand side. Then

$$
N^{\mathbf{p}-\mathbf{c}_k} u = N^{\mathbf{s}} u_j = N^{\mathbf{s}-\mathbf{c}_j} u
$$

for some $j \in \{1, \ldots, m\}$, hence $\mathbf{s} - \mathbf{p} + \mathbf{c}_k - \mathbf{c}_j \in \operatorname{Spread}(u)$. As $\mathbf{v}$ is orthogonal to $\operatorname{Spread}(u)$ by assumption, we have $\mathbf{v} \cdot (\mathbf{s} - \mathbf{p} + \mathbf{c}_k - \mathbf{c}_j) = 0$. On the other hand, $\mathbf{v} \cdot (\mathbf{s} - \mathbf{p}) > 0$, because $\mathbf{p}$ is a corner point of S with inner vector $\mathbf{v}$, and $\mathbf{v} \cdot \mathbf{c}_k \geq \mathbf{v} \cdot \mathbf{c}_j$ by the choice of k, so $\mathbf{v} \cdot (\mathbf{s} - \mathbf{p} + \mathbf{c}_k - \mathbf{c}_j) = \mathbf{v} \cdot (\mathbf{s} - \mathbf{p}) + \mathbf{v} \cdot \mathbf{c}_k - \mathbf{v} \cdot \mathbf{c}_j > 0$, a contradiction. It follows that $N^{\mathbf{p}-\mathbf{c}_k} u$ cannot appear in the denominator of $N^{\mathbf{s}} y$ for any $\mathbf{s} \in S \setminus \{\mathbf{p}\}$, therefore $N^{\mathbf{p}-\mathbf{c}_k} u \mid a_{\mathbf{p}}$. The claim follows with $\mathbf{i} = \mathbf{p} - \mathbf{c}_k$. $\square$

The lemma tells us for which choices of $W \subseteq \mathbb{Z}^r$ something nontrivial may happen. Let us illustrate this with an example.

EXAMPLE 1. *The equation*

$$
\begin{aligned}
(4k - 2n &+ 1)(k + n + 1)y(n, k) \\
&+ (8k^2 + 2kn + k + 6n^2 + 13n + 6)y(n, k+1) \\
&- 2(6k^2 + 2kn + 13k + 2n^2 + n + 6)y(n+1, k) = 0
\end{aligned}
$$

has the solution $y = (n^2 + 2k^2)/(k + n + 1)$. Its denominator is periodic, $\operatorname{Spread}(k + n + 1) = \binom{1}{-1}\mathbb{Z}$. Lemma 2 predicts the appearance of $u := k + n + 1$ (or at least some shifted version of it) in the coefficient of $y(n, k)$, because for the choice $W := \operatorname{Spread}(u) = \binom{1}{-1}\mathbb{Z}$, the point $\mathbf{p} = \binom{0}{0} \in S$ admits the choice $\mathbf{v} = \binom{1}{1}$ in accordance with the requirements imposed by the lemma. Note that no factor of the form $N^i K^j(k+n+1)$ occurs in the coefficients of $y(n, k+1)$ or $y(n+1, k)$, which does not contradict the lemma, because the points $\binom{0}{1}$ and $\binom{1}{0}$ lie on a line parallel to W (meaning $\binom{0}{1} - \binom{1}{0} = \binom{-1}{1} \in W$). This has the consequence that for these points, there does not exist a vector $\mathbf{v}$ with the required property.

Conversely, the factor $u' := 4k - 2n + 1$ cannot possibly appear in the denominator of a solution, because for $W' := \operatorname{Spread}(u') = \binom{1}{2}\mathbb{Z}$ we can take $\mathbf{p}' = \binom{1}{0}$ and $\mathbf{v}' = \binom{-2}{1}$, and according to the lemma, some factor of the form $N^i K^j(4k - 2n + 1)$ would have to appear in the coefficient of $y(n+1, k)$.

More generally, for any nontrivial good submodule W'' of $\mathbb{Z}^2$ other than W, Lemma 2 excludes the possibility of periodic factors whose spread is contained in W'', because such factors would have to leave a trace in at least one of the coefficients of the equation.

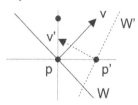

In the previous example, we could thus determine all the interesting modules W by just looking at the spreads of the factors of the coefficients of the equation. The following example indicates that this is not always sufficient.

EXAMPLE 2. *The equation*

$$(2k - 3n^2 - 8n - 5)y(n, k+1)$$
$$+ (k + 3n^2 + 5n + 4)y(n+1, k)$$
$$- (5k - 3n^2 - 11n - 7)y(n+1, k+1)$$
$$+ (2k - 3n^2 - 8n - 3)y(n+2, k) = 0$$

also has the solution $y = (n^2 + 2k^2)/(k+n+1)$. *Its denominator* $k+n+1$ *does not appear in any of the coefficients of the equation. This is because for its spread* $W = \binom{1}{-1}\mathbb{Z}$ *there are no suitable* $\mathbf{p} \in S$ *and* $\mathbf{v} \in \mathbb{R}^2$ *matching the conditions of the lemma because the points* $\binom{1}{0}, \binom{0}{1}$ *as well as the points* $\binom{2}{0}, \binom{1}{1}$ *lie on a line parallel to* W.

In summary, in order for W to be the spread of a factor that can appear in the denominator of a solution of (1), W must be contained in the spread of some coefficient of the equation (as in Ex. 1) or it must be parallel to one of the faces in the convex hull of the support S (as in Ex. 2). For every equation, we can thus determine some finitely many good submodules of $\mathbb{Z}^r$ of codimension one such that each possibly occurring spread W is contained in at least one of them.

3.1 A Normalizing Change of Variables

Let $\mathbb{Z}^r = V \oplus W$ be a decomposition of $\mathbb{Z}^r$ into good submodules. Our goal is to obtain denominator bounds with respect to W by applying the algorithm from last year [12] to $V \cong \mathbb{Z}^r/W$. It turns out that this can be done provided that W is sufficiently nondegenerate. In order to formulate the precise conditions on W without too much notational overhead, it seems convenient to make a change of coordinates.

Let invertible matrices $A = ((a_{i,j}))^r_{i,j=1} \in \mathbb{Q}^{r \times r}$ act on $\mathbb{K}(\mathbf{n})$ via

$$A \cdot y(n_1, \ldots, n_r) := y\big(a_{1,1}n_1 + a_{1,2}n_2 + \cdots + a_{1,r}n_r,$$
$$a_{2,1}n_1 + a_{2,2}n_2 + \cdots + a_{2,r}n_r,$$
$$\vdots$$
$$a_{r,1}n_1 + a_{r,2}n_2 + \cdots + a_{r,r}n_r\big).$$

We obviously have $A \cdot (p+q) = (A \cdot p) + (A \cdot q)$ and $A \cdot (pq) = (A \cdot p)(A \cdot q)$ for all $p, q \in \mathbb{K}(\mathbf{n})$. It can be checked that we also have

$$A \cdot (N^{\mathbf{s}} y) = N^{A^{-1}\mathbf{s}}(A \cdot y)$$

for every $A \in \mathbb{Z}^{r \times r}$ with $|\det A| = 1$ and every $\mathbf{s} \in \mathbb{Z}^r$ and every $y \in \mathbb{K}(\mathbf{n})$. It follows that $y \in \mathbb{K}(\mathbf{n})$ is a solution of (1) if and only if $\tilde{y} = A \cdot y$ is a solution of the transformed equation

$$\sum_{\mathbf{s} \in S} (A \cdot a_{\mathbf{s}}) N^{A^{-1}\mathbf{s}} \tilde{y} = A \cdot f,$$

or equivalently of

$$\sum_{\mathbf{s} \in \tilde{S}} \tilde{a}_{\mathbf{s}} N^{\mathbf{s}} \tilde{y} = \tilde{f},$$

where $\tilde{S} = \{A^{-1}\mathbf{s} : s \in S\}$, $\tilde{a}_{\mathbf{s}} := A \cdot a_{As}$ ($\mathbf{s} \in \tilde{S}$), and $\tilde{f} = A \cdot f$.

Now take $A \in \mathbb{Z}^{r \times r}$ with $|\det A| = 1$ such that the first t rows of A^{-1} form a basis of V and the last $r - t$ rows of A^{-1}

form a basis of W. Then the transformation just described maps the basis vectors of V to the first t unit vectors and the basis vectors of W to the last $r - t$ unit vectors. In other words, we can assume without loss of generality that V itself is generated by the first t unit vectors and W by the last $r - t$ unit vectors in $\mathbb{Z}^r$. We will make this assumption from now on, unless otherwise stated. Note that this convention implies for an irreducible polynomial $u \in \mathbb{K}[\mathbf{n}]$ that $\mathrm{Spread}(u) = W$ is equivalent to u being free of the variables $n_{t+1}, n_{t+2}, \ldots, n_r$ and aperiodic as element of $\mathbb{K}[n_1, \ldots, n_t]$.

From now on we will assume that W is a proper good submodule of $\mathbb{Z}^r$. This restriction is conform with our later application (see Algorithm 2) where we will choose $W := \mathrm{Spread}(u)$ for some irreducible $u \in \mathbb{K}[\mathbf{n}]$; since $u \notin \mathbb{K}$, this implies $W \neq \mathbb{Z}^r$. By applying, if necessary, a suitable power of N_1 on both sides of the equation (1) we can further assume without loss of generality that $\min\{s_1 : (s_1, \ldots, s_r) \in S\} = 0$, and we set $k := \max\{s_1 : (s_1, \ldots, s_r) \in S\}$. Moreover, we may assume $k > 0$: If $k = 0$, the variable n_1 in problem (1) is in fact a constant. Hence we can move n_1 into the constant field $\mathbb{K}$, and we can rename the remaining variables accordingly. This reduction can occur at most $r - 1$ times (otherwise this would imply $V = \{\mathbf{0}\}$ or equivalently $W = \mathbb{Z}^r$) and we eventually find a modified S with $k \geq 1$.

3.2 Bounding the Dispersion

With this transformation w.r.t. a proper good submodule W of $\mathbb{Z}^r$ and under the assumption that the extreme points (2) of S have certain properties, Theorem 2 below explains how one can bound the dispersion w.r.t. n_1 ($\mathrm{Disp}_1(u)$ as defined in Def. 1.2 in Section 2) of all factors u with $\mathrm{Spread}(u) \in W$ that occur in the denominator of a solution of (1). This result is a refinement of Lemma 2 from [12].

LEMMA 3. *Let* $u, v \in \mathbb{K}[\mathbf{n}] \setminus \{0\}$ *with* $\mathrm{Spread}(u) \subseteq W$ *and* $\mathrm{Spread}(v) \subseteq W$. *Then there is at most one* $(s_1, \ldots, s_t) \in \mathbb{Z}^r$ *s.t. there is* $(s_{t+1}, \ldots, s_r) \in \mathbb{Z}^{r-t}$ *with* $N^{(s_1, \ldots, s_r)}u = v$.

PROOF. Take $\mathbf{s}, \mathbf{s}'$ with $N^{\mathbf{s}}u = v = N^{\mathbf{s}'}u$. As $N^{\mathbf{s}-\mathbf{s}'}u = u$, it follows $\mathbf{s} - \mathbf{s}' \in W = \{0\}^t \times \mathbb{Z}^{r-t}$, and thus the first t components of $\mathbf{s}, \mathbf{s}'$ agree. $\square$

By the transformation in Section 3.1 it follows that for any irreducible $u \in \mathbb{K}[\mathbf{n}]$ with $\mathrm{Spread}(u) \subseteq W$ we have that $\mathrm{Disp}_1(u)$ is bounded. As a consequence, we have $s \in \mathbb{N} \cup \{-\infty\}$ for the s defined in (3) below.

THEOREM 2. *Let*

$$A = \{(s_1, \ldots, s_r) \in S : s_1 = 0\},$$
$$B = \{(s_1, \ldots, s_r) \in S : s_1 = k\}. \tag{2}$$

Suppose that no two elements of A *agree in the first* t *coordinates, and that the same is true for* B. *Let* a'_t *be those polynomials which contain all irreducible factors* u *of* a_t *with* $\mathrm{Spread}(u) \subseteq W$. *Let*

$$s := \max\{\mathrm{Disp}_1(a'_{\mathbf{s}}, N_1^{-k}a'_{\mathbf{t}}) : \mathbf{s} \in A \text{ and } \mathbf{t} \in B\}. \tag{3}$$

Then for any solution $y = p/q \in \mathbb{K}(\mathbf{n})$ *of* (1) *and any irreducible factors* u, v *of* q *with* $\mathrm{Spread}(u), \mathrm{Spread}(v) \subseteq W$ *we have* $\mathrm{Disp}_1(u, v) \leq s$.

PROOF. As S is not empty, A, B are nonempty. W.l.o.g. we may assume that the minimal element of A w.r.t. lexicographic order is the zero vector.

Suppose that there are irreducible factors u, v of q with $\text{Spread}(u) \subseteq W$, $\text{Spread}(v) \subseteq W$ and $d := \text{Disp}_1(u, v)$ such that $d > s$; take such u, v such that d is maximal (since there are only finitely many factors u, v in q and $\text{Disp}_1(u, v)$ is bounded, this is possible). W.l.o.g., we assume that $\gcd(v, N^{\mathbf{d}} u) \neq 1$ where the first entry in $\mathbf{d} \in \mathbb{Z}$ is d (otherwise we interchange u and v). Consider all the factors $N^{\mathbf{u}} u$ and $N^{\mathbf{v}} v$ occurring in q where the first entry in $\mathbf{u}$ and $\mathbf{v}$ is 0. Note that by Lemma 3 there are only finitely many choices of the first t components, so we can choose two such factors from q where the first t components of $\mathbf{u}$ are minimal and the first t components of $\mathbf{v}$ are maximal w.r.t. lexicographic order; these factors are denoted by u', v' respectively; note that $\gcd(v', N^{\mathbf{d}'} u') \neq 1$ for some $\mathbf{d}' \in \mathbb{Z}$ where the first entry is d.

• First suppose that u' divides one of the polynomials $a_{\mathbf{m}}$ with $\mathbf{m} \in A$. In this case we choose the polynomial $a_{\mathbf{w}}$ with $\mathbf{w} = (w_1, \ldots, w_r) \in B$ such that $(w_2, \ldots, w_t)$ is maximal w.r.t. lexicographic order (uniqueness is guaranteed by the assumption that no two elements from B agree in the first t components). We can write (1) in the form

$$N^{\mathbf{w}} y = \frac{1}{a_{\mathbf{w}}} \Big(f - \sum_{\mathbf{s} \in S \setminus \{\mathbf{w}\}} a_{\mathbf{s}} N^{\mathbf{s}} y \Big). \tag{4}$$

Now observe that the factor $N^{\mathbf{w}} v'$ does not occur in the denominator of any $N^{\mathbf{s}} y$ with $\mathbf{s} \in S \setminus \{\mathbf{w}\}$:

1. Suppose that there is $\mathbf{s} \in S \setminus B$ such that $N^{\mathbf{w}} v'$ occurs in $N^{\mathbf{s}} q$, i.e., $N^{\mathbf{w} - \mathbf{s}} v'$ is a factor of q. Since the first component of $\mathbf{w}$ is k ($\mathbf{w} \in B$) and the first component of $\mathbf{s}$ is smaller than k ($\mathbf{s} \notin B$), the first component of $\mathbf{w} - \mathbf{s}$ is positive. Moreover, since $\gcd(v', N^{\mathbf{d}'} u') \neq 1$, the factors v' and $N^{\mathbf{w} - \mathbf{s}} v'$ of q have distance larger than d in the first component; a contradiction to the maximality of d. Thus, if $N^{\mathbf{w}} v'$ is a factor in the denominator of $N^{\mathbf{s}} y$ with $\mathbf{s} \in S$, it follows that $\mathbf{s} \in B$.

2. Suppose that there is $\mathbf{s} \in B$ with $\mathbf{w} \neq \mathbf{s}$ such that $N^{\mathbf{w}} v'$ is a factor of $N^{\mathbf{s}} q$. Then $N^{\mathbf{w} - \mathbf{s}} v'$ is a factor of q. Since the first component of the vectors in B is k, but the first t components in total cannot be the same for two different vectors of B, it follows that the first entry in $\mathbf{w} - \mathbf{s}$ is zero and at least one of the others is non-zero; in particular, by the maximality assumption on $\mathbf{w}$ the first non-zero entry is positive. Hence we find $\mathbf{v}' = (0, v_2', \ldots, v_r') := \mathbf{v} + \mathbf{w} - \mathbf{s}$ such that $N^{\mathbf{v}'} v$ is a factor of q and such that $(v_2', \ldots, v_t')$ is larger than $(v_2, \ldots, v_t)$ w.r.t. lexicographic ordering; a contradiction to the choice of the vector $\mathbf{v}$.

Since $f, a_{\mathbf{s}} \in \mathbb{K}[\mathbf{n}]$ and $N^{\mathbf{w}} v'$ does not occur in the denominators of $N^{\mathbf{s}} y$ for any $\mathbf{s} \in S \setminus \{\mathbf{w}\}$, also the common denominator of the rational function $f - \sum_{\mathbf{s} \in S \setminus \{\mathbf{w}\}} a_{\mathbf{s}} N^{\mathbf{s}} y$ does not contain the factor $N^{\mathbf{w}} v'$. Finally, $N^{\mathbf{w}} v'$ cannot be a factor of $a_{\mathbf{w}}$: Since $\mathbf{m} \in A$, $\mathbf{w} \in B$ and $s < d$, we have $\text{Disp}_1(a_{\mathbf{m}}, N_1^{-k} a_{\mathbf{w}}) < d$. However, $\gcd(u', N^{\mathbf{d}'} v') \neq 1$ and $u' \mid a_{\mathbf{m}}$; thus $N^{\mathbf{w}} v' \mid a_{\mathbf{m}}$ would imply that $N_1^{-k} N^{\mathbf{w}} v' \mid N_1^{-k} a_{\mathbf{m}}$ and thus (note that the first component in $\mathbf{w}$ is $k \geq 0$) it would follow $\text{Disp}_1(a_{\mathbf{m}}, N_1^{-k} a_{\mathbf{w}}) \geq d$. Overall, the common denominator on the right side of (4) cannot contain the factor $N^{\mathbf{w}} v'$, and hence the denominator of $N^{\mathbf{w}} y$ is not divisible by $N^{\mathbf{w}} v'$. Thus the denominator of y, in particular q is not divisible by v'; a contradiction.

• Conversely, suppose that u' does not divide any of the polynomials $a_{\mathbf{s}}$ with $\mathbf{s} \in A$. Now let $\mathbf{w} = (0, w_2 \ldots, w_r) \in A$ such that $(w_2, \ldots, w_t)$ is minimal w.r.t. lexicographic ordering (again it is uniquely determined by the assumptions on A), and write (1) in the form (4); by our assumption stated in the beginning, $\mathbf{w}$ is just the zero vector $\mathbf{0}$. By analogous arguments as above (the roles of A and B, resp. u' and v', are exchanged) it follows that u' does not occur in the denominator of any $N^{\mathbf{s}} y$ with $\mathbf{s} \in S \setminus \{\mathbf{0}\}$. Hence as above, the common denominator of $f - \sum_{\mathbf{s} \in S \setminus \{\mathbf{0}\}} a_{\mathbf{s}} N^{\mathbf{s}} y$ does not contain the factor u'. Moreover, since u' does not divide any $a_{\mathbf{s}}$ from $\mathbf{s} \in A$, the factor u' does not occur in $a_{\mathbf{0}}$. In total, the factor u' is not part of the denominator on the right hand side of (4), but it is a factor of the denominator on the left hand side of (4); a contradiction. □

The following example illustrates that Theorem 2 is not always applicable.

EXAMPLE 3. *Fix* $W := \text{Spread}(k + n + 1) = \binom{1}{-1}\mathbb{Z}$ *and take* $V = \binom{0}{1}\mathbb{Z}$. *The problem from Example 1 is normalized by the change of variables* $n \to k$ *and* $k \to n - k$ *(i.e., a basis transformation* $\binom{0 \ 1}{1 \ -1}$ *with determinant* -1 *is chosen) and one obtains* $V' = \binom{1}{0}\mathbb{Z}$ *and* $W' = \binom{0}{1}\mathbb{Z}$. *This gives the new equation*

$$(n + 1)(-6k + 4n + 1)y(n, k)$$
$$+ (12k^2 - 14nk + 12k + 8n^2 + n + 6)y(n + 1, k)$$
$$- 2(6k^2 - 10nk - 12k + 6n^2 + 13n + 6)y(n + 1, k + 1) = 0$$

with the new structure set $S' = \{\binom{0}{0}, \binom{1}{0}, \binom{1}{1}\}$ *which now has the solution* $y = \frac{3k^2 - 4nk + 2n^2}{n+1}$ *where the denominator consists of the factor* $n + 1$ *with* $\text{Spread}(n + 1) = W'$. *As observed already in Example 1 one can predict the factor* $n + 1$ *(up to a shift in* n*) by exploiting Lemma 2. However, one cannot apply Theorem 2. For* S' *we get the sets* $A = \{\binom{0}{0}\}$ *and* $B = \{\binom{1}{0}, \binom{1}{1}\}$ *where in* B *the two vectors are the same in the first component but differ in the second component.*

3.3 Denominator Bounding Theorem

We are now working towards a denominator bounding theorem (Thm. 3 below) which says that if we rewrite the equation (1) into a new equation whose support contains some point $\mathbf{p}$ which is sufficiently far away from all the other points in the support, then we can read off a denominator bound from this new equation. We will need the following fact, which appears literally as Theorem 3 in [12] (with W, S' renamed to R^-, R^+ here in order to avoid a name clash with the meaning of W in the present paper).

LEMMA 4. *Let* $\mathbf{p}$ *be a corner point of* S *with border plane H and inner vector* $\mathbf{v}$. *Then for every* $s > 0$ *there exist finite sets*

$$R^- \subseteq \mathbb{Z}^r \cap \bigcup_{0 \leq e \leq s} (H + e\mathbf{v}) \ \text{and} \ R^+ \subseteq \mathbb{Z}^r \cap \bigcup_{e > s} (H + e\mathbf{v}),$$

and polynomials $b, b_{\mathbf{i}} \in \mathbb{K}[\mathbf{n}]$ *such that for any solution* $y \in \mathbb{K}(\mathbf{n})$ *of* (1) *we have*

$$N^{\mathbf{p}} y = \frac{b + \sum_{\mathbf{i} \in R^+} b_{\mathbf{i}} N^{\mathbf{i}} y}{\prod_{\mathbf{i} \in R^-} N^{\mathbf{i} - \mathbf{p}} a_{\mathbf{p}}}. \tag{5}$$

The sets R^- and R^+ and the polynomials b, b_i can be computed for a given s, S, $\mathbf{p}$, and $\mathbf{v}$ by Algorithm 2 from [12]. The next theorem provides a denominator bound with respect to W. It is an adaption of Theorem 4 from [12] to the present situation. We continue to assume the normalization $V = \mathbb{Z}^t \times \{0\}^{r-t}$, $W = \{0\}^t \times \mathbb{Z}^{r-t}$. The following figure illustrates the situation. The vector $\mathbf{v}$ is orthogonal to H but not necessarily to W, while the vector $\mathbf{v}'$ is orthogonal to W but not necessarily to H. Relation (5) separates $\mathbf{p}$ from the points in R^+ which are all below the plane $H + s\mathbf{v}$. The points in R^- are all between H and $H + s\mathbf{v}$.

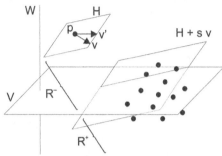

THEOREM 3. *Let $s \in \mathbb{N} \cup \{-\infty\}$ be such that for any solution $y = p/q \in \mathbb{K}(\mathbf{n})$ of (1) and any irreducible factors u, v of q with $\mathrm{Spread}(u), \mathrm{Spread}(v) \subseteq W$ we have $\mathrm{Disp}_1(u, v) \leq s$. Let $\mathbf{p}$ be a corner point of S for which there is an inner vector $\mathbf{v} = (v_1, \dots, v_r)$ with $v_1 \geq 1$ as well as an inner vector $\mathbf{v}'$ orthogonal to W. For these choices of s, $\mathbf{p}$, and $\mathbf{v}$, let R^-, R^+, b, b_i be as in Lemma 4. Let $a_{\mathbf{p}}'$ be the polynomial consisting of all the factors of $a_{\mathbf{p}}$ whose spread is contained in W. Then*

$$d := \prod_{\mathbf{s} \in R^-} N^{\mathbf{s} - 2\mathbf{p}} a_{\mathbf{p}}' \qquad (6)$$

is a denominator bound of (1) with respect to W.

PROOF. Let $y = p/q \in \mathbb{K}(\mathbf{n})$ be a solution of (1) and let u be an irreducible factor of q with multiplicity m and $\mathrm{Spread}(u) \subseteq W$. We have to show $u^m \mid d$. Lemma 2 applied to $\mathbf{p}$ and $\mathbf{v}'$ implies that there is some $\mathbf{i} \in \mathbb{Z}^r$ with $u' \mid q$ and $u' := N^{\mathbf{i}} u \mid a_{\mathbf{p}}$. By the choice of s we have $\mathrm{Disp}_1(u', u) \leq s$. Lemma 4 implies the representation

$$N^{\mathbf{p}} y = \frac{b + \sum_{\mathbf{i} \in R^+} b_i N^{\mathbf{i}} y}{\prod_{\mathbf{i} \in R^-} N^{\mathbf{i} - \mathbf{p}} a_{\mathbf{p}}}.$$

Because of $v_1 > 1$, every $\mathbf{i} \in R^+$ differs from $\mathbf{p}$ in the first coordinate by more than s. This implies that $N^{\mathbf{p}} u$ and hence that $N^{\mathbf{p}} u^m$ cannot appear in the denominator of $N^{\mathbf{i}} y$ for any $\mathbf{i} \in R^+$. But it does appear in the denominator of $N^{\mathbf{p}} y$, so it must appear as well in the denominator of the right hand side. The only remaining possibility is thus $N^{\mathbf{p}} u^m \mid \prod_{\mathbf{i} \in R^-} N^{\mathbf{i} - \mathbf{p}} a_{\mathbf{p}}$, and hence

$$u^m \mid \prod_{\mathbf{i} \in R^-} N^{\mathbf{i} - 2\mathbf{p}} a_{\mathbf{p}}.$$

Because of $\mathrm{Spread}(u') = \mathrm{Spread}(u) \subseteq W$, it follows that $u^m \mid d$. $\square$

3.4 A Denominator Bounding Algorithm

We now combine Theorems 2 and 3 to an algorithm for computing a denominator bound with respect to an arbitrary given W in situations where these theorems are applicable.

DEFINITION 3. *Let $\mathbf{p}, \mathbf{p}'$ be corner points of S and W some submodule of $\mathbb{Z}^r$.*

1. *The point $\mathbf{p}$ is called* useless *for W if there is an edge $(\mathbf{p}, \mathbf{s})$ in the convex hull of S with $\mathbf{p} - \mathbf{s} \in W$.*

2. *The pair $(\mathbf{p}, \mathbf{p}')$ is called* opposite *if there is a vector $\mathbf{v}$ such that $(\mathbf{s} - \mathbf{p}) \cdot \mathbf{v} \geq 0$ and $(\mathbf{p}' - \mathbf{s}) \cdot \mathbf{v} \geq 0$ for all $\mathbf{s} \in S$. Such a $\mathbf{v}$ is called a* witness vector *for the pair $(\mathbf{p}, \mathbf{p}')$.*

3. *The pair $(\mathbf{p}, \mathbf{p}')$ is called* useful *for W if it is opposite and neither $\mathbf{p}$ nor $\mathbf{p}'$ is useless for W.*

In the illustration below, the pair $(\mathbf{p}, \mathbf{p}')$ is opposite, with $\mathbf{v}$ being a witness vector. It is even a useful pair, because neither $\mathbf{p}$ nor $\mathbf{p}'$ is an endpoint of the edge of the convex hull of S which is parallel to W. In contrast, the corner point $\mathbf{q}$ is useless, because the edge $(\mathbf{q}, \mathbf{q}')$ is parallel to W.

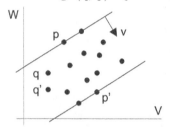

The definition of a useful pair is made in such a way that when a change of variables as described in Section 3.1 is applied which maps a witness vector of the pair to the first axis, then the sets A and B from Theorem 2 are such that $\mathbf{p} \in A$, $\mathbf{p}' \in B$ (because of the oppositeness), no two elements of A agree in the first $r - \dim W$ coordinates (because $\mathbf{p}$ is not useless), and the same is true for B (because $\mathbf{p}'$ is not useless).

Whether a pair $(\mathbf{p}, \mathbf{p}') \in S^2$ is useful or not can be found out by making an ansatz for the coefficients of a witness vector and solving the system of linear inequalities from the definition. The pair is useful if and only if this system is solvable, and in this case, any solution gives rise to a witness vector.

If for a given good submodule W we have found a useful pair, then we can compute a denominator bound with respect to W by the following algorithm.

ALGORITHM 1. Input: *An equation of the form (1), a proper good submodule W of $\mathbb{Z}^r$, a useful pair $(\mathbf{p}, \mathbf{p}')$ of S for W.* Output: *A denominator bound for (1) with respect to W.*

1   *Set $t := r - \dim W$.*
2   *Choose $\mathbf{v}_1, \mathbf{v}_2, \dots, \mathbf{v}_t \in \mathbb{Z}^r$ such that $\mathbf{v}_1$ is a witness*
3   *vector for $(\mathbf{p}, \mathbf{p}')$ and $\mathbb{Z}^r = V \oplus W$ where*
4   *V is the module generated by these vectors.*
5   *Perform a change of variables as described in*
6   *Section 3.1 such that $\mathbf{v}_i$ becomes the ith unit*
7   *vector in $\mathbb{Z}^r$, W becomes $\{0\}^t \times \mathbb{Z}^{r-t}$.*
8   *Determine A, B as in Theorem 2.*
9   *Compute $s \in \mathbb{N} \cup \{-\infty\}$ as defined in Theorem 2.*
10 *Choose an inner vector $\mathbf{v} \in \mathbb{R}^r$ for $\mathbf{p}$.*
11 *Compute R^- as defined in Lemma 4.*
12 *Compute d as defined in Theorem 3.*
13 *Apply the inverse change of variables to d, getting d'.*
14 *Return d'.*

The following variations can be applied for further improvements:

1. If the dimension of V is greater than 1, there might be different choices of witness vectors. Choosing different versions in line 2 might lead to different denominator bounds of W, say, $d_1, \ldots, d_k$. Then taking $d := \gcd(d_1, \ldots, d_k)$ may produce sharper denominator bound for (1) w.r.t. W.

2. Choosing different inner vectors in line 10 might lead to different sets R^- to write (5) and hence gives rise to different denominator bounds in (6). Taking the gcd of these denominator bounds may produce a refined version.

3. The coefficients $a_{\mathbf{s}}$ with $\mathbf{s} \in S$ are often available in factorized form. Then also the denominator bounds are obtained in factorized form, and the gcd-computations reduce to comparisons of these factors and bookkeeping of their multiplicities.

4. A COMBINED DENOMINATOR BOUND

As mentioned earlier, when setting $W = \{0\}$, one is able to derive an aperiodic denominator bound for equation (1). In this particular case, for each corner point $\mathbf{p}$ there is an other corner point $\mathbf{p}'$ such that $(\mathbf{p}, \mathbf{p}')$ is useful for W. Hence applying Algorithm 1 for any useful pair leads to an aperiodic denominator bound. In particular, running through all corner points and taking the gcd for all these candidates leads to a rather sharp aperiodic denominator bound for equation (1) which coincides with the output given in our previous investigation [12].

In the other extreme, when setting $W = \mathbb{Z}^r$, a denominator bound for (1) w.r.t. W would lead to a complete denominator bound for equation (1). However, in this case, we will fail to find a useful pair $(\mathbf{p}, \mathbf{p}')$, and in particular our Algorithm 1 is not applicable.

Our goal is to find a simultaneous denominator bound with respect to all W to which Algorithm 1 is applicable, i.e., for all W from the set

$$U := \{W \text{ good submodule of } \mathbb{Z}^r \mid \exists (\mathbf{p}, \mathbf{p}') \text{ useful for } W\}.$$

In general, this is an infinite set. But we can make use of the observations made after Example 2. Using Lemma 2, it turns out that instead of looping through all these infinitely many modules W, it is sufficient to consider those W which appear as spread of some factor in the coefficient of $a_{\mathbf{p}}$.

This argument even works for all W in the larger set

$$O := \{W \text{ good submodule of } \mathbb{Z}^r \mid$$

$$\exists (\mathbf{p}, \mathbf{p}') \text{ opposite with } \mathbf{p} \text{ not useless for } W\},$$

but since the $W \in O \setminus U$ do not satisfy the conditions of Theorem 2, we can only obtain partial information about their denominator bounds.

We propose the following algorithm.

ALGORITHM 2. Input: *An equation of the form* (1). *Output: A finite set of irreducible polynomials* $P = \{p_1, \ldots, p_k\}$, *and a nonzero* $d \in \mathbb{K}[\mathbf{n}]$ *such that for every solution* $y = \frac{p}{q} \in \mathbb{K}(\mathbf{n})$ *of* (1) *and every irreducible factor* u *of* q *with multiplicity* m *exactly one of the following holds:*
1. Spread$(u) \in U$ *and* $u^m \mid d$,

2. Spread$(u) \in O \setminus U$ *and* $\exists \mathbf{s} \in \mathbb{Z}^r, p \in P : N^{\mathbf{s}} u = p$,
3. Spread$(u) \notin O$.

```
1   d := 1; P := {}; C := {p ∈ S : p corner point of S}
2   forall q ∈ C do
3       forall u | a_q irreducible do
4           W := Spread(u)
5           if W ∈ U then
6               Compute a denominator bound d_0 w.r.t. W
7                   using an arbitrary useful pair for W.
8               d := lcm(d, d_0)
9           else if W ∈ O then
10              P := P ∪ {u}
11  return (P, d)
```

THEOREM 4. *The polynomial d computed by Algorithm 2 is a denominator bound with respect to any finite union of modules in U.*

PROOF. Let W be in U and $(\mathbf{p}, \mathbf{p}')$ be a useful pair with respect to W. Let $y = p/q$ be a solution of (1) and u be an irreducible factor of q with multiplicity m and Spread$(u) \subseteq W$. We have to show that $u^m \mid d$.

Since $\mathbf{p}$ is not useless, Lemma 2 implies that there is some $\mathbf{i} \in \mathbb{Z}^r$ with $N^{\mathbf{i}} u \mid a_{\mathbf{p}}$. This factor is going to be investigated in some iteration of the loop starting in line 3. The polynomial d_0 computed in this iteration is a denominator bound with respect to Spread$(N^{\mathbf{i}} u) = $ Spread(u). It follows that $u^m \mid d_0 \mid d$.

This proves the theorem when W itself is in U. If W is only a finite union of elements of U, the theorem follows from here by Lemma 1. □

For $W \in O \setminus U$, we can still apply Lemma 2 but Theorem 2 is no longer applicable. This prevents us from computing precise denominator bounds with respect to these W. However, using the set $P = \{p_1, \ldots, p_k\}$ returned by the algorithm we can at least say that for every denominator q of a solution $y = p/q$ of (1) there exist $m \in \mathbb{N}$ and a finite set $S' \subseteq \mathbb{Z}^r$ such that

$$d \prod_{\substack{p \in P \\ \mathbf{s} \in S'}} N^{\mathbf{s}} p^m \tag{7}$$

is a multiple of every divisor of q whose spread is contained in some finite union of modules in O. Appropriate choices S' and m can be found for instance by making an ansatz. Note also that the set P is usually smaller than the set of all periodic factors that occur in the coefficients $a_{\mathbf{s}}$ of (1). This phenomenon was demonstrated already in the second part of Example 2.

Summarizing, some part of the denominator is out of reach, namely all those parts of the denominator w.r.t. the modules from

$$\{W \text{ submodule of } \mathbb{Z}^r \mid (\mathbf{p}, \mathbf{p}') \text{ opposite for } W,$$

$$\text{both } \mathbf{p} \text{ and } \mathbf{p}' \text{ are useless for } W\},$$

some part of the denominator can be given up to possible shifts and multiplicities, and some part of the denominator bound is given explicitly by d.

The following improvements can be utilized.

1. As a preprocessing step, one should compute an aperiodic denominator bound for the equation (1) as described above. What remains is to recover the periodic factors. As a consequence, one can neglect all

irreducible factors u which are aperiodic and one can apply Theorem 3 where all aperiodic factors are removed from the polynomials $a'_\mathbf{p}$.

2. Choosing different useful pairs for a module W in line 9 might lead to different choices of denominator bounds, and taking their gcd may give rise to sharper denominator bounds of (1) w.r.t. W.

5. DISCUSSION

Typically the set O will contain all the submodules of $\mathbb{Z}^r$. Only when the convex hull of S happens to have two parallel edges on opposite sides, as is the case in Example 2, then modules W parallel to this edge do not belong to O. The set U will never contain all the submodules of $\mathbb{Z}^r$. Precisely those modules W which are parallel to an edge of the convex hull of S do not belong to U. Since the convex hull of S contains only finitely many edges, U will in some sense still contain almost all the submodules of $\mathbb{Z}^r$.

Depending on the origin of the equation, it may be that there is some freedom in the structure set S. For example, by multivariate guessing [13] or by creative telescoping [17, 10, 16] one can systematically search for equations with a prescribed structure set. In such situations, one can try to search for an equation with a structure set for which U and O cover as many spaces as possible.

If two equations with different structure sets are available, it may be possible to combine the two denominator bounds obtained by Algorithm 2 to a denominator bound with respect to the full space $\mathbb{Z}^r$.

EXAMPLE 4. *Consider the following system of equations:*

$$- (k+n+1)(2k+3n+1)y(n,k)$$
$$+ (k+n+4)(2k+3n+3)y(n,k+1)$$
$$- (k+n+2)(2k+3n+4)y(n+1,k)$$
$$+ (k+n+5)(2k+3n+6)y(n+1,k+1) = 0,$$
$$(n^2+n+1)(2k+3n+3)y(n,k+1)$$
$$- (n^2+5n+7)(2k+3n+4)y(n+1,k)$$
$$- (n^2+3n+3)(2k+3n+8)y(n+1,k+2)$$
$$+ (n^2+7n+13)(2k+3n+9)y(n+2,k+1) = 0.$$

Algorithm 2 applied to the first equation returns

$$d = (n+k+1)(n+k+2)(n+k+3)(3n+2k+1)$$

as a denominator bound with respect to any W except $\binom{1}{0}\mathbb{Z}$ and $\binom{0}{1}\mathbb{Z}$. Applied to the second equation, it returns

$$d = (n^2+n+1)((n+1)^2+(n+1)+1)(3n+2k+1)$$

as a denominator bound with respect to any W except $\binom{1}{1}\mathbb{Z}$ and $\binom{1}{-1}\mathbb{Z}$. The least common multiple of the two outputs is a simultaneous denominator bound with respect to any W.

Indeed, the system has the solution

$$\frac{1}{(n+k+1)(n+k+2)(n+k+3)(n^2+n+1)((n+1)^2+(n+1)+1)(3n+2k+1)}.$$

There is no hope for an algorithm which computes for any given single equation a denominator bound with respect to the full space $\mathbb{Z}^r$. This is because there are equations whose solution space contains rational functions with no finite common denominator. For instance, for every univariate polynomial p, we have that $1/p(n+k)$ is a solution of the equation

$$y(n+1,k) - y(n,k+1) = 0.$$

It would be interesting to characterize under which circumstances this happens, and to have an algorithm which finds a denominator bound with respect to $\mathbb{Z}^r$ in all other cases.

Acknowledgements. We thank all five referees for their careful reading and their critical comments.

6. REFERENCES

[1] S. A. Abramov. On the summation of rational functions. *Zh. vychisl. mat. Fiz*, pages 1071–1075, 1971.

[2] S. A. Abramov. Problems in computer algebra that are connected with a search for polynomial solutions of linear differential and difference equations. *Moscow Univ. Comput. Math. Cybernet.*, 3:63–68, 1989.

[3] S. A. Abramov and M. Barkatou. Rational solutions of first order linear difference systems. In *Proc. ISSAC'98*, pages 124–131, 1998.

[4] S. A. Abramov, A. Gheffar, and D. Khmelnov. Factorization of polynomials and gcd computations for finding universal denominators. In *Proc. CASC'10*, pages 4–18, 2010.

[5] S. A. Abramov and K. Yu. Kvashenko. Fast algorithms to search for the rational solutions of linear differential equations with polynomial coefficients. In *Proc. ISSAC'91*, pages 267–270, 1991.

[6] M. Barkatou. Rational solutions of matrix difference equations: The problem of equivalence and factorization. In *Proc. ISSAC'99*, pages 277–282, 1999.

[7] A. Bostan, F. Chyzak, T. Cluzeau, and B. Salvy. Low complexity algorithms for linear recurrences. In *Proc. ISSAC'06*, pages 31–39, 2006.

[8] M. Bronstein. On solutions of linear ordinary difference equations in their coefficient field. *J. Symb. Comput.*, 29:841–877, 2000.

[9] W. Y. C. Chen, P. Paule, and H. L. Saad. Converging to Gosper's algorithm. *Adv. in Appl. Math.*, 41(3):351–364, 2008.

[10] F. Chyzak. An extension of Zeilberger's fast algorithm to general holonomic functions. *Discrete Mathematics*, 217:115–134, 2000.

[11] M. van Hoeij. Rational solutions of linear difference equations. In *Proc. ISSAC'98*, pages 120–123, 1998.

[12] M. Kauers and C. Schneider. Partial denominator bounds for partial linear difference equations. In *Proc. ISSAC'10*, pages 211–218, 2010.

[13] M. Kauers. Guessing handbook. Technical Report 09-07, RISC-Linz, 2009.

[14] P. Paule. Greatest factorial factorization and symbolic summation. *J. Symb. Comput.*, 20:235–268, 1995.

[15] M. Petkovšek. Hypergeometric solutions of linear recurrences with polynomial coefficients. *Journal of Symbolic Computation*, 14(2-3):243–264, 1992.

[16] C. Schneider. A collection of denominator bounds to solve parameterized linear difference equations in $\Pi\Sigma$-extensions. In *Proc. SYNASC'04*, pages 269–282, 2004.

[17] D. Zeilberger. The method of creative telescoping. *J. Symb. Comput.*, 11:195–204, 1991.

Efficient Real Root Approximation

Michael Kerber
IST (Institute of Science and Technology) Austria
3400 Klosterneuburg, Austria
mkerber@ist.ac.at

Michael Sagraloff
Max-Planck-Institute for Informatics
66123 Saarbrücken, Germany
msagralo@mpi-inf.mpg.de

ABSTRACT

We consider the problem of approximating all real roots of a square-free polynomial f. Given isolating intervals, our algorithm refines each of them to a width at most 2^{-L}, that is, each of the roots is approximated to L bits after the binary point. Our method provides a certified answer for arbitrary real polynomials, only requiring finite approximations of the polynomial coefficient and choosing a suitable working precision adaptively. In this way, we get a correct algorithm that is simple to implement and practically efficient. Our algorithm uses the quadratic interval refinement method; we adapt that method to be able to cope with inaccuracies when evaluating f, without sacrificing its quadratic convergence behavior. We prove a bound on the bit complexity of our algorithm in terms of degree, coefficient size and discriminant. Our bound improves previous work on integer polynomials by a factor of $\deg f$ and essentially matches best known theoretical bounds on root approximation which are obtained by very sophisticated algorithms.

Categories and Subject Descriptors

G.1.5 [**Numerical Analysis**]: Roots of Nonlinear Equations; F.2.1 [**Analysis of Algorithms and Problem Complexity**]: Numerical Algorithms and Problems

General Terms

Algorithms, Reliability, Theory

Keywords

Root isolation, Root approximation, Quadratic Interval Refinement

1. INTRODUCTION

The problem of computing the real roots of a polynomial in one variable is one of the best studied problems in mathematics. If one asks for a *certified* method that finds all roots, it is common to write the solutions as a set of disjoint *isolating* intervals, each containing exactly one root; for that reason, the term *real root isolation* is common in the literature. Simple, though efficient methods for

this problem have been presented, for instance, based on Descartes' rule of signs [7], or on Sturm's theorem [9]. Recently, the focus of research shifted to polynomials with real coefficients which are approximated during the algorithm. It is worth remarking that this approach does not just generalize the integer case but has also lead to practical [11, 17] and theoretical [18] improvements of it.

We consider the related *real root refinement problem*: assuming that isolating intervals of a polynomial are known, *refine* them to a width of at most 2^{-L} (where $L \geq 0$ is an additional input parameter). Clearly, the combination of root isolation and root refinement, also called *strong root isolation*, yields a certified approximation of all roots of the polynomial to an absolute precision of 2^{-L} or, in other words, to L bits after the binary point in binary representation.

We present a solution to the root refinement problem for arbitrary square-free polynomial with real coefficients. Most of the related approaches are formulated in the REAL-RAM model where exact operations on real numbers are assumed to be available at unit costs. In contrast, our approach considers the coefficients as *bit-streams*, that is, it only works with finite prefixes of its binary representation, and we also quantify how many bits are needed in the worst case. The refinement uses the quadratic interval refinement method [1] (QIR for short), which is a quadratically converging hybrid of the bisection and secant method. We adapt the method to work with a increasing working precisions and use interval arithmetic to validate the correctness of the outcome. In this way, we obtain an algorithm that always returns a correct root approximation, is simple to implement on an actual computer (given that arbitrary approximations of the coefficients are accessible), and is adaptive in the sense that it might succeed with a much lower working precision than asserted by the worst-case bound.

We provide a bound on the bit complexity of our algorithm. Let

$$f(x) := \sum_{i=0}^{d} a_i x^i \in \mathbb{R}[x] \tag{1}$$

be a polynomial of degree $d \geq 2$ with leading coefficient $|a_d| \geq 1$ and $|a_i| < 2^\tau$ for all i, where $\tau \geq 1$. Given initial isolating intervals, our algorithm refines *one interval* to width 2^{-L} using

$$\tilde{O}(d(d\tau + R)^2 + dL)$$

bit operations and refines *all intervals* using

$$\tilde{O}(d(d\tau + R)^2 + d^2 L)$$

bit operations, where $R := \log(|\mathrm{res}(f, f')|)^{-1}$ and $\tilde{O}$ means that we ignore logarithmic factors in d, τ, and L. To do so, our algorithm requires the coefficients of f in a precision of at most

$$O(d\tau + R + L)$$

bits after the binary point. We remark that the costs of obtaining approximations for the coefficients are not included in this bound. For the analysis, we divide the sequence of QIR steps in the refinement process into a *linear sequence* where the method behaves like bisection in the worst case, and a *quadratic sequence* where the interval is converging quadratically towards the root, following the approach in [12]. We do not require any conditions on the initial intervals except that they are disjoint and cover all real roots of f; an initial *normalization phase* modifies the intervals to guarantee the efficiency of our refinement strategy.

We remark that, using the recently presented root solver from [18], obtaining initial isolating intervals can be done within $\tilde{O}(d(d+R)^2)$ bit operations using coefficient approximations of $O(d\tau+R)$ bits. Combined with that result, our complexity result also gives a bound on the strong root isolation problem.

The case of integer coefficients is often of special interest, and the problem has been investigated in previous work [12] for this restricted case. In that work, the complexity of root refinement was bounded by $\tilde{O}(d^4\tau^2+d^3L)$. We improve this bound to

$$\tilde{O}(d^3\tau^2+d^2L)$$

because R as defined above becomes negative for integer polynomials. The difference in the complexities is due to a different approach to evaluate the sign of f at rational points, which is the main operation in the refinement procedure: for an interval of size $2^{-\ell}$, the evaluation has a complexity of $\tilde{O}(d^2(\tau+\ell))$ when using exact rational arithmetic because evaluated function values can consist of up to $d(\tau+\ell)$ bits. However, we show that we can still compute the sign of the function value with certified numerical methods using the substantially smaller working precision of $O(d\tau+\ell)$.

Related work. The problem of accurate root approximation is omnipresent in mathematical applications; certified methods are of particular importance in the context of computations with algebraic objects, e.g., when computing the topology of algebraic curves [10, 6] or when solving systems of multivariate equations [3].

The idea of combining bisection with a faster converging method to find roots of continuous functions was first introduced in *Dekker's method* and elaborated in *Brent's method*; see [5] for a summary. However, these approaches assume exact arithmetic for their convergence results.

For polynomial equations, numerous algorithms are available, for instance, the *Jenkins-Traub algorithm* or *Durant-Kerner iteration*; although they usually approximate the real roots very fast in practice, general worst-case bounds on their arithmetic complexity are not available. In fact, for some variants, even termination cannot be guaranteed in theory; we refer to the survey [16] for extensive references on these and further methods.

The theoretical complexity of root approximation has been investigated by Pan [15]. Assuming all roots to be in the unit disc, he achieves a bit complexity of $\tilde{O}(d^3+d^2L)$ for approximating all roots to an accuracy of 2^{-L}, which matches our bound if L is the dominant input parameter. His approach even works for polynomials with multiple roots. However, as Pan admits in [16], the algorithm is difficult to implement and so is the complexity analysis when taking rounding errors in intermediate steps into account. Moreover, it appears unclear whether his bound can be improved if only a single root needs to be approximated.

We finally remark that a slightly simplified version of our approach (for integer coefficients) is included in the recently introduced CGAL[1]-package on algebraic computations [4]. Experimen-

---

[1]Computational Geometry Algorithms Library, www.cgal.org

Algorithm 1 EQIR: Exact Quadratic Interval Refinement

INPUT: $f \in \mathbb{R}[x]$ square-free, $I = (a,b)$ isolating, $N = 2^{2^i} \in \mathbb{N}$
OUTPUT: (J,N') with $J \subseteq I$ isolating for ξ and $N' \in \mathbb{N}$

1: **procedure** EQIR$(f, I = (a,b), N)$
2:     **if** $N = 2$, **return** (BISECTION(f,I),4).
3:     $\omega \leftarrow \frac{b-a}{N}$
4:     $m' \leftarrow a + \text{round}(N\frac{f(a)}{f(a)-f(b)})\omega \triangleright m' \approx a + \frac{f(a)}{f(a)-f(b)}(b-a)$
5:     $s \leftarrow \text{sign}(f(m'))$
6:     **if** $s = 0$, **return** $([m',m'],\infty)$
7:     **if** $s = \text{sign}(f(a))$ **and** $\text{sign}(f(m'+\omega)) = \text{sign}(f(b))$, **return** $([m',m'+\omega],N^2)$
8:     **if** $s = \text{sign}(f(b))$ **and** $\text{sign}(f(m'-\omega)) = \text{sign}(f(a))$, **return** $([m'-\omega,m'],N^2)$
9:     Otherwise, **return** $(I,\sqrt{N})$.

---

tal comparisons in the context of [3] have shown that the approximate version of QIR gives significantly better running times than its exact counterpart. These observations underline the practical relevance of our approximate version and suggest a practical comparison with state-of-the-art solvers mentioned above as further work.

Notation. Additional to f, d, τ, a_i, and R as above, we use the following terminology: We denote the complex roots of f by $z_1, \ldots, z_d$ numbered so that $z_1, \ldots, z_m$ are all the real roots. For each z_i, $\sigma_i = \sigma(z_i, f) := \min_{j \neq i} |z_i - z_j|$ denotes the *separation of z_i* and $\Sigma_f := \sum_{i=1}^n \log \sigma_i^{-1}$. An interval $I = (a,b)$ is called *isolating* for a root z_i if I contains z_i and no other root of f. We set $\text{mid}(I) = \frac{a+b}{2}$ for the *center* and $w(I) := b-a$ for the *width* of I.

Outline. We summarize the (exact) QIR method in Section 2. A variant using only approximate coefficients is described in Section 3. Its precision demand is analyzed in Section 4. Based on that analysis of a single refinement step, the complexity bound of root refinement is derived in Section 5.

Some technical proofs are left out for brevity. An appendix containing them is available from the authors' homepages [13].

2. REVIEW OF EXACT QIR

Abbott's QIR method [1, 12] is a hybrid of the simple (but inefficient) bisection method with a quadratically converging variant of the *secant method*. We refer to this method as EQIR, where "E" stands for "exact" in order to distinguish from the variant presented in Section 3. Given an isolating interval $I = (a,b)$ for a real root ξ of f, we consider the secant through $(a, f(a))$ and $(b, f(b))$ (see also Figure 1). This secant intersects the real axis in the interval I, say at x-coordinate m. For I small enough, the secant should approximate the graph of the function above I quite well and, so, $m \approx \xi$ should hold. An EQIR step tries to exploit this fact:

The isolating interval I is (conceptually) subdivided into N subintervals of same size, using $N+1$ equidistant grid points. Each subinterval has width $\omega := \frac{w(I)}{N}$. Then m', the closest grid point to m, is computed and the sign of $f(m')$ is evaluated. If that sign equals the sign of $f(a)$, the sign of $f(m'+\omega)$ is evaluated. Otherwise, $f(m'-\omega)$ is evaluated. If the sign changes between the two computed values, the interval $(m', m'+\omega)$ or the interval $(m'-\omega, m')$, respectively, is set as new isolating interval for ξ. In this case, the EQIR step is called *successful*. Otherwise, the isolating interval remains unchanged, and the EQIR step is called *failing*. See Algorithm 1 for a description in pseudo-code.

In [12], the root refinement problem is analyzed using the just

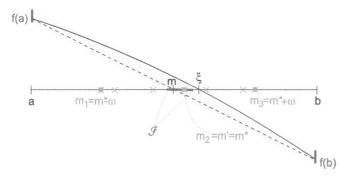

Figure 1: Illustration of an AQIR step for $N = 4$.

described EQIR method for the case of integer coefficients and exact arithmetic with rational numbers. For that, a sequence of EQIR steps is performed with $N = 4$ initially. After a successful EQIR step, N is squared for the next step; after a failing step, N is set to $\sqrt{N}$. If N drops to 2, a bisection step is performed, and N is set to 4 for the next step. In [12], a bound on the size of the interval is given, where every EQIR step will be successful proving that the method converges quadratically from this point on.

3. APPROXIMATE QIR

The most important numeric operation in an EQIR step is the computation of $f(x_0)$ for values $x_0 \in I$. Note that $f(x_0)$ is needed for determining the closest grid point m' to the secant (Step 4 of Algorithm 1), and its sign is required for checking for sign changes in subintervals (Steps 6-8).

What are the problems if f is a bitstream polynomial, so that $f(x_0)$ can only be evaluated up to a certain precision? First of all, $\frac{Nf(a)}{f(a)-f(b)}$ can only be computed approximately, too, which might lead to checking the wrong subinterval in the algorithm if m is close to the endpoint of a subinterval. Even more seriously, if $f(x_0) = 0$, its sign can, in general, not be evaluated using any precision, and even if we exclude this case, the evaluation of $f(x_0)$ can become costly if x_0 is too close to a root of f. The challenge is to modify QIR such that it can cope with the uncertainties in the evaluation of f, requires as low a precision as possible in a refinement step and still shows a quadratic convergence behavior eventually.

Bisection is a subroutine called in the QIR method if $N = 2$; before we discuss the general case, we first describe our variant of the bisection in the bitstream context. Note that we face the same problem: Writing mid(I) for the center of $I = (a,b)$, $f(\text{mid}(I))$ might be equal or almost equal to zero. We will overcome this problem by evaluating f at several x-coordinates "in parallel". For that, we subdivide I into 4 equally wide parts using the subdivision points $m_j := a + j \cdot \frac{b-a}{4}$ for $1 \le j \le 3$. We also assume that the sign of f at a is already known. We choose a starting precision ρ and compute $f(m_1), \dots, f(m_3)$ using interval arithmetic in precision ρ (cf. Section 4 for details). If fewer than 2 out of 3 signs have been determined using precision ρ, we set $\rho \leftarrow 2\rho$ and repeat the calculation with increased precision. Once the sign at at least 2 subdivision points is determined, we can determine a subinterval of at most half the size of I that contains ξ (Algorithm 2). We will refer to this algorithm as "bisection", although the resulting interval can also be only a quarter of the original size. Note that f can only become zero at one of the subdivision points which guarantees termination also in the bitstream context. Moreover, at least 2 of the 3 subdivision points have a distance of at least $\frac{b-a}{8}$ to ξ. This asserts that the function value at these subdivision points

---

Algorithm 2 Approximate Bisection

INPUT: $f \in \mathbb{R}[x]$ square-free, $I = (a,b)$ isolating, $s = \text{sign}(f(a))$
OUTPUT: $J \subseteq I$ isolating with $2 \cdot w(J) \le w(I)$.

1: **procedure** APPROXIMATE_BISECTION($f, I = (a,b), s$)
2:    $V \leftarrow [a + (i-1) \cdot \frac{b-a}{4}, i = 1, \dots, 5]$
3:    $S = [s, 0, 0, 0, -s]$
4:    $\rho \leftarrow 2$
5:    **while** S contains more than one zero **do**
6:       **for** i=2,...,4 **do**
7:          If $S[i] = 0$, set $S[i] \leftarrow \text{sign} \mathfrak{B}(f(V[i]), \rho)$
8:          $\rho \leftarrow 2\rho$
9:       Find v, w, such that $S[v] \cdot S[w] = -1 \wedge (v+1 = w \vee (v+2 = w \wedge S[v+1] = 0))$
10:      **return** $(V[v], V[w])$

---

is reasonable large and leads to an upper bound of the required precision (Lemma 5).

We next describe our bitstream variant of the QIR method that we call *approximate quadratic interval refinement*, or AQIR for short (see also Figure 1 for the illustration of an AQIR step for $N = 4$). Compared to the exact variant, we replace two substeps. In Step 4, we replace the computation of $\lambda := N \frac{f(a)}{f(a)-f(b)}$ as follows: For a working precision ρ, we evaluate $f(a)$ and $f(b)$ via interval arithmetic with precision ρ (blue vertical intervals in the above figure) and evaluate $N \frac{f(a)}{f(a)-f(b)}$ with interval arithmetic accordingly (cf. Section 4). Let $J = (c,d)$ denote the resulting interval (in Figure 1, $\mathscr{I} = a + J \cdot \frac{b-a}{N}$ is the intersection of the stripe defined by the interval evaluations of $f(a)$ and $f(b)$ with the real axis). If the width $w(J)$ of J is more than $\frac{1}{4}$, we set ρ to 2ρ and retry. Otherwise, let ℓ be the integer closest to mid(J) and set $m^* := a + \ell \cdot \frac{b-a}{N}$. For $m = a + \frac{f(a)}{f(a)-f(b)}(b-a)$ as before and $m_j := a + j \cdot \frac{b-a}{N}$ (red dots) for $j = 0, \dots, N$, the following Lemma shows that the computed $m^* = m_\ell$ indeed approximates m on the m_j-grid:

Lemma 1. *Let m be inside the subinterval $[m_j, m_{j+1}]$. Then, $m^* = m_j$ or $m^* = m_{j+1}$. Moreover, let $m' \in \{m_j, m_{j+1}\}$ be the point that is closer to m. If $|m - m'| < \frac{b-a}{4N}$, then $m^* = m'$.*

PROOF. Let $\lambda := N \frac{f(a)}{f(a)-f(b)}$ and J the interval computed by interval arithmetic as above, with width at most $\frac{1}{4}$. Since $m = f(a) + \lambda \frac{b-a}{N} \in [m_j, m_{j+1}]$, it follows that $j \le \lambda \le j+1$. By construction, $\lambda \in J$. Therefore, $|\lambda - \text{mid}(J)| \le \frac{1}{8}$ and, thus, it follows that mid(J) can only be rounded to j or $j+1$. Furthermore, for $m' = m_j$, $|m - m'| < \frac{b-a}{4N}$ implies that $|\lambda - j| < \frac{1}{4}$. It follows that $|\text{mid}(J) - j| < \frac{3}{8}$ by the triangle inequality, so mid(J) must be rounded to j. The case $m' = m_{j+1}$ is analogous. $\square$

The second substep to replace in the QIR method is to check for sign changes in subintervals in Steps 6-8. As before, we set $\omega := w(I)/N$. Instead of comparing the signs at m' and $m' \pm \omega$, we choose the seven subdivision points (red crosses in Figure 1)

$$m^* - \omega, m^* - \frac{7\omega}{8}, m^* - \frac{\omega}{2}, m^*, m^* + \frac{\omega}{2}, m^* - \frac{7\omega}{8}, m^* + \omega. \quad (2)$$

In case that $m^* = a$ or $m^* = b$, we only choose the 4 points of (2) that lie in I. For a working precision ρ, we evaluate the sign of f at all subdivision points using interval arithmetic. If the sign remains unknown for more than one point, we set ρ to 2ρ and retry. After the sign is determined for all except at most one of the points, we look for a sign change in the sequence. If such a sign change occurs, we set the corresponding interval I^* as isolating and call the AQIR step *successful*. Otherwise, we call the step *failing* and keep the old isolating interval. As in the exact case, we square up N after a successful step, and reduce it to its square root after a failing step. See Algorithm 3 for a complete description.

Note that, in case of a successful step, the new isolating interval I^* satisfies $\frac{1}{8N}w(I) \leq w(I^*) \leq \frac{1}{N}w(I)$. Also, similar to the bisection method, the function can only be zero at one of the chosen subdivision points, and the function is guaranteed to be reasonably large for all but one of them, which leads to a bound on the necessary precision (Lemma 7). The reader might wonder why we have chosen a non-equidistant grid involving the subdivision points $m^* \pm \frac{7}{8}\omega$. The reason is that these additional points allow us to give a success guarantee of the method under certain assumptions in the following lemma, which is the basis to prove quadratic convergence if the interval is smaller than a certain threshold (Section 5.2).

Lemma 2. *Let $I = (a,b)$ be an isolating interval for some root ξ of f, $s = \text{sign}(f(a))$ and m as before. If $|m - \xi| < \frac{b-a}{8N} = \frac{\omega}{8}$, then AQIR$(f,I,N,s)$ succeeds.*

PROOF. Let m^* be the subdivision point selected by the AQIR method. We assume that $m^* \notin \{a,b\}$; otherwise, a similar (simplified) argument applies. By Lemma 1 $m \in [m^* - \frac{3}{4}\omega, m^* + \frac{3}{4}\omega]$ and, thus, $\xi \in (m^* - \frac{7}{8}\omega, m^* + \frac{7}{8}\omega)$. It follows that the leftmost two points of (2) have a different sign than the rightmost two points of (2). Since the sign of f is evaluated for at least one value on each side, the algorithm detects a sign change and, thus, succeeds. $\square$

4. ANALYSIS OF AN AQIR STEP

The running time of an AQIR step depends on the maximal precision ρ needed in the two while loops (Step 5, Steps 11-14) of Algorithm 3. The termination criterion of both loops is controlled by evaluations of the form $\mathfrak{B}(E,\rho)$, where E is some polynomial expression and ρ is the current working precision.

We specify recursively what we understand by evaluating E in precision ρ with interval arithmetic. For that, we define $\text{down}(x,\rho)$ for $x \in \mathbb{R}$ and $\rho \in \mathbb{N}$ to be the maximal $x_0 \leq x$ such that $x_0 = \frac{k}{2^\rho}$ for some integer k. The same way $\text{up}(x,\rho)$ is the minimal $x_0 \geq x$ with x_0 of the same form. We extend this definition to arithmetic expressions by the following rules (we leave out ρ for brevity):

$$
\begin{aligned}
\text{down}(E_1 + E_2) &:= & \text{down}(E_1) + \text{down}(E_2) \\
\text{up}(E_1 + E_2) &:= & \text{up}(E_1) + \text{up}(E_2) \\
\text{down}(E_1 \cdot E_2) &:= & \text{down}(\min\{\text{down}(E_1)\text{down}(E_2), \text{up}(E_1)\text{up}(E_2), \\
&& \text{up}(E_1)\text{down}(E_2), \text{down}(E_1)\text{up}(E_2)\}) \\
\text{up}(E_1 \cdot E_2) &:= & \text{up}(\max\{\text{down}(E_1)\text{down}(E_2), \text{down}(E_1)\text{up}(E_2), \\
&& \text{up}(E_1)\text{down}(E_2), \text{up}(E_1)\text{up}(E_2)\}) \\
\text{down}(1/E_1) &:= & \text{down}(1/\text{up}(E_1)) \\
\text{up}(1/E_1) &:= & \text{up}(1/\text{down}(E_1))
\end{aligned}
$$

Finally, we define the interval $\mathfrak{B}(E,\rho) := [\text{down}(E,\rho), \text{up}(E,\rho)]$. By definition, the exact value of E is guaranteed to be contained in $\mathfrak{B}(E,\rho)$. We assume that polynomials $f \in \mathbb{R}[x]$ are evaluated according to the Horner scheme, and when evaluating $f(c)$ with precision ρ, we apply the above rules in each arithmetic step. The next lemma provides a worst case bound on the size of the resulting interval $\mathfrak{B}(f(c),\rho)$ under certain conditions; see [13] for a proof of Lemma 3. We also remark that, in an actual implementation, $\mathfrak{B}(E,\rho)$ is usually much smaller than the worst case bound derived here. Nevertheless, our complexity analysis is based on it.

Algorithm 3 Approximate Quadratic interval refinement

INPUT: $f \in \mathbb{R}[x]$ square-free, $I = (a,b)$ isolating, $N = 2^{2^i} \in \mathbb{N}$, $s = \text{sign}(f(a))$
OUTPUT: (J,N') with $J \subseteq I$ isolating and $N' \in \mathbb{N}$

1: **procedure** AQIR$(f, I = (a,b), N)$
2:     **if** $N = 2$, **return** (APPROXIMATE_BISECTION(f,I,s),4).
3:     $\omega \leftarrow \frac{b-a}{N}$
4:     $\rho \leftarrow 2$
5:     **while** $J \leftarrow \mathfrak{B}(N\frac{f(a)}{f(a)-f(b)}, \rho)$ has width $> \frac{1}{4}$, set $\rho \leftarrow 2\rho$
6:     $m^* \leftarrow a + \text{round}(\text{mid}(J)) \cdot \omega$
7:     **if** $m^* = a$, $s \leftarrow 4, V \leftarrow [m^*, m^* + \frac{1}{2}\omega, m^* + \frac{7}{8}\omega, m^* + \omega], S \leftarrow [s,0,0,0]$
8:     **if** $m^* = b$, $s \leftarrow 4, V \leftarrow [m^* - \omega, m^* - \frac{7}{8}\omega, m^* - \frac{1}{2}\omega, m^*], S \leftarrow [0,0,0,-s]$
9:     **if** $a < m^* < b$, $s \leftarrow 7, V \leftarrow [m^* - \omega, m^* - \frac{7}{8}\omega, m^* - \frac{1}{2}\omega, m^*, m^* + \frac{1}{2}\omega, m^* + \frac{7}{8}\omega, m^* + \omega], S \leftarrow [0,0,0,0,0,0,0]$
10:     $\rho \leftarrow 2$
11:     **while** S contains more than one zero **do**
12:         **for** i=1,...,s **do**
13:             If $S[i] = 0$, set $S[i] \leftarrow \text{sign}\,\mathfrak{B}(f(V[i]),\rho)$
14:         $\rho \leftarrow 2\rho$
15:     **If** $\exists v,w : S[v] \cdot S[w] = -1 \wedge (v+1 = w \vee (v+2 = w \wedge S[v+1] = 0))$ **return** $((V[v],V[w]),N^2)$
16:     **Otherwise, return** $(I, \sqrt{N})$

Lemma 3. *Let f be a polynomial as in (1), $c \in \mathbb{R}$ with $|c| \leq 2^\tau$, and $\rho \in \mathbb{N}$. Then,*

$$|f(c) - \text{down}(f(c),\rho)| \leq 2^{-\rho+1}(d+1)^2 2^{\tau d} \qquad (3)$$

$$|f(c) - \text{up}(f(c),\rho)| \leq 2^{-\rho+1}(d+1)^2 2^{\tau d} \qquad (4)$$

In particular, $\mathfrak{B}(f(c),\rho)$ has a width of at most $2^{-\rho+2}(d+1)^2 2^{\tau d}$.

We remark that, for the sake of simplicity, we decided to assume fixed-point arithmetic, that means, ρ determines the number of bits after the binary point. We refer the interested reader to [14, Thm. 12], where a corresponding result for floating-point arithmetic is given.

We analyze the required working precision of approximate bisection and of an AQIR step next. We exploit that, whenever we evaluate f at t subdivision points, $t-1$ of them have a certain minimal distance to the root in the isolating interval. The following lemma gives a lower bound on $|f(x_0)|$ for such a point x_0, given that it is sufficiently far away from any other root of f.

Lemma 4. *Let f be as in (1), $\xi = z_{i_0}$ a real root of f and x_0 a real value with distance $|x_0 - z_i| \geq \frac{\sigma_i}{4}$ to all real roots $z_i \neq z_{i_0}$. Then,*

$$|f(x_0)| > |\xi - x_0| \cdot 2^{-(2d+\tau+\Sigma_f)}.$$

(recall the notations from Section 1 for the definitions of σ_i and Σ_f)

PROOF. For each non-real root z_i of f, there exists a complex conjugate root $\bar{z}_i$ and, thus, we have $|x_0 - z_i| \geq \text{Im}(z_i) \geq \frac{\sigma_i}{2} > \frac{\sigma_i}{4}$ for all $i = m+1,\ldots,d$ as well. It follows that

$$|f(x_0)| = |a_d \prod_{i=1}^d (x_0 - z_i)| = |a_d| \cdot |\xi - x_0| \cdot \prod_{i=1,\ldots,d: i \neq i_0} |x_0 - z_i|$$

$$\geq |\xi - x_0| \cdot \frac{4}{\sigma_{i_0}} \cdot \prod_{i=1}^d \frac{\sigma_i}{4} > |\xi - x_0| \cdot 2^{-2d-\tau} \cdot 2^{-\Sigma_f},$$

where the last inequality uses that $|z_i| < 1 + \frac{\max|a_i|}{|a_d|} < 2^{\tau+1}$ by Cauchy's Bound [19] and, thus, $\sigma(z_{i_0}) \leq 2^{\tau+2}$. $\qquad\square$

We next analyze an approximate bisection step.

Lemma 5. *Let f be a polynomial as in (1), $I = (a,b)$ be an isolating interval for a root $\xi = z_{i_0}$ of f and $s = \mathrm{sign}(f(a))$. Then, Algorithm 2 applied on (f,I,s) requires a maximal precision of*

$$\rho_0 := 2\log(b-a)^{-1} + 4\log(d+1) + 4d + 10 + 2(d+1)\tau + 2\Sigma_f$$
$$= O(\log(b-a)^{-1} + d\tau + \Sigma_f),$$

and its bit complexity is bounded by $\tilde{O}(d(\log(b-a)^{-1} + d\tau + \Sigma_f))$.

PROOF. Consider the three subdivision points $m_j := a + j \cdot \frac{b-a}{4}$, where $1 \leq j \leq 3$, and an arbitrary real root $z_i \neq \xi$ of f. Note that $|m_j - z_i| > \frac{b-a}{4}$ because the segment from m_j to z_i spans at least over a quarter of (a,b). Moreover, $|\xi - m_j| \leq \frac{3}{4}(b-a)$, and so

$$\sigma_i \leq |\xi - z_i| \leq |\xi - m_j| + |m_j - z_i| \leq \frac{3}{4}(b-a) + |m_j - z_i| \leq 4|m_j - z_i|.$$

It follows that m_j has a distance to z_i of at least $\frac{\sigma_i}{4}$. Hence, we can apply Lemma 4 to each m_j, that is, we have $|f(m_j)| > |\xi - m_j| \cdot 2^{-(2d+\tau+\Sigma_f)}$. Since the signs of f at the endpoints of I are known, it suffices to compute the signs of f at two of the three subdivision points. For at least two of these points, the distance of m_j to ξ is at least $\frac{b-a}{8}$, thus, we have $|f(m_j)| > |b-a| \cdot 2^{-(2d+3+\tau+\Sigma_f)}$ for at least two points. Then, due to Lemma 3, we can use interval arithmetic with a precision ρ to compute these signs if ρ satisfies

$$2^{-\rho+2}(d+1)^2 2^{d\tau} \leq (b-a) \cdot 2^{-(2d+3+\tau+\Sigma_f)},$$

which is equivalent to $\rho \geq \frac{\rho_0}{2}$. Since we double the precision in each step, we will eventually succeed with a precision smaller than ρ_0. The bit complexity for an arithmetic operation with fixed precision ρ is $\tilde{O}(\rho + d\tau)$. Namely, since the absolute value of each subdivision point is bounded by $O(\tau)$, the results in the intermediate steps have magnitude $O(d\tau)$ and we consider ρ bits after the binary point. At each subdivision point, we have to perform $O(d)$ arithmetic operations for the computation of $f(m_j)$, thus, the costs for these evaluations are bounded by $\tilde{O}(d(d\tau + \rho))$. Since we double the precision in each iteration, the total costs are dominated by the last successful evaluation and, thus, we have to perform $\tilde{O}(d(\rho_0 + d\tau)) = \tilde{O}(d(\log(b-a)^{-1} + d\tau + \Sigma_f))$ bit operations. $\qquad\square$

We proceed with the analysis of an AQIR step. In order to bound the required precision, we need additional properties of the isolating interval.

Definition 6. *Let f be as in (1) and let $I := (a,b)$ be an isolating interval of a root ξ of f. We call I normal if*

- $I \subseteq (-2^{\tau+3}, 2^{\tau+3})$,

- $|p - z_i| > \frac{\sigma_i}{4}$ *for every $p \in I$ and $z_i \neq \xi$, and*

- $\min\{|f(a)|, |f(b)|\} \geq 2^{-(32d\tau + 2\Sigma_f - 5\log(b-a))}$.

In simple words, a normal isolating interval has a reasonable distance to any other root of f, and the function value at the endpoints is reasonably large. We will later see that it is possible to get normal intervals by a sequence of approximate bisection steps.

Lemma 7. *Let f be a polynomial as in (1), $I = (a,b)$ be a normal isolating interval for a root $\xi = z_{i_0}$ of f with $s = \mathrm{sign}(f(a))$, and let $N \leq 2^{2(\tau + 5\log(b-a))}$. Then, the AQIR step for (f,I,N,s) requires*

a precision of at most $\rho_{max} := 87d\tau + 4\Sigma_f - 14\log(b-a)$ and, therefore, its bit complexity is bounded by

$$\tilde{O}(d(d\tau + \Sigma_f - \log(b-a))).$$

Moreover, the returned interval is again normal.

PROOF. We have to distinguish two cases. For $N > 2$, we consider the two while-loops in Algorithm 3. In the first loop (Step 5), we evaluate $N\frac{f(a)}{f(a)-f(b)}$ via interval arithmetic, doubling the precision ρ until the width of the resulting interval J is less than or equal to $1/4$. The following considerations show that we can achieve this if ρ fulfills

$$2^{-\rho+1}(d+1)^2 2^{d\tau} \leq \frac{\min(|f(a)|, |f(b)|)}{32N}. \tag{5}$$

W.l.o.g., we assume $f(a) > 0$. If ρ fulfills the above condition, then, due to Lemma 3, $\mathfrak{B}(N \cdot f(a), \rho)$ is contained in the interval

$$[Nf(a) - \frac{|f(a)|}{32}, Nf(a) + \frac{|f(a)|}{32}] = Nf(a) \cdot [1 - \frac{1}{32N}, 1 + \frac{1}{32N}]$$

and $\mathfrak{B}(f(a) - f(b), \rho)$ is contained in $(f(a) - f(b)) \cdot [1 - \frac{1}{32N}, 1 + \frac{1}{32N}]$, where we used that $f(a)$ and $f(b)$ have different signs. It follows that $\mathfrak{B}(N\frac{f(a)}{f(a)-f(b)}, \rho)$ is contained in the interval $\frac{Nf(a)}{f(a)-f(b)} \cdot [(1 - \frac{1}{32N})/(1 + \frac{1}{32N}), (1 + \frac{1}{32N})/(1 - \frac{1}{32N})]$, and a simple computation shows that $N \cdot [(1 - \frac{1}{32N})/(1 + \frac{1}{32N}), (1 + \frac{1}{32N})/(1 - \frac{1}{32N})]$ has width less than $1/4$. Hence, since $\frac{f(a)}{f(a)-f(b)}$ has absolute value less than 1, $\mathfrak{B}(N\frac{f(a)}{f(a)-f(b)}, \rho)$ has width less than $1/4$ as well. The bound (5) on ρ also writes as

$$\rho \geq 7 + \log(d+1) + d\tau + \log N + \log\min(|f(a), f(b)|)^{-1},$$

and since we double ρ in each iteration, computing $N\frac{f(a)}{f(a)-f(b)}$ via interval arithmetic up to an error of $1/4$ is achieved with a precision

$$\rho < 14 + 2\log(d+1) + 2d\tau + 2\log N + 2\log\min(|f(a), f(b)|)^{-1}$$
$$< 11d\tau + 2\log N + 2\log\min(|f(a), f(b)|)^{-1}.$$

Because I is normal and because of the assumption on N we can bound this by

$$\rho < 11d\tau + 4(\tau + 5 - \log(b-a)) + 2(32d\tau + 2\Sigma_f - 5\log(b-a))$$
$$< 87d\tau + 4\Sigma_f - 14\log(b-a) = \rho_{max}.$$

We turn to the second while loop of Algorithm 3 (that is, Steps 11-14) where f is evaluated at the subdivision points $m^* - \omega, m^* - \frac{7\omega}{8}, \ldots, m^* + \omega$ as defined in (2). Since the interval is normal, we can apply Lemma 4 to each of the seven subdivision points. At least six of these points have distance $\geq \frac{b-a}{16N}$ to the root ξ and, thus, for these points, $|f|$ is larger than $\frac{b-a}{16N} \cdot 2^{-(2d+\tau+\Sigma_f)}$. Then, according to Lemma 5, it suffices to use a precision ρ that fulfills

$$2^{-\rho+1}(d+1)^2 2^{d\tau} \leq \frac{b-a}{16N} \cdot 2^{-(2d+\tau+\Sigma_f)}, \text{ or}$$

$$\rho \geq \rho_1 := 2\log(d+1) + (d+1)\tau + 2d + 5 + \Sigma_f + \log N - \log(b-a).$$

The same reasoning as above then shows that the point evaluation will be performed with a maximal precision of less than

$$2\rho_1 < 2(10d\tau + \Sigma_f + \log N - \log(b-a))$$
$$\leq 20d\tau + 2\Sigma_f + 4(\tau + 5 - \log(b-a)) - \log(b-a)$$
$$\leq 32d\tau + 2\Sigma_f - 5\log(b-a)$$

Algorithm 4 Normalization

INPUT: $f \in \mathbb{R}[t]$ a polynomial as in (1), $I_1 = (a_1, b_1), \ldots, I_m = (a_m, b_m)$ disjoint isolating intervals in ascending order, $s_1, \ldots, s_m$ with $s_k = \mathrm{sign}(f(\min I_k))$

OUTPUT: normal isolating intervals $J_1, \ldots, J_m$ with $z_k \in I_k \cap J_k$

1: **procedure** NORMALIZE$(f, I_1, \ldots, I_m)$
2:    **for** k=1,...,m-1 **do**
3:       **while** $\min I_{k+1} - \max I_k < 3 \max\{w(I_k), w(I_{k+1})\}$ **do**
4:          **if** $w(I_k) > w(I_{k+1})$
5:          **then** APPROXIMATE_BISECTION(f, I_k, s_k)
6:          **else** APPROXIMATE_BISECTION(f, I_{k+1}, s_{k+1})
7:    **for** k=1,...,m-1 **do**
8:       $d_k \leftarrow \min I_{k+1} - \max I_k$
9:       $J_k \leftarrow [a_k - d_{k-1}/3, b_k + d_k/3]$ $\triangleright$ enlarge I_k by more than $w(I_k)$ at both sides
10:    **return** $J_1, \ldots, J_m$

Algorithm 5 Root Refinement

INPUT: $f = \sum a_i x^i \in \mathbb{R}[t]$ a polynomial as in (1), isolating intervals $I_1, \ldots, I_m$ for *all* real roots of f in ascending order, $L \in \mathbb{Z}$

OUTPUT: isolating intervals $J_1, \ldots, J_m$ with $w(J_k) \leq 2^{-L}$

1: **procedure** ROOT_REFINEMENT$(f, L, I_1, \ldots, I_m)$
2:    $s_k := \mathrm{sign}(a_d) \cdot (-1)^{m-k+1}$ $\triangleright s_k = \mathrm{sign}(f(\min I_k))$
3:    $J_1, \ldots, J_m \leftarrow$ NORMALIZE$(f, I_1, \ldots, I_m)$
4:    **for** k=1,...,m **do**
5:       $N \leftarrow 4$
6:       **while** $w(J_k) > 2^{-L}$ **do** $(J_k, N) \leftarrow$ AQIR(f, J_k, N, s_k)
7:    **return** $J_1, \ldots, J_m$

---

which is bounded by ρ_{max}. Moreover, at the new endpoints a' and b', $|f|$ is at least

$$2^{-2\rho_1} \geq 2^{-(32d\tau + 2\Sigma_f - 5\log(b-a))} \geq 2^{-(32d\tau + 2\Sigma_f - 5\log(b'-a'))}$$

which proves that $I' = (a', b')$ is again normal.

It remains to treat the case $N = 2$, where a bisection step is performed. It is straight-forward to see with Lemma 5 that the required precision is bounded by ρ_{max}, and in an analogous way as for the point evaluations for $N > 2$, we can see that the resulting interval is again normal. By the same argument as in Lemma 5, the overall bit complexity of the AQIR step is bounded by $\tilde{O}(d\rho_{max})$.   □

5. ROOT REFINEMENT

We next analyze the complexity of our original problem: Given a polynomial f as in (1) and isolating intervals for all its real roots, refine the intervals to a size of at most 2^{-L}. Our refinement method consists of two steps. First, we turn the isolating intervals into normal intervals by applying bisections repeatedly. Second, we call the AQIR method repeatedly on the intervals until each has a width of at most 2^{-L}. Algorithm 5 summarizes our method for root refinement. We remark that depending on the properties of the root isolator used to get initial isolating intervals, the normalization can be skipped; this is for instance the case when using the isolator from [18]. We also emphasize that the normalization is unnecessary for the correctness of the algorithm; its purpose is to prevent the working precision in a single AQIR step of growing too high.

5.1 Normalization

The normalization (Algorithm 4) consists of two steps: first, the isolating intervals are refined using approximate bisection until the distance between two consecutive intervals is at least three times larger than the size of the larger of the two involved intervals. This ensures that all points in an isolating interval are reasonably far away from any other root of f. In the second step, each interval is enlarged on both sides by an interval of at least the same size as itself. This ensures that the endpoints are sufficiently far away from any root of f to prove a lower bound of f at the endpoints. W.l.o.g., we assume that the input intervals are contained in $(-2^{\tau+1}, 2^{\tau+1})$ because by Cauchy's bound [19], all roots are contained in that interval, so the leftmost and rightmost intervals can just be cut if necessary. Obviously, the resulting intervals are still isolating and disjoint from each other. Moreover, they do not become too small during the bisection process:

Lemma 8. *For $J_1, \ldots, J_m$ as returned by Alg. 4, $w(J_k) \geq \frac{1}{3}\sigma_k$.*

PROOF. After the first for-loop, the distance d_k between any two consecutive intervals I_k and I_{k+1} fulfills $d_k \geq 3 \max\{w(I_k), w(I_{k+1})\}$, thus $\sigma_k < w(I_k) + w(I_{k+1}) + d_k < 2d_k$. Hence, in the last step, each I_k is enlarged by at least $\sigma_k/6$ on each side. This proves that the corresponding enlarged intervals J_k have size $\sigma_k/3$ or more.   □

Lemma 9. *Algorithm 4 is correct, i.e., returns normal intervals.*

PROOF. Let $J_1, \ldots, J_m$ denote the returned intervals, and fix some interval J_k containing the root z_k of f. We have to prove the three properties of Definition 6. The first property is clear because the initial interval are assumed to lie in $(-2^{\tau+1}, 2^{\tau+1})$. In the proof of Lemma 8, we have already shown that I_k is eventually enlarged by at least $\sigma_k/6$ on each side. More precisely, the right endpoint of J_k has distance at least $d_k/3 > \sigma_{k+1}/6$ to J_{k+1}, and the left endpoint of J_k has distance at least $d_{k-1}/3 > \sigma_{k-1}/6$ to J_{k-1}. It follows that, for each $x_0 \in J_k$, we have $|x_0 - z_{k\pm1}| \leq \sigma_{k\pm1}/3$, respectively. Hence, the second property in Definition 6 is fulfilled.

For the third property of Definition 6, let e be one of the endpoints of J_k. We have just proved that the distance to every root z_i except z_k is at least $\frac{\sigma_i}{3}$ and $|e - z_k| \geq \sigma_k/6$. With an estimation similar as in the proof of Lemma 4, we obtain:

$$|f(e)| \geq \frac{\sigma_k}{6} \prod_{i \neq k} \frac{\sigma_i}{3} \geq \frac{1}{8} \cdot \frac{1}{4^{d-1}} 2^{-\Sigma_f} = 2^{-(2d + \Sigma_f + 1)},$$

and $2^{-(2d+\Sigma_f+1)} \geq 2^{-(24d\tau + 2\Sigma_f - 5\log(b-a))}$ because $\log(b-a) \leq \tau + 3 \leq 2d\tau$ and $-\Sigma_f \leq d\tau + 1 < 2d\tau$.   □

Lemma 10. *Algorithm 4 has a complexity of $\tilde{O}(d(\tau d + \Sigma_f)^2)$*

PROOF. As a direct consequence of Lemma 8, each interval I_k is only bisected $O(\tau + \log(\sigma_k)^{-1})$ many times because each starting interval is assumed to be contained in $(-2^{\tau+1}, 2^{\tau+1})$. So the total number of bisections adds up to $O(d\tau + \Sigma_f)$ considering all roots of f. Also, the size of the isolating interval I_k is lower bounded by $\frac{1}{3} \cdot \sigma_k = 2^{-O(\Sigma_f + d\tau)}$, so that one approximate bisection step has a complexity of $\tilde{O}(d(d\tau + \Sigma_f))$ due to Lemma 5.   □

5.2 The AQIR sequence

It remains to bound the cost of the calls of AQIR. We mostly follow the reasoning from [12]. We introduce the following convenient notation:

Definition 11. *Let $I_0 := I$ be a normal isolating interval for some real root ξ of f, $N_0 := 4$ and $s := \mathrm{sign}(\min I_0)$. The AQIR sequence $(S_0, S_1, \ldots, S_{v_\xi})$ is defined by*

$$S_0 := (I_0, N_0) = (I, 4) \quad S_i = (I_i, N_i) := \mathrm{AQIR}(f, I_{i-1}, N_{i-1}, s) \text{ for } i \geq 1,$$

where v_ξ is the first index such that the interval I_{v_ξ} has width at most 2^{-L}. We say that $S_i \overset{\text{AQIR}}{\to} S_{i+1}$ succeeds if $\text{AQIR}(f, I_i, N_i, s)$ succeeds, and that $S_i \overset{\text{AQIR}}{\to} S_{i+1}$ fails otherwise.

As in [12], we divide the AQIR sequence into two parts according to the following definition.

Definition 12. *Let ξ be a root of f. Define*

$$C_\xi := \frac{|f'(\xi)|}{8ed^3 2^\tau \max\{|\xi|, 1\}^{d-1}},$$

where $e \approx 2.71\ldots$ denotes the Eulerian number. For $(S_0, \ldots, S_{v_\xi})$ the AQIR sequence of ξ, define k the minimal index such that $S_k = (I_k, N_k) \overset{\text{AQIR}}{\to} S_{k+1}$ succeeds and $w(I_k) \leq C_\xi$. We call $(S_0, \ldots, S_k)$ linear sequence and $(S_k, \ldots, S_{v_\xi})$ quadratic sequence of ξ

Note that $C_\xi = \frac{1}{4} M_\xi$ as defined in [12], and that the linear sequence was called *initial sequence* therein. We renamed it to avoid confusion with the initial normalization phase in our variant.

Quadratic convergence. We start by justifying the name "quadratic sequence". Indeed, it turns out that all but at most one AQIR step in the quadratic sequence are successful, hence, N is squared in (almost) every step and therefore, the refinement factor of the interval is doubled in (almost) every step. The proof is mostly analogous to [12]. The following bound follows from considering the Taylor expansion of f at ξ in the expression for m (see also [13]).

Lemma 13. [12, Thm. 4.8] *Let (a,b) be isolating for ξ with width $\delta < C_\xi$ and m as in Lemma 2. Then, $|m - \xi| \leq \frac{\delta^2}{8C_\xi}$.*

Corollary 14. *Let I_j be an isolating interval for ξ of width $\delta_j \leq \frac{C_\xi}{N_j}$. Then, each call of the AQIR sequence*

$$(I_j, N_j) \overset{\text{AQIR}}{\to} (I_{j+1}, N_{j+1}) \overset{\text{AQIR}}{\to} \ldots$$

succeeds.

PROOF. We use induction on i. Assume that the first i AQIR calls succeed. Then, another simple induction shows that $\delta_{j+i} := w(I_{j+i}) \leq \frac{N_j \delta_j}{N_{j+i}} < \frac{C_\xi}{N_{j+i}}$, where we use that $N_{j+i} = N_{j+i-1}^2$. Then, according to Lemma 13, we have that

$$|m - \xi| \leq \delta_{j+i}^2 \frac{1}{8C_\xi} \leq \delta_{j+i} \frac{C_\xi}{N_{j+i}} \frac{1}{8C_\xi} = \frac{1}{8} \frac{\delta_{j+i}}{N_{j+i}},$$

with m as above. By Lemma 2, the AQIR call succeeds. $\square$

Corollary 15. [12, Cor. 4.10] *In the quadratic sequence, there is at most one failing AQIR call. (see [13] for a proof)*

Cost of the linear sequence. We bound the costs of refining the isolating interval of ξ to size C_ξ with AQIR. We first show that, on average, the AQIR sequence refines by a factor two in every second step. This shows in particular that refining using AQIR is at most a factor of two worse than refining using approximate bisection.

Lemma 16. *Let $(S_0, \ldots, S_\ell)$ denote an arbitrary prefix of the AQIR sequence for ξ, starting with the isolating interval I_0 of width δ. Then, the width of I_ℓ is not larger than $\delta 2^{-(\ell-1)/2}$.*

PROOF. Consider a subsequence $(S_i, \ldots, S_{i+j})$ of $(S_0, \ldots, S_\ell)$ such that $S_i \overset{\text{AQIR}}{\to} S_{i+1}$ is successful, but any other step in the subsequence fails. Because there are j steps in total, and thus $j-1$ consecutive

failing steps, the successful step must have used a N with $N \geq 2^{2^{j-1}}$. Because $2^{j-1} > \frac{j}{2}$, it holds that

$$w(I_{i+j}) \leq \frac{w(I_i)}{N} \leq w(I_i) 2^{-2^{j-1}} < w(I_i) 2^{-j/2}.$$

Repeating the argument for maximal subsequences of this form, we get that either $w(I_\ell) \leq w(I_0) 2^{-\ell/2}$ if the sequence starts with a successful step, or $w(I_\ell) \leq w(I_0) 2^{-(\ell-1)/2}$ otherwise, because the second step must be successful in this case. $\square$

We want to apply Lemma 7 to bound the bit complexity of a single AQIR step. The following lemma shows that the condition on N from Lemma 7 is always met in the AQIR sequence.

Lemma 17. *Let $(I_j, N_j) \overset{\text{AQIR}}{\to} (I_{j+1}, N_{j+1})$ be a call in an AQIR sequence and $I_j := (a, b)$. Then, $N_j \leq 2^{2(\tau+5-\log(b-a))}$.*

PROOF. We do induction on j. Note that $I_0 \subset (-2^{\tau+3}, 2^{\tau+3})$ by normality, hence $b - a \leq 2^{\tau+4}$. It follows that $2^{2(\tau+5-\log(b-a))} \geq 4 = N_0$. Assume that the statement is true for $j-1$. If the previous step $(I_{j-1}, N_{j-1}) \overset{\text{AQIR}}{\to} (I_j, N_j)$ is failing, then $N_j = \sqrt{N_{j-1}}$ and the isolating interval remains unchanged, so the statement is trivially correct. If the step is successful, then it holds that $(b-a) \leq \frac{2^{\tau+4}}{\sqrt{N_j}}$. By rearranging terms, we get that $N_j \leq 2^{2(\tau+4-\log(b-a))}$. $\square$

It follows inductively that the conditions of Lemma 7 are met for each call in the AQIR sequence because I_0 is normal by construction. Therefore, the linear sequence for a root ξ of f is computed with a bit complexity of

$$\tilde{O}((\tau + \log(C_\xi)^{-1}) d (\log(C_\xi^{-1}) + d\tau + \Sigma_f)) \qquad (6)$$

because $O(\tau + \log(C_\xi^{-1}))$ steps are necessary to refine the interval to a size smaller than C_ξ by Lemma 16, and the bit complexity is bounded by $\tilde{O}(d(\log(C_\xi^{-1}) + d\tau + \Sigma_f))$ with Lemma 7. It remains to bound $\log(C_\xi)^{-1}$; we do so by bounding the sum of all $\log(C_\xi)^{-1}$ with the following lemma.

Lemma 18. $\sum_{i=1}^m \log(C_{z_i})^{-1} = O(d(\tau + \log d) + R)$

PROOF. We can write the sum as

$$\sum_{i=1}^m \log(C_{z_i})^{-1} \leq O(d(\tau + \log d)) + d \cdot \log \text{Mea}(f) - \log |\prod_{i=1}^n f'(z_i)|$$

where $\text{Mea}(f)$ is the Mahler measure of f (see [12, Thm 4.5] for a more detailed calculation). It is known that $\log \text{Mea}(f) = O(\tau + \log d)$. For the last summand, we use the relation $\text{res}(f, f') = a_d^{d-1} \prod_{i=1}^n f'(z_i)$; see [2, Thm.4.16] [19, Thm.6.15]. It follows that

$$-\log |\prod_{i=1}^n f'(z_i)| = \log |a_d^{d-1}| - \log |\text{res}(f, f')| \leq (d-1)\tau + R. \quad \square$$

When we apply Lemma 18 to (6), we obtain a bound that depends on d, τ, Σ_f, and R. The next result shows that Σ_f is bounded by $\tilde{O}(d\tau + R)$. The proof is only sketched for brevity; a complete proof is given in [13].

Theorem 19. $\Sigma_f \in O(d(\tau + \log d) + R)$.

PROOF. The product of all σ_i's is a product of root differences, and corresponds to the nearest neighbor graph [8] of the roots of f. We would like to apply the Davenport-Mahler bound [9] on this product, but the preconditions of it are not satisfied. However, by exploiting simple properties of the nearest neighbor graph, we can define another root product P such that $2^{-\Sigma_f} \geq 2^{-5d(\tau+1)} P^6$ and such that the Davenport-Mahler bound is applicable to P. This yields that $\log \frac{1}{P} = O(d(\tau + \log d) + R)$. □

Lemma 20. *The linear sequences for all real roots are computed within a total bit complexity of $\tilde{O}(d(d\tau + R)^2)$.*

PROOF. The total cost of all linear sequences is bounded by

$$\tilde{O}(\sum_{i=1}^{d} (\tau + \log(C_{z_i}^{-1})) d (\log(C_{z_i}^{-1}) + d\tau + \Sigma_f)).$$

Using Theorem 19 and rearranging terms, we obtain

$$= \tilde{O}(d^2 \tau (d\tau + R) + d(d\tau + R) \sum \log(C_{z_i}^{-1}) + d(\sum \log(C_{z_i}^{-1}))^2)$$

which equals $\tilde{O}(d(d\tau + R)^2)$ with Lemma 18. □

Cost of the quadratic sequence. Let us fix some root ξ of f. Its quadratic sequence consists of at most $1 + \log L$ steps, because N is squared in every step (except for at most one failing step) and the sequence stops as soon as the interval is smaller than 2^{-L}. Since we ignore logarithmic factors, it is enough to bound the costs of one QIR step in the sequence. Clearly, since the interval is not smaller than 2^{-L} in such a step, we have that $\log(b-a)^{-1} \leq L$. Therefore, the required precision is bounded by $O(L + d\tau + \Sigma_f)$. It follows that an AQIR step performs up to $\tilde{O}(d(L + d\tau + \Sigma_f))$ bit operations.

Lemma 21. *The quadratic sequences for one real root is computed within a bit complexity of $\tilde{O}(d(L + d\tau + \Sigma_f))$.*

Total cost. We have everything together to prove the main result

Theorem 22. *Algorithm 5 performs root refinement within*

$$\tilde{O}(d(d\tau + R)^2 + dL)$$

bit operations for a single real root [2] of f, and within

$$\tilde{O}(d(d\tau + R)^2 + d^2 L)$$

for all real roots. The coefficients of f need to be approximated to $O(L + d\tau + \Sigma_f)$ bits after the binary point.

PROOF. We concentrate on the bound on all real roots; the case of a single root follows easily. By Lemma 10, the normalization requires $\tilde{O}(d(d\tau + \Sigma_f)^2) = \tilde{O}(d(d\tau + R)^2)$ bit operations. The linear subsequences of the AQIR sequence are computed in the same time by Lemma 20. The quadratic subsequences are computed with $\tilde{O}(d^2 L + d^3 \tau + d^2 \Sigma_f)$ bit operations by Lemma 21; the latter two terms are both dominated by $d(d\tau + R)^2$ which yields the complexity bound. The maximal number of required bits follows from Lemma 7 because the maximal required precision in any AQIR step is bounded by $O(L + d\tau + \Sigma_f)$. □

We remark without proof that, with little extra effort, the bound for a single root can be slightly improved to $\tilde{O}(d(d\tau + \Sigma_f)^2 + dL)$. For integer polynomials, $\operatorname{res}(f, f')$ is an integer and consequently $R < 0$. This improves the bound from [12] by a factor of d.

Corollary 23. *If f is a polynomial with integer coefficients, the bit complexity of Algorithm 5 is bounded by*

$$\tilde{O}(d^3 \tau^2 + d^2 L).$$

---

[2] In its initial formulation, Algorithm 5 assumes that isolating intervals are for *all* real roots are given. If only one isolating interval I_k for a root z_k is given, we have to normalize I_k first and, then, compute the signs of f at the endpoints of I. Due to space constraints, we omit the details for this relatively simple step.

6. REFERENCES

[1] J. Abbott. Quadratic Interval Refinement for Real Roots. Poster presented at the *2006 Intern. Symp. on Symbolic and Algebraic Computation (ISSAC 2006)*, 2006.

[2] S. Basu, R. Pollack, and M.-F. Roy. *Algorithms in Real Algebraic Geometry*. Springer, 2nd edition, 2006.

[3] E. Berberich, P. Emeliyanenko, and M. Sagraloff. An elimination method for solving bivariate polynomial systems: Eliminating the usual drawbacks. In *Workshop on Algorithm Engineering & Experiments (ALENEX)*, pages 35–47, 2011.

[4] E. Berberich, M. Hemmer, and M. Kerber. A generic algebraic kernel for non-linear geometric applications. Research report 7274, INRIA, 2010.

[5] J. Bus and T.J.Dekker. Two efficient algorithms with guaranteed convergence for finding a zero of a function. *ACM Trans. on Math. Software*, 1(4):330–345, 1975.

[6] J. Cheng, S. Lazard, L. Peñaranda, M. Pouget, F. Rouillier, and E. Tsigaridas. On the topology of real algebraic plane curves. *Mathematics in Computer Science*, 4:113–137, 2010.

[7] G. E. Collins and A. G. Akritas. Polynomial Real Root Isolation Using Descartes' Rule of Signs. In *Proc. of the 3rd ACM Symp. on Symbolic and Algebraic Computation (SYMSAC 1976)*, pages 272–275. ACM Press, 1976.

[8] D.Eppstein, M.S.Paterson, and F.F.Yao. On nearest-neighbor graphs. *Discrete and Computational Geometry*, 17(3):263–282, 1997.

[9] Z. Du, V. Sharma, and C. Yap. Amortized bound for root isolation via Sturm sequences. In *Symbolic-Numeric Computation*, Trends in Mathematics, pages 113–129. Birkhäuser Basel, 2007.

[10] A. Eigenwillig, M. Kerber, and N. Wolpert. Fast and exact geometric analysis of real algebraic plane curves. In *Proc. of the 2007 Intern. Symp. on Symbolic and Algebraic Computation (ISSAC 2007)*, pages 151–158, 2007.

[11] A. Eigenwillig, L. Kettner, W. Krandick, K. Mehlhorn, S. Schmitt, and N. Wolpert. A Descartes algorithm for polynomials with bit-stream coefficients. In *8th International Workshop on Computer Algebra in Scientific Computing (CASC 2005)*, volume 3718 of *LNCS*, pages 138–149, 2005.

[12] M. Kerber. On the complexity of reliable root approximation. In *11th International Workshop on Computer Algebra in Scientific Computing (CASC 2009)*, volume 5743 of *LNCS*, pages 155–167. Springer, 2009.

[13] M. Kerber and M. Sagraloff. Supplementary material for "Efficient Real Root Approximation", 2011. *http://www.mpi-inf.mpg.de/~msagralo/apx11.pdf*.

[14] K. Mehlhorn, R. Osbild, and M. Sagraloff. A general approach to the analysis of controlled perturbation algorithms. *CGTA*, 2011. to appear; for a draft, see *http://www.mpi-inf.mpg.de/~msagralo/cpgeneral.pdf*.

[15] V. Y. Pan. Optimal and nearly optimal algorithms for approximating polynomial zeros. *Computers and Mathematics with Applications*, 31(12):97–138, 1996.

[16] V. Y. Pan. Solving a polynomial equation: Some history and recent progress. *SIAM Review*, 39(2):187–220, 1997.

[17] F. Rouillier and P. Zimmermann. Efficient isolation of polynomial's real roots. *Journal of Compututational and Applied Mathematics*, 162(1):33–50, 2004.

[18] M. Sagraloff. On the complexity of real root isolation. arXiv:1011.0344v1, 2010.

[19] C. K. Yap. *Fundamental Problems in Algorithmic Algebra*. Oxford University Press, 2000.

Approximate Rational Solutions to Rational ODEs Defined on Discrete Differentiable Curves

Hongbo Li, Ruiyong Sun, Shoubin Yao, Ge Li
KLMM, AMSS, Chinese Academy of Sciences
Beijing 100190, China
hli@mmrc.iss.ac.cn, sunruiyong@126.com, yaoshoubin@163.com, liyoucun@126.com

ABSTRACT

In this paper, a new concept is proposed for discrete differential geometry: *discrete n-differentiable curve*, which is a tangent n-jet on a sequence of space points. A complete method is proposed to solve ODEs of the form

$$\mathbf{n}^{(m)} = \frac{\mathbf{F}(\mathbf{r}, \mathbf{r}', \ldots, \mathbf{r}^{(n)}, \mathbf{n}, \mathbf{n}', \ldots, \mathbf{n}^{(m-1)}, u)}{G(\mathbf{r}, \mathbf{r}', \ldots, \mathbf{r}^{(n)}, \mathbf{n}, \mathbf{n}', \ldots, \mathbf{n}^{(m-1)}, u)}, \qquad (0.1)$$

where $\mathbf{F}, G$ are respectively vector-valued and scalar-valued polynomials, where $\mathbf{r}$ is a discrete curve obtained by sampling along an unknown smooth curve parametrized by u, and where $\mathbf{n}$ is the vector field to be computed along the curve. Our Maple-13 program outputs an approximate rational solution with the highest order of approximation for given data and neighborhood size.

The method is used to compute rotation minimizing frames of space curves in CAGD. For one-step backward-forward chasing, a 6th-order approximate rational solution is found, and 6 is guaranteed to be the highest order of approximation by rational functions. The theoretical order of approximation is also supported by numerical experiments.

ACM Computing Classification: F.2.2 [Nonnumerical Algorithms and Problems]: Computations on discrete structures; G.1.7 [Ordinary Differential Equations]: One-step (single step) methods.

General Terms: Theory; algorithm.

Keywords: Discrete differentiable curve; rational ODE; approximate rational solution; rotation minimizing frame.

1. INTRODUCTION

Discrete differential geometry introduces differential geometric concepts to the study of polygons, meshes and simplicial complexes in computer graphics. In CAGD, however, it often occurs that only a sequence of space points is provided, together with some derivatives of the unknown smooth curve connecting the points. It is incorrect to assume that the connecting curve is piecewise linear.

ISSAC'11, June 8–11, 2011, San Jose, California, USA.
Copyright 2011 ACM 978-1-4503-0675-1/11/06 ...$10.00.

In this paper, we propose a different discretization of smooth objects for the purpose of fast approximate solving of ODEs defined on them. We define a *discrete n-differentiable curve* as a sequence of space points by sampling along an unknown smooth and parametrized curve, together with the derivatives up to order n of the curve with respect to the parameter at each sampled point. The sequence of sampling parameters need not be provided in practice.

There is no shortage of discrete differentiable curves in reality. When the parameter is the time, one can capture a moving object together with its velocity, even its acceleration, at a sequence of time instances using cameras, laser range finders, current meters, acceleration meters, etc., and obtain a discrete 1- or 2-differentiable curve. When the parameter is the arclength, one gets a discrete 1-differentiable curve composed of a sequence of points together with a tangent unit direction at each point. Such scenario occurs in Hermite interpolation.

Any smooth and parametric curve connecting points of a discrete differentiable curve and agreeing with the values of the derivatives at the points is called a *smooth filling* of the curve. In this paper, we always denote $\mathbf{f}' = d\mathbf{f}/du$ and $\mathbf{f}^{(i)} = d^i\mathbf{f}/du^i$ for function $\mathbf{f} = \mathbf{f}(u)$.

A *discrete m-jet* on a discrete curve refers to a sequence of $(m+1)$-tuples $(\mathbf{f}_0, \mathbf{f}_1, \ldots, \mathbf{f}_m)$ of vectors (or scalars) along the curve, such that there is a smooth filling of the curve, and an extension of $\mathbf{f}_0$ to a smooth function along the smooth filling, with the property that $\mathbf{f}_i$ for $1 \leq i \leq m$ at each discrete point is the i-th derivative of the extended $\mathbf{f}_0$ with respect to the parameter of the smooth filling. For example, a discrete n-differentiable curve $\mathbf{r}$ naturally contains a discrete n-jet $(\mathbf{r}, \mathbf{r}', \ldots, \mathbf{r}^{(n)})$, called the *tangent n-jet* of the curve [4].

An m-th order *ODE* defined on a discrete n-differentiable curve $\mathbf{r}$ refers to a vector-valued (or scalar-valued) equation on three objects: unknown m-jet $(\mathbf{f}, \mathbf{f}', \ldots, \mathbf{f}^{(m)})$, given tangent n-jet of the curve, and sampling parameter u:

$$\mathbf{F}(\mathbf{f}, \mathbf{f}', \ldots, \mathbf{f}^{(m)}, \mathbf{r}, \mathbf{r}', \ldots, \mathbf{r}^{(n)}, u) = 0. \qquad (1.2)$$

When $\mathbf{F}$ does not depend on u explicitly, the ODE is said to be *autonomous*. The *initial values* are the values of the $(m-1)$-jet $(\mathbf{f}, \mathbf{f}', \ldots, \mathbf{f}^{(m-1)})$ at the first sampled point.

ODEs defined on discrete curves have no counterparts in classical ODE theory. When (1.2) is taken as an ODE defined on the u-axis, then since $\mathbf{r}$ and its derivatives are unknown functions on the axis, the ODE is undefined. Although symbolic general solutions and numerical schemes to ODEs have been a subject of favor in computer algebra and computational mathematics [2], [3], no literature addresses the current problem.

A sequence of m-tuples $(\mathbf{g}, \mathbf{g}_1, \ldots, \mathbf{g}_{m-1})$ defined at every point of a discrete differentiable curve is said to be a *solution* to ODE (1.2), if on any smooth filling of the curve, there is a smooth function $\mathbf{f}$ satisfying (1.2), and at all sampled points, $\mathbf{f} = \mathbf{g}$ and $\mathbf{f}^{(i)} = \mathbf{g}_i$ for $1 \leq i \leq m - 1$.

Generally an ODE does not have such a solution, so we need to seek for its approximate solutions. For a discrete differentiable curve, assume that u_i is the sampling parameter of a sampled point $\mathbf{r}_i$, and $u_{i+1} - u_i$ is small.

Definition 1. An *approximate solution* to ODE (1.2) with *order of (one-step local) approximation k*, refers to a sequence of m-tuples $(\mathbf{g}, \mathbf{g}_1, \ldots, \mathbf{g}_{m-1})$ defined at every point of the discrete curve, such that on every smooth filling of the curve, between every two neighboring sampled points $\mathbf{r}_i, \mathbf{r}_{i+1}$, there is a smooth function $\mathbf{f}$ satisfying (1.2) and initial conditions $\mathbf{f} = \mathbf{g}$, $\mathbf{f}^{(j)} = \mathbf{g}_j$ for all $1 \leq j \leq m - 1$ at point $\mathbf{r}_i$, such that at point $\mathbf{r}_{i+1}$,

$$
\begin{aligned}
\mathbf{f} &= \mathbf{g} + o((u_{i+1} - u_i)^k), \\
\mathbf{f}^{(j)} &= \mathbf{g}_j + o((u_{i+1} - u_i)^{k-j}).
\end{aligned} \tag{1.3}
$$

The solution concept allows for computing exact or approximate solutions to ODEs defined on a discrete structure without interpolating the structure by smooth curves. A solution is a function in the discrete tangent n-jet, together with the initial values and the sampling parameter if it is provided, and is said to be *rational* if so is the function.

In this paper, we propose a complete method to both determine the existence of and find approximate rational solutions to rational ODEs on discrete curves. If the denominators are restricted to powers of a selected function, then all approximate rational solutions of this kind can be found.

The idea is to first find a power series solution to the ODE using Taylor expansion, a technique dating back to Euler and Newton [1], then convert the solution to a rational function by a loop procedure of applying rewriting rules and making Taylor expansions. The rewriting rules are independent of the ODE, are completely determined by the tangent jet, and are obtained by a triangulation process to data of the tangent jet at neighboring points.

One motivation of the research is to generate automatically an approximate formula for computing *rotation minimizing frames* (RMF) of space curves with the highest order of approximation. An RMF [5] along a space curve $\mathbf{r} = \mathbf{r}(u)$ is an orthonormal frame $\{\mathbf{r}; \mathbf{t}, \mathbf{n}, \mathbf{m}\}$ where $\mathbf{t}$ is the tangent direction, such that

$$
\mathbf{n}' \times \mathbf{t} = 0. \tag{1.4}
$$

RMFs are important tools in CAGD because of several attractive properties. In Frenet frame, $\mathbf{n}$ can be explicitly solved, and the solution involves the integration $\int \tau ds$ of the torsion along the arclength. On one hand, definition (1.4) requires the curve to be only first-order differentiable; on the other hand, the solution in Frenet frame requires the curve to be third-order differentiable so that τ exists. Moreover, the numerical integration is often not accurate enough. These considerations lead to the desire of finding approximate solutions involving $\mathbf{r}$ and $\mathbf{t}$ only.

By $(\mathbf{n} \cdot \mathbf{t})' = \mathbf{n}' \cdot \mathbf{t} + \mathbf{n} \cdot \mathbf{t}' = 0$, (1.4) can be written as

$$
\mathbf{n}' = -(\mathbf{n} \cdot \mathbf{t}')\mathbf{t}. \tag{1.5}
$$

This is an autonomous polynomial ODE. When $\mathbf{r}$ is sampled uniformly by unknown u, our program outputs a rational solution with 6-th order of approximation, and guarantees

that 6 is the highest order of approximation for all rational approximants based on three evenly sampled points.

2. POWER SERIES SOLUTIONS TO RATIONAL ODES ON DISCRETE CURVES

Consider a smooth space curve $\mathbf{r} = \mathbf{r}(u)$ and an unknown vector field $\mathbf{n} = \mathbf{n}(u)$ along the curve satisfying (0.1). Sample the curve to get a sequence of points $\mathbf{r}_1, \ldots, \mathbf{r}_q$ at sampling parameters $u_1, \ldots, u_q$. We make the following assumptions to ODE (0.1):

(i) $n, m \geq 1$.

(ii) If the ODE is non-autonomous, then the sampling parameters must be provided and are rational numbers.

(iii) The curve is non-singular at the u_i: $\mathbf{r}'(u_i) \neq 0$.

(iv) $\mathbf{n}$ has no pole for $u \in [u_1, u_q]$.

(v) $G \neq 0$ at the sampled points.

Suppose $u = u_{i+1} - u_i$ is sufficiently small so that it can be treated as a first-order infinitesimal. Let $\mathbf{r}, \mathbf{r}', \ldots, \mathbf{r}^{(n)}$ and $\mathbf{n}, \mathbf{n}', \ldots, \mathbf{n}^{(m)}$ be respective the values of these functions at u_{i+1}. Let the Taylor expansions of $\mathbf{r}, \mathbf{n}$ nearby u_i be

$$
\begin{aligned}
\mathbf{r} &= \mathbf{x}_0 + \mathbf{x}_1 u + \ldots + \mathbf{x}_k \frac{u^k}{k!} + o(u^k), \\
\mathbf{n} &= \mathbf{n}_0 + \mathbf{n}_1 u + \ldots + \mathbf{n}_l \frac{u^l}{l!} + o(u^l).
\end{aligned} \tag{2.6}
$$

Then $\mathbf{x}_0, \mathbf{x}_1, \ldots, \mathbf{x}_n$ are the values of $\mathbf{r}, \mathbf{r}', \ldots, \mathbf{r}^{(n)}$ at $\mathbf{r}_i$, and $\mathbf{n}_0, \mathbf{n}_1, \ldots, \mathbf{n}_{m-1}$ are the values of $\mathbf{n}, \mathbf{n}', \ldots, \mathbf{n}^{(m-1)}$ at $\mathbf{r}_i$.

For $1 \leq a \leq n$ and $1 \leq b \leq m$, substituting

$$
\begin{aligned}
\mathbf{r}^{(a)} &= \mathbf{x}_a + \mathbf{x}_{a+1} u + \ldots + \mathbf{x}_k \frac{u^{k-a}}{(k-a)!} + o(u^{k-a}), \\
\mathbf{n}^{(b)} &= \mathbf{n}_b + \mathbf{n}_{b+1} u + \ldots + \mathbf{n}_l \frac{u^{l-b}}{(l-b)!} + o(u^{l-b})
\end{aligned}
$$

into $G\mathbf{n}^{(m)} = \mathbf{F}$ and comparing the coefficients in u^j, we get a list of recursive formulas on $\mathbf{n}_c$ for $m \leq c \leq l = m + k - n$:

$$
\mathbf{n}_c = \frac{\mathbf{H}_c(\mathbf{x}_0, \mathbf{x}_1, \ldots, \mathbf{x}_{n+c-m}, \mathbf{n}_0, \mathbf{n}_1, \ldots, \mathbf{n}_{c-1}, u_i)}{G(\mathbf{x}_0, \mathbf{x}_1, \ldots, \mathbf{x}_n, \mathbf{n}_0, \mathbf{n}_1, \ldots, \mathbf{n}_{m-1}, u_i)}, \tag{2.7}
$$

where $\mathbf{H}_m = \mathbf{F}$, and for $c > m$, $\mathbf{H}_c$ is a vector-valued polynomial with rational coefficients.

Substituting (2.7) into (2.6), we get the following power series solution to (0.1): for all $0 \leq d < m$,

$$
\mathbf{n}^{(d)} = \sum_{i=0}^{m-d-1} \mathbf{n}_{i+d} \frac{u^i}{i!} + \sum_{i=m-d}^{l-d} \frac{\mathbf{H}_{i+d}}{G} \frac{u^i}{i!} + o(u^{l-d}). \tag{2.8}
$$

Suppose there is a fixed number h between 1 and n, such that only the data of the tangent h-jet of the curve are given. For example in (1.5), $h = 1$ but $n = 2$. Then $\mathbf{x}_{h+1}, \ldots, \mathbf{x}_k$ in the solution expressions are unknown. If the sampling parameters are not provided, then u is also unknown. The task is to eliminate these unknowns from the expressions, so that (2.8) involves only:

(a) $3(m + h + 1)$ coordinates of the vectors in

$$
\mathcal{I} := \{\mathbf{n}_0, \mathbf{n}_1, \ldots, \mathbf{n}_{m-1}, \mathbf{x}_0, \mathbf{x}_1, \ldots, \mathbf{x}_h\}; \tag{2.9}
$$

(b) $3(h + 1)$ infinitesimals which are coordinates of the following vectors, for all $0 \leq j \leq h$:

$$
\mathbf{r}^{(j)} - \mathbf{x}_j = \mathbf{x}_{j+1} u + \mathbf{x}_{j+2} \frac{u^2}{2!} + \ldots + \mathbf{x}_k \frac{u^{k-j}}{(k-j)!} + o(u^{k-j}); \tag{2.10}
$$

(c) u, if it is provided.

Denote by $\mathcal{D}$ the set of infinitesimals (2.10) if u is unknown, and add u into $\mathcal{D}$ otherwise.

There are various functions that can be used to express (2.8). Considering the computing cost of evaluating elementary functions, we restrict the scope of candidate functions to rational ones with coefficients in $Q(\mathcal{I})$, which is the field extension of rational numbers by adding the coordinates of (2.9). Henceforth this is the default coefficient field.

If all the $o(u^i)$ are overlooked, the problem of finding rational approximants is reduced to determining if all the coordinates of (2.8) are in $Q(\mathcal{I})(\mathcal{D})$. With the presence of infinitesimals, special care must be taken to rational functions, because if the denominator is an infinitesimal, its order must not be greater than that of the numerator.

Definition 2. Let

$$f = f_r u^r + f_{r+1} u^{r+1} + \ldots + f_p u^p + o(u^p), \qquad (2.11)$$

where $r \geq 0$, and f_r is an expression that is not identical to zero. Then r is called the *order* of infinitesimal of f, denoted by $f = O(u^r)$. p is called the *precision*, $p - r + 1$ is called the *effective length*, and $f_r u^r$ is called the *leading term* of the infinitesimal. If $f_r \in Q(\mathcal{I})$ and is guaranteed to be nonzero, this property is denoted by $f = \Theta(u^r)$. If $f_r = 1$, then f is said to be *monic*.

We make the following *rational function postulate* in converting the solution (2.8) to rational functions in $Q(\mathcal{I})(\mathcal{D})$:

The denominator is always $\Theta(u^r)$ for some r, and r is not greater than the order of infinitesimal of the numerator.

Lemma 1. Let $f_1 = O(u^{r_1})$ and $f_2 = O(u^{r_2})$ have precision p_1, p_2 and effective length e_1, e_2 respectively. Then
(1) $f_1 + f_2$ has effective length $\min(p_1, p_2) - \min(r_1, r_2) + 1$;
(2) $f_1 f_2$ has effective length $\min(e_1, e_2)$;
(3) when $r_1 \geq r_2$ and $f_2 = \Theta(u^{r_2})$, the Taylor expansion of f_1/f_2 has effective length $\min(e_1, e_2)$;
(4) for the above f_1, f_2, if there is an infinitesimal $f = \Theta(u^r)$ with $r \leq r_2$ and effective length $\geq \min(e_1, e_2)$, then the Taylor expansion of $(\frac{f_1}{f})/(\frac{f_2}{f})$ has effective length $\min(e_1, e_2)$.

Proof. Only item (3) needs attention. For $i = 1, 2$, let $f_i = u^{r_i}(f_{i0} + f_{i1}u + \ldots + f_{i(p_i - r_i)}u^{p_i - r_i}) + o(u^{p_i})$, where $f_{20} \neq 0$. Then the Taylor expansion of

$$\frac{f_1}{f_2} = u^{r_1 - r_2} \frac{f_{10} + f_{11}u + \ldots + f_{1(p_1 - r_1)}u^{p_1 - r_1}}{f_{20} + f_{21}u + \ldots + f_{2(p_2 - r_2)}u^{p_2 - r_2}} + o(u^{p_1 - r_2})$$

has precision $\min(r_1 - r_2 + p_2 - r_2, p_1 - r_2)$. Q.E.D.

Lemma 2. Let f be a monic 1st-order infinitesimal. Let $g = O(u^a)$, $h = \Theta(u^b)$ where $b \leq a$. Then the Taylor expansion of g/h has its terms in $Q(\mathcal{I})[g/f^b, h/f^b]$.

Proof. Let $h = cu^b + d$ where $c \neq 0$ and is in $Q(\mathcal{I})$, and where $d = o(u^b)$. Then

$$\frac{g}{h} = \frac{\frac{g}{f^b}}{\frac{h}{f^b}} = \frac{\frac{g}{f^b}}{c + (\frac{h}{f^b} - c)} = \frac{g}{cf^b} \sum_{i=0}^{\infty} (1 - \frac{h}{cf^b})^i. \qquad \text{Q.E.D.}$$

Monic 1st-order infinitesimals always exist. When u is provided, then it is a monic 1st-order infinitesimal. When u is unknown, then

$$v := \frac{(\mathbf{r} - \mathbf{x}_0) \cdot \mathbf{x}_1}{\mathbf{x}_1^2} = u + \frac{\mathbf{x}_1 \cdot \mathbf{x}_2}{2! \mathbf{x}_1^2} u^2 + \ldots + \frac{\mathbf{x}_1 \cdot \mathbf{x}_k}{k! \mathbf{x}_1^2} u^k + o(u^k) \qquad (2.12)$$

is a monic 1st-order infinitesimal.

Proposition 1. There exists a monic 1st-order infinitesimal $f \in Q(\mathcal{I})[\mathcal{D}]$, such that for any coordinate of an approximate rational solution to (0.1), there is a rational function

having the same order of approximation and of the form

$$g/f^r, \quad \text{where } g \in Q(\mathcal{I})[\mathcal{D}]. \qquad (2.13)$$

Proof. Set $f = u$ if u is provided, and $f = v$ in (2.12) otherwise. f has the longest effective length among all rational functions in $Q(\mathcal{I})(\mathcal{D})$. By the above two lemmas, we get the conclusion. Q.E.D.

In the next section, we will find a finite set of elements of the form (2.13), such that any approximate rational solution of the form (2.13) is a polynomial in the elements. Given a solution (2.8), its exponent r in (2.13) is automatically fixed by a term rewriting procedure based on these elements.

3. FINDING RATIONAL APPROXIMANTS

Given data at sampled point $\mathbf{r}_i$, by the Taylor expansions of the tangent h-jet at $\mathbf{r}_i$, a solution to (0.1) can be given at the next sampled point $\mathbf{r}_{i+1}$ but contains unknown data $\mathbf{x}_{h+1}, \ldots, \mathbf{x}_k$. Since a sampled point has two neighbors on the discrete curve as long as it is not at the boundary, data of the tangent h-jet at both points $\mathbf{r}_{i-1}, \mathbf{r}_{i+1}$ can be used in giving a rational approximant to the solution. Using data of the tangent h-jet at $\mathbf{r}_{i+1}$ to solve (0.1) at this point is called *one-step forward chasing*, while using data of the tangent h-jet at both points $\mathbf{r}_{i-1}, \mathbf{r}_{i+1}$ in the solving is called *one-step backward-forward chasing*.

There are all together 4 cases:
(1) One-step forward chasing with u provided.
(2) One-step forward chasing with u unknown.
(3) One-step backward-forward chasing with u provided.
(4) One-step backward-forward chasing with u unknown.

3.1 Forward chasing with u provided

In this case, (2.10) can be written as

$$\begin{aligned}
\frac{\mathbf{r} - \sum_{i=0}^{h} \mathbf{x}_i \frac{u^i}{i!}}{u^{h+1}} &= \sum_{i=0}^{k-h-1} \frac{\mathbf{x}_{h+i+1} u^i}{(h+i+1)!} + o(u^{k-h-1}), \\
\frac{\mathbf{r}' - \sum_{i=1}^{h} \mathbf{x}_i \frac{u^{i-1}}{(i-1)!}}{u^h} &= \sum_{i=0}^{k-h-1} \frac{\mathbf{x}_{h+i+1} u^i}{(h+i)!} + o(u^{k-h-1}), \\
\ldots \qquad & \qquad \ldots \\
\frac{\mathbf{r}^{(h)} - \mathbf{x}_h}{u} &= \sum_{i=0}^{k-h-1} \frac{\mathbf{x}_{h+i+1} u^i}{(i+1)!} + o(u^{k-h-1}).
\end{aligned}$$
$$(3.14)$$

Denote the left side by $\mathbf{g}_{h+1}, \mathbf{g}_h, \ldots, \mathbf{g}_1$ respectively.

Lemma 3. For any $h \geq 1$,

$$\begin{vmatrix}
\frac{1}{(h+1)!} & \frac{1}{(h+2)!} & \cdots & \frac{1}{(2h+1)!} \\
\frac{1}{h!} & \frac{1}{(h+1)!} & \cdots & \frac{1}{(2h)!} \\
\vdots & \vdots & \ddots & \vdots \\
\frac{1}{1!} & \frac{1}{2!} & \cdots & \frac{1}{(h+1)!}
\end{vmatrix} = \prod_{i=0}^{h} \frac{i!}{(h+i+1)!}.$$

Proof. Set $\mathbf{A}_{h+j} = \begin{vmatrix}
\frac{1}{(h+j)!} & \frac{1}{(h+j+1)!} & \cdots & \frac{1}{(2h+1)!} \\
\frac{1}{(h+j-1)!} & \frac{1}{(h+j)!} & \cdots & \frac{1}{(2h)!} \\
\vdots & \vdots & \ddots & \vdots \\
\frac{1}{(2j-1)!} & \frac{1}{(2j)!} & \cdots & \frac{1}{(h+j+1)!}
\end{vmatrix}.$

By $\frac{(i+1)!}{(i+j+1)!} - \frac{i!}{(i+j)!} = -j\frac{i!}{(i+j+1)!}$ and preliminary row transformations, we get $\mathbf{A}_{h+j} = \frac{(h+1-j)!}{(h+j)!}\mathbf{A}_{h+j+1}$, and the conclusion follows. Q.E.D.

Corollary 1. Assume $k \geq 2h+1$, and consider (3.14) as a system of equations with fixed precision $o(u^t)$, where $0 \leq t \leq k-h-1$.
(1) If $t \geq h$, then for any $0 \leq j \leq h$, $\mathbf{x}_{h+j+1}, \mathbf{x}_{h+j+2}u, \ldots,$ $\mathbf{x}_{2h+1}u^{h-j}$ each can be uniquely expressed as a Q-linear combination of $\mathbf{g}_1/u^j, \ldots, \mathbf{g}_{h+1}/u^j$ and $\mathbf{x}_{2h+2}u^{h+1-j}, \ldots,$ $\mathbf{x}_{h+t+1}u^{t-j}$ up to $o(u^{t-j})$.
(2) If $t < h$, then for any $0 \leq j \leq t$, $\mathbf{x}_{h+j+1}, \mathbf{x}_{h+j+2}u, \ldots,$ $\mathbf{x}_{h+t+1}u^{t-j}$ each can be expressed as a linear combination of the $\mathbf{g}_i/u^j$ up to $o(u^{t-j})$, where $h-t$ among the $h+1$ coefficients are free, and the others are fixed rational numbers.

Proof. Solving (3.14) for $\mathbf{x}_{h+1}, \mathbf{x}_{h+2}u, \ldots, \mathbf{x}_{2h+1}u^h$, we get the following linear solutions: for $0 \leq j \leq h$,

$$\mathbf{x}_{h+j+1}u^j = \mathbf{h}_j(\mathbf{g}_p, \mathbf{x}_{2h+2+q}u^{h+1+q} \,|\, 1 \leq p \leq h+1,$$
$$0 \leq q \leq k-2h-2) + o(u^{k-h-1}),$$
$$\tag{3.15}$$

where $\mathbf{h}_j$ is a multilinear function with rational coefficients.

When the order of approximation t satisfies $h \leq t \leq k-h-1$, (3.15) becomes that for all $0 \leq j \leq h$,

$$u^{-j}\mathbf{h}_j(\mathbf{g}_p, \mathbf{x}_{2h+1+q}u^{h+q} \,|\, 1 \leq p \leq h+1, 1 \leq q \leq t-h)$$
$$= \mathbf{x}_{h+j+1} + o(u^{t-j}).$$

When $t < h$, (3.15) becomes that for all $0 \leq j \leq t$,

$$u^{-j}\mathbf{h}_j(\mathbf{g}_p, 0 \,|\, 1 \leq p \leq h+1) = \mathbf{x}_{h+j+1} + o(u^{t-j}),$$

and for any $0 \leq i \leq h$, $u^{t-i-j+1}\mathbf{h}_i = o(u^{t-j})$. So for arbitrary rational functions λ_i of the form (2.13) where $f = u$,

$$\mathbf{x}_{h+j+1} + o(u^{t-j}) = u^{-j}(\mathbf{h}_j + \sum_{i=t+1}^h \lambda_i u^{t+1-i}\mathbf{h}_i). \quad (3.16)$$
$$\text{Q.E.D.}$$

For any $0 \leq j \leq t \leq \min(h, k-h-1)$, define the following rational function in u and the $\mathbf{g}_i$:

$$\hat{\mathbf{h}}_{j,t} := u^{-j}\mathbf{h}_j(\mathbf{g}_p, 0 \,|\, 1 \leq p \leq h+1), \quad (3.17)$$

by requiring its Taylor expansion to have precision $t-j$. Denote by $\mathcal{H}$ the set of $\hat{\mathbf{h}}_{j,t}$'s.

Proposition 2. Let the order of approximation $l-d$ be fixed in (2.8). Then for any approximate rational solution to (0.1), its coordinates are always equal to some polynomials in $Q(\mathcal{I})[u, \mathcal{H}]$ up to $o(u^{l-d})$. Either there does not exist any approximate rational solution, or there is a unique one in $Q(\mathcal{I})[u, \mathcal{H}]$ having the property that the order of infinitesimal of every term does not exceed $l-d$.

Proof. Let w be the Taylor expansion of a coordinate of (2.8), and let g/u^r be a rational approximant of w with order of approximation $l-d$, where $g \in Q(\mathcal{I})[u, \mathbf{g}\text{'s}] - Q(\mathcal{I})[u]$.

Let T be a term of g. Then T is in the form

$$T = \lambda u^q \mathbf{g}_{i_1}^{r_1} \mathbf{g}_{i_2}^{r_2} \ldots \mathbf{g}_{i_s}^{r_s}, \quad (3.18)$$

where (i) $\lambda \in Q(\mathcal{I})$, (ii) $\mathbf{g}_i = (g_{ix}, g_{iy}, g_{iz})$, and $\mathbf{g}_i^j$ denotes a monomial of total degree j in g_{ix}, g_{iy}, g_{iz}, (iii) $1 \leq i_1 < i_2 < \ldots < i_s \leq h+1$, (iv) all the exponents are positive.

By Lemma 1, the Taylor expansion of T is up to $o(u^{l-d+r})$, and the Taylor expansion of each $\mathbf{g}_i$ is up to $o(u^{l-d+r-q})$. Set $t-j = l-d+r-q$ in Corollary 1 to get a set of Q-linear relations of the $\mathbf{g}_i$ up to $o(u^t)$, and a set of algebraically independent linear combinations $\mathbf{h}_j(\mathbf{g}_i, 0 \,|\, 1 \leq i \leq h+1)$ of the $\mathbf{g}_i$ for $0 \leq j \leq \min(t, h)$. Then each $\mathbf{g}_i$, hence T, can be written as a polynomial in u and $\hat{\mathbf{h}}_{j,t}$.

Denote the new form of g when written as a polynomial in u and $\hat{\mathbf{h}}_{j,t}$ by $\hat{g}$. If there are two terms $\hat{T}_1, \hat{T}_2$ of $\hat{g}$ whose leading terms in their Taylor expansions are the same up to coefficient, then $\hat{T}_1, \hat{T}_2$ are infinitesimals of the same order, so by (3.18), they are monomials in variables u and the $\hat{\mathbf{h}}_{j,t}$ for only one t. Since these variables are algebraically independent, $\hat{T}_1, \hat{T}_2$ must be identical up to coefficient.

Let the order of infinitesimal of g be $r_g > r$. Let $\hat{T}$ be a term of $\hat{g}$ having the lowest order of infinitesimal r_T among all terms of $\hat{g}$. If $r_T < r_g$ then $\hat{T}$ must be canceled by some other terms in $\hat{g}$ with order of infinitesimal r_T, which is impossible because of the algebraic independence. So $r_T \geq r_g$. This proves $\hat{g}/u^r \in Q(\mathcal{I})[u, \mathcal{H}]$. The uniqueness comes from the fact that if $g/u^r \in Q(\mathcal{I})[u, \mathcal{H}]$ approximates zero with order of approximation $l-d$, then $r_g > r+l-d$. Q.E.D.

Corollary 2. Given a rational approximant $\mathbf{p} \in Q(\mathcal{I})[u, \mathcal{H}]$ with order of approximation r, then all the rational approximants with the same order of approximation and whose denominators are powers of u, can be found in the set

$$\mathbf{p} + u^{r+1}Q(\mathcal{I})[u, u^{-j}\mathbf{h}_j(\mathbf{g}_p, 0 \,|\, 1 \leq p \leq h+1), 0 \leq j \leq h].$$
$$\tag{3.19}$$

Let T be a term in the Taylor expansion w of a coordinate of (2.8), and let T have the lowest order of infinitesimal among all terms of w. Let $\mathbf{x}_i = (x_i, y_i, z_i)$ for $i > h$. Then T must be of the form

$$T = \lambda u^r \mathbf{x}_{h+1}^{p_1} \mathbf{x}_{h+2}^{p_2} \cdots \mathbf{x}_{h+s}^{p_s}, \quad (3.20)$$

where (i) $\lambda \in Q(\mathcal{I})$, (ii) $\mathbf{x}_i^a$ denotes a monomial of total degree a in x_i, y_i, z_i, (iii) $p_s > 0$ if $s > 0$.

If w has any rational approximant $\hat{w} \in Q(\mathcal{I})[u, \mathcal{H}]$ with order of approximation $l-d$, then the proof of Proposition 2 shows that T must be the leading term in the Taylor expansion of a unique term $\hat{T}$ in $\hat{w}$. Hence $s \leq h+1$.

Denote $c = l-d-r$. Then $\hat{T}$ must be of the form

$$\hat{T} = \lambda u^r \hat{\mathbf{h}}_{0,c}^{p_1} \hat{\mathbf{h}}_{1,c+1}^{p_2} \cdots \hat{\mathbf{h}}_{s-1,c+s-1}^{p_s}. \quad (3.21)$$

By $l-m = k-n$ and $c+s-1 \leq k-h-1$, for $\hat{T}$ to exist, the following must hold:

$$s \leq \min(n-h+d+r-m, h+1). \quad (3.22)$$

The following is the *term rewriting* procedure to determine the existence of and at the same time find the unique approximant in $Q(\mathcal{I})[u, \mathcal{H}]$ for input w, an infinitesimal of precision $l-d$ in (2.8).

Step 1. Set $W_0 := w$.
Step 2. For $1 \leq i \leq l-d+2$, do steps 3 and 4:
Step 3. For every term T of W_{i-1} containing u^{i-1} but not any u^j where $j \geq i$, if the corresponding $\hat{T}$ does not exist, which is due to either W_{i-1} being zero or violation of (3.22), then go to step 5.
Step 4. Let W_i be the Taylor expansion up to $o(u^{l-d})$ of W_{i-1} subtracting all the $\hat{T}$ obtained from the terms T of W_{i-1} in step 3.
Step 5. Set $e = i$.

Practically only term moving occurs before i reaches $m-d+1$. The construction of $\hat{T}$ suffices to guarantee the following conclusion:

Theorem 1. By the above term rewriting procedure, $e = l-d+2$ if and only if w has rational approximants with order of approximation $l-d$.

3.2 Forward chasing with u unknown

In this case, the role of u is replaced by v. Let $\mathbf{x}_1, \mathbf{e}_2, \mathbf{e}_3$ be an orthogonal frame. Then any vector $\mathbf{v}$ has coordinates $(\mathbf{v} \cdot \mathbf{x}_1/\mathbf{x}_1^2, \mathbf{v} \cdot \mathbf{e}_2/\mathbf{e}_2^2, \mathbf{v} \cdot \mathbf{e}_3/\mathbf{e}_3^2)$. Let the coordinates of $\mathbf{x}_i$ be (x_i, y_i, z_i). Then (2.12) is just the first coordinate of $\mathbf{r} - \mathbf{x}_0$:

$$v = u + \frac{x_2}{2!}u^2 + \ldots + \frac{x_k}{k!}u^k + o(u^k). \qquad (3.23)$$

In this section, we use the symbol $\mathbf{r} - \mathbf{x}_0$ to denote only its second and third coordinates with respect to $\mathbf{x}_1, \mathbf{e}_2, \mathbf{e}_3$. The meaning of $\mathbf{r}^{(j)} - \mathbf{x}_j$ for $j > 0$ is still as before: the three coordinates of the vector with respect to $\mathbf{x}_1, \mathbf{e}_2, \mathbf{e}_3$.

Lemma 4. For $p \geq 2$ and $q, r, s \geq 0$, where $q + s \leq k$, let
$$\mathbf{f}_{p,q} = \mathbf{x}_p \frac{u^q}{r!} + \mathbf{x}_{p+1}\frac{u^{q+1}}{(r+1)!} + \ldots + \mathbf{x}_{p+s}\frac{u^{q+s}}{(r+s)!} + o(u^{q+s}).$$
Then there exist vector-valued polynomials $\mathbf{p}_i$ such that

$$\frac{\mathbf{f}_{p,q}}{v^q} = \frac{\mathbf{x}_p}{r!} + \sum_{i=1}^{s}(\mathbf{x}_{p+i} + \mathbf{p}_i(\mathbf{x}_2, \ldots, \mathbf{x}_{p+i-1}))\frac{u^i}{(r+i)!} + o(u^s). \qquad (3.24)$$

Proof. The Taylor expansion of the monic 0th-order infinitesimal $(u/v)^q$ is a polynomial in the $x_{j+1}u^j$ up to $o(u^{k-1})$, while $\mathbf{f}_{p,q}/u^q$ is a polynomial in the $x_{j+p}u^j$ up to $o(u^s)$. As $p > 1$, the conclusion follows. Q.E.D.

In (2.10), for fixed $0 \leq j \leq h$, define $\mathbf{z}_{j,1} = (\mathbf{r}^{(j)} - \mathbf{x}_j)/v$, and denote the leading term of its Taylor expansion by $\mathbf{l}_{j,1}$. For $2 \leq i \leq h - j + 1$, define $\mathbf{z}_{j,i} = (\mathbf{z}_{j,i-1} - \mathbf{l}_{j,i-1})/v$, and denote the leading term of its Taylor expansion by $\mathbf{l}_{j,i}$. By Lemma 4, the leading term of $\mathbf{z}_{j,h-j+1}$ is $\mathbf{x}_{h+1}/(h-j+1)! + \mathbf{q}_j$, where $\mathbf{q}_j$ is a $Q(I)$-valued vector.

For $0 \leq j \leq h$, define

$$\mathbf{g}_{h-j+1} := \mathbf{z}_{j,h-j+1} - \mathbf{q}_j. \qquad (3.25)$$

They are rational functions in v and (2.10). We have

$$\begin{pmatrix} \mathbf{g}_{h+1} \\ \mathbf{g}_h \\ \vdots \\ \mathbf{g}_1 \end{pmatrix} = \mathbf{M}_{(h+1)\times(k-h)}\begin{pmatrix} 1 \\ u \\ \vdots \\ u^{k-h-1} \end{pmatrix} + o(u^{k-h-1}), \qquad (3.26)$$

where

$$\mathbf{M} = \begin{pmatrix} \frac{\mathbf{x}_{h+1}}{(h+1)!} & \frac{\mathbf{x}_{h+2}+\mathbf{p}_{0,h+1}^{[1]}(\mathbf{x}_{h+1})}{(h+2)!} & \cdots & \frac{\mathbf{x}_k+\mathbf{p}_{0,k-1}^{[1]}(\mathbf{x}_{h+1},\ldots,\mathbf{x}_{k-1})}{k!} \\ \frac{\mathbf{x}_{h+1}}{h!} & \frac{\mathbf{x}_{h+2}+\mathbf{p}_{1,h+1}^{[1]}(\mathbf{x}_{h+1})}{(h+1)!} & \cdots & \frac{\mathbf{x}_k+\mathbf{p}_{1,k-1}^{[1]}(\mathbf{x}_{h+1},\ldots,\mathbf{x}_{k-1})}{(k-1)!} \\ \vdots & \vdots & \ddots & \vdots \\ \frac{\mathbf{x}_{h+1}}{1!} & \frac{\mathbf{x}_{h+2}+\mathbf{p}_{h,h+1}^{[1]}(\mathbf{x}_{h+1})}{2!} & \cdots & \frac{\mathbf{x}_k+\mathbf{p}_{h,k-1}^{[1]}(\mathbf{x}_{h+1},\ldots,\mathbf{x}_{k-1})}{(h+1)!} \end{pmatrix}, \qquad (3.27)$$

and $\mathbf{p}_{j,h+i}^{[1]}$ is a vector-valued polynomial. Notice that the coefficient matrix of the $\mathbf{g}$'s in $\mathbf{x}_{h+1}, \mathbf{x}_{h+2}u, \ldots, \mathbf{x}_{2h+1}u^h$ is still the same as that of (3.14), hence invertible.

Do the following *triangulation* to $\mathbf{M}$, and to the $\mathbf{g}$'s accordingly so that relation (3.26) is always preserved:

Step 1. For $1 \leq i \leq h + 1$, multiply the i-th row by $(h - i + 2)!$. For $1 \leq i \leq h$, subtract the i-th row by the $(i+1)$-st row, then multiply the i-th row by $-1/(h-i+1)!$. Then all elements in the first column, except for the last one, are eliminated.

Step 2. Divide the first h rows by v and then make Taylor expansions to update all the columns of $\mathbf{M}$ by the powers of u. Now $\mathbf{M}$ is in the form

$$\begin{pmatrix} \frac{\mathbf{x}_{h+2}+\mathbf{p}_{0,h+1}^{[2]}(\mathbf{x}_{h+1})}{(h+3)!} & 2\frac{\mathbf{x}_{h+3}+\mathbf{p}_{0,h+2}^{[2]}(\mathbf{x}_{h+1},\mathbf{x}_{h+2})}{(h+3)!} & \cdots \\ \frac{\mathbf{x}_{h+2}+\mathbf{p}_{1,h+1}^{[2]}(\mathbf{x}_{h+1})}{(h+1)!} & 2\frac{\mathbf{x}_{h+3}+\mathbf{p}_{1,h+2}^{[2]}(\mathbf{x}_{h+1},\mathbf{x}_{h+2})}{(h+2)!} & \cdots \\ \vdots & \vdots & \ddots \\ \frac{\mathbf{x}_{h+2}+\mathbf{p}_{h-1,h+1}^{[2]}(\mathbf{x}_{h+1})}{3!} & 2\frac{\mathbf{x}_{h+3}+\mathbf{p}_{h-1,h+2}^{[2]}(\mathbf{x}_{h+1},\mathbf{x}_{h+2})}{4!} & \cdots \\ \frac{\mathbf{x}_{h+1}}{1!} & \frac{\mathbf{x}_{h+2}+\mathbf{p}_{h,h+1}^{[1]}(\mathbf{x}_{h+1})}{2!} & \cdots \end{pmatrix}$$

$$\begin{pmatrix} (k-h-1)\frac{\mathbf{x}_k+\mathbf{p}_{0,k-1}^{[2]}(\mathbf{x}_{h+1},\ldots,\mathbf{x}_{k-1})}{k!} & * \\ (k-h-1)\frac{\mathbf{x}_k+\mathbf{p}_{1,k-1}^{[2]}(\mathbf{x}_{h+1},\ldots,\mathbf{x}_{k-1})}{(k-1)!} & * \\ \vdots & \vdots \\ (k-h-1)\frac{\mathbf{x}_k+\mathbf{p}_{h-1,k-1}^{[2]}(\mathbf{x}_{h+1},\ldots,\mathbf{x}_{k-1})}{(h+2)!} & * \\ \frac{\mathbf{x}_{k-1}+\mathbf{p}_{h,k-2}^{[1]}(\mathbf{x}_{h+1},\ldots,\mathbf{x}_{k-2})}{h!} & \frac{\mathbf{x}_k+\mathbf{p}_{h,k-1}^{[1]}(\mathbf{x}_{h+1},\ldots,\mathbf{x}_{k-1})}{(h+1)!} \end{pmatrix}, \qquad (3.28)$$

where the $\mathbf{p}_{i,h+j}^{[2]}$ are vector-valued polynomials, and "$*$" denotes that the corresponding component is arbitrary.

Step 3. Subtract the first column by $(\frac{\mathbf{p}_{0,h+1}^{[2]}(\mathbf{g}_1)}{(h+2)!}, \frac{\mathbf{p}_{1,h+1}^{[2]}(\mathbf{g}_1)}{(h+1)!}, \ldots, \frac{\mathbf{p}_{h-1,h+1}^{[2]}(\mathbf{g}_1)}{3!}, 0)^T$, and then make Taylor expansions to update all the columns of $\mathbf{M}$ by the powers of u.

Step 4. Do steps 1 to 3 to the first $h \times (k-h-1)$ submatrix of $\mathbf{M}$, with corresponding changes to the multipliers in step 1 and subtractors in step 3. Repeat this process until the matrix size under consideration becomes either $0 \times (k-2h-1)$ if $k \geq 2h+1$, or $(2h+1-k) \times 0$ otherwise.

In the case of $k = 2h+1$, matrix $\mathbf{M}$ is ultimately changed into the following form:

$$\begin{pmatrix} \mathbf{x}_{2h+1} & * & \cdots \\ \mathbf{x}_{2h} & \alpha(h)\frac{\mathbf{x}_{2h+1}+\mathbf{p}_{1,2h}^{[h]}(\mathbf{x}_{h+1},\ldots,\mathbf{x}_{2h})}{(h+1)!} & \cdots \\ \vdots & \vdots & \ddots \\ \mathbf{x}_{h+2} & 3\frac{\mathbf{x}_{h+3}+\mathbf{p}_{h-1,h+2}^{[2]}(\mathbf{x}_{h+1},\mathbf{x}_{h+2})}{3!} & \cdots \\ \mathbf{x}_{h+1} & \frac{\mathbf{x}_{h+2}+\mathbf{p}_{h,h+1}^{[1]}(\mathbf{x}_{h+1})}{2!} & \cdots \\ * & * \\ * & * \\ \vdots & \vdots \\ \frac{6h}{h+2}\frac{\mathbf{x}_{2h+1}+\mathbf{p}_{h-1,2h}^{[2]}(\mathbf{x}_{h+1},\ldots,\mathbf{x}_{2h})}{(h+1)!} & * \\ \frac{\mathbf{x}_{2h}+\mathbf{p}_{h,2h-1}^{[1]}(\mathbf{x}_{h+1},\ldots,\mathbf{x}_{2h-1})}{h!} & \frac{\mathbf{x}_{2h+1}+\mathbf{p}_{h,2h}^{[1]}(\mathbf{x}_{h+1},\ldots,\mathbf{x}_{2h})}{(h+1)!} \end{pmatrix}, \qquad (3.29)$$

where $\alpha(h) \in Q$ is nonzero. Accordingly, the column of $\mathbf{g}$'s is changed into a column of rational functions in v and the $\mathbf{g}$'s, denoted by $\mathbf{h}_h, \ldots, \mathbf{h}_0$. The following conclusion is direct from the above construction.

Corollary 3. $\mathbf{h}_0 = \mathbf{g}_1$, and for $1 \leq j \leq h$, there exist vector-valued polynomials $\mathbf{q}_j(v, \mathbf{g}_1, \ldots, \mathbf{g}_j)$ such that

$$\mathbf{h}_j = (\beta(j)\mathbf{g}_{j+1} + \mathbf{q}_j(v, \mathbf{g}_1, \ldots, \mathbf{g}_j))/v^j, \qquad (3.30)$$

where $\beta(j) = (-1)^j(2j)!(2j+1)!/(j!)^2$.

Denote by $\mathcal{H}$ the set of rational functions $\hat{\mathbf{h}}_{j,t}$ for $0 \leq j \leq t \leq \min(h, k-h-1)$, where $\hat{\mathbf{h}}_{j,t} := \mathbf{h}_j$ by requiring its Taylor expansion to be up to $o(u^{t-j})$.

Theorem 2. Proposition 2 and Theorem 1 remain valid with u being replaced by v in the statements.

We see that division by v is computationally expensive in deriving $\mathcal{H}$. The number of divisions by v can be reduced when there exists an integer a between 1 and $h+1$, such that the Taylor expansions in solution (2.8) are polynomials in the coordinates of

$$\mathcal{V}_a := \{u, \mathbf{x}_{h+1}u^a, \mathbf{x}_{h+2}u^{a+1}, \ldots, \mathbf{x}_k u^{k-h-1+a}\}. \quad (3.31)$$

Lemma 5. For $\mathbf{f}_{p,q}$ in (3.24) and $1 \le t \le q \le p$, $\mathbf{f}_{p,q}/v^t$ up to $o(u^{q+s-t})$ is a polynomial in

$$u, \mathbf{x}_{h+1}, \ldots, \mathbf{x}_{p-q+t}, \mathbf{x}_{p-q+t+1}u^1, \ldots, \mathbf{x}_{p+s}u^{q+s-t}. \quad (3.32)$$

Proof. Since $\mathbf{f}_{p,q}/u^t$ up to $o(u^{q+s-t})$ is a polynomial in (3.32), and $(v/u)^t$ up to $o(u^{k-t})$ is a polynomial in $u, \mathbf{x}_{h+1}u^h, \ldots, \mathbf{x}_{p+s}u^{p+s-1}$, by $p-q+t \ge 1$, $(\mathbf{f}_{p,q}/u^t)/(v/u)^t$ up to $o(u^{q+s-t})$ must be a polynomial in (3.32). Q.E.D.

Consider the case of $\mathcal{V}_a$. For $0 \le j \le h$, define $\mathbf{g}_{h-j+1}$ as (3.25) multiplied by v^a. Do Taylor expansions to get

$$\begin{pmatrix} \mathbf{g}_{h+1} \\ \mathbf{g}_h \\ \vdots \\ \mathbf{g}_1 \end{pmatrix} = \mathbf{N}_{(h+1)\times(k-h)} \begin{pmatrix} 1 \\ 1 \\ \vdots \\ 1 \end{pmatrix} + o(u^b), \quad (3.33)$$

where $b = k-h-1+a$, and where $\mathbf{N}$ is the following matrix:

$$\begin{pmatrix} \frac{\mathbf{x}_{h+1}u^a}{(h+1)!} & \frac{\mathbf{x}_{h+2}u^{a+1}+\mathbf{p}_{0,h+1}^{[1]}(\mathcal{P}_{h+1})}{(h+2)!} & \cdots & \frac{\mathbf{x}_k u^b+\mathbf{p}_{0,k-1}^{[1]}(\mathcal{P}_{k-1})}{k!} \\ \frac{\mathbf{x}_{h+1}u^a}{h!} & \frac{\mathbf{x}_{h+2}u^{a+1}+\mathbf{p}_{1,h+1}^{[1]}(\mathcal{P}_{h+1})}{(h+1)!} & \cdots & \frac{\mathbf{x}_k u^b+\mathbf{p}_{1,k-1}^{[1]}(\mathcal{P}_{k-1})}{(k-1)!} \\ \vdots & \vdots & \ddots & \vdots \\ \frac{\mathbf{x}_{h+1}u^a}{1!} & \frac{\mathbf{x}_{h+2}u^{a+1}+\mathbf{p}_{h,h+1}^{[1]}(\mathcal{P}_{h+1})}{2!} & \cdots & \frac{\mathbf{x}_k u^b+\mathbf{p}_{h,k-1}^{[1]}(\mathcal{P}_{k-1})}{(h+1)!} \end{pmatrix}. \quad (3.34)$$

In (3.34), $\mathcal{P}_{h+i} := \{u, \mathbf{x}_{h+1}u^a, \mathbf{x}_{h+2}u^{a+1}, \ldots, \mathbf{x}_{h+i}u^{a+i-1}\}$, and $\mathbf{p}_{j,h+i}^{[1]}(\mathcal{P}_{h+i})$ is a vector-valued polynomial which as a univariate polynomial in u has degree $a+i$.

Do the following *triangulation* to $\mathbf{N}$, and to the column of $\mathbf{g}$'s accordingly so that (3.33) is always preserved:

Step 1. For $1 \le i \le h+1$, multiply the i-th row by $(h-i+2)!$. For $1 \le i \le h$, subtract the i-th row by the $(i+1)$-st row, then multiply the i-th row by $-1/(h-i+1)!$. The result of $\mathbf{N}$ is in the following form, where $w = k-h-1$:

$$\begin{pmatrix} 0 & \frac{\mathbf{x}_{h+2}u^{a+1}+\mathbf{p}_{0,h+1}^{[2]}(\mathcal{P}_{h+1})}{(h+2)!} & \cdots & w\frac{\mathbf{x}_k u^b+\mathbf{p}_{0,k-1}^{[2]}(\mathcal{P}_{k-1})}{k!} \\ 0 & \frac{\mathbf{x}_{h+2}u^{a+1}+\mathbf{p}_{1,h+1}^{[2]}(\mathcal{P}_{h+1})}{(h+1)!} & \cdots & w\frac{\mathbf{x}_k u^b+\mathbf{p}_{1,k-1}^{[2]}(\mathcal{P}_{k-1})}{(k-1)!} \\ \vdots & \vdots & \ddots & \vdots \\ \frac{\mathbf{x}_{h+1}u^a}{1!} & \frac{\mathbf{x}_{h+2}u^{a+1}+\mathbf{p}_{h,h+1}^{[1]}(\mathcal{P}_{h+1})}{2!} & \cdots & \frac{\mathbf{x}_k u^b+\mathbf{p}_{h,k-1}^{[1]}(\mathcal{P}_{k-1})}{(h+1)!} \end{pmatrix}. \quad (3.35)$$

Step 2. Subtract the second column of $\mathbf{N}$ by $\left(\frac{\mathbf{p}_{0,h+1}^{[2]}(v,\mathbf{g}_1)}{(h+2)!}, \frac{\mathbf{p}_{1,h+1}^{[2]}(v,\mathbf{g}_1)}{(h+1)!}, \ldots, \frac{\mathbf{p}_{h-1,h+1}^{[2]}(v,\mathbf{g}_1)}{3!}, 0\right)^T$, and then make Taylor expansions to update all the columns by the powers of u.

Step 3. Do steps 1 to 2 to the submatrix of $\mathbf{N}$ composed of the first h rows and the last $k-h-1$ columns, with corresponding changes to the multipliers in step 1 and subtractors in step 2. Repeat this process until the matrix size under consideration becomes either $0 \times (k-2h-1)$ if $k \ge 2h+1$, or $(2h+1-k) \times 0$ otherwise.

When $k = 2h+1$, matrix $\mathbf{N}$ is ultimately changed into a lower-right triangular form whose anti-diagonal entries are

$\mathbf{x}_{h+i}u^{a+i-1}$ for $i = 1, \ldots, h+1$. Accordingly, the column of $\mathbf{g}$'s is changed into a column of rational functions in v and the $\mathbf{g}$'s, denoted by $\mathbf{h}_h, \ldots, \mathbf{h}_0$.

Corollary 4. Each $\mathbf{g}_i$ as an infinitesimal has order a and effective length $k-h$. For $0 \le i \le h$, $\mathbf{h}_i$ has order $a+i$, effective length $k-h-i$, and precision $b = k-h-1+a$.

For $0 \le j \le t \le \min(h, k-h-1)$, define $\hat{\mathbf{h}}_{j,t} := \mathbf{h}_j$ by requiring its Taylor expansion to have effective length $t-j+1$, or equivalently, to have precision $a+t$. Denote the set of $\hat{\mathbf{h}}_{j,t}$'s by $\mathcal{H}$.

Theorem 3. If the Taylor expansions of solution (2.8) are polynomials in $\mathcal{V}_a$, then Proposition 2 and Theorem 1 remain valid if the following revisions are made:

(1) u is replaced by v everywhere in the statements;

(2) $T = \lambda u^r (\mathbf{x}_{h+1}u^a)^{p_1} (\mathbf{x}_{h+2}u^{a+1})^{p_2} \ldots (\mathbf{x}_{h+s}u^{a+s-1})^{p_s}$ is replaced by $\hat{T} = \lambda v^r \hat{\mathbf{h}}_{0,c}^{p_1} \hat{\mathbf{h}}_{1,c+1}^{p_2} \ldots \hat{\mathbf{h}}_{s-1,c+s-1}^{p_s}$ in the term rewriting procedure, where $c = l-d-r-\sum_{i=0}^{s-1}(a+i)p_{i+1}$ is the effective length of $\hat{\mathbf{h}}_{i,c+i}$ minus 1, for all $0 \le i \le s-1$.

Remark. In the term rewriting procedures of Theorems 1, 2 and 3, practically any $\hat{\mathbf{h}}_{j,t}$ can be replaced by $\hat{\mathbf{h}}_{j,k-h-1}$ as long as $t \le k-h-1$. Essentially the $\hat{\mathbf{h}}_{j,t}$ for different t's are only valuable to Proposition 2.

Example 1. Let there be given two neighboring sampled points $\mathbf{x}_0, \mathbf{r}$ on a space curve $\mathbf{r} = \mathbf{r}(s)$ and two unit tangent directions $\mathbf{x}_1, \mathbf{r}'$ at the two points. Let s be the unknown arclength from $\mathbf{x}_0$ to $\mathbf{r}$, and let $\mathbf{n}_0$ be a given unit normal direction at $\mathbf{x}_0$. In the coordinate system $\{\mathbf{x}_0; \mathbf{x}_1, \mathbf{n}_0, \mathbf{x}_1 \times \mathbf{n}_0\}$, let $\mathbf{r} = (v, y, z)$, $\mathbf{r}' = (t_x, t_y, t_z)$, and $\mathbf{x}_j = (x_j, y_j, z_j)$. All together there are 6 infinitesimals which are the coordinates of $\mathbf{r} - \mathbf{x}_0$ and $\mathbf{r}' - \mathbf{x}_1$, and their Taylor expansions are

$$\begin{aligned} \Delta x &= v &&= s + \frac{x_2}{2!}s^2 + \ldots + \frac{x_k}{k!}s^k + o(s^k), \\ \Delta y &= y &&= \frac{y_2}{2!}s^2 + \ldots + \frac{y_k}{k!}s^k + o(s^k), \\ \Delta z &= z &&= \frac{z_2}{2!}s^2 + \ldots + \frac{z_k}{k!}s^k + o(s^k); \\ \Delta t_x &= t_x - 1 &&= x_2 s + \frac{x_3}{2!}s^2 + \ldots + \frac{x_k}{(k-1)!}s^{k-1} + o(s^{k-1}), \\ \Delta t_y &= t_y &&= y_2 s + \frac{y_3}{2!}s^2 + \ldots + \frac{y_k}{(k-1)!}s^{k-1} + o(s^{k-1}), \\ \Delta t_z &= t_z &&= z_2 s + \frac{z_3}{2!}s^2 + \ldots + \frac{z_k}{(k-1)!}s^{k-1} + o(s^{k-1}). \end{aligned} \quad (3.36)$$

From $\mathbf{r}'^2 = 1$, we get that $t_x - 1 = \sqrt{1-t_y^2-t_z^2} - 1$ when Taylor-expanded is a polynomial in t_y, t_z, so the given Δt_x is redundant. In fact, by $\mathbf{r}^{(j+1)} \cdot \mathbf{x}_1 = (\mathbf{r}^{(j)} \cdot \mathbf{x}_1)'$ and induction, we can get that the Taylor expansion of the x-coordinate of $\mathbf{r}^{(j)} - \mathbf{x}_j$ up to $o(s^{k-j})$ for $1 \le j \le h$ is a polynomial in the (y, z)-coordinates of the $\mathbf{r}^{(i)} - \mathbf{x}_i$ for $1 \le i < j$. Hence all the given infinitesimals $(\mathbf{r}^{(j)} - \mathbf{x}_j) \cdot \mathbf{x}_1$ for $1 \le j \le h$ are redundant, and need be removed from the set $\mathcal{D}$.

Lemma 6. For any $2 \le p \le k$, $x_p s^{p-1}$ is a polynomial in $\mathbf{y}_i s^{i-1}$ for $1 \le i \le p-1$, where $\mathbf{y}_i := (y_i, z_i)$.

Proof. Substituting the Taylor expansion of $\mathbf{r}'$ into $\mathbf{r}'^2 = 1$, we get for all $j \ge 1$,

$$\begin{aligned} -\frac{x_{2j}}{(2j-1)!} &= \sum_{i=1}^{j-1} \frac{\mathbf{x}_{i+1} \cdot \mathbf{x}_{2j-i}}{i!(2j-i-1)!}, \\ -\frac{x_{2j+1}}{(2j)!} &= \frac{\mathbf{x}_{j+1}^2}{2(j!)^2} + \sum_{i=1}^{j-1} \frac{\mathbf{x}_{i+1} \cdot \mathbf{x}_{2j-i+1}}{i!(2j-i)!}. \end{aligned} \quad (3.37)$$

So $x_2 = 0$, and $x_3 = -\mathbf{x}_2^2 = -y_2^2 - z_2^2$. The conclusion holds trivially for $p = 2$. When multiplying the two equalities in (3.37) by $2j-1$ and $2j$ respectively, we get by induction that the conclusion holds for all $2 \le p \le k$. Q.E.D.

Consider RMF equation (1.5). We have $n = 2$, $h = m = 1$,

and by comparing the coefficients in powers of s, we get the following recursive relation of the solution $\mathbf{n}$: for all $p \geq 0$,

$$-\mathbf{n}_{p+1} = \sum_{\substack{i+j+t=p, \\ 0 \leq i,j,t \leq p}} \frac{p!}{i!j!t!}(\mathbf{n}_i \cdot \mathbf{x}_{j+2})\mathbf{x}_{t+1}. \qquad (3.38)$$

Corollary 5. (1) The Taylor expansion of v/s up to $o(s^{k-1})$ is a polynomial in the $\mathbf{y}_i s^{i-1}$ for $1 \leq i \leq k-1$. (2) The solution $\mathbf{n}$ when Taylor expanded up to $o(s^{k-1})$ is a polynomial in the $\mathbf{y}_i s^{i-1}$ for $1 \leq i \leq k$.

In coordinate system $\{\mathbf{x}_0; \mathbf{x}_1, \mathbf{n}_0, \mathbf{x}_1 \times \mathbf{n}_0\}$, we have $\mathbf{x}_0 = (0,0,0)$, $\mathbf{n}_0 = (0,1,0)$ and $\mathbf{x}_1 = (1,0,0)$. So $Q(\mathcal{I}) = Q$. The set $\mathcal{D}$ is composed of 5 given infinitesimals: v, $\mathbf{y} = (y,z)$ and $\mathbf{y}' = (t_y, t_z)$. By Corollary 5, the solution $\mathbf{n}$ up to $o(s^{k-1})$ is a polynomial in $\mathcal{V}_1$ of (3.31), where the $\mathbf{x}$'s are replaced by the $\mathbf{y}$'s. So by (3.33),

$$\begin{pmatrix} \mathbf{g}_2 \\ \mathbf{g}_1 \end{pmatrix} = \begin{pmatrix} \mathbf{y}/v \\ \mathbf{y}' \end{pmatrix} = \begin{pmatrix} \frac{\mathbf{y}_2 s}{2!} & \frac{\mathbf{y}_3 s^2}{3!} & \frac{(\mathbf{y}_4 + 2\mathbf{y}_2^2 \mathbf{y}_2)s^3}{4!} & \cdots \\ \frac{\mathbf{y}_2 s}{1!} & \frac{\mathbf{y}_3 s^2}{2!} & \frac{\mathbf{y}_4 s^3}{3!} & \cdots \end{pmatrix}$$

$$\begin{pmatrix} \frac{\mathbf{y}_k s^{k-1} + \mathbf{p}_k(\mathbf{y}_2 s, \ldots, \mathbf{y}_{k-2} s^{k-3})}{k!} \\ \frac{\mathbf{y}_k s^{k-1}}{(k-1)!} \end{pmatrix} \begin{pmatrix} 1 \\ \vdots \\ 1 \end{pmatrix} + o(s^{k-1}),$$
$$(3.39)$$

where the $\mathbf{p}_j$ for $4 \leq j \leq k$ are polynomials with rational coefficients. For example, $\mathbf{p}_4(\mathbf{y}_2 s) = 2(\mathbf{y}_2 s)^2 \mathbf{y}_2 s$.

For $k = 2h + 1 = 3$,

$$\begin{pmatrix} \mathbf{h}_1 \\ \mathbf{h}_0 \end{pmatrix} = \begin{pmatrix} 2\mathbf{g}_2 - \mathbf{g}_1 \\ \mathbf{g}_1 \end{pmatrix} = \begin{pmatrix} 0 & -\frac{\mathbf{y}_3 s^2}{6} \\ \mathbf{y}_2 s & \frac{\mathbf{y}_3 s^2}{2} \end{pmatrix} \begin{pmatrix} 1 \\ 1 \end{pmatrix} + o(s^2). \qquad (3.40)$$

Consider $k = 5$, *i.e.*, $l = k - 1 = 4$. By $t \leq k - h - 1 = 3$, the set $\mathcal{H}$ is composed of

$$\hat{\mathbf{h}}_{0,3} = \begin{pmatrix} t_y \\ t_z \end{pmatrix} = \mathbf{y}_2 s + \frac{\mathbf{y}_3}{2}s^2 + \frac{\mathbf{y}_4}{6}s^3 + \frac{\mathbf{y}_5}{24}s^4 + o(s^4),$$

$$\hat{\mathbf{h}}_{1,3} = \begin{pmatrix} h_y \\ h_z \end{pmatrix} = -\frac{\mathbf{y}_3}{6}s^2 + \frac{2(\mathbf{y}_2 \cdot \mathbf{y}_2)\mathbf{y}_2 - \mathbf{y}_4}{12}s^3$$
$$+ \left(\frac{(\mathbf{y}_2 \cdot \mathbf{y}_3)\mathbf{y}_2}{8} + \frac{(\mathbf{y}_2 \cdot \mathbf{y}_2)\mathbf{y}_3}{18} - \frac{\mathbf{y}_5}{40}\right)s^4 + o(s^4), \qquad (3.41)$$

together with

$$\hat{\mathbf{h}}_{0,2} = \mathbf{y}_2 s + \frac{\mathbf{y}_3}{2}s^2 + \frac{\mathbf{y}_4}{6}s^3 + o(s^3),$$
$$\hat{\mathbf{h}}_{0,1} = \mathbf{y}_2 s + \frac{\mathbf{y}_3}{2}s^2 + o(s^2),$$
$$\hat{\mathbf{h}}_{0,0} = \mathbf{y}_2 s + o(s), \qquad (3.42)$$
$$\hat{\mathbf{h}}_{1,2} = -\frac{\mathbf{y}_3}{6}s^2 + \frac{2(\mathbf{y}_2 \cdot \mathbf{y}_2)\mathbf{y}_2 - \mathbf{y}_4}{12}s^3 + o(s^3),$$
$$\hat{\mathbf{h}}_{1,1} = -\frac{\mathbf{y}_3}{6}s^2 + o(s^2).$$

By (3.38), $\mathbf{n}$ up to $o(s^4)$ equals

$$\begin{pmatrix} -y_2 s - \frac{y_3}{2}s^2 - \frac{y_4}{6}s^3 - \frac{y_5 + 2z_2(y_2 z_3 - z_2 y_3)}{24}s^4 \\ 1 - \frac{y_2^2}{2}s^2 - \frac{y_2 y_3}{2}s^3 - \left(\frac{y_2 y_4}{6} + \frac{y_3^2 + y_2^2 z_2^2}{8}\right)s^4 \\ -\frac{y_2 z_2}{2}s^2 - \frac{y_2 z_3}{6}s^3 - \frac{z_2 y_3}{3}s^3 - \frac{y_2 z_4 + 3(y_3 z_3 + y_4 z_2 + y_2^3 z_2 + y_2 z_2^3)}{24}s^4 \end{pmatrix}. \qquad (3.43)$$

By the term rewriting procedure in Theorem 3, we get the following approximate rational solution:

$$\mathbf{n} = \begin{pmatrix} -t_y + \frac{t_z(t_y h_z - t_z h_y)}{2} \\ 1 - \frac{t_y^2}{2} - \frac{t_y^2(t_y^2 + t_z^2)}{8} \\ -\frac{t_y t_z}{2} - \frac{t_y h_z - t_z h_y}{2} - \frac{t_y t_z(t_y^2 + t_z^2)}{8} \end{pmatrix} + o(s^4). \quad (3.44)$$

Furthermore, by

$$\begin{aligned} t_y &= \mathbf{r}' \cdot \mathbf{n}_0, \\ t_z &= \mathbf{r}' \cdot (\mathbf{x}_1 \times \mathbf{n}_0), \\ t_y^2 + t_z^2 &= 1 - (\mathbf{r}' \cdot \mathbf{x}_1)^2, \\ t_y h_z - t_z h_y &= \det(\mathbf{h}_0, \mathbf{h}_1) = 2\frac{\mathbf{x}_1 \cdot (\mathbf{r}' \times (\mathbf{r} - \mathbf{x}_0))}{\mathbf{x}_1 \cdot (\mathbf{r} - \mathbf{x}_0)}, \end{aligned}$$

(3.44) can be easily changed into a coordinate-free form.

When $k = 6$, the term rewriting procedure ends up with the conclusion that $\mathbf{n}$ cannot be expressed by $\mathbf{h}_0, \mathbf{h}_1$ up to $o(s^5)$. Hence, the highest order of approximation to $\mathbf{n}$ by rational functions in one-step forward chasing is 4.

3.3 Backward-forward chasing with u provided

Let there be three consecutive sampling parameters u_{i-1}, u_i, u_{i+1}. Denote $u = u_{i+1} - u_i$, and introduce ratio $\rho = (u_i - u_{i-1})/u \in Q$. Suppose that u and ρu are both first-order infinitesimals. For simplicity, in this paper we consider only the case $\rho = 1$: the sampling is *locally uniform* at u_i.

Denote $\mathbf{r}_{-1} = \mathbf{r}(u_{i-1})$, $\mathbf{x}_0 = \mathbf{r}(u_i)$, $\mathbf{r} = \mathbf{r}(u_{i+1})$, and for $1 \leq j \leq h$, denote $\mathbf{r}_{-1}^{(j)} = \mathbf{r}^{(j)}(u_{i-1})$, $\mathbf{x}_j = \mathbf{r}^{(j)}(u_i)$, $\mathbf{r}^{(j)} = \mathbf{r}^{(j)}(u_{i+1})$. For any integer j, denote

$$j_+ := 2[\frac{j}{2}], \quad j_- := 2[\frac{j+1}{2}] - 1. \qquad (3.45)$$

They are respectively the biggest even number and odd number that is not bigger than j.

The set $\mathcal{D}$ of given infinitesimals includes u if it is provided, together with the following, for all $0 \leq j \leq h$:

$$(\mathbf{r}^{(j)} - \mathbf{x}_j)_+ := \frac{\mathbf{r}^{(j)} + \mathbf{r}_{-1}^{(j)}}{2} - \mathbf{x}_j = \sum_{p=1}^{[\frac{k-j}{2}]} \mathbf{x}_{j+2p} \frac{u^{2p}}{(2p)!} + o(u^{k-j}),$$

$$(\mathbf{r}^{(j)} - \mathbf{x}_j)_- := \frac{\mathbf{r}^{(j)} - \mathbf{r}_{-1}^{(j)}}{2} = \sum_{p=1}^{[\frac{k-j+1}{2}]} \mathbf{x}_{j+2p-1} \frac{u^{2p-1}}{(2p-1)!} + o(u^{k-j}). \qquad (3.46)$$

The elements in (3.46) can be naturally divided into two subsets. The first subset, denoted by $\mathcal{D}_+$, is composed of

$$\begin{aligned} (\mathbf{r} - \mathbf{x}_0)_+ &= \sum_{i=1}^{[\frac{k}{2}]} \mathbf{x}_{2i} \frac{u^{2i}}{(2i)!} + o(u^k), \\ (\mathbf{r}' - \mathbf{x}_1)_- &= \sum_{i=1}^{[\frac{k}{2}]} \mathbf{x}_{2i} \frac{u^{2i-1}}{(2i-1)!} + o(u^{k-1}), \\ \cdots & \qquad \cdots \\ (\mathbf{r}^{(h_+)} - \mathbf{x}_{h_+})_+ &= \sum_{i=\frac{h_+}{2}+1}^{[\frac{k}{2}]} \mathbf{x}_{2i} \frac{u^{2i-h_+}}{(2i-h_+)!} + o(u^{k-h_+}), \\ (\mathbf{r}^{(h_-)} - \mathbf{x}_{h_-})_- &= \sum_{i=\frac{h_-+1}{2}}^{[\frac{k}{2}]} \mathbf{x}_{2i} \frac{u^{2i-h_-}}{(2i-h_-)!} + o(u^{k-h_-}). \end{aligned}$$
$$(3.47)$$

The second subset, denoted by $\mathcal{D}_-$, is composed of

$$\begin{aligned} (\mathbf{r} - \mathbf{x}_0)_- &= \sum_{i=1}^{[\frac{k+1}{2}]} \mathbf{x}_{2i-1} \frac{u^{2i-1}}{(2i-1)!} + o(u^k), \\ (\mathbf{r}' - \mathbf{x}_1)_+ &= \sum_{i=2}^{[\frac{k+1}{2}]} \mathbf{x}_{2i-1} \frac{u^{2i-2}}{(2i-2)!} + o(u^{k-1}), \\ \cdots & \qquad \cdots \end{aligned}$$

$$\left(\mathbf{r}^{(h_+)} - \mathbf{x}_{h_+}\right)_- = \sum_{i=\frac{h_+}{2}+1}^{\left[\frac{k+1}{2}\right]} \mathbf{x}_{2i-1} \frac{u^{2i-1-h_+}}{(2i-1-h_+)!} + o(u^{k-h_+}),$$

$$\left(\mathbf{r}^{(h_-)} - \mathbf{x}_{h_-}\right)_+ = \sum_{i=\frac{h_-+3}{2}}^{\left[\frac{k+1}{2}\right]} \mathbf{x}_{2i-1} \frac{u^{2i-1-h_-}}{(2i-1-h_-)!} + o(u^{k-h_-}).$$

$$(3.48)$$

When u is provided, denote $a = \left[\frac{k}{2}\right] - \left[\frac{h}{2}\right]$ and $b = k - h_+ - 2$. Write (3.47) as

$$\frac{(\mathbf{r}-\mathbf{x}_0)_+ - \sum_{i=1}^{\left[\frac{h}{2}\right]} \frac{\mathbf{x}_{2i}u^{2i}}{(2i)!}}{u^{h_++2}} = \sum_{i=1}^{a} \frac{\mathbf{x}_{h_++2i}u^{2i-2}}{(h_++2i)!} + o(u^b),$$

$$\frac{(\mathbf{r}'-\mathbf{x}_1)_- - \sum_{i=1}^{\left[\frac{h}{2}\right]} \frac{\mathbf{x}_{2i}u^{2i-1}}{(2i-1)!}}{u^{h_++1}} = \sum_{i=1}^{a} \frac{\mathbf{x}_{h_++2i}u^{2i-2}}{(h_++2i-1)!} + o(u^b),$$

$$\cdots \qquad \cdots$$

$$\frac{(\mathbf{r}^{(h_+)}-\mathbf{x}_{h_+})_+}{u^2} = \sum_{i=1}^{a} \frac{\mathbf{x}_{h_++2i}u^{2i-2}}{(2i)!} + o(u^b),$$

$$\text{(if } h=h_-)\quad \frac{(\mathbf{r}^{(h_-)}-\mathbf{x}_{h_-})_-}{u} = \sum_{i=1}^{a} \frac{\mathbf{x}_{h_++2i}u^{2i-2}}{(2i-1)!} + o(u^b),$$

$$(3.49)$$

and denote the left side by $\mathbf{g}_{(h+1)+}, \ldots, \mathbf{g}_{2+}, \mathbf{g}_{1+}$. The $\mathbf{x}_{h_++2i}$ for $1 \le i \le h+1$ can be solved linearly from (3.49) and written as rational functions in u and the $\mathbf{g}_{i+}$ up to some precisions. The $\hat{\mathbf{h}}_{j,t+}$ are defined just as in Subsection 3.1.

Let $p = \left[\frac{k+1}{2}\right] - \left[\frac{h+1}{2}\right]$, $q = k - h_- - 2$. Write (3.48) as

$$\frac{(\mathbf{r}-\mathbf{x}_0)_- - \sum_{i=1}^{\left[\frac{h+1}{2}\right]} \frac{\mathbf{x}_{2i-1}u^{2i-1}}{(2i-1)!}}{u^{h_-+2}} = \sum_{i=1}^{p} \frac{\mathbf{x}_{h_-+2i}u^{2i-2}}{(h_-+2i)!} + o(u^q),$$

$$\frac{(\mathbf{r}'-\mathbf{x}_1)_+ - \sum_{i=2}^{\left[\frac{h+1}{2}\right]} \frac{\mathbf{x}_{2i-1}u^{2i-2}}{(2i-2)!}}{u^{h_-+1}} = \sum_{i=1}^{p} \frac{\mathbf{x}_{h_-+2i}u^{2i-2}}{(h_-+2i-1)!} + o(u^q),$$

$$\cdots \qquad \cdots$$

$$\frac{(\mathbf{r}^{(h_-)}-\mathbf{x}_{h_-})_+}{u^2} = \sum_{i=1}^{p} \frac{\mathbf{x}_{h_-+2i}u^{2i-2}}{(2i)!} + o(u^q),$$

$$\text{(if } h=h_+)\quad \frac{(\mathbf{r}^{(h_+)}-\mathbf{x}_{h_+})_-}{u} = \sum_{i=1}^{p} \frac{\mathbf{x}_{h_-+2i}u^{2i-2}}{(2i-1)!} + o(u^q).$$

$$(3.50)$$

It is completely independent of (3.49). Denote the left side by $\mathbf{g}_{(h+1)-}, \ldots, \mathbf{g}_{2-}, \mathbf{g}_{1-}$. Solve the $\mathbf{x}_{h_-+2i}$ for $1 \le i \le h+1$ linearly from (3.50), and then obtain the $\hat{\mathbf{h}}_{j,t-}$. The $\hat{\mathbf{h}}_{j,t\pm}$ are then used in term rewriting to convert solution (2.8) to an approximate rational one, or determine the nonexistence.

3.4 Backward-forward chasing with u unknown

When u is unknown, v of (3.23) can be replaced by

$$v_- := (\mathbf{r}-\mathbf{x}_0)_- \cdot \mathbf{x}_1 = u + \frac{x_3}{3!}u^3 + \ldots + \frac{x_{k_-}}{(k_-)!}u^{k_-} + o(u^k).$$

$$(3.51)$$

In coordinate system $\{\mathbf{x}_0; \mathbf{x}_1, \mathbf{e}_2, \mathbf{e}_3\}$, the given $6(h+1)$ infinitesimals (3.46) are divided into 3 subsets:
(i) x-coordinates of the $(\mathbf{r}^{(2i)} - \mathbf{x}_{2i})_-$, $(\mathbf{r}^{(2j-1)} - \mathbf{x}_{2j-1})_+$;
(ii) (y,z)-coordinates of the $(\mathbf{r}^{(2i)} - \mathbf{x}_{2i})_-$, $(\mathbf{r}^{(2j-1)} - \mathbf{x}_{2j-1})_+$;
(iii) all coordinates of the $(\mathbf{r}^{(2i)} - \mathbf{x}_{2i})_+$, $(\mathbf{r}^{(2i-1)} - \mathbf{x}_{2i-1})_-$.

In set (i), the x_{h_-+2i} for $1 \le i \le h$ can be solved by the triangulation procedure in Subsection 3.2. The results are then used to solve the y_{h_-+2j}, z_{h_-+2j} from set (ii), and to

solve the $x_{h_++2j}, y_{h_++2j}, z_{h_++2j}$ from set (iii) by the same triangulation technique, for all $1 \le j \le h+1$. The $\hat{\mathbf{h}}_{j,t\pm}$ are obtained accordingly, and both Theorem 2 and Theorem 3 can be extended to the current case.

Example 2. In solving the RMF equation (1.5), when the unknown smooth curve is sampled uniformly by unknown parameter u, and the tangent vectors at the sampled points are given, then by one-step backward-forward chasing, an approximation rational solution with order of approximation 6 is found. When setting $k = l + 1 = 8$, then solution (3.38) cannot be converted to a rational one up to $o(u^7)$. So 6 is the maximal order of approximation by rational functions.

Numerical experiments on Matlab 7.0 are made to over 20 parametric curves with different sampling intervals u, e.g.,

$$A = \text{ curve of curvature and torsion both being } \tfrac{u}{1+u^2};$$
$$B = (u \sin u, u \cos u, ue^u).$$

Three approximate formulas with theoretical order of approximation $q = 4, 4, 6$ are compared in Table 1, the first being Wang's method [5], and the other two being formulas obtained from Examples 1 and 2 via Maple-13 coding of the triangulation and term rewriting procedures in this section.

Table 1: Errors by 3 RMF-computing formulas.

Curve	step-size	Wang [5]	Example 1	Example 2
A	2^{-4}	1.2331E-10	1.2331E-10	5.4171E-12
A	2^{-5}	1.9369E-12	1.9369E-12	2.1285E-14
A	2^{-6}	3.0303E-14	3.0303E-14	8.3268E-17
B	10^{-2}	5.8622E-12	1.1100E-09	7.8793E-14
B	10^{-3}	5.8896E-17	1.0987E-14	7.9147E-21
B	10^{-4}	5.8923E-22	1.0976E-19	7.9182E-28

The Taylor remainder estimate $O(u^{q+1})$ is not supported by the data at the first glance. However, When $u = a^{-p}$ tends to zero, the ratio $e(a^{-(p+1)})/e(a^{-p})$ of actual errors is about $a^{-(q+1)}$, firmly supporting the $O(u^{q+1})$ error bound:

Curve	step-size	Wang [5]	Example 1	Example 2
A	2^{-5}	0.0157	0.0157	0.0039
A	2^{-6}	0.0156	0.0156	0.0039
B	10^{-3}	1.0047E-5	9.8980E-6	1.0045E-7
B	10^{-4}	1.0005E-5	9.9897E-6	1.0004E-7

4. REFERENCES

[1] Y. Chang, G. Corliss. ATOMFT: solving ODEs and DAEs using Taylor series. *Comput. Math. Appl.* **28**: 209-233, 1994.

[2] R. Feng, X. Gao. A polynomial time algorithm for finding rational general solutions of first-order autonomous ODEs. *J. Symb. Comput.* **41**(7): 739–762, 2006.

[3] N. Shawagfeh, D. Kaya. Comparing numerical methods for the solutions of systems of ODEs. *Appl. Math. Letters* **17**: 323–328, 2004.

[4] P. Kim and P.J. Olver. Geometric integration via multi-space. *Regular and Chaotic Dynamics* **9** (2004) 213-226.

[5] W. Wang, B. Jütter, D. Zheng, Y. Liu. Computation of rotation minimizing frames. *ACM Trans. Graphics* **27**, 2008.

This paper is upported partially by NKBRSF 2011CB302404, NSFC 10871195, 10925105, 60821002, 50875027.

Sparse Differential Resultant*

Wei Li, Xiao-Shan Gao, Chun-Ming Yuan

KLMM, Institute of Systems Science, AMSS, Chinese Academy of Sciences, Beijing 100190, China

{liwei,xgao,cmyuan}@mmrc.iss.ac.cn

ABSTRACT

In this paper, the concept of sparse differential resultant for a differentially essential system of differential polynomials is introduced and its properties are proved. In particular, a degree bound for the sparse differential resultant is given. Based on the degree bound, an algorithm to compute the sparse differential resultant is proposed, which is single exponential in terms of the order, the number of variables, and the size of the differentially essential system.

Categories and Subject Descriptors

I.1.2 [**Computing Methodologies**]: Symbolic and Algebraic Manipulation - Algorithms for differential equations

General Terms

Algorithms, Theory

Keywords

Sparse differential resultant, differentially essential system, Chow form, degree bound, single exponential algorithm.

1. INTRODUCTION

The resultant, which gives conditions for a system of polynomial equations to have common solutions, is a basic concept in algebraic geometry and a powerful tool in elimination theory [2, 8, 16, 6, 19, 9, 24, 28]. The sparse resultant was introduced by Gelfand, Kapranov, and Zelevinsky as a generalization of the usual resultant [13]. Basic properties for the sparse resultant were given by Sturmfels and co-authors [23, 28, 29]. A Sylvester style matrix based method to compute sparse resultants was first given by Canny and Emiris [3, 10]. A determinant representation for the sparse resultant was given by D'Andrea [7].

* Partially supported by a National Key Basic Research Project of China (2011CB302400) and by a grant from NSFC (60821002).

The differential resultant for two nonlinear differential polynomials in one variable was studied by Ritt in [25, p.47]. General differential resultants were defined by Carrà Ferro using Macaulay's definition of algebraic resultants [4]. But, the treatment in [4] is not complete. For instance, the differential resultant for two generic differential polynomials with degrees greater than one is always zero if using the definition in [4]. Differential resultants for linear ordinary differential polynomials were studied by Rueda and Sendra in [27]. In [12], a rigorous definition for the differential resultant of $n+1$ generic differential polynomials in n variables was presented.

A generic differential polynomial with order o and degree d contains an exponential number of differential monomials in terms of o and d. Since most of the differential polynomials encountered in practice do not contain all of these monomials, it is useful to define the sparse differential resultant which can be considered as the differential analog for the algebraic sparse resultant [7, 10, 13, 28].

In this paper, the concept of sparse differential resultant for a differentially essential system consisting of $n + 1$ differential polynomials in n differential variables is introduced and its properties similar to that of the Sylvester resultant are proved. In particular, we give a degree bound for the sparse differential resultant, which also leads to a degree bound for the differential resultant. Based on the degree bound, we give an algorithm to compute the sparse differential resultant. The complexity of the algorithm in the worst case is single exponential of the form $O(n^{3.376}(s+1)^{O(n)}(m+1)^{O(ns^2l)})$, where s, m, n, and l are the order, the degree, the number of variables, and the size of the differentially essential system respectively. The sparseness is reflected in the quantity l.

In principle, the sparse differential resultant can be computed with any differential elimination method, and in particular with the change of order algorithms given by Boulier-Lemaire-Maza [1] and Golubitsky-Kondratieva-Ovchinnikov [14]. The differentially essential system already forms a triangular set when considering their constant coefficients as leading variables, and the sparse differential resultant is the first element of the characteristic set of the prime ideal generated by the differentially essential system under a different special ranking. Therefore, the change of order strategy proposed in [1, 14] can be used. In our case, due to the special structure of the differentially essential system, we can give specific bounds for the order and degree needed to compute the resultant, which allows us to reduce the problem to linear algebra directly and give explicit complexity bounds.

As preparations for the main results of the paper, we prove

several properties about the degrees of the elimination ideal and the generalized Chow form in the algebraic case, which are also interesting themselves.

The rest of the paper is organized as follows. In Section 2, we prove some preliminary results. In Section 3, we define the sparse differential resultant and give its properties. And in Section 4, we present an algorithm to compute the sparse differential resultant. In Section 5, we conclude the paper by proposing several problems for future research.

2. DEGREE OF ELIMINATION IDEAL AND GENERALIZED CHOW FORM

In this section, we will prove several properties about the degrees of elimination ideals and generalized Chow forms in the algebraic case, which will be used later in the paper. These properties are also interesting themselves.

2.1 Degree of elimination ideal

Let P be a polynomial in $K[\mathbb{X}]$ where $\mathbb{X} = \{x_1, \ldots, x_n\}$. We use $\deg(P)$ to denote the total degree of P. Let $\mathcal{I}$ be a prime algebraic ideal in $K[\mathbb{X}]$ with dimension d. We use $\deg(\mathcal{I})$ to denote the *degree* of $\mathcal{I}$, which is defined to be the number of solutions of the zero dimensional prime ideal $(\mathcal{I}, \mathbb{L}_1, \ldots, \mathbb{L}_d)$, where $\mathbb{L}_i = u_{i0} + \sum_{j=1}^{n} u_{ij} x_j$ $(i = 1, \ldots, d)$ are d generic primes [17]. That is,

$$\deg(\mathcal{I}) = |\mathbb{V}(\mathcal{I}, \mathbb{L}_1, \ldots, \mathbb{L}_d)|. \qquad (1)$$

Clearly, $\deg(\mathcal{I}) = \deg(\mathcal{I}, \mathbb{L}_1, \ldots, \mathbb{L}_i)$ for $i = 1, \ldots, d$. $\deg(\mathcal{I})$ is also equal to the maximal number of intersection points of $\mathbb{V}(\mathcal{I})$ with d hyperplanes under the condition that the number of these points is finite [18]. That is,

$$\deg(\mathcal{I}) = \max\{|\mathbb{V}(\mathcal{I}) \cap H_1 \cap \cdots \cap H_d| : H_i \text{ are affine}$$
$$\text{hyperplanes with } |\mathbb{V}(\mathcal{I}) \cap H_1 \cap \cdots \cap H_d| < \infty\} \qquad (2)$$

The relation between the degree of an ideal and that of its elimination ideal is give by the following result.

Theorem 2.1 *Let $\mathcal{I}$ be a prime ideal in $K[\mathbb{X}]$ and $\mathcal{I}_k = \mathcal{I} \cap K[x_1, \ldots, x_k]$ for any $1 \le k \le n$. Then $\deg(\mathcal{I}_k) \le \deg(\mathcal{I})$.*

Proof: Suppose $\dim(\mathcal{I}) = d$ and $\dim(\mathcal{I}_k) = d_1$. Two cases are considered:

Case (a): $d_1 = d$. Let $\mathbb{P}_i = u_{i0} + u_{i1}x_1 + \cdots + u_{ik}x_k$ $(i = 1, \ldots, d)$. Denote $\mathbf{u} = \{u_{ij} : i = 1, \ldots, d; j = 0, \ldots, k\}$. Then by [17, Theorem 1, p. 54], $\mathcal{J} = (\mathcal{I}_k, \mathbb{P}_1, \ldots, \mathbb{P}_d)$ is a prime ideal of dimension zero in $K(\mathbf{u})[x_1, \ldots, x_k]$ and has the same degree as $\mathcal{I}_k$. We claim that

1) $(\mathcal{I}, \mathbb{P}_1, \ldots, \mathbb{P}_d) \cap K(\mathbf{u})[x_1, \ldots, x_k] = \mathcal{J}$.

2) $(\mathcal{I}, \mathbb{P}_1, \ldots, \mathbb{P}_d)$ is a 0-dimensional prime ideal.

To prove 1), it suffices to show that whenever f is in the left ideal, f belongs to $\mathcal{J}$. Without loss of generality, suppose $f \in K[\mathbf{u}][x_1, \ldots, x_k]$. Then there exist $h_l, q_i \in K[\mathbf{u}][\mathbb{X}]$ and $g_l \in \mathcal{I}$ such that $f = \sum_l h_l g_l + \sum_{i=1}^{d} q_i \mathbb{P}_i$. Substituting $u_{i0} = -\sum_{j=1}^{k} u_{ik} x_k$ into the above equality, we get $\bar{f} = \sum_l \bar{h}_l g_l \in \mathcal{I}_k$ and $f \equiv \bar{f} \bmod(\mathbb{P}_1, \ldots, \mathbb{P}_d)$. So, $f \in \mathcal{J}$.

To prove 2), suppose $(\xi_1, \ldots, \xi_n)$ is a generic point of $\mathcal{I}$. Denote $U_0 = \{u_{10}, \ldots, u_{d0}\}$. Then $\mathcal{J}_0 = (\mathcal{I}, \mathbb{P}_1, \ldots, \mathbb{P}_d) \subseteq K(\mathbf{u}\backslash U_0)[\mathbb{X}, U_0]$ is a prime ideal of dimension d with a generic point $(\xi_1, \ldots, \xi_n, -\sum_{j=1}^{k} u_{1j}\xi_j, \ldots, -\sum_{j=1}^{k} u_{dj}\xi_j)$. Since

$d_1 = d$, there exist d elements in $\{\xi_1, \ldots, \xi_k\}$ algebraically independent over K. So by [16, p.168-169], $\mathcal{J}_0 \cap K(\mathbf{u}\backslash U_0)[U_0] = (0)$ and 2) follows.

Since $\mathcal{J}$ and $(\mathcal{I}, \mathbb{P}_1, \ldots; \mathbb{P}_d)$ are zero dimensional ideals, by [30, Proposition 9, p.7], $\deg(\mathcal{J}) \le \deg(\mathcal{I}, \mathbb{P}_1, \ldots, \mathbb{P}_d)$. So by (2), $\deg(\mathcal{I}) \ge |\mathbb{V}(\mathcal{I}, \mathbb{P}_1, \ldots, \mathbb{P}_d)| \ge \deg(\mathcal{J}) = \deg(\mathcal{I}_k)$.

Case (b): $d_1 < d$. Let $\mathbb{L}_i = u_{i0} + u_{i1}x_1 + \cdots + u_{in}x_n$ $(i = 1, \ldots, d - d_1)$. By [17, Theorem 1, p. 54], $\mathcal{J} = (\mathcal{I}, \mathbb{L}_1, \ldots, \mathbb{L}_{d-d_1}) \subseteq K(\mathbf{u})[\mathbb{X}]$ is a prime ideal of dimension d_1 and $\deg(\mathcal{J}) = \deg(\mathcal{I})$, where $\mathbf{u} = \{u_{ij} : i = 1, \ldots, d - d_1; j = 0, \ldots, n\}$. Let $\mathcal{J}_k = \mathcal{J} \cap K(\mathbf{u})[x_1, \ldots, x_k]$. We claim that $\mathcal{J}_k = (\mathcal{I}_k)$ in $K(\mathbf{u})[x_1, \ldots, x_k]$. Of course, $\mathcal{J}_k \supseteq (\mathcal{I}_k)$. Since both $\mathcal{J}_k$ and $(\mathcal{I}_k)$ are prime ideals and $\dim((\mathcal{I}_k)) = d_1$, it suffices to prove that $\dim(\mathcal{J}_k) = d_1$.

Let $\mathcal{J}_0 = (\mathcal{I}, \mathbb{L}_1, \ldots, \mathbb{L}_{d-d_1}) \subseteq K(\mathbf{u}\backslash U_0)[\mathbb{X}, U_0]$ with $U_0 = \{u_{10}, \ldots, u_{d-d_1, 0}\}$. Suppose $\{x_1, \ldots, x_{d_1}\}$ is a parametric set of $\mathcal{I}_k$. Similarly to the procedure of proving 2) in case (a), we can show that $\mathcal{J}_0 \cap K(\mathbf{u}\backslash U_0)[x_1, \ldots, x_{d_1}, U_0] = (0)$, and $\mathcal{J}_k \cap K(\mathbf{u})[x_1, \ldots, x_{d_1}] = (0)$ follows. So $\dim(\mathcal{J}_k) = d_1$.

Since $\dim(\mathcal{J}_k) = \dim(\mathcal{J})$, by case (a), we have $\deg(\mathcal{J}_k) \le \deg(\mathcal{J}) = \deg(\mathcal{I})$. And due to the fact that $\deg(\mathcal{J}_k) = \deg((\mathcal{I}_k)) = \deg(\mathcal{I}_k)$, $\deg(\mathcal{I}_k) \le \deg(\mathcal{I})$ follows. $\square$

In this article, we will use the following result.

Lemma 2.2 *[22, Proposition 1] Let $F_1, \ldots, F_m \in K[\mathbb{X}]$ be polynomials generating an ideal $\mathcal{I}$ of dimension r. Suppose $\deg(F_1) \ge \cdots \ge \deg(F_m)$ and let $D := \prod_{i=1}^{n-r} \deg(F_i)$. Then $\deg(\mathcal{I}) \le D$.*

2.2 Degree of algebraic generalized Chow form

Let $\mathcal{I}$ be a prime ideal in $K[\mathbb{X}]$ with dimension d,

$$\mathbb{P}_i = u_{i0} + \sum_{1 \le \alpha_1 + \cdots + \alpha_n \le m_i} u_{i, \alpha_1 \ldots \alpha_n} x_1^{\alpha_1} \cdots x_n^{\alpha_n} \ (i = 0, \ldots, d)$$

generic polynomials of degree m_i, and $\mathbf{u}_i$ the vector of coefficients of $\mathbb{P}_i$. Philippon [24] proved that

$$(\mathcal{I}, \mathbb{P}_0, \ldots, \mathbb{P}_d) \cap K[\mathbf{u}_0, \ldots, \mathbf{u}_d] = (G(\mathbf{u}_0, \ldots, \mathbf{u}_d)) \qquad (3)$$

is a prime principal ideal and $G(\mathbf{u}_0, \ldots, \mathbf{u}_d)$ is defined to be the *generalized Chow form* of $\mathcal{I}$, denoted by $G(\mathcal{I})$.

In this section, we will give the degree of the generalized Chow form in terms of the degrees of $\mathcal{I}$ and that of $\mathbb{P}_i$ by proving Theorem 2.4.

At first, we will give another description of the degree for a prime ideal. In (3), when $\mathbb{P}_i$ become generic primes

$$\mathbb{L}_i = v_{i0} + \sum_{j=1}^{n} v_{ij} x_j (i = 0, 1, \ldots, d),$$

the generalized Chow form becomes the usual *Chow form*, denoted by $\text{Chow}(\mathcal{I})$. That is

$$(\mathcal{I}, \mathbb{L}_0, \ldots, \mathbb{L}_d) \cap K[\mathbf{v}_0, \ldots, \mathbf{v}_d] = (\text{Chow}(\mathcal{I})) \qquad (4)$$

where $\mathbf{v}_i$ is the set of coefficients of $\mathbb{L}_i$. A basic property of Chow forms is that [17] for each i between 0 and d,

$$\deg(\mathcal{I}) = \deg_{\mathbf{v}_i} \text{Chow}(\mathcal{I}). \qquad (5)$$

In the following lemma, we will give the degree of an ideal intersected by a generic primal. To prove the lemma, we apply the following Bezout inequality (see [15] or [18]): Let V, W be affine algebraic varieties. Then

$$\deg(V \cap W) \le \deg(V) \cdot \deg(W). \qquad (6)$$

Lemma 2.3 *Let $\mathcal{I}$ be a prime ideal in $K[\mathbb{X}]$ with $\dim(\mathcal{I}) = d > 0$ and P a generic polynomial. Then $\deg(\mathcal{I}, P) = \deg(P) \cdot \deg(\mathcal{I})$.*

Proof: Firstly, we prove the lemma holds for $d = 1$. Let $\mathbf{v}$ be the vector of coefficients of P, $m = \deg(P)$, and $\mathcal{J} = (\mathcal{I}, P) \subset K(\mathbf{v})[\mathbb{X}]$. Then by [17, p. 110], $\mathcal{J}$ is a prime algebraic ideal of dimension zero. Let $\mathbb{L}_0$ be a generic prime with $\mathbf{u}_0$ the vector of coefficients. By (4), $(\mathcal{J}, \mathbb{L}_0) \cap K(\mathbf{v})[\mathbf{u}_0] = (\text{Chow}(\mathcal{J}))$. Here, we choose $\text{Chow}(\mathcal{J})$ to be an irreducible polynomial in $K[\mathbf{v}, \mathbf{u}_0]$. From (5), we have $\deg(\mathcal{J}) = \deg_{\mathbf{u}_0} \text{Chow}(\mathcal{J})$.

Let $\mathcal{M} = (\mathcal{I}, \mathbb{L}_0) \subset K(\mathbf{u}_0)[\mathbb{X}]$. Then $\mathcal{M}$ is a prime ideal of dimension zero with $\deg(\mathcal{M}) = \deg(\mathcal{I})$. And $(\mathcal{M}, P) \cap K(\mathbf{u}_0)[\mathbf{v}] = (G(\mathcal{M}))$ where $G(\mathcal{M}) \in K[\mathbf{v}, \mathbf{u}_0]$ is irreducible. Clearly, $G(\mathcal{M}) = c \cdot \text{Chow}(\mathcal{J})$ for some $c \in K^*$ and $G(\mathcal{M})$ can be factored as

$$G(\mathcal{M}) = A(\mathbf{u}_0) \prod_{\tau=1}^{\deg(\mathcal{I})} P(\xi_\tau),$$

where ξ_τ are all the elements of $\mathbb{V}(\mathcal{M})$ and $A(\mathbf{u}_0)$ is an extraneous factor lying in $K[\mathbf{u}_0]$. Now, specialize P to $\mathbb{L}_1^m$ where $\mathbb{L}_1 = u_{10} + \sum_{i=1}^n u_{1i} x_i$ is a generic prime. Then we have $\overline{G(\mathcal{M})} = A(\mathbf{u}_0) \prod_{\tau=1}^{\deg(\mathcal{I})} \mathbb{L}_1^m(\xi_\tau)$ and $\deg(\overline{G(\mathcal{M})}, \mathbf{u}_0) = \deg(\mathcal{J})$. Since $\text{Chow}(\mathcal{I}) = B(\mathbf{u}_0) \prod_{\tau=1}^{\deg(\mathcal{I})} \mathbb{L}_1(\xi_\tau)$ for some $B \in K[\mathbf{u}_0]$ is irreducible and $\overline{G(\mathcal{M})} \in K[\mathbf{u}_0, \mathbf{u}_1]$, there exists $g \in K[\mathbf{u}_0]^*$ such that $\overline{G(\mathcal{M})} = g \cdot (\text{Chow}(\mathcal{I}))^m$. So, $\deg(\overline{G(\mathcal{M})}, \mathbf{u}_0) \geq m \cdot \deg(\text{Chow}(\mathcal{I}), \mathbf{u}_0) = m \cdot \deg(\mathcal{I})$. And by Bézout inequality (6), $\deg(\mathcal{I}, P) \leq \deg(\mathcal{I}) \cdot \deg(P)$, so $\deg(\mathcal{I}, P) = \deg(\mathcal{I}) \cdot \deg(P)$.

For the case $d > 1$, let $\mathbb{L}_1, \ldots, \mathbb{L}_{d-1}$ be generic primes, then $\mathcal{I}_1 = (\mathcal{I}, \mathbb{L}_1, \ldots, \mathbb{L}_{d-1})$ is a prime ideal of dimension one and $\deg(\mathcal{I}_1) = \deg(\mathcal{I})$. By the case $d = 1$, $\deg(\mathcal{I}_1, P) = \deg(\mathcal{I}_1) \cdot \deg(P)$. So $\deg(\mathcal{I}, P) = \deg(\mathcal{I}, P, \mathbb{L}_1, \ldots, \mathbb{L}_{d-1}) = \deg(\mathcal{I}_1, P) = \deg(\mathcal{I}_1) \cdot \deg(P) = \deg(\mathcal{I}) \cdot \deg(P)$. $\square$

The following result generalizes Lemma 1.8 in [24].

Theorem 2.4 *Let $G(\mathbf{u}_0, \ldots, \mathbf{u}_d)$ be the generalized Chow form of a prime ideal $\mathcal{I}$ of dimension d w.r.t. $\mathbb{P}_0, \ldots, \mathbb{P}_d$. Then G is of degree $\deg(\mathcal{I}) \prod_{j \neq i} \deg(\mathbb{P}_j)$ in each set $\mathbf{u}_i$.*

Proof: It suffices to prove the result for $i = 0$.

If $d = 0$, then $G(\mathbf{u}_0) = \prod_{\tau=1}^{\deg(\mathcal{I})} \mathbb{P}_0(\xi_\tau)$, where $\xi_\tau \in \mathbb{V}(\mathcal{I})$. Clearly, $\deg(G, \mathbf{u}_0) = \deg(\mathcal{I})$.

We consider the case $d > 0$. Let $\mathcal{J}_0 = (\mathcal{I}, \mathbb{P}_1, \ldots, \mathbb{P}_d) \subset K[\mathbf{u}_1, \ldots, \mathbf{u}_d, \mathbb{X}]$ and $\mathcal{J} = (\mathcal{J}_0) \subset K(\mathbf{u}_1, \ldots, \mathbf{u}_d)[x_1, \ldots, x_n]$. Then $\mathcal{J}$ is a prime ideal of dimension zero and by Lemma 2.3, $\deg(\mathcal{J}) = \deg(\mathcal{I}) \prod_{i=1}^d \deg(\mathbb{P}_i)$. We claim that $G(\mathbf{u}_0, \ldots, \mathbf{u}_d)$ is also the generalized Chow form of $\mathcal{J}$, hence $\deg(G, \mathbf{u}_0) = \deg(\mathcal{J}) = \deg(\mathcal{I}) \prod_{i=1}^d \deg(\mathbb{P}_i)$. Since $G(\mathbf{u}_0, \ldots, \mathbf{u}_d)$ is the generalized Chow form of $\mathcal{I}$, we have $(\mathcal{I}, \mathbb{P}_0, \ldots, \mathbb{P}_d) \cap K[\mathbf{u}_0, \ldots, \mathbf{u}_d] = (G(\mathbf{u}_0, \ldots, \mathbf{u}_d)) = (\mathcal{J}_0, \mathbb{P}_0) \cap K[\mathbf{u}_0, \ldots, \mathbf{u}_d]$. Let $G_1(\mathbf{u}_0, \ldots, \mathbf{u}_d) \in K[\mathbf{u}_0, \ldots, \mathbf{u}_d]$ be the generalized Chow form of $\mathcal{J}$ and irreducible. Then $(\mathcal{J}, \mathbb{P}_0) \cap K(\mathbf{u}_1, \ldots, \mathbf{u}_d)[\mathbf{u}_0] = (G_1)$. So $G \in (G_1)$. But G, G_1 are irreducible polynomials in $K[\mathbf{u}_0, \ldots, \mathbf{u}_d]$, so $G = c \cdot G_1$ for some $c \in K^*$ and G is the generalized Chow form of $\mathcal{J}$. $\square$

3. SPARSE DIFFERENTIAL RESULTANT

In this section, we define the sparse differential resultant and prove its basic properties.

3.1 Definition of sparse differential resultant

Let $\mathcal{F}$ be an ordinary differential field and $\mathcal{F}\{\mathbb{Y}\}$ the ring of differential polynomials in the differential indeterminates $\mathbb{Y} = \{y_1, \ldots, y_n\}$. For any element $e \in \mathcal{F}\{\mathbb{Y}\}$, we use $e^{(k)} = \delta^k e$ to represent the k-th derivative of e and $e^{[k]}$ to denote the set $\{e^{(i)} : i = 0, \ldots, k\}$. Details about differential algebra can be found in [20, 26].

The following theorem presents an important property on differential specialization, which will be used later.

Theorem 3.1 *[12, Theorem 2.14] Let $\{u_1, \ldots, u_r\}$ be a set of differential indeterminates, and $P_i(\mathbb{U}, \mathbb{Y}) \in \mathcal{F}\{\mathbb{U}, \mathbb{Y}\}$ $(i = 1, \ldots, m)$ differential polynomials in the differential indeterminates $\mathbb{U} = (u_1, \ldots, u_r)$ and $\mathbb{Y} = (y_1, \ldots, y_n)$. Let $\mathbb{Y}^0 = (y_1^0, y_2^0, \ldots, y_n^0)$, where y_i^0 are in some differential extension field of $\mathcal{F}$. If $P_i(\mathbb{U}, \mathbb{Y}^0)$ $(i = 1, \ldots, m)$ are differentially dependent over $\mathcal{F}\langle \mathbb{U} \rangle$, then for any specialization $\mathbb{U}$ to $\mathbb{U}^0$ in $\mathcal{F}$, $P_i(\mathbb{U}^0, \mathbb{Y}^0)$ $(i = 1, \ldots, m)$ are differentially dependent over $\mathcal{F}$.*

To define the sparse differential resultant, consider $n + 1$ differential polynomials with differential indeterminates as coefficients

$$\mathbb{P}_i = u_{i0} + \sum_{k=1}^{l_i} u_{ik} M_{ik} \ (i = 0, \ldots, n) \qquad (7)$$

where $M_{ik} = (\mathbb{Y}^{[s_i]})^{\alpha_{ik}}$ is a monomial in $\{y_1, \ldots, y_n, \ldots, y_1^{(s_i)}, \ldots, y_n^{(s_i)}\}$ with exponent vector α_{ik} and $|\alpha_{ik}| \geq 1$. The set of exponent vectors $\mathbb{S}_i = \{\bar{0}, \alpha_{ik} : k = 1, \ldots, l_i\}$ is called the *support* of $\mathbb{P}_i$, where $\bar{0}$ is the exponent vector for the constant term. The number $|\mathbb{S}_i| = l_i + 1$ is called the *size* of $\mathbb{P}_i$. Note that s_i is the order of $\mathbb{P}_i$ and an exponent vector of $\mathbb{P}_i$ contains $n(s_i + 1)$ elements.

Denote $\mathbf{u} = \{u_{ik} : i = 0, \ldots, n; k = 1, \ldots, l_i\}$. Let $\eta_1, \ldots, \eta_n$ be n elements which are differentially independent over $\mathbb{Q}\langle \mathbf{u} \rangle$ and denote $\eta = (\eta_1, \ldots, \eta_n)$, where $\mathbb{Q}$ is the field of rational numbers. Let

$$\zeta_i = -\sum_{k=1}^{l_i} u_{ik}(\eta^{[s_i]})^{\alpha_{ik}} \ (i = 0, \ldots, n). \qquad (8)$$

Denote the differential transcendence degree by d.tr.deg. Then, we have

Lemma 3.2 *d.tr.deg $\mathbb{Q}\langle \mathbf{u} \rangle \langle \zeta_0, \ldots, \zeta_n \rangle / \mathbb{Q}\langle \mathbf{u} \rangle = n$ if and only if there exist n monomials $M_{r_i k_i}$ $(i = 1, \ldots, n)$ in (7) such that $r_i \neq r_j$ for $i \neq j$ and $M_{r_i k_i}(\eta) = (\eta^{[s_{r_i}]})^{\alpha_{r_i k_i}}$ are differentially independent over $\mathbb{Q}\langle \mathbf{u} \rangle$.*

Proof: " $\Leftarrow$ " Without loss of generality, we assume $r_i = i$ $(i = 1, \ldots, n)$ and $M_{i k_i}(\eta)$ $(i = 1, \ldots, n)$ are differentially independent. It suffices to prove that $\zeta_1, \ldots, \zeta_n$ are differentially independent over $\mathbb{Q}\langle \mathbf{u} \rangle$. Suppose the contrary, i.e. $\zeta_1, \ldots, \zeta_n$ are differentially dependent. Now specialize u_{ij} to $-\delta_{ik_i}$. By Theorem 3.1 and (8), $M_{ik_i}(\eta)$ $(i = 1, \ldots, n)$ are differentially dependent, which is a contradiction.

" $\Rightarrow$ " Suppose the contrary, i.e., $M_{r_i k_i}(\eta)$ $(i = 1, \ldots, n)$ are differentially dependent for any n different r_i and $k_i = 1, \ldots, l_{r_i}$. Since each ζ_{r_i} is a linear combination of $M_{r_i k_i}(\eta)$ $(k_i = 1, \ldots, l_{r_i})$, $\zeta_{r_1}, \ldots, \zeta_{r_n}$ are differentially dependent, contradicting that d.tr.deg $\mathbb{Q}\langle \mathbf{u} \rangle \langle \zeta_0, \ldots, \zeta_n \rangle / \mathbb{Q}\langle \mathbf{u} \rangle = n$. $\square$

Definition 3.3 *A set of differential polynomials of form (7) satisfying the condition in Lemma 3.2 is called a differentially essential system.*

A differential polynomial f of form (7) is called *quasi-generic* [12] if for each $1 \le i \le n$, f contains at least one monomial in $\mathcal{F}\{y_i\} \setminus \mathcal{F}$. Clearly, $n+1$ quasi-generic differential polynomials form a differentially essential system.

Now let $[\mathbb{P}_0, \ldots, \mathbb{P}_n]$ be the differential ideal generated by $\mathbb{P}_i$ in $\mathbb{Q}\langle \mathbf{u} \rangle \{\mathbb{Y}, u_{00}, \ldots, u_{n0}\}$. Then it is a prime differential ideal with a generic point $(\eta_1, \ldots, \eta_n, \zeta_0, \ldots, \zeta_n)$ and of dimension n. Clearly, $\mathcal{I} = [\mathbb{P}_0, \ldots, \mathbb{P}_n] \cap \mathbb{Q}\langle \mathbf{u} \rangle \{u_{00}, \ldots, u_{n0}\}$ is a prime differential ideal with a generic point $(\zeta_0, \ldots, \zeta_n)$. As a consequence of Lemma 3.2, we have

Corollary 3.4 *$\mathcal{I}$ is of codimension one if and only if $\{\mathbb{P}_0, \ldots, \mathbb{P}_n\}$ is a differentially essential system.*

Now suppose $\{\mathbb{P}_0, \ldots, \mathbb{P}_n\}$ is a differentially essential system. Since $\mathcal{I}$ is of codimension one, then by [26, line 14, p. 45], there exists an irreducible differential polynomial $R(\mathbf{u}; u_{00}, \ldots, u_{n0}) \in \mathbb{Q}\langle \mathbf{u} \rangle \{u_{00}, \ldots, u_{n0}\}$ such that

$$[\mathbb{P}_0, \ldots, \mathbb{P}_n] \cap \mathbb{Q}\langle \mathbf{u} \rangle \{u_{00}, \ldots, u_{n0}\} = \mathrm{sat}(R) \qquad (9)$$

where $\mathrm{sat}(R)$ is the saturation ideal of R. More explicitly, $\mathrm{sat}(R)$ is the whole set of differential polynomials having zero pseudo-remainders w.r.t. R under any ranking endowed on $u_{00}, \ldots, u_{n0}$. And by clearing denominators when necessary, we suppose $R \in \mathbb{Q}\{\mathbf{u}; u_{00}, \ldots, u_{n0}\}$ is irreducible and also denoted by $R(\mathbf{u}; u_{00}, \ldots, u_{n0})$. Let $\mathbf{u}_i = (u_{i0}, u_{i1}, \ldots, u_{il_i})$ be the vector of coefficients of $\mathbb{P}_i$ and denote $R(\mathbf{u}_0, \ldots, \mathbf{u}_n) = R(\mathbf{u}; u_{00}, \ldots, u_{n0})$. Now we give the definition of sparse differential resultant as follows:

Definition 3.5 *$R(\mathbf{u}_0, \ldots, \mathbf{u}_n) \in \mathbb{Q}\{\mathbf{u}_0, \ldots, \mathbf{u}_n\}$ in (9) is defined to be the sparse differential resultant of the differentially essential system $\mathbb{P}_0, \ldots, \mathbb{P}_n$.*

Example 3.6 *For $n = 2$, let $\mathbb{P}_0 = u_{00} + u_{01}y_1y_2$, $\mathbb{P}_1 = u_{10} + u_{01}y_1'y_2'$, and $\mathbb{P}_2 = u_{20} + u_{21}y_1'y_2$. Using differential elimination algorithms [5], we can show that $\mathbb{P}_1, \mathbb{P}_2, \mathbb{P}_3$ form a differentially essential system and their sparse differential resultant is $R = -u_{11}u_{20}^2u_{01}^2 - u_{01}u_{00}u_{21}^2u_{10} + u_{01}u_{11}u_{20}u_{21}u_{00}' - u_{11}u_{20}u_{00}u_{21}u_{01}'$.*

The following properties can be proved easily.

1. When all $\mathbb{P}_i$ become generic differential polynomials of the form $\mathbb{P}_i = u_{i0} + \sum_{1 \le |\alpha| \le m_i} u_{i,\alpha}(\mathbb{Y}^{[s_i]})^\alpha$, the sparse differential resultant is the differential resultant defined in [12].

2. R is the vanishing polynomial of $(\zeta_0, \ldots, \zeta_n)$ with minimal order in each u_{i0}. Since $R \in \mathbb{Q}\{\mathbf{u}; u_{00}, \ldots, u_{n0}\}$ is irreducible, $\mathrm{ord}(R, \mathbf{u}_i) = \mathrm{ord}(R, u_{i0})$.

3. Suppose $\mathrm{ord}(R, \mathbf{u}_i) = h_i \ge 0$ and denote $o = \sum_{i=0}^n h_i$. Given a vector $(q_0, \ldots, q_n) \in \mathbb{N}^{n+1}$ with $\sum_{i=0}^n q_i = q$, if $q < o$, then there is no polynomial P in $\mathrm{sat}(R)$ with $\mathrm{ord}(P, \mathbf{u}_i) = q_i$. And R is the unique irreducible polynomial in $\mathrm{sat}(R)$ with total order $q = o$ up to some $a \in \mathbb{Q}$. This property will be used in our algorithm to search for the sparse differential resultant.

Remark 3.7 *It is not easy to define the sparse differential resultant as the algebraic sparse resultant of $\mathbb{P}_i^{(k)}$ considered as polynomials in $y_i^{(j)}$. The reason is that it is difficult to check whether the supports of $\mathbb{P}_i$ and $\mathbb{P}_i^{(k)}$ satisfy the conditions for the existence of the algebraic sparse resultant [29]. Furthermore, the coefficients of $\mathbb{P}_i^{(k)}$ are not generic.*

3.2 Properties of sparse differential resultant

Following Kolchin [21], we introduce the concept of differentially homogenous polynomials.

Definition 3.8 *A differential polynomial $p \in \mathcal{F}\{y_0, \ldots, y_n\}$ is called differentially homogenous of degree m if for a new differential indeterminate λ, we have $p(\lambda y_0, \lambda y_1 \ldots, \lambda y_n) = \lambda^m p(y_0, y_1, \ldots, y_n)$.*

The differential analog of Euler's theorem related to homogenous polynomials is valid.

Theorem 3.9 *[21]* *$f \in \mathcal{F}\{y_0, y_1, \ldots, y_n\}$ is differentially homogenous of degree m if and only if*

$$\sum_{j=0}^n \sum_{k \in \mathbb{N}} \binom{k+r}{r} y_j^{(k)} \frac{\partial f(y_0, \ldots, y_n)}{\partial y_j^{(k+r)}} = \begin{cases} mf & r = 0 \\ 0 & r \ne 0 \end{cases}$$

Sparse differential resultants have the following property.

Theorem 3.10 *The sparse differential resultant is differentially homogenous in each $\mathbf{u}_i$ which is the coefficient set of $\mathbb{P}_i$.*

Proof: Similar to the proof of [12, Theorem 4.16], we can show that R satisfies the conditions of Theorem 3.9 for each $\mathbf{u}_i$. The proof is omitted due to the page limit. $\square$

Continue from Example 3.6. In this example, R is differentially homogenous of degree 2 in $\mathbf{u}_0$, of degree 1 in $\mathbf{u}_1$ and of degree 2 in $\mathbf{u}_2$ respectively.

In the following, we prove formulas for sparse differential resultants, which are similar to the Poisson type formulas for Chow forms and algebraic resultants [23]. Denote $\mathrm{ord}(R, \mathbf{u}_i)$ by h_i $(i = 0, \ldots, n)$. We have the following theorem.

Theorem 3.11 *Let $R(\mathbf{u}_0, \ldots, \mathbf{u}_n)$ be the sparse differential resultant of $\mathbb{P}_0, \ldots, \mathbb{P}_n$. Let $\deg(R, u_{00}^{(h_0)}) = t_0$. Then there exist $\xi_{\tau k}$ for $\tau = 1, \ldots, t_0$ and $k = 1, \ldots, l_0$ such that*

$$R = A \prod_{\tau=1}^{t_0} \left(u_{00} + \sum_{k=1}^{l_0} u_{0k}\xi_{\tau k} \right)^{(h_0)}, \qquad (10)$$

where A is a polynomial in $\mathcal{F}[\mathbf{u}_0^{[h_0]}, \ldots, \mathbf{u}_n^{[h_n]} \setminus u_{00}^{(h_0)}]$.

Proof: Now consider R as a polynomial in $u_{00}^{(h_0)}$ with coefficients in $\mathbb{Q}_0 = \mathbb{Q}(\cup_{l=0}^n \mathbf{u}_l^{[h_l]} \setminus \{u_{00}^{(h_0)}\})$. Then, in an algebraic extension field of $\mathbb{Q}_0$, we have

$$R = A \prod_{\tau=1}^{t_0} (u_{00}^{(h_0)} - z_\tau)$$

where $t_0 = \deg(R, u_{00}^{(h_0)})$. Note that z_τ is an algebraic root of $R(u_{00}^{(h_0)}) = 0$ and a derivative for z_τ can be naturally defined to make $\mathcal{F}\langle z_\tau\rangle$ a differential field. From $R(\mathbf{u}; \zeta_0, \ldots, \zeta_n) = 0$, if we differentiate this equality w.r.t. $u_{0k}^{(h_0)}$, then we have

$$\overline{\frac{\partial R}{\partial u_{0k}^{(h_0)}}} + \frac{\partial R}{\partial \zeta_0^{(h_0)}}(-\eta^{[s_0]})^{\alpha_{0k}} = 0 \qquad (11)$$

where $\overline{\frac{\partial R}{\partial u_{0k}^{(h_0)}}}$ and $\frac{\partial R}{\partial \zeta_0^{(h_0)}}$ are obtained by substituting u_{i0} by ζ_i in $\frac{\partial R}{\partial u_{0k}^{(h_0)}}$ and $\frac{\partial R}{\partial u_{00}^{(h_0)}}$ respectively.

Now multiply equation (11) by u_{0k} and for k from 1 to l_0 add all of the equations obtained together, then we get

$$\frac{\partial R}{\partial \zeta_0^{(h_0)}}\zeta_0 + \sum_{k=1}^{l_0} u_{0k}\overline{\frac{\partial R}{\partial u_{0k}^{(h_0)}}} = 0 \qquad (12)$$

Thus, the polynomial $G_1 = u_{00}\frac{\partial R}{\partial u_{00}^{(h_0)}} + \sum_{k=1}^{l_0} u_{0k}\frac{\partial R}{\partial u_{0k}^{(h_0)}}$ vanishes at $(u_{00}, \ldots, u_{n0}) = (\zeta_0, \ldots, \zeta_n)$. Since $\mathrm{ord}(G_1) \leq \mathrm{ord}(R)$ and $\deg(G_1) = \deg(R)$, there exists some $a \in \mathcal{F}$ such that $G_1 = aR$. Setting $u_{00}^{(h_0)} = z_\tau$ in both sides of G_1, we have $u_{00}R_{\tau 0} + \sum_{k=1}^{l_0} u_{0k}R_{\tau k} = 0$, where $R_{\tau k} = \frac{\partial R}{\partial u_{0k}^{(h_0)}}\big|_{u_{00}^{(h_0)}=z_\tau}$. Since R is irreducible as an algebraic polynomial in $u_{00}^{(h_0)}$, $R_{\tau 0} \neq 0$. Denote $\xi_{\tau k} = R_{\tau k}/R_{\tau 0}$. Thus, $u_{00} + \sum_{k=1}^{l_0} u_{0k}\xi_{\tau k} = 0$ under the condition $u_{00}^{(h_0)} = z_\tau$. Consequently, $z_\tau = -(\sum_{k=1}^{l_0} u_{0k}\xi_{\tau k})^{(h_0)}$ and (10) follows. $\square$

If $\mathbb{P}_0$ contains the linear terms y_i $(i = 1, \ldots, n)$, then the above result can be strengthened as follows.

Theorem 3.12 *Suppose $\mathbb{P}_0$ has the form*

$$\mathbb{P}_0 = u_{00} + \sum_{i=1}^{n} u_{0i}y_i + \sum_{i=n+1}^{l_0} u_{0i}(\mathbb{Y}^{[s_0]})^{\alpha_{0i}}. \qquad (13)$$

Then there exist $\xi_{\tau k}$ $(\tau = 1, \ldots, t_0; k = 1, \ldots, n)$ such that

$$R = A\prod_{\tau=1}^{t_0}\left(u_{00} + \sum_{i=1}^{n} u_{0i}\xi_{\tau i} + \sum_{i=n+1}^{l_0} u_{0i}(\xi_\tau^{[s_0]})^{\alpha_{0i}}\right)^{(h_0)}$$

$$= A\prod_{\tau=1}^{t_0}\mathbb{P}_0(\xi_\tau)^{(h_0)}, \quad \text{where } \xi_\tau = (\xi_{\tau 1}, \ldots, \xi_{\tau n}).$$

Moreover, ξ_τ $(\tau = 1, \ldots, t_0)$ lies on $\mathbb{P}_1, \ldots, \mathbb{P}_n$.

Proof: For the first part, from Theorem 3.11, it remains to show that for $i = n + 1$ to l_0, $\xi_{\tau i} = (\xi_\tau^{[s_0]})^{\alpha_{0i}}$. From equation (11), we have $\eta_j = \overline{\frac{\partial R}{\partial u_{0j}^{(h_0)}}}/\frac{\partial R}{\partial \zeta_0^{(h_0)}}$ and $(\eta^{[s_0]})^{\alpha_{0i}} = \overline{\frac{\partial R}{\partial u_{0i}^{(h_0)}}}/\frac{\partial R}{\partial \zeta_0^{(h_0)}}$. If $(\mathbb{Y}^{[s_0]})^{\alpha_{0i}} = \prod_{j=1}^{n}\prod_{k=0}^{s_0}(y_j^{(k)})^{(\alpha_{0i})_{jk}}$, then

$$\prod_{j=1}^{n}\prod_{k=0}^{s_0}((\overline{\frac{\partial R}{\partial u_{0j}^{(h_0)}}}/\frac{\partial R}{\partial \zeta_0^{(h_0)}})^{(k)})^{(\alpha_{0i})_{jk}} = \overline{\frac{\partial R}{\partial u_{0i}^{(h_0)}}}/\frac{\partial R}{\partial \zeta_0^{(h_0)}}.$$

It follows that

$$\prod_{j=1}^{n}\prod_{k=0}^{s_0}((\overline{\frac{\partial R}{\partial u_{0j}^{(h_0)}}}/\frac{\partial R}{\partial u_{00}^{(h_0)}})^{(k)})^{(\alpha_{0i})_{jk}} - \frac{\partial R}{\partial u_{0i}^{(h_0)}}/\frac{\partial R}{\partial u_{00}^{(h_0)}}$$

vanishes at $(u_{00}, \ldots, u_{n0}) = (\zeta_0, \ldots, \zeta_n)$. Since there exists some $a \in \mathbb{N}$, such that $G_i =$

$$\left(\frac{\partial R}{\partial u_{00}^{(h_0)}}\right)^a\left(\prod_{j=1}^{n}\prod_{k=0}^{s_0}((\frac{\partial R}{\partial u_{0j}^{(h_0)}}/\frac{\partial R}{\partial u_{00}^{(h_0)}})^{(k)})^{(\alpha_{0i})_{jk}} - \frac{\partial R}{\partial u_{0i}^{(h_0)}}/\frac{\partial R}{\partial u_{00}^{(h_0)}}\right)$$

is a polynomial in $\mathbb{Q}\{\mathbf{u}_0, \ldots, \mathbf{u}_n\}$, $G_i \in \mathrm{sat}(R)$. Now substituting $u_{00}^{(h_0+h)} = z_\tau^{(h)}$ for $h \geq 0$ into G_i, we obtain that $\xi_{\tau i} = \prod_{j=1}^{n}\prod_{k=0}^{s_0}((\xi_{\tau j})^{(k)})^{(\alpha_{0i})_{jk}} = (\xi_\tau^{[s_0]})^{\alpha_{0i}}$.

The proof of the second assertion is based on generalized differential Chow form introduced in [12] and is omitted. $\square$

As in algebra, the sparse differential resultant gives a necessary condition for a system of differential polynomials to have common solutions, as shown by the following theorem.

Theorem 3.13 *Let $\mathbb{P}_0, \ldots, \mathbb{P}_n$ be a differentially essential system of the form (7) and $R(\mathbf{u}_0, \ldots, \mathbf{u}_n)$ be their sparse differential resultant. Denote $\mathrm{ord}(R, \mathbf{u}_i) = h_i$ and $S_R = \frac{\partial R}{\partial u_{0i}^{(h_0)}}$. Suppose that when $\mathbf{u}_i$ $(i = 0, \ldots, n)$ are specialized to sets $\mathbf{v}_i$ which are elements in an extension field of $\mathcal{F}$, $\mathbb{P}_i$ are specialized to $\overline{\mathbb{P}}_i$ $(i = 0, \ldots, n)$. If $\overline{\mathbb{P}}_i = 0(i = 0, \ldots, n)$ have a common solution, then $R(\mathbf{v}_0, \ldots, \mathbf{v}_n) = 0$. Moreover, if $S_R(\mathbf{v}_0, \ldots, \mathbf{v}_n) \neq 0$, in the case that $\overline{\mathbb{P}}_i = 0(i = 0, \ldots, n)$ have a common solution ξ, then for each k, we have*

$$((\xi)^{[s_0]})^{\alpha_{0k}} = \frac{\partial R}{\partial u_{0k}^{(h_0)}}(\mathbf{v}_0, \ldots, \mathbf{v}_n)/S_R(\mathbf{v}_0, \ldots, \mathbf{v}_n). \quad (14)$$

Proof: Since $R(\mathbf{u}_0, \ldots, \mathbf{u}_n) \in [\mathbb{P}_0, \ldots, \mathbb{P}_n]$, $R(\mathbf{v}_0, \ldots, \mathbf{v}_n) \in [\overline{\mathbb{P}}_0, \ldots, \overline{\mathbb{P}}_n]$. So if $\overline{\mathbb{P}}_i = 0(i = 0, \ldots, n)$ have a common solution, then $R(\mathbf{v}_0, \ldots, \mathbf{v}_n)$ should be zero.

From equation (11), it is clear that the polynomial $\frac{\partial R}{\partial u_{0k}^{(h_0)}} + S_R \cdot (-\mathbb{Y}^{[s_0]})^{\alpha_{0k}} \in [\mathbb{P}_0, \ldots, \mathbb{P}_n]$. Thus, if ξ is a common solution of $\overline{\mathbb{P}}_i = 0$, then the polynomial $\frac{\partial R}{\partial u_{0k}^{(h_0)}}(\mathbf{v}_0, \ldots, \mathbf{v}_n) + S_R(\mathbf{v}_0, \ldots, \mathbf{v}_n) \cdot (-\mathbb{Y}^{[s_0]})^{\alpha_{0k}}$ vanishes at ξ. So (14) follows. $\square$

Again, if $\mathbb{P}_0$ contains the linear terms y_i $(i = 1, \ldots, n)$, then the above result can be strengthened as follows.

Corollary 3.14 *Suppose $\mathbb{P}_0$ has the form (13). If $R(\mathbf{v}_0, \ldots, \mathbf{v}_n) = 0$ and $S_R(\mathbf{v}_0, \ldots, \mathbf{v}_n) \neq 0$, then $\overline{\mathbb{P}}_i = 0$ have a common solution.*

Proof: From the proof of the above theorem, we know that for k from 1 to n,

$$A_k = \frac{\partial R}{\partial u_{0k}^{(h_0)}} + \frac{\partial R}{\partial u_{00}^{(h_0)}}(-y_k) \in [\mathbb{P}_0, \ldots, \mathbb{P}_n].$$

Clearly, A_k is linear in y_k. Suppose the differential remainder of $\mathbb{P}_i$ w.r.t. $A_1, \ldots, A_n$ in order to eliminate $y_1, \ldots, y_n$ is g_i, then $S_R^a\mathbb{P}_i \equiv g_i \mod [A_1, \ldots, A_n]$ for $a \in \mathbb{N}$. Thus, $g_i \in [\mathbb{P}_0, \ldots, \mathbb{P}_n] \cap \mathbb{Q}\langle\mathbf{u}\rangle\{u_{00}, \ldots, u_{n0}\} = \mathrm{sat}(R)$. So we have $S_R^b\mathbb{P}_i \equiv 0 \mod [A_1, \ldots, A_n, R]$ for some $b \in \mathbb{N}$. Now specialize $\mathbf{u}_i$ to $\mathbf{v}_i$ for $i = 0, \ldots, n$, then we have

$$S_R^b(\mathbf{v}_0, \ldots, \mathbf{v}_n) \cdot \overline{\mathbb{P}}_i \equiv 0 \mod [\overline{A}_1, \ldots, \overline{A}_n]. \quad (15)$$

Let $\xi_k = \frac{\partial R}{\partial u_{0k}^{(h_0)}}(\mathbf{v}_0, \ldots, \mathbf{v}_n)/S_R(\mathbf{v}_0, \ldots, \mathbf{v}_n)$ $(k = 1, \ldots, n)$, and denote $\xi = (\xi_1, \ldots, \xi_n)$. Then from equation (15), $\overline{\mathbb{P}}_i(\xi) = 0$. So, ξ is a common solution of $\overline{\mathbb{P}}_0, \ldots, \overline{\mathbb{P}}_n$. $\square$

4. AN ALGORITHM TO COMPUTE SPARSE DIFFERENTIAL RESULTANT

In this section, we give an algorithm to compute the sparse differential resultant with single exponential complexity.

4.1 Degree bounds for sparse differential resultants

In this section, we give an upper bound for the degree and order of the sparse differential resultant, which will be crucial to our algorithm to compute the sparse resultant.

Theorem 4.1 *Let* $\mathbb{P}_0, \ldots, \mathbb{P}_n$ *be a differentially essential system of form (7) with* $\operatorname{ord}(\mathbb{P}_i) = s_i$ *and* $\deg(\mathbb{P}_i, \mathbb{Y}) = m_i$. *Let* $R(\mathbf{u}_0, \ldots, \mathbf{u}_n)$ *be the sparse differential resultant of* $\mathbb{P}_i$ $(i = 0, \ldots, n)$. *Suppose* $\operatorname{ord}(R, \mathbf{u}_i) = h_i$ *for each* i. *We have*

1) $h_i \leq s - s_i$ *for* $i = 0, \ldots, n$ *where* $s = \sum_{i=0}^{n} s_i$.

2) R *can be written as a linear combination of* $\mathbb{P}_i$ *and their derivatives up to order* h_i. *Precisely,*

$$R(\mathbf{u}_0, \ldots, \mathbf{u}_n) = \sum_{i=0}^{n} \sum_{k=0}^{h_i} G_{ik} \mathbb{P}_i^{(k)} \qquad (16)$$

for some $G_{ik} \in \mathbb{Q}[\mathbf{u}_0^{[h_0]}, \ldots, \mathbf{u}_n^{[h_n]}, \mathbb{Y}^{[h]}]$ *where* $h = \max_i\{h_i + s_i\}$.

3) $\deg(R) \leq \prod_{i=0}^{n}(m_i + 1)^{h_i+1} \leq (m+1)^{ns+n+1}$, *where* $m = \max_i\{m_i\}$.

Proof: 1) Let $\theta_i = - \sum\limits_{1 \leq |\alpha| \leq m_i} u_{i\alpha}(\eta^{[s_i]})^{\alpha}$ $(i = 0, \ldots, n)$ where $\eta = (\eta_1, \ldots, \eta_n)$ is the generic point of the zero differential ideal $[0]$, and $\mathbb{W}_i = u_{i0} + \sum\limits_{1 \leq |\alpha| \leq m_i} u_{i\alpha}(\mathbb{Y}^{[s_i]})^{\alpha}$ is a generic polynomial of order s_i and degree m_i. Then from the property of differential resultants ([12, Theorem 1.3.]), we know the minimal polynomial of $(\theta_0, \ldots, \theta_n)$ is of order $s - s_i$ in each u_{i0}. Now specialize all the $u_{i\alpha}$ such that θ_i are specialized to the corresponding ζ_i. By the procedures in the proof of Theorem 3.1, we can obtain a nonzero differential polynomial vanishing at $(\zeta_0, \ldots, \zeta_n)$ with order not greater than $s - s_i$ in each variable u_{i0}. Since R is the minimal polynomial of $(\zeta_0, \ldots, \zeta_n)$, $\operatorname{ord}(R, \mathbf{u}_i) = \operatorname{ord}(R, u_{i0}) \leq s - s_i$.

2) Substituting u_{i0} by $\mathbb{P}_i - \sum\limits_{k=1}^{l_i} u_{ik}(\mathbb{Y}^{[s_i]})^{\alpha_{ik}}$ in the polynomial $R(\mathbf{u}; u_{00}, \ldots, u_{n0})$ for $i = 0, \ldots, n$, we get

$R(\mathbf{u}; u_{00}, \ldots, u_{n0})$
$= R(\mathbf{u}; \mathbb{P}_0 - \sum\limits_{k=1}^{l_0} u_{0k}(\mathbb{Y}^{[s_0]})^{\alpha_{0k}}, \ldots, \mathbb{P}_n - \sum\limits_{k=1}^{l_n} u_{nk}(\mathbb{Y}^{[s_n]})^{\alpha_{nk}})$
$= \sum_{i=0}^{n} \sum_{k=0}^{h_i} G_{ik} \mathbb{P}_i^{(k)} + T(\mathbf{u}, \mathbb{Y})$

for $G_{ik} \in \mathbb{Q}\{\cup_{i=0}^{n} \mathbf{u}_i, \mathbb{Y}\}$ and $T = R(\mathbf{u}; -\sum\limits_{k=1}^{l_0} u_{0k}(\mathbb{Y}^{[s_0]})^{\alpha_{0k}},$ $\ldots, -\sum\limits_{k=1}^{l_n} u_{nk}(\mathbb{Y}^{[s_n]})^{\alpha_{nk}}) \in [\mathbb{P}_0, \ldots, \mathbb{P}_n] \cap \mathbb{Q}\langle \mathbf{u} \rangle\{\mathbb{Y}\}$. Since $[\mathbb{P}_0, \ldots, \mathbb{P}_n] \cap \mathbb{Q}\langle \mathbf{u} \rangle\{\mathbb{Y}\} = [0]$, $T = 0$ and 2) is proved. Moreover, $(\mathbb{P}_0^{[h_0]}, \ldots, \mathbb{P}_n^{[h_n]}) \cap \mathbb{Q}[\mathbf{u}_0^{[h_0]}, \ldots, \mathbf{u}_n^{[h_n]}] = (R(\mathbf{u}_0, \ldots, \mathbf{u}_n))$.

3) Let $\mathcal{J}_0 = (\mathbb{P}_0^{[h_0]}, \ldots, \mathbb{P}_n^{[h_n]}) \subset \mathbb{Q}[\mathbf{u}_0^{[h_0]}, \ldots, \mathbf{u}_n^{[h_n]}, \widetilde{\mathbb{Y}}]$ where $\widetilde{\mathbb{Y}}$ are the y_i and their derivatives appearing in $\mathbb{P}_0^{[h_0]}, \ldots, \mathbb{P}_n^{[h_n]}$. By Lemma 2.2, $\deg(\mathcal{J}_0) \leq \prod_{i=0}^{n}\prod_{j=0}^{h_i}\deg(\mathbb{P}_i, \mathbb{Y} \cup \mathbf{u}_i) = \prod_{i=0}^{n}(m_i + 1)^{h_i+1}$ and $(R) = \mathcal{J}_0 \cap \mathbb{Q}[\mathbf{u}_0^{[h_0]}, \ldots, \mathbf{u}_n^{[h_n]}]$ is the elimination ideal of $\mathcal{J}_0$. Thus, by Theorem 2.1,

$$\deg(R) \leq \deg(\mathcal{J}_0) \leq \prod_{i=0}^{n}(m_i + 1)^{h_i+1}. \qquad (17)$$

Together with 1), 3) is proved. $\square$

The following theorem gives an upper bound for degrees of differential resultants, the proof of which is not valid for sparse differential resultants. In the following result, when we estimate the degree of R, only the degrees of $\mathbb{P}_i$ in $\mathbb{Y}$ are considered, while in Theorem 4.1, the degrees of $\mathbb{P}_i$ in both $\mathbb{Y}$ and u_{ik} are considered.

Theorem 4.2 *Let* F_i $(i = 0, \ldots, n)$ *be generic differential polynomials in* $\mathbb{Y} = \{y_1, \ldots, y_n\}$ *with order* s_i, *degree* $m_i = \deg(\mathbb{P}_i, \mathbb{Y})$, *and* $s = \sum_{i=0}^{n} s_i$. *Let* $R(\mathbf{u}_0, \ldots, \mathbf{u}_n)$ *be the differential resultant of* $F_0, \ldots, F_n$. *Then we have* $\deg(R, \mathbf{u}_k) \leq \frac{s-s_k+1}{m_k} \prod_{i=0}^{n} m_i^{s-s_i+1}$ *for each* $k = 0, \ldots, n$.

Proof: Without loss of generality, we consider $k = 0$.

By [12, Theorem 6.8], $\operatorname{ord}(R, \mathbf{u}_i) = s - s_i$ for each i and $R \in (F_0^{[s-s_0]}, \ldots, F_n^{[s-s_n]}) \subset \mathbb{Q}[\mathbb{Y}^{[s]}, \mathbf{u}_0^{[s-s_0]}, \ldots, \mathbf{u}_n^{[s-s_n]}]$. Let $\mathcal{I}^a = (F_1^{[s-s_1]}, \ldots, F_n^{[s-s_n]}) \subset \mathbb{Q}(\widetilde{\mathbf{u}})[\mathbb{Y}^{[s]}]$, where $\widetilde{\mathbf{u}} = \cup_{i=1}^{n} \mathbf{u}_i^{[s-s_i]}$. Clearly, $\mathcal{I}^a$ is a prime ideal of dimension $s - s_0$.

Let $\mathbb{P}_0, \ldots, \mathbb{P}_{s-s_0}$ be independent generic polynomials of degree m_0 in $\mathbb{Y}^{[s]}$ with $\mathbf{v}_i$ coefficients of $\mathbb{P}_i$. Denote $\widetilde{\mathbf{v}} = \cup_{i=0}^{s-s_0} \mathbf{v}_i \setminus \{v_{i0}\}$ where v_{i0} is the constant term of $\mathbb{P}_i$.

Suppose η is a generic point of $\mathcal{I}^a$. Let $\zeta_i = -\mathbb{P}_i(\eta) + v_{i0}$ and $\overline{\zeta_i} = -F_0^{(i)}(\eta) + u_{00}^{(i)}$ $(i = 0, \ldots, s-s_0)$. Clearly, ζ_i and $\overline{\zeta_i}$ are free of v_{i0} and $u_{00}^{(i)}$ respectively. Let $G(\mathbf{v}_0, \ldots, \mathbf{v}_{s-s_0}) = G(\widetilde{\mathbf{v}}; v_{00}, \ldots, v_{s-s_0,0}) \in \mathbb{Q}[\widetilde{\mathbf{u}}; \mathbf{v}_0, \ldots, \mathbf{v}_{s-s_0}]$ be the generalized Chow form of $\mathcal{I}^a$. Then $G(\widetilde{\mathbf{v}}; v_{00}, \ldots, v_{s-s_0,0})$ is the vanishing polynomial of $(\zeta_0, \ldots, \zeta_{s-s_0})$ over $\mathbb{Q}(\widetilde{\mathbf{u}}, \widetilde{\mathbf{v}})$. Now specialize $\mathbf{v}_i$ to the corresponding coefficients of $F_0^{(i)}$. Then ζ_i are specialized to $\overline{\zeta_i}$. By [16, p.168-169], there exists a nonzero polynomial $H(\mathbf{u}_0^{[s-s_0]}\setminus u_{00}^{[s-s_0]}; u_{00}, \ldots, u_{00}^{(s-s_0)}) \in \mathbb{Q}[\mathbf{u}_0^{[s-s_0]}, \ldots, \mathbf{u}_n^{[s-s_n]}]$ such that
  1) $H(\mathbf{u}_0^{[s-s_0]}\setminus u_{00}^{[s-s_0]}; \overline{\zeta_0}, \ldots, \overline{\zeta_{s-s_0}}) = 0$ and
  2) $\deg(H) \leq \deg(G)$.
So $H \in (F_0^{[s-s_0]}, \ldots, F_n^{[s-s_n]}) \cap \mathbb{Q}[\mathbf{u}_0^{[s-s_0]}, \ldots, \mathbf{u}_n^{[s-s_n]}] = (R)$. Thus, $\deg(R, \mathbf{u}_0^{[s-s_0]}) \leq \deg(H, \mathbf{u}_0^{[s-s_0]}) \leq \deg(G(\mathbf{v}_0, \ldots, \mathbf{v}_{s-s_0}))$. By Theorem 2.4, $\deg(G, \mathbf{v}_i) = \deg(\mathcal{I}^a)m_0^{s-s_0}$ for each i. Since $\mathcal{I}^a$ is generated by $(F_1^{[s-s_1]}, \ldots, F_n^{[s-s_n]})$ in $\mathbb{Q}(\widetilde{\mathbf{u}})[\mathbb{Y}^{[s]}]$, $\deg(\mathcal{I}^a) \leq \prod_{i=1}^{n} m_i^{s-s_i+1}$ by Lemma 2.2. So, $\deg(R, \mathbf{u}_0) \leq \frac{s-s_0+1}{m_0} \prod_{i=0}^{n} m_i^{s-s_i+1}$. $\square$

4.2 Algorithm

If a polynomial R is the linear combination of some known polynomials $F_i(i = 1, \ldots, s)$, that is $R = \sum_{i=1}^{s} H_i F_i$, then a general idea to estimate the computational complexity of R is to estimate the upper bounds of the degrees of R and $H_i F_i$ and to use linear algebra to find the coefficients of R.

For sparse differential resultant, we already gave its degree in Theorem 4.1. Now we will give the degrees of the expressions in the linear combination.

Theorem 4.3 *Let* $\mathbb{P}_0, \ldots, \mathbb{P}_n$ *be a differentially essential system with order* s_i *and degree* m_i *respectively. Denote* $s = \sum_{i=0}^{n} s_i$, $m = \max_{i=0}^{n}\{m_i\}$. *Let* $R(\mathbf{u}_0, \ldots, \mathbf{u}_n)$ *be the sparse differential resultant of* $\mathbb{P}_0, \ldots, \mathbb{P}_n$ *with* $\operatorname{ord}(R, \mathbf{u}_i) = h_i$ *for each* i. *Then we have* $\deg(G_{ik}\mathbb{P}_i^{(k)}) \leq (m+1)\deg(R) \leq (m+1)^{ns+n+2}$ *in formula (16)*.

Proof: By Theorem 4.1 and its proof, R can be written as $R(\mathbf{u}_0, \ldots, \mathbf{u}_n) = \sum_{i=0}^{n} \sum_{k=0}^{h_i} G_{ik}\mathbb{P}_i^{(k)}$.

To estimate the degree of $G_{ik}\mathbb{P}_i^{(k)}$, we need only to consider every monomial $M(\mathbf{u}; u_{00}, \ldots, u_{n0})$ in $R(\mathbf{u}_0, \ldots, \mathbf{u}_n)$. Consider one monomial $M = \mathbf{u}^\gamma \prod_{i=0}^n \prod_{k=0}^{h_i} (u_{i0}^{(k)})^{d_{ik}}$ with $|\gamma| = d$ and $d + \sum_{i=0}^n \sum_{k=0}^{h_i} d_{ik} \leq \deg(R)$, where $\mathbf{u}^\gamma$ represents a monomial in $\mathbf{u}$ and their derivatives with exponent vector γ. Using the substitution in the proof of Theorem 4.1, we have

$$M = \mathbf{u}^\gamma \prod_{i=0}^n \prod_{k=0}^{h_i} \left(\left(\mathbb{P}_i - \sum_{j=1}^{l_i} u_{ij} (\mathbb{Y}^{[s_i]})^{\alpha_{ij}} \right)^{(k)} \right)^{d_{ik}}.$$

When expanded, every term has total degree bounded by $d + \sum_{i=0}^n \sum_{k=0}^{h_i} (m_i + 1)d_{ik}$ in $\mathbf{u}_0^{[h_0]}, \ldots, \mathbf{u}_n^{[h_n]}$ and $\mathbb{Y}^{[h]}$ with $h = \max\{h_i + s_i\}$. Since $d + \sum_{i=0}^n \sum_{k=0}^{h_i} (m_i + 1)d_{ik} \leq (m+1)(d + \sum_{i=0}^n \sum_{k=0}^{h_i} d_{ik}) \leq (m+1)\deg(R)$, applying Theorem 4.1, the theorem is proved. $\square$

For a given system $f_0, \ldots, f_n \in \mathcal{F}\{y_1, \ldots, y_n\}$, let $\mathbf{v}_i$ be the set of coefficients of f_i and $\mathbb{P}(f_i)$ the differential polynomial of the form (7) with the same support as f_i. When $\mathbb{P}(f_i)$ form a differentially essential system, let $R(\mathbf{u}_0, \ldots, \mathbf{u}_n)$ be their sparse differential resultant. Then $R(\mathbf{v}_0, \ldots, \mathbf{v}_n)$ is defined to be the *sparse differential resultant of f_i*. The following result gives an effective differential Nullstellensatz under certain conditions.

Corollary 4.4 *Let $f_0, \ldots, f_n \in \mathcal{F}\{y_1, \ldots, y_n\}$ have no common solutions with $\mathrm{ord}(f_i) = s_i, s = \sum_{i=0}^n s_i$, and $\deg(f_i) \leq m$. If the sparse differential resultant of $f_0, \ldots, f_n$ is nonzero, then there exist $H_{ij} \in \mathcal{F}\{y_1, \ldots, y_n\}$ s.t. $\sum_{i=0}^n \sum_{j=0}^{s-s_i} H_{ij} f_i^{(j)} = 1$ and $\deg(H_{ij} f_i^{(j)}) \leq (m+1)^{ns+n+2}$.*

Proof: The hypothesis implies that $\mathbb{P}(f_i)$ form a differentially essential system. Clearly, $R(\mathbf{u}_0, \ldots, \mathbf{u}_n)$ has the property stated in Theorem 4.3, where $\mathbf{u}_i$ are coefficients of $\mathbb{P}(f_i)$. The result follows directly from Theorem 4.3 by specializing $\mathbf{u}_i$ to the coefficients of f_i. $\square$

Now, we give an algorithm **SDResultant** to compute sparse differential resultants. The algorithm works adaptively by searching R with an order vector $(h_0, \ldots, h_n) \in \mathbb{N}^{n+1}$ with $h_i \leq s - s_i$ by Theorem 4.1. Denote $o = \sum_{i=0}^n h_i$. We start with $o = 0$. And for this o, choose one vector $(h_0, \ldots, h_n)$ at a time. For this $(h_0, \ldots, h_n)$, we search for R from degree $D = 1$. If we cannot find an R with such a degree, then we repeat the procedure with degree $D + 1$ until $D > \prod_{i=0}^n (m_i + 1)^{h_i+1}$. In that case, we choose another $(h_0, \ldots, h_n)$ with $\sum_{i=0}^n h_i = o$. But if for all $(h_0, \ldots, h_n)$ with $h_i \leq s - s_i$ and $\sum_{i=0}^n h_i = o$, R cannot be found, then we repeat the procedure with $o + 1$. In this way, we need only to handle problems with the real size and need not to go to the upper bound in most cases.

Theorem 4.5 *Algorithm **SDResultant** computes sparse differential resultants with at most $O(n^{3.376}(s+1)^{O(n)}(m+1)^{O(nls^2)})$ $\mathbb{Q}$-arithmetic operations.*

Proof: In each loop of Step 3, the complexity of the algorithm is clearly dominated by Step 3.1.2., where we need to solve a system of linear equations $\mathcal{P} = 0$ over $\mathbb{Q}$ in $\mathbf{c}_0$ and $\mathbf{c}_{ij}$. It is easy to show that $|\mathbf{c}_0| = \binom{D+L-1}{L-1}$ and $|\mathbf{c}_{ij}| = \binom{(m+1)D-m_i-1+L+n(h+1)}{L+n(h+1)}$, where $L = \sum_{i=0}^n (h_i + 1)(l_i + 1)$. Then $\mathcal{P} = 0$ is a linear equation system with

---

Algorithm 1 — SDResultant$(\mathbb{P}_0, \ldots, \mathbb{P}_n)$

Input: A differentially essential system $\mathbb{P}_0, \ldots, \mathbb{P}_n$.
Output: The sparse differential resultant of $\mathbb{P}_0, \ldots, \mathbb{P}_n$.

1. For $i = 0, \ldots, n$, set $s_i = \mathrm{ord}(\mathbb{P}_i)$, $m_i = \deg(\mathbb{P}_i, \mathbb{Y})$, $\mathbf{u}_i = \mathrm{coeff}(\mathbb{P}_i)$ and $|\mathbf{u}_i| = l_i + 1$.
2. Set $R = 0$, $o = 0$, $s = \sum_{i=0}^n s_i$, $m = \max_i\{m_i\}$.
3. While $R = 0$ do
   3.1. For each vector $(h_0, \ldots, h_n) \in \mathbb{N}^{n+1}$ with $\sum_{i=0}^n h_i = o$ and $h_i \leq s - s_i$ do
      3.1.1. $U = \cup_{i=0}^n \mathbf{u}_i^{[h_i]}$, $h = \max_i\{h_i + s_i\}$, $D = 1$.
      3.1.2. While $R = 0$ and $D \leq \prod_{i=0}^n (m_i + 1)^{h_i+1}$ do
         3.1.2.1. Set R_0 to be a homogenous GPol of degree D in U.
         3.1.2.2. Set $\mathbf{c}_0 = \mathrm{coeff}(R_0, U)$.
         3.1.2.3. Set $H_{ij}(i = 0, \ldots, n; j = 0, \ldots, h_i)$ to be GPols of degree $(m+1)D - m_i - 1$ in $\mathbb{Y}^{[h]}, U$.
         3.1.2.4. Set $\mathbf{c}_{ij} = \mathrm{coeff}(H_{ij}, \mathbb{Y}^{[h]} \cup U)$.
         3.1.2.5. Set $\mathcal{P}$ to be the set of coefficients of $R_0(\mathbf{u}_0, \ldots, \mathbf{u}_n) - \sum_{i=0}^n \sum_{j=0}^{h_i} H_{ij}\mathbb{P}_i^{(j)}$ as an algebraic polynomial in $\mathbb{Y}^{[h]}, U$.
         3.1.2.6. Solve the linear equation $\mathcal{P} = 0$ in variables $\mathbf{c}_0$ and $\mathbf{c}_{ij}$.
         3.1.2.7. If $\mathbf{c}_0$ has a nonzero solution, then substitute it into R_0 to get R and go to Step 4., else $R = 0$.
         3.1.2.8. D:=D+1.
   3.2. o:=o+1.
4. Return R.

/*/ GPol stands for generic ordinary polynomial.

/*/ coeff(P, V) returns the set of coefficients of P as an ordinary polynomial in variables V.

$N = \binom{D+L-1}{L-1} + \sum_{i=0}^n (h_i + 1)\binom{(m+1)D-m_i-1+L+n(h+1)}{L+n(h+1)}$ variables and $M = \binom{(m+1)D+L+n(h+1)}{L+n(h+1)}$ equations. To solve it, we need at most $(\max\{M, N\})^\omega$ arithmetic operations over $\mathbb{Q}$, where ω is the matrix multiplication exponent and the currently best known ω is 2.376.

The iteration in Step 3.1.2. may go through 1 to $d_i = \prod_{i=0}^n (m_i + 1)^{h_i+1} \leq (m+1)^{ns+n+1}$, and the iteration in Step 3.1. at most will repeat $\prod_{i=0}^n (s - s_i + 1) \leq (s+1)^{n+1}$ times. And by Theorem 4.1, Step 3 may loop from $o = 0$ to ns. The whole algorithm needs at most

$$\sum_{o=0}^{ns} \sum_{\substack{h_i \leq s-s_i \\ \sum_i h_i = o}} \sum_{D=1}^{d_i} (\max\{M, N\})^{2.376}$$
$$\leq O(n^{3.376}(s+1)^{O(n)}(m+1)^{O(nls^2)})$$

arithmetic operations over $\mathbb{Q}$. In the above inequalities, we assume that $(m+1)^{ns+n+2} \geq ls + n(s+1)$ and use the fact that $l \geq (n+1)^2$, where $l = \sum_{i=0}^n (l_i + 1)$. Our complexity assumes an $O(1)$-complexity cost for all field operations over $\mathbb{Q}$. Thus, the complexity follows. $\square$

Remark 4.6 *Algorithm **SDResultant** can be improved by using a better search strategy. If D is not big enough, instead of checking $D + 1$, we can check $2D$. Repeating this procedure, we may find a k such that $2^k \leq \deg(R) \leq 2^{k+1}$. We then bisecting the interval $[2^k, q2^{k+1}]$ again to find the proper degree for R. This will lead to a better complexity, which is still single exponential.*

5. CONCLUSION AND PROBLEM

In this paper, the sparse differential resultant is defined and its basic properties are proved. In particular, degree bounds for the sparse differential resultant and the usual differential resultant are given. Based on these degree bounds, we propose a single exponential algorithm to compute the sparse differential resultant.

In the algebraic case, there exists a necessary and sufficient condition for the existence of sparse resultants in terms of the supports [29]. It is interesting to find such a condition for sparse differential resultants.

It is useful to represent the sparse resultant as the quotient of two determinants, as done in [7] in the algebraic case. In the differential case, we do not have such formulas, even in the simplest case of the resultant for two generic differential polynomials in one variable. The treatment in [4] is not complete. For instance, let f, g be two generic differential polynomials in one variable y with order one and degree two. Then, the differential resultant for f, g defined in [4] is zero, because all elements in the first column of the matrix $M(\delta, n, m)$ in [4, p.543] are zero. Furthermore, it is not easy to fix the problem.

The degree of the algebraic sparse resultant is equal to the mixed volume of certain polytopes generated by the supports of the polynomials [23] or [13, p.255]. A similar degree bound is desirable for the sparse differential resultant.

There exist very efficient algorithms to compute the algebraic sparse resultants ([10, 11]). How to apply the principles behind these algorithms to compute sparse differential resultants is an important problem.

6. REFERENCES

[1] F. Boulier, F. Lemaire, M.M. Maza. Computing Differential Characteristic Sets by Change of Ordering, *Journal of Symbolic Computation*, 45(1), 124-149, 2010.

[2] J.F. Canny. Generalized Characteristic Polynomials. *Journal of Symbolic Computation*, 9, 241-250, 1990.

[3] J.F. Canny and I.Z. Emiris. An Efficient Algorithm for the Sparse Mixed Resultant. In *Proc.AAECC*, LNCS 263, 89-104. Springer Verlag, 1993.

[4] G. Carrà-Ferro. A Resultant Theory for the Systems of Two Ordinary Algebraic Differential Equations. *AAECC*, 8, 539-560, 1997.

[5] S.C. Chou and X.S. Gao. Automated Reasoning in Differential Geometry and Mechanics: I. An Improved Version of Ritt-Wu's Decomposition Algorithm. *Journal of Automated Reasoning*, 10, 161-172, 1993.

[6] T. Cluzeau and E. Hubert. Rosolvent Representation for Regular Differential Ideals. *Appl. Algebra Engrg. Comm. Comput.*, 13, 395-425, 2003.

[7] C. D'Andrea. Macaulay Style Formulas for Sparse Resultants. *Trans. of AMS*, 354(7), 2595-2629, 2002.

[8] D. Eisenbud, F.O. Schreyer, and J. Weyman. Resultants and Chow Forms via Exterior Syzygies. *Journal of Amer. Math. Soc.*, 16(3), 537-579, 2004.

[9] M. Elkadi and B. Mourrain. A New Algorithm for the Geometric Decomposition of a Variety. *Proc. ISSAC'99*, 9-16, ACM Press, 1999.

[10] I.Z. Emiris and J.F. Canny. Efficient Incremental Algorithms for the Sparse Resultant and the Mixed Volume. *Journal of Symbolic Computation*, 20(2), 117-149, 1995.

[11] I.Z. Emiris and V.Y. Pan. Improved algorithms for computing determinants and resultants. *Journal of Complexity*, 21, 43-71, 2005.

[12] X.S. Gao, W. Li, C.M. Yuan, Intersection theory of Generic Differential Polynomials and Differential Chow Form. *Arxiv preprint*, arXiv:1009.0148, 1-50, 2010.

[13] I.M. Gelfand, M. Kapranov, and A. Zelevinsky. *Discriminants, Resultants and Multidimensional Determinants*. Boston, Birkhäuser, 1994.

[14] O. Golubitsky, M. Kondratieva, and A. Ovchinnikov. Algebraic Transformation of Differential Characteristic Decomposition from One Ranking to Another. *Journal of Symbolic Computation*, 44, 333-357, 2009.

[15] J. Heintz. Definability and Fast Quantifier Elimination in Algebraically Closed Fields. *Theoret. Comput. Sci.*, 24, 239-277, 1983.

[16] W.V.D. Hodge and D. Pedoe. *Methods of Algebraic Geometry, Volume I*. Cambridge Univ. Press, 1968.

[17] W.V.D. Hodge and D. Pedoe. *Methods of Algebraic Geometry, Volume II*. Cambridge Univ. Press, 1968.

[18] G. Jeronimo and J. Sabia. On the Number of Sets Definable by Polynomials. *Journal of Algebra*, 227, 633-644, 2000.

[19] J.P. Jouanolou. Le formalisme du rèsultant. *Advances in Mathematics*, 90(2), 117-263, 1991.

[20] E. R. Kolchin. *Differential Algebra and Algebraic Groups*. Academic Press, New York and London, 1973.

[21] E. R. Kolchin. A Problem on Differential Polynomials. *Contemporary Mathematics*, 131, 449-462, 1992.

[22] D. Lazard. Grönber Basis, Gaussian Elimination and Resolution of systems of Algebraic Equations. *Eurocal 83*, vol. 162 of *LNCS*, 146-157, 1983.

[23] P. Pedersen and B. Sturmfels. Product Formulas for Resultants and Chow Forms. *Mathematische Zeitschrift*, 214(1), 377-396, 1993.

[24] P. Philippon. Critères pour L'indíependance Algíebrique. *Inst. Hautes Ètudes Sci. Publ. Math.*, 64, 5-52, 1986.

[25] J.F. Ritt. *Differential Equations from the Algebraic Standpoint*. Amer. Math. Soc., New York, 1932.

[26] J.F. Ritt. *Differential Algebra*. Amer. Math. Soc., New York, 1950.

[27] S.L. Rueda and J.R. Sendra. Linear Complete Differential Resultants and the Implicitization of Linear DPPEs. *Journal of Symbolic Computation*, 45(3), 324-341, 2010.

[28] B. Sturmfels. Sparse Elimination Theory. In *Computational Algebraic Geometry and Commutative Algebra*, Eisenbud, D., Robbiano, L. eds. 264-298, Cambridge University Press, 1993.

[29] B. Sturmfels. On The Newton Polytope of the Resultant. *Journal of Algebraic Combinatorics*, 3, 207-236, 1994.

[30] A. Weil. *Foundations of Algebraic Geometry*. Amer. Math. Soc., New York, 1946.

An Automatic Parallelization Framework for Algebraic Computation Systems

Yue Li
Texas A&M University
yli@cse.tamu.edu

Gabriel Dos Reis
Texas A&M University
gdr@cse.tamu.edu

ABSTRACT

This paper proposes a non-intrusive automatic parallelization framework for typeful and property-aware computer algebra systems. Automatic parallelization remains a promising computer program transformation for exploiting ubiquitous concurrency facilities available in modern computers. The framework uses semantics-based static analysis to extract reductions in library components based on algebraic properties. An early implementation shows up to 5 times speed-up for library functions and homotopy-based polynomial system solver. The general framework is applicable to algebraic computation systems and programming languages with advanced type systems that support user-defined axioms or annotation systems.

Categories and Subject Descriptors

I.1.3 [**Symbolic and Algebraic Manipulation**]: Languages and Systems—*Special-purpose algebraic systems*; F.3.2 [**Logics and Meanings of Programs**]: Semantics of Programming Languages—*Program analysis*; D.3.3 [**Programming Languages**]: Language Constructs and Features

General Terms

Algorithms, Performance, Languages, Experimentation

Keywords

Automatic parallelization, computer algebra, user-defined axioms

1. INTRODUCTION

Concurrency offered by modern computers has the potential of enabling efficient scientific computation. However, by and large, development of scalable concurrent software remains a challenge. Furthermore, manual modification of *existing* programs to benefit from ubiquitous concurrency is just as elusive, left to a few highly trained programmers. In this paper, we propose an automatic parallelization framework for computer algebra systems that take properties of algebraic entities they manipulate seriously.

We previously reported [12] on the rich opportunity for parallelization in algebraic libraries such as those of the AXIOM family

systems. The intuition behind that work is that it is hard for a (well) structured algebraic algorithm not to reflect, in one way or the other, properties related to the entities it manipulates. Consequently, we built a semantics-based static analysis tool with the goal of detecting parallelizable reductions in algebraic libraries. In this paper, we show how to effectively exploit those findings, leading to an automatic parallelization framework.

The main thrust of this paper is a semantics-based source-to-source transformation. The transformation replaces sequential parallelizable reductions with their parallelized versions. It does not require the user to be an expert in parallel programming. Nor does it require write-access to the input program fragment, much less authorship. All that is needed is a description of algebraic properties of the input program fragment. The description language is an extension [12] of the "category" subset of the Spad programming language. For example, the content of a univariate polynomial with integer coefficients $P = \sum_0^n a_n X^n$ is the greatest common divisor of all the polynomial coefficients. It can be computed with a simple loop:

```
content(p: Polynomial(Integer)): Integer ==
  coefs : List(Integer) := coefficients(p)
  result : Integer := 0
  for c in  repeat
    result := gcd(result, c)
  return result
```

It is clear that this computation is a reduction of the *monoid operator* gcd over the coefficients of P. That suggests a computation strategy where pairs of coefficients are evaluated concurrently, and the results are themselves combined using the same divide-and-conquer pattern. That computation strategy corresponds to the following program:

```
content(p: Polynomial(Integer)): Integer ==
  coefs : List(Integer) := coefficients(p)
  result := parallelLeftReduce(gcd, coefs, 0)
  return result
```

where the function `parallelLeftReduce` performs reduction in parallel. Notice that while the example uses a polynomial with integer coefficients, all we need is a domain of computation where GCD computation makes sense and is effective, The function gcd remains a monoid operation, which we express in our extension to Spad [12] as:

```
forall(S: GcdDomain)
  assume MonoidOperator(S, gcd) with
    neutralValue = 0$S
```

The name `MonoidOperator` designates a category constructor that specifies what it means for an opetaor to be an monoid operator over a domain:

```
MonoidOperator(T: BasicType, op: (T, T) -> T): Category
  == AssociativeOperator(T, op) with
    neutralValue: T
```

The parameterized assumption statement instructs the reduction detector of the program transformation framework that it can assume (without having to conduct a proof) that gcd is a monoid operation over any GCD domain.

The contributions of this paper include:

1. Specification and implementation of semantics-based program analysis algorithms for detecting parallel reductions in user library code (section 3). The detection is guided by user provided assumptions.

2. Specification and implementation of program transformation algorithms for generating parallel reductions from the reductions identified in 1 (section 4).

3. Performance evaluation of our automatic parallelization framework using multicore PC and cluster (section 6). Experimental results show up to 5 times speed-up for some programs (section 6.3).

2. INTERNAL DATA STRUCTURES

The analysis and transformation algorithms operate on an internal representation (IR) of the user input program. The source code is first elaborated to IR. The result of the parallelization phase is translated back to Spad syntax, which is then compiled as if it was the original program. The abstract syntax for a subset of the IR is defined as follows:

$$
\begin{array}{lll}
name & x \\
type & \tau ::= & x(\tau^*) \mid (\tau^*) \to \tau \\
constant & c ::= & \mathrm{Constant}(x, \tau) \\
expression & e ::= & \mathrm{Funcall}(x, e^*, \tau) \\
& \mid & \mathrm{Variable}(x, \tau) \\
& \mid & \mathrm{Assign}(e, e) \\
& \mid & c \mid a \\
segment & g ::= & \mathrm{Segment}(e, e, e) \\
unnamed\ function & a ::= & \mathrm{Lambda}(\mathrm{Variable}(x, \tau)^*, s, \tau) \\
statement & s ::= & e \mid s^+ \\
& \mid & \mathrm{Declare}(x, \tau) \\
& \mid & \mathrm{For}(x, e, s) \\
& \mid & \mathrm{For}(x, g, s) \\
& \mid & \mathrm{While}(e, s) \\
& \mid & \mathrm{Return}(e) \\
& \mid & \mathrm{If}(e, s, s) \\
function & f ::= & \mathrm{FunDef}(x, \mathrm{Variable}(x, \tau)^*, S, \tau)
\end{array}
$$

A function definition node carries a name, a list of parameters, a definition body and a signature. A function call has an operator and optional operands. An anonymous function is a function definition without name. A variable is declared with its type. The iteration range of a for-loop is a sequence represented by either a container expression or an integer segment.

The reduction detection algorithms and the Ir manipulation algorithms several internal operators:

- *getIterationVariable*: retrieves the iteration variable from a for-loop.

- *getIterationSequence*: obtains the iteration sequence of a for-loop.

- *getLoopBody*: retrieves the body of a for-loop.

- *getOperator*: obtains the operator of a function call.

- *getOperands*: returns the operand list of a function call.

- *genAssign*: constructs an assignment.

- *genAnonymousFunction*: creates a lambda expression.

- *genFunCall*: builds a function call.

Figure 1 shows the IR for the body of the iterative content function definition. Each IR node represents an expression. The di-

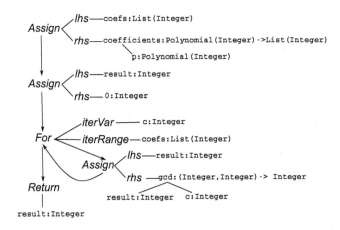

Figure 1: The internal representation of the content function body

rected edges between nodes indicate the control flow in a program. The undirected edges refer to the corresponding components of different IR nodes. The leaves of the IR nodes are expressions.

Type and user assumption information is used by the static analysis and program transformation algorithms. These information are stored in environments defined as follows:

$$
\begin{array}{lll}
TypeEnv & \Gamma ::= & [\,] \mid (x \mapsto \tau), \Gamma \\
property & p ::= & [\,] \mid (x \mapsto e), p \\
PropEnv & E ::= & [\,] \mid ((x, \tau, \tau) \mapsto p), E
\end{array}
$$

A type environment maps identifiers to their types. An entry of a property environment is a collection of all properties attached to an operator. Each entry in a property environment has an operator name, a signature, a defining type, and a list of properties. Each property maps a property name to a value. For instance, the property (*neutralValue*, 1) means the property *neutralValue* has value 1.

3. REDUCTION DETECTION

The reduction detector looks for semigroup operators, and also monoid operators. A reduction can be expressed as a *accumulation loop*, or a *library function call* to reduce, or an application of the *built-in reduce operator*. The detection algorithm is a semantics-based static analysis performed in two steps: (1) properties collection; followed by (2) reduction extraction. We summarize the algorithm for detecting accumulation loops in this section. Algorithms for detecting reduce call and built-in reduce operator are simpler. More in-depth discussion may be found in our previous work [12].

The detector first examines every user written assumption. The purpose is to derive all the algebraic properties attached to the operators. The derivation instantiates property categories according to a specific assumption. Algebraic property information is collected via the transitive closure of the instantiated categories. Consider the user assumption in section 1. Category `MonoidOperator` has two ancestor categories `AssociativeOperator` and `MagmaOperator`:

```
MagmaOperator(T: BasicType, op: (T,T) -> T): Category
  == Type
```

```
AssociativeOperator(T: BasicType,op: (T,T)->T): Category
  == MagmaOperator(T,op) with
    associativity:
      rule forall(a:T, b: T, c: T)
              op(a,op(b,c)) == op(op(a,b),c)
```

The definition of `MagmaOperator` means a binary operation on a domain satisfies the *magma operator* property. The `Associative-Operator` category contains a logical statement of the property that an operator is associative if it is a magma operator and follows the associativity rule. Category `MonoidOperator` is instantiated with type `Polynomial Integer` and operator `gcd`. Variable `neutralValue` is given value polynomial 0. The instantiated category has two ancestor categories `AssociativeOperator(Polynomial Integer,gcd)` and `MagmaOperator(Polynomial Integer,gcd)`. Therefore, the operator `gcd` carries all the properties of `MonoidOperator`, `AssociativeOperator` and `Magma-Operator`. At reduction extraction, the detector traverses the IR for the input source program. The extraction algorithm matches each IR node against the predefined parallel reduction patterns.

3.1 Detecting accumulation loop

One way for writing a reduction is to use an *accumulation loop*. The pattern of an accumulation loop is defined as a single for-loop of the following *recognizable form*:

$$\text{for i in l repeat s}^{+}$$

Variable i is the iteration variable of the loop, and l is a sequence. A new value from the sequence is yield at each iteration. The body of the loop is a sequence of statements s^{+}. Each statement s is an assignment a. An assignment a is of the form $v := f(X, e_1)$ or $v := f(e_2, X)$. Variable v is an accumulation variable. An accumulation variable has a linear occurrence on the right hand side of the assignment, and does not appear in sequence l. For each accumulation assignment, the same binary operator f has to be used consistently to accumulate values into v. The expression e is arbitrary, but must not mention v. The expression X is either the accumulation variable v, or of the form $f(X_1, e_1)$ or $f(e_1, X_1)$.

The pattern matching algorithm for accumulation loops is present in Algorithm 1. We start by preprocessing the input loop. The function *simplify* transforms an input loop using standard forward subexpression substitution [13]. The purpose of this preprocessing is to discover more "hidden" reductions. Consider the following code fragments:

```
a := 0                      a := 0
for i in 1..10 repeat       for i in 1..10 repeat
  r := i        -- local      a := a + i
  x := a        -- local
  a := x + r    -- global
```

the code on the left contains an accumulation loop. Without preprocessing, the loop is rejected during pattern matching. The reason is that the dependencies between each variable cause the violation of the recognizable form restriction. The preprocessed loop on the right is identified as an accumulation loop.

Each statement in an input loop is matched against the pattern of an accumulation assignment. This functionality is implemented

---

Algorithm 1 *isParallelAccumLoop?*(l: *Loop*, E: *PropEnv*, Γ: *TypeEnv*)

Require: l is an un-nested for-loop with body containing only assignments or definitions, E is a property environment, Γ is a type environment.

$l' \leftarrow simplify(l)$
$v \leftarrow getIterationVariable(l')$
$r \leftarrow getIterationSequence(l')$
$b \leftarrow getLoopBody(l')\}$
for s **in** b **do**
  if not *isAccumulationAssignment?*(s) **then**
    return false
for s **in** b **do**
  $v \leftarrow getAccumulationVariable(s)$
  if *dependsOn*(r, v) **then**
    return false
  for s' **in** b − {s} **do**
    if *dependsOn*(s', v) **then**
      return false
for s **in** b **do**
  $op \leftarrow getAccumulationOperator(s)$
  if *associative?*(op, Γ, E) = unknown **then**
    return unknown
return true

---

by the operator *isAccumulationAssignment?*. If each statement is an accumulation assignment, we continue checking that for each accumulation variable v, the iteration sequence and other assignments do not depend on v. The operator *getAccumulationVariable* takes out the variable at the left hand side of an accumulation statement. The operator *getAccumulationOperator* extracts the binary operator used in an accumulation statement, and *dependsOn* tests dependency between a statement and a variable, *i.e.*, whether the variable is read or written in the statement. Finally, the associativity of the accumulation operator in each statement is checked against user's assumption. The function *associative?* searches the property list of an accumulation operator for the associativity. If found, the function returns true, otherwise it returns unknown.

4. PROGRAM TRANSFORMATIONS FOR GENERATING PARALLEL REDUCTIONS

The transformation of an accumulation loop proceeds in several steps. First, we transform the body of the loop into a functional abstraction. This function computes the list of elements combined in the loop. Then parallel reduction is generated for combining the elements of the list. As an illustration, consider the following code for computing the n-th harmonic number:

```
harmonic(n: NonNegativeInteger): Fraction(Integer) ==
  h: Fraction(Integer) := 0
  for k in 1..n repeat
    h := h + 1/k
  return h
```

The transformation results in the following code:

```
harmonic(n: NonNegativeInteger): Fraction(Integer) ==
  h := parallelLeftReduce(+,_
        parallelMap((G768) +-> 1/G768,_
          [G769 for G769 in 1..n]),0)
  return h
```

In this example, a list of integer fractions [1, 1/2, ..., 1/n] are added to the accumulation variable h. In the transformed code, the list is computed in parallel with the function `parallelMap`. The library function applies the unary function (G768) +-> 1/G768 to each element of the sequence `[1..n]` in the loop iterator. The list is combined together by function `parallelLeftReduce`. The function performs a left associative reduction in parallel.

To parallelize reduce call and built-in reduce operator, we replace the reduce operator with parallel reduce function calls. Therefore, the parallelizations require to use parallel mapping and parallel reduction in the generated code.

4.1 A library for parallel mapping and reduction

We developed a small but sufficient Spad package `ParallelMapReduce` to provide the functionalities mentioned above. A package in the Spad language is a collection of function definitions. The interface of the package is shown below:

```
ParallelMapReduce(S:Type, R:Type):Public == Private where
  Public == with
    parallelMap      : (S -> R, List S) -> List R
    parallelRightReduce: ((S, R) -> R, List S, R) -> R
    parallelLeftReduce: ((R, S) -> R, List S, R) -> R
    ...
```

The package exports three functions `parallelMap`, `parallelRightReduce` and `parallelLeftReduce`. The definition of the package is parameterized by types S and R. The type parameter S is the element type of the list taken by parallel mapping and reduction. The type parameter R is the element type of the list returned by parallel mapping and the resultant type of the binary combination in a reduction. The expression `parallelMap(op, l)` applies op to the portions of l concurrently using threads. Functions `parallelRightReduce` and `parallelLeftReduce` are two parallel reduction operators. A parallel reduction takes a binary operator, a list and the neutral element of the binary operator. The elements of l are combined with the binary operator asynchronously. The function `parallelRightReduce` combines elements in a right associative way, *i.e.*, the accumulation variable is the right operand of the binary operator, and vice versa.

The input lists of parallel mapping and reduction are evenly split according to the number of working tasks. For parallel mapping, each task locally applies the same binary operator to the assigned piece of the original input list. In parallel reduction, each task performs sequential reduction on the assigned piece of the original input list. The local results are combined using a sequential reduction to produce the final result.

4.2 Transforming reductions

Different transformation algorithms are applied to reductions of different forms.

4.2.1 Accumulation loop

The algorithm for transforming accumulation loops is present in Algorithm 2. The correctness of the loop transformation is provided by the map-reduce programming model. Parallel mapping computes intermediate results which are consumed by parallel reduction. The transformation is done only if the accumulation operator is associative.

An accumulation loop with accumulation assignments in the body are first transformed to several accumulation loops. Each loop carries only one accumulation assignment. This is achieved through loop fission [2]. For instance, the loop on the left of the codes below is transformed to the two loops on the right:

Algorithm 2 *transformAccumLoop*($l : Loop, E : PropEnv, \Gamma : TypeEnv$)

Require: l is an accumulation loop with one accumulation assignment.

$v \leftarrow getIterationVariable(l)$
$s \leftarrow getIterationSequence(l)$
$b \leftarrow getLoopBody(l)$
$a \leftarrow getAccumulationVariable(b)$
$f \leftarrow getAccumulationOperator(b)$
Let $\alpha_1, \alpha_2, \alpha_3, \alpha_4$ be fresh variables
$let_1 \leftarrow genLet(\alpha_1, s)$
$g \leftarrow genAnonymousFunction(b, v)$
$\theta_2 \leftarrow genParallelMap(g, \alpha_1, \Gamma)$
$let_2 \leftarrow genLet(\alpha_2, \theta_2)$
$id \leftarrow getNeutralValue(f, E, \Gamma)$
if *leftAssociative?*(b) **then**
  $\theta_3 \leftarrow genLeftParallelReduce(f, \alpha_2, id, \Gamma)$
else
  $\theta_3 \leftarrow genRightParallelReduce(f, \alpha_2, id, \Gamma)$
$let_3 \leftarrow genLet(\alpha_3, \theta_3)$
$\theta_4 \leftarrow genFunCall(f, [v, \alpha_3], \Gamma)$
$let_4 \leftarrow genLet(v, \theta_4)$
return *forwardSubstitution*$([let_1, let_2, let_3, let_4])$

```
x := 0                    x := 0
y := 1                    y := 1
for i in 1..10 repeat     for i in 1..10 repeat
   x := x + i*i + i          x := x + i*i + i
   y := y * i             for i in 1..10 repeat
                             y := y * i
```

An accumulation loop is then transformed to a sequence of four assignments following Algorithm 2. The first assignment computes the list of elements produced by the loop iterator. The right hand side of the assignment is generated corresponding to iterators of different forms:

$$\alpha_1 := \begin{cases} e & \text{iterator: for } v \text{ in } e \\ [\alpha_0 \text{ for } \alpha_0 \text{ in } e_1..e_2] & \text{iterator: for } v \text{ in } e_1..e_2 \end{cases}$$

We use α_i to represent a fresh variable. Variable α_1 is passed to the next assignment. The right hand side of the next assignment calls parallelMap operator:

$$\alpha_2 := \text{parallelMap}(g, \alpha_1),$$

operator g is an unary anonymous function. The mapping of g over α_1 returns a list. The value of each element in the list is combined to the accumulation variable in the original accumulation loop. The parallel mapping is generated by function *genParallelMap*.

The third assignment reduces the binary accumulation operator f over the value of variable α_2. The result is assigned to variable α_3:

$$\alpha_3 := \begin{cases} \text{parallelRightReduce}(f, \alpha_2, c_i) & \text{for right reduction} \\ \text{parallelLeftReduce}(f, \alpha_2, c_i) & \text{for left reduction} \end{cases}$$

parallel reduction should be chosen following the associativity used in the original accumulation loop. The function *leftAssociative?* returns true, if the reduction is left associative. The operator f is given by function *getAccumulationOperator*. The constant c_i is the neutral element of operator f. The neutral value is obtained by calling function *getNeutralValue*, which looks up the assumption environment. The generations of function calls to the two parallel reductions are done using functions *genLeftParallelReduce* and *genRightParallelReduce*, respectively.

The last assignment combines the value of α_3 to the accumulation variable:

$$\nu := f(\nu, \alpha_3).$$

The accumulation variable ν is extracted from the accumulation loop via function *getAccumulationVariable*.

At the final step, we call subroutine *forwardSubstitution* over the assignment sequence. The function implements forward expression substitutions. This transformation simplifies the four generated assignments into an single assignment.

4.2.2 *Library function call and built-in reduce form*

The other two kinds of reduction are transformed using Algorithm 3. Both reductions are function applications, using left as-

---

Algorithm 3 *transformReduce*(e : *Funcall*, E : *PropEnv*, Γ : *TypeEnv*)

Require: e is a function application of `reduce` or the built-in reduce operator.
  op ← the operand of e which is a binary operator
  s ← the operand of e which is a sequence
  id ← *getNeutralValue*(op, E, Γ)
  return *genLeftParallelReduce*(op, s, id, Γ)

---

sociative reductions by default. Therefore, the operators of these reductions are simply replaced with `parallelLeftReduce`.

5. IMPLEMENTATION

The entire framework is implemented as a library in the OpenAxiom computer algebra system. A graphical description of the framework is shown in Figure 2.

5.1 Concurrency in OpenAxiom

The parallel mapping and reduction package is implemented using the concept of *futures* [10]. The interfaces of *futures* are follows:

```
Future(T: Type): Public == Private where
  Public ==
    future: (() -> T) -> %
    get: % -> T
    ...
```

`future(t)` creates a future by taking in a function `t`. Function `t` will be executed in the background. Type `Future` is parameterized by type T. Variable T is the return type of function `t`. Once a future value is created, `t` starts execution. `get(f)` retrieves the computed value from future `f`. If the function wrapped by `f` terminates when `get` is called, result will be returned immediately. Otherwise `get` waits until the function finishes.

6. EXPERIMENTS

The automatic parallelization framework was tested in several configurations, including a software regression test, a set of algebra library functions, and a polynomial homotopy continuation package. We measured the performance of the sequential programs and their parallelized versions on a desktop PC and a computation node of the Brazos cluster [1]. Both machines use a GNU/Linux operating system. The tests were conducted wit an SBCL-based build of the OpenAxiom system. The desktop PC has one Intel Core2 2.4GHz dual-core processor with 4GB memory. The cluster computation node we used has two quad-core Intel Xeon E5420 2.5GHz processors with 32GB memory. The sequential versions used as references are the original source codes. Each sequential program is parallelized using two, four and eight threads, respectively.

6.1 A software installation test

We started with parallelizing a software regression test which takes long time to complete. There are five reduce calls in the test. The first four compute simple algebraic extensions of lists of polynomials. The last one multiplies a list of five univariate polynomials of simple algebraic extension.

The sequential version took 684s to complete. The last reduction alone accounts for 646s. Since the last reduction only multiplies five polynomials, we only use two threads in parallelization. The parallelized code takes 592s, which is improved by (only) 15% comparing to the sequential version. The parallelized long running reduction costs 527s which is 19% improvement over its sequential version. For the first four reductions, it is unnecessary to generate parallel codes which introduce overheads. To avoid this, we plan an adaptive framework in the future which uses more analysis and parallelize codes selectively.

6.2 Algebra library functions

We applied the framework to a set of 22 library functions. The semantics of the functions is described in Table 1. Functions `vdet`, `Chebyshev1` and `Chebyshev2` are implemented by us, and others are from the algebra library shipped with the AXIOM system family. All the functions are tested with randomly generated inputs. Each of these functions directly or indirectly uses at least one reduction in any of the three forms. Figure 3 and Figure 4 show the execution times of both the sequential and parallel versions of the library functions on the desktop PC and cluster, respectively. The

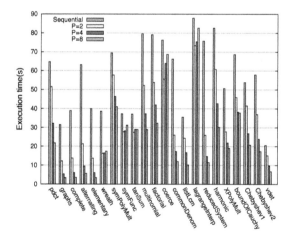

Figure 3: Execution times of library functions on the PC.

computed speed-ups are in Table 2.

The performance of a parallel reduction may be dominated by the administrative cost of spawning threads amd collecting intermediate results. Such cases include functions `pdct`, `commonDenom`, `listLcm` on cluster, and `symFunc`, `tanSum` and `coerce` on both machines. *e.g.*, in the parallel reduction of `pdct`, the final combination performs multiplications of large positive integers. The reductions too respectively 15s (38% of total execution time), 23s (65%) and 27s (79%) with two, four and eight threads on the cluster. The speed-ups of `pdct` are better on the desktop PC. The reason is that the large number multiplication is faster on desktop PC, which makes the final combination step less dominant. For instance, Multiplying 4000-bit positive integers is 6 times faster on the desktop machine than on the cluster node.

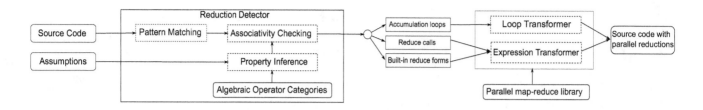

Figure 2: The workflow of the automatic parallelization framework.

Function name	Description
pdct	pdct takes in a partition of form $[a_1^{n_1}, ..., a_k^{n_k}]$, and computes $\prod_{i=1}^{k} n_i! a_i^{n_i}$.
graphs	graphs(n) is the cycle index of the group induced on the edges of a graph by applying the symmetric function to the n nodes.
complete	complete(n) computes the cycle index of the symmetric group of degree n.
alternating	alternating(n) computes the cycle index of the alternating group of degree n.
elementary	elementary(n) computes the n-th elementary symmetric function expressed in terms of power sums.
wreath	wreath(s1, s2) computes the cycle index of the wreath product of the two groups whose cycle indices are s1 and s2.
symPolyMult	multiplication between two symmetric polynomials.
symFunc	symFunc takes in a list of elements $[r_1, ..., r_n]$ of a ring. It returns the vector of the elementary symmetric functions in the r_i's: $[r_1 + ... + r_n, r_1 r_2 + ... + r_{n-1} r_n, ..., r_1 r_2 ... r_n]$.
tanSum	computes expansions of tangets of sums.
multinomial	multinomial(n,[m1,m2,...,mk]) computes the multinomial coefficient n!/(m1!m2!...mk!)
factorial	computes factorial n.
coerce	creates a permutation from a list of cycles.
reducedSystem	reducedSystem(A) returns a matrix B *s.t.* Ax = 0 and Bx = 0 have the same solutions in a ring.
commonDenom	computes a common denominator for a list of fraction integers.
listLcm	computes the least common multiply of a list of univariate polynomial integers.
harmonic	harmonic(n) compute the n-th harmonic number.
lagrangeInterp	computes the Largrange interpolation of a list of points.
XPolyMult	multiplies two generalized polynomials whose coefficients are not required to form a commutative ring.
boundOfCauchy	computes the Cauchy bound for the roots of the input polynomial.
Chebyshev1	evaluation of Chebyshev's first function $\theta(x) = \ln[\prod_{i=1}^{\pi(x)} p_i]$, where p_i is a prime, and π is the prime counting function.
Chebyshev2	evaluation of Chebyshev's second function $\psi(x) = \ln[lcm(1, 2, 3, ..., \lfloor x \rfloor)]$.
vdet	vdet(m) computes the determinant for a Vandermonde matrix m.

Table 1: OpenAxiom library functions used in the experiments.

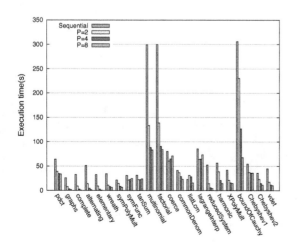

Figure 4: Execution times of library functions on the cluster.

Better speed-ups are obtained for a reduction if its sequential execution time increases rapidly with the size of the input list. Such as the functions graphs, complete, alternating, elementary, reducedSystem on both machines, and commonDenom on the desktop machine. Consider the super linear speed-ups of graphs. The reduction in this case uses addition over symmetric polynomials to sum elements in list of monomials. The addition operator first converts the two input polynomials to their internal representation. The internal representation is a list of monomials. The addition merges the two lists together in a sorted order. In the sequential code, merging two lists in sorted order iteratively has quadratic complexity. In the parallelized version, the monomial list obtained by each thread is much shorter. The local merge sort performed by each thread significantly saves the time as the execution time decreases quadratically when the input list becomes shorter. Moreover, the final combination adds up polynomials returned by the threads. Since each polynomial is a monomial list already in *sorted* order, this also significantly saves the computation time.

The execution of a function may be accelerated both by direct calls to parallel reductions functions, and by reductions present in

Function name	2_{PC}	4_{PC}	8_{PC}	2_{CL}	4_{CL}	8_{CL}
pdct	1.26	2.02	2.98	1.64	1.852	1.89
graphs	2.56	5.88	9.14	3.33	8.29	15.32
complete	2.82	6.43	11.77	3.63	12.28	34.92
alternating	2.96	6.62	11.16	3.66	11.86	32.59
elementary	2.92	6.61	11.49	3.61	12.13	34.19
wreath	2.36	2.34	2.21	3.10	4.23	5.34
symPolyMult	1.20	1.50	1.70	1.48	2.57	3.19
symFunc	1.34	1.32	1.20	1.43	1.38	1.26
tanSum	1.35	1.28	1.28	1.41	1.41	1.32
multinomial	1.52	2.13	2.75	2.24	3.40	3.59
factorial	1.47	1.89	2.45	2.16	3.32	3.57
coerce	1.37	1.19	1.11	1.32	1.23	1.13
reducedSystem	2.92	5.16	6.62	3.67	9.22	12.21
commonDenom	2.55	3.84	5.53	1.13	1.23	1.13
listLcm	1.46	2.12	3.48	0.74	0.82	1.46
harmonic	1.20	1.17	1.06	1.46	2.71	3.83
lagrangeInterp	1.36	1.93	2.73	1.33	1.33	1.17
XPolyMult	1.82	2.32	2.67	1.97	2.65	2.89
boundOfCauchy	1.50	1.80	1.82	1.33	2.41	4.52
Chebyshev1	1.30	2.00	2.6	1.45	1.53	1.51
Chebyshev2	1.57	2.43	3.34	1.54	2.46	3.11
vdet	1.56	2.45	3.73	2.54	3.88	4.29

Table 2: Speed-ups of the parallelized library functions on the PC and cluster with 2, 4 and 8 threads, respectively.

called functions. For instance, the function `wreath` contains a reduction using symmetric polynomial multiplication. The speed-ups shown in the results come from two sources: the parallel reduction itself, and the parallelized symmetric polynomial multiplication as the binary reduction operator. The latter contributes in a more significant way since multiplication is the most frequent computation in function `wreath`.

6.3 An application: concurrent homotopy continuation

We also developed a sequential polynomial homotopy library for solving polynomial systems. The parallelization framework is able to parallelize the path-following part of the source code. The homotopy library implements cheater's homotopy [11]. Linear system solving and evaluation in Newton's method use functions provided by OpenAxiom's algebra library.

This application is inspired by a recent work of Verschelde and Yoffe [18] on manually parallelizing various polynomial homotopy methods. Following a solution path is a task that can be done in parallel. We measured the performance and computed the speed-ups of the parallelized library on solving the 7-cyclic root problem. The system has 924 solution paths [6, 5]. Results on the desktop PC and the cluster node are shown in Table 3 and Table 4, respectively. On

Thread #	Execution Time(s)	Speedup(x)
Sequential	1370.47	1.00
2	727.82	1.88
4	790.19	1.73
8	778.32	1.76

Table 3: Performance of parallel homotopy continuations on the PC.

Thread #	Execution Time(s)	Speedup(x)
Sequential	1586.06	1.00
2	805.20	1.97
4	491.85	3.22
8	314.76	5.04

Table 4: Performance of parallel homotopy continuations on the cluster.

the desktop PC, we obtain good speed-up using two threads. We observed that the performance does not scale with more threads. This is due to contentions on limited computation resource. On the cluster node, we obtained good speed up using two and four threads. Speed up with eight threads is still far from ideal (8x). We believe this is because our preliminary parallel mapping and reduction library does not support advanced workload balancing strategies such as work-stealing, and thread pool. In the experiments where we use 8 threads, there are two threads which finish local computations much earlier than others do. The early finished threads return and exit instead of helping others to do more work.

7. RELATED WORK

The parallelization strategy presented in this paper is a map-reduce model [8]. In this model, programs are expressed in a functional style using a mapping followed by a reduction. Mapping and reduction are then automatically parallelized.

Most automatic parallelizations frameworks use program analysis, which are done at compile time, or at run time, or both. These analysis mainly focus on determining the parallelizability of loops. Static analysis such as GCD test [19] and Omega test [14] convert loops into linear systems. Dependence information is computed through linear system solving. Computation pattern matching is another way of parallelizing codes with specific formats. For instance, the range test [7] computes dependence information for loops whose iteration bounds are symbolic non-linear expressions. When the dependence information can not be determined at compile time, e.g., the behavior of loops depends on the values computed at run time, dynamic analysis is used to make decision at run time. For instance, the work of Salz and Mirchandaney [17] records the memory reference right before the execution of a loop. The information is used for computing dynamic dependence information. More recently, the hybrid analysis [16] and the sensitivity analysis [15] combine the information both from compile and run time, which proves to be a more precise way for capturing dependence information. The program analysis present in this paper is based on semantics pattern matching at compile time. This is due to the simple loop pattern used by reductions.

It is feasible to adapt our automatic parallelization framework to work for algebraic systems using other programming languages such as C++, Java and Aldor. One way to achieve the adaptation is through a type system or an annotation system which is able to provide algebraic semantic information from users. For instance, in C++ properties can be defined using *concepts* [9]. Java programmers can use *annotation* to provide extra information before declarations and definitions. Annotation in Java, however, must be written before definitions and declarations. Therefore, the user has to modify the original source code. By contrast, in our work, user assumptions may be written separately from the source code. The Fortress programming language [4] provides parallel execution by default for implicit parallelizable structures. Furthermore, properties may be specified using *traits*. At some point, a draft [3] of

Fortress specification allowed user-defined axioms. That capability was removed from recent Fortress language specification [4], and it does not seem to have even been implemented in released versions. Therefore, we cannot offer tangible point of comparison with Fortress.

8. CONCLUSION AND FUTURE WORK

We presented a set of algorithms and implementation of an automatic parallelization framework. The framework parallelizes reductions using algebraic semantics information in form of user-provided axioms. Experimental results show that the framework is capable of speeding up algebraic library functions as well as user applications which contain parallel reductions.

In the future, we would like to implement workload balancing such as work-stealing to improve the performance of parallel libraries. We plan on testing the framework with more real-world applications. Being able to parallelize reductions is only a start. It is important for us to support more implicit parallel structures *e.g.* recursions and nested loops, as well as to integrate more advanced automatic parallelization algorithms.

9. ACKNOWLEDGEMENTS

The authors thank the Texas A&M University Brazos HPC cluster for provinding computing resources to support the research reported here. This work was partially supported by NSF grant CCF-1035058.

10. REFERENCES

[1] Brazos HPC cluster. http://brazos.tamu.edu, Texas A&M University, 2011.

[2] Alfred V. Aho, Monica S. Lam, Ravi Sethi, and Jeffrey D. Ullman. *Compilers: Principles, Techniques, and Tools (2nd Edition)*. Addison-Wesley Longman Publishing Co., Inc., Boston, MA, USA, 2006.

[3] Eric Allen, David Chase, Joe Hallett, Victor Luchangco, JanWillem Maessen, Sukyoung Ryu, Guy L. Steele Jr., and Sam Tobin-Hochstadt. The fortress language specification version 1.0α. Technical report, Sun Labs, Oracle co., 2006.

[4] Eric Allen, David Chase, Joe Hallett, Victor Luchangco, JanWillem Maessen, Sukyoung Ryu, Guy L. Steele Jr., and Sam Tobin-Hochstadt. The fortress language specification version 1.0. Technical report, Sun Labs, Oracle co., 2008.

[5] Jörgen Backelin and Ralf Fröberg. How we proved that there are exactly 924 cyclic 7-roots. In *Proceedings of the 1991 international symposium on Symbolic and algebraic computation*, ISSAC '91, pages 103–111, New York, NY, USA, 1991. ACM.

[6] Göran Björck. Functions of modulus one on zp whose fourier transforms have constant modulus. In *Proceedings of Alfred Haar Memorial Conference*, 49, pages 193–197. Colloquia Mathematics Societatis János Bolyai, 1985.

[7] William Blume and Rudolf Eigenmann. The range test: a dependence test for symbolic, non-linear expressions. In *Proceedings of the 1994 conference on Supercomputing*, Supercomputing '94, pages 528–537, Los Alamitos, CA, USA, 1994. IEEE Computer Society Press.

[8] Jeffrey Dean and Sanjay Ghemawat. Mapreduce: simplified data processing on large clusters. In *Proceedings of the 6th conference on Symposium on Opearting Systems Design & Implementation - Volume 6*, pages 10–10, Berkeley, CA, USA, 2004. USENIX Association.

[9] Gabriel Dos Reis and Bjarne Stroustrup. Specifying c++ concepts. In *POPL '06: Conference record of the 33rd ACM SIGPLAN-SIGACT symposium on Principles of programming languages*, pages 295–308, New York, NY, USA, 2006. ACM.

[10] Robert H. Halstead, Jr. Multilisp: a language for concurrent symbolic computation. *ACM Trans. Program. Lang. Syst.*, 7(4):501–538, 1985.

[11] T. Y. Li, T. Sauer, and J. A. Yorke. The cheater's homotopy: an efficient procedure for solving systems of polynomial equations. *SIAM J. Numer. Anal.*, 26:1241–1251, October 1989.

[12] Yue Li and Gabriel Dos Reis. A quantitative study of reductions in algebraic libraries. In *PASCO '10: Proceedings of the 4th International Workshop on Parallel and Symbolic Computation*, pages 98–104, New York, NY, USA, 2010. ACM.

[13] Steven S. Muchnick. *Advanced compiler design and implementation*. Morgan Kaufmann Publishers Inc., San Francisco, CA, USA, 1997.

[14] William Pugh. The omega test: a fast and practical integer programming algorithm for dependence analysis. In *Proceedings of the 1991 ACM/IEEE conference on Supercomputing*, Supercomputing '91, pages 4–13, New York, NY, USA, 1991. ACM.

[15] Silvius Rus, Maikel Pennings, and Lawrence Rauchwerger. Sensitivity analysis for automatic parallelization on multi-cores. In *Proceedings of the 21st annual international conference on Supercomputing*, ICS '07, pages 263–273, New York, NY, USA, 2007. ACM.

[16] Silvius Rus, Lawrence Rauchwerger, and Jay Hoeflinger. Hybrid analysis: static & dynamic memory reference analysis. *Int. J. Parallel Program.*, 31:251–283, August 2003.

[17] Joel H. Salz, Ravi Mirchandaney, and Kay Crowley. Run-time parallelization and scheduling of loops. *IEEE Trans. Comput.*, 40:603–612, May 1991.

[18] Jan Verschelde and Genady Yoffe. Polynomial homotopies on multicore workstations. In *Proceedings of the 4th International Workshop on Parallel and Symbolic Computation*, PASCO '10, pages 131–140, New York, NY, USA, 2010. ACM.

[19] Michael Joseph Wolfe. *High Performance Compilers for Parallel Computing*. Addison-Wesley Longman Publishing Co., Inc., Boston, MA, USA, 1995.

The Minimum-Rank Gram Matrix Completion via Modified Fixed Point Continuation Method*

Yue Ma and Lihong Zhi
Key Laboratory of Mathematics Mechanization
AMSS, Beijing 100190, China
{yma, lzhi}@mmrc.iss.ac.cn

ABSTRACT

The problem of computing a representation for a real polynomial as a sum of minimum number of squares of polynomials can be casted as finding a symmetric positive semidefinite real matrix of minimum rank subject to linear equality constraints. In this paper, we propose algorithms for solving the minimum-rank Gram matrix completion problem, and show the convergence of these algorithms. Our methods are based on the fixed point continuation method. We also use the Barzilai-Borwein technique and a specific linear combination of two previous iterates to accelerate the convergence of modified fixed point continuation algorithms. We demonstrate the effectiveness of our algorithms for computing approximate and exact rational sum of squares decompositions of polynomials with rational coefficients.

Categories and Subject Descriptors: I.1.2 [Symbolic and Algebraic Manipulation]: Algorithms; G.1.6 [Numerical Analysis]: Global optimization

General Terms: algorithms, experimentation

Keywords: Gram matrix completion, nuclear norm minimization, Schur decomposition, sum of squares, fixed point iterative method

1. INTRODUCTION

Let $x = [x_1, \ldots, x_s]$ and $f(x) \in \mathbb{R}[x]$, then f is a sum of squares (SOS) in $\mathbb{R}[x]$ if and only if it can be written in the form

$$f(x) = m_d(x)^T \cdot W \cdot m_d(x), \tag{1}$$

in which $m_d(x)$ is a column vector of monomials of degree less than or equal to d and W is a real positive semidefinite matrix [42, Theorem 1] (see also [10]). W is also called a *Gram matrix* for f. If W has rational entries, then f is a sum of squares in $\mathbb{Q}[x]$.

*This material is based on work supported by a NKBRPC 2011CB302400, the Chinese National Natural Science Foundation under Grants 60821002/F02, 60911130369 and 10871194.

Problem 1 *Let $f \in \mathbb{Q}[x_1, \ldots, x_s]$ be a polynomial of degree $2d$, compute a representation for it as a sum of minimum number of squares of polynomials in $\mathbb{Q}[x_1, \ldots, x_s]$.*

The set of all matrices W for which (1) holds is an affine subspace of the set of symmetric matrices. If the intersection of this affine subspace with the cone of positive semidefinite (PSD) matrices is nonempty, then f can be written as a sum of squares. Since the components of $m_d(x)$ are not algebraically independent, W is in general not unique. Problem 1 can be restated as finding a Gram matrix with minimum rank satisfying a given set of constraints:

$$\left. \begin{array}{ll} \min & \mathrm{rank}(W) \\ s.t. & f(x) = m_d(x)^T \cdot W \cdot m_d(x) \\ & W \succeq 0,\, W^T = W \end{array} \right\} \tag{2}$$

For $s = 1$, Pourchet's main theorem [41] implies that every positive definite univariate polynomial in $\mathbb{Q}[x]$ is a sum of five squares in $\mathbb{Q}[x]$. Therefore, the minimum rank of the Gram matrix satisfying (2) is bounded by 5 for $s = 1$. For $s > 1$, Pfister's general theorem [40] shows that every positive definite polynomial in $\mathbb{R}[x_1, \ldots, x_s]$ is a sum of 2^s squares of rational functions in $\mathbb{R}(x_1, \ldots, x_s)$. It is well known that there exist positive semidefinite polynomials which cannot be written as sums of polynomial squares. However, as shown in [22], various exceptional SOS problems in the literature can be written as sums of less than 10 squares of polynomials after multiplying by suitable polynomials.

In general, the rank minimization is an intractable problem and is in fact provably NP-hard due to the combinatorial nature of the non-convex rank function [9]. In [12, 13, 43], they showed that $\mathrm{rank}(W)$ can be replaced by the nuclear norm of W, which is the best convex approximation of the rank function over the unit ball of matrices.

Expanding the right-hand side of the equality condition of (2), matching coefficients of the monomials, we obtain a set of linear equations which can be written as

$$\mathcal{A}(W) = b, \tag{3}$$

where $b = (b_1, \ldots, b_p) \in \mathbb{R}^p$ and b_i is the coefficient of the monomial $x^{\alpha_i} = x_1^{\alpha_{i,1}} \cdots x_s^{\alpha_{i,s}}$ in $f(x)$. The action of the linear operator $\mathcal{A} : \mathbb{S}^n \to \mathbb{R}^p$ on W is described by the inner product $\langle A_i, W \rangle := \mathrm{Tr}(A_i^T W)$ for $A_1, \ldots, A_p \in \mathbb{S}^n$. We use exponent tuples for indexing the matrices, then the entry in A_i with row index β_i and column index γ_i is equal to one if $\beta_i + \gamma_i = \alpha_i$ and zero otherwise. Therefore, there are at most n nonzero entries (being 1) in A_i, $i = 1, \ldots, p$. We use $\mathcal{A}^* : \mathbb{R}^p \to \mathbb{S}^n$ to denote the adjoint operator of $\mathcal{A}$.

The rank minimization problem (2) can be relaxed to a nuclear norm minimization problem

$$
\left.\begin{array}{ll}
\min & \|W\|_* \\
s.t. & \mathcal{A}(W) = b \\
& W \succeq 0,\, W^T = W
\end{array}\right\}
\tag{4}
$$

where the nuclear norm $\|W\|_*$ is defined as the sum of its singular values. The constraint $\mathcal{A}(W) = b$ can also be relaxed, resulting in either the problem

$$
\left.\begin{array}{ll}
\min & \|W\|_* \\
s.t. & \|\mathcal{A}(W) - b\|_2 \leq \epsilon \\
& W \succeq 0,\, W^T = W
\end{array}\right\}
\tag{5}
$$

or its Lagrangian version

$$
\min_{W \in \mathbb{S}_+^n} \ \mu\|W\|_* + \frac{1}{2}\|\mathcal{A}(W) - b\|_2^2,
\tag{6}
$$

where $\mathbb{S}_+^n$ is the set of symmetric positive semidefinite matrices and $\mu > 0$ is a parameter.

Prior work. In [1, 16, 25, 26, 27], they studied how to determine whether partially specified positive semidefinite matrices can be completed to fully specified matrices satisfying certain prescribed properties. A number of recent work has also shown that the low-rank solution can be recovered exactly via minimizing the nuclear norm under certain conditions [7, 8, 43, 44]. Notice that the nuclear norm of a symmetric positive semidefinite matrix is actually the trace, the nuclear norm minimization problem (4) is just a standard linear SDP problem which can be directly solved by interior-point methods in [4, 5, 13, 29, 45, 47] or projection methods in [18, 19, 23, 33, 37, 53] for large-scale SDP problems. Since most of these methods use second-order information, the memory requirement for computing descent directions quickly becomes too large as the problem size increases. Recently, several fast algorithms using only first-order information have been developed in [6, 14, 31, 32]. Moreover, some accelerated gradient algorithms were also proposed in [3, 20, 34, 35, 36, 49, 50] which have an attractive convergence rate of $O(1/k^2)$, where k is the iteration counter. These first-order methods, based on function values and gradient evaluation, cannot yield as high accuracy as interior point methods, but much larger problems can be solved since no second-order information needs to be computed and stored.

Main results. In this paper, we present two algorithms for solving the minimum-rank Gram matrix completion problem (4). Our algorithms are based on the fixed point continuation method (FPC). By modifying the shrinkage operator in FPC and using the Barzilai-Borwein (BB) technique to compute explicit dynamically updated step sizes, we get an algorithm, called modified fixed point continuation method with the Barzilai-Borwein technique (MFPC-BB). We prove the convergence of our algorithm under certain conditions.

We incorporate an accelerating technique in the MFPC-BB algorithm by computing the next iterate based not only on the previous one, but also on two previously computed iterates to get the AFPC-BB algorithm, which keeps its simplicity but shares the improved rate $O(1/k^2)$ of the optimal gradient method.

Numerical experiments demonstrate that modified FPC algorithms outperform SDP solvers SeDuMi [48] (in YALMIP [30]) and SDPNAL [53] for computing approximate and exact rational SOS of polynomials with rational coefficients, especially for large-scale sparse examples.

Structure of the paper. In Section 2, we derive the modified fixed point iterative algorithm for the minimum-rank Gram matrix completion problem. In Section 3, we establish the convergence result for our algorithm and prove that it converges to the optimal solution of problem (6). In Section 4, we introduce two techniques to accelerate the convergence of our algorithm and present MFPC-BB and AFPC-BB algorithms for solving problem (6). We demonstrate the performance and effectiveness of our algorithms through numerical examples for computing approximate and exact rational sum of squares decompositions of polynomials with rational coefficients in Section 5.

2. MODIFIED FIXED POINT ITERATIVE ALGORITHM

Let $f : \mathbb{R}^{n_1 \times n_2} \to \mathbb{R}$ be a convex function, the subdifferential of f at $X^* \in \mathbb{R}^{n_1 \times n_2}$ denoted by $\partial f(X^*)$ is the compact convex set defined by

$$
\partial f(X^*) := \{Z \in \mathbb{R}^{n_1 \times n_2} : f(Y) \geq f(X^*) + \langle Z, Y - X^* \rangle,
$$
$$
\forall\, Y \in \mathbb{R}^{n_1 \times n_2}\}.
$$

Following discussions in [28, Theorem 3.1] and [51], we derive the expression of the subdifferential of the nuclear norm at a symmetric matrix.

Theorem 1 Let $W \in \mathbb{S}^n$, then

$$
\partial\|W\|_* = \{Q^{(1)}Q^{(1)T} - Q^{(2)}Q^{(2)T} + Z : Q^{(i)T}Z = 0,
$$
$$
i = 1, 2, \ and \ \|Z\|_2 \leq 1\},
$$

where $Q^{(1)}$ and $Q^{(2)}$ are orthogonal eigenvectors associated with the positive and negative eigenvalues of W respectively.

PROOF. Suppose that the eigenvalues of a symmetric matrix W can be ordered as $\lambda_1 \geq \cdots \geq \lambda_t > 0 > \lambda_{t+1} \geq \cdots \geq \lambda_s$, $\lambda_{s+1} = \cdots = \lambda_n = 0$. Let $W = Q\Lambda Q^T$ be a Schur decomposition of W, where $Q \in \mathbb{R}^{n \times n}$ is an orthogonal matrix and $\Lambda = \mathrm{diag}(\lambda_1, \ldots, \lambda_n)$. These matrices can be partitioned as

$$
Q = \left(Q^{(1)}, Q^{(2)}, Q^{(3)}\right), \quad
\Lambda = \begin{pmatrix}
\Lambda^{(1)} & 0 & 0 \\
0 & \Lambda^{(2)} & 0 \\
0 & 0 & \Lambda^{(3)}
\end{pmatrix},
$$

with $Q^{(1)}, Q^{(2)}, Q^{(3)}$ having $t, s-t, n-s$ columns and being associated with $\Lambda^{(1)} = \mathrm{diag}(\lambda_1, \ldots, \lambda_t)$, $\Lambda^{(2)} = \mathrm{diag}(\lambda_{t+1}, \ldots, \lambda_s)$, and $\Lambda^{(3)} = \mathrm{diag}(\lambda_{s+1}, \ldots, \lambda_n)$, respectively.

Let $\lambda = (\lambda_1, \ldots, \lambda_n)^T$ and recall that

$$
\partial\|\lambda\|_1 = \{y \in \mathbb{R}^n : y_i = 1,\, i = 1, \ldots, t;\ y_j = -1,
$$
$$
j = t+1, \ldots, s;\ |y_k| < 1,\, k = s+1, \ldots, n\}.
$$

Let $Y \in \partial\|W\|_*$, by [28, Theorem 3.1], we have

$$
Y = Q\,\mathrm{diag}(d)\,Q^T,
$$

where $d \in \partial\|\lambda\|_1$. Therefore

$$
Y = Q^{(1)}Q^{(1)T} - Q^{(2)}Q^{(2)T} + Q^{(3)}DQ^{(3)T},
$$

where D is an $(n-s) \times (n-s)$ diagonal matrix with diagonal elements less than 1 in modulus.

Let $Z = Q^{(3)} D Q^{(3)T}$, we have $Q^{(i)T} Z = 0, i = 1, 2$. Let $\sigma_1(\cdot)$ denote the largest singular value of a given matrix, then we have

$$\|Z\|_2 = Q^{(3)} D Q^{(3)T} \leq \sigma_1(D) < 1,$$

which completes the proof. $\quad\square$

The optimality condition in [31, Theorem 2] can be generalized to the optimality condition for the constrained convex optimization problem (6).

Theorem 2 Let $f : \mathbb{S}^n \to \mathbb{R}$ be a proper convex function, i.e. $f < +\infty$ for at least one point and $f > -\infty$ for every point in its domain. Then W^* is an optimal solution to the problem

$$\min_{W \in \mathbb{S}^n_+} f(W) \qquad (7)$$

if and only if $W^* \in \mathbb{S}^n_+$, and there exists a matrix $U \in \partial f(W^*)$ such that

$$\langle U, V - W^* \rangle \geq 0, \text{ for all } V \in \mathbb{S}^n_+. \qquad (8)$$

PROOF. Suppose $U \in \partial f(W^*)$ and satisfies the inequality condition (8), then

$$f(V) \geq f(W^*) + \langle U, V - W^* \rangle, \quad \forall V \in \mathbb{S}^n_+,$$

we have $f(V) \geq f(W^*)$, for all $V \in \mathbb{S}^n_+$. This shows that W^* is an optimal solution of the problem (7).

Conversely, suppose W^* is the optimal solution of the problem (7), and (8) does not hold, i.e., for each $U \in \partial f(W^*)$,

$$\exists V \in \mathbb{S}^n_+, \text{ s.t. } \langle U, V - W^* \rangle < 0. \qquad (9)$$

Consider $Z(t) = tW^* + (1-t)V$, where $t \in [0, 1]$ is a parameter. Since $Z(t)$ is on the line segment between W^* and V, and $\mathbb{S}^n_+$ is a convex set, $Z(t) \in \mathbb{S}^n_+, \forall t \in [0, 1]$. By [46, Theorem 23.4], the one-sided directional derivative of f at $Z(1)$ with respect to the vector $W^* - V$ satisfies

$$f'(Z(t); W^* - V)|_{t=1} = f'(W^*; W^* - V)$$
$$= \sup\{\langle W, W^* - V \rangle : \forall W \in \partial f(W^*)\}$$
$$\geq \langle U, W^* - V \rangle > 0, \text{ by (9)}.$$

Therefore, for a small value $\epsilon > 0$, we have $f(Z(1-\epsilon)) < f(W^*)$, which is contradict to the fact that W^* is optimal to the problem (7). $\quad\square$

Based on above theorems, we can introduce a thresholding operator and extend the fixed point iterative scheme for solving (6).

Definition 1 Suppose $W = Q\Lambda Q^T$ is a Schur decomposition of a matrix $W \in \mathbb{S}^n$, where $\Lambda = \text{diag}(\lambda_1, \ldots, \lambda_n)$ and Q is a real orthogonal matrix. For any $\nu \geq 0$, the matrix thresholding operator $\mathcal{T}_\nu(\cdot)$ is defined as

$$\mathcal{T}_\nu(W) := Q\mathcal{T}_\nu(\Lambda)Q^T, \quad \mathcal{T}_\nu(\Lambda) = \text{diag}(\{\lambda_i - \nu\}_+),$$

where $t_+ = \max(0, t)$.

We should point out that the idea of using the eigenvalue decomposition of Y^k has also appeared in [49, Remark 3]. However, to our best knowledge, there exists no convergence analysis about the eigenvalue thresholding operator in the literature.

Let μ and τ be positive real numbers and X^0 be an initial starting matrix. For $k = 0, 1, 2, \cdots$, we compute

$$\begin{cases} Y^k &= X^k - \tau \mathcal{A}^*(\mathcal{A}(X^k) - b), \\ X^{k+1} &= \mathcal{T}_{\tau\mu}(Y^k), \end{cases} \qquad (10)$$

until a stopping criterion is reached.

Theorem 3 For the operator $\mathcal{A}$ defined by (3), suppose a matrix $W^* \in \mathbb{S}^n_+$ satisfies

1. $\|\mathcal{A}(W^*) - b\|_2 < \mu/n$ for a small positive number μ.

2. $W^* = \mathcal{T}_{\tau\mu}(h(W^*))$, where $h(\cdot) = I(\cdot) - \tau\mathcal{A}^*(\mathcal{A}(\cdot) - b)$ and $I(\cdot)$ is an identity operator.

Then W^* is the unique optimal solution of the problem (6).

PROOF. Let $\nu = \tau\mu$ and $Y^* = h(W^*) = W^* + E \in \mathbb{S}^n$, where $E = -\tau\mathcal{A}^*(\mathcal{A}(W^*) - b)$. We claim that $\mathcal{T}_\nu(Y^*)$ is the unique optimal solution to the following problem

$$\min_{W \in \mathbb{S}^n_+} \nu\|W\|_* + \frac{1}{2}\|W - Y^*\|_F^2, \qquad (11)$$

In fact, since the objective function $\nu\|W\|_* + \frac{1}{2}\|W - Y^*\|_F^2$ is strictly convex, there exists a unique minimizer, and we only need to prove that it is equal to $\mathcal{T}_\nu(Y^*)$. Without loss of generality, we assume that the eigenvalues of Y^* can be ordered as

$$\lambda_1(Y^*) \geq \cdots \geq \lambda_t(Y^*) \geq \nu > \lambda_{t+1}(Y^*) \geq \cdots > 0 >$$
$$\cdots \geq \lambda_s(Y^*), \lambda_{s+1}(Y^*) = \cdots = \lambda_n(Y^*) = 0.$$

We compute a Schur decomposition of Y^* as

$$Y^* = Q^{(1)}\Lambda^{(1)}Q^{(1)T} + Q^{(2)}\Lambda^{(2)}Q^{(2)T},$$

where $\Lambda^{(1)} = \text{diag}(\lambda_1, \ldots, \lambda_t)$, $\Lambda^{(2)} = \text{diag}(\lambda_{t+1}, \ldots, \lambda_s)$, $Q^{(1)}$ and $Q^{(2)}$ are block matrices corresponding to $\Lambda^{(1)}$ and $\Lambda^{(2)}$ respectively. Let $\widehat{X} = \mathcal{T}_\nu(Y^*)$, we have

$$\widehat{X} = Q^{(1)}(\Lambda^{(1)} - \nu I)Q^{(1)T},$$

therefore,

$$Y^* - \widehat{X} = \nu(Q^{(1)}Q^{(1)T} + Z), \quad Z = \nu^{-1}Q^{(2)}\Lambda^{(2)}Q^{(2)T}.$$

By definition, $Q^{(1)T}Z = 0$.

- If $\lambda_{t+1}(Y^*) \geq |\lambda_s(Y^*)|$, then $\|Z\|_2 = \lambda_{t+1}(Y^*)/\nu < 1$.

- Otherwise, let $y = (y_1, \ldots, y_p)^T = \mathcal{A}(W^*) - b \in \mathbb{R}^p$. Since $\mathcal{A}^*y = A_1y_1 + \cdots + A_py_p$ and there are at most n nonzero entries (being 1) in A_i, we have

$$\|E\|_F^2 = \tau^2\|\mathcal{A}^*y\|_F^2 \leq \tau^2 n^2(y_1^2 + \cdots + y_p^2) < \tau^2\mu^2.$$

Notice that $E \in \mathbb{S}^n$ and $W^* \in \mathbb{S}^n_+$, by [?, Theorem 8.1.5], we have

$$\|Z\|_2 = \frac{|\lambda_s(Y^*)|}{\nu} = \frac{\max\{|\lambda_1(E)|, |\lambda_n(E)|\}}{\nu} \leq \frac{\|E\|_F}{\nu} < 1.$$

Hence, according to Theorem 1, we have $Y^* - \widehat{X} \in \nu\partial\|\widehat{X}\|_*$, which means that $0 \in \nu\partial\|\widehat{X}\|_* + \widehat{X} - Y^*$. By Theorem 2, we immediately conclude that $\mathcal{T}_\nu(Y^*)$ is an optimal solution of the problem (11).

Since the objective function of the problem (6) is strictly convex, its optimal solution is also unique. If $W^* = \mathcal{T}_{\tau\mu}(Y^*)$, by Theorem 2, there exists a matrix $U \in \nu\partial\|W^*\|_* + W^* - Y^*$ such that

$$\langle U, V - W^* \rangle \geq 0, \quad \forall V \in \mathbb{S}_+^n.$$

Let $\widetilde{U} = U/\tau$, by substituting $\nu = \tau\mu$ and $Y^* = W^* - \tau\mathcal{A}^*(\mathcal{A}(W^*) - b)$ into the above subdifferential function, we have $\widetilde{U} \in \mu\partial\|W^*\|_* + \mathcal{A}^*(\mathcal{A}(W^*) - b)$ satisfying

$$\langle \widetilde{U}, V - W^* \rangle \geq 0, \quad \forall V \in \mathbb{S}_+^n.$$

By applying Theorem 2 once again, it is true that W^* is the optimal solution of the problem (6). $\square$

3. CONVERGENCE ANALYSIS

In this section, we analyze the convergence properties of the modified fixed point iterative scheme (10). We begin by recording two lemmas which establish the non-expansivity of the thresholding operator $\mathcal{T}_\nu(h(\cdot))$.

Lemma 1 *The thresholding operator $\mathcal{T}_\nu$ is non-expansive, i.e., for any $X_1, X_2 \in \mathbb{S}^n$,*

$$\|\mathcal{T}_\nu(X_1) - \mathcal{T}_\nu(X_2)\|_F \leq \|X_1 - X_2\|_F. \tag{12}$$

Moreover,

$$\|X_1 - X_2\|_F = \|\mathcal{T}_\nu(X_1) - \mathcal{T}_\nu(X_2)\|_F$$
$$\iff X_1 - X_2 = \mathcal{T}_\nu(X_1) - \mathcal{T}_\nu(X_2).$$

Lemma 2 *Suppose that the step size τ satisfies $\tau \in (0, 2/\|\mathcal{A}\|_2^2)$. Then the operator $h(\cdot) = I(\cdot) - \tau\mathcal{A}^*(\mathcal{A}(\cdot) - b)$ is non-expansive, i.e., for any $X_1, X_2 \in \mathbb{S}^n$,*

$$\|h(X_1) - h(X_2)\|_F \leq \|X_1 - X_2\|_F.$$

Moreover, we have

$$\|h(X_1) - h(X_2)\|_F = \|X_1 - X_2\|_F$$
$$\iff h(X_1) - h(X_2) = X_1 - X_2,$$

where $I(\cdot)$ is an identity operator.

The proof of these two lemmas follows the similar strategy presented in [31]. Instead of the inequality (3.3) in [31], we use the fact that for $X, Y \in \mathbb{S}^n$,

$$\mathrm{Tr}(XY) \leq \lambda(X)^T\lambda(Y),$$

where $\lambda(X), \lambda(Y)$ are the vectors of eigenvalues of X and Y respectively [28, Theorem 2.2].

We now claim that the modified fixed point iterations (10) converge to the optimal solution of the problem (6).

Theorem 4 *Let $\tau \in (0, 2/\|\mathcal{A}\|_2^2)$ and $W^* \in \mathbb{S}_+^n$ satisfy*

1. $\|\mathcal{A}(W^*) - b\|_2 < \mu/n$ *for a small positive number μ.*

2. $W^* = \mathcal{T}_{\tau\mu}(h(W^*))$, *where $h(\cdot) = I(\cdot) - \tau\mathcal{A}^*(\mathcal{A}(\cdot) - b)$.*

Then the sequence $\{X^k\}$ obtained via modified fixed point iterations (10) converges to W^*.

PROOF. Let $\nu = \tau\mu$. Since both $\mathcal{T}_\nu(\cdot)$ and $h(\cdot)$ are non-expansive, $\mathcal{T}_\nu(h(\cdot))$ is also non-expansive. Therefore, $\{X^k\}$ lies in a compact set and must have a limit point. Suppose $\widetilde{X} = \lim_{j \to \infty} X^{k_j}$ satisfying $\|\mathcal{A}(\widetilde{X}) - b\|_2 < \mu/n$. By $W^* = \mathcal{T}_\nu(h(W^*))$, we have

$$\|X^{k+1} - W^*\|_F = \|\mathcal{T}_\nu(h(X^k)) - \mathcal{T}_\nu(h(W^*))\|_F$$
$$\leq \|h(X^k) - h(W^*)\|_F \leq \|X^k - W^*\|_F,$$

which means that the sequence $\{\|X^k - W^*\|_F\}$ is monotonically non-increasing. Therefore

$$\lim_{k \to \infty} \|X^k - W^*\|_F = \|\widetilde{X} - W^*\|_F,$$

where $\widetilde{X}$ can be any limit point of $\{X^k\}$. By the continuity of $\mathcal{T}_\nu(h(\cdot))$, we have

$$\mathcal{T}_\nu(h(\widetilde{X})) = \lim_{j \to \infty} \mathcal{T}_\nu(h(X^{k_j})) = \lim_{j \to \infty} X^{k_j+1},$$

i.e., $\mathcal{T}_\nu(h(\widetilde{X}))$ is also a limit point of $\{X^k\}$. Therefore, we have

$$\|\mathcal{T}_\nu(h(\widetilde{X})) - \mathcal{T}_\nu(h(W^*))\|_F = \|\mathcal{T}_\nu(h(\widetilde{X})) - W^*\|_F$$
$$= \|\widetilde{X} - W^*\|_F.$$

Using Lemma 1 and Lemma 2 we obtain

$$\mathcal{T}_\nu(h(\widetilde{X})) - \mathcal{T}_\nu(h(W^*)) = h(\widetilde{X}) - h(W^*) = \widetilde{X} - W^*,$$

which implies $\mathcal{T}_\nu(h(\widetilde{X})) = \widetilde{X}$. By Theorem 3, $\widetilde{X}$ is the optimal solution to the problem (6), i.e., $\widetilde{X} = W^*$. Hence, we have

$$\lim_{k \to \infty} \|X^k - W^*\|_F = 0,$$

i.e., $\{X^k\}$ converges to its unique limit point W^*. $\square$

4. IMPLEMENTATION

This section provides implementation details of the modified FPC algorithm for solving the minimum-rank Gram matrix completion problem.

4.1 Evaluation of the eigenvalue thresholding operator

The main computational cost of the modified FPC algorithm is computing the Schur decompositions. Following the strategies in [6, 49], we use PROPACK [24] in Matlab to compute a partial Schur decomposition of a symmetric matrix.

PROPACK can not automatically compute only eigenvalues greater than a given threshold ν. To use this package, we must predetermine the number s_k of eigenvalues of Y^k to compute at the k-th iteration. Suppose $X^k = Q^{k-1}\Lambda^{k-1}(Q^{k-1})^T$, we set s_k equal to the number of diagonal entries of Λ^{k-1} that are no less than $\varepsilon_k\|\Lambda^{k-1}\|_2$, where ε_k is a small positive number. Notice that s_k is non-increasing. If s_k is too small, the non-expansive property (12) of the thresholding operator $\mathcal{T}_\nu$ may be violated. We increase s_k by 1 if the non-expansive property is violated 10 times [31].

4.2 Barzilai-Borwein technique

In [31], the authors always set the parameter $\tau = 1$ since their operator $\mathcal{A}$ is generated by randomly sampling a subset of p entries from matrices with i.i.d. standard Gaussian entries. For this linear map, the Lipschitz constant for the objective function of (6) is 1. According to Theorem 4, convergence for the Gram matrix completion problem is guaranteed provided that $\tau \in (0, 2/\|\mathcal{A}\|_2^2)$. This choice is, however, too conservative and the convergence is typically slow.

There are many ways to select a step size. For simplicity, we describe a strategy, which is based on the Barzilai-Borwein method [2], for choosing the step size τ_k. Let $g(\cdot) = \mathcal{A}^*(\mathcal{A}(\cdot) - b)$ and $g^k = \mathcal{A}^*(\mathcal{A}(X^k) - b)$. We perform the shrinkage iteration (10) along the negative gradient direction g^k of the smooth function $\frac{1}{2}\|\mathcal{A}(X^k) - b\|_2^2$, then apply the thresholding operator $\mathcal{T}_\nu(\cdot)$ to accommodate the non-smooth term $\|X\|_*$. Hence, it is natural to choose τ_k based on the function $\frac{1}{2}\|\mathcal{A}(X^k) - b\|_2$ alone. Let

$$\Delta X = X^k - X^{k-1}, \quad \Delta g = g^k - g^{k-1}.$$

The BB step provides a two-point approximation to the secant equation underlying quasi-Newton method, specifically,

$$\tau_k = \frac{\langle \Delta X, \Delta g \rangle}{\langle \Delta g, \Delta g \rangle}, \quad \text{or} \quad \tau_k = \frac{\langle \Delta X, \Delta X \rangle}{\langle \Delta X, \Delta g \rangle}.$$

In order to avoiding the parameter τ_k being either too small or too large, we take

$$\tau_k = \max\{\tau_{min}, \min\{\tau_k, \tau_{max}\}\},$$

where $0 < \tau_{min} < \tau_{max} < \infty$ are fixed parameters.

The idea of using the BB step to accelerate the convergence of gradient algorithms has also appeared in [52].

4.3 Algorithms

As suggested in [17, 31, 49], we adopt a continuation strategy to solve the problem (6). For the problem (6) with a target parameter $\bar{\mu}$ being a moderately small number, we propose solving a sequence of problems (6) defined by an decreasing sequence μ_k. When a new problem, associated with μ_{k+1}, is to be solved, the approximate solution for the current problem with μ_k is used as the starting point. We use the parameter η to determine the rate of reduction of the consecutive μ_k, i.e.,

$$\mu_{k+1} = \max(\eta\mu_k, \bar{\mu}), \quad k = 1, \ldots, L - 1.$$

Our modified fixed point continuation iterative scheme with the Barzilai-Borwein technique for solving (6) is outlined below.

Algorithm *MFPC-BB*

Input: ▸ Parameters $0 < \tau_{min} < \tau_0 < \tau_{max} < \infty$, $\mu_1 > \bar{\mu} > 0$, $\eta > 0$ and a tolerance $\epsilon > 0$

Output: ▸ A numeric Gram matrix.

- Set $X^0 = 0$.

- **For** $\mu = \mu_1, \ldots, \mu_L$, **do**

  1. Choose a step size τ_k via the BB technique such that $\tau_{min} \leq \tau_k \leq \tau_{max}$.
  2. Compute $Y^k = X^k - \tau_k \mathcal{A}^*(\mathcal{A}(X^k) - b)$ and a Schur decomposition of $Y^k = Q^k \Lambda^k (Q^k)^T$.
  3. Compute $X^{k+1} = Q^k \mathcal{T}_{\tau_k \mu_k}(\Lambda^k) (Q^k)^T$.

- **If** the stop criterion is true, **then return** X_{opt}.

- **end for**.

However, as shown in [3, 20, 49], the above algorithm may converge as $O(1/k)$. Very recently, alternative algorithms that could speed up the performance of the gradient method FPC have been proposed in [20, 49]. These algorithms rely on computing the next iterate based not only on the previous one, but also on two or more previously computed iterates. We incorporate this new accelerating technique in our MFPC-BB algorithm to solve the affine constrained low-rank Gram matrix completion problem (6). The accelerated algorithm, called AFPC-BB, keeps the simplicity of MFPC-BB but shares the improved rate $O(1/k^2)$ of the optimal gradient method.

Algorithm *AFPC-BB*

Input: ▸ Parameters $0 < \tau_{min} < \tau_0 < \tau_{max} < \infty$, $\mu_1 > \bar{\mu} > 0$, $\eta > 0$ and tolerance $\epsilon > 0$

Output: ▸ A numeric Gram matrix.

- Set $X^0 = 0, t_0 = 1$.

- **For** $\mu = \mu_1, \ldots, \mu_L$, **do**

  1. Choose a step size τ_k via the BB technique such that $\tau_{min} \leq \tau_k \leq \tau_{max}$.
  2. Compute $Z^k = X^k + \frac{t_{k-1} - 1}{t_k}(X^k - X^{k-1})$.
  3. Compute $Y^k = Z^k - \tau_k \mathcal{A}^*(\mathcal{A}(Z^k) - b)$ and a Schur decomposition of $Y^k = Q^k \Lambda^k (Q^k)^T$.
  4. Compute $X^{k+1} = Q^k \mathcal{T}_{\tau_k \mu_k}(\Lambda^k) (Q^k)^T$.
  5. Compute $t_{k+1} = \frac{1 + \sqrt{1 + 4t_k^2}}{2}$.

- **If** the stop criterion is true, **then return** X_{opt}.

- **end for**.

The following theorem shows that by performing the gradient step at the matrix Z^k instead of at the approximate solution X^k, the convergence rate of the MFPC-BB method can be accelerated to $O(1/k^2)$.

Theorem 5 *[20, 49] Let $\{X^k\}$ be the sequence generated by the AFPC-BB algorithm. Then for any $k > 1$, we have*

$$F(X^k) - F(X^*) \leq \frac{C\|X^* - X^0\|_F^2}{(k+1)^2},$$

where C is a constant, $F(X)$ is the objective function and X^* is the optimal solution of the problem (6).

5. NUMERICAL EXPERIMENTS

In this section, we report the performance of our modified FPC algorithms for writing a real positive semidefinite polynomial as a sum of minimum number of squares of polynomials. In our tests, we generate positive semidefinite matrices $W \in \mathbb{Q}^{n \times n}$ with rank r by sampling an $n \times r$ factor L with random integers ranging from -10 to 10, and setting $W = LL^T$. We construct the column vector $m_d(x)$ by choosing monomials in $x_1, \ldots, x_s$ of degree less than or equal to d for $2 \leq s \leq 4$ and $5 \leq d \leq 20$. Therefore, a positive semidefinite polynomial is obtained

$$f(x) = m_d(x)^T \cdot W \cdot m_d(x) \in \mathbb{Q}[x].$$

Replacing entries in W by parameters, expanding the right-hand side of the equality and matching coefficients of the

Problems				MFPC		MFPC-BB		AFPC-BB	
n	r	p	FR	# iter	error	# iter	error	# iter	error
100	10	579	1.6494	527	9.98e-4	434	9.97e-4	50	9.46e-4
200	10	1221	1.6011	797	9.99e-4	512	9.99e-4	59	9.84e-4
500	10	5124	0.9670	632	4.99e-3	499	4.99e-3	66	4.90e-3

Table 1: Comparison of MFPC, MFPC-BB and AFPC-BB, without using continuation technique.

monomials, we obtain a set of linear equations (3), which defines the linear map $\mathcal{A}$ from $\mathbb{S}^n$ to $\mathbb{R}^p$.

We know that an $n \times n$ symmetric matrix of rank r depends on $d_r = r(2n - r + 1)/2$ degrees of freedom. Let FR (degrees of freedom ratio) be d_r/p, where p is the number of linear constrains. If FR is large (close to 1), recovering W becomes harder as the number of measurements is close to the degree of freedom. Conversely, if FR is close to zero, recovering W becomes easier. Note that if $FR > 1$, there might have an infinite number of matrices with rank r satisfying given affine constraints.

The stopping criterion for the MFPC, MFPC-BB, AFPC-BB algorithms in our numerical experiments is given as follows:

$$\text{error} := \frac{\|\mathcal{A}(X_{\text{opt}}) - b\|_2}{\|b\|_2} < \epsilon, \qquad (13)$$

where ϵ is a moderately small number. Throughout the experiments, we choose the initial matrix $X^0 = 0$. For each test, we make an initial estimate of the value $L = \|\mathcal{A}\|_2^2$ which is the smallest Lipschitz constant of the gradient of $\frac{1}{2}\|\mathcal{A}X - b\|_2^2$. We set the Barzilai-Borwein parameters $\tau_{max} = 10/L$ and $\tau_{min} = 10^{-3}/L$. The thresholds 10 and 10^{-3} are found after some experiments.

We have implemented the MFPC-BB and AFPC-BB algorithms in MATLAB. All runs are conducted on a HP xw8600 workstation with an Inter Xeon(R) 2.67GHz CPU and 3.00 GB of RAM. The codes can be downloaded from http://www.mmrc.iss.ac.cn/~lzhi/Research/hybrid/FPCs/

5.1 Numerical experiments on random Gram matrix completion problems

In the first series of test, we set $\epsilon = 10^{-3}$ and compare the performance of the MFPC, MFPC-BB and AFPC-BB algorithms without continuation technique to solve problem (6) for randomly generated Gram matrix completion problems with moderate dimensions. In order to see the convergence behaviors of these algorithms clearly, we compute the full Schur decompositions at each iteration.

Table 1 reports the degree of freedom ratio FR, the number of iterations, and the error (13) of the three algorithms. Computational efficiency is measured by the number of iterations. As can be seen from this table, on the condition that these three algorithms achieve similar errors, MFPC-BB provides better performance with less number of iterations than MFPC, which shows that the Barzilai-Borwein technique is quite effective in accelerating the convergence of the MFPC algorithm. Moreover, AFPC-BB outperforms the other two algorithms greatly in terms of the number of iterations.

In Table 2, we report the performance of the AFPC-BB algorithm with continuation technique on randomly generated Gram matrix completion problems. We use PROPACK to compute partial eigenvalues and eigenvectors. For the con-

tinuation technique, we set the target parameter $\bar{\mu}$ to be $10^{-4}\|\mathcal{A}^*b\|$ and $\mu_1 = 1/4\|\mathcal{A}^*b\|$. The update strategy for μ_k is $\max(1/4\mu_{k-1}, \bar{\mu})$ until the stopping criterion is satisfied with $\epsilon = 10^{-3}$. The running time here and hereafter is shown in seconds. The rank of the Gram matrix is computed for the given tolerance 10^{-5} for all the following numerical experiments.

Problems				Results		
n	r	p	FR	# iter	rank	time
100	10	579	1.6494	76	10	1.48e+0
500	10	3309	1.4974	139	27	6.13e+1
1000	50	10621	4.5923	127	59	1.53e+2
1500	50	25573	2.8849	196	77	5.41e+2

Table 2: Numerical results for AFPC-BB, with continuation technique.

As indicated in this table, it takes the AFPC-BB algorithm fewer than 200 iterations and less than 10 minutes to reach convergence. For all problems in this set, FR is larger than 1. It is rather surprising that the low-rank Gram matrix can be recovered given only such a small number of affine constraints. To our best knowledge, nobody has considered solving matrix completion problems in this situation yet.

5.2 Exact rational sum of squares certificates

The numerical Gram matrix W returned by the AFPC-BB algorithm satisfies

$$f(x) \approx m_d(x)^T \cdot W \cdot m_d(x), \qquad W \succeq 0.$$

In order to derive an exact SOS decomposition of f, we might need to start with an approximate Gram matrix with high accuracy [21, 22, 38, 39] and convert it into a rational matrix.

Although first-order methods are often the only practical option for solving large-scale problems, it is rather difficult for them to achieve high accuracy. Therefore, we apply the structure-preserving Gauss-Newton iterations (see [21, 22]) to refine the low-rank Gram matrix W returned by the AFPC-BB algorithm: we choose a rank r which is less than or equal to the rank of W and compute the truncated $L^T DL$ decomposition of W to obtain an approximate SOS decomposition

$$f(x) \approx \sum_{i=1}^{r} (\sum_{\alpha} c_{i,\alpha} x^{\alpha})^2,$$

then apply the standard Gauss-Newton iteration to compute $\Delta c_{i,\alpha} x^{\alpha}$ such that

$$f(x) = \sum_{i=1}^{r} (\sum_{\alpha} c_{i,\alpha} x^{\alpha} + \Delta c_{i,\alpha} x^{\alpha})^2 + O(\sum_{i=1}^{r} (\sum_{\alpha} \Delta c_{i,\alpha} x^{\alpha})^2).$$

Examples				Results				Gauss-Newton iteration		
n	r	p	FR	solvers	rank	θ	time	rank	θ	time
100	5	579	0.8463	AFPC-BB	9	8.415e-1	1.75e+0	5	1.935e-9	2.98e+1
				SDPNAL	16	2.600e-1	1.50e+0	5	8.852e-10	2.63e+1
				SeDuMi	100	5.373e-2	4.03e+0	5	1.102e-10	3.22e+1
200	5	1221	0.8108	AFPC-BB	14	3.629e+0	1.07e+1	5	6.950e-10	4.02e+2
				SDPNAL	21	2.828e+0	1.06e+1	5	6.912e-10	5.57e+2
				SeDuMi	200	2.579e-1	5.56e+1	5	7.176e-10	1.10e+3
300	5	1932	0.7712	AFPC-BB	14	2.232e+1	2.32e+1	5	1.379e-9	5.61e+2
				SDPNAL	25	2.505e+0	2.69e+1	5	1.075e-9	7.05e+2
				SeDuMi	300	4.748e-1	2.62e+2	5	1.131e-9	6.89e+2
400	5	2610	0.7624	AFPC-BB	15	1.252e+1	6.23e+1	5	5.825e-7	1.22e+3
				SDPNAL	27	2.086e+0	8.69e+1	5	2.341e-8	5.03e+3
				SeDuMi	399	3.384e-1	4.88e+2	5	4.390e-8	5.03e+3
500	5	5124	0.4859	AFPC-BB	17	2.483e+1	5.33e+1	5	1.479e-5	7.92e+3
				SDPNAL	38	6.333e+0	2.53e+2	5	4.913e-8	1.84e+4
				SeDuMi	–	–	–			

Table 3: **Exact SOS certificates via AFPC-BB, SDPNAL, SeDuMi and Gauss-Newton iterations.**

Problems				AFPC-BB			SDPNAL		
n	r	p	FR	rank	θ	time	rank	θ	time
400	10	10078	0.3924	10	1.712e+1	2.46e+1	66	1.093e+1	1.43e+2
500	20	24240	0.4047	20	1.497e+1	4.48e+1	113	4.232e+1	6.72e+2
1000	10	27101	0.3673	10	2.207e+1	3.70e+2	99	8.801e+1	2.70e+3
1000	50	95367	0.5114	50	1.009e+1	6.56e+2	218	9.200e+1	9.92e+3
1500	10	45599	0.3280	10	3.310e+1	1.00e+3	121	3.408e+1	3.72e+4
1500	50	122742	0.6011	50	1.508e+1	3.84e+3	226	3.790e+1	1.36e+4

Table 4: **Exact SOS certificates via AFPC-BB and SDPNAL.**

The matrix W is updated accordingly to $W + \Delta W$ and the iteration is stopped when the backward error

$$\theta = \|f(x) - m_d(x)^T \cdot W \cdot m_d(x)\|_2$$

is less than the given tolerance. If it doesn't reach convergence after several Gauss-Newton iterations, we may increase the precision or use different r and try Gauss-Newton iterations again. Since these iterations may be run with multi-precision, it will be very expensive if r is large. This motivates us to find a Gram matrix with the minimum rank.

We notice that the AFPC-BB algorithm provides a low-rank Gram matrix to seed Gauss-Newton iterations while the SDP solver SeDuMi [48] (in YALMIP [30]) usually returns a Gram matrix with the maximum rank (see [11, Theorem 2.1]). It is interesting to notice that the newly developed SDP solver SDPNAL [53] can return a Gram matrix with relatively low rank.

In Table 3, we construct random examples with dense monomial vector $m_d(x)$ and compare the performance of the AFPC-BB algorithm with the SDP solvers SeDuMi and SDPNAL for recovering the low-rank Gram matrices. We also show the effectiveness of Gauss-Newton iterations run in Maple 13 with $Digits = 14$ in refining the numerical Gram matrix. The tolerance ϵ for the three solvers is set to 5×10^{-4} for all the numerical experiments, which is small enough to guarantee very good recoverability.

As indicated in this table, for the first four examples, we can use Gauss-Newton iterations (5.2) to refine the Gram matrices returned by all three algorithms to relatively high accuracy. After rounding every entry of the refined matrix to the nearest integer, we can easily recover a rational Gram matrix with rank 5 which gives the exact SOS representation of the nonnegative polynomial. However, when $n = 500$, Se-DuMi have troubles to recover the exact SOS decomposition for the given precision.

In Table 4, we construct random examples with sparse monomial vector $m_d(x)$, therefore, the degree of freedom ratio FR is reduced. It is surprising to notice that, without running Gauss-Newton iterations to achieve high accuracy, it is possible to recover the exact SOS representation of nonnegative polynomials directly from the numerical low-rank Gram matrix returned by the AFPC-BB algorithm. However, we are not yet able to recover exact SOS decompositions of polynomials directly from the matrices returned by SDPNAL, which have relatively large rank for the given tolerance.

Acknowledgments: We thank Ju Sun (National University of Singapore) for pointing out the reference [49]. We also thank all the referees for their useful comments.

6. REFERENCES

[1] BARRETT, W., JOHNSON, C. R., AND TARAZAGA, P. The real positive definite completion problem for a simple cycle. *Linear Algebra Appl. 192* (1993), 3–31.

[2] BARZILAI, J., AND BORWEIN, J. Two-point step size gradient methods. *IMA J. Numer. Anal. 8* (1988), 141–148.

[3] BECK, A., AND TEBOULLE, M. A fast iterative shrinkage-thresholding algorithm for linear inverse problems. *SIAM J. Imaging Sci. 2*, 1 (2009), 183–202.

[4] BURER, S., AND MONTEIRO, R. A nonlinear programming algorithm for solving semidefinite programs via low-rank factorization. *Math. Program. 95*, 2 (2003), 329–357.

[5] BURER, S., AND MONTEIRO, R. Local minima and convergence in low-rank semidefinite programming. *Math. Program. 103*, 3 (2005), 427–444.

[6] CAI, J.-F., CANDÈS, E. J., AND SHEN, Z. A singular value thresholding algorithm for matrix completion. *SIAM J. Optim. 20*, 4 (2010), 1956–1982.

[7] CANDÈS, E. J., AND RECHT, B. Exact matrix completion via convex optimization. *Found. Comput. Math. 9*, 6 (2009), 717–772.

[8] CANDÈS, E. J., AND TAO, T. The power of convex relaxation: near-optimal matrix completion. *IEEE Trans. Inform. Theory 56*, 5 (2010), 2053–2080.

[9] CHISTOV, A., AND GRIGORIEV, D. Complexity of quantifier elimination in the theory of algebraically closed fields. In *Proceedings of the Mathematical Foundations of Computer Science 1984* (London, UK, 1984), Springer-Verlag, pp. 17–31.

[10] CHOI, M., LAM, T., AND REZNICK, B. Sums of squares of real polynomials. *Symp. in Pure Math. 58*, 2 (1995), 103–126.

[11] DE KLERK, E., ROOS, C., AND TERLAKY, T. Initialization in semidefinite programming via a self-dual skew-symmetric embedding. *Oper. Res. Lett. 20*, 5 (1997), 213–221.

[12] FAZEL, M. *Matrix rank minimization with applications*. PhD thesis, Stanford University, 2002.

[13] FAZEL, M., HINDI, H., AND BOYD, S. A rank minimization heuristic with application to minimum order system approximation. In *Proceedings of the 2001 American Control Conference* (2001), pp. 4734–4739.

[14] GOLDFARB, D., AND MA, S. Convergence of fixed point continuation algorithms for matrix rank minimization. *Foundations of Computational Mathematics 11*, 2 (2011), 183–210.

[15] GOLUB, G. H., AND VAN LOAN, C. F. *Matrix computations*, third ed. Johns Hopkins Studies in the Mathematical Sciences. Johns Hopkins University Press, Baltimore, MD, 1996.

[16] GRONE, R., JOHNSON, C. R., DE SÁ, E. M., AND WOLKOWICZ, H. Positive definite completions of partial Hermitian matrices. *Linear Algebra Appl. 58* (1984), 109–124.

[17] HALE, E. T., YIN, W., AND ZHANG, Y. Fixed-point continuation for l_1-minimization: methodology and convergence. *SIAM J. Optim. 19*, 3 (2008), 1107–1130.

[18] HENRION, D., AND MALICK, J. Projection methods in convex optimization. *LAAS-CNRS Research Report 10730* (2010).

[19] HENRION, D., AND MALICK, J. Projection methods for conic feasibility problems; application to sum-of-squares decompositions. *Optimization Methods and Software 26*, 1 (2011), 23–46.

[20] JI, S., AND YE, J. An accelerated gradient method for trace norm minimization. In *Proceedings of the 26th Annual International Conference on Machine Learning* (New York, NY, USA, 2009), ICML '09, ACM, pp. 457–464.

[21] KALTOFEN, E., LI, B., YANG, Z., AND ZHI, L. Exact certification of global optimality of approximate factorizations via rationalizing sums-of-squares with floating point scalars. In *ISSAC '08: Proceedings of the twenty-first international symposium on Symbolic and algebraic computation* (New York, NY, USA, 2008), ACM, pp. 155–164.

[22] KALTOFEN, E., LI, B., YANG, Z., AND ZHI, L. Exact certification in global polynomial optimization via sums-of-squares of rational functions with rational coefficients, 2009. Accepted for publication in J. Symbolic Comput.

[23] KOČVARA, M., AND STINGL, M. On the solution of large-scale SDP problems by the modified barrier method using iterative solvers. *Math. Program. 109*, 2-3, Ser. B (2007), 413–444.

[24] LARSEN, R. PROPACK - software for large and sparse SVD calculations. Available from: http://soi.stanford.edu/~rmunk/PROPACK/.

[25] LAURENT, M. The real positive semidefinite completion problem for series-parallel graphs. *Linear Algebra Appl. 252* (1997), 347–366.

[26] LAURENT, M. Polynomial instances of the positive semidefinite and Euclidean distance matrix completion problems. *SIAM J. Matrix Anal. Appl. 22*, 3 (2000), 874–894.

[27] LAURENT, M. Matrix completion problems. *Encyclopedia of Optimization III (Interior - M)* (2001), 221–229.

[28] LEWIS, A. S. Convex analysis on the Hermitian matrices. *SIAM J. Optim. 6*, 1 (1996), 164–177.

[29] LIU, Z., AND VANDENBERGHE, L. Interior-point method for nuclear norm approximation with application to system identification. *SIAM J. Matrix Anal. Appl. 31* (2009), 1235–1256.

[30] LÖFBERG, J. YALMIP : A toolbox for modeling and optimization in MATLAB. In *Proc. IEEE CCA/ISIC/CACSD Conf.* (Taipei, Taiwan, 2004). URL: http://control.ee.ethz.ch/~joloef/yalmip.php.

[31] MA, S., GOLDFARB, D., AND CHEN, L. Fixed point and bregman iterative methods for matrix rank minimization. *Math. Program.* (2009), 1–33.

[32] MA, Y. The minimum-rank Gram matrix completion via fixed point continuation method (in Chinese). *Journal of Systems Science and Mathematical Sciences 30*, 11 (2010), 1501–1511.

[33] MALICK, J., POVH, J., RENDL, F., AND WIEGELE, A. Regularization methods for semidefinite programming. *SIAM J. Optim. 20*, 1 (2009), 336–356.

[34] NESTEROV, Y. A method of solving a convex programming problem with convergence rate $O(1/k^2)$. *Soviet Mathematics Doklady 27* (1983), 372–376.

[35] NESTEROV, Y. Smooth minimization of non-smooth functions. *Math. Program. 103*, 1 (2005), 127–152.

[36] NESTEROV, Y. Gradient methods for minimizing composite objective function. Tech. rep., 2007.

[37] NIE, J. Regularization methods for sum of squares relaxations in large scale polynomial optimization. Tech. rep., 2009. Available: http://arxiv.org/abs/0909.3551.

[38] PEYRL, H., AND PARRILO, P. A Macaulay 2 package for computing sum of squares decompositions of polynomials with rational coefficients. In *ProcSNC07* (2007), pp. 207–208.

[39] PEYRL, H., AND PARRILO, P. Computing sum of squares decompositions with rational coefficients. *Theoretical Computer Science 409* (2008), 269–281.

[40] PFISTER, A. Zur Darstellung definiter Funktionen als Summe von Quadraten. *Inventiones Math. 4*, 4 (1967), 229–236.

[41] POURCHET, Y. Sur la représentation en somme de carrés des polynômes à une indéterminée sur un corps de nombres algébriques. *Acta Arith. 19* (1971), 89–104.

[42] POWERS, V., AND WÖRMANN, T. An algorithm for sums of squares of real polynomials. *J. Pure Appl. Algebra 127*, 1 (1998), 99–104.

[43] RECHT, B., FAZEL, M., AND PARRILO, P. A. Guaranteed minimum-rank solutions of linear matrix equations via nuclear norm minimization. *SIAM Rev. 52*, 3 (2010), 471–501.

[44] RECHT, B., XU, W., AND HASSIBI, B. Necessary and sufficient conditions for success of the nuclear norm heuristic for rank minimization. In *CDC* (2008), pp. 3065–3070.

[45] RENNIE, J., AND SREBRO, N. Fast maximum margin matrix factorization for collaborative prediction. In *Proceedings of the 22nd international conference on Machine learning* (2005), ICML '05, pp. 713–719.

[46] ROCKAFELLAR, R. *Convex Analysis*. Princeton University Press, 1972.

[47] SREBRO, N., RENNIE, J., AND JAAKKOLA, T. Maximum-margin matrix factorization. In *Advances in Neural Information Processing Systems* (2005).

[48] STURM, J. Using SeDuMi 1.02, a MATLAB toolbox for optimization over symmetric cones. *Optimization Methods and Software 11/12* (1999), 625–653.

[49] TOH, K.-C., AND YUN, S. An accelerated proximal gradient algorithm for nuclear norm regularized linear least squares problems. Tech. rep., 2009. Available: http://www.optimization-online.org/DBHTML/2009/03/2268.html.

[50] TSENG, P. On accelerated proximal gradient methods for convex-concave optimization. *Submitted to SIAM J. Optim* (2008).

[51] WATSON, G. A. Characterization of the subdifferential of some matrix norms. *Linear Algebra Appl. 170* (1992), 33–45.

[52] WEN, Z., YIN, W., GOLDFARB, D., AND ZHANG, Y. A fast algorithm for sparse reconstruction based on shrinkage, subspace optimization, and continuation. *SIAM J. Sci. Comput. 32*, 4 (2010), 1832–1857.

[53] ZHAO, X.-Y., SUN, D., AND TOH, K.-C. A Newton-CG augmented Lagrangian method for semidefinite programming. *SIAM J. Optim. 20*, 4 (2010), 1737–1765.

Deflation and Certified Isolation of Singular Zeros of Polynomial Systems

Angelos Mantzaflaris and Bernard Mourrain
GALAAD, INRIA Méditerranée
BP 93, 06902 Sophia Antipolis, France
[FirstName.LastName]@inria.fr

ABSTRACT

We develop a new symbolic-numeric algorithm for the certification of singular isolated points, using their associated local ring structure and certified numerical computations. An improvement of an existing method to compute inverse systems is presented, which avoids redundant computation and reduces the size of the intermediate linear systems to solve. We derive a one-step deflation technique, from the description of the multiplicity structure in terms of differentials. The deflated system can be used in Newton-based iterative schemes with quadratic convergence. Starting from a polynomial system and a sufficiently small neighborhood, we obtain a criterion for the existence and uniqueness of a singular root of a given multiplicity structure, applying a well-chosen symbolic perturbation. Standard verification methods, based e.g. on interval arithmetic and a fixed point theorem, are employed to certify that there exists a unique perturbed system with a singular root in the domain. Applications to topological degree computation and to the analysis of real branches of an implicit curve illustrate the method.

Categories and Subject Descriptors

G.1.5 [**Mathematics of Computing**]: Roots of Nonlinear Equations; I.1.2 [**Computing Methodologies**]: Symbolic and Algebraic Manipulation—*Algebraic algorithms*

General Terms

Algorithms, Theory

Keywords

root deflation, multiplicity structure, dual space, inverse system, isolated point

1. INTRODUCTION

A main challenge in algebraic and geometric computing is singular point identification and treatment. Such problems naturally occur when computing the topology of implicit curves or surfaces [1], the intersection of parametric surfaces in geometric modeling. When algebraic representations are used, this reduces to solving polynomial systems. Several approaches are available: algebraic techniques such as Gröbner bases or border bases, resultants, subdivision algorithms[11], [14], homotopies, and so on. At the end of the day, a numerical approximation or a box of isolation is usually computed to identify every real root of the polynomial system. But we often need to improve the numerical approximation of the roots. Numerical methods such as Newton's iteration can be used to improve the quality of the approximation, provided that we have a simple root. In the presence of a multiple root, the difficulties are significantly increasing. The numerical approximation can be of very bad quality, and the methods used to compute this approximation are converging slowly (or not converging). The situation in practical problems, as encountered in CAGD for instance, is even worse, since the coefficients of the input equations are known, with some incertitude. Computing multiple roots of approximate polynomial systems seems to be an ill-posed problem, since changing slightly the coefficients may transform a multiple root into a cluster of simple roots (or even make it disappear).

To tackle this difficult problem, we adopt the following strategy. We try to find a (small) perturbation of the input system such that the root we compute is an exact multiple root of this perturbed system. In this way, we identify the multiplicity structure and we are able to setup deflation techniques which restore the quadratic convergence of the Newton system. The certification of the multiple root is also possible on the symbolically perturbed system by applying a fixed point theorem, based e.g. on interval arithmetic [17] or α-theorems ([6] and references therein).

Related work. In order to develop Newton-type methods that converge to multiple roots, deflation techniques which consist in adding new equations in order to reduce the multiplicity have already been considered. In [15], by applying a triangulation preprocessing step on the Jacobian matrix at the approximate root, minors of the Jacobian matrix are added to the system to reduce the multiplicity.

In [7], a presentation of the ideal in a triangular form in a good position and derivations with respect to the leading variables are used to iteratively reduce the multiplicity. This process is applied for p-adic lifting with exact computation.

In [8, 9], instead of triangulating the Jacobian matrix, the number of variables is doubled and new equations are introduced, which are linear in the new variables. They describe the kernel of the Jacobian matrix at the multiple root.

ISSAC'11, June 8–11, 2011, San Jose, California, USA.
Copyright 2011 ACM 978-1-4503-0675-1/11/06 ...$10.00.

In [3], this construction is related to the construction of the inverse system. The dialytic method of F.S. Macaulay [10] is revisited for this purpose. These deflation methods are applied iteratively until the root becomes regular, doubling each time the number of variables.

More recent algorithms for the construction of inverse systems are described e.g. in [12], reducing the size of the intermediate linear systems (and exploited in [18]), or in [13] using an integration method.

In [16], a minimization approach is used to reduce the value of the equations and their derivatives at the approximate root, assuming a basis of the inverse system is known.

In [20], the inverse system is constructed via Macaulay's method; tables of multiplications are deduced and their eigenvalues are used to improve the approximated root. They show that the convergence is quadratic at the multiple root.

Verification of multiple roots of (approximate) polynomial equations is a difficult task. The approach proposed in [17] consists of introducing perturbation parameters and to certifying the multiple root of nearby system by using a fixed point theorem, based on interval arithmetic. It applies only to cases where the Jacobian has corank equal to 1.

The univariate case. In preparation for the multivariate case, we review some techniques used to treat singular zeros of univariate polynomials, and we present our method on a univariate instance.

Let $g(x) \in \mathbb{K}[x]$ be a polynomial which attains at $x = 0$ a root of multiplicity $\mu > 1$. The latter is defined as the positive integer μ such that $d^\mu g(0) \neq 0$ whereas $g(0) = dg(0) = \cdots = d^{\mu-1} g(0) = 0$. Here we denote $d^k g(x) = \frac{d^k}{dx^k} g(x)/k!$ the normalized k-th order derivative.

We see that $\mathscr{D}_0 = \langle 1, d, \ldots, d^{\mu-1} \rangle$ is the maximal space of differentials which is stable under derivation, that vanish when applied to members of $\mathcal{Q}_0$, the $\langle x \rangle$-primary component of $\langle g \rangle$ at $x = 0$.

Consider now the symbolically perturbed equation

$$f_1(x, \varepsilon) = g(x) + \varepsilon_1 + \varepsilon_2 x + \cdots + \varepsilon_{\mu-1} x^{\mu-2} \qquad (1)$$

and apply every basis element of $\mathscr{D}_0$ to arrive to the new system $\boldsymbol{f}(x, \boldsymbol{\varepsilon}) = \left(f_1, df_1, \ldots, d^{\mu-1} f_1 \right)$ in $\mu - 1$ variables. The i-th equation is $f_i = d^{i-1} f_1 = d^{i-1} g + \sum_{k=i}^{\mu-1} \binom{k-1}{i-1} x^{k-i} \varepsilon_k$, i.e linear in $\boldsymbol{\varepsilon}$, the last one being $f_\mu = d^{\mu-1} g(x)$. This system deflates the root, as we see that the determinant of its Jacobian matrix at $(0, \boldsymbol{0})$ is

$$\det J_{\boldsymbol{f}}(0, \boldsymbol{0}) = \begin{vmatrix} \frac{d}{dx} f_1 & 1 & & 0 \\ \vdots & & \ddots & \\ \frac{d}{dx} f_{\mu-1} & 0 & & 1 \\ \frac{d}{dx} f_\mu & & 0 & \end{vmatrix} = \begin{matrix} -df_\mu(0) \\ = -\mu d^\mu g(0) \neq 0. \end{matrix}$$

Now suppose that ζ^* is an approximate zero, close to $x = \zeta$. We can still compute $\mathcal{D}_\zeta$ by evaluating $g(x)$ and the derivatives up to a threshold relative to the error in ζ^*. Then we can form (1) and use verification techniques to certify the root. Checking that the Newton operator is contracting shows the existence and unicity of a multiple root in a neighborhood of the input data. We are going to extend this approach, described in [17], to multi-dimensional isolated multiple roots.

Our approach. It consists of the following steps:

(a) Compute a basis for the dual space and of the local quotient ring at a given (approximate) singular point.

(b) Deflate the system by augmenting it with new equations derived from the dual basis, introducing adequate perturbation terms.

(c) Certify the singular point and its multiplicity structure for the perturbed system checking the contraction property of Newton iteration (e.g. via interval arithmetic).

In step (a), a dual basis at the singular point is computed by means of linear algebra, based on the integration approach of [13]. We describe an improvement of this method, which yields directly a triangular dual basis with no redundant computation. This method has the advantage to reduce significantly the size of the linear systems to solve at each step, compared to Macaulay's type methods [10, 8, 9, 3]. In the case of an approximate singular point, errors are introduced in coefficients of the basis elements. Yet a successful computation is feasible. In particular, the support of the basis elements is revealed by this approximate process.

In the deflation step (b), new equations and new variables are introduced in order to arrive to a new polynomial system where the singularity is obviated. The new variables correspond to perturbations of the initial equations along specific polynomials, which form a dual counterpart to the basis of the dual space. One of the deflated systems that we compute from the dual system is a square $n \times n$ system with a simple root. This improves the deflation techniques described in [8, 9, 3], which require additional variables and possibly several deflation steps. New variables are introduced only in the case where we want to certify the multiplicity structure. The perturbation techniques that we use extend the approach of [17] to general cases where the co-rank of the Jacobian matrix could be bigger than one. The verification step (c) is mostly a contraction condition, using e.g. techniques as in [17]. This step acts on the (approximate) deflated system, since verifying a simple solution of the deflated system induces a certificate of an exact singular point of (a nearby to) the initial system.

We are going to detail the different steps in the following sections, starting with notations in Sect. 2, dual basis in Sect. 3, deflation in Sect. 4, and certification in Sect. 5. In Sect. 6, we present and applications to the topology analysis of curves, and experimentation follows in the last section.

2. PRELIMINARY CONSIDERATIONS

We denote by $R = \mathbb{K}[\boldsymbol{x}]$ a polynomial ring over the field $\mathbb{K}$ of characteristic zero. Also, the *dual ring* R^* is the space of linear functionals $\Lambda : R \to \mathbb{K}$. It is commonly identified as the space of formal series $\mathbb{K}[[\boldsymbol{\partial}]]$ where $\boldsymbol{\partial} = (\partial_1, \ldots, \partial_n)$ are formal variables. Thus we view dual elements as formal series in differential operators at a point $\boldsymbol{\zeta} \in \mathbb{K}^n$. To specify that we use the point $\boldsymbol{\zeta}$, we also denote these differentials $\boldsymbol{\partial}_{\boldsymbol{\zeta}}$. When applying $\Lambda(\boldsymbol{\partial}_{\boldsymbol{\zeta}}) \in \mathbb{K}[[\boldsymbol{\partial}_{\boldsymbol{\zeta}}]]$ to a polynomial $g(\boldsymbol{x}) \in R$ we will denote by $\Lambda^{\boldsymbol{\zeta}}[g] = \Lambda^{\boldsymbol{\zeta}} g = \Lambda(\boldsymbol{\partial}_{\boldsymbol{\zeta}})[g(\boldsymbol{x})]$ the operation

$$\Lambda^{\boldsymbol{\zeta}}[g] = \sum_{\boldsymbol{\alpha} \in \mathbb{N}^n} \frac{\lambda_{\boldsymbol{\alpha}}}{\alpha_1! \cdots \alpha_n!} \cdot \frac{d^{|\boldsymbol{\alpha}|} g}{dx_1^{\alpha_1} \cdots dx_n^{\alpha_n}}(\boldsymbol{\zeta}), \qquad (2)$$

for $\Lambda(\boldsymbol{\partial}_{\boldsymbol{\zeta}}) = \sum \lambda_{\boldsymbol{\alpha}} \frac{1}{\alpha!} \boldsymbol{\partial}_{\boldsymbol{\zeta}}^{\boldsymbol{\alpha}} \in \mathbb{K}[[\boldsymbol{\partial}_{\boldsymbol{\zeta}}]]$. Extending this definition to an ordered set $\mathcal{D} = (\Lambda_1, \ldots, \Lambda_\mu) \in \mathbb{K}[[\boldsymbol{\partial}]]^\mu$, we shall denote $\mathcal{D}^{\boldsymbol{\zeta}}[g] = (\Lambda_1^{\boldsymbol{\zeta}} g, \ldots, \Lambda_\mu^{\boldsymbol{\zeta}} g)$. In some cases, it is convenient to use normalized differentials instead of $\boldsymbol{\partial}$: for any $\boldsymbol{\alpha} \in \mathbb{N}^n$, we denote $\boldsymbol{d}_{\boldsymbol{\zeta}}^{\boldsymbol{\alpha}} = \frac{1}{\alpha!} \boldsymbol{\partial}_{\boldsymbol{\zeta}}^{\boldsymbol{\alpha}}$. When $\boldsymbol{\zeta} = \boldsymbol{0}$, we have $\boldsymbol{d}_{\boldsymbol{0}}^{\boldsymbol{\alpha}} \boldsymbol{x}^{\boldsymbol{\beta}} = 1$ if $\boldsymbol{\alpha} = \boldsymbol{\beta}$ and 0 otherwise. More generally, $(\boldsymbol{d}_{\boldsymbol{\zeta}}^{\boldsymbol{\alpha}})_{\boldsymbol{\alpha} \in \mathbb{N}^n}$ is the dual basis of $((\boldsymbol{x} - \boldsymbol{\zeta})^{\boldsymbol{\alpha}})_{\boldsymbol{\alpha} \in \mathbb{N}^n}$.

For $\Lambda \in R^*$ and $p \in R$, let $p \cdot \Lambda : q \mapsto \Lambda(p\,q)$. We check that

$$(x_i - \zeta_i) \cdot \boldsymbol{\partial}_\zeta^\alpha = \frac{d}{d\partial_{i,\zeta}}(\boldsymbol{\partial}_\zeta^\alpha). \tag{3}$$

This property shall be useful in the sequel.

2.1 Isolated points and differentials

Let $\mathcal{I} = \langle f_1, \ldots, f_s \rangle$ be an ideal of R, $\boldsymbol{\zeta} \in \mathbb{K}^n$ a root of $\boldsymbol{f}$ and $m_\zeta = \langle x_1 - \zeta_1, \ldots, x_n - \zeta_n \rangle$ the maximal ideal at $\boldsymbol{\zeta}$. Suppose that $\boldsymbol{\zeta}$ is an isolated root of $\boldsymbol{f}$, then a minimal primary decomposition of $\mathcal{I} = \bigcap_{\mathcal{Q} \text{ prim.} \supset \mathcal{I}} \mathcal{Q}$ contains a primary component $\mathcal{Q}_\zeta$ such that $\sqrt{\mathcal{Q}_\zeta} = m_\zeta$ and $\sqrt{\mathcal{Q}'} \not\subset m_\zeta$ for the other primary components $\mathcal{Q}'$ associated to $\mathcal{I}$ [2].

As $\sqrt{\mathcal{Q}_\zeta} = m_\zeta$, $R/\mathcal{Q}_\zeta$ is a finite dimensional vector space. The multiplicity μ_ζ of $\boldsymbol{\zeta}$ is defined as the dimension of $R/\mathcal{Q}_\zeta$. A point of multiplicity one is called regular point, or simple root, otherwise we say that $\boldsymbol{\zeta}$ is a singular isolated point, or multiple root of $\boldsymbol{f}$. In the latter case we have $J_{\boldsymbol{f}}(\boldsymbol{\zeta}) = 0$.

We can now define the dual space of an ideal.

DEFINITION 2.1. *The dual space of $\mathcal{I}$ is the subspace of elements of $\mathbb{K}[[\boldsymbol{\partial}_\zeta]]$ that vanish on all the elements of $\mathcal{I}$. It is also called the orthogonal of $\mathcal{I}$ and denoted by $\mathcal{I}^\perp$.*

The dual space is known to be isomorphic to the quotient $R/\mathcal{I}$. Consider now the *orthogonal* of $\mathcal{Q}_\zeta$, i.e. the subspace $\mathscr{D}_\zeta$ of elements of R^* that vanish on members of $\mathcal{Q}_\zeta$, namely

$$\mathcal{Q}_\zeta^\perp = \mathscr{D}_\zeta = \{\Lambda \in R^* \,:\, \Lambda^\zeta[p] = 0, \, \forall p \in \mathcal{Q}_\zeta\}.$$

The following is an essential property that allows extraction of the local structure $\mathscr{D}_\zeta$ directly from the "global" ideal $\mathcal{I} = \langle \boldsymbol{f} \rangle$, notably by matrix methods outlined in Sect. 3.

PROPOSITION 2.2 ([13, TH. 8]). *For any isolated point $\boldsymbol{\zeta} \in \mathbb{K}$ of $\boldsymbol{f}$, we have $\mathcal{I}^\perp \cap \mathbb{K}[\boldsymbol{\partial}_\zeta] = \mathscr{D}_\zeta$.*

In other words, we can identify $\mathscr{D}_\zeta = \mathcal{Q}_\zeta^\perp$ with the space of polynomial differential operators that vanish at $\boldsymbol{\zeta}$ on every element of $\mathcal{I}$. Also note that $\mathscr{D}_\zeta^\perp = \mathcal{Q}_\zeta$.

The space $\mathscr{D}_\zeta$ has dimension μ_ζ, the multiplicity at $\boldsymbol{\zeta}$. As the variables $(x_i - \zeta_i)$ act on R^* as derivations (see (3)), $\mathscr{D}_\zeta$ is a space of differential polynomials in $\boldsymbol{\partial}_\zeta$, which is stable under derivation. This property will be used explicitly in constructing $\mathscr{D}_\zeta$ (Sect. 3).

DEFINITION 2.3. *The nilindex of $\mathcal{Q}_\zeta$ is the maximal integer $N \in \mathbb{N}$ s.t. $m_\zeta^N \not\subset \mathcal{Q}_\zeta$.*

It is directly seen that the maximal order of elements in $\mathscr{D}_\zeta$ is equal to N, also known as the *depth* of the space.

2.2 Quotient ring and dual structure

In this section we explore the relation between the dual ring and the quotient $R/\mathcal{Q}_\zeta$ where $\mathcal{Q}_\zeta$ is the primary component of the isolated point $\boldsymbol{\zeta}$. We show how to extract a basis of this quotient ring from the support of the elements of $\mathscr{D}_\zeta$ and how $\mathscr{D}_\zeta$ can be used to reduce any polynomial modulo $\mathcal{Q}_\zeta$.

It is convenient in terms of notation to make the assumption $\boldsymbol{\zeta} = \boldsymbol{0}$. This saves some indices, while it poses no constraint (since it implies a linear change of coordinates), and shall be adopted hereafter and in the next section.

Let $\text{supp}\,\mathscr{D}_0$ be the set of exponents of monomials appearing in $\mathscr{D}_0$, with a non-zero coefficient. These are of degree at most N, the nilindex of $\mathcal{Q}_0$. Since $(\forall \Lambda \in \mathscr{D}_0, \Lambda^0[p] = 0)$ iff $p \in \mathscr{D}_0^\perp = \mathcal{Q}_0$, we derive that $\text{supp}\,\mathscr{D}_0 = \{\boldsymbol{\alpha} \,:\, \boldsymbol{x}^\alpha \notin \mathcal{Q}_0\}$. In particular, we can find a basis of $R/\mathcal{Q}_0$ between the monomials $\{\boldsymbol{x}^\alpha \,:\, \boldsymbol{\alpha} \in \text{supp}\,\mathscr{D}\}$. This is a finite set of monomials, since their degree is bounded by the nilindex of $\mathcal{Q}_0$.

Given a monomial basis $\mathcal{B} = (\boldsymbol{x}^{\beta_i})_{i=1,\ldots,\mu}$ of $R/\mathcal{Q}_0$ and, for all monomials $\boldsymbol{x}^{\gamma_j} \notin \mathcal{Q}_0$, $j = 1, \ldots, s - \mu$, $s = \#\text{supp}\,\mathscr{D}_0$, with $\boldsymbol{x}^{\gamma_j} \notin \mathcal{B}$, the expression (normal form)

$$x^{\gamma_j} = \sum_{i=1}^{\mu} \lambda_{ij} \boldsymbol{x}^{\beta_i} \mod \mathcal{Q}_0 \tag{4}$$

of x^{γ_j} in the basis $\mathcal{B}$ then the dual elements [13, Prop. 13]

$$\Lambda_i(\boldsymbol{d}) = \boldsymbol{d}^{\beta_i} + \sum_{j=1}^{s-\mu} \lambda_{ij} \boldsymbol{d}^{\gamma_j}, \tag{5}$$

for $i = 1, \ldots, \mu$ form a basis of $\mathscr{D}_0$. We give a proof of this fact in the following lemma.

LEMMA 2.4. *The set of elements $\mathcal{D} = (\Lambda_i)_{i=1,\ldots,\mu}$ is a basis of $\mathscr{D}_0$ and the normal form of any $g(\boldsymbol{x}) \in R$ with respect to the monomial basis $\mathcal{B} = (\boldsymbol{x}^{\beta_i})_{i=1,\ldots,\mu}$ is*

$$NF(g) = \sum_{i=1}^{\mu} \Lambda_i^0[g]\, \boldsymbol{x}^{\beta_i}. \tag{6}$$

PROOF. First note that the elements of $\mathcal{D}$ are linearly independent, i.e. they form a basis. Now, by construction, $\sum_{i=1}^{\mu} \Lambda_i^0[\boldsymbol{x}^\alpha]\boldsymbol{x}^{\beta_i} = NF(\boldsymbol{x}^\alpha)$ for all $\boldsymbol{x}^\alpha \notin \mathcal{Q}_0$, e.g. $NF(\boldsymbol{x}^{\beta_i}) = \boldsymbol{x}^{\beta_i}$. Also, for $\boldsymbol{x}^\alpha \in \mathcal{Q}_0$, $\forall i$, $\Lambda_i^0(\boldsymbol{x}^\alpha) = 0$, since $\boldsymbol{\alpha} \notin \text{supp}\,\mathcal{D}$. Thus the elements of $\mathcal{D}$ compute $NF(\cdot)$ on all monomials of R, and (6) follows by linearity. We deduce that $\mathcal{D}$ generates the dual, as in Def. 2.1. $\square$

Computing the normal form of the border monomials of $\mathcal{B}$ via (6) also yields the border basis relations and the operators of multiplication in the quotient $R/\mathcal{Q}_0$ (see e.g. [5] for more properties).

If a graded monomial ordering is fixed and $\mathcal{B} = (\boldsymbol{x}^{\beta_i})_{i=1,\ldots,\mu}$ is the corresponding monomial basis of $R/\mathcal{Q}_0$, then $\boldsymbol{d}^{\beta_i}$ is the leading term of (5) w.r.t. the opposite ordering [9, Th. 3.1].

Conversely, if we are given a basis $\mathcal{D}$ of $\mathscr{D}_0$ whose coefficient matrix in the dual monomials basis $(\boldsymbol{d}^\alpha)_{\alpha \notin \mathcal{Q}_0}$ is $D \in \mathbb{K}^{\mu \times s}$, we can compute a basis of $R/\mathcal{Q}_0$ by choosing μ independent columns of D, say those indexed by $\boldsymbol{d}^{\beta_i}$, $i = 1, \ldots, \mu$. If $G \in \mathbb{K}^{\mu \times \mu}$ is the (invertible) matrix formed by these columns, then $D' := G^{-1}D$, is

$$D' = \begin{array}{c} \\ \Lambda_1' \\ \vdots \\ \Lambda_\mu' \end{array} \begin{array}{c} \overset{\beta_1 \quad \cdots \quad \beta_\mu \quad \gamma_1 \quad \cdots \quad \gamma_{s-\mu}}{\begin{bmatrix} 1 & & 0 & \lambda_{1,1} & \cdots & \lambda_{1,s-\mu} \\ & \ddots & & \vdots & & \vdots \\ 0 & & 1 & \lambda_{\mu,1} & \cdots & \lambda_{\mu,s-\mu} \end{bmatrix}} \end{array}, \tag{7}$$

i.e. a basis of the form (5). Note that an arbitrary basis of $\mathscr{D}$ does not have the above diagonal form, nor does it directly provide a basis for $R/\mathcal{Q}_0$.

For $t \in \mathbb{N}$, $\mathscr{D}_t$ denotes the vector space of polynomials of $\mathscr{D}$ of degree $\leq t$. The Hilbert function $h : \mathbb{N} \to \mathbb{N}$ is defined by $h(t) = \dim(\mathscr{D}_t)$, $t \geq 0$, hence $h(0) = 1$ and $h(t) = \dim \mathscr{D}$ for $t \geq N$. The integer $h(1) - 1 = \text{corank } J_{\boldsymbol{f}}$ is known as the *breadth* of $\mathscr{D}$.

3. COMPUTING LOCAL RING STRUCTURE

The computation of a local basis, given a system and a point, is done essentially by matrix-kernel computations, and consequently it can be carried out numerically, even when the point or even the system is inexact. Throughout the section we suppose $f \in R^m$ and $\zeta \in \mathbb{K}^n$ with $f(\zeta) = 0$.

Several matrix constructions have been proposed, that use different conditions to identify the dual space as a null-space. They are based on the *stability property* of the dual basis:

$$\forall \Lambda \in \mathscr{D}_t, \quad \frac{d}{d\partial_i}\Lambda \in \mathscr{D}_{t-1}, \quad i = 1, \ldots, n. \qquad (8)$$

We list existing algorithms that compute dual-space bases:
- As pointed out in (3), an equivalent form of (8) is: $\forall \Lambda \in \mathscr{D}_t, \Lambda[x_i f_j] = 0, \forall i,j = 1, \ldots, n$. Macaulay's method [10] uses it to derive the algorithm that is outlined in Sect. 3.1.
- In [12] they exploit (8) by forming the matrix D_i of the map $\frac{d}{d\partial_i} : \mathbb{K}[\boldsymbol{\partial}]_t \to \mathbb{K}[\boldsymbol{\partial}]_{t-1}$ for all $i = 1, \ldots, n$ and some triangular decomposition of the differential polynomials in terms of differential variables. This approach was used in [18] to reduce the row dimension of Macaulay's matrix, but not the column dimension. The closedness condition is also used in [21] to identify a superset of supp $\mathscr{D}_{t+1}$.
- The *integration method* in [13] "integrates" elements of a basis of $\mathscr{D}_t$, and obtains *a priori* knowledge of the form of elements in degree $t + 1$ (Sect. 3.2).

All methods are incremental, in the sense that they start by setting $\mathcal{D}_0 = (1)$ and continue by computing $\mathcal{D}_i$, $i = 1, \ldots, N, N+1$. When $\#\mathcal{D}_N = \#\mathcal{D}_{N+1}$ then $\mathcal{D}_N$ is a basis of $\mathscr{D}$, and N is the nilindex of $\mathcal{Q}$.

We shall review two of these approaches to compute a basis for $\mathscr{D}$, and then describe an improvement, that allows simultaneous computation of a monomial basis of the quotient ring while avoiding redundant computations.

3.1 Macaulay's dialytic matrices

This matrix construction is presented in [10, Ch. 4], a modern introduction is contained in [3], together with an implementation of the method in ApaTools[1].

The idea behind the algorithm is the following: An element of $\mathscr{D}$ is of the form $\Lambda(\boldsymbol{d}) = \sum_{|\boldsymbol{\alpha}| \leq N} \lambda_{\boldsymbol{\alpha}} \boldsymbol{d}^{\boldsymbol{\alpha}}$ under the condition: $\Lambda^{\boldsymbol{0}}$ evaluates to 0 at any $g \in \langle f \rangle$, i.e. $\Lambda^{\boldsymbol{0}}(g) = \Lambda^{\boldsymbol{0}}(\sum g_i f_i) = 0 \iff \Lambda^{\boldsymbol{0}}(x^{\boldsymbol{\beta}} f_i) = 0$ for all monomials $x^{\boldsymbol{\beta}}$. If we apply this condition recursively for $|\boldsymbol{\alpha}| \leq N$ we get a vector of coefficients $(\lambda_{\boldsymbol{\alpha}})_{|\boldsymbol{\alpha}| \leq N}$ in the (right) kernel of the matrix with rows indexed by constraints $\Lambda^{\boldsymbol{0}}[x^{\boldsymbol{\beta}} f_i] = 0$, $|\boldsymbol{\beta}| \leq N - 1$.

Note that the only requirement is to be able to perform derivation of the input equations and evaluation at $\zeta = \boldsymbol{0}$.

EXAMPLE 3.1. Let $f_1 = x_1 - x_2 + x_1^2$, $f_2 = x_1 - x_2 + x_2^2$. We also refer the reader to [3, Ex. 2] for a detailed demonstration on this instance. The matrices in order 1 and 2 are:

$$
\begin{array}{c}
\quad \begin{array}{ccc} 1 & d_1 & d_2 \end{array} \\
\begin{array}{c} f_1 \\ f_2 \end{array}
\begin{bmatrix} 0 & 1 & -1 \\ 0 & 1 & -1 \end{bmatrix},
\end{array}
\qquad
\begin{array}{c}
\quad\quad\quad \begin{array}{cccccc} 1 & d_1 & d_2 & d_1^2 & d_1 d_2 & d_2^2 \end{array} \\
\begin{array}{c} f_1 \\ f_2 \\ x_1 f_1 \\ x_1 f_2 \\ x_2 f_1 \\ x_2 f_2 \end{array}
\begin{bmatrix}
0 & 1 & -1 & 1 & 0 & 0 \\
0 & 1 & -1 & 0 & 0 & 1 \\
0 & 0 & 0 & 1 & -1 & 0 \\
0 & 0 & 0 & 1 & -1 & 0 \\
0 & 0 & 0 & 0 & 1 & -1 \\
0 & 0 & 0 & 0 & 1 & -1
\end{bmatrix}.
\end{array}
$$

[1]http://www.neiu.edu/~zzeng/apatools.htm

The kernel of the left matrix gives $\mathcal{D}_1 = (1, d_1 + d_2)$. Expanding up to order two, we get the matrix on the right, and $\mathcal{D}_2 = (1, d_1 + d_2, -d_1 + d_1^2 + d_1 d_2 + d_2^2)$. If we expand up to depth 3 we get the same null-space, thus $\mathcal{D} = \mathcal{D}_2$. $\square$

3.2 Integration method

This method is presented in [13]. It is an evolution of Macaulay's method, since the matrices are not indexed by all differentials, but just by elements based on knowledge of the previous step. This performs a computation adapted to the given input and results in smaller matrices.

For $\Lambda \in \mathbb{K}[\boldsymbol{\partial}]$, we denote by $\int_k \Lambda$ the element $\Phi \in \mathbb{K}[\boldsymbol{\partial}]$ with the property $\frac{d}{d\partial_k}\Phi(\boldsymbol{\partial}) = \Lambda(\boldsymbol{\partial})$ and with no constant term w.r.t. ∂_k.

THEOREM 3.2 ([13, TH. 15]). *Let $\langle \Lambda_1, \Lambda_2, \ldots, \Lambda_s \rangle$ be a basis of $\mathscr{D}_{t-1}$, that is, the subspace of $\mathscr{D}$ of elements of order at most $t-1$. An element $\Lambda \in \mathbb{K}[\boldsymbol{\partial}]$ with no constant term lies in $\mathscr{D}_t$ iff it is of the form:*

$$\Lambda(\boldsymbol{\partial}) = \sum_{i=1}^{s} \sum_{k=1}^{n} \lambda_{ik} \int_k \Lambda_i(\partial_1, \ldots, \partial_k, 0, \ldots, 0), \qquad (9)$$

for $\lambda_{ik} \in \mathbb{K}$, and the following two conditions hold:

(i) $\sum_{i=1}^{s} \lambda_{ik} \frac{d}{d\partial_l}\Lambda_i(\boldsymbol{\partial}) - \sum_{i=1}^{s} \lambda_{il} \frac{d}{d\partial_k}\Lambda_i(\boldsymbol{\partial}) = 0$,
for all $1 \leq k < l \leq n$.

(ii) $\Lambda^\zeta[f_k] = 0$, *for $k = 1, \ldots, m$.*

Condition (i) is equivalent to $\frac{d}{d\partial_k}\Lambda \in \mathscr{D}_{t-1}$, for all k. Thus the two conditions express exactly the fact that $\mathscr{D}$ must be stable under derivation and its members must vanish on $\langle f \rangle$.

This gives the following algorithm to compute the dual basis: Start with $\mathcal{D}_0 = \langle 1 \rangle$. Given a basis of $\mathscr{D}_{t-1}$ we generate the ns candidate elements $\int_k \Lambda_{i-1}(\partial_1, \ldots, \partial_k, 0, \ldots, 0)$. Conditions (i) and (ii) give a linear system with unknowns λ_{ik}. The columns of the corresponding matrix are indexed by the candidate elements. Then, the kernel of this matrix gives a basis of $\mathscr{D}_t$, which we use to generate new candidate elements. If for some t we compute a kernel of the same dimension as $\mathscr{D}_{t-1}$, then we have a basis of $\mathscr{D}$.

EXAMPLE 3.3. Consider the instance of Ex. 3.1. We have $f_1(\zeta) = f_2(\zeta) = 0$, thus we set $\mathcal{D}_0 = \{1\}$. Equation (9) gives $\Lambda = \lambda_1 d_1 + \lambda_2 d_2$. Condition (i) induces no constraints and (ii) yields the system

$$\begin{bmatrix} 1 & -1 \\ 1 & -1 \end{bmatrix} \begin{bmatrix} \lambda_1 \\ \lambda_2 \end{bmatrix} = 0 \qquad (10)$$

where the columns are indexed by d_1, d_2. We get $\lambda_1 = \lambda_2 = 1$ from the kernel of this matrix, thus $\mathcal{D}_1 = \{1, d_1 + d_2\}$.

For the second step, we compute the elements of $\mathcal{D}_2$, that must be of the form $\Lambda = \lambda_1 d_1 + \lambda_2 d_2 + \lambda_3 d_1^2 + \lambda_4(d_1 d_2 + d_2^2)$. Condition (i) yields $\lambda_3 - \lambda_4 = 0$, and together with (ii) we form the system

$$\begin{bmatrix} 0 & 0 & 1 & -1 \\ 1 & -1 & 1 & 0 \\ 1 & -1 & 0 & 1 \end{bmatrix} \begin{bmatrix} \lambda_1 \\ \vdots \\ \lambda_4 \end{bmatrix} = 0, \qquad (11)$$

with columns indexed by $d_1, d_2, d_1^2, d_1 d_2 + d_2^2$. We get two vectors in the kernel, the first yielding again $d_1 + d_2$ and a second one for $\lambda_1 = -1, \lambda_2 = 0, \lambda_3 = \lambda_4 = 1$, so we deduce that $-d_1 + d_1^2 + d_1 d_2 + d_2^2$ is a new element of $\mathcal{D}_2$.

In the third step we have

$$\Lambda = \lambda_1 d_1 + \lambda_2 d_2 + \lambda_3 d_1^2 + \lambda_4 (d_1 d_2 + d_2^2) + \tag{12}$$
$$\lambda_5 (d_1^3 - d_1^2) + \lambda_6 (d_2^3 + d_1 d_2^2 + d_1^2 d_2 - d_1 d_2),$$

condition (i) leads to $\lambda_3 - \lambda_4 + (\lambda_5 - \lambda_6)(d_1 + d_2) = 0$, and together with condition (ii) we arrive to a 4×6 matrix with two kernel elements that are already in $\mathcal{D}_2$. We derive that $\mathscr{D} = \langle \mathcal{D}_2 \rangle = \langle \mathcal{D}_3 \rangle$ and the algorithm terminates.

Note that for this example Macaulay's method ends with a matrix of size 12×10, instead of 4×6 in this approach. $\square$

3.3 Computing a primal-dual pair

In this section we provide a process that allows simultaneous computation of a basis pair $(\mathcal{D}, \mathcal{B})$ of $\mathscr{D}$ and $R/\mathcal{Q}$.

Computing a basis of $\mathscr{D}$ degree by degree involves duplicated computations. The successive spaces computed are $\mathscr{D}_1 \subset \cdots \subset \mathscr{D}_N = \mathscr{D}_{N+1}$. It is more efficient to produce only new elements $\Lambda \in \mathscr{D}_t$, independent in $\mathscr{D}_t/\mathscr{D}_{t-1}$, at step t.

Also, once a dual basis is computed, one has to transform it to the form (5), in order to identify a basis of $R/\mathcal{Q}$ as well. This transformation can be done a $posteriori$, by finding a sub-matrix of full rank and then performing Gauss-Jordan elimination over this sub-matrix, to reach matrix form (7).

We introduce a condition (iii) extending Th. 3.2, that addresses these two issues: It allows the computation of a total of μ independent elements throughout execution, and returns a "triangular" basis, e.g. a basis of $R/\mathcal{Q}$ is identified.

LEMMA 3.4. *Let* $\mathcal{D}_{t-1} = (\Lambda_1, \dots, \Lambda_k)$ *be a basis of* $\mathscr{D}_{t-1}$, *whose coefficient matrix is*

$$\begin{array}{c} \\ \Lambda_1 \\ \vdots \\ \Lambda_k \end{array} \begin{array}{cccccc} \boldsymbol{\beta}_1 \cdots \boldsymbol{\beta}_k & \gamma_1 & \cdots & \gamma_{s-k} \\ \left[\begin{array}{cccccc} 1 & * & * & * & \cdots & * \\ 0 & \ddots & * & \vdots & \vdots & \vdots \\ 0 & 0 & 1 & * & \cdots & * \end{array}\right] \end{array}, \tag{13}$$

yielding the monomial basis $\mathcal{B}_{t-1} = (\boldsymbol{x}^{\boldsymbol{\beta}_i})_{i=1,\dots,k}$. *Also, let* $\Lambda \in \mathbb{K}[\boldsymbol{\partial}]$ *be of the form* (9), *satisfying* (i-ii) *of Th. 3.2. If we impose the additional condition:*

(iii) $\Lambda^{\varsigma}[\boldsymbol{x}^{\boldsymbol{\beta}_i}] = 0$, $1 \leq i \leq k$,

then the kernel of the matrix implied by (i-iii) is isomorphic to $\mathscr{D}_t/\mathscr{D}_{t-1}$. *Consequently, it extends* $\mathcal{D}_{t-1}$ *to a basis of* $\mathscr{D}_t$.

PROOF. Let $\mathscr{K}$ be the kernel of the matrix implied by (i-iii), and let $\Lambda \in \mathbb{K}[\boldsymbol{\partial}]$ be a non-zero functional in $\mathscr{K}$. We have $\Lambda \in \mathscr{D}_t$ and $\Lambda^{\varsigma}[\boldsymbol{x}^{\boldsymbol{\beta}_i}] = 0$ for $i = 1, \dots, k$.

First we show that $\Lambda \notin \mathscr{D}_{t-1}$. If $\Lambda \in \mathscr{D}_{t-1}$, then $\Lambda = \sum_{i=1}^{k} \lambda_i \Lambda_i$. Take for i_0 the minimal i such that $\lambda_i \neq 0$. Then $\Lambda^{\varsigma}[\boldsymbol{x}^{\boldsymbol{\beta}_{i_0}}] = \lambda_{i_0}$, which contradicts condition (iii). Therefore, $\mathscr{K} \cap \mathscr{D}_{t-1} = \{0\}$, and $\mathscr{K}$ can be naturally embedded in $\mathscr{D}_t/\mathscr{D}_{t-1}$, i.e. $\dim \mathscr{K} \leq \dim \mathscr{D}_t - \dim \mathscr{D}_{t-1}$.

It remains to show that $\dim \mathscr{K}$ is exactly $\dim \mathscr{D}_t - \dim \mathscr{D}_{t-1}$. This is true, since with condition (iii) we added $k = \dim \mathscr{D}_{t-1}$ equations, thus we excluded from the initial kernel of (i-ii) (which is equal to $\mathscr{D}_t$) a subspace of dimension at most $k = \dim \mathscr{D}_{t-1}$, so that $\dim \mathscr{K} \geq \dim \mathscr{D}_t - \dim \mathscr{D}_{t-1}$.

We deduce that $\mathscr{K} \cong \mathscr{D}_t/\mathscr{D}_{t-1}$, thus a basis of $\mathscr{K}$ extends $\mathcal{D}_{t-1}$ to a basis of $\mathscr{D}_t$. $\square$

The above condition is easy to realize; it is equivalent to $\forall i, \boldsymbol{d}^{\boldsymbol{\beta}_i} \notin \text{supp}\, \Lambda$, which implies adding a row (linear constraint) for every i.

If we choose the elements of $\mathcal{B}$ with an opposite to total degree ordering, this constraint becomes $\lambda_{ik} = 0$ for some i, k, thus we rather remove the column corresponding to λ_{ik} instead of adding a row. Hence this lemma allows to shrink the kernel (but also the dimension) of the matrix and compute only new dual elements, which are reduced modulo the previous basis.

Let us explore our running example, to demonstrate the essence of this improvement.

EXAMPLE 3.5. We re-run Ex. 3.3 using Lem. 3.4.

In the initialization step $\mathcal{D}_0 = (1)$ is already in triangular form with respect to $\mathcal{B}_0 = \{1\}$. For the first step, we demand $\Lambda[1] = 0$, thus the matrix is the same as (10), yielding $\mathcal{D}_1 = (1, d_1 + d_2)$. We extend $\mathcal{B}_1 = \{1, x_2\}$, so that $\mathcal{D}_1$ is triangular with respect to $\mathcal{B}_1$.

In the second step we remove from (11) the second column, hence we are left a the 3×3 system in variables $\lambda_1, \lambda_3, \lambda_4$, yielding a single solution $-d_1 + d_1^2 + d_1 d_2 + d_2^2$. We extend $\mathcal{B}_1$ by adding monomial x_1: $\mathcal{B}_2 = \{1, x_2, x_1\}$.

For the final step, we search an element of the form (12) with $\Lambda[x_1] = \Lambda[x_2] = 0$, and together with (i-ii) we get:

$$\begin{bmatrix} 0 & 0 & 1 & -1 \\ 1 & -1 & 0 & 0 \\ 1 & 0 & -1 & 0 \\ 0 & 1 & 0 & 0 \end{bmatrix} \begin{bmatrix} \lambda_3 \\ \vdots \\ \lambda_6 \end{bmatrix} = 0.$$

We find an empty kernel, thus we recover the triangular basis $\mathcal{D} = \mathcal{D}_2$, which can be diagonalized to reach the form:

	1	d_2	d_1	d_1^2	$d_1 d_2$	d_2^2
Λ_1	1	0	0	0	0	0
Λ_2	0	1	0	1	1	1
Λ_3	0	0	1	-1	-1	-1

This diagonal basis is dual to the basis $\mathcal{B} = (1, x_2, x_1)$ of the quotient ring and also provides a normal form algorithm (Lem. 2.4) w.r.t. $\mathcal{B}$. In the final step we generated a 4×4 matrix, size smaller compared to all previous methods. $\square$

This technique for computing $\mathcal{B}$ can be applied similarly to other matrix methods, e.g. Macaulay's dialytic method.

If $h(t) - h(t-1) > 1$, i.e. there is more than one element in step t, then the choice of monomials to add to $\mathcal{B}$ is obtained by extracting a non-zero maximal minor from the coefficient matrix in $(\boldsymbol{d}^{\alpha})$. In practice, we will look first at the minimum monomials w.r.t. a fixed term ordering.

3.4 Approximate dual basis

In our deflation method, we assume that the multiple point is known approximately and we use implicitly Taylor's expansion of the polynomials at this approximate point to deduce the dual basis, applying the algorithm of the previous section. To handle safely the numerical problems which may occur, we utilize the following techniques:

- At each step, the solutions of linear system (9, i-iii) are computed via Singular Value Decomposition. Using a given threshold, we determine the numerical rank and an orthogonal basis of the solutions from the last singular values and the last columns of the right factor of the SVD.

- For the computation of the monomials which define the equations (3.4, iii) at the next step, we apply QR decomposition on the transpose of the basis to extract a non-zero maximal minor. The monomials indexing this minor are used to determine constraints (9, i-iii). A similar numerical technique is employed in [21], for Macaulay's method.

4. DEFLATION OF A SINGULAR POINT

We consider a system of equations $\boldsymbol{f} = (f_1, \ldots, f_s)$, $f_k \in \mathbb{R}[\boldsymbol{x}]$, which has a multiple root at $\boldsymbol{x} = \boldsymbol{\zeta}$. Also, let $\mathcal{B} = (\boldsymbol{x}^{\boldsymbol{\beta}_1}, \ldots, \boldsymbol{x}^{\boldsymbol{\beta}_\mu})$ be a basis of $R/\mathcal{Q}_{\boldsymbol{\zeta}}$ and $\mathcal{D} = (\Lambda_1, \ldots, \Lambda_\mu)$ its dual counterpart, with $\Lambda_1 = \boldsymbol{1}$.

We introduce a new set of equations starting from $\boldsymbol{f}$, as follows: add for every f_k the polynomial $g_k = f_k + p_k$, $p_k = \sum_{i=1}^\mu \varepsilon_{i,k}(\boldsymbol{x}-\boldsymbol{\zeta})^{\boldsymbol{\beta}_i}$ where $\boldsymbol{\varepsilon}_k = (\varepsilon_{k,1}, \ldots, \varepsilon_{k,\mu})$ is a new vector of μ variables.

Consider the system

$$\mathcal{D}\boldsymbol{g}(\boldsymbol{x}, \boldsymbol{\varepsilon}) = \left(\Lambda_1(\boldsymbol{\partial_x})[\boldsymbol{g}], \ldots, \Lambda_\mu(\boldsymbol{\partial_x})[\boldsymbol{g}]\right).$$

where $\Lambda^{\boldsymbol{x}}[g_k] = \Lambda_i(\boldsymbol{d_x})[g_k]$ is defined as in (2) with $\boldsymbol{\zeta}$ replaced by $\boldsymbol{x}$, i.e. we differentiate g_k but we do not evaluate at $\boldsymbol{\zeta}$. This is a system of μs equations, which we shall index $\mathcal{D}\boldsymbol{g}(\boldsymbol{x}, \boldsymbol{\varepsilon}) = (g_{1,1}, \ldots, g_{\mu,s})$. We have

$$g_{ik}(\boldsymbol{x}, \boldsymbol{\varepsilon}) = \Lambda_i^{\boldsymbol{x}}[f_k+p_k] = \Lambda_i^{\boldsymbol{x}}[f_k]+\Lambda_i^{\boldsymbol{x}}[p_k] = \Lambda_i^{\boldsymbol{x}}[f_k]+p_{i,k}(\boldsymbol{x}, \boldsymbol{\varepsilon}).$$

Notice that $p_{i,k}(\boldsymbol{\zeta}, \boldsymbol{\varepsilon}) = \Lambda_i^{\boldsymbol{\zeta}}[p_k] = \varepsilon_{i,k}$ because $\mathcal{D} = (\Lambda_1, .., \Lambda_\mu)$ is dual to $\mathcal{B}$.

As the first basis element of $\mathcal{D}$ is $\boldsymbol{1}$ (the evaluation at the root), the first s equations are $\boldsymbol{g}(\boldsymbol{x}, \boldsymbol{\varepsilon}) = 0$.

Note that this system is under-determined, since the number of variables is $\mu s + n$ and the number of equations is μs. We shall provide a systematic way to choose n variables and purge them (or better, set them equal to zero).

This way we arrive to a square system $\mathcal{D}\boldsymbol{g}(\boldsymbol{x}, \tilde{\boldsymbol{\varepsilon}})$ (we use $\tilde{\boldsymbol{\varepsilon}}$ for the remaining $\mu s - n$ variables) of size $\mu s \times \mu s$. We shall prove that this system vanishes on $(\boldsymbol{\zeta}, \boldsymbol{0})$ and that $J_{\mathcal{D}\boldsymbol{g}}(\boldsymbol{\zeta}, \boldsymbol{0}) \neq 0$.

By linearity of the Jacobian matrix we have

$$J_{\mathcal{D}\boldsymbol{g}}(\boldsymbol{x}, \boldsymbol{\varepsilon}) = J_{\mathcal{D}\boldsymbol{f}}(\boldsymbol{x}, \boldsymbol{\varepsilon}) + J_{\mathcal{D}\boldsymbol{p}}(\boldsymbol{x}, \boldsymbol{\varepsilon})$$
$$= [\, J_{\mathcal{D}\boldsymbol{f}}(\boldsymbol{x})\,|\,\boldsymbol{0}\,] + [\, J_{\mathcal{D}\boldsymbol{p}}^{\boldsymbol{x}}(\boldsymbol{x}, \boldsymbol{\varepsilon})\,|\,J_{\mathcal{D}\boldsymbol{p}}^{\boldsymbol{\varepsilon}}(\boldsymbol{x}, \boldsymbol{\varepsilon})\,],$$

where $J_{\mathcal{D}\boldsymbol{p}}^{\boldsymbol{x}}(\boldsymbol{x}, \boldsymbol{\varepsilon})$ (resp. $J_{\mathcal{D}\boldsymbol{p}}^{\boldsymbol{\varepsilon}}(\boldsymbol{x}, \boldsymbol{\varepsilon})$) is the Jacobian matrix of $\mathcal{D}\boldsymbol{p}$ with respect to $\boldsymbol{x}$ (resp. $\boldsymbol{\varepsilon}$).

LEMMA 4.1. *The Jacobian $J_{\mathcal{D}\boldsymbol{p}}^{\boldsymbol{\varepsilon}}(\boldsymbol{x}, \boldsymbol{\varepsilon})$ of the linear system $\mathcal{D}\boldsymbol{p} = (p_{1,1}, \ldots, p_{\mu,s})$ with $p_{i,k}(\boldsymbol{\varepsilon}_k) = \Lambda_i^{\boldsymbol{x}}[p_k](\boldsymbol{x}, \boldsymbol{\varepsilon}_k)$ evaluated at $(\boldsymbol{x}, \boldsymbol{\varepsilon}) = (\boldsymbol{\zeta}, \boldsymbol{0})$ is the identity matrix of dimension μs.*

PROOF OF LEMMA 4.1. First note that the system is block separated, i.e. every $p_{i,k}$ depends only on variables $\boldsymbol{\varepsilon}_k$ and not on all $\boldsymbol{\varepsilon} = (\boldsymbol{\varepsilon}_1, \ldots, \boldsymbol{\varepsilon}_s)$. This shows that $J_{\mathcal{D}\boldsymbol{p}}^{\boldsymbol{\varepsilon}}(\boldsymbol{x}, \boldsymbol{\varepsilon})$ is block diagonal, $J_{\mathcal{D}\boldsymbol{p}}^{\boldsymbol{\varepsilon}}(\boldsymbol{x}, \boldsymbol{\varepsilon}) = \mathrm{diag}(J_1, \ldots, J_\mu)$. Now we claim that these blocks are all equal to the identity matrix. To see this, consider their entry $\frac{d}{d\varepsilon_{k,j}} p_{i,k}$ for $i, j = 1, .., \mu$, which is

$$\frac{d}{d\varepsilon_{k,j}} \Lambda_i^{\boldsymbol{\zeta}}[p_k] = \Lambda_i^{\boldsymbol{\zeta}}[\frac{d}{d\varepsilon_{k,j}} p_k] = \Lambda_i^{\boldsymbol{\zeta}}[\boldsymbol{x}^{\boldsymbol{\beta}_j}] = \begin{cases} 1 & ,i = j \\ 0 & ,\text{otherwise} \end{cases},$$

since $\frac{d}{d\varepsilon_{k,j}} p_k = \frac{d}{d\varepsilon_{k,j}}(\boldsymbol{x}^{\boldsymbol{\beta}_j}\varepsilon_{k,j}) = \boldsymbol{x}^{\boldsymbol{\beta}_j}$. $\square$

LEMMA 4.2. *The $\mu s \times n$ Jacobian matrix $J_{\mathcal{D}\boldsymbol{f}}(\boldsymbol{x})$ of the system $\mathcal{D}\boldsymbol{f}(\boldsymbol{x}) = (f_1, \ldots, f_{\mu n})$ is of full rank n at $\boldsymbol{x} = \boldsymbol{\zeta}$.*

PROOF OF LEMMA 4.2. Suppose that the matrix is rank-deficient. Then there is a non-trivial vector in its kernel,

$$J_{\mathcal{D}\boldsymbol{f}}(\boldsymbol{\zeta}) \cdot \boldsymbol{v} = \boldsymbol{0}.$$

The entries of $\boldsymbol{v}$ are indexed by ∂_i. This implies that a non-zero differential $\Delta = v_1\partial_1 + \cdots + v_n\partial_n$ of order one satisfies

the following relations: $(\Delta\Lambda_i)^{\boldsymbol{\zeta}}[f_j] = 0, i = 1, \ldots, \mu, j = 1, \ldots, s$. By the standard derivation rules, we have

$$\frac{d}{d\partial_k}(\Delta\Lambda_i) = v_k\Lambda_i + \Delta\frac{d}{d\partial_k}\Lambda_i,$$

for $i = 1, \ldots, \mu, , k = 1, \ldots, n$. Since $\mathscr{D}$ is stable under derivation, $\frac{d}{d\partial_k}\Lambda_i \in \mathscr{D}$. We deduce that the vector space spanned by $\langle \mathscr{D}, \Delta\mathscr{D} \rangle$ is stable under derivation and vanishes on $\boldsymbol{f}$ at $\boldsymbol{\zeta}$. By Proposition 2.2, we deduce that $\Delta\mathscr{D} \subset \mathscr{D}$. This is a contradiction, since Δ is of degree 1 and the elements in $\mathscr{D}$ are of degree $\leq N$. $\square$

The columns of $J_{\mathcal{D}\boldsymbol{g}}(\boldsymbol{x}, \boldsymbol{\varepsilon})$ are indexed by the variables $(\boldsymbol{x}, \boldsymbol{\varepsilon})$, while the rows are indexed by the polynomials g_{ik}. We construct the following systems:

(a) Let $\mathcal{D}\boldsymbol{f}^I$ be a subsystem of $\mathcal{D}\boldsymbol{f}$ s.t. the corresponding n rows of $J_{\mathcal{D}\boldsymbol{f}}(\boldsymbol{\zeta})$ are linearly independent (Lem. 4.2). We denote by $I = \{(i_1, k_1), \ldots, (i_n, k_n)\}$ their indices.

(b) Let $\mathcal{D}\tilde{\boldsymbol{g}}(\boldsymbol{x}, \tilde{\boldsymbol{\varepsilon}})$ be the square system formed by removing the variables $\varepsilon_{k_1,i_1}, \ldots, \varepsilon_{k_n,i_n}$ from $\mathcal{D}\boldsymbol{g}(\boldsymbol{x}, \boldsymbol{\varepsilon})$. Therefore the Jacobian $J_{\mathcal{D}\tilde{\boldsymbol{g}}}(\boldsymbol{x}, \tilde{\boldsymbol{\varepsilon}})$ derives from $J_{\mathcal{D}\boldsymbol{g}}(\boldsymbol{x}, \boldsymbol{\varepsilon})$, after purging the columns indexed by $\varepsilon_{k_1,i_1}, \ldots, \varepsilon_{k_n,i_n}$ and it's (i_j, k_j)−th row becomes $[\nabla(\Lambda_{i_j}^{\boldsymbol{x}}\tilde{g}_{i_j,k_j})^T|\,\boldsymbol{0}\,]$.

THEOREM 4.3 (DEFLATION THEOREM 1). *Let $\boldsymbol{f}(\boldsymbol{x})$ be a n−variate polynomial system with an μ−fold isolated zero at $\boldsymbol{x} = \boldsymbol{\zeta}$. Then the $n \times n$ system $\mathcal{D}\boldsymbol{f}^I(\boldsymbol{x}) = 0$, defined in (a), has a simple root at $\boldsymbol{x} = \boldsymbol{\zeta}$.*

PROOF. By construction, $\boldsymbol{\zeta}$ is a solution of $\mathcal{D}\boldsymbol{f}^I(\boldsymbol{x}) = 0$. Moreover, the indices I are chosen such that $\det J_{\mathcal{D}\boldsymbol{f}^I}(\boldsymbol{\zeta}) \neq 0$. This shows that $\boldsymbol{\zeta}$ is a simple (thus isolated) root of the system $\mathcal{D}\boldsymbol{f}^I(\boldsymbol{x}) = 0$. $\square$

EXAMPLE 4.4. In our running example, we expand the rectangular Jacobian matrix of 6 polynomials in (x_1, x_2). Choosing the rows corresponding to f_1 and $(d_1 - d_2^2 - d_1d_2 - d_1^2)[f_1]$, we find a non-singular minor, hence the resulting system $(f_1, 2x_1)$ has a regular root at $\boldsymbol{\zeta} = (0, 0)$. $\square$

The deflated system $\mathcal{D}\boldsymbol{f}^I(\boldsymbol{x}) = 0$ is a square system in n variables. Contrarily to the deflation approach in [8, 3], we do not introduce new variables and one step of deflation is sufficient. The trade-off is that here we assume that exact dual elements are pointed at by indices I, so as to be able to compute the original multiple root with high accuracy.

On the other hand, when the coefficients are machine numbers, an exact multiple root is unlikely to exist. In the following theorem, we introduce new variables that will allow us later to derive an approximate deflation method.

THEOREM 4.5 (DEFLATION THEOREM 2). *Let $\boldsymbol{f}(\boldsymbol{x})$ be a n−variate polynomial system with a μ−fold isolated root at $\boldsymbol{x} = \boldsymbol{\zeta}$. The square system $\mathcal{D}\tilde{\boldsymbol{g}}(\boldsymbol{x}, \tilde{\boldsymbol{\varepsilon}}) = 0$, as defined in (b), has a regular isolated root at $(\boldsymbol{x}, \tilde{\boldsymbol{\varepsilon}}) = (\boldsymbol{\zeta}, \boldsymbol{0})$.*

PROOF. Computing approximate dual basis at $\boldsymbol{\zeta}$ we get

$$\mathcal{D}\tilde{\boldsymbol{g}}(\boldsymbol{\zeta}, \boldsymbol{0}) = (\Lambda_1^{\boldsymbol{\zeta}}[\boldsymbol{f}], \ldots, \Lambda_\mu^{\boldsymbol{\zeta}}[\boldsymbol{f}]) = 0.$$

Moreover, by construction of $\mathcal{D}\tilde{\boldsymbol{g}}$ we get, up to a row permutation, the following structure in the Jacobian determinant:

$$\pm\det J_{\mathcal{D}\tilde{\boldsymbol{g}}}(\boldsymbol{\zeta}, \boldsymbol{0}) = \det \begin{vmatrix} J_1 & 0 \\ J_2 & I \end{vmatrix} = \det J_1 \neq 0,$$

where $J_1 = J_{\mathcal{D}f^I}(\zeta)$. This shows that $(\zeta, 0)$ is regular and thus isolated point of the algebraic variety defined by $\mathcal{D}\tilde{g}(x, \tilde{\varepsilon}) = 0$. □

Nevertheless, this deflation does differ from the deflation strategy in [8, 3]. There, new variables are added that correspond to coefficients of differential elements, thus introducing a perturbation in the dual basis.. This is suitable for exact equations, but, in case of perturbed data, the equations do not actually define a true singular point. In our method, we perturb the equations, keeping a fixed structure of a multiple root. Consequently, the certification of a root concerns a nearby system, within controlled error bounds, that attains a true multiple point, as it shall be described in the next section.

We mention that it would also be possible to use the equations (9, i-iii) to construct a deflated system on the differentials and to perturb the approximate dual structure.

5. VERIFYING APPROXIMATE SINGULAR POINTS

In real-life applications it is common to work with approximate inputs. Also, there is the need to (numerically) decide if an (approximate) system possesses a single (real) root in a given domain, notably for use in subdivision-based algorithms, e.g. [14, 11].

In the regular case, Smale's α−theory, extending Newton's method, can be used to answer this problem, also partially extended to singular cases in [6], using zero clustering. Another option is Rump's Theorem, also based on Newton theory. In our implementation we use this latter approach, since it is suitable for inexact data and suits best with the perturbation which is applied. In particular, it coincides with the numerical scheme of [17] in the univariate case.

The certification test is based on the verification method of Rump [17, Th. 2.1], which we rewrite in our setting:

THEOREM 5.1 ([17] RUMP'S THEOREM). *Let $f \in R^n$ be a polynomial system and $\zeta^* \in \mathbb{R}^n$ a real point. Given an interval domain $Z \in \mathbb{IR}^n$ containing $\zeta^* \in \mathbb{R}^n$, and an interval matrix $M \in \mathbb{IR}^{n \times n}$ whose i-th column M_i satisfies $\nabla f_i(Z) \subseteq M_i$ for $i = 1 \ldots, n$, then the following holds: If the interval domain*

$$V_f(Z, \zeta^*) := -J_f(\zeta^*)^{-1} f(\zeta^*) + (I - J_f(\zeta^*)^{-1} M) Z \quad (14)$$

is contained in the interior of Z, then there is a unique $\zeta \in Z$ with $f(\zeta) = 0$ and the Jacobian $J_f(\zeta) \in M$ is non-singular.

This theorem is applied to the system of 4.5, using an (approximate) structure $\mathcal{D}$. The resulting range of the ε−parameters encloses a system that attains a single multiple root of that structure. Hence the domain for ε−variables reflects the distance of the approximate system from a precise system with local structure $\mathcal{D}$, see Ex. 7.2.

6. GEOMETRY AROUND A SINGULARITY

As a final step in analyzing isolated singularities, we show how the local basis can be used to compute the topological degree around the singular point. If the latter is a singular point of a real algebraic curve, one can deduce the number of curve (half-)branches that touch the point.

Topological degree computation. Let $f(x)$ be a square n−variate system with an μ−fold isolated zero at $x = \zeta$.

The topological degree $\mathrm{tdeg}_\zeta(f)$ at $x = \zeta$ is the number of times that the (Gauss) map $G_\zeta : S_\zeta(\epsilon) \to \mathbb{S}^{n-1}$, $G_\zeta(x) := f(x)/\|f(x)\|$, with domain on then ball $S_\zeta(\epsilon)$, wraps around the sphere $\mathbb{S}^{n-1}$. This integer remains invariant if we replace spheres by any other compact oriented manifold [4].

To a functional $\Lambda \in \mathbb{R}[\partial]$, we associate the quadratic form

$$Q_\Lambda : R/\mathcal{Q} \times R/\mathcal{Q} \to \mathbb{R} \quad, \quad (x^{\beta_i}, x^{\beta_j}) \mapsto \Lambda[x^{\beta_i + \beta_j}] \quad (15)$$

for $R/\mathcal{Q} = \langle x^{\beta_1}, \ldots, x^{\beta_\mu} \rangle$. The signature of this (symmetric and bi-linear) form is the sum of signs of the diagonal entries of any diagonal matrix representation of it.

PROPOSITION 6.1 ([4, TH. 1.2]). *If Q_Φ, $\Phi \in \mathcal{D}$ is any bi-linear symmetric form such that $\Phi^\zeta[\det J_f(x)] > 0$, then*

$$\mathrm{tdeg}_\zeta(f) = sgn(Q_\Phi). \quad (16)$$

This signature is independent of the bi-linear form used.

We can use this result to compute the topological degree at $x = \zeta$ using the dual structure at ζ. Since a basis $\mathcal{D}$ is available we set $\Phi = \pm \Lambda_i$, for some basis element that is not zero on $\det J_f(x)$. Indeed, such an element can be retrieved among the basis elements, since $\det J_f \notin \langle f \rangle$, see [5, Ch. 0].

In practice it suffices to generate a random element of $\mathcal{D}$, compute its matrix representation $[\Phi(x^{\beta_i + \beta_j})]_{ij}$, and then extract the signature of Q_Φ.

Branches around a singularity. In the context of computing with real algebraic curves, the identification of singular points is only the first step towards determining the local topology. As a second step, one needs to calculate the number of half-branches attached to the singular point ζ, hereafter denoted $\mathrm{Br}(f, \zeta)$. This information is encoded in the topological degree.

An implicit curve in n−space is given by all points satisfying $f(x) = 0$, $f = (f_1, \ldots, f_{n-1})$. Consider $p(x) = (x_1 - \zeta_1)^2 + \cdots + (x_n - \zeta_n)^2$, and $g(x) = \det J_{(f,p)}(x)$. Then ([19] and references therein):

$$\mathrm{Br}(f, \zeta) = 2\,\mathrm{tdeg}_\zeta(f, g). \quad (17)$$

This implies an algorithm for $\mathrm{Br}(f, \zeta)$. First compute the primal-dual structure of (f, g) at ζ and then use Prop. 6.1 to get $\mathrm{tdeg}_\zeta(f, g)$, see Ex. 7.3.

7. EXPERIMENTATION

Our method is developed in MAPLE. It uses our modified integration technique to compute (approximate) dual basis and derive the augmented system of Th. 4.5. Then Rump's method is used to verify the root. Macaulay's method is also implemented for testing purposes.

EXAMPLE 7.1. Let, as in [7, 9], $f_1 = 2x_1 + 2x_1^2 + 2x_2 + 2x_2^2 + x_3^2 - 1$, $f_2 = (x_1 + x_2 - x_3 - 1)^3 - x_1^3$, and $f_3 = 2x_1^3 + 2x_2^2 + 10x_3 + 5x_3^2 + 5)^3 - 1000x_1^5$.

Point $(0, 0, -1)$ occurs with multiplicity equal to 18, in depth 7. The final matrix size with our method is 206×45, while Macaulay's method ends with a 360×165 matrix.

If the objective is to deflate as efficiently as possible, then one can go step by step: First compute a basis of $\mathcal{D}_1$ and stop the process. We get the evaluation **1** and 2 first order functionals, which we apply to f_1. We arrive to $(\mathbf{1}[f_1], (d_2 - d_1)[f_1], (d_1 + d_3)[f_1]) = (f_1, -4x_1 + 4x_2, 2 + 4x_1 + 2x_3)$ and we check that the Jacobian determinant is 64, thus we have a deflated system only with a partial local structure. □

EXAMPLE 7.2. Consider the equations ([3, DZ3]): $f_1 = 14x_1 + 33x_2 - 3\sqrt{5}(x_1^2 + 4x_1x_2 + 4x_2^2 + 2) + \sqrt{7} + x_1^3 + 6x_1^2x_2 + 12x_1x_2^2 + 8x_2^3$, $f_2 = 41x_1 - 18x_2 - \sqrt{5} + 8x_1^3 - 12x_1^2x_2 + 6x_1x_2^2 - x_2^3 + 3\sqrt{7}(4x_1x_2 - 4x_1^2 - x_2^2 - 2)$ and take an approximate system $\tilde{f}$ with those coefficients rounded to 6 digits. A 5−fold zero of f rounded to 6 digits is $\zeta^* = (1.50551, .365278)$.

Starting with the approximate system and with a tolerance of .001, we compute the basis $\mathcal{D} = (1, d_1 + .33d_2, d_1^2 + .33d_1d_2 + .11d_2^2, d_1^3 + .33d_1^2d_2 + .11d_1d_2^2 + .03d_2^3 - 1.54d_2, d_1^4 + .33d_1^3d_2 + .11d_1^2d_2^2 + .03d_1d_2^3 + .01d_2^4 - 1.54d_1d_2 - 1.03d_2^2)$ having 4 correct digits, w.r.t. the initial exact system, and the primal counterpart $\mathcal{B} = (1, x_1, x_1^2, x_1^3, x_1^4)$.

We form the deflated system (b), with $I = \{(3,1), (5,1)\}$, i.e. the 3rd and 5th dual element on f_1 have non-null Jacobian. By adding 8 new variables, the system is perturbed as: $g_{1,1} = \tilde{f}_1 + \varepsilon_{1,1} + \varepsilon_{1,2}(x_1 - \zeta_1^*) + \varepsilon_{1,4}(x_1 - \zeta_1^*)^3$, $g_{2,1} = \tilde{f}_2 + \sum_{i=1}^{5} \varepsilon_{2,i}(x_1 - \zeta_1^*)^{i+1}$ and their derivation w.r.t. $\mathcal{D}$.

We consider a box Z with center $= \zeta^*$ and length $= .004$ at each side. Also, we allow a range $E = [-.004, .004]^8$ for the variables $\tilde{\varepsilon}$. Applying 5.1 we get a verified inclusion $V_g(Z \times E, (\zeta^*, \mathbf{0}))$ inside $Z \times E$ and we deduce that a unique specialization $\tilde{\varepsilon} \in E$ "fits" the approximate system $\tilde{f}$ to the multiplicity structure $\mathcal{D}$.

Indeed, one iteration of Newton's method on $g(x, \varepsilon)$ gives $\zeta = (1.505535473, .365266196)$ and corresponding values for $\varepsilon_0 \in E$, such that ζ is a 9−digit approximation of the multiple root of the perturbed system $g(x, \varepsilon_0)$. □

EXAMPLE 7.3. Consider the implicit curve $f(x, y) = 0$, in xy−plane, with $f(x, y) = x^4 + 2x^2y^2 + y^4 + 3x^2y - y^3$, that looks like this ⚘. We search for the number of half-branches attached to $\zeta = (0, 0)$. We compute $g(x, y) = J_{(f, x^2 + y^2)} = 18xy^2 - 6x^3$, and then the multiplicity structure of (f, g) at ζ, and we arrive to the monomial basis $\mathcal{B} = (1, y, x, y^2, xy, x^2, y^3, xy^2, x^2y)$. Among the 9 elements of the dual basis, we find $\Phi = d_y^3 + \frac{3}{8}d_y^4 + \frac{1}{8}d_x^2d_y^2 + \frac{3}{8}d_x^4$, having value $\Phi^0[\det J_{(f,g)}(x)] = 54 > 0$ on the Jacobian determinant.

Using $\mathcal{B}$ and (6), we get the 9×9 matrix representation of Q_Φ (15) with ij−th entry $\Phi^0[x^{\beta_i + \beta_j}]$, and we compute $\text{tdeg}_\zeta(f, g) = \text{sgn}\, Q_\Phi = 3$, thus $\text{Br}(f, (0, 0)) = 6$. □

In Table 1 we run dual basis computation on the benchmark set of [3]. Multiplicity, matrix sizes at termination step and computation time is reported. One sees that there is at least an order of gain in the running time.

Sys.	μ	integration		Macaulay	
cmbs1	11	33×23	0.18s	105×56	1.55s
cmbs2	8	21×17	0.08s	60×35	0.48s
mth191	4	10×9	0.03s	30×20	0.14s
decker2	4	5×5	0.02s	20×15	0.10s
Ojika2	2	6×5	0.02s	12×10	0.04s
Ojika3	4	24×9	0.07s	60×35	0.59s
KSS	16	565×65	8.59s	630×252	70.03s
Caprasse	4	34×13	0.28s	60×35	2.34s
Cyclic-9	4	321×33	1.04s	495×220	31.40s
DZ1	131	1450×394	14m	4004×1365	220m
DZ2	16	73×33	0.68s	360×165	25.72s
DZ3	5	12×6	0.04s	30×21	0.79s

Table 1: Benchmark systems from [3].

Acknowledgements. The authors are grateful to anonymous reviewers for comments and suggestions. This research has received funding from the EU's 7th FP [FP7/2007-2013], Marie Curie ITN SAGA, grant n° [PITN-GA-2008-214584].

8. REFERENCES

[1] L. Alberti, B. Mourrain, & J. Wintz. Topology and arrangement computation of semi-algebraic planar curves. *CAGD*, 25:631–651, 2008.

[2] M.F. Atiyah & I.G. MacDonald. *Introduction to Commutative Algebra*. Addison-Wesley, 1969.

[3] B. H. Dayton & Z. Zeng. Computing the multiplicity structure in solving polynomial systems. In *Proc. of ISSAC '05,*, pp. 116–123, 2005. ACM.

[4] D. Eisenbud & H.I. Levine. An algebraic formula for the degree of a C^∞ map germ. *The Annals of Mathematics*, 106(1):pp. 19–44, 1977.

[5] M. Elkadi & B. Mourrain. *Introduction à la résolution des systèmes d'équations algébriques*, vol. 59 of *Mathématiques et Applications*. Springer, 2007.

[6] M. Giusti, G. Lecerf, B. Salvy, & J.-C. Yakoubsohn. On location and approximation of clusters of zeros: Case of embedding dimension 1. *FoCM*, 7:1–58, 2007.

[7] G. Lecerf. Quadratic newton iteration for systems with multiplicity. *FoCM*, 2:247–293, 2002.

[8] A. Leykin, J. Verschelde, & Zhao A. Newton's method with deflation for isolated singularities of polynomial systems. *TCS*, 359(1-3):111 – 122, 2006.

[9] A. Leykin, J. Verschelde, & A. Zhao. Higher-order deflation for polynomial systems with isolated singular solutions. *IMA Math. & its Appl.* 146, pp. 79–97, 2008.

[10] F.S. Macaulay. *The algebraic theory of modular systems*. Cambridge Univ. Press, 1916.

[11] A. Mantzaflaris, B. Mourrain, & E. Tsigaridas. Continued fraction expansion of real roots of polynomial systems. In *Proc. of SNC '09*, pp. 85–94, 2009.

[12] M. G. Marinari, T. Mora, & H.M. Möller. Gröbner duality and multiplicities in polynomial system solving. In *Proc. of ISSAC '95*, pp. 167–179, 1995.

[13] B. Mourrain. Isolated points, duality and residues. *J. of Pure & App. Alg.*, 117-118:469 – 493, 1997.

[14] B. Mourrain & J. P. Pavone. Subdivision methods for solving polynomial equations. *JSC*, 44:292–306, 2009.

[15] T. Ojika, S. Watanabe, & T. Mitsui. Deflation algorithm for multiple roots of a system of nonlinear equations. *J. of Math. An. & Appls.*, 96(2):463–479, 1983.

[16] S.R. Pope & A. Szanto. Nearest multivariate system with given root multiplicities. *JSC*,44(6):606-625,2009.

[17] S. Rump & S. Graillat. Verified error bounds for multiple roots of systems of nonlinear equations. *Num. Algs.*, 54:359–377, 2010.

[18] H. J. Stetter. Analysis of zero clusters in multivariate polynomial systems. In *Proc. of ISSAC '96*, pp. 127–136, New York, NY, USA, 1996. ACM.

[19] Z. Szafraniec. Topological degree and quadratic forms. *J. of Pure & App. Alg.*, 141(3):299 – 314, 1999.

[20] X. Wu & L. Zhi. Determining singular solutions of polynomial systems via symbolic-numeric reduction to geometric involutive form, MM Research Preprints, 27 (2008), pp. 104–122. (accepted for publication in *JSC*).

[21] Z. Zeng. The closedness subspace method for computing the multiplicity structure of a polynomial system. *Contemporary Math.* 496, pp. 347–362. AMS. RI, 2009.

Space-efficient Gröbner Basis Computation without Degree Bounds

Ernst W. Mayr
Technische Universität München
Boltzmannstr. 3
D-85748 Garching
mayr@in.tum.de

Stephan Ritscher
Technische Universität München
Boltzmannstr. 3
D-85748 Garching
ritsches@in.tum.de

ABSTRACT

The computation of a Gröbner basis of a polynomial ideal is known to be exponential space complete. We revisit the algorithm by Kühnle and Mayr using recent improvements of various degree bounds. The result is an algorithm which is exponential in the ideal dimension (rather than the number of indeterminates).

Furthermore, we provide an incremental version of the algorithm which is independent of the knowledge of degree bounds. Using a space-efficient implementation of Buchberger's S-criterion, the algorithm can be implemented such that the space requirement only depends on the size of the representation and the Gröbner basis degrees of the *problem instance* (instead of the worst case), and thus is much lower in average.

Categories and Subject Descriptors

I.1.2 [**Symbolic and Algebraic Manipulation**]: Algorithms; G.4 [**Mathematics of Computing**]: Algorithm design and analysis—*space efficiency*

General Terms

Algorithms, Performance, Theory

Keywords

multivariate polynomial, Gröbner basis, polynomial ideal, ideal dimension, space complexity, S-criterion, Macaulay matrix

1. INTRODUCTION

Most algorithms for the computation of Gröbner bases of polynomial ideals are based on Buchberger's algorithm [3] (translated in [4]). They start from an arbitrary basis and add new polynomials contained in the ideal until the basis is a Gröbner basis. The latter is checked using the so-called S-criterion by Buchberger. The algorithms mostly vary in

the ways to come up with new polynomials, the intermediate reductions which help to keep the size of the basis small, and the avoidance of unnecessary checks.

Another approach was taken by Kühnle and Mayr in [17]. They estimated apriori how large the Gröbner basis could become and therefore avoided the S-criterion. Since the size of the Gröbner basis is much larger in the worst case than in the average case, this approach is of purely theoretical interest. Still, the idea of using methods of linear algebra for Gröbner basis computations reappeared in the fastest known algorithms F4 [10] and F5 [11] by Faugère. The corresponding reduction of the representation problem to linear algebra using the so-called Macaulay matrix was already used by Hermann [12] who proved the first degree bound for the representation problem.

2. MAIN RESULTS

In this paper we obtain two primary results. First, we revisit the analysis of the algorithm by Kühnle and Mayr. Due to new degree bounds for the representation problem [13] and the Gröbner basis degree (submitted for the JSC special issue ISSAC 2010), we prove tighter space bounds which are only exponential in the ideal dimension.

THEOREM 1. *Let $I \subsetneq \mathbb{Q}[x_1, \ldots, x_n]$ be an ideal of dimension r generated by polynomials $F = \{f_1, \ldots, f_s\}$ of degrees bounded by d, and fix an admissible monomial ordering $\prec$ represented by a rational weight matrix $W \in \mathbb{Q}^{n \times n}$. If q bounds the bitsize of all numerators and denominators in W and F, it is possible to compute the reduced Gröbner basis G of I w.r.t. $\prec$ in space $O(n^8 2^{4r} \log^2(sdq))$.*

Moreover, we show how to realize the S-polynomial check space-efficient using a system of linear equations. So we are able to provide an incremental version of the algorithm whose complexity depends on the Gröbner basis and representation degrees of the instance rather than the worst case. On the one hand, this is comparable to F4 and F5 while still providing space bounds for the computation, on the other hand, it provides a simple way of proving further complexity bounds using new degree bounds.

THEOREM 2. *Let I be an ideal in the ring $\mathbb{Q}[x_1, \ldots, x_n]$, let I be generated by polynomials $F = \{f_1, \ldots, f_s\}$, and fix an admissible monomial ordering $\prec$ represented by a rational weight matrix $W \in \mathbb{Q}^{n \times n}$. If q bounds the bitsize of all numerators and denominators in W and F, it is possible to compute a Gröbner basis G of I w.r.t. $\prec$ in space $O(\log^2(sD^n q))$ where D bounds the representation degrees of the S-polynomials of the elements of the Gröbner basis.*

Both algorithms assume the multitape Turing machine model which is detailed in section 3.3.

Note that the results are not limited to polynomial rings over $\mathbb{Q}$. The main results are formulated in full generality in theorems 25 and 26.

3. PRELIMINARIES

In the following, we define notation and introduce concepts used throughout the paper. For a more detailed introduction into polynomial algebra, the reader may consult the text books [6] and [7] or [14] and [15].

3.1 Polynomial Algebra

Consider the ring $\mathbb{K}[X]$ of polynomials in the variables $X = \{x_1, \ldots, x_n\}$. The *(total) degree* of a monomial $x^\alpha = x_1^{\alpha_1} \cdots x_n^{\alpha_n}$ is $\deg(x^\alpha) = \alpha_1 + \ldots + \alpha_n$. The *support* of a polynomial $f = \sum_{\alpha \in \mathbb{N}^n} f_\alpha x^\alpha$ is $\operatorname{supp}(f) = \{x^\alpha : f_\alpha \neq 0\}$ and, by definition, it is always finite. By convention, the coefficient of x^α in a polynomial f will always be denoted by f_α. $\langle f_1, \ldots, f_s \rangle$ denotes the *ideal* $I = \{\sum_{i=1}^s a_i f_i : a_i \in \mathbb{K}[X]\}$ generated by polynomials $f_1, \ldots, f_s \in \mathbb{K}[X]$.

Throughout the paper, we assume some arbitrary but fixed *admissible* monomial ordering $\prec$. This means that $\prec$ is a total ordering of the monomials, $x^\alpha \succ 1$ for all $x^\alpha \neq 1$, and $x^\alpha \prec x^\beta$ implies $x^{\alpha+\gamma} \prec x^{\beta+\gamma}$. Since the monomial ordering will be fixed, we will not keep track of it in the notation. The largest monomial occurring in a polynomial f is called its *leading monomial* and denoted by $\operatorname{lm}(f) = \max_\prec(\operatorname{supp}(f))$. The coefficient of the leading monomial is called *leading coefficient* $\operatorname{lc}(f)$. For an ideal I, we write $\operatorname{lm}(I)$ for the ideal $\langle \operatorname{lm}(f) : f \in I \rangle$.

A polynomial h is *reducible* w.r.t. a set of polynomials F iff $\operatorname{supp}(h) \cap \langle \operatorname{lm}(F) \rangle \neq \emptyset$. With $x^\beta \in \operatorname{supp}(h) \cap \langle \operatorname{lm}(F) \rangle$ and $f \in F$ such that $x^\gamma \operatorname{lm}(f) = x^\beta$, h reduces to $h - \frac{h_\beta}{\operatorname{lc}(f)} x^\gamma f$.

A finite set G is a *Gröbner basis* of I if $\langle G \rangle = I$ and $\langle \operatorname{lm}(G) \rangle = \operatorname{lm}(I)$. G is called *reduced* iff $\operatorname{lc}(g) = 1$ and g is irreducible w.r.t. $G \setminus \{g\}$ for all $g \in G$

$\operatorname{nf}_I(h)$ denotes the *normal form* of $h \in \mathbb{K}$ which, for a fixed monomial ordering, is the unique irreducible polynomial in the coset $h + I$. If G is a Gröbner basis of I, every chain of reductions starting from h terminates after finitely many steps in $\operatorname{nf}_I(h)$. The set of all normal forms is denoted by N_I. Since the normal forms are unique, the sum $\mathbb{K}[X] = I \oplus N_I$ is direct.

The *dimension* $\dim(I)$ of a polynomial ideal I can be defined in various equivalent ways. A very common definition in computer algebra is the following:

Let $U \subseteq X$ be such that $I \cap \mathbb{K}[U] = \{0\}$. Such U is called *independent set*. The ideal dimension equals the cardinality $\#U$ of a maximal independent set U, i.e.

$$\dim(U) = \max\{\#U : U \subseteq X, I \cap \mathbb{K}[U] = \{0\}\}.$$

Other well-known definitions of the ideal dimension are via the maximal length of a chain of prime ideals in the factor ring or the degree of the Hilbert polynomial. We will not make explicit use of this definition but cite results which require ideals of a particular dimension.

Finally, recall the well-known structure of reduced Gröbner bases and Buchberger's S-polynomial criterion.

LEMMA 3 (CF. [17]). *Each ideal I in $\mathbb{K}[X]$ has a unique reduced Gröbner basis $G = \{x^\alpha - \operatorname{nf}_I(x^\alpha) \in \mathbb{K}[X] : x^\alpha$*

minimally reducible w.r.t. I}. Here $x^\alpha \in \mathbb{K}[X]$ is minimally reducible w.r.t. I if it is reducible w.r.t. I but none of its proper divisors is reducible w.r.t. I.

LEMMA 4. *Let I be an ideal in $\mathbb{K}[X]$, $G = \{g_1, \ldots, g_t\}$ a basis of I, and $\prec$ be an admissible monomial ordering. Then G is a Gröbner basis of I w.r.t. $\prec$ iff $I = \langle G \rangle$ and*

$$S(g_k, g_l) = \sum_{i=1}^t a_i g_i$$

for some $a_i \in \mathbb{K}[X]$ with $\operatorname{lm}(a_i g_i) \preceq \operatorname{lm}(S(g_k, g_l))$ and all $i, k, l = 1, \ldots, t$.

PROOF. See [6], §2.9. □

3.2 Degree Bounds

The algorithm needs two types of degree bounds: bounds for the representation degree and bounds for the Gröbner basis degree:

DEFINITION 5 (GRÖBNER BASIS DEGREE). *For the reduced Gröbner basis G of an ideal $I \subseteq \mathbb{K}[X]$ (w.r.t. an admissible monomial ordering $\prec$) the Gröbner basis degree of I (w.r.t. $\prec$) is $\max\{\deg(g) : g \in G\}$.*

DEFINITION 6 (REPRESENTATION DEGREE). *Let F be a basis of an ideal $I \subseteq \mathbb{K}[X]$ and $h \in I$ be an ideal member. Then the representation degree of h and F is*

$$\min\left\{ d \in \mathbb{N} : h = \sum_{f \in F} a_f f \text{ with} \right.$$
$$\left. a_f \in \mathbb{K}[X], \deg(a_f f) \leq d \text{ for all } f \in F \right\}.$$

For both types, recent research tightened the bounds by considering the ideals parameterized by their dimension.

The representation problem was first approached by Hermann in [12]. Recently, Kratzer gave a dimension-dependent bound:

THEOREM 7 (KRATZER 2008). *Let I be an ideal of dimension $\dim(I) = r$ in the polynomial ring $\mathbb{K}[X]$ over an infinite field $\mathbb{K}$, and let I be generated by polynomials $F = \{f_1, \ldots, f_s\}$ of maximal degree d and $h \in I$. Then there is a representation $h = \sum_{i=1}^s a_i f_i$ with*

$$\deg(a_i f_i) \leq \deg(h) + \left(d\Big((n+1) \right.$$
$$\left. \max\left\{\deg(h), (n+2)^2 \left(d^\mu + 1\right)^{\mu+2}\right\} + 1\right)^{n-r} \Big)^{2^r}$$

for $\mu = \min\{n, s\}$ and $i = 1, \ldots, s$.

PROOF. See [13], theorem 5. □

For the Gröbner basis degree, Dubé proved a simple upper bound in [9]. His construction was improved by us making it dimension-dependent.

THEOREM 8 (M-R 2011). *Let I be an ideal of dimension r in the polynomial ring $\mathbb{K}[X]$ over an infinite field $\mathbb{K}$, let I be generated by polynomials $F = \{f_1, \ldots, f_s\}$ of degrees $d_1 \geq \ldots \geq d_s$, and fix some admissible monomial ordering. Then the degree of the reduced Gröbner basis G is bounded by*

$$\deg(G) \leq 2\left[\frac{1}{2}\left((d_1 \cdots d_{n-r})^{2(n-r)} + d_1\right)\right]^{2^r}.$$

PROOF. The first publication [19] was slightly corrected and submitted for publication in the JSC special issue IS-SAC 2010. □

3.3 Space Bounds for Turing Machines

As model for sequential computations we use an offline multitape Turing machine with separated input, output, and working tapes. The input tape is read-only, the output tape is write-only and the working tapes read-write. We say the Turing machine is $f(n)$-space bounded if the sum of lengths of the working tapes is $f(n)$ for inputs of length n. Assuming $f(n) \geq \log(n)$, the Turing machine can only have $2^{O(f(n))}$ distinct states which bounds the time of any terminating computation and the length of the respective output.

Since we are interested in space bounds only, machines with $k > 1$ working tapes can be simulated by a machine with 1 working tape without (space) overhead.

Note that this machine model is a standard model and commonly used for the derivation of *sublinear* space bounds.

In the case of Gröbner basis computation, the complexity seems to be dominated by the size of the output which can be exponential in the working space. However, one can easily come up with problems with little output and the same space complexity (e.g. the computation of the Gröbner basis degree).

3.4 Boolean Circuits

Boolean circuits are a common machine model for parallel computations.

DEFINITION 9. *A Boolean circuit C is a directed acyclic graph. The nodes with in-degree zero are* input nodes, *the nodes with out-degree zero are* output nodes *and have in-degree one. The inner nodes (also called* gates*) are labeled by the binary operations AND, OR, and the unary operation NOT. The number of nodes is called* size *of the circuit and denoted by* size(C), *the longest path in the graph (from an input node to an output node) is called* depth *and denoted by* depth(C).

Since all gates are labeled by unary respectively binary operations, the in-degree of the circuit is bounded (actually by 2) while the out-degree is arbitrary. The input of the circuit is an assignment of Boolean values to the input nodes. The values of the gates are determined by the operations indicated by their labels applied to the values of their predecessor nodes. The output nodes inherit the values of their predecessors. Since the graph is acyclic, this recursive evaluation is well-defined and unique for given input values. By numbering the n input and m output nodes, one can view C as a function $C : \{0, 1\}^n \mapsto \{0, 1\}^m$. Since the gates are viewed as independent processing units, the depth of the circuit is a measure of the time the (parallel) evaluation takes.

Using a topological ordering, one can encode the circuit C in a straight-forward way as string in $\{0, 1\}^*$. This string will be denoted by $\overline{C}$. Note that $|\overline{C}| \geq c \cdot \text{size}(C) \cdot \log(\text{size}(C))$ for some $c > 0$ if the output depends on all input bits. This is because the representation of a node index takes $\Theta(\log(\text{size}(C)))$ bits and only a constant number of indices have to be stored per node (namely the indices of the predecessors).

DEFINITION 10. *A problem $P : \{0, 1\}^* \longrightarrow \{0, 1\}^*$ is realized by a family of Boolean circuits $(C_n)_{n \in \mathbb{N}}$ iff $C_n(y) =$ $P_n(y)$ for all inputs $y \in \{0, 1\}^n$ of length n. Here, the restriction $P_n = P|_{\{0,1\}^n}$ is assumed to have a fixed output length (otherwise it must be padded to the maximal length).*

Up to now, there is a big difference between Turing machines and families of Boolean circuits. While the description of a Turing machine is finite, a family of Boolean circuits can have an independent definition for each input length. This non-uniformity causes an unbalance of the computing power when comparing space-bounded Turing machines and depth-bounded circuits.

DEFINITION 11. *A family of Boolean circuits $(C_n)_{n \in \mathbb{N}}$ is $O(f(n))$-uniform iff $\overline{C_n}$ can be computed by a $O(f(n))$ space-bounded Turing machine.*

DEFINITION 12. *The class of all problems which can be realized by a family of $O(\log(n))$-uniform Boolean circuits $(C_n)_{n \in \mathbb{N}}$ with depth$(C_n) = O(\log^k(n))$ and size$(C_n) = n^{O(1)}$ is denoted by NC^k.*

Be aware that the definitions of the class NC^k in literature vary slightly. Sometimes, uniformity is not required or a slightly different kind of uniformity is chosen.

Uniform Boolean circuits can be easily simulated by Turing machines. The depth of the circuit, which is a measure of the parallel computation time, determines the space requirements of the Turing machine.

THEOREM 13 (BORODIN 1977). *Let $(C_n)_{n \in \mathbb{N}}$ be a family of $O(f(n))$-uniform Boolean circuits with depth$(C_n) = O(f(n))$ for some function $f(n) \geq \log(n)$. Then $(C_n)_{n \in \mathbb{N}}$ can be simulated by a Turing machine in space $O(f(n))$.*

PROOF. See [1], theorem 4. □

Efficient implementations of basic ring operations were studied by Borodin et al. in [2] who introduced the concept of well-endowed rings for this purpose.

DEFINITION 14. *Let R be a ring and $\alpha : R \longrightarrow \mathbb{N}$ be a length function, i.e. $\alpha(a + b) \leq \max\{\alpha(a), \alpha(b)\} + O(1)$ and $\alpha(a \cdot b) \leq \alpha(a) + \alpha(b) + O(\log(\max\{\alpha(a), \alpha(b)\}))$. Then $R_n = \{r \in R : \alpha(r) \leq n\}$. (l, r) is a representation of (R, α) iff $l : \mathbb{N} \longrightarrow \mathbb{N}$ and $r_n : \{0, 1\}^{l(n)} \longrightarrow R_n$ such that $R_n \subseteq r_n(\{0, 1\}^{l(n)})$. It is called succinct iff $l(n) = n^{O(1)}$, i.e. all ring elements of length n can be represented as strings of bitsize polynomial in n. The representation is uniform iff, for arbitrary $k \in \mathbb{N}$, a $(l(n) + k)$-bit representation of any element of R_n can be computed in NC^1 (i.e. with depth $O(\log(l(n) + k))$). If (R, α) has a succinct uniform representation such that addition is in NC^0 and multiplication is in NC^1, the ring is called well-endowed.*

The ring operations of well-endowed rings are fast enough such that the complexity of the considered algorithms is not essentially influenced. Also many operations on the fields of fractions can be computed efficiently. This yields to the following definition.

DEFINITION 15. *Let R be a well-endowed domain. Then its field of fractions $\mathbf{Q}(R)$ is also called well-endowed.*

For linear algebra, the rational numbers play a vital role which are the field of fractions of integers. Borodin et al. gathered all the facts in order to show they are well-endowed.

LEMMA 16. *Using the* balanced p-ary representation *for* $p \geq 3$, *the addition of two integers is in* NC^0, *the multiplication of two integers in balanced p-ary representation is in* NC^1, *and hence* $\mathbb{Z}$ *is well-endowed. Moreover, conversion from binary to balanced 4-ary representation is in* NC^0 *and conversion from balanced 4-ary representation to binary representation is in* NC^1.

PROOF. See [2]. □

Independently, Chiu used the Chinese remainder representation and efficient conversions to show that integer comparison can be realized efficiently.

LEMMA 17 (CHIU 1995). *The comparison of two integers in binary representation is in* NC^1.

PROOF. See [5], §3.3. □

Using Chiu's result and Borodin's NC^1-circuit for iterated addition, a comparison circuit for scalar products in NC^1 using binary representation can be constructed. Applying theorem 13, this can be simulated by a logspace-bounded Turing machine. However note that the comparison of two integers is trivially in logspace and thus Chiu's result is not needed.

COROLLARY 18. *Given vectors* $u, v, w \in \mathbb{Z}^n$ *with q-bit entries, $u \cdot w < v \cdot w$ can be decided by a $O(\log(nq))$ space-bounded Turing machine.*

For rational vectors, first multiply each vector with the product of all denominators using the circuit for iterated multiplication in NC^2 (see [2]). The bitsize of the input blows up by a factor of $O(n)$ which can be neglected due to the logarithm in the formula of the space complexity.

COROLLARY 19. *Given vectors* $u, v, w \in \mathbb{Q}^n$ *with q-bit entries, $u \cdot w < v \cdot w$ can be decided by a $O(\log^2(nq))$ space-bounded Turing machine.*

A rather surprising result of complexity theory is about solving systems of linear equations. Borodin et al. [2] constructed a family of Boolean circuits that solves various problems for linear systems over a well-endowed field in NC^2.

THEOREM 20 (BORODIN ET AL. 1983). *Let* $\mathcal{A} \in \mathbb{K}^{n \times n}$ *be a matrix over a well-endowed field. Then the computation of its determinant, characteristic polynomial, rank, and adjoint matrix are in* NC^2.

PROOF. See [2], corollary 4.3, proposition 2.1, and proposition 2.2. □

The rank of a matrix can be determined from the characteristic polynomial since the corank equals the exponent of the highest power of the indeterminate that divides the characteristic polynomial. In order to compute the rank of a rectangular rational matrix, multiply it with its transpose to obtain a square matrix with the same rank. Finally, the adjoint matrix can be computed by a polynomial number of uniform determinant computations. Thus all these algorithms are in NC^2. Again, applying theorem 13 yields space bounded Turing machines for the respective problems.

COROLLARY 21. *Let* $n \geq m$, $\mathcal{A} \in \mathbb{K}^{n \times m}$ *a matrix over a well-endowed field with q-bit numerators and denominators. Then the computation of its rank and adjoint matrix, and, if $n = m$, its determinant and characteristic polynomial are in space $O(\log^2(nq))$.*

4. GRÖBNER BASIS COMPUTATION

The following exposition extends the results by Kühnle and Mayr in [17]. The goal is to compute Gröbner bases on Turing machines with low space complexity. The algorithm by Kühnle and Mayr requires exponential space and is therefore asymptotically optimal. The matching lower bound was given by Mayr and Meyer in [18]. However, the algorithm's time and space complexity essentially depends only on the degree bounds by Hermann [12] and Dubé [9] which are used in order to turn a polynomial equation into a system of linear equations.

Note that — just like in [17] — we require a monomial ordering given by a rational weight matrix. This is a proper restriction since not all monomial orderings can be represented this way. However all common monomial orderings can be represented by a rational weight matrix. Moreover, one can approximate any monomial ordering up to an arbitrary degree with a rational weight matrix.

4.1 Reduction to Linear Algebra

Kühnle and Mayr came up with a way to compute normal forms efficiently. This is central to the following and thus will be explained in detail. Let I be the ideal in $\mathbb{K}[X]$ whose Gröbner basis shall be computed and assume it is generated by polynomials $f_1, \ldots, f_s$. Since $h - \mathrm{nf}_I(h) \in I$ for any polynomial $h \in \mathbb{K}[X]$, there exists a representation

$$h - \mathrm{nf}_I(h) = \sum_{i=1}^{s} a_i f_i \qquad \text{with } a_1, \ldots, a_s \in \mathbb{K}[X]. \quad (1)$$

Their idea was to rewrite this equation as linear system and apply the result from corollary 21. First assume $\deg(a_i f_i) \leq D$ for $i = 1, \ldots, s$ and worry about D later. Name the coefficients by

$$a_i = \sum_{|\alpha| \leq D - \deg(f_i)} \mathbf{a}_{i,\alpha} x^\alpha, \qquad \text{for } i = 1, \ldots, s,$$

$$f_i = \sum_{|\beta| \leq \deg(f_i)} f_{i,\beta} x^\beta, \qquad \text{for } i = 1, \ldots, s,$$

$$h = \sum_{|\gamma| \leq D} h_\gamma x^\gamma, \qquad \text{and}$$

$$\mathrm{nf}_I(h) = \sum_{|\gamma| \leq D} \mathbf{y}_\gamma x^\gamma.$$

Then (1) is equivalent to

$$h_\gamma - \mathbf{y}_\gamma = \sum_{i=1}^{s} \sum_{\substack{|\alpha| \leq D - \deg(f_i) \\ |\beta| \leq \deg(f_i) \\ \alpha + \beta = \gamma}} \mathbf{a}_{i,\alpha} f_{i,\beta} \text{ for all } \gamma \in \mathbb{N}^n, |\gamma| \leq D.$$

$$(2)$$

Note that the unknowns of the system are printed in bold letters. Rewrite the system in matrix form

$$h - \mathcal{E} \cdot \mathbf{y} = \mathcal{F} \cdot \mathbf{a}$$

where $h = (h_\gamma)_{|\gamma| \leq D}$, $\mathbf{y} = (\mathbf{y}_\gamma)_{|\gamma| \leq D}$,

$$\mathbf{a} = (\mathbf{a}_{i,\alpha})_{\substack{i=1,\ldots,s \\ |\alpha| \leq D - \deg(f_i)}},$$

$\mathcal{E}$ is the identity matrix of size $\binom{D+n}{n}$, and $\mathcal{F}$ is the corresponding coefficient matrix. If it is possible to compute the coefficients of $\mathcal{F}$ efficiently, one can apply corollary 21 to

$$\begin{pmatrix} \mathcal{F} & \mathcal{E} \end{pmatrix} \cdot \begin{pmatrix} \mathbf{a} \\ \mathbf{y} \end{pmatrix} = h \qquad (3)$$

and thereby solve (1).

DEFINITION 22. *Let I be an ideal in $\mathbb{K}[X]$ generated by polynomials $F = \{f_1, \dots, f_s\}$ and fix an admissible monomial ordering $\prec$. For any given $D \in \mathbb{N}$ and $h \in \mathbb{K}[X]$, the w.r.t. $\prec$ minimal polynomial $\tilde{h} = \sum_{|\alpha| \leq D} \mathbf{y}_\alpha x^\alpha$ for which (2) is solvable is denoted by $\mathrm{nf}_F(h, D) = \tilde{h}$. If $\mathrm{nf}_F(h, D) \neq h$, h is called D-reducible w.r.t. F.*

Note that contrary to other definitions of reducibility and normal forms, F may be an arbitrary ideal basis here, and not necessarily a Gröbner basis. For sufficiently large D, $\mathrm{nf}_{F,D}(h) = \mathrm{nf}_G(h)$ where G is a Gröbner basis of $\langle F \rangle$. Thus D-reducibility and reducibility are equivalent. For arbitrary D, however, D-reducibility does not imply reducibility, nor the other way round.

LEMMA 23 (KÜHNLE, MAYR 1996). *Let I be an ideal in the polynomial ring $\mathbb{K}[X]$ over a well-endowed field $\mathbb{K}$, let I be generated by polynomials $F = \{f_1, \dots, f_s\}$, and fix an admissible monomial ordering $\prec$ represented by a rational weight matrix $W \in \mathbb{Q}^{n \times n}$. For any given $D \in \mathbb{N}$ and $h \in \mathbb{K}[X]$, it is possible to compute $\mathrm{nf}_F(h, D)$. If q bounds the bitsize of all numerators and denominators in W, F, and h, the algorithm is in space $O(\log^2(sD^nq))$.*

PROOF. (from [17], §3 and §4) The idea is to find a special maximal minor of (2) respectively its matrix form (3) which corresponds to the w.r.t. $\prec$ minimal solution of the system, i.e. $\mathrm{nf}_F(h, D)$. The caveat, of course, is the space consumption. Storing the whole matrix is prohibitive, but even storing which of the $\binom{D+n}{n}$ rows respectively $O(sD^n)$ columns belong to the minor requires too much storage. Thus this has to be avoided in a clever way. It is also necessary to tackle the computation of the indices of $\mathcal{F}$ in (3).

For the first problem, the solution lies in the choice of a special minor. Fix an ordering in which one can enumerate the rows (respectively columns) with little space requirement (postpone the choice of the ordering for a moment). Then there is a canonical maximal minor for which the index set of rows respectively columns is lexicographically minimal. For this minor, one can "locally" compute whether a row (respectively column) belongs to the minor. It suffices to compare the rank of the minor of the first $k - 1$ rows (respectively columns) and the minor of the first k rows (respectively columns) differ. The k-th row (respectively k-th column) belongs to the minor iff both ranks differ. Using corollary 21, one can determine both ranks in space $O(\log^2(sD^nq))$.

Next consider the order of the columns and rows. Remember that the columns correspond to the variables $\mathbf{a}_{i,\alpha}$ and $\mathbf{y}_\gamma$. The desired solution $\tilde{h} = \mathrm{nf}_F(h, D)$ is minimal w.r.t. $\prec$ which means that the coefficients $\mathbf{y}_\gamma$ corresponding to large monomials of $\tilde{h}$ are zero. Choosing columns for the minor corresponds to choosing the non-zero variables of the solution. By the greedy computation of the minor and the Steinitz exchange lemma, the variables which should be zero have to be in the last columns. Thus the columns will be ordered with the variables $\mathbf{a}_{i,\alpha}$ first (in arbitrary order) and the $\mathbf{y}_\alpha$ following in increasing order w.r.t. $\prec$. This guarantees that the solution $\tilde{h}$ which will be computed from the

above minor is minimal w.r.t. $\prec$. It turns out that the order or the rows is arbitrary.

For the above construction, it is necessary to enumerate the all monomials up to degree D ordered by $\prec$ (this also can be used if an arbitrary order is required). Assume that the algorithm only stores the current monomial. The next term will be found in an exhaustive search which requires the storage of two more monomials, the enumeration monomial and the smallest monomial found during the enumeration which is greater than the current monomial. This needs space $O(n \log(D))$. By corollary 19 and since $\prec$ is represented by a matrix, the comparison of two monomials w.r.t. $\prec$ can be done in space $O(\log^2(nD))$.

Last but not least, consider the matrix $\mathcal{F}$. Given a row index γ and a column index (i, α), the corresponding matrix coefficient is $f_{i,\beta}$ if $\beta = \gamma - \alpha \geq 0$ and 0 otherwise. So it suffices to write down α, β, γ, and i which can be done in space $O(n \log(D) + \log(s))$. Since the matrix dimensions of the linear system are $O(sD^n)$, corollary 21 and the intermediate space requirements yield the stated complexity. $\square$

4.2 Degree Bounds

The key for turning lemma 23 into an algorithm which computes a Gröbner basis is lemma 3. The remaining pieces of the jigsaw are a suitable degree bound and a way to enumerate the minimally reducible monomials.

Kühnle and Mayr bound the degree of the minimally reducible monomials by Dubé's degree bound. Then they represent the monomial ordering as single rational weight function (on the appearing monomials) and bound the degree of a normal form by estimating the length of the reduction w.r.t. the reduced Gröbner basis. This yields

LEMMA 24 (KÜHNLE, MAYR 1996). *Let I be an ideal in $\mathbb{K}[X]$ and fix an admissible monomial ordering $\prec$ represented by a non-negative rational weight matrix $W \in \mathbb{Q}^{n,n}$. Let B be a bound on all numerators and denominators of the entries of W and assume its Gröbner basis degree is bounded by $\deg(\mathrm{GB}(I)) \leq G$. Then the degree of the normal form of a polynomial $h \in \mathbb{K}[X]$ w.r.t. I is bounded by*

$$\deg(\mathrm{nf}_I(h)) \leq \deg(h)^n n^{n^2} B^{2n^2+2n} G^{n^2+1}.$$

PROOF. See [17], section 2. $\square$

While lemma 24 is necessary for the computation of arbitrary normal forms, it can be avoided for the computation of Gröbner bases. In this case, degree bounds like Dubé's or the dimension-dependent analogon, theorem 8, apply not only to the minimally reducible monomials but also to their normal forms. In the following theorem, the main result of [17] will be improved by applying the dimension-dependent bounds by Kratzer and ourselves. Later, the degree bounds will be replaced by an incremental algorithm with a S-polynomial criterion.

THEOREM 25. *Let $\mathbb{K}$ be a well-endowed field and $I \subsetneq \mathbb{K}[X]$ be an ideal of dimension r generated by polynomials $F = \{f_1, \dots, f_s\}$ of degrees bounded by d, and fix an admissible monomial ordering $\prec$ represented by a rational weight matrix $W \in \mathbb{Q}^{n \times n}$. If q bounds the bitsize of all numerators and denominators in W and F, it is possible to compute the reduced Gröbner basis G of I w.r.t. $\prec$ in space $O(n^8 2^{4r} \log^2(sdq))$.*

PROOF. (improving on [17], §5) By lemma 3, the leading monomials of the elements of a reduced Gröbner basis are minimally reducible, i.e. they are reducible but none of their divisors is. Then the Gröbner basis polynomials are obtained as difference of the leading monomial and its normal form w.r.t. I. Hence it suffices to enumerate all monomials $x^\alpha \in \mathbb{K}[X]$ up to the maximal Gröbner basis degree D_1 and check for each, whether it is D_2-reducible for a suitable D_2, but all the divisors $x_k^{-1} x^\alpha$ $(k = 1, \ldots, n)$ are D_2-irreducible. This check is done using lemma 23.

In order to obtain the abovementioned space bound, we remember theorem 8 which states that

$$\deg(G) \leq 2 \left[\frac{1}{2} \left(d^{2(n-r)^2} + d \right) \right]^{2^r} := D_1 \,,$$

where G is the reduced Gröbner basis of I. Furthermore, $x^\alpha - \mathrm{nf}_I(x^\alpha) \in G$ yields $\deg(\mathrm{nf}_I(x^\alpha)) \leq \deg(G)$. Now D_2 must be large enough to ensure that $\mathrm{nf}_F(x^\alpha, D_2) = \mathrm{nf}_I(x^\alpha)$ for all monomials $x^\alpha \in \mathbb{K}[X]$ up to degree D_1. The corresponding representation degree is bounded by Kratzer's theorem 7 (with $\mu = \min\{n, s\}$). Since

$$D_1 \geq (n+2)^2 \left(d^\mu + 1 \right)^{\mu+2} \,,$$

we set

$$D_2 := D_1 + \left(d \left((n+1)D_1 + 1 \right)^{n-r} \right)^{2^r} .$$

The complexity is dominated by the computation of normal forms and thus can be derived from lemma 23 as

$$O(\log^2(s D_2^n q)) = O(\log^2(s D_1^{n(n-r)2^r} q)) =$$
$$= O(\log^2(s d^{n(n-r)^3 2^{2r}} q)) = O(n^8 2^{4r} \log^2(sdq)).$$

$\square$

This result also follows as a corollary from theorem 26. However, it was proved here directly in order to make the presentation easier to understand and to underline the improvements over [17].

4.3 The S-Polynomial Criterion

The algorithm in theorem 25 always uses the worst case degree bounds. Thus the size of the linear system only depends on the degrees of the input polynomials and the ideal dimension. In the worst case, this is optimal because the membership problem is exponential space complete (shown by Mayr, Meyer in [18]). Still, for most instances this complexity can be avoided as the improvement of the original result by Kühnle and Mayr indicates. For further improvements, this will be done blindly — i.e. without the knowledge of better degree bounds — by increasing D step by step. As soon as the Gröbner basis is complete, the calculation can be aborted. Unfortunately the result is not necessarily reduced. Our contribution is the proof that this can be done space-efficiently using S-polynomials.

Given an ideal I in $\mathbb{K}[X]$ generated by polynomials $F = \{f_1, \ldots, f_s\}$, remember the structure lemma 3 for the reduced Gröbner basis of I. It claims that $x^\alpha - \mathrm{nf}_I(x^\alpha)$ is an element of the Gröbner iff x^α is minimally reducible w.r.t. I. The idea is to approximate this by

$$G = \{x^\alpha - \mathrm{nf}_I(x^\alpha, D) \in \mathbb{K}[X] : \alpha \in \mathbb{N}^n,$$
$$x^\alpha \text{ is minimally } D\text{-reducible w.r.t. } F, |\alpha| \leq D\}$$

and check the Gröbner basis using lemma 4. With $g_\alpha = x^\alpha - \mathrm{nf}_I(x^\alpha, D)$ for all $\alpha \in \mathbb{N}^n$, this means to consider

$$S(g_\alpha, g_\beta) = \sum_{g_\gamma \in G} a_{\alpha,\beta,\gamma} g_\gamma$$
$$g_\alpha, g_\beta \in G,$$
$$\mathrm{lm}(a_{\alpha,\beta,\gamma} g_\gamma) \preceq \mathrm{lm}(S(g_\alpha, g_\beta)) \text{ for } i = 1, \ldots, s, \text{ and} \quad (4)$$
$$f_i = \sum_{g_\gamma \in G} b_{i,\gamma} g_\gamma \qquad a_{\alpha,\beta,\gamma}, b_{i,\gamma} \in \mathbb{K}[X].$$

Note the last set of equation which verifies that G generates I. As before, the space efficient linear algebra methods of corollary 21 can be applied if the degrees of $a_{\alpha,\beta,\gamma}$ and $b_{i,\gamma}$ are bounded by D. Let

$$M = \{\alpha \in \mathbb{N}^n : |\alpha| \leq D,$$
$$x^\alpha \text{ minimally } D\text{-reducible w.r.t. } F\}$$

and

$$S(g_\alpha, g_\beta) = h_{\alpha,\beta} = \sum_{|\varepsilon| \leq 2D} h_{\alpha,\beta,\varepsilon} x^\varepsilon \quad \text{for } \alpha, \beta \in M,$$
$$a_{\alpha,\beta,\gamma} = \sum_{|\zeta| \leq D} \mathbf{a}_{\alpha,\beta,\gamma,\zeta} x^\zeta \qquad \text{for } |\alpha|, |\beta|, |\gamma| \leq D,$$
$$g_\gamma = \sum_{|\eta| \leq D} g_{\gamma,\eta} x^\eta \qquad \text{for } |\gamma| \leq D,$$
$$f_i = \sum_{|\varepsilon| \leq 2D} f_{i,\varepsilon} x^\varepsilon \qquad \text{for } i = 1, \ldots, s, \text{ and}$$
$$b_{i,\gamma} = \sum_{|\zeta| \leq D} \mathbf{b}_{i,\gamma,\zeta} x^\zeta \qquad \text{for } i = 1, \ldots, s, |\gamma| \leq D,$$

(4) yields a system of linear equations

$$h_{\alpha,\beta,\varepsilon} = \sum_{|\gamma| \leq D} \sum_{\substack{|\zeta| \leq D \\ |\eta| \leq D \\ \zeta+\eta=\varepsilon}} \mathbf{a}_{\alpha,\beta,\gamma,\zeta} g_{\gamma,\eta} \quad \forall \alpha, \beta \in M, |\varepsilon| \leq 2D$$

$$\mathbf{a}_{\alpha,\beta,\gamma,\zeta} = 0 \qquad \begin{aligned} &\forall \alpha, \beta \in M \\ &\forall |\gamma|, |\zeta| \leq D : \\ &\quad x^\gamma x^\zeta \succ \mathrm{lm}(h_{\alpha,\beta}) \end{aligned}$$

$$\mathbf{a}_{\alpha,\beta,\gamma,\zeta} = 0 \qquad \begin{aligned} &\forall \alpha, \beta \in M_D \\ &\forall |\gamma|, |\zeta| \leq D : \gamma, \zeta \notin M \end{aligned}$$

$$f_{i,\varepsilon} = \sum_{|\gamma| \leq D} \sum_{\substack{|\zeta| \leq D \\ |\eta| \leq D \\ \zeta+\eta=\varepsilon}} \mathbf{b}_{i,\gamma,\zeta} g_{\gamma,\eta} \quad \forall i = 1, \ldots, s, |\varepsilon| \leq 2D$$

$$\mathbf{b}_{i,\gamma,\zeta} = 0 \qquad \begin{aligned} &\forall i = 1, \ldots, s, |\zeta| \leq D \\ &\forall |\gamma| \leq D : \gamma \notin M \end{aligned}$$

(5)

With $h = (h_{\alpha,\beta,\varepsilon})_{\substack{|\alpha|,|\beta| \in M \\ |\varepsilon| \leq 2D}}$, $\mathbf{a} = (\mathbf{a}_{\alpha,\beta,\gamma,\zeta})_{\substack{|\alpha|,|\beta| \in M \\ |\gamma|,|\zeta| \leq D}}$, $f = (f_{i,\varepsilon})_{\substack{i=1,\ldots,s \\ |\varepsilon| \leq 2D}}$, and $\mathbf{b} = (\mathbf{b}_{i,\gamma,\zeta})_{\substack{i=1,\ldots,s \\ |\gamma|,|\zeta| \leq D}}$, one can write (5) in matrix form

$$\begin{pmatrix} \mathcal{G} & 0 \\ \mathcal{E}_1 & 0 \\ \mathcal{E}_2 & 0 \\ 0 & \mathcal{F} \\ 0 & \mathcal{E}_3 \end{pmatrix} \cdot \begin{pmatrix} \mathbf{a} \\ \mathbf{b} \end{pmatrix} = \begin{pmatrix} h \\ 0 \\ 0 \\ f \\ 0 \end{pmatrix}. \quad (6)$$

It remains to show, how $\mathcal{G}$, $\mathcal{F}$, $\mathcal{E}_1$, $\mathcal{E}_2$, and $\mathcal{E}_3$ can be computed efficiently.

THEOREM 26. *Let I be an ideal in the polynomial ring $\mathbb{K}[X]$ over a well-endowed field $\mathbb{K}$, let I be generated by polynomials $F = \{f_1, \ldots, f_s\}$, and fix an admissible monomial ordering $\prec$ represented by a rational weight matrix $W \in \mathbb{Q}^{n \times n}$. If q bounds the bitsize of all numerators and denominators in W and F, it is possible to compute a Gröbner basis G of I w.r.t. $\prec$ in space $O(\log^2(sD^n q))$ where D bounds the representation degrees of the S-polynomials of the elements of the Gröbner basis.*

PROOF. The algorithm starts with

$$D = \max\{\deg(f_i) : i = 1, \ldots, s\}$$

and doubles D after each step. For each value of D, it solves (5) respectively (6) using corollary 21. If the system is solvable, then

$$G = \{x^\alpha - \mathrm{nf}_I(x^\alpha, D) \in \mathbb{K}[X] : \alpha \in \mathbb{N}^n,$$
$$x^\alpha \text{ is minimally } D\text{-reducible w.r.t. } F, |\alpha| \leq D\}$$

is a Gröbner basis of I. In this case, the algorithm terminates with computing these polynomials by solving the smaller system (2) and the enumeration technique of theorem 25. Thus the complexity is dominated by the part that solves (5) for the largest value of D.

It was already discussed how to check whether a monomial is minimally D-reducible and how to compare two monomials w.r.t. $\prec$. Thus one can enumerate the set M and it is legal to index the matrices by indices from M. First consider the matrices $\mathcal{E}_1$, $\mathcal{E}_2$, and $\mathcal{E}_3$. One can choose all of them to be square matrices whose only non-zero entries are on the diagonal. The entry on the diagonal corresponding to a variable $\mathbf{a}_{\alpha,\beta,\gamma,\zeta}$ respectively $\mathbf{b}_{i,\gamma,\zeta}$ is 1 if the conditions of the respective line of (5) are fulfilled and 0 otherwise. Here the computation of $\mathrm{lm}(h_{\alpha,\beta})$ remains. It suffices to be able to compute the coefficients of the S-polynomial $h_{\alpha,\beta,\varepsilon}$. Then the leading monomial can be determined by enumerating all monomials and remembering the largest with non-zero coefficient. For the computation of $h_{\alpha,\beta,\varepsilon}$, observe $\mathrm{lm}(g_\alpha) = x^\alpha$ and $\mathrm{lm}(g_\beta) = x^\beta$ since x^α and x^β both are D-reducible w.r.t. F. So one can compute $x^\delta = \gcd(x^\alpha, x^\beta) = x^{\alpha \wedge \beta}$ and therefore

$$h_{\alpha,\beta} = \mathrm{S}(g_\alpha, g_\beta) = g_{\beta,\beta} x^{\beta-\delta} g_\alpha - g_{\alpha,\alpha} x^{\alpha-\delta} g_\beta =$$
$$= x^{\beta-\delta} g_\alpha - x^{\alpha-\delta} g_\beta.$$

The coefficients of $\mathcal{F}$ and $\mathcal{G}$ are $g_{\gamma,\eta}$ or zero. Which of both is the case can be determined analogously to lemma 23.

In total, there are $O(sD^{4n})$ variables and equations. So corollary 21 yields a complexity of $O(\log^2(sD^{4n} q))$ where the constant in the exponent can be dropped due to the logarithm and the O-notation. $\square$

5. CONCLUSION

It is well-known that the computation of Gröbner bases is exponential space complete. Up to now, the sharpest upper bound [17] was exponential in the number of variables. Using recent improvements regarding bounds for the Gröbner basis degree and the representation degree, we were able to give a tighter analysis of the algorithm by Kühnle and Mayr

yielding a space complexity which is exponential in the ideal dimension only.

This bound is competitive with the best known (sequential) time bounds (cf. [16]) which are double exponential. Such time bounds can be derived from the space bounds by the reasoning from section 3.3.

Note that this bound is effective, since the ideal dimension can be computed in polynomial space (cf. [8] and [13]). This obviously does not affect the total complexity (in O-notation).

Moreover, the authors of [16] use the uniform cost model which neglects the growth of coefficients. For Gröbner basis computations, these can grow double exponentially, as well, such that the cost model is not realistic. Our analysis is based on the construction of well-endowed rings and thus inherently respects the growth of coefficients.

Finally, we provide an adaptive version of the algorithm. The key tool is a space-efficient implementation of the S-polynomial criterion. Contrasting the previous work, this algorithm only needs exponential time in the worst case and performs better on nice instances.

This algorithm can be used in order to derive new complexity results. Now it is only necessary to derive bounds for the representation degree and the Gröbner basis degree and plug them into theorem 26. Note that this does *not* affect the algorithm itself - it only proves a bound for its complexity.

6. REFERENCES

[1] A. Borodin. On relating time and space to size and depth. *SIAM Journal on Computing*, 6(4):733–744, 1977.

[2] A. Borodin, S. Cook, and N. Pippenger. Parallel computation for well-endowed rings and space-bounded probabilistic machines. *Information and Control*, 58(1-3):113–136, 1983.

[3] B. Buchberger. *Ein Algorithmus zum Auffinden der Basiselemente des Restklassenringes nach einem nulldimensionalen Polynomideal*. PhD thesis, Universität Innsbruck, Austria, 1965.

[4] B. Buchberger. Bruno Buchberger's PhD thesis 1965: An algorithm for finding the basis elements of the residue class ring of a zero dimensional polynomial ideal. *Journal of Symbolic Computation*, 41(3-4):475–511, 2006.

[5] A. Y. Chiu. *Complexity of Parallel Arithmetic Using the Chinese Remainder Representation*. PhD thesis, The University of Wisconsin-Milwaukee, WI, USA, 1995.

[6] D. A. Cox, J. B. Little, and D. O'Shea. *Ideals, Varieties, and Algorithms*. Springer New York, 1992.

[7] D. A. Cox, J. B. Little, and D. O'Shea. *Using Algebraic Geometry*. Springer, 2005.

[8] A. Dickenstein, N. Fitchas, M. Giusti, and C. Sessa. The membership problem for unmixed polynomial ideals is solvable in single exponential time. *Discrete Applied Mathematics*, 33(1-3):73–94, 1991.

[9] T. W. Dubé. The Structure of Polynomial Ideals and Gröbner Bases. *SIAM Journal on Computing*, 19(4):750–773, 1990.

[10] J. C. Faugère. A new efficient algorithm for computing

Gröbner bases (F4). *Journal of Pure Applied Algebra*, 139:61–88, 1999.

[11] J. C. Faugère. A new efficient algorithm for computing Gröbner bases without reduction to zero (F5). In *Proceedings of the 2002 International Symposium on Symbolic and Algebraic Computation*, pages 75–83. ACM, 2002.

[12] G. Hermann. Die Frage der endlich vielen Schritte in der Theorie der Polynomideale. *Mathematische Annalen*, 95(1):736–788, 1926.

[13] M. Kratzer. Computing the dimension of a polynomial ideal and membership in low-dimensional ideals. Master's thesis, Technische Universität München, Germany, October 2008.

[14] M. Kreuzer and L. Robbiano. *Computational Commutative Algebra 1*. Springer, 2000.

[15] M. Kreuzer and L. Robbiano. *Computational Commutative Algebra 2*. Springer, 2005.

[16] T. Krick and A. Logar. Membership problem, Representation problem and the Computation of the Radical for one-dimensional Ideals. In *Effective Methods in Algebraic Geometry*, pages 203–216. Birkhauser, 1991.

[17] K. Kühnle and E. W. Mayr. Exponential space computation of Gröbner bases. In *Proceedings of the 1996 international symposium on Symbolic and algebraic computation*, pages 63–71. ACM New York, NY, USA, 1996.

[18] E. W. Mayr and A. R. Meyer. The complexity of the word problems for commutative semigroups and polynomial ideals. *Advances in Mathematics*, 46(3):305–329, 1982.

[19] E. W. Mayr and S. Ritscher. Degree bounds for Gröbner bases of low-dimensional polynomial ideals. In *Proceedings of the 2010 International Symposium on Symbolic and Algebraic Computation*, pages 21–27. ACM, 2010.

Division Polynomials for Jacobi Quartic Curves [*]

Dustin Moody
National Institute of Standards and Technology (NIST)
100 Bureau Drive
Gaithersburg, MD, 20899-8930, USA
dbmoody25@gmail.com

ABSTRACT

In this paper we find division polynomials for Jacobi quartics. These curves are an alternate model for elliptic curves to the more common Weierstrass equation. Division polynomials for Weierstrass curves are well known, and the division polynomials we find are analogues for Jacobi quartics. Using the division polynomials, we show recursive formulas for the n-th multiple of a point on the quartic curve. As an application, we prove a type of mean-value theorem for Jacobi quartics. These results can be extended to other models of elliptic curves, namely, Jacobi intersections and Huff curves.

Categories and Subject Descriptors

I.1.2 [**Symbolic and Algebraic Manipulation**]: Algorithms—*Algebraic Algorithms*

General Terms

Algorithms, Theory

Keywords

Algorithms, Elliptic Curves, Division Polynomials

1. INTRODUCTION

Elliptic curves have been an object of study in mathematics for well over a century. Recently elliptic curves have proven useful in applications such as factoring [16] and cryptography [15],[19]. The traditional way of writing the equation of an elliptic curve is to use its Weierstrass form:

$$y^2 + a_1 xy + a_3 y = x^3 + a_2 x^2 + a_4 x + a_6.$$

In the past several years, other models of elliptic curves have been introduced. Such models include Edwards curves [2],

[6], Jacobi intersections and Jacobi quartics [3], [4],[17], Hessian curves [13], and Huff curves [8], [14], among others. These models sometimes allow for more efficient computation on elliptic curves or provide other features of interest to cryptographers. In particular, Jacobi quartics provide resistance to side channel attacks, and they also have the most efficient unified point addition formulae [3], [10].

In this paper we find division polynomials for Jacobi quartics, although the ideas can be extended to Jacobi intersections and Huff curves. Division polynomials for Weierstrass curves are well known, and play a key role in the theory of elliptic curves. They can be used to find a formula for the n-th multiple of the point (x, y) in terms of x and y, as well as determining when a point is an n-torsion point on a Weierstrass curve. Division polynomials are also a crucial ingredient in Schoof's algorithm to count points on an elliptic curve over a finite field [22]. In addition, they have been used to perform efficient computations on elliptic curves, see for example [5], [9].

Hitt, McGuire, and Moloney recently have found formulas for division polynomials of twisted Edwards curves [11], [18]. The division polynomials we find are the analogues for Jacobi quartic curves. We illustrate a recursive formula for the n-th multiple of a point using these division polynomials. We are also able to prove some properties of these division polynomials. As an illustration, we show how they can be used to find the mean value of a certain collection of points related to the discrete logarithm problem.

This paper is organized as follows. In section 2 we review Jacobi quartics, and in section 3 we examine their division polynomials. As an application, in section 4 we look at a certain mean value theorem. We conclude in section 5 with some remarks and open questions.

2. THE JACOBI QUARTIC

One model for elliptic curves is known as Jacobi quartics. For a background on these curves, see [3], [4], [17]. We recall only the basic facts. For the remainder of this paper, let K be a field whose characteristic is not 2 or 3. Any elliptic curve with a point of order 2 can be put into Jacobi quartic form, with equation

$$J_{d,e} : y^2 = ex^4 - 2dx^2 + 1,$$

where we require $e(d^2 - e) \neq 0$, with $d, e \in K$. The identity element is $(0, 1)$, and the point $(0, -1)$ has order 2. The inverse of a point (x, y) is $(-x, y)$. There are two points at infinity, whose coordinates can be written in projective coordinates (with $z = 0$). The addition formula on $J_{d,e}$ is

---

[*]A full version of this paper is available as *Divison Polynomials for Alternate Models of Elliptic Curves* at http://eprint.iacr.org/2010/630

given by

$$(x_1, y_1) + (x_2, y_2) = \left(\frac{x_1 y_2 + y_1 x_2}{1 - e(x_1 x_2)^2}, \right.$$

$$\left. \frac{(1 + e(x_1 x_2)^2)(y_1 y_2 - 2 d x_1 x_2) + 2 e x_1 x_2 (x_1^2 + x_2^2)}{(1 - e(x_1 x_2)^2)^2} \right).$$

This addition formula can be efficiently implemented, which is one of the primary advantages of writing an elliptic curve in this form [10]. Another is that this addition formula protects against side-channel attacks [3], [17]. There is a birational transformation from a Jacobi quartic curve to a curve in Weierstrass form with a point of order 2. The map

$$(r, s) = \left(2 \frac{3(y+1) - dx^2}{3x^2}, 4 \frac{(y+1) - dx^2}{x^3} \right),$$

sends the points of the curve $J_{d,e}$ with $x \neq 0$ to the Weierstrass curve

$$s^2 = r^3 - \frac{4}{3}(d^2 + 3e)r - \frac{16}{27}d(d^2 - 9e).$$

Under this transformation, the identity point $(0, 1)$ corresponds to ∞, and the point of order two $(0, -1)$ goes to the point $(4d/3, 0)$. The inverse from the Weierstrass curve $s^2 = r^3 + ar + b$, with point of order 2 $(p, 0)$ is given by

$$(x, y) = \left(\frac{2(r - p)}{s}, \frac{(2r + p)(r - p)^2 - s^2}{s^2} \right),$$

with the image being the Jacobi quartic $J_{d,e}$ with $d = 3p/4$, and $e = -(3p^2 + 4a)/16$. The points $\infty, (p, 0)$ are exceptional, and get sent to $(0, 1)$ and $(0, -1)$ respectively.

3. DIVISION POLYNOMIALS

3.1 Division polynomials for Weierstrass curves

We begin by recalling the standard division polynomials for Weierstrass curves. We write $[n](x, y)$ to denote the n-th multiple of a point (x, y).

THEOREM 1. *Let E be given by $y^2 = x^3 + ax + b$, over a field whose characteristic is not 2. Then for any point (x, y) and $n \geq 2$*

$$[n](x, y) = \left(\frac{\phi_n(x, y)}{\psi_n^2(x, y)}, \frac{\omega_n(x, y)}{\psi_n^3(x, y)} \right).$$

The functions $\phi_n, \omega_n,$ and ψ_n in $\mathbb{Z}[x, y]$ are defined recursively by

$$\psi_0 = 0$$
$$\psi_1 = 1$$
$$\psi_2 = 2y$$
$$\psi_3 = 3x^4 + 6ax^2 + 12bx - a^2$$
$$\psi_4 = 4y(x^6 + 5ax^4 + 20bx^3 - 5a^2x^2 - 4abx - 8b^2 - a^3)$$
$$\psi_{2n+1} = \psi_{n+2}\psi_n^3 - \psi_{n-1}\psi_{n+1}^3 \text{ for } n \geq 2$$
$$\psi_{2n} = \frac{\psi_n}{2y}\left(\psi_{n+2}\psi_{n-1}^2 - \psi_{n-2}\psi_{n+1}^2\right) \text{ for } n \geq 3,$$

and

$$\phi_n = x\psi_n^2 - \psi_{n+1}\psi_{n-1}$$
$$\omega_n = \frac{1}{4y}\left(\psi_{n+2}\psi_{n-1}^2 - \psi_{n-2}\psi_{n+1}^2\right).$$

PROOF. These formulas are well-known. For example, see [23] or [24] for details. □

The polynomial ψ_n is called the n-th *division polynomial* of E. It is easy to see that a point $P = (x, y)$ satisfies $[n]P = \infty$ if and only if $\psi_n(x) = 0$. Division polynomials are an important tool for finding multiples of points. In fact, they have been used to speed up computation of point multiplication in some cases (see for example [5], [9]). They also play a key role in Schoof's algorithm for counting the number of points on an elliptic curve over a finite field [22].

3.2 Division polynomials for Jacobi quartics

We now perform a similar calculation for Jacobi quartics. The division polynomials we find allow us to perform arithmetic on the Jacobi quartic with only the x-coordinate along with one multiplication by the y-coordinate. For convenience, let $h(x) = ex^4 - 2dx^2 + 1$, so the curve equation for $J_{d,e}$ is $y^2 = h(x)$.

THEOREM 2. *Let $F_1 = 1, G_1 = 1, F_2 = -2,$ and $G_2 = ex^4 - 1$. Let $P_1 = 1, Q_1 = 1, P_2 = e^2x^8 - 4dex^6 + 6ex^4 - 4dx^2 + 1$, and $Q_2 = (ex^4 - 1)^2$. Write $[n](x, y) = (x_n, y_n)$. Then there are polynomials $F_n(x), G_n(x), P_n(x),$ and $Q_n(x)$ such that*

$$(x_{2k}, y_{2k}) = \left(xy\frac{F_{2k}(x)}{G_{2k}(x)}, \frac{P_{2k}(x)}{Q_{2k}(x)} \right),$$

$$(x_{2k+1}, y_{2k+1}) = \left(x\frac{F_{2k+1}(x)}{G_{2k+1}(x)}, y\frac{P_{2k+1}(x)}{Q_{2k+1}(x)} \right).$$

The $F_n, G_n, P_n,$ and Q_n can all be calculated recursively:

$$F_{2k+1} = 2hF_{2k}G_{2k-1}G_{2k} - F_{2k-1}(G_{2k}^2 - ex^4hF_{2k}^2),$$
$$G_{2k+1} = G_{2k-1}(G_{2k}^2 - ex^4hF_{2k}^2),$$

$$F_{2k+2} = 2F_{2k+1}G_{2k}G_{2k+1} - F_{2k}(G_{2k+1}^2 - ex^4F_{2k+1}^2),$$
$$G_{2k+2} = G_{2k}(G_{2k+1}^2 - ex^4F_{2k+1}^2),$$

and

$$P_{2k+1} = 2G_{2k}^2 P_{2k}Q_{2k-1}(G_{2k}^2 + ex^4hF_{2k}^2)$$
$$\quad - P_{2k-1}Q_{2k}(G_{2k}^2 - ex^4hF_{2k}^2)^2,$$
$$Q_{2n+1} = Q_{2k-1}Q_{2k}(G_{2k}^2 - ex^4hF_{2k}^2)^2,$$

$$P_{2k+2} = 2hG_{2k+1}^2 P_{2k+1}Q_{2k}(G_{2k+1}^2 + ex^4F_{2k+1}^2)$$
$$\quad - P_{2k}Q_{2k+1}(G_{2k+1}^2 - ex^4F_{2k+1}^2)^2,$$
$$Q_{2k+2} = Q_{2k}Q_{2k+1}(G_{2k+1}^2 - ex^4F_{2k+1}^2)^2,$$

for $k \geq 1$.

PROOF. The proof is along the same lines as what was done for Edwards curves in [11],[18]. In turn, these authors credit Abel [1]. We use induction on n. For $n = 1$ the claim is trivially true,

$$(x_1, y_1) = \left(x\frac{F_1(x)}{G_1(x)}, y\frac{P_1(x)}{Q_1(x)} \right).$$

For $n = 2$, the addition formula yields

$$(x_2, y_2) = \left(-\frac{2xy}{ex^4 - 1}, \frac{(1 + ex^4)(y^2 - 2dx^2) + 4ex^4}{(ex^4 - 1)^2} \right).$$

By the defining curve equation, we have that $y^2 = ex^4 - 2dx^2 + 1$, so y_2 can be rewritten as

$$y_2 = \frac{e^2x^8 - 4dex^6 + 6ex^4 - 4dx^2 + 1}{(ex^4 - 1)^2}.$$

Thus $(x_2, y_2) = (xyF_2/G_2, P_2/Q_2)$. We now assume the result holds true for all n.

Given two points (r_1, s_1) and (r_2, s_2) on $J_{d,e}$, let $(r_+, s_+) = (r_1, s_1) + (r_2, s_2)$ and $(r_-, s_-) = (r_1, s_1) - (r_2, s_2)$. Then by the addition formula, we have

$$r_+ + r_- = \frac{2r_1 s_2}{1 - e(r_1 r_2)^2}$$

and

$$s_+ + s_- = \frac{2s_1 s_2(1 + e(r_1 r_2)^2)}{(1 - e(r_1 r_2)^2)^2}.$$

If we substitute in $(r_1, s_1) = (x_n, y_n)$, and $(r_2, s_2) = (x, y)$ we obtain

$$x_{n+1} = \frac{2x_n y}{1 - e(xx_n)^2} - x_{n-1},$$

and

$$y_{n+1} = \frac{2y_n y(1 + e(xx_n)^2)}{(1 - e(xx_n)^2)^2} - y_{n-1}.$$

Assume first that $n = 2k$ is even, so then

$$x_{2k+1} = \frac{2xh\frac{F_{2k}}{G_{2k}}}{1 - ex^4 h\frac{F_{2k}^2}{G_{2k}^2}} - x\frac{F_{2k-1}}{G_{2k-1}}$$
$$= x\left(\frac{2hF_{2k}G_{2k-1}G_{2k} - F_{2k-1}(G_{2k}^2 - ex^4 hF_{2k}^2)}{G_{2k-1}(G_{2k}^2 - ex^4 hF_{2k}^2)}\right),$$

and

$$y_{2k+1} = \frac{2y\frac{P_{2k}}{Q_{2k}}(1 + ex^4 h\frac{F_{2k}^2}{G_{2k}^2})}{(1 - ex^4 h\frac{F_{2k}^2}{G_{2k}^2})^2} - y\frac{P_{2k-1}}{Q_{2k-1}}$$
$$= y\left(\frac{2G_{2k}^2 P_{2k}Q_{2k-1}(G_{2k}^2 + ex^4 hF_{2k}^2)}{Q_{2k-1}Q_{2k}(G_{2k}^2 - ex^4 hF_{2k}^2)^2}\right.$$
$$\left. - \frac{P_{2k-1}Q_{2k}(G_{2k}^2 - ex^4 hF_{2k}^2)^2}{Q_{2k-1}Q_{2k}(G_{2k}^2 - ex^4 hF_{2k}^2)^2}\right).$$

When $n = 2k + 1$ is odd

$$x_{2k+2} = \frac{2xy\frac{F_{2k+1}}{G_{2k+1}}}{1 - ex^4\frac{F_{2k+1}^2}{G_{2k+1}^2}} - xy\frac{F_{2k}}{G_{2k}}$$
$$= xy\left(\frac{2F_{2k+1}G_{2k}G_{2k+1} - F_{2k}(G_{2k+1}^2 - ex^4 F_{2k+1}^2)}{G_{2k}(G_{2k+1}^2 - ex^4 F_{2k+1}^2)}\right),$$

and

$$y_{2k+2} = \frac{2y^2\frac{P_{2k+1}}{Q_{2k+1}}(1 + ex^4\frac{F_{2k+1}^2}{G_{2k+1}^2})}{(1 - ex^4\frac{F_{2k+1}^2}{G_{2k+1}^2})^2} - \frac{P_{2k}}{Q_{2k}}$$
$$= \frac{2hG_{2k+1}^2 P_{2k+1}Q_{2k}(G_{2k+1}^2 + ex^4 F_{2k+1}^2)}{Q_{2k+1}Q_{2k}(G_{2k+1}^2 - ex^4 F_{2k+1}^2)^2}$$
$$- \frac{P_{2k}Q_{2k+1}(G_{2k+1}^2 - ex^4 F_{2k+1}^2)^2}{Q_{2k+1}Q_{2k}(G_{2k+1}^2 - ex^4 F_{2k+1}^2)^2}.$$

This proves the recurrence relations given in the statement of the theorem hold.

Alternatively, if we let $\alpha_n = F_n/G_n$ and $\beta_n = P_n/Q_n$, then the above can be rewritten as follows: for n odd,

$$x_{n+1} = xy\left(\frac{2\alpha_n}{1 - ex^4\alpha_n^2} - \alpha_{n-1}\right),$$

$$y_{n+1} = \frac{2h\beta_n(1 + ex^4\alpha_n^2)}{(1 - ex^4\alpha_n^2)^2} - \beta_{n-1}.$$

When n is even,

$$x_{n+1} = x\left(\frac{2h\alpha_n}{1 - ex^4 h\alpha_n^2} - \alpha_{n-1}\right),$$

and

$$y_{n+1} = y\left(\frac{2\beta_n(1 + ex^4 h\alpha_n^2)}{(1 - ex^4 h\alpha_n^2)^2} - \beta_{n-1}\right).$$

$\square$

There are some common factors that can be cancelled in the numerators and denominators of F_n/G_n and P_n/Q_n. Also, the degrees of the $F_n, G_n, P_n,$ and Q_n grow exponentially. By removing these common factors our new division polynomials will have degrees that only grow quadratically. The next proposition shows what these are.

THEOREM 3. *Let* $f_1 = 1, g_1 = 1, f_2 = -2,$ *and* $g_2 = ex^4 - 1$. *Let* $p_1 = 1, q_1 = 1, p_2 = e^2 x^8 - 4dex^6 + 6ex^4 - 4dx^2 + 1,$ *and* $q_2 = (ex^4 - 1)^2$. *For* $n > 2$, *define* $f_n, g_n, p_n,$ *and* q_n *by*

$$f_{2k} = \frac{2f_{2k-1}g_{2k-2}g_{2k-1} - f_{2k-2}(g_{2k-1}^2 - ex^4 f_{2k-1}^2)}{g_{2k-2}^2},$$

$$f_{2k+1} = \frac{2hf_{2k}g_{2k-1}g_{2k} - f_{2k-1}(g_{2k}^2 - ex^4 hf_{2k}^2)}{g_{2k-1}^2},$$

$$g_{2k} = \frac{g_{2k-1}^2 - ex^4 f_{2k-1}^2}{g_{2k-2}},$$

$$g_{2k+1} = \frac{g_{2k}^2 - ex^4 hf_{2k}^2}{g_{2k-1}},$$

and

$$p_{2k} = \frac{2hg_{2k-1}^2 p_{2k-1}q_{2k-2}(g_{2k-1}^2 + ex^4 f_{2k-1}^2)}{g_{2k-2}^2 q_{2k-1}}$$
$$- \frac{p_{2k-2}q_{2k-1}(g_{2k-1}^2 - ex^4 f_{2k-1}^2)^2}{g_{2k-2}^2 q_{2k-1}},$$

$$p_{2k+1} = \frac{2g_{2k}^2 p_{2k}q_{2k-1}(g_{2k}^2 + ex^4 hf_{2k}^2)}{g_{2k-1}^2 q_{2k}}$$
$$- \frac{p_{2k-1}q_{2k}(g_{2k}^2 - ex^4 hf_{2k}^2)^2}{g_{2k-1}^2 q_{2k}},$$

$$q_{2k} = \frac{(g_{2k-1}^2 - ex^4 f_{2k-1}^2)^2}{q_{2k-2}},$$

$$q_{2k+1} = \frac{(g_{2k}^2 - ex^4 hf_{2k}^2)^2}{q_{2k-1}}.$$

Then the f_n, g_n, p_n *and* q_n *are even polynomials in* x *and satisfy*

$$(x_{2k}, y_{2k}) = \left(xy\frac{f_{2k}(x)}{g_{2k}(x)}, \frac{p_{2k}(x)}{q_{2k}(x)}\right),$$

$$(x_{2k+1}, y_{2k+1}) = \left(x\frac{f_{2k+1}(x)}{g_{2k+1}(x)}, y\frac{p_{2k+1}(x)}{q_{2k+1}(x)} \right).$$

Before we give the proof, we prove a lemma. It will be needed in the proof of Theorem 3 as well as for some of the identities of the Jacobi division polynomials. Most importantly, it gives a simpler recurrence for the f_n (and p_n).

LEMMA 1. *For $n \geq 1$, the functions f_n, g_n, p_n, and q_n from Theorem 3 satisfy*

$$g_{2k}^2 - hf_{2k}^2 = -f_{2k-1}f_{2k+1}, \tag{1}$$

and as a result

$$f_{2k+1} = \frac{hf_{2k}^2 - g_{2k}^2}{f_{2k-1}},$$

and for $n > 1$

$$f_{2k-1}^2 - g_{2k-1}^2 = hf_{2k-2}f_{2k}, \tag{2}$$

so therefore

$$f_{2k} = \frac{f_{2k-1}^2 - g_{2k-1}^2}{hf_{2k-2}}.$$

Also $q_n = g_n^2$ and

$$p_{2k} = \frac{2hp_{2k-1}(g_{2k-1}^2 + ex^4 f_{2k-1}^2) - p_{2k-2}g_{2k}^2}{q_{2k-2}},$$

$$p_{2k+1} = \frac{2p_{2k}(g_{2k}^2 + ex^4 hf_{2k}^2) - p_{2k-1}g_{2k+1}^2}{q_{kn-1}}.$$

PROOF. First note that by definition, we have

$$\begin{aligned} f_{2k+1}g_{2k-1} &= \frac{2hf_{2k}g_{2k-1}g_{2k} - f_{2k-1}(g_{2k}^2 - ex^4 hf_{2k}^2)}{g_{2k-1}}, \\ &= \frac{2hf_{2k}g_{2k-1}g_{2k} - f_{2k-1}g_{2k-1}g_{2k+1}}{g_{2k-1}}, \tag{3} \\ &= 2hf_{2k}g_{2k} - f_{2k-1}g_{2k+1}. \end{aligned}$$

We now use induction. For $k = 1$, a direct computation checks that both sides of (1) are equal to $e^2x^8 - 6ex^4 + 8dx^2 - 3$. The expression $g_{2k}^2 - hf_{2k}^2 + f_{2k-1}f_{2k+1}$ can be rewritten as

$$\frac{g_{2k}^2}{g_{2k-2}^2 g_{2k-1}^2}\Big(-f_{2k-1}^2(g_{2k-2}^2 - ex^4 hf_{2k-2}^2)$$
$$+ g_{2k-1}^2(g_{2k-2}^2 - hf_{2k-2}^2)$$
$$+ 2hf_{2k-2}f_{2k-1}g_{2k-2}g_{2k-1} \Big).$$

By the induction hypothesis, $g_{2k-2}^2 - hf_{2k-2}^2 = -f_{2k-3}f_{2k-1}$, and we also have $g_{2k-2}^2 - ex^4 hf_{2k-2}^2 = g_{2k-3}g_{2k-1}$ so this last expression becomes

$$\frac{f_{2k-1}g_{2k}^2}{g_{2k-2}^2 g_{2k-1}}\Big(2hf_{2k-2}g_{2k-2} - f_{2k-1}g_{2k-3} - g_{2k-1}f_{2k-3} \Big).$$

By (3) (with $k-1$ in place of k), we see that this is equal to 0. This shows $g_{2k}^2 - hf_{2k}^2 + f_{2k-1}f_{2k+1} = 0$, which was to be proved.

To prove (2) we also use induction. For $k = 2$ both sides are equal to $8(ex^4 - 2dx^2 + 1)(ex^4 - 1)(-e^2x^8 + 4dex^6 - 6ex^4 + 4dx^2 - 1)$. We can rewrite $f_{2k-1}^2 - g_{2k-1}^2 - hf_{2k-2}f_{2k}$

as

$$\frac{g_{2k-1}^2}{g_{2k-3}^2 g_{2k-2}^2}\Big(g_{2k-2}^2(f_{2k-3}^2 - g_{2k-3}^2)$$
$$- 2hf_{2k-3}f_{2k-2}g_{2k-3}g_{2k-2} \tag{4}$$
$$+ hf_{2k-2}^2(g_{2k-3}^2 - ex^4 f_{2k-3}^2) \Big).$$

Using the induction hypothesis and the identity $g_{2k-3}^2 - ex^4 f_{2k-3}^2 = g_{2k-4}g_{2k-2}$ then equation (4) becomes

$$\frac{hf_{2k-2}g_{2k-1}^2}{g_{2k-3}^2 g_{2k-2}}\Big(f_{2k-4}g_{2k-2} - 2f_{2k-3}g_{2k-3} + f_{2k-2}g_{2k-4} \Big). \tag{5}$$

But

$$\begin{aligned} f_{2k-2}g_{2k-4} &= \frac{2f_{2k-3}g_{2k-4}g_{2k-3} - f_{2k-4}(g_{2k-3}^2 - ex^4 f_{2k-3}^2)}{g_{2k-4}} \\ &= 2f_{2k-3}g_{2k-3} - f_{2k-4}g_{2k-2}, \end{aligned}$$

so (5) is equal to 0, showing $f_{2k-1}^2 - g_{2k-1}^2 - hf_{2k-2}f_{2k} = 0$.

Finally, we verify that $q_n = g_n^2$. For $n = 1$ and 2, this is clearly true. Now assume that $q_n = g_n^2$. Then by definition $q_{n+1} = g_{n+1}^2 g_{n-2}^2 / q_{n-2}$. By the induction hypothesis, $g_{n-2}^2 = q_{n-2}$ which proves $q_{n+1} = g_{n+1}^2$. Using this, combined with the definition of the g_n, the formulas for the p_n are straightforward and we omit the details. $\square$

We now give the proof of Theorem 3.

PROOF. Note the similarities in the definitions of F_n and f_n, G_n and g_n, P_n and p_n, and finally between Q_n and q_n. Since the f_n and g_n are just the F_n and G_n with their common factors canceled then $F_n/G_n = f_n/g_n$. Likewise $P_n/Q_n = p_n/q_n$. It is clear that f_n, g_n, p_n, and q_n are all even using the recursion formulas combined with the fact that $f_1, f_2, g_1, g_2, p_1, p_2, q_1$, and q_2 are all even.

We first show that the g_n are polynomials. Let γ be a root of g_{2k-2}, and $\delta \in \overline{K}$ such that (γ, δ) is a point on $J_{d,e}$. It follows that $[2k-2](\gamma, \delta)$ is a point at infinity R. Using the addition law for projective coordinates (given in [3]), $(x, y) + R = (\pm 1/\sqrt{e}x, \pm y/\sqrt{e})$. As a result, we see

$$x_{2k-1}(\gamma) = \frac{1}{e\gamma^2} = \gamma^2 \frac{f_{2k-1}^2(\gamma)}{g_{2k-1}^2(\gamma)}.$$

This is equivalent to γ being a root of $g_{2k-1}^2 - ex^4 f_{2k-1}^2$. As γ was arbitrary, then this shows $g_{2k-2}|g_{2k-1}^2 - ex^4 f_{2k-1}^2$. Similarly, if $g_{2k-1}(\gamma) = 0$ then by the same reasoning we have

$$x_{2k}^2(\gamma) = \frac{1}{e\gamma^2} = \gamma^2 h(\gamma) \frac{f_{2k}^2(\gamma)}{g_{2k}^2(\gamma)}.$$

Thus γ is a root of $g_{2k}^2 - ex^4 hf_{2k}^2$ as desired. We conclude that the g_n are polynomials in x.

We now show that the f_n are polynomials in x. By Lemma 1, $f_{2k+1} = (hf_{2k}^2 - g_{2k}^2)/f_{2k-1}$. Let γ be a root of f_{2k-1}. Then by the addition law, we have $x_{2k}(\gamma) = \pm\gamma$. Squaring this relation yields

$$\gamma^2 = \gamma^2 h(\gamma) \frac{f_{2k}^2(\gamma)}{g_{2k}^2(\gamma)},$$

which shows γ is a root of $g_{2k}^2 - hf_{2k}^2$, and hence f_{2k+1} is a polynomial.

Similarly, by Lemma 1 we have that $f_{2k} = \frac{f_{2k-1}^2 - g_{2k-1}^2}{h f_{2k-2}}$.
Now if $f_{2k-2}(\gamma) = 0$ for some $\gamma \neq 0$, then $x_{2k-1}(\gamma) = \pm\gamma$.
Squaring this yields

$$\gamma^2 = \gamma^2 \frac{f_{2k-1}^2(\gamma)}{g_{2k-1}^2(\gamma)},$$

and we see that γ is a root of $f_{2k-1}^2 - g_{2k-1}^2$, so f_{2k-2} divides $f_{2k-1}^2 - g_{2k-1}^2$.

If γ is a root of $h = ex^4 - 2dx^2 + 1$, then $(\gamma, 0)$ is a point on the curve $J_{d,e}$, and it is easy to check that $[2](\gamma, 0) = (0, -1), [3](\gamma, 0) = (-\gamma, 0)$, and $[4](\gamma, 0) = (0, 1)$. So then

$$x_{2k-1}^2(\gamma) = \gamma^2 = \gamma^2 \frac{f_{2k-1}^2(\gamma)}{g_{2k-1}^2(\gamma)},$$

so γ is a root of $f_{2k-1}^2 - g_{2k-1}^2$, and hence h divides $f_{2k-1}^2 - g_{2k-1}^2$. This shows that f_{2k} is a polynomial in x.

To see q_n is a polynomial in x, we appeal to Lemma 1. As g_n is a polynomial, and $q_n = g_n^2$, then q_n is a polynomial as well. The proof that p_n is a polynomial is much more cumbersome to write down, although the technique is the same. Consequently, we omit it. $\square$

We list the division polynomials for $n = 3$ and 4:

$$f_3 = -e^2 x^8 + 6ex^4 - 8dx^2 + 3,$$

$$g_3 = -3e^2 x^8 + 8dex^6 - 6ex^4 + 1,$$

$$p_3 = e^4 x^{16} - 8de^3 x^{14} + 28e^3 x^{12} - 56de^2 x^{10}$$
$$+ 2e(32d^2 + 3e)x^8 - 56dex^6 + 28ex^4 - 8dx^2 + 1,$$

$$q_3 = (-3e^2 x^8 + 8dex^6 - 6ex^4 + 1)^2,$$

$$f_4 = -4(ex^4 - 1)(-e^2 x^8 + 4dex^6 - 6ex^4 + 4dx^2 - 1),$$

$$g_4 = -e^4 x^{16} + 20e^3 x^{12} - 64de^2 x^{10} + (64d^2 + 26e^2)ex^8$$
$$- 64dex^6 + 20ex^4 - 1,$$

$$p_4 = e^8 x^{32} - 16 de^7 x^{30} - 560 de^6 x^{26} + \cdots - 16 dx^2 + 1,$$

$$q_4 = g_4{}^2.$$

We call the f_n the Jacobi quartic division polynomials, as they satisfy the following corollary.

COROLLARY 1. For $n > 2$, the point (x, y), with $xy \neq 0$, satisfies $[n](x, y) = (0, \pm 1)$ if and only if we have $f_n(x) = 0$.

PROOF. This is immediate from Theorems 2 and 3. Note that $[n](x, y) = (0, 1)$ if and only if $[n](x, -y) = (0, -1)$. $\square$

An advantage of our division polynomials is that the n-th one can be computed from the previous two rounds, i.e., f_n and g_n only depend on $f_{n-1}, g_{n-1}, f_{n-2}$, and g_{n-2}. The division polynomials for Weierstrass curves given in Theorem 1 require the previous $n/2$ rounds of computation. We now show some of the properties of these latter Jacobi division polynomials, beginning with their degrees.

PROPOSITION 1. For odd n,

$$\frac{f_n(x)}{g_n(x)} = \frac{e^{(n^2-1)/4} x^{n^2-1} + \cdots}{n e^{(n^2-1)/4} x^{n^2-1} + \cdots},$$

$$\frac{p_n(x)}{q_n(x)} = \frac{e^{(n^2-1)/2} x^{2(n^2-1)+\cdots}}{(n e^{(n^2-1)/4} x^{n^2-1} + \cdots)^2},$$

where $+\cdots$ indicates lower powers of x. For even n, we have

$$\frac{f_n(x)}{g_n(x)} = -n \frac{e^{(n^2-4)/4} x^{n^2-4} + \cdots}{e^{n^2/4} x^{n^2} + \cdots},$$

$$\frac{p_n(x)}{q_n(x)} = \frac{e^{n^2/2} x^{2n^2} + \cdots}{(e^{n^2/4} x^{n^2} + \cdots)^2}.$$

PROOF. The proof of the leading terms of the quotient f_n/g_n and p_n/q_n is a straightforward exercise in induction. We only give the proof for f_n/g_n, and skip the proof for p_n/q_n. We first establish that for odd n,

$$f_n = (-1)^{(n-1)/2} e^{(n^2-1)/4} x^{n^2-1} + \cdots,$$

$$g_n = (-1)^{(n-1)/2} n e^{(n^2-1)/4} x^{n^2-1} + \cdots,$$

while for even n

$$f_n = (-1)^{n/2} n e^{(n^2-4)/4} x^{n^2-4} + \cdots,$$

$$g_n = -(-1)^{n/2} e^{n^2/4} x^{n^2} + \cdots.$$

Note that for $n = 1$ and 2 this is clearly true. For even n, if we include only the leading terms we have

$$f_{n+1} = \frac{(ex^4)(n^2 e^{(n^2-4)/2} x^{2(n^2-4)}) - (e^{n^2/2} x^{2n^2})}{(-1)^{(n-2)/2} e^{(n^2-2n)/4} x^{n^2-2n}}$$
$$= -(-1)^{n/2} e^{(n^2+2n)/4} x^{n^2+2n} + \cdots$$
$$= (-1)^{(n+1-1)/2} e^{((n+1)^2-1)/4} x^{(n+1)^2-1} + \cdots.$$

Similarly, when n is odd we have

$$f_{n+1} = \frac{(e^{(n^2-1)/2} x^{2(n^2-1)}) - (n^2 e^{(n^2-1)/2} x^{2(n^2-1)})}{(ex^4)((-1)^{(n-1)/2}(n-1) e^{(n^2-2n-3)/4} x^{n^2-2n-3})}$$
$$= (n+1)(-1)^{(n+1)/2} e^{((n+1)^2-4)/4} x^{(n+1)^2-4} + \cdots.$$

This shows the leading term of f_n is as desired for n even or odd. Now for $n = 2k$, we have

$$g_{n+1} = \frac{e^{2k^2} x^{8k^2} - ex^4(ex^4)(4k^2) e^{2k^2-2} x^{8k^2-8}}{(-1)^{k-1}(2k-1) e^{k^2-k} x^{4k^2-4k}}$$
$$= (-1)^k (2k+1) e^{k^2+k} x^{4k^2+4k} + \cdots$$
$$= (-1)^{(n+1-1)/2}(n+1) e^{((n+1)^2-1)/4} x^{(n+1)^2-1} + \cdots.$$

Also for $n = 2k+1$,

$$g_{n+1} = \frac{(2k+1)^2 e^{2k^2+2k} x^{8k^2+8k} - ex^4 e^{2k^2+2k} x^{8k^2+8k}}{(-1)^{k+1} e^{k^2} x^{4k^2}}$$
$$= (-1)^k e^{k^2+2k+1} x^{4k^2+8k+4} + \cdots$$
$$= -(-1)^{(n+1)/2} e^{n^2/4} x^{n^2} + \cdots,$$

which shows the leading term of g_n is as claimed. $\square$

We include some functional equations for the Jacobi division polynomials.

PROPOSITION 2. For odd n,

$$g_n(x) = (-1)^{(n-1)/2} e^{(n^2-1)/4} x^{n^2-1} f_n\left(\frac{1}{\sqrt{ex}}\right),$$

269

while for even n,

$$f_n(x) = (-1)^{(n+2)/2} e^{(n^2-4)/4} x^{n^2-4} f_n\left(\frac{1}{\sqrt{ex}}\right),$$

$$g_n(x) = (-1)^{n/2} e^{n^2/4} x^{n^2} g_n\left(\frac{1}{\sqrt{ex}}\right).$$

We also have

$$p_n(x) = e^{(n^2-1)/2} x^{2(n^2-1)} p_n\left(\frac{1}{\sqrt{ex}}\right),$$

for odd n, and

$$p_n(x) = e^{n^2/2} x^{2n^2} p_n\left(\frac{1}{\sqrt{ex}}\right),$$

for even n.

PROOF. Recall that f_n, g_n, and p_n are even, so the square roots in the formulae make sense. We use induction to prove Proposition 2. The results are all easily verified for $n = 1, 2$. We first verify the functional equation for g_n when $n = 2k$ is even:

$$(-1)^k e^{k^2} x^{4k^2} g_{2k}\left(\frac{1}{\sqrt{ex}}\right)$$

$$= (-1)^k e^{k^2} x^{4k^2} \frac{g_{2k-1}^2 - ex^4 f_{2k-1}^2}{g_{2k-2}}\left(\frac{1}{\sqrt{ex}}\right),$$

$$= (-1)^k e^{k^2} x^{4k^2} \frac{\frac{f_{2k-1}^2}{e^{2k^2-2k}x^{8k^2-8k}} - \frac{g_{2k-1}^2}{e^{2k^2+1}x^{8k^2-8k+4}}}{\frac{(-1)^{k-1} g_{2k-2}}{e^{(k-1)^2} x^{4(k-1)^2}}},$$

$$= \frac{g_{2k-1}^2 - ex^4 f_{2k-1}^2}{g_{2k-2}},$$

which is $g_{2k}(x)$ as desired.

Also for $n = 2k$,

$$(-1)^{k+1} e^{k^2-1} x^{4k^2-4} f_{2k}\left(\frac{1}{\sqrt{ex}}\right)$$

$$= (-1)^{k+1} e^{k^2-1} x^{4k^2-4} \frac{f_{2k-1}^2 - g_{2k-1}^2}{h f_{2k-2}}\left(\frac{1}{\sqrt{ex}}\right),$$

$$= (-1)^{k+1} e^{k^2-1} x^{4k^2-4} \frac{\frac{g_{2k-1}^2}{e^{2k^2-2k}x^{8k^2-8k}} - \frac{f_{2k-1}^2}{e^{2k^2-2k}x^{8k^2-8k}}}{\frac{h}{ex^4} \frac{f_{2k-2}}{(-1)^k e^{k^2-2k}x^{4k^2-8k}}},$$

$$= \frac{g_{2k-1}^2 - f_{2k-1}^2}{h f_{2k-2}},$$

$$= f_{2k}.$$

Finally, we show the functional equation relating f_n and g_n for odd $n = 2k+1$. We leave the proof of the functional equation for p_n to the reader. We have

$$(-1)^k e^{k^2+k} x^{4k^2+4k} f_{2k+1}\left(\frac{1}{\sqrt{ex}}\right)$$

$$= (-1)^k e^{k^2+k} x^{4k^2+4k} \frac{h f_{2k}^2 - g_{2k}^2}{f_{2k-1}}\left(\frac{1}{\sqrt{ex}}\right),$$

$$= (-1)^k e^{k^2+k} x^{4k^2+4k} \frac{\frac{h}{ex^4} \frac{f_{2k}^2}{e^{2k^2-2}x^{8k^2-8}} - \frac{g_{2k}^2}{e^{2k^2}x^{8k^2}}}{\frac{g_{2k-1}}{(-1)^{k-1}e^{k^2-k}x^{4k^2-4k}}},$$

$$= \frac{g_{2k}^2 - ex^4 h f_{2k}^2}{g_{2k-1}},$$

$$= g_{2k+1},$$

which was to be proved. Note these functional equations impose certain symmetries on the coefficients of the Jacobi division polynomials. □

4. MEAN VALUE THEOREMS

4.1 Weierstrass and Edwards mean value theorems

Let K be an algebraically closed field of characteristic not equal to 2 or 3. Let $E : y^2 = x^3 + Ax + B$ be an elliptic curve defined over K, and $Q = (x_Q, y_Q) \neq \infty$ a point on E. Let $P_i = (x_i, y_i)$ be the n^2 points such that $[n]P_i = Q$, where $n \in \mathbb{Z}$, (char $(K),n)=1$. The P_i are known as the n-division points of Q. In [7], Feng and Wu showed that

$$\frac{1}{n^2}\sum_{i=1}^{n^2} x_i = x_Q, \qquad \frac{1}{n^2}\sum_{i=1}^{n^2} y_i = n y_Q.$$

This shows the mean value of the x-coordinates of the n-division points of Q is equal to x_Q, and $n y_Q$ for the y-coordinates.

In [21] a similar formula was established for elliptic curves in twisted Edwards form. Let Q be a point on a twisted Edwards curve. Let $P_i = (x_i, y_i)$ be the n^2 points such that $[n]P_i = Q$. If n is odd, then

$$\frac{1}{n^2}\sum_{i=1}^{n^2} x_i = \frac{1}{n}x_Q, \qquad \frac{1}{n^2}\sum_{i=1}^{n^2} y_i = \frac{(-1)^{(n-1)/2}}{n} y_Q.$$

If n is even, then

$$\frac{1}{n^2}\sum_{i=1}^{n^2} x_i = 0 = \frac{1}{n^2}\sum_{i=1}^{n^2} y_i.$$

4.2 Jacobi quartic mean value theorem

We now give a mean value theorem for the x-coordinates of Jacobi quartics.

THEOREM 4. *Let $Q \neq (0, \pm 1)$ be a point on $J_{d,e}$. Let $P_i = (x_i, y_i)$ be the n^2 points such that $[n]P_i = Q$. Then*

$$\frac{1}{n^2}\sum_{i=1}^{n^2} x_i = \frac{1}{n}x_Q,$$

if n is odd and

$$\frac{1}{n^2}\sum_{i=1}^{n^2} x_i = 0,$$

if n is even.

We first need a result showing how we can combine mean value results for n-division points and m-division points to obtain one for the mn-division points.

PROPOSITION 3. *Fix m and n. Suppose we have that $\sum_{i=1}^{m^2} x_{P_i} = c_m x_Q$ and $\sum_{i=1}^{m^2} y_{P_i} = d_m y_Q$ for some constants c_m, d_m which depend only on m, whenever the P_i, $i = 1, 2, \cdots, m^2$ are points such that $[m]P_i = Q$, for some $Q \neq (0, 0)$. Similarly, suppose we have that $\sum_{i=1}^{n^2} x_{R_i} = e_n x_S$ and $\sum_{i=1}^{n^2} y_{R_i} = f_n y_S$ for some constants e_n, f_n which* depend only on n, where the R_i, $i = 1, 2, \cdots, n^2$ are points such that $[n]R_i = S$, for some $S \neq (0,0)$.

Then given $(mn)^2$ points $T_1, T_2, \cdots, T_{(mn)^2}$ on $J_{d,e}$ such that $[mn]T_i = U$ for some $U \neq (0,0)$, we have that $\sum_{i=1}^{(mn)^2} x_{T_i} = c_m e_n x_U$ and $\sum_{i=1}^{(mn)^2} y_{T_i} = d_m f_n y_U$.

PROOF. Consider the set of points $\{[m]T_1, [m]T_2, \cdots, [m]T_{(mn)^2}\}$. Each element $[m]T_i$ satisfies $[n]([m]T_i) = U$. So this set must be equal to the same set of n^2 points V that satisfy $[n]V = U$. Call this set $\{V_1, V_2, \cdots, V_{n^2}\}$. For each V_j, there are at most m^2 elements of the T_i which satisfy $[m]T_i = V_j$. As each T_i must satisfy $[m]T_i = V_j$ for some j, this partitions our original set of the $(mn)^2$ points T_i into n^2 subsets of m^2 points. Then by assumption, we have

$$\sum_{i=1}^{(mn)^2} x_{T_i} = \sum_{i=1}^{n^2} c_m x_{V_i} = c_m e_n x_U,$$

and

$$\sum_{i=1}^{(mn)^2} y_{T_i} = \sum_{i=1}^{n^2} d_m y_{V_i} = d_m f_n y_U.$$

$\square$

For example, fix an elliptic curve and suppose we know the mean value of the x-coordinates of the 3-division points, or $\sum_{i=1}^{9} x_i = 3x_Q$. Similarly if know the same for the 5-division points, $\sum_{i=1}^{25} x_i = 5x_Q$, then by Proposition 3 we know the mean value for the 15-division points. It will be $\sum_{i=1}^{225} x_i = 15x_Q$.

Now we give the proof of Theorem 4.

PROOF. We first examine the case when n is odd. By definition, the solutions of $\left(x\frac{f_n(x)}{g_n(x)}, y\frac{p_n(x)}{q_n(x)}\right) = (x_Q, y_Q)$ are exactly the (x_i, y_i). By proposition 1, we can rewrite this x-coordinate relation as

$$x\left(e^{(n^2-1)/4} x^{n^2-1} + 0x^{n^2-2} + \cdots\right) = x_Q(ne^{(n^2-1)/4} x^{n^2-1} + \cdots)$$

or

$$e^{(n^2-1)/4}\left(x^{n^2} - nx_Q x^{n^2-1} + \cdots\right) = 0.$$

This must be equal to the polynomial $e^{(n^2-1)/4} \prod_{i=1}^{n^2}(x - x_i)$, so we can conclude that

$$\sum_{i=1}^{n^2} x_i = nx_Q.$$

This proves the mean value of the x-coordinate is as claimed when n is odd.

We now look at the case when $n = 2$. By the addition formula it is clear that if $[2](x, y) = Q$, then $[2](-x, -y) = Q$ as well. So the four points P_i with $[2]P_i = Q$ can be written as $(x_1, y_1), (x_2, y_2), (-x_1, -y_1)$, and $(-x_2, -y_2)$. The result for $n = 2$ is immediate. Now by Proposition 3, and the result for odd n, Theorem 4 is true for even n as well. $\square$

We remark that Theorem 4 was proved for points $Q \neq (0, \pm 1)$. For $Q = (0, \pm 1)$, recall that $(x_i, y_i) \neq (0, \pm 1)$ is an n-division point of Q if and only if $f_n(x_i) = 0$. Recall that for odd n, f_n is an even function of x and so

$$f_n(x) = \prod_{i=1}^{n^2-1}(x - x_i) = x^{n^2-1} + 0x^{n^2-2} + \cdots,$$

and hence $\sum_{i=1}^{n^2-1} x_i = 0$. When we consider Q as the last n-division point of Q, then we have $\sum_{i=1}^{n^2} x_i = 0$.

We are unable to prove, but conjecture the following mean-value theorem for the y-coordinates of the n-division points on a Jacobian quartic:

$$\frac{1}{n^2}\sum_{i=1}^{n^2} y_i = y_Q,$$

for n odd, and

$$\frac{1}{n^2}\sum_{i=1}^{n^2} y_i = 0,$$

for n even. The proof techniques in [7], [21] do not work for Jacobi quartic curves. The Weierstrass result uses properties of the Weierstrass $\wp(z)$ function, which we do not have a Jacobi quartic analogue for. In the Edwards case, the result is obtained by the obvious symmetry of x and y in the defining curve equation.

Note that in our proof above, we showed the conjecture is true for $n = 2$. Hence, by Proposition 3, the even result follows immediately once it is true for odd n. Also note that the y-coordinate mean value theorem is equivalent to showing

$$\sum_{i=1}^{n^2} \frac{g_n(x_i)}{f_n(x_i)} = n^2,$$

for odd n because $y_i \frac{f_n(x_i)}{g_n(x_i)} = y_Q$.

5. CONCLUSION

In this paper we looked at division polynomials for Jacobi quartics. Using them we were able to find a formula for the n-th multiple of a point. We also proved some of the properties of these division polynomials, and a type of mean-value theorem. In the extended version of this paper ([20]) we show how to extend these results to other models of elliptic curves, namely, Huff curves and Jacobi intersections. This includes results for the division polynomials and related mean-value theorems.

Some directions for future study would be to find division polynomials for the remaining models of elliptic curves, such as Hessian curves. It would also be interesting to see if the formulas derived in this paper could be used to perform efficient scalar multiplication, as has been done in some cases with Weierstrass curves. This is the most important computation in elliptic curve cryptography and the subject of much research. We leave this for a future project.

6. ACKNOWLEDGMENTS

The author would like to thank Hongfeng Wu for his thoughtful discussions which helped improve this paper.

7. REFERENCES

[1] N. Abel. *Oeuvres Completes*. Nouvelle Edition, Oslo, 1881.

[2] D. Bernstein, P. Birkner, M. Joye, T. Lange, and C. Peters. Twisted Edwards curves. In *Progress in cryptology—AFRICACRYPT 2008 proceedings*, LNCS vol 5023, pages 389–405. Springer, 2008.

[3] O. Billet, and M. Joye. The Jacobi model of an elliptic curve and side-channel analysis. In *Applied Algebra, Algebraic Algorithms and Error-Correcting Codes 2003 proceedings*, LNCS vol 2643, pages 34–42. Springer, 2003.

[4] D. Chudnovsky, and G. Chudnovsky. Sequences of numbers generated by addition in formal groups and new primality and factorization tests. *Advances in Applied Mathematics*, 7: 385–434, 1986.

[5] V.S. Dimitrov, and P.K. Mishra. Efficient Quintuple Formulas for Elliptic Curves and Efficient Scalar Multiplication Using Multibase Number Representation. In *International Conference on Information Security 2007 proceedings*, LNCS vol 4779, pages 390–406. Springer, 2007.

[6] H. Edwards. A normal form for elliptic curves. *Bulletin of the AMS*, 44: 393–422, 2007.

[7] R. Feng, and H. Wu. A mean value formula for elliptic curves. Available at http://eprint.iacr.org/2009/586.pdf, 2009.

[8] R. Feng, and H. Wu. Elliptic curves in Huff's model. Available at http://eprint.iacr.org/2010/390.pdf, 2010.

[9] P. Giorgi, L. Imbert and T. Izard. Optimizing elliptic curve scalar multiplication for small scalars. In *Mathematics for Signal and Information Processing proceedings*, SPIE vol 7444, page 7444N. 2009.

[10] H. Hisil, K. Wong, G. Carter, and E. Dawson. Faster group operations on elliptic curves. In *Australasian Information Security Conference proceedings*, 98:7–19, 2009.

[11] L. Hitt, G. Mcguire, and R. Moloney. Division polynomials for twisted Edwards curves. Available at http://arxiv.org/abs/0809.2182, 2008.

[12] G. Huff. Diophantine problems in geometry and elliptic ternary forms. *Duke Math. J.*, 15: 443-453, 1948.

[13] M. Joye, and J. Quisquater. Hessian elliptic curves and side-channel attacks. In *Workshop on Cryptographic Hardware and Embedded Systems proceedings*, LNCS vol 2162, pages 402–410. Springer, 2001.

[14] M. Joye, M. Tibouchi, and D. Vergnaurd. Huff's model for elliptic curves. In *Algorithmic Number Theory Symposium (ANTS-IX) proceedings*, LNCS vol 6197, pages 234–250. Springer, 2010.

[15] N. Koblitz. Elliptic curve cryptosystems. *Math. Comp.*, 48:203–209, 1987.

[16] H. Lenstra. Factoring integers with elliptic curves. *Ann. Math.*, 126 (2): 649–673, 1987.

[17] P. Liardet, and N. Smart. Preventing SPA/DPA in ECC systems using the Jacobi form. In *Workshop on Cryptographic Hardware and Embedded Systems*, LNCS vol 2162, pages 391–401. Springer, 2001.

[18] G. McGuire, and R. Moloney. Two Kinds of Division Polynomials For Twisted Edwards Curves. Available at http://arxiv.org/abs/0907.4347, 2009.

[19] V. Miller. Use of elliptic curves in cryptography. In *Advances in Cryptology - CRYPTO '85 proceedings*, 218: 417–426, Springer, 1986.

[20] D. Moody. Division Polynomials for Alternate Models of Elliptic Curves. Available at eprint.iacr.org/2010/630.pdf

[21] D. Moody. Mean value formulas for twisted Edwards curves. Available at eprint.iacr.org/2010/142.pdf, 2010.

[22] R. Schoof. Counting points on elliptic curves over finite fields. *J. Théor. Nombres Bordeaux*, 7: 219–254, 1995.

[23] J. Silverman. *The arithmetic of elliptic curves.* Springer-Verlag, 1986.

[24] L. Washington. *Elliptic curves (Number theory and cryptography), 2nd edition.* Chapman & Hall, 2008.

Computing a Structured Gröbner Basis Approximately

Kosaku Nagasaka
Graduate School of Human Development and Environment, Kobe University,
3-11 Tsurukabuto, Nada-ku, Kobe 657-8501 JAPAN
nagasaka@main.h.kobe-u.ac.jp

ABSTRACT

There are several preliminary definitions for a Gröbner basis with inexact input since computing such a basis is one of the challenging problems in symbolic-numeric computations for several decades. A structured Gröbner basis is such a basis defined from the data mining point of view: how to extract a meaningful result from the given inexact input when the amount of noise is not small or we do not have enough information about the input. However, the known algorithm needs a suitable (unknown) information on terms required for a variant of the Buchberger algorithm. In this paper, we introduce an improved version of the algorithm that does not need any extra information in advance.

Categories and Subject Descriptors

I.1 [**Symbolic and algebraic manipulation**]: Miscellaneous

General Terms

Algorithms

Keywords

Gröbner Bases, Symbolic-Numeric Computations, Inexact

1. INTRODUCTION

Computing a Gröbner basis for polynomials with inexact coefficients is one of the challenging problems for several decades in symbolic-numeric computations since for the given inexact coefficients we have to operate with a priori errors whether we compute a basis by exact arithmetic or not. Hence the known results are widely studied from their different points of view: numerical analysis, comprehensive Gröbner system and computational time.

The difficulties for computing a Gröbner basis by floating-point numbers are studied by Stetter [26] and Traverso and Zanoni [28] and several numerical analyses are given by Sasaki and Kako [21, 20, 22]. However, their results are not applicable if we do not have enough information on a priori errors. On the other hand, computing a comprehensive Gröbner system [29] for polynomials with parameters instead of inexact coefficients does not need any information on a priori errors. However, in general, a comprehensive Gröbner system has a huge number of segments and its computation time is quite slow (see [17] for example) though Weispfenning [30] tried to decrease the time-complexity by using only a single parameter to represent the inexact parts and there are several improvements in computing comprehensive Gröbner systems (see [11, 27, 10, 16, 8] and citations therein). Moreover, even if we can deal with the large number of segments, we are not able to determine which segment is preferable for the input since in general we do not have any information on a priori errors. There are also studies [23, 24] for computing a Gröbner basis for polynomials with exact coefficients, using floating-point numbers. They use stabilization techniques [25] by which we can compute a numerical sequence of Gröbner bases with exact inputs and the sequence converges to the exact result. However, their algorithms can not deal with a priori errors since the stabilization techniques are designed for exact inputs only.

Therefore, roughly speaking, the known methods above can not extract a meaningful result from the given inexact input if we do not have any information on a priori errors. To overcome this problem, we go back to the starting point "When do we compute a Gröbner basis with inexact inputs?" and reach the following resolution from the data mining point of view. The present author thinks that we compute it when it seems that there are some (nontrivial) algebraic structures on inexact data or we wish to have this hypothesis. Hence the author introduced the concept of structured Gröbner basis [19] by which we find a Gröbner basis with lower entropy (unfortunately enlarged by some errors), which may be hidden by a priori errors. Here "structured" means that we limit perturbations on coefficients to being under some constraints to prevent the inexact inputs from being far from the originals since we should not create but mine the hidden results.

However, the former algorithm needs a suitable (unknown) information on terms required for a variant of the Buchberger algorithm hence it is useless. In this paper, we introduce an improved version of the algorithm that does not need any extra information in advance.

After the preliminary section below, we introduce an improved algorithm for computing a structured Gröbner basis approximately in Section 3. Its theoretical background and the proofs of correctness of the algorithm are also given in Section **3**. In Section **4**, we give some useful remarks with numerical examples.

2. NOTATIONS AND FORMER WORK

We assume that we compute a Gröbner basis or its variants for the ideal $I \subseteq \mathbb{C}[\vec{x}]$ generated by a polynomial set $F = \{f_1, \ldots, f_k\} \subset \mathbb{C}[\vec{x}]$ where $\mathbb{C}[\vec{x}]$ is the polynomial ring in variables $\vec{x} = x_1, \ldots, x_\ell$ over the complex number field $\mathbb{C}$.

As in the studies [14, 1, 3] for SLRA (Structured Low Rank Approximation) and its variant, we define a structured polynomial set. Consider a mapping $\mathfrak{S}_i$ $(i = 1, \ldots, k)$ from a parameter space $\mathbb{C}^{n_i}$ to a set of polynomials $\mathbb{C}[\vec{x}]$. A polynomial set $F = \{f_1, \ldots, f_k\}$ is called $\mathfrak{S}$-structured if each element $f_i(\vec{x})$ of the set is in the image of $\mathfrak{S}_i$, i.e., if there exists a parameter $\vec{p_i} \in \mathbb{C}^{n_i}$, such that $f_i(\vec{x}) = \mathfrak{S}_i(\vec{p_i})$. We note that the choice of mappings are limited by the SLRA solver used in the algorithm. In fact, our preliminary implementation is only compatible with some simple linear mappings.

As in the studies computing a Gröbner basis by using the reduced row echelon form (RREF for short, [13, 2, 6, 7, 12, 5, 18]), we consider the linear map $\phi_{\mathcal{T}} : \mathbb{C}[\vec{x}]_{\mathcal{T}} \to \mathbb{C}^{1 \times m_{\mathcal{T}}}$ such that $\phi_{\mathcal{T}}(t_i) = \vec{e_i}$ where $\mathbb{C}[\vec{x}]_{\mathcal{T}}$ is the submodule of $\mathbb{C}[\vec{x}]$ generated by an ordered set (the left-most element is the highest) of terms $\mathcal{T} = \{t_1, \ldots, t_{m_{\mathcal{T}}}\}_{\succ}$ and $\vec{e_i}$ $(i = 1, \ldots, m_{\mathcal{T}})$ denotes the canonical basis of $\mathbb{C}^{1 \times m_{\mathcal{T}}}$. We note that "term" and "monomial" are not the same and we denote a *power product* of variables by "term". The coefficient vector $\vec{p}$ of $p(\vec{x}) \in \mathbb{C}[\vec{x}]$ is defined to be satisfying $\vec{p} = \phi_{\mathcal{T}}(p)$ and $p(\vec{x}) = \phi_{\mathcal{T}}^{-1}(\vec{p})$. With a fixed $\mathcal{T}$, we consider the following subset $F_{\mathcal{T}}$ of I.

$$F_{\mathcal{T}} = \left\{ \sum_{i=1}^{k} s_i(\vec{x}) f_i(\vec{x}) \;\middle|\; s_i(\vec{x}) f_i(\vec{x}) \in_{\mathfrak{S}_i} \mathbb{C}[\vec{x}]_{\mathcal{T}}, \; s_i(\vec{x}) \in \mathbb{C}[\vec{x}] \right\}$$

where $s_i(\vec{x}) f_i(\vec{x}) \in_{\mathfrak{S}_i} \mathbb{C}[\vec{x}]_{\mathcal{T}}$ denotes that this inclusion relation is satisfied for any image of $\mathfrak{S}_i$. The Buchberger algorithm guarantees that $G \subseteq F_{\mathcal{T}}$ if $\mathcal{T}$ has a large enough number of elements (however, note that $\mathcal{T}$ must include some required elements depending on the term order). To compute a Gröbner basis for I, we construct the matrix $\mathcal{M}_{\mathcal{T}}(F)$ whose each row vector $\vec{p} = \phi_{\mathcal{T}}(p)$ is corresponding to each element of $p(\vec{x}) \in \mathcal{P}_{\mathcal{T}}(f_i)$ for each $f_i(\vec{x}) \in F$ where

$$\mathcal{P}_{\mathcal{T}}(f_i) = \{ t_j \times f_i(\vec{x}) \in_{\mathfrak{S}_i} \mathbb{C}[\vec{x}]_{\mathcal{T}} \mid t_j = \phi_{\mathcal{T}}^{-1}(\vec{e_j}), \\ j = 1, \ldots, m_{\mathcal{T}} \}.$$

By this definition, $F_{\mathcal{T}}$ and the linear space $\mathcal{V}_{\mathcal{T}}$ generated by the row vectors of $\mathcal{M}_{\mathcal{T}}(F)$ are isomorphic. We note that the row space of $\mathcal{M}_{\mathcal{T}}(F)$ defined above is unique for the given $\mathcal{T}$ and F and have the following properties.

LEMMA 1 (LEMMA 1 IN [18]).
Let $\overline{\mathcal{M}_{\mathcal{T}}(F)}$ be the reduced row echelon form of $\mathcal{M}_{\mathcal{T}}(F)$. For any $g(\vec{x}) \in F_{\mathcal{T}}$, $\overline{\mathcal{M}_{\mathcal{T}}(F)}$ has a row vector $\vec{p}$ satisfying $\mathrm{ht}(g) = \mathrm{ht}(\phi_{\mathcal{T}}^{-1}(\vec{p}))$. ◁

LEMMA 2 (LEMMA 2 IN [18]).
Let $\overline{\mathcal{M}_{\mathcal{T}}(F)}$ be the reduced row echelon form of $\mathcal{M}_{\mathcal{T}}(F)$. If $\mathcal{T}$ has a large enough number of elements, the following $G_{\mathcal{T}}$ is a Gröbner basis for I w.r.t. the term order of $\mathcal{T}$.

$$G_{\mathcal{T}} = \left\{ \phi_{\mathcal{T}}^{-1}(\vec{p}) \;\middle|\; \vec{p} \text{ is a row vector of } \overline{\mathcal{M}_{\mathcal{T}}(F)} \right\}. \quad ◁$$

We give some remarks on the SLRA problem: given a structure specification $\mathcal{S} : \mathbb{R}^{n_\alpha} \to \mathbb{R}^{m \times n}$, a parameter vector $\vec{p} \in \mathbb{R}^{n_\alpha}$, a vector norm $\|\cdot\|$, and an integer r, $0 < r < \min\{m, n\}$, find a vector $\vec{p^*}$ such that

$$\min_{\vec{p^*}} \|\vec{p} - \vec{p^*}\| \text{ and } \mathrm{rank}(\mathcal{S}(\vec{p^*})) \leq r.$$

This problem is NP-hard except for a few special cases (see [15] for details). In general, we can compute a local optimum by the lift-and-project method or solvers for the STLS problem (Structured Total Least Squares) under some convergent conditions (see Chapter 5 in [1]) and easily extended to complex numbers (see Chapter 2 in [14]). We note that the difference between the SLRA and STLS problems is the objective rank deficiency and the STLS problem is a special case of the SLRA problem with $r = \min\{m, n\} - 1$.

2.1 Structured Gröbner Basis

For the sake of completeness, we present the following definition, algorithm and numerical example of structured Gröbner basis, introduced in [19] by the present author.

DEFINITION 1 (STRUCTURED GRÖBNER BASIS).
We say G is a $\mathfrak{S}$-structured Gröbner basis for F with tolerance $\varepsilon \in \mathbb{R}_{\geq 0}$, rank deficiency $d \in \mathbb{Z}_{\geq 0}$ and set of terms $\mathcal{T}$ if they satisfy the following conditions:

1. *G is a Gröbner basis for the ideal generated by the following $F_{st} = \{f_{st,1}, \ldots, f_{st,k}\} \in \mathbb{C}[\vec{x}]$.*

2. *F and F_{st} are $\mathfrak{S}$-structured polynomial sets, i.e., there exists parameters $\vec{p_i}, \vec{p_{st_i}} \in \mathbb{C}^{n_i}$, such that $f_i(\vec{x}) = \mathfrak{S}_i(\vec{p_i})$ and $f_{st,i}(\vec{x}) = \mathfrak{S}_i(\vec{p_{st_i}})$.*

3. *$\|(\vec{p_1} \ldots \vec{p_k}) - (\vec{p_{st_1}} \ldots \vec{p_{st_k}})\| = \varepsilon$ where $\|\cdot\|$ denotes a suitable vector norm.*

4. *$\mathcal{T}$ has all the terms required for computing Gröbner bases for F and F_{st} hence G is a subset of $F_{\mathcal{T}}$ of F_{st}. (Note that this is implicitly introduced in the original.)*

5. *$\mathrm{rank}(\mathcal{M}_{\mathcal{T}}(F_{st})) = \mathrm{rank}(\mathcal{M}_{\mathcal{T}}(F)) - d$.* ◁

ALGORITHM 1 (𝔖-STRUCTURED GRÖBNER BASIS).
Input: *$F = \{f_1(\vec{x}), \ldots, f_k(\vec{x})\} \subset \mathbb{C}[\vec{x}]$, a term order $\succ$ and a structure specification $\mathfrak{S}$.*

Output: *a $\mathfrak{S}$-structured Gröbner basis G for F with the tolerance ε, the rank deficiency d, the set of terms $\mathcal{T}$ and $\mathfrak{S}$-structured polynomial set F_{st}, or failed.*

1. *Compute a numerical Gröbner basis $\tilde{G}$ for the ideal generated by F, by some known algorithms and determine a suitable set of terms $\mathcal{T}$ based on the result.*

2. *Construct $\mathcal{M}_{\mathcal{T}}(F) \in \mathbb{C}^{n \times m}$, compute its non-zero singular values σ_i $(i = 1, \ldots, r_{org})$ and determine a suitable rank deficiency d (Take the largest d such that $\sigma_{r_{org}-d+1}/\sigma_{r_{org}-d} < 10^{-2}$ for example). If there is no such d found, output failed.*

3. *By a solver for the SLRA problem, find a $\mathfrak{S}$-structured polynomial set F_{st} with the rank deficiency d satisfying $\mathrm{rank}(\mathcal{M}_{\mathcal{T}}(F_{st})) = \mathrm{rank}(\mathcal{M}_{\mathcal{T}}(F)) - d$ and compute the tolerance ε. If there is no such F_{st} found, output failed.*

4. *Compute a numerical Gröbner basis G for the ideal generated by F_{st}, by some known algorithms and output $\{G, \varepsilon, d, \mathcal{T}, F_{st}\}$.* ◁

EXAMPLE 1   (STRUCTURED GRÖBNER BASIS).

We compute a $\mathfrak{S}$-structured Gröbner basis approximately w.r.t. the lexicographic order for the following polynomial set F.

$$F = \{x^3 + x^2y^2, x^2y^2 - y^3,$$
$$- x^2y + 1.000001x^2 + xy^2 + 0.999999y^2\}.$$

This is the following polynomial set F_δ with $\delta = 10^{-6}$, which is introduced by Sasaki and Kako (Example 5,[20]).

$$F_\delta = \{x^3 + x^2y^2, \ x^2y^2 - y^3, \ -x^2y + (1+\delta)x^2 + xy^2 + (1-\delta)y^2\}.$$

In this case, by the algorithm (appGröbner, [20]) with initial precision $\varepsilon_{Init} = 10^{-16}$ and approximate-zero threshold $\varepsilon_Z = 10^{-15}$, we get the following Gröbner basis and the set of terms $\mathcal{T}$.

$$G_{az} = \{1.0x^2 - 2.000001y^3 + 0.999998y^2,$$
$$1.0xy^2 + 1.000001y^3, \ 1.0y^4 - 1.000001y^3\},$$

$$\mathcal{T} = \{x^4y^4, \ x^4y^3, \ x^4y^2, \ x^4y, \ x^3y^5, \ x^3y^4, \ x^3y^3, \ x^3y^2,$$
$$x^3y, \ x^3, \ x^2y^5, \ x^2y^4, \ x^2y^3, \ x^2y^2, \ x^2y, \ x^2, \ xy^6,$$
$$xy^5, \ xy^4, \ xy^3, \ xy^2, \ y^6, \ y^5, \ y^4, \ y^3, \ y^2\}.$$

We construct $\mathcal{M}_{\mathcal{T}}(F) \in \mathbb{C}^{30 \times 26}$ and determine the rank deficiency $d = 4$ since we get the following singular values and we have $\sigma_{26-4+1}/\sigma_{26-4} = 1.47591 \times 10^{-6}$.

$$\{2.12971, 1.84588, \ldots \ (18 \ \text{elements snipped}) \ \ldots,$$
$$0.282599, 0.238185, 3.51538 \times 10^{-7}, 3.04624 \times 10^{-7},$$
$$1.66608 \times 10^{-16}, 1.66608 \times 10^{-16}\}.$$

We take the following structure specification $\mathfrak{S}$. Although their head coefficients p_1, p_3, p_5 can be zeros, structures of $F_{\mathcal{T}}$, $\mathcal{P}_{\mathcal{T}}(f_i)$ and $\mathcal{M}_{\mathcal{T}}(F)$ are invariant by their definitions.

$$\mathfrak{S}_1 : \qquad (p_1 \ p_2) \ \mapsto \ p_1x^3 + p_2x^2y^2,$$
$$\mathfrak{S}_2 : \qquad (p_3 \ p_4) \ \mapsto \ p_3x^2y^2 + p_4y^3,$$
$$\mathfrak{S}_3 : \quad (p_5 \ p_6 \ p_7 \ p_8) \ \mapsto \ p_5x^2y + p_6x^2 + p_7xy^2 + p_8y^2.$$

By the lift-and-project method for the SLRA problem, we get the following $\mathfrak{S}$-structured polynomial set F_{st} with tolerance $\varepsilon = 7.2326 \times 10^{-7}$ in 2-norm, such that $\text{rank}(\mathcal{M}_{\mathcal{T}}(F_{st})) = \text{rank}(\mathcal{M}_{\mathcal{T}}(F)) - d$.

$$F_{st} = \{1.00000023x^3 + 0.9999998x^2y^2,$$
$$1.00000018x^2y^2 - 0.9999998y^3,$$
$$- 0.99999968x^2y + 1.00000073x^2$$
$$+ 1.00000027xy^2 + 0.99999932y^2\}.$$

Finally, by the algorithm (appGröbner, [20]), we get the following $\mathfrak{S}$-structured Gröbner basis for F.

$$G = \{1.0x^2 - 0.99999802y^5 - 0.99999908y^4 + 0.99999859y^2,$$
$$1.0xy^2 + 0.99999954y^4, \ 1.0y^6 - 1.0000006y^3\}.$$

We note that this result is compatible to the following comprehensive Gröbner system for F if we think that δ represents a priori errors. The result reveals the basis for $\delta = 0$ hidden by a priori errors.

$$\begin{cases} \{x^2 - y^5 - y^4 + y^2, xy^2 + y^4, y^6 - y^3\} & (\delta = 0), \\ \{2x^2 + xy^2 - y^3, xy^3 + y^3, y^4 - y^3\} & (\delta = 1), \\ \{x^3 + y^3, x^2y + y^3 - 2y^2, xy^2 + y^3, y^4 - y^3\} & (\delta = -1), \\ \{(1+\delta)^2x^2 + 2xy^2 - 2\delta y^3 + (1-\delta^2)y^2, & (\delta^3 \neq \delta). \\ \quad -(1-\delta)(xy^2 + y^3), y^4 - y^3\} & \end{cases}$$

$\triangleleft$

2.2   The Problem to be Solved

Algorithm 1 computes a suitable set of terms $\mathcal{T}$ by some known numerical Gröbner basis algorithms. In the exact case, this guarantees that the resulting G is a subset of $F_{\mathcal{T}}$ hence G is a Gröbner basis since we have $F = F_{st}$. However, in the inexact case, we may have $F \neq F_{st}$ and $\tilde{G}$ may include a posteriori numerical errors hence $\mathcal{T}$ may not have a large enough number of elements for computing G. Moreover, most of numerical Gröbner basis algorithms rewrite nonzero small numbers with zero (approximate zero rewriting) though such small numbers may become larger in F_{st}. This causes a big problem since each structured Gröbner basis depends on the set of terms $\mathcal{T}$ hence the resulting G may not be meaningful.

Moreover, for polynomials in more than two variables or polynomials of higher degrees, it becomes difficult to determine a suitable set of terms $\mathcal{T}$ since most of generated syzygies during computations in Step 1 becomes unreliable. This forces us to use much larger $\mathcal{T}$ hence the lift-and-project method has to operate with a huge matrix and its convergence speed becomes very slow. Therefore, in the former study [19], finding a method to determine a suitable set of terms $\mathcal{T}$ in terms of $\mathfrak{S}$-structured Gröbner basis for the input is one of the open questions. In this paper, we give a resolution for this problem.

3.   SUITABLE SET OF TERMS

For computing a Gröbner basis in the usual manner, we may not take care of terms used in the algorithm since we just need to compute S-polynomials and do monomial reductions as polynomials. Except F_4 and its variants, any special treatment on terms may not be required. In fact, such information (a set of terms used in the algorithm) is made just as a byproduct of computing S-polynomials and monomial reductions. However, for computing a $\mathfrak{S}$-structured Gröbner basis, we have to determine a suitable set of terms in advance and any S-polynomial is not required at this time. This is a big difference between them. Our approach is basically based on the Buchberger algorithm with variants of F_4 [6] and sugar selection strategy [9]. However, at this point, we do not need to compute any S-polynomials hence we focus on their head terms only and will not compute residual terms nor their coefficients.

The following algorithm computes a set of terms required for computing the reduced S-polynomial of $f_i(\vec{x})$ and $f_j(\vec{x})$ of the specified critical pair $\{i, j\}$, where "terms required" means that we can computes the reduced S-polynomial by computing the reduced row echelon form of $\mathcal{M}_{\mathcal{T}}(F)$, by Lemma 1.

ALGORITHM 2   (SET OF TERMS FOR CRITICAL PAIR).

Input: *a critical pair $\{i, j\}$ and a set of polynomials $\{\{t_1, \mathcal{T}_1\}, \ldots, \{t_k, \mathcal{T}_k\}\}$ where $\mathcal{T}_i$ denotes the set of terms required for computing $f_i(\vec{x})$ whose head term is t_i.*

Output: *a set of terms required for computing the reduced S-polynomial of $f_i(\vec{x})$ and $f_j(\vec{x})$.*

1. *For $h \in \{1, \ldots, k\}$,*
   $\mathcal{T}_{\lhd h} := \{t \in \mathcal{T}_h \mid t \succeq t_h\}$ *and* $\mathcal{T}_{\rhd h} := \{t \in \mathcal{T}_h \mid t \prec t_h\}$.
2. $\mathcal{T}_\lhd := (\text{lcm}(t_i, t_j)/t_i)\mathcal{T}_{\lhd i} \cup (\text{lcm}(t_i, t_j)/t_j)\mathcal{T}_{\lhd j}$ *and*
   $\mathcal{T} := \mathcal{T}_\rhd := (\text{lcm}(t_i, t_j)/t_i)\mathcal{T}_{\rhd i} \cup (\text{lcm}(t_i, t_j)/t_j)\mathcal{T}_{\rhd j}$.

3. While $\mathcal{T} \neq \phi$ do

   3-1. $t \in \mathcal{T}$ and $\mathcal{T} := \mathcal{T} \setminus \{t\}$.

   3-2. For $h \in \{1, \ldots, k\}$ s.t. $t_h | t$, if $(t/t_h)\mathcal{T}_h \setminus (\mathcal{T}_\lhd \cup \mathcal{T}_\rhd) \neq \phi$ then $\mathcal{T}_\lhd := \mathcal{T}_\lhd \cup (t/t_h)\mathcal{T}_{\lhd h}$, $\mathcal{T}_\rhd := \mathcal{T}_\rhd \cup (t/t_h)\mathcal{T}_{\rhd h}$, $\mathcal{T} := \mathcal{T} \cup (t/t_h)\mathcal{T}_{\rhd h}$ and continue the while loop.

4. output $\mathcal{T}_\lhd \cup \mathcal{T}_\rhd$. $\lhd$

THEOREM 1 (CORRECTNESS OF ALGORITHM 2).
Algorithm 2 terminates and outputs a set of terms required for computing the specified S-polynomial. $\lhd$

PROOF OF THEOREM 1. The union of $\mathcal{T}_\lhd$ and $\mathcal{T}_\rhd$ in Step 2 is corresponding to a set of terms required for computing the S-polynomial of the critical pair $\{i, j\}$ and each term t in $\mathcal{T}$ is corresponding to a monomial of S-polynomial to be reduced. Each loop iteration in Step 3 is corresponding to a monomial reduction since the condition $t_h | t$ is that S-polynomial has a term can be reduced by $f_h(\vec{x})$. Moreover, the initial set $\mathcal{T}$ is finite and each term order of additional elements in Step 3-2 is less than t. Therefore, by Lemma 1 this algorithm terminates and outputs a set of terms required for computing the specified S-polynomial. $\square$

By this algorithm we can follow the Buchberger algorithm without computing any S-polynomials concretely. However, we still need to compute their head terms. For computing head terms we use the following algorithm which is a variant of Gaussian elimination with partial pivoting and unitary transformations (e.g. Householder or Givens rotations) where $\|\cdot\|_2$ denotes the 2-norm.

ALGORITHM 3 (GAUSSIAN ELIMINATION VARIANT).

Input: $A = (a_{ij}) \in \mathbb{C}^{n \times m}$ and a threshold $\varepsilon_a \in \mathbb{R}_{\geq 0}$.

Output: *a variant of reduced row echelon form R and a unitary matrix Q s.t. $QA = R$ with pivot set P.*

1. $k := h := 1$, $P = \phi$ and $Q \in \mathbb{C}^{n \times n}$ be the unit matrix.

2. While $k \leq n$ and $h \leq m$ do

   2-1. Determine $\mu \geq k$ s.t. $|a_{\mu,h}| = \max_{i \geq k} |a_{i,h}|$, for $j = 1, \ldots, m$ swap $a_{\mu,j}$ for $a_{k,j}$ and update Q.

   2-2. If $\|(a_{k,h}\ a_{k+1,h}\ \cdots\ a_{n,h})\|_2 \geq \varepsilon_a$ do

      2-2-1. Construct a unitary matrix U zeroing $a_{k+1,h}$, $\ldots$, $a_{n,h}$ by $a_{k,h}$ and $Q := UQ$.

      2-2-2. $A := UA$.

      2-2-3. $P := P \cup \{(k,h)\}$ and $k := k + 1$.

   2-3. $h := h + 1$.

3. Outputs $R := A$ and Q with P. $\lhd$

Though Algorithm 3 outputs a quasi upper triangular matrix R, we do not need the lower triangular part of R since they may be generated by a priori error. To make this simple, we define the mappings φ_U and φ_L as follows. Let $R = (r_{ij})$ and P be the resulting matrix and pivot set computed by Algorithm 3 with ε_a. We define $\varphi_U(R) = R - E$ and $\varphi_L(R) = E$ where

$$E = (e_{ij}) \in \mathbb{C}^{n \times m}, \quad e_{ij} = \begin{cases} r_{ij} & (\forall (k,h) \in P, i > k \\ & \text{or } \exists (i,h) \in P, j < h) \\ 0 & \text{(otherwise)} \end{cases}.$$

LEMMA 3. *Let R be the resulting matrix by Algorithm 3 with ε_a. We have $\|\varphi_L(R)\|_2 < \varepsilon_a \sqrt{m}$ or $\|\varphi_L(R)\|_2 = 0$.* $\lhd$

PROOF OF LEMMA 3. $\varphi_L(R)$ is corresponding to the parts of R that are zeroed by pivots in Step 2-2-2 or skipped in Step 2-2. Hence if $\varepsilon_a = 0$, $\varphi_L(R)$ is the zero matrix and the lemma is valid. If not, basically we have $\|\varphi_L(R)\|_2 < \varepsilon_a \sqrt{m}$ since the Frobenius norm is always larger than or equal to the 2-norm. Moreover, unitary transformations in Step 2-2-2 and 2-1 (swapping can be done by unitary matrices) preserve 2-norm and non-zero elements of $\varphi_L(R)$ and $\varphi_U(R)$ are disjoint by these transformations after being skipped. Therefore, we have $\| \varphi_L(R) \|_2 < \varepsilon_a \sqrt{m}$ for $\varepsilon_a \neq 0$ and $\|\varphi_L(R)\|_2 = 0$ for $\varepsilon_a = 0$. $\square$

The above lemma gives us an upper bound that the given matrix for Algorithm 3 becomes a matrix having the same rank of $\varphi_U(R)$. However, for computing a structured Gröbner basis, we have to calculate all the head terms of F_{st} that is not known at the beginning. Hence we have to guarantee that the set of terms required for F_{st} is a subset of that for F. The following lemma gives us a sufficient condition for this in part (see the examples for its efficiency).

LEMMA 4. *For matrices $A, B \in \mathbb{C}^{n \times m}$, let $\{Q_A, R_A, P_A\}$ and $\{Q_B, R_B, P_B\}$ be the resulting sets of matrices satisfying $Q_A A = R_A$ and $Q_B B = R_B$ by Algorithm 3 for A with $\varepsilon_a = \varepsilon_A$ and B with $\varepsilon_a = \varepsilon_B$, respectively. If the following two conditions are satisfied*

(1) $\forall (k_A, h) \in P_A, \ |r_{A,k_A,h}| \geq \sigma_A |r_{A,k_A j}| \ \ (h < j \leq m)$,

(2) $\forall (k_B, h) \in P_B, \ |r_{B,k_B h}| > (1 + \sigma_A^{-1})^\mu \times$
$$(\|A - B\|_2 + \|\varphi_L(R_A)\|_2 + \|\varphi_L(R_B)\|_2),$$

we have $\forall (k_B, h) \in P_B, \exists (k_A, h) \in P_A$, where μ is the number of elements of $\{(k_A, h_A) \in P_A \mid h_A < h\}$ and $r_{A,ij}$ and $r_{B,ij}$ denote the (i,j) elements of $\varphi_U(R_A)$ and $\varphi_U(R_B)$, respectively. $\lhd$

PROOF OF LEMMA 4. Let E_{AB} be the matrix such that $B = A + E_{AB}$. Consider the relation $\varphi_U(R_B) = U\varphi_U(R_A) + E$ where U is unitary and $\|E\|_2 \leq \|E_{AB}\|_2 + \|\varphi_L(R_A)\|_2 + \|\varphi_L(R_B)\|_2$ since we have $\varphi_U(R_B) = Q_B Q_A^{-1} \varphi_U(R_A) + Q_B Q_A^{-1} \varphi_L(R_A) + Q_B E_{AB} - \varphi_L(R_B)$ and Q_A and Q_B are unitary. We denote the (i,j) elements of U and E by u_{ij} and e_{ij}, respectively.

Suppose that the lemma is not valid hence there exists k_B and h such that $(k_B, h) \in P_B$ and $(k_A, h) \notin P_A$ for any integer k_A. Let h be the smallest integer with this property. If $h = 1$ we must have $|r_{B,11}| \leq \|E\|_2$ since $r_{A,11} = 0$, however this is not satisfied since we have $|r_{B,11}| > (\|A - B\|_2 + \|\varphi_L(R_A)\|_2 + \|\varphi_L(R_B)\|_2)$. Hence we have $h > 1$ and $|u_{k_B 1}||r_{A,11}| \leq \|E\|_2$.

Let $\pi(k_A) = h$ for any $(k_A, h) \in P_A$ and $\max_h(k_A)$ be the maximum k_A of $\{(k_A, h_A) \in P_A \mid h_A < h\}$. For $i \leq \max_h(k_A)$, we firstly show (note that we already have this for $i = 1$)

$$|u_{k_B i}||r_{A,i\pi(i)}| \leq \|E\|_2 (1 + \sigma_A^{-1})^{i-1}.$$

We assume that this relation is valid for $i = 1, \ldots, \bar{i} - 1$. By the mathematical induction, we have for $i = \bar{i}$ since we have

$$
\begin{aligned}
0 = |r_{B,k_B\pi(\bar{i})}| &= |\textstyle\sum_{s=1}^{n} u_{k_Bs} r_{A,s\pi(\bar{i})} + e_{k_B\pi(\bar{i})}| \\
&= |\textstyle\sum_{s=1}^{\bar{i}} u_{k_Bs} r_{A,s\pi(\bar{i})} + e_{k_B\pi(\bar{i})}| \\
&\Downarrow
\end{aligned}
$$

$$
\begin{aligned}
|u_{k_B\bar{i}}||r_{A,\bar{i}\pi(\bar{i})}| &\leq \textstyle\sum_{s=1}^{\bar{i}-1} |u_{k_Bs}||r_{A,s\pi(\bar{i})}| + \|E\|_2 \\
&\leq \textstyle\sum_{s=1}^{\bar{i}-1} \sigma_A^{-1} |u_{k_Bs}||r_{A,s\pi(s)}| + \|E\|_2 \\
&\leq \textstyle\sum_{s=1}^{\bar{i}-1} \sigma_A^{-1} \|E\|_2 \,(1 + \sigma_A^{-1})^{s-1} + \|E\|_2 \\
&\leq \|E\|_2 \,(1 + \sigma_A^{-1})^{\bar{i}-1}.
\end{aligned}
$$

Therefore, we have

$$
\begin{aligned}
|r_{B,k_Bh}| &= |\textstyle\sum_{i=1}^{n} u_{k_Bi} r_{A,ih} + e_{k_Bh}| \\
&\leq \textstyle\sum_{i=1}^{\max_h(k_A)} |u_{k_Bi}||r_{A,ih}| + |e_{k_Bh}| \\
&\leq \textstyle\sum_{i=1}^{\max_h(k_A)} \sigma_A^{-1} |u_{k_Bi}||r_{A,i\pi(i)}| + |e_{k_Bh}| \\
&\leq \textstyle\sum_{i=1}^{\max_h(k_A)} \sigma_A^{-1} \|E\|_2 \,(1 + \sigma_A^{-1})^{i-1} + \|E\|_2 \\
&\leq \|E\|_2 \,(1 + \sigma_A^{-1})^{\mu}.
\end{aligned}
$$

However, this is a contradiction and the lemma is valid. $\qquad\square$

LEMMA 5. *Let Q and R be the resulting matrices by Algorithm 3, satisfying $QM_{\mathcal{T}}(F) = R$. We can compute sugars of corresponding polynomials of row vectors of R.* ◁

PROOF OF LEMMA 5. Let $q_i = (q_{ij})$ and $\vec{r_i}$ be the i-th row vectors of Q and R, respectively, and $\vec{f_i}$ be the i-th coefficient vector such that $M_{\mathcal{T}}(F) = (\vec{f_1} \ldots \vec{f_n})^t \in \mathbb{C}^{n \times m}$. By the definition of $M_{\mathcal{T}}(F)$, for any $\vec{f_i}$, there exist t and $f_j(\vec{x})$ satisfying $\phi^{-1}(\vec{f_i}) = tf_j(\vec{x})$ and the sugar of $tf_j(\vec{x})$ is $\mathrm{tdeg}(t) + \mathrm{tdeg}(f_j)$. Therefore, the sugar of corresponding polynomial of $\vec{r_i}$ can be computed by taking the maximum of sugars $\vec{f_j}$ for non-zero elements q_{ij}. $\qquad\square$

As in the definition of $F_{\mathcal{T}}$, we introduce some notations with structure specification $\mathfrak{S}_i$. By $\mathrm{supp}_{\mathfrak{S}_i}(f_i)$ we denote the union of sets of terms of $f_i(\vec{x})$ for all the images of $\mathfrak{S}_i$. By $\mathrm{ht}_{\mathfrak{S}_i}(f_i)$ we denote the highest order term in the set of head terms of $\mathfrak{S}_i(\vec{p_i})$ for $\vec{p_i} \in \mathbb{C}^{n_i}$ w.r.t. the specified term order. $\mathrm{tdeg}_{\mathfrak{S}_i}(f_i)$ is also defined in the same manner.

ALGORITHM 4   (SUITABLE SET OF TERMS).

Input: $F = \{f_1(\vec{x}), \ldots, f_k(\vec{x})\}$, a term order $\succ$, a structure specification $\mathfrak{S}$ and a threshold $\varepsilon_r \in \mathbb{R}_{\geq 0}$.

Output: a suitable set of terms $\mathcal{T}$ for F, $\succ$ and $\mathfrak{S}$ and the maximum threshold ε_a.

1. $L := \big\{ \{\mathrm{ht}_{\mathfrak{S}_i}(f_i), \mathrm{supp}_{\mathfrak{S}_i}(f_i), \mathrm{tdeg}_{\mathfrak{S}_i}(f_i)\} \,\big|\, f_i \in F \big\}$, $\varepsilon_a := 0$, $\mathcal{T} = \phi$ and $\mathcal{C}$ be the set of critical pairs without using any criteria.

2. While $\mathcal{C} \neq \phi$ do

   2-1. $\{i,j\} \in \mathcal{C}$ and $\mathcal{C} := \mathcal{C} \setminus \{i,j\}$ by the sugar strategy (third values of tuples in L are sugars).

   2-2. By Algorithm 2, compute a set of terms required for computing the reduced S-polynomial of the pair $\{i,j\}$ with L and let $\mathcal{T}_{ij}$ be the resulting set.

   2-3. If $\mathcal{T}_{ij} \subset \mathcal{T}$, continue the while loop. Otherwise, $\mathcal{T} := \mathcal{T} \cup \mathcal{T}_{ij}$. Output the theoretical upper bound [4] if $\#\mathcal{T}$ is not smaller than the bound.

   2-4. Construct a matrix $M_{\mathcal{T}}(F)$ and compute its singular values $\sigma_{ij,1} \geq \sigma_{ij,2} \geq \cdots \geq \sigma_{ij,r_{ij}} > 0$.

   2-5. Find the largest singular value $\sigma_{ij,h}$ of $M_{\mathcal{T}}(F)$ such that $\sigma_{ij,h+1} < \varepsilon_r\,\sigma_{ij,h}$ ($h = 1, \ldots, r_{ij} - 1$) and $\varepsilon_a := \max\{\varepsilon_a, \min\{\sigma_{ij,h}/\sqrt{m}, \sigma_{ij,h+1}/\sqrt{\varepsilon_r}\}\}$ where m denotes the number of columns of $M_{\mathcal{T}}(F)$. If there is no such $\sigma_{ij,h}$ found, let ε_a be 0.

   2-6. By Algorithm 3 with ε_a, compute matrices Q, R and pivot set P satisfying $QM_{\mathcal{T}}(F) = R$.

   2-7. For each element (p_k, p_h) in P do

      2-7-1. Let t_{ij} be the p_h-th element in $\mathcal{T}$ and s_{ij} be the sugar of the p_k-th row vector of R.

      2-7-2. If L does not have the tuple whose first element divides t_{ij}, $L := L \cup \{\{t_{ij}, \mathcal{T}', s_{ij}\}\}$ where $\mathcal{T}'$ is the set of terms required for the p_k-th row vector of R from $M_{\mathcal{T}'}(F)$ (cf. the proof of Lemma 5), and update $\mathcal{C}$ without using any criteria.

3. Output $\mathcal{T}$ and ε_a. ◁

In the worst case, Algorithm 4 outputs the theoretical upper bound [4] for which we do not have to prove that $\mathcal{T}$ is a set of terms required for computing a Gröbner basis w.r.t. $\succ$ for F_{st} since the structures and degrees of F and F_{st} are the same hence the bound does not change. We note that we use a threshold $\min\{\sigma_{ij,h}/\sqrt{m}, \sigma_{ij,h+1}/\sqrt{\varepsilon_r}\}$ in Step 2-5, however this is not optimal but only follows from the experimental data. Moreover, Algorithm 4 does not use any criterion for updating the critical pairs since this is required by the following theorem.

THEOREM 2   (STABILITY OF SET OF TERMS).
Suppose that Algorithm 4 with $\varepsilon_r > 0$ terminates without reaching the upper bound and let $\mathcal{T}$ and ε be the resulting set of terms and the threshold, respectively. Then, $\mathcal{T}$ is a set of terms required for computing a Gröbner basis w.r.t. $\succ$ for F_{st} such that $A = \mathcal{M}_{\mathcal{T}}(F)$ with $\varepsilon_A = \varepsilon$ and $B = \mathcal{M}_{\mathcal{T}}(F_{st})$ with $\varepsilon_B = 0$ satisfy the conditions of Lemma 4. ◁

PROOF OF THEOREM 2. For F, let $L_{A_1}, L_{A_2}, \ldots, L_{A_r}$ be the sequence of L generated in the algorithm for which the algorithm computes the monotonically increasing sequence $\mathcal{T}$, and $A_1, A_2, \ldots, A_r = A$ be the corresponding sequences of $\mathcal{M}_{\mathcal{T}}(F)$ constructed from $L_{A_1}, L_{A_2}, \ldots, L_{A_r}$, respectively. For F_{st}, let $L_{B_1}, L_{B_2}, \ldots, L_{B_{\bar{r}}}$ be the sequence of L generated in the algorithm for which the algorithm computes the monotonically increasing sequence $\mathcal{T}$, and $B_1, B_2, \ldots, B_{\bar{r}}$ be the corresponding sequences of $\mathcal{M}_{\mathcal{T}}(F_{st})$ constructed from $L_{B_1}, L_{B_2}, \ldots, L_{B_{\bar{r}}}$, respectively. We note that we may have $r \neq \bar{r}$ and $B_{\bar{r}} \neq B$ and for any $i \geq 2$, A_{i-1} an B_{i-1} are submatrices of A_i and B_i, respectively. We denote the head terms of A_i and B_i computed by Algorithm 3 by P_{A_i} and P_{B_i}, respectively and note that they are the pivots of A_i and B_i. We use the notation $\mathrm{ht}(L) = \{\,t \mid \{t, \mathcal{T}, s\} \in L\}$.

We have $P_B \subset P_A = P_{A_r}$ and A_i is a submatrix of A which has the same structure of B by the conditions. If we have $\mathrm{ht}(L_{B_i}) = \mathrm{ht}(L_{A_i})$ for all i, the theorem is valid since this means that A_i and B_i have the same structure. We suppose that there exists $i > 1$ such that $\mathrm{ht}(L_{B_i}) \neq \mathrm{ht}(L_{A_i})$ since $\mathrm{ht}(L_{A_1}) = \mathrm{ht}(L_{B_1})$, and let $\bar{i}$ be the smallest integer satisfying this property. Since $\mathrm{ht}(L_{B_{\bar{i}-1}}) = \mathrm{ht}(L_{A_{\bar{i}-1}})$ and $\mathrm{ht}(L_{B_{\bar{i}}}) \neq \mathrm{ht}(L_{A_{\bar{i}}})$, $B_{\bar{i}-1}$ is a submatrix of $A_{\bar{i}-1}$ and $P_{B_{\bar{i}-1}} \neq P_{A_{\bar{i}-1}}$. However, we have $P_B \subset P_A$ by Lemma 4 and $B_{\bar{i}-1}$ is a submatrix of B (note again that A and B have the same structure) and the threshold $\varepsilon_B = 0$ hence the basis of B includes the bases of $B_{\hat{i}-1}$. This means that there exists L_{A_i} satisfying $\text{ht}(L_{B_{\hat{i}}}) \subset \text{ht}(L_{A_i})$ and let $\hat{i}$ be the smallest integer satisfying this property. Any S-polynomial corresponding to $t \in \text{ht}(L_{B_{\hat{i}}})$, $t \notin \text{ht}(L_{B_{\hat{i}-1}})$ is computed in A_i ($i > \hat{i}$) that are submatrices of A since we do not use any criteria for updating critical pairs. Hence, for any $L_{B_{\hat{i}}}$ there exists L_{A_i} satisfying $\text{ht}(L_{B_{\hat{i}}}) \subset \text{ht}(L_{A_i})$ and $B_{\hat{i}}$ is a submatrix of B. Therefore, we have $\text{ht}(L_{B_{\hat{r}}}) \subset \text{ht}(L_{A_r})$, and the resulting $\mathcal{T}$ for $B_{\hat{r}}$ is a subset of that for A_r. $\qquad\square$

We note that the above proof is not applicable if we use some criteria for the critical pairs since we may not have A_i for some pairs that must be computed in B_i in this case. To cover this situation, we need the following additional conditions.

THEOREM 3 (STABILITY OF SET OF TERMS II).
Under the conditions in Theorem 2 except using the usual criteria for updating critical pairs. $\mathcal{T}$ is a set of terms required for computing a Gröbner basis w.r.t. $\succ$ for F_{st} if A and B additionally satisfy that the numbers of pivots of A and B are the same and the head terms of resulting L in the algorithm is a subset of corresponding terms of pivots of A. $\qquad\triangleleft$

PROOF OF THEOREM 3. We use the same notations in the proof of Theorem 2. The additional conditions guarantee that $\text{ht}(L_{A_r}) \subset P_B = P_A$ by Lemma 4. This means that there is no L_{A_i} such that $\exists t \in \text{ht}(L_{A_i})$, $t \notin \text{ht}(L_{B_r})$. Therefore, ignoring critical pairs in the sequence L_{A_i} are also ignored in the sequence L_{B_i}. Hence, the resulting $\mathcal{T}$ for $B_{\hat{r}}$ is a subset of that for A_r. $\qquad\square$

COROLLARY 1. *Algorithm 4 with $\varepsilon_r = 0$ terminates and outputs a set of terms required for computing a Gröbner basis w.r.t. $\succ$ for F in the exact manner.* $\qquad\triangleleft$

PROOF OF COROLLARY 1. In Step 2-5, there is no singular value satisfying $\sigma_{ij,h+1} < \varepsilon_r \, \sigma_{ij,h}$ hence we have $\varepsilon_a = 0$. Therefore, by Lemmas 1, 3 and 5 and Theorem 1, Algorithm 4 just follows the Buchberger algorithm with the sugar selection strategy by RREF (see also [13, 2, 6, 7, 12, 5, 18]). $\qquad\square$

4. STRUCTURED GRÖBNER BASIS

We have the algorithms in the previous section to compute a suitable set of terms for computing a $\mathfrak{S}$-structured Gröbner basis in advance. In this section, we combine the above algorithms to compute a $\mathfrak{S}$-structured Gröbner basis as follows.

ALGORITHM 5 (NEW $\mathfrak{S}$-STRUCTURED GRÖBNER BASIS).

Input: $F = \{f_1(\vec{x}), \ldots, f_k(\vec{x})\} \subset \mathbb{C}[\vec{x}]$, a term order $\succ$, a structure specification $\mathfrak{S}$ and a threshold ε_r.

Output: a $\mathfrak{S}$-structured Gröbner basis G for F with the tolerance ε, the rank deficiency d, the set of terms $\mathcal{T}$ and $\mathfrak{S}$-structured polynomial set F_{st}, or failed.

1. By Algorithm 4 with ε_r, determine a suitable set of terms $\mathcal{T}$ and the maximum threshold ε_a.

2. Construct $\mathcal{M}_\mathcal{T}(F) \in \mathbb{C}^{n \times m}$, compute its non-zero singular values σ_i ($i = 1, \ldots, r_{org}$) and determine a suitable rank deficiency d: take the largest d such that

$\sigma_{r_{org}-d} \leq \sqrt{m}\varepsilon_a < \sigma_{r_{org}-d-1}$. *If there is no such d found, output failed.*

3. *By a solver for the SLRA problem, find a $\mathfrak{S}$-structured polynomial set F_{st} with the rank deficiency d satisfying $\text{rank}(\mathcal{M}_\mathcal{T}(F_{st})) = \text{rank}(\mathcal{M}_\mathcal{T}(F)) - d$ and compute the tolerance ε. If there is no such F_{st} found, output failed.*

4. *By Algorithm 6, compute a numerical Gröbner basis G for F_{st}.*

5. *If the resulting matrix R by Algorithm 3 in Algorithm 6 satisfies the conditions of Lemma 4, G is a $\mathfrak{S}$-structured Gröbner basis and output $\{G, \varepsilon, d, \mathcal{T}, F_{st}\}$. Otherwise, output failed.* $\qquad\triangleleft$

We note that the rank deficiency condition, $\sigma_{r_{org}-d} \leq \sqrt{m}\varepsilon_a < \sigma_{r_{org}-d-1}$ in Step 2 is not optimal but only follows from the experimental data and Lemma 3.

ALGORITHM 6 (GRÖBNER BASIS BY RREF).

Input: $F = \{f_1(\vec{x}), \ldots, f_k(\vec{x})\} \subset \mathbb{C}[\vec{x}]$, a term order $\succ$, a structure specification $\mathfrak{S}$ and a set of terms $\mathcal{T}$.

Output: a Gröbner basis G for F.

1. *Construct $\mathcal{M}_\mathcal{T}(F) \in \mathbb{C}^{n \times m}$.*

2. *By Algorithm 3 with $\varepsilon_a = 0$, compute matrices Q, R satisfying $Q\mathcal{M}_\mathcal{T}(F) = R$ and pivot set P.*

3. $G := \phi$ and $\mathcal{T}_G = \{p_h\text{-th element of } \mathcal{T} \mid (p_k, p_h) \in P\}$.

4. *For each $(p_k, p_h) \in P$, $G := G \cup \{\phi_\mathcal{T}^{-1}(p_k\text{-th row vector of } R)\}$ if there is no $t \in \mathcal{T}_G$ satisfying $t \neq t_{p_h}$ and $t \mid t_{p_h}$ where t_{p_h} is the p_h-th element of $\mathcal{T}$.*

5. *Output G.* $\qquad\triangleleft$

5. REMARKS

We introduced the set of algorithms to compute a $\mathfrak{S}$-structured Gröbner basis. To understand the algorithms and their efficiency, we show some examples below. We note again our premise in this paper: we do not have enough information on a priori errors. One may think that the desired outputs in the following examples are the Gröbner bases of exact polynomials with integer coefficients. However, such integer coefficients may not be the exact inputs but only candidates including just the inexact inputs.

EXAMPLE 2. *We compute a $\mathfrak{S}$-structured Gröbner basis with $\varepsilon_r = 10^{-2}$ w.r.t. the lexicographic order for the following polynomial set F in Example 1 to compare the results.*

$$F = \{x^3 + x^2y^2, x^2y^2 - y^3, \\ - x^2y + 1.000001x^2 + xy^2 + 0.999999y^2\}.$$

We take the following structure specification $\mathfrak{S}$.

$$\mathfrak{S}_1 : \qquad (p_1 \, p_2) \mapsto p_1 x^3 + p_2 x^2 y^2,$$
$$\mathfrak{S}_2 : \qquad (p_3 \, p_4) \mapsto p_3 x^2 y^2 + p_4 y^3,$$
$$\mathfrak{S}_3 : (p_5 \, p_6 \, p_7 \, p_8) \mapsto p_5 x^2 y + p_6 x^2 + p_7 xy^2 + p_8 y^2.$$

In this case, by Algorithm 4 with $\varepsilon_r = 10^{-2}$ and using the usual criteria for updating critical pairs, we get the following set of terms $\mathcal{T}$ and $\varepsilon_a = 6.11037 \times 10^{-6}$.

$$\mathcal{T} = \{x^5y^2, x^5y, x^5, x^4y^4, x^4y^3, x^4y^2, x^4y, x^4, x^3y^5, x^3y^4, \\ x^3y^3, x^3y^2, x^3y, x^3, x^2y^6, x^2y^5, x^2y^4, x^2y^3, x^2y^2, x^2y, \\ x^2, xy^6, xy^5, xy^4, xy^3, xy^2, y^6, y^5, y^4, y^3, y^2\}.$$

This set of terms is larger than that of Example 1. However, the result of Example 1 is not guaranteed by Theorem 3 though we can not determine its correctness. We construct $\mathcal{M}_\mathcal{T}(F) \in \mathbb{C}^{40\times31}$ and determine the rank deficiency $d = 4$ since we get the following singular values and $\sigma_{28} \le \sqrt{31} \times 6.11037 \times 10^{-6} \approx 3.40211 \times 10^{-5} < \sigma_{27}$.

$$\{3.99631, 3.40895, \ldots \text{ (22 elements snipped)} \ldots,$$
$$0.551857, 0.52158, 0.427668, 6.11037 \times 10^{-7},$$
$$5.51469 \times 10^{-7}, 4.85337 \times 10^{-16}, 1.69376 \times 10^{-16}\}.$$

By the lift-and-project method for the SLRA problem, we get the following $\mathfrak{S}$-structured polynomial set F_{st} with tolerance $\varepsilon = 7.14286 \times 10^{-7}$ in 2-norm, such that $\mathrm{rank}(\mathcal{M}_\mathcal{T}(F_{st}))$ $= \mathrm{rank}(\mathcal{M}_\mathcal{T}(F)) - d$. We note that we show only limited number of figures for each coefficient.

$$F_{st} = \{1.00000028x^3 + 0.9999997x^2y^2,$$
$$1.00000029x^2y^2 - 0.9999997y^3,$$
$$- 0.99999979x^2y + 1.00000079x^2$$
$$+ 1.00000021xy^2 + 0.99999921y^2\}.$$

In this case, the conditions in Theorem 3 are not satisfied since $(1 + \sigma_A^{-1}) \approx 2$ and $\max \mu = 26$. We apply Algorithm 4 to the resulting F_{st}. The resulting set of terms for F_{st} and $\mathcal{T}$ for F are the same hence by Algorithm 6, we get the following $\mathfrak{S}$-structured Gröbner basis for F. We note that the left-and-project method only computes a numerical rank deficient matrix hence we ignore tiny elements in the absolute value in Algorithm 3.

$$G = \{1.0x^2 + 0.9999984y^2 + 1.0524686xy^2 + 0.5227041y^3$$
$$+ 1.0624003xy^3 + 0.2390588y^4 + 0.4902203xy^4$$
$$+ 0.07823411y^5 + 0.1865897xy^5 - 0.03248369y^6$$
$$+ 0.01583228xy^6, \ 1.0y^6 - 1.0000006y^3,$$
$$1.0xy^2 + 0.1374344y^3 + 0.9999994y^4 - 0.1374343y^6\}.$$

We note that the resulting $\mathfrak{S}$-structured Gröbner basis is not reduced since reducing all the redundant monomials can not be done by unitary transformations. ◁

The above example poses a problem. One may think that the resulting structured Gröbner basis does not have the approximate zero $(x,y) = (-1.0, 1.0)$ while the original system has it accurately hence the algorithm may not be efficient. This is partially correct but partially incorrect. We note again that it is difficult to say which system is better since we can not know the desired exact system. Even if the desired system has the approximate zero $(x,y) = (-1.0, 1.0)$, our algorithm is still efficient. To get $y = 1.0$ in this case, we must have $y^6 - y^3 = (y-1)(y^5 + y^4 + y^3)$ in the ideal. However, the row space of $\mathcal{M}_\mathcal{T}(F)$ before the lift-and-project method has polynomials whose head term is y^5. This means that one of roots of $y^6 - y^3$ has disappeared. Our method recovered this information. On the other hand, the following example is very simple. Our method derives a consistent system from an inconsistent system.

EXAMPLE 3. We compute a $\mathfrak{S}$-structured Gröbner basis with $\varepsilon_r = 10^{-1}$ w.r.t. the graded lexicographic order for the following polynomial set F.

$$F = \{0.002 + 1.01x^2 - 2.09y^2, 3.06xy + 4.03x^2y,$$
$$0.504x^2 + 1.504xy + 2.04x^2y - 1.02y^2\}.$$

We take the following structure specification $\mathfrak{S}$.

$$\mathfrak{S}_1 : \quad (p_1 \ p_2 \ p_3) \quad \mapsto \quad p_1 + p_2x^2 + p_3y^2,$$
$$\mathfrak{S}_2 : \quad (p_4 \ p_5) \quad \mapsto \quad p_4xy + p_5x^2y,$$
$$\mathfrak{S}_3 : \quad (p_6 \ p_7 \ p_8 \ p_9) \quad \mapsto \quad p_6x^2 + p_7xy + p_8x^2y + p_9y^2.$$

In this case, by Algorithm 4 with $\varepsilon_r = 10^{-1}$ and using the usual criteria for updating critical pairs, we get the following set of terms $\mathcal{T}$ and $\varepsilon_a = 0.0927818$.

$$\mathcal{T} = \{x^2y, \ y^3, \ x^2, \ xy, \ y^2, \ y, \ 1\}.$$

We construct $\mathcal{M}_\mathcal{T}(F) \in \mathbb{C}^{4\times7}$ and determine the rank deficiency $d = 1$ since we get the following singular values and $\sigma_4 \le \sqrt{7} \times 0.0927818 \approx 0.245478 < \sigma_3$.

$$\{5.75329, 2.52696, 2.14761, 0.0293402\}.$$

By the lift-and-project method for the SLRA problem, we get the following $\mathfrak{S}$-structured polynomial set F_{st} with tolerance $\varepsilon = 0.0333776$ in 2-norm, such that $\mathrm{rank}(\mathcal{M}_\mathcal{T}(F_{st}))$ $= \mathrm{rank}(\mathcal{M}_\mathcal{T}(F)) - d$. We note that we show only limited number of figures for each coefficient and the constant term of the first polynomial may be numerical error.

$$F_{st} = \{9.3459 \times 10^{-16} + 1.01198x^2 - 2.08901y^2,$$
$$3.04856xy + 4.03864x^2y,$$
$$0.49605x^2 + 1.52686xy + 2.02274x^2y - 1.02398y^2\}.$$

In this case, the conditions in Theorem 3 are satisfied. Hence by Algorithm 6, we get the following $\mathfrak{S}$-structured Gröbner basis for F, which is not reduced.

$$G = \{1.0x^2 - 2.06428y^2,$$
$$1.0y^3 + 0.0238244x^2 + 0.365673xy - 0.0491802y^2\}.$$

◁

As in the above examples, we still need hard work in the conditions in Theorem 3 and numerical instability. Algorithms and theorems in this paper assume that we can get a rank deficient matrix by some SLRA solver. In fact, we use the left-and-project method. However, these methods only can compute a numerical candidate matrix hence we still have to operate a posteriori error in Algorithm 6. With this, for computing a $\mathfrak{S}$-structured Gröbner basis, the following open questions are postponed to future work: 1) a better method for our SLRA problem, 2) numerical analyses for computing a Gröbner basis by RREF with floating-point numbers, 3) improvements on the conditions of Lemma 4 for finding a suitable set of terms $\mathcal{T}$, and 4) a method to compute an optimal $\mathfrak{S}$-structured numerical Gröbner basis w.r.t. the given tolerance ε.

The preliminary implementation on *Mathematica* 7.0, used in this paper can be found at the following URL.
http://wwwmain.h.kobe-u.ac.jp/~nagasaka/
                        research/snap/issac11.nb

Acknowledgements

The author wishes to thank the anonymous reviewers for their constructive comments. This work was supported in part by Japanese Ministry of Education, Culture, Sports, Science and Technology under Grant-in-Aid for Young Scientists, MEXT KAKENHI (22700011).

6. REFERENCES

[1] P. Boito. *Structured Matrix Based Methods for Approximate GCD*. Ph.D. Thesis. Department of Mathematics, University of Pisa, Italia, 2007.

[2] M. Byröd, K. Josephson, and K. Åström. Fast optimal three view triangulation. In Y. Yagi, I. S. Kweon, S. B. Kang, and H. Zha, editors, *Asian Conference on Computer Vision*, 2007.

[3] M. T. Chu, R. E. Funderlic, and R. J. Plemmons. Structured low rank approximation. *Linear Algebra Appl.*, 366:157–172, 2003. Special issue on structured matrices: analysis, algorithms and applications (Cortona, 2000).

[4] T. W. Dubé. The structure of polynomial ideals and Gröbner bases. *SIAM J. Comput.*, 19(4):750–775, 1990.

[5] C. Eder and J. Perry. F5c: A variant of faugère's f5 algorithm with reduced Gröbner bases. *Journal of Symbolic Computation*, 45(12):1442 – 1458, 2010. MEGA'2009.

[6] J.-C. Faugére. A new efficient algorithm for computing Gröbner bases (F_4). *J. Pure Appl. Algebra*, 139(1-3):61–88, 1999.

[7] J.-C. Faugère. A new efficient algorithm for computing Gröbner bases without reduction to zero (F_5). In *Proceedings of the 2002 International Symposium on Symbolic and Algebraic Computation*, pages 75–83 (electronic), New York, 2002. ACM.

[8] J.-C. Faugère and Y. Liang. Artificial discontinuities of single-parametric Gröbner bases. *J. Symb. Comput.*, (in press, 8 pages), 2010.

[9] A. Giovini, T. Mora, G. Niesi, L. Robbiano, and C. Traverso. "one sugar cube, please" or selection strategies in the buchberger algorithm. In *Proceedings of the 1991 international symposium on Symbolic and algebraic computation*, ISSAC '91, pages 49–54, New York, NY, USA, 1991. ACM.

[10] M. Kalkbrener. On the stability of Gröbner bases under specializations. *J. Symbolic Comput.*, 24(1):51–58, 1997.

[11] D. Kapur, Y. Sun, and D. Wang. A new algorithm for computing comprehensive Gröbner systems. In *Proceedings of the 2010 International Symposium on Symbolic and Algebraic Computation*, ISSAC '10, pages 29–36, New York, NY, USA, 2010. ACM.

[12] A. Kondratyev, H. J. Stetter, and S. Winkler. Numerical computation of Gröbner bases. In *Proceedings of CASC2004 (Computer Algebra in Scientific Computing)*, pages 295–306, 2004.

[13] D. Lazard. Gröbner bases, Gaussian elimination and resolution of systems of algebraic equations. In *Computer algebra (London, 1983)*, volume 162 of *Lecture Notes in Comput. Sci.*, pages 146–156. Springer, Berlin, 1983.

[14] P. Lemmerling. *Structured total least squares: analysis, algorithms and applications*. Ph.D. Thesis. Faculty of Applied Sciences, K.U. Leuven, Belgium, 1999.

[15] I. Markovsky. Structured low-rank approximation and its applications. *Automatica J. IFAC*, 44(4):891–909, 2008.

[16] A. Montes and M. Wibmer. Gröbner bases for polynomial systems with parameters. *J. Symb. Comput.*, 45(12):1391–1425, 2010.

[17] K. Nabeshima. A speed-up of the algorithm for computing comprehensive Gröbner systems. In *ISSAC 2007: Proceedings of the 2007 international symposium on Symbolic and algebraic computation*, pages 299–306, New York, NY, USA, 2007. ACM.

[18] K. Nagasaka. A study on Gröbner basis with inexact input. In *Proceedings of CASC 2009*, volume 5743 of *Lecture Notes in Comput. Sci.*, pages 247–258. Springer, Berlin, 2009.

[19] K. Nagasaka. Extracting a Gröbner basis from inexact input (preprint, 15 pages). 2010.

[20] T. Sasaki and F. Kako. Computing floating-point Gröbner bases stably. In *Proceedings of SNC 2007*, pages 180–189. ACM, New York, 2007.

[21] T. Sasaki and F. Kako. Floating-point Gröbner basis computation with ill-conditionedness estimation. In *Proceedings of ASCM 2007*, volume 5081 of *Lecture Notes in Comput. Sci.*, pages 278–292. Springer, Berlin, 2008.

[22] T. Sasaki and F. Kako. Term cancellations in computing floating-point Gröbner bases. In *Proceedings of CASC 2010*, volume 6244 of *Lecture Notes in Comput. Sci.*, pages 220–231, Berlin, 2010. Springer.

[23] K. Shirayanagi. An algorithm to compute floating point Gröbner bases. In *Proceedings of the Maple summer workshop and symposium on Mathematical computation with Maple V : ideas and applications*, pages 95–106, Cambridge, MA, USA, 1993. Birkhauser Boston Inc.

[24] K. Shirayanagi. Floating point Gröbner bases. In *Selected papers presented at the international IMACS symposium on Symbolic computation, new trends and developments*, pages 509–528, Amsterdam, The Netherlands, The Netherlands, 1996. Elsevier Science Publishers B. V.

[25] K. Shirayanagi and M. Sweedler. A theory of stabilizing algebraic algorithms. *Technical Report 95-28*, pages 1–92, 1995. http://www.ss.u-tokai.ac.jp/s̃hirayan/msitr95-28.pdf.

[26] H. J. Stetter. Approximate Gröbner bases – an impossible concept? In *Proceedings of SNC 2005 (Symbolic-Numeric Computation)*, pages 235–236, 2005.

[27] A. Suzuki and J. Sato. A simple algorithm to compute comprehensive Gröbner bases using Gröbner bases. In *ISSAC 2006*, pages 326–331. ACM, New York, 2006.

[28] C. Traverso and A. Zanoni. Numerical stability and stabilization of Groebner basis computation. In *ISSAC 2002: Proceedings of the 2002 international symposium on Symbolic and algebraic computation*, pages 262–269, New York, NY, USA, 2002. ACM.

[29] V. Weispfenning. Comprehensive Gröbner bases. *J. Symbolic Comput.*, 14(1):1–29, 1992.

[30] V. Weispfenning. Gröbner bases for inexact input data. In *Proceedings of CASC 2003 (Computer Algebra in Scientific Computing)*, pages 403–411, 2002.

Randomized Preconditioning of the MBA Algorithm [*]

Victor Y. Pan
Department of Math and
Computer Science
Lehman College of CUNY
Bronx, NY 10468 USA
victor.pan@lehman.cuny.edu
http://comet.lehman.cuny.edu/vpan/

Guoliang Qian
Department of Computer
Science
The Graduate Center of CUNY
New York, NY 10036 USA
gqian@gc.cuny.edu

Ai-Long Zheng
Department of Mathematics
The Graduate Center of CUNY
New York, NY 10036 USA
azheng@yahoo.com

ABSTRACT

MBA algorithm inverts a structured matrix in nearly linear arithmetic time but requires a serious restriction on the input class. We remove this restriction by means of randomization and extend the progress to some fundamental computations with polynomials, e.g., computing their GCDs and AGCDs, where most effective known algorithms rely on computations with matrices having Toeplitz-like structure. Furthermore, our randomized algorithms fix rank deficiency and ill conditioning of general and structured matrices. At the end we comment on a wide range of other natural extensions of our progress and underlying ideas.

CATEGORIES AND SUBJECT DESCRIPTORS:

F.2.1 [ANALYSIS OF ALGORITHMS AND PROBLEM COMPLEXITY]: Numerical Algorithms and Problems–Computations on matrices

G.1.0 [NUMERICAL ANALYSIS]: General
Conditioning (and ill-conditioning)

GENERAL TERMS: Algorithms

1. INTRODUCTION

Some effective numerical algorithms such as the MBA algorithm in [17], [2] and Gohberg-Koltracht's [12] invert a structured, e.g, Toeplitz or Hankel matrix or its largest nonsingular leading block, in nearly linear arithmetic time but fail unless the matrix has generic rank profile, that is unless its $k \times k$ leading blocks are nonsingular for $k \leq \operatorname{rank} M$.

This restriction is mild in symbolic implementation over a field of a large cardinality and can be relaxed with randomized regularization (see, e.g., [16], [20, Chapter 5]), but it is quite vexing in numerical computations, in which case the algorithms are prone to numerical stability problems [1].

---

[*]Supported by PSC CUNY Awards 62230–0040 and 63153–0041

One can try to counter them with randomization, but its formal support is elusive, and the current numerical methods of choice run in quadratic time, relying, e.g, on the displacement transformation techniques proposed in [18] and made practical in [11] (see our Remark 2.1). Our randomized methods relax the cited restriction to accelerate the known numerical algorithms by order of magnitude and, furthermore, reduce computations with rank deficient or ill conditioned general or structured matrices to computations with well conditioned matrices of full rank.

For structured matrix computations our work implies the decrease of the running time of these algorithms from quadratic to nearly linear. The progress is immediately translated to some fundamental polynomial computations such as computing polynomial GCDs and AGCDs (see [3], the full version of our paper, and the references therein). Our algorithms also precondition and regularize various other fundamental computations with general and structured matrices (see [22]–[24] and the references therein).

At end we comment on a much wider range of natural extensions of our methods and underlying ideas.

The results of our extensive tests (the contribution of the second and the third authors) are in good accordance with our formal analysis (see Section 7 and our full paper).

2. DEFINITIONS

Hereafter "expected to be" and "likely to be" mean "with a probability near one"; "op" stands for "arithmetic operation".

2.1 General matrices

We use standard definitions of matrix computations [13]. $\mathbb{K}^{h \times k}$ is the algebra of $h \times k$ matrices with the hk entries from a field $\mathbb{K}$, e.g. from the fields of complex numbers $\mathbb{C}$, real numbers $\mathbb{R}$, or rational numbers $\mathbb{Q}$.

$M^{(k)}$ is the $k \times k$ leading principal (that is northwestern) submatrix of a matrix M. M^T is its transpose, and M^H is its Hermitian transpose. $M^H = M^T$ for a real matrix M. An $m \times n$ matrix M of a rank ρ has *generic rank profile* if all its leading blocks $M^{(k)}$ of size $k \times k$ for $k \leq \rho$ are nonsingular. If in addition $\rho = \min\{m, n\}$, then the matrix is *strongly nonsingular*.

$(M_1 \mid M_2 \mid \ldots \mid M_h)$ (resp. $\operatorname{diag}(M_1, M_2, \ldots, M_h)$) is the $1 \times h$ block matrix (resp. $h \times h$ block diagonal matrix) with h blocks (resp. diagonal blocks) $M_1, M_2, \ldots, M_h$.

$I = I_k$ is the $k \times k$ identity matrix $(\mathbf{e}_1 \mid \ldots \mid \mathbf{e}_k)$, with the columns $\mathbf{e}_1, \ldots, \mathbf{e}_k$. $J = J_k$ is the $k \times k$ reflection matrix

$(\mathbf{e}_k \mid \ldots \mid \mathbf{e}_1)$, with the columns $\mathbf{e}_k, \ldots, \mathbf{e}_1$. $I\mathbf{v} = \mathbf{v}$; $J\mathbf{v} = (v_i)_{i=k}^1$ for any vector $\mathbf{v} = (v_i)_{i=1}^k$; $J^2 = I$.

$\mathcal{R}(M) = \{\mathbf{z} : \mathbf{z} = M\mathbf{y}$ over all vectors $\mathbf{y}\}$ is the range of a matrix M. $\mathcal{N}(M) = \{\mathbf{x} : M\mathbf{x} = \mathbf{0}\}$ is its *null space*, made up of its *null vectors* $\mathbf{x}$. $\rho = \operatorname{rank} M = \dim(\mathcal{R}(M))$ is the rank of a matrix M, $\nu = \dim(\mathcal{N}(M))$ is its nullity. $\nu + \rho = n$ for an $m \times n$ matrix M where $m \geq n$.

A matrix U is unitary (orthonormal) if $U^H U = I$. $M = S_M \Sigma_M T_M^H$ is SVD of a $k \times l$ matrix M of a rank ρ if $\Sigma_M = \operatorname{diag}(\widehat{\Sigma}_M, O_{k-\rho, l-\rho})$, $\widehat{\Sigma}_M = \operatorname{diag}(\sigma_j(M))_{j=1}^\rho$, S_M and T_M are square unitary matrices, $S_M S_M^H = S_M^H S_M = I_k$, $T_M T_M^H = T_M^H T_M = I_l$, $\sigma_j = \sigma_j(M)$ is the jth largest singular value of M, $\sigma_j = 0$ for $j > \rho$, $\|M\| = \|M\|_2 = \sigma_1$ is its 2-norm.

$X = M^{[I]}$ is a left inverse of a matrix M if $XM = I$ and its right inverse if $MX = I$. $\Sigma_M^+ = \operatorname{diag}(\widehat{\Sigma}_M^{-1}, O_{k-\rho, l-\rho})$. $M^+ = T_M \Sigma_M^+ S_M^H$ is the generalized Moore–Penrose inverse of M. $\sigma_\rho = 1/\|M^+\|$. M^+ equals $(M^H M)^{-1} M^H$ (resp. $M^H (M M^H)^{-1}$) and is a left (resp. right) inverse $M^{[I]}$ if M has full column (resp. row) rank.

$\operatorname{cond} M = \|M\| \, \|M^+\| = \sigma_1/\sigma_\rho$ is the *condition number* of a matrix M (a fundamental concept of numerical matrix computations). $M^+ = M^{-1}$ and $\operatorname{cond} M = \|M\| \, \|M^{-1}\|$ for a nonsingular matrix M. For a matrix M having a positive rank ρ, the smallest positive singular value σ_ρ equals the distance $\|M - B\|$ to a nearest matrix B of rank $\rho - 1$.

In solving a linear system of equations and matrix inversion, $\operatorname{cond} M$ is close to the ratio of the output and input error norms [13], [14], and the backward error analysis closely links the impact of rounding errors on the output to the impact of input errors. Thus one must perform computations with extended precision to yield a meaningful output where a matrix M is *ill conditioned*, that is where its condition number is large in the context. Otherwise the matrix M is called *well conditioned*. Ill (resp. well) conditioned matrices of full rank lie near (resp. far from) rank deficient matrices.

2.2 Random matrices

Hereafter $|\Delta|$ is the cardinality of a set Δ. *Sampling* from it is the selection of its elements at random and independently of each other. A matrix is *random* if its entries are sampled from a fixed set Δ. Sampling is *uniform* if it is done under the uniform probability distribution on the set Δ.

DEFINITION 2.1. $F_X(y) = Probability\{X \leq y\}$ for a real random variable X is the cumulative distribution function (CDF) of X evaluated at y. We write $r = \operatorname{rank} A$ for a random $m \times n$ matrix A if $\operatorname{rank} A = r$ with probability one, and in this case we also write $F_A(y) = F_{\sigma_r(A)}(y)$. A matrix is a Gaussian random matrix with a mean μ and a variance σ^2 if it is filled with independent real Gaussian random variables, all having mean μ and variance σ^2. We have $\operatorname{rank} W = \min\{h, k\}$ for such $h \times k$ matrices W. They form a set (not an algebra) $\mathcal{G}_{\mu,\sigma}^{h \times k}$. We write $F_{h,k,\mu,\sigma}(y) = F_W(y)$.

THEOREM 2.1. *[7], [25], [29]. Suppose k values $\hat{x}_1, \ldots, \hat{x}_k$ have been uniformly sampled from a finite set Δ, and suppose $p(x_1, \ldots, x_k)$ is a nonzero k-variate polynomial of a total degree d. Then $Probability\{p(\hat{x}_1, \ldots, \hat{x}_k) = 0\} \leq d/|\Delta|$.*

2.3 Toeplitz-like matrices

$m \times n$ Toeplitz matrix $T = (t_{i-j})_{i,j=1}^{m,n}$ is defined by the $m + n - 1$ entries in their first row and first column. $Z_f = (z_{ij}^{(f)})_{i=1}^n$ for a scalar f is the unit f-circulant matrix, $z_{i+1,i}^{(f)} =$

1, $i = 1, \ldots, n-1$, $z_{1,n}^{(f)} = f$, $z_{i,j}^{(f)} = 0$ if $i \neq j - 1 \mod n$. $Z_f(\mathbf{v})$ denotes the Toeplitz matrix $\sum_{i=1}^n v_i Z_f^{i-1}$, defined by its first column $\mathbf{v} = (v_i)_{i=1}^n$. $Z_0(\mathbf{v})$ (resp. $(Z_0(\mathbf{v}))^T$) is a lower (resp. an upper) triangular Toeplitz matrix. $Z_f(\mathbf{v})$ is an f-circulant matrix if $f \neq 0$ and circulant if $f = 1$.

Call $\mathcal{L}(M) = \Delta_{A,B}(M) = M - AMB$ the Stein displacement of a matrix M for two operator matrices A and B. $\operatorname{dr}(M) = \operatorname{rank}(\mathcal{L}(M))$ is the *displacement rank* of M. M is a *Toeplitz-like* matrix if its displacement rank $\operatorname{dr}(M)$ is small (in the context) for $A = Z_e$, $B = Z_f^T$ and two scalars e, f. $\operatorname{dr}(T) \leq 2$ for a Toeplitz matrix T. For an $n \times n$ matrix L of a rank r there are pairs of $n \times r$ matrices G and H such that $L = GH^T$. If $L = \mathcal{L}(M)$ such a pair is called a *displacement generator* of length r for a matrix M.

THEOREM 2.2. *[20, Example 4.4.1]. Assume scalars e and f such that $ef \neq 1$, an $n \times n$ matrix M, and a pair of $n \times l$ matrices $G = (\mathbf{g}_j)_{j=1}^l$ and $H = (\mathbf{h}_j)_{j=1}^l$. Then $M = \sum_{j=1}^l Z_e(\mathbf{g}_j)(Z_f(\mathbf{h}_j))^T$ if and only if $\Delta_{Z_e, Z_f^T}(M) = GH^T$.*

THEOREM 2.3. *[20, Section 4.6.4]. If $L = G_l H_l^T$ for $G_l, H_l \in \mathbb{K}^{n \times l}$ and if $\operatorname{rank} L = r$, then in $O(nl^2)$ ops one can compute matrices $G_r, H_r \in \mathbb{K}^{n \times r}$ such that $L = G_r H_r^T$.*

THEOREM 2.4. *[20, Section 1.5]. For any 5-tuple of compatible matrices $\{A, B, C, M, N\}$ we have $\Delta_{A,C}(MN) = \Delta_{A,B}(M)N + AMB\Delta_{B^{-1},C}(N)$ if B is a nonsingular matrix, whereas $\Delta_{A,C}(MN) = \Delta_{A,B}(M)N - AM\Delta_{B,C^{-1}}(N)C$ if C is a nonsingular matrix.*

FACT 2.1. *[20, Theorem 1.5]. The displacement ranks $\operatorname{dr}_{\text{out}}$ and the lengths of displacement generators $\operatorname{dl}_{\text{out}}$ of matrix sums, products (cf. Theorem 2.4), transposes, inverses, and blocks can be bounded in terms of the displacement ranks $\operatorname{dr}_{\text{in}}^{(1)}, \ldots, \operatorname{dr}_{\text{in}}^{(h)}$ and the lengths of displacement generators $\operatorname{dl}_{\text{in}}^{(1)}, \ldots, \operatorname{dl}_{\text{in}}^{(h)}$ of the h input matrices where $h = 1$ in the cases of inverses, transposes, and blocks, $\operatorname{dr}_{\text{out}} \leq \sum_{i=1}^h \operatorname{dr}_{\text{in}}^{(i)} + \delta$ and $\operatorname{dl}_{\text{out}} \leq \sum_{i=1}^h \operatorname{dl}_{\text{in}}^{(i)} + \delta$, $\delta \leq 2$ in the case of blocks; $\delta = 0$ in the other cases. The displacement generators of sums and transposes having these lengths can be generated with using no ops.*

REMARK 2.1. *Theorem 2.4 reveals the impact of multiplication of structured matrices on the operator matrices and therefore on matrix structure. This simple but powerful resource remained unnoticed until 1989, when it was first explored in [18]. That paper proposed to control matrix structure by applying proper multipliers and to exploit this power systematically for devising effective algorithms for computations with structured matrices. E.g., JH and HJ are Toeplitz (resp. Toeplitz-like) matrices if H is a Hankel (resp. Hankel-like) matrix, JT and TJ are Hankel (resp. Hankel-like) matrices if T is a Toeplitz (resp. Toeplitz-like) matrix. By combining the unit Hankel multiplier J with Vandermonde multipliers $V = (x_i^j)_{i,j=1}^{m,n}$ and V^T one can relate the four matrix structures of Toeplitz, Hankel, Vandermonde or Cauchy types to each other, so that any successful algorithm for matrices with one of these structures can be immediately extended to the matrices with the three other structures. Practically valuable extensions by means of such displacement transforms keep appearing since [11].*

THEOREM 2.5. *Based on displacement representation one*

(a) can multiply an $n \times n$ matrix M_0 by a vector by using $O(r_0 n \log n)$ ops [20, Section 2.4] and

(b) only needs $O(r_1 r_2 n \log n)$ ops to compute a displacement generator $\{G, H\}$ of the product $M_1 M_2$ (such that G and H are in $\mathbb{C}^{n \times (r_1 r_2)}$ and $\Delta_{Z_{e(i)}, Z_{f(i)}}(M_1 M_2) = G H^T$, provided $f(1) = e(2)$, $e(i) f(i) \neq 1$, $\mathrm{rank}(\Delta_{Z_{e(i)}, Z_{f(i)}}(M_i)) = r_i$, and the matrices M_i are given with displacement generators of lengths r_i for $i = 1, 2$ [20, Theorem 1.5.4].

(c) If such a matrix M_1 has generic rank profile, then one can compute its rank ρ and the inverse of its leading $\rho \times \rho$ block $M_1^{(\rho)}$ by using $O(\rho \log^2 \rho)$ ops, by applying the MBA algorithm in Section 4 [17], [2], [20, Chapter 5].

3. EXPRESSING NULL VECTORS VIA MATRICES OF FULL RANK

The following result in [22] on additive preprocessing $M \to C = M + UV^H$ reduces the computations with rank deficient matrices to computations with matrices of full rank.

THEOREM 3.1. *Suppose $M \in \mathbb{K}^{m \times n}$, $U \in \mathbb{K}^{m \times r}$, $V \in \mathbb{K}^{n \times r}$, $\mathrm{rank}\, M = n - r$, $m \geq n > r > 0$, and the matrix $C = M + UV^T$ has full column rank. Then $\mathcal{R}(C^{[I]} U) = \mathcal{N}(M)$.*

THEOREM 3.2. *Suppose $M \in \mathbb{R}^{m \times n}$, $U \in \mathcal{G}_{0,1}^{m \times q}$, $V \in \mathcal{G}_{0,1}^{n \times q}$, $C = M + UV^T$, $\mathrm{rank}\, M = n - r$, $m \geq n > r > 0$, and $n \geq q > 0$. Then (a) $\mathrm{rank}\, C < n$ for $q < r$, $\mathrm{rank}\, C$ is likely to equal n for $q \geq r$; (b) $\mathrm{cond}\, C$ is likely to be of order $\mathrm{cond}\, M$ if $q \geq r$ and if the matrix M is scaled so that its norm is neither large nor small (e.g., $\|M\| \approx 1$).*

Parts (a) follows from Theorem 2.1. Part (b) is proved in Section 6.

The theorems express the rank, nullity, and null vectors of a rank deficient matrix M in terms of matrices expected to have full rank; these expressions extend to the numerical rank, numerical nullity (that is the minimum rank and the maximum nullity of nearby matrices), and singular vectors associated with small singular values of the nearby ill conditioned matrices $M + E$ of full rank where $\|E\|/\|M\|$ is small. (For a rank deficient matrix M and random E we expect that $\mathrm{cond}(M + E)$ grows to infinity as $\|E\| \to 0$.)

REMARK 3.1. *For a structured input matrix M additive preprocessing $M \to C = M + UV^T$ increases the values $dr(M)$ and $dl(M)$ by δ in $O(r)$, $r = \mathrm{rank}(UV^T)$. δ is in $O(1)$ (a constant) where the matrices M, U and V have consistent structure [20, Section 1.5]. For such matrices Theorems 3.1 and 3.2 are extended, except for part (b) of Theorem 3.2; its unproved extension has been supported by our extensive experiments in the case of Toeplitz matrices U and V.*

The power of augmentation $M \to K = \begin{pmatrix} V \\ M \end{pmatrix}$ is similar to the power of additive preprocessing.

THEOREM 3.3. *[23]. Assume an $m \times n$ matrix M of a rank $\rho < n$, an $r \times n$ matrix V, $r = n - \rho$, $K = (V^T \mid M^T)^T$, $\mathrm{rank}\, K = n$, and $B = K^{[I]}(I_r \mid O)^T$. Then (a) $\mathcal{N}(M) = \mathcal{R}(B)$. (b) Furthermore, let $M = S_M \Sigma_M T_M^T$ be SVD, $\Sigma_M = \mathrm{diag}(\mathrm{diag}(\sigma_j(M))_{j=1}^{\rho}, O)$. Write $\mathrm{diag}(I_r, S_M^T) K T_M = \begin{pmatrix} A \\ O \end{pmatrix}$ and $A = \begin{pmatrix} V_0 & V_1 \\ \widehat{\Sigma}_M & O \end{pmatrix}$. Then we have the following estimate,*

$\mathrm{cond}\, K \leq (\frac{1}{\sigma_\rho(M)} + \frac{1}{\sigma_r(V_1)} + \frac{\|V_0\|}{\sigma_\rho(M)\sigma_r(V_1)}) \|K\|$.

(c) Let $\|M\| = \|V\|$, $\kappa = \mathrm{cond}\, M$, $\kappa_1 = \|V\|/\sigma_r(V_1)$. Then $\mathrm{cond}\, K \leq \sqrt{2}(\kappa + \kappa_1 + \kappa \kappa_1)$. (d) If $V \in \mathbb{C}_{0,\sigma}^{r \times n}$, then $F_{V_1}(y) \leq 2.35 y \sqrt{n}/\sigma$ and (e) the matrix K is column rank deficient with probability zero.

PROOF. Verify part (a) by inspection. Furthermore, we have $\|A^{-1}\| \leq \|\widehat{\Sigma}_M^{-1}\| + \|V_1^{-1}\| + \|\widehat{\Sigma}_M^{-1}\| \|V_1^{-1}\| \|V_0\|$ because $A^{-1} = \begin{pmatrix} O & \widehat{\Sigma}_M^{-1} \\ V_1^{-1} & -V_1^{-1} V_0 \widehat{\Sigma}_M^{-1} \end{pmatrix}$. Substitute $\|\widehat{\Sigma}_M^{-1}\| = \frac{1}{\sigma_\rho(M)}$, $\|V_1^{-1}\| = \frac{1}{\sigma_r(V_1)}$, $\|A^{-1}\| = \frac{1}{\sigma_n(A)} = \frac{1}{\sigma_n(K)}$, and $\mathrm{cond}\, K = \|K\|/\sigma_n(K)$. Part (b) follows and implies part (c). Deduce part (d) from Theorems 5.2 and 5.4 (part (c)) for $W = V$, $H = T_M(O \mid I_r)^T$. Deduce part (e) from part (d). $\square$

REMARK 3.2. *We can reverse direction and reduce the solution of a nonsingular linear system $A\mathbf{y} = \mathbf{b}$ to computing a null vector of a matrix $(A \mid \eta\mathbf{b})$ for a nonzero scalar η of our choice (see [23], [24] on nontrivial numerical details).*

4. THE MBA ALGORITHM

The MBA algorithm inverts a strongly nonsingular matrix $M = \begin{pmatrix} M_{00} & M_{01} \\ M_{10} & M_{11} \end{pmatrix}$ for $M \in \mathbb{K}^{n \times n}$, $M_{00} \in \mathbb{K}^{n \times j}$, $r = n - j$, $|n - 2j| \leq 1$, based on recursive extension of the block factorizations

$$M = \begin{pmatrix} I_j & O_{j,r} \\ M_{10} M_{00}^{-1} & I_r \end{pmatrix} \begin{pmatrix} M_{00} & M_{01} \\ O_{r,j} & S_{n,j} \end{pmatrix}, \quad (4.1)$$

$$M^{-1} = \begin{pmatrix} M_{00}^{-1} & -M_{00}^{-1} M_{01} S_{n,j}^{-1} \\ O_{r,j} & S_{n,j}^{-1} \end{pmatrix} \begin{pmatrix} I_k & O_{j,r} \\ -M_{10} M_{00}^{-1} & I_r \end{pmatrix}. \quad (4.2)$$

Here $S_{n,j} = M_{11} - M_{10} M_{00}^{-1} M_{01}$ (the jth *Schur complement* in M) is a pivot block in block Gaussian elimination, $S_{n,j}^{-1}$ is the trailing (southeastern) block of the matrix M^{-1}. Hereafter $S_{j+h,j}$ denotes the jth Schur complement in $M^{(j+h)}$ for $h \geq 0$, and we write $S_{j,0} = M^{(j)}$.

THEOREM 4.1. *[20, Theorem 5.2.4]. $S_{j+h,j} = S_{n,j}^{(h)}$.*

The MBA algorithm recursively applies the above block triangular factorization steps balanced in size to the matrices M_{00}^{-1} and $S_{n,j}^{-1}$ until it arrives at 1×1 matrices. In virtue of Theorem 4.1 it inverts only Schur complements $S_{j+h,j}$ in the leading blocks $M^{(j+h)}$. They are nonsingular for a strongly nonsingular input M. The algorithm yields the inverses $(M^{(j)})^{-1}$ by extending factorization (4.2) from M to $M^{(j+h)}$, and it can also compute $\det M = (\det M_{00}) \det S_{n,j}$.

For a structured matrix M represented with a displacement generator of a small length l, the algorithm operates with displacement generators representing the input, output and auxiliary matrices. Based on Theorem 2.3 and Fact 2.1 one can keep the lengths of all displacement generators in $O(l)$ and compute a shortest displacement generator for the inverse of a Toeplitz-like matrix M by using $O(l^2 n \log^2 n)$ ops. We readily extend the algorithm to rectangular matrices having generic rank profile.

THEOREM 4.2. *See (4.1) for $M_{00} = M^{(k)}$. Suppose a matrix M of a rank ρ has generic rank profile. Then (a) the matrix $M^{(j)}$ is nonsingular if and only if $j \leq \rho$. If it is, then (b) the matrix $S_{j+h,j}$ is nonsingular if and only if $j + h \leq \rho$; furthermore, (c) $j = \rho$ if and only if $S_{n,j} = O$.*

$j \leq \rho < j+h$ if a matrix $S_{j+h,j=S_{n,j}^{(h)}}$ is singular. The MBA algorithm detects singularity when it arrives at a singular one-by-one matrix. Then the algorithm outputs the rank $\rho = \operatorname{rank} M = j$. We have $\mathcal{N}(M) = \mathcal{R}(G)$ where $G = \begin{pmatrix} -M_{00}^{-1} M_{01} \\ I_{n-\rho} \end{pmatrix}$, $M = \begin{pmatrix} M_{00} & M_{01} \\ M_{10} & M_{11} \end{pmatrix}$ and $M_{00} = M^{(\rho)}$. Toeplitz-like structure of M is extended to the matrix G.

In numerical computations with rounding errors, rank deficient, e.g., singular matrices typically turn into ill conditioned matrices of full rank, lying near rank deficient ones. The MBA algorithm is vulnerable to singularity and ill conditioning of leading blocks of an input matrix, but it encounters no numerical problems where the matrix has both generic rank profile and *generic conditioning profile*, that is has its leading blocks $M^{(j)}$ nonsingular and well conditioned if and only if $j \leq \rho$. Here are some supporting results.

THEOREM 4.3. *Write* $N_- = \max_{j=1}^n \|(M^{(j)})^{-1}\|$. *Write* $\kappa_+ = \|M\| N_-$. *Then* $\operatorname{cond} D \leq (1+\kappa_+)\kappa_+$ *for every diagonal block* D *in recursive block factorization (4.2) of a strongly nonsingular matrix* M.

PROOF. For the blocks M_{00} of M and S^{-1} of M^{-1} we surely have $\|M_{00}\| \leq \|M\|$, $\|M_{00}^{-1}\| \leq N_-$, and $\|S^{-1}\| \leq \|M^{-1}\| \leq N_-$. We also have $\|S\| = \|M_{11} - M_{01} M_{00}^{-1} M_{01}\| \leq \|M\| + N_- \|M\|^2$. Now the claimed bound follows from Theorem 4.1. □

THEOREM 4.4. *Suppose a matrix* M *has generic rank profile. Then* $\sigma_{j+1}(M) \leq \|S_{n,j}\|$.

PROOF. Recall equation (4.1) for $M_{00} = M^{(j)}$, replace the block M_{11} by $M_{11} - S_{n,j}$, and observe that the Schur complement $\tilde{S}_{n,j}$ in the resulting matrix $\tilde{M}$ vanishes. □

It follows that the numerical rank of M does not exceed j if the norm $\|S_{n,j}\|$ is small.

Given a rank deficient or ill conditioned matrix M, we regularize and precondition it to support the MBA algorithm. We deduce from Theorem 2.1 that random general and structured matrices in $\mathbb{C}$, $\mathbb{R}$ and all fields of large cardinalities are likely to have generic rank profile and thus to support the MBA symbolic algorithm, and we can handle even the unlikely case of a bad input with the recipes below and in [20, Sections 5.6 and 5.7], based on Theorem 2.1 (applied in any field $\mathbb{K}$) and [13, Theorem 8.1.7] (in the fields $\mathbb{K} \supseteq \mathbb{Q}$).

THEOREM 4.5. *[16]. Assume a field* $\mathbb{K}$ *and three matrices* $M \in \mathbb{K}^{k \times l}$, $Z_0(\mathbf{w}) \in \mathbb{K}^{k \times k}$ *and* $Z_0(\mathbf{z}) \in \mathbb{K}^{l \times l}$ *where* $\rho = \operatorname{rank} M$, $\mathbf{w} = (w_i)_{i=1}^k$, $\mathbf{z} = (z_i)_{i=1}^l$, $w_1 = z_1 = 1$, *and the other* $k + l - 2$ *coordinates of the vectors* $\mathbf{w}$ *and* $\mathbf{z}$ *are uniformly sampled from a set* $\Delta \subseteq \mathbb{K}$. *Then the matrix* $(Z_0(\mathbf{w}))^T M Z_0(\mathbf{z})$ *has generic rank profile with a probability at least* $1 - (\rho + 1)\rho/|\Delta|$; *for* $\rho = m = n$ *it is strongly nonsingular with a probability at least* $1 - (n+1)n/|\Delta|$.

THEOREM 4.6. *[4, Section 2.13]. Let a matrix* $M \in \mathbb{K}^{k \times l}$ *have full column rank* l *for* $\mathbb{K} \supseteq \mathbb{Q}$, *e.g.* $\mathbb{K} = \mathbb{R}$. *Then the matrix* $M^H M \in \mathbb{K}^{l \times l}$ *is strongly nonsingular, whereas the matrix* $TM \in \mathbb{K}^{l \times l}$ *is strongly nonsingular with a probability at least* $1 - (l+1)l/|\Delta|$ *provided* T *is an* $l \times k$ *Toeplitz matrix with entries uniformly sampled from a set* $\Delta \subseteq \mathbb{K}$.

Preprocessing in Theorems 4.5 and 4.6 should yield generic rank profile for general and structured rectangular matrices.

For matrices M of full column rank in $\mathbb{K} \supseteq \mathbb{Q}$, Theorem 4.6 defines deterministic preprocessing that ensures generic rank profile. Moreover, $\operatorname{cond}(M^H M)^{(k)} \leq \operatorname{cond}(M^H M) \leq \operatorname{cond}^2 M$ in virtue of [13, Theorem 8.1.7]. This implies generic conditioning profile unless $\operatorname{cond}^2 M$ is too large in the context. The symmetrization $M \to M^H M$ (as well as $M \to MM^H$) loses its power where M is a rank deficient matrix, but based on Theorems 3.2 or 3.3 we can relax the full rank assumption and also support application of the MBA algorithm to overdetermined linear systems of equations and to computation of null vectors of rank deficient matrices.

In the next sections we prove preconditioning power of randomized preprocessing of Theorem 4.6.

5. CONDITIONING OF RANDOM MATRICES AND OF RANDOMIZED MATRIX PRODUCTS

Gaussian random matrices (cf. Definition 2.1) tend to be well conditioned [6], [9], and even perturbations by such a matrix A is expected to make a matrix M well conditioned if the norms $\|A\|$ and $\|M\|$ have the same order [26]. Let us recall some relevant results.

THEOREM 5.1. *[8, Theorem II.7]. Let* $A \in \mathcal{G}_{0,\sigma}^{n \times n}$. *Then* $F_{\|A\|}(y) \geq 1 - \exp(-x^2/2)$ *for* $x = y/\sigma - 2\sqrt{n} \geq 0$.

THEOREM 5.2. *[26, Theorem 3.3]. Suppose* $M \in \mathbb{R}^{m \times n}$, $A \in \mathcal{G}_{\mu,\sigma}^{n \times n}$ $W = A + M$, $l = \min\{m,n\}$, *and* $y \geq 0$. *Then* $F_W(y) \leq 2.35 \, y\sqrt{l}/\sigma$.

THEOREM 5.3. *[26, Theorem 3.1]; see [28] for a factor* $\sqrt{\log n}$ *improvement. Under the assumptions of Theorem 5.2, let* $\|M\| \leq \sqrt{l}$, $\mu = 0$, $\sigma \leq 1$. *Then* $F_{\operatorname{cond} W}(y) \geq 1 - (14.1 + 4.7\sqrt{(2 \ln y)/n})n/(y\sigma)$ *for all* $y \geq 1$.

Next we extend these estimates to the products of fixed and random matrices.

THEOREM 5.4. *Suppose two matrices* $G \in \mathbb{R}^{q \times m}$ *and* $H \in \mathbb{R}^{n \times r}$ *have full ranks* $r_G = \operatorname{rank} G$ *and* $r_H = \operatorname{rank} H$. *Write* $r' = \min\{r_G, n\}$ *and* $r'' = \min\{r_H, m\}$. *Let* $W \in \mathcal{G}_{\mu,\sigma}^{m \times n}$ *for two scalars* μ *and* $\sigma > 0$. *Let* $y \geq 0$. *Then*
(a) $\operatorname{rank}(GW) = r'$, $\operatorname{rank}(WH) = r''$ *with probability one*,
(b) $F_{GW}(y) \leq F_{r_G,n,\mu,\sigma}(y/\sigma_{r'})$, *and*
(c) $F_{WH}(y) \leq F_{m,r_H,\mu,\sigma}(y/\sigma_{r''})$.

PROOF. Part (a) follows from Theorem 2.1. Assume SVD $G = S_G \Sigma_G T_G^H$, $\Sigma_G = \operatorname{diag}(\widehat{\Sigma}_G, O)$, $\widehat{\Sigma}_G = \operatorname{diag}(\sigma_j(G))_{j=1}^{r_G}$. Then $\bar{W} = T_G^H W \in \mathcal{G}_{\mu,\sigma}^{m \times n}$ because T_G is a unitary matrix. Obtain a matrix $\tilde{W}$ by deleting the $m - r_G$ zero rows of the matrix $S_G^H GW = \Sigma_G \bar{W}$. The matrices $\tilde{W}$ and GW share their positive singular values because S_G is a unitary matrix. We have $\tilde{W} = \widehat{\Sigma}_G \widehat{W}$ where $\widehat{W} \in \mathcal{G}_{\mu,\sigma}^{r_G \times n}$ is a block submatrix of $\bar{W}$. Clearly, scaling by the diagonal matrix $\widehat{\Sigma}_G$ can decrease the smallest positive singular value $\sigma_{r'}(\tilde{W})$ of the matrix $\tilde{W}$ by at most a factor $\sigma_{r'}(G)$. This proves part (b), which implies part (c) because $\sigma_j(WH) = \sigma_j((WH)^T) = \sigma_j(H^T W^T)$ for all j. □

THEOREM 5.5. *Under the assumptions of Theorem 5.4, write* $G_i = (I_i \mid O)G$, $r(G_i) = \operatorname{rank} G_i$ *for* $i = 1, \ldots, q$; $H_j = H(I_j \mid O)^T$ *and* $r(H_j) = \operatorname{rank} H_j$ *for* $j = 1, \ldots, r$.

Then for all i and j we have

(a) $\operatorname{rank}(G_i W) = \min\{r(G_i), n\}$ *and with probability one* $\operatorname{rank}(W H_j) = \min\{r(H_j), m\}$,

(b) $F_{(GW)^{(i)}}(y) \le F_{r(G_i), n, \mu, \sigma}(y/\sigma_{r(G_i)})$, *and*

(c) $F_{(WH)^{(j)}}(y) \le F_{m, r(H_j), \mu, \sigma}(y/\sigma_{r(H_j)})$.

PROOF. For every i (resp. j) the theorem is reduced to Theorem 5.4 where we replace G by G_i, r_G by $r(G_i)$, and W by $W(I_i \mid O)^T$ (resp. H by H_j, r_H by $r(H_j)$, and W by $(I_j \mid O)W$). $\square$

Combined with Theorem 5.1 the latter theorem implies probabilistic upper bounds of order $\operatorname{cond} G$ (resp. $\operatorname{cond} H$) on the condition numbers of all leading blocks of the matrix GW (resp. WH) and also implies

COROLLARY 5.1. *Under the assumptions of Theorem 5.4, suppose the matrices G and H have generic rank profile and $\sigma \ne 0$. Then with probability one the matrices GW and WH have generic rank profile.*

Our results imply that $\max_k \operatorname{cond}(\tilde{M}^{(k)})$ is expected to have order $\operatorname{cond} M$ provided $M \in \mathbb{R}^{n \times n}$, $\tilde{M}$ is WM or MW, and $W \in \mathcal{G}_{0,1}^{n \times n}$. Therefore multiplicative preprocessing $M \to \tilde{M}$ is expected to yield generic rank and conditioning profiles for well conditioned matrices M of full rank.

To support application of the MBA algorithm to such matrices M, we would need to extend these results to the case of random matrices W having structure consistent with the structure of the matrix M.

We can readily extend the proof of the regularization results based on Theorem 2.1, but not of our randomized preconditioning results, which rely on the Smoothed Analysis in [26] and on Theorems 5.2 and 5.3. Like that analysis they hold where the multipliers and preprocessors U, V, and W are general Gaussian random matrices. No extension of the proofs in [26] and Theorems 5.2 and 5.3 to structured (e.g., Toeplitz) matrices W is known, but such extensions have consistent empirical support from our tests with random Toeplitz matrices W and even with circulant matrices W filled with integers one and -1 chosen at random.

Our alternative randomized preprocessing policies in the next section handle both regularization and preconditioning problems even where the matrix M is rank deficient and ill conditioned as long as it has a small nullity and a small numerical nullity. See [24, Sections 8 and 10] on deterministic and randomized preconditioning methods that cover structured and general matrices with a large nullity. In contrast the maps $M \to \tilde{M}$ (for $\tilde{M} = MW$ and $\tilde{M} = WM$, square matrices M and W, and random W) promise no progress because $\operatorname{cond} \tilde{M} \ge (\operatorname{cond} M)/\operatorname{cond}(W^{-1})$ and $\operatorname{cond}(W^{-1}) = \operatorname{cond} W$ tends to be not very large for random matrices W (cf. Theorem 5.3).

6. RANDOMIZED ADDITIVE PREPROCESSING IS EXPECTED TO BE PRECONDITIONING

We are going to prove strong preconditioning power of randomized additive preprocessing. See [24] on proving similar power of randomized augmentation.

Suppose $M \in \mathbb{C}^{n \times n}$, $U, V \in \mathbb{R}^{n \times r}$, the matrices M and $R = M + UV^H$ are nonsingular, and $0 < r < n$.

Let us prove that additive preprocessing $M \implies C = M + UV^T$ is likely to precondition quite a general class of ill conditioned matrices M assuming Gaussian random matrices U and V with a variance σ^2 of order $\|M\|^2$. We first reduce the study of ill conditioned input matrix M to the case of a nearby singular matrix $\tilde{M}$; then based on its SVD we factorize the auxiliary matrices.

Proceeding orderly, let $\tilde{M} = M + E$ be the matrix of a rank $\rho = n - r$ obtained by setting to zero the singular values $\sigma_j(M)$ for $j > n - r$ in the SVD $M = S\Sigma T^H$, $\|E\| = \sigma_{n-r+1}(M)$. Write $C = M + UV^H$ and $\tilde{C} = \tilde{M} + UV^H = C + E$, assume that the matrices C and $\tilde{C}$ are nonsingular and recall that $\operatorname{cond} \tilde{C} \le \frac{1+\delta}{1-\delta \operatorname{cond} C} \operatorname{cond} C$ provided $\delta = \frac{\|E\|}{\|C\|}$ and $\delta \operatorname{cond} C < 1$ [13, Section 5.5.5]. Next assume that the value δ is small and write $\tilde{C} = \tilde{M} + UV^H$. In the rest of this section we estimate the ratio $\frac{\operatorname{cond} \tilde{C}}{\operatorname{cond} \tilde{M}} = \frac{\sigma_{n-r}(\tilde{M})}{\sigma_1(\tilde{M})} \operatorname{cond} \tilde{C}$, which closely approximates the value $\frac{\sigma_{n-r}(M)}{\sigma_1(M)} \operatorname{cond} C$; to simplify the notation we drop the character "tilde" and write M and C instead of $\tilde{M}$ and $\tilde{C}$ assuming that $\operatorname{rank} M = n - r$ and $C = M + UV^H$. Our next theorem is readily verified.

THEOREM 6.1. *Let $M = S\Sigma T^H$ be full SVD of an $n \times n$ matrix M of a rank ρ where $\rho < n$, S and T are unitary matrices, $S, T \in \mathbb{C}^{n \times n}$, $\Sigma = \operatorname{diag}(\Sigma_M, O_{r,r})$ is an $n \times n$ diagonal matrix, $r = n - \rho$, and $\Sigma_M = \operatorname{diag}(\sigma_j)_{j=1}^{\rho}$ is the $\rho \times \rho$ diagonal matrix of the positive singular values of the matrix M. Suppose $U \in \mathbb{C}^{n \times r}$, $V \in \mathbb{C}^{n \times r}$, and let the $n \times n$ matrix $C = M + UV^H$ be nonsingular. Write*

$$S^H U = \begin{pmatrix} U_\rho \\ U_r \end{pmatrix}, \quad T^H V = \begin{pmatrix} V_\rho \\ V_r \end{pmatrix}, \quad R_U = \begin{pmatrix} I_\rho & U_\rho \\ O & U_r \end{pmatrix},$$

$R_V = \begin{pmatrix} I_\rho & V_\rho \\ O & V_r \end{pmatrix}$ *where U_r and V_r are nonsingular $r \times r$ matrices. Then $R_U \Sigma R_V^H = \Sigma$, $R_U \operatorname{diag}(O_{\rho,\rho}, I_r) R_V^H = S^H UV^H T$, so that*

$$C = S R_U \operatorname{diag}(\Sigma_M, I_r) R_V^H T^H. \quad (6.1)$$

THEOREM 6.2. *Under the assumptions of Theorem 6.1 let $p = \|R_U^{-1}\| \, \|R_V^{-1}\|$. Then (a) $p \ge \frac{\|C^{-1}\|}{\|M^+\|} = \frac{\sigma_{n-r}(M)}{\sigma_n(C)}$ and*

(b) $1 \le p^2 \le (1+(1+\|U\|^2)\|U_r^{-1}\|^2)(1+(1+\|V\|^2)\|V_r^{-1}\|^2)$.

PROOF. First invert matrix equation (6.1) and obtain that $C^{-1} = T R_V^{-H} \operatorname{diag}(\Sigma_M^{-1}, I_r) R_U^{-1} S^H$. Consequently $\|C^{-1}\| \le \|T\| \, \|R_V^{-H}\| \, \|\operatorname{diag}(\Sigma_M^{-1}, I_r)\| \, \|R_U^{-1}\| \, \|S^H\|$. Now substitute $\|T\| = \|S^H\| = 1$ and $\|\operatorname{diag}(\Sigma_M^{-1}, I_r)\| = 1/\sigma_{n-r}(M) = \|M^+\|$ (recall that $\sigma_{n-r}(M) \le 1$ by assumption), and obtain part (a). Combine the equations $R_U^{-1} = \begin{pmatrix} I_\rho & -U_\rho U_r^{-1} \\ O & U_r^{-1} \end{pmatrix}$ and $R_V^{-1} = \begin{pmatrix} I_\rho & -V_\rho V_r^{-1} \\ O & V_r^{-1} \end{pmatrix}$ and obtain part (b). $\square$

We can bound the ratio $\frac{\|C\|}{\|M\|}$ from above and below by scaling the matrices M, U and V, e.g., $\frac{1}{2} \le \frac{\|C\|}{\|M\|} \le \frac{3}{2}$ if $\|M\| = 2\|UV^H\| = 1$. It remains to deduce a probabilistic upper bound on the value $p \ge \frac{\|C^{-1}\|}{\|M^+\|}$.

We first choose two matrices $\bar{U}, \bar{V} \in \mathcal{G}_{k,\sigma}^{n,r}$ where the ratio k/σ is large, e.g., where $k = 2n\sigma$, so that we expect that all the entries lie near the value k and therefore $\|\bar{U}\bar{V}^H\| \approx k^2 rn$. Then we scale both matrices $\bar{U}$ and $\bar{V}$ by a factor f such that

$2f^2\|\bar{U}\bar{V}^H\| = 1$, expecting that $f \approx 1/(2k\sqrt{rn})$, and define the matrices $U = f\bar{U}$ and $V = f\bar{U}$ such that $2\|UV^H\| = 1$, expecting that $\|U\| \approx \|V\| \approx 1/2$.

Finally the following theorem supplies probabilistic upper bounds on the norms $\|U_r^{-1}\| = \frac{1}{\sigma_r(U_r)}$ and $\|V_r^{-1}\| = \frac{1}{\sigma_r(V_r)}$.

Theorem 6.3. *Let U, V, U_r, and V_r denote the four matrices in Theorem 6.1, suppose $m = n$ and Theorem 5.4 holds (a) for $r_G = r$, $G = (O \mid I_r)S^H$, and $W = U$ (in this case $GW = U_r$) as well as (b) for $r_G = r$, $G = (O \mid I_r)T^H$, $W = V$ (in this case $GW = V_r$). Then we have (a) $F_{U_r}(y) \leq 2.35\, y\sqrt{r}/\sigma$ and (b) $F_{V_r}(y) \leq 2.35\, y\sqrt{r}/\sigma$.*

Proof. Apply part (a) of Theorem 5.4 for $r_G = r$, $G = (O \mid I_r)S^H$, and $W = U$ to obtain $F_{U_r}(y) \leq \frac{2.35 y\sqrt{r}}{\sigma_r((O\mid I_r)S^H)\sigma}$. $\sigma_r((O \mid I_r)S^H) = 1$ because S^H is a unitary matrix. Substitute this equation into the above bound on $F_{U_r}(y)$ and obtain part (a) of Theorem 6.3. Similarly prove part (b). $\square$

Remark 6.1. *For $r = 1$ the matrices U and V turn into Gaussian random vectors, whereas U_r and V_r turn into the scalar products of these vectors with some fixed vectors having norm one. Then $F_{U_r}(y) \leq \sqrt{\frac{2}{\pi}}\frac{y}{\sigma}$ and $F_{V_r}(y) \leq \sqrt{\frac{2}{\pi}}\frac{y}{\sigma}$ (see [26, Lemma A.2]).*

Corollary 6.1. *Under assumptions of Theorem 6.3 the matrix C is singular with probability zero.*

Proof. Theorem 6.3 implies that the matrices U_r and V_r are singular with probability zero. Therefore the corollary follows from equation (6.1). $\square$

One can deduce from Theorem 2.1 that the matrix C is likely to be nonsingular where the entries of the matrices U and V have been uniformly sampled from a set of a large cardinality in any ring.

Theorems 6.2 and 6.3 and Corollary 6.1 together imply that under the assumed randomization and scaling, the matrix C is expected to be nonsingular and to have condition number of order $\frac{\sigma_1(M)}{\sigma_{n-r}(M)}$, versus $\operatorname{cond} M = \frac{\sigma_1(M)}{\sigma_n(M)}$.

The small neighborhood of a singular matrix $M \in R^{n \times n}$ having a positive nullity r is mostly filled with nonsingular ill conditioned matrices $\tilde{M}$ having numerical nullity r. By extending the above analysis we obtain that the additive preprocessing $\tilde{M} \to \tilde{C} = M + UV^T$ with $U, V \in \mathcal{G}_{0,\mu}^{n\times r}$ is expected to map $\tilde{M}$ into a nonsingular matrix $\tilde{C}$ having condition number of order $\frac{\sigma_1(M)}{\sigma_{n-r}(M)} \approx \frac{\sigma_1(\tilde{M})}{\sigma_{n-r}(\tilde{M})}$. Thus the map is expected to be preconditioning, and if so, then the Sherman–Morrison–Woodbury formula $M^{-1} = C^{-1} + C^{-1}UG^{-1}V^HC^{-1}$, $G = I_r - V^HC^{-1}U$, [13, page 50] would reduce the inversion of the ill conditioned matrix $\tilde{M}$ (as well as the solution of a linear system $\tilde{M}\mathbf{x} = \mathbf{b}$) to similar operations with the better conditioned matrices $\tilde{C}$ and G.

The reduction requires highly accurate computation of the $r \times r$ matrix G, but by applying iterative refinement we can still dramatically decrease the overall time cost of inverting the matrix M and solving a linear system $M\mathbf{y} = \mathbf{b}$ (see [23]). Similar progress can be obtained based on randomized augmentation (see [24]). The cited deterministic and randomized preconditioning methods in [24, Sections 8 and 10], which cover the matrices having a large numerical nullity, employ neither Sherman–Morrison–Woodbury formula nor iterative refinement.

Theorems 6.2 and 6.3 and Corollary 6.1 can be extended to show that the matrix C tends to have generic rank and conditioning profiles as long as all leading blocks have nullity and numerical nullity at most r.

Indeed assume matrices U and V in $\mathcal{G}_{0,1}^{n\times r}$ and a matrix M scaled so that its norm is neither large nor small. Then also the $k \times k$ leading principal blocks $C^{(k)}$ of the matrix C for all k, $k = 1, \dots, n$, are expected to have condition numbers of order at most $\frac{\sigma_1(M)}{\sigma_{n-\min\{k,r\}}(M)}$.

To deduce this bound write $C^{(k)} = (I_k, O)C(I_k, O)^T = (I_k, O)M(I_k, O)^T + U_kV_k^H = M^{(k)} + U_kV_k^H$ where $U_k = (I_k, O)U$ and $V_k = (I_k, O)V$. Then write $\rho_k = \operatorname{rank} A^{(k)}$, $k' = k - \rho_k$, $U_{k'} = U_k(I_{k'}, O)^T$, $V_{k'} = V_k(I_{k'}, O)^T$, $U_k = U_{k'} + W_k$, $V_k = V_{k'} + Z_k$, and $C_k' = M^{(k)} + U_kV_{k'}^T$. Next extend factorization (6.1) and other results of this section from the matrix pair $\{M, C\}$ to the matrix pair $\{M^{(k)}, C_k'\}$. Finally deduce that the transition $C_k' \longrightarrow C$, that is addition of the scaled product $W_kZ_k^H$ of two random matrices to the matrix C_k', is not likely to increase the condition number $\operatorname{cond} C_k'$ substantially (if it increases at all) (cf. [27, Section 4, case 3]).

We remark that the class of matrices with small nullities and numerical nullities is large. In particular the ratio $\frac{\sigma_1(M)}{\sigma_{n-r}(M)}$ is large only for matrices M lying near the algebraic variety $\mathbb{V}_r$ of matrices M of ranks at most $n - r - 1$, that is such that $\sigma_{n-r}(M) = 0$. Such a variety is empty where $r = n - 1$ and generally has dimension $n^2 - (r+1)^2$.

Finally, preprocessing $M \to C = M + UV^T$ for $U, V \in \mathcal{G}_{\mu,\sigma}^{n\times r}$ and a small integer r little afffects the structure of the matrix M because $\operatorname{dr}(C) \leq \operatorname{dr}(M) + r$.

7. NUMERICAL EXPERIMENTS

Our numerical experiments with random Toeplitz and Toeplitz-like matrices (the contribution of the second and the third authors) have been performed in the Graduate Center of the City University of New York on a Dell server with a dual core 1.86 GHz Xeon processor and 2G memory running Windows Server 2003 R2. The test Fortran code was compiled with the GNU gfortran compiler within the Cygwin environment. Random numbers were generated with the random_number intrinsic Fortran function, assuming the uniform probability distribution over the range $\{x : -1 \leq x < 1\}$.

Conditioning tests.

We computed the condition numbers of $n \times n$ random real and complex Toeplitz matrices for $n = 2^k$, $k = 5, 6, \dots$ whose entries had real and imaginary parts sampled at random in the same range $[-1, 1)$. We performed 100 tests for each dimension n and represented the test results for complex inputs in Table 1, omitting similar results for real Toeplitz matrices because of the space limitation. The table displays the minimum, mean and maximum of the computed condition numbers $\|M\|_1 \|M^{-1}\|_1$ for $n \times n$ Toeplitz matrices M. (The 1-norms $\|M\|_1$ and $\|M^{-1}\|_1$ were easier to compute, and we consistently had $1 \leq \|M\|_1/\|M\|_2 < 10$, $1 \leq \|M^{-1}\|_1/\|M^{-1}\|_2 < 3$ for $n = 2^k$, $k = 5, 6, 7, 8, 9, 10$.)

Solution of Toeplitz-like linear systems with randomized preconditioning.

We solved 1000 linear systems of equations $M\mathbf{x} = \mathbf{b}$ for each input class with vectors $\mathbf{b}$ having random coordinates from the range $[-1, 1)$ and matrices M specified below. We specially created Toeplitz-like input for which the MBA algorithm failed, and we fixed the problem by means of randomized circulant preconditioners.

Input Matrices:

$M = \begin{pmatrix} M_k & A \\ B & C \end{pmatrix}$ is an $n \times n$ matrix, M_k is a $k \times k$ matrix, A, B, and C are random Toeplitz matrices such that $\|A\| \approx \|B\| \approx \|C\| \approx \|M_k\| \approx 1$, $n = 2^s$, $s = 5, 6, 7, 8, 10$, and $k = n/2$. $M_k = c(T \mid TS)$ for random Toeplitz matrices T of size $k \times (k-4)$ and S of size $(k-4) \times h$ for a positive scalar c such that $\|M_k\| \approx 1$. (M_k were Toeplitz-like matrices with nullity four.)

For multiplicative preconditioners C we use $n \times n$ circulant multipliers, each defined by its first column with the n entries $+1$ and -1 chosen at random.

Table 2 shows the test results for the solution of linear systems of equations where we apply the MBA algorithm to the systems $M\mathbf{y} = \mathbf{b}$ and $CM\mathbf{y} = C\mathbf{b}$. The table displays the minimum, maximum and average values (mean) of the relative residual norm $\|CM\mathbf{x} - C\mathbf{b}\|/\|C\mathbf{b}\|$. We show these data obtained before we performed iterative refinement and after the first and sometimes also the third step of it. We continued iterative refinement until we decreased the output residual norms to the level of 10^{-14}. The column **iter** shows the numbers of steps of iterative refinement.

Due to the singularity of the leading block M_k, the relative residual norms in the output of the MBA algorithm performed without preconditioning stayed in the range $[10, 10^8]$ and were too large to allow iterative refinement of the computed solution. With our randomized structured preconditioning, however, these norms were always small enough to allow rapid iterative refinement to the level achieved in Gaussian elimination with partial pivoting.

We observed limited growth of the relative residual norm of the output as the input size grew.

We represented the input matrices M and performed our tests with double precision, but then repeated the computations for the entries of the matrix M truncated to the single precision. In this case double-precision multipication by our multipliers was error-free. The residual norms remained essentially at the same level as for the double precision input, so that the impact of rounding errors at the elimination stage dominated their impact at the stage of multiplication by preconditioners.

Table 1: condition numbers $\mathrm{cond}_1(M)$ of random complex Toeplitz matrices M

n	min	mean	max
256	9.1×10^2	9.2×10^3	1.3×10^5
512	2.3×10^3	3.0×10^4	2.4×10^5
1024	5.6×10^3	7.0×10^4	1.8×10^6
2048	1.7×10^4	1.8×10^5	4.2×10^6
4096	4.3×10^4	2.7×10^5	1.9×10^6
8192	8.8×10^4	1.2×10^6	1.3×10^7

8. DISCUSSION

Our randomized additive preprocessing and augmentation are expected to regularize and precondition computations

Table 2: residual norms of the solutions of Toeplitz-like linear systems

n	iter	min	max	mean
32	0	7.8×10^{-15}	1.6×10^{-10}	3.6×10^{-12}
32	1	8.3×10^{-16}	5.7×10^{-12}	7.4×10^{-14}
64	0	5.9×10^{-14}	1.6×10^{-9}	2.4×10^{-11}
64	1	1.7×10^{-15}	7.3×10^{-13}	4.9×10^{-14}
128	0	3.1×10^{-13}	1.9×10^{-8}	3.5×10^{-10}
128	1	5.2×10^{-15}	1.3×10^{-10}	1.6×10^{-12}
256	0	2.7×10^{-12}	3.6×10^{-9}	1.7×10^{-10}
256	1	8.8×10^{-15}	2.8×10^{-12}	1.6×10^{-13}
1024	0	4.0×10^{-10}	3.8×10^{-9}	1.5×10^{-9}
1024	1	1.2×10^{-13}	5.1×10^{-13}	2.3×10^{-13}

with rank deficient and ill conditioned general and structured input matrices and thus to accelerate substantially the known algorithms such as the MBA numerical algorithm for structured matrices. The resulting speedup is immediately extended to some fundamental computations with polynomials, e.g., computing their GCDs and AGCDs. This can be a sample work in symbolic computations involving numerical methods (cf. [19], [4], [20], [10], [5], [15]). We refer the reader to [22]–[24], and the references therein on various further applications of our randomized preprocessing to fundamental computations with general and structured matrices.

There is a number of ideas behind our current progress, and we expect to reveal a wide area of their applications when we combine them with other known and new effective techniques.

Here is a sample tentative direction, partly motivated by the observed power of matrix augmentation, which increases the number of constraints versus the original system of equations. The computation of AGCDs can be reduced to solving (by means of the SNTLN techniques) any of the two distinct nonlinear systems of equations, based on the Bezout and Sylvester representation of the GCD problem. In both cases we deal with matrix structures of Toeplitz–Hankel type, belonging to the MBA domain [3]. By following the Principle of Arming with Constraints (PAC) in [21], we can combine the two systems of constraints into a single system with the hope to improve global convergence of Newton's iteration when we apply it to this larger system.

The proposal of the PAC in [21] was also motivated by the observed efficiency of root-finders for a univariate polynomial of a degree n where they reduced the root-finding task to employing a larger Army of n Constraints, based on solving the Vieta's equations, convolution equation, or approximating the eigenvectors of the associated companion or generalized companion matrices. In a sense this principle reverses the direction of the Gröbner basis and elimination techniques that reduce the solution of a system of multivariate polynomial equations to root-finding for a univariate polynomial.

Enlarging the set of constraints should help resisting random impacts that otherwise could more easily push the iterations astray from their convergence course. The PAC explains the power of the SNTLN techniques and generalizes them as well as the cited ad hoc examples of root-finders and matrix augmentation to suggest a systematic method for enhancing global convergence power of iterative algorithms.

The paper [21] also proposes a more limited idea for the simplification of root-finding as well as the computation of GCDs and AGCDs in the important case where the degree of one of the two polynomials is small. In that case as well as for Newton's refinement of splitting out a linear or quadratic factor of a polynomial, one must solve the associated nonsingular Sylvester linear system of n equations, and [21] proposes to reduce this task to computing the associated partial fraction decompositions.

This recipe enables the solution of such linear systems by using $O(n)$ ops versus order of $n \log^2 n$ numerically unstable ops or n^2 numerically stable ops, required for solving a nonsingular Sylvester linear systems of n equations whose matrix is defined by a pair of polynomials of degrees k and $n - k$, respectively, for an unrestricted k.

9. REFERENCES

[1] J. R. Bunch, Stability of Methods for Solving Toeplitz Systems of Equations, *SIAM Journal on Scientific and Statistical Computing*, **6(2)**, 349–364, 1985.

[2] R. R. Bitmead, B. D. O. Anderson, Asymptotically Fast Solution of Toeplitz and Related Systems of Linear Equations, *Linear Algebra and Its Applications*, **34**, 103–116, 1980.

[3] D. A. Bini, P. Boito, A Fast Algorithm for Approximate Polynomial GCD Based on Structured Matrix Computations, *Operator Theory: Advances and Applications*, **199**, 155–173, Birkhäuser Verlag, 2010.

[4] D. Bini, V. Y. Pan, *Polynomial and Matrix Computations, Volume 1: Fundamental Algorithms*, Birkhäuser, Boston, 1994.

[5] D. A. Bini, V. Y. Pan, and J. Verschelde (editors), Special Issue on Symbolic–Numerical Algorithms, *Theoretical Computer Science*, **409, 2**, 155–157, 2008.

[6] J. Demmel, The Probability That a Numerical Analysis Problem Is Difficult, *Math. of Computation*, **50**, 449–480, 1988.

[7] R. A. Demillo, R. J. Lipton, A Probabilistic Remark on Algebraic Program Testing, *Information Processing Letters*, **7, 4**, 193–195, 1978.

[8] K. R. Davidson, S. J. Szarek, Local Operator Theory, Random Matrices, and Banach Spaces, in *Handbook on the Geometry of Banach Spaces* (W. B. Johnson and J. Lindenstrauss editors), pages 317–368, North Holland, Amsterdam, 2001.

[9] A. Edelman, Eigenvalues and Condition Numbers of Random Matrices, *SIAM J. on Matrix Analysis and Applications*, **9, 4**, 543–560, 1988.

[10] I. Z. Emiris, B. Mourrain, V. Y. Pan, Guest Editors, Special Issue on Algebraic and Numerical Algorithms, *Theoretical Computer Science*, **315, 2–3**, 307–672, 2004.

[11] I. Gohberg, T. Kailath, V. Olshevsky, Fast Gaussian Elimination with Partial Pivoting for Matrices with Displacement Structure, *Math. of Computation*, **64**, 1557–1576, 1995.

[12] I. Gohberg, I. Koltracht, Efficient Algorithm for Toeplitz plus Hankel Matrices, *Integral Equations and Operator Theory*, **12**, 136–142, 1989.

[13] G. H. Golub, C. F. Van Loan, *Matrix Computations*, The Johns Hopkins University Press, Baltimore, Maryland, 1996 (third edition).

[14] N. J. Higham, *Accuracy and Stability in Numerical Analysis*, SIAM, Philadelphia, 2002 (second edition).

[15] I. S. Kotsireas, B. Mourrain, V. Y. Pan (editors), Special Issue on Symbolic and Numerical Algorithms, *Theor. Computer Science*, **412, 16**, 1443–1544, 2011.

[16] E. Kaltofen, B. D. Saunders, On Wiedemann's Method for Solving Sparse Linear Systems, *Proceedings of AAECC–5, Lecture Notes in Computer Science*, **536**, 29–38, Springer, Berlin, 1991.

[17] M. Morf, Doubling Algorithms for Toeplitz and Related Equations, *Proc. IEEE Intern. Conf. ASSP*, 954–959, IEEE Press, Piscataway, New Jersey, 1980.

[18] V. Y. Pan, On Computations with Dense Structured Matrices, *Math. of Computation*, **55(191)**, 179–190, 1990. Also in Proceedings of International Symposium on Symbolic and Algebraic Computation (ISSAC'89), 34-42, ACM Press, New York, 1989.

[19] V. Y. Pan, Complexity of Computations with Matrices and Polynomials, *SIAM Review*, **34, 2**, 225–262, 1992.

[20] V. Y. Pan, *Structured Matrices and Polynomials: Unified Superfast Algorithms*, Birkhäuser/Springer, Boston/New York, 2001.

[21] V. Y. Pan, Acceleration of Newton's Polynomial Factorization: Army of Constraints, Convolution, Sylvester Matrices, and Partial Fraction Decomposition, Tech. Report TR 2011004, *Ph.D. Program in Computer Science, Graduate Center, CUNY*. Available at http://www.cs.gc.cuny.edu/tr/techreport.php?id=352

[22] V. Y. Pan, G. Qian, Randomized Preprocessing of Homogeneous Linear Systems, *Linear Algebra and Its Applications*, **432**, 3272–3318, 2010.

[23] V. Y. Pan, G. Qian, On Solving Linear Systems with Randomized Augmentation, Tech. Report TR 2010009, *Ph.D. Program in Comp. Sci., Graduate Center, CUNY*, 2010. Available at http://www.cs.gc.cuny.edu/tr/techreport.php?id=352

[24] V. Y. Pan, G. Qian, A. Zheng, Randomized Preconditioning of Linear Systems of Equations, Tech. Report TR 2010012, *Ph.D. Program in Computer Science, Graduate Center, CUNY*, 2010. Available at http://www.cs.gc.cuny.edu/tr/techreport.php?id=352

[25] J. T. Schwartz, Fast Probabilistic Algorithms for Verification of Polynomial Identities, *Journal of ACM*, **27, 4**, 701–717, 1980.

[26] A. Sankar, D. Spielman, S.-H. Teng, Smoothed Analysis of the Condition Numbers and Growth Factors of Matrices, *SIAM Journal on Matrix Analysis*, **28, 2**, 446–476, 2006.

[27] X. Wang, Affect of Small Rank Modification on the Condition Number of a Matrix, *Computer and Math. (with Applications)*, **54**, 819–825, 2007.

[28] M. Wschebor, Smoothed Analysis of $\kappa(a)$, *J. of Complexity*, **20**, 97–107, 2004.

[29] R. E. Zippel, Probabilistic Algorithms for Sparse Polynomials, *Proceedings of EUROSAM'79, Lecture Notes in Computer Science*, **72**, 216–226, Springer, Berlin, 1979.

Fast Fourier Transforms over Poor Fields

Alexey Pospelov

Computer Science Department, Saarland University
Saarbrücken, Germany
pospelov@cs.uni-saarland.de

ABSTRACT

We present a new algebraic algorithm for computing the discrete Fourier transform over arbitrary fields. It computes DFTs of infinitely many orders n in $O(n \log n)$ algebraic operations, while the complexity of a straightforward application of the known FFT algorithms can be $\Omega(n^{1.5})$ for such n. Our algorithm is a novel combination of the classical FFT algorithms, and is never slower than any of the latter.

As an application we come up with an efficient way of computing DFTs of high orders in finite field extensions which can further boost polynomial multiplication algorithms. We relate the complexities of the DFTs of such orders with the complexity of polynomial multiplication.

Categories and Subject Descriptors

F.2.1 [**Analysis of Algorithms and Problem Complexity**]: Numerical Algorithms and Problems—*Computation of transforms, Computations in finite fields, Computations on polynomials*; G.4 [**Mathematical Software**]: Algorithm design and analysis, Efficiency; I.1.2 [**Symbolic and Algebraic Manipulation**]: Algorithms—*Algebraic algorithms, Analysis of algorithms*

General Terms

Algorithms, Performance, Theory

Keywords

Fast Fourier transforms, complexity of polynomial multiplication, algebraic complexity, finite fields

1. INTRODUCTION

The discrete Fourier transform (DFT) is a map which evaluates a given polynomial at distinct roots of unity of the same order. The applications of the DFT are very broad, ranging from spectral analysis and data compression to fast integer and polynomial multiplication. The latter involves

the DFTs over *arbitrary* fields, which is the main topic of this paper.

DFTs of specific lengths can be computed efficiently by so-called fast Fourier transforms (FFTs). The most popular FFT is the Cooley-Tukey algorithm [10], whose idea traces back to Gauss. It is used as an important building block for the fast integer and polynomial multiplication algorithms [24, 23, 6, 12, 11]. However, there exist certain limitations which make the Cooley-Tukey FFT algorithm in its original form not suitable for the improvement of the currently known upper bounds for the mentioned problems [20].

There exist DFTs over some fields, where all known FFT methods fail, e.g., the DFTs of prime lengths over *arbitrary* fields. However, if the *ground field*, that is, the field, over which we are considering the DFT, has extra roots of unity of special order, then the DFTs of prime lengths can be computed efficiently. This was proved first in the celebrated paper by Rader [22], and generalized for arbitrary lengths by Bluestein in [4]. These algorithms are not applicable over the *poor* ground fields, *i.e.,* fields lacking extra roots of unity.

1.1 Background

In what follows k will always stand for a field.

Let R be a ring. For an integer $n > 0$, $\omega \in R$ is called an *n-th root of unity* if $\omega^n = 1$. It is called a *principal n-th root of unity* if, additionally, for $1 \le \nu < n$, $1 - \omega^\nu$ is not a zero divisor in R. If R contains a principal n-th root of unity, then the characteristic of R is coprime with n.

If $\omega \in R$ is an n-th principal root of unity then

$$\sum_{i=0}^{n-1} \omega^{ij} = \begin{cases} 0, & \text{if } j \not\equiv 0 \pmod{n}, \\ n, & \text{if } j \equiv 0 \pmod{n}. \end{cases} \qquad (1)$$

If $m \mid n$, then $\omega^{\frac{n}{m}}$ is a principal m-th root of unity. If $\omega \in R$ is a principal n-th root of unity, then $\omega^{-1} = \omega^{n-1}$ is also a principal n-th root of unity in R.

Let R be a ring with a principal n-th root of unity ω. The *discrete Fourier transform* (of length n with respect to ω) of the vector $a := (a_0, \ldots, a_{n-1}) \in R^n$, is the vector $\tilde{a} := (\tilde{a}_0, \ldots, \tilde{a}_{n-1}) \in R^n$, where

$$\tilde{a}_i := \sum_{j=0}^{n-1} a_j \omega^{ij}. \qquad (2)$$

This linear map will be denoted by $\mathrm{DFT}_n^\omega : R^n \to R^n$, such that $\tilde{a} = \mathrm{DFT}_n^\omega(a)$.

We call k *poor* with respect to an integer $n > 0$, if the DFT of length n is defined over k, but the only primitive roots of unity in k are those whose orders divide n.

By (1), we have $\mathrm{DFT}_n^{\omega^{-1}}(\mathrm{DFT}_n^{\omega}(a)) = na$, for all $a \in R^n$. As mentioned before, n is coprime with the characteristic of R, therefore $a = \frac{1}{n}\mathrm{DFT}_n^{\omega^{-1}}(\mathrm{DFT}_n^{\omega}(a))$, and $\frac{1}{n}\mathrm{DFT}_n^{\omega^{-1}}$ is the inverse map for DFT_n^{ω}. This map will be denoted by $\mathrm{IDFT}_n^{\omega} := \frac{1}{n}\mathrm{DFT}_n^{\omega^{-1}}$.

Let x be a variable over R, and $a := (a_0, \ldots, a_{n-1})$ be the vector of coefficients of $a(x) := \sum_{i=0}^{n-1} a_i x^i \in R[x]/(x^n - 1)$. The DFT of order n with respect to ω *of the polynomial* $a(x)$ is the vector $\tilde{a} := (\tilde{a}_0, \ldots, \tilde{a}_{n-1}) = \mathrm{DFT}_n^{\omega}(a) \in R^n$. Note that

$$\tilde{a}_i = a(\omega^i) = a(x) \bmod (x - \omega^i), \qquad 0 \le i < n. \quad (3)$$

We will ambiguously write $\tilde{a} = \mathrm{DFT}_n^{\omega}(a(x))$, and reuse the introduced notation for $\mathrm{DFT}_n^{\omega} : R[x]/(x^n - 1) \to R^n$. We will also reuse the notation $\mathrm{IDFT}_n^{\omega} : R^n \to R[x]/(x^n - 1)$ for the inverse isomorphism. The context will always make this notation each time unambiguos.

It follows from the Chinese Remainder Theorem, that DFT_n^{ω} is an isomorphic map $R[x]/(x^n - 1) \to R^n$. In particular, if the DFT of length n is defined over R, then for all $a(x), b(x) \in R[x]/(x^n - 1)$, their product (in $R[x]/(x^n - 1)$) can be computed via 3 DFTs of length n and a multiplication in R^n, *i.e.*, n multiplications in R via

$$a(x)b(x) = \mathrm{IDFT}_n^{\omega^{-1}}(\mathrm{DFT}_n^{\omega}(a(x)) \cdot \mathrm{DFT}_n^{\omega}(b(x))). \quad (4)$$

1.2 Computational model

In this paper we study *algebraic complexity* of computations.

Let R be a ring, $x_1, \ldots, x_n$ be *input variables* over R, and $f_1, \ldots, f_m \in R[x_1, \ldots, x_n]$ be rational functions over R. A *division-free algebraic algorithm* for $f_1, \ldots, f_m$ is a sequence $\phi = (\phi_{-n+1}, \ldots, \phi_0, \ldots, \phi_\ell)$, such that

- For $-n+1 \le i \le 0$, $\phi_i = x_{n+i}$. The function associated with ϕ_i is $f_{\phi_i}(x_1, \ldots, x_n) = x_{n+i}$;

- For $1 \le i \le \ell$, $\phi_i = u_i \circ_i v_i$, where $\circ_i \in \{+, -, \cdot\}$, and $u_i, v_i \in \{\phi_j\}_{j=-n+1}^{i-1} \cup R$. If $u_i = c_{u_i} \in R$, then the function associated with u_i is $f_{u_i}(x_1, \ldots, x_n) = c_{u_i}$, and let f_{v_i} be defined in the same way if $v_i \in R$. The function associated with ϕ_i is then

$$f_{\phi_i}(x_1, \ldots, x_n) = f_{u_i}(x_1, \ldots, x_n) \circ_i f_{v_i}(x_1, \ldots, x_n);$$

- For each $1 \le \mu \le m$, $f_\mu \in (f_{\phi_{-n+1}}, \ldots, f_{\phi_\ell})$.

ℓ is called the (algebraic) *complexity* of ϕ. The minimal complexity of an algebraic algorithm for a family of rational functions is called *algebraic complexity* of this family.

Algebraic complexity assumes that each binary algebraic operation over R has unit cost. This metric is more abstract than, e.g., bit-complexity, but it also benefits from being less dependent on a particular computer architecture or implementation, see [5, p. 2] for more discussion on this topic.

1.3 Fast Fourier transforms

There are many algorithms for fast computation of the DFT called fast Fourier transforms (FFTs). For a good review of theoretical developments and generalizations we recommend [8], and for numerous algorithms we refer the reader to [18]. In this section we outline the most important approaches which lead under rather general conditions to a qualitative boost for the computation of the DFT.

In what follows ω_i stands for an i-th principal root of unity for a natural i. Algebraic complexity of the DFT of length n over k will be denoted by $D_k(n)$. For any n we have

$$D_k(n) \le 2n^2 - 3n + 1. \quad (5)$$

This follows directly from the trivial computation procedure according to (2) (we do not have to multiply by ω_n^{ij}, if i or j equals 0).

1.3.1 Factorization-based algorithms

The first approach lies behind the prime-factor algorithm (also called the Good-Thomas FFT) [14, 27] and the Cooley-Tukey FFT [10], [8, Sect. 4.1], [18, Sect. 4.2] algorithms, and gives an $O(n \log n)$ upper bound for the complexity of the computation of the DFT of *smooth* lengths n.[1]

The Cooley-Tukey FFT algorithm reduces the DFT of length

$$n = n_1^{d_1} \cdots n_s^{d_s} \quad (6)$$

to nd_σ/n_σ DFTs of length n_σ, for $1 \le \sigma \le s$, and at most $n \log n$ multiplications by powers of ω_n, called *twiddle factors*. Therefore,

$$D_k(n) \le n \sum_{\sigma=1}^{s} \frac{d_\sigma}{n_\sigma} D_k(n_\sigma) + n \log n.$$

For a power of 2 it gives a better bound:

$$D_k(2^d) \le \frac{3}{2} n \log n - n + 1. \quad (7)$$

If $n_1, \ldots, n_s$ in (6) are pairwise coprime and $d_\sigma = 1$, for $1 \le \sigma \le s$, then the prime-factor algorithm [14, 27] allows to get rid of the multiplications by twiddle factors:

$$D_k(n) \le n \sum_{\sigma=1}^{s} \frac{D_k(n_\sigma)}{n_\sigma}.$$

This comes at the expense of memory indexing, which can dominate the algebraic cost [26, 7]. However, this is not a matter of algebraic complexity.

Many variants of these algorithms and their combinations are widely accessible in the literature. However, all of them are only efficient if n does not have large prime factors.

1.3.2 Convolution-based algorithms

Rader's FFT algorithm [22], [8, Sect. 4.2], [18, Sect. 4.3] reduces the DFT of a prime order p over k to a cyclic convolution of order $p-1$, $2p-2$ additions, and $p-2$ multiplications by powers of ω. The convolution can be computed by 3 DFTs of order $N = p-1$ or $N \ge 2p-3$, if such a DFT is defined over k, N multiplications by polynomials in ω_p and ω_N, and $p-1$ multiplications by $\frac{1}{N}$. For a fixed p, one of the three DFTs is applied to a constant sequence. Therefore, it may be precomputed, but we will still count its cost:

$$D_k(p) \le 3D_k(N) + N + 4p - 5, \ N = p-1 \text{ or } N \ge 2p-3. \quad (8)$$

Therefore, if $D_k(N) = O(N \log N)$, and $N = O(p)$, then $D_k(p) = O(p \log p)$. Note that the necessary condition to apply Rader's FFT algorithm is the existence of $\omega_N \in k$.

Bluestein's algorithm [4], [8, Sect. 4.3] is applicable for arbitrary orders n. It requires however that $\omega_{2n} \in k$. In this

---

[1] n is called *A-smooth*, if all prime divisors of n do not exceed A. A set of integers is called *smooth*, if there exists such $A = O(1)$, that each integer from the set is A-smooth.

case it is possible to reduce the DFT of order n to a cyclic convolution of order n and $4n-3$ multiplications by powers of ω_{2n}. The convolution can be computed by 3 DFTs of order $N \geq 2n-1$, N multiplications by polynomials in ω_{2n}, and n scalar multiplications by $\frac{1}{N}$. Therefore,

$$D_k(n) \leq 3D_k(N) + N + 5n - 3, \quad N \geq 2n-1. \quad (9)$$

We mention finally that the enabling conditions for Rader's and Bluestein's FFT algorithms do not hold for all k. For example, in $k = \mathbb{Q}(\omega_n)$, for $n \geq 3$, which is the simple extension of $\mathbb{Q}$ with $\omega_n \in \mathbb{C}$, we have $\omega_{2n} \notin k$, and $\omega_{n'} \notin k$, for $n' \in \{n-1\} \cup [2n-3, \infty)$.

1.3.3 DFT over finite fields

A completely different technique is based on properties of finite fields. By carefully picking $I \subset \{0, \ldots, n-1\}$, $f_I(x) := \prod_{i \in I}(x - \omega^i)$ can be a relatively sparse polynomial. In this case we can compute first $a_I(x) := a(x) \bmod f_I(x)$, and then compute the values of $a_I(x)$ at $\{\omega^i\}_{i \in I}$. The Wang-Zhu's algorithm [28] recursively partitions the set of indexes $\{0, \ldots, n-1\}$ in a smart way so that all f_I's are sparse over a finite field. This leads to the upper bound

$$D_{\mathbb{F}_{p^d}}(p^d - 1) \leq \frac{1}{2}p^d(d^2 + 1),$$

which is $D_{\mathbb{F}_{p^d}}(n) = O(n \log^2 n)$, if we denote $n = p^d - 1$. This way is slower than the desired $O(n \log n)$, but it is independent of the prime decomposition of n and of the existence of special roots of unity in $\mathbb{F}_{p^d}$.

Another way to achieve an $O(n \log^2 n)$ algorithm for the computation of the DFT of order $n = p^d - 1$ over $\mathbb{F}_{p^d}$ is due to Preparata and Sarwate [21]. Their technique is based on modeling the approximate complex field arithmetic over finite fields.

1.4 Polynomial multiplication

A classical problem in computer algebra and algebraic complexity theory is the complexity of polynomial multiplication over arbitrary fields. The goal is an algorithm of the smallest algebraic complexity which computes the coefficients of the product of two polynomials over k.

The DFT plays a key role in the design of fast polynomial and integer multiplications algorithms, see [5, Sect. 2.1, 2.2], [13, Ch. 8]. The well-known Schönhage-Strassen algorithm for integer and polynomial multiplication [24], Schönhage's version for the polynomial multiplication over fields of characteristic 2 [23], the Cantor-Kaltofen algorithm for polynomial multiplication over arbitrary algebras [6], all use the DFT to reduce the multiplication of two degree n polynomials to $\sim 2 \lceil \sqrt{n} \rceil$ multiplications of degree $\sim \lceil \sqrt{n} \rceil$ polynomials. This leads to the rough recursive inequality

$$P_k(n) \leq 2\lceil \sqrt{n} \rceil P_k(\lceil \sqrt{n} \rceil) + O(D_k(n)), \quad (10)$$

where $P_k(n)$ denotes the algebraic complexity of multiplication of two degree n polynomials, and $D_k(n)$ stands for the algebraic complexity of the DFT of order n over k. The solution $P_k(n) = O(n \log n \log \log n)$ is currently the best known upper bound for the complexity of polynomial multiplication over generic fields. Over fields which are reach enough on roots of unity, the $O(n \log n)$ upper bound for the same problem is easily derived by a DFT-based algorithm via (4), [5, Sect. 2.1]. Improving the quality of the FFT procedures used in these algorithms is a known way

to improve performance and memory requirements of such polynomial multiplication algorithms, see, e.g., [15].

Fürer's algorithm for integer multiplication [12] uses DFT with recursive integer multiplications to reduce the multiplication of two length n integers to $O\left(\frac{n}{\log n \log \log n}\right)$ multiplications of length $\lceil \log^2 n \rceil$ integers. Denoting by $I(n)$ the bit complexity of multiplication of two length n integers, the complexity of Fürer's algorithm implies

$$I(n) = O\left(D_{\mathbb{C}}(n) + \frac{n}{\log n \log \log n} I(\lceil \log^2 n \rceil)\right).$$

The solution is $I(n) = n \log n \cdot 2^{O(\log^* (n))}$, where $\log^* n$ is the iterated logarithm[2], the best currently known upper bound for $I(n)$. A different approach of the same complexity for the multiplication of integers was proposed in [11]. The latter algorithm is also based on the DFT.

A cousin problem is the complexity of multiplication in finite field extensions. Elements of the finite field with q^n elements $\mathbb{F}_{q^n}$ can be represented as polynomials of degree $n-1$ over $\mathbb{F}_q$. The problem is to find an efficient procedure for the multiplication in $\mathbb{F}_{q^n}$, where all operations of unit cost are binary arithmetical operations over $\mathbb{F}_q$. Afanassiev and Davydov proved in [1] the upper bounds of $O(n \log^{\log_2 3} n)$ and $O(n \log n)$ for several instances of this problem. The backbone of their algorithm are the FFTs over finite fields.

Because of the obvious similarities and multiple links between these problems and their existing solutions, the natural question is if the Fürer's (or a better) upper bound can be proved for the complexity of polynomial multiplication. Further reduction of a polynomial multiplication to more multiplications of polynomials of smaller degrees would improve the Schönhage-Strassen's upper bound, which is a long-standing open problem [24, 19]. However, there are several obstacles on this way. Over the rational field the complexity of a DFT-based polynomial multiplication algorithm cannot be substantially smaller than Schönhage-Strassen's upper bound, see [20] for more discussion on this topic.

The idea of all of the mentioned fast multiplication algorithms can be generalized as follows [20]. To multiply two degree $n-1$ polynomials over k, represent the inputs as polynomials of degree m over an algebraic ring extension $R \supset k$, such that $[R : k] \cdot m = n$. R and m are chosen in such a way that the DFT of order m is defined over R, and is computable in $O(n \log n)$ steps over k. An important detail about the Schönhage-Strassen, Schönhage's, and the Cantor-Kaltofen algorithms is that the DFT of order m there has complexity $O(m \log m)$ over R, and all necessary operations in R can be computed in $O([R : k])$ operations over k.

Over a field of characteristic $p > 0$ an algebraic ring extension $R \supset k$ of degree l admits the DFT of order $m = p^l - 1$. If the latter were computable in $O(ml \log(ml))$ operations over k, similarly as in (10) this would lead to

$$P_k(n) \leq \left\lceil \frac{2n}{\log n} \right\rceil P_k(\lceil \log n \rceil) + O(n \log n),$$

which results in $P_k(n) = O(n \log n)$. Even a weaker version would do: for some constant c, R should admit the DFT of order $\Omega(l^c)$, and there should be a way to reduce degree n polynomial multiplication to roughly $dn^{1-1/c}$ degree $\lceil n^{1/c} \rceil$

---

[2]Iterated logarithm is a very slowly growing function defined as $\log^* 1 := 0$, and $\log^*(n+1) := 1 + \log^*(\lfloor \log n \rfloor)$.

polynomial multiplications, and $d < c$; the DFT should have complexity $O(l^c \log l)$ over k. We will show that our algorithm comes close to this goal.

1.5 Summary of results

We present an algorithm for the computation of DFTs which is a novel combination of Cooley-Tukey's, Rader's and Bluestein's FFT methods. Its algebraic complexity for the DFTs of infinitely many lengths n is $O(n \log n)$, while the complexity of former methods can be $\Omega(n^{1.5})$ for such n. For general n our algorithm is never slower than any of the previously known methods, since any of the latter can naturally be used as its subroutine.

We apply the new algorithm for the computation of DFTs over finite field extensions. We pose two open questions, either being answered positively would result in a desired $O(n \log n)$ algorithm for degree n polynomial multiplication over arbitrary fields of characteristic different from 0 and 2.

2. FAST FOURIER TRANSFORMS OVER POOR FIELDS

2.1 Motivating example

Let $p > 2$ be a prime, $m := 1 + \lceil \log p \rceil$, and $n := 2^m p$. Note that

$$2p \le 2^m < 4p, \quad \tfrac{1}{2}\log n + \tfrac{1}{2} \le m = \left\lfloor \tfrac{1}{2}\log n + 1 \right\rfloor. \quad (11)$$

Consider the simple extension of $\mathbb{Q}$ with a primitive n-th root of unity $\omega_n \in \mathbb{C}$, $k := \mathbb{Q}(\omega_n)$. We have $k \cong \mathbb{Q}[x]/\Phi_n(x)$, where $\Phi_n(x)$ is the cyclotomic polynomial of order n and degree $\phi(n)$.[3] Note that k is poor with respect to n.

We can use the prime-factor algorithm (see Sect. 1.3.1) to reduce the DFT of order n to p DFTs of order 2^m, and 2^m DFTs of order p (since p is odd, $(2^m, p) = 1$):

$$D_k(n) \le p D_k(2^m) + 2^m D_k(p). \quad (12)$$

Then we can use the Cooley-Tukey FFT algorithm to compute p DFTs of order 2^m with the algebraic cost (7). At this point no factorization-based FFT algorithm can be applied to compute 2^m DFTs of prime order p, and the naive quadratic algorithm (5) for the DFTs of order p together with (11) gives

$$D_k(n) \le p\left(\tfrac{3}{2}2^m m - 2^m + 1\right) + 2^m(2p^2 - 3p + 1) = \Theta(n^{\frac{3}{2}}).$$

We cannot use Rader's and Bluestein's FFT algorithms for the DFT of length n since it is composite and $\omega_{2n} \notin k$. However we can combine them with the Cooley-Tukey FFT.

Starting again with (12), we will compute the DFTs of order p with Rader's FFT algorithm. Since $2^m > 2p - 3$, we can set $N = 2^m$ in (8): $D_k(p) \le 3D_k(2^m) + 2^m + 4p - 5$. Together with (12), (7), and (11) this leads to the upper bound

$$D_k(n) < \tfrac{39}{4}n\log n + \tfrac{37}{2}n.$$

Therefore, $D_k(n) = O(n \log n)$.

---

[3]Recall that $\Phi_n(x) = \prod_{(i,\,n)=1}(x - \omega^i)$, where $\omega \in \mathbb{C}$ is a primitive n-th root of unity. $\Phi_n(x)$ is irreducible over $\mathbb{Q}$ and has integer coefficients. *Euler's totient function* $\phi(n)$ gives the number of natural numbers less than n and coprime with n.

2.2 The algorithm

Our ultimate goal is to compute the DFT of length n over k with respect to an n-th primitive root of unity $\omega_n \in k$. The only primitive roots of unity in k we are relying on are the m-th primitive roots of unity $\omega_m \in k$, for all $m \mid n$. Their existence is implied by the existence of ω_n.

It is well known [22] that a cyclic convolution of length n can be computed as a part of a cyclic convolution of order $N \ge 2n - 1$. In our algorithm we will fetch cyclic convolutions of length n from cyclic convolutions of length $N \ge n + 1$. This step requires the following novel tool.

LEMMA 1. *Let $n, \Delta \in \mathbb{N}$, so that $1 \le \Delta \le n - 2$. A cyclic convolution of length n can be computed from a cyclic convolution of length $n + \Delta$, and a product of two polynomials in $k[x]/x^{n-\Delta-1}$, with at most $2(n - \Delta - 1)$ additions in k.*

PROOF. Let the convolution of $a := (a_0, \ldots, a_{n-1}) \in k^n$ and $b := (b_0, \ldots, b_{n-1}) \in k^n$, be $c := (c_0, \ldots, c_{n-1}) \in k^n$, i.e., $c_i = \sum_{\substack{0 \le j,\, l \le n-1 \\ j+l \equiv i \pmod{n}}} a_j b_l$, $i = 0, 1, \ldots, n-1$. Set

$$a' := (a_0, \underbrace{0, \ldots, 0}_{\Delta \text{ times}}, a_1, \ldots, a_{n-1}) \in k^{n+\Delta},$$

$$b' := (b_0, \ldots, b_{n-1}, b_0, \ldots, b_{\Delta-1}) \in k^{n+\Delta}.$$

We will also denote

$$\bar{a}(x) := \sum_{i=0}^{n-\Delta-2} a_{i+1}x^i, \quad \bar{b}(x) := \sum_{i=0}^{n-\Delta-2} (b_{i+\Delta} - b_i)x^i. \quad (13)$$

Let $c' = (c'_0, \ldots, c'_{n+\Delta-1})$ be the convolution of a' with b'. Note that $c_i = c'_i$ for $0 \le i \le \Delta$. For $\Delta + 1 \le i \le n - 1$, we have

$$c'_i = a_0 b_i + \sum_{j=1}^{i-\Delta} a_j b_{i-j-\Delta} + \sum_{j=i-\Delta+1}^{n-1} a_j b_{(i-j) \bmod n}$$

$$= c_i - \underbrace{\sum_{j=1}^{i-\Delta} a_j (b_{i-j} - b_{i-j-\Delta})}_{=:\bar{c}_i}.$$

Note that $\bar{c}_i$ is exactly the coefficient at $x^{i-\Delta-1}$ in the product $\bar{a}(x)\bar{b}(x)$, as defined in (13). Therefore, the computation of the c_i's can be performed by

- Computing $b_{i+\Delta} - b_i$, for $i = 0, 1, \ldots, n - \Delta - 2$,
- Computing the coefficients of

$$\bar{c}(x) := \bar{a}(x)\bar{b}(x) \pmod{x^{n-\Delta-1}},$$

- Computing c', the cyclic convolution of length $n + \Delta$ of a' with b',
- Computing $c_i = c'_i + \bar{c}_i$, for $i = \Delta+1, \Delta+2, \ldots, n-1$,

and the statement follows. $\square$

COROLLARY 1. *Let the DFT of order $N = 2n - m$ be defined over k, for $2 \le m < n$. The cyclic convolution of length n over k can be computed in at most*

$$3D_k(N) + O(n) + O(m \log m \log \log m)$$

operations over k, of which at most $N + O(m \log m)$ multiplications are not by twiddle factors.

PROOF. By Lemma 1, a cyclic convolution of length n can be computed by a cyclic convolution of length N, at most $2m - 2 = O(n)$ additions in k, and computing a product of two degree $m - 2$ polynomials. The cyclic convolution of length N can be computed with 3 DFTs of order N (since the latter are defined) and $N \leq 2n$ multiplications in k. The statement follows then from the Schönhage-Strassen [24] and Schönhage's [23] polynomial multiplication algorithms, whose complexity is $O(m \log m \log \log m)$ additions and $O(m \log m)$ multiplications in k for computing the product of two degree m (and $m - 2$) polynomials. $\square$

Remark 1. If we put $\Delta \geq n - 1$ in Lemma 1 the convolution of a and b will be simply a part of the convolution of a' and b', see [22]. The proof of this fact is actually contained in the proof of Lemma 1.

W.l.o.g. we will assume in (6) that

$$d_i > 0, \quad n_i < n_j, \quad (n_i, n_j) = 1, \quad \text{for } 1 \leq i < j \leq s. \quad (14)$$

By the Cooley-Tukey and the Good-Thomas FFTs, we reduce $\mathrm{DFT}_n^{\omega_n}$ to nd_σ/n_σ DFTs of length n_σ, for $1 \leq \sigma \leq s$. The overhead of this reduction is at most $n \log n$ multiplications by powers of ω_n, see Sect. 1.3.1.

We compute the DFTs of length n_σ in the ascending order of σ. The DFTs of length n_1 are always computed by the naive procedure with the quadratic complexity upper bound (5). Each DFT of order n_σ can either be computed by the naive algorithm again, or can be reduced to a cyclic convolution of length N_σ, where

$$N_\sigma = n_1^{\delta_1} \cdots n_{\sigma-1}^{\delta_{\sigma-1}}, \quad 0 \leq \delta_i \leq d_i, \quad 1 \leq i < \sigma, \quad (15)$$

using Rader's or Bluestein's reductions, see Sect. 1.3.2. We will call a particular method used in our algorithm for computing $\mathrm{DFT}_{n_\sigma}^{\omega_{n_\sigma}}$, a *strategy* for n_σ.

The strategies for n_σ with $\sigma \geq 2$ are selected by the following process. Let the algorithm compute all DFTs of order n_i with complexities L_i for $1 \leq i < \sigma$.

We define the set

$$\mathcal{N}_\sigma = \{N_\sigma : \text{as defined in (15)}\} \cap [n_\sigma - 1, \infty). \quad (16)$$

If $\mathcal{N}_\sigma$ is empty, we choose for n_σ the direct strategy. If n_σ is prime and $\mathcal{N}_\sigma \neq \varnothing$, we define for $N_\sigma = \prod_{i=1}^{\sigma-1} n_i^{\delta_i} \in \mathcal{N}_\sigma$,

$$L'_R(N_\sigma) := 3N_\sigma \Big(\sum_{i=1}^{\sigma-1} \Big(\delta_i \Big(\frac{L_i - 1}{n_i} + 1 \Big) + \frac{1}{n_i^{\delta_i}} \Big) - 1 \Big) \\ + N_\sigma + 4n_\sigma - 5, \quad (17)$$

If $N_\sigma = n_\sigma - 1$, or $N_\sigma \geq 2n_\sigma - 3$, we set $L_R(N_\sigma) := L'_R(N_\sigma)$. Otherwise,

$$L_R(N_\sigma) := L'_R(N_\sigma) \\ + 2(2n_\sigma - N_\sigma - 3) + M_k(2n_\sigma - N_\sigma - 4), \quad (18)$$

where $M_k(j)$ is the algebraic complexity of multiplication of two degree j polynomials in $k[x]/x^{j+1}$. $L_R(N_\sigma)$ is the complexity of computing the DFT of length n_σ via Rader's reduction to a cyclic convolution of length N_σ, with prime-factor and Cooley-Tukey's reductions to the DFTs of lengths $n_1, \ldots, n_{\sigma-1}$. Note that $L_R(N_\sigma) - L'_R(N_\sigma)$ is the overhead implied by choosing $N_\sigma < 2n_\sigma - 3$. If n_σ is composite or $\mathcal{N}_\sigma = \varnothing$, we set $L_{\sigma, R} = \infty$, otherwise

$$L_{\sigma, R} := \min_{N_\sigma \in \mathcal{N}_\sigma} L_R(N_\sigma).$$

$L_{\sigma, R}$ is the algebraic complexity of the DFT of order n_σ over k, computed by reducing it to a cyclic convolution of length N_σ via Rader's algorithm and Lemma 1 in the best possible way with respect to (6) and (14). Note that we use only the principal roots of unity in k whose existence is guaranteed by the existence of $\omega_n \in k$.

In the same way we define the complexity of the computation of the DFT of length n_σ using Bluestein's reduction. If $2 \mid n_1^{d_1} \cdots n_{\sigma-1}^{d_{\sigma-1}}$, and $\mathcal{N}_\sigma \neq \varnothing$, we define for each $N_\sigma = \prod_{i=1}^{\sigma-1} n_i^{\delta_i} \in \mathcal{N}_\sigma \setminus \{n_\sigma - 1\}$,

$$L'_B(N_\sigma) := 3N_\sigma \Big(\sum_{i=1}^{\sigma-1} \Big(\delta_i \Big(\frac{L_i - 1}{n_i} + 1 \Big) + \frac{1}{n_i^{\delta_i}} \Big) - 1 \Big) \\ + N_\sigma + 5n_\sigma - 3. \quad (19)$$

If $N_\sigma \geq 2n_\sigma - 1$, we set $L_B(N_\sigma) := L'_B(N_\sigma)$. Otherwise,

$$L_B(N_\sigma) := L'_B(N_\sigma) \\ + 2(2n_\sigma - N_\sigma - 1) + M_k(2n_\sigma - N_\sigma - 2). \quad (20)$$

If $n_1^{d_1} \cdots n_{\sigma-1}^{d_{\sigma-1}}$ is odd, or $\mathcal{N}_\sigma \setminus \{n_\sigma - 1\}$ is empty, we set $L_{\sigma, B} = \infty$, otherwise

$$L_{\sigma, B} := \min_{N_\sigma \in \mathcal{N}_\sigma \cap [n_\sigma, \infty)} L_R(N_\sigma).$$

Finally we set

$$L_\sigma = \min\{2n_\sigma^2 - 3n_\sigma + 1, L_{\sigma, R}, L_{\sigma, B}\},$$

and choose the strategy for n_σ accordingly. Note that in case of using Rader's and Bluestein's reductions the algorithm needs at least N_σ multiplications other than by twiddle factors for the computation of the DFT of length n_σ.

2.3 Complexity analysis

We will denote algebraic complexity *of the introduced algorithm* computing the DFT of order n over k by $L_k(n)$. The algorithm starts with the decomposition (6) of n by the Cooley-Tukey FFT algorithm, and computes all nd_1/n_1 DFTs of order n_1 by the direct formulas (2). The DFTs of order n_σ are computed by the algorithm in L_σ operations over k. Therefore,

$$L_k(n) < 2nd_1 n_1 + n \sum_{\sigma=2}^{s} \frac{d_\sigma L_\sigma}{n_\sigma} + n \log n. \quad (21)$$

Note that if the direct strategy is used for some n_σ with $\sigma \geq 2$, then $L_k(n) = \Omega\big(n(d_\sigma n_\sigma + \log n)\big)$. We will be interested primarily in such n, that all strategies for n_σ with $\sigma \geq 2$ can use Rader's or Bluestein's reductions. Therefore, the DFT of order n will eventually be reduced to a number of DFTs of order n_1 with a reasonable overhead. In what follows, we assume that in (6) we have for some $c = O(1)$,

$$\prod_{i=1}^{\sigma-1} n_i^{d_i} \geq 2n_\sigma - c, \quad 2 \leq \sigma \leq s, \quad \text{and } 2 \mid n_1. \quad (22)$$

In Section 3 we will show that such n appear naturally in finite field extensions. Furthermore, the upper bounds for the DFT of such orders can be used to speed up the polynomial multiplication over fields of positive characteristic.

In what follows, all considerations are made for the factorization (6) with (14) and (22).

LEMMA 2. *Let $L_i \leq An_i \log n_i + Bn_i + C$, for some constants A, B, $C > 0$, for all $2 \leq i < \sigma$. If the DFTs of length n_σ are computed by the Rader's or Bluestein's reductions to the cyclic convolutions of length $2n_\sigma - c \leq N_\sigma \leq En_\sigma$, then*

$$L_\sigma \leq 3(A + B + C + 1)E \cdot n_\sigma \log n_\sigma$$
$$+ \big(3(A + B + C + 1)E \log E + 1\big) \cdot n_\sigma$$
$$+ c^2 + 2c - 4.$$

PROOF. From (17), (18), (19), (20) we have

$$L_\sigma \leq 3N_\sigma \sum_{i=1}^{\sigma-1} \frac{L_i \delta_i}{n_i} + 3N_\sigma \log N_\sigma - 2N_\sigma + 5n_\sigma - 3$$
$$+ \max\big\{2(2n_\sigma - N_\sigma - 1) + M_k(2n_\sigma - N_\sigma - 1), 0\big\}. \quad (23)$$

We set the upper bounds for the L_i into (23) and use the following simple facts to complete the proof:

$$2n_\sigma - N_\sigma - 1 \leq c - 1,$$
$$M_k(c - 1) \leq (c - 1)^2,$$
$$N_\sigma \log N_\sigma \leq En_\sigma \log n_\sigma + E \log E \cdot n_\sigma,$$
$$\sum_{i=1}^{\sigma-1} \delta_i \log n_i = \sum_{i=1}^{\sigma-1} \log n_i^{\delta_i} = \log \prod_{i=1}^{\sigma-1} n_i^{\delta_i} = \log N_\sigma,$$
$$\sum_{i=1}^{\sigma-1} \frac{\delta_i}{n_i} < \sum_{i=1}^{\sigma-1} \delta_i \leq \log N_\sigma. \quad \square$$

It is clear from the flow of the algorithm, that explicit upper bounds for generic n might be difficult to prove. However, for specific n, we can prove that our algorithm is an FFT algorithm as it is usually defined in literature, *i.e.*, its complexity is $O(n \log n)$ for the computation of the DFT of order n. There are infinitely many such n, for which the classical algorithms have higher order of complexity than $n \log n$.

THEOREM 1. *Let the DFT of order n be defined over k, and let (22) hold with $c \leq 6$. Let E be the minimal real number, such that $\mathcal{N}_\sigma \cap [1, En_\sigma] \neq \varnothing$, for all $2 \leq \sigma \leq s$, where $\mathcal{N}_\sigma$ is as in (16). Then for $\ell(E) = \max\{1, \log E\}$,*

$$D_k(n) \leq L_k(n) \leq \big(6^s E^s \ell^s(E)(2n_1 + s) + 1\big)n \log n.$$

PROOF. We have $L_1 < 2n_1^2$. Since $n_1 \geq 2$, we may also use that $L_1 \leq (2n_1) \cdot n_1 \log n_1$. By Lemma 2, for n_2 we have $A = 2n_1$, $B = C = 0$, and thus

$$L_2 \leq 3(2n_1 + 1)En_2 \log n_2$$
$$+ \big(3(2n_1 + 1)E \log E + 1\big)n_2 + c^2 + 2c - 4.$$

(14) implies that $n_2 \geq 3$. Along with $c \leq 6$, this leads to $L_2 \leq (6(2n_1 + 2)E\ell(E)) \cdot n_2 \log n_2$. Applying this argument $\sigma - 1$ times we arrive for $1 \leq \sigma \leq s$ at

$$L_\sigma \leq \big(6^\sigma(2n_1 + \sigma)E^\sigma \ell^\sigma(E)\big) \cdot n_\sigma \log n_\sigma.$$

Finally, since $L_k(n) \leq n \sum_{\sigma=1}^{s} \frac{d_\sigma L_\sigma}{n_\sigma} + n \log n$, the statement follows from the following:

$$\sum_{\sigma=1}^{s} \frac{d_\sigma L_\sigma}{n_\sigma} \leq \big(6^s(2n_1 + s)E^s \ell^s(E)\big) \sum_{\sigma=1}^{s} \log n_\sigma^{d_\sigma}$$
$$= \big(6^s(2n_1 + s)E^s \ell^s(E)\big) \log n.$$

Note that here we have used the trivial facts that $n_1 \geq 2$ and $\ell(E) \geq 1$. $\square$

COROLLARY 2. *If in (6), $s = O(1) = n_1$, and in Theorem 1, $E = O(1)$, then $D_k(n) = O(n \log n)$. In this setting, the constant in the upper bound for $D_k(n)$ will not depend on the value of n_2, which can be $\Omega(\sqrt{n})$.*

Example 1. Now we generalize the example of Section 2.1. Let m and p be as defined in (11). Let $n_1 := 2^m p$, and p_1 be a prime such that $2p_1 \leq n_1 < 4p_1$ (by Chebyshev's theorem p_1 always exists, see, e.g., [3, Sect. 8-2]). We define $n_\sigma := n_{\sigma-1} p_{\sigma-1}$, where $p_\sigma \in (\frac{n_{\sigma-1}}{4}, \frac{n_{\sigma-1}}{2}]$ are primes for $2 \leq \sigma \leq s$. Finally, let $n := n_s$, and $k := \mathbb{Q}(\omega_n)$. In Theorem 1 we have $E = 2$, thus

$$D_k(n) \leq L_k(n) \leq 12^s(4 + s)n \log n.$$

This upper bound does not depend on m, therefore n can be arbitrarily big. On the other hand, $n = n_{\sigma-1} p_{\sigma-1}$ contains a prime divisor $p_{\sigma-1} > \sqrt{n}/4$, which makes the complexity of the Cooley-Tukey FFT algorithm $\Theta(n^{1.5})$.

Our algorithm can be applied for computing the DFT over a field of prime characteristic. We will show this on the example of a field k of characteristic $p \geq 3$, which contains a finite field with $q := p^{2^m}$ elements. The DFT of order $n \mid q - 1$ is defined over k since the multiplicative group of $\mathbb{F}_q$ is cyclic.

THEOREM 2. *Let k be a field of characteristic $p \geq 3$, $m \geq \log(p + 1)$, $q = p^{2^m}$, and $\mathbb{F}_q \subseteq k$. For any $0 \leq s \leq \frac{m}{2}$, the DFT of length*

$$n = n(s) := 2^{m+1} \cdot \frac{p-1}{2} \cdot \prod_{\sigma=0}^{s} \frac{p^{2^\sigma} + 1}{2} \quad (24)$$

is defined over k, and

$$D_k(n) \leq L_k(n) = O(48^s \cdot sn \log n). \quad (25)$$

The number of required multiplications other than by twiddle factors is at most $s(s + 1)n$.

PROOF. Since $n \mid q - 1$ for all such s, the DFT of length n is defined over k. We will prove the statement by applying Theorem 1 for the decomposition (24) of n. We will prove that the valid parameters are $E = 4$ and $c = 1$.

To align (24) with the notation of (6) we will denote $n_1 = 2$, $d_1' = m + 1$, $n_2' = \frac{p-1}{2}$, $n_3' = \frac{p+1}{2}$, $d_2 = d_3 = 1$, $n_\sigma = \frac{p^{2^{\sigma-3}} + 1}{2}$, and $d_\sigma = 1$, for $4 \leq \sigma \leq s + 2$. Note that $n = n_1^{d_1'} n_2'^{d_2} n_3'^{d_3} n_4^{d_4} \cdots n_{s+2}^{d_{s+2}}$.

Let $n_2' = n_2 \cdot 2^j$, $n_3' = n_3 \cdot 2^l$, for odd n_2 and n_3. Since $n_3' = n_2' + 1$, exactly one of n_2' and n_3' is even, and $j + l > 0$. For $d_1 := d_1' + j + l$, we have $n = \prod_{\sigma=1}^{s+2} n_\sigma^{d_\sigma}$. Furthermore, n_2 and n_3 are odd and coprime by construction and for $4 \leq \sigma \leq s + 2$:

$$n_\sigma = 1 + n_2' \cdot n_3' \cdot \prod_{i=4}^{\sigma-1} n_i = 1 + 2^{j+l-1} \prod_{i=1}^{\sigma-1} n_i^{d_i}, \quad 4 \leq \sigma \leq s.$$

Therefore, $n_1, \ldots, n_s$ are pairwise coprime. By swapping n_2 with n_3 if needed we can finally align this factorization of n with (14).

Since $m \geq \log(p + 1)$, we have $2n_2 < 2^m$. Therefore, to compute a DFT of orders n_2 the algorithm can choose $i = \lceil \log(2n_2 - 1) \rceil \leq m$, so that $2^{i-1} < 2n_2 - 1 \leq 2^i$, and $N_2 := 2^i$. The same can be done for n_3. Note that in this case $E = 4$, $n/n_2^{d_2}$ and $n/n_3^{d_3}$ are even, and we can use

294

Bluestein's reduction without extra polynomial multiplications. Therefore, $c = 0$ in (22).

For n_σ with $\sigma \geq 4$, we have $2n_\sigma - 2 = 2^{\sigma-1} \prod_{i=2}^{\sigma-1} n_i$, therefore we can use Bluestein's reduction with $N_\sigma = 2n_\sigma - 2$, one multiplication of two degree 0 polynomials over k, i.e., just one field multiplication, and 2 additions. Therefore, we can assume for this case $E = 2$ and $c = 2$.

We have shown that $E \leq 4$, $c \leq 2$, and (25) follows from Theorem 1.

The number of multiplications other than by twiddle factors in the computation of the DFT of length n_σ for $\sigma \geq 2$ is at most $2\sigma n_\sigma - 1$. (In fact, it is at most $2\sigma n_\sigma - 2$, since the additional multiplication needed by Lemma 1 to restore the convolution of length n from the convolution of length $2n - 2$ can be replaced by two multiplications by twiddle factors and one subtraction. Adding these values to (25) will not increase the upper bound.) There are n/n_σ DFTs of length n_σ computed in the algorithm, therefore, the account of n_σ is less than $2\sigma n$ multiplications other than by twiddle factors. Since the DFTs of order n_1 are computed without such multiplications, and there are $s + 1$ reductions via Bluestein's algorithm, the total number of such multiplications is at most $s(s+1)n$. $\square$

Remark 2.   1. With a little modification, we can prove the statement of Theorem 2 for any $n' \mid n(s)$.

2. Theorem 2 remains valid if we replace everywhere p with p^l, for some integer $l > 0$.

3. We can improve (25) by reducing all DFTs of length $n_\sigma < 2^{m+1}$ to the DFTs of orders 2^d for carefully chosen d. This is possible, since $2n_\sigma - 1 < 2^{m+2} \leq n_1^{d_1}$, and provides lower complexity estimates than the reduction to a cyclic convolution of length $2n_\sigma - 2$.

4. The upper bounds of Theorems 1 and 2 in the part depending on s are very rough. A bit more involved technical argument provides better bounds, both for the general case, and for specific n (see, e.g., Section 2.1 and Example 1). In particular, in Theorem 2, if p is constant, the upper bound can easily be reduced to $O(12^s sn \log n)$, as we used $E = 4$ only for the DFTs of orders n_2 and n_3. For the rest of the factors, E can be assigned the value 2.

3. POLYNOMIAL MULTIPLICATION

Theorem 2 implies that for any constant $c > 0$ and integer l, there exists an extension K of a field k of characteristic $p \geq 3$, such that for $m = [K : k]$:

- $l \leq m < 2l$,

- K admits the DFT of length $n = \Omega(m^c)$, and

- $D_K(n) = O(n \log n)$.

LEMMA 3. *For each $n' \leq n(s)/(p-1)$, as in (24), there exists a divisor $N' \mid n$, such that $n' \leq N' \leq 2(1 + \frac{1}{p-1})n'$.*

PROOF. Let $s, q \geq 3$ be natural numbers, let $\ell > \log q$, and $Q := \frac{q^{2^s}-1}{q-1} = \prod_{i=0}^{s-1} \left(q^{2^i} + 1 \right)$, $N := 2^\ell Q$. We will show first, that for any $n \leq Q/q$, there exists a divisor $Q_n \mid Q$, such that $n \leq Q_n < q \left(1 + \frac{1}{q-1}\right) n$.

Let $m = \lceil \log_q n \rceil$. We have $n \leq q^m < qn \leq Q$. Let $m = \sum_{i=0}^{s-1} \alpha_i 2^i$, be the binary representation of n. We set $Q_n := \prod_{i=0}^{s-1} \left(q^{2^i} + 1 \right)^{\alpha_i}$. We have

$$Q_n \leq \prod_{i=0}^{s-1} \left(1 + \frac{1}{q^{2^i}}\right) \cdot \prod_{i=0}^{s-1} q^{2^i \alpha_i}$$
$$< \left(1 + \frac{1}{q-1}\right) \cdot q^m < q\left(1 + \frac{1}{q-1}\right)n,$$

and $Q_n \geq \prod_{i=0}^{s-1} q^{2^i \alpha_i} = q^m \geq n$.

It follows that for any $n \leq N/q$, there exists $N'_n \mid N$, such that $n \leq N'_n \leq 2q\left(1 + \frac{1}{q-1}\right)n$. Now if for some i, $2^i n \leq N'_n < 2^{i+1}n$, the desired divisor of N is $N' := 2^{\ell-i}Q_n$, for which $n \leq N' \leq 2\left(1 + \frac{1}{q-1}\right)n$. $\square$

Remark 3. By setting a sufficiently large p^l instead of p according to p. 2 of Remark 2, we can make the upper bound of Lemma 3 arbitrarily close to $2N'$.

If $p \equiv 1 \pmod 4$, then $K := \mathbb{F}_{p^{2^m}}$ can be represented as $\mathbb{F}_p[x]/(x^{2^m} - a)$, where a is a nonsquare in $\mathbb{F}_p$, [9, Theor. 6].[4] Furthermore, if a is primitive in $\mathbb{F}_p$, then the order of x in K is $2^m(p-1)$, [2, Chap. V, Theor. 19], [16, Theor. 2.3.4, Cor. 2.3.6], [17, Theor. 3.7.5]. In other words, x is a principal $(2^m(p-1))$-th root of unity in K, and multiplication by its powers can be performed in K with at most 2^s multiplications in $\mathbb{F}_p$. The same upper bound holds trivially for the complexity of addition of two K-elements.

The twiddle factors used in our algorithm are the powers of the $(2^{m-s}(p^{2^s}-1))$-th root of unity $\omega(x) \in K$. Such $\omega(x)$ can be represented as the product $x^s \cdot \omega'(x)$, where $\omega'(x)$ is the lift in K of a primitive element in $\mathbb{F}_{p^{2^s}}$. Note that any power of $\omega'(x)$ has at most 2^s nonzero monomials in K, since it always belongs to $\mathbb{F}_{p^{2^s}}$. We can assume that $\omega'(x)$ is precomputed, or we can add the search for $\omega'(x)$ into the algorithm. The complexity of the latter is $O(2^{s/3})$, see [25], and it does not affect much the upper bounds for the complexity of the DFT. Therefore, multiplication of a degree 2^m polynomial by a power of $\omega'(x)$ can be performed in $O(2^{m+s})$ operations over k. Finally, multiplications by powers of $\omega(x)$ can be performed via multiplications by a power of x and a power of $\omega'(x)$, which can be performed altogether in $O(2^{m+s})$ multiplications in k.

Let $c > 0$ be fixed. We want to proceed as follows: given two degree n polynomials $a(x)$ and $b(x)$ over $k \supseteq \mathbb{F}_p$, take an extension $K \supset k$ of degree 2^m such that the DFT of length $N := \Theta(2^{mc})$ is defined over K, and $2n \leq N < 4(1 + \frac{1}{p-1})n$ (N is picked according to Lemma 3). Then $a(x)$ and $b(x)$ are represented as polynomials of degree N over K. We compute their DFTs, perform N multiplications of degree 2^m polynomials, and compute the inverse DFT to fetch the coefficients of $a(x)b(x)$. The cost of this procedure is roughly

$$P_k(n) \leq \left(4\left(1 + \frac{1}{p-1}\right) + c^2\right)n^{1-\frac{1}{c}}P_k(\lceil n^{\frac{1}{c}}\rceil) + O(n \log n).$$

About $c^2 n^{1-\frac{1}{c}}$ multiplications come from the multiplications other than by twiddle factors. The solution of the above inequality is therefore inferior to the upper bound of

---

[4]If $p \equiv 3 \pmod 4$, we can start with $\mathbb{F}_{p^2}$ according to p. 2 of Remark 2.

Schönhage-Strassen algorithm. However, these multiplications are not completely arbitrary, one of the multiplicands is always an output of the DFT of twiddle factors. They could probably be computed in a more efficient way than via reduction to the general polynomial product.

THEOREM 3. *For $c \geq 5$, if the multiplications other than by twiddle factors in the above procedure can be performed in $O(n^{\frac{1}{c}})$ time, or their number can be reduced to at most $\alpha c n^{1-\frac{1}{c}}$, for some fixed $\alpha < 1$, then the complexity of degree n polynomial multiplication over an arbitrary field of characteristic $p \geq 3$ is $O(n \log n)$.*

4. FINAL NOTES

Our combination of the known FFT techniques extends the set of orders n for which the DFT can be computed in $O(n \log n)$ field operations. Brief software experiments showed that our algorithm is faster than some dedicated methods for DFTs of specific orders over finite fields. If such orders are useful in other applications one could think about an efficient software implementation. Another challenge is the validity of the conjectures in Theorem 3.

The author would like to thank Markus Bläser for the attention to this work and anonymous reviewers for numerous important improvement suggestions.

One referee pointed out a concern regarding the claimed $\Omega(n^{1.5})$ complexity bound of the known techniques for the DFT of certain lengths n and mentioned a way to compute the DFT of order n in $O(n \log n \log \log n)$ for an arbitrary n via fast evaluation/interpolation on a geometric sequence. In response to this we would like to note that such complexity is indeed achievable over any field of characteristic *other than* 2 by the following simple trick. If a $2n$-th primitive root of unity is not in k, we can consider an extension of degree 2 and use Bluestein's reduction. The complexity upper bound will be the product of the complexity of polynomial multiplication and the complexity of arithmetics in the field extension. The first is $O(n \log n \log \log n)$ for the multiplication of two degree $O(n)$ polynomials, and the second is $O(1)$ since the extension degree is 2.

This work is supported by the Cluster of Excellence "Multimodal Computing and Interaction" at Saarland University.

5. REFERENCES

[1] V. B. Afanassiev and A. A. Davydov. Finite field towers: Iterated presentation and complexity of arithmetic. *Finite Fields Appl.*, 8(2):216–232, 2002.

[2] A. A. Albert. *Fundamental Concepts of Higher Algebra*. Univ. of Chicago Press, Chicago, 1956.

[3] G. E. Andrews. *Number theory*. Dover Pub., 1994.

[4] L. I. Bluestein. A linear filtering approach to the computation of the discrete Fourier transform. *Northeast Electronics Research and Engineering Meeting Record*, 10:218–219, 1968.

[5] P. Bürgisser, M. Clausen, and M. A. Shokrollahi. *Algebraic Complexity Theory*. Springer, 1997.

[6] D. G. Cantor and E. Kaltofen. On fast multiplication of polynomials over arbitrary algebras. *Acta Inf.*, 28(7):693–701, 1991.

[7] S. C. Chan and K. L. Ho. On indexing the prime-factor fast Fourier transform algorithm. *IEEE Trans. Circuits and Systems*, 38(8):951–953, 1991.

[8] M. Clausen and U. Baum. *Fast Fourier Transforms*. BI-Wissenschaftsverlag, Mannheim, 1993.

[9] S. D. Cohen. The explicit construction of irreducible polynomials over finite fields. *Des. Codes Cryptogr.*, 2(2):169–174, 1992.

[10] J. W. Cooley and J. W. Tukey. An algorithm for the machine calculation of complex Fourier series. *Math. Comp.*, 19:297–301, 1965.

[11] A. De, P. P. Kurur, C. Saha, and R. Saptharishi. Fast integer multiplication using modular arithmetic. In *STOC 2008*, pages 499–506. ACM, New York, NY, USA, 2008.

[12] M. Fürer. Faster integer multiplication. In *STOC 2007*, pages 57–66. ACM, New York, NY, USA, 2007.

[13] J. von zur Gathen and J. Gerhard. *Modern Computer Algebra*. Cambridge University Press, New York, NY, USA, second edition, 2003.

[14] I. J. Good. The interaction algorithm and practical Fourier analysis. *J. R. Statist. Soc. B*, 20(2):361–372, 1958. Addendum, *ibid.*, 22(2):373–375, 1960.

[15] J. van der Hoeven. The truncated Fourier transform and applications. In *ISSAC 2004*, pages 290–296. ACM, New York, NY, USA, 2004.

[16] D. Jungnickel. *Finite Fields: Structure and Arithmetics*. Wissenschaftsverlag, Mannheim, 1992.

[17] R. Lidl and H. Niederreiter. *Finite Fields*. Cambridge University Press, 2008.

[18] H. J. Nussbaumer. *Fast Fourier Transform and Convolution Algorithms*, volume 2 of *Springer Series in Information Sciences*. Springer, 1981.

[19] V. Y. Pan. Simple multivariate polynomial multiplication. *J. Symb. Comput.*, 18(3):183–186, 1994.

[20] A. Pospelov. Faster polynomial multiplication via discrete Fourier transforms. To appear in *CSR 2011*, volume 6651 of Lecture Notes in Computer Science. Springer, 2011.

[21] F. P. Preparata and D. V. Sarwate. Computational complexity of Fourier transforms over finite fields. *Math. Comp.*, 31(139):740–751, 1977.

[22] C. M. Rader. Discrete Fourier transforms when the number of data samples is prime. *Proc. IEEE*, 56:1107–1108, 1968.

[23] A. Schönhage. Schnelle Multiplikation von Polynomen über Körpern der Charakteristik 2. *Acta Inf.*, 7:395–398, 1977.

[24] A. Schönhage and V. Strassen. Schnelle Multiplikation großer Zahlen. *Computing*, 7:281–292, 1971.

[25] I. Shparlinski. On finding primitive roots in finite fields. *Theoret. Comput. Sci.*, 157(2):273–275, 1996.

[26] C. Temperton. Implementation of a self-sorting in-place prime factor FFT algorithm. *J. Comput. Phys.*, 58:283–299, 1985.

[27] L. H. Thomas. Using a computer to solve problems in physics. In Applications of Digital Computers, Ginn and Co., Boston, MA, 1963.

[28] Y. Wang and X. Zhu. A fast algorithm for Fourier transform over finite fields and its VLSI implementation. *IEEE J. Sel. Areas Commun.*, 6(3):572–577, 1988.

Normalization of Row Reduced Matrices

Soumojit Sarkar
soumojitsarkar@gmail.com

Arne Storjohann
astorjoh@uwaterloo.ca

David R. Cheriton School of Computer Science
University of Waterloo, Ontario, Canada N2L 3G1

ABSTRACT

This paper gives gives a deterministic algorithm to transform a row reduced matrix to canonical Popov form. Given as input a row reduced matrix R over $\mathsf{K}[x]$, K a field, our algorithm computes the Popov form in about the same time as required to multiply together over $\mathsf{K}[x]$ two matrices of the same dimension and degree as R. We also show that the problem of transforming a row reduced matrix to Popov form is at least as hard as polynomial matrix multiplication.

Categories and Subject Descriptors

G.4 [**Mathematical Software**]: Algorithm Design and Analysis; I.1.2 [**Symbolic and Algebraic Manipulation**]: Algorithms; F.2.1 [**Analysis of Algorithms and Problem Complexity**]: Numerical Algorithms and Problems

General Terms

Algorithms

Keywords

Popov form, Polynomial matrices

1. INTRODUCTION

This paper considers the problem of lattice reduction, or row reduction, for matrices over the ring $\mathsf{K}[x]$ of univariate polynomials with coefficients from a field K. Row reduction of a matrix A over $\mathsf{K}[x]$ is the problem of finding a basis with row degrees as small as possible for the lattice $\mathcal{L}(A)$ generated by all $\mathsf{K}[x]$-linear combinations of rows of A. For the following example, recall that a matrix $U \in \mathsf{K}[x]^{n \times n}$ is unimodular precisely when $\det U$ is a nonzero constant from K. Two matrices $A, R \in \mathsf{K}[x]^{n \times n}$ are *left equivalent* (i.e., the rows of A and R generate the same lattice) if and only if $A = UR$ for $U \in \mathsf{K}[x]^{n \times n}$ a unimodular matrix. We remark that in the literature some authors (for example [4]) prefer to consider the equivalent but transposed situation of column reduction, where the unimodular transform on the right.

EXAMPLE 1. *Let us indicate a polynomial of degree t with $[t]$. The following shows the degree structure in a particular matrix $A \in \mathsf{K}[x]^{4 \times 4}$, a row reduced form R of A, and the unimodular matrix U such that $A = UR$.*

$$A = \begin{bmatrix} [13] & [13] & [12] & [12] \\ [13] & [13] & [12] & [12] \\ [13] & [13] & [12] & [12] \\ [13] & [13] & [12] & [12] \end{bmatrix}$$

$$= \begin{bmatrix} [12] & [11] & [11] & [9] \\ [12] & [11] & [11] & [9] \\ [12] & [11] & [11] & [9] \\ [12] & [11] & [11] & [9] \end{bmatrix} \overset{U}{} \begin{bmatrix} [1] & [1] & [1] & [1] \\ [2] & [2] & [2] & [2] \\ [2] & [2] & [2] & [2] \\ [4] & [4] & [4] & [4] \end{bmatrix} \overset{R}{}$$

Let $A \in \mathsf{K}[x]^{n \times n}$ be nonsingular. A fast Las Vegas probabilistic algorithm for computing a reduced basis R of A is given in [6]. Our main contribution in this paper is a deterministic algorithm that computes the canonical Popov reduced basis P, together with the unimodular matrix U such that $A = UP$, in about the same time as required to multiply together two polynomial matrices of the same dimension and degree as A. To clearly state our contributions, and to compare with previous work, we recall from [8, page 385] the precise definition of a row reduced form and the normalization conditions required for a row reduced form to be in canonical Popov form.

Let v be a row vector over $\mathsf{K}[x]$. The degree of v, denoted by $\deg v$, is the maximal degree of all entries. The *pivot index* of v, denoted by $\text{piv}(v)$ is the index of the rightmost entry of degree $\deg v$. The *leading coefficient* vector $\text{LC}(v)$ over K is obtained by taking the coefficient of $x^{\deg v}$ of all entries of v. Let A be a matrix over $\mathsf{K}[x]$. The degree of A, denoted by $\deg A$, is the maximal degree of its rows. The leading coefficient matrix of A, denoted by $\text{LC}(A)$, is the matrix over K formed by taking the leading coefficient of each row of A.

DEFINITION 2. *A nonsingular matrix*

$$P = \begin{bmatrix} p_{11} & p_{12} & \cdots & p_{1n} \\ p_{21} & p_{22} & \cdots & p_{2n} \\ \vdots & \vdots & \ddots & \vdots \\ p_{n1} & p_{n2} & \cdots & p_{nn} \end{bmatrix} = \begin{bmatrix} \underline{\vec{p}_1} \\ \underline{\vec{p}_2} \\ \vdots \\ \underline{\vec{p}_n} \end{bmatrix} \in \mathsf{K}[x]^{n \times n}$$

is row reduced *if* $\text{LC}(P)$ *is nonsingular. If, in addition, P satisfies the following normalization conditions it is in* Popov form.

(i) The pivot indices $\text{piv}(\vec{p}_1), \ldots, \text{piv}(\vec{p}_n)$ *are distinct.*

(ii) The pivot entries $p_{1,\mathrm{piv}(\vec{p}_1)},\ldots,p_{n,\mathrm{piv}(\vec{p}_n)}$ are monic.

(iii) $\deg \vec{p}_i \leq \deg \vec{p}_{i+1}$ for $1 \leq i < n$, and if $\deg \vec{p}_i = \deg \vec{p}_{i+1}$ then $\mathrm{piv}(\vec{p}_i) < \mathrm{piv}(\vec{p}_{i+1})$.

(iv) Nonpivot entries have degree less than that of the pivot entry in the same column.

If P satisfies only condition (i) it is said to be in weak Popov form *[9]*.

Any nonsingular $A \in \mathsf{K}[x]^{n \times n}$ has a unique decomposition $A = UP$ with U unimodular and P in Popov form. The Popov form is a canonical form for left equivalence which has row degrees as small as possible, in particular, $\deg P \leq \deg A$. We also remark that the multi-sets of row degrees of row reduced forms that are left equivalent are identical.

EXAMPLE 3. *Consider the row reduced form R from Example 1. The following shows the possible degree structure in a weak Popov form W of R, and in the canonical Popov form P of R. The pivot entries in each row have been underlined.*

$$
\begin{array}{ccc}
R & W & P \\[4pt]
\begin{bmatrix}
[1] & [1] & [1] & [1] \\
[2] & [2] & [2] & \underline{[2]} \\
[2] & [2] & [2] & \underline{[2]} \\
[4] & [4] & [4] & \underline{[4]}
\end{bmatrix}
\rightarrow
\begin{bmatrix}
[1] & [1] & [1] & \underline{[1]} \\
[1] & [2] & [2] & \underline{[1]} \\
\underline{[2]} & [1] & \underline{[1]} & [1] \\
\underline{[3]} & \underline{[4]} & [3] & [3]
\end{bmatrix}
\rightarrow
\begin{bmatrix}
[1] & [1] & [1] & \underline{[1]} \\
\underline{[2]} & [1] & [1] & [0] \\
\underline{[1]} & [2] & \underline{[2]} & [0] \\
[1] & \underline{[4]} & \underline{[1]} & [0]
\end{bmatrix}
\end{array}
$$

Algorithms and complexity analysis for computing row reduced forms of matrices over $\mathsf{K}[x]$ are given in [9, 6, 10, 4], see also the references in [10]. In this paper, cost estimates will be given in terms of field operations from K, and we use ω for the exponent of matrix multiplication: two $n \times n$ matrices over a commutative ring can be multiplied in $O(n^\omega)$ operations from the ring.

Let $A \in \mathsf{K}[x]^{n \times n}$ be nonsingular with $\deg A = d$. The deterministic algorithm in [9] computes the Popov form P of A in time $O(n^3 d^2)$. The algorithm in [9] is inherently iterative and does not seem amenable to a recursive approach which might introduce fast matrix and polynomial arithmetic. In [6] a Las Vegas randomized algorithm is given to compute a row reduced form of A with expected running time $O^\sim(n^\omega d)$, which is about the same time as required to multiply together two polynomial matrices of the same dimension and degree as A. Our first contribution in this paper is to give an $O^\sim(n^\omega d)$ deterministic algorithm to transform a row reduced matrix (such as produced by the algorithm in [6]) to Popov form. To the best of our knowledge, a transformation from row reduced from to Popov form in this time bound was not previously know. Note that in the particular case when all rows of a row reduced form R are equal, we can transform R to Popov form P in time $O(n^\omega d)$ using the identity $P = \mathrm{LC}(R)^{-1} R$. Our effort in this paper is devoted to the more subtle case when the row degrees of R are distinct.

On the one hand, for many applications a non canonical row reduced form R of A will suffice. In particular, a row reduced form gives a basis for $\mathcal{L}(A)$ that has row degrees as small as possible, and will satisfy the highly useful *predictable degree* property [8]: for polynomials $u_1, \ldots, u_n \in \mathsf{K}[x]$, we have $\deg u_1 \vec{p}_1 + \cdots + u_n \vec{p}_n = \max_i \{\deg u_i + \deg \vec{p}_i\}$.

On the other hand, computing the Popov form has some obvious advantages. Being canonical, equality of two lattices

over $\mathsf{K}[x]$ can be determined by checking that their Popov basis are identical. If asked for a basis for a lattice over $\mathsf{K}[x]$, returning the Popov instead of only a row reduced form is analogous to a computer algebra system returning the normalized (i.e., monic) gcd of two scalar polynomials. Indeed, given two nonsingular matrices $A, B \in \mathsf{K}[x]^{n \times n}$, the Popov basis P of the lattice generated by the rows of A and B gives a canonical matrix greatest common right divisor of A and B: A and B can be expressed as $A = U_1 P$ and $B = U_2 P$ for polynomial matrices U_1 and U_2 for which there exists polynomial matrices V_1 and V_2 such that $V_1 U_1 + V_2 U_2 = I_n$.

To illustrate the analogy between the Popov form and the normalized monic gcd, it is useful to consider the definition of Popov form used in [4], which, up to a (unique) row permutation, is identical to the classical one we have given in Definition 2: condition (iii) is replaced with the condition that $\mathrm{piv}(\vec{p})_i = i$, that is, the rows are permuted so that the pivots are on the diagonal. Following [4, Definition 2.1], a row reduced matrix P as in (1) is in Popov form precisely when $\mathrm{LC}(P)$ is lower triangular and the normalization condition $\mathrm{LC}(P^T) = I_n$ is satisfied. Given the Popov form P of A, we can exploit the normalization condition $\mathrm{LC}(P^T) = I_n$ to get a fast algorithm that computes $U = AP^{-1}$ deterministically.

Producing a canonical form is also advantageous from an algorithmic point of view: a randomized Las Vegas algorithm for computing the Popov form P, instead of an arbitrary row reduced form R, will always return the same result even if different random choices are made. Many randomized algorithms require that the field K be large enough to ensure a positive probability of success. For example, the algorithm for row reduction in [6] first performs a random shift of variable $x \to x - \gamma$ to ensure that x does not divide $\det A$. To ensure a probability of success at least $1/2$ in the worst case, γ should be chosen form a subset of K of size at least $2nd$. If $\#\mathsf{K}$ is too small, a common technique is to work over a small algebraic extension $\bar{\mathsf{K}}$ of K that contains sufficiently many elements. However, a row reduced form R of $A \in \mathsf{K}[x]^{n \times n}$ may be over $\bar{\mathsf{K}}[x]$ if computed over $\bar{\mathsf{K}}[x]$. Nonetheless, even if we pass over an algebraic extension, the Popov form P must be over the ground field: $A \in \mathsf{K}[x]^{n \times n} \to \bar{R} \in \bar{\mathsf{K}}[x]^{n \times n} \to P \in \mathsf{K}[x]^{n \times n}$.

Our algorithm to transform R to P proceeds in two phases as illustrated in Example 3: first we transform R to a weak Popov form W, then we transform W to Popov form P. The first phase uses a careful modification of the LUP decomposition algorithm described in [1], and the second phase utilizes the fast minimal approximant basis algorithm of [6].

The rest of this paper is organized as follows. Section 2 recalls some facts about row reduced bases. Section 3 gives the algorithm to transform a row reduced form to weak Popov form. Section 4 gives an algorithm to go from weak Popov to Popov form. Section 5 gives the deterministic algorithm to produce the decomposition $A = UP$. Section 6 concludes, and offers a simple reduction of the problem of polynomial matrix multiplication to that of transforming a row reduced form to Popov form. Actually, we show that even the problem of transforming a matrix in weak Popov form to Popov form is as hard as polynomial matrix multiplication.

Cost model

Algorithms are analysed by bounding the number of required field operations from a field K on an algebraic random access machine; the operations $+$, $-$, $\times$ and "divide by a nonzero" involving two field elements have unit cost.

We use ω to denote the exponent of matrix multiplication: two $n \times n$ matrices over a ring R can be multiplied with $O(n^\omega)$ ring operations from R. We use M for polynomial multiplication: let $\mathsf{M} : \mathbb{Z}_{\geq 0} \to \mathbb{R}_{>0}$ be such that polynomials in $\mathsf{K}[x]$ of degree bounded by d can be multiplied using at most $\mathsf{M}(d)$ field operations from K. We refer to [5] for more details and references about ω and M. We assume that $2 < \omega \leq 3$, and that $\mathsf{M}(ab) \leq \mathsf{M}(a)\mathsf{M}(b)$ for $a, b \in \mathbb{Z}_{>1}$. Some of our complexity estimates will explicitly make the assumption that $\mathsf{M}(t) \in O(n^{\omega-1})$. This assumption states that if fast matrix multiplication techniques are used, then fast polynomial multiplication should also be used.

Given two polynomials $a, b \in \mathsf{K}[x]$ with b nonzero, we denote by $\mathrm{Rem}(a, b)$ and $\mathrm{Quo}(a, b)$ the unique polynomials such that $a = \mathrm{Quo}(a, b)\, b + \mathrm{Rem}(a, b)$ with $\deg \mathrm{Rem}(a, b) < \deg b$. If a and b have degree bounded by d then both the Rem and Quo operation have cost $O(\mathsf{M}(d))$, and if b is a power of x both operations are free in our cost model. If the first argument of Rem or Quo is a matrix or vector the intention is to apply the function elementwise to the entries.

It will be useful to define an additional function B to bound the cost of the extended gcd operation, as well as other gcd-related computations. We can take either $\mathsf{B}(d) = \mathsf{M}(d)\log d$ or $\mathsf{B}(d) = d^2$. Then the extended gcd problem with two polynomials in $\mathsf{K}[x]$ of degree bounded by d can be solved in time $O(\mathsf{B}(d))$.

2. PRELIMINARIES

Row reduced and Popov forms are defined for matrices of arbitrary shape and rank profile. In this paper, we restrict ourselves to matrices of full row rank. The following definition generalizes Definition 2 to the case of full row rank matrices.

DEFINITION 4. *A full row rank matrix*

$$
P = \begin{bmatrix} p_{11} & p_{12} & \cdots & p_{1m} \\ p_{21} & p_{22} & \cdots & p_{2m} \\ \vdots & \vdots & \ddots & \vdots \\ p_{n1} & p_{n2} & \cdots & p_{nm} \end{bmatrix} = \begin{bmatrix} \vec{p}_1 \\ \vec{p}_2 \\ \vdots \\ \vec{p}_n \end{bmatrix} \in \mathsf{K}[x]^{n \times m}
$$

is row reduced *if* $\mathrm{LC}(P)$ *has full row rank* n. *If, in addition, P satisfies the following normalization conditions then it is in* Popov form.

(i) *The pivot indices* $\mathrm{piv}(\vec{p}_1), \ldots, \mathrm{piv}(\vec{p}_n)$ *are distinct.*

(ii) *The pivot entries* $p_{1,\mathrm{piv}(\vec{p}_1)}, \ldots, p_{n,\mathrm{piv}(\vec{p}_n)}$ *are monic.*

(iii) $\deg \vec{p}_i \leq \deg \vec{p}_{i+1}$ *for* $1 \leq i < n$, *and if* $\deg \vec{p}_i = \deg \vec{p}_{i+1}$ *then* $\mathrm{piv}(\vec{p}_i) < \mathrm{piv}(\vec{p}_{i+1})$.

(iv) $\deg p_{k,\mathrm{piv}(\vec{p}_i)} < \deg p_{i,\mathrm{piv}(\vec{p}_i)}$ *for* $k \in \{1, 2, \ldots, i-1, i+1, i+2, \ldots, n\}$, $1 \leq i \leq n$.

If P satisfies only condition (i) it is said to be in weak Popov form *[9].*

The following lemma recalls an essential feature of row reduced bases.

LEMMA 5. *[8, Theorem 6.3-13] If $R \in \mathsf{K}[x]^{n \times m}$ is row reduced and $v = \begin{bmatrix} v_1 \cdots v_n \end{bmatrix} \in \mathsf{K}[x]^{1 \times n}$, then $\deg vR = \max_i\{\deg v_i + \deg \mathrm{Row}(R, i)\}$.*

In the following lemma, we use $\bar{*}$ to denote a square nonsingular matrix over K, and $*^d$ to denote a rectangular matrix over $\mathsf{K}[x]$ of degree bounded by d. The next lemma follows as a corollary of Lemma 5.

LEMMA 6. *Let $R, \bar{R} \in \mathsf{K}[x]^{n \times m}$ be full row rank and row reduced matrices that are left equivalent. If both R and $\bar{R}$ have rows ordered such that degrees are nondecreasing, then the degrees of the rows of R and $\bar{R}$ are the same. Furthermore, if $d_1, d_2, \cdots, d_k$ is the nondecreasing sequence of distinct degrees of the rows of R, then*

$$
\overset{T}{\begin{bmatrix} \bar{*} & & & \\ *^{d_2-d_1} & \bar{*} & & \\ \vdots & \vdots & \ddots & \\ *^{d_k-d_1} & *^{d_k-d_2} & \cdots & \bar{*} \end{bmatrix}} \overset{R}{\begin{bmatrix} R^{[d_1]} \\ R^{[d_2]} \\ \vdots \\ R^{[d_k]} \end{bmatrix}} = \overset{\bar{R}}{\begin{bmatrix} \bar{R}^{[d_1]} \\ \bar{R}^{[d_2]} \\ \vdots \\ \bar{R}^{[d_k]} \end{bmatrix}}
$$

where the block decomposition is conformal, and $R^{[d_i]}$ denotes the submatrix of R comprised of the rows of degree d_i.

In the following corollary, let

$$
X = \begin{bmatrix} x^{d_k-d_1} I & & & \\ & x^{d_k-d_2} I & & \\ & & \ddots & \\ & & & x^{d_k-d_k} I \end{bmatrix} \in \mathsf{K}[x]^{n \times n},
$$

where the dimension of the diagonal block $x^{d_k-d_i} I$ corresponds to the row dimension of $R^{[d_i]}$, $1 \leq i \leq n$.

COROLLARY 7. *Let R, $\bar{R}$ and T be as in Lemma 6, and X be as in (1). Then $L := \mathrm{LC}(x^{d_k} XTX^{-1}) \in \mathsf{K}^{n \times n}$, with $L\,\mathrm{LC}(R) = \mathrm{LC}(\bar{R})$.*

PROOF. The result can be seen most easily by passing over the ring of Laurent polynomials. Note that

$$
(XTX^{-1})XR = X\bar{R},
$$

with all rows in XR and $X\bar{R}$ of degree d_k, and $XTX^{-1} = L + O(x^{-1})_{x \to \infty}$ for $L \in \mathsf{K}^{n \times n}$. $\square$

In the next section our goal is to find a matrix T as in Lemma 6 such that $W = TR \in \mathsf{K}[x]^{n \times n}$ is in weak Popov form. The following lemma, a corollary of Corollary 7, states that it is sufficient to solve this transformation to weak Popov form for a scalar input matrix, namely for $\mathrm{LC}(R) \in \mathsf{K}^{n \times n}$.

LEMMA 8. *Let $R \in \mathsf{K}[x]^{n \times m}$ have full row rank, be row reduced, and have rows ordered so that degrees are nondecreasing. If $\bar{T} \in \mathsf{K}^{n \times n}$ is a unit lower triangular such that $\bar{W} = \bar{T}\,\mathrm{LC}(R) \in \mathsf{K}^{n \times n}$ is in weak Popov form, then $T := X^{-1}\bar{T}X \in \mathsf{K}[x]^{n \times n}$ is unimodular and $W = TR \in \mathsf{K}[x]^{n \times n}$ is in weak Popov form.*

EXAMPLE 9. *The following partially specified matrix*

$$
R = \begin{bmatrix} 73x+56 & 68x+24 & 65x+90 & 3x+16 \\ 78x^2+\cdots & 59x^2+\cdots & 69x^2+\cdots & 3x^2+\cdots \\ 60x^2+\cdots & 41x^2+\cdots & 83x^2+\cdots & 5x^2+\cdots \\ 75x^4+\cdots & 94x^4+\cdots & 70x^4+\cdots & 3x^4+\cdots \end{bmatrix}
$$

is row reduced, where $\mathsf{K} = \mathbb{Z}/(97)$. *The following shows a transformation of* $\mathrm{LC}(R)$ *to weak Popov form* $\bar{W}$.

$$
\begin{array}{ccc}
\bar{T} & \mathrm{LC}(R) & \bar{W} \\
\begin{bmatrix} 1 & & & \\ 96 & 1 & & \\ 89 & 71 & 1 & \\ 3 & 38 & 33 & 1 \end{bmatrix} &
\begin{bmatrix} 73 & 68 & 65 & 3 \\ 78 & 59 & 69 & 3 \\ 60 & 41 & 83 & 5 \\ 75 & 94 & 70 & 3 \end{bmatrix} =
\begin{bmatrix} 73 & 68 & 65 & 3 \\ 5 & 88 & & 4 \\ 67 & & & \\ & & & 3 \end{bmatrix}
\end{array}
$$

If we set

$$
T = \begin{array}{ccc}
X^{-1} & \bar{T} & X
\end{array}
$$
$$
T = \begin{bmatrix} x^{-3} & & & \\ & x^{-2} & & \\ & & x^{-2} & \\ & & & 1 \end{bmatrix}
\begin{bmatrix} 1 & & & \\ 96 & 1 & & \\ 89 & 71 & 1 & \\ 3 & 38 & 33 & 1 \end{bmatrix}
\begin{bmatrix} x^3 & & & \\ & x^2 & & \\ & & x^2 & \\ & & & 1 \end{bmatrix}
$$
$$
= \begin{bmatrix} 1 & & & \\ 96x & 1 & & \\ 89x & 71 & 1 & 0 \\ 3x^3 & 38x^2 & 33x^2 & 1 \end{bmatrix},
$$

then $W = TR$ *is in weak Popov form with* $\bar{W} = \mathrm{LC}(W)$.

3. ROW REDUCED TO WEAK POPOV

Our goal is to transform a row reduced matrix to weak Popov form. By Lemma 8, it will be sufficient to handle the scalar case, that is, given a full row rank $R \in \mathsf{K}^{n \times m}$, compute a unit lower triangular transformation matrix $T \in \mathsf{K}^{n \times n}$ such that TR is in weak Popov form. Our approach is to compute a decomposition $R = LUP$ where L is unit lower triangular, U is upper triangular, and P is a permutation matrix. We accomplish this using a modification of the well known LUP decomposition algorithm described in [1, Page 236]. The following lemma gives the idea of our approach.

LEMMA 10. *Let* $R \in \mathsf{K}^{n \times m}$ *have full row rank, and let* $R = LUP$ *be an* LUP *decomposition of* R. *If* $(p_1, \ldots, p_n)$ *is such that* p_i *is the index of integer* i *in the permuted tuple* $(1, 2, \ldots, m)P$, *then* $(UP)_{i,p_i}$ *is nonzero and entries in* UP *below* $(UP)_{i,p_i}$ *are zero,* $1 \le i \le n$. *Furthermore, if* $(UP)_{i,p_i}$ *is the rightmost nonzero entry in row* i *of* UP *for* $1 \le i \le n$, *then* $L^{-1}R = UP$ *is in weak Popov form.*

The following example is based on Example 9.

EXAMPLE 11. *The following shows an* LUP *decomposition of a nonsingular* $R \in \mathbb{Z}_{97}^{4 \times 4}$.

$$
\begin{array}{cccc}
& L & U & P
\end{array}
$$
$$
R = \begin{bmatrix} 1 & & & \\ 1 & 1 & & \\ 34 & 26 & 1 & \\ 1 & 74 & 64 & 1 \end{bmatrix}
\begin{bmatrix} 3 & 65 & 73 & 68 \\ & 4 & 5 & 88 \\ & & 67 & 0 \\ & & & 3 \end{bmatrix}
\begin{bmatrix} & & & 1 \\ & & 1 & \\ 1 & & & \\ & 1 & & \end{bmatrix}
$$
$$
= \begin{bmatrix} 73 & 68 & 65 & 3 \\ 78 & 59 & 69 & 3 \\ 60 & 41 & 83 & 5 \\ 75 & 84 & 70 & 3 \end{bmatrix}.
$$

Now observe that $\bar{T}$ *and* $\bar{W}$ *in Example 9 are equal to* L^{-1} *and* UP, *respectively. But not every* LUP *decomposition leads to transformation to weak Popov form. For example,* R *has generic rank profile and so can be decomposed as the product of a unit lower triangular and upper triangular matrix.*

For $i = 1, 2, \ldots, n$, the iterative LUP decomposition algorithm chooses a nonzero pivot element in row i of the work matrix, postmultiplies the work matrix by a permutation P_i, swapping column i with a latter column, if needed, to ensure the pivot entry is located in column i, and zeroes out entries below the pivot entry by premultiplying the work matrix with a matrix L_i that is unit lower triangular with all entries zero except for possibly column i. Setting and $L := (L_n \cdots L_2 L_1)^{-1}$, $P := (P_1 P_2 \cdots P_n)^{-1}$ and U to be the final work matrix, gives an LUP decomposition. To ensure that the LUP decomposition produced will lead to a transformation to weak Popov form we need to specify how the pivot entries are chosen. Initialize a tuple $D = (1, 2, \ldots, n)$. After each row is processed the tuple D should be updated as $D := DP_i$. The pivot in row i is chosen to be the nonzero entry from among the last $n - i + 1$ entries of row i of the work matrix for which the corresponding component of D is maximal.

EXAMPLE 12. *Let* R *be as in Example 11. Initialize* $D = (1, 2, 3, 4)$. *The first pivot we select is the right most element of the first row of* R. *This gives*

$$
\begin{array}{ccc}
L_1 & R & P_1
\end{array}
$$
$$
R_1 = \begin{bmatrix} 1 & & & \\ -1 & 1 & & \\ -34 & & 1 & \\ -1 & & & 1 \end{bmatrix}
\begin{bmatrix} 73 & 68 & 65 & 3 \\ 78 & 59 & 69 & 3 \\ 60 & 41 & 83 & 5 \\ 75 & 84 & 70 & 3 \end{bmatrix}
\begin{bmatrix} & & & 1 \\ & 1 & & \\ & & 1 & \\ 1 & & & \end{bmatrix}
$$
$$
= \begin{bmatrix} 3 & 68 & 65 & 73 \\ & 88 & 4 & 5 \\ & 57 & 7 & 3 \\ & 16 & 5 & 2 \end{bmatrix}.
$$

The updated D *is* $D = (4, 2, 3, 1)$. *The next pivot is thus chosen to be the third element of row 2 of* R_1. *The next elimination step gives*

$$
\begin{array}{ccc}
L_2 & R_1 & P_2
\end{array}
$$
$$
R_2 = \begin{bmatrix} 1 & & & \\ & 1 & & \\ & -26 & 1 & \\ & -74 & & 1 \end{bmatrix}
\begin{bmatrix} 3 & 68 & 65 & 73 \\ & 88 & 4 & 5 \\ & 57 & 7 & 3 \\ & 16 & 5 & 2 \end{bmatrix}
\begin{bmatrix} 1 & & & \\ & & & 1 \\ & & 1 & \\ & 1 & & \end{bmatrix}
$$
$$
= \begin{bmatrix} 3 & 65 & 68 & 73 \\ & 4 & 88 & 5 \\ & & & 67 \\ & & 3 & 20 \end{bmatrix}.
$$

and D *is updated to* $D = (4, 3, 2, 1)$.

When applied to a full row rank $n \times m$ matrix, the base cases of the fast LUP decomposition algorithm will consist in computing an LUP decomposition of a nonzero $1 \times m$ matrix B which corresponds to the last m columns of a row of the work matrix, $1 \le m \le n$. By modifying the algorithm as follows, it will produce the same output as the iterative version with pivoting as specified above.

- Initialize $D = (1, 2, \ldots, n)$ at the start of the algorithm.

- At each base case involving a $B \in \mathsf{K}^{1 \times m}$, compute the unique LUP decomposition $B = LUP$ which has P^{-1} equal to the permutation that interchanges column 1 and j, with j chosen so that $D[n - m + j]$ is maximal from among all j with $B[j]$ nonzero, $1 \le j \le m$. Update D by interchanging $D[n-m+1]$ and $D[n-m+j]$.

```
ReducedToWeakPopov(R, n, m, d)
```

Input: A row reduced matrix $R \in \mathsf{K}[x]^{n \times m}$ with rank n and $d = \deg R$.

Output: W, a weak Popov form of R.

1. [Compute scalar transformation]
   Row permute R so that degrees are nondecreasing.
   $\bar{R} := \mathrm{LC}(R)$;
   $L, U, P :=$ an LUP decomposition of $\bar{R}$ with
   $\qquad\qquad$ pivots chosen as described above;

2. [Apply transformation]
   Let d_i be the degree of row i of R, $1 \le i \le n$.
   $X := \mathrm{Diag}(x^{d_1}, x^{d_2}, \ldots, x^{d_n})$;
   $\bar{T} := L^{-1}$;
   $W := X(\bar{T}(X^{-1}R))$;
   return W

Figure 1: Algorithm `ReducedToWeakPopov`

We obtain the following result as a corollary of Lemma 8 and [1, Theorem 6.4].

THEOREM 13. *Algorithm* `ReducedToWeakPopov` *is correct. The cost of the algorithm is $O(mn^{\omega - 1}d)$ operations from K.*

4. WEAK POPOV TO POPOV

In this section we show how to transform a full rank matrix $W \in \mathsf{K}[x]^{n \times m}$ that is in weak Popov form to Popov form. The following lemma observes that we can restrict our attention to the square nonsingular case.

LEMMA 14. *Let $W \in \mathsf{K}[x]^{n \times m}$ have rank n and be in weak Popov form. If B is the submatrix of W comprised of the columns containing pivot entries, and $T \in \mathsf{K}[x]^{n \times n}$ is a unimodular matrix such that TB is in Popov form, then TW is the Popov form of W.*

PROOF. Without loss of generality, up to a row permutation, assume W satisfies conditions (i) and (ii) of Definition 4. Then we can observe that the iterative algorithm of [9, Section 7] to transform W to Popov form P will maintain $\mathrm{piv}(\mathrm{Row}(W, i)) = \mathrm{piv}(\mathrm{Row}(P, i))$ for $1 \le i \le n$. Now, if $\bar{P}$ is the submatrix of P comprised of the columns containing the pivot entries, then $\bar{P}$ satisfies all conditions of Definition 2 and is in Popov form. Thus $\bar{P}$ is the Popov form TB of B. The result follows. $\square$

The next lemma follows directly from Definition 2.

LEMMA 15. *Let $P \in \mathsf{K}[x]^{n \times n}$ be nonsingular and in Popov form, and let c_i equal to the degree of the pivot entry in column i, $1 \le i \le n$. Set $X := \mathrm{Diag}(x^{d-c_1}, \ldots, x^{d-c_n})$, where $d = \deg P$. If Q is the permutation matrix such that QP has pivot entries located on the diagonal, then QPX is in Popov form with every row of degree d.*

EXAMPLE 16. *The following shows the column shift of the Popov form from Example 1.*

$$
QPX = \begin{bmatrix} & & \overset{Q}{1} & \\ & & & 1 \\ & 1 & & \\ 1 & & & \end{bmatrix} \overset{P}{\begin{bmatrix} [1] & [1] & [1] & [1] \\ [2] & [1] & [1] & \overline{[0]} \\ \overline{[1]} & [2] & [2] & [0] \\ [1] & \underline{[4]} & \overline{[1]} & [0] \end{bmatrix}} \overset{X}{\begin{bmatrix} x^2 & & & \\ & 1 & & \\ & & x^2 & \\ & & & x^3 \end{bmatrix}}
$$

$$
= \overset{QPX}{\begin{bmatrix} \underline{[4]} & [1] & [3] & [3] \\ \overline{[3]} & \underline{[4]} & [3] & [3] \\ [3] & \overline{[2]} & \underline{[4]} & [3] \\ [3] & [1] & \overline{[3]} & \underline{[4]} \end{bmatrix}}.
$$

The next lemma follows from Definition 2.

LEMMA 17. *If $R \in \mathsf{K}[x]^{n \times n}$ be a row reduced matrix with every row of degree d, then $\mathrm{LC}(R)^{-1}R$ is the Popov form of R and all its pivot elements are along the diagonal of the matrix.*

The following corollary of Lemmas 15 and 17 now shows how we may transform the problem of computing the Popov form of a weak Popov form to that of computing a row reduced basis of a suitably shifted matrix.

THEOREM 18. *Let $B \in \mathsf{K}[x]^{n \times n}$ be nonsingular and in weak Popov form, and let c_i equal to the degree of the pivot entry in column i, $1 \le i \le n$. Let T be the unimodular matrix such that $P = TB$ is in Popov form, and let Q be the permutation matrix such that pivot entries in QP are on the diagonal. Set $d = \deg B$ and $X := \mathrm{Diag}(x^{d-c_1}, \ldots, x^{d-c_n})$. If $U \in \mathsf{K}[x]^{n \times n}$ is a unimodular matrix such that $R = UBX$ is row reduced, then $T := Q^{-1}\mathrm{LC}(UBX)^{-1}U \in \mathsf{K}[x]^{n \times n}$. Moreover, $\deg T \le d$.*

PROOF. By Lemma 15 the matrix QPX will be in Popov form with all rows of degree d. Since QT is a unimodular matrix, $QP \equiv_L B$ and so also $QPX \equiv_L BX$. Since the Popov form QPX has all rows of degree d, the left equivalent reduced form UBX will also have all rows of degree d. Lemma 17 now shows that the following diagram commutes.

$$
\begin{array}{ccc}
B & \xrightarrow{\text{Postmul. by } X} & BX \\
{\scriptstyle\text{Premul. by } QT}\downarrow & & \downarrow{\scriptstyle\text{Premul. by } \mathrm{LC}(UBX)^{-1}U} \\
QP & \xrightarrow{\text{Postmul. by } X} & QPX
\end{array}
$$

The claim that $T = Q^{-1}\mathrm{LC}(R)^{-1}U$ follows.

Now consider the degree of T. Since $P = TB$ is the Popov form of B, we have $\deg P \le \deg B = d$. The predictable degree property (Lemma 5) now implies that $\deg T \le d$. $\square$

The final ingredient is the transformation of the matrix BX of Theorem 18 to row reduced form. To accomplish this we use a minimal approximant basis computation as described by [3, Theorem 5.2]. We will use algorithm **PM-Basis** of [6] to compute an order $3d+1$ minimal approximant $M \in \mathsf{K}[x]^{2n \times 2n}$ for the matrix

$$
G = \begin{bmatrix} BX \\ \hline -I_n \end{bmatrix} \in \mathsf{K}[x]^{2n \times n}. \tag{1}
$$

Recall that M is a nonsingular row reduced matrix that gives a basis for the lattice $\{w \in \mathsf{K}[x]^{1 \times n} \mid wG \equiv 0 \bmod x^{3d+1}\}$. We obtain the following result.

LEMMA 19. *Let B and X be as in Theorem 18. If M is a minimal approximant basis of order $3d+1$ for G shown in (1), and $\left[\begin{array}{c|c} \bar{U} & \bar{R} \end{array}\right]$ is the submatrix of M comprised of the rows of degree bounded by d, with $\bar{U}$ of column dimension n, then $\bar{U}$ is unimodular and $\bar{R}$ is a row reduced form of BX.*

PROOF. First note that the degree bounds $\deg \bar{U} \leq d$, $\deg \bar{R} \leq d$ and $\deg BX \leq 2d$, together with $\left[\begin{array}{c|c} \bar{U} & \bar{R} \end{array}\right] G \equiv 0 \bmod x^{3d+1}$, imply that

$$\left[\begin{array}{c|c} \bar{U} & \bar{R} \end{array}\right] \left[\begin{array}{c} BX \\ -I_n \end{array}\right] = 0. \qquad (2)$$

We will show in succession that the following hold:

(a) $\bar{U}$ has at most n rows.

(b) $\bar{U}$ is nonsingular.

(c) $\bar{U}$ is unimodular.

Using (c) together with (2) (i.e., $\bar{U}(BX) = \bar{R}$) shows that $\bar{R}$ is left equivalent to BX with all rows of $\bar{R}$ of degree d. Since the Popov form of BX has all rows of degree d, $\bar{R}$ must be a row reduced form of BX.

Claim (a): Since the rows of M are linearly independent, the row dimension of $\bar{U}$ can't be more than the dimension of the nullity of G, which is n.

Claim (b): From Theorem 18 we have $\left[\begin{array}{c|c} U & R \end{array}\right] G = 0$, with $\deg U, \deg R \leq d$. Since M is minimal approximant basis, all n linearly independent rows of $\left[\begin{array}{c|c} U & R \end{array}\right]$ must be generated by $\left[\begin{array}{c|c} \bar{U} & \bar{R} \end{array}\right]$. Since U is nonsingular and $\bar{U}$ has at most n rows, $\bar{U}$ must also be nonsingular.

Claim (c): From (2) we have $\bar{U} BX = \bar{R}$. Since $\bar{U}$ is nonsingular by claim (c), $\bar{R}$ is nonsingular also. The Popov form of BX has all rows of degree d, so $\deg \det BX nd$. Since $\deg \bar{R} \leq d$, we have $\deg \det \bar{R} \leq nd$. Finally, using $\bar{U} BX = \bar{R}$ gives that $\deg \det \bar{U} \leq \deg \det \bar{R} - \deg \det BX \leq 0$, showing that $\bar{U}$ is unimodular. $\square$

Algorithm WeakToPopov is shown in Figure 2. By [6, Theorem 2.4], M is computed in $O(n^\omega \, \mathsf{B}(d))$ field operations from K. We obtain the following result.

THEOREM 20. *Algorithm WeakToPopov is correct. The cost of the algorithm is $O(n^\omega \, \mathsf{B}(d) + mn^{\omega-1} \, \mathsf{M}(d))$ field operations from K.*

5. POPOV DECOMPOSITION OF NONSINGULAR MATRICES

Let $A \in \mathsf{K}[x]^{n \times n}$ be nonsingular of degree d. In this section we put together the results of the previous sections and give a deterministic algorithm to produce the decomposition $A = UP$ where P is the Popov form of A and U is unimodular.

Once the Popov form P has been computed, we can recover U as $U = AP^{-1}$. Let $X = \mathrm{Diag}(x^{c_1}, \ldots, x^{c_n})$, where c_i is the degree of the pivot entry in column i of P, $1 \leq i \leq n$. The Popov form P of A also satisfies $\deg P \leq \deg Ad$, and by Lemma 5, each row of U must also have degree bounded

---

WeakToPopov(W, n, m, d)

Input: A weak Popov form $W \in \mathsf{K}[x]^{n \times m}$ of rank n and degree d.
Output: P, the Popov form of W.

1. [Extract pivot columns and scale]
   $B :=$ submatrix of W comprised of the columns containing pivot entries;
   Let c_i be the degree of the pivot in column i of B.
   $X := \mathrm{Diag}(x^{d-c_1}, x^{d-c_2}, \ldots, x^{d-c_n})$;

2. [Minimal approximant basis computation]
   $G := \left[\begin{array}{c|c} BX & -I_n \end{array}\right]^T \in \mathsf{K}[x]^{2n \times n}$;
   $\delta := (0, \ldots, 0)$, of length $2n$;
   $M := \mathrm{PM\text{-}Basis}(G, 3d+1, \delta)$;
   $\left[\begin{array}{c|c} U & R \end{array}\right] :=$ the rows of M that have degree bounded by d;

3. [Recover the Popov form of W]
   $T := \mathrm{LC}(R)^{-1} U$;
   $P := TW$;
   Permute rows of P so that (iii) of Def. 4 holds;
   return P

Figure 2: Algorithm WeakToPopov

by d. Now note that

$$
\begin{aligned}
U &= AP^{-1} \\
&= (AX^{-1})(PX^{-1})^{-1} \\
&= \left(y^{-d} \overbrace{y^d (AX^{-1})|_{x=1/y}}^{D} \overbrace{((PX^{-1})|_{x=1/y})^{-1}}^{B} \right) \Big|_{y=1/x}
\end{aligned}
$$

where D and B are over $\mathsf{K}[y]$. Since $\deg U \leq d$ and since $B(0)$ is invertible, we have $y^d U(y^{-1}) = \mathrm{Rem}(DB^{-1}, y^{d+1})$.

Algorithm NonsingularPopovDecomp shown in Figure 3 uses the scheme described above the compute U from P and A. Algorithm RowReduce used in phase 1 is described in [7]. RowReduce is a deterministic variant of the Las Vegas randomized algorithm for row reduction in [6] that, unlike the algorithm from [6], avoids the need to know *a a priori* or choose randomly an $\alpha \in \mathsf{K}$ such that $x - \alpha$ does not divide $\det A$. By [7, Theorem 36], the cost of computing R in phase 1 is $O(n^\omega (\log n)^2 \, \mathsf{B}(d))$ field operations from K. The only computations in phase 2 requiring field operations is the computation of $\mathrm{Rem}(B^{-1}, y^{d+1})$ and the product $D \, \mathrm{Rem}(B^{-1}, y^{d+1})$. Since the constant coefficient of B is a permutation of I_n, the inverse of B up to order y^{d+1} can be computed using Newton iteration in time $O(n^\omega \, \mathsf{M}(d))$. We obtain the following result as a corollary of Theorems 13 and 20.

THEOREM 21. *Algorithm NonsingularPopovDecomp is correct. The cost of the algorithm is $O(n^\omega (\log n)^2 \, \mathsf{B}(d))$ field operations from K. This result assumes that $\mathsf{B}(t) \in O(t^{\omega-1})$.*

6. CONCLUSIONS AND FUTURE WORK

Given that the Popov form P has the same set of row degrees as a reduced form R, and only requires some ad-

---

```
NonsingularPopovDecomp(A, n, d)
```

Input: A nonsingular matrix $A \in \mathsf{K}[x]^{n \times n}$ of degree d.
Output: $P, U \in \mathsf{K}[x]^{n \times n}$, with P the Popov form of A
and $A = UP$.

1. [Compute the Popov form]
   $R := \mathtt{RowReduce}(A, n, d);$
   $W := \mathtt{ReducedToWeakPopov}(R, n, n, \deg R);$
   $P := \mathtt{WeakToPopov}(W, n, n, \deg W);$

2. [Compute U]
   $X := \mathrm{Diag}(x^{c_1}, \ldots, x^{c_n})$, where $c_i = \deg \mathrm{Col}(P, i);$
   $B := (PX^{-1})|_{x=1/y};$
   $D := y^d(AX^{-1})|_{x=1/y};$
   $E := y^{-d} \mathrm{Rem}(D \, \mathrm{Rem}(B^{-1}, y^{d+1}), y^{d+1});$
   $U := E|_{y=1/x};$
   return P, U

Figure 3: Algorithm `NonsingularPopovDecomp`

ditional normalization conditions to be satisfied, a natural question that arises is if the transformation from R to P is at least as hard as polynomial matrix multiplication: we answer this question affirmatively with a reduction similar to the well known reduction [1, Page 246] of scalar matrix multiplication to triangular matrix inversion.

Let $A, B \in \mathsf{K}[x]^{n \times n}$ have degree bounded by d. The following matrix C with degree bounded by $2d + 1$ is row reduced since it is in weak Popov form:

$$C := \begin{bmatrix} x^{d+1}I_n & B \\ -x^{d+1}A & x^{2d+1}I_n \end{bmatrix} \in \mathsf{K}[x]^{2n \times 2n}.$$

The Popov form P of C is obtained as follows:

$$\begin{bmatrix} I & \\ \hline A & I \end{bmatrix} \overset{C}{\begin{bmatrix} x^{d+1}I & B \\ \hline -x^{d+1}A & x^{2d+1}I \end{bmatrix}} = \overset{P}{\begin{bmatrix} x^{d+1} & B \\ \hline & AB + x^{2d+1}I \end{bmatrix}}.$$

We obtain the following result.

THEOREM 22. *If we have an algorithm (algebraic* RAM*) for transforming a nonsingular $2n \times 2n$ row reduced matrix of degree $2d+1$ to Popov form with $P(n, d)$ operations from* K, *then two $n \times n$ matrices of degree d over $\mathsf{K}[x]$ can be multipied together with $P(n, d)$ operations from* K.

Our algorithms for transforming from row reduced to weak Popov, and from weak Popov to Popov, worked for rectangular input matrices of full row rank. Currently, our deterministic algorithm for computing the Popov decomposition requires the input matrix to be square and nonsingular. Randomization can be used to extend the algorithm to matrices of arbitrary shape and rank, but our ultimate goal is to obtain a deterministic algorithm for the general case.

7. REFERENCES

[1] A. V. Aho, J. E. Hopcroft, and J. D. Ullman. *The Design and Analysis of Computer Algorithms.* Addison-Wesley, 1974.

[2] B. Beckermann and G. Labahn. A uniform approach for the fast computation of matrix–type Padé approximants. *SIAM Journal on Matrix Analysis and Applications*, 15(3):804–823, 1994.

[3] B. Beckermann, G. Labahn, and G. Villard. Shifted normal forms of polynomial matrices. In S. Dooley, editor, *Proc. Int'l. Symp. on Symbolic and Algebraic Computation: ISSAC '99*, pages 189—196. ACM Press, New York, 1999.

[4] B. Beckermann, G. Labahn, and G. Villard. Normal forms for general polynomial matrices. *Journal of Symbolic Computation*, 41(6):708–737, 2006.

[5] J. von zur Gathen and J. Gerhard. *Modern Computer Algebra*. Cambridge University Press, 2 edition, 2003.

[6] P. Giorgi, C.-P. Jeannerod, and G. Villard. On the complexity of polynomial matrix computations. In R. Sendra, editor, *Proc. Int'l. Symp. on Symbolic and Algebraic Computation: ISSAC '03*, pages 135–142. ACM Press, New York, 2003.

[7] S. Gupta, S. Sarkar, A. Storjohann, and J. Valeriote. Triangular x-basis decompositions and derandomization of linear algebra algorithms over $\mathsf{K}[x]$. *Journal of Symbolic Computation*. Accepted for publication.

[8] T. Kailath. *Linear Systems*. Prentice Hall, Englewood Cliffs, N.J., 1980.

[9] T. Mulders and A. Storjohann. On lattice reduction for polynomial matrices. *Journal of Symbolic Computation*, 35(4):377–401, 2003.

[10] G. Villard. Computing Popov and Hermite forms of polynomial matrices. In Y. N. Lakshman, editor, *Proc. Int'l. Symp. on Symbolic and Algebraic Computation: ISSAC '96*, pages 251–258. ACM Press, New York, 1996.

Numeric-Symbolic Exact Rational Linear System Solver*

B. David Saunders, David Harlan Wood, and Bryan S. Youse
Dept. of Computer and Information Sciences, University of Delaware
Newark, Delaware, USA
saunders@udel.edu, wood@udel.edu, bryouse@udel.edu

ABSTRACT

An iterative refinement approach is taken to rational linear system solving. Such methods produce, for each entry of the solution vector, a rational approximation with denominator a power of 2. From this the correct rational entry can be reconstructed. Our iteration is a numeric-symbolic hybrid in that it uses an approximate numeric solver at each step together with a symbolic (exact arithmetic) residual computation and symbolic rational reconstruction. The rational solution may be checked symbolically (exactly). However, there is some possibility of failure of convergence, usually due to numeric ill-conditioning. Alternatively, the algorithm may be used to obtain an extended precision floating point approximation of *any* specified precision. In this case we cannot guarantee the result by rational reconstruction and an exact solution check, but the approach gives evidence (not proof) that the probability of error is extremely small. The chief contributions of the method and implementation are (1) confirmed continuation, (2) improved rational reconstruction, and (3) faster and more robust performance.

Categories and Subject Descriptors

G.4 [**Mathematical Software**]: Algorithm Design and Analysis; I.1.4 [**Symbolic and Algebraic Manipulation**]: Applications

General Terms

Algorithms, Design, Performance

Keywords

iterative refinement, rational linear system, rational reconstruction

*Research supported by National Science Foundation Grants CCF-0830130, CCF-108063

1. INTRODUCTION

We address the problem of solving $Ax = b$ for a vector $x \in \mathbb{Q}^n$, given $A \in \mathbb{Q}^{m \times n}$ and $b \in \mathbb{Q}^m$. We will restrict ourselves to square ($m = n$), nonsingular matrices with integer entries of length d bits or fewer. This is the core problem. Also, in this paper we are concerned with dense matrices, which is to say, matrices that do not have so many zero entries that more specialized sparse matrix techniques should be applied. We do anticipate that the refined numeric-symbolic iterative approach presented here will also apply effectively to sparse systems.

We present a method which is a refinement of the numeric-symbolic method of Wan[27, 26]. Earlier work of Geddes and Zheng[10] showed the effectiveness of the numeric-symbolic iteration, but used higher precision (thus higher cost) steps in the residue computation. However, Wan's method has had only sporadic success as deployed in the field (in the LinBox[22] library). Here we present a new *confirmed continuation method* which is quite robust and effective. In general, numerical numerical iteration methods are intended to extend the number of correct digits in the partial solution x'. The confirmed continuation method verifies that these new digits overlap the previous iteration's partial solution. This is our assurance of progress, rather than the less reliable matrix condition number small norm of residual, $|b - Ax'|$, which is used in prior methods [27, 26, 20, 12]. Evidence from data suggests that the new version solves a larger class of problems, is more robust, and provides the fastest solutions for many dense linear systems.

Standard non-iterative methods such as Gaussian elimination in its various forms suffer from extreme expression swell when working in exact integer or rational number arithmetic. In fact, the solution vector x itself is typically a larger object than the inputs. When elimination is used, typically $O(n^2)$ large intermediate values are typically created, with concomitant large time and memory cost.

In view of such expression swell, it is remarkable that iterative methods provide for solution in $n^{3+o(1)}$ time and $n^{2+o(1)}$ space when input entry lengths are constant. (The factor $n^{o(1)}$ absorbs any factors logarithmic in n.) There are two contending approaches.

A classical approach for finding rational number solutions to linear systems is Dixon's modular method[6] which begins by solving the system modulo a prime, p, and proceeds to a p-adic approximation of the solution by Hensel lifting, and finishes with reconstruction of the rational solution from p-adic approximants of sufficient length.

The second approach is a numeric-symbolic combination introduced by Wan in his thesis[27, 26]. Out focus is on extending Wan's method to to a larger class of problems where the size of residuals is too pessimistic.

Historically, the idea of solving exact linear systems to arbitrarily high accuracy by numerical iterative refinement (earlier referred to as binary-cascade iterative-refinement process, BCIR) is attributed to H. Wozniakowski by Wilkinson[28]. Wozniakowski is also acknowledged in a 1981 paper by Kielbasinski[12]. This 1981 paper emphasized "using the lowest sufficient precision in the computation of residual vectors." The required precision was allowed to vary at each iterative step. The case when doubling the working precision suffices to compute sufficiently accurate residuals was also treated soon after in [20]. An important limitation of these early papers was the assumption that the condition number of the matrix A is known. In practice, the system's condition number is rarely known and estimators can fail drastically.

Wan introduced two innovations into iterative refinement. The first innovation is that knowledge of condition numbers is not required. Instead, the accuracy of intermediate approximation vectors is estimated by the computed residuals, $|b - Ax'|$. Wan's second innovation was to compute these residuals exactly, rather than in variable precision or double precision as in the two earlier papers. Accurate residuals are essential, of course, for the correctness of subsequent iterative steps. However, residuals, even exact residuals, do not always correctly assess the accuracy of approximate solutions.

Thus, Wan's approach is basically to iterate with a series of approximate numerical solutions, each contributing its possibly differing number of correct bits, and to do exact computation of the current residual (via truncation and scaling) at each iteration in preparation for the next. The exactly computed residual is used to estimate the number of reliable bits in the current numeric approximation, and to provide the required accuracy of the residual that is to be input into the next iterative step. The final step in Wan's method, just as in Dixon's method, is that rational construction of the solution is undertaken only after a sufficiently accurate (dyadic, in this case) rational approximation is obtained.

One may say that, as input to the rational reconstruction, Dixon's method produces a Laurent series in powers of the prime p and numeric-symbolic iteration produces a Laurent series in powers of $1/2$. A bound is computed for the maximum length of the series necessary to assure rational reconstruction. Both of these methods have the same asymptotic complexity.

Reconstruction earlier in the process can be tried and will succeed if the rational numbers in the solution have smaller representations than the *a priori* bound. This is not done in the current implementation of Wan's method. Steffy studies this case in [21]. We offer a variant of rational reconstruction which recognizes potential early termination. But we distinguish these speculative results from the results that are *guaranteed* from known properties of the output and length of the Laurent series. Speculative results are be checked to see if they satisfy the original linear system.

One advantage of numeric-symbolic iteration is that it obtains the most significant digits first. One can stop short of the full rational reconstruction and instead take as the output the floating point values at any desired precision. A disadvantage of numeric-symbolic iteration is that it does require the numeric solver to obtain at least a few bits of accuracy at each iteration to be able to continue. Thus it is subject to failure due to ill-conditioning.

Wan's method has been implemented in LinBox[22, 7]. Some uses of linear system solving, for instance in Smith Normal Form computation, proceed by trying Wan's method and, if it fails, resorting to Dixon's. Unfortunately, past experience is that the numeric-symbolic iteration fails more often than not in this context. The confirmed continuation algorithm variant reported here is designed to significantly increase the success rate.

In section 2, we discuss Dixon's and Wan's iterations in more detail. Then in section 3 we describe our confirmed continuation method. In section 4 the rational reconstruction phase is discussed in detail. Finally our experiments are reported in section 5.

2. BACKGROUND

Here is a unified skeleton of Dixon's p-adic method and the numeric (dyadic) iteration for rational linear system solution. To unify the notation note that a rational number x may be written as a Laurent series $x = \sum_{i=k}^{\inf} x_i p^i$, where either p is a prime (p-adic expansion) or $p = 1/2$ (dyadic expansion). It will be convenient to think of the dyadic expansion in e bit chunks, in other words, use $p = 2^{-e}$. We specify that each x_i is integer and $0 \le x_i < p$ in the p-adic case, $0 \le x_i < 1/p$ in the dyadic case. In either case let $x \bmod p^l$ denote $\sum_{i=k}^{l-1} x_i p^i$. This will allow us to use the same modular language when discussing p-adic or dyadic expansions.

The skeleton of iterative refinement schemes to compute a solution x to $Ax = b$ is then the following.

1. Compute B such that $B = A^{-1} \bmod p$. That is, $A * B = I \bmod p$. The needed functionality of the object is, that for various vectors r, it can be used to accurately compute $A^{-1}r \bmod p$ in n^2 arithmetic steps. For instance, B could be represented by an LU decomposition of A.

2. By Cramer's rule the solution vector can be represented by quotients of $n \times n$ minors of (A, b). Compute a bound H (for instance the Hadamard bound) for these determinants. Let $k = \lceil \log_q(H) \rceil$, where $q = p$ if doing p-adic expansion and $q = 1/p$ if doing dyadic expansion. $2k$ terms of expansion are needed, in the worst case, to reconstruct the rational numbers in the solution vector.

3. Let $r_0 = b, y_0 = 0$. For i in $0..2k$ do the following:

    (a) $y_i = A^{-1}r_i \bmod p$.

    (b) $r_{i+1} = (r_i - Ay_i)/p$. Do this computation modulo p^2 at least. Since $r_i - Ay_i = 0 \bmod p$, after the division, r_{i+1} is the correct residual modulo p.

    (c) $y = y + y_i p^i$.

    Each of these steps corrects for the preceding residual by computing y to one more p-adic digit of accuracy. In other words $y = A^{-1}b \bmod p^{2k}$.

4. Apply rational reconstruction to y, p^{2k} to obtain x, the vector of rational numbers solution.

When p is a prime, this is Dixon's method. When $p = (1/2)^{30}$ this is essentially Wan's numeric-symbolic iterative scheme. The method succeeds so long as this is possible at each iteration. Thus there is the possibility of failure due to insufficient numeric accuracy in the iteration not present in Dixon's method. On the other hand, it is possible to exploit whatever amount of accuracy is achieved at each step, which could be more or fewer than 30 bits. In other words, there is no need to use the same power of $1/2$ at each iteration. Wan's iteration (and others) adjust the number of bits used at each iteration to the accuracy of the solver.

The trick to this is to know the accuracy of the solver. The condition number and/or the norm of the residual (absolute and/or relative) have been used as guidance here. The residual norm idea is basically that in step 3b if $r_{i+1} = r_i - A r_i$ is smaller by e bits than r_i, then also the first e bits of y_i are likely to be accurate. As is well known, this is not always the case.

The first contribution of our approach is to replace the use of the residual norm with an overlap confirmed continuation principle. Suppose it is believed that e bits are accurate. The residual norm based iteration would define y_i as w mod 2^{-e}. Thus $w = y_i + 2^{-e}q, (q \leq 1)$ and q is discarded[1]. Instead, we choose the exponent e' of $1/2$ used at each iteration slightly conservatively. Let $e' = e - 1$ and use the decomposition $w = y_i + 2^{-e'}q$. We take a little less in y_i so as to be able to make use of q. Since we believe the numeric solver gave us e bits of accuracy, the first bit in each entry of q is presumably accurate. Thus y_{i+1} should agree with q in the leading bits. When this happens we say we have a *confirmed continuation*. When it fails, we recognize that w was not accurate to e bits, and make an adjustment as described in the next section.

Confirmed continuation is a heuristic, since when it succeeds we do not know with certainty that the solution is accurate. It will succeed very well when the numeric solver is unbiased and the intuition is that it will still do very well when there is bias. Let $A \in \mathbb{Z}^{n \times n}$ and let B be a representation of A^{-1}. Suppose B is unbiased, which means that, for any $b \in \mathbb{Z}^n, s \in \mathbb{Z}$, if $y = Bb$ mod 2^s and $y \neq A^{-1}b$ mod s then the direction of $B(b - Ay)$ is uniformly random. Observe that if B is unbiased then the probability is $1/2^n$ of a false one bit continuation confirmation. This is just the observation that there are 2^n patterns of n bits. This is a rather weak justification for our confirmed continuation heuristic since solvers are rarely if ever unbiased. However, in practice the heuristic is proving to be effective, allowing continuation in some cases in which the residual norm is discouragingly large.

In the next section our confirmed continuation method is described in more detail including the exploitation of techniques to discover the solution sooner when the actual numerators and denominator are smaller than the *a priori* bounds. This is variously called output sensitivity or early termination [5, 18]. Output sensitivity has been used primarily with Dixon's algorithm. The only study of it we know for numeric-symbolic iteration is [21].

---

[1] It is a central idea of Wan's approach to do this truncation so that the next residual may be computed *exactly*.

3. CONFIRMED CONTINUATION AND OUTPUT SENSITIVITY

Our variant on iterative refinement uses the same basic structure as previous implementations. That is, the system is solved numerically in a loop, with the solution at each iteration contributing some bits to the dyadic numerators and common denominator. Specifically, we call the solution in a step of the iteration $\hat{x}$, and divide it into two parts. $\hat{x}_{int}$ contains the higher order bits and is incorporated into the dyadic estimate. $\hat{x}_{frac}$ contains the lower order bits and is unused in Wan's algorithm. The residual vector obtained by applying A to $\hat{x}_{int}$ provides the right-hand side for the next iteration. The loop ends when it is determined the dyadic approximants contain enough information to reconstruct the true rational solution. This determination is made by checking against a pre-computed bound on the size of the rationals.

Algorithm 1 Overlap: Confirmed continuation iterative refinement to solve $Ax = b$

Input: $A \in \mathbb{Z}^{n \times n}, b \in \mathbb{Z}^n, k$. Output: $x \in \mathbb{Z}^n, 0 < q \in \mathbb{Z}$ such that $Ax = qb$.

Compute A^{-1}.   {Numeric LU decomposition}
$N_{1..n} \leftarrow 0$.   {dyadic numerators}
$D \leftarrow 1$.   {common denominator}
loopbound $\leftarrow 2 \times \prod_{i=1}^{n} \|A_i\| \times b_{\max}$.
$r \leftarrow b$.   {Residue of intermediate solutions}
$s \leftarrow 52 - \textbf{bitlength}(n \times \|A\|_\infty \times \|b\|_\infty)$.
thresh $\leftarrow \frac{1}{2^k}$.   {Threshold for overlap confirmation}
$\hat{x} \leftarrow A^{-1}r$.
while $D <$ loopbound **do**
    $\hat{x}_{int} \leftarrow \lfloor \hat{x} \times 2^s + 0.5 \rfloor$.
    $\hat{x}_{frac} \leftarrow \hat{x} - \hat{x}_{int}$.
    $r \leftarrow r \times 2^s - A\hat{x}_{int}$.   {Update residual}
    $\hat{x} \leftarrow A^{-1}r$.
    if $\|\hat{x} - \hat{x}_{frac}\|_\infty >$ thresh **then**
        Shrink s, repeat iteration.
    else
        $N_{1..n} \leftarrow N_{1..n} \times 2^s + \hat{x}_{int}$.   {Update dyadics}
        $D \leftarrow D \times 2^s$.
        if $r = 0$ **then**
            Return: N, D as x, d.
        end if
    end if
end while
Return: $x, d \leftarrow$ Algorithm 3 (N, D).

To ensure the accuracy of the numeric solver's solution at each iteration, we verify there is overlap between the current iteration's numeric solution and the discarded fractional portion of the previous solution. Overlap is demonstrated in the conditional statement where prospective solution $\hat{x}$ is checked against $\hat{x}_{frac}$, the leftover bits from the previous iteration. The vectors are subtracted and the maximal absolute value in the difference set is checked against a threshold $\frac{1}{2^k}$ to ensure k overlapping bits. In practice, we find one bit of overlap (i.e. $k = 1$) suffices to confirm continuation except for very small n.

Once this verification step is successful, we are able to explore seeking more bits of accuracy from the numeric solver. We treat the value s as an adjustable bit-shift length. Each numeric solution $\hat{x}$ is multiplied by 2^s in order to split into

$\hat{x}_{int}$ and $\hat{x}_{frac}$. That is, it is bit-shifted left by s. Likewise when we update the dyadic numerators N, we shift them left by s, then add the new information to the now zeroed lower s bits.

The value of s is at our disposal and allows the algorithm to adapt to changing accuracy from the numeric solver. Ideally it will hug the true number of accurate bits in the intermediate results as closely as possible. As long as some bits of accuracy are provided in each solve, the iteration can continue. Within the bounds of a 52-bit mantissa of a double-precision floating point number, we seek to maximize the shift length to minimize the number of iteration steps. Program speed is the foremost improvement provided by the confirmed continuation method as compared to the residual-norm based iterative refinement.

Finding a good shift length s is a matter of starting at 1 and iteratively doubling until no overlap is evident or the hard ceiling of 52 is reached. The absence of overlap is an indication that we obtained fewer than s bits of numeric accuracy, and we must back off. Required to do this is a copy of the last successful $\hat{x}$. From this we must repeat the extraction of bits using a smaller s, recompute residual, r, and finally solve against this adjusted right-hand side. We use a binary search to determine the maximum value of s that produces overlap, which sits between the failed shift length and the last successful shift length. Algorithm 1 omits these details for brevity, simply initializing s to a sensible starting point.

If the step applying A to $\hat{x}_{int}$ is done in double precision and produces values that cannot fit into the mantissa of a double floating point number, this operation computes an inexact residual. The next iteration would then be solving the wrong problem. This error is detected by neither the norm-based approaches nor the overlap method, since both approaches only guard against numerical inaccuracy of the partial solutions themselves. If the numeric solver itself is accurate, repeated divergence from the problem we intend to solve will be undetected. The algorithm completes after sufficiently many iterations, and reports dyadic estimates that have no hope of being reconstructed into the correct rational solution to the original problem.

To avoid this error, we employ big-integer arithmetic (using GMP) in the residual update, but only when necessary, specifically when $\|A\|_{\infty} \times \|\hat{x}_{int}\|_{\infty} \geq 2^{52}$, which is a conservative condition.

The matrix norm is computed beforehand, so it costs only $O(n)$ work per iteration to compute the vector norm. The flexibility of this approach both prevents the aforementioned divergent behavior and allows for the use of quicker, double precision computation of the exact residual in many cases. Our experience is that for borderline problems that require some bignum residual computation, the need is rare amongst iterations.

Sometimes the numerators and denominator of the final rational solution are significantly smaller than the worst case bound computed *a priori*. When this is the case, it is possible to obtain dyadic approximants of sufficient length to reconstruct the solution before the iterative refinement would normally end. Our early termination strategy is designed to improve running time for these cases. It is sketched in Algorithm 2.

The core iterative refinement loop is still in place, but every so often it is stopped to attempt a rational reconstruction

---

Algorithm 2 Ov-ET: Confirmed continuation iterative refinement w/ Early Termination to solve $Ax = b$

This is Algorithm 1, replacing the while loop (iterative refinement) with:
bound $\leftarrow \prod_{i=1}^{n} \|A_i\|_2$.　　　　{Hadamard bound}
while bound $<$ loopbound **do**
　　while $D <$ bound **do**
　　　　while loop in Algorithm 1.
　　end while
　　bound $\leftarrow \sqrt{bound \times loopbound}$.
　　$i \leftarrow$ **random**$(1..n)$.　　　{Select random element}
　　if Algorithm 3 (N_i, D) is **success then**
　　　　if $x, d \leftarrow$ Algorithm 3 (N, D) is **success then**
　　　　　　Return: x, d.
　　　　end if
　　end if
end while
Return: $x, d \leftarrow$ Algorithm 3 (N, D).

---

from the current dyadic approximation. Specifically it is initially stopped at the halfway point to the worst case bound, that is, as soon as D is larger than the Hadamard bound for $\det(A)$, which is the initial value of *bound* in Algorithm 2. A single-element rational reconstruction is attempted using a random element from the numerator vector N and denominator D. Success here provides encouragement for attempting a full vector reconstruction with all elements of N, which is then performed. Success on the vector reconstruction provides a speculative or guaranteed solution, depending on the reconstructed denominator and length of the dyadic approximation. After a solution verification, we terminate here, potentially saving many iterations.

Upon failure to rationally reconstruct the solution on an early attempt the *bound* is set to the bitwise half-way point between itself and *loopbound*, the point at which iterative refinement would end without early termination. The new value of *bound* serves as the next checkpoint for an early termination attempt. This is a binary search that keeps reporting "higher" after failed guesses. The strategy ensures the number of attempts is logarithmic in the number of iterations required. Also reconstruction attempts are of increasing density as the full iteration bound is approached, which address the expectation that successful early termination becomes increasingly likely. We remark that van Hoeij and Monagan [25] and Steffy [21] also use a logarithmic number of iterations but with increasing density of trials at the low numbered iterations rather than at the end as we do. Either approach ensures good asymptotic behaviour. Which is better in practice is an open question. For good performance in practice, One might use a more uniform spacing of reconstruction trials with frequency such that reconstruction cost does not exceed a specified fraction of overall cost.

4. DYADIC RATIONAL TO RATIONAL RECONSTRUCTION

In an earlier section we made a point of the similarity between numeric approximation and p-adic approximation. When it comes to the rational reconstruction, both may be expressed in terms of extended Euclidean algorithm remainder sequences. However there is a difference. In rational reconstruction from a residue and modulus, the a remainder serves as numerator and the coefficient of the residue as denominator of the approximated rational. The coefficient of the modulus is ignored. In contrast, for dyadic to rational reconstruction we use the two coefficients for the rational and the remainder serves to measure the error of approximation as we explain next.

First consider a single entry of the solution vector. The input to the reconstruction problem is a dyadic n/d (with d a power of 2) together with a known bound B for the denominator of the approximated rational a/b. Let us say that a/b is *well approximated* by n/d if $|a/b - n/d| < 1/2d$. By this definition, n/d can never well approximate the midpoint between $(n \pm 1)/d$ and n/d. But this midpoint has larger denominator, and the rational reconstruction process described below never finds a/b when $b > d$ in any case. In the system solving application, the rational reconstruction would fail but the next iteration would compute a/b exactly and terminate with residual 0.

Proposition 1. *If two distinct fractions a/b and p/q are well approximated by n/d then $d < bq$.*

The proposition follows from the fact that $1 \le |pb - aq|$ (nonzero integer) and the triangle inequality: $1/qb \le |p/q - a/b| \le |p/q - n/d| + |n/d - a/b| < 1/2d + 1/2d = 1/d$,

Proposition 2. *If a/b is well approximated by n/d and $d \ge bB$, then no other fraction with denominator bounded by B is well approximated. Also n/d well approximates at most one rational with denominator bound B when $d \ge B^2$.*

Proposition 4 follows from the previous proposition since $bq \le bB$, when p/q is a second well approximated fraction with denominator bounded by B.

This allows for a *guaranteed* early termination (output sensitive) strategy in the numeric-symbolic iteration. In the Dixon method, early termination is a probabilistic matter (the prime used is chosen at random). It cannot be so in numeric-symbolic iteration, because there is no randomness used.

Reconstruction of the sought fraction a/b is done with the extended Euclidean algorithm remainder sequence of n, d. Define this to be (r_i, q_i, p_i) such that $r_i = q_i n - p_i d$, with $q_0 = p_1 = 1$ and $q_i = p_0 = 0$. We have altered the usual treatment slightly so that p_i and q_i are positive (and strictly increasing) for $i > 1$, while the remainders alternate in sign and decrease in absolute value. Let Q be defined by Euclidean division on the remainders: $|r_{i-1}| = Q|r_i| + r$, with $0 \le r < |r_i|$. Then the recursion is $r_{i+1} = Qr_i + r_{i-1}$, $p_{i+1} = Qp_i + p_{i-1}$, and $q_{i+1} = Qq_i + q_{i-1}$. Also the determinants $p_i q_{i+1} - p_{i+1} q_i$ are alternately 1 and -1. See e.g. [9] for properties of remainder sequences and continued fractions.

Proposition 3. *The coefficients p, q in a term (r, q, p) of the remainder sequence define a rational p/q well approximated by n/d and denominator bounded by B if and only if $2|r| < q \le B$.*

This follows from $r = qn - pd$ so that $|r|/qd = |p/q - n/d| < 1/2d$ (and $q \le B$ by hypothesis).

Proposition 4. *Given n, d, B, let (r, q, p) be the last term such that $q < B$ in the remainder sequence of n, d. This term defines the best approximated B bounded fraction p/q of any term in the remainder sequence.*

When n/d well approximates a rational a/b and $d < bB$ then $a/b = p/q$, i.e. is defined by this term of the remainder sequence.

This follows because $|r|$ is decreasing and q increasing in the remainder sequence. The claim that the rational will be found in the remainder sequence follows from Theorem 4.4 in [26]. Half extended gcd computation computation $((r, q)$ rather than $(r, q, p))$ lowers the cost, with p computed post hoc only for the term of interest.

When this last term below the bound defines a well approximated rational p/q, i.e. $2|r| < q$, we say we have a "guaranteed" reconstruction. When that is not the case, it is still possible that we have found the correct rational. As mentioned in the previous section, sometimes by good luck this leads to successful solutions even when the iteration has not proceeded far enough to have a guaranteed well approximated answer.

Thus we may offer the last approximant from the remainder sequence with denominator bounded by B. It is speculative if $d > bB$ and guaranteed to be the unique solution otherwise. It is never necessary to go beyond $d = B^2$. As the experiments attest, trial reconstructions during the numeric iteration process, can be effective at achieving early termination. The vector reconstruction described next helps keep the cost of these trials low.

To construct a solution in the form of a vector of numerators $x \in \mathbb{Z}^n$ and common denominator q from a vector of $n \in \mathbb{Z}^n$, and common (power of 2) denominator d, we can often avoid reconstructing each entry separately with a remainder sequence computation. We compute x_i as $x_i = [n_i q/d]$. In other words, x_i is the quotient in the division $n_i q = x_i d + r$, with $-d/2 < r < d/2$. The error of the approximation is then $x_i/q - n_i/d| = r/qd$. If this error is bounded by $1/2d$, x_i/q is well approximated by n/d. Thus we have a well approximated result if and only if $2r < q$. When single division fails to produce a well approximated x_i/q, resort to a full remainder sequence. This leads to the following algorithm.

The first loop discovers new factors of the common denominator as it goes along. In practice one or two full reconstructions are needed and the remainder are done by the single division before the if statement. The backward propagation of new factors is delayed to the second loop, to avoid a quadratic number of multiplications. In the worst case this algorithm amounts to n gcd computations. In the best case it is one gcd and $n-1$ checked divisions with remainder. Experimentally we have encountered essentially the best case, with a very few full gcd computations.

A rational reconstruction algorithm presented in another paper of this proceedings achieves a better asymptotic complexity than that of n independent scalar rational reconstructions [2]. That concerns reconstruction from residues and modulus and may be adaptable to the dyadic to rational setting.

To our knowledge, prior algorithms do not assume n/d well approximates (to accuracy $1/2d$) and so do not exploit the guarantee of uniqueness as we do, particularly when using the early termination strategy. However, Cabay [4] gave a guarantee of early termination based on a sufficiently long

Algorithm 3 Vector DyadicToRational

Input: $N \in \mathbb{Z}^n, D \in \mathbb{Z}$. Output: $x \in \mathbb{Z}^n, 0 < d \in \mathbb{Z}$, flag, such that flag is "fail" or N/D well approximates x/d and flag is "speculative" or "guaranteed".

$d \leftarrow 1$.

for i from 1 to n **do**
  $x_i \leftarrow [N_i q/d]$.
  if x_i fails the well approximation test **then**
    x_i, d_i, flag = ScalarDyadicToRational(N_i, D).
    if flag = "fail", return "fail".
    Compute the factorizations $d = a_i g, d_i = b_i g$, where $g = \gcd(d, d_i)$. The new common denominator is $d \leftarrow a_i d_i$, so set $x_i \leftarrow x_i \times a_i$. Prior numerators must be multiplied by b_i. Enqueue b_i for that later.
  end if
end for

$B \leftarrow 1$.

for i from n down to 1 **do**
  $x_i \leftarrow x_i \times B$;
  if $b_i \neq 1$ **then**
    $B \leftarrow B \times b_i$.
  end if
end for

return x, d, flag. [If any scalar reconstruction was speculative, flag = "speculative", otherwise flag = "guaranteed".]

---

sequence of iterations resulting in the same reconstructed rational. This was in the context of Chinese remaindering, but should apply to Hensel lifting and numeric-symbolic iteration as well. Note that our guarantee comes from a single reconstruction, not a series. Steffy exploits speculative reconstructions as we do and gives a guaranteeing condition based on the error of the approximation [21, lemma 2.6]. Note that our overlap heuristic provides evidence on the error that is independent of a condition number estimation. It could be useful to accept reconstructions earlier in the iteration using Steffy's condition and our measure of the error. We have not yet experimented with this.

5. EXPERIMENTS

For test matrices, we use the following 8 matrix families $H_n, J_n, Q_n, S_n, m_n, M_n, R_n, Z_n$ described next.

H_n: The inverse of the $n \times n$ Hilbert matrix. This is a famously ill-conditioned matrix. The condition number of H_n

$$\kappa(H_n) = \|H_n\|_2 \|H_n^{-1}\|_2 \approx c \, 33.97^n/\sqrt{n}$$

where c is a constant, is quoted in[1]. We find that our numeric solvers – both the residual norm based and the overlap confirmed continuation approach – can handle this matrix only up to $n = 11$. On the other hand, Dixon's p-adic iteration can handle any size, provided p is chosen large enough to insure the nonsingularity of H_n mod p. For instance, Dixon does the $n = 100$ case in 12 seconds. This class is introduced only to illustrate the potential for numeric solver failure due to ill-condition.

J_n: This matrix is twice the $n \times n$ Jordan block for the eigenvalue $1/2$. We multiply by 2 to get an integer matrix. It is a square matrix with 1's on the diagonal, and 2's on the first subdiagonal. Numerical computations for matrices with repeated eigenvalues are notoriously difficult. The inverse matrix contains $(-2)^j$ on the j-th subdiagonal. For

Examples of numeric failure to converge			
matrix	Dixon	Wan	Overlap
J_{994}	2.27	1.77	**0.0850**
J_{995}	2.23	fail	**0.0920**
J_{1022}	2.40	fail	**0.100**
J_{1023}	**2.38**	fail	fail
J_{2000}	**13.3**	fail	fail
Q_{500}	2.07	fail	**0.81**
Q_{1000}	15.0	fail	**7.29**
Q_{2000}	121	fail	**70.3**
Q_{4000}	1460	fail	**633**

Table 1: Dixon is p-adic iteration, Wan is numeric-symbolic iteration using residual norm based continuation, Overlap is the confirmed continuation of this paper. Times are in seconds.

$n > 1023$, the matrix J_n^{-1} is not representable in double precision (infinity entries), and for smaller n it poses numerical challenges.

Table 1 shows that the numeric-symbolic solvers are faster than the p-adic lifting when they work, but they have difficulties with J_n.

For reasons we do not completely understand, on another machine the thresholds at which the solvers have convergence problems are different than in Table 1. We suspect it has to do with a different LAPACK version. On that machine, for n larger than 54, Wan's residual norm based solver is discouraged by the first residual and gives up.

For n larger than 1023, infinities (numbers not representable in double precision) defeat all numeric solving. The bottom left entry of J_n^{-1} is 2^{n-1} which is not representable when $n \geq 1024$. However, the overlap solver fails at $n = 1023$. Although the inverse matrix itself is just barely representable, some numbers which occur in the matrix-vector products are not representable in this case.

Q_n: Let $Q_n = DLD$, where L is the $n \times n$ Lehmer matrix[23, 14], with elements $L_{i,j} = \min(i,j)/\max(i,j)$, and D is the diagonal matrix with $D_{i,i} = i$. Thus Q is an integral Brownian matrix[11] with $Q_{i,j} = \min(i,j)^2$ ("Q" is for quadratic). A closed form expression, $\det(Q_n) = 2^{-n}(2n)!/n!$ follows from[13].

Note that $Lx = b$ iff $x = Dy$ and $Qy = Db$ (also $De_1 = e_1$). Being an integer matrix, Q fits in our experimental framework while rational L does not.

Table 1 includes Q_n measurements concerning numeric difficulties. In his recent experiments, Steffy[21] used the Lehmer matrix as an example where Dixon's method works but numeric-symbolic iteration does not. We include it here because it shows a striking difference between residual norm based continuation and overlap confirmed continuation in numeric-symbolic iteration. In fact, Wan's code in LinBox fails on Q_n for $n > 26$.

The examples of Q_n, along with the remaining five classes of examples, are used for our performance study shown in Table 2. These test cases are in many collections of matrices used for testing. A notable such collection[3] is maintained by John Burkardt.

Three of our test matrices (Q_n, m_n, and M_n) are Brownian matrices[11] in that they have have a "echelon" structure: that is, the elements obey $b_{i,j+1} = b_{i,j}, j > i$, and $b_{i+1,j} =$

$b_{i,j}, i > j$, for all i, j. Many Brownian matrices have known closed form results for inverses, determinants, factorization, etc. One source of special results is the following observation[11]. If the matrix P is taken to be a Jordan block corresponding to a repeated eigenvalue of -1, then PBP^T is tridiagonal if and only if B is Brownian.

S_n: The $n \times n$ Hadamard matrix using Sylvester's definition. $S_1 = (1), S_{2n} = \begin{pmatrix} S_n & S_n \\ S_n & -S_n \end{pmatrix}$. This definition results in n being a power of two. The determinant of S_n equals $n^{n/2}$, which is sharp for the Hadamard bound. Thus, for any integral right hand side, the solution is a dyadic rational vector. This provides a test of early termination due to a zero residual.

Algorithm performance comparisons				
Matrix	Dixon	Wan	Overlap	Ov-ET
S_{512}	0.728	0.711	0.0723	**0.0721**
m_{500}	1.28	1.34	**0.273**	0.273
M_{500}	1.46	fail	1.06	**0.562**
Q_{500}	2.41	fail	2.98	**1.39**
R_{500}	1.09	1.04	1.05	**0.931**
Z_{500}	0.793	0.864	0.584	**0.580**
S_{1024}	4.58	4.75	0.380	**0.371**
m_{1000}	8.83	10.8	**2.24**	2.24
M_{1000}	10.2	fail	8.56	**4.42**
Q_{1000}	**16.6**	fail	24.5	17.4
R_{1000}	7.25	fail	6.87	**6.48**
Z_{1000}	6.04	6.38	**4.41**	4.46
S_{2048}	32.3	36.6	**2.08**	2.10
m_{2000}	72.0	89.6	17.1	**17.0**
M_{2000}	82.8	fail	75.0	**37.8**
Q_{2000}	**137**	fail	243	167
R_{2000}	54.6	fail	53.7	**49.3**
Z_{2000}	45.4	52.15	35.8	**34.1**
S_{4096}	255	297	**11.7**	11.7
m_{4000}	579	783	**138**	138
M_{4000}	628	fail	658	**319**
Q_{4000}	**1519**	fail	3274	2294
R_{4000}	**380**	fail	393	397
Z_{4000}	340	439	318	**271**
S_{8192}	2240	2517	**77.6**	82.6
m_{8000}	mem	6802	**1133**	1138
M_{8000}	mem	fail	6170.6	**3049**
Q_{8000}	mem	fail	33684	**27367**
R_{8000}	mem	fail	**2625**	2710
Z_{8000}	mem	5771	2584	**2474**

Table 2: Dixon, Wan, and Overlap columns are as in Table 1. Ov-ET is Overlap with with early termination enabled. "mem" denotes out of memory. Times are in seconds.

m_n: The $n \times n$ matrix with $m_{i,j} = \min(i, j)$. Because this a Brownian matrix[11], PBP^T is tridiagonal, and in this case, the tridiagonal matrix is the identity matrix. Thus, determinant of m_n is 1, so the solution is integral for any integral right hand side. This is another case where early termination due to zero residual is expected. But the entries in the inverse are larger than in the Hadamard matrix case, so more iterations may be needed for this example.

M_n: The $n \times n$ matrix with $M_{i,j} = \max(i, j)$. The determinant of this matrix is $(-1)^{n+1}n$, so the solution vector has denominator much smaller than the Hadamard bound predicts. The determinant of M_n is found by reversing its rows and columns, which does not change its determinant. The result is a Brownian matrix. Its tridiagonal form using the matrix P is the identity matrix — except for the value $(-1)^n n$ in the upper left corner.

The previous three test cases can benefit from early termination. Q_n and the following 2 are expected to benefit less from output sensitivity.

R_n: An $n \times n$ matrix with random entries in $(-100, 100)$.

Z_n: An $n \times n$ $\{0, 1\}$-matrix with probability $1/2$ of a 1 in a given position. This is meant to represent some commonly occurring applications. The LinBox library is often used to compute Smith forms of incidence matrices, where invariant factor computation involves solving linear systems with random right hand sides.

Reported are run times on a 3.0 GHz Intel Pentium D processor in a Linux 2.6.32 environment. All codes used are in LinBox, svn revision 3639, and will be included in the next LinBox release. The experiments were run with right hand sides being e_1, the first column of the identity matrix. This provides a direct comparison to Steffy's examples [21] and in some cases allows checking a known solution formula. But for Q_n, M_n, and Z_n, the right hand sides used are random with entries in $(-100, 100)$. This is to create an interesting early termination situation in the case of Q_n and M_n (where the solution for rhs e_1 is obtained in the first iteration). For Z_n it is in view of the expected application.

S_{2^k} and m_n are examples where the determinant is a power of two and considerably less than the Hadamard bound. Thus an early termination due to a perfect dyadic expansion with residual zero can occur and no rational reconstruction is needed. Both forms of the Overlap algorithm verify this. The current implementation of Wan's method does not check for an exactly zero residual, though there no reason it could not. The determinant (thus the denominator of solution vector) of S_n is $n = 2^k$ and the Hadamard bound is considerably larger, $n^{n/2}$. Output sensitive termination due to zero residual accounts for the factor of 10 or more speedups. The determinant of m_n is 1 and the Hadamard bound is larger than that of S_n. For right hand side e_1 the solution vector is $2e_2 - e_1$ so that essentially no iteration is required if early termination (Dixon) or zero residual detection (Overlap) is used. In these cases all the time is in matrix factorization which is about 4 times more costly modulo a prime (Dixon) than numerically using LAPACK (Overlap). The Wan's implementation lacks the early termination so does a full iteration. That more than offsets the faster matrix factorization than in Dixon making Wan's the slowest on the m_n family.

M_n and Q_n results show early termination saving a factor of about 2, the most available with sufficient dyadic approximation for a guaranteed rational reconstruction. Further speedup is possible from very early speculative reconstructions. We have not explored this.

In the data for the random entry matrix, R_n, and random $\{0, 1\}$-matrix, Z_n, we see variable speedups up to a factor of 1.8 over Dixon's p-adic lifting, sometimes aided a bit by early termination. Significant early termination is not generally expected for these matrix families.

The overlap method should work well with sparse numeric solvers (both direct and iterative) for sparse matrices as well. In that case performance asymptotically better than obtained with Dixon's method can be expected. The significant symbolic competition will be the method of Eberly, et al[8]. We intend to explore the sparse matrix problem in the future. To this end we have made a LinBox interface to call MATLAB functions.

6. REFERENCES

[1] Bernhard Beckermann. The condition number of real Vandermonde, Krylov and positive definite Hankel matrices. *Numerische Mathematik*, 85:553–577, 1997.

[2] C. Bright and A. Storjohan. Vector rational number reconstruction. In *ISSAC '11*. ACM, 2011.

[3] John Burkardt. TEST MAT Test Matrices. http://people.sc.fsu.edu/~jburkardt/c_src/test_mat/ test_mat.html.

[4] Stanley Cabay. Exact solution of linear equations. In *Proceedings of the second ACM symposium on Symbolic and algebraic manipulation*, SYMSAC '71, pages 392–398, New York, NY, USA, 1971. ACM.

[5] Z. Chen and A. Storjohann. A BLAS based C library for exact linear algebra on integer matrices. In *Proc. of ISSAC'05*, pages 92–99. ACM Press, 2005.

[6] J. D. Dixon. Exact solution of linear equations using *p*-adic expansion. *Numer. Math.*, pages 137–141, 1982.

[7] J-G. Dumas, T. Gautier, M. Giesbrecht, P. Giorgi, B. Hovinen, E. Kaltofen, B. D. Saunders, W. Turner, and G. Villard. Linbox: A generic library for exact linear algebra. In *ICMS'02*, pages 40–50, 2002.

[8] W. Eberly, M. Giesbrecht, P. Giorgi, A. Storjohann, and G. Villard. Solving sparse rational linear systems. In *Proc. of ISSAC'06*, pages 63–70. ACM Press, 2006.

[9] Joachim Von Zur Gathen and Jurgen Gerhard. *Modern Computer Algebra*. Cambridge University Press, New York, NY, USA, 2 edition, 2003.

[10] Keith O. Geddes and Wei Wei Zheng. Exploiting fast hardware floating point in high precision computation. In J. Rafael Sendra, editor, *ISSAC*, pages 111–118. ACM, 2003.

[11] M. J. C. Gover and S. Barnett. Brownian matrices: properties and extensions. *International Journal of Systems Science*, 17(2):381–386, 1986.

[12] Andrzej Kiełbasiński. Iterative refinement for linear systems in variable-precision arithmetic. *BIT*, 21(1):97–103, 1981.

[13] E. Kilic and P. Stanica. The Lehmer matrix and its recursive analogue. *Journal of Combinatorial Mathematics and Combinatorial Computing*, 74(2):195–205, 2010.

[14] D. H. Lehmer. Solutions to problem E710, proposed by D. H. Lehmer: The inverse of a matrix, November 1946.

[15] Robert T. Moenck and John H. Carter. Approximate algorithms to derive exact solutions to systems of linear equations. In *Proceedings of the International Symposium on on Symbolic and Algebraic Computation*, pages 65–73, London, UK, 1979. Springer-Verlag.

[16] Michael B. Monagan. Maximal quotient rational reconstruction: an almost optimal algorithm for rational reconstruction. In Jaime Gutierrez, editor, *ISSAC*, pages 243–249. ACM, 2004.

[17] Teo Mora, editor. *Symbolic and Algebraic Computation, International Symposium ISSAC 2002, Lille, France, July 7-10, 2002, Proceedings*. ACM, 2002.

[18] T. Mulders and A. Storjohann. Certified dense linear system solving. *Jounal of symbolic computation*, 37(4), 2004.

[19] Victor Y. Pan and Xinmao Wang. Acceleration of euclidean algorithm and extensions. In Mora [17], pages 207–213.

[20] Alicja Smoktunowicz and Jolanta Sokolnicka. Binary cascades iterative refinement in doubled-mantissa arithmetics. *BIT*, 24(1):123–127, 1984.

[21] Daniel Steffy. Exact solutions to linear systems of equations using output sensitive lifting. *ACM Communications in Computer Algebra*, 44(4):160–182, 2010.

[22] The LinBox Team. LinBox, a C++ library for exact linear algebra. http://www.linalg.org/.

[23] John Todd. *Basic Numerical Mathematics, Vol. 2: Numerical Algebra*. Birkhäuser, Basel, and Academic Press, New York, 1977.

[24] Silvio Ursic and Cyro Patarra. Exact solution of systems of linear equations with iterative methods. *SIAM Journal on Algebraic and Discrete Methods*, 4(1):111–115, 1983.

[25] Mark van Hoeij and Michael B. Monagan. A modular gcd algorithm over number fields presented with multiple extensions. In Mora [17], pages 109–116.

[26] Zhengdong Wan. *Computing the Smith Forms of Integer Matrices and Solving Related Problems*. PhD thesis, University of Delaware, Newark, DE, 2005.

[27] Zhengdong Wan. An algorithm to solve integer linear systems exactly using numerical methods. *Journal of Symbolic Computation*, 41:621–632, 2006.

[28] James H. Wilkinson. *Rounding Errors in Algebraic Processes*. Dover Publications, Incorporated, 1994.

Algebraic Analysis on Asymptotic Stability of Continuous Dynamical Systems

Zhikun She, Bai Xue, Zhiming Zheng

LMIB and School of Mathematics and Systems Science, Beihang University, China

zhikun.she@buaa.edu.cn, xuebai0402@163.com, zzheng@pku.edu.cn

ABSTRACT

In this paper we propose a mechanisable technique for asymptotic stability analysis of continuous dynamical systems. We start from linearizing a continuous dynamical system, solving the Lyapunov matrix equation and then check whether the solution is positive definite. For the cases that the Jacobian matrix is not a Hurwitz matrix, we first derive an algebraizable sufficient condition for the existence of a Lyapunov function in quadratic form without linearization. Then, we apply a real root classification based method step by step to formulate this derived condition as a semi-algebraic set such that the semi-algebraic set only involves the coefficients of the pre-assumed quadratic form. Finally, we compute a sample point in the resulting semi-algebraic set for the coefficients resulting in a Lyapunov function. In this way, we avoid the use of generic quantifier elimination techniques for efficient computation. We prototypically implemented our algorithm based on DISCOVERER. The experimental results and comparisons demonstrate the feasibility and promise of our approach.

Categories and Subject Descriptors

I.1 [**Symbolic and algebraic manipulation**]: Applications, Algorithms; J.7 [**Computers in other systems**]: Real time

General Terms

Verification, Theory, Algorithms

Keywords

Lyapunov matrix equations, Lyapunov functions, semi-algebraic sets, real root classification

1. INTRODUCTION

Stability analysis [11] plays a very important role in the analysis and design of control systems, for instance, in gyroscopic systems [7], power systems [15] and biological systems [31]. A sufficient condition for verifying asymptotic stability of continuous dynamical systems is the existence of a Lyapunov function [11]. In cases where the differential equations are polynomial, due to decidability of the theory of real-closed fields [30], there is an algorithm that, for a given polynomial with parametric coefficients, decides whether there are instantiations of these parameters resulting in a Lyapunov function. However, all the existing decision procedures (e.g., implemented in the software packages QEPCAD [3] or REDLOG [5]), while being able to solve impressively difficult examples, are not efficient enough to be able to solve this problem in practice. Thus, Weber and his co-authors [32] have pointed out that finding constructive and efficient ways for generating appropriate Lyapunov functions is one possible future direction.

In addition to quantifier elimination [8, 10, 28, 24], there are two other methods for computing Lyapunov functions for differentiable equations in the literature. One is the Gröbner bases method, by choosing the parameters in Lyapunov function in an optimal way [6]. The other one is the sums of squares decomposition [20, 16] based method by using the relaxation to linear matrix inequalities [17].

In this paper, we propose a mechanisable technique for asymptotic stability analysis of continuous dynamic systems.

We start with the linearization of continuous dynamical systems. That is, for a given continuous dynamical system, we linearize this system, solve the Lyapunov matrix equation and then use the Descartes rule to check whether the solution is positive definite.

For the cases that stability cannot be verified by linearization, that is, the Jacobian matrix is not a Hurwitz matrix (e.g., the Jacobian matrix has more than one pair of conjugated purely imaginary eigenvalues or at least one eigenvalue equal to zero), we first construct a sufficient condition for the existence of a Lyapunov function in quadratic form without linearization. Based on this condition, we apply a real root classification method to eliminate variables step by step, arriving at a semi-algebraic set which only involves the coefficients of the pre-assumed quadratic form. Then we compute a sample point in the resulting semi-algebraic set for the coefficients. Note that since a special structure is considered in our procedure, we can avoid using generic quantifier elimination techniques for efficiency.

We prototypically implemented our algorithms based on the semi-algebraic system solver DISCOVERER [33] with manual intervention. The computation results and comparisons demonstrate the feasibility and promise of our approach.

Our current algorithms can be extended for stability analysis of parametric systems with applications to biological systems [31, 28, 23] by solving a parametric semi-algebraic system. In addition, our algebraic approach can also be extended for computing Lyapunov functions beyond quadratic forms after modifications.

Moreover, our algorithms can be extended for stability analysis of switched hybrid systems [14] by computation of common and multiple Lyapunov functions [18, 9, 1]

Note that we have used a relaxation-and-checking scheme for nonlinear dynamical systems in [24]. That is, we first linearize the system and check whether there is a positive definite quadratic form such that its derivative according to linearization is semi-negative definite; then, we use the quantifier elimination method to check whether the sampling quadratic form is a Lyapunov function of the nonlinear system. However, in this present paper, we first derive an algebraizable sufficient condition for the existence of a Lyapunov function without linearization; then, we formulate the first condition as a semi-algebraic set by applying the Descartes rule and the second derived condition as a semi-algebraic set by applying a real root classification based method; finally, we solve the resulting semi-algebraic system. Thus, our current approach has two advantages: one is that it will work for more cases since it does not require checking on sampling quadratic forms and thus does not lose the possible solutions; the other is that it is more efficient since it avoids the quantifier elimination method used in [24].

The structure of the paper is as follows: After introducing some preliminaries about continuous dynamical systems in Subsection 2.1, we start with the classical Lyapunov matrix equation based method in Subsection 2.2; Then, we present our real root classification based method in Section 3 for computing Lyapunov functions in quadratic form, and analyze the method theoretically in Section 4. After a brief introduction to our implementation in Section 5, we experimentally evaluate our algorithms with comparisons in Section 6; We conclude the paper in Section 7.

2. STABILITY ANALYSIS OF CONTINUOUS DYNAMICAL SYSTEMS

2.1 Preliminaries

Consider an autonomous polynomial system of form

$$\dot{\vec{x}} = f(\vec{x}) \tag{1}$$

where $\vec{x} = (x_1, \cdots, x_n)^T$, $f = (f_1, \cdots, f_n)^T$, and $f_i : \mathbb{R}^n \mapsto \mathbb{R}$ is a polynomial in $\mathbb{Q}[\vec{x}]$. A point $\vec{x}^*$ is an equilibrium if $f(\vec{x}^*) = \vec{0}$. Without loss of generality, we assume that the origin is one of its equilibria if its equilibrium exists. If not specified, we denote psf the system (1) with an equilibrium at the origin. Moreover, for a given psf, the asymptotic stability means the asymptotic stability of the origin in the Lyapunov sense [7], which can be assured by the existence of a Lyapunov function [7] defined as follows.

DEFINITION 1. *Given an autonomous polynomial system psf and a neighborhood $\mathbf{U}$ of the origin, a Lyapunov function (or, LF) with respect to psf is a continuously differentiable function $V : \mathbf{U} \mapsto \mathbb{R}$ such that*

1. *$V(\vec{x})$ is positive definite (i.e., $V(\vec{x}) \geq 0$ and $V(\vec{x}) = 0$ if and only if $\vec{x} = \vec{0}$);*

2. *$\frac{d}{dt}V(\vec{0}) = 0$ and $\frac{d}{dt}V(\vec{x}) < 0$ whenever $\vec{x} \neq \vec{0}$.*

2.2 Lyapunov Matrix Equation based Approach

For a given nonlinear system $\dot{\vec{x}} = f(\vec{x})$, let us consider its linearization about the origin

$$\dot{\vec{x}} = A\vec{x}, \text{ where } A = \frac{\partial f}{\partial \vec{x}}(\vec{0}).$$

As we know, for every eigenvalue of $A = (a_{i,j})_{n \times n}$, if its real part is less than zero, that is, A is a Hurwitz matrix, then the origin is asymptotically stable.

For checking whether A is a Hurwitz matrix, we use the following lemma.

LEMMA 1. *[11] A is a Hurwitz matrix if and only if for any given positive definite symmetric matrix Q, there exists a positive definite symmetric matrix P that satisfies the Lyapunov matrix equation $PA + A^TP = -Q$. Moreover, if A is Hurwitz, then P is the unique solution of the Lyapunov matrix equation.*

Let Q be the unit matrix I. Due to Theorem 1, if there is a positive definite P such that $PA + A^TP = -I$, then A is a Hurwitz matrix and $V(\vec{x}) = \vec{x}^TP\vec{x}$ is a Lyapunov function.

Due to the uniqueness of the solution to the Lyapunov matrix equation when A is a Hurwitz matrix, we can first solve the Lyapunov matrix equation which is linear and then check whether the solution is positive definite.

For checking positive definiteness, we first recall the following lemma, which is a consequence of the Descartes rule. Note that we prefer the Descartes rule since it can be used to check semi-positive definiteness required for computing multiple Lyapunov functions, which will be our future work.

LEMMA 2. *For a real polynomial $h(\lambda) = \lambda^n + c_{n-1}\lambda^{n-1} + \cdots + c_0$, suppose that all its roots are real. Then all the roots are positive if and only if for all $1 \leq i \leq n$, $(-1)^i c_{n-i} > 0$.*

Let $P = (p_{i,j})_{n \times n}$ be a symmetric matrix and $h(\lambda) = \lambda^n + c_{n-1}(\vec{p})\lambda^{n-1} + \cdots + c_0(\vec{p})$ be its characteristic polynomial, where $\vec{p} = (p_{1,1}, \cdots, p_{n,n})$ and $c_i(\vec{p})$ $(i \in \{0, \cdots, n-1\})$ is a polynomial over $p_{1,1}, \cdots, p_{n,n}$. We have Algorithm 1 for verifying asymptotic stability of a given psf as follows.

Clearly, Algorithm 1 is simpler than the one proposed in [24] due to the fact that we here solve linear equations instead of solving a semi-algebraic system. But, this Lyapunov matrix equation based method is not our major focus since there are also many other efficiently classical criteria for stability analysis of linearization, for example, Routh-Hurwitz and Liénard-Chipard criteria [8, 10, 31, 28].

However, all these efficient classical criteria mentioned above still do not work for the cases that the system is stable but its Jacobian matrix A is not a Hurwitz matrix, e.g., A has more than one pair of conjugated purely imaginary eigenvalues or at least one eigenvalue equal to zero. We will in the next section directly work on such a nonlinear system by computing Lyapunov functions.

3. REAL ROOT CLASSIFICATION BASED ALGEBRAIC APPROACH

As mentioned in Subsection 2.2, Algorithm 1 will return "Unknown" for the cases that the system is stable but the matrix A in its linearization is not a Hurwitz matrix. In

Algorithm 1 Lyapunov matrix equation based method

Input: A given differential system $\dot{\vec{x}} = f(\vec{x})$.
Output: Asymptotically Stable or Unknown.
1: let $P = (p_{i,j})_{n \times n}$ with $p_{i,j} = p_{j,i}$ be a parametric matrix and compute its characteristic polynomial to get the parametric coefficients $c_i(\vec{p})$, $i \in \{0, \cdots, n-1\}$.
2: compute the linearization system to get A.
3: solve the Lyapunov matrix equation $A^T P + PA = -I$ for P.
4: **if** P is unique **then**
5:     check whether P satisfies $c_i(\vec{p}) > 0$ for all $i \in \{0, \cdots, n-1\}$.
6:     **if** yes **then**
7:         return $V = \vec{x}^T P \vec{x}$ as a Lyapunov function, associated with "Asymptotically Stable".
8:     **else**
9:         return Unknown.
10:     **end if**
11: **else**
12:     return Unknown.
13: **end if**

this section, without linearization, we will construct a sufficient condition for the existence of a Lyapunov function in quadratic form, and then apply a real root classification based method to compute a Lyapunov function, which can avoid the use of generic quantifier elimination techniques.

For a psf, let $V(\vec{x})$ be a quadratic form and represent $\dot{V} = \frac{d}{dt}V(\vec{x}) = (\nabla V(\vec{x}))^T \cdot f(x)$ as $\sum_{i=2}^m v_i(\vec{x})$, where m is the degree of $\dot{V}(\vec{x})$ and $v_i(\vec{x})$ is a homogeneous polynomial of degree i. Before constructing a sufficient condition for the existence of a Lyapunov function in quadratic form, we need the following theorem with detailed proof since we cannot find the proof in the literature.

THEOREM 1. *Let $p = p(\vec{x})$ be a polynomial of degree $m \geq 2$. If $p(\vec{x})$ is positive definite, then for every polynomial $q(\vec{x})$ of form $\sum_{i=m+1}^k q_i(\vec{x})$, where $q_i(\vec{x})$ is a homogeneous polynomial of degree i, there is a a neighborhood $\mathbb{U}$ of $\vec{x} = \vec{0}$ such that the sum $p(\vec{x}) + q(\vec{x})$ is positive definite in $\mathbb{U}$.*

PROOF. First, we transform the Cartesian coordinates $(x_1, \cdots, x_n)$ to polar coordinates $(r, \theta_1, \cdots, \theta_{n-1})$. Letting

$$\begin{cases} x_1 = r\cos\theta_1 \\ x_2 = r\sin\theta_1\cos\theta_2 \\ \cdots \\ x_n = r\sin\theta_1\sin\theta_2 \cdots \sin\theta_{n-2}\sin\theta_{n-1} \end{cases},$$

where $0 \leq r < +\infty$, $0 \leq \theta_1, \cdots, \theta_{n-2} \leq \pi$, $0 \leq \theta_{n-1} \leq 2\pi$, we get $p(r, \vec{\theta}) = r^2\phi_2(\vec{\theta}) + r^3\phi_3(\vec{\theta}) + \cdots + r^m\phi_m(\vec{\theta})$ and $q(r, \vec{\theta}) = \sum_{i=m+1}^k r^i\phi_i(\vec{\theta})$, where $\vec{\theta} = (\theta_1, \cdots, \theta_{n-1})$.

Letting $\Omega_1 = \{\vec{\theta} : 0 \leq \theta_1, \cdots, \theta_{n-2} \leq \pi, 0 \leq \theta_{n-1} \leq 2\pi\}$ and $f(r, \vec{\theta}) = p(r, \vec{\theta}) + q(r, \vec{\theta})$, it is sufficient to only prove that there is an $l > 0$ such that $f(r, \vec{\theta})$ is positive definite in $\{(r, \vec{\theta}) : 0 < r < l, \vec{\theta} \in \Omega_1\}$.

Since $p(r, \vec{\theta})$ is positive definite, there is no $\vec{\theta} \in \Omega_1$ such that $\phi_2(\vec{\theta}) = 0, \cdots$, and $\phi_m(\vec{\theta}) = 0$. Let $\Omega_{i-1} = \{\vec{\theta} : \phi_2(\vec{\theta}) = 0, \cdots, \phi_{i-1}(\vec{\theta}) = 0\}$, where $3 \leq i \leq m-1$.

Clearly, for every $2 \leq i \leq m-1$, Ω_{i-1} is compact, $\Omega_{i-1} \subseteq \Omega_{i-2} \subseteq \cdots \subseteq \Omega_2 \subseteq \Omega_1$ and there is an index I such that $2 \leq I \leq m-1$, $\Omega_I = \emptyset$ and $\Omega_{I-1} \neq \emptyset$.

We can get a subset ω' from the set $\omega = \{2, \cdots, I\}$ using the following strategy: (1) let $s := I - 1$ and $\omega' := \omega$; (2) if $s \geq 2$ and there exists a k such that $\Omega_s = \Omega_k$, where $1 \leq k < s$, then $\omega' := \omega' \setminus \{s\}$, $s := s - 1$ and return to (2). Denote ω' as $\{I_1, \cdots, I_j, I_{j+1}\}$, where $I_1 < \cdots < I_{j+1}$. Clearly, $I_1 = 1$, $I_{j+1} = I$ and for each $k = 2, \cdots, j+1$ and for each s satisfying $I_{k-1} < s < I_k$, $\phi_s(\vec{\theta}) \equiv 0$ in $\Omega_{I_{k-1}}$.

For all $\vec{\theta} \in \Omega_{I_j}$, $p(r, \vec{\theta}) = r^I(\phi_I(\theta) + r\phi_{I+1}(\theta) + \cdots)$. Due to the assumption that $p(r, \vec{\theta})$ is positive definite, for all $\vec{\theta} \in \Omega_{I_j}$, $\phi_I(\vec{\theta}) > 0$. Since Ω_{I_j} is compact, there exists a $\varepsilon_I > 0$ such that $\phi_I(\vec{\theta}) \geq \varepsilon_I$. Thus, there is an open set H_{I_j} such that $\Omega_{I_j} \subsetneq H_{I_j}$ and for all $\vec{\theta} \in H_{I_j}$, $\phi_I(\vec{\theta}) \geq \frac{\varepsilon_I}{2}$.

Due to the assumption that $p(r, \vec{\theta})$ is positive definite, $\phi_{I_j}(\vec{\theta}) \geq 0$ in $\Omega_{I_{j-1}}$. So, for all $\vec{\theta} \in H_{I_j} \cap \Omega_{I_{j-1}}$, $p(r, \vec{\theta}) = r^{I_j}(\phi_{I_j}(\theta) + r^{I_{j+1}-I_j}\phi_{I_{j+1}}(\theta) + \cdots) \geq r^{I_j}(\frac{\varepsilon_I}{2} + r\phi_{I+1}(\vec{\theta}) + \cdots)$. Thus, there exists $r_{I_{j+1}} > 0$ such that $f(r, \vec{\theta})$ is positive definite in $\{(r, \theta) : 0 < r < r_{I_{j+1}}, \theta \in H_{I_j} \cap \Omega_{I_{j-1}}\}$.

Let $\Omega'_{I_{j-1}} = \Omega_{I_{j-1}} \setminus H_{I_j}$. Then, $\phi_{I_j}(\vec{\theta}) \neq 0$ in $\Omega'_{I_{j-1}}$. Due to the assumption that $p(r, \vec{\theta})$ is positive definite, $\phi_{I_j}(\vec{\theta}) > 0$ in $\Omega'_{I_{j-1}}$. Since $\Omega'_{I_{j-1}}$ is also compact, there exists a $\varepsilon_{I_j} > 0$ such that $\phi_{I_j}(\vec{\theta}) \geq \varepsilon_{I_j}$. Thus, there is an open set $H_{I_{j-1}}$ such that $\Omega'_{I_{j-1}} \subsetneq H_{I_{j-1}}$ and for all $\vec{\theta} \in H_{I_{j-1}}$, $\phi_{I_j}(\vec{\theta}) \geq \frac{\varepsilon_{I_j}}{2}$.

According to the assumption that $p(r, \vec{\theta})$ is positive definite, $\phi_{I_{j-1}}(\vec{\theta}) \geq 0$ in $\Omega_{I_{j-2}}$. So, for all $\vec{\theta} \in H_{I_{j-1}} \cap \Omega_{I_{j-2}}$, $p(r, \vec{\theta}) = r^{I_{j-1}}(\phi_{I_{j-1}}(\theta) + r^{I_j-I_{j-1}}\phi_{I_j}(\theta) + \cdots) \geq r^{I_{j-1}}(\frac{\varepsilon_{I_j}}{2} + r\phi_I(\vec{\theta}) + \cdots)$. Thus, there exists $r_{I_j} > 0$ such that $f(r, \vec{\theta})$ is positive definite in $\{(r, \theta) : 0 < r < r_{I_j}, \theta \in H_{I_{j-1}} \cap \Omega_{I_{j-2}}\}$.

Due to deduction, we can prove that there exist an open set H_{I_i} and $r_{I_{i+1}} > 0$ such that $f(r, \vec{\theta})$ is positive definite in $\{(r, \theta) : 0 < r < r_{I_3}, \theta \in H_{I_i} \cap \Omega_{I_{i+1}}\}$, where $i = 2, \cdots, j-1$.

According to the assumption that $p(r, \vec{\theta})$ is positive definite, $\phi_{I_2}(\vec{\theta}) > 0$ in $\Omega \setminus \cup_{k=1}^{j-1}(\Omega_{I_k} \cap H_{I_{k+1}})$. Since $\Omega \setminus \cup_{k=1}^{j-1}(\Omega_{I_k} \cap H_{I_{k+1}})$ is also compact, there exists a $\varepsilon_{I_2} > 0$ such that $\phi_{I_2}(\vec{\theta}) \geq \varepsilon_{I_2}$ for all $\vec{\theta} \in \Omega \setminus \cup_{k=1}^{j-1}(\Omega_{I_k} \cap H_{I_{k+1}})$. Thus, there exists $r_{I_2} > 0$ such that $f(r, \vec{\theta})$ is positive definite in $\{(r, \vec{\theta}) : 0 < r < r_2, \vec{\theta} \in \Omega \setminus \cup_{k=1}^{j-1}(\Omega_{I_k} \cap H_{I_{k+1}})\}$.

So, letting $r_0 = \min\{r_{I_2}, \cdots, r_{I_{j+1}}\}$, $f(r, \vec{\theta})$ is positive definite in $\{(r, \vec{\theta}) : 0 < r < r_0, \vec{\theta} \in \Omega\}$. $\square$

Now we can construct a sufficient condition for the existence of a Lyapunov function in quadratic form as follows.

THEOREM 2. *Supposed $V = V(\vec{x}) : \mathbb{R}^n \to \mathbb{R}$ is a polynomial in quadratic form such that*

1. $V(\vec{x})$ is positive definite, and

2. there exists a positive even number $m_c \leq m$ such that

    (a) $\forall\vec{x}[\vec{x} \neq \vec{0} \Rightarrow \sum_{i=2}^{m_c} v_i(\vec{x}) \neq 0]$, and

    (b) $\exists\vec{y} \neq \vec{0}[\sum_{i=2}^{m_c} v_i(\vec{y}) < 0 \wedge \sum_{i=2}^{m_c} v_i(-\vec{y}) < 0]$.

Then V is a Lyapunov function for psf.

PROOF. Due to the condition (a), $\vec{0}$ is the unique solution of $\sum_{i=2}^{m_c} v_i(\vec{x}) = 0$. We want to prove that for all $\vec{x} \neq \vec{0}$, $\sum_{i=2}^{m_c} v_i(\vec{x}) < 0$.

Suppose there is a point $\vec{x} \neq 0$ such that $\sum_{i=2}^{m_c} v_i(\vec{x}) > 0$. Letting $g(t) = \vec{y} + t(\vec{x} - \vec{y})$, where $g(0) = \vec{y}$ and $g(1) = \vec{x}$, we have $\sum_{i=2}^{m_c} v_i(g(0)) < 0$ and $\sum_{i=2}^{m_c} v_i(g(1)) > 0$. So there exists a $t' \in (0,1)$ such that $\sum_{i=2}^{m_c} v_i(g(t')) = 0$, implying that $\vec{y} + t'(\vec{x} - \vec{y}) = \vec{0}$. Similarly, there is a $t'' \in (0,1)$ such that $-\vec{y} + t''(\vec{x} + \vec{y}) = \vec{0}$. Thus, $\vec{x} = \vec{y} = \vec{0}$, contradicting the assumption that $\vec{x} \neq 0$. So, for all $\vec{x} \neq \vec{0}$, $\sum_{i=2}^{m_c} v_i(\vec{x}) < 0$.

Since all terms in $\dot{V}(\vec{x}) - \sum_{i=2}^{m_c} v_i(\vec{x})$ have degree greater than m_c, form Theorem 1, there is a neighborhood $\mathbb{U}$ of the origin such that for all $\vec{x} \in \mathbb{U} \setminus \{\vec{0}\}$, $\dot{V}(\vec{x}) < 0$.

Since $V = V(\vec{x})$ is positive definite, $V = V(\vec{x})$ is a LF. $\square$

In Theorem 2, let $V(\vec{x})$ be $L(\vec{x}, \vec{p}) = \vec{x}^T P \vec{x}$, where $P = (p_{ij})_{n \times n}$ is symmetric and $\vec{p} = (p_{1,1}, \cdots, p_{n,n})$. Then $\dot{V}(\vec{x}) = 2\vec{x}^T P f(\vec{x})$. In addition, let $\sum_{i=2}^{m_c} v_i(\vec{x})$ be $\dot{L}_{m_c}(\vec{x}, \vec{p})$. For P, let $h(\lambda) = \lambda^n + c_{n-1}(\vec{p})\lambda^{n-1} + \cdots + c_0(\vec{p})$ be its characteristic polynomial.

To compute a V satisfying the condition in Theorem 2 is equivalent to computing a $\vec{p}$ such that P is positive definite and $\dot{L}_{m_c}(\vec{x}, \vec{p})$ satisfies the conditions (a) and (b).

However, it is difficult to directly compute such a $\vec{p}$. We try to under-approximatively relax the conditions in Theorem 2 – in the sense that every solution of the relaxation is also a solution of the original conditions and it is easier to solve the relaxation than the original conditions – as follows:

1. According to Subsection 2.2, to compute a $\vec{p}$ such that P is positive definite is equivalent to finding a $\vec{p}$ such that $\Lambda_0(\vec{p}) = \bigwedge_{i=1}^{n} (-1)^i[c_{n-i}(\vec{p}) > 0]$ holds.

2. For solving the condition (a), we first transform it to the following equivalent form

$$\left[\forall \vec{x}[x_1 \neq 0 \Rightarrow \dot{L}_{m_c}(\vec{x}, \vec{p}) \neq 0] \right]$$
$$\wedge \left[\forall \vec{x}[x_2 \neq 0 \Rightarrow \dot{L}_{m_c}(0, x_2, \cdots, x_n, \vec{p}) \neq 0] \right]$$
$$\wedge \cdots$$
$$\wedge \left[\forall \vec{x}[x_n \neq 0 \Rightarrow \dot{L}_{m_c}(0, \cdots, 0, x_n, \vec{p}) \neq 0] \right],$$

denoted as $\bigwedge_{i=1}^{n} \phi_i(\vec{p})$. Assume that for each $\phi_i(\vec{p})$, $i = 1, \ldots, n$, we have a real root classification based method to get an under-approximative constraint $\Lambda_{1,i}^{m_c}(\vec{p})$ only involving $\vec{p}$, which will be discussed later in this section. Then, we have $\bigwedge_{i=1}^{n} \Lambda_{1,i}^{m_c}(\vec{p})$, denoted as $\Lambda_1^{m_c}(\vec{p})$.

3. For solving the condition (b), we simply use the point $\vec{y}_0 = (1, 0, \cdots, 0)$ to get the constraint

$$[\dot{L}_{m_c}((1, 0, \cdots, 0), \vec{p}) < 0 \wedge \dot{L}_{m_c}((-1, 0, \cdots, 0), \vec{p}) < 0],$$

denoted as $\Lambda_2^{m_c}(\vec{p})$. Note that such a simplification will not lose information, which will be analytically stated in Section 4.

Thus, we can get a conjunction $\Lambda_0 \bigwedge \Lambda_1^{m_c} \bigwedge \Lambda_2^{m_c}$. Note that the conjunction $\Lambda_0 \bigwedge \Lambda_1^{m_c} \bigwedge \Lambda_2^{m_c}$ can be transformed to a set of semi-algebraic sets and the computation of a sample point in a semi-algebraic set by SASsolver will be discussed in Section 5. Thus, we arrive at Algorithm 2 for computing a Lyapunov function as follows.

Now the problem is how to use a real root classification based technique to get our under-approximatively constraint $\Lambda_1^{m_c}$ required in Algorithm 2.

We start with the following two preparations for solving $\forall x_i[x_j \neq 0 \Rightarrow g(x_1, \cdots, x_i, \vec{p}) \Delta 0]$, where $j \in \{1, \cdots, i\}$, $g(x_1, \cdots, x_i, \vec{p})$ is a polynomial and $\Delta \in \{<, \leq, \neq\}$.

Algorithm 2 Real root classification based method

Input: A given psf $\dot{\vec{x}} = f(\vec{x})$.
Output: Asymptotically Stable or Unknown.
1: choose a quadratic form $V = \vec{x}^T P \vec{x}$.
2: compute the characteristic polynomial $h(\lambda)$ of P and the conjunction $\Lambda_0(\vec{p})$.
3: compute $\dot{V}$ and let m be its degree.
4: **for** $m_c = 2 : 2 : m$ **do**
5:     compute $\dot{L}_{m_c}(\vec{x}, \vec{p})$.
6:     compute the conjunctions $\Lambda_1^{m_c}(\vec{p})$ and $\Lambda_2^{m_c}(\vec{p})$.
7:     apply SASsolver to the conjunction $\Lambda_0 \bigwedge \Lambda_1^{m_c} \bigwedge \Lambda_2^{m_c}$.
8:     **if** SASsolver returns a sample point over $\vec{p}$ **then**
9:         put it into V, return V as a Lyapunov function, associated with "Asymptotically Stable", and halt.
10:    **else**
11:        **if** SASsolver returns a list of intervals over $\vec{p}$ **then**
12:            return "Asymptotically Stable" and halt.
13:        **end if**
14:    **end if**
15: **end for**
16: return Unknown.

---

1. First, if x_i appears in $g(x_1, \cdots, x_i, \vec{p})$, we use the real root classification in [33] to get a sufficient and necessary condition $\delta_{i,j,1}$ – which can be an empty set – such that $\{g(x_1, \cdots, x_i, \vec{p}) = 0, x_j \neq 0\}$ has no solution about x_i. $\delta_{i,j,1}$ can be formulated as a disjunction of conjunctions (i.e., $\delta_{i,j,1} = \vee_{m=1}^{k_{i,j}} \delta_{i,j,m,1}$), where for each conjunction $\delta_{i,j,m,1}$, its conjuncts are of form $h_{i,j,m,l}(x_1, \cdots, x_{i-1}, \vec{p}) \Delta 0$, where $\Delta \in \{=, <, \leq, \neq\}$ and $l = 1, \cdots, k_{i,j,m}$. We can also denote it as $rrc(i, j, g)$. Note that this real root classification has been contained in the Maple package and will be discussed in Section 5.

2. Second, letting $\vec{x}_0 \in \mathbb{R}^i$ be the point with $x_j = 1$ and $x_l = 0$ for $l \neq j$, we use $\vec{x}_0$ to get the constraint $\delta_{i,j,2} = [g(\vec{x}_0, \vec{p}) < 0 \wedge g(-\vec{x}_0, \vec{p}) < 0]$. Clearly, according to the proof of Theorem 2, $\forall x_i[x_j \neq 0 \Rightarrow g(x_1, \cdots, x_i, \vec{p}) < 0]$ holds if and only if $\delta_{i,j,1} \wedge \delta_{i,j,2}$ holds. Note that since under-approximation is considered, in order to make $\forall x_i[x_j \neq 0 \Rightarrow g(x_1, \cdots, x_i, \vec{p}) \leq 0]$ hold, it is enough to require $\forall x_i[x_j \neq 0 \Rightarrow g(x_1, \cdots, x_i, \vec{p}) < 0]$ hold.

After the above two preparations, we formulate $\delta_{i,j,1} \wedge \delta_{i,j,2}$ as a disjunction of conjunctions (i.e., $\bigvee_{m=1}^{k'_{i,j}} \delta'_{i,j,k}$) and denote it as $ve(i, j, g)$. Similarly, for each conjunction $\delta'_{i,j,k}$, its conjuncts are of form $h'_{i,j,m,l}(x_1, \cdots, x_{i-1}, \vec{p}) \Delta 0$, where $\Delta \in \{=, <, \leq, \neq\}$ and $l = 1, \cdots, k'_{i,j,m}$. Notice that the variable x_i does not appear in $ve(i, j, g)$, implying that x_i has been eliminated.

If there exists $\vec{p}_0$ such that $[x_j \neq 0 \Rightarrow \delta'_{i,j,k}]$ holds, then $\forall x_i[x_j \neq 0 \Rightarrow g(x_1, \cdots, x_i, \vec{p}_0)] \Delta 0]$ holds, which can be obtained from Lemma 4 in Section 4.

Based on the above two preparations, we will use Algorithm 3 to get an under-approximation $\delta_{i,j}$ for $\forall x_i[x_j \neq 0 \Rightarrow \bigvee_{t=1}^{k} \bigwedge_{q=1}^{l_t} g_{t,q}(x_1, \cdots, x_i, \vec{p}] \Delta 0]$, where $\Delta \in \{=, <, \leq, \neq\}$, which can also be assured by Lemma 4 in Section 4.

Based on Algorithm 3, for the conjunct $\phi_i = \forall \vec{x}[x_1 \neq 0 \Rightarrow \dot{L}_{m_c}(\vec{x}, \vec{p}) \neq 0]$, we can eliminate the variables $x_n, \ldots, x_1$ step by step, arriving at the under-approximation $\Lambda_{1,1}^{m_c}$ which

Algorithm 3 Computing the under-approximation $\delta_{i,j}$

Input: $\forall x_i[x_j \neq 0 \Rightarrow \bigvee_{t=1}^{k} \bigwedge_{q=1}^{l_t} g_{t,q}(x_1, \cdots, x_i, \vec{p})\Delta 0]$.
Output: an under-approximative constraint $\delta_{i,j}$.
1: **for** $t = 1 : 1 : k$ **do**
2:   **for** $q = 1 : 1 : l_t$ **do**
3:     **if** x_i does not appear in $g_{t,q}(x_1, \cdots, x_i, \vec{p})$ **then**
4:       let $\delta_{j,t,q} = [g_{t,q}(x_1, \cdots, x_i, \vec{p})\Delta 0]$;
5:     **else**
6:       **if** Δ in $g_{t,q}(x_1, \cdots, x_i, \vec{p})\Delta 0$ is "=" **then**
7:         formulate $g_{t,q}(x_1, \cdots, x_i, \vec{p})$ as $\sum_{d=0}^{t} g_{t,q,d}(x_1, \cdots, x_{i-1}, \vec{p})x_i^d$ and let $\delta_{j,t,q} = [\bigwedge_{d=0}^{t} g_{t,q,d}(x_1, \cdots, x_{i-1}, \vec{p}) = 0]$;
8:       **else**
9:         **if** $\Delta \in \{<, \leq\}$ **then**
10:           let $\delta_{j,t,q} = ve(i, j, g_{t,q}(x_1, \cdots, x_i, \vec{p}))$;
11:         **else**
12:           let $\delta_{j,t,q} = rrc(i, j, g_{t,q}(x_1, \cdots, x_i, \vec{p}))$;
13:         **end if**
14:       **end if**
15:     **end if**
16:   **end for**
17: **end for**
18: formulate $\bigvee_{t=1}^{k} \bigwedge_{q=1}^{l_t} \delta_{j,t,q}$ as $\bigvee_{t=1}^{k'}[\bigwedge_{q=1}^{l'_t} g'_{t,q}(x_1, \cdots, x_{i-1}, \vec{p})\Delta 0]$, denoted by $\delta_{i,j}$;
19: **return** $\delta_{i,j}$.

---

only involves $\vec{p}$. This description is formalized as Algorithm 4 as follows.

Algorithm 4 Computing the under-approximation $\Lambda_{1,1}^{m_c}$

Input: the conjunct $\phi_1(\vec{p}) = \forall \vec{x}[x_1 \neq 0 \Rightarrow \dot{L}_{m_c}(\vec{x}, \vec{p}) \neq 0]$.
Output: the under-approximative constraint $\Lambda_{1,1}(\vec{p})$.
1: let $g(x_1, \cdots, x_n, \vec{p}) = \dot{L}_{m_c}(\vec{x}, \vec{p})$;
2: let $\delta_{n,1}^{m_c} = rrc(n, 1, g(x_1, \cdots, x_n, \vec{p}))$ and formulate it as $\bigvee_{t=1}^{k}\left[\bigwedge_{q=1}^{l_t} g_{t,q}(x_1, \cdots, x_{n-1})\Delta 0\right]$;
3: **for** $i = n - 1 : -1 : 1$ **do**
4:   use Algorithm 3 for the input $\forall x_i[x_1 \neq 0 \Rightarrow \delta_{i+1,1}^{m_c}]$ to get $\delta_{i,1}^{m_c}$;
5: **end for**
6: **return** $\Lambda_{1,1}^{m_c} = \delta_{1,1}^{m_c}$.

If there exists $\vec{p}_0$ such that $\Lambda_{1,1}^{m_c}(\vec{p}_0)$ holds, then $\forall \vec{x}[x_1 \neq 0 \Rightarrow \dot{L}_{m_c}(\vec{x}, \vec{p}_0) \neq 0]$ holds, which can be obtained from Lemma 5 in Subsection 4.

Similarly, for each conjunct ϕ_i, we can relax it to an under-approximative constraint $\Lambda_{1,i}^{m_c}$.

So we obtain the under-approximative constraint $\Lambda_1^{m_c} = \bigwedge_{i=1}^{n} \Lambda_{1,i}^{m_c}$ and finish explaining our real root classification based approach.

Next, we will use an example to illustrate Algorithm 2, associated with Algorithm 4.

EXAMPLE 1. *Consider the system [11]:*

$$\begin{cases} \dot{x_1} = -x_1 - \dfrac{3}{2}x_1^2 x_2^3 \\ \dot{x_2} = -x_2^3 + \dfrac{1}{2}x_1^2 x_2^2 \end{cases}.$$

Let $V(\vec{x}) = L(\vec{x}, \vec{p}) = \vec{x}^T P \vec{x}$, where $P = \begin{pmatrix} 1 & \frac{b}{2} \\ \frac{b}{2} & a \end{pmatrix}$ and

$\vec{p} = (a, \frac{b}{2})^T$, *then $\frac{d}{dt}V(\vec{x}) = -2x_1^2 - bx_1x_2 - 2ax_2^4 - bx_1x_2^3 + ax_1^2x_2^3 + \frac{1}{2}bx_1^3x_2^2 - 3x_1^3x_2^3 - \frac{3}{2}bx_1^2x_2^4$. *According to Algorithm 2,*

1. *P is positive definite $\Leftrightarrow \Lambda_0 = [a > \frac{b^2}{4}]$.*

2. *When $m_c = 2$, $\dot{L}_2(\vec{x}, \vec{p}) = -2x_1^2 - bx_1x_2$. According to the Algorithm 4, there is no condition over x_1, a and b such that $\{\dot{L}_2(\vec{x}, \vec{p}) = 0, x_1 \neq 0\}$ has no solution. Thus, we get $\delta_{2,1}^2 = \emptyset$, implying that we cannot get a Lyapunov function.*

3. *When $m_c = 4$, $\dot{L}_4(\vec{x}, \vec{p}) = -2x_1^2 - bx_1x_2 - bx_1x_2^3 - 2ax_2^4$.*

   (a) *According to Algorithm 4,*

      i. *for the conjunct $\forall \vec{x}[x_1 \neq 0 \Rightarrow \dot{L}_4(\vec{x}, \vec{p}) \neq 0]$, we get $\Lambda_{1,1}^4 = [b^2 - 4a > 0 \wedge a \neq 0 \wedge b \neq 0 \wedge 16a - b^2 \neq 0 \wedge 32a + b^2 \neq 0 \wedge -768b^2a^2 - 27b^4 - 6b^4a - 27b^4a^2 + 4096a^3 - b^6 > 0] \bigvee[b = 0 \wedge a \neq 0] \bigvee(16a - b^2 = 0 \wedge b \neq 0 \wedge a \neq 0 \wedge -768b^2a^2 - 27b^4 - 6b^4a - 27b^4a^2 + 4096a^3 - b^6 > 0] \bigvee[32a + b^2 = 0 \wedge b \neq 0 \wedge a \neq 0 \wedge -768b^2a^2 - 27b^4 - 6b^4a - 27b^4a^2 + 4096a^3 - b^6 > 0]$.*

      ii. *for the conjunct $\forall \vec{x}[x_2 \neq 0 \Rightarrow \dot{L}_4(0, x_2, \vec{p}) \neq 0]$, we get $\Lambda_{1,2}^4 = [a \neq 0]$.*

   (b) *$\Lambda_1^4 = \Lambda_{1,1}^4 \wedge \Lambda_{1,2}^4$ and $\Lambda_2^4 = [-\dot{L}_4(1, 0, \vec{p}) > 0 \wedge -\dot{L}_4(-1, 0, \vec{p}) > 0]$, where Λ_2^4 is always true.*

   (c) *Formulate $\Lambda_0 \wedge \Lambda_1^4 \wedge \Lambda_2^4$ to a set of semi-algebraic sets $\{\{-768b^2a^2 - 27b^4 - 6b^4a - 27b^4a^2 + 4096a^3 - b^6 > 0, b^2 - 4a > 0, a \neq 0, b \neq 0, 16a - b^2 \neq 0, 32a + b^2 \neq 0\}, \{b = 0, -768b^2a^2 - 27b^4 - 6b^4a - 27b^4a^2 + 4096a^3 - b^6 > 0, a \neq 0\}, \{16a - b^2 = 0, -768b^2a^2 - 27b^4 - 6b^4a - 27b^4a^2 + 4096a^3 - b^6 > 0, a \neq 0, b \neq 0\}, \{32a + b^2 = 0, -768b^2a^2 - 27b^4 - 6b^4a - 27b^4a^2 + 4096a^3 - b^6 > 0, a \neq 0, b \neq 0\}\}$.*

   (d) *For each semi-algebraic set, compute a sample point by SASsolver. Among these sample points, take the sample point $\vec{p}_0 = (1, 0)$, implying the system is asymptotically stable and $V(\vec{x}) = x_1^2 + x_2^2$ is a Lyapunov function.*

□

Note that in Algorithm 2, in order to reduce the computational complexity, especially for high dimensional systems, we pre-choose a quadratic form with fewer parameters instead use a general quadratic function. For the cases that "Unknown" is returned for this pre-chosen quadratic form, we will then try a form with more parameters.

4. THEORETICAL ANALYSIS OF OUR APPROACH

In this section, we will analytically evaluate Algorithm 2. Specifically, we want to prove the following three statements:

1. The simplification for solving the condition (b) will not lose information;

2. For each $i \in \{1, \ldots, n\}$, the solution set of $\Lambda_{1,i}^{m_c}$ is a subset of the solution set of ϕ_i;

3. If there exists $\vec{p}_0$ such that $\Lambda_0 \wedge \Lambda_1^{m_c} \wedge \Lambda_2^{m_c}$ holds, then $V(\vec{x}, \vec{p}_0)$ is a Lyapunov function.

Let $\vec{y}_0 = (1, 0, \cdots, 0)$ and

$$\Omega_1 = \{\vec{p} : \forall \vec{x}[\vec{x} \neq \vec{0} \Rightarrow \dot{L}_{m_c}(\vec{x}, \vec{p}) \neq 0]\},$$
$$\Omega_2 = \{\vec{p} : \exists \vec{y} \neq \vec{0}[\dot{L}_{m_c}(\vec{y}, \vec{p}) < 0 \wedge \dot{L}_{m_c}(-\vec{y}, \vec{p}) < 0]\},$$
$$\Omega_3 = \{\vec{p} : \vec{p} \in \Omega_1 \wedge \vec{p} \in \Omega_2\},$$
$$\Omega_4 = \{\vec{p} : \vec{p} \in \Omega_1 \wedge \dot{L}_{m_c}(\vec{y}_0, \vec{p}) < 0 \wedge \dot{L}_{m_c}(-\vec{y}_0, \vec{p}) < 0\}.$$

For proving the first statement, it is enough to prove that:

LEMMA 3. $\Omega_3 = \Omega_4$.

PROOF. From the proof of Theorem 2, if $\vec{p}_0 \in \Omega_3$, then $\forall \vec{x}[\vec{x} \neq \vec{0} \Rightarrow \dot{L}_{m_c}(\vec{x}, \vec{p}_0) < 0]$, implying that $\dot{L}_{m_c}(\vec{y}_0, \vec{p}_0) < 0$ and $\dot{L}_{m_c}(-\vec{y}_0, \vec{p}_0) < 0$. Thus $\vec{p}_0 \in \Omega_4$ and $\Omega_3 \subseteq \Omega_4$. Similarly, if $\vec{p}_0 \in \Omega_4$, then $\forall \vec{x}[\vec{x} \neq \vec{0} \Rightarrow \dot{L}_{m_c}(\vec{x}, \vec{p}_0) < 0]$, implying that $\vec{p}_0 \in \Omega_2$. Thus $\Omega_4 \subseteq \Omega_3$.
So $\Omega_3 = \Omega_4$. $\square$

For proving the second statement, we first prove Lemma 4, which implies that our real root classification based method will result in under-approximation.

LEMMA 4. Let each $g_{t,q}(x_1, \cdots, x_i, \vec{p})$ be a polynomial and suppose that $\delta_{i,j,t,q} = rrc(i, j, g_{t,q})$. For all $\vec{p}_0$ such that

$$\forall x_1 \cdots \forall x_{i-1}[x_j \neq 0 \Rightarrow \bigvee_t \bigwedge_q [\delta_{i,j,t,q}|_{\vec{p}=\vec{p}_0} \wedge g_{t,q}(\vec{z}_0, \vec{p}_0) < 0$$
$$\wedge g_{t,q}(-\vec{z}_0, \vec{p}_0) < 0]]$$

holds, where $\vec{z}_0$ satisfies $z_j = 1$ and $z_l = 0$ if $l \neq j$, the constraint $\forall x_1 \cdots \forall x_i[x_j \neq 0 \Rightarrow \vee_t \wedge_q g_{t,q}(x_1, \ldots, x_i, \vec{p}_0)\Delta_{t,q}0]$ holds, where $\Delta_{t,q} \in \{<, \leq\}$.

PROOF. Suppose that $\vec{p}_0$ makes $\forall x_1 \cdots \forall x_{i-1}[x_j \neq 0 \Rightarrow \vee_t \wedge_q [\delta_{i,j,t,q}|_{\vec{p}=\vec{p}_0} \wedge g_{t,q}(\vec{z}_0, \vec{p}_0) < 0 \wedge g_{t,q}(-\vec{z}_0, \vec{p}_0) < 0]]$ hold. Letting $S_{t,q} = \{(x_1, \ldots, x_{i-1}) : [x_j \neq 0 \Rightarrow [\delta_{i,j,t,q}|_{\vec{p}=\vec{p}_0} \wedge g_{t,q}(\vec{z}_0, \vec{p}_0) < 0 \wedge g_{t,q}(-\vec{z}_0, \vec{p}_0) < 0]]\}$ and $S_t = \{(x_1, \ldots, x_{i-1}) : [x_j \neq 0 \Rightarrow \wedge_q[\delta_{i,j,t,q}|_{\vec{p}=\vec{p}_0} \wedge g_{t,q}(\vec{z}_0, \vec{p}_0) < 0 \wedge g_{t,q}(-\vec{z}_0, \vec{p}_0) < 0]]\}$, then $S_t = \cap_q S_{t,q}$ and $\cup_t S_t = \mathbb{R}^{i-1}$. Letting $S'_{t,q} = \{(x_1, \ldots, x_{i-1}) : \forall x_i[x_j \neq 0 \Rightarrow g_{t,q}(x_1, \ldots, x_i, \vec{p}_0) < 0]\}$, it is sufficient to prove: $S_{t,q} = S'_{t,q}$.
Since $\delta_{i,j,t,q} = rrc(i, j, g_{t,q})$ is the sufficient and necessary condition obtained by using real root classification such that $\forall x_i[x_j \neq 0 \Rightarrow g_{t,q}(x_1, \cdots, x_i, \vec{p}) \neq 0]$ holds, $\{(x_1, \ldots, x_{i-1}) : [x_j \neq 0 \Rightarrow \delta_{i,j,t,q}|_{\vec{p}=\vec{p}_0}]\}$ equals $\{(x_1, \ldots, x_{i-1}) : \forall x_i[x_j \neq 0 \Rightarrow g_{t,q}(x_1, \cdots, x_i, \vec{p}_0) \neq 0]\}$. Thus, $\{(x_1, \ldots, x_{i-1}) : [x_j \neq 0 \Rightarrow [\delta_{i,j,t,q}|_{\vec{p}=\vec{p}_0} \wedge g_{t,q}(\vec{z}_0, \vec{p}_0) < 0 \wedge g_{t,q}(-\vec{z}_0, \vec{p}_0) < 0]]\}$ equals $\{(x_1, \ldots, x_{i-1}) : \forall x_i[x_j \neq 0 \Rightarrow [g_{t,q}(x_1, \cdots, x_i, \vec{p}_0) \neq 0 \wedge g_{t,q}(\vec{z}_0, \vec{p}_0) < 0 \wedge g_{t,q}(-\vec{z}_0, \vec{p}_0) < 0]]\}$.
According to the proof of Theorem 2, $\{(x_1, \ldots, x_{i-1}) : \forall x_i[x_j \neq 0 \Rightarrow [g_{t,q}(x_1, \cdots, x_i, \vec{p}_0) \neq 0 \wedge g_{t,q}(\vec{z}_0, \vec{p}_0) < 0 \wedge g_{t,q}(-\vec{z}_0, \vec{p}_0) < 0]]\}$ equals $\{(x_1, \ldots, x_{i-1}) : \forall x_i[x_j \neq 0 \Rightarrow g_{t,q}(x_1, \ldots, x_i, \vec{p}_0) < 0]\}$. Thus, $S_{t,q} = S'_{t,q}$.
Since $\cup_t \cap_q S'_{t,q} = \cup_t \cap_q S_{t,q} = \mathbb{R}^{i-1}$, $\forall x_1 \cdots \forall x_i[x_j \neq 0 \Rightarrow \vee_t \wedge_q g_{t,q}(x_1, \ldots, x_i, \vec{p}_0) < 0]$ holds, implying that $\forall x_1 \cdots \forall x_i[x_j \neq 0 \Rightarrow \vee_t \wedge_q g_{t,q}(x_1, \ldots, x_i, \vec{p}_0)\Delta_{t,q}0]$ holds, where $\Delta_{t,q} \in \{<, \leq\}$. [1] $\square$

Based on Lemma 4, we have the following lemma.

LEMMA 5. For all $\vec{p}_0$ such that $\Lambda_{1,1}^{m_c}$ holds, where $\Lambda_{1,1}^{m_c}$ is the output of Algorithm 4 with the input $\forall \vec{x}[x_1 \neq 0 \Rightarrow \dot{L}_{m_c}(\vec{x}, \vec{p}) \neq 0]$, $\forall \vec{x}[x_1 \neq 0 \Rightarrow \dot{L}_{m_c}(\vec{x}, \vec{p}_0) \neq 0]$ holds.

[1] From Algorithm 3 and the proof of Lemma 4, we notice that the under-approximation is used only when $\Delta_{t,q}$ is $\leq$.

PROOF. According to Algorithm 4, $\delta_{1,1} = \Lambda_{1,1}^{m_c}$. If $\vec{p}_0$ makes $\Lambda_{1,1}^{m_c}$ holds, from Lemma 4, $\vec{p}_0$ makes $\forall x_1[x_1 \neq 0 \Rightarrow \delta_{2,1}]$ hold. Moreover, we can deductively prove that for $i = 2, \cdots, n-1$, if $\vec{p}_0$ makes $\forall x_1 \cdots \forall x_{i-1}[x_1 \neq 0 \Rightarrow \delta_{i,1}]$ hold, then $\vec{p}_0$ makes $\forall x_1 \cdots \forall x_i[x_1 \neq 0 \Rightarrow \delta_{i+1,1}]$ hold. Since $\delta_{n,1}$ is the sufficient and necessary condition over the parameters $x_1, \cdots, x_{i-1}, \vec{p}$ obtained by using real root classification such that $\{x_1 \neq 0, \dot{L}_{m_c}(\vec{x}, \vec{p}) = 0\}$ has no solution about x_n, $\forall \vec{x}[x_1 \neq 0 \Rightarrow \dot{L}_{m_c}(\vec{x}, \vec{p}_0) \neq 0]$ holds. $\square$

Similarly, we have the following lemma.

LEMMA 6. For $i = 2, \ldots, n$, for all $\vec{p}_0$ such that $\Lambda_{1,i}^{m_c}$ holds, where $\Lambda_{1,i}^{m_c}$ is the output of Algorithm 4 with the input $\phi_i(\vec{p})$, $\phi_i(\vec{p}_0)$ holds.

Thus, we finish the proof of the second statement. The third statement is guaranteed by the following theorem.

THEOREM 3. For all $\vec{p}_0$ such that $\Lambda_0 \bigwedge \Lambda_1^{m_c} \bigwedge \Lambda_2^{m_c}$ holds, $V(\vec{x}, \vec{p}_0)$ is a Lyapunov function.

PROOF. If $\vec{p}_0$ makes $\Lambda_0 \bigwedge \Lambda_1^{m_c} \bigwedge \Lambda_2^{m_c}$ hold, then

1. from Lemma 2, $V(\vec{x}, \vec{p}_0)$ is positive definite.

2. according to Lemmas 5 and 6, $\bigwedge_{i=1}^n \phi_i(\vec{p}_0)$ holds. Since the constraint $\forall \vec{x}[\vec{x} \neq \vec{0} \Rightarrow \dot{L}_{m_c}(\vec{x}, \vec{p}) \neq 0]$ is equivalent to $\bigwedge_{i=1}^n \phi_i$, $\forall \vec{x}[\vec{x} \neq 0 \Rightarrow \dot{L}_{m_c}(\vec{x}, \vec{p}_0) \neq 0]$ holds.

3. $[\dot{L}_{m_c}(y, \vec{p}_0) < 0 \wedge \dot{L}_{m_c}(-y, \vec{p}_0) < 0]$ holds, where $y = (1, 0, \ldots, 0)$.

Thus, from Theorem 2, $V(\vec{x}, \vec{p}_0)$ is a Lyapunov function. $\square$

5. IMPLEMENTATION

We implemented our algorithms based on DISCOVERER[2], which is a solver to a semi-algebraic system that is defined as a set of form $g(\vec{x}, \vec{p})\Delta 0$, where $\vec{x} \in \mathbb{R}^n$, $\vec{p} \in \mathbb{R}^d$, $g(\vec{x}, \vec{p})$ is a polynomial in $\mathbb{Q}[\vec{x}, \vec{p}]$ and $\Delta \in \{=, <, \leq, \neq\}$.

Simply speaking, our implementation consists of the following two main steps:

1. The first main step is to use a real root classification based method to eliminate the variables $x_n, \cdots, x_1$ one by one. In particular, in order to get a sufficient and necessary condition over $x_1, \cdots, x_{i-1}, x_{i+1}, \cdots, x_n, \vec{p}$ such that $\{g(\vec{x}, \vec{p}) = 0, x_j \neq 0\}$ has no solution about the variable x_i, where $i, j \in \{1, \cdots, n\}$, we orderly call the commands $tofind$ and $Tofind$, which are implemented in DISCOVERER [33] by using real root classification and can return a sufficient and necessary condition over $x_1, \cdots, x_{i-1}, x_{i+1}, \cdots, x_n$, and $\vec{p}$ such that $\{g(\vec{x}, \vec{p}) = 0, x_j \neq 0\}$ has exactly N distinct real solutions, where N is a non-negative integer. Note that due to the special structure that $g(\vec{x}, \vec{p}) = 0$ can be regard as a univariate polynomial equation over x_i and N is required to be 0 during our discussions, this sufficient and necessary condition can be efficiently obtained by DISCOVERER.

2. The second main step is to solve the resulting conjunction using SASsolver. Specifically, after getting the conjunction which only involves the parameters

[2] http://www.is.pku.edu.cn/~xbc/DISCOVERER.html.

$\vec{p}$, we reformulate this conjunction as a set of semi-algebraic sets and then compute a sample point in each semi-algebraic set by using `SASsolver`, which is implemented using an adaptive partial cylindrical algebraic decomposition [2]. Here, for a given semi-algebraic system, `SASsolver` returns a sample point which is a solution, or a list of rational intervals in which there is only one solution, or an empty set which means that there is no solution to this semi-algebraic system.

6. EXPERIMENTAL EVALUATION

In this section, we test the implementation of our Algorithms 1 and 2 on some examples with comparisons.

EXAMPLE 2. *Consider the system [24]:*

$$\begin{cases} \dot{x} = -x - 2xy^2 \\ \dot{y} = -y^3 + x^2 y \end{cases}.$$

Suppose $V(\vec{x}) = ax^2 + bxy + cy^2$. Algorithm 1 returns Unknown. However, by Algorithm 2, $V(\vec{x}) = x^2 + y^2$ is a Lyapunov function. □

EXAMPLE 3. *Consider the system [24]:*

$$\begin{cases} \dot{x} = -x + y + xz^2 - x^3 \\ \dot{y} = x - y + z^2 - y^3 \\ \dot{z} = -yz - z^3 \end{cases}.$$

Supposed $V(\vec{x}) = x^2 + ay^2 + bz^2$. Algorithm 1 returns Unknown. However, by Algorithm 2, $V(\vec{x}) = x^2 + y^2 + z^2$ is a Lyapunov function. □

EXAMPLE 4. *Consider the system:*

$$\begin{cases} \dot{x} = -y - x^3 + z^4 x \\ \dot{y} = x - y^3 \\ \dot{z} = -z + x^3 z \end{cases}.$$

Suppose $V(\vec{x}) = ax^2 + by^2 + cz^2 + dyz$. Algorithm 1 returns Unknown. However, by Algorithm 2, $V(\vec{x}) = x^2 + y^2 + z^2$ is a Lyapunov function. □

EXAMPLE 5. *Consider the system:*

$$\begin{cases} \dot{x_1} = -x_1^3 + x_1^2 x_3 x_4 \\ \dot{x_2} = -x_2 - 3x_3 + 2x_4 + x_3^2 x_4^2 \\ \dot{x_3} = 3x_2 - x_3 - x_4 \\ \dot{x_4} = -2x_2 + x_3 - x_4 \end{cases}.$$

Suppose $V(\vec{x}) = x_1^2 + ax_2^2 + bx_3^2 + cx_4^2 + dx_2 x_3$. Algorithm 1 returns Unknown. However, by Algorithm 2, $V(\vec{x}) = x_1^2 + x_2^2 + x_3^2 + x_4^2 + \frac{1}{2} x_2 x_3$ is a Lyapunov function. □

EXAMPLE 6. *This is a six-dimensional system:*

$$\begin{cases} \dot{x}_1 = x_4 x_2 + x_4^3 x_3 - x_1^3 \\ \dot{x}_2 = -x_2^3 + x_6^3 - 3x_4 x_1 \\ \dot{x}_3 = -3x_4 x_1 - x_5^3 - x_3 \\ \dot{x}_4 = x_2^3 x_1 - x_4 + x_1 x_3 \\ \dot{x}_5 = -x_6^4 - x_5 + x_5^2 x_3 \\ \dot{x}_6 = -x_2 x_6^2 - x_6 + x_3^4 \end{cases}.$$

Let $V(x_1, \dots, x_6) = ax_1^2 + bx_2^2 + cx_3^2 + dx_4^2 + ex_5^2 + fx_6^2$. Algorithm 1 returns Unknown. However, by Algorithm 2, $V(x_1, x_2, x_3, x_4, x_5, x_6) = 3x_1^2 + x_2^2 + x_3^2 + 3x_4^2 + x_5^2 + x_6^2$ is a Lyapunov function. □

For Example 2, 3, 4, 5 and 6, after applying REDLOG to check whether there is a solution of the parameters in the same pre-assumed $V(\vec{x})$ resulting in a Lyapunov function defined in a certain neighborhood of the origin, our computer with 2GB memory ran out of memory since every example has at least 6 total variable. For example, Example 2 has 6 total variables (i.e., a, b, c, r, x, y) and Example 4 has 8 total variables (i.e., a, b, c, d, r, x, y, z), where r is used to represent the radius of a potential neighborhood of the origin.

For Example 2, 3, 4, 5 and 6, we apply QEPCAD and the program terminates abnormally.

Moreover, the asymptotic stability of Examples 4, 5 and 6 cannot be verified by Algorithms in [24] since the sample points cannot form Lyapunov functions. Especially, for Example 5, even though we use our current obtained solution as a sample, after applying REDLOG to the constraint

$$\exists r \forall \vec{x} [[r > 0 \wedge \sum_{i=1}^4 x_i^2 < r^2 \wedge \sum_{i=1}^4 x_i^2 > 0] \implies \dot{V}(\vec{x}) < 0],$$

the program cannot terminate within four hours. Similarly, after applying QEPCAD to the constraint

$$\forall \vec{x} [[r > 0 \wedge \sum_{i=1}^4 x_i^2 < r^2 \wedge \sum_{i=1}^4 x_i^2 > 0] \implies \dot{V}(\vec{x}) < 0],$$

the program terminates abnormally. These phenomena imply that the method in [24] is less efficient and powerful than our current approach.

Further, according to the theory described in [16, 29], we try to use a bilinear programming solver [12, 13] to obtain a feasible $V(\vec{x})$ such that:

$$V(\vec{x}) - l_1(\vec{x}) \in \sum_n,$$

$$- [(1 - V(\vec{x})) s_1(\vec{x}) + \frac{\partial V(\vec{x})}{\partial \vec{x}} f(\vec{x}) s_2(\vec{x}) + l_2(\vec{x})] \in \sum_n$$

where $\sum_n$ is a set of polynomials in n variables that can be formulated as SOS, $s_i \in \sum_n (i = 1, 2)$ and $l_i(\vec{x}) (i = 1, 2)$ are given positive definite polynomials. Pre-assuming all polynomials to be quadratic polynomials except $l_i(\vec{x}) (i = 1, 2)$, the program returns "PENBMI failed" for Example 4 and 5 in several seconds; and for Example 6, the program returns "PENBMI failed" after three hours. Moreover, for these three examples, we also tried using polynomials beyond quadratic ones but the program still cannot return a feasible solution in three hours.

7. CONCLUSIONS

In this paper, we first proposed an algebraic approach for analyzing asymptotic stability of continuous dynamical systems. That is, without linearization, we use a real root classification based method to arrive at a semi-algebraic set which only involves the coefficients of the pre-assumed quadratic form and solve the resulting semi-algebraic set for the coefficients to get a Lyapunov function. In this way, we avoid the use of generic quantifier elimination techniques.

We prototypically implemented our algorithms based on DISCOVERER with manual intervention and tested it on several examples. Compared to the generic quantifier elimination techniques [3, 5], the method in [24] and the SOS based method [16], the computation results show that our current algorithms are more efficient and powerful in practice.

Our short-term goal is to optimize our algorithms with complexity analysis of algorithms [24, 27, 25] and make them fully automatic. Our long-term goal is to verify the stability of general nonlinear hybrid systems [4] by computing multiple Lyapunov functions [1], multiple Lyapunov-like functions [22] or transition systems [21, 19, 26].

Acknowledgments

This work was supported by NSFC-61003021 and Beijing Nova Program. The authors are most grateful for the numerous inspiring discussions with Dr. Stefan Ratschan.

8. REFERENCES

[1] M. S. Branicky. Multiple Lyapunov functions and other analysis tools for switched and hybrid systems. *IEEE Trans. on Auto. Contr.*, 43(4): 475–482, 1998.

[2] G. E. Collins, H. Hong. Partial cylindrical algebraic decomposition for quantifier elimination. *J. Symb. Comput.*, 12: 299–328, 1991.

[3] C. W. Brown. QEPCAD B: a system for computing with semi-algebraic sets via cylindrical algebraic decomposition. *SIGSAM Bull*, 38(1): 23–24, 2004.

[4] R. A. Decarlo, M. S. Branicky, S. Pettersson. Perspective and results on the stability annd stabilizability of hybrid systems. *In Proc. of the IEEE*, 88(7): 1069–1081, 2000.

[5] A. Dolzmann, T. Sturm. REDLOG: computer algebra meets computer logic. *SIGSAM Bull*, 31(2): 2–9, 1997.

[6] F. Forsman. Construction of Lyapunov functions using Gröbner bases. In *Proc. of IEEE Conf. on Decision and Control*, 798–799, 1991.

[7] W. Hahn. Stability of Motion. Springer, 1967.

[8] H. Hong, R. Liska, S. Steinberg. Testing stability by quantifier elimination. *J. Symb. Comput.*, 24(2): 161–187, 1997.

[9] M. Johansson, A. Rantzer. Computation of piecewise quadaratic Lyapunov functions for hybrid systems. *IEEE Trans. on Auto. Contr.*, 43(4): 555–559, 1998.

[10] M. El Kahoui, A. Weber. Deciding Hopf bifurcations by quantifier elimination in a software-component architecture. *J. Symb. Comput.*, 30(2): 161–179, 2000.

[11] H. K. Khalil. Nonlinear Systems. Prentice Hall, 2002.

[12] M. Kočvara, M. Stingl. PENBMI User's Guide. Avaiable from http://www.penopt.com, 2005.

[13] J. Löfberg. YALMIP: A toolbox for modeling and optimization in MATLAB. In *Proceedings of the CACSD Conference*. Available from http://control.ee.ethz.ch/ joloef/yalmip.php, 2004.

[14] J. Lunze and F. Lamnabhi-Lagarrigue, editors. Handbook of Hybrid Systems Control: Theory, Tools, Applications. Cambridge University Press, 2009.

[15] M. A. Pai. Power System Stability by Lyapunov's Method. North Holland Publishing company, 1981.

[16] A. Papachristodoulou, S. Prajna. On the construction of Lyapunov functions using the sum of squares decomposition. In: *IEEE CDC 2002*.

[17] P. A. Parrilo. Semidefinite programming relaxations for semialgebraic problems. *Mathematical Programming (Series B)*, 96(2): 293–320, 2003.

[18] S. Pettersson, B. Lennartson. An LMI approach for stability analysis of nonlinear systems. In *Proc. of the 4th European Control Conference*, 1997.

[19] A. Podelski, S. Wagner. Model checking of hybrid systems: From reachability towards stability. In J. Hespanha and A. Tiwari, editors, *Hybrid Systems: Computation and Control*, LNCS 3927, Springer, 2006.

[20] S. Prajna, A. Papachristodoulou, P. A. Parrilo. Introducing SOSTOOLS: A general purpose sum of squares programming solver. In *Proc. of the IEEE Conf. on Decision and Control*, 2002.

[21] S. Ratschan, Z. She. Safety verification of hybrid systems by constraint propagation-based abstraction refinement. *ACM Transactions on Embedded Computing Systems*, 6(1), 2007.

[22] S. Ratschan, Z. She. Providing a basin of attraction to a target region of polynomial systems by computation of Lyapunov-like functions. *SIAM J. Control Optim.*, 48(7): 4377–4394, 2010.

[23] Z. She, Y. Ran, B. Xue, Z. Zheng. On the Algebraization of Asymptotic Stability Analysis for Differential Systems. In *Proc. of the 11th IASTED CA*, pp. 68–74, ACTA Press, 2009.

[24] Z. She, B. Xia, R. Xiao, Z. Zheng. A semi-algebraic approach for asymptotic stability analysis. *Nonlinear Analysis: Hybrid system*, 3(4): 588–596, 2009.

[25] Z. She, B. Xia, Z. Zheng. Condition number based complexity estimate for solving polynomial systems. *J. Comput. Appl. Math*, 235(8): 2670–2678, 2011.

[26] Z. She, Z. Zheng. Tightened reachability constraints for the verification of linear hybrid systems. *Nonlinear Analysis: Hybrid Systems*, 2(4): 1222-1231, 2008.

[27] Z. She, Z. Zheng. Condition number based complexity estimate for solving local extrema. *J. Comput. Appl. Math*, 230(1): 233–242, 2009.

[28] T. Sturm, A. Weber, E. O. Abdel-Rahman, M. El Kahoui. Investigating algebraic and logical algorithms to solve Hopf bifurcation problems in algebraic biology. *Math. Comput. Sci.*, 2(3): 493–515, 2009.

[29] W. Tan, A. Packard. Stability region analysis using polynomial and composite polynomial Lyapunov functions and sum-of-squares programming. *IEEE Trans. on Automatic Control*, 53(2): 565–571, 2008.

[30] A. Tarski. A Decision Method for Elementary Algebra and Geometry. Univ. of California Press, 1951.

[31] D. Wang, B. Xia. Stability analysis of biological systems with real solution classification. In *ISSAC*, ACM Press, New York, pp. 354–361, 2005.

[32] Andreas Weber, Thomas Sturm, Werner M. Seiler, Essam O. Abdel-Rahman. Parametric Qualitative Analysis of Ordinary Differential Equations: Computer Algebra Methods for Excluding Oscillations. In *CASC2010*, pp. 267–279, 2010.

[33] L. Yang, B. Xia. Automated deduction in real geometry. In *Geometric Computation*, pp. 248–298, World Scientific, 2004.

Univariate Real Root Isolation in an Extension Field

Adam Strzeboński
Wolfram Research Inc.,100 Trade Centre Drive,
Champaign, IL 61820, U.S.A.
adams (AT) wolfram.com

Elias P. Tsigaridas
Computer Science Department
Aarhus University, Denmark
elias (AT) cs.au.dk

ABSTRACT

We present algorithmic, complexity and implementation results for the problem of isolating the real roots of a univariate polynomial in $B_\alpha \in L[y]$, where $L = \mathbb{Q}(\alpha)$ is a simple algebraic extension of the rational numbers. We revisit two approaches for the problem. In the first approach, using resultant computations, we perform a reduction to a polynomial with integer coefficients and we deduce a bound of $\widetilde{\mathcal{O}}_B(N^{10})$ for isolating the real roots of B_α, where N is an upper bound on all the quantities (degree and bitsize) of the input polynomials. In the second approach we isolate the real roots working directly on the polynomial of the input. We compute improved separation bounds for the roots and we prove that they are optimal, under mild assumptions. For isolating the real roots we consider a modified Sturm algorithm, and a modified version of DESCARTES' algorithm introduced by Sagraloff. For the former we prove a complexity bound of $\widetilde{\mathcal{O}}_B(N^8)$ and for the latter a bound of $\widetilde{\mathcal{O}}_B(N^7)$. We implemented the algorithms in C as part of the core library of MATHEMATICA and we illustrate their efficiency over various data sets. Finally, we present complexity results for the general case of the first approach, where the coefficients belong to multiple extensions.

Categories and Subject Descriptors: F.2 [Theory of Computation]: Analysis of Algorithms and Problem Complexity; I.1 [Computing Methodology]: Symbolic and algebraic manipulation: Algorithms

Keywords real root isolation, algebraic polynomial, field extension, separation bounds, Sturm, Descartes' rule of sign

General Terms Algorithms, Experimentation, Theory

1. INTRODUCTION

Real root isolation is a very important problem in computational mathematics. Many algorithms are known for isolating the real roots of a polynomial with integer or rational coefficients that are either based solely on operations with rational numbers, [8, 13, 24, 29] and references therein,

or they follow a numerical, but certified approach, [25, 33] and references therein. In this paper we consider a variation of the problem in which the coefficients of the polynomial are polynomial functions of a real algebraic number, that is they belong to a simple algebraic extension of the rationals.

> **Problem 1.** *Let α be a real algebraic number with isolating interval representation $\alpha \cong (A, \mathfrak{I})$, where $A = \sum_{i=0}^{m} a_i x^i$, $\mathfrak{I} = [\mathsf{a}_1, \mathsf{a}_2]$, $\mathsf{a}_{1,2} \in \mathbb{Q}$ and $\deg(A) = m$ and $\mathcal{L}(A) = \tau$. Let $B_\alpha = \sum_{i=0}^{n} b_i(\alpha) y^i \in \mathbb{Z}(\alpha)[y]$ be square-free, where $b_i(x) = \sum_{j=0}^{\eta_i} c_{i,j} x^j \in \mathbb{Z}[x]$, $\mathcal{L}(c_{i,j}) \leq \sigma$, and $\eta_i < m$, for $0 \leq i \leq d$. What is the Boolean complexity of isolating the real roots of B_α?*

Rump [31], see also [30], presented an algorithm for the problem that is an extension of Collins and Loos [6] algorithm for integral polynomials. Johnson [17] presented and compared various algorithms for Problem 1. He considered a norm based algorithm that reduces the problem to root isolation of integral polynomial (this is the approach that we consider in Sec. 3) and extended three algorithms used for integral polynomials, i.e. Sturm (we present it in Sec. 4.2), the algorithm based on derivative sequence and Rolle's theorem [6], and the algorithm based on Descartes' rule of sign [5] (we present a modified version in Sec. 4.3). Johnson and Krandick [16] modified the latter and managed to replace exact arithmetic, when possible, with certified floating point operations; a novelty that speeds up considerably the computations. Along the same lines, Rouillier and Zimmermann [29] presented an optimal in terms of memory used algorithm for integral polynomials that exploits adaptive multiprecision techniques that could be used for Problem 1, if we approximate the real algebraic number up to a sufficient precision. In a series of works [11, 12, 22] a bitstream version of Descartes' algorithm was introduced. The coefficients of the input polynomial are considered to be real numbers that we can approximate up to arbitrary precision. We use the most recent version of this approach, which is due to Sagraloff [32], to tackle Problem 1. Last but not least, let us also mention the numerical algorithms due to Pan [25] and Schönhage [33], that could be also used if approximate α in our problem up to a sufficient precision.

Rioboo [28] considered various symbolic algorithms for operations with real algebraic numbers, based on quasi Sylvester sequences. These algorithms could be used for Problem 1, and they are closely connected with the Sturm algorithm that we present (Sec. 4.2). However, we use different subalgorithms for sign evaluations and solving polynomials. The focus in [28] is on efficient implementation of the real closure in AXIOM.

Problem 1 is closely related to real root isolation of of triangular systems and regular chains. In [4, 20, 38, 39] algorithms and implementations are presented for isolating the real roots of triangular polynomial systems, based on interval arithmetic and the so-called *sleeve* polynomials. In the case of two variables the problem at study is similar to Problem 1. In this line of research the coefficients of the algebraic polynomial are replaced with sufficiently refined intervals, hence obtaining upper and lower bounds (i.e. a sleeve) for the polynomial. Isolation is performed using evaluations and exclusion predicates that involve the non-vanishing of the derivative. To our knowledge there is no complexity analysis of the algorithms. Nevertheless in [4] evaluation bounds are presented, which are crucial for the termination of the algorithm, based on separation bounds of polynomial systems. However, the systems used for the bounds involve the derivative of the polynomial (this is needed for the exclusion criterion), which is not the case for our approach. In [3] the problem of real root isolation of 0-dim square-free regular chains is considered. A generalization of Vincent-Collins-Akritas (or Descartes) algorithm is used to isolate the real roots of of polynomials with real algebraic numbers as coefficients. This approach is similar to the direct strategy that we study. To our knowledge the authors do not present a complexity analysis since they focus on efficient algorithms and implementation in MAPLE.

We revisit two approaches for isolating the real roots of a square-free polynomial with coefficients in a simple algebraic extension of the rational numbers. The first, indirect, approach (Sec. 3), already presented in [17], is to find a polynomial with integer coefficients which is zero at all roots of B_α, isolate its real roots, and identify the intervals which contain the roots of B_α. We compute (aggregate) separation bounds for the resulting polynomial (Lem. 7), that are slightly better than the ones in [31], and prove that the complexity of the algorithm is $\widetilde{\mathcal{O}}_B(N^{10})$, where N is an upper bound on all the quantities (degrees and bitsizes) of the input. The second approach (Sec. 4.1) is to isolate the roots of the input polynomial directly, using either the Sturm's algorithm or Sagraloff's modified Descartes algorithm. We analyze the worst-case asymptotic complexity of the algorithms and we obtained a bound of $\widetilde{\mathcal{O}}_B(N^8)$ and $\widetilde{\mathcal{O}}_B(N^7)$, respectively. We obtain these complexity bounds by estimating improved separation bounds for the roots (Sec. 4.1 and Lem. 9), that we also prove that they are optimal (Sec. 4.4). The bounds are better than the previously known ones [17, 30] by a factor of N. We empirically compare the performance of the indirect approach and the direct approach based on Sagraloff's modified Descartes algorithm. The algorithms were implemented in C as part of the core library of MATHEMATICA, and we illustrate their behavior on various datasets (Sec. 5). The complexity bounds that we present are many factors better that the previously known ones. However, a fair and explicit comparison with the bounds in [17] is rather difficult, if possible at all, since, besides the improved separation bounds that we present, the complexity bounds of many subalgorithms that are used have been dramatically improved over the last 20 years, and it is not clear how to take this into account in the comparison.

Finally, we present a generalization of the first approach to the case where the input polynomials are univariate, but with coefficients that belong to multiple extensions (Sec. 6). We derive (aggregate) separation bounds for this case (Lem. 12) and we sketch the overall complexity of the algorithm. The bounds are single exponential with respect to the number of extensions.

Notation. $\mathcal{O}_B$ means bit complexity and the $\widetilde{\mathcal{O}}_B$-notation means that we are ignoring logarithmic factors. For $A = \sum_{i=1}^{d} a_i x^i \in \mathbb{Z}[x]$, $\deg(A)$ denotes its degree. $\mathcal{L}(A)$ denotes an upper bound on the bitsize of the coefficients of A, including a bit for the sign. For $a \in \mathbb{Q}$, $\mathcal{L}(a) \geq 1$ is the maximum bitsize of the numerator and the denominator.

If $\alpha_1, \ldots, \alpha_d$ are the distinct, possible complex, roots of A, then $\Delta_i = |\alpha_i - \alpha_{c_i}|$, where α_{c_i} is the roots closest to α_i. $\Delta(A) = \min_i \Delta_i(A)$ is the separation bound, that is the smallest distance between two (real or complex, depending on the context) roots of A. By $\Sigma(A) = -\sum_{i=1}^{n} \lg \Delta_i(A)$, we denote the numbers of bits needed to represent isolating rational numbers for all the roots of A.

Given two polynomials, possible multivariate, f and g, then $\mathrm{res}_x(f, g)$ denotes their resultant with respect to x.

2. PRELIMINARIES

Real algebraic numbers are the real roots of univariate polynomials with integer coefficients; let their set be $\mathbb{R}_{\mathsf{alg}}$. We represent them in the so-called *isolating interval representation*. If $\alpha \in \mathbb{R}_{\mathsf{alg}}$ then the representation consists of a square-free polynomial with integer coefficients, $A \in \mathbb{Z}[x]$, that has α as a real root, and an isolating interval with rational endpoints, $\mathcal{I} = [a_1, a_2]$, that contains α and no other root of the polynomial. We write $\alpha \cong (A, \mathcal{I})$.

The following proposition provides various bounds for the roots of a univariate polynomial. Various versions of the proposition could be found in e.g. [8, 10, 36]. We should mention that the constants that appear are not optimal. For multivariate bounds we refer to [15].

Proposition 1. *Let f be a univariate polynomial of degree p. If γ_i are the distinct real roots of f, then it holds*

$$|\gamma_i| \leq 2\|f\|_\infty \leq 2^{\tau+1}, \tag{1}$$

$$-\lg \Delta(f) \leq -\frac{1}{2} \lg |3 \operatorname{disc}(f_{red})| + \frac{p+2}{2} \lg(p) +$$
$$(p-1)\lg\|f_{red}\|_2 \tag{2}$$
$$\leq 2p \lg p + p\tau,$$

$$-\sum_i \lg \Delta_i(f) \leq -\frac{1}{2} \lg |\operatorname{disc}(f_{red})| + \frac{p^2-p-2}{2} +$$
$$(2p-1)\lg\|f_{red}\|_2 \tag{3}$$
$$\leq 3p^2 + 3p\tau + 4p \lg p,$$

where f_{red} is the square-free part of f, and the second inequalities hold if we consider $f \in \mathbb{Z}[x]$ and $\mathcal{L}(f) = \tau$.

Proposition 2. *Let $f \in \mathbb{Z}[x]$ have degree p and bitsize τ. We compute the isolating interval representation of its real roots and their multiplicities in $\widetilde{\mathcal{O}}_B(p^5 + p^4\tau + p^3\tau^2)$ [32, 35]. The endpoints of the isolating intervals have bitsize $\mathcal{O}(p^2 + p\tau)$ and $\mathcal{L}(f_{red}) = \mathcal{O}(p + \tau)$, where f_{red} is the square-free part of f. If $N = \max\{p, \tau\}$ then complexity bound for isolation becomes $\widetilde{\mathcal{O}}_B(N^5)$.*

Proposition 3. *[9, 14] Given a real algebraic number $\alpha \cong (f, [\mathsf{a}, \mathsf{b}])$, where $\mathcal{L}(\mathsf{a}) = \mathcal{L}(\mathsf{b}) = \mathcal{O}(p^2 + p\tau)$, and $g \in \mathbb{Z}[x]$, such that $\deg(g) = q$, $\mathcal{L}(g) = \sigma$, we compute $\mathrm{sign}(g(\alpha))$ in bit complexity $\widetilde{\mathcal{O}}_B(pq \max\{\tau, \sigma\} + p \min\{p, q\}^2 \tau)$.*

For the proofs of the following results the reader may refer to [9]. Let $f, g \in (\mathbb{Z}[x])[y]$ such that $\deg_x(f) = p$, $\deg_x(g) = q$, $\deg_y(f), \deg_y(g) \leq d$, $\tau = \max(\mathcal{L}(f), \mathcal{L}(g))$. By $\mathbf{SR}(f, g\,;\mathsf{a})$ we denote the evaluation of the signed polynomial remainder sequence of f and g with respect to x over a, and by $\mathbf{SR}_j(f, g\,;\mathsf{a})$ the j-th element in this sequence.

Proposition 4. *We can compute $\mathrm{res}(f, g)$ w.r.t. x or y in $\widetilde{\mathcal{O}}_B(pq \max\{p, q\} d\tau)$.*

Proposition 5. *We compute $\mathbf{SR}(f, g\,;\mathsf{a})$, where $\mathsf{a} \in \mathbb{Q} \cup \{\infty\}$ and $\mathcal{L}(\mathsf{a}) = \sigma$, in $\widetilde{\mathcal{O}}_B(pq \max\{p, q\} d \max\{\tau, \sigma\})$. For the polynomials $\mathbf{SR}_j(f, g\,;\mathsf{a}) \in \mathbb{Z}[y]$, except for f, g, we have $\deg_y(\mathbf{SR}_j(f, g\,;\mathsf{a})) = \mathcal{O}((p + q)d)$ and $\mathcal{L}(\mathbf{SR}_j(f, g\,;\mathsf{a})) = \mathcal{O}(\max\{p, q\}\tau + \min\{p, q\}\sigma)$.*

3. REDUCTION TO INTEGER COEFFICIENTS

3.1 Some useful bounds

The roots of B_α in Problem 1 are algebraic numbers, hence they are roots of a polynomial with integer coefficients. We estimate bounds on the degree and the bitsize of this polynomial, and we will use them to analyze the Boolean complexity of the real root isolation algorithm.

Consider a real algebraic number $\alpha \in \mathbb{R}_{\mathrm{alg}}$, in isolating interval representation $\alpha \cong (A, \mathfrak{I})$, where $A = \sum_{i=0}^{m} a_i x^i$, $\mathfrak{I} = [\mathsf{a}_1, \mathsf{a}_2]$, $\mathsf{a}_{1,2} \in \mathbb{Q}$ and $\deg(A) = m$ and $\mathcal{L}(A) = \tau$. Since A is square-free, has m, possible complex, roots, say $\alpha_1, \alpha_2, \ldots, \alpha_m$ and after a (possible) reordering let $\alpha = \alpha_1$.

Let $B_\alpha \in \mathbb{Z}(\alpha)[y]$, be a univariate polynomial in y, with coefficients that are polynomials in α with integer coefficients. More formally, let $B_\alpha = \sum_{i=0}^{n} b_i(\alpha) y^i$, where $b_i(x) = \sum_{j=0}^{\eta_i} c_{ij} x^j$ and $\eta_i < m$, $0 \leq i \leq d$. The restriction $\eta_i < m$ comes from the fact that $\mathbb{Z}(\alpha)$ is a vector space of dimension[1] m and the elements of one of its bases are $1, \alpha, \ldots, \alpha^{m-1}$. Finally, let $\mathcal{L}(B_\alpha) = \max_{i,j} \mathcal{L}(c_{ij}) = \sigma$. We assume that B_α is a square-free.

Our goal is to isolate the real roots of B_α (Problem 1). Since B_α has algebraic numbers as coefficients, its roots are algebraic numbers as well. Hence, there is a polynomial with integer coefficients that has as roots the roots of B_α, and possible other roots as well. To construct this polynomial, e.g. [8, 17, 19], we consider the following resultant w.r.t. x

$$R(y) = \mathrm{res}_x(B(x, y), A(x)) = (-1)^{mn} a_m^\eta \prod_{j=1}^{m} B(\alpha_j, y), \quad (4)$$

where $\eta = \max\{\eta_i\}$, and $B(x, y) \in \mathbb{Z}[x, y]$ is obtained from B_α after replacing all the occurrences of α with x. Interpreting the resultant using the Poisson formula, $R(y)$ is the product of polynomials $B(\alpha_j, y)$, where j ranges over all the roots of A. Our polynomial $B_\alpha \in \mathbb{Z}(\alpha)[y]$ is the factor in this product for $j = 1$. Hence, R has all the roots that B_α has and maybe more.

---

[1]If A is the minimal polynomial of α then the dimension is exactly m. In general it is not (computational) easy to compute the the minimal polynomial of a real algebraic number, thus we work with a square-free polynomial that has it as real root.

Remark 6. *Notice that $R(y)$ is not square-free in general. For example consider the polynomial $B_\alpha = y^4 - \alpha^2$, where α is the positive root of $A = x^2 - 3$. In this case $R(y) = \mathrm{res}_x(A(x), B(x, y)) = \mathrm{res}_x(x^2 - 3, y^2 - x^2) = (y^4 - 3)^2$.*

Using Prop. 14 and by taking into account that $\eta_i < m$, we get $\deg(R) \leq mn$ and $\mathcal{L}(R) \leq m(\tau + \sigma) + 2m \lg(4mn)$. We may also write $\deg(R) = \mathcal{O}(mn)$ and $\mathcal{L}(R) = \widetilde{\mathcal{O}}(m(\sigma + \tau))$.

In order to construct an isolating interval representation for the real roots of B_α, we need a square-free polynomial. This polynomial, $C(y) \in \mathbb{Z}[y]$, is a square factor of $R(y)$, and so it holds $\deg(C) \leq mn$ and $\mathcal{L}(C) \leq m(\tau + \sigma) + 3m \lg(4mn)$, where the last inequality follows from Mignotte's bound [23].

Using the Prop. 1, we deduce the following lemma:

Lemma 7. *Let B_α be as in Problem 1. The minimal polynomial, $C \in \mathbb{Z}[x]$, of the, possible complex, roots of B_α, γ_i, has degree $\leq mn$ and bitsize $\leq m(\tau + \sigma) + 3m \lg(4mn))$ or $\widetilde{\mathcal{O}}(m(\tau + \sigma))$. Moreover, it holds*

$$|\gamma_i| \leq 2^{m(\tau+\sigma)+2m\lg(4mn)}, \quad (5)$$

$$-\lg \Delta(C) \leq m^2 n(\tau + \sigma + 4\lg(4mn)), \quad (6)$$

$$-\sum_i \lg \Delta_i(C) \leq 3m^2 n(n + \tau + \sigma + 6\lg(4mn)), \quad (7)$$

$$|\gamma_i| \leq 2^{\widetilde{\mathcal{O}}(m(\tau+\sigma))}, \quad (8)$$

$$-\lg \Delta(C) = \widetilde{\mathcal{O}}(m^2 n(\tau + \sigma)), \quad (9)$$

$$\Sigma(C) = -\sum_i \lg \Delta_i(C) = \widetilde{\mathcal{O}}(m^2 n(n + \tau + \sigma)). \quad (10)$$

3.2 The algorithm

The indirect algorithm for Problem 2, follows closely the procedure described in the previous section to estimate the various bounds on the roots of B_α. First, we compute the univariate polynomial with integer coefficients, R, such that the set of its real roots includes those of B_α. We isolate the real roots of R and we identify which ones are roots of B_α.

Let us present in details the three steps and their complexity. We compute R using resultant computation, as presented in (4). For this we consider B as a bivariate polynomial in $\mathbb{Z}[x, y]$ and we compute $\mathrm{res}_x(B(x, y), A(x))$, using Prop. 4. Since $\deg_x(B) < m$, $\deg_y(B) = n$, $\mathcal{L}(B) = \sigma$, $\deg_x(A) = m$, $\deg_y(A) = 0$ and $\mathcal{L}(A) = \tau$, this computation costs $\widetilde{\mathcal{O}}_B(m^3 n(\sigma + \tau))$, using Prop. 4.

Now we isolate the real roots of R. This can be done in $\widetilde{\mathcal{O}}_B(m^4 n^3(mn^2 + mn\tau + n^2\sigma + m\tau^2 + m\sigma^2 + m\tau\sigma))$, by Prop. 2. In the same complexity bound we can also compute the multiplicities of the real roots, if needed [14].

The rational numbers that isolate the real roots of R have bitsize bounded by $\widetilde{\mathcal{O}}(m^2 n(n + \sigma + \tau))$, which is also a bound on the bitsize of all of them, as Prop. 1 and Lem. 7 indicate.

It is possible that R can have more roots that B_α, thus it remains to identify which real roots of R are roots of B_α. For sure all the real roots of B_α are roots of R. Consider a real root γ of R and its isolating interval $[\mathsf{c}_1, \mathsf{c}_2]$. If γ is a root of B_α, then since B_α is square-free, by Rolle's theorem it must change signs if we evaluate it over the endpoints of the isolating interval of γ. Hence, in order to identify the real roots of R that are roots of B_α it suffices to compute the sign of B_α over all the endpoints of the isolating intervals.

We can improve the step that avoids the non-relevant roots of R by applying the algorithm for chainging the ordering of a bivariate regular chain [26]. However, currently, this step is not the bottleneck of the algorithm so we do not elaborate further.

Consider an isolating point of R, say $\mathsf{c}_j \in \mathbb{Q}$, of bitsize s_j. To compute the sign of the evaluation of B_α over it, we proceed as follows. First we perform the substitution $y = \mathsf{c}_j$, and after clearing denominators, we get a number in $\mathbb{Z}[\alpha]$, for which we want to compute its sign. This is equivalent to consider the univariate polynomial $B(x, \mathsf{c}_j)$ and to compute its sign if we evaluate it over the real algebraic number α. We have $\deg(B(x, \mathsf{c}_j)) = \mathcal{O}(m)$ and $\mathcal{L}(B(x, \mathsf{c}_j)) = \widetilde{\mathcal{O}}(\sigma + ns_j)$. Hence the sign evaluation costs $\widetilde{\mathcal{O}}_B(m^3\tau + m^2\sigma + m^2ns_j)$ using Prop. 3. Summing up over all s_j's, there are $\mathcal{O}(mn)$, and taking into account that $\sum_j s_j = \widetilde{\mathcal{O}}(m^2n(\sigma + \tau + n))$ (Lem. 7), we conclude that the overall complexity of identifying the real roots of B_α is $\widetilde{\mathcal{O}}_B(m^4n^3 + m^4n\tau + m^3n\sigma + m^4n^2(\sigma + \tau))$.

The overall complexity of the algorithm is dominated by that of real solving. We can state the following theorem:

Theorem 8. *The complexity of isolating the real roots of $B \in \mathbb{Z}(\alpha)[y]$ using the indirect method is $\widetilde{\mathcal{O}}_B(m^4n^3(mn^2 + mn\tau + n^2\sigma + m\tau^2 + m\sigma^2 + m\tau\sigma))$. If $N = \max\{m, n, \sigma, \tau\}$, then the previous bounds become $\widetilde{\mathcal{O}}_B(N^{10})$.*

If the polynomial B_α is not square-free then we can apply the algorithm of [37] to compute its square-free factorization and then we apply the previous algorithm either to the square-free part or to each polynomial of the square-free factorization. The complexity of the square-free factorization is $\widetilde{\mathcal{O}}_B(m^2n(\sigma^2 + \tau^2) + mn^2(\sigma + \tau))$, and does not dominate the aforementioned bound.

4. TWO DIRECT APPROACHES

The computation of R, the polynomial with integer coefficients that has the real roots of B_α is a costly operation that we usually want to avoid. If possible, we would like to try to solve the polynomial B_α directly, using one of the well-known subdivision algorithms, for example STRUM or DESCARTES and BERNSTEIN, specially adopted to handle polynomials that have coefficients in an extension field. In practice, this is accomplished by obtaining, repeatedly improved, approximations of the real algebraic number α and subsequently apply DESCARTES or BERNSTEIN for polynomials with interval coefficients, e.g. [16, 29].

The fact that we compute the roots using directly the representation of B_α allows us to avoid the complexity induced by the conjugates of α. This leads to improved separation bounds, and to faster algorithms for real root isolation.

4.1 Separation bounds for B_α

We compute various bounds on the roots of B_α based on the first inequalities of Prop. 1. For this we need to compute a lower bound for $|\mathsf{disc}(B_\alpha)|$ and an upper bound for $\|B_\alpha\|_2$.

First we compute bounds on the coefficients on B_α. Let $\alpha_1 = \alpha, \alpha_2, \ldots, \alpha_m$ be the roots of A. We consider the resultants

$$r_i := \mathtt{res}_x(A(x), z - b_i(x)) = \mathtt{res}_x\left(A(x), z - \sum_{j=0}^{\eta_i} c_{i,j}x^j\right) \in \mathbb{Z}[z] \ .$$

It holds that

$$r_i(z) = a_m^\eta \prod_{k=1}^m (z - b_i(\alpha_k)) \ ,$$

where $\eta = \max\{\eta_i\} < m$. The roots of r_i are the numbers $b_i(\alpha_k)$, where k runs over all the roots of A. We use Prop. 14 to bound the degree and bitsize of r_i. The degree of r_i is bounded by m and their coefficient are of bitsize $\leq m\sigma + m\tau + 5m\lg(m)$. Using Cauchy's bound, we deduce

$$2^{-m\sigma - m\tau - 5m\lg(m)} \leq |b_i(\alpha_k)| \leq 2^{m\sigma + m\tau + 5m\lg(m)} \ , \quad (11)$$

for all i and k. To bound $|\mathsf{disc}(B_\alpha)|$ we consider the identity

$$\begin{aligned} \mathsf{disc}(B_\alpha) &= (-1)^{\frac{1}{2}n(n-1)} \frac{1}{b_n(\alpha)} \mathtt{res}_y(B_\alpha, \partial B_\alpha(y)/\partial y) \\ &= (-1)^{\frac{1}{2}n(n-1)} \frac{1}{b_n(\alpha)} R_B(\alpha) \ , \end{aligned}$$

where the resultant, $R_B \in \mathbb{Z}[\alpha]$, can be computed as the determinant of the Sylvester matrix of B_α and $\partial B_\alpha(y)/\partial y$, evaluated over α.

The Sylvester matrix is of size $(2n-1) \times (2n-1)$, the elements of which belong to $\mathbb{Z}[\alpha]$. The determinant consists of $(2n-1)!$ terms. Each term is a product of $n-1$ polynomials in α of degree at most $m-1$ and bitsize at most σ, times a product of n polynomials in α of degree at most $m-1$ and bitsize at most $\sigma + \lg n$. The first product results a polynomial of degree $(n-1)(m-1)$ and bitsize $(n-1)\sigma + (n-1)\lg m$. The second product results polynomials of degree $n(m-1)$ and bitsize $n\sigma\lg n + n\lg m$. Thus, any term in the determinant expansion is a polynomial in α of degree at most $(2n-1)(m-1)$, or $\mathcal{O}(mn)$, and bitsize at most $4(2n-1)\sigma\lg(mn)$ or $\widetilde{\mathcal{O}}(n\sigma)$. The determinant itself, is a polynomial in α of degree at most mn and of bitsize $4(2n-1)\sigma\lg(mn) + (2n-1)\lg(2n-1) \leq 5(2n-1)\sigma\lg(mn) = \widetilde{\mathcal{O}}(n\sigma)$.

To compute a bound on $R_B(\alpha)$ we consider R_B as a polynomial in $\mathbb{Z}[y]$, and we compute a bound on its evaluation over α. For this we use resultants. It holds

$$D = \mathtt{res}_x(A(x), y - R_B(x)) = a_m^{\deg(R_B)} \prod_{i=1}^m (y - R_B(\alpha_i)) \ .$$

We notice that the roots of $D \in \mathbb{Z}[x]$ are the evaluations of R_B over the roots of A. So it suffices to compute bounds on the roots of D. Using Prop. 14 we deduce that $\deg(D) \leq m$ and $\mathcal{L}(D) \leq 13mn\sigma\lg(mn) + mn\tau$ or $\mathcal{L}(D) = \widetilde{\mathcal{O}}(mn(\sigma+\tau))$. Using Cauchy bound, refer to Eq. (1), we conclude that

$$2^{-13mn\sigma\lg(mn) - mn\tau} \leq |R_B(\alpha)| \leq 2^{13mn\sigma\lg(mn) + mn\tau} \ .$$

Using this inequality and (11), we can bound $|\mathsf{disc}(B_\alpha)|$, i.e.

$$2^{-13mn\sigma\lg(mn) - 2mn\tau} \leq |\mathsf{disc}(B_\alpha)| \leq 2^{13mn\sigma\lg(mn) + 2mn\tau} \ . \quad (12)$$

It remains to bound $\|B_\alpha\|_2$. Using Eq. (11) we get

$$\|B_\alpha\|_2^2 \leq \sum_{i=0}^n (b_i(\alpha))^2 \leq (n+1)\, 2^{2m(\sigma + \tau + 5\lg(m))} \ .$$

The previous discussion leads to the following lemma

Lemma 9. *Let B_α be as in Problem 1, and ξ_i be its roots. Then, it holds*

$$|\xi_i| \leq 2^{m(\tau+\sigma+5\lg m)} , \tag{13}$$

$$-\lg\Delta(B_\alpha) \leq 12mn(\sigma\lg(mn) + \tau + 5\lg m) , \tag{14}$$

$$-\sum_i \lg\Delta_i(B_\alpha) \leq 14mn(\sigma\lg(mn) + \tau + 5\lg m) , \tag{15}$$

or

$$|\xi_i| \leq 2^{\widetilde{\mathcal{O}}(m(\tau+\sigma))} , \tag{16}$$

$$-\lg\Delta(B_\alpha) = \widetilde{\mathcal{O}}(mn(\tau+\sigma)) , \tag{17}$$

$$\Sigma(B_\alpha) = -\sum_i \lg\Delta_i(B_\alpha) = \widetilde{\mathcal{O}}(mn(\tau+\sigma)) . \tag{18}$$

4.2 The STURM algorithm

Let us first study the STURM algorithm. We assume B_α as in Problem 1 to be square-free. To isolate the real roots of B_α using the STURM algorithm, we need to evaluate the Sturm sequence of $B(\alpha, y)$ and its derivative with respect to y, $\partial B(\alpha, y)/\partial y$, over various rational numbers. For the various bounds needed we will use Lem. 9.

The number of steps that a subdivision-based algorithm, and hence STURM algorithm, performs to isolate the real roots of a polynomial depends on the separation bound. To be more specific, the number of steps, $(\#T)$, that STURM performs is $(\#T) \leq 2r + r\lg\mathsf{B} + \Sigma(B_\alpha)$ [8, 10], where r is the number of real roots and B is an upper bound on the real roots. Using (14) and (15) we deduce that $(\#T) = \widetilde{\mathcal{O}}(mn(\tau+\sigma))$.

To complete the analysis of the algorithm it remains to compute the complexity of each step, i.e. the cost of evaluating the Sturm sequence over a rational number, of the worst possible bitsize. The latter is induced by the separation bound, and in our case is $\widetilde{\mathcal{O}}(mn(\tau+\sigma))$.

We consider B as polynomial in $\mathbb{Z}[x, y]$ and we evaluate the Sturm-Habicht sequence of B and $\frac{\partial B}{\partial y}$, over rational numbers of bitsize $\widetilde{\mathcal{O}}(mn(\tau+\sigma))$. The cost of this operation is $\widetilde{\mathcal{O}}_B(m^2n^4(\tau+\sigma))$ (Prop. 5).

It produces $\mathcal{O}(n)$ polynomials in $\mathbb{Z}[x]$, of degrees $\mathcal{O}(mn)$ and bitsize $\widetilde{\mathcal{O}}(n\tau + n\sigma)$. For each polynomial we have to compute its sign if we evaluate it over α. Using Prop. 3 each sign evaluation costs $\widetilde{\mathcal{O}}_B(m(m^2 + n^2)\tau + mn^2\sigma)$, and so the overall cost is $\widetilde{\mathcal{O}}_B(mn(m^2 + n^2)\tau + mn^3\sigma)$. If we multiply the latter bound with the number of steps, $\widetilde{\mathcal{O}}(mn(\tau+\sigma))$, we get the following theorem.

Theorem 10. *The complexity of isolating the real roots of $B \in \mathbb{Z}(\alpha)[y]$ using the STURM algorithm is $\widetilde{\mathcal{O}}_B(m^2n^2(m^2 + n^2)(\tau^2 + \sigma^2))$, or $\widetilde{\mathcal{O}}_B(N^8)$, where $N = \max\{m, n, \sigma, \tau\}$.*

4.3 A modif ed DESCARTES algorithm

We consider Sagraloff's modified version of Descartes' algorithm [32], that applies to polynomials with bitstream coefficients. We also refer the reader to [12, 21].

As stated in Problem 1, let α be a real root of $A = \sum_{i=0}^m a_i x^i \in \mathbb{Z}[x]$, where $a_m \neq 0$ and $|a_i| < 2^\tau$ for $0 \leq i \leq m$, and let $B_\alpha = \sum_{i=0}^n b_i(\alpha)y^i \in \mathbb{Z}[\alpha][y]$, where $b_i = \sum_{j=0}^{\eta_i} c_{i,j}x^j \in \mathbb{Z}[x]$, $\eta_i < m$ and $|c_{i,j}| < 2^\sigma$ for $0 \leq i \leq n$ and $0 \leq j \leq \eta_i$, where we also assume that B_α is square-free.

Let $\xi_1, \ldots, \xi_n$ be all (complex) roots of B, and $\Delta_i(B_\alpha) := \min_{j\neq i}|\xi_j - \xi_i|$. By Theorem 19 of [32], the complexity of

isolating real roots of B_α is

$$\widetilde{\mathcal{O}}_B(n(\Sigma(B_\alpha) + n\tau_B)^2) ,$$

where $\left|\frac{b_i(\alpha)}{b_n(\alpha)}\right| \leq 2^{\tau_B}$ and $\Sigma(B_\alpha) = -\sum_{i=1}^n \lg(\Delta_i(B_\alpha))$. From Lem. 9 we get that

$$\Sigma(B_\alpha) \leq 14mn(\tau + \sigma\lg(mn)) + n\lg n = \widetilde{\mathcal{O}}(mn(\tau+\sigma)) . \tag{19}$$

To compute a bound on τ_B, we use Eq. (11). It holds $\left|\frac{b_i(\alpha_k)}{b_n(\alpha_k)}\right| \leq 2^{2m\sigma+2m\tau+6m\lg(m)}$, for all i and k. Hence,

$$\tau_B \leq 2m\sigma + 2m\tau + 6m\lg(m) = \widetilde{\mathcal{O}}(m(\sigma+\tau)) . \tag{20}$$

Finally, by combining (19) and (20), we deduce that the cost of isolating real roots of B is

$$\widetilde{\mathcal{O}}_B(n(\Sigma(B_\alpha) + n\tau_B)^2) = \widetilde{\mathcal{O}}_B(n(mn\tau + mn\sigma)^2) = \widetilde{\mathcal{O}}_B(m^2n^3(\sigma^2 + \tau^2)) .$$

If $N = \max\{m, n, \sigma, \tau\}$, then the bound becomes $\widetilde{\mathcal{O}}_B(N^7)$.

It remains to estimate the cost of computing the successive approximations of $b_i(\alpha)/b_n(\alpha)$. The root isolation algorithm requires approximations of $b_i(\alpha)/b_n(\alpha)$ to accuracy of $\mathcal{O}(\Sigma(B_\alpha) + n\tau_B)$ bits after the binary point. Since $|b_i(\alpha)/b_n(\alpha)| \leq 2^{\tau_B}$, to approximate each fraction, for $0 \leq i \leq n-1$, to accuracy L, it is sufficient to approximate $b_i(\alpha)$, for $0 \leq i \leq n$, up to precision $\mathcal{O}(L + \tau_B)$. Hence, the algorithm requires approximation of $b_i(\alpha)$, for $0 \leq i \leq n$, to precision $\mathcal{O}(\Sigma(B)+n\tau_B)$. By inequality (11), $|b_i(\alpha)| \geq 2^{-\tau_B}$, and therefore it is sufficient to approximate $b_i(\alpha)$ to accuracy $\mathcal{O}(\Sigma(B_\alpha) + n\tau_B)$.

Approximation of $c_{i,j}\alpha^j$ to accuracy of L bits requires approximation of α to accuracy of $L + \lg|c_{i,j}| + \lg(j) + (j-1)\lg|\alpha| \leq L + \sigma + \lg(m) + (m-1)(\tau+1) = \widetilde{\mathcal{O}}(L + \sigma + m\tau)$ bits. Hence the accuracy of approximations of α required by the algorithm is

$$\mathcal{O}(\Sigma(B_\alpha) + n\tau_B) = \widetilde{\mathcal{O}}(mn(\sigma+\tau)) .$$

By Lemmata 4.4, 4.5 and 4.11 of [18], the bit complexity of approximating α to accuracy L is

$$\widetilde{\mathcal{O}}(m^4\tau^2 + m^2L) .$$

Therefore, the bit complexity of computing the required approximations of $b_i(\alpha)/b_n(\alpha)$ is

$$\widetilde{\mathcal{O}}(m^4\tau^2 + m^2mn(\sigma+\tau)) = \widetilde{\mathcal{O}}(m^3(m\tau^2 + n\sigma + n\tau)) .$$

Theorem 11. *The bit complexity of isolating the real roots of B_α of Problem 1 using the modified Descartes' algorithm in [32] is $\widetilde{\mathcal{O}}_B(m^2n^3(\sigma^2 + \tau^2) + m^3(m\tau^2 + n\sigma + n\tau))$, or $\widetilde{\mathcal{O}}_B(N^7)$, where $N = \max\{m, n, \sigma, \tau\}$.*

4.4 Almost tight separation bounds

Let α be the root of $A(x) = x^m - ax^{m-1} - 1$, in $(a, a+1)$, for $a \geq 3$, $m \geq 3$. Then the Mignotte polynomial $B_\alpha(y) = y^n - 2(\alpha^k y - 1)^2$, where $k = \lfloor(m-1)/2\rfloor$, has two roots in $(1/\alpha^k - h, 1/\alpha^k + h)$, where $h = \alpha^{-k(n+2)/2} < a^{-(m-2)(n+2)/4}$.

If $a \leq 2^\tau$ and $\tau = \Omega(\lg(mn))$, then $-\lg\Delta(B_\alpha) = \Omega(mn\tau)$, which matches the upper bound in (15) of Lem. 9. This quantity, $\Omega(mn\tau)$, is also a tight lower bound for the number of steps that an subdivision based algorithm performs, following the arguments used in [13] to prove a similar bound for polynomials with integer coefficients.

n	Algorithm	$m=2$	$m=3$	$m=5$	$m=10$	$m=20$
10	ICF	0.003	0.006	0.013	0.082	0.820
	BMD	0.002	0.002	0.003	0.006	0.019
20	ICF	0.004	0.010	0.048	1.49	2.80
	BMD	0.008	0.008	0.010	0.017	0.053
50	ICF	0.014	0.044	0.271	8.29	20.5
	BMD	0.046	0.050	0.061	0.079	0.213
100	ICF	0.047	0.173	1.09	33.1	108
	BMD	0.165	0.206	0.137	0.246	0.546
200	ICF	0.144	0.612	4.90	141	626
	BMD	0.746	0.701	1.00	0.824	1.55

Table 1. Randomly generated polynomials

n	Algorithm	$m=2$	$m=3$	$m=5$	$m=10$	$m=20$
10	ICF	0.011	0.008	0.032	0.208	1.75
	BMD	0.007	0.007	0.009	0.010	0.015
20	ICF	0.019	0.041	0.193	1.50	13.9
	BMD	0.075	0.071	0.080	0.088	0.106
50	ICF	0.122	0.270	1.51	25.8	338
	BMD	1.78	1.63	1.83	1.90	2.27
100	ICF	0.834	2.17	16.1	365	10649
	BMD	54.7	51.3	56.0	74.7	92.4
200	ICF	7.53	31.2	246	8186	> 36000
	BMD	2182	3218	3830	4280	4377

Table 2. Generalized Laguerre polynomials

n	Algorithm	$m=2$	$m=3$	$m=5$	$m=10$	$m=20$
10	ICF	0.017	0.012	0.035	0.285	2.09
	BMD	0.015	0.013	0.011	0.015	0.008
20	ICF	0.029	0.069	0.262	2.23	18.3
	BMD	0.059	0.052	0.069	0.039	0.027
50	ICF	0.137	0.356	2.04	45.4	429
	BMD	1.84	1.35	1.29	0.703	0.561
100	ICF	0.808	2.84	24.6	674	8039
	BMD	47.0	38.6	32.0	23.3	8.38
200	ICF	8.48	35.1	348	11383	> 36000
	BMD	3605	2566	2176	927	565

Table 3. Generalized Wilkinson polynomials

n	Algorithm	$m=3$	$m=5$	$m=10$	$m=20$
10	ICF	0.003	0.008	0.049	0.594
	BMD	0.010	0.006	0.014	0.036
20	ICF	0.006	0.027	0.288	8.83
	BMD	0.015	0.020	0.049	0.137
50	ICF	0.041	0.441	12.2	777
	BMD	0.112	0.147	0.321	0.854
100	ICF	0.866	11.6	729	28255
	BMD	0.702	0.868	2.32	5.99
200	ICF	35.7	684	23503	> 36000
	BMD	3.12	5.30	13.8	46.1

Table 4. Mignotte polynomials

5. IMPLEMENTATION AND EXPERIMENTS

We compare implementations of two methods of real root isolation for square-free polynomials over simple algebraic extensions of rationals. The first method, *ICF* (for Integer Continued Fractions), performs reduction to integer coefficients described in Section 3.2. For isolating roots of polynomials with integer coefficients it uses the MATHEMATICA implementation of the Continued Fractions algorithm [1]. The second method, *BMD* (for Bitstream Modified Descartes), uses Sagraloff's modified version of Descartes' algorithm ([32], see Section 4.3). The algorithm has been implemented in C as a part of the MATHEMATICA system.

For the experiments we used a 64-bit Linux virtual machine with a 3 GHz Intel Core i7 processor and 6 GB of RAM. The timings are in given seconds. Computations that did not finish in 10 hours of CPU time are reported as > 36000.

Randomly generated polynomials. For given values of m and n each instance was generated as follows. First, univariate polynomials of degree m with uniformly distributed random 10-bit integer coefficients were generated until an irreducible polynomial which had real roots was obtained. A real root r of the polynomial was randomly selected as the extension generator. Finally, a polynomial in $\mathbb{Z}[r,y]$ of degree n in y and degree $m-1$ in r with 10-bit random integer coefficients was generated. The results of the experiments are given in Table 1. Each timing is an average for 10 randomly generated problems.

Generalized Laguerre Polynomials. This example compares the two root isolation methods for generalized Laguerre polynomials $L_n^\alpha(x)$, where α was chosen to be the smallest root of the Laguerre polynomial $L_m(x)$. Note that $L_n^\alpha(x)$ has n positive roots for any positive α and $L_m(x)$ has m positive roots, so this example maximizes the number of real roots of both the input polynomial with algebraic number coefficients and the polynomial with integer coefficients obtained by *ICF*. The results of the experiment are given in Table 2.

Generalized Wilkinson Polynomials. This example uses the following generalized Wilkinson polynomials $W_{n,\alpha}(x) := \prod_{k=1}^{n}(x - k\alpha)$, where α is the smallest root of the Laguerre polynomial $L_m(x)$. The timings are presented in Table 3.

Mignotte Polynomials. The variant of Mignotte polynomials used in this example is given by $M_{n,\alpha}(x) := y^n - 2(\alpha^k y - 1)^2$, where α is the root of $A_m(x) := x^m - 3x^{m-1} - 1$ in $(3, 4)$, $m \geq 3$ and $k = \lfloor (m-1)/2 \rfloor$ (see Section 4.4). The results of the experiment are given in Table 4.

The experiments suggest that for low degree extensions *ICF* is faster than *BMD*, but in all experiments as the degree of extension grows *BMD* becomes faster than *ICF*. Another fact worth noting is that *ICF* depends directly on the extension degree m, since it isolates roots of a polynomial of degree mn. On the other hand, the only part of *BMD* that depends directly on m is computing approximations of coefficients, which in practice seems to take a very small proportion of the running time. The main root isolation loop depends only on the geometry of roots, which depends on m only through the worst case lower bound on root separation. Indeed, in all examples the running time of *ICF* grows substantially with m, but the running time of *BMD* either grows at a much slower pace or, in case of generalized Wilkinson polynomials, it even decreases with m (because the smallest root α of $L_m(x)$, and hence the root separation of $W_{n,\alpha}(x)$, increase with m). The superiority of the direct approach was also observed in [17].

6. MULTIPLE EXTENSIONS

In this section we consider the problem of real root isolation of a polynomials with coefficients in multiple extensions. We tackle the problem using a reduction to a polynomial with integer coefficients. The technique could be considered as a generalization of the one presented in Sec. 3.

We use $\mathbf{x}^{\mathbf{e}}$ to denote the monomial $x_1^{e_1} \cdots x_n^{e_\ell}$, with $\mathbf{e} = (e_1, \ldots, e_\ell) \in \mathbb{N}^\ell$. For a polynomial $f = \sum_{j=1}^{m} c_j \mathbf{x}^{\mathbf{e}_j} \in \mathbb{Z}[\mathbf{x}]$, let $\{\mathbf{e}_1, \ldots, \mathbf{e}_m\} \subset \mathbb{N}^\ell$ be the support of f; its Newton polytope Q is the convex hull of the support. By $(\#Q)$ we denote the integer points of the polytope Q, i.e. $(\#Q) = |Q \cap \mathbb{Z}^\ell|$.

Problem 2. *Let α_j, where $1 \leq j \leq \ell$, be a real algebraic numbers. Their isolating interval representation is $\alpha_j \cong (A_j, \mathfrak{I}_j)$, where $A_j = \sum_{i=0}^{m} a_i x_j^i$, $\mathfrak{I}_j = [\mathsf{a}_{j,1}, \mathsf{a}_{j,2}]$, $\mathsf{a}_{1,2} \in \mathbb{Q}$, $\deg(A_j) = m$, and $\mathcal{L}(A_j) = \tau$. Let*

$$B_\alpha = \sum_{i=0}^{n} b_i(\alpha_1, \ldots, \alpha_\ell)\, y^i \in \mathbb{Z}(\alpha)[y],$$

be square-free, where $b_i(\mathbf{x}) = \sum_{\mathbf{e}} c_{ij}\, \mathbf{x}^{\mathbf{e}} \in \mathbb{Z}[\mathbf{x}]$, $\mathcal{L}(c_{i,j}) \leq \sigma$, for $0 \leq i \leq d$, and for $\mathbf{e} = (e_1, \ldots, e_\ell)$, it holds $e_j \leq \eta < m$, What is the Boolean complexity of isolating the real roots of B_α?

We denote by $\mathbf{a}_i$ the coefficients of A_i, where $1 \leq i \leq \ell$, and by $\mathbf{c}$ the coefficients of B. We compute separation bounds following the technique introduced [15].

We consider the zero dimensional polynomial system (S) : $A_1(\mathbf{x}) = \cdots = A_\ell(\mathbf{x}) = A_{\ell+1}(\mathbf{x}) = 0$, where $A_k(\mathbf{x}) = \sum_{i=0}^{m} a_{k,i} x_k^i = 0$, $1 \leq k \leq \ell$, and $A_{\ell+1} = B(\mathbf{x}, y) = \sum_{i=0}^{n} b_i(x_1, \ldots, x_\ell)\, y^i = 0$. We should mention that we make the assumption that B does not become identically zero when $\alpha_1, \ldots, \alpha_l$ are replaced with some set of their conjugates (otherwise the resultant is zero).

We hide variable y, that is we consider (S) as an overdetermined system of $\ell + 1$ equations in ℓ variables. We consider the resultant, R, with respect to $x_1, \ldots, x_\ell$, that is we eliminate these variables, and we obtain a polynomial $R \in \mathbb{Z}[\mathbf{a}_1, \ldots, \mathbf{a}_\ell, \mathbf{c}, y]$. We interpret the resultant using the Poisson formula [7], see also [27], i.e.

$$R(y) = \mathtt{res}_x(A_1, \ldots, A_\ell, B) = \prod B(\alpha_{1,i_1}, \ldots, \alpha_{\ell,i_\ell}, y) ,$$

and $R(y) \in (\mathbb{Z}[\mathbf{a}_1, \ldots, \mathbf{a}_\ell, \mathbf{c}])[y]$. Similar to the single extension case, B_α, is among the factors of R, hence it suffices to compute bounds for the roots of $R(y)$.

We consider R as a univariate polynomial in y. The resultant is a homogeneous polynomial in the coefficients of (S), we refer to e.g. [7, 27] for more details and to [15] for a similar application. To be more specific, the structure of the coefficients of R is

$$R(y) = \cdots + \varrho_k\, \mathbf{a}_1^{\mathsf{M}_1} \cdots \mathbf{a}_\ell^{\mathsf{M}_\ell}\, \mathbf{c}^{\mathsf{M}_{\ell+1}-k} (y^i)^k + \cdots ,$$

where $1 \leq k \leq \mathsf{M}_{\ell+1} = m^\ell$, and i is a number in $\{1, \ldots, n\}$. The semantics of $\mathbf{a}_i^{\mathsf{M}_i}$ are that it is a monomial in the coefficients of A_i of total degree M_i. Similarly, $\mathbf{c}^{\mathsf{M}_{\ell+1}-k}$ stands for a monomial in the coefficients of B of total degree $\mathsf{M}_{\ell+1} - k$. Moreover, $\mathsf{M}_i \leq \ell\eta m^{\ell-1} < \ell(m-1)m^{\ell-1} < \ell m^\ell$. The degree of R with respect to y is at most $n\,\mathsf{M}_{\ell+1} = nm^\ell$.

Since $|a_{i,j}| \leq 2^\tau$, it holds

$$\lg \prod_{i=i}^{\ell} |\mathbf{a}_i|^{\mathsf{M}_i} \leq \tau \ell^2 m^\ell . \tag{21}$$

Similarly, since $|c_{i,j}| \leq 2^\sigma$, we get

$$\lg |\mathbf{c}|^{\mathsf{M}_{\ell+1}-k} \leq \sigma(m^\ell - k) \leq \sigma m^\ell . \tag{22}$$

Finally, $|\varrho_k| \leq \prod_{i=1}^{\ell+1} (\#Q_i)^{\mathsf{M}_i}$ [34], where $(\#Q_i)$ is the number of integer points of the Newton polytope of the polynomial A_i. We let $A_{\ell+1} = B$. It is $(\#Q_i) = m + 1$ for

---

$1 \leq i \leq \ell$, so $\prod_{i=1}^{\ell} (\#Q_i)^{\mathsf{M}_i} \leq (m+1)^{\ell(m-1)m^{\ell-1}} \leq m^{\ell m^\ell}$, and $(\#Q_{\ell+1}) \leq (\ell(m-1)+n)^{\ell+1} + \ell + 1$. Hence,

$$\begin{aligned}
(\#Q_i)^{\mathsf{M}_{\ell+1}} &\leq \left((\ell(m-1)+n)^{\ell+1} + \ell + 1 \right)^{m^\ell} \\
&\leq (2\ell m + n)^{(\ell+1)m^\ell} \leq (\ell m n)^{\ell m^\ell} ,
\end{aligned}$$

and so for every k

$$\lg |\varrho_k| \leq \lg \prod_{i=1}^{\ell+1} (\#Q_i)^{\mathsf{M}_i} \leq 2\ell m^\ell \lg(mn\ell) . \tag{23}$$

By combining (21), (22) and (23) we can bound the coefficients of R and its square-free factors. Using also Prop. 1 we get the following lemma.

Lemma 12. *Let B_α be as in Problem 2. The minimal polynomial, C_ℓ of the, possible complex, roots of B_α, γ_i, has degree $\leq n m^\ell$ and bitsize $\leq m^\ell(\tau\ell^2 + \sigma + 3\ell \lg(mn\ell))$ or $\widetilde{\mathcal{O}}(m^\ell(\ell^2\tau + \sigma))$. Moreover, it holds*

$$|\gamma_i| \leq 2^{m^\ell(\ell^2\tau + \sigma + 2\ell \lg(mn\ell))} , \tag{24}$$

$$-\lg \Delta(C_\ell) \leq m^{2\ell} n(\ell^2\tau + \sigma + 4\ell \lg(mn\ell)) , \tag{25}$$

$$-\sum_i \lg \Delta_i(C_\ell) \leq m^{2\ell} n(\ell^2\tau + \sigma + n + 6\ell \lg(mn\ell)) \tag{26}$$

$$|\gamma_i| \leq 2^{\widetilde{\mathcal{O}}(m^\ell(\ell^2\tau + \sigma))} , \tag{27}$$

$$-\lg \Delta(C_\ell) = \widetilde{\mathcal{O}}(m^{2\ell} n(\ell^2\tau + \sigma)) , \tag{28}$$

$$-\sum_i \lg \Delta_i(C_\ell) = \widetilde{\mathcal{O}}(m^{2\ell} n(\ell^2\tau + \sigma + n)) . \tag{29}$$

Remark 13. *To match exaclty the bounds derived in Lem. 7 one should use for M_i the more accurate inequality $\mathsf{M}_i < \ell(m-1)m^{\ell-1}$.*

We can isolate the real roots of C_ℓ in $\widetilde{\mathcal{O}}_B(n^5 m^{5\ell} + n^4 m^{5\ell} \tau \ell^2 + n^4 m^{4\ell} \sigma + + n^3 m^{5\ell} \tau^2 \ell^4 + + n^3 m^{3\ell} \sigma^2)$. That is we get a single exponential bound with respect to the number of the real algebraic numbers involved.

Acknowledgement

ET is partially supported by an individual postdoctoral grant from the Danish Agency for Science, Technology and Innovation, and also acknowledges support from the Danish National Research Foundation and the National Science Foundation of China (under the grant 61061130540) for the Sino-Danish Center for the Theory of Interactive Computation, within which part of this work was performed.

References

[1] A. G. Akritas and A. Strzeboński. A comparative study of two real root isolation methods. *Nonlinear Analysis: Modelling and Control*, 10:297–304, 2005.

[2] S. Basu, R. Pollack, and M-F.Roy. *Algorithms in Real Algebraic Geometry*, volume 10 of *Algorithms and Computation in Mathematics*. Springer-Verlag, 2nd edition, 2006.

[3] F. Boulier, C. Chen, F. Lemaire, and M. Maza. Real root isolation of regular chains. In *Proc. Asian Symposium on Computer Mathematics (ASCM)*, pages 1–15, 2009.

[4] J.-S. Cheng, X.-S. Gao, and C.-K. Yap. Complete numerical isolation of real roots in zero-dimensional triangular systems. *J. Symbolic Computation*, 44:768–785, July 2009.

[5] G. Collins and A. Akritas. Polynomial real root isolation using Descartes' rule of signs. In *SYMSAC '76*, pages 272–275, New York, USA, 1976. ACM Press.

[6] G. E. Collins and R. Loos. Polynomial real root isolation by differentiation. In *Proc. of the 3rd Int'l Symp. on Symbolic and Algebraic Computation*, SYMSAC '76, pages 15–25, New York, NY, USA, 1976. ACM.

[7] D. Cox, J. Little, and D. O'Shea. *Using Algebraic Geometry*. Number 185 in GTM. Springer, New York, 2nd edition, 2005.

[8] J. H. Davenport. Cylindrical algebraic decomposition. Technical Report 88–10, School of Mathematical Sciences, University of Bath, England, URL: http://www.bath.ac.uk/masjhd/, 1988.

[9] D. I. Diochnos, I. Z. Emiris, and E. P. Tsigaridas. On the asymptotic and practical complexity of solving bivariate systems over the reals. *J. Symbolic Computation*, 44(7):818–835, 2009. (Special issue on ISSAC 2007).

[10] Z. Du, V. Sharma, and C. K. Yap. Amortized bound for root isolation via Sturm sequences. In D. Wang and L. Zhi, editors, *Int. Workshop on Symbolic Numeric Computing*, pages 113–129, School of Science, Beihang University, Beijing, China, 2005.

[11] A. Eigenwillig. *Real root isolation for exact and approximate polynomials using Descartes´ rule of signs*. PhD thesis, Doktorarbeit, Universität des Saarlandes, Saarbrücken, 2008.

[12] A. Eigenwillig, L. Kettner, W. Krandick, K. Mehlhorn, S. Schmitt, and N. Wolpert. A Descartes Algorithm for Polynomials with Bit-Stream Coefficients. In V. Ganzha, E. Mayr, and E. Vorozhtsov, editors, *CASC*, volume 3718 of *LNCS*, pages 138–149. Springer, 2005.

[13] A. Eigenwillig, V. Sharma, and C. K. Yap. Almost tight recursion tree bounds for the Descartes method. In *Proc. Annual ACM ISSAC*, pages 71–78, New York, USA, 2006.

[14] I. Z. Emiris, B. Mourrain, and E. P. Tsigaridas. Real Algebraic Numbers: Complexity Analysis and Experimentation. In P. Hertling, C. Hoffmann, W. Luther, and N. Revol, editors, *Reliable Implementations of Real Number Algorithms: Theory and Practice*, volume 5045 of *LNCS*, pages 57–82. Springer Verlag, 2008. (also available in www.inria.fr/rrrt/rr-5897.html).

[15] I. Z. Emiris, B. Mourrain, and E. P. Tsigaridas. The DMM bound: Multivariate (aggregate) separation bounds. In S. Watt, editor, *Proc. 35th ACM Int'l Symp. on Symbolic & Algebraic Comp. (ISSAC)*, pages 243–250, Munich, Germany, July 2010.

[16] J. Johnson and W. Krandick. Polynomial real root isolation using approximate arithmetic. In *Proc. Int'l Symp. on Symbolic and Algebraic Comp. (ISSAC)*, pages 225–232. ACM, 1997.

[17] J. R. Johnson. *Algorithms for Polynomial Real Root Isolation*. PhD thesis, The Ohio State University, 1991.

[18] M. Kerber. On the complexity of reliable root approximation. In V. P. Gerdt, E. W. Mayr, and E. V. Vorozhtsov, editors, *CASC*, volume 5743 of *Lecture Notes in Computer Science*, pages 155–167. Springer, 2009.

[19] R. Loos. Computing in algebraic extensions. In B. Buchberger, G. E. Collins, R. Loos, and R. Albrecht, editors, *Computer Algebra: Symbolic and Algebraic Computation*, pages 173–187. Springer-Verlag, 1983.

[20] Z. Lu, B. He, Y. Luo, and L. Pan. An algorithm of real root isolation for polynomial system. In D. Wang and L. Zhi, editors, *Proc. 1st ACM Int'l Work. Symbolic Numeric Computation (SNC)*, pages 94–107, 2005.

[21] K. Mehlhorn and S. Ray. Faster algorithms for computing Hong's bound on absolute positiveness. *J. Symbolic Computation*, 45(6):677 – 683, 2010.

[22] K. Mehlhorn and M. Sagraloff. A deterministic algorithm for isolating real roots of a real polynomial. *J. Symbolic Computation*, 46(1):70–90, 2011.

[23] M. Mignotte. *Mathematics for Computer Algebra*. Springer-Verlag, New York, 1991.

[24] B. Mourrain, M. Vrahatis, and J. Yakoubsohn. On the complexity of isolating real roots and computing with certainty the topological degree. *J. Complexity*, 18(2), 2002.

[25] V. Pan. Univariate polynomials: Nearly optimal algorithms for numerical factorization and rootfinding. *J. Symbolic Computation*, 33(5):701–733, 2002.

[26] C. Pascal and E. Schost. Change of order for bivariate triangular sets. In *Proc. 31th ACM Int'l Symp. on Symbolic & Algebraic Comp. (ISSAC)*, pages 277–284, New York, NY, USA, 2006.

[27] P. Pedersen and B. Sturmfels. Product formulas for resultants and Chow forms. *Math. Zeitschrift*, 214:377–396, 1993.

[28] R. Rioboo. Towards faster real algebraic numbers. *J. Symb. Comput.*, 36(3-4):513–533, 2003.

[29] F. Rouillier and Z. Zimmermann. Efficient isolation of polynomial's real roots. *J. of Computational and Applied Mathematics*, 162(1):33–50, 2004.

[30] S. Rump. On the sign of a real algebraic number. In *SYMSAC '76: Proc. of the 3rd ACM Symposium on Symbolic and Algebraic Computation*, pages 238–241, New York, USA, 1976.

[31] S. M. Rump. Real root isolation for algebraic polynomials. *ACM SIGSAM Bulletin*, 11(2):327–336, 1977.

[32] M. Sagraloff. On the complexity of real root isolation. *CoRR*, abs/1011.0344, 2010.

[33] A. Schönhage. The fundamental theorem of algebra in terms of computational complexity. Manuscript. Univ. of Tübingen, Germany, 1982.

[34] M. Sombra. The height of the mixed sparse resultant. *Amer. J. Math.*, 126:1253–1260, 2004.

[35] E. P. Tsigaridas. Improved complexity bounds for real root isolation using Continued Fractions. *Arxiv preprint arXiv:1010.2006*, 2010.

[36] E. P. Tsigaridas and I. Z. Emiris. On the complexity of real root isolation using Continued Fractions. *Theor. Comput. Sci.*, 392:158–173, 2008.

[37] M. van Hoeij and M. Monagan. A modular GCD algorithm over number fields presented with multiple extensions. In *Proc. Annual ACM ISSAC*, pages 109–116, July 2002.

[38] B. Xia and L. Yang. An algorithm for isolating the real solutions of semi-algebraic systems. *J. Symbolic Computation*, 34:461–477, November 2002.

[39] B. Xia and T. Zhang. Real solution isolation using interval arithmetic. *Comput. Math. Appl.*, 52:853–860, September 2006.

[40] C. Yap. *Fundamental Problems of Algorithmic Algebra*. Oxford University Press, New York, 2000.

APPENDIX

Proposition 14. *Let $B = \sum_{i,j} c_{i,j} x^i y^j \in \mathbb{Z}[x,y]$ of degree n with respect to y and of degree η with respect to x, and of bitsize σ. Let $A = \sum_{i=0}^{m} a_i x^i \in \mathbb{Z}[x]$ of degree m and bitsize τ. The resultant of B and A with respect to x is univariate polynomial in y of degree at most mn and bitsize at most $m\sigma + \eta\tau + m\lg(n+1) + (m+\eta)\lg(m+\eta)$ or $\widetilde{\mathcal{O}}(m\sigma + \eta\tau)$.*

Proof: The proof follows closely the proof in [2, Prop. 8.15] that provides a bound for general multivariate polynomials. We can compute the resultant of $B(x,y)$ and $A(x)$ with respect to x from the determinant of the Sylvester matrix, by considering them as univariate polynomial in x, with coefficients that are polynomial in y, which is

$$
\begin{pmatrix}
b_\eta & b_{\eta-1} & \dots & b_0 & & & \\
 & b_\eta & b_{\eta-1} & \dots & b_0 & & \\
 & & \ddots & & \ddots & & \ddots \\
 & & & b_\eta & b_{\eta-1} & \dots & b_0 \\
a_m & a_{m-1} & \dots & a_0 & & & \\
 & a_m & a_{m-1} & \dots & a_0 & & \\
 & & \ddots & & \ddots & & \ddots \\
 & & & a_m & a_{m-1} & \dots & a_0
\end{pmatrix}
\begin{matrix}
x^{m-1}B \\ x^{m-2}B \\ \vdots \\ x^0 B \\ x^{\eta-1}A \\ x^{\eta-2}A \\ \vdots \\ x^0 A
\end{matrix}
$$

where $b_k = \sum_{i=0}^{n} c_{i,k} y^i$.

The resultant is a factor of the determinant of the Sylvester matrix. The matrix is of size $(\eta+m) \times (\eta+m)$, hence the determinant consists of $(\eta+m)!$ terms. Each term is a product of m univariate polynomials in y, of degree n and bitsize σ, times the product of n numbers, of bitsize τ. The first product results in polynomials in y of degree at most mn and bitsize at most $m\sigma + m\lg(n+1)$; since there are at most $(n+1)^m$ terms with bitsize at most $m\sigma$ each. The second product results in numbers of bitsize at most $\eta\tau$. Hence each term of the determinant is, in the worst case a univariate polynomial in y of degree m and bitsize $m\sigma + \eta\tau + m\lg(n+1)$. We conclude that the resultant is of degree at most mn in y and of bitsize $m\sigma + \eta\tau + m\lg(n+1) + (m+\eta)\lg(m+\eta)$ or $\widetilde{\mathcal{O}}(m\sigma + \eta\tau)$. □

Verification and Synthesis Using Real Quantifier Elimination

Thomas Sturm
Max-Planck-Institut für Informatik
66123 Saarbrücken, Germany
sturm@mpi-inf.mpg.de

Ashish Tiwari*
SRI International
Menlo Park, CA 94025
tiwari@csl.sri.com

ABSTRACT

We present the application of real quantifier elimination to formal verification and synthesis of continuous and switched dynamical systems. Through a series of case studies, we show how first-order formulas over the reals arise when formally analyzing models of complex control systems. Existing off-the-shelf quantifier elimination procedures are not successful in eliminating quantifiers from many of our benchmarks. We therefore automatically combine three established software components: virtual substitution based quantifier elimination in Reduce/Redlog, cylindrical algebraic decomposition implemented in Qepcad, and the simplifier Slfq implemented on top of Qepcad. We use this combination to successfully analyze various models of systems including adaptive cruise control in automobiles, adaptive flight control system, and the classical inverted pendulum problem studied in control theory.

Categories and Subject Descriptors: I.1.2 [Symbolic and Algebraic Manipulation]: Algorithms; I.1.4 [Symbolic and Algebraic Manipulation]: Applications; I.6.4 [Simulation and Modeling]: Model Analysis

General Terms: Algorithms, Experimentation, Verification

Keywords: Formal verification, Safety, Stability, Lyapunov functions, Inductive invariants, Controller synthesis

1. INTRODUCTION

Physical processes in the world around us are often modeled using the real numbers. The temperature of a room, the speed of a car, the angle of descent of an airplane, relative population of a species, protein concentration in a cell, blood glucose concentration in a human, and the amount of a chemical in a tank are a few of the countless quantities that arise in science and engineering and that are modeled using real-valued variables. Many of these physical quantities are being controlled by computer software implementing sophisticated control algorithms. The resulting system – consisting of a physical plant and a software controller – is called a *cyber-physical system*. These systems are often employed in safety-critical applications. Before a newly designed complex system, such as a new flight-control system or a modern automobile cruise control module, can be certified and deployed, it is imperative to guarantee its correctness. One of the most pressing needs today is to develop tools that can formally analyze, and possibly also correctly synthesize, such systems.

The current practice in verification of cyber-physical systems is based on performing extensive (numerical) simulation and testing. However, simulation-based methods are incomplete – how do we know that the system has been tested enough? In the past few years, there has been an extensive push for extending formal verification approaches to also verify physical and cyber-physical systems. Broadly speaking, these techniques can be classified as follows:
(a) *reach-set methods* that compute the set of all reachable states of the system, either exactly [21], or approximately [34]
(b) *abstraction-based methods* that first abstract the system and then analyze the abstraction [33]
(c) *certificate-based methods* that directly search for certificates of correctness (such as inductive invariants and Lyapunov functions) of systems [30, 23, 26, 22, 18]

While all these techniques have had some success, the certificate-based methods are turning out to be particularly effective in proving deep properties of complex systems. At the core of all certificate-based methods, and also many of the other verification methods above, lie reasoning engines that perform inferences in the theory of reals.

During the past 40 years significant advances have been made in tools and techniques for performing quantifier elimination in the first-order theory of reals (QE). For practical purposes, substitution methods [35, 37] and their implementation in `redlog` [12] play a prominent role for formulas where the degrees of the quantified variables are small. For general formulas, partial cylindrical algebraic decomposition (CAD) and its implementation in the `qepcad` package is an important tool [8, 2, 9, 6]. Another efficient implementation of CAD exists in the commercial computer algebra system Mathematica, and a less mature one in `redlog`. For both, substitution methods and CAD, simplification of quantifier-free results is important [13, 7]. This is particularly true for substitution methods. While these methods typically have

*Research partially funded by DARPA under contract FA8650-10-C-7078, NSF grants CSR-0917398 and SHF:CSR-1017483, and NASA grant NNX08AB95A.

been referred to as *virtual substitution*, recently the term *substitute-and-simplify*[1] has been coined, which adequately describes the equal relevance of the core elimination method and the simplification aspect.

In this paper we reduce a class of verification and synthesis problems that arise when analyzing cyber-physical systems to quantifier elimination problems over the reals. It turns out that the corresponding formulas are computationally too hard to be solved by the established software. Our approach here is to automatically combine several systems to a fully automatic procedure suitable for our purposes.

The goal of this paper is threefold:
(1) Present the application of quantifier elimination to the verification and synthesis of switched and hybrid dynamical systems
(2) Present some benchmarks and details on how they were generated so that the larger community can benefit from the availability of real benchmarks and improvements in the technology for performing quantifier elimination can be calibrated[2]
(3) Present a novel combination of tools and techniques for performing quantifier elimination that is more scalable and promising than any of its components

In Section 2 we describe the design and the architecture of our software. In Sections 3 we present several verification and synthesis case studies that are challenging for most of the existing analysis tools, but that we were able to successfully solve using the certificate-based approach implemented using quantifier elimination. In Section 4 we summarize and evaluate our results.

2. A META-QE PROCEDURE FOR CONTROL THEORY

To start with, let us recall some basic asymptotic complexity results for real quantifier elimination, the substitute-and-simplify method, and CAD. For simplicity, we restrict ourselves to prenex formulas. In the worst case, the running time of real QE is asymptotically bounded from both above and below by a double exponential function in the length of the input formula [35, 10]. With CAD the relevant complexity parameter is the number of variables, where it makes no difference whether or not they are quantified. With substitution methods, in contrast, the quantification significantly contributes to the complexity: The procedure is doubly exponential only in the number of quantifier alternations. For a fixed number of quantifer alternations the number of quantifiers contributes only singly exponential to the complexity, and unquantified variables contribute only polynomially [35, 37].

While the substitution method is appealing from the complexity standpoint, it is limited in its applicability to formulas of low degree in the quantified variables. More precisely, assuming w.l.o.g that all right-hand sides of real constraints are 0 and that all left-hand sides are expanded to distributive polynomials, the maximal total degree in the quantified variables must not exceed 2. Moreover, with the successive elimination of the quantifiers from the inside to the outside, the degrees of outer quantifiers possibly increase so that before elimination it is not even predictable whether or not

the elimination procedure will succeed. In principle, substitution methods can be generalized to arbitrary degrees [37, 36], but these extensions have not been implemented so far, and it is unclear whether or not they are practical.

Our first idea is to apply substitute-and-simplify as long as there occur no degree violations, and then to use CAD for the remaining problem. Obviously, we benefit from the advantages of the substitution method wrt. complexity at the beginning, and later on we possibly enter CAD with a formula where several variables have already been eliminated. In addition, the quantifier-free formula establishing the final result will be generated by CAD, yielding another advantage: It is well-known that elimination results of CAD, in contrast to most other real QE methods, are very concise, nonredundant, and intuitively interpretable. In this raw form, our approach has been available within `redlog` and mentioned in several presentations by the first author since 2005. The CAD used then was always that of `redlog`.

Our present work refines this idea in several ways. First, we use `qepcad` instead of `redlog`'s own CAD. This improves performance of the overall method. Second, `qepcad` is not used directly after a degree violation. Before invoking `qepcad`, we apply `slfq` to the quantifier-free part of the intermediate result. `slfq` is a simplifier for quantifier-free formulas over the reals that uses multiple `qepcad` calls on subformulas in a divide-and-conquer approach [7]. Simplification using `slfq` significantly reduces the size of the intermediate formula generated by the substitution method and makes `qepcad` run much faster. Third, when using `qepcad` to eliminate quantifiers, we distribute existential quantifiers over top-level disjunctions and solve several smaller QE problems, $\exists \vec{x} : \phi_i$, in place of one large QE problem $\exists \vec{x} : \vee_i \phi_i$. This optimization is frequently usable in our application since all our input formulas are of the form "exists-forall", and substitution methods turn out to successfully eliminate all the universal variables and some of the existential variables. Recall that the successive elimination of existential quantifiers via substitution methods systematically yields comprehensive disjunctions. Hence, the result produced by the substitution method is often of the form $\exists \vec{x} : \vee_i \phi_i$, enabling the optimization above. Note also that `slfq` preserves this form unless it is particularly successful. A more important benefit of this optimization is the following: If `qepcad` fails due to limited time or space on some of the subproblems, the disjunction of the elimination results for the successful subproblems still yields a sufficient (although not necessary) quantifier-free condition for the original question. In our application, this partial result is still enough to successfully complete the analysis task; see the example in Section 3.1.

To complete the picture, we can also automatically use the CAD of Mathematica instead of `qepcad`. However, we did not observe any significant advantage of Mathematica on our benchmarks and, hence, we do not discuss it further. Finally, `qepcad` itself can optionally spawn `Singular` [11] processes to speed up its Gröbner basis computations. We systematically made use of this feature and observed that this considerably improved our computation times.

All relevant software components, i.e., Reduce/`redlog`, `slfq`, `qepcad`, and `Singular`, as well as all the benchmarks discussed in this paper (and many others), are freely available on the Web [32]. Using the current head version of Reduce, the process communication described here should run out-of-the-box using default installations of `slfq`, `qep-`

---

[1] In an ISSAC 2010 presentation by C. Zengler
[2] The website [32] contains all benchmark described in this paper and many others, too.

cad, and Singular. The system can be used either in batch or interactively. With interactive use, Reduce serves as the interface, and all results obtained from external components are available there for further processing.

We also experimented with using *generic* quantifier elimination [14], which makes some nondegeneracy assumptions during the initial substitute-and-simplify elimination step. The assumptions made were found to not influence the final outcome, especially in those cases where there was a "robust" verification proof; see Section 3.2 for more discussion.

All computations described here have been carried out on an Intel Xeon E5630 2.53GHz single-core processor (x86_64 arch) with 4G RAM running Ubuntu Linux 2.6.32-26.

3. CERTIFICATE-BASED TECHNIQUES

Given a system, say modeled using differential equations, and given a property, the *verification problem* asks whether the system satisfies the property. Given an incomplete system and given a property, the *synthesis problem* asks whether the system can be completed so that it satisfies the property. A *certificate* for a verification problem (respectively, synthesis problem) is a (Boolean or real valued) function on the state space of the system such that existence of such a function is sufficient, and perhaps even necessary, condition for the verification problem (synthesis problem) to have a positive answer. For example, a Lyapunov function is a certificate for stability verification, and an inductive invariant (also known as barrier certificate) is a certificate for safety verification. A controlled Lyapunov function (respectively, controlled inductive invariant) is a certificate for a synthesis problem whose goal is stability (safety).

Certificate-based methods tranform the verification problem (respectively, the synthesis problem) into a search for an appropriate certificate. The space of certificates is unbounded, and hence, we bound the search for a certificate by fixing the *form* of the certificate. For example, for stability verification, we can restrict search to quadratic Lyapunov functions.

Formally defining certificates for different verification and synthesis problems is beyond the scope of this paper. In each subsequent section, we precisely define a different verification or synthesis problem and then define a certificate for that problem. The search for a certificate is cast as an ∃∀ problem. The overall approach is shown in Figure 1.

3.1 Adaptive Cruise Control: Proving Collision Avoidance

Here, we prove collision avoidance for two cars under cruise control. The rear car uses a cruise control law that actively adjusts its acceleration based on its own velocity, acceleration, the relative velocity of the leading car, and the gap between the two cars. Proving collision avoidance means showing that the two cars will not collide assuming that the cruise control is activated in a safe initial configuration.

The cruise control law is taken from the leader control developed in [16] and also discussed in [24] and [30]; see also the Berkeley Path project [4]. Let gap, v_f, v, and a, respectively, represent the gap between the two cars, the velocity of the leading car, and the velocity and acceleration of the rear car. The dynamics of the velocity of the rear car

and the gap are given by

$$
\begin{aligned}
\frac{dv}{dt} &= a, \quad a \in [-5, 2] \\
\frac{dgap}{dt} &= v_f - v
\end{aligned}
\tag{1}
$$

The restriction of a to be in the range $[-5, 2]$ comes from the physical constraint on the braking and accelerating capability of the car. The dynamics of the acceleration a of the rear car are assumed to be determined by the following control law

$$
\dot{a} = -3a - 3(v - v_f) + (gap - (v + 10)) \tag{2}
$$

The dynamics of the leading car are given by

$$
\frac{dv_f}{dt} = a_f, \quad a_f \in [-5, 2] \tag{3}
$$

Note that we do not assume any particular acceleration profile for the leading car. Thus, the leading car can behave nondeterministically as long as its acceleration remains within the $[-5, 2]$ range.

We wish to find the initial states such that if we activate the above cruise control law in those states, then the control law will guarantee that there will be no collision. The initial states we are interested in are of the form

$$
Init := (gap = 10 \land a = 0 \land v_f = c_1 \land v = c_2) \tag{4}
$$

where c_1, c_2 are parameters. The set of *safe* (collision-free) states is defined by

$$
\texttt{safe} := (gap > 0) \tag{5}
$$

How to prove collision avoidance for the above (parametric) system? We use the *certificate-based approach* for verification [18, 23, 30, 28]. The idea behind proving safety is to discover an invariant set, *Inv*, such that
(1) all initial states in *Init* are also in *Inv*, and
(2) all states in *Inv* are in `safe`, and
(3) the system dynamics cannot force the system to go out of the set *Inv*
Such a set *Inv* is a *certificate* for safety. The problem is that we do not know *Inv*. We can discover *Inv* by fixing its form. Let us assume a linear form for *Inv*, that is,

$$
p := c_3 v + c_4 v_f + c_5 a + gap + c_6, \quad Inv := (p \geq 0) \tag{6}
$$

Let *Inv'* denote the constraints imposed by physical reality,

$$
Inv' := (a \in [-5, 2] \land a_f \in [-5, 2] \land v \geq 0 \land v_f \geq 0) \tag{7}
$$

Now, the three conditions for *Inv* to be a certificate for safety can be encoded in the following formula

$$
\begin{aligned}
\phi_1 &:= (Init \land Inv' \Rightarrow Inv) \\
\phi_2 &:= (Inv \land Inv' \Rightarrow (gap > 0)) \\
\phi_3 &:= (p = 0 \land Inv' \Rightarrow \frac{dp}{dt} \geq 0)
\end{aligned}
\tag{8}
$$

where dp/dt can be symbolically computed using the definition of p in Equation (6) and the dynamics in Equation (1) and Equation (2) as

$$
\frac{dp}{dt} := c_3 a + c_4 a_f + \tag{9}
$$
$$
c_5(-3a - 4v + 3v_f + gap - 10) + (v_f - v)
$$

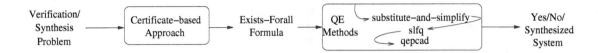

Figure 1: Overall approach for verification and synthesis using quantifier elimination.

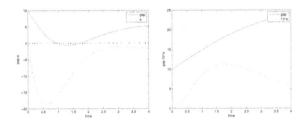

Figure 2: Simulation of the adaptive cruise control system. (Left) Plot of gap, a: The cars collide (gap becomes negative) even though the initial conditions $v = 30, vf = 15$ satisfy the precondition under which safety was established. This occurs because the assumption $a \geq -5$ is also violated. **(Right)** Plot of $gap, 10a$: The assumptions always hold, and cars do not collide. The initial conditions $v = 15, vf = 20$ satisfy the precondition for safety.

Thus, we can find the conditions on the initial velocities c_1, c_2 that will guarantee collision avoidance by eliminating quantifiers from the following formula (File acc7.red [32])

$$\exists c_3, c_4, c_5, c_6 : \forall v, v_f, gap, a, a_f : (\phi_1 \wedge \phi_2 \wedge \phi_3) \qquad (10)$$

where ϕ_1, ϕ_2, ϕ_3 are as defined in Equation (8) expanded using the definitions given in Equation (4), Equation (6), Equation (7), and Equation (9).

Analysis Results

We use `redlog`, `qepcad`, and `slfq` to eliminate quantifiers from Formula (10) and to then simplify it. Virtual substitution implemented in `redlog` is able to eliminate all but one quantified variable, namely c_5, from the above formula, but it returns a huge formula that is a disjunction of 584 subformulas and contains 33365 atomic formulas (nested to depth 13). The simplifier `slfq` fails to simplify this formula. Since `slfq` fails on the 34th disjunct, we simplify the first 33 disjuncts using `slfq` under the assumption that $c_1 > 0$ and $c_2 > 0$ and obtain $c_2^2 - 30c_2 - 75 \leq 0$, which is, surprisingly, independent of c_1 and c_5. Since we have discarded some disjuncts, the actual equivalent formula would have been $c_2^2 - 30c_2 - 75 \leq 0 \vee \psi$ for some ψ. This means that, if the initial velocity of the rear car is at most 32, then we are guaranteed to be safe. (There may be other cases, too, when we would be safe, since we have lost some solutions in the approximation.) We can verify that our results are correct by instantiating c_1 and c_2 by the respective conditions and proving the implications, which are immediately proved by `redlog` (File acc7-verify.red [32]).

Why is this result interesting? It is because we have established collision freedom without making any assumption on the dynamics of the leading car. So, the leading car is free to choose any driving profile, and the control law would guar-

antee safety. However, there is one caveat. We have assumed that the physical constraints (in Equation (7)) remain true always. We have not proved that those constraints would not be violated. In fact, let us consider a scenario in which the leading car starts at velocity of 15m/s (decelerating at -3m/s^2), and the rear car starts at velocity 30 m/s at a distance of 10m behind it. Since the velocity 30 is less than 32, we expect that the two cars will not collide. However, a simulation plot in Figure 2 (left) shows that the cars collide. This occurs because, even before the cars collide, the physical constraint ($a \geq -5$) is violated. In the simulation shown in Figure 2 (right), the physical constraints are not violated and there is no collision. So, what we have actually proved is the following fact.

PROPOSITION 1. *If the rear car follows the control law in Equation (2) and the dynamics of the leading and rear car are given by Equation (1) and Equation (3), and the cars start in any initial configuration where $gap = 10$, $a = 0$, $0 \leq v \leq 32$, $0 \leq v_f$, then either one of the physical constraints in Equation (7) is violated or the cars never collide.*

3.2 1-D Robot: Synthesizing Safe Switching Logic

Consider a robot moving in a 1-dimensional space. Let x denote the position of the robot and v denote its velocity. Suppose we can control the robot by controlling the force we apply on it: we can either force the robot to have an acceleration of $+1$ units or -1 units. Thus, the robot has two modes with the following dynamics:

$$\text{Mode}_1 : \frac{dx}{dt} = v, \frac{dv}{dt} = 1 \quad \text{Mode}_2 : \frac{dx}{dt} = v, \frac{dv}{dt} = -1 \quad (11)$$

We wish to switch between these two modes so that the robot remains within a specified range, say $70 \leq x \leq 80$. We assume that initially the robot is in a state such that $74 \leq x \leq 76$ and $v = 0$.

$$\phi_{\text{safe}} := 70 \leq x \wedge x \leq 80$$
$$\phi_{\text{init}} := 74 \leq x \wedge x \leq 76 \wedge v = 0 \qquad (12)$$

It is clear that we have to switch to Mode_1 before x reaches 70 and we have to switch to Mode_2 before x reaches 80. A recent paper [27] proposed a certificate-based method to solve this "switching logic synthesis problem" by deciding formulas in the theory of reals. Specifically, quantifier elimination is used to find a *controlled inductive invariant*, which is any set, say defined by $V_1 \geq 0 \wedge V_2 \geq 0$, that satisfies the following formula:

$$(\phi_{\text{init}} \Rightarrow V_1 \geq 0 \wedge V_2 \geq 0) \wedge$$
$$(V_1 \geq 0 \wedge V_2 \geq 0 \Rightarrow \phi_{\text{safe}}) \wedge \qquad (13)$$
$$(V_1 = 0 \wedge V_2 \geq 0 \Rightarrow (\frac{dV_1}{dt}\Big|_{\text{Mode}_1} \geq 0 \vee \frac{dV_1}{dt}\Big|_{\text{Mode}_2} \geq 0))$$
$$(V_2 = 0 \wedge V_1 \geq 0 \Rightarrow (\frac{dV_2}{dt}\Big|_{\text{Mode}_1} \geq 0 \vee \frac{dV_2}{dt}\Big|_{\text{Mode}_2} \geq 0))$$

where $dV_1/dt|_{\text{Mode}_1}$ denotes the derivative of V_1 in Mode_1.

Suppose that we are given the following forms for V_1, V_2:

$$\begin{aligned} V_1 &:= v^2 + c_2 v + c_3 x + c_4 \\ V_2 &:= -v^2 - c_2 v - c_3 x + c_5 \end{aligned} \quad (14)$$

where c_2, c_3, c_4, c_5 are some (unknown) constants. For these choices of V_1 and V_2, we can symbolically compute the derivatives dV_1/dt and dV_2/dt in the two modes using the dynamics in Equation (11).

We can determine if there exist constants $c_2, \ldots, c_5$ that will make Formula (13) true by deciding the formula

$$\exists c_2, c_3, c_4, c_5 : \forall x, v : \phi \quad (15)$$

where ϕ is the formula in Equation (13) with subexpressions replaced by their definitions given in Equation (12), Equation (14), and $dV_i/dt|_{\text{Mode}_j}$ replaced by the symbolic value of dV_i/dt in Mode_j (File thermo-two-fail.red [32]).

Analysis Results

Using virtual substitution we can eliminate the inner universally quantified variables and get an equivalent constraint on the unknowns $c_2 \ldots, c_5$. If we existentially quantify these variables and ask qepcad if the formula is satisfiable, it fails. However, slfq is able to simplify the formula to false – in 1.03 seconds and using 604 qepcad calls – indicating that there is no controlled inductive invariant of this form.

We retry using a different template for V_1 and V_2:

$$\begin{aligned} V_1 &:= c_1 x - v^2 + c_2 p + c_3 \\ V_2 &:= -c_1 x - v^2 + c_2 p + c_4 \end{aligned} \quad (16)$$

Using these new forms for V_1 and V_2 we get a new $\exists\forall$ formula (File thermo-two-orig.red [32]). In this case, we succeed: redlog successfully eliminates the universal variables quickly, but the resulting constraint on c_1, c_2, c_3, c_4 is not easy to check for satisfiability. Even slfq fails to simplify the constraints. But looking at the constraints and using one of the disjuncts, $c_1 = 2$, as an assumption, slfq successfully simplifies the formula in 120 milliseconds using 296 qepcad calls, to

$$\begin{aligned} c_2 = 0 \ &\wedge\ c_4 \geq 76 c_1 \ \wedge\ 4 c_4 + c_2^2 - 320 c_1 \leq 0 \ \wedge \\ c_3 + 74 c_1 &\geq 0 \ \wedge\ 4 c_3 + c_2^2 + 280 c_1 \leq 0 \end{aligned}$$

Thus, we find that $c_1 = 2$, $c_2 = 0$, $c_4 = 156$, $c_3 = -144$ is a possible solution and, hence, we get the inductive controlled invariant,

$$2x - v^2 - 144 \geq 0 \ \wedge\ -2x - v^2 + 156 \geq 0$$

A simulation of the system that maintains this invariant is shown in Figure 3 (left).

We finally see if we can do better using more general quadratic templates. Let us use the following template

$$V_1 := -v^2 - c_1 (x - 75)^2 + c_2, \quad (17)$$

which is motivated by the desire to bound the absolute values of v and $x - 75$. Using this template, we can expand the formula in Equation (13) to get another quantifier elimination problem (File thermo-two-quad.red [32]). This new problem is considerably simpler as redlog immediately returns after successfully eliminating the universal variables v and x. The condition on a, b is simplified by slfq in 60 milliseconds (using 37 qepcad calls) to

$$c_1 > 0 \wedge c_2 \leq 25 c_1 \wedge c_2 \geq c_1 \wedge c_1 c_2 \leq 1$$

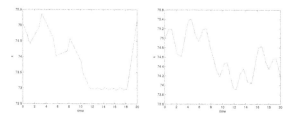

Figure 3: Simulation of the synthesized robot controller. (Left) Plot of x using the controller synthesized from a linear-quadratic controlled invariant. (Right) Plot of x using the controller synthesized from the quadratic controlled invariant. In both cases, the controller switches modes as soon as the boundary of the invariant is reached, which ensures that x remains in the safe interval $[70, 80]$.

Thus, by choosing $c_2 = 1$ and $c_1 = 1/25$, we get the following controlled inductive invariant

$$-v^2 - (x - 75)^2 / 25 + 1 \geq 0$$

A simulation of the controller generated using this controlled inductive invariant is shown in Figure 3 (right).

Using an ostensibly more "complex" template here leads to a "simpler" QE problem. One reason why the complex template is better is that it leads to a more "robust" proof – even if the model of the system were to change slightly (the coefficients were to be perturbed), there would still be invariants of the complex quadratic form, whereas there may not be an invariant of the simpler linear-quadratic form. While quantifier elimination is a hard problem, it could still be successful in verifying systems that are "well-designed" since such systems are more likely to be robust, and hence have small (easy) proofs [15].

3.3 Adaptive Flight Control: Proving Stability

We consider the problem of verifying the stability of a closed loop model of an adaptive flight control system.

The roll, pitch, and yaw rates of an airplane are controlled by setting the angles on the respective actuators – ailerons, elevators, and rudder. The task of the flight controller is to set the actuators so that the airplane reaches some desired roll, pitch, and yaw state. A typical proportional-integral (PI) controller is used for this purpose. However, recently there is renewed interest in evaluating *adaptive* controllers because of their potential to successfully control a damaged or aging aircraft.

Let w_e denote the error between the desired state and the current state of the airplane. In general, w_e (and other state variables that we will consider below) will be a vector (consisting of the error in roll, pitch, yaw); however, for simplicity (and also since the proof generalizes from a scalar to a vector), we let w_e be a scalar. Let intw_e denote the integral of w_e. The state variables w_e and intw_e are required to describe the standard PI controller. The adaptation term is modeled using three additional variables: β, L, and L^*, where β are the kernel functions, L are the weights learned by the adaptation procedure, and L^* are the optimal weights. Again we will assume that these are scalars in our analysis here. The dynamics of the system are given by

$$\frac{d\mathtt{intw}_e}{dt} = \mathtt{w}_e$$

$$\frac{d\mathtt{w}_e}{dt} = -10\mathtt{intw}_e - 5\mathtt{w}_e + (L - L^*)\beta$$

$$\frac{dL}{dt} = (-1000\mathtt{intw}_e - 2200\mathtt{w}_e)\beta$$

$$\frac{dL^*}{dt} = 0 \qquad (18)$$

The dynamics of L describe the (neural) learning law used to update the current model of the plant damage. For further details on the actual model and the simplifications used to obtain the model above, we refer the reader to [31].

We are interested in showing that the error $\mathtt{w}_e$ eventually falls below a certain threshold. We prove this by showing that whenever the error is greater than that threshold, a certain positive semidefinite function will decrease. We assume that we are given a template for the positive semidefinite function, namely,

$$V := \mathtt{w}_e{}^2 + b\mathtt{intw}_e{}^2 + c(L - L^*)^2 \qquad (19)$$

where b, c are unknown constants that we need to find. We cannot prove that the error $\mathtt{w}_e$ will eventually be bounded without making further assumptions. Specifically, we first assume that the absolute value of $\mathtt{intw}_e$ is bounded and also assume that the absolute value of the term $(L - L^*)\beta$ is bounded. Under these assumptions, the formula ϕ defined below says that V always decreases whenever $\mathtt{w}_e{}^2 \geq 1$:

$$\phi := (\mathtt{intw}_e{}^2 \leq 1 \wedge (L - L^*)^2\beta^2 \leq 1 \wedge \mathtt{w}_e{}^2 \geq 1)$$
$$\Rightarrow \frac{dV}{dt} < 0 \qquad (20)$$

where dV/dt can be computed using the definition of V and the dynamics given above as

$$\frac{dV}{dt} := 2\mathtt{w}_e(-5\mathtt{w}_e - 10\mathtt{intw}_e + (L - L^*)\beta) + 2b\mathtt{intw}_e\mathtt{w}_e +$$
$$2c(L - L^*)(-1000\mathtt{intw}_e - 2200\mathtt{w}_e)\beta$$

Thus, we get the quantified formula $\exists b, c : b > 0 \wedge c > 0 \wedge \forall \mathtt{w}_e, \mathtt{intw}_e, L, L^*, \beta : \phi$ in File adaptive-simpl.red [32].

Using virtual substitution of redlog, we successfully eliminate all the universal quantifiers except $\mathtt{w}_e$ to get an equivalent formula on $b, c, \mathtt{w}_e$. This formula is a conjunction of 48 subformulas and contains 1081 atomic formulas, nested to a depth of 10. We simplify it using slfq under the assumption that $b > 0 \wedge c > 0$ and get the following simplified formula after 27.45 seconds of system time and 1897 qepcad calls:

$$b - 14 < 3200c < 16 - b \wedge 6 - b < 1200c < b - 4$$

The variable $\mathtt{w}_e$ is eliminated automatically. Thus, for example, we can choose $b = 10$ and $c = 1/600$. This proves that, under the assumptions made, the error $\mathtt{w}_e$ is always eventually bounded.

The choice of bounds on the assumptions may seem arbitrary. In fact, we can formulate the problem by replacing the concrete values for the bounds by symbolic constants and get the following formula.

$$\phi := (\mathtt{intw}_e{}^2 \leq e \wedge (L - L^*)^2\beta^2 \leq d \wedge \mathtt{w}_e{}^2 \geq a)$$
$$\Rightarrow \frac{dV}{dt} < 0 \qquad (21)$$

The $\exists\forall$ formula obtained from quantifying the above formula is contained in File adaptive-hard.red [32]. Eliminating quantifiers from this formula proceeds as before, and redlog successfully eliminates all universal quantifiers except $\mathtt{w}_e$. However, slfq is unable to simplify the resulting formula (in 30 minutes of real time).

Finally consider the case when only the kernel functions used by the learning module (β) are known to be bounded. Under this assumption, we wish to search for a nonincreasing positive semidefinite function of the form,

$$V := a\mathtt{intw}_e{}^2 + (\mathtt{w}_e + b\mathtt{intw}_e)^2 + c(L - L^*)^2 \quad (22)$$

where a, b, c are unknown constants to be determined such that the resulting function V is nonincreasing. This is stated in the following formula, under the assumption that β remains bounded.

$$\phi := (\beta^2 \leq 1 \Rightarrow \frac{dV}{dt} \leq 0); \qquad (23)$$

where the derivative of V is easily calculated using the definition of V in Equation (22) and the dynamics of the system defined in Equation (18). Thus, we get the quantified formula $\forall \mathtt{w}_e, \mathtt{intw}_e, \beta, L, L^* : \phi$ in File adaptive-final.red [32]. Virtual substitution is successful in eliminating all the quantified variables. This quantifier-free formula is simplified by slfq in 60 milliseconds and using 29 qepcad calls to

$$11b = 5 \wedge 1000c = b \wedge$$
$$(a + 2b^2 - 10b - 20)a + (b^2 - 10b + 45)b^2 \leq 100(b - 1)$$

which suggests $b = 5/11, c = 1/2200, a = 5$ as one possible solution. (In fact, a can be any number in the interval $[3, 21]$). This proves bounded stability of the adaptive PI controller assuming that the kernel functions remain bounded.

3.4 Inverted Pendulum: Synthesizing Stable Controller

A classic problem in control pertains to maintaining an inverted pendulum around its unstable equilibrium by controlling the force on the cart on which the pendulum is mounted. The state of the inverted pendulum can be described using four continuous variables, the position x of the cart, the velocity v of the cart, the angular deviation θ of the pendulum from its unstable equilibrium point $\theta = 0$, and the angular velocity ω of the pendulum. The dynamics of the inverted pendulum are obtained by balancing forces and can be rewritten in state space form as

$$\frac{dx}{dt} = v$$

$$\frac{dv}{dt} = \frac{(F - ml\omega^2\sin(\theta) + mg\cos(\theta)\sin(\theta))}{(M + m - m\cos(\theta)\cos(\theta))}$$

$$\frac{d\theta}{dt} = \omega \qquad (24)$$

$$\frac{d\omega}{dt} = (g\sin(\theta) + \cos(\theta)\frac{dv}{dt})/l$$

where $g = 10$ is the acceleration due to gravity, $m = 0.5$ is the mass of the pendulum, $M = 0.5$ is the mass of the cart, $l = 0.3$ is the length of the pendulum, and F is the force on the cart.

Since we cannot perform quantifier elimination on formulas containing trigonometric functions, and since we know that θ remains close to 0, we approximate the trigonometric functions by the first few terms of their Taylor expansions. We assume that we have three modes available to us to control the pendulum depending on the force F we apply: we can choose $F = 2$, or $F = -2$, or $F = 0$. After substituting the values for the parameters and Taylor approximations of the trigonometric functions, we get the following equations for the dynamics of θ and ω.

$$\frac{d\theta}{dt} = \omega \tag{25}$$
$$\frac{d\omega}{dt} = 50\theta - \omega^2\theta/2 - 100\theta^3/3 + 3\omega^2\theta^3/4$$
$$+ F(10/3 - 5\theta^2 + 5\theta^4/3)$$

where $F \in \{+2, 0, -2\}$ in the three modes.

We wish to keep the pendulum inside a safe region, namely,

$$\mathtt{safe} := (20\theta^2 \leq 1)$$

The goal is to design a controller that will take the system to the region $\mathtt{safe}$ and keep it there. The controller takes the form of logical conditions for switching between the three modes. Assume that initially the pendulum is in a state that satisfies the constraint $-1 \leq 20\theta \leq 1 \wedge \omega = 0$.

We solve the problem by synthesizing an inductive controlled invariant for the problem. We assume that the user specifies the following template for searching for a controlled invariant $V \geq 0$ where

$$V := -\theta^2 - b\omega^2 + c$$

Thus, we need to find b, c such that $V \geq 0$ becomes an inductive controlled invariant. This happens when the formula ϕ becomes valid:

$$\phi := \phi_1 \wedge \phi_2 \wedge \phi_3$$
$$\phi_1 := ((-1 \leq 20\theta \leq 1 \wedge \omega = 0) \Rightarrow$$
$$(-\theta^2 - \omega^2 b + c \geq 0));$$
$$\phi_2 := (-\theta^2 - \omega^2 b + c \geq 0 \Rightarrow 1 \geq 20\theta^2);$$
$$\phi_3 := (-\theta^2 - \omega^2 b + c = 0 \Rightarrow$$
$$(\left.\frac{dV}{dt}\right|_{\mathrm{Mode}_1} \geq 0 \vee \left.\frac{dV}{dt}\right|_{\mathrm{Mode}_2} \geq 0 \vee \left.\frac{dV}{dt}\right|_{\mathrm{Mode}_3} \geq 0))$$

where dV/dt in the three modes is easily computed symbolically. This way we get the universally quantified formula $\forall \theta, \omega : \phi$ with free variables b, c (File inverted-pend.red [32]).

We use virtual substitution of $\mathtt{redlog}$ to eliminate the inner universal variables. It successfully eliminates θ, but it fails to eliminate ω. Neither $\mathtt{qepcad}$ succeeds in reasonable time (5 minutes user time) to eliminate ω, nor $\mathtt{slfq}$ is successful in simplifying the formula. However, the formula produced by $\mathtt{redlog}$ has a conjunct $c \geq 1/400$. We pick an arbitrary value, $1/100$, for c that is greater than $1/400$. Now the quantifier elimination problem is much simpler (File inverted-pend-easy.red [32]) and after virtual substitution eliminates θ, $\mathtt{qepcad}$ is able to eliminate ω in 190 milliseconds to give the constraint $4801b - 300 \geq 0$ on b. Thus, we get the following controlled inductive invariant for the inverted pendulum system:

$$-\theta^2 - (300/4801)\omega^2 + (1/100) \geq 0$$

Using this controlled invariant, we can now synthesize an algorithm for switching between the three modes of the system so that the system remains inside the set $\mathtt{safe}$. A sample simulation of the synthesized system is shown in Figure 4.

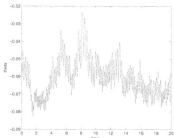

Figure 4: Inverted pendulum simulation. Plot of θ when a mode switching controller is synthesized using the generated controlled invariant. By switching mode as soon as the boundary of the controlled invariant is reached, we guarantee that θ remains inside the safe set.

4. RELATED WORK AND CONCLUSION

Quantifier elimination has been applied earlier to solve nonlinear control system design [20]. However, this early work focused only on continuous (and not switched) systems, and moreover only on simple properties. Properties like safety and stability were not considered – partly because they cannot be captured as semialgebraic sets in a sound and complete way. We give up completeness and generate an $\exists\forall$ formula that is only sufficient for the verification or synthesis problem. Consequently, whenever the $\exists\forall$ formula is valid, we successfully verify the system (or synthesize a correct system), but when the formula is not valid, it does not mean the system is faulty (or unsynthesizable).

The classical way of proving stability by finding Lyapunov functions is an instance of certificate-based verification. In this classical approach, the search for a Lyapunov function of a particular form is reduced to solving an $\exists\forall\phi$ formula, where ϕ is an *atomic* fact. Numerical techniques in the form of semidefinite programming exist for solving such problems [22, 5]. The work on barrier certificates [23] moves this overall approach from stability to safety.

There is plenty of work on certificate-based verification of hybrid systems [30, 26, 18], but none of it has used CAD or substitute-and-simplify methods and instead relied on approximate methods to eliminate quantifiers. In a recent paper [29], we used $\mathtt{qepcad}$ to solve $\exists\forall$ formulas arising from certificate-based synthesis. This paper builds upon [29] by proposing certificate-based analysis as a uniform approach for verification and synthesis, presenting several different benchmarks, and solving them using a combination of symbolic tools for quantifier elimination and simplification. Recently, Anai [1] used a combination of numerical methods (sum-of-squares) and symbolic quantifier elimination methods to solve problems arising in control, and such an integration is left for future work here.

It might be noteworthy that there has been considerable theoretical research on real quantifier elimination beyond the methods discussed here [17, 25, 3]. Most unfortunately, this appears not to have led to practically applicable software so far. An interesting step towards making alternative approaches practically useful has been made in [19] recently.

In summary, the *certificate-based approach* for verification and synthesis is a promising technique for formal analysis of complex cyber-physical systems. Its success is, however, crucially dependent on real quantifier elimination methods.

Certificate-based approach reduces verification and synthesis problems for continuous and switched systems to first-order formulas over the reals. An automatic combination of various software components for quantifier elimination and simplification was used to successfully process the first-order formulas. Our case studies described here provide an interesting set of benchmarks for real quantifier elimination.

Acknowledgments

We would like to thank Andreas Weber for encouraging and supporting the first author in visiting SRI.

5. REFERENCES

[1] H. Anai. A symbolic-numeric approach to nonlinear dynamical system analysis, 2010. SIAM/MSRI workshop on hybrid method. for symb.-numeric comp.

[2] D. S. Arnon, G. E. Collins, and S. McCallum. Cylindrical algebraic decomposition I: The basic algorithm. *SIAM J. Computing*, 13(4):865–877, 1984.

[3] S. Basu, R. Pollack, and M.-F. Roy. On the combinatorial and algebraic complexity of quantifier elimination. *J. of the ACM*, 43(6):1002–1045, 1996.

[4] California PATH: Partners for advanced transit and highways. http://www.path.berkeley.edu/.

[5] S. Boyd, L. El Ghaoui, E. Feron, and V. Balakrishnan. *Linear matrix inequalities in system and control theory*. SIAM, 1994.

[6] C. W. Brown. QEPCAD B: a program for computing with semi-algebraic sets using CADs. *ACM SIGSAM Bulletin*, 37(4):97–108, 2003.

[7] C. W. Brown and C. Gross. Efficient preprocessing methods for quantifier elimination. In *CASC*, volume 4194 of *LNCS*, pages 89–100. Springer-Verlag, 2006.

[8] G. E. Collins. Quantifier elimination for real closed fields by cylindrical algebraic decomposition – preliminary report. *ACM SIGSAM Bulletin*, 8(3):80–90, Aug. 1974.

[9] G. E. Collins and H. Hong. Partial cylindrical algebraic decomposition for quantifier elimination. *J. Symbolic Computation*, 12(3):299–328, Sept. 1991.

[10] J. H. Davenport and J. Heintz. Real quantifier elimination is doubly exponential. *J. of Symbolic Computation*, 5(1–2):29–35, Feb.–Apr. 1988.

[11] W. Decker et al. SINGULAR 3-1-2 — A computer algebra system for polynomial computations, 2010. http://www.singular.uni-kl.de.

[12] A. Dolzmann and T. Sturm. Redlog: Computer algebra meets computer logic. *ACM SIGSAM Bulletin*, 31(2):2–9, June 1997.

[13] A. Dolzmann and T. Sturm. Simplification of quantifier-free formulae over ordered fields. *J. of Symbolic Computation*, 24(2):209–231, Aug. 1997.

[14] A. Dolzmann, T. Sturm, and V. Weispfenning. A new approach for automatic theorem proving in real geometry. *J. Automated Reasoning*, 21(3), 1998.

[15] D. Gayme, M. Fazel, and J. C. Doyle. Complexity in automation of SOS proofs: An illustrative example. In *45th IEEE Conf. on Decision and Control*, 2006.

[16] D. Godbole and J. Lygeros. Longitudinal control of the lead car of a platoon. *IEEE Transactions on Vehicular Technology*, 43(4):1125–35, 1994.

[17] D. Grigoriev. Complexity of deciding Tarski algebra. *Journal of Symbolic Computation*, 5(1-2):65–108, 1988.

[18] S. Gulwani and A. Tiwari. Constraint-based approach for analysis of hybrid systems. In *Proc. 20th CAV*, volume 5123 of *LNCS*, pages 190–203. Springer, 2008.

[19] H. Hong and M. Safey El Din. Variant real quantifier elimination: algorithm and application. In *ISSAC*, pages 183–190. ACM, 2009.

[20] M. Jirstrand. Nonlinear control system design by quantifier elimination. *J. Symb. Comput.*, 24(2):137–152, 1997.

[21] G. Lafferriere, G. J. Pappas, and S. Yovine. Symbolic reachability computations for families of linear vector fields. *J. Symbolic Computation*, 32(3):231–253, 2001.

[22] P. A. Parrilo. SOS methods for semi-algebraic games and optimization. In *HSCC 2005*, volume 3414 of *LNCS*, page 54. Springer, 2005.

[23] S. Prajna, A. Jadbabaie, and G. J. Pappas. A framework for worst-case and stochastic safety verification using barrier certificates. *IEEE Trans. on Automatic Control*, 52(8):1415–1428, 2007.

[24] A. Puri and P. Varaiya. Driving safely in smart cars. In *Proc. 1995 American Control Conference*, 1995.

[25] J. Renegar. On the computational complexity and geometry of the first-order theory of the reals. *Journal of Symbolic Computation*, 13(3):255–352, Mar. 1992.

[26] S. Sankaranarayanan, H. Sipma, and Z. Manna. Constructing invariants for hybrid systems. In *HSCC*, volume 2993 of *LNCS*, pages 539–554. Springer, 2004.

[27] A. Taly, S. Gulwani, and A. Tiwari. Synthesizing switching logic using constraint solving. In *VMCAI*, volume 5403 of *LNCS*, pages 305–319. Springer, 2009.

[28] A. Taly and A. Tiwari. Deductive verification of continuous dynamical systems. In *FSTTCS*, volume 4 of *LIPIcs*, pages 383–394, 2009.

[29] A. Taly and A. Tiwari. Switching logic synthesis for reachability. In *EMSOFT*, 2010.

[30] A. Tiwari. Approximate reachability for linear systems. In *Proc. 6th HSCC*, volume 2623 of *LNCS*, pages 514–525. Springer, 2003.

[31] A. Tiwari. Bounded verification of adaptive flight control systems. In *Proc. AIAA Infotech@Aerospace*, 2010. AIAA-2010-3362.

[32] A. Tiwari. Certificate-based verification: Tools and benchmarks, 2011. http://www.csl.sri.com/~tiwari/existsforall/.

[33] A. Tiwari and G. Khanna. Series of abstractions for hybrid automata. In *HSCC*, volume 2289 of *LNCS*, pages 465–478. Springer, 2002.

[34] C. J. Tomlin, I. Mitchell, A. M. Bayen, and M. Oishi. Computational techniques for the verification of hybrid systems. *Proc. of the IEEE*, 91(7), 2003.

[35] V. Weispfenning. The complexity of linear problems in fields. *J. of Symbolic Computation*, 5(1&2):3–27, 1988.

[36] V. Weispfenning. Quantifier elimination for real algebra—the cubic case. In *Proc. ISSAC*, pages 258–263. ACM Press, New York, 1994.

[37] V. Weispfenning. Quantifier elimination for real algebra—the quadratic case and beyond. *Applicable Alg. in Eng. Comm. Comp.*, 8(2):85–101, 1997.

A Generalized Criterion for Signature Related Gröbner Basis Algorithms [*]

Yao Sun, Dingkang Wang
Key Laboratory of Mathematics Mechanization
Academy of Mathematics and Systems Science, Chinese Academy of Sciences
Beijing 100190, China
sunyao@amss.ac.cn, dwang@mmrc.iss.ac.cn

ABSTRACT

A generalized criterion for signature related algorithms to compute Gröbner basis is proposed in this paper. Signature related algorithms are a popular kind of algorithms for computing Gröbner basis, including the famous F5 algorithm, the F5C algorithm, the extended F5 algorithm and the GVW algorithm. The main purpose of current paper is to study in theory what kind of criteria is correct in signature related algorithms and provide a generalized method to develop new criteria. For this purpose, a generalized criterion is proposed. The generalized criterion only relies on a general partial order defined on a set of polynomials. When specializing the partial order to appropriate specific orders, the generalized criterion can specialize to almost all existing criteria of signature related algorithms. For *admissible* partial orders, a proof is presented for the correctness of the algorithm that is based on this generalized criterion. And the partial orders implied by the criteria of F5 and GVW are also shown to be admissible in this paper. More importantly, the generalized criterion provides an effective method to check whether a new criterion is correct as well as to develop new criteria for signature related algorithms.

Categories and Subject Descriptors

I.1.2 [**Symbolic and Algebraic Manipulation**]: Algorithms

General Terms

Algorithms, Theory

Keywords

Gröbner basis, F5, signature related algorithm, generalized criterion.

---

[*]The authors are supported by NKBRPC 2011CB302400, NSFC 10971217 and 60821002/F02.

1. INTRODUCTION

Gröbner basis was first proposed by Buchberger in 1965. Since then, many important improvements have been made to speed up the algorithms for computing Gröbner basis [3, 4, 14, 15, 19, 10, 11]. One important improvement is that Lazard pointed out the connection between a Gröbner basis and linear algebra [18]. This idea is also implemented as XL type algorithms by Courtois et al. [5] and Ding et al. [7]. Up to now, F5 is one of the most efficient algorithms for computing Gröbner basis. The concept of signatures for polynomials was also introduced by Faugère in [11]. Since F5 was proposed in 2002, it has been widely investigated and several variants of F5 have been presented, including the F5C algorithm [9] and F5 with extended criteria [16]. Proofs and other extensions of F5 are also investigated in [20, 8, 1, 2, 21, 22, 23]. Gao et al. proposed an incremental signature related algorithm G2V to compute Gröbner basis in [12], and presented an extended version GVW in [13].

The common characteristics of F5, F5C, extended F5 and GVW are (1) each polynomial has been assigned a *signature*, and (2) both the criteria and the reduction process depend on the signatures of polynomials. So all these algorithms are signature related algorithms. The only difference among the algorithms is that their criteria are different.

By studying these criteria carefully, we find that all of these criteria work almost in a same way. Suppose f and g are two polynomials with signatures and the S-pair of f and g is denoted by (t_f, f, t_g, g) where t_f and t_g are power products such that the leading power product of $t_f f$ and $t_g g$ are the same. Then a *necessary* condition of existing criteria to reject this S-pair is that, there exists some known polynomial h such that h's signature is a factor of $t_f f$'s or $t_g g$'s signature. However, this condition is not sufficient to make the criteria correct. Thus, existing criteria use different extra conditions to ensure correctness. With this insight, we generalize these extra conditions to a partial order defined on a set of polynomials, and then propose a generalized criterion for signature related algorithms. When specializing the partial order to appropriate specific orders, the generalized criterion can specialize to almost all existing criteria of signature related algorithms. We will discuss the specializations in detail.

Unfortunately, not all partial orders can make the generalized criterion correct. We proved that the generalized criterion is correct if the partial order is *admissible*. Moreover, we show that the partial orders implied by the criteria of F5 and GVW are both admissible, so the proof in this paper is also valid for the correctness of F5 and GVW.

The significance of the generalized criterion is to show what kind of criteria for signature related algorithms is correct and provide a generalized method to check or develop new criteria. Specifically, when a new criterion is presented, if it can be specified from the generalized criterion by using an admissible partial order, then this new criterion is definitely correct. It is also possible for us to develop some new criteria by using an admissible partial order in the generalized criterion. From the proof in this paper, we know that any admissible partial order can develop a new criterion for signature related algorithms in theory, but not all of these criteria can reject almost all useless critical pairs. Therefore, we claim that if the admissible partial order is in fact a total order, then almost all useless computations can be avoided. The proof for the claim will be included in our future works.

The paper is organized as follows. Section 2 gives the generalized criterion and describes how this generalized criterion specializes to the criteria of F5 and GVW. Section 3 proves the correctness of the generalized criterion. Section 4 develops a new criterion by using an admissible partial order in the generalized criterion. Concluding remarks follow in Section 6.

2. GENERALIZED CRITERION

2.1 Generalized criterion

Let $R = \mathrm{K}[x_1, \cdots, x_n]$ be a polynomial ring over a field K with n variables. Suppose $\{f_1, \cdots, f_m\}$ is a finite subset of R. We want to compute a Gröbner basis for the ideal

$$I = \langle f_1, \cdots, f_m \rangle = \{p_1 f_1 + \cdots + p_m f_m \mid p_1, \cdots, p_m \in R\}$$

with respect to some term order on R.

Let $\mathbf{f} = (f_1, \cdots, f_m) \in R^m$, and consider the following R-module of $R^m \times R$:

$$\mathbf{M} = \{(\mathbf{u}, f) \in R^m \times R \mid \mathbf{u} \cdot \mathbf{f} = f\}.$$

Let $\mathbf{e}_i$ be the i-th unit vector of R^m, i.e. $(\mathbf{e}_i)_j = \delta_{ij}$ where δ_{ij} is the Kronecker delta. Then the R-module $\mathbf{M}$ is generated by $\{(\mathbf{e}_1, f_1), \cdots, (\mathbf{e}_m, f_m)\}$. The R-module $\mathbf{M}$ was first introduced to describe signature related algorithms by Gao et al. in [12, 13].

Fix *any* term order $\prec_1$ on R and *any* term order $\prec_2$ on R^m. We must emphasize that the order $\prec_2$ may or may not be related to $\prec_1$ in theory, although $\prec_2$ is usually an extension of $\prec_1$ to R^m in implementation. For sake of convenience, we shall use the following convention for leading power products:

$$\mathrm{lpp}(f) = \mathrm{lpp}_{\prec_1}(f) \text{ and } \mathrm{lpp}(\mathbf{u}) = \mathrm{lpp}_{\prec_2}(\mathbf{u}),$$

for any $f \in R$ and any $\mathbf{u} \in R^m$. We make the convention that if $f = 0$ then $\mathrm{lpp}(f) = 0$ and $0 \prec_1 t$ for any non-zero power product t in R; similarly for $\mathrm{lpp}(\mathbf{u})$. In the following, we use $\prec$ to represent $\prec_1$ and $\prec_2$, if no confusion occurs. Most of the terminologies on "module" in this paper can be found in Chapter 5 of [6].

For any $(\mathbf{u}, f) \in \mathbf{M}$, we call $\mathrm{lpp}(\mathbf{u})$ the **signature** of $(\mathbf{u}, f)$, which is the same as the signature used in F5.

Given a finite set $B \subset \mathbf{M}$, consider a **partial order** "$\leq$" defined on B, where "$\leq$" has:

1. Reflexivity: $(\mathbf{u}, f) \leq (\mathbf{u}, f)$ for all $(\mathbf{u}, f) \in B$.

2. Antisymmetry: $(\mathbf{u}, f) \leq (\mathbf{v}, g)$ and $(\mathbf{v}, g) \leq (\mathbf{u}, f)$ imply $(\mathbf{u}, f) = (\mathbf{v}, g)$, where $(\mathbf{u}, f), (\mathbf{v}, g) \in B$.

3. Transitivity: $(\mathbf{u}, f) \leq (\mathbf{v}, g)$ and $(\mathbf{v}, g) \leq (\mathbf{w}, h)$ imply $(\mathbf{u}, f) \leq (\mathbf{w}, h)$, where $(\mathbf{u}, f), (\mathbf{v}, g), (\mathbf{w}, h) \in B$.

In the rest of this paper, we *do not* care about the *equality* case, so we always use "<", which means "$\leq$" without equality.

Based on a partial order, we give a generalized criterion for signature related algorithms.

Definition 2.1 (generalized rewritable criterion) *Given a set $B \subset \mathbf{M}$ and a partial order "<" defined on B. We say $t(\mathbf{u}, f)$, where $(\mathbf{u}, f) \in B$, f is nonzero and t is a power product in R, is **generalized rewritable** by B (**gen-rewritable** for short), if there exists $(\mathbf{u}', f') \in B$ such that*

1. $\mathrm{lpp}(\mathbf{u}')$ divides $\mathrm{lpp}(t\mathbf{u})$, and

2. $(\mathbf{u}', f') < (\mathbf{u}, f)$.

In subsection 2.3, we will show how the generalized criterion specializes to some exiting criteria. In next subsection, we describe how this generalized criterion is applied to reject redundant critical pairs.

2.2 Algorithm with generalized criterion
Let

$$G = \{(\mathbf{v}_1, g_1), \cdots, (\mathbf{v}_s, g_s)\} \subset \mathbf{M}$$

be a finite subset. We call G an **S-Gröbner basis**[1] for $\mathbf{M}$ ("S" short for signature related), if for any $(\mathbf{u}, f) \in \mathbf{M}$ with $f \neq 0$, there exists $(\mathbf{v}, g) \in G$ such that

1. $\mathrm{lpp}(g)$ divides $\mathrm{lpp}(f)$, and

2. $\mathrm{lpp}(t\mathbf{v}) \preceq \mathrm{lpp}(\mathbf{u})$, where $t = \mathrm{lpp}(f)/\mathrm{lpp}(g)$.

If G is an S-Gröbner basis for $\mathbf{M}$, then the set $\{g \mid (\mathbf{v}, g) \in G\}$ is a Gröbner basis of the ideal $I = \langle f_1, \cdots, f_m \rangle$. The reason is that for any $f \in \langle f_1, \cdots, f_m \rangle$, there exist $p_1, \cdots, p_m \in R$ such that $f = p_1 f_1 + \cdots + p_m f_m$. Let $\mathbf{u} = (p_1, \cdots, p_m)$. Then $(\mathbf{u}, f) \in \mathbf{M}$ and hence there exists $(\mathbf{v}, g) \in G$ such that $\mathrm{lpp}(g)$ divides $\mathrm{lpp}(f)$ by the definition of S-Gröbner basis.

Suppose $(\mathbf{u}, f), (\mathbf{v}, g) \in \mathbf{M}$ are two pairs with f and g both nonzero. Let $t = \mathrm{lcm}(\mathrm{lpp}(f), \mathrm{lpp}(g))$, $t_f = t/\mathrm{lpp}(f)$ and $t_g = t/\mathrm{lpp}(g)$. If $\mathrm{lpp}(t_f \mathbf{u}) \succeq \mathrm{lpp}(t_g \mathbf{v})$, then

$$[t_f(\mathbf{u}, f), t_g(\mathbf{v}, g)]$$

is called a **critical pair** of $(\mathbf{u}, f)$ and $(\mathbf{v}, g)$. The corresponding **S-polynomial** is $t_f(\mathbf{u}, f) - c t_g(\mathbf{v}, g)$ where $c = \mathrm{lc}(f)/\mathrm{lc}(g)$. Please keep in mind that, for any critical pair $[t_f(\mathbf{u}, f), t_g(\mathbf{v}, g)]$, we always have $\mathrm{lpp}(t_f \mathbf{u}) \succeq \mathrm{lpp}(t_g \mathbf{v})$. Also notice that t_f (or t_g) here does not mean it only depends on f (or g). For convenience, we say $[t_f(\mathbf{u}, f), t_g(\mathbf{v}, g)]$ is a critical pair of B, if both $(\mathbf{u}, f)$ and $(\mathbf{v}, g)$ are in B.

Given a critical pair $[t_f(\mathbf{u}, f), t_g(\mathbf{v}, g)]$, there are three possible cases, assuming $c = \mathrm{lc}(f)/\mathrm{lc}(g)$:

1. If $\mathrm{lpp}(t_f \mathbf{u} - c t_g \mathbf{v}) \neq \mathrm{lpp}(t_f \mathbf{u})$, then we say $[t_f(\mathbf{u}, f), t_g(\mathbf{v}, g)]$ is **non-regular**.

2. If $\mathrm{lpp}(t_f \mathbf{u} - c t_g \mathbf{v}) = \mathrm{lpp}(t_f \mathbf{u})$ and $\mathrm{lpp}(t_f \mathbf{u}) = \mathrm{lpp}(t_g \mathbf{v})$, then $[t_f(\mathbf{u}, f), t_g(\mathbf{v}, g)]$ is called **super regular**.

---

[1]S-Gröbner basis is a simpler version of *strong Gröbner basis* defined in [13], so the GVW algorithm computes an S-Gröbner basis. We proved in another paper that F5 also computes an S-Gröbner basis.

3. If $\mathrm{lpp}(t_f\mathbf{u}) \succ \mathrm{lpp}(t_g\mathbf{v})$, then we call $[t_f(\mathbf{u}, f), t_g(\mathbf{v}, g)]$ **genuine regular** or **regular** for short.

We say a **critical pair** $[t_f(\mathbf{u}, f), t_g(\mathbf{v}, g)]$ **is gen-rewritable** if *either* $t_f(\mathbf{u}, f)$ *or* $t_g(\mathbf{v}, g)$ is gen-rewritable.

We now state the signature related Gröbner basis algorithm that is based on the generalized criterion.

GB algorithm with generalized criterion (GBGC)
Input: $(\mathbf{e}_1, f_1), \cdots, (\mathbf{e}_m, f_m)$
Output: An S-Gröbner basis for $M = \langle (\mathbf{e}_1, f_1), \cdots, (\mathbf{e}_m, f_m) \rangle$
begin
$\quad G \longleftarrow \{(\mathbf{e}_i, f_i) \mid i = 1, \cdots, m\}$
$\quad CPairs \longleftarrow \{[t_f(\mathbf{u}, f), t_g(\mathbf{v}, g)] \mid (\mathbf{u}, f), (\mathbf{v}, g) \in G\}$
$\quad G \longleftarrow G \cup \{(f_j\mathbf{e}_i - f_i\mathbf{e}_j, 0) \mid 1 \le i < j \le m\}$ (✳)
$\quad$ while $CPairs \ne \emptyset$ do
$\quad\quad [t_f(\mathbf{u}, f), t_g(\mathbf{v}, g)] \longleftarrow$ any critical pair in $CPairs$ (★)
$\quad\quad CPairs \longleftarrow CPairs \setminus \{[t_f(\mathbf{u}, f), t_g(\mathbf{v}, g)]\}$
$\quad\quad$ if $[t_f(\mathbf{u}, f), t_g(\mathbf{v}, g)]$ is **regular** and
$\quad\quad\quad$ is **not gen-rewritable** by G
$\quad\quad$ then
$\quad\quad\quad c \longleftarrow \mathrm{lc}(f)/\mathrm{lc}(g)$
$\quad\quad\quad (\mathbf{w}, h) \longleftarrow$ reduce $t_f(\mathbf{u}, f) - ct_g(\mathbf{v}, g)$ by G
$\quad\quad\quad$ if $h \ne 0$,
$\quad\quad\quad$ then
$\quad\quad\quad\quad CPairs \longleftarrow CPairs \cup \{\text{critical pair of}$
$\quad\quad\quad\quad\quad (\mathbf{w}, h) \text{ and } (\mathbf{w}', h') \mid (\mathbf{w}', h') \in G \text{ and } h' \ne 0\}$
$\quad\quad\quad\quad G \longleftarrow G \cup \{(h\mathbf{e}_i - f_i\mathbf{w}, 0) \mid i = 1, \cdots, m\}$ (✳)
$\quad\quad\quad$ end if
$\quad\quad\quad G \longleftarrow G \cup \{(\mathbf{w}, h)\}$
$\quad\quad$ end if
$\quad$ end while
$\quad$ return G
end

For the above algorithm, please notice that

1. The gen-rewritable criterion uses a partial order defined on G. While new elements are added to G, the partial order on G needs to be updated simultaneously. Fortunately, most partial orders can be updated automatically.

2. For the line ended with (★), we emphasize that any critical pair can be selected, while some other algorithm, such as GVW, always selects the critical pair with minimal signature.

3. $(\mathbf{w}, h)$ is the reduction result of $t_f(\mathbf{u}, f) - ct_g(\mathbf{v}, g) \in M$, we will later show that $(\mathbf{w}, h)$ is an element of M. So we have $\mathbf{w} \cdot \mathbf{f} = h$ where $\mathbf{f} = (f_1, \cdots, f_m)$.

4. We add the elements of the form $(\mathbf{u}, 0)$ into G in the lines ended with (✳) to enhance the gen-rewritable criterion. Notice that $(f_j\mathbf{e}_i - f_i\mathbf{e}_j) \cdot \mathbf{f} = 0$ and $(h\mathbf{e}_i - f_i\mathbf{w}) \cdot \mathbf{f} = hf_i - f_i h = 0$ where $\mathbf{f} = (f_1, \cdots, f_m)$, so both $(f_j\mathbf{e}_i - f_i\mathbf{e}_j, 0)$ and $(h\mathbf{e}_i - f_i\mathbf{w}, 0)$ are elements in M. Moreover, G is always a subset of M.

5. The S-polynomial of $[t_f(\mathbf{u}, f), t_g(\mathbf{v}, g)]$ is considered only when $[t_f(\mathbf{u}, f), t_g(\mathbf{v}, g)]$ is *regular*, which means $\mathrm{lpp}(t_f\mathbf{u}) \succ \mathrm{lpp}(t_g\mathbf{v})$ and $\mathrm{lpp}(t_f\mathbf{u}) = \mathrm{lpp}(t_f\mathbf{u} - ct_g\mathbf{v})$. So for each element, say $(\mathbf{u}, f)$, in the set G, only $(\mathrm{lpp}(\mathbf{u}), f)$ is really used throughout the algorithm. For sake of efficiency, it suffices to record $(\mathrm{lpp}(\mathbf{u}), f)$ for each $(\mathbf{u}, f) \in G$ in the practical implementation.

Next let us see the reduction process in the above algorithm. There are several ways to define the reduction process [13, 16, 11]. We emphasize that any of these definitions can be used in the above algorithm. Here we use a similar definition as that in [11]. Given $(\mathbf{u}, f) \in \mathbf{M}$ and $B \subset \mathbf{M}$, $(\mathbf{u}, f)$ is said to be **reducible** by B, if there exists $(\mathbf{v}, g) \in B$ such that $g \ne 0$, $\mathrm{lpp}(g)$ divides $\mathrm{lpp}(f)$, $\mathrm{lpp}(\mathbf{u}) \succ \mathrm{lpp}(t\mathbf{v})$ and $t(\mathbf{v}, g)$ is *not* gen-rewritable by B where $t = \mathrm{lpp}(f)/\mathrm{lpp}(g)$. If $(\mathbf{u}, f)$ is reducible by some $(\mathbf{v}, g) \in B$, we say $(\mathbf{u}, f)$ **reduces** to $(\mathbf{u}, f) - ct(\mathbf{v}, g) = (\mathbf{u} - ct\mathbf{v}, f - ctg)$ by $(\mathbf{v}, g)$ where $c = \mathrm{lc}(f)/\mathrm{lc}(g)$ and $t = \mathrm{lpp}(f)/\mathrm{lpp}(g)$. This procedure is called a one-step reduction. Next, we can repeat this process until it is not reducible by B anymore. Clearly, if both $(\mathbf{u}, f)$ and $(\mathbf{v}, g)$ are elements in $\mathbf{M}$, then the reduction result $(\mathbf{u} - ct\mathbf{v}, f - ctg)$ is also an element in $\mathbf{M}$.

In the algorithm GBGC, we say a partial order "$<$" defined on G is **admissible**, if for any critical pair $[t_f(\mathbf{u}, f), t_g(\mathbf{v}, g)]$, which is regular and not gen-rewritable by G when it is being selected from $CPairs$ and whose corresponding S-polynomial is reduced to $(\mathbf{w}, h)$ by G, we always have $(\mathbf{w}, h) < (\mathbf{u}, f)$ after updating "$<$" for $G \cup \{(\mathbf{w}, h)\}$. We emphasize that in the above definition of admissible, the relation $(\mathbf{w}, h) < (\mathbf{u}, f)$ is essential and $(\mathbf{w}, h)$ may not be related to other elements in G.

With the above definition, it is easy to verify whether a partial order is admissible. In next subsection, we will show that the partial orders implied by the criteria of F5 and GVW are both admissible.

The following theorem shows the algorithm GBGC is correct if the partial order used in the generalized criterion is admissible.

Theorem 2.2 *Let* $\mathbf{M} = \langle (\mathbf{e}_1, f_1), \cdots, (\mathbf{e}_m, f_m) \rangle$ *be an R-module in* $R^m \times R$. *Then an S-Gröbner basis for* M *can be constructed by the algorithm GBGC, if the algorithm GBGC terminates in finite steps and the partial order in the generalized criterion is admissible.*

2.3 Specializations

In this subsection, we focus on specializing the generalized criterion to the criteria of F5 and GVW by using appropriate admissible partial orders in the algorithm GBGC. By saying "specialize" here, we mean that the critical pairs detected/rejected by the criteria of F5 or GVW can also be detected/rejected by the generalized criterion.

2.3.1 Criteria of F5

First, we list the criteria of F5 by current notations. In F5, the order $\prec_2$ on R^m is obtained by extending $\prec_1$ to R^m in a *position over term* fashion with $\mathbf{e}_1 \succ_2 \cdots \succ_2 \mathbf{e}_m$.

Definition 2.3 (syzygy criterion) *Given a set* $B \subset \mathbf{M}$, *we say* $t(\mathbf{u}, f)$, *where* $(\mathbf{u}, f) \in B$ *with* $\mathrm{lpp}(\mathbf{u}) = x^\alpha \mathbf{e}_i$, f *is nonzero and* t *is a power product in* R, *is* **F5-divisible** *by* B, *if there exists* $(\mathbf{u}', f') \in B$ *with* $\mathrm{lpp}(\mathbf{u}') = x^\beta \mathbf{e}_j$, *such that*

1. $\mathrm{lpp}(f')$ *divides* tx^α, *and*

2. $\mathbf{e}_i \succ \mathbf{e}_j$.

Definition 2.4 (rewritten criterion) *Given a set* $B \subset \mathbf{M}$, *we say* $t(\mathbf{u}, f)$, *where* $(\mathbf{u}, f) \in B$ *and* t *is a power product in* R, *is* **F5-rewritable** *by* B, *if there exists* $(\mathbf{u}', f') \in B$ *such that*

1. lpp($\mathbf{u}'$) *divides* lpp($t\mathbf{u}$), *and*

2. ($\mathbf{u}', f'$) *is added to B later than* ($\mathbf{u}, f$).

In F5, given a critical pair $[t_f(\mathbf{u}, f), t_g(\mathbf{v}, g)]$ of B, if either $t_f(\mathbf{u}, f)$ or $t_g(\mathbf{v}, g)$ is F5-divisible or F5-rewritable by B, then this critical pair is redundant.

Next, we show how to specialize the generalized criterion to both syzygy criterion and rewritten criterion at the same time. For this purpose, we choose the following partial order defined on G which can be updated automatically when a new element is added to G: we say $(\mathbf{u}', f') < (\mathbf{u}, f)$ where $(\mathbf{u}', f'), (\mathbf{u}, f) \in G$, if

1. $f' = 0$ and $f \neq 0$,

2. otherwise, ($\mathbf{u}', f'$) is added to G later than ($\mathbf{u}, f$).

The above partial order "<" is admissible in the algorithm GBGC. Because for any critical pair $[t_f(\mathbf{u}, f), t_g(\mathbf{v}, g)]$, which is regular and not gen-rewritable by G when it is being selected from *CPairs* and whose corresponding S-polynomial is reduced to $(\mathbf{w}, h)$ by G, the pair $(\mathbf{w}, h)$ is always added to G later than $(\mathbf{u}, f)$ no matter h is 0 or not.

At last, we show how the generalized criterion specializes to the rewritten criterion and syzygy criterion. For the rewritten criterion, the specialization is obvious by the definition of "<". For the syzygy criterion, if $t(\mathbf{u}, f)$, where $(\mathbf{u}, f) \in G$ with lpp($\mathbf{u}$) $= x^\alpha \mathbf{e}_i$ and $f \neq 0$, is F5-divisible by some $(\mathbf{u}', f') \in G$ with lpp($\mathbf{u}'$) $= x^\beta \mathbf{e}_j$, we have lpp(f') divides $t x^\alpha$ and $\mathbf{e}_i \succ \mathbf{e}_j$. According to the algorithm GBGC, since $f' \neq 0$, we have $(f' \mathbf{e}_i - f_i \mathbf{u}', 0) \in G$ and lpp($f' \mathbf{e}_i - f_i \mathbf{u}'$) $=$ lpp(f')$\mathbf{e}_i$ divides $t x^\alpha \mathbf{e}_i$. So $t(\mathbf{u}, f)$ is gen-rewritable by $(f' \mathbf{e}_i - f_i \mathbf{u}', 0) \in G$ by definition.

With a similar discussion, the generalized criterion can also specialize to the criteria in [16], since the extended F5 algorithm in that paper only differs from the original F5 in the order $\prec_2$ on R^m.

2.3.2 Criteria of GVW

First, we rewrite the criteria of GVW by current notations.

Definition 2.5 (First Criterion) *Given a set $B \subset \mathbf{M}$. We say $t(\mathbf{u}, f)$, where $(\mathbf{u}, f) \in B$, f is nonzero and t is a power product in R, is **GVW-divisible** by B, if there exists $(\mathbf{u}', f') \in B$ such that*

1. lpp($\mathbf{u}'$) *divides* lpp($t\mathbf{u}$), *and*

2. $f' = 0$.

Definition 2.6 (Second Criterion) *Given a set $B \subset \mathbf{M}$. We say $t(\mathbf{u}, f)$, where $(\mathbf{u}, f) \in B$ and t is a power product in R, is **eventually super top-reducible** by B, if $t(\mathbf{u}, f)$ is reducible and reduced to $(\mathbf{w}, h)$ by B, and there exists $(\mathbf{u}', f') \in B$ such that*

1. lpp($\mathbf{u}'$) *divides* lpp($\mathbf{w}$),

2. lpp(f') *divides* lpp(h), *and*

3. $\frac{\text{lpp}(\mathbf{w})}{\text{lpp}(\mathbf{u}')} = \frac{\text{lpp}(h)}{\text{lpp}(f')}$ *and* $\frac{\text{lc}(\mathbf{w})}{\text{lc}(\mathbf{u}')} = \frac{\text{lc}(h)}{\text{lc}(f')}$.

In GVW, given a critical pair $[t_f(\mathbf{u}, f), t_g(\mathbf{v}, g)]$ of B, if $t_f(\mathbf{u}, f)$ is GVW-divisible or eventually super top-reducible by B, then this critical pair is redundant. The GVW algorithm also has a third criterion.

Third Criterion *If there are two critical pairs $[t_f(\mathbf{u}, f), t_g(\mathbf{v}, g)]$ and $[\bar{t}_f(\bar{\mathbf{u}}, \bar{f}), \bar{t}_g(\bar{\mathbf{v}}, \bar{g})]$ of B such that lpp($t_f \mathbf{u}$) $=$ lpp($\bar{t}_f \bar{\mathbf{u}}$), then at least one of the critical pairs is redundant.*

Next, in order to specialize the generalized criterion to the above three criteria at the same time, we use the following partial order defined on G which can also be updated automatically when a new element is added to G: we say $(\mathbf{u}', f') < (\mathbf{u}, f)$ where $(\mathbf{u}', f'), (\mathbf{u}, f) \in G$, if one of the following two conditions holds:

1. lpp($t'f'$) $<$ lpp(tf), where $t' = \frac{\text{lcm}(\text{lpp}(\mathbf{u}), \text{lpp}(\mathbf{u}'))}{\text{lpp}(\mathbf{u}')}$ and $t = \frac{\text{lcm}(\text{lpp}(\mathbf{u}), \text{lpp}(\mathbf{u}'))}{\text{lpp}(\mathbf{u})}$ such that lpp($t'\mathbf{u}'$) $=$ lpp($t\mathbf{u}$).

2. lpp($t'f'$) $=$ lpp(tf) and ($\mathbf{u}', f'$) is added to G later than ($\mathbf{u}, f$).

The above partial order "<" is admissible in the algorithm GBGC. Because for any critical pair $[t_f(\mathbf{u}, f), t_g(\mathbf{v}, g)]$, which is regular and not gen-rewritable by G when it is being selected from *CPairs* and whose corresponding S-polynomial is reduced to $(\mathbf{w}, h)$ by G, we always have lpp($t_f \mathbf{u}$) $=$ lpp($\mathbf{w}$) and lpp($t_f f$) $>$ lpp(h).

At last, let us see the three criteria of GVW.

For the first criterion, if $t(\mathbf{u}, f)$ is GVW-divisible by some $(\mathbf{u}', f') \in G$, then $t(\mathbf{u}, f)$ is also gen-rewritable by $(\mathbf{u}', f') \in G$ by definition.

For the second criterion, if $t(\mathbf{u}, f)$, where $(\mathbf{u}, f) \in G$, is eventually super top-reducible by G, then $t(\mathbf{u}, f)$ is reduced to $(\mathbf{w}, h)$ and there exists $(\mathbf{u}', f') \in G$ such that lpp($\mathbf{u}'$) divides lpp($\mathbf{w}$), lpp(f') divides lpp(h), $\frac{\text{lpp}(\mathbf{w})}{\text{lpp}(\mathbf{u}')} = \frac{\text{lpp}(h)}{\text{lpp}(f')}$ and $\frac{\text{lc}(\mathbf{w})}{\text{lc}(\mathbf{u}')} = \frac{\text{lc}(h)}{\text{lc}(f')}$. Then we have lpp($t'\mathbf{u}'$) $=$ lpp($\mathbf{w}$) $=$ lpp($t\mathbf{u}$) and lpp($t'f'$) $=$ lpp(h) $<$ lpp(tf), which means $(\mathbf{u}', f') < (\mathbf{u}, f)$. So $t(\mathbf{u}, f)$ is gen-rewritable by $(\mathbf{u}', f') \in G$.

For the third criterion, we have lpp($t_f \mathbf{u}$) $=$ lpp($\bar{t}_f \bar{\mathbf{u}}$). First, if $(\mathbf{u}, f) < (\bar{\mathbf{u}}, \bar{f})$, then $\bar{t}_f(\bar{\mathbf{u}}, \bar{f})$ is gen-rewritable by $(\mathbf{u}, f)$ and hence $[\bar{t}_f(\bar{\mathbf{u}}, \bar{f}), \bar{t}_g(\bar{\mathbf{v}}, \bar{g})]$ is redundant; the reverse is also true. Second, if $(\mathbf{u}, f) = (\bar{\mathbf{u}}, \bar{f})$, one of the two critical pairs should be selected earlier from *CPairs*, assuming $[t_f(\mathbf{u}, f), t_g(\mathbf{v}, g)]$ is selected first. If $[t_f(\mathbf{u}, f), t_g(\mathbf{v}, g)]$ is regular and not gen-rewritable, then its S-polynomial is reduced to $(\mathbf{w}, h)$ and $(\mathbf{w}, h)$ is added to G by the algorithm GBGC. Since "<" is admissible, we have $(\mathbf{w}, h) < (\mathbf{u}, f)$. Thus, when $[\bar{t}_f(\bar{\mathbf{u}}, \bar{f}), \bar{t}_g(\bar{\mathbf{v}}, \bar{g})]$ is selected afterwards, it will be redundant, since $\bar{t}_f(\bar{\mathbf{u}}, \bar{f})$ is gen-rewritable by $(\mathbf{w}, h)$. Otherwise, if $[t_f(\mathbf{u}, f), t_g(\mathbf{v}, g)]$ is not regular, or it is regular and gen-rewritable, then $[t_f(\mathbf{u}, f), t_g(\mathbf{v}, g)]$ is redundant. Anyway, at least one of the critical pairs is redundant in the algorithm.

3. PROOFS FOR THE CORRECTNESS OF THE GENERALIZED CRITERION

To prove the main theorem (Theorem 2.2) of the paper, we need the following definition and lemmas.

In this section, we always assume that $\mathbf{M}$ is an R-module generated by $\{(\mathbf{e}_1, f_1), \cdots, (\mathbf{e}_m, f_m)\}$. Let $(\mathbf{u}, f) \in \mathbf{M}$, we say $(\mathbf{u}, f)$ has a **standard representation** w.r.t. a set $B \subset \mathbf{M}$, if there exist $p_1, \cdots, p_s \in R$ and $(\mathbf{v}_1, g_1), \cdots, (\mathbf{v}_s, g_s) \in B$ such that

$$f = p_1 g_1 + \cdots + p_s g_s,$$

where lpp($\mathbf{u}$) $\succeq$ lpp($p_i \mathbf{v}_i$) and lpp(f) $\succeq$ lpp($p_i g_i$) for $i = 1, \cdots, s$. Clearly, if $(\mathbf{u}, f)$ has a standard representation w.r.t. B, then there exists $(\mathbf{v}, g) \in B$ such that lpp(g) divides lpp(f) and lpp($\mathbf{u}$) $\succeq$ lpp($t\mathbf{v}$) where $t =$ lpp(f)/lpp(g).

We call this property to be the **basic property** of standard representations.

Lemma 3.1 *Let G be a finite subset of $\mathbf{M}$ and $\{(\mathbf{e}_1, f_1),$ $\cdots, (\mathbf{e}_m, f_m)\} \subset G$. For an element $(\mathbf{u}, f)$ in $\mathbf{M}$, $(\mathbf{u}, f)$ has a standard representation w.r.t. G, if for any critical pair $[t_g(\mathbf{v}, g), t_h(\mathbf{w}, h)]$ of G with $\mathrm{lpp}(\mathbf{u}) \succeq \mathrm{lpp}(t_g\mathbf{v})$, the S-polynomial of $[t_g(\mathbf{v}, g), t_h(\mathbf{w}, h)]$ always has a standard representation w.r.t. G.*

PROOF. For $(\mathbf{u}, f) \in \mathbf{M}$, we have $\mathbf{u} \cdot \mathbf{f} = f$ where $\mathbf{f} = (f_1, \cdots, f_m) \in R^m$. Assume $\mathbf{u} = p_1\mathbf{e}_1 + \cdots + p_m\mathbf{e}_m$ where $p_i \in R$. Clearly, $f = p_1 f_1 + \cdots + p_m f_m$. Notice that $\mathrm{lpp}(\mathbf{u}) \succeq \mathrm{lpp}(p_i\mathbf{e}_i)$ for $i = 1, \cdots, m$. If $\mathrm{lpp}(f) \succeq \mathrm{lpp}(p_i f_i)$, then we have already got a standard representation for $(\mathbf{u}, f)$ w.r.t. G. Otherwise, we will prove it by the classical method. Let $T = \max\{\mathrm{lpp}(p_i f_i) \mid i = 1, \cdots, m\}$, then $T \succ \mathrm{lpp}(f)$ holds by assumption. Consider the equation

$$f = \sum_{\mathrm{lpp}(p_i f_i) = T} \mathrm{lc}(p_i)\mathrm{lpp}(p_i) f_i + \sum_{\mathrm{lpp}(p_j f_j) \prec T} p_j f_j$$

$$+ \sum_{\mathrm{lpp}(p_i f_i) = T} (p_i - \mathrm{lc}(p_i)\mathrm{lpp}(p_i)) f_i. \qquad (1)$$

The leading power products in the first sum should be canceled, since we have $T \succ \mathrm{lpp}(f)$. So the first sum can be rewritten as a sum of S-polynomials, that is

$$\sum_{\mathrm{lpp}(p_i f_i) = T} \mathrm{lc}(p_i)\mathrm{lpp}(p_i) f_i = \sum \bar{c} t(t_g g - c t_h h),$$

where $(\mathbf{v}, g), (\mathbf{w}, h) \in G$, $\bar{c} \in K$, $t_g(\mathbf{v}, g) - c t_h(\mathbf{w}, h)$ is the S-polynomial of $[t_g(\mathbf{v}, g), t_h(\mathbf{w}, h)]$, $\mathrm{lpp}(t\, t_g g) = \mathrm{lpp}(t\, t_h h) = T$ and $\mathrm{lpp}(\mathbf{u}) \succeq \mathrm{lpp}(t\, t_g\mathbf{v}) \succeq \mathrm{lpp}(t\, t_h\mathbf{w})$ such that we have $\mathrm{lpp}(t(t_g g - c t_h h)) \prec T$. By the hypothesis of the lemma, the S-polynomial $(t_g\mathbf{v} - c t_h\mathbf{w}, t_g g - c t_h h)$ has a standard representation w.r.t. G, that is, $t_g g - c t_h h = \sum q_i g_i$, where $(\mathbf{v}_i, g_i) \in G$, $\mathrm{lpp}(\mathbf{u}) \succeq \mathrm{lpp}(t\, t_g\mathbf{v}) \succeq \mathrm{lpp}(t\, q_i\mathbf{v}_i)$ and $\mathrm{lpp}(t_g g - c t_h h) \succeq \mathrm{lpp}(q_i g_i)$. Substituting these standard representations back to the original expression of f in (1), we get a new representation for f. Let $T^{(1)}$ be the maximal leading power product of the polynomials appearing in the right side of the new representation. Then we have $T \succ T^{(1)}$. Repeat the above process until $T^{(s)}$ is the same as $\mathrm{lpp}(f)$ for some s after finite steps. Finally, we always get a standard representation for $(\mathbf{u}, f)$. $\square$

Lemma 3.2 *Let G be a finite subset of $\mathbf{M}$ and $\{(\mathbf{e}_1, f_1),$ $\cdots, (\mathbf{e}_m, f_m)\} \subset G$. Then G is an S-Gröbner basis for $\mathbf{M}$, if for any critical pair $[t_f(\mathbf{u}, f), t_g(\mathbf{v}, g)]$ of G, the S-polynomial of $[t_f(\mathbf{u}, f), t_g(\mathbf{v}, g)]$ always has a standard representation w.r.t. G.*

PROOF. By using Lemma 3.1, for any $(\mathbf{u}, f) \in \mathbf{M}$, $(\mathbf{u}, f)$ has a standard representation w.r.t. G. According to the basic property of standard representations, G is an S-Gröbner basis for $\mathbf{M}$. $\square$

Before giving a full proof of Theorem 2.2, we introduce the following definitions first.

Suppose $[t_f(\mathbf{u}, f), t_g(\mathbf{v}, g)]$ and $[t_{f'}(\mathbf{u}', f'), t_{g'}(\mathbf{v}', g')]$ are two critical pairs, we say $[t_{f'}(\mathbf{u}', f'), t_{g'}(\mathbf{v}', g')]$ is **smaller** than $[t_f(\mathbf{u}, f), t_g(\mathbf{v}, g)]$ if one of the following conditions holds:

(a). $\mathrm{lpp}(t_{f'}\mathbf{u}') \prec \mathrm{lpp}(t_f\mathbf{u})$.

(b). $\mathrm{lpp}(t_{f'}\mathbf{u}') = \mathrm{lpp}(t_f\mathbf{u})$ and $(\mathbf{u}', f') < (\mathbf{u}, f)$.

(c). $\mathrm{lpp}(t_{f'}\mathbf{u}') = \mathrm{lpp}(t_f\mathbf{u})$, $(\mathbf{u}', f') = (\mathbf{u}, f)$ and $\mathrm{lpp}(t_{g'}\mathbf{v}') \prec \mathrm{lpp}(t_g\mathbf{v})$.

(d). $\mathrm{lpp}(t_{f'}\mathbf{u}') = \mathrm{lpp}(t_f\mathbf{u})$, $(\mathbf{u}', f') = (\mathbf{u}, f)$, $\mathrm{lpp}(t_{g'}\mathbf{v}') = \mathrm{lpp}(t_g\mathbf{v})$ and $(\mathbf{v}', g') < (\mathbf{v}, g)$.

Let D be a set of critical pairs. A critical pair in D is said to be **minimal** if there is no critical pair in D smaller than this critical pair. Remark that the order "smaller" defined on the critical pairs is also *a partial order*, i.e. some critical pairs may not be comparable. Thus, the minimal critical pair in D may not be unique, but we can always find one if D is finite.

Now, we can give the proof of the main theorem.

PROOF OF THEOREM 2.2. Let G_{end} denote the set returned by the algorithm GBGC. According to the hypotheses, G_{end} is finite, and we also have $\{(\mathbf{e}_1, f_1), \cdots, (\mathbf{e}_m, f_m)\} \subset G_{end}$ by the algorithm GBGC.

To show G_{end} is an S-Gröbner basis for $\mathbf{M}$, we will take the following strategy.

Step 1: Let $Todo$ be the set of *all* the critical pairs of G_{end}, and $Done$ be an empty set.

Step 2: Select a minimal critical pair $[t_f(\mathbf{u}, f), t_g(\mathbf{v}, g)]$ in $Todo$.

Step 3: For such $[t_f(\mathbf{u}, f), t_g(\mathbf{v}, g)]$, we will prove the following two facts.

(F1). The S-polynomial of $[t_f(\mathbf{u}, f), t_g(\mathbf{v}, g)]$ has a standard representation w.r.t. G_{end}.

(F2). If $[t_f(\mathbf{u}, f), t_g(\mathbf{v}, g)]$ is *super regular* or *regular*, then $t_f(\mathbf{u}, f)$ is gen-rewritable by G_{end}.

Step 4: Move $[t_f(\mathbf{u}, f), t_g(\mathbf{v}, g)]$ from $Todo$ to $Done$, i.e. $Todo \longleftarrow Todo \setminus \{[t_f(\mathbf{u}, f), t_g(\mathbf{v}, g)]\}$ and $Done \longleftarrow Done \cup \{[t_f(\mathbf{u}, f), t_g(\mathbf{v}, g)]\}$.

We can repeat **Step 2, 3, 4** until $Todo$ is empty. Please notice that for every critical pair in $Done$, it always has property (F1). Particularly, if this critical pair is super regular or regular, then it has properties (F1) and (F2). When $Todo$ is empty, all the critical pairs of G_{end} will lie in $Done$, and hence, all the corresponding S-polynomials have standard representations w.r.t. G_{end}. Then G_{end} is an S-Gröbner basis by Lemma 3.2.

Step 1, 2, 4 are trivial, so we next focus on showing the facts in **Step 3**.

Take a minimal critical pair $[t_f(\mathbf{u}, f), t_g(\mathbf{v}, g)]$ in $Todo$. And this critical pair must appear in the algorithm GBGC. Suppose such pair is selected from the set $CPairs$ in some loop of the algorithm GBGC and G_k denotes the set G at the beginning of the same loop. For such $[t_f(\mathbf{u}, f), t_g(\mathbf{v}, g)]$, it must be in one of the following cases:

C1: $[t_f(\mathbf{u}, f), t_g(\mathbf{v}, g)]$ is *non-regular*.

C2: $[t_f(\mathbf{u}, f), t_g(\mathbf{v}, g)]$ is *super regular*.

C3: $[t_f(\mathbf{u}, f), t_g(\mathbf{v}, g)]$ is *regular* and is *not* gen-rewritable by G_k.

C4: $[t_f(\mathbf{u}, f), t_g(\mathbf{v}, g)]$ is *regular* and $t_f(\mathbf{u}, f)$ is gen-rewritable by G_k.

C5: $[t_f(\mathbf{u}, f), t_g(\mathbf{v}, g)]$ is *regular* and $t_g(\mathbf{v}, g)$ is gen-rewritable by G_k.

Thus, to show the facts in **Step 3**, we have two things to do: First, show (F1) holds in case **C1**; Second, show (F1) and (F2) hold in cases **C2**, **C3**, **C4** and **C5**. We make the following claims under the condition that $[t_f(\mathbf{u}, f), t_g(\mathbf{v}, g)]$ is minimal in *Todo*. The proofs of these claims will be presented after the current proof.

Claim 1: Given $(\bar{\mathbf{u}}, \bar{f}) \in \mathbf{M}$, if $\mathrm{lpp}(\bar{\mathbf{u}}) \prec \mathrm{lpp}(t_f\mathbf{u})$, then $(\bar{\mathbf{u}}, \bar{f})$ has a standard representation w.r.t. G_{end}.

Claim 2: If $[t_f(\mathbf{u}, f), t_g(\mathbf{v}, g)]$ is super regular or regular and $t_f(\mathbf{u}, f)$ is gen-rewritable by G_{end}, then the S-polynomial of $[t_f(\mathbf{u}, f), t_g(\mathbf{v}, g)]$ has a standard representation w.r.t. G_{end}.

Claim 3: If $[t_f(\mathbf{u}, f), t_g(\mathbf{v}, g)]$ is regular and $t_g(\mathbf{v}, g)$ is gen-rewritable by G_{end}, then $t_f(\mathbf{u}, f)$ is also gen-rewritable by G_{end}.

Claim 2 plays an important role in the whole proof. Since **Claim 2** shows that (F2) implies (F1) in the cases **C2**, **C3**, **C4** and **C5**, it suffices to show $t_f(\mathbf{u}, f)$ is gen-rewritable by G_{end} in these cases.

Next, we proceed for each case respectively.

C1: $[t_f(\mathbf{u}, f), t_g(\mathbf{v}, g)]$ is *non-regular*. Consider the S-polynomial $(t_f\mathbf{u} - ct_g\mathbf{v}, t_f f - ct_g g)$ where $c = \mathrm{lc}(f)/\mathrm{lc}(g)$. Notice that $\mathrm{lpp}(t_f\mathbf{u} - ct_g\mathbf{v}) \prec \mathrm{lpp}(t_f\mathbf{u})$ by the definition of non-regular, so **Claim 1** shows $(t_f\mathbf{u} - ct_g\mathbf{v}, t_f f - ct_g g)$ has a standard representation w.r.t. G_{end}, which proves (F1).

C2: $[t_f(\mathbf{u}, f), t_g(\mathbf{v}, g)]$ is *super regular*, i.e. $\mathrm{lpp}(t_f\mathbf{u} - ct_g\mathbf{v}) = \mathrm{lpp}(t_f\mathbf{u})$ and $\mathrm{lpp}(t_f\mathbf{u}) = \mathrm{lpp}(t_g\mathbf{v})$ where $c = \mathrm{lc}(f)/\mathrm{lc}(g)$. Let $\bar{c} = \mathrm{lc}(\mathbf{u})/\mathrm{lc}(\mathbf{v})$. Notice that $\bar{c} \neq c$, since $\mathrm{lpp}(t_f\mathbf{u} - ct_g\mathbf{v}) = \mathrm{lpp}(t_f\mathbf{u})$. Then we have $\mathrm{lpp}(t_f\mathbf{u} - \bar{c}t_g\mathbf{v}) \prec \mathrm{lpp}(t_f\mathbf{u})$ and $\mathrm{lpp}(t_f f - \bar{c}t_g g) = \mathrm{lpp}(t_f f)$. So **Claim 1** shows $(t_f\mathbf{u} - \bar{c}t_g\mathbf{v}, t_f f - \bar{c}t_g g)$ has a standard representation w.r.t. G_{end}, and hence, there exists $(\mathbf{w}, h) \in G_{end}$ such that $\mathrm{lpp}(h)$ divides $\mathrm{lpp}(t_f f - \bar{c}t_g g) = \mathrm{lpp}(t_f f)$ and $\mathrm{lpp}(t_f\mathbf{u}) \succ \mathrm{lpp}(t_f\mathbf{u} - \bar{c}t_g\mathbf{v}) \succeq \mathrm{lpp}(t_h\mathbf{w})$ where $t_h = \mathrm{lpp}(t_f f)/\mathrm{lpp}(h)$. Consider the critical pair of $(\mathbf{u}, f)$ and $(\mathbf{w}, h)$, say $[\bar{t}_f(\mathbf{u}, f), \bar{t}_h(\mathbf{w}, h)]$. Since $\mathrm{lpp}(h)$ divides $\mathrm{lpp}(t_f f)$, then $\bar{t}_f$ divides t_f, $\bar{t}_h$ divides t_h and $\frac{\mathrm{lpp}(t_f)}{\mathrm{lpp}(\bar{t}_f)} = \frac{\mathrm{lpp}(t_h)}{\mathrm{lpp}(\bar{t}_h)}$. So $[\bar{t}_f(\mathbf{u}, f), \bar{t}_h(\mathbf{w}, h)]$ is regular, and is smaller than $[t_f(\mathbf{u}, f), t_g(\mathbf{v}, g)]$ in fashion (a) if $\bar{t}_f \neq t_f$ or in fashion (c) if $\bar{t}_f = t_f$, which means $[\bar{t}_f(\mathbf{u}, f), \bar{t}_h(\mathbf{w}, h)]$ lies in *Done* and $\bar{t}_f(\mathbf{u}, f)$ is gen-rewritable by G_{end}. Then $t_f(\mathbf{u}, f)$ is also gen-rewritable by G_{end}, since $\bar{t}_f$ divides t_f.

C3: $[t_f(\mathbf{u}, f), t_g(\mathbf{v}, g)]$ is *regular* and *not* gen-rewritable by G_k. According to the algorithm GBGC, the S-polynomial $t_f(\mathbf{u}, f) - ct_g(\mathbf{v}, g)$ is reduced to $(\mathbf{w}, h)$ by G_k where $c = \mathrm{lc}(f)/\mathrm{lc}(g)$, and $(\mathbf{w}, h)$ will be added to the set G_k afterwards. Notice that $G_k \subset G_{end}$ and $(\mathbf{w}, h) \in G_{end}$. Since "$<$" is an admissible partial order, we have $(\mathbf{w}, h) < (\mathbf{u}, f)$ by definition. Combined with the fact $\mathrm{lpp}(\mathbf{w}) = \mathrm{lpp}(t_f\mathbf{u})$, so $t_f(\mathbf{u}, f)$ is gen-rewritable by $(\mathbf{w}, h) \in G_{end}$.

C4: $[t_f(\mathbf{u}, f), t_g(\mathbf{v}, g)]$ is *regular* and $t_f(\mathbf{u}, f)$ is gen-rewritable by G_k. Then $t_f(\mathbf{u}, f)$ is also gen-rewritable by G_{end}, since $G_k \subset G_{end}$.

C5: $[t_f(\mathbf{u}, f), t_g(\mathbf{v}, g)]$ is *regular* and $t_g(\mathbf{v}, g)$ is gen-rewritable by G_k. $t_g(\mathbf{v}, g)$ is also gen-rewritable by G_{end}, since $G_k \subset G_{end}$. Then **Claim 3** shows $t_f(\mathbf{u}, f)$ is gen-rewritable by G_{end} as well.

Theorem 2.2 is proved. $\square$

We give the proofs for the three claims below.

PROOF OF **Claim 1**. According to the hypothesis, we have $(\bar{\mathbf{u}}, \bar{f}) \in \mathbf{M}$ and $\mathrm{lpp}(\bar{\mathbf{u}}) \prec \mathrm{lpp}(t_f\mathbf{u})$. So for any critical pair

$[t_{f'}(\mathbf{u}', f'), t_{g'}(\mathbf{v}', g')]$ of G_{end} with $\mathrm{lpp}(\bar{\mathbf{u}}) \succeq \mathrm{lpp}(t_{f'}\mathbf{u}')$, we have $[t_{f'}(\mathbf{u}', f'), t_{g'}(\mathbf{v}', g')]$ is smaller than $[t_f(\mathbf{u}, f), t_g(\mathbf{v}, g)]$ in fashion (a) and hence lies in *Done*, which means the S-polynomial of $[t_{f'}(\mathbf{u}', f'), t_{g'}(\mathbf{v}', g')]$ has a standard representation w.r.t. G_{end}. So Lemma 3.1 shows that $(\bar{\mathbf{u}}, \bar{f})$ has a standard representation w.r.t. G_{end}. $\square$

PROOF OF **Claim 2**. We have that $[t_f(\mathbf{u}, f), t_g(\mathbf{v}, g)]$ is minimal in *Todo* and $t_f(\mathbf{u}, f)$ is gen-rewritable by G_{end}. Let $c = \mathrm{lc}(f)/\mathrm{lc}(g)$. Then $(\bar{\mathbf{u}}, \bar{f}) = (t_f\mathbf{u} - ct_g\mathbf{v}, t_f f - ct_g g)$ is the S-polynomial of $[t_f(\mathbf{u}, f), t_g(\mathbf{v}, g)]$. Since $[t_f(\mathbf{u}, f), t_g(\mathbf{v}, g)]$ is super regular or regular, we have $\mathrm{lpp}(\bar{\mathbf{u}}) = \mathrm{lpp}(t_f\mathbf{u})$. Next we will show that $(\bar{\mathbf{u}}, \bar{f})$ has a standard representation w.r.t. G_{end}. The proof is organized as follows.

First: We show that there exists $(\mathbf{u}_0, f_0) \in G_{end}$ such that $(\mathbf{u}_0, f_0) < (\mathbf{u}, f)$, $t_f(\mathbf{u}, f)$ is gen-rewritable by $(\mathbf{u}_0, f_0)$ and $t_0(\mathbf{u}_0, f_0)$ is *not* gen-rewritable by G_{end} where $t_0 = \mathrm{lpp}(t_f\mathbf{u})/\mathrm{lpp}(\mathbf{u}_0)$.

Second: For such $(\mathbf{u}_0, f_0)$, we show that $\mathrm{lpp}(\bar{f}) \succeq \mathrm{lpp}(t_0 f_0)$ where $t_0 = \mathrm{lpp}(t_f\mathbf{u})/\mathrm{lpp}(\mathbf{u}_0)$.

Third: We prove that $(\bar{\mathbf{u}}, \bar{f})$ has a standard representation w.r.t. G_{end}.

Proof of the **First** fact. By hypothesis, suppose $t_f(\mathbf{u}, f)$ is gen-rewritable by some $(\mathbf{u}_1, f_1) \in G_{end}$, i.e. $\mathrm{lpp}(\mathbf{u}_1)$ divides $\mathrm{lpp}(t_f\mathbf{u})$ and $(\mathbf{u}_1, f_1) < (\mathbf{u}, f)$. Let $t_1 = \mathrm{lpp}(t_f\mathbf{u})/\mathrm{lpp}(\mathbf{u}_1)$. If $t_1(\mathbf{u}_1, f_1)$ is not gen-rewritable by G_{end}, then $(\mathbf{u}_1, f_1)$ is the one we are looking for. Otherwise, there exists $(\mathbf{u}_2, f_2) \in G_{end}$ such that $t_1(\mathbf{u}_1, f_1)$ is gen-rewritable by $(\mathbf{u}_2, f_2)$. Notice that $t_f(\mathbf{u}, f)$ is also gen-rewritable by $(\mathbf{u}_2, f_2)$ and we have $(\mathbf{u}, f) > (\mathbf{u}_1, f_1) > (\mathbf{u}_2, f_2)$. Let $t_2 = \mathrm{lpp}(t_f\mathbf{u})/\mathrm{lpp}(\mathbf{u}_2)$. We next discuss whether $t_2(\mathbf{u}_2, f_2)$ is gen-rewritable by G_{end}. In the better case, $(\mathbf{u}_2, f_2)$ is the needed one if $t_2(\mathbf{u}_2, f_2)$ is not gen-rewritable by G_{end}; while in the worse case, $t_2(\mathbf{u}_2, f_2)$ is gen-rewritable by some $(\mathbf{u}_3, f_3) \in G_{end}$. We can repeat the above discussions for the worse case. Finally, we will get a chain $(\mathbf{u}, f) > (\mathbf{u}_1, f_1) > (\mathbf{u}_2, f_2) > \cdots$. This chain must terminate, since G_{end} is finite and "$>$" is a partial order defined on G_{end}. Suppose $(\mathbf{u}_s, f_s)$ is the last one in the above chain. Then $t_f(\mathbf{u}, f)$ is gen-rewritable by $(\mathbf{u}_s, f_s)$ and $t_s(\mathbf{u}_s, f_s)$ is not gen-rewritable by G_{end} where $t_s = \mathrm{lpp}(t_f\mathbf{u})/\mathrm{lpp}(\mathbf{u}_s)$.

Proof of the **Second** fact. From the **First** fact, we have that $t_0(\mathbf{u}_0, f_0)$ is *not* gen-rewritable by G_{end} where $t_0 = \mathrm{lpp}(t_f\mathbf{u})/\mathrm{lpp}(\mathbf{u}_0)$. Next, we prove the **Second** fact by contradiction. Assume $\mathrm{lpp}(\bar{f}) \prec \mathrm{lpp}(t_0 f_0)$. Let $c_0 = \mathrm{lc}(\bar{\mathbf{u}})/\mathrm{lc}(\mathbf{u}_0)$. Then we have $\mathrm{lpp}(\bar{\mathbf{u}} - c_0 t_0 \mathbf{u}_0) \prec \mathrm{lpp}(\bar{\mathbf{u}}) = \mathrm{lpp}(t_0 \mathbf{u}_0)$ and $\mathrm{lpp}(\bar{f} - c_0 t_0 f_0) = \mathrm{lpp}(t_0 f_0)$. So $(\bar{\mathbf{u}} - c_0 t_0 \mathbf{u}_0, \bar{f} - c_0 t_0 f_0)$ has a standard representation w.r.t. G_{end} by **Claim 1**, and hence, there exists $(\mathbf{w}, h) \in G_{end}$ such that $\mathrm{lpp}(h)$ divides $\mathrm{lpp}(\bar{f} - c_0 t_0 f_0) = \mathrm{lpp}(t_0 f_0)$ and $\mathrm{lpp}(t_0 \mathbf{u}_0) \succ \mathrm{lpp}(\bar{\mathbf{u}} - c_0 t_0 \mathbf{u}_0) \succeq \mathrm{lpp}(t_h \mathbf{w})$ where $t_h = \mathrm{lpp}(t_0 f_0)/\mathrm{lpp}(h)$. Next consider the critical pair of $(\mathbf{u}_0, f_0)$ and $(\mathbf{w}, h)$, say $[\bar{t}_0(\mathbf{u}_0, f_0), \bar{t}_h(\mathbf{w}, h)]$. Since $\mathrm{lpp}(h)$ divides $\mathrm{lpp}(t_0 f_0)$, then $\bar{t}_0$ divides t_0, $\bar{t}_h$ divides t_h and $\frac{\mathrm{lpp}(t_0)}{\mathrm{lpp}(\bar{t}_0)} = \frac{\mathrm{lpp}(t_h)}{\mathrm{lpp}(\bar{t}_h)}$. So $[\bar{t}_0(\mathbf{u}_0, f_0), \bar{t}_h(\mathbf{w}, h)]$ is regular, and is smaller than $[t_f(\mathbf{u}, f), t_g(\mathbf{v}, g)]$ in fashion (a) if $\bar{t}_0 \neq t_0$ or in fashion (b) if $\bar{t}_0 = t_0$, which means $[\bar{t}_0(\mathbf{u}_0, f_0), \bar{t}_h(\mathbf{w}, h)]$ lies in *Done* and $\bar{t}_0(\mathbf{u}_0, f_0)$ is gen-rewritable by G_{end}. Moreover, since $\bar{t}_0$ divides t_0, $t_0(\mathbf{u}_0, f_0)$ is also gen-rewritable by G_{end}, which contradicts with the property that $t_0(\mathbf{u}_0, f_0)$ is *not* gen-rewritable by G_{end}. The **Second** fact is proved.

Proof of the **Third** fact. According to the second fact, we have $\mathrm{lpp}(\bar{f}) \succeq \mathrm{lpp}(t_0 f_0)$ where $t_0 = \mathrm{lpp}(t_f\mathbf{u})/\mathrm{lpp}(\mathbf{u}_0)$.

Let $c_0 = \mathrm{lc}(\bar{\mathbf{u}})/\mathrm{lc}(\mathbf{u}_0)$. We have $\mathrm{lpp}(\bar{\mathbf{u}} - c_0 t_0 \mathbf{u}_0) \prec \mathrm{lpp}(\bar{\mathbf{u}})$ and $\mathrm{lpp}(\bar{f} - c_0 t_0 f_0) \preceq \mathrm{lpp}(\bar{f})$. So $(\bar{\mathbf{u}}, \bar{f}) - c_0 t_0 (\mathbf{u}_0, f_0) = (\bar{\mathbf{u}} - c_0 t_0 \mathbf{u}_0, \bar{f} - c_0 t_0 f_0)$ has a standard representation w.r.t. G_{end} by **Claim 1**. Notice that $\mathrm{lpp}(\bar{\mathbf{u}}) = \mathrm{lpp}(t_0 \mathbf{u}_0)$ and $\mathrm{lpp}(\bar{f}) \succeq \mathrm{lpp}(t_0 f_0)$. So after adding $c_0 t_0 f_0$ to both sides of the standard representation of $(\bar{\mathbf{u}}, \bar{f}) - c_0 t_0 (\mathbf{u}_0, f_0)$, then we will get a standard representation of $(\bar{\mathbf{u}}, \bar{f})$ w.r.t. G_{end}.

Claim 2 is proved. □

PROOF OF **Claim 3**. Since $t_g(\mathbf{v}, g)$ is gen-rewritable by G_{end} and $\mathrm{lpp}(t_g \mathbf{v}) \prec \mathrm{lpp}(t_f \mathbf{u})$, by using a similar method in the proof of the First and Second facts in **Claim 2**, we have that there exists $(\mathbf{v}_0, g_0) \in G_{end}$ such that $t_g(\mathbf{v}, g)$ is gen-rewritable by $(\mathbf{v}_0, g_0)$, $t_0(\mathbf{v}_0, g_0)$ is not gen-rewritable by G_{end} and $\mathrm{lpp}(t_g g) \succeq \mathrm{lpp}(t_0 g_0)$ where $t_0 = \mathrm{lpp}(t_g \mathbf{v})/\mathrm{lpp}(\mathbf{v}_0)$.

If $\mathrm{lpp}(t_g g) = \mathrm{lpp}(t_0 g_0)$, then the critical pair of $(\mathbf{u}, f)$ and $(\mathbf{v}_0, g_0)$, say $[\bar{t}_f(\mathbf{u}, f), \bar{t}_0(\mathbf{v}_0, g_0)]$, must be regular and smaller than the critical pair $[t_f(\mathbf{u}, f), t_g(\mathbf{v}, g)]$ in fashion (a) or (d), which means $[\bar{t}_f(\mathbf{u}, f), \bar{t}_0(\mathbf{v}_0, g_0)]$ lies in $Done$ and $\bar{t}_f(\mathbf{u}, f)$ is gen-rewritable by G_{end}. Since $\mathrm{lpp}(t_0 g_0) = \mathrm{lpp}(t_g g) = \mathrm{lpp}(t_f f)$, then $\bar{t}_f$ divides t_f, and hence, $t_f(\mathbf{u}, f)$ is gen-rewritable by G_{end} as well.

Otherwise, $\mathrm{lpp}(t_g g) \succ \mathrm{lpp}(t_0 g_0)$ holds. Let $c = \mathrm{lc}(\mathbf{v})/\mathrm{lc}(\mathbf{v}_0)$, we have $\mathrm{lpp}(t_g \mathbf{v} - c t_0 \mathbf{v}_0) \prec \mathrm{lpp}(t_g \mathbf{v})$ and $\mathrm{lpp}(t_g g - c t_0 g_0) = \mathrm{lpp}(t_g g)$. Then $(t_g \mathbf{v} - c t_0 \mathbf{v}_0, t_g g - c t_0 g_0)$ has a standard representation w.r.t. G_{end} by **Claim 1**, and hence, there exists $(\mathbf{w}, h) \in G_{end}$ such that $\mathrm{lpp}(h)$ divides $\mathrm{lpp}(t_g g - c t_0 g_0) = \mathrm{lpp}(t_g g)$ and $\mathrm{lpp}(t_h \mathbf{w}) \preceq \mathrm{lpp}(t_g \mathbf{v} - c t_0 \mathbf{v}_0) \prec \mathrm{lpp}(t_g \mathbf{v})$ where $t_h = \mathrm{lpp}(t_g g)/\mathrm{lpp}(h)$. Notice that $\mathrm{lpp}(t_h h) = \mathrm{lpp}(t_g g) = \mathrm{lpp}(t_f f)$. The critical pair of $(\mathbf{u}, f)$ and $(\mathbf{w}, h)$, say $[\bar{t}_f(\mathbf{u}, f), \bar{t}_h(\mathbf{w}, h)]$, must be regular and smaller than the critical pair $[t_f(\mathbf{u}, f), t_g(\mathbf{v}, g)]$ in fashion (a) or (c), which means $[\bar{t}_f(\mathbf{u}, f), \bar{t}_h(\mathbf{w}, h)]$ lies in $Done$ and $\bar{t}_f(\mathbf{u}, f)$ is gen-rewritable by G_{end}. Since $\mathrm{lpp}(h)$ divides $\mathrm{lpp}(t_g g) = \mathrm{lpp}(t_f f)$, then $\bar{t}_f$ divides t_f, and hence, $t_f(\mathbf{u}, f)$ is gen-rewritable by G_{end} as well.

Claim 3 is proved. □

4. DEVELOPING NEW CRITERIA

Based on the generalized criterion, to develop new criteria for signature related algorithms, it suffices to choose appropriate admissible partial orders. For example, we can develop a new criterion by using the following admissible partial order implied by GVW's criteria: that is, $(\mathbf{u}', f') < (\mathbf{u}, f)$, where $(\mathbf{u}, f), (\mathbf{u}', f') \in G$, if one of the following two conditions holds.

1. $\mathrm{lpp}(t' f') < \mathrm{lpp}(t f)$ where $t' = \frac{\mathrm{lcm}(\mathrm{lpp}(\mathbf{u}), \mathrm{lpp}(\mathbf{u}'))}{\mathrm{lpp}(\mathbf{u}')}$ and $t = \frac{\mathrm{lcm}(\mathrm{lpp}(\mathbf{u}), \mathrm{lpp}(\mathbf{u}'))}{\mathrm{lpp}(\mathbf{u})}$ such that $\mathrm{lpp}(t' \mathbf{u}') = \mathrm{lpp}(t \mathbf{u})$.

2. $\mathrm{lpp}(t' f') = \mathrm{lpp}(t f)$ and $(\mathbf{u}', f')$ is added to G later than $(\mathbf{u}, f)$.

Recently, we notice Huang also uses a similar order in [17].

Applying this admissible partial order in the algorithm GBGC, we get a new algorithm (named by NEW). This algorithm can be considered as an improved version of GVW. To test the efficacy of the new criterion, we implemented the algorithm NEW on Singular (version 3-1-2), and use two strategies for selecting critical pairs in our implementation.

Minimal **S**ignature Strategy: $[t_f(\mathbf{u}, f), t_g(\mathbf{v}, g)]$ is selected from $CPairs$ if there does *not* exist $[t_{f'}(\mathbf{u}', f'), t_{g'}(\mathbf{v}', g')] \in CPairs$ such that $\mathrm{lpp}(t_{f'} \mathbf{u}') \prec \mathrm{lpp}(t_f \mathbf{u})$;

Minimal **D**egree Strategy: $[t_f(\mathbf{u}, f), t_g(\mathbf{v}, g)]$ is selected from

$CPairs$ if there does *not* exist $[t_{f'}(\mathbf{u}', f'), t_{g'}(\mathbf{v}', g')] \in CPairs$ such that $\deg(\mathrm{lpp}(t_{f'} f')) \prec \deg(\mathrm{lpp}(t_f f))$.

The proof in Section 3 ensures the algorithm NEW is correct by using any of the above strategies.

In the following table, we use (s) and (d) to refer the two strategies respectively. The order $\prec_1$ is graded reverse lex order and $\prec_2$ is extended from $\prec_1$ in the following way: $x^\alpha \mathbf{e}_i \prec_2 x^\beta \mathbf{e}_j$, if either $\mathrm{lpp}(x^\alpha f_i) \prec_1 \mathrm{lpp}(x^\beta f_j)$, or $\mathrm{lpp}(x^\alpha f_i) = \mathrm{lpp}(x^\beta f_j)$ and $i > j$. This order $\prec_2$ has also been used in [13, 22]. The examples are selected from [13] and the timings are obtained on Core i5 4×2.8 GHz with 4GB memory running Windows 7.

Table 1: *#all.*: number of all critical pairs generated in the computation; *#red.*: number of critical pairs that are really reduced in the computation; *#gen.*: number of non-zero generators in the Gröbner basis in the last iteration but before computing a reduced Gröbner basis. "Katsura5 (22)" means there are 22 non-zero generators in the reduced Gröbner basis of Katsura5.

	NEW(s)	NEW(d)	NEW(s)	NEW(d)
	Katsura5 (22)		Katsura6 (41)	
#all.	351	378	1035	1275
#red.	39	40	73	78
#gen.	27	28	46	51
time(sec.)	1.400	1.195	7.865	5.650
	Katsura7 (74)		Katsura8 (143)	
#all.	3160	3160	11325	11325
#red.	121	121	244	244
#gen.	80	80	151	151
time(sec.)	38.750	29.950	395.844	310.908
	Cyclic5 (20)		Cyclic6 (45)	
#all.	1128	2080	18528	299925
#red.	56	78	231	834
#gen.	48	65	193	775
time(sec.)	2.708	2.630	106.736	787.288

From the above table, we can see that the new criterion can reject redundant critical pairs effectively. We also notice that the timings are influenced by the strategies of selecting critical pairs. For some examples, the algorithm with minimal signature strategy has better performance. The possible reason is that less critical pairs are generated by this strategy. For other examples, the algorithm with minimal degree strategy cost less time. The possible reason is that, although the algorithm with the minimal degree strategy usually generates more critical pairs, the critical pairs which are really needed to be reduced usually have lower degrees.

5. CONCLUSIONS AND FUTURE WORKS

Signature related algorithms are a popular kind of algorithms for computing Gröbner basis. A generalized criterion for signature related algorithms is proposed in this paper. Almost all existing criteria of signature related algorithms can be specialized by the generalized criterion, and we show in detail that this generalized criterion can specialize to the criteria of F5 and GVW by using appropriate admissible orders. We also proved that if the partial order is admissible, the generalized criterion is always correct no matter which computing order of the critical pairs is used. Since the generalized criterion can specialize to the criteria of F5 and GVW, the proof in this paper also ensures the correctness of F5 and GVW for any computing order of critical pairs.

The significance of this generalized criterion is to describe what kind of criterion is correct in signature related algorithms. Moreover, the generalized criterion also provides an effective approach to check and develop new criteria for signature related algorithms, i.e., if a new criterion can be specialized from the generalized criterion by using an admissible partial order, it must be correct; when developing new criteria, it suffices to choose admissible partial orders in the generalized criterion. We also develop a new effective criterion in this paper. We claim that if the admissible partial order is in fact a total order, then the generalized criterion can reject almost all useless critical pairs. The proof of the claim will be included in future works.

However, there are still some open problems.

Problem 1: Is the generalized criterion still correct if the partial order is not admissible? We do know some partial orders will lead to wrong criteria. For example, consider the following partial order which is not admissible: we say $(\mathbf{u}', f') < (\mathbf{u}, f)$, where $(\mathbf{u}, f), (\mathbf{u}', f') \in G$, if $f' = 0$ and $f \neq 0$; otherwise, $(\mathbf{u}', f')$ is added to G *earlier* than $(\mathbf{u}, f)$. The above partial order leads to a wrong criterion. The reason is that $(\mathbf{e}_1, f_1), \cdots, (\mathbf{e}_m, f_m)$ are added to G earlier than others, so using this partial order, the generalized criterion will reject almost all critical pairs generated later, which definitely leads to a wrong output unless $\{(\mathbf{e}_1, f_1), \cdots, (\mathbf{e}_m, f_m)\}$ itself is an S-Gröbner basis.

Problem 2: Does the S-Gröbner basis always exist for the module generated by any $\{(\mathbf{e}_1, f_1), \cdots, (\mathbf{e}_m, f_m)\}$? The existence of S-Groebner basis is the prerequisite of the termination of GBGC as well as GVW, since GVW also computes an S-Gröbner basis. Our experiments show GBGC always terminates in finite steps, so the S-Gröbner bases always exist for these examples.

Problem 3: Does the algorithm GBGC always terminate in finite steps? We have tested many examples, and we have not found a counterexample that GBGC does not terminate.

Acknowledgements
We would like to thank Shuhong Gao and Mingsheng Wang for constructive discussions, and the anonymous reviewers for their helpful comments.

6. REFERENCES
[1] M. Albrecht and J. Perry. F4/5. Preprint, arXiv:1006.4933v2 [math.AC], 2010.

[2] A. Arri and J. Perry. The F5 criterion revised. Preprint, arXiv:1012.3664v3 [math.AC], 2010.

[3] B. Buchberger. A criterion for detecting unnecessary reductions in the construction of Gröbner basis. In Proceedings of EUROSAM'79, Lect. Notes in Comp. Sci., Springer, Berlin, vol. 72, 3-21, 1979.

[4] B. Buchberger. Gröbner-bases: an algorithmic method in polynomial ideal theory. Reidel Publishing Company, Dodrecht - Boston - Lancaster, 1985.

[5] N. Courtois, A. Klimov, J. Patarin, and A. Shamir. Efficient algorithms for solving overdefined systems of multivariate polynomial equations. In Proceedings of EUROCRYPT'00, Lect. Notes in Comp. Sci., Springer, Berlin, vol. 1807, 392-407, 2000.

[6] D. Cox, J. Little, and D. O'Shea. Using algebraic geometry. Springer, New York, second edition, 2005.

[7] J. Ding, J. Buchmann, M.S.E. Mohamed, W.S.A.E. Mohamed, and R.-P. Weinmann. MutantXL. In Proceedings of the 1st international conference on Symbolic Computation and Cryptography (SCC08), Beijing, China, 16-22, 2008.

[8] C. Eder. On the criteria of the F5 algorithm. Preprint, arXiv:0804.2033v4 [math.AC], 2008.

[9] C. Eder and J. Perry. F5C: a variant of Faugère's F5 algorithm with reduced Gröbner bases. J. Symb. Comput., vol. 45(12), 1442-1458, 2010.

[10] J.-C. Faugère. A new effcient algorithm for computing Gröbner bases (F_4). J. Pure Appl. Algebra, vol. 139(1-3), 61-88, 1999.

[11] J.-C. Faugère. A new effcient algorithm for computing Gröbner bases without reduction to zero (F_5). In Proceedings of ISSAC'02, ACM Press, New York, USA, 75-82, 2002. Revised version downloaded from fgbrs.lip6.fr/jcf/Publications/index.html.

[12] S.H. Gao, Y.H. Guan, and F. Volny. A new incremental algorithm for computing Gröbner bases. In Proceedings of ISSAC'10, ACM Press, New York, USA, 13-19, 2010.

[13] S.H. Gao, F. Volny, and M.S. Wang. A new algorithm for computing Gröbner bases. Cryptology ePrint Archive, Report 2010/641, 2010.

[14] R. Gebauer and H.M. Moller. Buchberger's algorithm and staggered linear bases. In Proceedings of SYMSAC'86, ACM press, New York, USA, 218-221, 1986.

[15] A. Giovini, T. Mora, G. Niesi, L. Robbiano and C. Traverso. "One sugar cube, please" or selection strategies in the Buchberger algorithm. In Proceedings of ISSAC'91, ACM Press, New York, USA, 49-54, 1991.

[16] A. Hashemi and G. Ars. Extended F5 criteria. J. Symb. Comput., vol. 45(12), 1330-1340, 2010.

[17] L. Huang. A new conception for computing Gröbner basis and its applications. Preprint, arXiv:1012.5425v2 [cs.SC], 2010.

[18] D. Lazard. Gröbner bases, Gaussian elimination and resolution of systems of algebraic equations. In Proceeding of EUROCAL'83, Lect. Notes in Comp. Sci., Springer, Berlin, vol. 162, 146-156, 1983.

[19] H.M. Möller, T. Mora, and C. Traverso. Gröbner bases computation using syzygies. In Proceedings of ISSAC'92, ACM Press, New York, USA, 320-328, 1992.

[20] T. Stegers. Faugère's F5 algorithm revisited. Cryptology ePrint Archive, Report 2006/404, 2006.

[21] Y. Sun and D.K. Wang. The F5 algorithm in Buchberger's style. To appear in J. Syst. Sci. Complex., arXiv:1006.5299v2 [cs.SC], 2010.

[22] Y. Sun and D.K. Wang. A new proof for the correctness of the F5 algorithm. Preprint, arXiv:1004.0084v4 [cs.SC], 2010.

[23] A. Zobnin. Generalization of the F5 algorithm for calculating Gröbner bases for polynomial ideals. Programming and Computer Software, vol. 36(2), 75-82, 2010.

Generating Subfields

Mark van Hoeij[*]
Florida State University
Tallahassee, FL 32306
hoeij@math.fsu.edu

Jürgen Klüners[†]
Mathematisches Institut
der Universität Paderborn
Universität Paderborn
Warburger Str. 100
33098 Paderborn, Germany
klueners@math.uni-
paderborn.de

Andrew Novocin
Laboratoire LIP (U. Lyon,
CNRS, ENS Lyon, INRIA,
UCBL)
46 Allée d'Italie
69364 Lyon Cedex 07, France
andy@novocin.com

ABSTRACT

Given a field extension K/k of degree n we are interested in finding the subfields of K containing k. There can be more than polynomially many subfields. We introduce the notion of generating subfields, a set of up to n subfields whose intersections give the rest. We provide an efficient algorithm which uses linear algebra in k or lattice reduction along with factorization. Our implementation shows that previously difficult cases can now be handled.

Categories and Subject Descriptors

I.1.2 [**Symbolic and Algebraic Manipulation**]: Algorithms; G.4 [**Mathematics of Computing**]: Mathematical Software

General Terms

Algorithms

Keywords

Symbolic Computation, Subfields, Lattice Reduction

1. INTRODUCTION

Let K/k be a finite separable field extension of degree n and α a primitive element of K over k with minimal polynomial $f \in k[x]$. We explore the problem of computing subfields of K which contain k. We prove that all such subfields (there might be more than polynomially many) can be expressed as the intersections of at most n particular subfields which we will call the 'generating subfields'. We give an efficient algorithm to compute these generating subfields.

---

[*]Supported by NSF Grant number 0728853 and 1017880
[†]Research supported by the Deutsche Forschungsgemeinschaft

Previous methods progress by solving combinatorial problems on the roots of f, such as [4, 5, 8, 13]. Similar to our algorithm [11] starts by factoring f over K and then tries to find all subfield polynomials (see Definition 2.5) by a combinatorial approach. Such approaches can be very efficient, but in the worst cases they face a combinatorial explosion. The paper [14] proceeds by factoring resolvent polynomials of degree bounded by $\binom{n}{\lfloor n/2 \rfloor}$. By introducing the concept of generating subfields we restrict our search to a small number of target subfields. This new fundamental object allows for polynomial time algorithms.

We can find the generating subfields whenever we have a factorization algorithm for f over K or any $\tilde{K}/K$ and the ability to compute a kernel in k. For $k = \mathbb{Q}$ this implies a polynomial-time algorithm as factoring over $\mathbb{Q}(\alpha)$ and linear algebra over $k = \mathbb{Q}$ are polynomial time. When one desires all subfields we give such an algorithm which is additionally linear in the number of subfields.

For the number field case we are interested in a specialized and practical algorithm. Thus we replace exact factorization over $\mathbb{Q}(\alpha)$ by a p-adic factorization and the exact kernel computation by approximate linear algebra using the famous LLL algorithm for lattice reduction [15]. We take advantage of some recent practical lattice reduction results [18] and tight theoretical bounds to create an implementation which is practical on previously difficult examples.

ROADMAP: The concept of the principal and generating subfields are introduced in Section 2.1. In Section 2.2 we explain how to compute all subfields in a running time which is linearly dependent on the number of subfields. For the number field case we will use the LLL algorithm and this case is handled in detail in Section 3. Finally we compare our approach with the state of the art in Section 4.

NOTATIONS: For a polynomial g we let $\| g \|$ be the ℓ_2 norm on the coefficient vector of g. For a vector $\mathbf{v}$ we let $\mathbf{v}[i]$ be the ith entry. Unless otherwise noted $\| \cdot \|$ will represent the ℓ_2 norm.

2. A GENERAL ALGORITHM

2.1 Generating subfields

In this section we introduce the concept of a generating set of subfields and prove some important properties. Let $\tilde{K}$ be a field containing K. We remark that we can choose $\tilde{K} = K$, but in some case it might be better to choose a larger $\tilde{K}$ from an algorithmic point of view. E.g. in the number field case we choose a p-adic completion (see Section 3). Let $f = f_1 \cdots f_r$ be the factorization of f over $\tilde{K}$ where the $f_i \in \tilde{K}[x]$ are irreducible and $f_1 = x - \alpha$. We define the fields $\tilde{K}_i := \tilde{K}[x]/(f_i)$ for $1 \leq i \leq r$. We denote elements of K as $g(\alpha)$ where $g \in k[x]$ is a polynomial of degree $< n$, and define for $1 \leq i \leq r$ the embedding

$$\phi_i : K \to \tilde{K}_i, \qquad g(\alpha) \mapsto g(x) \bmod f_i.$$

Note that ϕ_1 is just the identity map $\mathrm{id} : K \to \tilde{K}$. We define for $1 \leq i \leq r$:

$$L_i := \mathrm{Ker}(\phi_i - \mathrm{id}) = \{g(\alpha) \in K \mid g(x) \equiv g(\alpha) \bmod f_i\}.$$

The L_i are closed under multiplication, and hence fields, since $\phi_i(ab) = \phi_i(a)\phi_i(b) = ab$ for all $a, b \in L_i$.

THEOREM 2.1. *If L is a subfield of K/k then L is the intersection of L_i, $i \in I$ for some $I \subseteq \{1, \ldots, r\}$.*

PROOF. Let f_L be the minimal polynomial of α over L. Then f_L divides f since $k \subseteq L$, and $f_L = \prod_{i \in I} f_i$ for some $I \subseteq \{1, \ldots, r\}$ because $L \subseteq \tilde{K}$. We will prove

$$L = \{g(\alpha) \in K \mid g(x) \equiv g(\alpha) \bmod f_L\} = \bigcap_{i \in I} L_i.$$

If $g(\alpha) \in L$ then $h(x) := g(x) - g(\alpha) \in L[x]$ is divisible by $x - \alpha$ in $K[x]$. The set of polynomials in $L[x]$ divisible by $x - \alpha$ is the principal ideal (f_L) by definition of f_L. Then $h(x) \equiv 0 \bmod f_L$ and hence $g(x) \equiv g(\alpha) \bmod f_L$. Conversely, $g(x) \bmod f_L$ is in $L[x] \pmod{f_L}$ because division by f_L can only introduce coefficients in L. So if $g(x) \equiv g(\alpha) \bmod f_L$ then $g(\alpha) \in K \cap L[x] = L$.

By separability and the Chinese remainder theorem, one has $g(x) \equiv g(\alpha) \bmod f_L$ if and only if $g(x) \equiv g(\alpha) \bmod f_i$ (i.e. $g(\alpha) \in L_i$) for every $i \in I$. □

LEMMA 2.2. *The set $S := \{L_1, \ldots, L_r\}$ is independent of the choice of $\tilde{K}$.*

PROOF. Let $f = g_1 \cdots g_s \in K[x]$ be the factorization of f into irreducible factors over K. Suppose that f_i divides g_l. Let L resp. L_i be the subfield corresponding to g_l resp. f_i. Assume $g(\alpha) \in L$, in other words $g(x) \equiv g(\alpha) \bmod g_l$. Then $g(x) \equiv g(\alpha) \bmod f_i$ because f_i divides g_l. Hence $g(\alpha) \in L_i$.

Conversely, assume that $g(\alpha) \in L_i$. Now $h(x) := g(x) - g(\alpha)$ is divisible by f_i, but since $h(x) \in L_i[x] \subseteq K[x]$ it must also be divisible by g_l since g_l is irreducible in $K[x]$ and divisible by f_i. So $g(x) \equiv g(\alpha) \bmod g_l$ in other words $g(\alpha) \in L$. It follows that $L = L_i$. □

DEFINITION 2.3. *We call the fields $L_1, \ldots, L_r$ the principal subfields of K/k. A set S of subfields of K/k is called a generating set of K/k if every subfield of K/k can be written as $\bigcap T$ for some $T \subseteq S$. Here $\bigcap T$ denotes the intersection of all $L \in T$, and $\bigcap \emptyset$ refers to K. A subfield L of K/k is called a generating subfield if it satisfies the following equivalent conditions*

1. *The intersection of all fields L' with $L \subsetneq L' \subseteq K$ is not equal to L.*

2. *There is precisely one field $L \subsetneq \tilde{L} \subseteq K$ for which there is no field between L and $\tilde{L}$ (and not equal to L or $\tilde{L}$).*

The field $\tilde{L}$ in condition 2. is called *the field right above L*. It is clear that $\tilde{L}$ is the intersection in condition 1., so the two conditions are equivalent.

The field K is a principal subfield but not a generating subfield. A maximal subfield of K/k is a generating subfield as well. Theorem 2.1 says that the principal subfields form a generating set. By condition 1., a generating subfield can not be obtained by intersecting larger subfields, and must therefore be an element of every generating set. In particular, a generating subfield is also a principal subfield.

If S is a generating set, and we remove every $L \in S$ for which $\bigcap \{L' \in S | L \subsetneq L'\}$ equals L, then what remains is a generating set that contains only generating subfields. It follows that

PROPOSITION 2.4. *S is a generating set if and only if every generating subfield is in S.*

Suppose that K/k is a finite separable field extension and that one has polynomial time algorithms for factoring over K and linear algebra over k (for example when $k = \mathbb{Q}$). Then applying Theorem 2.1 with $\tilde{K} = K$ yields a generating set S with $r \leq n$ elements in polynomial time. We may want to minimize r by removing all elements of S that are not generating subfields, then $r \leq n - 1$.

The computation of the principal subfields L_i reduces to linear algebra when we know a factorization of f over K. In this case we get a k-basis of L_i by a simple kernel computation. In the number field case, the factorization of f over K could be slow, in which case we prefer to use a larger field $\tilde{K} \supsetneq K$ where the factorization is faster. In Section 3 this is done for $k = \mathbb{Q}$, but this can be generalized to an arbitrary global field. Then we let $\tilde{K}$ be some completion of K. This reduces the cost of the factorization, however, one now has to work with approximations for the factors f_i of f, which means that we get approximate (if $\tilde{K}$ is the field of p-adic numbers then this means modulo a prime power) linear equations. Solving approximate equations involves LLL in the number field case and [2, 7] in the function field case.

2.2 All subfields

Now suppose that one would like to compute all subfields of K/k by intersecting elements of a generating set $S = \{L_1, \ldots, L_r\}$. We present an algorithm with complexity proportional to the number of subfields of K/k. Unfortunately there exist families of examples where this number is more than polynomial in n. Note that we have represented our subfields $k \leq L_i \leq K$ as k-vector subspaces of K. This allows the intersection $L_1 \cap L_2$ to be found with linear algebra as the intersection of two subspaces of a vector space. To each subfield L of K/k we associate a tuple $e = (e_1, \ldots, e_r) \in \{0, 1\}^r$, where $e_i = 1$ if and only if $L \subseteq L_i$.

Algorithm AllSubfields
Input: A generating set $S = \{L_1, \ldots, L_r\}$ for K/k.
Output: All subfields of K/k.

1. Let $e := (e_1, \ldots, e_r)$ be the associated tuple of K.

2. ListSubfields := $[K]$.

3. Call NextSubfields$(S, K, e, 0)$.

4. Return ListSubfields.

The following function returns no output but appends elements to ListSubfields, which is used as a global variable. The input consists of a generating set, a subfield L, its associated tuple $e = (e_1, \ldots, e_r)$, and the smallest integer $0 \le s \le r$ for which $L = \bigcap \{L_i \mid 1 \le i \le s, \, e_i = 1\}$.

Algorithm NextSubfields
Input: S, L, e, s.

For all i with $e_i = 0$ and $s < i \le r$ **do**

1. Let $M := L \cap L_i$.

2. Let $\tilde{e}$ be the associated tuple of M.

3. **If** $\tilde{e}_j \le e_j$ for all $1 \le j < i$ **then** append M to ListSubfields and call NextSubfields$(S, M, \tilde{e}, i)$.

DEFINITION 2.5. *Let L be a subfield of K/k. Then the minimal polynomial f_L of α over L is called the **subfield polynomial** of L.*

REMARK 2.6. *Let $g \in K[x]$ be a monic polynomial. Then the following are equivalent:*

1. *$g = f_L$ for some subfield L of K/k.*

2. *$f_1 \mid g \mid f$ and $[\mathbb{Q}(\alpha) : \mathbb{Q}(\text{coefficients}(g))] = \deg(g)$.*

3. *$f_1 \mid g \mid f$ and the $\mathbb{Q}$–vector space $\{h(x) \in \mathbb{Q}[x] \mid \deg(h) < \deg(f), h \mod g = h \mod f_1\}$ has dimension $\deg(f)/\deg(g)$.*

REMARK 2.7. *For each subfield L, we can compute subfield polynomial f_L with linear algebra. Testing if $L \subseteq M$ then reduces to testing if f_L is divisible by f_M. For many fields K this test can be implemented efficiently by choosing a non-archimedian valuation v of K with residue field $\mathbf{F}$ such that the $f \mod v$ (the image of f in $\mathbf{F}[x]$) is defined and separable. Then f_L is divisible by f_M in $K[x]$ if and only if the same is true mod v, since both are factors of a polynomial f whose discriminant does not vanish mod v.*

Subfields that are isomorphic but not identical are considered to be different in this paper. Let m be the number of subfields of K/k. Since S is a generating set, all subfields occur as intersections of $L_1, \ldots, L_r$. The condition in Step (3) in Algorithm NextSubfields holds if and only if M has not already been computed before. So each subfield will be placed in ListSubfields precisely once, and the total number of calls to Algorithm NextSubfields equals m. For each call, the number of i's with $e_i = 0$ and $s < i \le r$ is bounded by r, so the total number of intersections calculated in Step (1) is $\le rm$. Step (2) involves testing which L_j contain M. Bounding the number of j's by r, the number of subset tests is $\le r^2 m$. One can implement Remark 2.7 to keep the cost of each test low.

THEOREM 2.8. *Given a generating set for K/k with r elements, Algorithm AllSubfields returns all subfields by computing at most rm intersections and at most $r^2 m$ subset tests, where m is the number of subfields of K/k.*

2.3 Quadratic subfields

In this section we will show that, although there might be more than polynomially many subfields, the set of quadratic subfields of K/k can be computed in polynomial time (Theorem 2.9 below). The main goal in this section is not the theorem itself, rather, the main goal is to illustrate a theoretical application of our "generating subfields" framework (Theorem 2.9 had already been proven by Hendrik Lenstra (private communication) using a different approach.)

Let $Q(K/k)$ denote the subfield generated over k by $\{a \in K \mid a^2 \in k\}$, and let C_2 denote the cyclic group of order 2. If $K = Q(K/k)$, in other words the Galois group of f is C_2^s for some s, then $n = 2^s$ and f splits over K into linear factors $f_1 \cdots f_n$ where $f_1 = x - \alpha$. Furthermore, there are precisely $n - 1$ generating subfields $L_2, \ldots, L_n$ and n principal subfields $L_1, \ldots, L_n$ where $L_1 = K$.

Conversely, suppose there are n principal subfields. Every principal subfield corresponds to at least one factor of f over K, and hence to precisely one factor since f has degree n. So f must split into linear factors, and each L_i corresponds to precisely one linear factor f_i. Then the minimal polynomial of α over L_i is $f_1 f_i$ when $i \in \{2, \ldots, n\}$. The degree of $f_1 f_i$ is 2, so there are $n - 1$ subfields of index 2, which implies that the Galois group is C_2^s for some s.

THEOREM 2.9. *If factoring over K and linear algebra over k can be done in polynomial time then all quadratic subfields of K/k can be computed in polynomial time.*

The principal subfields of $Q(K/k)$ are subfields of index 2, and hence correspond to automorphisms of $Q(K/k)$ over k of order 2. This way it is not difficult to show that the quadratic subfields of $Q(K/k)$ can be computed in polynomial time; for the above theorem it suffices to prove that the following algorithm computes $Q(K/k)$ in polynomial time.

Algorithm Q
Input: A separable field extension K/k where $K = k(\alpha)$.
Output: $Q(K/k)$.

1. Let $n := [K : k]$. If n is odd then return k.

2. Compute the set S of generating subfields.

3. If K/k has $n - 1$ distinct subfields of index 2 then return K.

4. Choose a generating subfield $L_i \in S$ with index > 2, and let $\tilde{L}_i$ be the field right above L_i, so $L_i \subsetneq \tilde{L}_i := \bigcap \{L_j \in S \mid L_i \subsetneq L_j\}$.

5. If $[\tilde{L}_i : L_i] = 2$ then return $Q(\tilde{L}_i/k)$, otherwise return $Q(L_i/k)$.

In the first call to Algorithm Q, we can compute a generating set in Step (2) in polynomial time using Theorem 2.1 with $\tilde{K} := K$. For the recursive calls we use:

REMARK 2.10. *If S is a generating set for K/k and if L is a subfield of K/k, then $\{L \bigcap L' \mid L' \in S\}$ is a generating set of L/k.*

For Step (3) see the remarks before Theorem 2.9. If we reach Step (4) then $K \ne Q(K/k)$. The field L_i in Step (4) exists by Lemma 2.11 below. Let $\tilde{L}_i$ be the field right above L_i. If $[\tilde{L}_i : L_i] = 2$ then $\tilde{L}_i \neq K$ so the algorithm terminates.

Let $a \in Q(K/k)$. We may assume that $a^2 \in k$. Now $\tilde{L}_i$ is contained in any subfield L' of K/k that properly contains L_i. So if $a \notin L_i$ then $L_i(a)$ contains $\tilde{L}_i$ and hence equals $\tilde{L}_i$ since $[\tilde{L}_i : L_i(a)] = 2$. Then $a \in \tilde{L}_i$. We conclude $Q(K/k) \subseteq \tilde{L}_i$. If $[\tilde{L}_i : L_i] \neq 2$ then the assumption $a \notin L_i$ leads to a contradiction since $L_i(a)$ can not contain $\tilde{L}_i$ in this case. So $Q(K/k) \subseteq L_i$ in this case, which proves that Step (5) is correct.

LEMMA 2.11. *If K/k does not have $n-1$ distinct subfields of index 2 then there exists a generating field of index > 2.*

PROOF. Assume that every generating (and hence every maximal) subfield has index 2. So the subfields of index 2 form a generating set. Let G be the automorphism group of K/k. If K/L_i and K/L_j are Galois extensions, then so is $K/(L_i \cap L_j)$ since $L_i \cap L_j$ is the fixed field of the group generated by the Galois groups of K/L_i and K/L_j. If $[K : L_i] = 2$ then K/L_i is Galois. Let k' be the intersection of all subfields L_i of index 2. Then K/k' is Galois. However, k' must equal k, otherwise the set of subfields of index 2 can not be a generating set. It follows that K/k is Galois.

If n is not a power of 2, then there exists a maximal subfield of odd index. If $n = 2^s$ with $s > 1$ then the Galois group must have an element of order 4 (G can not be C_2^s since the number of subfields of index 2 is not $n-1$). This element of order 4 corresponds to a linear factor f_i of f in $K[x]$. Let L_i be its corresponding principal subfield. Then L_i is contained in m maximal subfields where m is either 1 or 3. Let $\check{f}_i$ be the minimal polynomial of α over L_i. If $m = 3$ then every irreducible factor of $\check{f}_i/(x - \alpha)$ corresponds to a subfield of index 2. This is a contradiction since f_i divides $\check{f}_i/(x - \alpha)$. $\square$

3. THE NUMBER FIELD CASE

3.1 Introduction

In this section we describe an algorithm for producing a generating set when $K = \mathbb{Q}(\alpha)$. Factoring f over K, though polynomial time, may be slow, thus we design an algorithm that uses an approximation of a p-adic factorization and LLL instead. We show that when the algorithm terminates[1], it returns the correct output.

For a prime number p, let $\mathbb{Q}_p$ denote the field of p-adic numbers, $\mathbb{Z}_p$ the ring of p-adic integers, and $\mathbf{F}_p = \mathbb{Z}/(p)$. We choose a prime number p with these three properties: p does not divide the leading coefficient of $f \in \mathbb{Z}[x]$, the image $\bar{f}$ of f in $\mathbf{F}_p[x]$ is separable, and has at least one linear factor which we denote $\bar{f}_1$ (asymptotically, the probability that a randomly chosen prime p has these properties is $\geq 1/n$, where equality holds when K/k is Galois).

By factoring $\bar{f}$ in $\mathbf{F}_p[x]$ and applying Hensel lifting, we obtain a factorization of $f = f_1 \cdots f_r$ over $\mathbb{Q}_p$ where f_1 has degree 1. By mapping $\alpha \in K$ to the root α_1 of f_1 in $\mathbb{Q}_p$ we obtain an embedding $K \to \mathbb{Q}_p$, and so we can view K as a subfield of $\check{K} := \mathbb{Q}_p$.

The advantage of taking $\mathbb{Q}_p$ (instead of K) for $\check{K}$ is that it saves time on factoring f over $\check{K}$. Since p does not divide the

---

[1] a bound for the running time can be obtained in a similar way as in [3]

denominators of the coefficients of f, the factors $f_1, \ldots, f_r$ of f over $\mathbb{Q}_p$ lie in $\mathbb{Z}_p[x]$. We can not compute these factors with infinite accuracy, but only to some finite accuracy a, meaning that $f_1, \ldots, f_r$ are only known modulo p^a.

For each of the factors, f_i, we will need to find the principal subfield L_i which was defined in Section 2.1 as the kernel of $\phi_i - \text{id}$. To do this we will make use of a knapsack-style lattice in the style of [18]. To get the best performance we would like to design a lattice such that boundably short vectors correspond with elements in L_i.

A natural approach would be to use $1, \alpha, \ldots, \alpha^{n-1}$ as a basis, and search for linear combinations whose images under $\phi_i - \text{id}$ are 0 (mod p^a). However, we will use a different basis. Denote $\mathbb{Z}[\alpha]_{<n} := \mathbb{Z} \cdot \alpha^0 + \cdots + \mathbb{Z} \cdot \alpha^{n-1}$ (note: if f is monic then this is simply $\mathbb{Z}[\alpha]$ but we do not assume that f is monic). Then the basis $\frac{1}{f'(\alpha)}, \ldots, \frac{\alpha^{n-1}}{f'(\alpha)}$ of $\frac{1}{f'(\alpha)} \cdot \mathbb{Z}[\alpha]_{<n}$ allows us to prove more practical bounds (this phenomena has also been observed in other contexts [6]). Using this basis of K we prove the existence of a $\mathbb{Q}$-basis of L_i which has a bounded representation. We delay the proof of this theorem until section 3.4.

THEOREM 3.1. *Let L_i, the target principal subfield, have degree m_i over $\mathbb{Q}$. For $\beta \in \frac{1}{f'(\alpha)} \cdot \mathbb{Z}[\alpha]_{<n}$ with $\beta = \sum b_i \frac{\alpha^i}{f'(\alpha)}$ we associate the vector $\mathbf{v}_\beta := (b_0, \ldots, b_{n-1})$. Then there exists m_i linearly independent algebraic numbers $\beta_1, \ldots \beta_{m_i} \in L_i \cap \frac{1}{f'(\alpha)} \cdot \mathbb{Z}[\alpha]_{<n}$ each with $\|\mathbf{v}_{\beta_k}\| \leq n^2 \|f\|_2$.*

3.2 The computation of a principal subfield

Now we can continue the description of the computation of the principal subfield L_i corresponding to the factor f_i of degree d_i. As mentioned before we will represent our elements in the basis $\frac{1}{f'(\alpha)}, \ldots, \frac{\alpha^{n-1}}{f'(\alpha)}$. Each of these basis elements will be represented as the column of an identity matrix to which we attach entries for the image of that basis element under $\phi_i - \text{id}$. Since these images are only known modulo p^a we must also adjoin columns which allow for this modular reduction. Suppose the degree of f_i is d_i, then our lattice is spanned by the columns of the following $(n + d_i) \times (n + d_i)$ integer matrix:

$$B_i := \begin{pmatrix} 1 & & & & & \\ & \ddots & & & & \\ & & 1 & & & \\ c_{0,0} & \cdots & c_{0,n-1} & p^a & & \\ \vdots & \ddots & \vdots & & \ddots & \\ c_{d_i-1,0} & \cdots & c_{d_i-1,n-1} & & & p^a \end{pmatrix} \quad (1)$$

where $c_{k,j}$ is the kth coefficient of $\frac{x^j}{f'(x)} \bmod f_i - \frac{x^j}{f'(x)} \bmod f_1$ reduced modulo p^a. To interpret a vector $\mathbf{v}$ in the column space of this matrix we take the first n entries $b_0, \ldots, b_{n-1}$ and then compute $(\sum b_j \alpha^j)/f'(\alpha)$. A vector corresponding to an element in L_i will have its final d_i entries be 0 modulo p^a. Thus Theorem 3.1 shows us that the lattice generated by columns of B_i contains a dimension m_i sublattice which has a small basis. This allows us to use the new sub-lattice reduction techniques of [18] on B_i. Thus, rather than standard LLL, we use `LLL_with_removals` which performs lattice reduction but removes any vectors in the final position whose G-S norm is above a given bound. The following lemma is derived from [15] and justifies these removals.

LEMMA 3.2. *Given a basis* $\mathbf{b}_1, \ldots, \mathbf{b}_d$ *of a lattice* Λ, *and let* $\mathbf{b}_1^*, \ldots, \mathbf{b}_d^*$ *be the output of Gram-Schmidt orthogonalization. If* $\| \mathbf{b}_d^* \| > B$ *then any vector in* L *with norm* $\leq B$ *is a* $\mathbb{Z}$-*linear combination of* $\mathbf{b}_1, \ldots, \mathbf{b}_{d-1}$.

This technique is common and is used in [10, 18]. As the removal condition requires Gram-Schmidt norms we can state that LLL reduced bases tend to be numerically stable for Gram-Schmidt computations so a floating point Gram-Schmidt computation could be used for efficiency (see [19]). Also FLINT 1.6 [9] has an LLL with removals routine which takes a bound and returns the dimension of the appropriate sub-lattice.

In this way using `LLL_with_removals` with the bound from Theorem 3.1 will allow us to reduce the dimension. In Figure 1 we give a practical algorithm which will create a basis of a subfield of K which is highly likely to be L_i. We will use $D := \text{diag}\{1, \ldots, 1, C, \ldots, C\}$ as a matrix for scaling the last d_i rows of B_i by a scalar C. Since the vectors guaranteed by Theorem 3.1 come from L_i we know that the final d_i entries must be 0. Thus multiplication on the left by D and removals will eventually ensure that vectors with zero entries are found by LLL.

Input: f_i
Output: h_k which probably generate L_i

1. Create lattice B_i from equation (1)
2. $A := $ `LLL_with_removals`$(B_i, n^2 \| f \|)$
3. $m := \dim(A)$
4. while $\exists l > n, j$ such that $A[l, j] \neq 0$:
5. $A := D \cdot A$
6. $A := $ `LLL_with_removals`$(A, n^2 \| f \|)$
7. $m := \dim(A)$
8. if $m \nmid n$ increase precision repeat `principal`
9. for $1 \leq k \leq m$:
10. $h_k := \sum_{j=1}^{n} \frac{A[j,k]x^{j-1}}{f'(x)}$

Figure 1: principal algorithm

Using LLL on the matrix entire B_i will suffice for this paper. However, in practice the d_i final rows of B_i can also be reduced one at a time. In this way one could potentially arrive at a solution without needing all rows of B_i. Such an approach is seen in [18] and could be adapted to this situation.

The algorithm in figure 1 will produce m p-adic polynomials h_k, which are likely to correspond with algebraic numbers which generate L_i as a $\mathbb{Q}$-vector space. It is possible that m is not m_i but some other divisor of n. In particular, if the p-adic precision is not high enough then there could be entries in the lattice basis which are 0 modulo p^a but not exactly 0. In that case one of the h_k would not be from L_i. Even so the $\mathbb{Q}$-vector space generated by the h_k must at least contain L_i. The reason is that at least m_i linearly independent algebraic numbers from L_i remain within the lattice after `LLL_with_removals` thanks to the bound of Theorem 3.1 and Lemma 3.2.

Theorem 3.1 can also be used to make a guess for a starting precision of p^a. Since any reduced basis has Gram-Schmidt norms within a factor 2^{n+d_i} of the successive minima and the determinant of B_i is $p^{a \cdot d_i}$ then we should ensure than $p^{a \cdot d_i}$ is at least $(2^{n+d_i} n^2 \| f \|)^n$.

3.3 Confirming a principal subfield

In this section we will assume that we have elements in approximate p-adic form which are likely to generate a principal subfield (in other words, the output of the algorithm in Figure 1). Our goal is to certify that the elements indeed generate the target L_i. We give an algorithm which will construct the subfield polynomial g, of L_i or return failure, in which case more p-adic precision is needed. We choose the subfield polynomial as it will provide a proof that we have a principal subfield and can be stored in a relatively compact way thanks to our new basis. Of course other representations and proofs are possible.

From here on our algorithmic objective will be to output the minimal polynomial $g \in L_i[x]$ of alpha over L_i. This g is the subfield polynomial of L_i and its coefficients generate L_i. We know m elements h_k modulo p^a, we know that $m|n$ and that $\phi_i - \text{id}(h_k) \equiv 0$ modulo p^a for each k. Recall that the h_k were from columns of a lattice basis A. First we will create a p-adic candidate subfield polynomial which we then subject to 3 certification checks.

Candidate g: Create an index set $T := \{j | \phi_j(h_k) \equiv \text{id}(h_k) \mod p^a \forall h_k\}$, that is find the p-adic factors of f which also agree with f_1 on the elements corresponding to the basis from A. T will contain at least 1 and i. Now let $g_{\text{cand}} := \prod_{j \in T} f_j \mod p^a$. This is done in steps 1–5 of Figure 2

Input: $h_1 \ldots h_m, f_1, \ldots f_r \in \mathbb{Q}_p[x]$, $f \in \mathbb{Z}[x]$ precision a
Output: g subfield poly, or `fail`

1. $T := \{\}$
2. for each $1 \leq j \leq r$:
3.   if $(h_k \mod f_j = h_k \mod f_1) \mod p^a \forall k$ then:
4. $T := T \cup j$
5. $g_{\text{cand}} := \text{lc}(f) \cdot \prod_{j \in T} f_j \mod p^a$
     where $\text{lc}(f)$ is the leading coefficient of f
6. Create lattice M using (2)
7. $M := $ LLL(M)
8. $g_{\text{temp}} = 0$
9. for each coefficient g_k of x^k in g_{cand}:
10.   create M_{g_k} lattice using (3)
11.   **Check 1** find $\mathbf{v}$ in LLL(M_{g_k})
         with $\mathbf{v}[n+1] = 0$ and $\mathbf{v}[n+2] = 1$
12. $g_{\text{temp}} := g_{\text{temp}} + \sum_{j=1}^{n} \frac{\mathbf{v}[j]\alpha^{j-1}}{f'(\alpha)} x^k$
13. $g_{\text{cand}} := g_{\text{temp}} \in \mathbb{Q}(\alpha)[x]$
14. **Check 2** ensure $g_{\text{cand}} | f$ exactly
15. **Check 3** ensure $(h_k \mod g_{\text{cand}} = h_k \mod f_1) \forall k$
16. return $g := g_{\text{cand}}$

Figure 2: final_check algorithm

Check 1: Let $\Lambda(A) \subseteq \frac{\mathbb{Z}[\alpha]_{<n}}{f'(\alpha)}$ be the lattice generated by the algebraic numbers corresponding with columns of A. We now attempt to find an exact representation of g_{cand} by converting each coefficient into an algebraic number in $\Lambda(A) \cap \frac{\mathbb{Z}[\alpha]_{<n}}{f'(\alpha)}$. We'll do this by attempting to find linear combinations of h_k which exactly equal each coefficient of g_{cand}.

Note that this g_{cand} is a polynomial with p-adic coefficients, these coefficients can be quickly Hensel lifted using the fact that $f = g \cdot (f/g) \mod p^a$ if more precision is needed. Now we want to express these coefficients in the basis $\frac{\mathbb{Z}[\alpha]_{<n}}{f'(\alpha)} \cap \Lambda(A)$. To do this we will use a lattice basis similar to A with a slight adjustment. Rather than finding algebraic numbers whose images under $\phi_i - \text{id}$ are zero, we'll

find combinations of the h_k whose p-adic valuations match a coefficient of g_{cand}.

Lets call $\mathbf{v}_{h_k}$ the coefficient vector of h_k, and the corresponding p-adic valuation $c_j := h_k(\alpha_1)$ (that is, h_k modulo f_1). Also we pick a large scalar constant C (to ensure that LLL works on reducing the size of the p-adic row). We let the columns of the new matrix be $(\mathbf{v}_{h_j}, C \cdot c_j)^T$, and the column $(0, \ldots, 0, C \cdot p^a)$.

$$M := \begin{pmatrix} \mathbf{v}_{h_1}^T & \cdots & \mathbf{v}_{h_m}^T & \mathbf{0} \\ C \cdot c_1 & \cdots & C \cdot c_m & C \cdot p^a \end{pmatrix} \quad (2)$$

A vector in the column space of this matrix is a representation of a combination of the elements from h_k along with a p-adic valuation of that element. Now for each coefficient we'll use this matrix to find a combination which matches that coefficient. In practice we LLL-reduce M before adjoining data from the coefficients of g_{cand}, but here we present an augmented M without altering the columns first (for clarity).

For each coefficient g_k of g_{cand} augment each column of M with a zero, then adjoin a new column $(0, \ldots, 0, C \cdot g_k, 1)^T$. This is what the coefficient matching matrix looks like:

$$M := \begin{pmatrix} \mathbf{v}_{h_1}^T & \cdots & \mathbf{v}_{h_m}^T & \mathbf{0} & \mathbf{0} \\ C \cdot c_1 & \cdots & C \cdot c_m & C \cdot p^a & C \cdot g_k \\ 0 & \cdots & 0 & 0 & 1 \end{pmatrix} \quad (3)$$

Run LLL on this matrix (provided C is large enough) then find the vector which has its final two entries as $0, 1$, the first n entries are an expression of g_k in $\frac{\mathbb{Z}[\alpha]_{<n}}{f'(\alpha)}$. If this works for every coefficient of g_{cand} then the check has passed.

Check 2: Ensure that $g_{cand} | f$ in $\mathbb{Q}(\alpha)[x]$.

Check 3: Ensure that $h_k \mod g_{cand} = h_k \mod f_1$ for each h_k.

THEOREM 3.3. *If all checks pass then the $\mathbb{Q}$-linear combination of the elements corresponding to the lattice basis A generate L_i the target principal subfield, and g_{cand} is the subfield polynomial of L_i.*

PROOF. By construction of g_{cand} and A we know that the span over $\mathbb{Q}$ of the elements corresponding to A, the h_k, contains L_i. Let's call this span V, so $L_i \subseteq V$. Since g_{cand} divides f and f_i divides g_{cand} then $h \mod g_{cand} = h \mod f_1$ implies $h \mod f_i = h \mod f_1$. By check 1 this implies that $V \subseteq L_i$ thus the span over $\mathbb{Q}$ of the elements from the lattice is L_i.

Now $x - \alpha, f_i | g_{cand} \mod p^a$ and $g_{cand} | f$ exactly then $f_i | g_{cand}$ and $(x - \alpha) | g_{cand}$ exactly. Now by Remark 2.6 we know g_{cand} is the subfield polynomial of L_i. $\square$

If check 1 fails then perhaps try a larger constant C, otherwise if any check fails increase the p-adic precision via Hensel lifting and try again.

3.4 Bounds for the coefficients

The only aim of this section is to prove Theorem 3.1. The techniques described in this section are not used in the algorithm.

In order to get our desired bounds it is useful to introduce the notation of a codifferent, see [16, Chapter 4.2] for more details.

LEMMA 3.4. *Let $f \in \mathbb{Z}[x]$ be primitive and irreducible, with degree n. Let α be a root of f. Let $\mathcal{O}_K$ be the ring of*

integers in $K = \mathbb{Q}(\alpha)$ *and let $\mathcal{O}_K^*$ be the* co-different *which is defined as:*

$$\mathcal{O}_K^* = \{a \in K | \forall_{b \in \mathcal{O}_K} \operatorname{Tr}(ab) \in \mathbb{Z}\}.$$

Then

$$\mathcal{O}_K^* \subseteq \frac{1}{f'(\alpha)} \mathbb{Z}[\alpha]_{<n} \quad (4)$$

.

PROOF. Let $a \in \mathcal{O}_K^*$, so $\operatorname{Tr}(ab) \in \mathbb{Z}$ for any $b \in \mathcal{O}_K$. The content of a polynomial $g = c_0 x^0 + \cdots + c_d x^d \in K[x]$ is defined as the fractional ideal $c(g) = \mathcal{O}_K c_0 + \cdots + \mathcal{O}_K c_d$. Let $g_1 = x - \alpha$ and $g_2 = f/g_1$. Gauss' lemma says $c(g_1)c(g_2) = c(g_1 g_2)$. Then $c(g_1)c(g_2) = c(f) = \mathcal{O}_K$, ($f$ is primitive) and since g_1 has a coefficient equal to 1 it follows that $c(g_2) \subseteq \mathcal{O}_K$, in other words $g_2 \in O_K[x]$. Now $ag_2 \in a \cdot \mathcal{O}_K[x]_{<n}$ and by definition of $\mathcal{O}_K^*$ we see that $\operatorname{Tr}(ag_2) \in \mathbb{Z}[x]_{<n}$. So

$$\operatorname{Tr}(ag_2) = \operatorname{Tr}(a \frac{f(x)}{x - \alpha}) = \sum a_i \frac{f(x)}{x - \alpha_i} \in \mathbb{Z}[x]_{<n}$$

where a_i and α_i denote the conjugates of a and α. Evaluating the right-hand side at $x = \alpha = \alpha_1$ gives $af'(\alpha) \in \mathbb{Z}[\alpha]_{<n}$ and hence $a \in 1/f'(\alpha) \cdot \mathbb{Z}[\alpha]_{<n}$. $\square$

Now suppose that we have an $\beta \in \mathcal{O}_K^*$, then we can write

$$f'(\alpha)\beta = \sum_{i=0}^{n-1} b_i \alpha^i \text{ with } b_i \in \mathbb{Z}. \quad (5)$$

In our applications β is an element of a principal subfield and we would like to bound the size of b_i. In the following we need the complex embeddings and some norms of algebraic numbers.

DEFINITION 3.5. *Let $K = \mathbb{Q}(\alpha)$ be a number field of degree n and f be the minimal polynomial of α. Then we denote by $\phi_1, \ldots, \phi_n : K \to \mathbb{C}, \alpha \mapsto \alpha_i$ the n complex embeddings, where $\alpha_1, \ldots, \alpha_n$ are the complex roots of f. We assume that $\alpha_1, \ldots, \alpha_{r_1}$ are real and the complex roots are ordered such that $\alpha_{r_1+i} = \bar{\alpha}_{r_1+r_2+i}$ for $1 \leq i \leq r_2$.*

For $\beta \in K$ we define the norms

$$\|\beta\|_1 := \sum_{i=1}^n |\phi_i(\beta)| \text{ and } \|\beta\|_2 := \sqrt{\sum_{i=1}^n |\phi_i(\beta)|^2}.$$

Note the well known estimates:

$$\|\beta\|_2 \leq \|\beta\|_1 \leq \sqrt{n}\|\beta\|_2.$$

We are able to give the promised bounds.

LEMMA 3.6. *Let β be given as in (5) with coefficient vector $b := (b_0, \ldots, b_{n-1})$. Then we have $\|b\|_2 \leq n\|\beta\|_1\|f\|_2 \leq n^{1.5}\|\beta\|_2\|f\|_2$.*

PROOF. Let $h(x) := \sum_{i=0}^{n-1} b_i x^i$. Let $\alpha_i := \phi_i(\alpha)$ and $\beta_i := \phi_i(\beta)$, then we get: $h(\alpha_i) = \beta_i f'(\alpha_i)$ for $1 \leq i \leq n$. Using Lagrange interpolation we get:

$$h(x) = \sum_{i=1}^n \beta_i f'(\alpha_i) \frac{f(x)/(x - \alpha_i)}{f'(\alpha_i)} \leq \sum_{i=1}^n \beta_i \frac{f(x)}{x - \alpha_i}.$$

Now:

$$\|b\|_2 = \|h\|_2 = \sum_{i=1}^n |\beta_i| \|f/(x - \alpha_i)\|_2$$

$$\leq \max_i \|f/(x-\alpha_i)\|_2 \sum_{i=1}^n |\beta_i| \leq n\|f\|_2\|\beta\|_1,$$

$\|f/(x-\alpha_i)\|_2 \leq n\|f\|_2$ is proved in [17, cor4.7]. The second estimate follows then trivially from $\|\cdot\|_1 \leq \sqrt{n}\|\cdot\|_2$. $\square$

Now our goal is the following. Let L be a principal subfield of degree m which we would like to compute. We want to find a $\mathbb{Q}$-basis of L represented in our $\frac{1}{f'(\alpha)}\mathbb{Z}[\alpha]_{<n}$–basis. Note that $\mathcal{O}_L^* \subseteq \mathcal{O}_K^* \subseteq \frac{1}{f'(\alpha)}\cdot\mathbb{Z}[\alpha]_{<n}$. In order to apply Lemma 3.6 we need to bound $\|\beta_i\|_2$ for m linearly independent elements $\beta_1,\ldots,\beta_m \in L$. We will use the following theorem.

THEOREM 3.7 (BANASZCZYK). *Let $\Lambda \subset \mathbb{R}^m$ be a lattice and denote by $\Lambda^* := \{y \in \mathbb{R}^m \mid \forall x \in \Lambda : \langle x,y\rangle \in \mathbb{Z}\}$ the dual lattice. Furthermore denote by λ_i, λ_i^* the i-th successive minima of Λ, Λ^*, respectively. Then $\lambda_i\lambda_{m+1-i}^* \leq m$ for $1 \leq i \leq m$.*

The proof can be found in [1, Theorem 2.1]. In our application we have that $\lambda_1 = \sqrt{m}$, so we get the upper bound $\lambda_m^* \leq \sqrt{m}$. There are canonical ways to map number fields to lattices, but we have the slight problem that the bilinear form $L \times L \to \mathbb{Q}, (x,y) \mapsto \mathrm{Tr}(xy)$ is not positive definite, if L has non-real embeddings. We assume the same order of the complex embeddings of L as in Definition 3.5, so we have $m = r_1 + 2r_2$ (recall that $m = [L:\mathbb{Q}]$). Defining $\gamma_i = \phi_i(\gamma)$ and $\delta_i = \phi_i(\delta)$ we get:

$$\mathrm{Tr}(\gamma\delta) = \sum_{i=1}^m \gamma_i\delta_i.$$

The corresponding scalar product looks like:

$$\langle\gamma,\delta\rangle := \sum_{i=1}^m \gamma_i\bar{\delta}_i.$$

For totally real number fields L those two notions coincide and then we get that the dual lattice equals $\mathcal{O}_L^*$ and we can apply Theorem 3.7 directly to get the desired bounds. First we introduce the canonical real lattice $\Lambda := \Psi(\mathcal{O}_L) \subseteq \mathbb{R}^m$ associated to $\langle\gamma,\delta\rangle$ via

$$\Psi : L \to \mathbb{R}^m, \qquad (6)$$

$$\beta \mapsto (\beta_1,\ldots,\beta_{r_1}, \sqrt{2}\Re(\beta_{r_1+1}),\ldots,\sqrt{2}\Re(\beta_{r_1+r_2}),$$
$$\sqrt{2}\Im(\beta_{r_1+1}),\ldots,\sqrt{2}\Im(\beta_{r_1+r_2})).$$

Note that now the standard scalar product of $\mathbb{R}^m$ coincides with the (complex) scalar product defined above. This is the reason for the weight $\sqrt{2}$ in the above definition. Denote by $\langle\cdot,\cdot\rangle_1$ the standard scalar product of $\mathbb{R}^m$. Furthermore denote by

$$\langle x,y\rangle_2 := \sum_{i=1}^{r_1+r_2} x_iy_i - \sum_{i=r_1+r_2+1}^m x_iy_i.$$

Then we have

$$\langle\gamma,\delta\rangle = \langle\Psi(\gamma),\Psi(\delta)\rangle_1 \text{ and } \mathrm{Tr}(\gamma\delta) = \langle\Psi(\gamma),\Psi(\delta)\rangle_2.$$

Now we are able to compare our two dual objects, the dual lattice Λ^* of Λ corresponding to $\langle\cdot,\cdot\rangle_1$ and the codifferent.

LEMMA 3.8. *Using the above notations. Then $\theta : \mathbb{R}^m \to \mathbb{R}^m$,*

$$(x_1,\ldots,x_m) \mapsto (x_1,\ldots,x_{r_1+r_2},-x_{r_1+r_2+1},\ldots,-x_m)$$

induces an isomorphism $\Lambda^* \to \Psi(\mathcal{O}_L^*)$ of $\mathbb{Z}$-modules.

PROOF. θ is linear and has the property

$$\langle x,y\rangle_1 = \langle x,\theta(y)\rangle_2 \text{ for all } x,y \in \mathbb{R}^m.$$

We need to show that $\theta(\Lambda^*) = \Psi(\mathcal{O}_L)$. Note that θ^2 is the identity and therefore this is equivalent to $\theta(\Psi(\mathcal{O}_L)) = \Lambda^*$. Denote by $\omega_1,\ldots,\omega_m$ a $\mathbb{Z}$-basis of $\mathcal{O}_L$. Then $\Lambda = \mathbb{Z}\Psi(\omega_1) + \ldots + \mathbb{Z}\Psi(\omega_m)$. Choose $\gamma \in \mathcal{O}_L^*$ arbitrarily. Then $\mathrm{Tr}(\omega_i\gamma) \in \mathbb{Z}$ for $1 \leq i \leq m$ and therefore

$$\langle\Psi(\omega_i),\theta(\Psi(\gamma))\rangle_1 = \langle\Psi(\omega_i),\Psi(\gamma)\rangle_2 = \mathrm{Tr}(\omega_i\gamma) \in \mathbb{Z}.$$

Therefore $\theta(\Psi(\gamma)) \in \Lambda^*$ and we have shown $\theta(\Psi(\mathcal{O}_L^*)) \subseteq \Lambda^*$. Denote by $\tau_1,\ldots,\tau_m \in \mathcal{O}_L^*$ the dual basis of $\omega_1,\ldots,\omega_m$. Because of duality (e.g. see [16, Proof of Prop. 4.14]) we know that $\mathrm{disc}(\tau_1,\ldots,\tau_m) = \mathrm{disc}(\omega_1,\ldots,\omega_m)^{-1} = d_L^{-1}$. Furthermore $\theta(\Psi(\tau_i))$ $(1 \leq i \leq m)$ are linearly independent elements of Λ^* and the discriminant of the $\mathbb{Z}$–module generated by those elements is $|d_L^{-1}|$ since the corresponding determinants differ by a power of -1 because we have to consider the twists between our two bilinear forms. Therefore we know a subset $\theta(\Psi(\mathcal{O}_L^*)) \subseteq \Lambda^*$ which has the correct lattice discriminant. Therefore we get equality. $\square$

Now we are able to get our bound by applying Lemma 3.8 and Theorem 3.7.

LEMMA 3.9. *Let L be a number field of degree m. Then $\mathcal{O}_L^*$ contains m $\mathbb{Q}$–linearly independent elements $\gamma_1,\ldots,\gamma_m$ such that $\|\gamma_i\|_2 \leq \sqrt{m}$ for $1 \leq i \leq m$.*

PROOF. As before let $\Lambda := \Psi(\mathcal{O}_L)$, where Ψ is defined in (6). Now we claim that the first successive mimimum λ_1 equals $\sqrt{m}$ by taking the element $\Psi(1)$. Let $\gamma \in \mathcal{O}_L$ and $\gamma \neq 0$. Then

$$1 \leq |\mathrm{Norm}(\gamma)| = \left(\prod_{i=1}^m |\gamma_i|^2\right)^{1/2} \leq \left(\frac{\sum_{i=1}^m |\gamma_i|^2}{m}\right)^{m/2}$$

$$= \left(\frac{\langle\Psi(\gamma),\Psi(\gamma)\rangle_1}{m}\right)^{m/2},$$

where the inequality is the one between geometric and arithmetic means. Now we get that $\langle\Psi(\gamma),\Psi(\gamma)\rangle_1 \geq m$ which finishes the proof that $\lambda_1 = \sqrt{m}$.

Applying Theorem 3.7 we find m linearly independent elements $y_1,\ldots,y_m \in \Lambda^*$ with euclidean length bounded by $m/\sqrt{m} = \sqrt{m}$. By using Lemma 3.8 we find elements $\theta(y_i) \in \Psi(\mathcal{O}_L^*)$ which have the same euclidean length. By choosing $\gamma_i := \Psi^{-1}(\theta(y_i))$ for $1 \leq i \leq m$ we finish our proof. $\square$

Now we are able to prove our theorem. Note that the field L takes the role of the principal subfield L_i in the statement.

PROOF OF THEOREM 3.1. Using Lemma 3.9 we find m_i linearly independent elements β_j in $\mathcal{O}_L^*$ with 2-norm bounded by $\sqrt{m_i}$. When we interpret those elements in K, we get n/m_i copies of the complex embeddings, which gives that the 2-norm as elements of K bounded by $\sqrt{n}$. Now apply Lemma 3.6. $\square$

4. AN EXAMPLE

The aim of this section is to compare our algorithm with the previous state of the art. We want to indicate that our approach can be useful in practice. The algorithm most efficient in practice at the time of this paper is based on [12]. That algorithm uses a combinatorial approach in order to find block systems corresponding to a subfield. The drawback of that algorithm is that it might have to test exponentially many possibilities before it finds the right block system.

Our algorithm is more robust, in the sense that there is no risk of an exponentially large computation time due to a combinatorial problem. We compare our algorithm with [12] by taking an example which was given in [12].

We use the degree 60 field generated by a root of the polynomial

$f(t) := t^{60} + 36t^{59} + 579t^{58} + 5379t^{57} + 30720t^{56} + 100695t^{55} + 98167t^{54} - 611235t^{53} - 2499942t^{52} - 1083381t^{51} + 15524106t^{50} + 36302361t^{49} - 22772747t^{48} - 205016994t^{47} - 194408478t^{46} + 417482280t^{45} + 954044226t^{44} + 281620485t^{43} - 366211766t^{42} - 1033459767t^{41} - 8746987110t^{40} - 15534020046t^{39} + 23906439759t^{38} + 104232578583t^{37} + 31342660390t^{36} - 364771340802t^{35} - 547716092637t^{34} + 583582152900t^{33} + 2306558029146t^{32} + 998482693677t^{31} - 3932078004617t^{30} - 5195646620046t^{29} + 2421428069304t^{28} + 10559164336236t^{27} + 3475972372302t^{26} - 22874708335419t^{25} - 33428241525914t^{24} + 21431451023271t^{23} + 90595197659892t^{22} + 50882107959528t^{21} - 67090205528313t^{20} - 117796269461541t^{19} - 74369954660792t^{18} + 25377774560496t^{17} + 126851217660123t^{16} + 104232393296166t^{15} - 29072256729168t^{14} - 83163550972215t^{13} - 24296640395870t^{12} + 14633584964262t^{11} + 8865283658688t^{10} + 5364852154893t^{9} - 15657021718837t^{8} - 7601782249737t^{7} - 21061322895551t^{6} + 33693566195437t^{5} + 3717661159674t^{4} + 1754791133184t^{3} + 573470363592t^{2} + 74954438640t + 3285118944$

which is the splitting field of the polynomial $t^5 + t^4 - 2t^3 + t^2 + t + 1$. The Galois group of this polynomial is the alternating group A_5 and therefore all elements have order $1, 2, 3,$ or 5.

For lower degree examples, the algorithm from [12] is generally faster, however, to compute this degree 60 example, it needed some assistance to prevent the combinatorial problem from becoming prohibitively large. Our algorithm is more robust in the sense that it handles such examples without difficulties or assistance. The algorithm [12], with some assistance, took a couple of hours for this example. On the same machine, our algorithm (without assistance) can find each principal subfield in 3–5 seconds. One can construct examples where the difference in running time becomes exponentially larger. For example, construct an S_5-example of degree 120. Our algorithm is sufficiently robust to handle such degrees.

5. REFERENCES

[1] W. Banaszczyk. New bounds in some transference theorems in the geometry of number. *Math. Ann*, 296:625–635, 1993.

[2] Bernhard Beckermann and George Labahn. A uniform approach for the fast computation of matrix-type pade approximants. *SIAM J. Matrix Anal. Appl.*, 15:804–823, July 1994.

[3] Karim Belabas, Mark van Hoeij, Jürgen Klüners, and Allan Steel. Factoring polynomials over global fields. *J. Théor. Nombres Bordeaux*, 21:15–39, 2009.

[4] D. Casperson and J. McKay. Symmetric functions, m-sets, and Galois groups. *Math. Comput.*, 63:749–757, 1994.

[5] Henri Cohen and Francisco Diaz y Diaz. A polynomial reduction algorithm. *Séminaire de Théorie des Nombres de Bordeaux 2*, 3:351–360, 1991.

[6] Xavier Dahan and Éric Schost. Sharp estimates for triangular sets. In *Proceedings of the 2004 international symposium on Symbolic and algebraic computation*, ISSAC '04, pages 103–110, New York, NY, USA, 2004. ACM.

[7] H. Derksen. An algorithm to compute generalized Padé-Hermite forms. Preprint, Catholic University Nijmegen, 1994.

[8] J Dixon. Computing subfields in algebraic number fields. *J. Austral. Math. Soc. Series A*, 49:434–448, 1990.

[9] W. Hart. FLINT. open-source C-library http://www.flintlib.org.

[10] Mark Van Hoeij. Factoring polynomials and the knapsack problem. *J. Number Theory*, 95:167–189, 2002.

[11] A. Hulpke. Block systems of a Galois group. *Exp. Math.*, 4(1):1–9, 1995.

[12] J. Klüners. *Über die Berechnung von Automorphismen und Teilkörpern algebraischer Zahlkörper.* Dissertation, Technische Universität Berlin, 1997.

[13] J. Klüners. On computing subfields - a detailed description of the algorithm. *Journal de Théorie des Nombres de Bordeaux*, 10:243–271, 1998.

[14] D. Lazard and A. Valibouze. Computing subfields: Reverse of the primitive element problem. In A. Galligo F. Eyssete, editor, *MEGA-92, Computational algebraic geometry*, volume 109, pages 163–176. Birkhäuser, Boston, 1993.

[15] A. K. Lenstra, H. W. Lenstra Jr., and L. Lovász. Factoring polynomials with rational coefficients. *Math. Ann.*, 261:515–534, 1982.

[16] Władisław Narkiewicz. *Elementary and Analytic Theory of Algebraic Numbers.* Springer, 2004.

[17] M. v. Hoeij and V. Pal. Isomorphisms of algebraic number fields. arXiv:1012.0096v2, 2010.

[18] Mark van Hoeij and Andrew Novocin. Gradual sub-lattice reduction and a new complexity for factoring polynomials. In *LATIN*, pages 539–553, 2010.

[19] G. Villard. Certification of the QR factor R, and of lattice basis reducedness. In *Proceedings of the 2007 International Symposium on Symbolic and Algebraic Computation (ISSAC'07)*, pages 361–368, 2007.

A Simple But Exact and Efficient Algorithm for Complex Root Isolation*

Michael Sagraloff
Max Planck Institute for Informatics
Saarbrücken, Germany
msagralo@mpi-inf.mpg.de

Chee K. Yap
Courant Institute of Mathematical Sciences
New York University, New York
yap@cs.nyu.edu

ABSTRACT

We present a new exact subdivision algorithm CEVAL for isolating the complex roots of a square-free polynomial in any given box. It is a generalization of a previous real root isolation algorithm called EVAL. Under suitable conditions, our approach is applicable for general analytic functions. CEVAL is based on the simple Bolzano Principle and is easy to implement exactly. Preliminary experiments have shown its competitiveness.

We further show that, for the "benchmark problem" of isolating all roots of a square-free polynomial with integer coefficients, the asymptotic complexity of both algorithms EVAL and CEVAL matches (up a logarithmic term) that of more sophisticated real root isolation methods which are based on Descartes' Rule of Signs, Continued Fraction or Sturm sequences. In particular, we show that the tree size of EVAL matches that of other algorithms. Our analysis is based on a novel technique called δ-clusters from which we expect to see further applications.

Categories and Subject Descriptors

G.1.5 [**Numerical Analysis**]: Roots of Nonlinear Equations; F.2.1 [**Analysis of Algorithms and Problem Complexity**]: Numerical Algorithms and Problems

General Terms

Algorithms, Reliability, Theory

Keywords

exact root isolation, complexity of complex root isolation, Bolzano methods, subdivision algorithms, evaluation-based root isolation

---

*The full paper is available from http://www.mpi-inf.mpg.de/~msagralo/ or http://cs.nyu.edu/exact/.

1. INTRODUCTION

Root finding might be called the *Fundamental Problem of Algebra*, after the Fundamental Theorem of Algebra [40, 42, 47]. The literature on root finding is extremely rich, with a large classical literature. The work of Schönhage [40] marks the beginning of complexity-theoretic approaches to the Fundamental Problem. Pan [33] provides a history of root-finding from the complexity view point; see McNamee [23] for a general bibliography. The root finding problem can be studied as two distinct problems: root isolation and root refinement. In the complexity literature, the main focus is on what we call the **benchmark problem**, that is, isolating all the complex roots of a polynomial f of degree n with integer coefficients of at most L bits. Let $T(n, L)$ denote the (worst case) bit complexity of this problem. There are three variations on this benchmark problem:

- We can ask for only the real roots. Special techniques apply in this important case. E.g., Sturm [12, 21, 36], Descartes [9, 13, 15, 20, 28, 37], and continued fraction methods [1, 41, 44].

- We can seek the arithmetic complexity of this problem, that is, we seek to optimize the number $T_A(n, L)$ of arithmetic operations.

- We can add another parameter $p > 0$, and instead of isolation, we may seek to approximate each of the roots to p relative or absolute bits.

Schönhage achieved a bound of $T(n, L) = \widetilde{O}(n^3 L)$ for the benchmark isolation problem where $\widetilde{O}$ indicates the omission of logarithmic factors. This bound has remained intact. Pan and others [33] gave theoretical improvements in the sense of achieving $T_A(n, L) = \widetilde{O}(n^2 L)$ and $T(n, L) = T_A(n, L) \cdot \widetilde{O}(n)$, thus achieving record bounds simultaneously in both bit complexity and arithmetic complexity. Theoretical algorithms designed to achieve record bounds for the benchmark problem have so far not been used in practice. Moreover, the benchmark problem is inappropriate for some applications. For instance, we may only be interested in the first positive root (as in ray shooting in computer graphics), or in the roots in some specified neighborhood. In the numerical literature, there are many algorithms that are widely used and effective in practice but lack a guarantee on the global behavior (cf. [33] for discussion). Some "global methods" such as the Weierstrass or Durant-Kerner method that simultaneously approximate all roots seem ideal for the benchmark problem and work well in practice, but their convergence and/or complexity analysis are open. Thus, the benchmark complexity, despite its theoretical usefulness, has limitation as sole criterion in evaluating the usefulness of root isolation algorithms.

There are two sub-literature on "practical" root isolation algorithms: (1) One is the exact computation literature, providing algorithms used in various algebraic applications and computer algebra systems. Such exact algorithms have a well-developed complexity analysis and there is considerable computational experience especially in the context of cylindrical algebraic decomposition. The favored root isolation algorithms here, applied to the benchmark problem, tend to lag behind the theoretical algorithms by a factor of nL. Nevertheless, current experimental data justify their use [17, 37]. (2) The other is the numerical literature mentioned above. Although numerical algorithms traditionally lack any exactness guarantees, they have many advantages that practitioners intuitively understand: compared to algebraic methods, they are easier to implement and their complexity is more adaptive. Hence, there is a growing interest in constructing numerical algorithms that are exact and efficient.

§1. The Subdivision Approach.

Among the exact root isolation algorithms, the subdivision paradigm is widely used. It is a generalization of binary search in which we search for roots in a given domain (say a box $B_0 \subseteq \mathbb{C}$). Its principle action is a simple **subdivision phase** where we keep subdividing boxes into 4 congruent subboxes until each box B satisfies a predicate $C_{stop}(B)$. Typically, $C_{stop}(B) \equiv C_{out}(B) \vee C_{in}(B)$ where $C_{out}(B)$ is an **exclusion predicate** whose truth implies that B has no roots, and $C_{in}(B)$ is an **inclusion predicate** whose truth implies that B contains a unique root. Subdivision methods have the advantage of being "local": they can restrict computational effort to the given box B_0, and may terminate quickly if there few or no roots in B_0.

Exact implementation of $C_{stop}(B)$ can be based on algebraic properties such as generalized Sturm sequences [47, Chap. 7]. Unfortunately, algebraic predicates are expensive. Since finding a root is metaphorically like "finding a needle in a hay stack", an efficient exclusion predicate C_{out} can be highly advantageous. Numerical exclusion predicates have been used in Dedieu, Yakoubsohn and Taubin [11, 43, 46] but the inclusion predicate in these papers are inexact, based on an arbitrary ϵ-cutoff: $C_{in}(B) \equiv size(B) < \epsilon$. *Our paper will exploit numerical exclusion and inclusion predicates to yield exact subdivision algorithms.*

§2. Three Principles for Subdivision.

We compare three general principles used in subdivision algorithms for real root isolation: theory of Sturm sequences, Descartes' rule of sign, and the Bolzano principle. The latter principle is simple and intuitive: *if a continuous real function $f(x)$ satisfies $f(a)f(b) < 0$, then there is a point c between a and b such that $f(c) = 0$. Furthermore, if f is differentiable and f' does not vanish on (a, b), then this root is unique in (a, b).* Modern algorithmic treatment of the Descartes method began with Collins and Akritas [9]. In recent years, algorithms based on the first two principles have been called (respectively) **Sturm method** and the **Descartes method**. By analogy, algorithms based on the third principle may be classified under the **Bolzano method** [7, 8, 26]. Note that the Bolzano principle is an analytic one, while Sturm is algebraic (Descartes seems to have

an intermediate status). Johnson [17] has shown empirically that the Descartes method is more efficient than Sturm. Rouillier and Zimmermann [37] implemented a highly efficient exact real root isolation algorithm based on Descartes method. Since their theoretical bounds are indistinguishable, any practical advantage of Descartes over Sturm must be derived from the fact that the predicates in the Descartes method are cheaper. We believe that Bolzano methods have a similar advantage over Descartes. Such evidence is provided in a recent empirical study of Kamath [18] where a version of CEVAL is compared with several algorithms, including the well-known MPSOLVE of Bini and Fiorentini [3, 4]. Bolzano methods also have the advantage of greater generality: *The Bolzano method is applicable to the much larger class of complex analytic functions. Our CEVAL algorithm can be adapted to such functions under mild conditions.*

§3. Complexity Analysis.

All complexity analysis is for the benchmark problem of isolating all roots of a polynomial $f(z)$. There are two complexity measures for subdivision algorithms: the subdivision tree size $S(n, L)$ and the bit complexity $P(n, L)$ of the subdivision predicates. Clearly, $T(n, L) \leq S(n, L)P(n, L)$. But the analysis in this paper shows that $T(n, L)$ may be smaller than $S(n, L)P(n, L)$ by a factor of n. For the Sturm method, Davenport [10] has shown that for isolating all real roots of $f(x)$, we have $S(n, L) = O(n(L + \log n))$. This is optimal if $L \geq \log n$ [15]. The tree size in the Descartes method was only recently proven to be $O(n(L + \log n))$ [15] matching the Sturm bound. In this paper, we will prove that the tree size in the Bolzano method is $\widetilde{O}(n(L + \log n))$ for real roots. Furthermore, in our extension of the Bolzano method for complex roots the corresponding tree size is $\widetilde{O}(n^2(L + \log n))$. Despite this larger tree size, we prove that both real and complex Bolzano have $\widetilde{O}(n^4 L^2)$ bit complexity, matching Descartes and Sturm.

Our complexity analysis of Bolzano methods is novel, and it opens up the exciting possibility of analysis of similar subdivision algorithms as in meshing of algebraic surfaces [5, 22, 35]. Perhaps it is no surprise that Bolzano methods could outperform the more sophisticated algebraic methods in practice. *What seems surprising from our analysis is that Bolzano methods could also match (up to a logarithmic factor) the theoretical complexity of algebraic methods as well.*

§4. Contributions of this paper.

1. Our complex root isolation algorithm (CEVAL) is a contribution to the growing literature on exact algorithms based on numerical techniques and subdivision. The algorithm is simple and practical. Preliminary implementation shows that it is competitive with the highly regarded MPSOLVE.

2. This paper provides a rather sharp complexity analysis of EVAL. Somewhat surprisingly, the worst-case bit-complexity of this simple algorithm can match (up to logarithmic-factors) those of sophisticated methods like Sturm or Descartes.

3. We further show that the more general CEVAL also achieves the same bit complexity as EVAL (despite the fact that the tree size of CEVAL may be quadratically larger).

4. Our analysis is based on the novel technique of δ-clusters. We expect to see other applications of cluster analysis. This is a contribution to the general challenge of analyzing the complexity of numerical subdivision algorithms.

§5. Overview of Paper.

Section 2 reviews related work. The algorithm is presented in Section 3. In Section 4, we sketch our approach of δ-cluster from which we derive the complexity analysis of EVAL and CEVAL. In this conference paper, we summarize the most important results and provide sketches of the main proofs and techniques. Full proofs and further details on our δ-cluster analysis technique and 8-point test may be found in the full paper [39] on our homepages. Our original paper [39] only has the 8-point version of CEVAL, not the simplified version described below.

2. PRIOR WORK

The main distinction among the various subdivision algorithms is the choice[1] of tests or predicates. One approach is based on doing root isolation on the boundary of the boxes. Pinkert [34] and Wilf [45] (see also [47, Chap. 7]) use Sturm-like sequences, while Collins and Krandick [19] considered the Descartes method. Such approaches are related to topological degree methods [29], which go back to Brouwer (1924). But root isolation on boundary of subdivision boxes and topological degrees computations are relatively expensive and unnecessary: as shown in this paper, weaker but cheaper predicates may be more effective. This key motivation for our present work came from subdivision algorithms for curve approximation where a similar phenomenon occurs [22]. We next review several previous work that are most closely related to our paper.

§6. Work of Pan, Yakoubsohn, Dedieu and Taubin.

Pan [30, 31, 32, 33] describes a subdivision algorithm with the current record asymptotic complexity bound. Pan regards his work as a refinement of Weyl's Exclusion Algorithm (1924). Weyl is also the basis for Henrici and Gargantini (1969) and Renegar (1987) (see [33]). The predicates are based on estimating the distance from the midpoint of a box B to the nearest zero of the input polynomial $f(z)$. Turan (1968) provides such a bound up to a constant factor, say 5. Pan further reduces this factor to $(1 + \epsilon)$ (for a small $\epsilon > 0$) by applying the Graeffe iteration to $f(z)$. Finally, he combines the exclusion test with Newton-like accelerations to achieve the bound of $O(n^2 \ln n \ln(hn))$, where h is the cut-off depth of subdivision. Pan noted that *"there remains many open problems on the numerical implementation of Weyl's algorithm and its modification"* [33, p. 216]; in particular, *"proximity tests should be modified substantially to take into account numerical problems ... and controlling the precision growth"* [33, p. 193].

The approach of Yakoubsohn and Dedieu [11, 46] is much simpler than Pan's. Their algorithm keeps subdividing boxes until each box B satisfies an exclusion predicate $C_{out}(B)$, or B is smaller than an arbitrary cut-off $\epsilon > 0$. For any analytic function f, their predicate $C_{out}(B)$ is "$M^f(z, r\sqrt{2}) > 0$" where B is a square centered at z of length $2r$, and

$$M^f(z,t) := |f(z)| - \sum_{k \geq 1} \frac{|f^{(k)}(z)|}{k!} t^k. \qquad (1)$$

It is easy to see that if $C_{out}(B)$ holds, then B has no roots of f. Taubin [43] introduce exclusion predicates that can be viewed as the linearized form of $M^f(z,t)$ or a Newton

---

[1] We use the terms "predicate" and "test" interchangeably.

correction term. He shows their effectiveness in approximating (rasterizing) surfaces. These algorithms are useful in practice, but the use of ϵ-cutoff does not constitute a true inclusion predicate in the sense on §1: at termination, we have a collection of non-excluded ϵ-boxes, none of which is guaranteed to isolate a root.

§7. The Eval Algorithm.

The starting point for this paper is a simple algorithm for real root isolation. Suppose we want to isolate the roots of a real analytic function $f : \mathbb{R} \to \mathbb{R}$ in the interval $I_0 = [a, b]$. Assume f has only simple roots in I_0. For any interval I with center $m = m(I)$ and width $w = w(I)$, we introduce two interval predicates using the function in (1):

$$\begin{array}{rcl} C_0(I) & \equiv & M^f(m, w/2) > 0 \\ C_1(I) & \equiv & M^{f'}(m, w/2) > 0 \end{array} \Bigg\} \qquad (2)$$

Clearly, $C_0(I)$ is an exclusion predicate. Note that if $C_1(I)$ holds, then f has at most one zero in I. Thus, $C_1(I)$ in combination with the following **root confirmation test**

$$f(a)f(b) < 0, \qquad \text{where } I = [a, b], \qquad (3)$$

constitutes an inclusion predicate. Here is the algorithm:

EVAL(I_0):
    Check the endpoints of I_0, and output them if they are zeros of f
    Let Q be a queue of intervals, initialized as $Q \leftarrow \{I_0\}$
    While Q is non-empty:
        Remove I from Q.
1.   If $C_0(I)$ holds, discard I.
2.   Else if $C_1(I)$ holds,
3.   If I passes the confirmation test (3), output I.
4.   Else, discard I.
5.   Else
6.   If $f(m) = 0$, output $[m, m]$ where $m = m(I)$.
7.   Split I at m and put both subintervals into Q.

Termination and correctness are easy to see (e.g., [7]). Output intervals either have the exact form $[m, m]$ or are regarded as open intervals (a, b). This algorithm is easy to implement exactly if we assume that all intervals are represented by dyadic numbers.

Mitchell [26] seems to be the first to explicitly describe EVAL, but as he assumes approximate floating point arithmetic, he does not check if $f(m) = 0$ at the midpoint m. He attributes ideas to Moore [27]. The second author of the present paper initiated the complexity investigation of EVAL (and its extension for multiple roots) as the 1-D analogue of the surface meshing algorithm of Plantinga-Vegter [5, 22, 35]. In [7], we succeeded in obtaining a bound of $O(n^3(L + \log n))$ when EVAL is applied to the benchmark problem. The proof involves several highly technical tools, but the approach is based on the novel concept of **continuous amortization**. The idea is to bound the tree size in terms of an integral $\int_I \frac{dx}{F(x)}$ where $F(x)$ is a suitable "stopping function". Recently, Burr and Krahmer [6] simplified the choice of $F(x)$, obtaining a tree size bound $O(n(L + \ln n))$ for EVAL. Such a bound is optimal for $L \geq \ln n$ (see [15]), and matches the bounds in the present paper, as well as those for Descartes and Sturm methods. But they require f' to be square-free. Our present paper uses a different analysis to obtain a slightly weaker bound of

$O(n(L+\ln n)(\ln L+\ln n))$, but we do not require the square-freeness of f'. Furthermore, our analysis extends to the complex root isolation algorithm CEVAL. Our upper bound for the bit complexity of CEVAL matches those of EVAL, Sturm and Descartes method.

3. THE COMPLEX ROOT ALGORITHM

In this section, we describe CEVAL, the complex analogue of EVAL. In fact, we describe two versions of CEVAL, and only prove the correctness of the simpler version here. The algorithm in described in way that allows a straightforward exact implementation.

Notation. For the rest of this paper, we fix a square-free polynomial $f \in \mathbb{C}[z]$ of degree n. For $m \in \mathbb{C}$ and $r > a$ real value, we denote $D_r(m)$ the disk of **radius** $r(D) = r$ centered at $m(D) = m$. For $\xi, \mu \in \mathbb{C}$, we write "$\xi \leq \mu$" if $\mathrm{Re}(\xi) \leq \mathrm{Re}(\mu)$ and $\mathrm{Im}(\xi) \leq \mathrm{Im}(\mu)$. A subset $B \subseteq \mathbb{C}$ is called a **box** if $B = B(\xi, \mu) := \{z \in \mathbb{C} : \xi \leq z \leq \mu\}$ for some $\xi \leq \mu$. We further define $m(B) := (\xi + \mu)/2$ the **midpoint** and $w(B) := \max\{|\mathrm{Re}(\mu - \xi)|, |\mathrm{Im}(\mu - \xi)|\}$ the **width** of B. Its **radius** $r(B)$ is defined as the radius of the smallest disk centered in $m(B)$ and containing B. Obviously, $\bar{r}(B) := 3w(B)/4$ is an upper bound on $r(B)$. We can split a box B into four congruent subboxes, called the **children** of B. The boundary of a region $R \subseteq \mathbb{C}$ is denoted ∂R (R is usually a disk or a box). A connected region R is said to be **isolating** if it contains exactly one zero of $f(z)$.

§8. Complex Analogues of C_0 and C_1 Predicates.

For $m \in \mathbb{C}$ and $K, r > 0$, we define the **test function** $t^f(m,r)$ and the **predicate** $T_K^f(m,r)$ as follows:

$$t^f(m,r) := \sum_{k \geq 1} \left| \frac{f^{(k)}(m)}{f(m)} \right| \frac{r^k}{k!} \tag{4}$$

$$T_K^f(m,r) \equiv t^f(m,r) < \frac{1}{K} \tag{5}$$

Since f is fixed in this paper, we simply write $T_K(m,r)$ for $T_K^f(m,r)$. When f' is used in place of f, we simply write $T'_K(m,r)$ for $T_K^{f'}(m,r)$. Moreover, for a disk D, we may write $T_K(D)$ for $T_K(m(D), r(D))$, etc. We remark that the success of $T_K^f(m,r)$ implies the success of $T_{K'}^f(m,r)$ for any $K' \leq K$ and $r' \leq r$, and $T_K^f(m,r)$ is equivalent to $T_K^{f(m+rz/\lambda)}(0,\lambda)$ with $\lambda \in \mathbb{R}$ an arbitrary positive real value.

LEMMA 1   (EXCLUSION-INCLUSION PROPERTIES). *Consider any disk $D = D_r(m)$:*
(i) If $T_1(D)$ holds, the closure $\overline{D}$ of D has no root of f.
(ii) If $T_1(D)$ fails, the disc $D_{2nr}(m)$ has some root of f.
(iii) If $T'_{\sqrt{2}}(D)$ holds, $\overline{D}$ has at most one root of f.

Proof. See [2, 39] for proofs of (i) and (iii). We show the contrapositive of (ii): let $z_1, \dots, z_n$ denote the roots of f and suppose that $D_{2nr}(m)$ contains no root. Then,

$$\left| \frac{f^{(k)}(m)}{f(m)} \right| = \left| \sum'_{i_1,\dots,i_k} \frac{1}{(m - z_{i_1})\dots(m - z_{i_k})} \right|$$

$$\leq \Sigma_k(m) := \left(\sum_{i=1}^n \left| \frac{1}{m - z_i} \right| \right)^k \leq \left(\frac{1}{2r} \right)^k, \tag{6}$$

where the prime means that the i_j's ($j = 1 \dots k$) are chosen to be distinct. Hence, it follows that

$$\sum_{k \geq 1} \left| \frac{f^{(k)}(m)}{f(m)} \right| \frac{r^k}{k!} < \sum_{k \geq 1} \frac{1}{k!} \left(\frac{1}{2} \right)^k = e^{\frac{1}{2}} - 1 < 1$$

and, thus, $T_1(D)$ holds.   **Q.E.D.**

Part (i) of the lemma shows that $T_1(D)$, in analogy to $C_0(I)$, is an exclusion predicate for $D = D_r(m)$. Part (ii) shows that the negation of $T_1(D)$ is a root confirmation test like (3), albeit for the enlarged disc $D^+ := D_{2nr}(m)$. Part (iii) shows that $T'_{\sqrt{2}}(D)$ plays the role of the predicate $C_1(I)$. From (ii) and (iii) we could derive an inclusion predicate for B.

The next lemma gives lower bounds on the size of discs that pass our tests. The bounds are in terms of the **separation** $\sigma(\xi) := \min_{j \neq i} |z_j - \xi|$ of a root $\xi := z_i$ of f, and the **separation** $\sigma(f) := \min_i \sigma(z_i)$ **of** f.

LEMMA 2. *Consider a disk D and a root $\xi := z_i$ of f:*
(i) If $r(D) \leq \sigma(f)/(4n^2)$, then $T_1(D)$ or $T'_{\sqrt{2}}(D)$ holds.
(ii) If D contains ξ and $r \leq \sigma(\xi)/(4n^2)$, then $T'_{\sqrt{2}}(D)$ holds.
(iii) If D contains ξ and $r \leq \sigma(\xi)/(8n^3)$, then D^+ is isolating.

Proof. For (i), suppose that $r(D) \leq \sigma(f)/(4n^2)$ and both $\overline{T_1(D)}$ and $T'_{\sqrt{2}}(D)$ do not hold. Then, according to Lemma 1 (ii), $D_{2nr(D)}(m)$ must contain a root z of f. The same result applied to f' shows that $D_{2nr(D)}(m)$ also contains a root z' of f'. It follows that $|z - z'| < 4nr(D) \leq \sigma(f)/n \leq \sigma(z)/n$ contradicting the fact [13, 47] that $D_{\sigma(z)/n}(z)$ does not contain any root of the derivative f'. Part (ii) follows from (i) since $\xi \in D$ implies that $T_1(D)$ does not hold. Part (iii) is a direct consequence of (ii).   **Q.E.D.**

§9. Simplified Complex Root Isolation.

We are ready to present a complex version of EVAL. Call a disk $D_r(m)$ **well-isolating** if $D_r(m)$ and $D_{2r}(m)$ are both isolating. The property we exploit is that if D and D' are both well-isolating with non-empty intersection, then they share a common root in $D \cap D'$. Our algorithm produces well-isolated disks:

Simplified CEVAL(B_0, f):
  Input: Box B_0, and square-free polynomial $f(z)$ of degree n.
  Output: List $\mathcal{L}$ of disjoint well-isolating disks, centered in B_0.

  $Q \leftarrow \{B_0\}$. $\mathcal{L} \leftarrow \emptyset$.
  While Q is non-empty:
      Remove B from Q. Let $m = m(B)$, $\bar{r} = \frac{3}{4}w(B) > r(B)$.
1.   If $T_1(m, \bar{r})$ holds, discard B.
2.   Else if $T'_{\sqrt{2}}(m, 4n\bar{r})$ holds:
2.1   If $D_{2n\bar{r}}(m)$ intersects any disk D' in $\mathcal{L}$,
2.2   replace D' by the smaller of $D_{2n\bar{r}}(m)$ and D'.
2.3   Else insert $D_{2n\bar{r}}(m)$ into $\mathcal{L}$.
3.   Else
          Split B into four children and insert them into Q.

Correctness of our algorithm is based on three claims:

THEOREM 3   (CORRECTNESS).
(i) The algorithm halts: indeed, no box of width less than $\sigma(f)/(12n^3)$ is subdivided.
(ii) $\mathcal{L}$ is a list of well-isolating disks, each centered in B_0.
(iii) Every root of $f(z)$ in B_0 is isolated by some disk in $\mathcal{L}$.

Proof. Claim (i) is true because Lemma 2(i) implies that the tests in Steps 1 or 2 must pass when $4n\bar{r} \leq \sigma(f)/(4n^2)$, and by definition $\bar{r} = 3w(B)/4$. To see (ii), observe that the disc $D_{2n\bar{r}}(m)$ is inserted into $\mathcal{L}$ in Steps 2.2 or 2.3. The m and $\bar{r}$ in Step 2.1 have the properties that $T_1(m,\bar{r})$ fails and $T'_{\sqrt{2}}(m, 4n\bar{r})$ succeeds. Then, Lemma 1(ii,iii) implies that $D_{2n\bar{r}}(m)$ is well-isolating. To see (iii), observe that boxes $B \subseteq B_0$ are discarded in Steps 1 or 2.2 of the algorithm: Step 1 is justified by Lemma 1(i) and Step 2.2 is justified because of the above-noted property of well-isolating disks. **Q.E.D.**

§10. The Eight Point Test.

Instead of relying on Lemma 1(ii) for root confirmation, we offer another root confirmation test that is closer in spirit to the sign-change idea in (3), and which could be generalized for analytic functions. The idea is to look at the 8 compass points (N,S,E,W, NE, SE, NW, SW) on the disk $D_{4r}(m)$ as illustrated in Figure 1. These compass points divide the boundary $\partial D_{4r}(m)$ of the disk into 8 arcs $A_0, \ldots, A_7$ where $A_j := \{m + 4re^{\mathbf{i}\theta} : j\pi/4 \leq \theta < (j+1)\pi/4\}$.

We rewrite the function $f(z)$ as $f(x + \mathbf{i}y) = u(x,y) + \mathbf{i}v(x,y)$, where $z = x + \mathbf{i}y$, $\mathbf{i} = \sqrt{-1}$ and u and v are the real and imaginary part of f. So $f(x+\mathbf{i}y) = 0$ iff $u(x,y) = 0$ and $v(x,y) = 0$. Since the roots are simple, the u- and v-curves intersect at right angles. We say that there is an **arcwise** u**-crossing** at A_j if $u(m+4re^{\mathbf{i}j\pi/4}) \cdot u(m+4re^{\mathbf{i}(j+1)\pi/4}) < 0$ or $u(m+4re^{\mathbf{i}j\pi/4}) = 0$.

If r is sufficiently small, then we want to detect roots in $D_r(m)$ by arcwise u- and v-crossings. More precisely: we say $D_{4r}(m)$ passes the **8-Point test** if there are exactly two arcwise u-crossings at A_j, A_k, $(j < k)$ and exactly two arcwise v-crossings at $A_{j'}, A_{k'}$ $(j' < k')$, and these **interleave** in the sense that either $0 \leq j < j' < k < k' < 8$ or $0 \leq j' < j < k' < k < 8$.

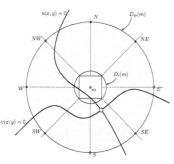

Figure 1: 8 compass points.

We introduce the following novel test to confirm the existence of ordinary roots.

THEOREM 4 (SUCCESS OF 8-POINT TEST). *Suppose $T'_6(m, 4r)$ holds and the 8-point test is applied to $D_{4r}(m)$.*
(i) If $D_{4r}(m)$ fails the test, then $D_r(m)$ is non-isolating.
(ii) If $D_{4r}(m)$ passes the test, then $D_{4r}(m)$ is isolating.

Using the 8-point test, we devise an alternative to the simplified CEVAL. This **8-point Ceval** is described in the full version [39] of this paper including the proof of Theorem 4 which is non-trivial. The cardinal points (N,S,E,W) are dyadic assuming the center and radius are dyadic; however the ordinal points (NE,SE,SW,NW) are irrational. Hence for exact implementation, we show how the correctness of the 8-Point test is preserved if we use rational points that are slightly perturbed versions of ordinal points. The 8-point test has independent interest: (a) For analytic functions, we no longer have Lemma 1(ii) for root confirmation, but some kind of 8-point test is applicable. More precisely,

the tests $T_K^f(m,r)$ can be considered for arbitrary analytic function, and the same argumentation as in the case of polynomials shows the correctness of Lemma 1(i),(iii) and Theorem 4. (b) We can use it to "confirm" the output from pure-exclusion algorithms such as Yakoubsohn-Dedieu's in §6. The asymptotic complexity of these two forms of CEVAL for the benchmark problem are the same. This is due to the fact that there exists a corresponding result to Lemma 2 for the 8-point test.

4. COMPLEXITY ANALYSIS

In this section, we analyze the complexity of EVAL and the simplified CEVAL. For this purpose, we use the benchmark problem of isolating all roots of a square-free polynomial of degree n with L-bit integer coefficients. The initial start box for CEVAL may be assumed to be $B_0 = B(-2^L(1 + \mathbf{i}), 2^L(1 + \mathbf{i}))$. For EVAL, we can start with the interval $I_0 = (-2^{-L}, 2^L)$. According to Cauchy's bound [47], B_0 contains all complex roots $z_1, \ldots, z_n \in \mathbb{C}$ of f (thus, I_0 all real roots of f). Throughout the following considerations, let $\mathcal{T}^{CE}$ and $\mathcal{T}^{EV}$ denote the subdivision trees induced by CEVAL and EVAL, respectively.

§11. Cluster Analysis and Tree Size.

In (6), we have already seen that $\Sigma_k(m) := (\sum_i \frac{1}{|m - z_i|})^k = (\Sigma_1(m))^k$ constitutes an upper bound on $\frac{|f^{(k)}(m)|}{|f(m)|}$ for all $k \geq 1$. Furthermore, $\Sigma_1(m) < \nu$ for a $\nu > 0$ implies that $\sum_{k \geq 1} |\frac{f^{(k)}(m)}{f(m)}| \frac{r^k}{k!} < e^{\nu r} - 1$ and, thus,

$$T_K^f(m,r) \text{ holds if } \Sigma_1(m) < \frac{1}{r}\ln\left(1 + \frac{1}{K}\right). \quad (7)$$

Now let us consider an arbitrary box B of depth h in the subdivision process, that is, B has width $w(B) = w_h := 2^{L+1-h}$. Let $\bar{r} = \bar{r}(B) = 3w(B)/4$ be the upper bound on the radius of B used in the CEVAL algorithm. If the midpoint $m(B)$ of B fulfills $|m(B) - z_i| > 2n \cdot \bar{r}$ for all $i = 1, \ldots, n$, then $\Sigma_1(m(B)) < \frac{1}{2\bar{r}} < \frac{\ln 2}{\bar{r}}$, thus $T_1(m(B), \bar{r})$ holds according to the above consideration and B is discarded. It follows that, for each root z_i, there exist at most $O(n^2)$ disjoint boxes B of the same size with $|m(B) - z_i| \leq 2n\bar{r}$. Hence, in total, at most $O(n^3)$ boxes are retained at each subdivision level h. From this straightforward observation we immediately derive the upper bound $O(n^3)$ on the width of $\mathcal{T}^{CE}$. For EVAL, a similar argumentation shows that $O(n^2)$ intervals are retained at each subdivision level. This consideration is based on a pretty rough estimation of $\Sigma_1(m)$ which assumes that, from a given point m, the distances to all roots z_i are nearly of the same minimal value. In order to improve the latter estimate, we introduce the concept of δ-**clusters** of roots, where δ is an arbitrary positive real value. We will show that, outside some "smaller" neighborhood of the roots of f, the sum $\Sigma_1(m)$ is sufficiently small to guarantee the success of our exclusion predicate T_1:

THEOREM 5. *For arbitrary $\delta > 0$, there exist disjoint, axes-parallel, open boxes $B_1, \ldots, B_k \subset \mathbb{C}$ $(k \leq n^2)$ such that:*
(i) $\mathcal{B} := \bigcup_{i=1,\ldots,k} B_i$ covers all roots $z_1, \ldots, z_n$.
(ii) $\mathcal{B}$ covers an area of less than or equal to $4n^2\delta^2$.
(iii) For each point $m \notin \mathcal{B}$, we have $\Sigma_1(m) \leq \frac{2(1+\ln\lceil n/2 \rceil)}{\delta}$.

Proof. We only provide a sketch of the proof and refer the reader to the full paper [39] for a complete reasoning. The roots $z_1, \ldots, z_n$ are first projected onto the real axes defining a multiset (elements may appear several times) $R_{\mathtt{Re}} = \{x_1, \ldots, x_n\}$ in $\mathbb{R}$. The latter points are now partitioned into disjoint multisets $R_1, \ldots, R_l$ such that the following properties are fulfilled:

(a) Each R_i is a so called δ-**cluster** which is defined as follows: The corresponding δ-**interval**

$$I_\delta(R_i) = (\mathrm{cg}(R_i) - \delta|R_i|, \mathrm{cg}(R_i) + \delta|R_i|),$$

with $\mathrm{cg}(R_i) = \frac{\sum_{x \in R_i} x}{|R_i|}$ the **center of gravity** of R_i, contains all elements of R_i. In addition, we can order the elements of R_i in way such that their distances to the right boundary of $I_\delta(R_i)$ are at least $\delta, 2\delta, \ldots, |R_i|\delta$, respectively, and the same for the left boundary of $I_\delta(R_i)$.

(b) The δ-intervals $I_\delta(R_i)$ are pairwise disjoint.

The construction of a partition of $R_{\mathtt{Re}}$ with the above properties is rather simple: We start with the trivial partition of $R_{\mathtt{Re}}$ into n δ-clusters each consisting of one element of $R_{\mathtt{Re}}$. An easy computation shows that the union of two δ-clusters for which (b) is not fulfilled is again a δ-cluster. Thus, we iteratively merge δ-clusters whose corresponding δ-intervals overlap until (b) is eventually fulfilled. It is now easy to see that, for each $x \in \mathbb{R} \backslash \bigcup_i I_\delta(R_i)$, the inequality $\sum_j \frac{1}{|x - x_j|} \leq \frac{2(1 + \ln\lceil n/2 \rceil)}{\delta}$ holds.

In a second step, we project the roots of f onto the imaginary axes defining a multiset $R_{\mathtt{Im}}$ for which we proceed in exactly the same manner as for $R_{\mathtt{Re}}$. Let $S_1, \ldots, S_{l'}$ be the corresponding partition of $R_{\mathtt{Im}}$, then the overlapping of the stripes $\mathtt{Re}(z) \in I_\delta(R_i)$ and $\mathtt{Im}(z) \in I_\delta(S_j)$ defines $k \leq n^2$ boxes $B_1, \ldots, B_k$ covering an area of total size $4n^2\delta^2$ or less. Now, for each $m \notin \mathcal{B} = \bigcup_i B_i$, either $\mathtt{Re}(m) \notin \bigcup_i I_\delta(R_i)$ or $\mathtt{Im}(m) \notin \bigcup_i I_\delta(S_i)$. In the first case, we have

$$\Sigma_1(m) \leq \sum_{j=1}^n \frac{1}{|\mathtt{Re}(m) - \mathtt{Re}(z_j)|} \leq \frac{2(1 + \ln\lceil n/2 \rceil)}{\delta}.$$

The case $\mathtt{Im}(m) \notin \bigcup_j I_\delta(S_j)$ is treated in exactly the same manner. **Q.E.D.**

We now apply the above theorem to

$$\delta := r \cdot \frac{(1 + \ln\lceil n/2 \rceil)}{\ln 2} = \frac{3w(B)(1 + \ln\lceil n/2 \rceil)}{4\ln 2}$$

and use (7). It follows that, for all m outside a union of boxes covering an area of size $w(B)^2 \cdot O((n\ln n)^2)$, we have $\Sigma_1(m) < \frac{1}{r}\ln 2$. Thus, at any level in the subdivision process, only $O((n\ln n)^2)$ boxes are retained. For EVAL, we can apply the real counterpart of Theorem 5 which says that there exist $k \leq n$ disjoint intervals $I_1, \ldots, I_k$ that cover the projections of all z_i onto the real axes, the total size of all intervals is $\leq 2n\delta$, and $\Sigma_1(m) \leq \frac{2(1 + \ln\lceil n/2 \rceil)}{\delta}$ for each m located outside all I_j. It follows that the width of $\mathcal{T}^{EV}$ can be bounded by $O(n\ln n)$. A more refined argument even shows that, at a subdivision level h, the width of the tree adapts itself to the number k_h of roots z_i with separation $\sigma(z_i) \leq 16n^3 w_h = 2^{L+5-h}n^3$ related to the width $w_h = 2^{L+1-h}$ of the boxes at that level. We refer the reader to the full paper for the non-trivial proof. We fix this result:

THEOREM 6. *Let $h \in \mathbb{N}_0$ be an arbitrary subdivision level and k_h be the number of roots z_i with $\sigma(z_i) \leq 16n^3 w_h =$*

$2^{L+5-h}n^3$. *Then, the width of $\mathcal{T}^{CE}$ at level h is upper bounded by*

$$16k_{h-1}^2(17 + \ln\lceil k_{h-1}/2 \rceil) = O(k_{h-1}^2(\ln k_{h-1})^2)$$

and the width of $\mathcal{T}^{EV}$ is upper bounded by

$$4k_{h-1}(17 + \ln\lceil k_{h-1}/2 \rceil) = O(k_{h-1}\ln k_{h-1}).$$

In order to translate the above result on the treewidth into a bound on the treesize in terms of the degree n and the bit-size L, we have to derive an estimate for k_h. The main idea is to apply the generalized Davenport-Mahler bound [12, 13] to the roots of f. In a first step, we partition the set $R = \{z_1, \ldots, z_n\}$ of roots into disjoint sets $R_1, \ldots, R_l$ such that $|R_{i_0}| \geq 2$ for each $i_0 = 1, \ldots, n$ and $|z_i - z_j| \leq 2^{L+5-h}n^3 \cdot |R_{i_0}| \leq 2^{L+5-h}n^4$ for all pairs $z_i, z_j \in R_{i_0}$: Starting with the set $R_1 := \{z_1\}$, we can iteratively add roots to R_1 that have distance $\leq 2^{L+5-h}n^3$ to at least one root within R_1. When there is no further root to add, we proceed with a root z_i not contained in R_1 and construct a set R_2 from $\{z_i\}$ in the same manner, etc; see [39].

In a second step, we consider a directed graph $\mathcal{G}_i$ on each R_i which connects consecutive points of R_i in ascending order of their absolute values. We define $\mathcal{G} := (R, E)$ as the union of all $\mathcal{G}_i$. Then $\mathcal{G}$ is a directed graph on R with the following properties:

1. each edge $(\alpha, \beta) \in E$ satisfies $|\alpha| \leq |\beta|$,

2. $\mathcal{G}$ is acyclic, and

3. the in-degree of any node is at most 1.

Now, the generalized Davenport-Mahler bound applies:

$$\prod_{(\alpha, \beta) \in E} |\alpha - \beta| \geq \frac{1}{((n+1)^{1/2}2^L)^{n-1}} \cdot \left(\frac{\sqrt{3}}{n}\right)^{\#E} \cdot \left(\frac{1}{n}\right)^{n/2}$$

As each set R_i contains at least 2 roots, we must have $\#E \geq k_h/2$. Furthermore, for each edge $(\alpha, \beta) \in E$, we have $|\alpha - \beta| \leq 16n^4 w_h = 2^{L+5-h}n^4$, thus,

$$\left(2^{L+5-h}n^4\right)^{\frac{k_h}{2}} \geq \frac{1}{((n+1)^{1/2}2^L)^{n-1}} \cdot \left(\frac{\sqrt{3}}{n}\right)^{k_h} \cdot \left(\frac{1}{n}\right)^{n/2}$$

$$> \frac{1}{(n+1)^n 2^{nL}} \cdot \left(\frac{3}{n^2}\right)^{k_h/2} > n^{-n-k_h}2^{-n(L+1)}.$$

A simple computation then shows that

$$k_h < \frac{16n(L + \ln n)}{h - 2L} \quad \forall h > h_0 := \max(2L, \lceil 64\ln n + L \rceil). \tag{8}$$

In particular, the bound $O(n(L + \ln n))$ on the depth of the subdivision tree immediately follows. Namely, if $k_{h+1} < 1$, then $k_h = 0$ and, thus, $\sigma(f) < 2^{L+4-h}n^3 < 12w_h n^3$. But this implies that, at subdivision level h, no box is further subdivided (Theorem 3). For $h \leq h_0$, the trivial inequality $k_h \leq n$ holds. Now, we can derive our bound on the tree size by summing up the number of nodes over all subdivision levels, where we use Theorem 6 and the bound (8) for k_h. A similar computation also applies to the tree induced by the EVAL algorithm; see [39] for details.

THEOREM 7. *Let f be a square-free polynomial of degree n with integer coefficients of bit-size $\leq L$. Then,*
(i) the subdivision tree $\mathcal{T}^{CE}$ has size $\widetilde{O}(n^2 L)$.
(ii) the subdivision tree $\mathcal{T}^{EV}$ has size $\widetilde{O}(nL)$.

§12. Bit Complexity.

For the bit complexity analysis of CEVAL, we consider the computational costs at a node (box B) of depth h. So B has width $w(B) = w_h = 2^{L+1-h}$. In order to evaluate $T_1^f(m(B), \bar{r})$ and $T_{\sqrt{2}}^{f'}(m(B), 2n\bar{r})$, where $\bar{r} = \frac{3}{4}w(B)$ bounds the radius $r(B)$ of B, we compute

$$f_B(z) = f(m(B) + w(B) \cdot z)$$

and test whether $T_1^{f_B(z)}(0, 3/4)$ or $T_{\sqrt{2}}^{f_B'(z)}(0, 3n)$ holds. Notice that the latter two tests are equivalent to $T_1^f(m(B), \bar{r})$ and $T_{\sqrt{2}}^{f'}(m(B), 4n\bar{r})$, respectively. We first bound the costs for computing $f_B(z)$: For a polynomial $g(z) := \sum_{i=0}^n g_i z^i$ with binary fractions $g_i = m_i \cdot 2^{-\tau_i}$, $m_i \in \mathbb{Z}$ and $\tau_i \in \mathbb{N}_0$, as coefficients, we say that g **has bitsize** $\tau(g)$ if multiplication of g by the common denominator $2^{\max_i \tau_i}$ of all g_i leads to an integer polynomial with coefficients of at most $\tau(g)$ bits. For our starting box B_0, the polynomial $f_{B_0}(z) = f(2^{L+1}z)$ has bitsize $O(nL)$ because of the scaling operation $z \mapsto 2^{L+1}z$. We incrementally compute $f_{B'}$ from f_B via the substitution $z \mapsto (z \pm 1 \pm \mathbf{i})/2$, where B' is one of the four children of B. Hence, the bitsize of $f_{B'}$ increases by at most n compared to the bitsize of f_B. It follows that, for a box B at subdivision level h, f_B has bitsize $\tau_B = O(n(L+h))$. $f_{B'}$ is computed from f_B by first substituting z by $z/2$ followed by a Taylor shift by 1 and then by $\mathbf{i}$, that is, $z \mapsto z \pm 1 \pm \mathbf{i}$. A Taylor shift by $\mathbf{i}$ can be realized as a Taylor shift by 1 combined with two scalings by $\mathbf{i}$, using the identity $f(z + \mathbf{i}) = f(\mathbf{i}(-\mathbf{i}z + 1))$. The scalings by $\mathbf{i}$ are easy. Using asymptotically fast Taylor shift [16], each shift by 1 requires $\widetilde{O}(n(n + \tau_B)) = O(n^2(L + h))$ bit operations.

To evaluate the polynomials in the predicates $T_1^{f_B(z)}(0, 3/4)$ and $T_{\sqrt{2}}^{f_B'(z)}(0, 3n)$, we have to compute the value of a polynomial of bitsize $O(n(L+h))$ at a point of bit size $O(1)$ and $O(\log n)$, respectively. Therefore, $\widetilde{O}(n(L+h))$ bit operations suffice and so the overall bit complexity for a box of depth h is $\widetilde{O}(n^2(L+h))$. An analogous argument shows that, for an interval I at level h (i.e., $w(I) = 2^{L+1-h}$), EVAL requires $\widetilde{O}(n^2(L+h))$ bit operations as well. Thus, the bit complexity at each node is bounded by $\widetilde{O}(n^3L)$ since $h = O(n(L+\ln n))$.

For EVAL, the claimed bit complexity of $\tilde{O}(n^4L^2)$ follows easily by multiplying the bound $\tilde{O}(nL)$ from Theorem 7 on the number of nodes with the bound $\widetilde{O}(n^3L)$ on the bit operations at each node. Furthermore, a simple computation (see [39]) combining our results on the width of $\mathcal{T}^{CE}$ and the costs at each node at any subdivision level h leads to the overall bit complexity of $\tilde{O}(n^4L^2)$ for CEVAL. It is worth noting that the larger tree size of $\mathcal{T}^{CE}$ (compared to $\mathcal{T}^{EV}$) does not effect the overall bit complexity. Intuitively, most of the nodes of $\mathcal{T}^{CE}$ are at subdivision levels where the computational costs are considerably smaller than the worst case bound $\tilde{O}(n^3L)$.

THEOREM 8. *For a square-free polynomial f of degree n with integer coefficients with absolute value bounded by 2^L, the algorithms* CEVAL *and* EVAL *isolate the complex (real) roots of f with a number of bit operations bounded by $\widetilde{O}(n^4L^2)$.*

5. CONCLUSION

This paper introduced CEVAL, a new complex root isolation algorithm, continuing a line of recent work to develop exact subdivision algorithms based on the Bolzano principle. The primitives in such algorithms are simple to implement and extendible to analytic functions. Our 8-Point CEVAL algorithm has been implemented in Kamath's thesis [18] using the `Core Library` [48], and compares favorably to Yakoubsohn's algorithm and MPSOLVE [3, 4].

The complexity of CEVAL is theoretically competitive with that of known exact practical algorithms for real root isolation. It is somewhat unexpected that our simple evaluation-based algorithms can match those based on sophisticated primitives like Descartes or Sturm methods. Another surprise is that the complex case has (up to $\widetilde{O}$-order) the bit complexity of the real case despite its larger subdivision tree.

Our complexity analysis introduces new ideas including a technique of root clusters which has proven to have other applications [24] as well. One open problem is to sharpen our complexity estimates (only logarithmic improvements can be expected).

The Descartes method had been successfully extended to the bitstream model [14, 25] in which the coefficients of the input polynomial are given by a bitstream on-demand. It has useful applications in situations where the coefficients are algebraic numbers (e.g., in cylindrical algebraic decomposition). Recent work [38] shows that the CEVAL algorithm also extends to bitstream polynomials.

6. REFERENCES

[1] A. G. Akritas and A. Strzeboński. A comparative study of two real root isolation methods. Nonlinear Analysis:Modelling and Control, 10(4):297–304, 2005.

[2] E. Berberich, P. Emeliyanenko, and M. Sagraloff. An elimination method for solving bivariate polynomial systems: Eliminating the usual drawbacks. ALENEX 2011, pp. 35-47, Jan 22, 2011. San Francisco.

[3] D. A. Bini. Numerical computation of polynomial zeroes by means of Aberth's method. Numerical Algorithms, 13:179–200, 1996.

[4] D. A. Bini and G. Fiorentino. Numerical Computation of Polynomial Roots Using MPSolve Version 2.2. Dipart. di Matematica, Univ. di Pisa. Jan 2000. `ftp://ftp.dm.unipi.it/pub/mpsolve/MPSolve-2.2.tgz`.

[5] M. Burr, S. Choi, B. Galehouse, and C. Yap. Complete subdivision algorithms, II: Isotopic meshing of singular algebraic curves. ISSAC'08, pp. 87–94. Accepted Special JSC Issue.

[6] M. Burr and F. Krahmer. SqFreeEVAL: An (almost) optimal real-root isolation algorithm. CoRR, abs/1102.5266, 2011.

[7] M. Burr, F. Krahmer, and C. Yap. Continuous amortization: A non-probabilistic adaptive analysis technique. ECCC, TR09(136), Dec 2009.

[8] M. Burr, V. Sharma, and C. Yap. Evaluation-based root isolation, Feb. 2009. In preparation.

[9] G. E. Collins and A. G. Akritas. Polynomial real root isolation using Descartes' rule of signs. In R. D. Jenks, ed., ACM Symp. on Symb. and Alg. Comp., pp. 272–275. ACM Press, 1976.

[10] J. H. Davenport. Computer algebra for cylindrical algebraic decomposition. Tech. Rep., Royal Inst. of Tech., Dept. of Numerical Analysis & Comp. Sci., Stockholm, Sweden, 1985.

[11] J.-P. Dedieu and J.-C. Yakoubsohn. Localization of an

algebraic hypersurface by the exclusion algorithm. AAECC, 2:239–256, 1992.

[12] Z. Du, V. Sharma, and C. Yap. Amortized bounds for root isolation via Sturm sequences. In D. Wang and L. Zhi, eds., Symbolic-Numeric Computation, pp. 113–130. Birkhäuser, Basel, 2007. Proc. SNC 2005.

[13] A. Eigenwillig. Real Root Isolation for Exact and Approximate Polynomials Using Descartes' Rule of Signs. Ph.D. thesis, Univ. of Saarland, May 2008.

[14] A. Eigenwillig, L. Kettner, W. Krandick, K. Mehlhorn, S. Schmitt, and N. Wolpert. A Descartes algorithm for polynomials with bit stream coefficients. In 8th Comp.Algebra in Sci.Computing (CASC), pp. 138–149. Springer, 2005. LNCS 3718.

[15] A. Eigenwillig, V. Sharma, and C. Yap. Almost tight complexity bounds for the Descartes method. ISSAC'06, pp. 71–78, 2006.

[16] J. Gerhard. Modular algorithms in symbolic summation and symbolic integration. LNCS 3218, Springer, 2004.

[17] J. Johnson. Algorithms for polynomial real root isolation. In B. Caviness and J. Johnson, eds., Quantifier Elimination and Cylindrical Algebraic Decomposition, pp. 269–299. Springer, 1998.

[18] N. Kamath. Subdivision algorithms for complex root isolation: Empirical comparisons. Master's thesis, Oxford Univ., Oxford Computing Lab, Aug. 2010.

[19] W. Krandick and G. E. Collins. An efficient algorithm for infallible polynomial complex root isolation. In ISSAC 97, pp. 189–194, 1992.

[20] W. Krandick and K. Mehlhorn. New bounds for the Descartes method. JSC, 41(1):49–66, 2006.

[21] T. Lickteig and M.-F. Roy. Sylvester-Habicht sequences and fast Cauchy index computation. J. Symbolic Comp., 31:315–341, 2001.

[22] L. Lin and C. Yap. Adaptive isotopic approximation of nonsingular curves: the parametrizability and non-local isotopy approach. In 25th SoCG, pp. 351–360, 2009. To appear, Special Issue of DCG.

[23] J. McNamee. A bibliography on roots of polynomials. J. Comput. Appl. Math., 47:391–394, 1993. Online at http://www.elsevier.com/homepage/sac/cam/mcnamee.

[24] K. Mehlhorn and R. Osbild and M. Sagraloff. A General Approach to the Analysis of Controlled Perturbation Algorithms. CGTA, 2011. To appear.

[25] K. Mehlhorn and M. Sagraloff. Isolating real roots of real polynomials. In ISSAC 09, 2009.

[26] D. P. Mitchell. Robust ray intersection with interval arithmetic. In Graphics Interface'90, pp. 68–74, 1990.

[27] R. E. Moore. Interval Analysis. Prentice Hall, Englewood Cliffs, NJ, 1966.

[28] B. Mourrain, F. Rouillier, and M.-F. Roy. The Bernstein basis and real root isolation. In Goodman, Pach, and Welzl, eds., Comb. and Comp. Geom., No. 52 MSRI Pub., pp. 459–478. Cambridge Press, 2005.

[29] B. Mourrain, M. N. Vrahatis, and J. C. Yakoubsohn. On the complexity of isolating real roots and computing with certainty the topological degree. J. Complexity, 18:612–640, 2002.

[30] V. Y. Pan. New techniques for approximating complex polynomial zeros. Proc. 5th ACM-SIAM Symp. on Discrete Algorithms (SODA94), pp. 260–270, 1994.

[31] V. Y. Pan. Optimal (up to polylog factors) sequential and parallel algorithms for approximating complex polynomial zeros. 27th STOC, pp. 741–750, 1995.

[32] V. Y. Pan. On approximating polynomial zeros: Modified quadtree (Weyl's) construction and improved Newton's iteration. RR No. 2894, INRIA Sophia-Antipolis, 1996.

[33] V. Y. Pan. Solving a polynomial equation: some history and recent progress. SIAM Review, 39(2):187–220, 1997.

[34] J. R. Pinkert. An exact method for finding the roots of a complex polynomial. ACM Trans. on Math. Software, 2:351–363, 1976.

[35] S. Plantinga and G. Vegter. Isotopic approximation of implicit curves and surfaces. In Eurographics Symp. on Geom. Processing, pp. 245–254, 2004. ACM Press.

[36] D. Reischert. Asymptotically fast computation of subresultants. In ISSAC 97, pp. 233–240, 1997.

[37] F. Rouillier and P. Zimmermann. Efficient isolation of [a] polynomial's real roots. J. Comput. and Applied Math., 162:33–50, 2004.

[38] M. Sagraloff. A general approach to isolating roots of a bitstream polynomial. Mathematics in Computer Science (MCS), 2011. To appear.

[39] M. Sagraloff and C. K. Yap. An efficient exact subdivision algorithm for isolating complex roots of a polynomial and its complexity analysis, July 2009. Full paper from http://cs.nyu.edu/exact/ or http://www.mpi-inf.mpg.de/~msagralo/.

[40] A. Schönhage. The fundamental theorem of algebra in terms of computational complexity, 1982. Manuscript , Dept. of Math., U. of Tübingen. Updated 2004.

[41] V. Sharma. Complexity of real root isolation using continued fractions. Th. Comp. Sci., 409(2), 2008.

[42] S. Smale. The fundamental theorem of algebra and complexity theory. Bull. (N.S.) AMS, 4(1):1–36, 1981.

[43] G. Taubin. Rasterizing algebraic curves and surfaces. IEEE Comp. Graphics and Applic., 14(2):14–23, 1994.

[44] E. Tsigaridas and I. Emiris. On the complexity of real root isolation using continued fractions. Theor. Computer Science, 392:158–173, 2008.

[45] H. S. Wilf. A global bisection algorithm for computing the zeros of polynomials in the complex plane. J. ACM, 25(3):415–420, 1978.

[46] J.-C. Yakoubsohn. Numerical analysis of a bisection-exclusion method to find zeros of univariate analytic functions. J. of Complexity, 21:652–690, 2005.

[47] C. K. Yap. Fundamental Problems of Algorithmic Algebra. Oxford Univ. Press, 2000.

[48] J. Yu, C. Yap, Z. Du, S. Pion, and H. Bronnimann. Core 2: A library for Exact Numeric Computation in Geometry and Algebra. In 3rd ICMS, pp. 121–141. 2010. LNCS 6327.

Author Index